Revised Second Edition

Masterplots

1,801 Plot Stories and Critical Evaluations
of the World's Finest Literature

Revised Second Edition

Volume 7
Los – Myr
3733 – 4356

Edited by
FRANK N. MAGILL

Story Editor, Revised Edition
DAYTON KOHLER

Consulting Editor, Revised Second Edition
LAURENCE W. MAZZENO

SALEM PRESS
Pasadena, California   Englewood Cliffs, New Jersey

Editor in Chief: Dawn P. Dawson

Consulting Editor: Laurence W. Mazzeno	*Managing Editor:* Christina J. Moose
Project Editors: Eric Howard	*Research Supervisor:* Jeffry Jensen
Juliane Brand	*Research:* Irene McDermott
Acquisitions Editor: Mark Rehn	*Proofreading Supervisor:* Yasmine A. Cordoba
Production Editor: Cynthia Breslin Beres	*Layout:* William Zimmerman

∞ The paper used in these volumes conforms to the American National Standard for Permanence of Paper for Printed Library Materials, Z39.48-1984.

Library of Congress Cataloging-in-Publication Data
Masterplots / edited by Frank N. Magill; consulting editor, Laurence W. Mazzeno. — Rev. 2nd ed.
    p.   cm.
Expanded and updated version of the 1976 rev. ed.
Includes bibliographical references and indexes.
1. Literature—Stories, plots, etc. 2. Literature—History and criticism. I. Magill, Frank Northen, 1907-1997. II. Mazzeno, Laurence W.
PN44.M33   1996
809—dc20   96-23382
ISBN 0-89356-084-7 (set)   CIP
ISBN 0-89356-091-x (volume 7)

Revised Second Edition
Third Printing

LIST OF TITLES IN VOLUME 7

Revised Second Edition

THE LOST WEEKEND

Type of work: Novel
Author: Charles Reginald Jackson (1903-1968)
Type of plot: Psychological realism
Time of plot: October, 1936
Locale: New York City
First published: 1944

Principal characters:
DON BIRNAM, an alcoholic
WICK, his brother
HELEN, his friend

The Story:

Three days after his last drinking binge, Don Birnam sat alone in the apartment he shared with his younger brother Wick. Wick had gone to meet their friend Helen at a concert after failing to persuade Don that he should join them. After a short time alone, Don became agitated and impulsively decided to drink again. Taking money Wick had left for the maid, he went to Sam's bar. While looking in the mirror he conceived a short story called "In a Glass" based on his own sensitive youth and subsequent adult failures. He returned home and watched from hiding as Wick left for a long weekend in the country, a trip originally planned to help Don's recovery. Again alone in the apartment, Don reflected on all the broken promises he had made to the brother who was now supporting him. After another drink he became elated and decided to go out. Borrowing money from a laundrywoman, he proceeded to a bar in Greenwich Village. He began to drink and to imagine himself more sophisticated than the other patrons, but, on a sudden whim, he stole a woman's handbag. Just as he was congratulating himself on his performance as a thief, the doorman apprehended him and pushed him into the street. In acute embarrassment, he rushed home and drank in search of oblivion.

Don awoke, not knowing if it were morning or early evening. He realized he was off on another binge and would not be able to stop until he was physically unable to get liquor. He reflected on his career as an alcoholic and remembered with disgust his pretensions of the previous night. He knew too well that he was anything but a worldly sophisticate. Furthermore, who would want to read the short story he now self-contemptuously dismissed as a tale of "a punk and a drunk"? He understood himself; he realized his basic immaturity; he knew drink led only to misery, yet he felt no hope of ever stopping. Changes of scenery, trips abroad, psychiatry—nothing helped; he always drank again.

Don bought a bottle and returned home for "safe" drinking. After fantasizing himself as a great pianist, he grew restless and ventured out again. Eventually, he wandered back to Sam's bar. Over drinks, he told Gloria, the hostess, an involved lie that he was a rich man with a frigid wife. Gloria agreed to meet him after work, and he came home to drink and wait. He began to reminisce, eventually recalling his expulsion from a fraternity for suspected homosexuality. Overwhelmed with self-pity, he gulped liquor until he passed out.

Don awoke to an empty bottle, cursing himself for drinking the last drop the previous night. He knew he must have more liquor, but somehow he had lost all his money. Faint and sick, he took his typewriter to a pawnbroker, amazed that he could walk so far. Finding the door locked, he staggered dozens of blocks down the busy avenue, but every pawnshop was closed for a holiday. Exhausted, he fled home and borrowed liquor money from the grocer. After a soothing drink, he reflected that his quest to pawn his typewriter would make a good story—but to whom could he tell it? He had no friends left; drinking had made him a pariah. Abruptly deciding that he needed to get more liquor while he was able, he left the apartment. Distracted by trying to appear sober before his neighbors, he fell down two flights of stairs and knocked himself unconscious.

This time he awoke in the alcoholic ward of the hospital with a black eye and a fractured skull. Men with delirium tremens babbled and moaned around him. The doctor on duty treated him with detached impersonality. Bim, an aggressively homosexual male nurse, seemed to be both taunting and propositioning him. Don refused further treatment and signed himself out of the hospital. Somehow he had lost his money again, but Sam accepted his watch in exchange for a bottle. Gloria upbraided him for missing their date, but Don did not even remember making it. He went home, determined to stay there and drink quietly. After pretending to be a literature professor and Shakespearean actor, he passed out and had a long, vivid dream. He awoke weeping, drained his bottle, and passed out again.

He came to with no liquor and no hope of getting any. Whisperings came out of nowhere; then other auditory and visual hallucinations occurred. Don sat suffering for hours, tortured by the ringing of the telephone. He knew the caller was Helen, the woman who once loved and now pitied him, but he could not bring himself to answer. Hours later, Helen found him trembling in a chair and took him to her apartment. She cleaned and fed him, but he still had to face delirium. Don watched in horror as a bat attacked and devoured a mouse, but Helen showed him it was a hallucination. She reassured Wick by phone that Don was recovering.

The next morning, Don still craved alcohol. After failing to manipulate Helen's maid into opening the liquor closet, he considered murdering the woman, but instead stole Helen's fur and pawned it for five dollars. On the way to the store, he discovered all of his lost money in the breast pocket of his suit—during blackouts he had put it there for safekeeping, but forgot it each time. Now he had plenty of cash; he bought six pints and returned home. Wick was back from the country but temporarily out of the apartment. Don hid two bottles in the toilet tank, hung two more out the window, put one in the bookcase for Wick to confiscate, and gulped the last one. Drunk again, he reflected that he was home and safe; his ordeal was over. Why, he wondered, did everyone make such a fuss?

Critical Evaluation:

The Lost Weekend is both a psychologically realistic study of an alcoholic personality and an intensely dramatic narrative. Author Charles Jackson demonstrates that he is adept at various modern fiction techniques, and his protagonist Don Birnam—like the intelligent, sensitive alcoholics in the works of F. Scott Fitzgerald and Ernest Hemingway—transcends the nineteenth century stereotype of alcoholics as villains or lowlifes. Jackson, however, also diverges sharply from Fitzgerald and Hemingway's tendency to treat alcoholism as a somewhat noble and artistic reaction to the cruel bourgeois world. Don's "modern" sensibilities serve only as fuel for the flame of alcoholic rationalization, and the real life of the alcoholic is revealed in *The Lost Weekend* as being the furthest thing from noble.

The Lost Weekend has many autobiographical elements; Jackson admitted that all but two of the plot points in the story were taken from his own experiences, and he clearly understands the terror, loneliness, and hopelessness of the drinker. His accomplishment is even more noteworthy because he is working against type. On the surface, Don Birnam is the antithesis of the hopeless drunk: He is sensitive, articulate, well-dressed, and from a good family. Unlike the typical problem drinker in literature, Don never denies that he is an alcoholic. He is acutely aware of his other psychological problems, yet self-knowledge is no help. He has drunk himself out of society and into an unhealthy dependent relationship with his younger brother and his former fiancée, and he teeters on the brink of destitution and institutionalization. He is not a romantic hero; he is only a constant source of frustration and sometimes a real danger to himself and to everyone around him.

Psychoanalysis was popular in the 1930's, and Jackson incorporates many psychoanalytic interpretations of human behavior into Don's tortured reflections. Glimpses of Freudian staples (narcissism, arrested adolescence, latent homosexuality, sibling rivalry, passive aggression, the Oedipus complex) abound. Don is haunted by mirrors, beset with portentous dreams. Yet *The Lost Weekend* transcends all Freudian paradigms, and Don's problems defy any neat psychiatric solutions. Following the lead of Alcoholics Anonymous, Jackson portrays alcoholism as a spiritual illness ultimately impossible to deal with on logical terms. The loss of friends and livelihood and his trip to the alcoholic ward show that Don has passed a crucial milestone in the progression from periodic to chronic alcoholism, and, for all his grandiose philosophizing, the standard alcoholic's abyss awaits him.

The Lost Weekend's grim tone and gritty realism were considered rather sordid in 1944, but the book was generally well-received by contemporary reviewers. Soon after its publication, it was made into a popular movie starring Ray Milland, with a new "happy" ending provided by Jackson himself. Perhaps in part due to its popular success, literary critics have largely ignored the novel in discussions of alcoholism in twentieth century literature, preferring to dwell upon the tragic hero-drunks of Fitzgerald and Hemingway and the densely symbolic *Under the Volcano* (1947) by Malcolm Lowry, who made the trials of his alcoholic protagonist stand for nothing less than the throes of the modern world.

Whatever one thinks of Jackson's decision to focus on the harsh reality of Don's predicament, the author's sure sense of craft is enough to assure its place in modern literature. Using an objective third-person perspective, incorporating seamless flashbacks and bursts of stream-of-consciousness, the narrative achieves the immediacy of a first-person narrative without sacrificing the ability to venture outside the knowledge of the central character. The reader is able to follow the protagonist even when Don forgets where he has been; the careful reader can spot the inconsistencies in Don's self-analysis. Thus both narrator and reader understand Don's past, and have a surer sense of his future, than Don himself could possibly achieve. Jackson succeeds in making Don as sympathetic, and yet as revolting and exasperating to the reader who knows his innermost thoughts, as Don is to the other players in the novel, who only see him on his surface. By stripping all romantic and symbolic pretension from the enigma of alcoholism, Jackson has arguably accomplished one of the finest literary presentations of the alcoholic character.

Richard A. Hill

Bibliography:
Alcoholics Anonymous. 1st ed. New York: Works, 1939. This landmark text examines alcoholism from the layperson's perspective; Jackson cited it later as a primary source for the view of alcoholic progression in *The Lost Weekend*. Basically a spiritual guide for the recovering alcoholic, many first-person accounts in the story section parallel Don Birnam's sordid adventures and downward spiral.
Crowley, John W. *The White Logic: Alcoholism and Gender in American Modernist Fiction.* Amherst: University of Massachusetts Press, 1994. Excellent discussion of drinking in Amer-

ican fiction, with historical background and literary antecedents to the modern age. A heavily annotated chapter on *The Lost Weekend* includes biographical information on Jackson and puts the novel in perspective as a postscript to the novels of the 1920's and 1930's featuring the "heroic drunk."

Gilmore, Thomas B. *Equivocal Spirits: Alcoholism and Drinking in Twentieth Century Literature.* Chapel Hill: University of North Carolina Press, 1987. Carries the discussion of alcoholism in literature to the postmodern 1960's and 1970's. *The Lost Weekend* is largely ignored, but Gilmore discusses Jackson and Don Birnam as a backdrop to praise of Malcolm Lowry's "more compelling and complex" alcoholic hero in *Under the Volcano*.

Spectorsky, A. C. Review of *The Lost Weekend*, by Charles Reginald Jackson. *Book Week*, January 30, 1944, 4. In this contemporary analysis, Spectorsky discusses the unique and "spectacular" writing techniques employed by Jackson. Though he admits the book is shocking, it is never so for shock value alone; rather Jackson aims at "accuracy and the complete truth."

Wilson, Edmund. Review of *The Lost Weekend. The New Yorker* 19 (February 5, 1944): 78. Another contemporary review that generally praises the novel, but Wilson ultimately finds the story a disappointment because of its lack of dramatic climax.

THE LOST WORLD

Type of work: Poetry
Author: Randall Jarrell (1914-1965)
First published: 1965

The Lost World is the last book Randall Jarrell prepared for publication, and it is considered his finest work. The lost world of the title is, first of all, the world of childhood, inevitably lost as the child grows into adulthood. Innocence is lost to experience, ignorance to knowledge, and immediate reality to habit and routine. Childhood can only be recovered in memory and given limited immortality in works of art. Individual consciousness is extinguished in death, the final loss of the world for everyone. The earth, too, is finite, but this knowledge brings wisdom, which also depends on recovering the child's way of viewing the world with what Jarrell calls "interest." It evokes what he calls "adoration" for life and empathy for all things that die.

In the title poem, "The Lost World," Jarrell remembers his own childhood, when he lived for a while with his grandparents, Pop and Mama, and his great-grandmother, Dandeen, in Hollywood, California. The poem is divided into three sections. In the first, "Children's Arms," Jarrell recalls himself as a boy of twelve, coming home from school on Friday to begin his weekend. He passes a Hollywood lot, where a papier-mâché dinosaur and a pterodactyl look over the fence of the movie set for *The Lost World*. When he gets home, the boy arms himself with his homemade bow and arrows, ready to climb to his tree house and begin his real life of make-believe.

At the beginning of adolescence, the boy is already losing his innocence. He wakes up Saturday morning trying to remember his dream of a wolf and a tall girl. Then he accompanies Pop to the adult world of work, where he realizes that "the secret the grown-ups share, is what to do to make money." That evening the boy escapes back into childhood when he listens to Pop's stories about his own childhood. In "A Night with Lions," part 2 of "The Lost World," Jarrell remembers his young aunt, who took him with her when she visited a friend who owned the Metro-Goldwyn-Mayer lion. He confesses his "dream discovery" that his breath comes faster whenever he hears someone with her voice. She gives him the image he will seek to find in the woman he marries, compelling him into adulthood.

In "A Street off Sunset," part 3 of "The Lost World," Jarrell recounts the boy's growing knowledge of good and evil. On Sunday evening, he is reading a book about a mad scientist, who is planning to destroy the world. Forced to go to bed, he puts his arms around Mama, Pop, and Dandeen, and they put theirs around him. Caring for one another is the good that contrasts with the evil of the scientist. The boy claims not to believe in God, but in bed he listens to a woman preaching on the radio. He imagines her holding out her arms to release people from the "bonds of sin, of sleep."

The next morning he finishes his book as he gets ready for school. Good is victorious over evil. After school, though, he learns that issues of good and evil are not always clear. Dandeen tells him her memories of the Civil War, and he watches Mama wring the neck of a chicken, its headless body "lunging and reeling" in "great flopping circles." He realizes this could happen to him. With renewed worry about the scientist, he asks Pop if someone could really destroy the world. Pop reassures him that no one can.

In contrast to the focus on childhood in "The Lost World," Jarrell portrays adulthood in "Hope." The child has grown up to become a husband and the father of his own child. It is two o'clock in the morning of Christmas Eve. The man's wife and son are asleep. Noticing the fir tree, covered in artificial snow, on top of a pile of presents, he says "a man is a means." He works to make money for his family. Dissatisfied with his life, he says he would rather live in the squirrel's nest in the dream his son is having. He remembers wanting to tell his wife his nightmare about "the God Fish," who told him the story of Sleeping Beauty. In their version, however, she wakes when the prince kisses her, only to turn over and go back to sleep. She sleeps inside the wife/mother. The boy, the prince, inside the husband/father would like to recover the girl in his wife. He considers waking her, but he imagines she would only tell him that he is dreaming. Then he thinks—"later on, who knows?"

Like the wife in "Hope," most of the adults in *The Lost World* sleep through life, unless something wakes them to the repressed knowledge of their own mortality. Such is the speaker of "Next Day." An affluent, middle-aged housewife, she has everything she wished for as a girl: a husband, a house, and children. Having attended the funeral of a friend on the previous day, she has become acutely aware of her age. She is bewildered that the boy putting groceries in her car does not see her. She remembers when the world looked at her and its "mouth watered." She realizes now that she is not "exceptional." Her dead friend's face and body could be her face and body. Even though her life is "commonplace and solitary," she is afraid it will change, like her friend's.

Anxiety about death is also the subject of "In Montecito." When the speaker, who lives in this fashionable suburb of Santa Barbara, is "visited" one midnight by a "scream with breasts," he thinks of the recent death of an acquaintance, Greenie Taliaferro. In his nightmare, the scream comes from a billboard that contractors are tearing down. They strip off the "lips, let the air out of the breasts." Greenie's life is as temporary as the billboard, and Montecito is a place of death-in-life. In spite of money, or because of it, existence there is static, sterile, and suffocating. When the inhabitants pass from their sleep of life into the annihilation of death, they disappear into the "Greater Montecito" that "surrounds Montecito like the echo of a scream."

In "The One Who Was Different," Jarrell reveals that staying awake in life depends on the acceptance of death. The speaker is attending the funeral of Miss I——, who considered herself different from others but who suffers the common human fate. Having been around the world twice, she lies in her casket, ready for the next trip—the trip to the grave. She has lived in the "earnest expectation" of life after death, but the speaker states that life is only a "temporary arrangement of the matter." At this point, the speaker notices a child waiting "eagerly" to look at death, another secret that grown-ups share. The child looks, not with "sympathy or empathy" but with "interest"—"Without me." Interest is objective and reveals what is, rather than being subjective and revealing what one wishes. The speaker knows this. He wishes he could have made Miss I—— see that those who make up their minds about death, if they accept mortality, could live in a state of "interest" and experience life as what it is and as it is—a kind of dream, or poem.

Most of Jarrell's adults have lost the capacity to experience the immediate reality of life because they have repressed or denied the reality of death and gone to sleep in the habits and routines of adulthood. Two poems in *The Lost World*, taken from one of Jarrell's children's books, *The Bat Poet* (1964), represent the child's way of experiencing life with "interest." "Bats" is a verbal rendition of a mother bat flying back and forth at night feeding on insects, while her baby clings to her. At dawn, she returns to her rafter, where she sleeps with her wings folded "about her sleeping child." In a similar poem, "The Bird of Night," an owl flies back and forth while all living creatures "hold their breath." Both poems re-create immediate reality.

In "The Mockingbird," also from *The Bat Poet*, Jarrell relates the child's way of experiencing life to that of the poet; the poet, the adult who has stayed awake, recovers life from death in memory and re-creates it in imagination. All day the mockingbird, an image of the poet, drives away other birds, even a black cat. Then, as the sun goes down and the moon rises—that juncture of life and death—the mockingbird imitates life. A thrush, then a thrasher, then a jay is heard, as well as the meowing of a cat. The mockingbird has made "the world he drove away" his "own." The listener cannot tell which is the mockingbird, which the world. Art and reality are one.

In order to recover and transform experience—the "cheeping" and "squeaking" of experience become "singing" in the poem—the poet must see life not only with "interest" but also with "sympathy or empathy." These feelings are the subject of "In Galleries," which portrays three museum guards. The first represents indifference, the opposite of interest; the second represents sympathy and feeling for someone or something; and the third, who is a mute, represents empathy, the feeling with, becoming one with, someone or something. With a "rapt smile," the third guard takes out a magnifying glass and shows the visitor that in the painting of the woman holding the death of the world in her arms the "something" on the man's arm is "the woman's tear." Under this guard's guidance, empathy occurs. The visitor "and the guard and the man and the woman are dumbly one."

In "The Old and the New Masters," Jarrell speculates as to the likely result for the earth, and the life it nourishes, if the human race fails to develop empathy. He refers to Georges de la Tour's painting *St. Sebastian Mourned by St. Irene* to illustrate the old masters' view of suffering: "no one breathes/ As the sufferers watch the sufferer." Everyone has empathy with the sufferer because everyone is a sufferer. Jarrell refers to Hugo van der Goes' *Nativity* to illustrate the old masters' view of "adoration." In this painting, everything is fixed on the world's "small, helpless, human center"—the Christ child. For Jarrell, Christ represents the living, suffering body of the world.

Without adoration, the pure joy of beholding the miracle of being, there can be no empathy. The new masters paint a world that has lost adoration and empathy. At first, they put the crucifixion in a corner of the canvas. The Christ disappears from their paintings altogether. Finally, in a painting of the universe, the last master places a "bright spot" in a corner to represent "the small radioactive planet men called Earth." This passage is Jarrell's prophecy of the final loss of the world.

In "Thinking of the Lost World," Jarrell returns to the scene of his childhood in Hollywood, where he finds smog instead of sunshine. His bow and arrows are lost, and the planks of his tree house have been burned as firewood, but he realizes that age is like childhood and that the lost world still lives in his memory. In happiness, he holds in his hands—"Nothing: the nothing for which there's no reward." Life is a dream, a poem, that ends.

James Green

Bibliography:
Bryant, J. A., Jr. *Understanding Randall Jarrell.* Columbia: University of South Carolina Press, 1986. A good introduction to all of Jarrell's work. Treats *The Lost World* in chapter 5.
Ferguson, Suzanne. *The Poetry of Randall Jarrell.* Baton Rouge: Louisiana State University Press, 1971. The first book-length critical study of Jarrell's work. Includes an extensive analysis of *The Lost World.*
Flynn, Richard. *Randall Jarrell and the Lost World of Childhood.* Athens: University of Georgia Press, 1990. Detailed analysis of poems from *The Lost World.* Considers all of Jarrell's work in the context of his interest in childhood.

Pritchard, William H. *Randall Jarrell: A Literary Life*. 1st ed. New York: Farrar, Straus & Giroux, 1990. The first biography of Jarrell. Discusses the interaction of Jarrell's life and work. Chapter 10 treats *The Lost World*.

Quinn, Mary Bernetta. *Randall Jarrell*. Boston: Twayne, 1981. Contains useful information about Jarrell's childhood and provides analysis of "In Galleries" and "The Old and the New Masters."

LOVE FOR LOVE

Type of work: Drama
Author: William Congreve (1670-1729)
Type of plot: Comedy of manners
Time of plot: Seventeenth century
Locale: London
First performed: 1695; first published, 1695

> *Principal characters:*
> SIR SAMPSON LEGEND, a foolish old gentleman
> VALENTINE, his son, an indigent gallant
> BENJAMIN, another son, a sailor
> FORESIGHT, an old man given to astrology
> ANGELICA, his niece
> PRUE, his daughter
> MRS. FORESIGHT, his young second wife
> MISTRESS FRAIL, her sister

The Story:

Young Valentine Legend, having squandered all of his money in riotous living, was destitute and deeply in debt. With no property left but his books, he declared his intention of becoming a playwright, for his love for Angelica had indeed compelled him to take desperate measures. On hearing of his intention, Jeremy, his knavish manservant, showed alarm and said that Valentine's family would surely disown him.

Among Valentine's creditors was Trapland, a lecherous old scrivener who persisted in dunning him. When Valentine, who had been joined by his friend Scandal, subtly threatened Trapland with blackmail concerning a wealthy city widow, the old man suddenly forgot the money owed him.

Sir Sampson Legend's steward told Valentine that he could be released from all debts by signing over his rights as Sir Sampson's heir to Ben, his younger brother. If he signed, he would receive four thousand pounds in cash. In the meantime, Foresight, an old fool given to the science of prognostication, recalled Prue, his bumpkin daughter, from the country. Foresight planned to marry her to Ben Legend.

Angelica, wealthy, young, and clever, reproved her uncle for his belief in astrology. Irate, Foresight threatened to end her friendship with Valentine. Angelica, piqued, insinuated that Mrs. Foresight, the old man's young second wife, was not true to him.

Sir Sampson Legend, a great teller of tall tales of world travel, arranged with Foresight for the marriage of Ben and Prue. When Sir Sampson playfully hinted to Foresight that Mrs. Foresight might not be a faithful wife, Foresight threatened to break off the marriage agreement. Sir Sampson quickly made amends.

Valentine, seeking Angelica, encountered his father at Foresight's house. He was indignant when his father disowned him as a son, and he begged his father to change his mind about the conditions under which he could be freed of debt.

When Mrs. Foresight rebuked her sister for her indiscretion in frequenting the haunts of gamesters and gallants, Mistress Frail revealed her knowledge of Mrs. Foresight's own indiscretions. Mistress Frail then declared her intention of marrying Ben and enlisted her sister's aid in the project. Prue, meanwhile, found herself charmed by Tattle, a voluble young dandy. When Mrs. Foresight and Mistress Frail encouraged Tattle to court Prue, he was mystified because he knew of the marriage arranged between Prue and Ben. Even so, he gave Prue a lesson in the art of love, a lesson that progressed as far as her bedchamber. Tattle, having grown tired of dalliance with the rude country girl, was relieved when Prue's nurse found them.

Ben, returning from a sea voyage, declared that marriage did not interest him at the moment, but he visibly changed his mind when Mistress Frail flattered him. Left alone, he and Prue expressed dislike for each other. Ben declared that he talked to Prue only to obey his father.

Scandal, in Valentine's behalf, ingratiated himself with Foresight by pretending a knowledge of astrology. His scheme having succeeded, he convinced Foresight that it was not in the stars for Valentine to sign over his inheritance or for Ben and Prue to marry. Attracted to Mrs. Foresight, Scandal hoodwinked old Foresight in order to pay gallant attentions to his young wife. Ben and Mistress Frail confessed their love and decided to marry.

Scandal had reported that Valentine was ill, so Angelica went to his lodgings. In spite of Scandal's insistence that her acknowledgment of love for Valentine would cure the young man, she quickly detected a trick and departed. Sir Sampson and a lawyer named Buckram arrived to get Valentine's signature on the documents they had prepared. Jeremy insisted that Valentine was out of his mind. Buckram said that the signature would be invalid under the circumstances, but Sir Sampson forced his way into his son's presence. Valentine, pretending complete lunacy, called himself Truth and declared that he would give the world the lie. After the frightened Buckram left, Valentine showed clarity of mind, but, when the lawyer was called back, Valentine again seemed to lapse into lunacy.

Mistress Frail, having learned that there was little chance of Ben's getting the whole estate, broke off their engagement. Sir Sampson, frustrated by Valentine, decided to marry and beget a new heir. Mrs. Foresight plotted with Jeremy to marry Mistress Frail, disguised as Angelica, to Valentine during one of his fits of madness. When Jeremy revealed the scheme to Valentine and Scandal, the friends, in their turn, planned to marry Mistress Frail to Tattle by means of another disguise.

After Valentine had confessed his feigned madness to Angelica, she expressed disappointment. She decided to test his love of her. She then went to Sir Sampson, learned his new state of mind, and suggested that he and she go through with a mock marriage ceremony in order to bring Valentine to his senses. When foolish Sir Sampson suggested that they actually get married so that she could inherit his estate, Angelica said that his plan would not be advisable because the papers leaving the estate to Ben were already drawn up.

Jeremy tricked foolish Tattle into believing that he, disguised as a friar, might marry Angelica, who would be disguised as a nun. Prue, forsaken by Tattle, asserted that she would marry Robin, the butler, who had professed his love for her.

Mistress Frail, thinking that she was marrying Valentine, and Tattle, thinking that he was marrying Angelica, were thus tricked into wedlock. Told by Angelica that she intended to marry his father, Valentine in despair declared that he was ready to sign over his inheritance. Impressed by this indication of his love for her, Angelica tore up the bond, which Sir Sampson had given her, and she brought the doting old man to his senses by revealing that she had always intended to marry Valentine. Sir Sampson and old Foresight consoled each other; they admitted that they had acted like fools.

Critical Evaluation:

As a genre, dramatic comedy has always had its stock characters: the cunning servant; the foolish, foppish socialite; the wrong-headed, demanding parent; the thwarted lovers. Comedy also has familiar plot devices: multiple stories, disguises, intrigues, and misapprehensions. William Congreve's third comedy, *Love for Love*, generally considered one of his finest, is certainly no exception regarding such conventions. The plot is relatively simple and not particularly original. It does have elements reminiscent of William Shakespeare's drama (the theme of madness, for example, recalls, with comic irony, *Hamlet*, 1600-1601, and *King Lear*, 1605-1606) or Ben Jonson's dark comedies of humours (evidenced by Foresight's obsession with astrology or Sir Sampson's avarice and lechery), not to mention earlier Restoration plays. Congreve, however, creates from these derivative elements a play with distinctly late Restoration characteristics, language, and attitudes. The play enjoyed great popularity during its time and has remained entertaining. *Love for Love* is enlightening as well, for in it Congreve takes up an array of issues, including wit, fashion, sexual conduct, marriage, and family.

Love for Love is a comedy of manners, a play about social behavior, social language, and social intrigue. Its characters are two-dimensional, their ideas without any apparent substance, their actions silly and self-centered. What appears to be most important, as the opening scene between Valentine and Jeremy indicates, is one's ability to turn a witty phrase and to dupe others. Congreve's play is more than just a frenetic piece of stagecraft with characters running to and fro. At the heart of the play, there lies a set of questions that are emblematized by Valentine's role as "Truth" during his feigned madness: What is true? What is true friendship? What is true knowledge? What is true love? What is the truth of human relationships? Can one honestly navigate through a world based on deception and self-interest? These questions dominate the play's characters, language, events, and structure.

Congreve reveals his answers through three sets of contrasting characters, their contrasting actions, and their contrasting levels of social success. In this way, he leads the audience to recognize the distinctions between true wit (intelligence and judgment) and false wit (accidental cleverness or duplicity), and between true love (self-sacrifice) and false love (self-love or self-interest).

The rustics Prue and Ben enter the play honest and straightforward, but this honesty prevents them from effectively operating in society. Ben blusters around and then simply goes back to sea. Prue eagerly learns the deceitful ways and the sexual freedoms of a society woman, but she lacks the discretion needed to control them. Unmanageable truth serves neither one of these characters.

The second set of characters includes the city gallants, both male and female. Each believes himself or herself a social expert, a wit, and a skillful lover, but the truth is somewhat different. Scandal's attitude toward and relationships with women are cynical and selfish. Tattle's sexual escapades and his flippant attitude toward women, evidenced by his treatment of Prue, make him vulnerable to the machinations of those more cunning than he. Bored and unhappy Mrs. Foresight is false to her husband and her lover. Mercenary Mistress Frail is interested only in attaching herself to a man with a fortune. Each one is victimized by his or her own deception and self-deception.

The two fathers in the play also fall into this category of wise fools. Foresight looks for wisdom in the stars, but he cannot see his wife's infidelity. Unlike his counterpart's extraterrestrial focus, Sir Sampson's vision is limited to the terrestrial, namely his estate, his sons, and his own body. Both men are locked in their own limited, failed visions, excluded from true human relationships. Both are also manipulated and disdained by those around them.

Much of *Love for Love*'s highly complicated plot—the intrigues, the manipulations, the stratagems to gain money, sex, or power—is generated by these secondary characters. Motivated by egotism, vanity, greed, and revenge, they fracture their world (and the play). As represented by these characters, human relationships are, at worst, predatory, and at best ambiguous and fragile. Everyone seems to be speaking his or her own language, a point that Congreve intensifies with a variety of figurative images—nautical, astrological, zoological, religious, and legal—and acting according to a set of rules with no heart and no basis in moral truth. Those who believe themselves masters of the game are ultimately victimized by it; those who cannot, or will not, play the game according to its rules withdraw from it.

These three categories of characters are only one dimension of Congreve's play, however, for amid all the frenetic scheming of the others stand two characters, Valentine and Angelica. In a sense, the play has a double emphasis: Alongside the darkly satirical look at the foolishness of society and its mavens exists the love story of its hero and heroine. Valentine and Angelica are nevertheless very much a part of the world they inhabit. Valentine has at least one illegitimate child, he has foolishly lost his fortune to fashionable living, and he tries to trick his way out of the situation. Angelica is witty, disrespectful, cruel, and not above plotting an intrigue herself. These two characters occupy the middle ground between corruption and perfection: They are wise, witty, and worldly, and yet they are recoverable. Despite all of his faults, Valentine remains true to his love for Angelica—he is willing to martyr himself for her—and she remains true to him.

The sentimentality of their final declaration of love may seem incongruous with the rest of the action, but the ending is of a piece with both the play's social satire and its underlying moral plot, and the reformation of a rake. Angelica ("angel") puts Valentine ("lover") to the test in order to teach him, as well as the other characters, what true love is. Their blending of true wit and true love finally rewards the couple with both the greatest social and personal success: She has her fortune, he will inherit his father's estate, and they will have their marriage. Their union even converts the cynical Scandal from his misbehavior and his misconceptions. Ultimately, the title of the play sums up its social satire and its moral lesson: Love for love's sake.

"Critical Evaluation" by Judith Burdan

Bibliography:
Hoffman, Arthur W. *Congreve's Comedies*. Victoria, B.C., Canada: University of Victoria, English Literary Studies, 1993. Chapter on *Love for Love* focuses on the roles of Valentine and Angelica as romantic hero and heroine, and on Sir Sampson as blocking agent. Shows how Congreve skillfully employs allusions to biblical, classical, and Shakespearean traditions.

Markley, Robert. *Two-Edg'd Weapons: Style and Ideology in the Comedies of Etherege, Wycherley, and Congreve*. Oxford, England: Clarendon Press, 1988. Argues that Congreve is stylistically a transitional figure between earlier satirical comedies and the later sentimental comedies.

Novak, Maximillian E. *William Congreve*. New York: Twayne, 1971. A good, basic overview of Congreve's life and works. Discusses his various works, with a chapter on *Love for Love*, and the intellectual, artistic, and moral debates of his period. Useful annotated bibliography of critical works from the seventeenth to the twentieth century.

Van Voris, W. H. *The Cultivated Stance: The Designs of Congreve's Plays*. Dublin: Dolmen Press, 1965. Discusses Congreve's social, philosophical, and aesthetic values. Argues that *Love for Love* represents a chaotic world populated by monsters driven by vanity and self-interest. Valentine and Angelica's love brings about order, but only ambiguously.

Williams, Aubrey. *An Approach to Congreve*. New Haven, Conn.: Yale University Press, 1979. Asserts that the world represented on the Restoration stage appears chaotic but is actually ordered by providential design. Finds in *Love for Love* a pattern of testing, trial, and judgment, at the center of which Angelica stands as judge and reward.

LOVE IN A WOOD
Or, St. James's Park

Type of work: Drama
Author: William Wycherley (1641?-1715)
Type of plot: Comedy of manners
Time of plot: Seventeenth century
Locale: London
First performed: 1671; first published, 1672

Principal characters:
> MR. RANGER, a young man-about-town
> LYDIA, his cousin and betrothed
> MR. VALENTINE, a gallant lately returned to London
> CHRISTINA, his betrothed
> MR. VINCENT, a confidant of all the lovers
> ALDERMAN GRIPE, an elderly usurer
> MISTRESS MARTHA, his daughter
> LADY FLIPPANT, his sister, in London to find a husband
> SIR SIMON ADDLEPLOT, an indomitable fortune hunter
> MR. DAPPERWIT, a fop and a would-be gentleman
> MRS. JOYNER, a matchmaker and procuress
> MRS. CROSSBITE, a blackmailer and procuress
> LUCY, her daughter

The Story:

Lady Flippant, a widow disappointed in her efforts to find a new husband, berated her matchmaker, Mrs. Joyner, for not finding a wealthy young man to relieve her impecunious position. The lady's brother, Alderman Gripe, had grown tired of her foppish visitors, especially the witless Mr. Dapperwit. At the suggestion of the cozening Mrs. Joyner and the double-dealing Dapperwit, Sir Simon Addleplot disguised himself and gained employment as a clerk to the miserly Gripe in order to woo the usurer's daughter, Mistress Martha, and through her secure her father's fortune. Not realizing that he had been gulled into masquerading as Jonas the clerk, Sir Simon was also duped into believing that he was loved by Lady Flippant, who was really enamored of Dapperwit.

Together with Mr. Vincent, his friend and confidant, Mr. Ranger was about to go into St. James's Park in search of amorous adventure when he was discovered by his cousin and betrothed, Lydia. He avoided her, however, and dined with the gulled Sir Simon, Dapperwit, and Lady Flippant for the diversion of watching the work of Mrs. Joyner, who had already made twenty crowns through introductions and would obtain a hundred if Sir Simon got Mistress Martha or fifty if he got Lady Flippant. The widow spurned Sir Simon, flirted with Dapperwit, and hinted at matrimony to both Ranger and Vincent.

Later, all promenaded through St. James's Park in the hope of discovering one another's intrigues. Lydia, recognizing Ranger, ran into the house of her friend Christina in order to avoid a compromising meeting with her betrothed. Ranger pursued her, only to become enamored of Christina, who was faithfully waiting the return to London of her fiancé, Mr. Valentine. In order to help Lydia, Christina pretended to be the young woman he had pursued from the park. Once her little act was over, she sent the impertinent young man away. Ranger, in despair because he had not learned the fair unknown's name, had no idea that Lydia had heard his gallant speeches to Christina.

Ranger went to the home of his friend Vincent. Valentine, in danger of his life from a rival, was in hiding there, for he wished no one to know of his return from France before his loved one did. The concealed Valentine overheard Ranger ask the name of the young woman whom he had pursued into her apartment. When Vincent said that the apartment was Christina's, Valentine became convinced that his beloved had been untrue to him.

In contrast to this sequence of mistaken and confused identities, the busy Mrs. Joyner was more positive in identifying Lucy, the daughter of her friend Mrs. Crossbite, as the object of hypocritical old Gripe's lust. The solicitous mother, pleased with this development, ordered her recalcitrant daughter to give up her love for Dapperwit. Dapperwit, thinking to cure Ranger's melancholy over Christina, brought him to see Lucy, but the girl repulsed Dapperwit for his infidelity and what she thought was his intention of procuring her for Ranger. The jilted fop recovered his spirits, however, when he received a message delivered by Jonas, the supposed clerk, which held out the promise of a later assignation that might, Dapperwit hoped, lead to a wedding.

As the gallants departed, the ever-busy Mrs. Joyner brought the furtive Alderman Gripe to see Lucy. His hasty lust frightened her, however, and she screamed. Though he dickered in true miserly fashion, Gripe was coerced into paying five hundred pounds hush money to Mrs. Crossbite. Lady Flippant, at the same time, was making advances to the defenseless Dapperwit, and the nimble-footed lovers, Ranger and Lydia, were busy at double deception. Lydia denied that she had been in the park jealously searching for him; Ranger assured her that he had called for her as he had promised.

The Gripe household was in an uproar. The sly old man was busily attempting to hide his shame and regain his money, and Mrs. Joyner virtuously pretended horror at the treatment he had received at the hands of Mrs. Crossbite. Jonas, meanwhile, made love to Lady Flippant, who protested only after she learned that her seducer was really Sir Simon Addleplot, the man she hoped eventually to marry. So the poor man, undone by his own deceit, lost Mistress Martha through his dissembling ways and Dapperwit's roguery.

To test Ranger, Lydia sent him a letter to which she signed Christina's name, asking the gallant to meet her that evening at St. James's Gate. The wronged Christina had since learned of her lover's return, and Valentine was at that time trying to reassure himself of her innocence. Overhearing Ranger's new plans unsettled him again, though his eavesdropping on a conversation between Christina and Vincent and then on one between Christina and her supposed lover finally set his mind at rest. Lydia also confessed her part in this lovers' plot and counterplot, and the two couples, thus reunited, decided that matrimony was the only sure solution to love's equation.

The false lovers found no such easy solution, however, so addle-witted and dapper-plotted had their intrigues become. Sir Simon, still passing as Jonas, escorted Mistress Martha to Dapperwit. He thought their embraces inopportune and inappropriate, but his arrangements for a parson, a supper, and a reception in nearby Mulberry Garden were not completely wasted. Propelled to the same garden by the two scheming procuresses, Alderman Gripe married Lucy to be revenged on his son-in-law, Dapperwit, who had taken a bride six months pregnant. In the end, Sir Simon took widowed Lady Flippant as his wife, just as she had intended. Thus were all the honest ladies made wives and all the bawds made honest in St. James's Park.

Critical Evaluation:

The first of three satiric comedies, *Love in a Wood: Or, St. James's Park* shows brilliantly the genius of William Wycherley, who gained his insight as an intimate in high society on both sides of the English Channel. It was this play that gained for the young man the king's favor and the love of the king's mistress, the duchess of Cleveland.

As Wycherley uses the phrase, "in a wood" means "confused"; such a description might apply as well to the audience and readers of this play as to the characters in it, for by the end there are no less than five marriages, one accomplished and four in prospect. The unusually large quantity of couples, the complicated intrigues in which they indulge, and the various unravelings that are required, keep the play bustling with physical and dramatic movement. It is, however, a movement less controlled than in the playwright's later satiric masterpieces, *The Country Wife* (1675) and *The Plain-Dealer* (1676).

The play contains many of the motifs of deception that were to become standard in Restoration comedy: disguises, mistaken identity, hiding, and overheard and misinterpreted conversations, all of which create confusion between appearance and reality. Valentine, for instance, hears an apparently compromising report of Christina and concludes that she is unfaithful; Gripe frantically attempts to maintain the pretense of Puritan piety and respectability; Sir Simon poses as a clerk, and then discovers to his consternation that Martha refuses to believe he is a knight. Critics have pointed out that Wycherley uses the metaphor of light and darkness to dramatize social reality and inner reality; it is significant that most of the crucial revelations take place in the darkness, where truth can safely come out.

The characters are standard types: a fool, a hypocrite, a fop, a lecherous widow, and a wench, which make up the "low" plot, and a set of "realistic" lovers and a set of "ideal" ones, which make up the "high" plot. Wycherley skillfully uses Mrs. Joyner, on the one hand, and Vincent, on the other, to serve as go-betweens for the various characters and to lend coherence to the many strands of the action. Of course, Mrs. Joyner, the functionary of the low plot, helps only to increase the confusion, in accordance with the dictates of her financial interest; Vincent, on the other hand, with an earnest regard for the truth, does his best to clear up misunderstandings. The high plot characters profit by the unraveling, while the others, despite the prospect of their marriages, only succeed in duping themselves or in making the best of a bad bargain.

Like other Restoration comedies, *Love in a Wood* creates a highly realistic and immediate sense of contemporary London: Scenes unfold in places like Mulberry Garden and St. James's Park, and the dialogue is peppered with contemporary allusions and jokes. Like other comic dramatists of the period, Wycherley treats love as a battle between the sexes (metaphors of war and hunting abound), with women usually having the upper hand. Wycherley is distinctive, however, in his caustic wit and his cynical attitude toward human relationships. Aggression, lust, greed, and mistrust seem to be the main drives governing the behavior of his characters. Dissimulation is accepted as the norm, so the complicated intrigues of the plot are as much an indication of the necessary condition of life as of the development of a comic drama. The marriages of the low plot characters are motivated by either financial interest (and in the case of Sir Simon and Lady Flippant, a mistaken view of financial interest) or revenge. Lydia and Ranger seem to be on firmer ground, but the jealousy of the one and the philandering of the other are not, despite Ranger's protestations of reform, very reassuring. Only the marriage between Valentine and Christina, which is based on genuine love and honesty, seems to have any hopeful prospects; their relationship, however, (note Wycherley's choice of names) seems too idealized to be credible in this setting. Thus the exception only proves Wycherley's rule about love and marriage in Restoration London.

Bibliography:

Holland, Norman. *The First Modern Comedies*. Bloomington: Indiana University Press, 1959. Chapter on *Love in a Wood* focuses on Wycherley's structuring of the novel's intrigues and analyzes the play as a combination of high plot and low plot.

McCarthy, B. Eugene. *William Wycherley: A Biography*. Athens: Ohio University Press, 1979. A general biography. Discusses *Love in a Wood* in some detail as the product of a dramatist who lived and worked in a very specific social climate. Gives some attention to influences on Wycherley's writing of the play.

Rogers, Katharine M. *William Wycherley*. New York: Twayne, 1972. Provides production history as well as a discussion of Wycherley's borrowings from Pedro Calderón de la Barca's *Mornings in April and May* (c. 1637). Points out that although *Love in a Wood* is Wycherley's first play, it shows distinct elements of the moral awareness that would distinguish the playwright from his contemporaries.

Thompson, James. *Language in Wycherley's Plays*. Tuscaloosa: University of Alabama Press, 1984. Uses language theory as well as Restoration philosophies of language to discuss *Love in a Wood* as a good-humored comedy that employs a wide range of linguistic styles for a broadly comic rather than satiric effect.

Zimbardo, Rose A. *Wycherley's Drama*. New Haven, Conn.: Yale University Press, 1965. Introduces the idea of Wycherley's plays as English forms of classical satire. Discusses *Love in a Wood* as a pastoral tale transferred from the mythical forests of Arcadia to London's St. James's Park. Suggests that Wycherley's satiric effects add spice to what is basically a Renaissance play.

LOVE IN THE TIME OF CHOLERA

Type of work: Novel
Author: Gabriel García Márquez (1928-   )
Type of plot: Psychological realism
Time of plot: Late nineteenth and early twentieth centuries
Locale: Colombia, South America
First published: El amor en los tiempos del cólera, 1985 (English translation, 1988)

> *Principal characters:*
> FLORENTINO ARIZA, who is in love with Fermina
> FERMINA DAZA, a strong-willed woman
> DR. JUVENAL URBINO, her husband
> LORENZO DAZA, her father
> TRANSITO ARIZA, Florentino's mother
> LOTARIO THUGUT, Florentino's employer at the telegraph office
> DON LEO LOAYZA XII, Florentino's uncle
> JEREMIAH DE SAINT-AMOUR, a friend of Dr. Juvenal Urbino
> THE YOUNG DR. JUVENAL URBINO, son of Fermina and Dr. Juvenal
>   Urbino
> LUCRETIA DEL REAL DEL OBISPO, the young Dr. Urbino's wife
> HILLDEBRANDA SANCHEZ, Fermina's cousin

The Story:

Dr. Juvenal Urbino had been called to the residence of his friend Jeremiah de Saint-Amour, who had taken his own life the previous evening. From a letter that his friend had left him, Urbino learned that Saint-Amour had spent his final night with a female companion and that he was actually a fugitive who had indulged in cannibalism. Devastated by the knowledge, Urbino found his whole day unsettled. Late that afternoon, he fell to his death while trying to retrieve his parrot from his tree. Dr. Urbino's funeral took place the next day. After the funeral, and after years of waiting, one of the guests, Florentino Ariza, told Dr. Urbino's wife Fermina Daza that he loved her.

The relationship between Florentino and Fermina had begun more than fifty years earlier. Florentino, then working at a telegraph office, had delivered a message to Lorenzo Daza and fallen in love with Fermina, whom he saw in the sewing room. After this, Florentino daily sat on a bench in the park across from the Daza house, reading poetry but mostly waiting to see Fermina. After a brief correspondence between them, Fermina agreed to marry him and, after two years of secret courtship, they began to plan the wedding.

When Fermina's father discovered the plan, he took his daughter to Valledupar, the home of his relatives, where she found a sympathetic friend in her cousin Hilldebranda Sanchez. With Hilldebranda's help, Fermina continued to correspond with Florentino over the telegraph. Lorenzo realized that he could not control his daughter and gave her her freedom. In the midst of preparing for her wedding, however, Fermina in an abrupt about-face called off the engagement.

Eventually, she met Dr. Juvenal Urbino, a new doctor in the city who had just returned from his studies in Paris. He was committed to fighting cholera, and when Fermina was diagnosed as possibly having the disease, Urbino visited her house. Although he found her in perfect health, he returned repeatedly to the Daza household to see her. Initially, Fermina resisted the doctor's suit, but her cousin Hilldebranda finally persuaded Fermina to marry Urbino.

When he learned that Fermina would marry Dr. Urbino, Florentino was devastated, especially because he realized that the two did not love each other. To escape this painful situation, Florentino went on a voyage down the Magdalena River. On the journey, he lost his virginity and realized that sexual passion could temporarily block out his pain over losing Fermina. When he returned to the city, he had an affair with the Widow Nazaret, and after that he went from one woman to another.

Florentino's behavior at this point became enigmatical. On the one hand, he had decided to devote his life to winning back Fermina; he went to work for his Uncle Leo, who was president of the board of directors and manager of the River Company of the Caribbean, and advanced steadily. On the other hand, to cope with having lost Fermina, he became obsessed with other women.

At the same time, Fermina became disillusioned with her marriage. She saw that there was no passion between her and Urbino and that her husband fell far short of what a real man should be. Urbino was at heart a weak person whose social success depended largely on his family's name. Moreover, Fermina discovered that her husband was having an affair with Barbara Lynch, wife of a Presbyterian minister. Urbino's full confession of the affair infuriated her. She was further outraged when she learned that Juvenal had confessed his affair to the priest, whereas a real man as she saw it would have denied everything. She left her husband for two years to live with her cousin Hilldebranda, but when Juvenal finally came for her, she rejoiced, for then he was acting like a man.

After his Uncle Leo's retirement from the navigation company, Florentino became president of the board of directors and general manager. The promotion certainly elevated his social status, but it also frightened Florentino because it meant that he, like his uncle, must grow old and die. He therefore began a final affair, this time with America Vicuna, a fourteen-year-old girl for whom he acted as guardian and who reminded him of Fermina.

This affair ended when Florentino heard the bells tolling the death of an important citizen in the city. He returned to the city, learned that Dr. Juvenal Urbino had died, and told Fermina that he still loved her and that she was the only woman he had ever loved. At first, she maintained the distance that the years had put between them. Only when she lost her will to live did she allow Florentino back into her life, telling him that she wanted to escape everything associated with her marriage. He thereupon arranged a boat trip, which allowed him to be alone with Fermina. On the journey, Fermina realized that she loved Florentino. Florentino for his part not only saw his lifelong quest fulfilled, he also overcame his fear of mortality as he realized that only through love could he transcend the time and eminence of death that remained the only obstacles in his romance with Fermina.

Critical Evaluation:

Gabriel García Márquez is perhaps the most important Latin American writer of the second half of the twentieth century. His novels and stories are distinguished by a vivacity of style that clearly sets them apart from the pessimism often associated with early twentieth century Western literature. Yet his characters' acute sensitivity to the passage of time clearly shows the influence of one of the greatest twentieth century American writers, William Faulkner.

García Márquez's *Love in the Time of Cholera* can, in fact, be viewed as a novel both of tradition and of its own time. The story is a traditional love story focusing on two lovers who overcome many obstacles before they are united. Beyond that, however, the novel addresses the question of time and the related fear of death in a universe in which God's existence no longer seems assured. *Love in the Time of Cholera* represents the author's response to the notion that death is inescapable and final. García Márquez uses a framed plot, the interweaving narratives of Florentino and Fermina, and symbolism to assert that passionate love can transcend time and death.

The frame emphasizes the seeming inescapability of death. García Márquez begins the novel with the death of Jeremiah de Saint-Amour, who has committed suicide at the age of sixty because he can no longer fully enjoy human passion. García Márquez next presents the death of Dr. Juvenal Urbino, who proclaims his passion for Fermina at the moment of his death. After that, the narrative moves back in time to the stories of Florentino and Fermina. Only toward the end of the novel does García Márquez return to the deaths of Saint-Amour and Urbino, both of which in turn remind the now-elderly Florentino of his own inescapable death. With this frame, García Márquez establishes a tension between death and love and suggests that there is no escape from death.

Throughout the novel, constant references to cholera remind the characters as well as the reader of death. Regardless of Urbino's efforts to find a cure for cholera, the disease remains a fatal presence. Further, in an interesting bit of symbolism, when Dr. Urbino and his wife Fermina celebrate the transition from the nineteenth century to the twentieth by riding in a hot-air balloon, they see below them the bodies of people who have been killed in the latest political uprising. The message is clear: Death is ever-present and inescapable.

Yet the interweaving of the narratives of the two lovers reminds the readers that passionate love is not merely a constant in this novel but the only thing that allows the two main characters to transcend death. Florentino's passionate love for Fermina sustains him through a series of sexual encounters that he uses to cope with the pain of having been rejected by her; likewise, Fermina's love for Florentino, although she does not admit to it until old age, sustains her through the years of marriage to Urbino, who falls far short of being the man that she had hoped he would be. Following the funeral of her husband Juvenal Urbino, Fermina spends the night in bed unable to think about anyone but Florentino. Clearly, though she may have denied it to herself, she has loved Florentino since the moment of their separation. The fact, too, that the lovers' narrative continues beyond the deaths of Urbino and Saint-Amour—and that their romance is renewed—actually constitutes a journey beyond death that corresponds to Florentino and Fermina's final cruise down the Magdalena River, when Florentino does transcend his own mortality. Love is the constant that García Márquez uses to oppose that other constant, death.

García Márquez also uses symbolism to suggest the power of human passion over death. For instance, the smell of almonds, referred to in the opening line of the novel, is always associated with unrequited love and, throughout the novel, emphasizes the enduring presence of love in the midst of death. Although he may have indulged in cannibalism—symbolizing utter human depravity—Saint-Amour ("saint of love") is redeemed because he has lived and died for love. Indeed, in this novel, passionate love is sacred. Emphasizing this association, García Márquez often links love with the Holy Spirit: Romantic passion is as holy as God's love for humanity. It is therefore significant that the deaths of Saint-Amour and Urbino occur on Pentecost Sunday, the Christian holiday commemorating the outpouring of the Holy Spirit. During his boat trip down the Magdalena River (water traditionally being associated with life and renewal), Florentino's moment of transcendence is related to the "grace of the Holy Spirit." In an almost mystical moment in the final page of the novel, giving the captain of the riverboat the impression that "life, more than death, has no limits," Florentino and Fermina seem to have stepped beyond mortality. A masterpiece of Western literature, *Love in the Time of Cholera* is a romance that goes beyond a simple love story to assert, through plot, character, and symbol, that life need not be limited by death.

Richard Logsdon

Bibliography:
Bloom, Harold, ed. *Modern Critical Views: Gabriel García Márquez.* New York: Chelsea House, 1989. An excellent collection of critical essays on the works of García Márquez. Proves a good overview of the themes and literary trends that shaped García Márquez's works.
Castronovo, David. *"Love in the Time of Cholera* by Gabriel García Márquez." *America* 159, no. 6 (September 10, 1988): 146-148. Discusses in particular the versatility and variety of *Love in the Time of Cholera.*
Garris, Robert. *"Love in the Time of Cholera* by García Márquez." *The Hudson Review* 41, no. 4 (June, 1990): 759-760. A discussion of the novel's style that finds the work "robust, energetic, and meditative." Points out that love and death are treated as comic and absurd.
McNerney, Kathleen. *Understanding Gabriel García Márquez.* Columbia: University of South Carolina Press, 1989. A useful study that attempts to interpret the works of García Márquez in the light of modern and contemporary European and Latin American literature.
Mose, K. E. A. *Defamiliarization in the Work of Gabriel García Márquez.* Lewiston, N.Y.: E. Mellen Press, 1989. An interesting consideration of the figures of speech employed by García Márquez to "defamiliarize" his subject and present the familiar in an unfamiliar fashion.

THE LOVE SUICIDES AT SONEZAKI

Type of work: Drama
Author: Chikamatsu Monzaemon (Sugimori Nobumori, 1653-1725)
Type of plot: Tragedy
Time of plot: Eighteenth century
Locale: Osaka, Japan
First performed: Sonezaki shinjū, 1703 (English translation, 1961)

Principal characters:

O HATSU, a popular geisha
TOKUBEI, her lover, an apprentice
KYŪEMON, Tokubei's uncle and employer
KUHEIJI, Tokubei's friend, also in love with O Hatsu
GIHEI, a wealthy countryman

The Story:

Gihei, a rich man from the country, was trying to decide how to spend the evening in Osaka. Two friends urged him to hire O Hatsu, the famous geisha or courtesan for the evening. She begged off, however, and remained with her maids, meanwhile thinking about her lover Tokubei, a clerk, who had been neglecting her. To her great joy, he arrived a short time later, but with word that Kyūemon, his uncle and employer, had arranged for his marriage to an heiress and that his aunt had already received and spent the dowry. When Tokubei refused to marry the young woman, the dowry had to be returned. Tokubei had managed to collect the money but later lent it to his friend Kuheiji. Now Kyūemon wanted Tokubei to leave Osaka.

O Hatsu, in spite of this disturbing news, was happy once more; she had feared Tokubei no longer loved her. While the lovers were talking, Kuheiji and a group of his friends appeared. When Tokubei asked for the money owed him, Kuheiji pretended to know nothing about the loan. Desperately, Tokubei attacked Kuheiji, whose friends joined the fight and overwhelmed Tokubei. During the uproar Gihei returned and compelled O Hatsu to go off with him.

Not knowing what had happened to Tokubei, O Hatsu was afraid that he had been killed in the quarrel. When Kyūemon arrived, she went outside to speak to him. Saying that she was a bad influence on the young man and that she was not truly in love with him, Kyūemon begged her to give up Tokubei. He also asked where Tokubei could be found. O Hatsu insisted that her love was real, and that she was ignorant of her lover's whereabouts. Kyūemon went inside, but O Hatsu, still fearful, remained in the street.

She was still standing there when a shabby Tokubei appeared. As she told him of Kyūemon's visit, Kuheiji and his gang reappeared and insisted that O Hatsu join them. She was able to hide Tokubei under the porch while she sat above him on a step, and from his hiding place he was able to communicate his understanding by fondling her foot tenderly. It developed that Kuheiji had come to ransom O Hatsu, using Tokubei's money. O Hatsu, seeing no solution but suicide, managed to convey her resolve to Tokubei through her conversation with Kuheiji. Kuheiji, the braggart, went away to close the deal, and O Hatsu was forced to withdraw without talking to Tokubei again.

That night O Hatsu stole away secretly to meet Tokubei, and the lovers fled to the woods of Sonezaki. Meanwhile, Kuheiji and his servant, while discussing the plan to gain O Hatsu and malign Tokubei, had been overheard by Kyūemon. After confronting the evil Kuheiji, Kyūemon went in haste to find the lovers. He was too late. They had already committed suicide together.

Critical Evaluation:

Of the three literary giants who appeared simultaneously on the Japanese literary scene during the early half of the Tokugawa Period (1600-1867), Chikamatsu Monzaemon was the playwright. He wrote the books (called jōruri) for puppet theater, which came into its own in Osaka because of the happy appearance of Chikamatsu, a great chanter (Takemoto Gidayū), a talented *samisen* accompanist (Takezawa Gon'emon) who put Chikamatsu's words to music, and a superb puppeteer (Tatsumatsu Hachirobei) who boldly appeared on the stage with his puppets and yet, through sheer artistry, made the audience forget his physical presence in the movements of the puppets he manipulated. Chikamatsu also wrote for the *Kabuki* theater then centered in Kyoto and Edo (now Tokyo). Chikamatsu's dramatic works fall into two classes according to the subject matter treated: the historical and the domestic, the latter dealing with contemporary events and with people chiefly of the merchant, or common, class. The Love Suicides at Sonezaki was the first of the domestic plays written by Chikamatsu. He was fifty years old at the time. First staged in Osaka in 1703, it is a dramatization, with additions, of an actual occurrence in Osaka earlier that same year. Originally written for the puppet theater, it was soon presented also on the Kabuki stage as well. The play remains popular.

Although Chikamatsu has been called the most Western of the great Japanese dramatists, two obstacles—one cultural, the other artistic—confront the Western reader who attempts to understand and appreciate Chikamatsu's dramas. The cultural gulf that separates the contemporary Western reader from the eighteenth century Japanese characters frequently seems too great to bridge and, since the West has almost no tradition of adult puppet theater, or even any highly stylized, ritualized drama comparable to Kabuki theater, it is most difficult to visualize theatrically the plays on the basis of translated texts. Even so, moments of great feeling and dramatic power come through to interest and move the Western reader. Perhaps Chikamatsu's most accessible play is his first domestic tragedy, *The Love Suicides at Sonezaki.*

The story established the basic plot line for all of Chikamatsu's later domestic tragedies. A young tradesman and a prostitute fall in love. He is unable to "ransom" her (purchase her "contract") and so, frustrated, the lovers eventually commit suicide together. Although the persistent choice of a prostitute for a heroine (an accurate reflection of social conditions) may strike the modern Western reader as peculiar, Chikamatsu's antiheroic characterizations seem quite modern. It is through Chikamatsu's domestic plays that realism can be said to have come to Japanese theater. Caught between intense human emotion (*ninjo*) and a rigid social morality (*giri*), the characters are inevitably destroyed by circumstances that are essentially beyond their control. Tokubei is weak, volatile, erratic, and foolishly trusting; O Hatsu is, from the beginning, the more heroic—she decides on suicide long before he does and urges him to it. He vacillates and postures; she offers him her strength and example. Ultimately the only choice for them is suicide; they carry it out with great courage and mutual devotion, thereby achieving a tragic dignity. If the social context of their behavior is not completely clear and their fatalistic attitudes seem psychologically obscure, the purity of their love and the nobility of their suicides are convincing and touching. In the reading and the presentation, the high point of the dramatic in *The Love Suicides at Sonezaki*, as in all the shinju plays, is the poetic lovers' journey (*michiyuki*) to their appointed end.

Although Chikamatsu uses the love-suicide formula with greater flexibility, subtlety, and complexity in later plays, the poetic immediacy and dramatic impact of *The Love Suicides at*

Sonezaki have kept it a permanent favorite with the Japanese public. *The Love Suicides at Sonezaki* began a theatrical vogue (in addition to Chikamatsu, many other Japanese playwrights exploited the formula), and it produced widespread public reaction. Originally stimulated by a real incident, it and its successors provoked so many real-life love-suicides that in 1722 the government felt it necessary to ban the production of any play that contained the word *shinjū* in its title.

Bibliography:
Chikamatsu Monzaemon. *Major Plays of Chikamatsu*. Translated by Donald Keene. New York: Columbia University Press, 1961. Pages 1 to 38 provide biographical and social background on Chikamatsu and deal with such issues as the structure of the plays and moral issues involved.
Gerstle, C. Andrew. *Circles of Fantasy: Convention in the Plays of Chikamatsu*. Cambridge, Mass.: Harvard University Press, 1986. Pages 113 to 129 provide a brief synopsis and history of the play, then turn to a discussion of the love-suicide as a dramatic form. Includes a detailed analysis of the structure and dynamics of the play, especially the *michiyuki*, or final journey to death.
Kato, Shuichi. *The Years of Isolation*. Vol. 2 in *A History of Japanese Literature*. Translated by David Chibbet. New York: Kodansha International, 1983. Pages 85 to 93 deal with the contrast between the celebration of the lover's death and the celebration of the warrior's death in Japanese literature. Examines the *michiyuki* scene in the play.
Keene, Donald. *World Within Walls: Japanese Literature of the Pre-Modern Era, 1600-1867*. New York: Holt, Rinehart and Winston, 1976. Pages 244 to 274 place the play in the context of the author's entire oeuvre. Points out the importance of the themes of love and money, which provide the tension that drives the play. He also discusses the themes of *giri* (obligation) and *ninjo* (human feeling) that provide dramatic conflict.
Kirkwood, Kenneth P. *Renaissance in Japan: A Cultural Survey of the Seventeenth Century*. Rutland, Vt.: Charles E. Tuttle, 1970. Pages 224 to 312 include a biographical sketch of the author and a discussion of specific works by him. Covers the historical event that provided the basis for the play and a discussion of the phenomenon of lovers' suicides in Japanese literature.

THE LOVER

Type of work: Novel
Author: Marguerite Duras (1914-1996)
Type of plot: New Novel
Time of plot: Late 1920's through 1940's
Locale: Indochina and France
First published: L'Amant, 1984 (English translation, 1985)

>   *Principal characters:*
>   THE NARRATOR, the novel's protagonist and author
>   HER MOTHER
>   HER OLDER BROTHER
>   HER YOUNGER BROTHER
>   HER LOVER, a wealthy young Chinese man

The Story:

A man told the narrator that she was more beautiful now that she was old and her face was ruined than she had been as a young woman. While thinking about this unusual comment, the narrator began to remember her unhappy family and her scandalous first love affair. Abruptly she changed in age. No longer an old woman, she was now once again fifteen-and-a-half, riding a ferry across the Mekong River in what was then French Indochina.

As a girl, she attended both the state boarding school in Saigon and a French high school because her mother was ambitious for her future. All of the family's hopes and chances for success depended on her; she had two brothers, but unfortunately, both were unreliable. The older brother was a drug addict who stole from his own family and had such a negative effect on his two siblings that he was eventually sent back to France. The younger brother had a different problem: He was simply too sensitive and weak to achieve worldly success.

Telling her story, the narrator shifted fluidly between the present and the past, referring to old photographs and memories as though she were thumbing through a family album. In one photo, taken when she was still a fifteen-year-old virgin, she had the face of a sexually experienced woman. In another memory, she recalled a favorite outfit that also made her appear prematurely worldly. She wore it the day she met the young Chinese man who became her first lover.

When she was very young, she knew that she wanted to be a writer, but her mother discouraged her. A math degree was much more practical for a girl who was going to have to support her family. She earned an income, however, in a way that her mother had not foreseen. She became essentially a prostitute, accepting money from her lover in return for sleeping with him.

Although her lover was older, wealthier, and had many sexual experiences to her none, her power over him was far greater than his over her. She felt intense sexual desire for him, but no love. He, on the other hand, genuinely loved her, and was acutely aware that his feelings were not matched by hers. She reveled in her ability to give less to him than she got in return, and also in the knowledge that she could have this same power over other men.

Their first sexual encounter took place in Cholon, the Chinese district of Saigon. Their lovemaking was characterized by his tears and her joyous discovery of physical pleasure.

Once the affair became known to her family, they treated him rudely, as he expected. He bought them expensive dinners in restaurants, and they refused to speak to him. Rudeness to the contrary, her mother, in general, approved of the affair. Although it had ruined the narrator's chances of marrying within the local white community, it had also resulted in money for the family. One day, however, her mother's fragile mental stability collapsed. Her mother locked her in her room, and, in a frenzy, proceeded to beat her.

She began spending the night with her lover instead of sleeping at the boarding school. When she was caught she was not punished, but instead was allowed to come and go as she pleased. She was European, so she was granted special privileges not allowed to the native-born Indochinese students. Official sanction did not stop the nasty things that were said about her by the teachers and other students, but the sight of a large diamond ring on her engagement ring finger did, even though everyone knew she was not actually engaged.

Her romance unraveled after the illness of her lover's father. After recovering, the father made plans to send her away to France, so that his son could forget her and begin the search for a suitable Chinese bride. In her usual contrary fashion, she sided with the father rather than with her lover, who was by then desperately in love with her. Eventually, however, her lover realized that it was best that she leave Indochina. Even if they were somehow miraculously to be married, she would still inevitably abandon him.

The way her lover touched her body changed. She began to seem more like his child than his lover, and so he became more tender and less ravenously passionate. The change intensified once the date for her voyage to France was set. He became physically unable to make love to her. Despairing, they tried to stop seeing each other, but could not.

In a scene much like their first meeting, her lover came to see her sail away, watching her from inside his long, black car. Later, she heard that he had obeyed his father and married a rich Chinese woman. She wondered how long it was before her lover could bear to make love to his new wife, and if he did so thinking of her. After many years her questions received a kind of answer. Near the end of his life, the lover visited Paris, the city in which she lived. Over the telephone he told her that he had always loved her and would always love her, even unto death.

Critical Evaluation:

The Lover has a complex structure that is disguised by its simple sentences and unadorned vocabulary. The novel's time period shifts between the past and the present, so that the narrator is sometimes an old woman and sometimes an adolescent girl. Similarly, Marguerite Duras writes both in the first person and in the third, which allows the narrator to experience her story as both a participant and a bystander. Repetition is also a favorite strategy. Phrases and even entire scenes are repeated. Major events are also chopped into fragments and intercut with one another. For example, the story of the narrator's first sexual experience is told twice, each time interrupted by other memories. Interestingly, Duras is also known as a filmmaker, and the fragmentation of *The Lover* gives the novel the feel of a film montage (a juxtaposition of several shots that creates a single impression).

At times, Duras departs totally from the novel's main story and introduces completely unrelated characters, such as the social hostesses she knew in Paris during World War II. These digressions challenge the reader to account for their presence. The book's strongly autobiographical nature is one plausible reason for them. Memoirs not uncommonly appear meandering and unfocused. Another reason has been suggested by the writer Barbara Probst Solomon, who has noted that the digressions tend to occur around emotionally charged moments in the love story. She has theorized that the seemingly unrelated material breaks up the main action of the novel in order to hide facts and emotions that Duras did not want to reveal.

Whatever real-life events Duras may have left out of *The Lover*, the novel gives the impression of frankness and courage. The narrator defies the conventions of romantic love as well as traditional gender roles. Not only is she merely fifteen years of age at the beginning of her relationship with the lover, but also she is the seducer rather than the seduced. Duras does not condemn the narrator's prostitution, nor the fact that her sexual pleasure is inextricably linked to the money her lover gives her.

Duras also reverses standard roles in her handling of racial issues. When the couple first meet, it is the European narrator who is poor and rides the bus, and her Chinese lover who is a millionaire's son riding in a chauffeured limousine. In a more conventional story, it would be the girl's family who refused to allow their daughter to marry across racial lines. Instead, the lover's father opposes the match, so much so that he pays for the narrator's passage back to France. Through these and other inversions, Duras suggests that class takes precedence over race; skin color is less important than wealth.

This unconventional portrayal of race and class has been controversial. Some critics have accused Duras of implying that it was the French colonizers, not the resident peoples, who were exploited when portions of Indochina were a French colony. For example, the family's poverty resulted primarily from a bad real estate deal in which the mother was swindled because she did not know that farmable land was sold only to those who bribed the local officials. Duras also has come under fire for the political views she expresses in *The Lover*. In one passage, she equates communists with the collaborators who aided the Germans during the occupation of France in World War II. Again, she has been accused of rewriting history, especially given her own background as a former communist who worked against collaborators during the war. She also has been criticized for the novel's sympathetic portrayal of the Fernandezes, who are described as collaborators. As infuriating as these passages are to some readers, they can be classified as part of the novel's general strategy of inverting conventions and confounding expectations.

The debate over *The Lover* is typical of Duras' career. Critical opinion of her work has been intensely divided. There are those, sometimes called "Durasophiles," who have strongly praised her writings for their redefinition of the feminine, especially in matters of sexuality and worldview. Some of them have gone as far as to adopt her writing style in their analyses of her work. The opposing camp has been dubbed "Durasophobes." They have tended to fall into two groups: those who have thought that Duras pushes the definition of the feminine so far that it becomes masculine, and those who have felt that she does not push it far enough.

Despite the lack of agreement among critics, *The Lover* won France's prestigious Prix Goncourt in 1984. Announcement of the prize immediately boosted sales of the book, which was translated into more than forty languages. Sales of *The Lover* also benefited from its inherently sensational subject matter—subject matter that allowed the book to be marketed as the sexual confessions of a famous writer and filmmaker. The novel's success also resulted in its being produced as a motion picture. Although Duras worked on the screenplay, she was disappointed in the film. As a result, she wrote *The North China Lover* (1991), another autobiographical novel centered on the same love affair.

The Lover has been beneficial to Duras in terms of increasing the availability of Duras' other written works. As a result of the novel's being so commercially successful, earlier Duras works have been, for example, translated into English. Her books have been exposed to a much wider reading public, who for the first time may properly judge the written work of Marguerite Duras for themselves.

Kelly Fuller

Bibliography:

Annan, Gabriele. "Saigon Mon Amour." *New York Review of Books*, June 27, 1985, 11-12. Concisely restates many of the major critical arguments both for and against the novel.

Callahan, Anne. "Vagabondage: Duras." In *Remains to Be Seen: Essays on Marguerite Duras*, compiled by Sanford Scribner Ames. New York: Peter Lang, 1988. Readable scholarly essay that celebrates *The Lover* as a groundbreaking work of feminist erotica. Part of a section that includes three other essays on *The Lover*.

Glassman, Deborah N. *Marguerite Duras: Fascinating Vision and Narrative Cure*. London: Associated University Presses, 1991. Contains an interesting discussion of *The Lover* that relates the novel's visual imagery to Duras' film-making style. Quotes Duras extensively in French, with English translations.

Schuster, Marilyn R. *Marguerite Duras Revisited*. New York: Twayne, 1993. Outstanding overview of Duras scholarship and Duras' work. Explains why Duras is an important figure in French culture, and how her written works are related to one another.

Solomon, Barbara Probst. "Indochina Mon Amour." *The New Republic*, September 9, 1985, 26-32. Strong, opinionated political analysis of *The Lover*. Memorably describes Duras' political views, their impact on her work, and her involvement in the French Resistance during World War II.

LOVE'S LABOUR'S LOST

Type of work: Drama
Author: William Shakespeare (1564-1616)
Type of plot: Comedy of manners
Time of plot: Sixteenth century
Locale: Navarre, Spain
First performed: c. 1594-1595; revised presentation, 1597; first published, 1598

Principal characters:
　FERDINAND, king of Navarre
　BEROWNE,
　LONGAVILLE, and
　DUMAINE, lords of Navarre
　DON ADRIANO DE ARMADO, a foolish Spaniard
　COSTARD, a clown
　THE PRINCESS OF FRANCE
　ROSALINE,
　MARIA, and
　KATHARINE, ladies attending the princess
　JAQUENETTA, a country wench

The Story:

　　The king of Navarre had taken a solemn vow and forced three of his attending lords to take it also. This vow was that for three years they would fast and study, enjoy no pleasures, and see no ladies. None of the three noblemen wanted to take the vow; Berowne, in particular, felt that it would be impossible to keep his promise. He pointed out this fact to the king by reminding him that the princess of France was approaching the court of Navarre to present a petition from her father, who was ill. The king agreed that he would be compelled to see her, but he added that in such cases the vow must be broken by necessity. Berowne foresaw that "necessity" would often cause the breaking of their vows.

　　The only amusement the king and his lords would have was provided by Costard, a clown, and by Don Adriano de Armado, a foolish Spaniard attached to the court. Armado wrote the king to inform him that Costard had been caught in the company of Jaquenetta, a country wench of dull mind. Since all attached to the court had been under the same laws of abstinence from earthly pleasures, Costard was remanded to Armado's custody and ordered to fast on bran and water for one week. The truth was that Armado also loved Jaquenetta. He feared the king would learn of his love and punish him in the same manner.

　　The Princess of France arrived with her three attendants. All were fair, and they expected to be received at the palace in the manner due their rank. The king, however, sent word that they would be housed at his lodge, since under the terms of his vow no lady could enter the palace. The princess, furious at being treated in this fashion, scorned the king for his bad manners. When she presented the petition from her father, she and the king could not agree because he vowed he had not received certain monies she claimed had been delivered to him.

　　At that first meeting, although each would have denied the fact, eight hearts were set to beating faster. The king viewed the princess with more than courteous interest. Berowne, Longaville, and Dumaine, his attendants, looked with love on the princess' ladies in waiting, Rosaline, Maria, and Katharine. A short time later Berowne sent a letter to Rosaline, with Costard as his messenger. Costard had also been given a letter by Armado, to be delivered to Jaquenetta. Costard, who was illiterate, mixed up the letters, giving Jaquenetta's to Rosaline and Rosaline's to the country wench.

Berowne had been correct in thinking the vow to leave the world behind would soon be broken. Hiding in a tree, he heard the king read aloud a sonnet that proclaimed his love for the princess. Later the king, in hiding, overheard Longaville reading some verses he had composed to Maria. Longaville, in turn, concealed himself and listened while Dumaine read a love poem inscribed to Katharine. Then each one in turn stepped out from hiding to accuse the others of breaking their vows. Berowne all that time had remained hidden in the tree. Thinking to chide them for their broken vows, he revealed himself at last and ridiculed them for their weakness, at the same time proclaiming himself the only one able to keep his vow. Costard and Jaquenetta then brought to the king the letter Berowne had written Rosaline, which Costard had mistakenly delivered to Jaquenetta.

All confessed that they had broken their vows. Berowne provided an excuse for all when he declared that one could learn much by studying women and the nature of love; thus, they were still devoting themselves to study. Having, in a fashion, saved face, the four determined to woo the ladies in earnest, and they made plans to entertain their loves with revels and dances.

Each lover sent his lady an anonymous token to wear in his honor. The ladies learned from a servant who the lovers were. The ladies played a joke on their suitors, who came in disguise to woo them. The women masked themselves and exchanged the tokens. The men arrived, also masked and disguised as Russians. Each man tried to make love to the lady wearing his token, but each was spurned and ridiculed. The ladies would not dance or sing, but would only mock the bewildered gentlemen.

Finally the suitors departed, hurt and indignant at the treatment they had received. Before long they returned in their own dress. The ladies, also unmasked, told of the lunatic Russians who had called on them. The men confessed their plot and forswore all such jokes forever, but the ladies did not stop teasing them. Since each man had made love to the wrong woman because of the exchange of tokens, the ladies pretended to be hurt that each man had broken his vows of love and constancy. The suitors suffered greatly for the sake of the ladies' merriment. Then the suitors learned that the ladies had anticipated the suitors' coming in disguise and thus had planned a joke of their own.

The king ordered a play presented for the entertainment of all. In the midst of the gaiety word came that the princess' father, the king of France, had died. She had to sail for home immediately, accompanied by her attendants. When the king and his lords pleaded with the ladies to stay in Navarre and marry them, the ladies refused to accept their serious protestations of love; they had jested too much to be believed. Each man vowed that he would remain faithful, only to be reminded of the former vows he had broken. Then each lady made a condition which, if met, would reward her lover a year hence. The king must retire for twelve months to a hermitage and there forsake all worldly pleasures. If at the end of that time he still loved the princess, she would be his. In the same fashion the other three lords must spend a year in carrying out the wishes of their sweethearts. Even the foolish Armado was included in the plan. He joined the others, announcing that Jaquenetta would not have him until he spent three years in honest work. Thus all the swains tried with jests and fair speech to win their ladies, but without success. Now as the price of their folly they had to prove in earnest that they deserved the hearts of their beloveds.

Critical Evaluation:

The exuberant language of *Love's Labour's Lost* has made it, in the words of Anne Barton, "the most relentlessly Elizabethan of all Shakespeare's plays." At times the dazzling wordplays have been deemed too clever, complex, and convoluted to make for a play that translates well to a modern audience. Yet audiences continue to sense, if not always completely comprehend, the wit and consequent fun inherent in the language—and it is on the issues of language that appreciation of the play ultimately rests.

Several factors give the play a special status in the William Shakespeare canon. It is one of the few Shakespeare plays for which an original source has not been found. For a comedy, it is also unusual that in spite of at least five possible couplings, it does not end in the traditional marriage or multiple marriages. The happy ending is suspended and left to the future, with the agreement of the couples to meet a year later. It is highly unusual that death plays such a direct role in the outcome of the play. Given the artificial motivation for the beginning of the plot, however, as well as the heavily verbal middle, it is not surprising that it takes the extreme intrusion of death to jolt the characters back to reality.

Critical attention has focused largely on Shakespeare's satire of the men's behavior. The king of Navarre's plan is patently absurd. In wishing to take a vow to separate himself from women and from pleasure and to dwell only on study, Ferdinand is plainly rejecting life's realities. In his forcing his attendants to take the vow with him and in their agreeing to take it, the entire trustworthiness of vows is put at stake. The vows are, naturally, soon challenged by the intrusion into the king's withdrawn world of the princess of France and her attendants.

What follows largely justifies the complaints of those who find the plot weak. Little happens to move the story forward—love letters are misdirected and sonnets and verses are read. The games of words are followed by games of wooing, with some of the usual comic stage business of disguises and mistaken identities used to prolong the courtship. When the representatives of the outside world seem to have been thoroughly drawn into the king's artificial world of games, the startling news of the death of the king of France shatters this fragile and illusory world built on words. As a commentary on the insubstantiality of language, the play is strong. As drama, the vows of love from it are not as strong.

Love's Labour's Lost is often excused as an early play, suggesting but not itself exhibiting some of the greater characterizations that came later. The cynical Berowne and the quick-witted Rosaline, for example, seem to foreshadow Benedick and Beatrice in *Much Ado About Nothing* (c. 1598-1599). There is a hint of the substantial subplots so common in Shakespeare with the clowns and comic characters. Don Adriano de Armado, Costard, and Jaquenetta, for example, serve to reflect on the foolishness and self-deception of the main male characters.

With this play it may be helpful to remember that actual performances have often been comical and fun. A reading may be laborious, and some of the language difficult to grasp. The easygoing silliness of the play in performance, however, can be rewarding. The play may have been written specifically to be performed for a small, highly educated audience. Discussions about the precise dating of the play have relied on the numerous historical references in it. More than usual, Shakespeare seems to have chosen names that evoked real people of the time, a theatrical device that would appeal only to those in the know. Although not based on any specific sources, the play evokes the Petrarchan conventions and the exaggerated language of love so popular in the writings of courtiers of the time. *Love's Labour's Lost* is also remarkable for its large number of puns and other wordplay.

With this early play, Shakespeare seems to have fused form and content. In satirizing the unrealistic idealization of learning, in examining the reliability and trustworthiness of that fallible vehicle for expression—language—Shakespeare draws on his considerable stock of verbal tricks and games to make the point. Although all the labor that the men put into their verse and their trickery to express their love for the women seems lost at the end, it is a temporary loss. What the women ask for, ironically enough, is that the men fulfill the vows that they undertook in the first place. Words may be inadequate, but there are practically no other means, especially for a playwright, for expression. The unexpected ending, with its promise of fulfillment, seems to be a challenge to make the promise of words of love become true in deeds of love.

"Critical Evaluation" by Shakuntala Jayaswal

Bibliography:
Barber, C. L. "The Folly of Wit and Masquerade in *Love's Labour's Lost*." In *Shakespeare's Festive Comedy: A Study of Dramatic Form and Its Relation to Social Custom*. Princeton, N.J.: Princeton University Press, 1959. An influential study of the relationship between holiday rituals and the comedies. Sees the games in this play as providing necessary festive release.
Barton, Anne. Introduction to *Love's Labor's Lost*. In *The Riverside Shakespeare*. Boston: Houghton Mifflin, 1974. An introduction to the play's textual history and an explication of language and themes by a premier Oxonian Shakespeare scholar.
Carroll, William C. *The Great Feast of Language in "Love's Labour's Lost."* Princeton, N.J.: Princeton University Press, 1976. Argues that the play does not pit art against nature but rather shows their connection and interdependence. Includes a discussion of the songs at the play's end.
Gilbert, Miriam. *Love's Labour's Lost*. Manchester, England: Manchester University Press, 1993. Describes a select group of productions of the play. The variety of possible interpretations is revealed in the description of productions.
Roesen, Bobbyann. "*Love's Labour's Lost*." *Shakespeare Quarterly* 4, no. 4 (October, 1953): 411-426. Examines the contrast between the artificial and the real in the play. Explains the movement toward reality as necessary for love.
Wilson, John Dover. "*Love's Labour's Lost*: The Story of a Conversion." In *Shakespeare's Happy Comedies*. Evanston, Ill.: Northwestern University Press, 1962. Explains how one's low opinion of the play may change after watching a performance. Compares the high spirits of the play to a Mozart opera and is an example of understanding the difference between reading and watching a play.

LOVING

Type of work: Novel
Author: Henry Green (Henry Vincent Yorke, 1905-1973)
Type of plot: Domestic
Time of plot: World War II
Locale: Ireland
First published: 1945

> *Principal characters:*
> CHARLEY RAUNCE, an English butler
> MRS. TENNANT, Raunce's employer
> MRS. JACK TENNANT, Mrs. Tennant's daughter-in-law
> EDITH, a maid in love with Raunce
> ALBERT, Raunce's assistant

The Story:

The great mansion owned by Mrs. Tennant was thrown into turmoil by the death of old Eldon, the butler. In the servants' quarters, no one knew quite what arrangements would be made after his death. The mansion and its inhabitants formed an isolated bit of England in Ireland. None of the servants could guess what Mrs. Tennant, who was a widow and very vague, might do in rearranging their duties. Only the footman, Charley Raunce, kept any purpose in his behavior.

Immediately after Eldon's death, Raunce went into the butler's room and took two small notebooks, one filled with the butler's monthly accounts and the other containing a set of special memoranda about visitors to the mansion, information that had helped the old man to obtain generous tips from Mrs. Tennant's guests. That same day, Raunce went to his mistress and asked for the post of butler. She agreed to give him the post, but without any extra pay. Raunce knew, however, that by juggling the accounts he could make up whatever pay raise he deemed sufficient. That evening, he solidified his position by successfully taking over the old butler's place at the head of the table in the servants' dining room.

Edith and Kate were the two upstairs maids in the Tennant mansion. Raunce insisted that Edith, with whom he was in love, continue her practice of bringing the butler his morning tea. The housekeeper, Mrs. Burch, was scandalized but was forced to give in. Raunce's usurpation of the old butler's position immediately upon the latter's death soon appeared a minor matter, because a scandal rocked the mansion within a few days. Mrs. Tennant's daughter-in-law, Mrs. Jack, was found in bed with a neighbor, Captain Davenport. The discovery was made by Edith, who went to open the curtains and to lay out Mrs. Jack's clothes in the morning. Although Mrs. Tennant was unaware of her daughter-in-law's indiscretion, the episode created consternation and nervousness in the servants' quarters.

To add to the uneasiness among the servants, a blue sapphire ring belonging to Mrs. Tennant disappeared. Mrs. Tennant, who was always losing valuables, did not blame the servants, but the loss made them feel ill at ease. A few days afterward, Mrs. Tennant and her daughter-in-law went to England to visit Jack Tennant, who had been given a few days' leave from military duty. The English servants almost gave their notice when they learned that they were being left in sole charge of the mansion, for they were well aware of the unfriendly attitudes of the Irish in the countryside and were also in fear of an invasion of the district by German troops. Raunce had a great sense of duty as well as a realization of what a good place he had; he prevailed upon the servants to remain, despite the general dissatisfaction.

In Mrs. Tennant's absence, Raunce paid court to Edith and discovered that she was in love with him. They spent many pleasant hours together, for Raunce was kept from his duties by a sore throat and Edith spent much of her time nursing him. Like the other servants, they were worried by the absence of their mistress and by their failure to find Mrs. Tennant's missing ring. Edith finally found it, but she and Raunce were at a loss to know where to keep it until Mrs. Tennant's return. They decided to hide it in the upholstering of a chair. Much to their dismay, the ring was taken from the chair. Shortly after they discovered its loss a second time, an investigator from an insurance company called at the mansion. All the servants refused to answer his questions; his presence during their mistress' absence bothered them, and they did not know what to say in order to protect her and her interests. The investigator left in a suspicious mood, saying that his company would not pay for the loss. After his departure, the servants discovered that the initials of the insurance company were like those of the militant, revolutionary Irish Republican Army. The discovery almost panicked them completely. Only the thought of military service and short rations in England kept them from giving up their jobs immediately.

In the remaining days before Mrs. Tennant's return, Edith learned that Mrs. Tennant's grandchildren and the cook's nephew had found the sapphire ring while playing. Not realizing the value of the piece of jewelry, the youngsters had taken it out and hidden it on the lawn. By pretending to want it as a wedding present from one of the little girls, Edith persuaded the child to bring it to her.

When Mrs. Tennant returned, the ring was restored to her, and the matter of its loss and the ugliness of the insurance investigator soon became matters of the past, almost forgotten after Raunce's helper, a young lad named Albert, gave his notice and left the mansion. Albert left because Mrs. Tennant had implied that he had taken the ring in the first place. He went back to England to enter the military service and become an aerial gunner.

Raunce grew restless by the realization, brought home to him by Albert's departure, that he had no part in the war effort. He also felt remorseful because his mother, who was exposed to the bombings by the Germans, refused to come to Ireland to live with her son and Edith after their marriage. These influences, coupled with the many dissensions among the servants and the domestic crises that were occurring at the mansion, assumed larger and larger proportions as he thought about them. At last, he admitted to Edith that he was dissatisfied and wanted to leave. His announcement made Edith unhappy, for she thought at first that he was trying to cancel their wedding plans.

When he had convinced her that he wanted her to go with him, they decided that, unlike good servants, they would leave without giving notice to Mrs. Tennant. One night, they eloped and went back to England to be married and to live.

Critical Evaluation:

Henry Green, despite his publishing ten novels between 1926 and 1952, is the least-known English novelist of high artistic quality of that period. He was a part-time novelist, spending most of his time in business, writing his novels seemingly as a diversion. He tended to avoid promoting himself as a writer. There is also the matter of the technical oddity of his work. In *Loving*, for example, he emulates some of the satirical insights of Evelyn Waugh (with whom he associated at Oxford), but in addition there is a kind of bizarre whimsy that goes beyond Waugh. Often, there is a strange lyric quality in Green's prose that is unsettling because it seems to appear from nowhere, in a way that is reminiscent of Ford Madox Ford. His work bothers readers because it never quite settles down, in terms of its tone, into a clearly identifiable point of view. Readers are left unsure of how to respond to the work, morally and emotionally. Green's rather stubborn determination to record conversations in the rawest natural form adds to the confusion. It is not simply that his working-class characters use a slangy, demotic language that is full of eccentricities and unfamiliar figures of speech, but also that the same occurs with his upper-class characters. He is determined not to compromise the veracity of regional, occupational, or class language. Most writers, even when they are re-creating the peculiarities of spoken language, tend to edit carefully in order not to confuse readers. Green seems not to care if everything is clearly understood. The conversations are often made more difficult by the maddeningly furtive intimacies, off-handed asides, and associations of ideas that people who know each other well and are living in close, constant contact indulge in unmindfully. His characters are talking, in a sense, to themselves, and have no idea that they are in a novel and ought to make things a bit clearer to the reader. Green, in this sense, is an innovator. He adds to this experimental style in using punctuation sparingly and by refusing to separate changes of time, place, and subject. There is a kind of "run-on" consciousness that brings an improvisational, seemingly unliterary informality to a novel that is, in fact, a very clever, mannered performance.

Loving is probably Green's best work, and it manifests much of his skill as a writer. What looks like an obvious tale of eccentric English behavior accumulates density not so much out of complicated plot or characterization as out of charming aimlessness. An upper-class English household, servants and all, is found in a great country house in the Republic of Ireland during World War II. The situation is ripe with the possibility for minor comedy or for tragedy, depending upon the loosely manic manner in which the household conducts itself under worries about the war, staff jealousies, love affairs, and an exaggerated fear of the Irish Republican Army, which is supposed to be lurking somewhere.

The young maids have some sense, but many of the servants take the least reasonable conclusion for granted. The infidelity of Captain Jack's young wife, missing jewels, a throttled peacock, and the unfounded rumors surrounding the war being fought far from provincial Ireland make for madness. The book is, ultimately, a comedy—the butler runs off with one of the maids, to live, as the last line announces tersely, "happily ever after"—but what gives it aesthetic texture is the way in which Green makes a dreamworld of it. This is partly the result of Green's ability to make characters out of caricatures. Raunce is the typically dishonest butler, but Green manages to give this sometimes cocky, middle-aged man credibility in his odd love affair with Edith, in his worrying concern for his duties, in his sense of the social hierarchy of the house, in his strange, enfeebling illness, and in his paranoia. There is a fragility and tenderness in him that shows itself not only in his courtship of Edith but also in his concern for his mother, who is back in England facing the bombs.

What makes *Loving* more than simply a joke of modest proportion is, in the first instance, its strangely uncommitted tone, which makes it difficult to decide if one is to take the work lightly or if disaster is going to strike. Second, the novel rises above modest accomplishment in its dreamlike language of description of landscape and of the house and its architectural extravagances. The dreamlike description makes this lonely haven from the war seem a fairy-tale world in which anything can happen. The joke is that ultimately very little does, but the enchantment is so complete that one hardly cares. The novel is masterful in its sharp but elegiac insights into a fading world of class hierarchy that will hardly survive the war. There is in the novel a sense of things passing. It is a lovely shaggy-dog story.

"Critical Evaluation" by Charles Pullen

Bibliography:

Allen, Walter. *The Modern Novel: In Britain and the United States*. New York: E. P. Dutton, 1964. Discusses Green in the context of the British gentlemanly tradition in the modern novel.

Burgess, Anthony. *The Novel Now: A Guide to Contemporary Fiction*. New York: W. W. Norton, 1967. Speaks of Green as an experimental writer.

Green, Henry. *Surviving: The Uncollected Writings of Henry Green*. Edited by Matthew Yorke. London: Chatto & Windus, 1992. Green stopped writing novels in 1952, but he continued to write occasional journalism, which is collected in this book. As a bonus there is a perceptive introduction by John Updike, who admits that he was deeply influenced by Green.

Holmesland, Oddvar. *A Critical Introduction to Henry Green's Novels*. New York: Macmillan, 1986. A sensible discussion of Green's ideas of life and how they affect his work.

Karl, Frederick R. *A Reader's Guide to the Contemporary English Novel*. New York: Farrar, Straus & Giroux, 1972. A good place to start; examines the novels in readable language and puts Green in the context of his fellow writers.

Odom, Keith. *Henry Green*. Boston: Twayne, 1978. A volume of the Twayne series. Direct and sensible, with an emphasis on sociological influences.

THE LOWER DEPTHS

Type of work: Drama
Author: Maxim Gorky (Aleksey Maksimovich Peshkov, 1868-1936)
Type of plot: Naturalism
Time of plot: Late nineteenth century
Locale: Russia
First performed: 1902; first published, 1902 as *Na dne* (English translation, 1912)

> *Principal characters:*
> KOSTILYOFF, the landlord
> VASSILISA, his wife
> NATASHA, her sister
> VASKA, a young thief
> KLESHTCH, a locksmith
> ANNA, his wife
> NASTYA, a streetwalker
> THE BARON, a former nobleman
> LUKA, a tramp
> SATINE, a cardsharp
> THE ACTOR, an alcoholic

The Story:

The cellar resembled a cave, with only one small window to illuminate its dank recesses. In a corner, thin boards partitioned off the room of Vaska, the young thief. In the kitchen lived Kvashnya, a vendor of meat pies, the decrepit Baron, and the streetwalker, Nastya. All around the room were bunks occupied by other lodgers.

Nastya, her head bent down, was absorbed in reading a novel entitled *Fatal Love*. The Baron, who lived largely on her earnings, seized the book and read its title aloud. Then he banged Nastya over the head with it and called her a lovesick fool. Satine raised himself painfully from his bunk at the noise. His memory was vague, but he knew he had been beaten up the night before, and the others told him he had been caught cheating at cards. The Actor stirred in his bed on top of the stove. He predicted that some day Satine would be beaten to death.

The Actor awakened enough to remind the Baron to sweep the floor. The landlady was strict and made them clean every day. The Baron loudly announced that he had to go shopping. He and Kvashnya left to make the day's purchases.

The Actor climbed down from his bunk and declared that the doctor had told him he had an organism poisoned by alcohol. Sweeping the floor would be bad for his health. Anna coughed loudly in her bunk. She was dying of consumption and there was no hope for her. Her husband, Kleshtch, was busy at his bench, where he fitted old keys and locks. Anna sat up to call her husband. Kvashnya had left her some dumplings in the pot, and she offered them to her husband. Kleshtch agreed there was no use feeding a dying woman, and so with a clear conscience he ate the dumplings.

The Actor helped Anna down from her high bed and out to the draughty hall. The sick woman was wrapped in rags. As they went through the door, the landlord, Kostilyoff, nearly knocked them down.

Kostilyoff looked around the dirty cellar and glanced several times at Kleshtch, working at his bench. Loudly, the landlord said that the locksmith occupied too much room for two roubles a month and that henceforth the rent would be two roubles and a half. Then Kostilyoff edged toward Vaska's room and inquired furtively if his wife had been in. He had good reason to suspect that Vassilisa was sleeping with Vaska.

At last, Kostilyoff got up the courage to call Vaska. The thief came out and denounced the landlord for not paying his debts, saying that Kostilyoff still owed seven roubles for a watch he had bought. Ordering Kostilyoff to produce the money immediately, Vaska sent him roughly out of the room.

The others admired Vaska for his courage and urged him to kill Kostilyoff and marry Vassilisa; then he could be landlord. Vaska thought over the idea for a time but decided that he was too soft-hearted to be a landlord. Besides, he was thinking of discarding Vassilisa for her sister Natasha. Satine asked Vaska for twenty kopecks, which the thief was glad to give; he was afraid Satine would want a rouble next.

Natasha came in with Luka. She put him in the kitchen to sleep with the three already there. Luka was a merry fellow who began to sing, but he stopped when all the others objected. The whole group sat silent when Vassilisa came in, saw the dirty floor, and gave orders for an immediate sweeping. She looked over the new arrival, Luka, and asked to see his passport. Because he had none, he was more readily accepted by the others. Miedviedeff, who was a policeman and Vassilisa's uncle, entered the cellar to check up on the lodging. He began to question Luka, but when the tramp called him sergeant, Miedviedeff left him alone.

That night, Anna lay in her bunk while a noisy, quarrelsome card game went on. Luka talked gently to the consumptive woman as Kleshtch came from time to time to look at her. Luka remarked that her death would be hard on her husband, but Anna accused Kleshtch of causing her death. She looked forward to the rest and peace she had never known. Luka assured her she would be at peace after her death.

The card players became louder and Satine was accused of cheating. Luka quieted the rioters; they all respected him even though they thought him a liar. He told Vaska that he would be able to reform in Siberia, and he assured the Actor that at a sanatorium he could be cured of alcoholism. Vassilisa came in, and when the others left, she offered Vaska three hundred roubles if he would kill Kostilyoff and set her free. That would leave Vaska free to marry Natasha, who at the moment was recovering from a beating from her jealous sister. Vaska was about to refuse when Kostilyoff entered in search of his wife. He was extremely suspicious, but Vaska pushed him out of the cellar.

A noise on top of the stove revealed that Luka had overheard everything. He was not greatly disturbed and warned Vaska not to have anything to do with the vicious Vassilisa. Walking over to Anna's bunk, Luka saw that she was dead. When they got Kleshtch out of the saloon, he came to look at the body of his dead wife. The others told him that he would have to remove the body, because in time dead people smell. Kleshtch agreed to take her outside. The Actor began to cavort in joy, talking excitedly. He had made up his mind to go to the sanatorium for his health. Luka had told him he could even be cured at state expense.

In the back yard that night, as Natasha was telling romantic stories to the crowd, Kostilyoff came out and gruffly ordered her in to work. When she went in, Vassilisa poured boiling water on her feet. Vaska went to rescue her and knocked Kostilyoff down, and in the ensuing brawl Kostilyoff was killed. As the crowd slunk away, Vassilisa immediately accused Vaska of murder. Natasha thought that Vaska had murdered Kostilyoff for the sake of Vassilisa. Natasha was almost in delirium as she wandered about accusing Vaska of murder and calling for revenge.

In the excitement, Luka wandered off, and he was never seen again. Vaska escaped a police search. Natasha went to the hospital. In the lodging, things went on much as they had before. Satine cheated at cards, and the Baron tried to convince the others of his former affluence. They all agreed that Luka was a kind old man but a great liar.

During a bitter quarrel with Nastya, the Baron stepped out in the yard. Satine and the others struck up a bawdy song. They broke off when the Baron hurried back to announce that the Actor had hanged himself. Satine thought the suicide was too bad—it broke up the song.

Critical Evaluation:

Maxim Gorky's exceptionally well-crafted play, *The Lower Depths*, is a transitional piece between the nineteenth and twentieth century literary masterpieces. As such, it shares in the best of both worlds. The play is constructed with a nineteenth century eye toward dramatic structure at the same time that it treats contemporary socio-political themes. Among the most important of these is the issue of freedom versus slavery, a frequent topic of conversation—implicit or explicit—among the denizens of *The Lower Depths*, a cellar-like rooming house accommodating a varied group of inhabitants. Also threading its way through the play is the naturalistic assumption of predestination, which forces the audience to ask—without really expecting an answer—whether the Actor was foredoomed to alcoholism, whether Anna was destined to die of tuberculosis and leave her husband penniless because of medical and burial expenses, and whether Satine was the only one who recognized how low *The Lower Depths* were. Many more such questions arise, but all serve only to illustrate the essential slavery of the characters to the lower depths of the socio-economic system and their lack of freedom to rise above it.

This theme is also reinforced by the poetic imagery in the play, which revolves around references to light and dark, clean and dirty. The interior of the cellar rooming house, for example, is dark, but ideas and hopes are light. Conventional associations of good with light or white, and bad with dark or black abound. The conventional system gets turned on its head when the Actor begins to view death by suicide as a hope for his salvation, whereby death becomes white. Yet throughout the play, dark or black retains its traditional connotation of hopelessness and doom.

Gorky's use of light-dark imagery is particularly evident in being amalgamated into another effective literary device that he uses most strikingly—the device called foreshadowing or prescience, a subtle hint or prophecy of events to manifest themselves in the future. Anna's death, for example, which occurs at the end of Act II, is already predicted in Act I. The Actor's death is suggested in the middle of Act III, although he does not commit suicide until the end of Act IV. Natasha foresees an apocalyptic doom in Act III that does not come to pass until Act IV. In fact, the Actor senses his own fate at the beginning of Act IV although it does not occur until the end of that act. In the resolution of this precisely structured play, only Luka and Satine go unaccounted for; the rest play out their roles as though programmed. Yet the impact is undeniable, and the two escapees do not really escape, because they bear responsibility for the fate of others. The victims survive spiritually—despite death or other devastation—as reminders of the inexorable workings of the socio-economic system. It could be said that the end was prophesied from the beginning and that Gorky merely worked out the details, but those details were sufficiently compelling to support a revolution and sustain a remarkable play.

Bibliography:

Borras, F. M. *Maxim Gorky the Writer: An Interpretation.* Oxford, England: Clarendon Press, 1967. One of the more astute interpretations of Gorky's works, especially of his novels and plays, including *The Lower Depths*. Borras emphasizes Gorky's artistic achievements rather than focusing on biographical or political issues.

Hare, Richard. *Maxim Gorky: Romantic Realist and Conservative Revolutionary*. London: Oxford University Press, 1962. The first substantial study of Gorky in English since Alexander Kaun's 1932 book. Hare combines the political aspects of Gorky's biography with critical analysis of his works. Includes an analysis of *The Lower Depths* (pp. 56-61).

Kaun, Alexander. *Maxim Gorky and His Russia*. New York: Jonathan Cape and Harrison Smith, 1931. This first book on Gorky in English is supported by firsthand knowledge of the writer. Covers literary and nonliterary aspects of Russia's literary life and of the atmosphere in Gorky's time.

Levin, Dan. *Stormy Petrel: The Life and Work of Maxim Gorky*. East Norwalk, Conn.: Appleton-Century-Crofts, 1965. A general source that covers his entire life, thus completing Kaun's study. Levin discusses *The Lower Depths* on pages 86-95.

Muchnic, Helen. "Circe's Swine: Plays by Gorky and O'Neill." *Russian Writers: Notes and Essays*. New York: Random House, 1971. A comparative study of Gorky's *The Lower Depths* and O'Neill's *The Iceman Cometh*, with some keen insights.

Weil, Irwin. *Gorky: His Literary Development and Influence on Soviet Intellectual Life*. New York: Random House, 1966. The most scholarly book on Gorky in English, skillfully combining biography with critical analysis. *The Lower Depths* is discussed on pages 37-43.

LUCASTA POEMS

Type of work: Poetry
Author: Richard Lovelace (1618-1658)
*First published: Lucasta: Epodes, Odes, Sonnets, Songs &c. to Which Is Added Aramantha,
a Pastorall,* 1649; *Lucasta: Posthume Poems of Richard Lovelace, Esq.,* 1659

To most readers, Richard Lovelace is remembered for two lines each of two songs. He voiced for all those spirits who have suffered in prison, who have thought or composed thoughts in jails, the perfect expression of the free will in "Stone Walls doe not a Prison make,/ Nor I'ron bars a Cage," and he expressed his own high standards as a gentleman, soldier, scholar, and poet in lines which he wrote when going off to war: "I could not love thee (Deare) so much,/ Lov'd I not Honour more." A Royalist by birth and politics, the poet lost a modest fortune upholding his own high standards: He suffered imprisonment twice, and his entire life he spent surrounded by war's tragedies. He lost his father and a brother in battle, and he and his remaining brothers fought valorously for England (he attained the rank of colonel). His poetry, of limited popularity, was virtuous and modest in extreme and, as critics hasten to point out, the most moral written by the Cavalier poets. His most famous series, *Lucasta* (from *lux casta,* light of virtue), is his testimonial.

No conclusive evidence has yet come to light concerning the Lucasta of Lovelace's first volume, though it is now certain that this idealized figure was not Lucy Sacheverell. The woman to whom he addressed most of his early poems may have been a Lucas, however; hence the play on words.

Lovelace wrote in the age of the "conceit," that witty and often barbed line popularized by John Donne, but he must always rank in second place in its use. His two famous songs, written also in an age of words set to music, surpass those of his betters, but on moral grounds: "To Althea, from Prison," demonstrates Lovelace's indomitable spirit and "To Lucasta, Going to the Warres," his incorruptible soul. Lovelace was an amateur poet, a man of action whose education made of him a man of parts; he is often compared to Sir Philip Sidney, "A Scholar, Souldier, Lover, and a Saint," as one epitaph verse reads.

The diversified poetry within *Lucasta* indicates that Lovelace followed in that great tradition of the Renaissance gentleman. His varied activities and tastes led sometimes to the exercise of a talent thinly spread, to poor taste, but especially to haste—Lovelace's literary sin. His first volume lacked care, proofreading (evident even at a time of variable spellings, indifferent typography, and fanciful punctuation), not to mention chronological arranging, collating of stanzas, and other matters so necessary to professional work. Despite these weaknesses, Lovelace was well regarded. As a contemporary said of him, "He writes very well for a gentleman." His noble sentiments attracted readers.

Only twenty-seven copies of the 1649 *Lucasta*, available in the seventeenth century for a few pence, are now known to be extant. The portrait included makes one wonder at the extravagant praise of Lovelace's looks. The volume's poetry is courtly, exuberant, and at times pleasingly fanciful, although often amateurish in tone and style. This slender book of some sixty poems is dedicated to Lady Anne Lovelace, wife of his cousin John. This woman is not to be thought of as Lucasta. A group of commendatory poems follows the dedication, by his brothers Francis and Dudley, the latter, ten years later, the compiler of Lovelace's posthumous poems. The most interesting poem in this commendatory group is by the author's friend and fellow poet, Andrew Marvell, who suggests the verses will please the ladies more than the critics, those

"Word-peckers, Paper-rats, Book-scorpions."

The poems proper begin with two songs, both dedicated to ideal or Platonic love and both related to going overseas and fighting. Of the sixty, about a third were set to music and may still be found in books of "Ayres." Most of the poems conform to the seventeenth-century pattern of odes written on memorable days or for sad occasions, pastorals, sonnets, satires, and elegies. An interesting example of the latter is one of the poet's earliest poems, written when he was twenty and addressed to Princess Katherine "borne, christened, buried in one day." The interesting contrasts of birth and death, swaddling and winding clothes, joy and sorrow, with the overtones of pomp and circumstance befitting her royal lineage make of this poem a study in contrasts.

In addition to these varied types of poems, Lovelace wrote at least one acted play, *The Scholar* (1636) the prologue and epilogue of which appear in his first collection. Another play, *The Soldier* (1640), a tragedy, was never acted because of the closing of the theaters in 1642. During the period of the Protectorate, songs by Lovelace were probably sung in the masques, which were dramas produced privately for an aristocratic audience.

Lovelace prepared his second book, *Lucasta: Posthume Poems*, before his death, although it remained for his brother to bring out the volume. It is dedicated to Sir John Lovelace, an indication this time of his patronage. The first poem, "To Lucasta: Her Reserved Looks," epitomizes the gay-sad theme so prevalent among the Cavaliers, even at death:

> Lucasta, frown and let me die,
> But smile and see I live;
> The sad indifference of your Eye
> Both kills, and doth reprieve.
> You hide our fate within its screen,
> We feel our judgment ere we hear:
> So in one Picture I have seen
> An Angel here, the Devil there.

The poems in this volume show a mature writer, even a practiced one, and the salutary effect of careful editing by Dudley Lovelace assisted by Eldred Revett, makes this edition a more appealing one for the modern reader. Although the volume does not contain as many songs, the same types of poems appear, forty-four in all, with a series of translations from Latin and French appended. There is also a group of nature verses on "The Ant," "The Grasshopper," "The Falcon," "The Spider," "The Snail," and others.

Thought by the critics to be devoid of playful talent, Lovelace disputes the charge effectively in the poem "A Black Patch on Lucasta's Face," a sonnet in which a bee "Mistook her glorious Face for Paradise," and the plaster placed on the sting serves as "the sweet little Bees large Monument."

It may be significant that Lovelace's longest poems, in the first volume a pastoral titled "Amarantha" and in the second a satire, "On Sanazar's Being Honoured with Six Hundred Duckets by the Clarissimi of Venice," display the courtier as a gallant and then as a cynic. In the later poem Lovelace sees woman as something less than perfect, but so much gentler is this knight than the other Cavalier poets that he would almost fit Chaucer's famous description of knightly grace.

From the sentiments expressed in a group of elegies in which the poet's friends lament his death, the character of Lovelace was exemplary. Such expressions were a literary convention, of course, but so much of what is said rings true of his life that a backward glance reveals in epitome a man of his age. His brother, revealing something of a family talent, wrote the concluding lines to Richard Lovelace's literary epitaph, lines in which the tragedy of premature death—"Snatcht the bright Jewell from the Case"—is softened by bright memory:

> And now, transform'd, he doth arise
> A Constellation in the Skies,
> Teaching the blinded World the way,
> Through Night, to startle into Day:
> And shipwrackt shades, with steady hand
> He steers unto th' Elizian Land.

Lovelace will be remembered as long as readers continue to appreciate perfect, sincere lyrics about beauty, love, honor, and the lessons of life.

Bibliography:

Hartmann, C. H. *The Cavalier Spirit and Its Influence on the Life and Work of Richard Lovelace.* New York: E. P. Dutton, 1925. Biographical and historical study of the poet and his times. Comments on the publication of *Lucasta* and *Lucasta: Posthume Poems,* and provides critical analysis of a number of individual lyrics.

Seeling, Sharon Cadman. "'My Curious Hand or Eye': The Wit of Richard Lovelace." In *The Wit of Seventeenth Century Poetry*, edited by Claude Summers and Ted-Larry Pebworth. Columbia: University of Missouri Press, 1995. Discusses several of Lovelace's works as examples of the poet's understanding of issues involving gender and audience; notes the significance of male-female power relationships in his works.

Skelton, Robin. *Cavalier Poets.* London: Longmans, Green, 1960. A chapter on Lovelace discusses his wit and explores reasons for his emphasis on the ideal and on idyllic situations; compares him to other Cavalier poets, citing his facility with language as a special strength.

Weidhorn, Manfred. *Richard Lovelace.* New York: Twayne, 1970. Biographical and critical study intended for the general reader. Includes chapters on Lovelace's philosophy, his interests, and his sociopolitical views. Insightful commentary on the Lucasta poems included in a general discussion of Lovelace's merits as a Cavalier poet of the seventeenth century.

Wilkinson, C. H., ed. Introduction to *The Poems of Richard Lovelace*, by Richard Lovelace. Oxford, England: Clarendon Press, 1930. Excellent biographical sketch, and critical commentary on both volumes, emphasizing the biographical background for many of the poems. Corrects errors in earlier scholarly discussions.

THE LUCK OF ROARING CAMP AND OTHER SKETCHES

Type of work: Short fiction
Author: Bret Harte (1836-1902)
First published: 1870

Few authors ever achieve the astonishing literary success that Bret Harte did during his lifetime. His enormously popular stories of California life were in great demand by magazine editors all over the country, and the *Atlantic Monthly* offered the unprecedented amount of ten thousand dollars for the sole rights to one year of Harte's literary production.

Such enormous popularity is, however, seldom consistent with a lasting literary reputation. Harte reached his artistic maturity at the age of thirty-one and the quality of his work began to decline five years later. During these few years, however, Harte produced some stories of genuine literary value, most of which are collected in *The Luck of Roaring Camp and Other Sketches*. It is therefore mainly on this volume that Harte's literary reputation rests.

Harte's vision of life goes far to explain the meteoric popularity of his stories. The local color and picturesque characters he chose, and the trick endings he devised, added to the attraction but were surface attractions. The heart of his success lay in his ability to convey his particular vision of life to his readers. Harte was, essentially, an optimist and an uplifter. This does not mean that he believed in a shallow doctrine of social or moral reform. Rather, he believed in the potential goodness of human beings and in the possibility of redemption for every sinner. Harte saw life as a purgatory for the human soul, a test whose ultimate goal is salvation. He also thought that salvation could be achieved in this life, although, paradoxically, frequently at the cost of death. Rather than being an end of the trial, death was to be seen as the final consummation of the trial. Redemption for Harte was an act of selfless heroism, love, and devotion. Such an act could lift individuals above the petty world of grasping self-interest and redeem them from the sin of self-involvement. This is the spirit that pervades Harte's most memorable stories.

This spirit raises Harte's best characters from local stereotypes and picturesque caricatures to people of real feeling and semiheroic stature. Mark Twain explained that "Bret Harte got his California and his Californians by unconscious absorption, and put both of them into his tales alive." Harte wove the experiences of his people into his private theme of redemption and thereby gave them life. The people Harte wrote about were people seeking salvation from themselves, people who longed to wipe their past clean, and people who had come west to lose their identity, as is indicated by the fact that very few of his characters retained their given names. His characters had had their identities and pasts wiped clean with names like Cherokee Sal, Kentuck, Yuba Bill, Tennessee's Partner, and the Duchess. Such people were ripe for redemption by virtue of their self-dissatisfaction. To be saved, one must first have sinned.

This theme is at the core of Harte's most successful stories. In the title story of the collection, "The Luck of Roaring Camp," which first appeared in the *Overland Monthly* in 1868, a dissolute prostitute works out her salvation by giving birth to a baby and dying. The miners in the camp work out their salvation by giving the baby love and generous gifts to make up for the absence of a mother. One miner, Kentuck, works out his salvation by giving his life in a futile attempt to save the baby. The baby, of course, is incidental because of its innocence. What matters is that the baby brought out the generous qualities of the people whose lives it touched and thereby redeemed them from their own pettiness. In the second story of the collection, "The Outcasts of Poker Flat," a gambler and two prostitutes are saved from themselves by their devotion to a pair of innocent youngsters who had eloped. In the third story, "Miggles," a pretty young woman is redeemed by her devotion to a helpless invalid. The theme of love's power to save invests Harte's best stories with human interest. This was the source of Harte's uplift, optimism, and popularity.

Harte's weaknesses, which can be attributed to this same source, include frequent lapses into sentimentality and his use of illusory glamour and romance to gloss over the sharp frictions and discordances of everyday life. In "Brown of Calaveras," the image of gambler Jack Hamlin riding off into the rosy sunset after having handsomely refused to run away with a man's beautiful young wife certainly strikes one as unnecessarily romantic and sentimental. The theme of redemption through love and death lends itself too easily to theatrical, facile endings.

At his best, however, Harte avoids these pitfalls. A story's sentimentality is usually balanced by his ironic, humorous narrative style. In his most memorable stories, Harte employs an ironic prose that maintains a distance between himself and his subject matter. This skillful prose is clear and restrained, giving his fiction a sweet-sour flavor that blends well with his vision of life and convinces the reader that his characters do not deserve sympathy until they succeed in redeeming themselves. It reminds readers that his characters are human and subject to human failings. Yet Harte is never self-righteous. On the contrary, he is deeply sympathetic in his treatment of character, realizing human limitations as well as human virtues. In his preface to *The Luck of Roaring Camp*, he wrote:

> I might have painted my villains of the blackest dye. . . . I might have made it impossible for them to have performed a virtuous or generous action, and have thus avoided that moral confusion which is apt to rise in the contemplation of mixed motives and qualities. But I should have burdened myself with responsibility of their creation, which . . . I did not care to do.

Even in his preface, Harte's use of irony is skillful. Actually, he was a shrewd judge of character and had a particular talent for "the contemplation of mixed motives and qualities."

Harte put this talent to good use in his sketches. He was an admirable craftsman in blending virtue and vice, humor and pathos, the ridiculous and the sublime. He had a good eye for contrasts, particularly for the contrast between nature and human nature. Harte saw the ambivalences in both. On the one hand, he saw nature as serene, remote, and passionless; on the other, it could be violent, deadly, and passionate. In Harte's stories, the moods of nature are usually in juxtaposition with the moods of his characters. In "The Luck of Roaring Camp," for example, nature becomes still for a moment at the birth and the first cry of the baby. Later, when everything in the human realm seems calm and settled, a flood overwhelms the mining camp and takes several lives, including the baby's. The same occurs in "The Outcasts of Poker Flat." When the gambler, the thief, and the two prostitutes are driven out of town, everything is calm, but when these four begin to find some measure of peace, a snowstorm overtakes them and their two innocent companions.

It has been pointed out that Harte's literary techniques were borrowed from such writers as Washington Irving and Charles Dickens. To be sure, Harte did adapt techniques from Eastern and European writers, and he had developed out of the Romantic tradition. Yet to focus on what Harte borrowed from other writers is to miss the point. Harte was essentially an Easterner who had come west for his literary materials and who transformed his adopted techniques through his own personal values, limitations, and vision of life.

Both Harte's virtues and weaknesses as a storyteller derive from his optimistic vision of human redemption. While his bittersweet endings are patently stylized and there is a tendency to overuse sentiment, Harte creates endings with a good measure of dramatic impact. Then, too, he frequently balances the sentiment and glamour with a healthy humor and irony. Harte was an effective stylist, and his sentences are sharp and lucid. Moreover, Harte focused on human interest and local-color, thus paving the way for a school of regional fiction. Harte's talent for characterization and caricature blended well with his style of writing, creating a fortunate fusion of form and content. For these many reasons, he retains an assured place in a minor tradition.

Bibliography:

Morrow, Patrick. *Bret Harte: Literary Critic*. Bowling Green, Ohio: Bowling Green State University Popular Press, 1979. Emphasizes Harte's strong technical control and craftsmanship in his short stories. Discusses the way he fashioned stories with local color out of tall tales and barroom ballads.

Pattee, Fred Lewis. *The Development of the American Short Story: An Historical Survey*. New York: Harper & Brothers, 1923. Good discussion of Harte's contributions to the short story: a sense of humor, use of paradox and antithesis, and creation of local atmosphere and individualized character types.

Rhode, Robert D. *Setting in the American Short Story of Local Color: 1865-1900*. The Hague: Mouton, 1975. Argues that in Harte's best stories, setting is related to character as a stimulus to create new attitudes, a contrast to affect moral nature, and a sign of providence or symbol of a character's life.

Rourke, Constance. *American Humor: A Study of the National Character*. Garden City, N.Y.: Doubleday Anchor Books, 1931. Claims that Harte created tragicomedy and for the first time introduced a philosophic strain into American comedy. Points out that although his stories were sometimes sentimental and humor sometimes gave way to pathos, Harte always included a flicker of satire.

Stegner, Wallace. Introduction to *The Outcasts of Poker Flat and Other Tales*, by Bret Harte. New York: New American Library, 1961. Notes that Harte's characters do not strike the reader as lifelike but are, rather, clearly defined. Points out that Harte learned from Dickens how to combine apparently incompatible qualities to create a striking paradox.

LUCKY JIM

Type of work: Novel
Author: Kingsley Amis (1922-1995)
Type of plot: Social satire
Time of plot: Mid-twentieth century
Locale: An English provincial college
First published: 1954

Principal characters:
JAMES "JIM" DIXON, a young history lecturer
MARGARET PEEL, one of his colleagues
PROFESSOR WELCH, Dixon's superior
MRS. WELCH, his wife
BERTRAND WELCH, their son and a painter
JULIUS GORE-URQUHART, a rich patron of the arts
CHRISTINE CALLAGHAN, his niece
CAROL GOLDSMITH, the wife of another history lecturer
JOHNS, a musician and member of the Welch circle

The Story:

Jim Dixon's predicament was twofold: He had a job as a lecturer at a provincial English college, in medieval history, which he did not really want but was trying hard to keep, and, without quite knowing why, he had become involved with Margaret Peel, a younger but better established colleague. For the renewal of his contract, Jim depended on the mercurial opinion of Professor Welch, a seedy, absentminded historian of independent means in whose country house Margaret was recuperating from an attempted suicide, the apparent result of being jilted by Catchpole, Jim's erstwhile but since departed rival.

Jim tried to improve his professional standing by writing an absurd article on medieval shipbuilding techniques, agreeing to give a lecture for the college's annual festival, and accepting an invitation to a cultural weekend of madrigal singing and art talk at Welch's home. There he met the professor's son, Bertrand, a London artist, and Bertrand's extremely attractive girlfriend, Christine Callaghan; he disliked them both at first sight, especially Bertrand. Despite Jim's efforts to the contrary, the result of the weekend was deeper involvement with Margaret and further damage to his job. After an overdose of culture, he sneaked out to a pub, got drunk, made an unsuccessful though solicited pass at Margaret, and went to sleep with a lighted cigarette, as a result of which he burned a rug, a table, and the bedclothes in the Welches' guest room. With the surprising help of Christine, he partially concealed the fire damage, but Margaret found them hiding the charred table and used this as a lever to manipulate Jim into asking her to the college's annual dress ball.

Bertrand and Christine came to the ball, as did Christine's uncle, Julius Gore-Urquhart, a rich devotee of the arts. Bertrand was hoping through Christine to secure a position as Gore-Urquhart's private secretary. Gore-Urquhart had brought Carol Goldsmith, whose husband was also a history lecturer, to the ball. Telling Jim that she had been having an affair with Bertrand, Carol advised him to drop Margaret and pursue Christine. With both Margaret and Bertrand devoting full and fawning attention to Gore-Urquhart, Jim persuaded Christine to leave with him, and they arranged to meet again.

Margaret came to Jim's room the next morning, furious at having been left at the dance; when he told her he was through with her, she went into hysterics. The following day, he accompanied Professor Welch home to dinner. There Mrs. Welch confronted him with the bedclothes, about which he confessed and apologized, and Bertrand confronted him about Christine. Left alone with Margaret, he found himself, without much resistance, falling back into his old, ambiguous relationship with her; she did not object. When he met Christine for tea, they agreed not to see each other again, for she was involved with Bertrand in the same way he was involved with Margaret.

The following evening, Jim—sporting a black eye after a fight with Bertrand over having met Christine—gave his public lecture. Under the influence of a few stiff drinks beforehand, he turned the lecture, which he had planned as an encomium to Welch's prejudices, into a condemnation of them; he parodied a number of people, including Welch, and fell into a drunken stupor just as he was finally beginning to speak for himself and attack Welch's values directly.

After word came that he was to be fired, Jim met Catchpole, who had been in Wales, and discovered that the latter had never really been involved with Margaret and that her suicide attempt was a hoax carefully planned to entrap them both. Gore-Urquhart offered him the London job Bertrand had been seeking, and Christine, having broken up with Bertrand, became free. As the novel ends, Jim was beginning a new job in a new city with the promise of a new and better romance.

Critical Evaluation:

According to French philosopher Henri Bergson, the basis of laughter is the mechanization of gesture, movement, or language; it results from a substitution of the artificial for the natural so that the actions, attitudes, or speech of humans takes on some aspect of the mechanical. The moral function of comedy is to scorn by laughter the mechanical, which impedes freedom and evolution, and thus to laud the natural and flexible, which allow men to survive and improve. Laughter is itself an expression of the naturalness and freedom comedy lauds.

Despite its oversimplification, Bergson's theory provides a perspective from which to view Kingsley Amis' *Lucky Jim*. In it, characters are laughable and immoral to the extent that they resemble machines in their behavior, moral to the extent that they are or become natural. Laughter itself in the novel is the expression of naturalness, of feelings unfettered by social convention or individual pretension.

Welch and his son are major cases in point. Their speech, to which Amis devotes much care, and their gestures are mechanized by cliché and affectation. This point is developed by a controlling metaphor. The jerky movements of Welch's car are compared implicitly and explicitly to his conversational habits. His passengers are in constant jeopardy because he confuses his driving with his talking and often lets the course of his conversation dictate the direction of his car. Amis exploits the analogy by describing Welch's speech in terms stemming from automation and by making his driving and his car important to the plot. Bertrand's speech is similarly automatic; it is a jibe at one of Bertrand's speech mannerisms and not Dixon's refusal to stop seeing Christine that leads Bertrand to hit Dixon. The same sclerosis of speech and manner is seen in varying degrees in Margaret, Johns (who continually informs on Jim), and Mrs. Welch; in each case, mannerism becomes automatic, to that extent risible, and, to Dixon, dangerous.

Central to the novel is the irony that these automaton characters are each devoted in a mechanical way to theories that extol the natural and oppose what is modern, urban, and industrial. These worshipers of "integrated village-type community life," homemade music, handicrafts, and other ostensibly "natural" ways are, in fact, inflexible, nonadaptive, and hence neither free nor natural. In this portrayal, Amis comments on a major trend of modern thought and art, the preference for the simplicities of a preindustrial past over the present. He makes Welch and his circle precise examples of what they supposedly detest above all else— mechanization—and locates what they value—freedom and naturalness—in the enemy camp. The strategy is effective, and it suggests that morality is a matter not of time and place but of humans, not of theory but of practice, and not of doctrine but of instinct.

Naturalness and freedom are problematical for Jim and Christine, but in a different way. Both of them—Jim in particular—expend considerable energy trying to live up to the Welches and what they represent. Their failure to do so, and the fact that they are naturally resistant to mechanization, is the source of both a different, unsatirical humor and their salvation. Jim wants to get away from Margaret and go to London. Instead, he tries to regulate his smoking, put on the face his superiors expect of him, talk as if he were a Cambridge don, and get along with Margaret; he tries but cannot, and his failures are magnificently funny. They lead to trouble, which leads him to discover what he really wants and therefore away from the automatization. Special emphasis is placed on his speech, his face, and his laughter. In the Merrie Old England lecture, he begins by trying to assume the ideas and gestures he thinks, correctly, that Welch expects of him; these, however, detach themselves from him, and he ends the lecture speaking for himself.

There is a spectrum of characters in the novel, arranged according to the degree to which they have become mechanized in speech, gesture, and attitude—and perhaps more important, the degree to which the mechanization is separable from their existences as human beings. Welch has become a thing; his mechanized gestures have totally usurped his being. Jim Dixon is also mechanical at times and is trying hard to be more so, but his automatic gestures are merely encrustations, clearly separable from and finally the victims of his human self.

Bibliography:
Bradford, Richard. *Kingsley Amis*. London: Edward Arnold, 1989. A brief but incisive volume, in which Bradford argues that most critics have failed to grasp the complex nature and intentions of Amis' work. Concludes by labeling him a "comic misfit" inspired by the novelist and essayist G. K. Chesterton and the poet A. E. Housman.
Gardner, Philip. *Kingsley Amis*. Boston: Twayne, 1981. Dated because it does not cover Amis' entire career, but still a reliable introduction to his earlier novels, stories, and poetry.
McDermott, John. *Kingsley Amis: An English Moralist*. New York: St. Martin's Press, 1989. An important study emphasizing not only the moral seriousness of Amis' work but also its generally underrated intellectual and aesthetic range. McDermott examines why *Lucky Jim* was so successful upon publication and why it remains popular.
Moseley, Merritt. *Understanding Kingsley Amis*. Columbia: University of South Carolina Press, 1993. A basic, accessible survey, in which the author describes *Lucky Jim* as "one of the key books of the English 1950's" and goes on to place it in the context of Amis' subsequent work. Includes a good bibliography.
Salwak, Dale. *Kingsley Amis: Modern Novelist*. New York: Harvester Wheatsheaf, 1992. An extended, sympathetic biographical and critical study written with Amis' assistance. *Lucky Jim* is considered independently and in the context of Amis' subsequent development, particularly in relation to the dark later novel *Jake's Thing* (1978). Salwak declares that Dixon is so appealing because his adventures allow us to "break free from well-ordered, sensible lives."

THE LUSIADS

Type of work: Poetry
Author: Luís de Camões (c. 1524-1580)
Type of plot: Epic
Time of plot: Fifteenth century
Locale: Europe, Africa, and Asia
First published: Os Lusíades, 1572 (English translation, 1655)

> *Principal characters:*
> VASCO DA GAMA, Portuguese sea captain and explorer
> VENUS, goddess of love, patroness of the Portuguese
> BACCHUS, god of revelry, patron of Asia

The Story:

The gods and goddesses, called together by Jove, assembled on Olympus. When they had taken their places, Jove announced to them that the Fates had decreed that the men of Lusitania, or Portugal, should outdo all the great conquerors of ancient times by sailing around Africa to Asia, there to become the rulers of a new continent. Of all the assembled pantheon only Bacchus, who looked upon Asia as his own, dissented. Venus, however, friendly toward the Portuguese, took their side, aided by Mars.

Vasco da Gama was the captain chosen to head the voyage of exploration. Having sailed southward to the Cape of Good Hope, the Portuguese ships made their way around it and then sailed northward along the African coast, until they arrived at the island of Mozambique. The natives of that island pretended friendliness but tried to ambush the sailors when they put ashore for water; fortunately, the Portuguese escaped. Leaving the island behind, da Gama sailed northward along the African coast in search of India. He tried to land on another coast, but there, too, the natives were unfriendly. When they tried to lay an ambush, Venus interceded on behalf of da Gama and his men.

Guided by Mercury, da Gama set sail for a point still farther north. Arriving off Mombassa, the Portuguese ships dropped sails and anchors. The king of Mombassa made the Portuguese welcome to his domain, as Jove had told Venus he would, and gave the men of Portugal needed supplies. While paying a visit to da Gama's ship, the king asked the Portuguese leader to tell him about Portugal's history and the history of the voyage thus far. Da Gama was only too glad to give an account of his long and troublesome voyage and to tell of his nation's history.

Da Gama told the king where Portugal lay on the map of Europe and related how the Moors had at one time overrun the land. He described the great battles of Portuguese kings against the Moors: how the first Alphonso had first pushed the Moors back toward the shores of the Mediterranean and how his grandson, also named Alphonso, had continued the wars against the Moors and defeated with a small army five hosts of Moors under five Moorish kings. The second Alphonso was succeeded by Sancho, who, continuing the wars against the Moors, drove them from Europe and then fought against them in the Holy Land. Da Gama also told of the wars between the Spanish kings and the descendants of the great Alphonsos.

After ending his narrative of the martial history of Portugal, da Gama described his own adventures since leaving the mouth of the Tagus River. He told how his ships had sailed past the Canary Islands, past the Hesperides, and past the mouth of the mighty Congo. He told the king of the strange waterspouts they had seen, the terrible storms they had endured, and the awesome sea creatures they had met. He related how they had tried to make friends of the people of the African coast by giving them odd knickknacks and how the Africans in return had tried to kill them after pretending friendship. Da Gama told of the experiences of one of his men, Veloso, who had wandered too far inland and had almost been killed by Africans, and how Veloso had claimed that he returned quickly only because he thought the ships in danger.

Da Gama also narrated his adventure with the spirit of the Cape of Good Hope. The spirit appeared to the Portuguese as his ships sighted the cape and told them that they were the first men to sail in those waters. In return for their daring, the spirit prophesied, some of them would have to die, and that many of these men who followed them would also die for venturing so far into strange lands. The spirit said that he was one of the Titans who had fought against Jove and that his name had been Adamastor. The Titan had pursued a nymph, a chase which ended when divine wrath changed him into a range of mountains forming the cape at Africa's foot. Da Gama next told of the plague that had struck his crew, of the shortage of drinking water, of the loss of necessary food through spoilage. He also told of battles and ambushes in which the Portuguese fought with unfriendly natives of the east African coast.

After hearing his account of Portuguese history and da Gama's fabulous voyage, the king thought he could not do enough to show his friendliness toward the great men who represented Portugal. The Mombassans sent a pilot to da Gama and also the provisions and water necessary for a voyage across the Indian Ocean to the city of Calcutta. Bacchus, meanwhile, was furious at the success of da Gama and his ships. Determined to prevent Asia from falling into the hands of the Portuguese, Bacchus went into the depths of the sea to the court of Neptune, there to seek the aid of the sea god. He told Neptune that the men of Portugal were despoiling his kingdom and that the Portuguese spoke of the ruler of the sea only in terms of insolence. Neptune, angered at the report, sent storms to destroy their ships, but Venus interceded once more on behalf of the Portuguese and saved them from the storms unleashed by Neptune.

The Portuguese, arriving on the Indian coast, landed on the shore near Calcutta. One of the first to meet the men of Portugal was a Mohammedan who was glad to see them because he himself was from the northwestern part of Africa. He sent word to the Emperor of Malabar, informing him of the white strangers and of the distance they had traveled. The emperor quickly gave audience to da Gama, who told the ruler that he wished to trade for products of the eastern lands. Arrangements went forward to exchange Portuguese goods for spices and other products of India. The Mohammedan peoples in India became aroused and tried to bribe the king's council to halt the trading. Failing in that plan, they tried to delay da Gama's departure, for they hoped to destroy the Portuguese ships in battle with a fleet sailing from Arabia. Da Gama outwitted his enemies, however, and set out on the return voyage before the Arabian fleet had arrived.

As the Portuguese ships sailed westward toward home, Venus moved an island into their path. Needing a rest from their travels, da Gama and his men anchored off the island and went ashore. There, under the guidance of Venus, nymphs charmed away the hours for the sailors, and the goddess herself took da Gama to a castle high on a hill and showed him a vision of the future in which he saw later Portuguese—Albuquerque, Sampoyo, Noronia, and others—completing the conquest of Asia for their king and nation.

Critical Evaluation:

Descended from an ancient Galician family, Luís de Camões was distantly related to the hero of his epic narrative. In addition, the author had covered part of Vasco da Gama's route when he went to the Orient as an agent of the crown. On his return trip from Macao, Camões was shipwrecked, saving nothing but a faithful Javanese slave and the manuscripts of *The Lusiads*. The poem was the product of a man of action during a period of great national activity, at a time when the national spirit of Portugal had reached a high point. In the epic tradition, the poem finds the gods of Olympus siding for and against the Portuguese heroes; there is a descent into the underworld of Neptune. The famous weapon in this poem, a feature of epics, is the Portuguese ships' cannon. All of the other hallmarks of the epic are present, too, for those who seek them.

The Lusiads is one of the world's noted epics. It is dedicated to Portugal, and its author, Luís de Camões, is regarded as a symbol of that country. A poem of distant enterprise, one of whose themes is "man against the sea," *The Lusiads* also contains a fund of historic, geographic, cultural, and scientific information. It presents a panorama of interesting personalities, such as kings, navigators, conquistadors, missionaries, and Asian monarchs. The poem is thus much more than a glorification of Vasco de Gama's discovery of India and more than a jingoistic puffing-up of Portugal's sixteenth century conquests in Asia, Africa, and Brazil.

Camões selected da Gama's 1497-1499 voyage only as the literary center of his work. This voyage is used merely to tell the real story—that of the "Lusiads," or the men of Portugal. These men founded a new nation in Spain's northwest corner, following the battle of Ourique in 1139, when they placed five blue shields on their flag in the form of a cross. Celebrating Christ's five wounds and the five Moorish kings killed at Ourique, this symbol was carried southward in an anti-Islamic crusade until Portugal's continental limits were reached in 1252.

No element was missing in Portuguese history for Camões to write his epic, for Portugal's epic was achieved at home and, after 1415, abroad by kings, counselors, princes, saints, and all the heroes capable of conceiving, molding, and effecting a titanic enterprise. The common man, however, is its truest hero, for Camões wrote, "I sing the noble Lusitanian breast," thus making an entire people his collective hero.

After the Moorish wars were completed, Portugal was blessed by key Portuguese such as the scholarly King Diniz, who consolidated the new country by peopling southern Portugal, planting pine forests to build ships, developing agriculture, and founding Coimbra University. By 1415, Portugal was a compact, military nation on Europe's western edge with a martial aristocracy and hardy peasantry of Celtic-Swabian stock that unblushingly believed in the superiority of its religion, culture, and race. A geographic outpost of Europe, fanatically Christian, Portugal launched its ships into the uncharted seas, "never before navigated," ending medieval geography and rolling back the "Sea of Darkness." Its tiny caravels and galleons were commanded by Knights of Christ clad in chain mail, bearing the symbol of the Sacred Heart, and carrying huge, two-handed swords. Camões' epic had as its stated purpose the destruction of Islam at its distant sources.

Having rounded the Cape of Good Hope and discovered India in 1497-1499, Portugal's conquistadors continued the traditional Spanish-Portuguese vendetta against "the Moors" throughout the Indian Ocean. *The Lusiads* exults in their killing, burning, and looting as they took the spice trade from "the obscene Ismaelites." They tried to capture Mecca and Medina so as to ransom the Holy Sepulcher in Jerusalem; they conquered most of the outlets to the Indian Ocean; they reached China seven years before Cortez reached Mexico. They seized and destroyed what they believed was the Dalada, or Holy Tooth of Buddha, and they plundered the tombs of the emperors of China, but their missionaries evangelized from the interior of Brazil to Japan. At the height of Portuguese Empire, Camões' flag of "five azures in a cross designed" flew in Brazil, many regions of Africa including the interior of the area around the Congo, the coasts of Arabia, Persia, Malaya, parts of Indonesia, and over countless islands. It has been said that the empire of Camões' poem comprised thirty-two foreign kingdoms, 433 overseas garrison towns, and many isolated fortresses, even though Portugal itself comprised less than one percent of Europe's land area and had perhaps one million people.

The Lusiads has been translated into many languages. It was written during Camões' seventeen years as a private soldier in Asia, where research opportunities were scant; yet, it is filled with mythological allusions, some of which are so obscure that professional classicists have to consult their texts in order to explain them. The astronomy of *The Lusiads*, for example, is accurate despite sixteenth century limitations, while Camões' descriptions of the eternal correlation of sea and sky, of the ocean's surface, and of weather conditions has been praised by naturalists. The most diverse elements enter into the complex structure of *The Lusiads*, including the flora and religions of India's subcontinent. The poem's nautical aspects have also been praised, often by professional seamen. Camões also intentionally archived elements of phonetics, grammar, spelling, and meter, for which reason his poem has been called simultaneously a poem and a museum. The poem's thought soars above its polished surfaces, or even its complex symbolism. Camões was a religious writer, who must be considered a poet of the Counter-Reformation, and who depicted the great conquistadors Almeida and Albuquerque as missionaries who carried war to pagan lands. Camões was a person of unusual piety, and has been likened to "a Christian poet at the foot of the Cross of Calvary." His deepest admiration is reserved for the fanatic young King Sebastian of Portugal, the so-called "Portuguese Quijote," who died on a rash crusade against Islam in Africa's interior, and whom Camões considered the perfect epitome of a "Lusiad."

Camões also expressed his views on individual behavior, exalting virtues such as honesty, selflessness, and intrepidity in death. His heroes were always heroes of duty and honor, and he felt that death was happier than birth because there was one safe port—"to believe in Christ." He pilloried jealousy, greed, selfishness, cruelty (except against Infidels), and materialism, and it has been said that *The Lusiads* is written in letters of gold on a whiteness of marble, as Portugal's epitaph and testament.

The Lusiads remains a bond of unity between the peoples of the Portuguese world, whether in continental Portugal itself, on the adjacent islands of Madeira and the Azores, or in Brazil, Angola, Mozambique, Macao, Timor, and even the enclave of Goa, lost to India in 1961. Camões' subtle influence on national behavior patterns is visible not only in "the unpleasing portraits of the poet that grace the walls of Portuguese taverns," as Aubrey Bell stated, but because he is studied in the classrooms of Portugal, its colonies, and Brazil. His memory, not that of a great king or warrior, was used as a symbol of nationality when Portugal recovered its independence from Spain in 1640. It may be argued that there is no country that pays a greater homage to any of its national poets than Portugal does to Camões. Thus, the greatest influence of *The Lusiads* was felt after its author's death, and the epic remains a living force wherever its language is spoken.

"Critical Evaluation" by William Freitas

Bibliography:
Bowra, C. M. "Camões and the Epic of Portugal." In *From Virgil to Milton*. New York: St. Martin's Press, 1967. An explication of *The Lusiads* as an epic poem, a poem of the ideal in manhood. Demonstrates Camões' indebtedness to classical tradition and especially to Homer, Vergil, and Ariosto.

Burton, Richard Francis. *Camões: His Life and His Lusiads*. London: Bernard Quartich, 1881. Biography, history of Portugal up to the death of the poet, geography, annotations, bibliography.

Freitas, William. *Camões and His Epic: A Historic, Geographic, and Cultural Survey*. Stanford, Calif.: Institute of Hispanic American and Luso-Brazilian Studies, Stanford University, 1963. Uses *The Lusiads* as a source for information on Portugal's clashes with the nations of Islam, Africa, and India. Twenty illustrations, including portraits and maps.

O'Halloran, Colin M. *History and Heroes in the "Lusiads": A Commemoration Essay on Camões*. Lisbon: Comissão Executiva do IV Centenário da Publicaçao de "Os Lusiades," 1974. Discusses the poem as a record of and tribute to Portugal's national drive to conquer new lands and to win Christian converts. Accessible, although all the quotations from the poem are in Portuguese.

THE LUTE

Type of work: Drama
Author: Gao Ming (c. 1303-c. 1370)
Type of plot: Opera
Time of plot: c. 200
Locale: Honan Province, China
First performed: c. 1367; first published, c. 1367 as *Pi-pa ji* (English translation, 1980)

> *Principal characters:*
> Ts'AI JUNG, a young scholar
> CHAO WU-NIANG, his wife
> CHANG, a neighbor
> THE HONORABLE MR. NIU, the prime minister
> MISS NIU, his daughter

The Story:

Ts'ai Jung had been married for only two months when the local government recommended him as a candidate for the Imperial Examination. His father insisted on his making the trip to the capital, for the examination would give the young scholar an opportunity to distinguish himself and bring honor to his family. Ts'ai himself would rather have stayed home and fulfilled his duties as a son. However, fearing that his unwillingness to leave his parents, who were infirm with age, would be interpreted as selfish love for his wife, Ts'ai reluctantly took his departure, after entrusting his family to the care of his neighbor Chang, an old man.

Ts'ai easily won the first place in the examination. The emperor took such a fancy to the young scholar that he ordered him to be married to the daughter of Mr. Niu, the prime minister. The imperial order came as a happy solution to the prime minister; he had a problem in his daughter, who had sworn never to marry unless the man was a genius who passed first in the Imperial Examination. Here, at last, was a young man who met the requirement; consequently, no one paid attention to Ts'ai's protestations that he already had a wife and that his only ambition was to serve his parents. He was married a second time, against his wishes. Further restrictions were imposed on his freedom when he was ordered to live in the prime minister's house.

Ts'ai's second wife was as intelligent and sympathetic as she was beautiful, and she could see that her husband was unhappy in his new surroundings. He loved her, but he was also homesick. He had no knowledge that Ch'en-liu, his home district, had been stricken with famine. Nor did he know what a strain it was for his first wife, Chao Wu-niang, to support his parents during that terrible time. She sold her clothes and jewels to save the aged couple from starvation, while she herself lived on chaff. Their neighbor Chang also shared with them whatever rice he had.

No word came from Ts'ai. When the mother succumbed to sorrow, hunger, and disease, Chang lent them the money to buy a coffin. When the father died a short time later, Chao Wu-niang did not want to trouble the kind neighbor for another loan. She cut her hair and tried to get a little money from its sale. Before any buyer came, however, she was discovered in the street by Chang, who bought another coffin for her. Because she could not hire a gravedigger, she tried to raise a tumulus with her own hands. At last she fell asleep from fatigue, her fingers bleeding from her hard labor. While she slept, spirits came to finish the grave for her. Carrying a *pi-pa*, an instrument like a guitar, and portraits of the deceased parents, done by herself, which she exhibited while begging for alms, she set out for the capital in search of her husband.

Ts'ai had never for a moment forgotten his parents and first wife. He was duped when a swindler arrived with invented news from his family. Relieved to hear that they were all well and safe, Ts'ai asked the same man to deliver a letter to his parents, together with gold and pearls. The villain disappeared.

After a long period of anxious waiting, Ts'ai decided to go and see for himself how his family fared. He had the wholehearted support of his second wife, who intended to go with him to perform daughterly duties for his parents. The prime minister refused to grant permission, however; he wanted to keep his daughter and son-in-law close to him. When his daughter kept pestering him with supplications, he finally agreed to send a servant to Ch'en-liu to bring Ts'ai's parents and first wife to the capital, where they would live in his house as guests.

One day Chao Wu-niang came to a temple where a special mass was being celebrated. She had arrived in the capital, but she did not wish to see her husband until she was sure that he had not hardened his heart against her. She sang to the *pi-pa* a song on the virtue of filial piety, but the pilgrims and worshipers were not as generous in giving alms as she had expected. After she had hung up the portraits and begun to say prayers for the deceased parents, Ts'ai appeared to pray for his parents, whom he believed to be on their way to the capital. Chao Wu-niang immediately left the temple. Ts'ai failed to see her, but he found the picture and took it home with him.

The prime minister's daughter, in anticipation of the arrival of her parents-in-law, was looking for an intelligent woman to serve as a maid for the old couple. Chao Wu-niang, applying for the position, won the sympathy of the young mistress with her story of long suffering and the purpose of her journey to the capital. Chao Wu-niang used an anagram for her husband's name, but the other could not fail to see who the unfortunate woman really was. She immediately addressed her as sister and together the two devised a stratagem to test Ts'ai's heart.

The picture Chao Wu-niang had left in the temple was now hanging in Ts'ai's study. Chao Wu-niang wrote a poem on the back, criticizing in a loving tone her husband's conduct. Ts'ai had not looked carefully at the picture, nor did he know that a servant had hung it up. Now, returning from his office, he saw it again. The two faces bore a strange resemblance to his parents, but he was puzzled by their emaciated and ragged looks. Then he discovered the poem, apparently a satire at his expense. His first reaction was anger. He asked his wife whether she had any knowledge of the person who had ventured into his study and scribbled an unjust attack on him. Chao Wu-niang was summoned, and the whole story was told.

The prime minister was finally won over, and Ts'ai took his two wives to Ch'en-liu to worship at his parents' graves. All three were honored by the emperor as examples of virtuous conduct. The happiest man on the scene was the neighbor Chang, who derived more satisfaction from the reunion of Ts'ai's family than he did from the material rewards he now received.

Critical Evaluation:

The Lute is Gao Ming's only surviving opera. It is also the only Southern ch'uan-ch'i (telling of the remarkable) of the Yüan period (1280-1368) to be declared worthy of the highest praise. This judgment was rendered by none other than Chu Yüan-chang, who became the founder and emperor of the Ming dynasty (1368-1644). Other qualified persons have supported this view, although others have disagreed, expressing their dissatisfaction with the diction and lack of modal harmony. These judgments may be questioned, but there is no mistaking the flaws in the plot: the parents' ignorance of their son's success and marriage and his failure to recognize his father's calligraphy when the swindler presents the forged letter to him.

The title of Gao's opera includes a word for a stringed instrument called the *pi-pa*. This term has been translated into English as "guitar" or "lute." Although the Western guitar is a member of the lute family, neither of these terms is very correct. The Chinese *pi-pa* is not really like either one. It has a shallow pear-shaped body, a short fretted neck, and only four strings. A guitar has a deep body shaped something like an hourglass, a long neck, and six strings. The *pi-pa* is meant to be emblematic of the hardships and the sufferings of Ts'ai's first wife, Chao Wu-niang, during her journey to the capital to rejoin her husband. She is obliged to sing to the accompaniment of her *pi-pa* to obtain food and lodging. For her to walk such a long distance unchaperoned requires remarkable courage.

The Western theater typically classifies dramas as tragedies, comedies, and tragicomedies, but the Chinese theater has no such categories. A didactic theater, the Chinese opera deals largely with kinds of persons: saintly immortals, filial sons, chaste wives, obedient grandsons, young scholars, young beauties, wise judges, martial knights, and so on. In Western terms *The Lute* is a tragicomedy, the main line of the action being tragic but nevertheless ending happily, like a comedy. From the Chinese point of view, the story is a moral fable and an exemplum of filial piety, neighborliness, ancestor worship, scholarly ambition, government service, class conflict, political power, polygyny without jealousy, married love, separation, suffering, death, heroic courage, reunion, and harmony, all according to Confucian ethics.

In the Chinese view filial piety stems from the concept of *li*, or ceremony. It includes not merely acts but above all motives and intentions, as measured by the rules of propriety, from which genuine etiquette and politeness come. According to ancient texts, filial piety is the root of all virtue, and that from which all teaching comes. The path of filial piety leads to ancestor worship. The latter comes into play with the deaths of family members, beginning with the painting of the funeral portraits and the burial ceremony to the display of the ancestral tablets. On certain occasions the living pay homage to the dead by displaying their tablets and funeral portraits, by prayers offered to their spirits, and by offerings of food and paper money. It has been alleged by some that ancestor worship has been what binds the Chinese into a nation.

One of the most important goals of the ancient Chinese was to lead a life that would glorify and honor one's parents while avoiding any action that might shame them. For living parents, one way of assuring the former is to have a son become an advanced scholar by competing successfully in the government civil service examinations. This would typically lead to an important official post. Parents who had a son who had become an advanced scholar would advertise the fact by setting up a double flagpole in front of their door. All of the complexity of the theme of filial piety is clearly and suspensefully developed in Gao's great work.

"Critical Evaluation" by Richard P. Benton

Bibliography:
Birch, Cyril. "Some Concerns and Methods of the Ming *Ch'uan-ch'i* Drama." In *Studies in Chinese Literary Genres*, edited by Cyril Birch. Berkeley: University of California Press, 1974. A background essay on the Southern drama of the Ming dynasty.

_____. "Tragedy and Melodrama in Early *Ch'uan-ch'i* Plays: *Lute Song* and *Thorn Hairpin* Compared." *Bulletin of the School of Oriental Studies* 36 (1973): 228-247. An investigation of the genre.

Crump, James I. *Chinese Theater in the Days of Kublai Khan*. Tucson: The University of

Arizona Press, 1980. Describes the social milieu and the conditions and methods of theatrical performances. Presents three plays of the Yüan period in English translations of unusual quality.

_____. "Elements of Yüan Opera." *Journal of Asian Studies* 17 (1958): 417-434. Meticulous analysis and statistics regarding the form and content of *tsa-chü*, or northern style drama, of the Yüan period.

Dolby, William. *History of Chinese Drama*. London: Paul Elek, 1976. A full survey of the history of Chinese drama, which includes an English translation of *The Lute*'s scene xxxvii.

Mulligan, Jean, trans. *The Lute: Kao Ming's P'i-p'a chi*. New York: Columbia University Press, 1980. An outstanding English translation. All the speeches, songs, and stage directions are fully translated. Also, speeches which in the Chinese text are in parallel prose or poetic meter are identified.

LYSISTRATA

Type of work: Drama
Author: Aristophanes (c. 450-c. 385 B.C.E.)
Type of plot: Satire
Time of plot: Fifth century B.C.E.
Locale: Athens
First performed: Lysistratē, 411 B.C.E. (English translation, 1812)

Principal characters:
> LYSISTRATA, an Athenian woman
> CLEONICE, her friend
> LAMPITO, a Spartan woman
> MYRRHINÉ, a Greek woman
> A MAGISTRATE
> CINESIAS, a Greek husband
> OLD MEN OF ATHENS, the chorus

The Story:

The Second Peloponnesian War was in progress when Lysistrata summoned women from Athens, Sparta, and all other Greek cities involved in the war. She wished them to consider a plan she had carefully thought out for ending hostilities between Athens and Sparta. The women arrived, curious about the purpose of the meeting. Since their husbands were all away at war, they were well inclined toward any scheme that would bring them back to them.

Lysistrata declared that the war would end immediately if all the Greek women refused to sleep with their husbands until the fighting stopped. The women at first objected strenuously, but Lampito, a Spartan woman, liked the idea. The others finally agreed to try the plan, but they did so without enthusiasm. Over a bowl of Thracian wine, Lysistrata led her companions in an oath binding them to charm their husbands and their lovers but not to sleep with them unless forced. Most of the women then returned to their native lands to begin their continent lives. Lysistrata went to the Acropolis, the citadel of Athens, for while the younger women had been meeting with Lysistrata, the older women had marched upon the Acropolis and seized it. The old men of the city laid wood around the base of the Acropolis and set fire to it with the intention of smoking the women out, in response to which the women threatened to throw water on the old men from their pots and, during a particularly heated exchange, actually did so.

When a magistrate and his men attempted to break open a gate of the citadel, Lysistrata, who had taken command, emerged and suggested that the magistrate use common sense. The indignant magistrate ordered his Scythians to seize Lysistrata and bind her hands, but the Scythians advanced reluctantly and were soundly trounced by the fierce women.

Asked why they had seized the Acropolis, the women replied that they had done so to possess the treasury. Now that they controlled the money, they believed that the war must soon end, since it took money to wage war.

The old men were deeply wounded in their pride when Lysistrata declared that the women had assumed all civil authority and would henceforth provide for the safety and welfare of Athens. The magistrate could not believe his ears when he heard Lysistrata say that the women had grown impatient with the incompetence of their husbands in matters that concerned the commonweal. For rebuking the women, the magistrate received potfuls of water poured on his head. When the ineffectual old men declared they would never submit, the women answered that the old men were worthless and that all they had been able to do was legislate the city into trouble.

Despite their brave talk and their bold plan, however, the women proved to be weak in the flesh, and disaffection thinned their ranks. Some, caught as they deserted, offered various excuses in the hope of getting away from the strictures imposed by Lysistrata's oath. One woman simulated pregnancy by placing the sacred helmet of Athena under her robe. Some of the women claimed to be frightened by the holy snakes and by the owls of the Acropolis. As a last desperate measure, Lysistrata resorted to a prophecy favorable to their project, and the women reluctantly returned to their posts.

When the husband of Myrrhiné, one of Lysistrata's companions, returned from the war and sought his wife, Lysistrata directed Myrrhiné to be true to her oath. The husband, Cinesias, begged Myrrhiné to come home, using various appeals, but without success. Although Myrrhiné consented to his request for a moment of dalliance with her, she put him off. At last, ignoring his pleas, she retired into the citadel.

A messenger arrived from Sparta, where Lampito and her cohorts had been successful, with the news that the men of Sparta were prepared to sue for peace. As the magistrate arranged for a peace conference, the women looked on the old men of Athens with restored kindness, which cooled their ire.

On their arrival in Athens, the Spartan envoys were so desperate for the favors of their wives that they were ready to agree to any terms. Lysistrata rebuked the Spartans and the Athenians for warring with each other; they had, she declared, a common enemy in the barbarians and they shared many traditions. While she spoke, a nude maiden, representing the goddess of peace, was brought before the frustrated men. Lysistrata reminded the men of both countries that they had previously been allies, and she insisted that war between the two was illogical. The men, their eyes devouring the nude maiden, agreed with everything Lysistrata said, but when she asked for terms of agreement there was immediate contention, with each side asking for conditions unsatisfactory to the other.

The women, seeing that appeal to reason was futile, prepared a feast for the envoys and filled them with intoxicating liquors. Sated, and eager for further physical satisfaction, the men signed a peace agreement and left hastily with their wives for their homes.

Critical Evaluation:

Lysistrata is the most frequently produced Greek drama in twentieth century theater, for reasons that are not hard to determine, for the play deals openly with sex, feminism, and pacifism—all major preoccupations of the late twentieth century. In fact, a popular slogan of the 1960's, "Make Love, Not War," sums up Aristophanes' message in this comedy. It is clear, however, that many later times have taken up *Lysistrata* largely for its ideology rather than for its intrinsic value as a play.

By contrast with other Aristophanes plays on similar themes, *Lysistrata* seems rather thin in imagination. Undoubtedly the basic assumption of the comedy—that women could achieve peace and governmental reform through sexual abstinence—was an ancient idea even in Aristophanes' time. *The Acharnians* (425 B.C.E.) and *The Peace* (421 B.C.E.) present novel, if bizarre, methods of achieving peace, while *The Thesmophoriazusae* (411 B.C.E.) and *The Ecclesiazusae* (392 B.C.E.?) show women in a funnier, more satirical light. Twentieth century audiences as a rule appreciate directness and simplicity and in many instances do not object to a certain lack of originality, but they probably would dislike a satirical treatment of Lysistrata, who is both a militant feminist and a pacifist.

In structure, the drama is straightforward. The problem is simple: The women are tired of living without their husbands because of war. Out of the solution they devise—teasing their husbands but withholding sex from them until the men settle the war out of sheer frustration—everything else in the play follows. The women capture the treasury; the old men try to force the women into submission; when force fails the two sides hold an inconclusive debate in which the magistrate, a chief warmonger, is first decked out like a woman and then as a corpse; the women begin to defect from their oath of chastity, but with strenuous effort Lysistrata whips them back into shape; and finally the Athenian and Spartan men agree to negotiate for peace. When those negotiations fail, the diplomats are tricked into a peace settlement through feasting and drinking. Once the problem has been established, almost all of the consequent action is predictable yet it amuses nevertheless. Perhaps the funniest idea in the play is that diplomats should never negotiate when they are sober: Cleverness and greed are inimical to peace, whereas drink and festivity promote good will.

Sex—particularly the battle of the sexes—is a traditional subject for comedy, and Greek comedy in fact evolved in part from phallic farce. The play's central idea—that women take over the affairs of state—would have seemed irresistibly comic to Aristophanes and his audience. The slapstick and banter between the chorus of old men and the chorus of women simply restate the age-old contest between male and female.

Yet *Lysistrata* carries a more important theme than sexuality, which is merely used as a weapon to bring about peace. At the time this play was first produced in 411 B.C.E., Athens had been through twenty hard years of war with Sparta, and the conflict was not to end for another seven years. The seriousness of the war is brought out very forcefully when Lysistrata tells the magistrate that sons have perished in battle and that many young women will never find mates because of this. The fact that the chorus consists of old men underscores the point that many Athenian youths had died in the Peloponnesian War. Here the drama reveals Aristophanes' true feelings about the war with no trace of buffoonery. The dramatist clearly regards Lysistrata as a heroine and not as a butt for humor. When men have failed so thoroughly to govern the affairs of the city, he says, it is time for others to take over. All the while Aristophanes and his audience are fully aware of women's weaknesses. In essence, the playwright is scolding the Athenian men and telling them that if they cannot put an end to the war after twenty years, they might as well give up.

Lysistrata was originally presented as a musical comedy, with songs, choreography, colorful costumes, and masks. The actors were all male, as in the Shakespeare theater. This type of presentation tended to soften the strength of Aristophanes' biting wit, and it gave the play an air of spectacle, of festivity. Aristophanes had the keen comic wit of a Bernard Shaw, but it was employed in a different medium and style, and used for opposite social ends.

"Critical Evaluation" by James Weigel, Jr.

Bibliography:

Bowie, A. M. *Aristophanes: Myth, Ritual, and Comedy.* Cambridge, England: Cambridge University Press, 1993. An interesting structural anthropological approach that places Aristophanes' plays in their contemporary context. The analysis of *Lysistrata* includes a discussion of earlier myths and rituals that demonstrate feminist power.

Dover, K. J. *Aristophanic Comedy.* Berkeley: University of California Press, 1972. A tribute to

Artistophanes' plays in their cultural context by a distinguished classical Greek scholar. A separate chapter on *Lysistrata* provides a synopsis and examines the lyrics and characters. Also includes a discussion of war and incorporates useful notes on transliteration.

Reckford, Kenneth J. *Aristophanes' Old-and-New Comedy*. Chapel Hill: University of North Carolina Press, 1987. Six essays on interpreting Aristophanes. The author, who views *Lysistrata* as living theater, offers unusual staging possibilities and discusses the play within the context of loyalty to comic truths, ritual, and sexual equality. Lengthy bibliography included.

Solomos, Alexis. *The Living Aristophanes*. Ann Arbor: University of Michigan Press, 1974. The author, the director who first staged all of Aristophanes' plays at the classic theater at Epidaurus, discusses *Lysistrata* as Aristophanes' first attempt at comedy as popular entertainment. Argues that Aristophanes was indulging his theatrical fancies rather than moralizing as a social reformer.

Spatz, Lois. *Aristophanes*. Boston: Twayne, 1978. Sound introduction to Aristophanes' plays. A separate chapter on *Lysistrata* examines the political and historical background, secondary role of women in Athenian society, and the elusive and idyllic quest for peace. Also includes chronology, notes, and selected bibliography.

THE MABINOGION

Type of work: Novel
Author: Unknown
Type of plot: Folklore
Time of plot: The Middle Ages
Locale: Arthurian Britain, primarily Wales
First published: 1838-1849 (tales from *The White Book of Rhydderch*, 1300-1325 and *The Red Book of Hergest*, 1375-1425)

Principal characters:
>PWYLL, the prince of Dyved
>RHIANNON, his wife
>PRYDERI, their son
>KICVA, Pryderi's wife
>BENDIGEID VRAN, the king of the Island of the Mighty and Llyr's son
>BRANWEN, Llyr's daughter
>MATHOLWCH, the king of Ireland and Branwen's husband
>MANAWYDAN, another of Llyr's sons and Pryderi's stepfather
>KING MATH
>GWYDION, one of King Math's warriors
>LLEW LLAW GYFFES, Gwydion's favorite son
>BLODEUWEDD, Llew Llaw Gyffes' elfwife
>MACSEN WLEDIG, the emperor of Rome
>LLUDD, the king of Britain
>LLEVELYS, his brother and the king of France
>KING ARTHUR
>KILHWCH, one of King Arthur's knights
>YSBADDADEN, a crafty giant
>OLWEN, his daughter and Kilhwch's beloved
>RHONABWY, a dreamer
>OWAIN, the new Knight of the Fountain
>PEREDUR, one of King Arthur's knights
>GERINT, another of King Arthur's knights and later a king
>ENID, his wife

The Stories:
"Pwyll, Prince of Dyved." Pwyll, the prince of Dyved, was caught stealing a dying deer. In order to redeem himself, Pwyll agreed to exchange lands and appearances with the chieftain who had caught him and to slay the chieftain's enemy after a year's time. That year, each prince ruled the other's land wisely and well, and each remained faithful to his own true wife. At the year's end, Pwyll slew the enemy, returned home on good terms with the other prince, and eventually gained the other's lands. From a hill one day, Pwyll saw a lovely lady ride by. She eluded him three times, but on the fourth, he spoke to her. She told him that her name was Rhiannon and invited him to her castle a year from that day. Pwyll went with his men, subdued her other suitor, and won the lady. Some time thereafter, Rhiannon bore a son who disappeared the first night after his birth. The women on watch accused her of killing it, and Pwyll made her

pay a heavy penance. Meanwhile, a farmer had taken the baby from a monster. Eventually, he restored the boy to Pwyll, who then released his wife from her penance and named his son Pryderi.

"Branwen, Daughter of Llyr." Bendigeid Vran, son of Llyr and king of the Island of the Mighty, made a pact with Matholwch, king of Ireland, and gave him his sister Branwen to wed. When the king of Ireland suffered an insult at the hands of one of Bendigeid Vran's men, Bendigeid Vran made good the loss; but because of the insult, Matholwch and Branwen were made to suffer heavily at the hands of the Irishmen. Bendigeid Vran learned of their treatment, sailed to Ireland, and made war on the Irish. Both sides suffered great losses. Bendigeid Vran was killed by a poisoned spear; his last request was that his head be buried in the White Mount in London. Branwen died of sorrow. Finally, only seven of Bendigeid Vran's men were left alive to bury the head of their chief, and only five pregnant Irish women.

"Manawydan, Son of Llyr." Two of the men left living after the war in Ireland were Pryderi and Manawydan, the brother of Bendigeid Vran. These two men went to live on Pryderi's lands and Manawydan married Pryderi's mother. The two men and their wives—for Pryderi had a wife named Kicva—lived pleasantly until the countryside was magically laid desolate and everyone else had disappeared. They left their lands and tried to earn a living at various trades, but they were always driven off by their envious competitors. When they returned to their own lands, Pryderi and his mother entered a magic castle that vanished with them. Manawydan then tried farming, and again his crops were magically desolated. Determined to get to the bottom of the mystery, Manawydan stayed up to watch his last field. When he saw thousands of mice ravaging the field, he caught one and declared that he would hang it. Pryderi's wife, along with three churchmen, tried to dissuade him, but he was still determined to hang the mouse. At last, the third churchman disclosed himself as the one who had cursed Manawydan and his friends in revenge for an insult from Pryderi's father years before. He promised to restore everything, including Pryderi and his mother, if Manawydan would release the mouse. Manawydan insisted that the magician never touch his lands again, and he returned the mouse, who happened to be the churchman's wife. Everything was restored, and the four companions returned to their former happiness.

"Math, Son of Mathonwy." Gwydion's brother, Gilvaethwy, loved King Math's footmaiden, Goewin. Hoping to secure the maiden for his brother, Gwydion tricked Pryderi into exchanging some pigs for twelve phantom steeds and twelve phantom greyhounds. Pryderi and his men pursued them. While King Math and his men were preparing to fight this army, Gwydion and his brother raped the footmaiden before they returned to the fight and won the battle for King Math. The king then punished the brothers by turning them into animals for three years. After his penance, Gwydion had two sons. Their mother cursed Gwydion's favorite son, named Llew Llaw Gyffes, by saying that he would never have a human wife. To thwart this curse, King Math and Gwydion created for him an elfwife, Blodeuwedd, out of flowers. The wife proved unfaithful by taking a lover. Determined to get rid of her husband, she asked him how he might be killed. He foolishly told her; in turn, she told her lover, who tried to kill Llew Llaw Gyffes. Gwydion's son did not die, however, but was turned into an eagle. Gwydion then searched for his son, found him, and restored him to his former shape. Gwydion and Llew Llaw Gyffes then took revenge on the wife and her lover by turning her into an owl and killing him.

"The Dream of Macsen Wledig." Macsen Wledig, the Emperor of Rome, dreamed one night of a lovely maiden in a strange and wonderful land. Awakening, he sent his messengers all over the world in search of her. After wandering in many lands, they found her in a castle in Britain, and they guided the Emperor to her. He found everything as it had been in his dream. The maiden accepted him. For her maiden portion, he gave her father the island of Britain and had three castles built for her. Macsen Wledig lived with his wife in Britain for seven years. Meanwhile, the Romans had chosen a new emperor, who sent a note to Wledig warning him not to return. Wledig then marched on Gaul, fought his way through Italy, and reconquered Rome.

"Lludd and Llevelys." Three plagues ravaged Britain. The first was a crafty foreign people; the second was a yearly midnight scream that made everything barren; and the third was the habitual disappearance of food at the king's court. Lludd, the great king of Britain, asked help from his wise and well-beloved brother, Llevelys, who was king of France. Llevelys told him to mash insects in water and sprinkle the solution over the foreigners to kill them. To get rid of the screaming dragon, Lludd would have to lure it with mead, put it in a sack, and bury it in a stone coffer. To keep the food, Lludd would have to capture a magician who put everyone to sleep. The king performed these tasks, and Britain was rid of the plagues.

"Kilhwch and Olwen." Kilhwch's stepmother had spitefully prophesied that Kilhwch would not have a woman until he won Olwen, the daughter of Ysbaddaden, a crafty and powerful giant. Kilhwch, who had fallen in love with Olwen without having seen her, set out immediately for King Arthur's court, where King Arthur accepted the young man as his knight. Kilhwch then set out to seek Ysbaddaden; all King Arthur's gallant warriors went with him. After a long journey, Kilhwch met Olwen, the most beautiful woman he had ever seen. He and King Arthur's men proceeded to Ysbaddaden's court to ask for Olwen. After fighting for three days and wounding the giant three times, Kilhwch learned that he could win Olwen and slay her father after performing forty nearly impossible tasks for the giant. By dint of brute force, cunning, and magic, Kilhwch, King Arthur, and his men succeeded in completing the tasks. Kilhwch then slew Ysbaddaden, married Olwen, and lived happily ever after.

"The Dream of Rhonabwy." While seeking a man who had ravaged the land, Rhonabwy and his companions found themselves in a dark hall where the floors were covered with dung. After trying to talk to the strange people inhabiting the hall and failing, Rhonabwy lay down on an ox-skin and began to dream. He dreamed of the heroic Arthurian age when men were demigods who lived in splendor in a land where life was full. He found himself in King Arthur's court watching a game between King Arthur and Owain. While the game was in progress, three servants informed Owain that his ravens were being killed by King Arthur's men, but the king insisted that the game continue. Owain told his men to raise his banner, whereupon the ravens revived and began to slaughter the men. Three servants came to tell King Arthur how his men were being killed, but Owain insisted that the game continue. At last, the king begged Owain to call off the ravens. He did so, and there was peace. Many men then brought tribute to King Arthur. At that point, Rhonabwy awakened.

"The Lady of the Fountain." While at King Arthur's court, Owain learned from Kynon of a powerful Knight of the Fountain who overthrew all challengers. Upon being taunted by Kai, Owain went in search of this knight, challenged him, and slew him. With the help of a maiden, Owain then escaped the angry townsmen who were seeking to avenge the death of their lord, and he married the dead knight's wife. He ruled the land well for three years. Meanwhile, King Arthur and his knights had come in search of Owain. King Arthur's men arrived at the fountain and challenged the new Knight of the Fountain but were overthrown by him. The king and Owain were finally reunited, and Owain returned to King Arthur's court after promising his wife that he would return at the end of three years. Owain was reminded of his promise when his wife came to King Arthur's court and removed the ring that she had given him as a token by which to remember her. Then Owain went in search of his wife. After restoring a lady's kingdom, killing a serpent about to destroy a lion, saving the maiden who had aided him six years earlier, and killing her tormentors, Owain was restored to his wife. Another feat was defeating and transforming the Black Oppressor. Thereafter, Owain and his wife lived happily at King Arthur's court.

"Peredur, Son of Evrawg." Peredur lived a sheltered life with his mother; nevertheless, he grew up strong and swift. Although his mother did not want him to become a knight, nothing could keep him from fulfilling his desire. When he prepared to leave his mother and journey to King Arthur's court, she instructed him in the chivalric code. Peredur was an ungainly sight as he entered King Arthur's court, for he was still awkward and naïve. Nevertheless, he soon showed his prowess in battle, and through many adventures, he acquired polish and skill in the arts of hunting, war, and love. Many reports of his strength and bravery reached King Arthur's ears. Peredur spent his time defending and loving maidens, restoring kingdoms to the wronged, avenging insults, killing monsters and evil men, protecting the weak, and ridding the land of plagues. In short, he was a matchless knight. In the course of his adventures, he inadvertently caused a kingdom to wither and grow barren, but he restored it to fertility by dint of strength and courage. In the end, he rid the land of seven evil witches.

"Gerint, Son of Erbin." While King Arthur and his men were hunting, Gerint rode with the Queen and her maids. When a dwarf insulted Gerint and one of the maids, the knight challenged the dwarf's lord to a contest and defeated him. Afterward, Gerint restored a kingdom to its proper lord and won the king's daughter, Enid, as his wife. Gerint then traveled back to King Arthur's court and received a stag head for his reward. In time, Gerint went with Enid to rule the land, after inheriting a kingdom from his father. He devoted more time to his wife than he did to jousts or battles, and his subjects complained bitterly. When Enid learned of their grievance, she inadvertently told him. In anger, Gerint set out on a journey with his wife to prove his strength and valor. He performed superhuman feats and slaughtered belligerent knights and caitiffs in vast numbers, but he nearly died in the attempt. Finally, having proved himself to his wife and subjects, he returned home to rule once more.

Critical Evaluation:

These tales had a long oral tradition before they were written down, perhaps as early as the twelfth or thirteenth century. Strictly speaking, *The Mabinogion* is the first four tales in the collection of Lady Charlotte Guest, which was published in 1838-1839. The entire collection of tales furnishes some of the best-known characters and motifs of European romance. The stories have unity, assurance of style, skillful dialogue, accurate delineation of character, rich color, and a noble perspective of life. Their author or authors were artists well trained in nuances and subtleties of language. No one has ever doubted that the Welsh were skilled storytellers. So were the Bretons and Icelandic bards, and their talent has left indelible impressions upon Western literature. *The Mabinogion*, in particular, has contributed significant and ancient folkloric themes as well as some of the earliest lore of Britain.

The unknown author of "Kilhwch and Olwen," one of the most artistic and enthusiastic contributors in *The Mabinogion*, creates a world of magic, color, and vigorous action. He narrates the story of the Celtic hero, Kilhwch, who seeks a giant's daughter for his wife. The plot is a typical quest with a list of forty tasks that Kilhwch must accomplish before he wins Ysbaddaden's daughter, Olwen. The tasks or quests are not so important as the assemblage of attendant persons to Kilhwch, which include his cousin Arthur. Arthur and his company form a nucleus for the later Arthurian Round Table. Appearing in this story too, is the giant herdsman, a familiar motif in folklore, one to surface in other romances.

An important contribution to medieval romance generally is that richness of color that vibrates in the Welsh narrative. Olwen wears a robe of flame-red silk and necklace of red gold set with pearls and rubies. The author states her hair was yellower "than the flower of the broom," her cheeks redder "than the reddest foxgloves." Wherever she walks, white flowers spring up behind her. Kilhwch rides with two greyhounds in collars of red gold; his purple mantle has a red-gold apple in each corner.

"The Dream of Rhonabwy," one of the early dream visions in Celtic literature, lacks such movement and character description but has more realism. The dream deals with Arthur's battles against the Saxons; the main incident is the game played between Arthur and Owain with its conflict between the former's men and the latter's ravens. Norman-French themes combine with older Irish and Welsh ones here with possible foreshadowing of Morgain la Fe (Modron), a shape-shifting figure who weaves her way through various Continental romances bringing magic birds, healing plasters, rings, and curative waters to innumerable heroes in time of need.

The last three stories in *The Mabinogion* are often compared to three similar works by Chrétien de Troyes. Much critical debate has been carried on between the Celticists, those who feel Welsh tradition underlies the spread of Arthurian material on the Continent, and the Continentalists, who assert that the latter influenced Welsh stories. As Gwyn Jones notes, opinion is swinging toward the Celticists because of evidence from linguistics, comparative folklore, and methods of composition in the Middle Ages. Nevertheless, parallels between "The Lady of the Fountain," "Peredur, Son of Evrawg" and "Gerint, Son of Erbin" on the one hand, and Chrétien's similar verse romances on the other, are considerable; perhaps the Welsh authors and the French romancer worked from a lost common source.

The characters in the three Welsh tales may lack depth, and the actions themselves may be insufficiently motivated, but Owain, Gerint, and Peredur partake of entertaining adventures. If the narratives lack the meaning and skillful joining of incident found in Chrétien's poems, this seems purposeful rather than due to bungling artistry. In addition, many of the tales in *The Mabinogion* are probably retellings of material whose origins may have been forgotten, if indeed they were ever known. Bits of ancient Irish stories, Norman-French fragments, and archaic traditions in Welsh make up their subject matter; the Welsh tellers contributed the color and vigor of action. The audience must have loved this excess color in garments, tapestries, ornaments, and armor, and the innumerable battles and adventures, whether these were smoothly connected or not. Cohesive unity was not the authors' intent, as it was that of Chrétien de Troyes.

The familiar world of hunting, fighting, shape-shifting, and magic is there; so is Arthur presiding over a court rich with armor, jewels, beautiful ladies, and brave knights. The nebulous sixth century "battle leader," as the Latin chronicler Nennius described Arthur, may have been only a local chieftain leading somewhat limited skirmishes in southwest Britain, but in *The Mabinogion* he returns to literature a powerful and glorious king. He presides over an extensive court, and important kings from all over the Western world come to pay him homage. Whether he lived or not, this is the hero England needed and remembers. The Welsh tales of *The Mabinogion* helped immeasurably in clothing him and his famous knights with splendor, regardless of possible influences from other sources.

"Critical Evaluation" by Muriel B. Ingham

Bibliography:
Ford, Patrick K. *The "Mabinogi" and Other Medieval Welsh Tales*. Berkeley: University of

California Press, 1972. Traces history of various translations of the Welsh myths. Includes a map of Wales, a glossary, and a guide to Welsh pronunciations. Designed to inform students and general readers alike.

Graves, Robert. *The White Goddess*. 3d ed. Winchester, Mass.: Faber & Faber, 1959. This amended and enlarged edition celebrates the poetic myth in great detail. Hails Rhiannon as "white goddess."

Jones, Gwyn. *Kings, Beasts, and Heroes*. Oxford, England: Oxford University Press, 1972. Portions of text present an excellent condensed overview of *The Mabinogion*. Focuses on Culhwch and Olwen, as well as Arthur. More than twenty-two illustrations.

Laynard, John. *A Celtic Quest: Sexuality and Soul in Individuation*. Edited by Anne S. Bosch. New York: Spring Publications, 1975. Explains *The Mabinogion* and related stories in psychological and behavioral terms. Uses allegory to show the characters' relationship to areas of the psyche. Places emphasis on the dichotomy between the nurturing mother figure and the devouring, animalistic mother.

The Mabinogion. Translated by Gwyn Jones and Thomas Jones. London: J. M. Dent, 1949. Excellent adaptation of the Welsh myths. Discusses the four branches of the Mabiniogi and its seven related stories in thorough detail. Advocates the literary merit of the mythological legends.

MAC FLECKNOE

Type of work: Poetry
Author: John Dryden (1631-1700)
Type of plot: Mock-heroic
Time of plot: Late 1670's
Locale: London, England
First published: 1682

> *Principal characters:*
> FLECKNOE, a minor poet and dramatist, monarch of dullness
> SHADWELL, his chosen successor
> HERRINGMAN, captain of the honor guard
> SIR FORMAL TRIFLE, character from a Shadwell drama

The Story:

Flecknoe, the monarch of dullness, sensed the approaching end of his long reign and began to reflect on an appropriate successor. He planned to crown a new monarch before death overcame him. In order to secure a proper succession, he was willing, even eager, to abdicate. Fortunately, candidates were numerous; among his numerous poetic sons, many were suitably dull and stupid. Yet with little hesitation, he concluded that Shadwell most resembled himself in dullness and was therefore the ideal choice. Even Shadwell's portly, rotund appearance was an element favorable to his selection. In a speech musing on the selection, Flecknoe praised Shadwell for his nonsensical, obscure, tautological verses. Depicting Shadwell as potentially a greater monarch, he portrayed his own reign as merely a precursor to a more gloriously dull age. Flecknoe remembered Shadwell's previous participation in low forms of entertainment, like lute playing, public spectacles, and dances. Flecknoe concluded, however, that Shadwell's dramas best qualified him as the chosen monarch of dunces.

The site selected for the coronation was the Barbican, an area surrounding a ruined Roman watchtower located in the northern part of London. A run-down portion of the city, it had become the site of brothels and of the Nursery, a school for young actors. It was associated with inferior forms of entertainment. Instead of practicing roles created by John Fletcher and Ben Jonson, young actors were schooled in punning and coarse humor like that found in the comedies of Shadwell. In order to fulfill the prophecy of Thomas Dekker, a minor Elizabethan dramatist, that a mighty prince would reign in the area, Flecknoe erected a throne on the site, made from piles of his own printed works that no one would buy.

Once news of the coronation had spread through the area, other inferior poetasters and dunces began to assemble themselves before the throne. Their procession led through streets covered not with imperial carpets, but with loose pages from the unsold books of Shadwell and others like him. Caught up in the enthusiasm, the throng of poetasters expressed their approval with shouts of acclamation.

In his coronation oath, Shadwell swore to maintain true dullness and to wage perpetual war with truth and sense. As tokens of his office, he received a mug of ale in his left hand and a copy of Flecknoe's play *Love's Kingdom* in his right. These replaced the ball and scepter used in actual coronations as symbols of secular rule and regal power. Instead of the laurel wreath connoting achievement in art, a wreath featuring sleep-inducing opium poppies crowned his head, and at the conclusion, twelve owls, symbols of stupidity, were released to fly aloft.

Following the coronation Flecknoe delivered a prophetic speech that included advice about writing. Believing that Shadwell would prove even duller than he had been, Flecknoe urged Shadwell to trust his own gifts, not labor to be dull. When writing plays, he should model both witty characters and fops on himself, for they would all appear identical to the audience. He should avoid vain claims about imitating Ben Jonson or successful Restoration dramatists like Sir George Etheredge; instead he should rely on obscure poetasters as models. Lacking any ability to create Jonson's array of characters of humor, he had fashioned characters who were all inclined in one direction, toward dullness. His inclination toward farce, coarse physical humor, and obscene language showed that he had little in common with his betters like Jonson and Sir Charles Sedley. Indeed, it would be better if he abandoned major literary genres like drama and satire altogether, since his efforts in these literary forms produced effects in the audience opposite to that intended. Instead, he should turn his attention to inferior forms such as anagrams, pattern poems, acrostics, and songs.

As his speech was drawing to a close, a trap door opened and Flecknoe sank down, but an upward wind bore his mantle aloft. Like the prophet Elija's mantle descending upon Elisha, Flecknoe's mantle rose upward and landed upon Shadwell.

Critical Evaluation:

John Dryden was the first acknowledged master of poetic satire in English. Of his three major satires, *Mac Flecknoe*, consisting of 217 lines of rhymed iambic pentameter, was the first to be composed. The poem is a mock-epic attack against Thomas Shadwell (1642-1692), a rival playwright. It may stand as an example of many similar works that grew out of dramatic rivalry. The satire has been the subject of intensive scholarly and critical study because many puzzles and ambiguities concerning it remain unresolved. Neither the date of composition nor the occasion of writing the work is known with assurance, and some of the poem's numerous topical allusions are unidentified.

The work was published anonymously in 1682, but from contemporary references, was known to have circulated in manuscript before its unauthorized publication. Dryden made no written acknowledgment of his authorship until after Shadwell's death in 1692 but to contemporaries the authorship was no secret. Scholarly evidence suggests that it was written between 1676, the date of the latest Shadwell drama cited in the text, and 1678, the most probable year for Richard Flecknoe's death.

Dryden's reasons for attacking Shadwell at the time also remain obscure. Undeniably, the two dramatists disagreed on literary and political questions. In the political controversies of the time, Dryden sided with the Tory supporters of the king, and Shadwell allied himself with the Whigs. In prefaces to his plays, Shadwell portrayed himself as a follower of Ben Jonson, whose comedies of humor featured characters influenced by humors, or quirks of personality, that motivated their actions. Dryden preferred the comedies of wit and intrigue that were the dominant forms during the Restoration. Yet Dryden could hardly have perceived Shadwell as a threat to himself. Several clumsy poetic lampoons on Dryden have been attributed to Shadwell, but none appears to have preceded *Mac Flecknoe*. Scholars have attempted to discover passages in Shadwell's published works that may have given offense to Dryden, and some of the scholars' suggestions may be considered plausible but not clearly established occasions for Dryden's satire.

The poem employs the mock-epic or mock-heroic mode of satire, making low nonsense and dullness ridiculous by juxtaposing them with solemn, important matters like imperial Rome or the question of monarchical succession. Placing literary dunces within the exalted context of a coronation ceremony and dignifying the event with comparisons to religious prophets and allusions to the Roman Empire at its zenith serve to deflate the satiric victims by drawing attention to the differences between the exalted and the lowly. The satire achieves a devastating attack on Shadwell and other poets through an ironic inversion of values. It also establishes by implication a reliable set of critical guidelines for poets.

While achieving these ends of satire, it also creates a rich and complex tone of poetic vigor, largely through allusion, wit, irony, and humor. While it might be expected that the theme of a declining monarch seeking to abdicate and naming a successor would lend itself to a somber tone, the poem belies the expectation. As a character, Flecknoe conveys a tone of gaiety and exuberance through his speeches, which make up more than half the poem's length.

Undeniably the satire is in some measure a lampoon, a personal attack on Shadwell. It goes beyond exposing literary ineptness, clearly present in Shadwell's works, to attack his personal appearance and habits, and there is no reason to assume that Dryden had reform of his victim in mind. Shadwell's obesity is cited as an indication of thoughtlessness, and his known habit of taking opium becomes an allusion in the coronation scene. Even his frequent acknowledgments of literary debts to Ben Jonson and to contemporaries like Sir Charles Sedley are presented as evidence of plagiarism. Other personal details, like Shadwell's skill at playing the lute and his family association with Ireland, are introduced for the sake of ridicule. Unlike the tone of invective, or railing denunciation, commonly found in the satires of Juvenal, Dryden seeks the fine raillery through the exposure of excesses, in the manner of Horatian satire. Shadwell's excesses are assailed as comical, not criminal.

Beyond vexing and discrediting a rival dramatist, however, the satire upholds canons of neoclassic criticism. One perceives Dryden's sense of a hierarchy of values in the overall plan of the work. To the neoclassic critic, Augustan Rome, source of numerous allusions, represented the apex of literary art. From a neoclassic perspective, modern poets did best by schooling themselves in Roman literature, being guided by the critical maxims of Horace. Through these means modern vernacular literatures might equal that of Rome, but few believed it possible for moderns to surpass the literary achievement of Rome. In addition, neoclassic criticism assumed a hierarchy in literary genres, with drama near the top and such contrived lyric forms as acrostics and pattern poems near the bottom.

Yet the emphasis on hierarchies, apparent in the framework of the satire, remains somewhat in the background. A more pervasive literary technique for establishing neoclassic canons is the use of polarities or dichotomies, opposed terms, with one embraced, the other rejected. The all-important neoclassic standards of "nature" and "art" serve to condemn Shadwell's unnatural railing at arts he does not understand and his producing works that never rise to the level of art. "Wit" is the antithesis of "dullness," "sense" of "nonsense." The ideals, with their opposites, are frequently repeated to enforce the neoclassic insistence on lucid reasoning and felicitous expression in literature.

In genres, drama and satire are juxtaposed to songs and acrostics. In verse forms, the iambic pentameter line, the English meter nearest epic verse in Latin, is superior to meters of ordinary lyrics. In the contrasts between kingdoms, the Roman Aeneas and Ascanius, his chosen successor, draw attention to the triviality of Flecknoe and Shadwell. The kingdom of letters has its giants and pygmies as well. Among the literary figures of an earlier age, Ben Jonson and John Fletcher are contrasted to Thomas Dekker, James Shirley, and Thomas Heywood. Among Dryden's English contemporaries, George Etheredge and Sir Charles Sedley represent dramatic achievement beyond the ken of Shadwell and Flecknoe. As in other critical works of Dryden, one perceives not only the emphasis on neoclassicism but also numerous references to English authors. These references reflect a nascent sense of English literary history.

Stanley Archer

Bibliography:
Dryden, John. *Poems 1681-1684.* Edited by H. T. Swendenberg and Vinton A. Dearing. Berkeley: University of California Press, 1972. The standard edition of Dryden. Traces the background and origin of the poem, identifies allusions, references, and ambiguities with thoroughness and accuracy.

Jack, Ian. *Augustan Satire: Intention and Idiom in English Poetry, 1660-1750.* Oxford, England: Clarendon Press, 1952. Devotes a chapter to *Mac Flecknoe*, analyzing the satire as a mock epic. Emphasizes the personal elements in the attack on Shadwell.

Miner, Earl. *Dryden's Poetry.* Bloomington: Indiana University Press, 1967. Explores theatrical elements in the poem and its fundamental metaphors. Identifies the monarchical, religious, and aesthetic metaphors as central to the meaning and poetic effect.

Swedenberg, H. T., Jr., ed. *Essential Articles for the Study of John Dryden.* London: Frank Cass, 1966. Includes three articles on *Mac Flecknoe.* Two explore dating and authorship; one traces Dryden's debt to Abraham Cowley's *Davideis.*

Winn, James Anderson. *John Dryden and His World.* New Haven, Conn.: Yale University Press, 1987. In his critical biography of Dryden, Winn provides an extended account of Dryden's controversy with Shadwell. Includes a brief analysis of the satire.

MACBETH

Type of work: Drama
Author: William Shakespeare (1564-1616)
Type of plot: Tragedy
Time of plot: Eleventh century
Locale: Scotland
First performed: 1606; first published, 1623

Principal characters:
MACBETH, a Scottish thane
LADY MACBETH, his wife
DUNCAN, the king of Scotland
MALCOLM, his son
BANQUO, a Scottish chieftain
MACDUFF, a rebel lord

The Story:

On a lonely heath in Scotland, three weird witches sang their riddling runes and said that soon they would meet Macbeth. Macbeth, the noble thane of Glamis, had recently been victorious in a great battle against Vikings and Scottish rebels. For his brave deeds, King Duncan decided to confer upon him the lands of the rebellious thane of Cawdor.

On his way to see the king, Macbeth and his friend Banquo met the three witches on the dark moor. The wild and frightful women greeted Macbeth by first calling him thane of Glamis, then thane of Cawdor, and finally, king of Scotland. Finally, they prophesied that Banquo's heirs would reign in Scotland in years to come. When Macbeth tried to question the three hags, they vanished.

Macbeth thought very little about the strange prophecy until he met one of Duncan's messengers, who told him that he was now thane of Cawdor. This piece of news stunned Macbeth, but Banquo thought the witches' prophecy was an evil ruse to whet Macbeth's ambition and trick him into fulfilling the prophecy. Macbeth did not heed Banquo's warning; hearing the witches call him king had gone deep into his soul. He pondered over the possibility of becoming a monarch and set his whole heart on the attainment of this goal. If he could be thane of Cawdor, perhaps he could rule all of Scotland as well. As it was now, Duncan was king, and he had two sons who would rule after him. The problem was great. Macbeth shook off his dreams and accompanied Banquo to greet Duncan.

Duncan was a kind, majestic, gentle, and strong ruler; Macbeth was fond of him. When Duncan however mentioned that his son, Malcolm, would succeed him on the throne, Macbeth saw the boy as an obstacle in his own path; he hardly dared admit to himself how this impediment disturbed him. Duncan announced that he would spend one night of a royal procession at Macbeth's castle. Lady Macbeth, who was even more ambitious than her husband, saw Duncan's visit as a perfect opportunity for Macbeth to become king. She determined that he should murder Duncan and usurp the throne.

That night there was much feasting in the castle. After everyone was asleep, Lady Macbeth told her husband of her plan for the king's murder. Horrified, Macbeth at first refused to do the deed, but when his wife accused him of cowardice and dangled bright prospects of his future before his eyes, Macbeth finally succumbed. He stole into the sleeping king's chamber and plunged a knife into his heart.

The murder was blamed on two grooms whom Lady Macbeth had smeared with Duncan's blood while they were asleep. Yet suspicions were aroused in the castle. The dead king's sons fled—Malcolm to England and Donalbain to Ireland—and when Macbeth was proclaimed king, Macduff, a nobleman who had been Duncan's close friend, suspected him of the bloody killing.

Macbeth began to have horrible dreams; his mind was never free from fear. Often he thought of the witches' second prophecy, that Banquo's heirs would hold the throne, and the prediction tormented him. Macbeth was so determined that Banquo should never share in his own hard-earned glory that he resolved to murder Banquo and his son, Fleance.

Lady Macbeth and her husband gave a great banquet for the noble thanes of Scotland. At the same time, Macbeth sent murderers to waylay Banquo and his son before they could reach the palace. Banquo was slain in the scuffle, but Fleance escaped. Meanwhile, in the large banquet hall, Macbeth pretended great sorrow that Banquo was not present. Banquo was however present in spirit, and his ghost majestically appeared in Macbeth's own seat. The startled king was so frightened that he almost betrayed his guilt when he saw the apparition, but he was the only one to see it. Lady Macbeth quickly led him away and dismissed the guests.

More frightened than ever at the thought of Banquo's ghost having returned to haunt him and of Fleance who had escaped but might one day claim the throne, Macbeth determined to seek solace from the witches on the dismal heath. They assured Macbeth that he would not be overcome by man born of woman, nor until the forest of Birnam came to Dunsinane Hill. They also warned him to beware of Macduff. When Macbeth asked if Banquo's children would reign over the kingdom, the witches disappeared. The news they gave him had brought him cheer, however. Macbeth now felt he need fear no man, since all were born of women, and certainly the great Birnam forest could not be moved by human power.

Macbeth heard that Macduff was gathering a hostile army in England that was to be led by Duncan's son Malcolm, who was determined to avenge his father's murder. So terrified was Macbeth that he resolved to murder Macduff's wife and children in order to bring the rebel to submission. After this slaughter, however, Macbeth was more than ever tormented by fear; his twisted mind had almost reached the breaking point, and he longed for death to release him from his nightmarish existence.

Before long, Lady Macbeth's strong will broke as well. Dark dreams of murder and violence drove her to madness. The horror of her crimes and the agony of being hated and feared by all of Macbeth's subjects made her so ill that her death seemed imminent.

On the eve of Macduff's attack on Macbeth's castle, Lady Macbeth died, depriving her husband of all the support and courage she had been able to give him in the past. Rallying, Macbeth summoned strength to meet his enemy. Yet Birnam wood was moving, for Malcolm's soldiers were hidden behind cut green boughs, which from a distance appeared to be a moving forest. Macduff, enraged by the slaughter of his innocent family, was determined to meet Macbeth in hand-to-hand conflict.

Macbeth went out to battle filled with the false courage given him by the witches' prophecy that no man born of woman would overthrow him. Meeting Macduff, Macbeth began to fight him, but when he found out that Macduff had been ripped alive from his mother's womb, Macbeth fought with waning strength, all hope of victory gone. With a flourish, Macduff severed the head of the bloody King of Scotland. The prophecy was fulfilled.

Critical Evaluation:

Not only is *Macbeth* by far the shortest of William Shakespeare's great tragedies, but it is also anomalous in some structural respects. Like *Othello* (1604) and only a very few other Shakespearean plays, *Macbeth* is without the complications of a subplot. Consequently, the action moves forward in a swift and inexorable rush. More significantly, the climax—the murder of Duncan—takes place very early in the play. As a result, attention is focused on the various consequences of the crime rather than on the ambiguities or moral dilemmas that had preceded and occasioned it.

In this, the play differs from *Othello*, where the hero commits murder only after long plotting, and from *Hamlet* (1600-1601), where the hero spends most of the play in moral indecision. It is more like *King Lear* (1605-1606), where destructive action flows from the central premise of the division of the kingdom. Yet *Macbeth* differs from that play, too, in that it does not raise the monumental, cosmic questions of good and evil in nature. Instead it explores the moral and psychological effects of evil in the life of one man. For all the power and prominence of Lady Macbeth, the drama remains essentially the story of the lord who commits regicide and thereby enmeshes himself in a complex web of consequences.

When Macbeth first enters, he is far from the villain whose experiences the play subsequently describes. He has just returned from a glorious military success in defense of the crown. He is rewarded by the grateful Duncan, with preferment as thane of Cawdor. This honor, which initially qualifies him for the role of hero, ironically intensifies the horror of the murder Macbeth soon thereafter commits.

His fall is rapid, and his crime is more clearly a sin than is usually the case in tragedy. It is not mitigated by mixed motives or insufficient knowledge. Moreover, the sin is regicide, an action viewed by the Renaissance as exceptionally foul, since it struck at God's representative on earth. The sin is so boldly offensive that many have tried to find extenuation in the impetus given Macbeth by the witches. However, the witches do not control behavior in the play. They are symbolic of evil and prescient of crimes which are to come, but they neither encourage nor facilitate Macbeth's actions. They are merely a poignant external symbol of the ambition that is already within Macbeth. Indeed, when he discusses the witches' prophecy with Lady Macbeth, it is clear that the possibility has been discussed before.

Nor can the responsibility be shifted to Lady Macbeth, despite her goading. In a way, she is merely acting out the role of the good wife, encouraging her husband to do what she believes to be in his best interests. She is a catalyst and supporter, but she does not make the grim decision, and Macbeth never tries to lay the blame on her.

When Macbeth proceeds on his bloody course, there is little extenuation in his brief failure of nerve. He is an ambitious man overpowered by his high aspirations, yet Shakespeare is able to elicit feelings of sympathy for him from the audience. Despite the evil of his actions, he does not arouse the distaste audiences reserve for such villains as Iago and Cornwall. This may be because Macbeth is not evil incarnate but a human being who has sinned. Moreover, audiences are as much affected by what Macbeth says about his actions as by the deeds themselves. Both substance and setting emphasize the great evil, but Macbeth does not go about his foul business easily. He knows what he is doing, and his agonizing reflections show a man increasingly losing control over his own moral destiny.

Although Lady Macbeth demonstrated greater courage and resolution at the time of the murder of Duncan, it is she who falls victim to the physical manifestations of remorse and literally dies of guilt. Macbeth, who starts more tentatively, becomes stronger, or perhaps more inured, as he faces the consequences of his initial crime. The play examines the effects of evil on Macbeth's character and on his subsequent moral behavior. The later murders flow naturally out of the first. Evil breeds evil because Macbeth, to protect himself and consolidate his position, is forced to murder again. Successively, he kills Banquo, attempts to murder Fleance, and brutally exterminates Macduff's family. As his crimes increase, Macbeth's freedom seems to decrease, but his moral responsibility does not. His actions become more cold-blooded as his options disappear.

Shakespeare does not allow Macbeth any moral excuses. The dramatist is aware of the notion that any action performed makes it more likely that the person will perform other such actions. The operation of this phenomenon is apparent as Macbeth finds it increasingly easier to rise to the gruesome occasion. However, the dominant inclination never becomes a total determinant of behavior, so Macbeth does not have the excuse of loss of free will. It does however become ever more difficult to break the chain of events that are rushing him toward moral and physical destruction.

As he degenerates, he becomes more deluded about his invulnerability and more emboldened. What he gains in will and confidence is counterbalanced and eventually toppled by the iniquitous weight of the events he set in motion and felt he had to perpetuate. When he dies, he seems almost to be released from the imprisonment of his own evil.

"Critical Evaluation" by Edward E. Foster

Bibliography:
Bradley, A. C. *Shakespearean Tragedy*. London: Macmillan, 1905. A classic study. Chapters on *Macbeth* deal with fundamental issues of evil, flawed nobility of character, and tragic choice; Bradley's eloquent prose helps the reader appreciate the grandeur of the subject.
Harbage, Alfred. *William Shakespeare: A Reader's Guide*. New York: Farrar, Straus & Giroux, 1963. An excellent introduction to Shakespeare's plays, accessible to the general reader while providing masterful analyses of selected plays. Discussion of *Macbeth* gives a scene-by-scene synopsis, illuminated by wide-ranging, sensitive, analytical commentary.
Holland, Norman. *The Shakespearean Imagination*. New York: Macmillan, 1964. Informative, readable discussions of Shakespeare's major plays based on a series of educational television lectures. Introductory chapters provide a good background to the beliefs and values of Shakespeare's times. The chapter on *Macbeth* discusses elements of the play such as theme, characterization, atmosphere, and imagery.
Long, Michael. *Macbeth*. Boston: Twayne, 1989. An excellent introduction to the play as well as original critical commentary. Includes chapters on stage history, literary counterparts and antecedents, and dramatic symbols, as well as scene-by-scene analysis. Long characterizes Macbeth's tragedy as both Christian and classical, a story of radical isolation from humanity.
Shakespeare, William. *Macbeth*. Edited by Alan Sinfield. Houndsmills, England: Macmillan, 1992. Contains a dozen articles on *Macbeth* that together provide a good idea of the intellectual issues, political concerns, and style of postmodernist criticism not only of this play but also of literature in general. Includes a useful introduction and summative chapter endnotes, plus an annotated bibliography.

MCTEAGUE
A Story of San Francisco

Type of work: Novel
Author: Frank Norris (1870-1902)
Type of plot: Naturalism
Time of plot: 1890's
Locale: San Francisco and Death Valley
First published: 1899

> *Principal characters:*
> McTEAGUE, a dentist
> TRINA, his wife
> MARCUS SCHOULER, McTeague's friend and Trina's cousin

The Story:

McTeague, born in a small mining town, worked with his unambitious father in the mines; yet, his mother saw in her son a chance to realize her own dreams. The opportunity to send him away for a better education came a few years after McTeague's father had died. A traveling dentist was prevailed upon to take the boy as an apprentice.

McTeague learned something of dentistry, but he was too stupid to understand much of it. When his mother died and left him a small sum of money, he set up his own practice in an office-bedroom in San Francisco. McTeague was easily satisfied. He had his concertina for amusement and enough money from his practice to keep him well supplied with beer.

In the flat above McTeague lived his friend Marcus Schouler. Marcus was in love with his cousin Trina Sieppe, whom he brought to McTeague for some dental work. While they were waiting for McTeague to finish with a patient, the cleaning woman sold Trina a lottery ticket.

McTeague immediately fell in love with Trina. Marcus, realizing his friend's attachment, rather enjoyed playing the martyr, setting aside his own love in order that McTeague might feel free to court Trina. He invited the dentist to go with him to call on the Sieppe family. From that day on, McTeague was a steady visitor at the Sieppe home. To celebrate their engagement, McTeague took Trina and her family to the theater. Afterward, they returned to McTeague's flat and found the building in an uproar. Trina's lottery ticket had won five thousand dollars.

In preparation for their wedding, Trina was furnishing a flat across from McTeague's office. When she decided to invest her winnings and collect the monthly interest, the dentist was disappointed, for he had hoped to spend the money on something lavish and exciting. Trina's wishes, however, prevailed. With that income and McTeague's earnings, as well as the little that Trina earned from her hand-carved animals, the McTeagues could be assured of a comfortable life.

Marcus slowly changed in his attitude toward his friend and his cousin. One day, he accused McTeague of stealing Trina's affection for the sake of the five thousand dollars. In his fury, he struck at his old friend with a knife. McTeague was not hurt, but his anger was thoroughly aroused.

In the early months after their wedding, McTeague and Trina were extremely happy. Trina was tactful in the changes she began to make in her husband. Generally, she improved his manners and appearance. They both planned for the time when they could afford a home of their own. As a result of those plans, they had their first real quarrel. McTeague wanted to rent a nearby house, but Trina objected to the high rent. Her thriftiness was slowly turning into miserliness. When McTeague, unknown to her, rented the house, she refused to move or to contribute to the payment of the first month's rent which signing of the lease entailed.

Some days later, they went on a picnic to which Marcus was also invited. Outwardly, he and McTeague had settled their differences, but jealousy still rankled in Marcus. When some wrestling matches were held, Marcus and the dentist were the winners in their bouts. It now remained for the two winners to compete. No match for the brute strength of McTeague, Marcus was thrown. Furious, he demanded another match. In that match, Marcus suddenly leaned forward and bit off the lobe of the dentist's ear. McTeague broke Marcus' arm in his anger.

Marcus soon left San Francisco. Shortly thereafter, an order from City Hall disbarred McTeague from his practice because he lacked college training; Marcus had informed the authorities. Trina and McTeague moved from their flat to a tiny room on the top floor of the building, for the loss of McTeague's practice had made Trina more niggardly than ever. McTeague found a job making dental supplies. Trina devoted almost every waking moment to her animal carvings. She allowed herself and the room to become slovenly, she begrudged every penny they spent, and when McTeague lost his job, she insisted that they move to even cheaper lodgings. McTeague began to drink, and drinking made him vicious. When he was drunk, he would pinch or bite Trina until she gave him money for more whiskey.

The new room into which they moved was filthy and cramped. McTeague grew more and more surly. One morning, he left to go fishing and failed to return. That night, while Trina was searching the streets for him, he broke into her trunk and stole her hoarded savings. After his disappearance, Trina learned that the paint she used on her animals had infected her hand. The fingers of her right hand were amputated.

Trina took a job as a scrubwoman, and the money she earned together with the interest from her five thousand dollars was sufficient to support her. Now that the hoard of money that she had saved was gone, she missed the thrill of counting over the coins, and so she withdrew the whole of her five thousand dollars from the bank and hid the coins in her room. One evening, there was a tap on her window. McTeague was standing outside, hungry and without a place to sleep. Trina angrily refused to let him in. A few evenings later, drunk and vicious, he broke into a room she was cleaning. When she refused to give him any money, he beat her until she fell unconscious. She died early the next morning.

McTeague took her money and went back to the mines, where he fell in with another prospector. McTeague, however, was haunted by the thought that he was being followed. One night, he stole away from his companion and started south across Death Valley. The next day, as he was resting, he was suddenly accosted by a man with a gun. The man was Marcus.

A posse had been searching for McTeague ever since Trina's body had been found, and as soon as Marcus heard about the murder, he volunteered for the manhunt. While the two men stood facing each other in the desert, McTeague's mule ran away, carrying a canteen bag of water on its back. Marcus emptied his gun to kill the animal, but its dead body fell on the canteen bag, and the water was lost. The five thousand dollars was also lashed to the back of the mule. As McTeague went to unfasten it, Marcus seized him. In the struggle, McTeague killed his enemy with his bare hands. Yet, as he slipped to the ground, Marcus managed to snap one handcuff to McTeague's wrist and the other to his own. McTeague looked stupidly around, at the hills about a hundred miles away, and at the dead body to which he was helplessly chained. He was trapped in the parching inferno of the desert that stretched away on every side.

Critical Evaluation:

McTeague presents a unique challenge to the critic. It is a gripping story of the relentless pressures of heredity and environment that distort the soul; it is also a melodrama with stereotyped characters, lurid action, and a creaking machinery of symbols that includes everything from dental equipment to snarling dogs. Despite its weaknesses, *McTeague* is exactly what Alfred Kazin has said it is: "The first great tragic portrait in America of an acquisitive society." Frank Norris' novel initiates the literary treatment of a theme that eventually informed significant American literary works such as Theodore Dreiser's *An American Tragedy* (1925) and Arthur Miller's *Death of a Salesman* (1949).

McTeague himself is a crude but well-meaning hulk of a man whose gentle temper suggests "the draft horse, immensely strong, stupid, docile, obedient." His brutishness is under control as long as he can putter with his dentistry and sleep off his steam beer in the dental chair. Once he succumbs to the erotic impulse that his wife Trina generates in him, however, McTeague is sucked into a world of feelings that undermine the fragile self-control that his undisturbed life made possible. Once he and Trina marry, McTeague becomes vulnerable to her avarice and to Marcus' jealousy and envy. These destructive emotions release the underlying primitiveness of McTeague's character. When Marcus bites McTeague's earlobe during the wrestling match at the family picnic, the gentle "draft horse" rises with "the hideous yelling of a hurt beast, the squealing of a wounded elephant. . . . It was something no longer human; it was rather an echo from the jungle." For Norris, a man is fundamentally an animal, his world ruled by harsh laws of survival.

McTeague's brutalization is tragic because the humanity he had achieved was so touching in its vulnerability. He is also strikingly innocent of avarice. Although the release of McTeague's brutish animal quality results in two slayings, Norris suggests greater dehumanization in the mad greed of Trina's counting her gold coins. McTeague becomes an animal, but Marcus and Trina defy nature in the hideousness of their moral and psychological deformity.

It is in this unsubtly implied theme that the melodramatic elements of the novel undermine its power. Norris succeeds nevertheless in conveying the irony that the nonbrutes in an acquisitive society are more lethal than the brutes. McTeague comes from a nonurban world, and it is a testimony to his instincts for self-preservation that he flees back to the mountains after killing Trina. She, Marcus, and others in the novel are all shaped by the city and its acquisitive and artificial environment, and they are all annihilated violently to dramatize the hopelessness of their origins.

Perhaps Norris overdoes the pettiness and petit bourgeois traits of Trina's family. He also may be accused of anti-Semitism in his portrayal of the character Zerkov. Yet the shallowness of the characterizations serves a symbolic purpose. All of these people are what they are because their environment is a kind of hell, a swarming, competitive world. If Norris indulges in harsh stereotypes, it is because society produces them. "I never truckled. . . . I told them the truth. They liked it or they didn't like it. What had that to do with me?" This was Norris' literary creed, and he adhered to it relentlessly in other naturalist works of social criticism such as *The Octopus* (1901) and *The Pit* (1903). Even in situations that unobservant readers might dismiss as sentimentalism, Norris preserves his sardonic and tough-minded view of the world. The budding love affair between old Mister Grannis and Miss Baker, which reads like a contrast to the deteriorating marriage of McTeague and Trina, is, in reality, a bitter comment on the frustrations of isolation in the congested city. These two old people have conducted their romance through the wall that separates their room for so long that their final coming together is a cruelly ironic comment on the life they have never lived.

The central symbol in *McTeague* is gold. Everyone craves it: Maria, the servant, is full of stories about the ancestral gold plate of her family. She captivates Zerkov with descriptions of it and steals gold fillings from McTeague's dental parlor. Trina counts her gold coins into the night, deriving a fiercer erotic joy from this than from the bear hugs of her husband. Marcus covets Trina's lottery winnings and finally brings about his own death in struggling over the gold with McTeague in the middle of Death Valley. Only McTeague is indifferent to the glitter of gold. For him, it is merely a tool of his trade. When he runs off with Trina's money, he is motivated not by greed, as all critics of the novel agree, but by revenge.

Erich von Stroheim made a famous film version of *McTeague* and called it *Greed*. He is said to have followed *McTeague* page by page, "never missing a paragraph." Any reader of *McTeague* will agree that Norris moves through his story with what Kenneth Rexroth has called "a rentless photographic veracity." Scene after scene unfolds with a visual precision and crispness that leave an indelible impression on the mind and do much to dispel the reservations that the melodramatic action arouses. There is a relentless and powerful movement in these pictures. From the opening scenes describing McTeague on a Sunday in his cozy dental office slumbering or lazily playing his concertina, to the violent closing scene of the novel in which McTeague and Marcus are locked in a violent death struggle in the middle of the greatest wasteland in America, the reader is swept steadily along to increasingly arresting visual involvements. The eye wins over the mind. The environment is rendered with a revelatory concreteness that reveals its central power in the novel.

"Critical Evaluation" by Peter A. Brier

Bibliography:
Campbell, Donna M. "Frank Norris' 'Drama of a Broken Teacup': The Old Grannis-Miss Baker Plot in *McTeague*." *American Literary Realism 1870-1910* 26, no. 1 (Fall, 1993): 40-49. Argues that this subplot illustrates the difficulties involved in the intersection of three styles of late nineteenth century writing: realism, naturalism, and women's local color fiction.
Dawson, Hugh J. "McTeague as Ethnic Stereotype." *American Literary Realism 1870-1910* 20, no. 1 (Fall, 1987): 34-44. Discusses the relation of the title character to stereotypes of the Irish. Briefly mentions use of other ethnic stereotypes in the characters of Zerkow, the Sieppes, and Maria Macapa.
Hochman, Barbara. *The Art of Frank Norris, Storyteller*. Columbia: University of the Missouri Press, 1988. Discounts naturalism as the organizing principle of the novel. Instead, argues that fear of loss is the common ground. Shows how various characters struggle to protect themselves from loss through strategies such as habit and obsession.
McElrath, Joseph R., Jr. *Frank Norris Revisited*. New York: Twayne, 1992. An excellent starting point for students of Norris. The chapter on McTeague discusses Émile Zola and naturalism, Victorian sexuality, and the structure and themes of the novel.
Pizer, Donald. *The Novels of Frank Norris*. Bloomington: Indiana University Press, 1966. Claims Norris' themes are inseparable form the leading controversy of the time: religion versus science. The chapter on *McTeague* traces the influence of Zola and naturalism, explicates the gold symbolism in the novel, and analyzes the structure, characters, and setting.

MADAME BOVARY

Type of work: Novel
Author: Gustave Flaubert (1821-1880)
Type of plot: Psychological realism
Time of plot: Mid-nineteenth century
Locale: France
First published: 1857 (English translation, 1886)

Principal characters:
    CHARLES BOVARY, a provincial doctor
    EMMA, his wife
    LÉON DUPUIS, a young lawyer
    RODOLPHE BOULANGER, a wealthy landowner

The Story:

Charles Bovary was a student of medicine who married for his own advancement a woman much older than himself. She made his life miserable with her nagging and groundless suspicions. One day, Charles was called to the bedside of Monsieur Rouault, who had a broken leg, and there he met the farmer's daughter, Emma, a beautiful but restless girl whose early education in a French convent had given her an overwhelming thirst for broader experience. Charles found his patient an excellent excuse to see Emma, whose charm and grace had captivated him. His whining wife, Héloise, however, soon began to suspect the true reason for his visits to the Rouault farm. She heard rumors that in spite of Emma's peasant background, the girl conducted herself like a gentlewoman. Angry and tearful, Héloise made Charles swear that he would not visit the Rouault home again. Unexpectedly, Héloise's fortune was found to be nonexistent. There was a violent quarrel over her deception, followed by a stormy scene between her and Charles' parents, which brought on an attack of an old illness. Héloise died quickly and quietly.

Charles felt guilty because he had so few regrets at his wife's death. At old Rouault's invitation, he went once more to the farm and again fell under the spell of Emma's charms. As old Rouault watched Charles fall more deeply in love with his daughter, he decided that the young doctor was dependable and perfectly respectable. He forced the young man's hand, telling Charles he could have Emma in marriage and giving the couple his blessing.

During the first weeks of marriage, Emma occupied herself with changing their new home. She busied herself with every household task she could think of to keep herself from being utterly disillusioned. Emma realized that even though she had thought she was in love with Charles, she did not feel the rapture that should have come with marriage. All the romantic books she had read had led her to expect more from marriage than she received, and the dead calm of her feelings was a bitter disappointment. Indeed, the intimacy of marriage disgusted her. Instead of a perfumed, handsome lover in velvet and lace, she found herself tied to a dull-witted husband who reeked of medicines and drugs.

As she was about to give up all hope of finding any joy in her new life, a noble patient whom Charles had treated invited them to a ball at his chateau. At the ball, Emma danced with a dozen partners, tasted champagne, and received compliments on her beauty. The contrast between the life of the Bovarys and that of the nobleman was painfully evident. Emma became more and

3813

more discontented with Charles. His futile and clumsy efforts to please her only made her despair at his lack of understanding. She sat by her window, dreamed of Paris, moped, and became ill.

Hoping a change would improve her condition, Charles took Emma to Yonville, where he set up a new practice and Emma prepared for the birth of a child. When her daughter was born, Emma's chief interest in the child was confined to laces and ribbons for her clothes. The child was sent to a wet nurse, where Emma visited her, and where, accidentally, she met Léon Dupuis, a law clerk bored with the town and seeking diversion. Charmed with the youthful mother, he walked home with her in the twilight, and Emma found him sympathetic to her romantic ideas about life. Later, Léon visited the Bovarys in company with Homais, the town chemist. Homais held little soirees at the local inn, to which he invited the townsfolk. There, Emma's acquaintance with Léon ripened. The townspeople gossiped about the couple, but Charles Bovary was not acute enough to sense the nature of the interest Emma took in Léon.

Bored with Yonville and tired of loving in vain, Léon went to Paris to complete his studies. He left Emma brokenhearted and deploring her weakness in not having given herself to Léon. She fretted in her boredom and once more made herself ill, but she had not time to become as melancholy as before because a stranger, Rodolphe Boulanger, came to town. One day, he brought his farm tenant to Charles for bloodletting. Rodolphe, an accomplished lover, saw in Emma a promise of future pleasure. Emma realized that if she gave herself to him, her surrender would be immoral. Nevertheless, she rationalized her doubts by convincing herself that nothing as romantic and beautiful as love could be sinful.

Emma began to deceive Charles, meeting Rodolphe, riding over the countryside with him, and listening to his urgent avowals of love. Finally, she succumbed to his persuasive appeals. She felt guilty at first but later identified herself with adulterous heroines of fiction and believed that, like them, she had known true romance. Sure of her love, Rodolphe no longer found it necessary to continue to behave like a gentle lover; he stopped being punctual for his meetings with Emma, and though he continued to see her, she began to suspect that his passion was dwindling.

Charles had become involved in Homais' attempt to cure a boy of a clubfoot with a machine Charles had designed. Both Homais and Charles were convinced that the success of their operation would raise their future standing in the community. After weeks of torment, however, the boy contracted gangrene, and his leg had to be amputated. Homais' reputation was undamaged, for he was by profession a chemist, but Bovary, a doctor, was looked on with suspicion. His practice began to fall away.

Disgusted with Charles' failure, Emma, trying to hold Rodolphe, began to spend money recklessly on jewelry and clothes, bringing her husband deeply into debt. She finally secured Rodolphe's word that he would take her away, but on the very eve of what was to be her escape, she received from him a letter in which he hypocritically repented of what he called their sin. Distraught at the realization that she had lost him, she almost threw herself from the window but was saved when Charles called to her. She became gravely ill with brain fever and lay near death for several months.

Emma's convalescence was slow, but she was finally well enough to go to Rouen to the theater. The tender love scenes behind the footlights made Emma breathless with envy. Once more, she dreamed of romance. In Rouen, she met Léon Dupuis again. This time, Léon was determined to possess Emma. He listened to her complaints with sympathy, soothed her, and took her driving. Emma, whose thirst for romance still consumed her, yielded herself to Léon with regret that she had not done so before.

Charles Bovary grew concerned over his increasing debts. Adding to his own financial worries, the death of his father had left his mother in ignorance about the family estate. Emma used the excuse of procuring a lawyer for her mother-in-law to visit Léon in Rouen, where he had set up a practice. At his suggestion, she secured a power of attorney from Charles, a document that left her free to spend his money without his knowing of her purchases.

In despair over his debts, the extent of which Emma had only partly revealed, Charles took his mother into his confidence and promised to destroy Emma's power of attorney. Deprived of her hold over Charles' finances and unable to repay her debts, Emma threw herself on Léon's mercy without any regard for caution. Her corruption and her addiction to pleasure had become complete, but Emma began to realize that she had brought her lover down with her. She no longer respected him, and she scorned his faithfulness when he was unable to give her money she needed to pay her bills. When her name was posted publicly for a debt of several thousand francs, the bailiff prepared to sell Charles' property to settle her creditors' claims. Charles was out of town when the debt was posted, and Emma, in one final act of self-abasement, appealed to Rodolphe for help. He, too, refused to lend her money.

Knowing that the framework of lies with which she had deceived Charles was about to collapse, Emma Bovary resolved to die a heroine's death. She swallowed arsenic bought at Homais' shop. Charles, returning from his trip, arrived too late to save her from a slow, painful death.

Pitiful in his grief, Charles could barely endure the sounds of the hammer as her coffin was nailed shut. Later, feeling that his pain over Emma's death had grown less, he opened her desk, to find there the carefully collected love letters of Léon and Rodolphe. Broken with the knowledge of his wife's infidelity, scourged with debt, and helpless in his disillusionment, Charles died soon after his wife, leaving a legacy of only twelve francs for the support of his orphaned daughter.

Critical Evaluation:

Gustave Flaubert's genius lay in his infinite capacity for taking pains, and *Madame Bovary*, so true in its characterizations, so vivid in its setting, so convincing in its plot, is ample testimony to the realism of his work. This novel was one of the first of its type to come out of France, and its truth shocked contemporary readers. Condemned on the one hand for picturing the life of a romantic adulteress, he was acclaimed on the other for the honesty and skill with which he handled his subject. Flaubert does not permit Emma Bovary to escape the tragedy she brings on herself. Emma finds diversion from the monotony of her life, but she finds it at the loss of her own self-respect. The truth of Emma's struggle is universal and challenging.

Since the time of Charles Baudelaire, many critics have noted, either approvingly or disapprovingly, Flaubert's application of an accomplished and beautifully sustained style to a banal subject matter in *Madame Bovary*. In Flaubert's own time, many readers objected to an adulterous heroine as not only banal but vulgar as well. Baudelaire, however, offered the telling defense against this criticism in his acknowledgment that the logic of the work as a whole provides an indictment of the immoral behavior.

Flaubert himself viewed his book as "all cunning and stylistic ruse." His intention was to write "a book about nothing, a book with no exterior attachment . . . a book that would have almost no subject." Flaubert's goals, however, were not as purely aesthetic as they might initially seem, for he did not mean to eschew significance entirely. Rather, he meant that any subject matter, no matter how trivial, could be raised to art by language and pattern. Like Stendhal and Honoré de Balzac, Flaubert believed that quotidian matters could be treated seriously, but he goes further than his predecessors in refusing to provide narrative guidance and interpretation.

Erich Auerbach observed that Flaubert seems simply to pick scenes that are significant and endow them with a language that allows them to be interpreted. As a result, many commentators have seen Flaubert as the first modern novelist, even a precursor of the antinovelist, because of his unwillingness to deal with subject matter in the traditional, narrative manner. Certainly, he represents a break with the past, for although he retains the story, he makes the novel, in his own words, into "a coloration, a nuance."

At the heart of the novel is a provincial dreamer, a romantic who distorts her environment and ultimately destroys herself with wish fulfillments born of the desperate boredom of her circumscribed situation. Her romantic illusions are, however, not so much the theme of the novel as they are the prime example of human stupidity, which is reflected by all the characters. Charles is trapped by his complacency as much as Emma is by her vain imaginings. The surrounding figures, more types than fully developed characters, represent contemporary failures—the irresponsible seducer, the usurer, the inadequate priest, the town rationalist. All are isolated from those around them by their personal obsessions or deficiencies, and all contribute to the overwhelming stagnation that smothers Emma.

Martin Furnell has divided the novel into three parts, each of which is controlled by an action and a dominant image. In the first part, Emma marries Charles; here the dominant image is in her visit to Le Vaubyessard. The marriage is the central fact of her discontent, while the visit ostensibly provides her with a view of the opulent life she so desperately craves. In the second part of the novel, where she is seduced by the conscienceless landowner Rodolphe, the dominant image is the Comices Agricoles, the elaborate fair with its rustic and vulgar trappings. To Emma, as she is succumbing to Rodolphe, the Comices Agricoles is the very symbol of the limitations of her life. Naturally, she is not capable of consciously making such an interpretation. If she were, her perception might save her. What she does not realize is that her affair is as banal as the fair. The third part of the novel, which describes her seduction by Léon, has as its dominant image the meeting in Rouen Cathedral. The cathedral becomes both church and boudoir, populated not only by images of saints but also by a statue of Diane de Poitiers, a notable adulteress. Once again, Emma reaches out to the grand but is compromised by her own limitations and those of her situation.

The dominant images, which reveal the ambiguity as well as the frustration of her predicament, are reinforced and refined by a series of recurrent, minor images. A striking example is the plaster statue of a curé that deteriorates as Emma is progressively debased. The image is extended by a contract of the curé's statue with a statue of Cupid: love and sexuality rise as the holy man disintegrates. Later, the damage to the curé's foot reminds the reader of Charles' peasant boots, which resemble a clubfoot, and of the amputation of Hippolyte's leg as a result of Charles' desperate desire to please Emma. As these complex images recur, they bind together the varieties of stupidity and vanity.

Even more revolutionary than the use of imagery is the point of view, the series of perspectives from which Flaubert narrates the story. He does not assume the stance of the distanced observer but repeatedly shifts the point of view to avail himself of multiple angles of vision. The narrative begins and ends with scenes focused on Charles. Although Flaubert never allows Charles a first-person presentation, readers see the beginning of the novel and, indeed, are introduced to Emma from Charles' perspective. The readers finally return to view the debris of the conclusion from the vantage point of this uncomprehending victim.

Most of the novel is seen from Emma's perspective, but there is such a deft playing off of

Emma's perceptions against the narrator's control that the reader is able to analyze her perceptions in a broader context rather than simply accept them as fact. The details of Charles' eating habits, for example, become to Emma and the reader a sign of his bovinity, while at the same time, to the reader only, they are a sign of Emma's discontent. Looking out from Emma's or Charles' eyes, interpretations emerge that are beyond the mental capacity of either character. Flaubert presents what they perceive as a means of representing what they fail to perceive. An advantage of this method is that, while the reader becomes aware of Emma's shortcomings, a sympathy develops. The reader recognizes the oppressiveness of Emma's circumstances, the triviality of her evil, and the relative sensitivity of her kind of stupidity.

Apparently subjective presentations, controlled and ordered by Flaubert's selection of image and detail, reveal what the characters themselves do not understand. Emma's romantic idealism is the prime example. If Flaubert cannot make tragedy out of these ingredients, he can quite powerfully describe, in his miniscule characters, personal and social frustration on a grand scale.

"Critical Evaluation" by Edward E. Foster

Bibliography:
Bloom, Harold, ed. *Emma Bovary.* New York: Chelsea House, 1994. Includes excerpts from reviews and articles (some contemporaneous with the novel), as well as ten essays that analyze the heroine in light of twentieth century and feminist perspectives and understanding. Extensive bibliography.
_____, ed. *Gustave Flaubert's "Madame Bovary."* New York: Chelsea House, 1988. An excellent and balanced collection of some of the best and most provocative essays published in the last third of the twentieth century. Topics range from thematic to linguistic and from deconstructionist to psychoanalytical.
Fairlie, Alison. *Flaubert: "Madame Bovary."* London: Arnold, 1962. A well-written, sensitive, and insightful interpretation that provides a thorough examination of the themes, characters, narrative structure, style, and importance of the masterpiece.
Gans, Eric. *"Madame Bovary": The End of Romance.* Boston: Twayne, 1989. A brief but very good introduction that covers the work's essential points, influence, and critical reception. Also places it in its historical and sociological context.
Giraud, Raymond, ed. *Flaubert: A Collection of Critical Essays.* Englewood Cliffs, N.J.: Prentice-Hall, 1964. Includes essays dealing with Flaubert's literary theories and his other works. Also reprints several stimulating pieces on the novel (two not translated elsewhere) that include a perceptive reading by the poet Charles Baudelaire and thoughtful character analyses by Martin Turnell and Jean Rousset.

MADEMOISELLE DE MAUPIN

Type of work: Novel
Author: Théophile Gautier (1811-1872)
Type of plot: Sentimental
Time of plot: Early nineteenth century
Locale: France
First published: 1835-1836 (English translation, 1889)

Principal characters:
  MONSIEUR D'ALBERT, a young aesthete
  ROSETTE, his mistress
  THÉODORE DE SÉRANNES, in reality MADEMOISELLE MADELAINE DE
    MAUPIN

The Story:

D'Albert was a young Frenchman of twenty-two, handsome, artistic, well-educated, and well-versed in the affairs of the world. He loved beauty, especially female beauty. All his life he had dreamed of women, but he had never met the woman of his dreams, who was to combine the beauty of a Rubens' nude with that of a Titian. It was little wonder that he had not found her.

Another thing lacking in d'Albert's life was a mistress. One day, his friend de C—— offered to take him around the town and discourse on the various ladies of his acquaintance so that d'Albert could make a choice. The expedition was a delightful one, as de C—— seemed to have precise and full information not only on the outward circumstances of every beauty but also on the very quality of her mind. After some hesitation, d'Albert finally decided to lay siege to Rosette, a beautiful young woman who he thought the most likely to bring his romantic and poetic mind down to earth.

It did not take d'Albert long to win Rosette's love, and they were soon acknowledged lovers. Rosette was pliable, versatile, and always entertaining. She did not leave d'Albert alone long enough for him to indulge in musing daydreams. Variety was the spice of their love.

For five months, they were the happiest of lovers, but then d'Albert began to tire of Rosette. When she noticed that his ardor was cooling, Rosette knew that she must do something different if she wished to keep his love. If he were growing tired of her in the solitary life they were leading, perhaps he would regain his interest if he saw her among a group of people. For this reason, Rosette took d'Albert to her country estate for a visit. There she planned parties, dinners, and visits to keep him amused, but he remained bored.

One day, an old friend of Rosette arrived, an extremely handsome young man named Théodore de Sérannes, whose conversation, riding, and swordsmanship all entranced d'Albert. The two men met every day and went hunting together, and the more d'Albert saw of Théodore the more fascinated he became. Before long, d'Albert realized that he was in love with Théodore.

He was in love with a man, yet he always thought of him as a woman. D'Albert's mind grew sick with the problem of Théodore's true identity. Some days he was sure that Théodore was a woman in disguise. Then, seeing him fencing or jumping his horse, he would be forced to conclude that Théodore was a man. He knew that Rosette was also in love with Théodore, but her infatuation kept her from noticing d'Albert's interest in the same young man.

One day, d'Albert mentioned that his favorite play was William Shakespeare's *As You Like It* (1599-1600). The rest of the company immediately decided to present the play. At first, Rosette was chosen for the part of Rosalind, the heroine who dresses as a man to escape from her uncle, but when she refused to wear men's clothes, the part was given to Théodore.

As soon as d'Albert saw Théodore dressed in women's clothes, he guessed rightly that Théodore really was a woman. What he did not know was that Théodore, whose real name was Madelaine de Maupin, had decided that she would have nothing to do with men until she had found a good and noble lover. She knew that as a woman she would have no chance to see men as they really were, and so she had devised the scheme of learning about them by dressing as a man. Nevertheless, she had found perfidy and falseness in every man she met. She had watched with amusement while d'Albert fell in love with her, and she had guessed the tortures of his mind at not being able to decide whether she was male or female.

As the rehearsals of the play went on, the parallels between the play and real life became ever more amusing to both d'Albert and Mademoiselle de Maupin. At last, after the play had been presented, d'Albert wrote Mademoiselle de Maupin a letter, in which he told her he was sure she was a woman and that he loved her deeply.

She took so long to reply to his letter that d'Albert again became afraid that she really was a man. One night, however, as d'Albert stood at a window, a hand gently touched his shoulder. He looked around and beheld Mademoiselle de Maupin dressed in her costume as Rosalind. He was struck dumb with amazement. Mademoiselle de Maupin told him that since he was the first man to have seen through her disguise, he should be the first to have her as a woman.

That night, d'Albert learned that she was truly the woman of his dreams. In the morning he found himself alone. Mademoiselle de Maupin had gone, leaving a letter in which she told d'Albert and Rosette that they would never see her again. She wrote separately to d'Albert, telling him that they had known one perfect night. She had answered his dream, and to fulfill a dream once was enough. She ended her letter by telling d'Albert to try to console Rosette for the love she had wasted on the false Théodore and by hoping that the two would be very happy for many years to come.

Critical Evaluation:

Théophile Gautier's *Mademoiselle de Maupin* shocked contemporaries by its unrestrained sensuality. Yet the novel is primarily concerned not with sexual desire but with the quest for an ideal lover. For d'Albert, the pleasures of the spirit hold no appeal. His orientation toward love is aesthetic, just as his evaluations of objects are artistic. The major episodes in the novel are organized around critical moments in d'Albert's quest for ideal beauty. His discouragement initially stems from his failure to find a woman who lives up to his requirements. His affair with Rosette deepens his despair because, even though he finds her sexually exciting, she does not embody ideal beauty. He frequently laments the shortcoming of a world that lacks the embodiment of his conception of perfect beauty. He seeks that beauty in vain until he finds Mademoiselle de Maupin. Yet when he does possess her, it is for only one night. She leaves him because, as she explains, the human tendency to satiety would invariably cause their happy relationship to deteriorate. The renewal of his relationship with Rosette is a compromise with reality. He rationalizes that his demands may be too extreme and that Rosette can mitigate his suffering.

Like d'Albert, Madelaine seeks the living embodiment of an ideal, but for her it is the character of a loved one that is important. Whereas d'Albert's desires are physical, Madelaine's are ethical. Her demands seem, however, equally extreme, though they are only vaguely described. Rosette's passion for Théodore, the male identity that Madelaine has adopted, demonstrates precisely the kind of love that would bring Madelaine happiness. Rosette's passion for Théodore is so absolute that it requires little requital. Assuming a male disguise, Madelaine discovers that men are fundamentally cynical in their treatment of women. Madelaine wants spiritual love and intense passion, which seems to be precisely what men avoid. At the end of the novel, Madelaine disappears, still hoping to find the ideal lover.

Much of the tension in the novel arises from the emphasis on the ambivalence of human sexuality. The physical duality of Madelaine/Théodore's identity reflects an inner ambiguity of traditional notions of gender. Madelaine's powerful sexual nature and forcefully articulated opinions are traditionally associated with masculinity, but her beauty and emotional sensitivity are portrayed as feminine. Gender confusion extends to the other characters as well. Rosette, who conforms to a traditionally feminine role in her relationship with d'Albert, actively seduces Théodore. D'Albert is told that he dresses in a feminine manner and finds himself looking on Rosette as a Platonic friend. Although d'Albert values physical beauty, he finds himself most attracted to Madelaine's keen mind. In fact, Madelaine provides a counterpoint to many of d'Albert theories. Although d'Albert desires her as a second half, she actually mirrors his own sexual ambivalence.

The triangular relationships in the novel place happiness beyond reach. The dynamics of the triangle depend on tensions and oppositions, attractions and connections. The comic triangle of William Shakespeare's *As You Like It*, acted out by Rosette's guests, mirrors and complicates the relationships. Madelaine playing Rosalinde is disguised as the youth Ganymede to test her lover Orlando. While disguised as Ganymede, Rosalinde attracts the unwelcome attention of Phoebe. This situation mirrors her own: As Théodore she attracts the attention of Rosette and as Madelaine she appeals to d'Albert. Rosette, as the page Isabel, pursues Ganymede much as she pursues Théodore/Madelaine. D'Albert's confusion mirrors that of Orlando. On seeing Madelaine dressed as Rosalinde for the play, both d'Albert and Rosette question her true identity.

The plot traces the protagonists' explorations of their own identities. Since the novel's narrative structure is self-conscious, the explorations of self in the text draw attention to the fiction of fixed identity. D'Albert's identity doubles his own ironic narration. He fantasizes and then critiques his fantasies, and then criticizes that self-reflexive impulse itself. The play acting, both in the character's rendition of *As You Like It* and in their interaction with each other in the novel, allows the characters to question ambiguities of identity. Gautier frequently resorts to masks and mirrors to express the duality of human existence. Metamorphosis, borrowed from Shakespeare's play as well as from Ovid's *Metamorphoses* (c. 8 C.E.), prominently figures as literary allusion and overarching theme.

Mademoiselle de Maupin is not only the most beautifully written of Gautier's novels but the most sustained profession of his creed. Many of Gautier's theories of art appear in the preface and text, where he derides utility in art and declares that nothing is beautiful unless it is useless. The preface ultimately became the credo of the art-for-art's-sake movement, with its insistence on the sovereignty of art, independent of moral and social conditions. The love of palpable, external beauty is a primary feature of Gautier's work and the novel reads as a series of vivid visual descriptions. His taste for Greek sculpture and Gothic architecture is apparent as well as the rich allusions to literary precursors. A painter's eye for visual form and color contribute to the stylistic beauty of Gautier's prose.

According to Gautier, the artist combines masculine and feminine traits to translate the image of feminine beauty into art. The desire for an androgynous union of male and female surfaces in the novel as well. D'Albert would like to combine the awareness of beauty with the state of being beautiful. The relationship between art and sexuality is a central issue of the novel. D'Albert's quest as both artist and lover reenacts the Romantic quest to overcome the split between self and another. Théodore/Madelaine as a work of art is not so easily appropriated by his/her observer. There is no simple identity to be unmasked. Constant transformation and veiled appearances dramatize the endless process of aesthetic creativity. The equivocal position of Madelaine, her ability to arouse a double passion, suggests that beauty may be loved independently of sex. Despite the lengthy passages analyzing the Romantic soul, which verge on parody, Gautier emphasizes the confining nature of sexual stereotypes, elaborates the notion of endlessly evolving beauty, and explores the nature of love, pleasure, and desire.

"Critical Evaluation" by Pamela Pavliscak

Bibliography:

Lloyd, Rosemary. "Rereading *Mademoiselle de Maupin.*" *Orbis Litterarum: International Review of Literary Studies* 41, no. 1 (1986): 19-32. Provides a valuable overview of previous discussions, many of which are only available in French. Traces the many literary allusions in the text and places the novel within the larger tradition of explorations of human sexuality.

Richardson, Joanna. *Théophile Gautier, His Life and Times.* London: M. Reinhardt, 1958. The most comprehensive biography of Gautier in English, combining biographical detail with textual evaluation. Proposes the novel as an example of the art-for-art's-sake principle outlined in the author's preface.

Scott, David. *Pictorialist Poetics: Poetry and the Visual Arts in Nineteenth-Century France.* Cambridge, England: Cambridge University Press, 1988. Argues that the aesthetic theory and literary practice of the nineteenth century combined to produce a new conception of literature's potential. Examines Gautier's preoccupation with the visual arts, as both critic and artist, and its impact on his literary efforts.

Smith, Albert B. *Ideal and Reality in the Fictional Narratives of Théophile Gautier.* Gainesville: University of Florida Press, 1969. One of the only books in English devoted to Gautier's prose. Smith offers a detailed analysis of *Mademoiselle de Maupin*, as well as a broad discussion of Gautier's aesthetic philosophy and literary style.

Spenser, Michael C. *The Art Criticism of Théophile Gautier.* Geneva: Librarie Droz, 1969. Explores the concept of the microcosm in Gautier's art criticism and fiction. Spenser considers the preface to *Mademoiselle de Maupin* to have been the inception of his cult of metaphysical and sensual beauty.

THE MADWOMAN OF CHAILLOT

Type of work: Drama
Author: Jean Giraudoux (1882-1944)
Type of plot: Parable
Time of plot: A little before noon in the spring of next year
Locale: The Chaillot district of Paris
First performed: 1945; first published, 1945 as *La Folle de Chaillot* (English translation, 1947)

> *Principal characters:*
> COUNTESS AURELIA, the Madwoman of Chaillot
> MME CONSTANCE, the Madwoman of Passy
> MLLE GABRIELLE, the Madwoman of St. Sulpice
> MME JOSEPHINE, the Madwoman of La Concorde
> THE RAGPICKER
> THE PRESIDENT
> THE BARON
> THE BROKER
> THE PROSPECTOR

The Story:

A mighty syndicate of financiers wished to exploit the untouched deposits of oil under the streets of Paris, and they ignored humanity, beauty, and truth in the process. The free souls of Paris opposed them and eventually triumphed by literally removing the syndicate from the scene.

On the one side were the President, the Prospector, the Baron, the Press Agent, the Broker, and the Ladies of the Street. On the other side were the Waiter, the Little Man, the Street Singer, the Flower Girl, the Shoelace Peddler, the Ragpicker, and other folk. In the middle, and significantly devoted to the gentle souls, was the Madwoman of Chaillot, aided by her compatriots, the Madwomen of Passy, St. Sulpice, and La Concorde. The capitalistic forces functioned as well-oiled machinery; they were devoid of characteristics that would set them apart or elicit for them the least bit of empathic reaction. The people of Paris were all recognizable types, but each possessed some quality of individuality.

The Madwoman encountered the President, the Baron, the Prospector, and the Broker at a sidewalk café in the Chaillot district. Her friends were all aware that something terrible was afoot and informed her of the plot to drill for oil beneath the streets. The Prospector sent his agent with a bomb to destroy the city architect, the only obstacle to the drilling. Pierre, the young assassin, was rescued by the Policeman as he was about to throw himself into the river rather than carry out his task. He was revived and convinced by the Madwoman that life is really worth living.

It was apparent to the Madwoman that the only way to combat the materialistic interests was to annihilate them. She and her friends had little chance of opposing them if commonly interpreted methods of justice were used, so she decided upon an infallible plan and sent her confederates scurrying about on errands to help her carry it out.

She retired to her quarters in the Rue de Chaillot to receive the delegation of capitalists. They answered her invitation because she had informed them that a large deposit of oil rested under her basement. To prove it, she prepared a sample; a bottle of mixed kerosene and mange cure was waiting for the Prospector, who professed to be able to detect the existence of oil deposits by merely sniffing the air.

Some years before, the Madwoman had rescued a Sewer Man who had promised to show her a secret entrance from her basement into the sewers of Paris. She summoned him and he pressed the stone concealing the entrance. The other Madwomen, Mme Constance, who took her invisible lap dog with her everywhere; Mlle Gabrielle, who talked to nonexistent friends; and Mme Josephine, who was an expert at jurisprudence because her brother-in-law was a lawyer, all arrived for a delightful tea scene. They were mad, but that fact in no way prejudiced the trial that followed.

Mme Josephine was called upon to conduct a court, for it was only just and proper that the financiers have a fair hearing before they were sent to oblivion. The Ragpicker agreed to speak in their defense, and a damning testimony it was, with money at the root of their materialistic evil. The verdict of the tribunal was unanimous; the accused were guilty on all charges. The Madwoman was authorized to proceed with the extermination.

The guests began to arrive, and in a wonderful scene of comic irony each group in turn was sent through the door into the sewer. First came the President, next the Prospector, then the Press Agent, and so on until all, like sheep, had followed the infallible nose of the Prospector down the dark stairway, never to return again.

Immediately all the wrongs of the world were righted. The pigeons flew again; the air was pure; the sky was clear; grass sprouted on the pavements; complete strangers were shaking hands. Humanity had been saved, and the friends of friendship thanked the Madwoman, the triumphant feminine force.

Critical Evaluation:

In *The Madwoman of Chaillot*, Jean Giraudoux orchestrates three of his recurring themes: the inscrutability of woman, the love of humanity, and the abhorrence of materialism. For one who is familiar with all of Giraudoux's plays, the antiwar theme is implied in the latter. Stylistically, Giraudoux employs two of his favorite devices: the fantastic parable and the duality of character. The resulting impact of *The Madwoman of Chaillot* is that it possesses a remarkable unity of form and idea, the unifying theme being the writer's love and faith in the triumph of the human entity in a time of despair. Giraudoux knew something about living in a time of despair.

A very important aspect of *The Madwoman of Chaillot* involves the time of its composition: The play was written by Giraudoux toward the end of the period during which the Germans occupied Paris (from June, 1940, to August, 1944) during World War II. Giraudoux died in the winter of 1943-1944, months before the Allies' invasion of Normandy and the Germans' departure from the city.

Although the play makes no clear mention of the war and there are no direct references to the terrible deprivations suffered by Parisians throughout the Occupation, the play premiered during the first theater season after the liberation of France. Critical responses to this work therefore have frequently been influenced by the knowledge that Giraudoux's attitude toward his own country's defeat and the Occupation was far from positive. For this reason, many have continued to see in the play a commentary on France's ability to resist the fascist oppression of the Nazis. Such an interpretation, which helped make this play a worldwide success, is dependent on an awareness of the period during which the play was written and of the playwright's sympathies, because the script itself seems curiously quiet about such issues.

The Madwoman of Chaillot offers a blend of fantasy and realism in presenting its setting, characters, and story. For example, Chaillot, which is the area located directly across the Seine from the Eiffel Tower, seems, in the play, a timeless place. There are few references to everyday life, and little appears on stage to suggest any specific part of the actual neighborhood. The play lacks any authentic sense of geography: This Chaillot is a charming, bustling neighborhood filled with funny and interesting people who seem to come and go quite freely. Most of the characters are referred to not by name but by who they are or what they do—the Ragpicker, the Baron, and the Policeman, for example. The majority of the more than forty characters who populate *The Madwoman of Chaillot* appear to be self-consciously playing their parts in a highly theatricalized environment. Against the fantastical backdrop, only a few characters stand out as genuine individuals, notably the Madwomen, who claim particular Paris neighborhoods as their domains: Mme Constance of Passy; Mlle Gabrielle of St. Sulpice; Mme Josephine of La Concorde; and the Countess Aurelia, the Madwoman of Chaillot.

The play's theme is that society is redeemed by those it chooses to label insane. The mad are portrayed in the play as charmingly nonconformist, resistant, and enterprisingly clever. The madness of Countess Aurelia, for example, is liberating in its bold honesty and candor. She is allowed to make whatever remarks she wishes—after all, the woman is crazy—but consistently throughout the play, her comments, even with all their amusing idiosyncrasies, seem to contain the truth. Eccentric and suspended in a sweeter, happier past, the Madwoman of Chaillot becomes a worthy opponent to those forces who would destroy the beauty of Paris and of the life that may be lived there.

The plot to convert the enchanting city into an oil field is led by a group of highly disagreeable men who lust after money. These characters are painted with broad, often stereo-typical strokes: They are quite similar and operate as an effective unit. Opposed to these evil, titled plutocrats and vile money-grubbers are the Waiter, the Ragpicker, the Flower Girl, the Street Singer, the Shoelace Peddler—in other words, the many, varied people who inhabit the play's magical Chaillot. Much of the conflict in the play pits these interesting individuals against the devious, faceless businessmen.

Between these two extremes stands Countess Aurelia, who mediates between the juxtaposed realities of the people and the businessmen. Her attempt to convince Pierre that life is wonderful provides her with her first opportunity to express the play's view of life—that it is worth living. Later, when the trial begins in the Madwoman's basement, she is able to add that what is worth living is worth protecting. The scene in which the enemies of human existence, who wish to turn the city into an ugly, money making machine, are lured into the Paris sewers dramatizes the play's message that if people are willing to fight for what is beautiful, the world will become a better place. No sooner have the villains disappeared than Paris is transfigured.

Although Giraudoux should not be considered a feminist, his play carefully contrasts the materialistic world—led by males—with the sensibilities associated with females. Rather than succumb to the enticements of finances and money, the Madwoman of Chaillot is triumphant in maintaining her values. In this idealized setting, the appreciation of beauty and truth conquers the excesses of capitalism.

As noted above, Giraudoux's fanciful drama scored a major success when it premiered. It was admiringly received by critics and audiences not only in Paris but also in London, New York, and other major theater centers all over the world. Wherever it was produced, it enjoyed long runs and revivals throughout the 1950's and 1960's. By the 1970's, however, audiences seemed to find *The Madwoman of Chaillot* somewhat dated, even naïve, and literary critics, who had once been interested in Giraudoux, lost interest in him. This play, certainly the dramatist's best-known work, is still produced in France and elsewhere, but it is often regarded as charming but lightweight fare. Perhaps its sense of whimsy and its rather straightforward way of dramatizing how complex problems might be solved seem too simple for modern theatergoers.

"Critical Evaluation" by Kenneth Krauss

Bibliography:

Body, Jacques. *Jean Giraudoux: The Legend and the Secret.* Translated by James Norwood. Rutherford, N.J.: Fairleigh Dickinson University Press, 1991. A fascinating series of essays draws important connections between the author's life and his major plays, especially *The Madwoman of Chaillot.* Offers a wealth of informative facts regarding the play's composition and posthumous production.

Cohen, Robert. *Giraudoux: Three Faces of Destiny.* Chicago: University of Chicago Press, 1968. An excellent analysis of Giraudoux's dramatic works and their philosophical implications. The chapter on *The Madwoman of Chaillot* is especially helpful for its discussion of how the playwright's dramatic style and techniques fit his plays' intellectual and emotional content.

Lemaitre, Georges Édouard. *Jean Giraudoux: The Writer and His Work.* New York: Ungar, 1971. A good overview of Giraudoux's career. Offers an accurate picture of how the playwright was regarded until the early 1970's.

Raymond, Agnes. *Jean Giraudoux: The Theatre of Victory and Defeat.* Amherst: University of Massachusetts Press, 1966. Particularly notable for its assessment of the playwright's political ideas and the historical context in which his major works were developed. The chapter on *The Madwoman of Chaillot* provides information on how the German Occupation affected the writing of the play.

Reilly, John H. *Jean Giraudoux.* Boston: Twayne, 1978. A comprehensive survey of Giraudoux's dramatic works. Reilly sees *The Madwoman of Chaillot* as one of the high points of the playwright's career.

MAGGIE
A Girl of the Streets

Type of work: Novel
Author: Stephen Crane (1871-1900)
Type of plot: Naturalism
Time of plot: Late nineteenth century
Locale: New York
First published: 1893

>*Principal characters:*
>MAGGIE
>JIMMY, her brother
>PETE, Jimmy's friend and Maggie's lover
>THE MOTHER

The Story:

In the slums of New York City, Maggie and her two brothers grew up in the squalor and corruption, both moral and physical, of that poverty-stricken area. Her father usually came home from work drunk, and her mother, too, was fond of the bottle. The children were neglected. When the drunken parents ranted at each other, the children hid in terror under the table or the bed.

Somehow Maggie managed to remain untouched by that sordidness. Her younger brother died. Jimmy, her older brother, went to work after their father died. He fought, drank, and had many affairs with women. From time to time, he was hounded by some of the women, who demanded support for themselves and the illegitimate children he had fathered. Jimmy brushed them aside.

When Jimmy brought his best friend home with him, Maggie fell in love. Pete, a bartender, was handsome, flashy, and exciting. One night, he took her out to show her the nightlife of the city. Maggie's wonder knew no bounds, for to her the experience was the height of luxury. On the doorstep, she allowed Pete to kiss her good-night. Pete was disappointed but not discouraged. He took Maggie out again. The next time, she surrendered and went to live with him.

Pete soon grew tired of Maggie, however, and she was compelled to return home. In furious indignation, her mother ordered her out of the house. She had done everything, the mother insisted, to bring Maggie up to be a fine, decent girl. She had been an excellent mother and had spared no pains to keep her daughter on the path of virtue. Now her daughter would be dead to her. The neighbors joined in, denouncing Maggie. Jimmy, the seducer of other men's sisters, became indignant. He and a companion went to the bar where Pete worked, intent upon beating him up. When they failed, Jimmy contented himself by shrugging his shoulders and condemning his sister.

Maggie was homeless and penniless. She went to see Pete, but he sent her away, irritated and fearful lest he should lose his job. She turned to prostitution, plying her trade by night, accosting poor and wealthy alike, but she did not have much luck. One night, she walked forlornly and unsuccessfully in the waterfront district. Resignedly she trudged on, toward the pier and the black, murky depths of the river.

A short time later, Jimmy came home from one of his prolonged absences. Maggie, the mother wailed, was dead. With the neighbors around her, she sobbed and moaned. What the

Lord had given the Lord had taken away, the neighbors told her. Uncomforted, Maggie's mother shrieked that she forgave her daughter; she forgave Maggie her sins.

Critical Evaluation:

Stephen Crane's *Maggie: A Girl of the Streets* reveals a governing social determinism that exonerates the denizens of the Bowery from the hypocritical moral judgments they pronounce on Maggie, and that serves as the basis for an attack on false values. Viewed in this context, *Maggie* conforms to many of the tenets of literary naturalism. When the term naturalism is applied to literature, it signifies a philosophical orientation; more specifically, it reflects the presence of a determinism that is either biological or environmental. In other words, the careers of naturalistic protagonists are determined by their inherited traits and by their environments. Caught up in the web of these forces, the protagonists cannot be held responsible for their actions, since they have little, if any, freedom of will. Consequently, the naturalistic work manifests an ethical orientation that is neither moral nor immoral, but amoral. Naturalism is distinguished from realism by several other features as well: a focus on the lower classes, an attack on false values, a reformist agenda, imagery that is either animalistic or mechanistic, and a plot of decline that often leads to catastrophe through a deterministic sequence of causes and effects.

The setting, imagery, and plot of *Maggie* manifest the operation of a governing social determinism that serves as a springboard for Crane's attack on both romantic idealism in works about the slum and on the moral posturing of the church and the Bowery inhabitants. Rum Alley is a sordid, Darwinian landscape of violent people engaged in a brutal struggle for survival. Children are disgorged onto the slum streets from dark doorways where they must fend for themselves. Working conditions in the local factories are bleak. Lacking an education and any positive role models in her life, Maggie turns to the stage melodrama and the popular romance for her values. They give rise to her dream of a perfect lover who will rescue her from the Bowery. They also instill in her the false beliefs that virtue triumphs over vice, and that poverty in ennobling. In the last analysis, Maggie's dream proves as fatal as it is illusory, for in the savage environment of the Bowery, the romantic ideals she inherits from the slum novel and theatrical melodrama have negative survival value.

The bestial, martial, and romantic imagery associated with the principal characters also reflects the social determinism of *Maggie*. Maggie's deluded romanticism is reinforced by the imagery Crane employs to describe her impression of Pete, who appears to her as a glowing sun, a knight in shining armor who has come to her rescue, when, in reality, he is nothing more than a dandified street thug. Similarly, Maggie's fatal incompatibility with her environment is revealed by the images Crane uses to describe her. For example, she is compared to a flower that sprouts from the mud, her soul unstained by the dirt and grime of Rum Alley. By contrast, the images used to describe Pete and Jimmy reflect the extent of their adaptation to their environment. They and their friends fight with the savagery of a pack of dogs. The animalistic imagery is significant, for it reinforces the work's naturalistic orientation; humans are viewed as extensions of the animal kingdom engaged in a Darwinian struggle for survival.

A plot of decline leading to catastrophic closure is further evidence of a governing social determinism in *Maggie*. The initial chapters establish the violent environment of the Bowery. Succeeding chapters contrast Pete and Jimmy's adaptation to this sordid milieu with Maggie's ardent desire to escape from it. Chapters 6 and 7 chronicle her attempts to realize her dream of escape. Ensuing chapters document the moral backlash and rejection of Maggie by the denizens of the Bowery, and the consequent narrowing of her options, leading to closure and death. First she is rejected by Pete, who claims she is not good enough for him. Forced to pursue a life of prostitution, she is subsequently disowned by her mother, who condemns her thankless disobedience, and shunned by Jimmy for bringing shame upon the family. Turning finally to the church, Maggie is rejected by the priest, who is not willing to risk his respectability to save her soul. The novel assails the hypocrisy of the priest who offers condemnation instead of compassion, who claims to help people, yet turns a deaf ear to their pleas for help, and whose moral posturing encourages others to adopt a similar stance. These characters are not to be blamed for their moral hypocrisy, however, because their harsh environment forces them to act immorally while keeping up moral appearances in order to survive.

By parodying the sentimental romance, theatrical melodrama, and slum novel to which his audience was addicted, Crane forced his readers to take a closer look at the unsavory conditions of slum life. *Maggie* also exerted an influence on future generations of writers, from Frank Norris and Theodore Dreiser to Dashiell Hammett and Ernest Hemingway, as a result of its many new elements: a focus on the social dregs, the prostitutes, sweat shops, factories, and slums; a terse, laconic style and vernacular dialogue; its subversion of old Victorian sexual taboos and its frank depiction of the sexual needs that drive humans; its portrayal of characters as biological and social pawns with little intellect but great physical attributes; a narrative technique that combined an objective, documentary style with a riot of irony, and that featured an impressionistic approach in which mood and tone were privileged over theme and character. In the final analysis, the novel's impact may be assessed by the fact that its publication in 1893 helped give birth to a new mode of storytelling, known as American literary naturalism.

"Critical Evaluation" by Stephen G. Brown

Bibliography:
Gandal, Keith. "Stephen Crane's *Maggie* and the Modern Soul." *English Literary History* 60, no. 3 (Fall, 1993): 759-785. Argues that the novel is not about Maggie's moral decline but her loss of self-confidence and self-defensiveness. Asserts that Maggie fails not in trying to redeem her sinful nature—the old story of the fallen woman—but in overcoming self-doubt and cowardice, making it a modern psychological tale.
Golemba, Henry. "'Distant Dinners' in Stephen Crane's *Maggie:* Representing 'The Other Half.'" *Essays in Literature* 21, no. 2 (Fall, 1994): 235-250. Crane uses food imagery to suggest the realist's problem. By feeding the reader's taste for detail, the writer plays into the gluttonous, base, modern social tendencies he exposes.
Gullason, Thomas A., ed. *Maggie: A Girl of the Streets*, by Stephen Crane. New York: W. W. Norton, 1979. Contains the 1893 text as well as biographical and literary background period reviews, and important critical essays on the work's structure, technique, and subject matter.
Irving, Katrina. "Gendered Space, Racialized Space: Nativism, the Immigrant Woman, and Stephan Crane's Maggie." *College Literature* 20, no. 3 (October, 1993): 30-43. Asserts that immigrants posed a threat to late nineteenth century American society, especially women prostitutes such as Maggie, who must die before diluting "native" stock.
Sweeney, Gerard M. "The Syphilitic World of Stephen Crane's *Maggie*." *American Literary Realism* 24, no. 1 (Fall, 1991): 79-85. Discusses how Crane reveals the diseased condition of Maggie's world, its syphilis and alcoholism. His tough realism suggests Maggie is fortunate to escape through early death.

THE MAGIC MOUNTAIN

Type of work: Novel
Author: Thomas Mann (1875-1955)
Type of plot: Philosophical
Time of plot: 1907-1914
Locale: Davos, Switzerland
First published: Der Zauberberg, 1924 (English translation, 1927)

Principal characters:

HANS CASTORP, a German engineer
JOACHIM ZIEMSSEN, his cousin
SETTEMBRINI, a patient at Davos-Platz
NAPHTA, Settembrini's friend
CLAVDIA CAUCHAT, Hans's friend
MYNHEER PEEPERKORN, a Dutch planter from Java

The Story:

Hans Castorp had been advised by his doctor to go to the mountains for a rest. Accordingly, he decided to visit his cousin, Joachim Ziemssen, a soldier by profession, who was a patient in the International Sanatorium Berghof at Davos-Platz in the mountains of Switzerland. He planned to stay there for three weeks and then return to his home in Hamburg. Hans had just passed his examinations and was now a qualified engineer; he was eager to get started in his career. His cousin's cure at the sanatorium was almost complete. Hans thought Joachim looked robust and well.

At the sanatorium, Hans soon discovered that the ordinary notions of time did not exist. Day followed day almost unchangingly. He met the head of the institution, Dr. Behrens, as well as the other patients, who sat in particular groups at dinner. There were two Russian tables, for example, one of which was known to the patients as the bad Russian table. A couple who sat at that table had the room next to Hans. Through the thin partitions, he could hear them—even in the daytime—chase each other around the room. Hans was rather revolted, inasmuch as he could hear every detail of their lovemaking.

One patient interested him greatly, a merry Russian woman, supposedly married, named Clavdia Cauchat. Every time she came into the dining room she banged the door, which annoyed Hans a great deal. Hans also met the Italian Settembrini, a humanist writer and philosopher. Settembrini introduced him to a Jew, Naphta, who turned out to be a converted Jesuit and a cynical absolutist. Because the two men spent their time in endless discussions, Settembrini finally left the sanatorium to take rooms where Naphta lodged in the village.

From the very first day of his arrival, Hans felt feverish and a bit weak. His three weeks were almost up when he decided to take a physical examination, which revealed that he had tuberculosis. So he stayed on as a patient. One day, defying orders, he went out skiing and was caught in a snowstorm. The exposure aggravated his condition.

His interest in Clavdia was heightened when he learned that Dr. Behrens, who liked to dabble in art, had painted her picture. The doctor gave Hans an X-ray plate of Clavdia's skeletal structure. Hans kept the plate on the bureau in his room. Hans spent most of his free time with Joachim or with Settembrini and Naphta. The Italian and the Jesuit were given to all sorts of ideas, and Hans became involved in a multitude of philosophical discussions on the duration of time, God, politics, astronomy, and the nature of reality. Joachim, who was rather humorless and unimaginative, did not enjoy those talks, but Hans, since he himself had become a patient at the sanatorium, felt more at home and was not quite as attached to Joachim as he had been. Besides, it was Clavdia who interested him. On the occasion of a carnival, when some of the restrictions of the sanatorium were lifted, Hans told her that he loved her. She thought him foolish and refused his proposal of marriage. The next day she left for Russia. Hans was in despair and became listless. Joachim grew impatient with the progress of his cure when the doctor told him that he was not yet well and would have to remain on the mountain for six more months. Wanting to rejoin his regiment, Joachim, in defiance of the doctor's injunctions, left the sanatorium. The doctor told Hans that he could leave too; but Hans knew that the doctor was angry when he said it, and therefore he remained.

Before long Joachim returned, his condition now so serious that his mother was summoned to the sanatorium. He died shortly afterward. Clavdia Cauchat also returned. She had been writing to the doctor, and Hans had heard of her from time to time, but she did not return alone. She had found herself a protector, an old Dutchman named Mynheer Peeperkorn, an earthy, hedonistic planter from Java. Hans became very friendly with Peeperkorn, who soon learned that the young engineer was in love with Clavdia. The discovery did not affect their friendship at all, and the friendship lasted until the Dutchman died.

For a time, the guests amused themselves with spiritualist séances. A young girl, a new arrival at the sanatorium, claimed that she was able to summon anyone from the dead. Hans took part in one meeting and asked that Joachim be called back from the dead. Dr. Krokowski, the psychologist at the sanatorium, was opposed to the séances and broke up the sessions. Then Naphta and Settembrini got into an argument. A duel was arranged between the two dialecticians. When the time came, the Italian said he would fire into the air. When he did so, Naphta became more furious than ever. Realizing that Settembrini would not shoot at him, Naphta turned the pistol on himself and pulled the trigger. He fell face downward in the snow and died.

Hans Castorp had come to the sanatorium for a visit of three weeks. His stay turned out to last more than seven years. During that time he saw many deaths and many changes in the institution. He became an old patient, not just a visitor. The sanatorium became another home in the high, thin air of the mountaintop. For him time, as measured by minutes, or even years, no longer existed. Time belonged to the flat, busy world below.

Then an Austrian archduke was assassinated. Newspapers suddenly brought the world to the International Sanatorium Berghof, with news of war and troops movements. Some of the patients remained in neutral Switzerland. Others packed to return home. When Hans Castorp said good-bye to Settembrini, who was his best friend among the old patients, the disillusioned humanist wept at their parting. Hans was going back to Germany to fight. Time, the tragic hour of his generation, had overtaken him at last, and the sanatorium was no longer his refuge. Dodging bullets and bombs in a frontline trench, he disappeared into the smoky mists that hid the future of Europe.

Critical Evaluation:

The Magic Mountain, begun in 1912 but written largely after World War I, was actually planned as a novella, inspired by Thomas Mann's own brief stay at a sanatorium at Davos-Platz, Switzerland. In fact, his early novella *Tristan* (1903) lays much of the groundwork for the later novel, which grew in bulk and complexity to become a veritable mirror of European society in the period leading up to World War I. It comes directly out of the tradition of the German *Bildungsroman*, or novel of development, in which a relatively unformed character is exposed to various aspects of life and a range of influences. In a gradual process, that character achieves form, false goals are cast aside and the true calling and, even more important, the right relationship to life, discovered. Hans Castorp is just such a character when he arrives from the flatlands for a brief visit at Berghof. Mann emphasizes his bourgeois background and the lack of firm convictions and direction in his life. For Mann, the North German type—Hans is from Hamburg—always represented the solid, respectable middle-class life. Yet Hans is also something of a quester, curious and adventuresome in the spiritual and intellectual realms. He observes the new world of the sanatorium intently and becomes involved with the personalities there, inquiring and holding long conversations. The narrative voice of the novel, as in most of Mann's works, has a certain ironic distance, but the pace of the work is very much tied to Castorp's own experience of events and temporal rhythms. The three weeks of his planned visit stretch out to seven years, and the work becomes the record of the growth of his character in a microcosm of European society.

Mann's style developed out of the nineteenth century realist school, and he observes and describes reality with minute care. Yet in his major novels, his style becomes increasingly symbolic and the structure increasingly expressive of symbolic values. Thus, the individual character development of Castorp reflects the problems of European thought as a whole, and the various ideas to which he is exposed represent various intellectual and spiritual currents of the epoch. Castorp initially falls prey to a fascination with death, a dangerous attraction to the irresponsible freedom of the mountain world, the temptation to turn inward and to fall in love with sickness. He studies the illness whose symptoms he himself soon exhibits. He visits the "moribundi" and has long talks with Behrens and Krokowski, two of the doctors. Here life is seen as a process of decay, and even the intellect and the emotions are reduced to unconscious urges according to the new psychology of Sigmund Freud. Castorp crystallizes these ideas in his feverish love for Clavdia Cauchat, who represents the Russian temperament—the urge to lose oneself, to give in to the emotions, to live life for the sake of life. She is contrasted to Settembrini, the Italian intellectual, educator, and humanist who is an optimist and believes in the perfectibility of humanity by reason. He opposes the fascination with death that Castorp manifests. Settembrini is also contrasted to Naphta, his intellectual opponent, who is an irrationalist, a Jew turned Jesuit, with a highly Nietzschean viewpoint. He is a pessimist, deriding Settembrini's optimism and ridiculing his arguments as inconsistent. In actuality, neither figure means or is meant to convert Castorp; their arguments cancel each other, as does so much else in the novel. Castorp finds his own position midway between the various opposing forces. This occurs primarily in the chapter "Snow." If the magic mountain is a timeless realm above the immediate concerns of the world, "Snow" is a hermetic world within that realm. Castorp loses his way in a snowstorm and, exhausted and in danger of death, has a vision in which he sees juxtaposed an idyllic world of tropical paradise, peopled by gentle and happy folk, with a temple in which a terrible ritual of human sacrifice is being performed. This symbolizes the two poles of human life, and Castorp's response is clear and decisive: Life is inseparably bound up with death, and the horrible is real and cannot be denied, but for the sake of goodness and love, human beings must not grant death dominion over their thoughts.

It is after this chapter that the figure of Mynheer Peeperkorn for a time dominates the novel, a figure of great vitality, simple in his thoughts, but of powerful personality. He is in love with his life force and terrified of losing it, and therefore he eventually commits suicide rather than face decay. He, like the other figures, represents an aspect of contemporary European thought and attitudes. Indeed, his traits, like those of Settembrini and Naphta, were drawn from life, from figures known to Mann. Thus the novel has something of the autobiographical and represents a stage in Mann's own thought. In the realm he has constructed, all these aspects—fictional *Bildungsroman*, intellectual autobiography, and symbolic portrait of the prewar era—merge. This is made possible in part by the very foundation of the novel, the mountain. The small community is elevated above the flatlands, in the rarefied Alpine air, remote from the problems of the world and the demands of everyday life. Time is dissolved, the rhythm of the novel moves from sequences of hours to days, weeks, months, and finally years, all rendered indistinguishable by the precise daily routine. In this world outside of time, Hans can grow, can hover between conflicting opinions. Here he has freedom, most essentially in the "Snow" chapter, where even space is obliterated. Yet in contrast to the earlier romantic outlook, this elevated position of freedom in isolation is not seen as a good thing, for though it provides an aesthetic space in which ideal development can occur, it is divorced from life. Life is the value that Hans's development finally leads him to affirm—life, with its horror as well as its beauty. When the European world saw itself plunged into World War I, Thomas Mann saw himself jolted out of his apolitical aesthetic stance. Therefore it is only fitting that Hans Castorp, too, must come down from the mountain to the world of time and action, even if only to be lost among the havoc of a world at war.

"Critical Evaluation" by Steven C. Schaber

Bibliography:
Hatfield, Henry. *From "The Magic Mountain": Mann's Later Masterpieces*. Ithaca, N.Y.: Cornell University Press, 1979. The chapter *"The Magic Mountain"* provides a concise and broad introduction to the novel in the context of Mann's other later works; a good place to start for beginners. Includes some discussion of contemporary critical opinion and politics.
Heller, Erich. *Thomas Mann: The Ironic German*. South Bend, Ind.: Regnery/Gateway, 1979. The chapter "Conversation on the Magic Mountain" is a delightfully informative study of the novel in the form of a dialogue. Perhaps Heller's best-known statement on Mann's work and a key to further study. Magisterial.
Ridley, Hugh. *The Problematic Bourgeois: Twentieth-Century Criticism on Thomas Mann's "Buddenbrooks" and "The Magic Mountain."* Columbia, S.C.: Camden House, 1994. A study of the reception of these two major novels in both literary and political history. Places the works in the contexts of the debate over modernism and of psychological and philosophical criticism.
Weigand, Hermann J. *"The Magic Mountain": A Study of Thomas Mann's Novel "Der Zauberberg."* Chapel Hill: University of North Carolina Press, 1964. Though published first in 1933, this study still offers much to the beginning student of Mann's novel. Provides a close reading with an especially interesting discussion of Germanness in the pre-World War I epoch.
Ziolkowski, Theodore. *Dimensions of the Modern Novel*. Princeton, N.J.: Princeton University Press, 1969. The chapter "Thomas Mann: The Magic Mountain" provides a careful reading of the form, content, and substance in the novel, paying special attention to the narrator and his attitudes toward time. Useful connections to other German novels of so-called high modernism.

THE MAGICIAN OF LUBLIN

Type of work: Novel
Author: Isaac Bashevis Singer (1904-1991)
Type of plot: Psychological realism
Time of plot: Late nineteenth century
Locale: Poland
First published: Der Kuntsnmakher fun Lublin, 1959 (English translation, 1960)

Principal characters:
YASHA MAZUR, a magician
ESTHER MAZUR, his wife
MAGDA ZBARSKI, his assistant and his mistress
ZEFTEL LEKACH, a deserted wife, also his mistress
EMILIA CHRABOTZKY, a widow whom Yasha loves

The Story:

At his home in Lublin, Yasha Mazur, a magician, got out of bed and ate the breakfast that his wife Esther had prepared. Again, he assured her that he had never been unfaithful, even on long trips such as that from which he had just returned. However, while he sat in a tavern drinking beer and discussing women, his thoughts turned to the woman with whom he was presently in love, Emilia Chrabotzky, who wanted him to convert to Catholicism, marry her, and move to Italy. Yasha could not get Emilia out of his mind, but he was reluctant to leave his childless wife, who had made Yasha the center of her life. Moreover, though, unlike his wife, he was careless in religious matters, Yasha was hesitant about rejecting his faith and his people.

Again, Yasha set off on his travels. Near Piask, he spent the night with the unattractive Magda, her mother Elzbieta Zbarski, who treated Yasha like a son-in-law, and Magda's unsavory brother, Bolek, who hated Yasha. The next day, Yasha went to Piask to visit yet another mistress, Zeftel Lekach, whose husband had disappeared after his escape from prison. Yasha spent the evening with a gang of thieves, his longtime friends, who were awed by his skills, especially his ability to pick locks, and once again urged him to join them and make a fortune.

While Yasha and Magda were on their way to Warsaw, a storm broke, and they took refuge in a prayer house. Yasha again worried about abandoning his religion. In Warsaw, however, he had to deal with a more urgent matter: his performance schedule. As usual, he learned that he would be working for very low wages. Perhaps, he thought, Emilia was right in thinking that he should go abroad.

When he saw the beautiful Emilia, Yasha could not resist agreeing to her terms. He would become a Catholic, marry her, and take her to Italy, along with her consumptive daughter Halina and her servant Yadwiga. Privately, however, he wondered where he would find the money. At a play with Emilia, Yasha became so depressed that he considered repenting, but the impulse passed. When Emilia again refused to allow him into her bed, he became even more despondent.

Back at his own apartment, Yasha enjoyed being coddled by Magda. Just as he sat down to dinner, however, Zeftel turned up at his door. Although Magda was furious, Yasha left to accompany Zeftel to the house where she was staying, fearing that the white slaver who had taken her in would take advantage of her. When he got there, however, Yasha soon found himself in a friendly conversation, and he spent most of the night with the white slaver and his female accomplice.

Suddenly recalling that Yadwiga had told him about a rich old man who kept his money in a safe in his apartment, Yasha went to steal the money he needed. However, he found himself unable to pick the lock, and, when he jumped from the balcony of the apartment, he hurt his foot. Pursued by a watchman, he again took refuge in a prayer house. This time, he joined in the prayers, convinced that he must return to God and Judaism.

Even though Yasha's foot was now so bad that he feared he would not be able to perform, he refused to call a doctor. Instead, he limped off to tell Emilia that he had no money for the trip. Then, to Yasha's horror, a policeman stopped by to warn Emilia that the thief might have designs on her, since a notebook with her name in it had been left in the old man's apartment. Certain that he would eventually be arrested, Yasha told Emilia what he had done, but, to his amazement, she responded by rebuking him for bungling the job.

In despair, Yasha wandered into a synagogue where Lithuanian Jews were holding a service. If he were to return to Judaism, Yasha mused, he would not settle for a form so worldly. Only the strictest kind of observance could prevent him from sinning.

Back at his apartment, Yasha discovered that Magda had strangled the three animals that he used in his magic act and then hanged herself. After Magda's body was removed, Yasha could not remain in his apartment, and he had himself driven to a hotel. However, because he had not brought his identification papers, he was turned away. Certainly, he thought, Zeftel would help him out. At the white slaver's house, however, Yasha received his second shock of the night. Zeftel and the white slaver were in bed together. Yasha interpreted this as a sign: God had left him nowhere to go but to God.

Three years later, Yasha the magician had become Reb Jacob the Penitent. He was back in Lublin, walled up in a tiny cell in the courtyard of his house. His foot had healed, but spiritually he was still in pain, every day remembering yet another sin for which he must be punished. Esther kept begging him to come out, and strangers broke into his meditations to ask for his prayers, to discuss theology, or just to mock him.

One day, an old friend visited with news of the world Yasha had left behind. Elzbieta was dead; Bolek was in prison; and Zeftel was married to the white slaver and running a brothel in Argentina. Irrationally, Yasha felt responsible for all of these disasters. In a long letter to him, however, Emilia said that she, not he, was to blame for their affair and assured him that she and her daughter were both well and happy. Although Emilia had married again, she counted her days with Yasha as the happiest in her life. She insisted that Yasha was basically a good, kind man and urged him not to be so hard on himself. Finally, Emilia said that she, her daughter, and even the professor thought of Yasha with affection, and that, in Warsaw, he was widely admired once again.

Critical Evaluation:

Writing in Yiddish about Yiddish-speaking Jewish communities in Poland, Isaac Bashevis Singer established the reputation that in 1978 won for him the Nobel Prize in Literature. Although later works about Holocaust survivors in America have won high praise, in setting, plot, and characterization *The Magician of Lublin* is typical of the fiction which brought Singer his initial fame and ensured his lasting popularity.

The plot of *The Magician of Lublin* is not as simple as it seems. It begins as a picaresque novel; Singer establishes an interesting character and then follows him on his travels, pointing out how, through trickery, his protagonist manages to survive, though not always unharmed. However, there is a second story line in the novel, a second journey involving the same character. Even while he pursues fame, fortune, and Emilia, Yasha, without realizing it, is traveling in quest of God.

The historical setting of the novel also involves a duality of perspective. The villages Singer describes appear to be self-sufficient, insulated from the outside world. Within them, the characters may quarrel and reconcile, suffer and survive, but actually their lives move in a pattern as inevitable as the seasons, as old as their religious heritage. Even a rebel like Yasha Mazur knows this; he counts time not only by the coming of spring but also by the coming of Shabuoth.

However, *The Magician of Lublin* contains reminders that this apparent permanence is, in fact, an illusion. When the villagers talk about the power of czarist Russia, they are not aware of what Singer's readers know: that, within a few decades, there will be no czar in Russia. When they arrange marriages and plan the futures of their children, they have no way of knowing that a half century later, a set of conscienceless criminals will murder Jews by the millions, wipe out their villages, and destroy their way of life. One's knowledge of this historical fact, in particular, contributes to the poignancy of novels which, on the surface, are comic or perhaps tragicomic in tone.

Singer's characterization, too, is more complex than one might think. Yasha's women, for example, are initially presented almost as stereotypes: Esther, the devout and devoted wife; Magda, the girl so unattractive that she cannot catch a husband; Zeftel, the vulnerable, deserted wife; Emilia, the widow who, though desperately in love, is virtuous. In the course of the novel, however, Emilia and Zeftel prove to be more practical than sentimental; Magda reveals a capacity for tragic intensity; and Esther discards her dignity in a vain attempt to get Yasha back into her bed.

Yasha, too, begins as a stereotype, in his case as a folk hero. There is nothing he cannot do, no feat of magic he cannot perform, no lock he cannot pick, no acrobatic stunt that is too much for him, no woman who does not adore him, no role he cannot play. Later, however, Yasha is perceived as less perfect than his admirers thought him to be. In one way or another, all of his mistresses desert him, and when he attempts burglary, not only does he fail to pick a simple lock, but he also falls and injures his foot. It can be argued, of course, that it is not a matter of Yasha's having been overrated; it is that God chose to humble him in order to bring Yasha back to God.

Clearly, it is the meaning of this change in Yasha which is crucial to any interpretation of *The Magician of Lublin*. It has been suggested that Reb Jacob the Penitent is as foolish as the original Yasha, for surely, as the rabbi suggests, a sensible man would search for a mean between two extremes. However, it seems more likely that, instead of rebuking his ascetic protagonist, Singer understands his need to retreat from the world. By nature, Yasha is not moderate; his imagination is as excessive as his appetites. It is not surprising then that, for him, there is no middle way, such as that represented by the practical Catholic, Emilia, or the worldly Lithuanian Jews. For Yasha, there are only two possibilities: the street or the synagogue. His God is uncompromising. Singer may be suggesting that, unpalatable as the idea may be to modern minds, this is the very nature of God.

Rosemary M. Canfield Reisman

Bibliography:
Alexander, Edward. *Isaac Bashevis Singer: A Study of the Short Fiction.* Boston: Twayne, 1980. Sees *The Magician of Lublin* as marking a new direction for Singer. Instead of the Jewish community, his subject is the individual, in this case the artist, as he vacillates between freedom and faith.

Allentuck, Marcia, ed. *The Achievement of Isaac Bashevis Singer*. Carbondale: Southern Illinois University Press, 1969. A collection of essays on Singer's works. Particularly helpful is one by Cyrena N. Pondrom, pointing out various opinions as the meaning of Yasha's penitence.

Friedman, Lawrence S. *Understanding Isaac Bashevis Singer*. Columbia: University of South Carolina Press, 1988. Discusses the theme of identity in *The Magician of Lublin*. A good starting point for the study of Singer.

Lee, Grace Farrell. *From Exile to Redemption: The Fiction of Isaac Bashevis Singer*. Carbondale: Southern Illinois University Press, 1987. A chronological study of Singer's works, intended to show how his views altered with the years. A perceptive section on *The Magician of Lublin* focuses on symbolism.

Malin, Irving, ed. *Critical Views of Isaac Bashevis Singer*. New York: New York University Press, 1969. A number of essays on various subjects. J. S. Wolkenfeld's "Isaac Bashevis Singer: The Faith of His Devils and Magicians" compares the moral choices of several major characters, including Yasha.

THE MAGNIFICENT AMBERSONS

Type of work: Novel
Author: Booth Tarkington (1869-1946)
Type of plot: Social realism
Time of plot: 1873-early twentieth century
Locale: A city in the Midwest
First published: 1918

>
> *Principal characters:*
> GEORGE AMBERSON MINAFER, the protagonist
> ISABEL AMBERSON MINAFER, his mother
> GEORGE AMBERSON, his uncle
> FANNY MINAFER, his aunt
> EUGENE MORGAN, a prosperous industrialist
> LUCY MORGAN, his daughter

The Story:

Major Amberson created the family fortune in the 1870's. When Isabel, his daughter, was about twenty years old, she was courted by two men: Wilbur Minafer, a quiet businessman, and Eugene Morgan, a debt-ridden lawyer. Morgan destroyed his chances in a drinking incident on the Amberson estate. Isabel married Wilbur, and their only child was George Amberson Minafer. Isabel spoiled her wild boy. George treated others with contempt and was once expelled from a prep school for his bad behavior. The townspeople hoped to see George get his comeuppance.

When George was an eighteen-year-old college student, a ball was held in his honor at the Amberson mansion. Here George met Eugene Morgan, his mother's former suitor, and fell in love with his nineteen-year-old daughter, Lucy. Eugene had left town at the time Isabel dismissed him, become an inventor, and returned to town twenty years later to manufacture horseless carriages. George informed Lucy that he had no career plans. During their sleigh ride the next day, George attempted to embarrass the inventor by racing his sleigh past Morgan's inoperative horseless carriage. George's sleigh crashed, and he and Lucy had to hitch a ride back into town on the new vehicle. After George returned home for summer vacation, he renewed his relationship with Lucy. When she and her father attended one of the Major's weekly Sunday dinners, the latter revealed that Isabel and Eugene had once been engaged. On the night before George returned to college, Isabel told him of Wilbur's declining health. His father was deeply worried because he and George's uncle, George Amberson, had tied up much of the family's assets in a company owned by their friends, an investment that was turning sour.

During the following summer, George proposed to Lucy when he heard a false rumor that she was engaged to Fred Kinney. Though she declined to say either yes or no at that time, she promised to settle the matter before he returned to school. On George's final night before returning to college, Lucy still left their relationship unsettled. She told him that they were "almost" engaged. While back at college, Isabel wrote George that she had gotten the ailing Wilbur to take a vacation and that his uncle, Sydney Amberson, and his wife had taken their one-third share of the Amberson fortune. Then Wilbur died, and his business failure left Uncle George and Fanny broke. George Minafer gave his father's insurance money to Fanny as compensation. After George's graduation from college, he was horrified to see five new houses on the family estate—the Major's attempt to recoup the family fortune. George became increasingly hostile to both Eugene Morgan and his automobiles. Lucy refused to go beyond their "almost" engagement because George, unlike her father, refused to pursue a career. George then insulted Eugene Morgan during a Sunday dinner. Angered by his differences with Lucy and by a rumor that Isabel had always been in love with Eugene, George confronted the rumormonger, Mrs. Johnson, and then barred the industrialist from his house. George then told Isabel that he had to protect the Amberson name from scandal, and bullied her into ceasing all contact with Eugene Morgan. George subsequently told Lucy that he and Isabel were to leave the country indefinitely.

Then the Amberson holdings fell into decay, the Major's new houses proved a failure, and Uncle George and Fanny invested heavily in an ill-fated headlight invention. Against Uncle George's advice, Fanny secretly staked all of her money on the scheme. After several years abroad, George brought his mother back when she was gravely ill. As she lay dying, George refused to let Eugene see his old flame one last time. Isabel later told her son that she had wanted to see Morgan once more. With Isabel's demise, the Major lost all interest in business. When Fanny told George that the gossip had died out soon after his departure, George then feared that his interference had been a grave error. Then the headlight scheme collapsed, and Uncle George revealed that Isabel had never received a deed for her house. When Major Amberson died, the Amberson estate was bankrupt, and Sydney and Amelia, having taken the best part of it, then refused to help. Uncle George was awarded a consulship in another city, while George was to room with Fanny and study law. When Fanny confessed that she was destitute, George had to accept a dangerous job involving explosives in order to support her. The growing city quickly effaced all traces of the Ambersons, and George felt the humiliation the townspeople had long ago desired. George was then seriously injured by an automobile. When Eugene was away on business, he discovered that both he and Lucy had had a vision of Isabel. His subsequent visit to a psychic and a second vision of Isabel suggested to him that she wanted him to help George. Upon returning home, Eugene rushed to George's hospital room and found Lucy and Fanny already there. George begged his forgiveness, and Eugene realized that he could regain his connection with Isabel by helping her son.

Critical Evaluation:

Perhaps more than any other American writer of the twentieth century, Booth Tarkington demonstrates the insecure position of an author in relation to his critics. Born into an upper-middle-class Indianapolis family and educated at Purdue and Princeton universities, Tarkington went on to become one of the most popular and critically acclaimed writers of the early twentieth century. During this period, his plays were readily produced and his short stories and novels regularly published. Critical reception was no less favorable, with the novels *The Magnificent Ambersons* (1918) and *Alice Adams* (1921) both receiving Pulitzer Prizes. Although postwar critics have virtually ignored Tarkington, his well-wrought tales are important examples of social realism. They chart the development of an industrial giant, the United States.

Tarkington is primarily a regional writer, his major works depicting the social upheaval of industrialism and its effects upon Midwest locales and their inhabitants in the industrial era. *The Magnificent Ambersons* is no exception. Initially published in 1918, Tarkington reissued the novel in the 1920's as part of the *Growth* trilogy, which also includes *The Turmoil* (1915) and *The Midlander* (1923). Like the other realist writers of his time, Tarkington effectively employs physical detail to depict a palpable and often gritty reality. In *The Magnificent Ambersons*, much of the story takes place in the early years of the twentieth century. Tarkington re-creates the immediate past for the readers of 1918 by opening the novel with a lengthy discussion of the changing fashions—from clothing fads to the particular jargon of George Minafer's social stratum. The most striking example of Tarkington's brand of realism is the smoke created by the burning of soft coal. Though little more than a nuisance at the beginning of the novel, it obscures and eventually engulfs the Amberson estate when the latter goes bankrupt, casting a pall on the once mighty family. In Tarkington's skillful hands, a seemingly minor detail comes to symbolize for the Ambersons a dark future they can neither recognize nor accept. Told in a conventional third-person narration, Tarkington's tale charts the transition of a large Midwestern town (presumably Indianapolis, although it is never stated) into a modern city. Specifically, the novel deals with characters who are wedded to the past (the Ambersons) and those who look forward to the future (the Morgans). George Amberson Minafer, the protagonist and Major Amberson's only grandchild, is clearly linked to an earlier age in the novel. As a nine-year-old child, George reigns like a feudal lord over the growing town, rebelling against any kind of authority and thrashing his perceived enemies. Indeed, the "F.O.T.A." clubroom contains a representation of a shield and battle axes. His chivalric tendencies are also reflected in his ultimately disastrous efforts to protect his mother's reputation. Calling those who are not of his own class "riff-raff," Tarkington's protagonist fully embodies an aristocratic old order, one who prefers a horse to the horseless carriage. Significantly, George wins Lucy only when he sheds this veneer of nobility and adopts her father's work ethic. Clearly, Tarkington rejects an American aristocracy.

In its broadest terms, *The Magnificent Ambersons* depicts the rags-to-riches-to-rags scenario that is the dark side of the American success story. The novel's central theme is the necessity of adapting to change in a time of transition. Simply put, Major Amberson's empire crumbles because he and his family fail to accommodate change. In contrast to the old guard, Eugene Morgan heralds change and is its most visible exponent. Indeed, he nurtures its most potent symbol, the automobile. Irony is the means by which Tarkington explores this theme. This is evident in specific incidents, but irony is also a factor in the larger structure of the book. When George attempts to show his bravado by racing past Eugene Morgan's machine, the destruction of the sleigh ironically leaves the former little choice but to ride in the horseless carriage he sought to mock. The irony is compounded when this scene is compared with George's more successful stunts as a child. In addition to demonstrating George's lack of growth, Tarkington increases the irony by having his protagonist defeated by the embodiment of the future in the book, Eugene Morgan. Even more ironic is the automobile accident that lands George in the hospital. From the "princely terror" who whipped the hardware man in the third chapter, George has now become the hapless victim in chapter 34—felled by the very "riff-raff" he so vigorously disdained. Most ironic of all is the economic context of the Ambersons' rise and fall: They build their empire in a time of great hardship and lose it in a period of booming prosperity. Critics have faulted the novel for what they regard as its sentimental and overly optimistic ending, but Tarkington's conclusion serves two important purposes. First, it brings to a close the moral education of George Minafer. Having lost his aristocratic status and having received his deserved punishment, he is ready to adopt the American work ethic. Second, Tarkington's adept engineering of the final reconciliation brings about a merging of the old and the new.

Cliff Prewencki

Bibliography:
Cournos, John, and Sybil Norton. *Famous Modern American Novelists.* New York: Dodd,

Mead, 1952. Contains a brief biography of Tarkington and a useful synopsis of the *Growth* trilogy.

Fennimore, Keith J. *Booth Tarkington*. New York: Twayne, 1974. Perhaps the best book on Tarkington for the general reader, one that offers a good overview of the author and his novels, a useful chronology, and an excellent annotated bibliography. Emphasizes the interaction between the aristocrats and the upstarts in *The Magnificent Ambersons*.

Gray, Donald J. Introduction to *The Magnificent Ambersons*, by Booth Tarkington. Bloomington: Indiana University Press, 1989. Provides a valuable overview of the novel as well as an overview of Tarkington's prolific career. Claims that the author is less concerned with psychological than social realism.

Noe, Marcia. "Failure and the American Mythos: Tarkington's *The Magnificent Ambersons*." *Midamerica* 15 (1988): 11-18. Contends that failure is a prominent theme in American literature and that this novel is Tarkington's most thorough treatment of that theme. Holds that George's failure as an aristocrat is an essential element in the novel in that it paves the way for his moral growth.

Woodress, James Leslie. *Booth Tarkington: Gentleman from Indiana*. Philadelphia: J. B. Lippincott, 1955. An old but valuable biography that includes insightful analyses of the author's plays as well as the novels. Highlights the importance of work as the foundation of Tarkington's moral vision and the purifying power of a woman's love in *The Magnificent Ambersons*.

MAGNIFICENT OBSESSION

Type of work: Novel
Author: Lloyd C. Douglas (1877-1951)
Type of plot: Domestic realism
Time of plot: Early twentieth century
Locale: Detroit and Europe
First published: 1929

Principal characters:
> DR. WAYNE HUDSON, a famous brain surgeon
> HELEN BRENT HUDSON, the doctor's second wife
> JOYCE HUDSON, the doctor's daughter and Helen's school friend
> ROBERT MERRICK, a physician
> NANCY ASHFORD, the superintendent at the Hudson Clinic

The Story:

The staff at the Hudson Clinic was worried about the head of the hospital, Dr. Wayne Hudson. The doctor had suddenly become nervous and haggard, a bad condition for an eminent practicing surgeon, and his staff tried to advise the doctor to take six months away from his work. The doctor himself surprised his staff by announcing that he was about to marry his daughter's school friend, Miss Helen Brent. The couple were married within a short time and went to live at the doctor's lakeside cottage. Soon afterward, a shocking tragedy occurred at the lake. Dr. Hudson drowned because the inhalator that might have saved his life had been dispatched across the lake to resuscitate a wealthy young playboy, Robert Merrick.

While he was recuperating from his experience, young Merrick believed that the doctors and the nurses at the Hudson Clinic resented him. He did not yet know that it was at the expense of the life of the hospital's chief surgeon that he himself was alive. He questioned the superintendent of the clinic, Nancy Ashford, who had been in love with her chief, Doctor Hudson, but Miss Ashford did not give him a satisfactory answer. Later, overhearing a conversation, Merrick discovered why the people at the hospital seemed to despise him. He talked again to Nancy Ashford, who told him the only way he could ever make amends would be to take Dr. Hudson's place in life by becoming a great surgeon.

After weeks of pondering on the idea of going to medical school, Merrick decided that he would try to fill Dr. Hudson's place. When he went back to Nancy Ashford to tell her of his plans, she told him the story of the doctor's many philanthropies. She also gave him a book which the doctor had written in code. After many days and nights of perseverance, the young man managed to break the cipher. When he had done so, it seemed to him that the doctor, whom he had come to look upon as an ideal, had been a lunatic, for the book was a strange, mystic tract about doing good. From Nancy Ashford, he learned that the deceased doctor had been a great mystic, believing that his gift as a surgeon came to him from what he called the Major Personality. That power was earned by doing good unknown to others, philanthropy that would aid the recipient in leading a valuable life of service. During the next few years, Merrick attended the state medical school. One night, as he sat studying, he suddenly felt a call to go to a nightclub where he knew Joyce Hudson, the doctor's daughter, was to be. After rescuing her from a drunken scene, he took her home. There he met the doctor's widow.

That semester, Merrick almost failed at medical school. Discouraged with his own efforts, he decided to experiment with the knowledge he had gained from the dead surgeon's manuscript. He aided a fellow student, Dawson, who was about to leave school because he lacked funds. Immediately, he felt renewed hope and plunged into his work with enthusiasm. Helen Hudson, the doctor's widow, had gone to Europe, where she remained for three years. Near the end of that time, she discovered that the cousin who was handling her affairs was dishonest. Needing funds, she wrote to Nancy Ashford to ask if her stock in the Hudson Clinic could be sold. Nancy told Merrick, now a doctor at the clinic. He sent Helen twenty-five thousand dollars and sold some of the stock for her. Toward the end of her stay in Europe, Helen met Mrs. Dawson, wife of the medical student whom Merrick had helped through medical school. Merrick had asked Mrs. Dawson to learn something of Helen's financial losses so that he might put her affairs in order. After telling Mrs. Dawson her troubles, Helen discovered an envelope Mrs. Dawson had addressed to Merrick. Helen promptly disappeared.

Merrick went to the cousin who was managing Helen's financial affairs. The man had robbed Helen of about one hundred thousand dollars. Merrick made good the loss and sent the man out of the country, bringing no charges against him because he was related to Helen. Before the cousin left, he learned Merrick's theory of personality projection and made up his mind to lead an honest life.

Tired from overwork, Merrick took a vacation in the country for several weeks. Then he returned to his laboratory and began a program of hard work. His meals were returned to the kitchen almost untouched. His labors were at last successful, for he perfected a scalpel that automatically cauterized by means of electricity. The device opened a new field of brain surgery because it prevented hemorrhage as it cut into the tissue.

About Christmas, Helen returned to the United States. In Detroit, she went to her trust company and asked to see the shares of stock that they held in her name. As she suspected, they had been transferred from Merrick. When she left the bank, she did not know whether to feel thankful or insulted. Helen went from the bank to the Hudson Clinic, where she asked to see Merrick immediately. Her confusion was even greater when he told her he could not take back the money. He tried to explain the transfer of her stock, but she was in no mood for explanations. As he took her to the door, they met her stepdaughter. Joyce complicated the tense situation by proposing a theater party for the next day. In order not to create gossip, both Helen and Merrick agreed to go to dinner and the theater afterward. As he helped Helen into the taxi, Merrick managed to murmur that he loved her.

The next evening at dinner, Merrick asked Helen not to tell all that had been done for a needy Italian family at Assisi. He added that the philanthropy would thereby lose its value if the story were told.

The following summer, Merrick went to Europe to visit eminent surgeons in Vienna and to demonstrate his cauterizing scalpel to them. While he was in Paris, he heard that Helen had been injured in a train wreck near Rome. Hurrying to Rome, he operated on the injured woman and saved her life. Then, in quixotic fashion, he left Rome before anyone could tell her who had performed the delicate operation. Helen guessed Merrick's identity, however, from the few words he had mumbled in her presence. Weeks later, when she discovered that he was planning to visit her, Helen, ashamed of her previous attitude toward his interest in her affairs, arranged to leave for the United States. Yet Merrick flew to Le Havre ahead of her, arranged for their marriage, and met her on the dock. When she saw him waiting, she walked into his arms. She did not have to be told why he had come.

Critical Evaluation:

Critics never understood the popularity of Lloyd C. Douglas' novels, condemning them for trite language, superficial characterization, and thin ideas. By Douglas' death in 1951, more than seven million copies of his books had been sold. Of those, one and a half million were of his first novel, *Magnificent Obsession*. He was the highest-selling author in American publishing history in his time. Toward the close of the twentieth century, he often does not even have an entry in a standard dictionary of literary biography. Therefore, what made him such a popular novelist for the two decades in which he wrote must be determined.

For almost three decades prior to publishing *Magnificent Obsession*, Douglas was a minister in several Lutheran and Congregational pulpits. As he moved from pulpit to pulpit, from Washington, D.C., to Ann Arbor to Akron to Los Angeles, his theology became increasingly liberal but his rhetoric stayed the same. His vivid narratives held crowds spellbound, and he achieved some fame in religious circles for his lectures, essays, and sermons. Before beginning his writing career, he often commented that he would like to try his hand at a novel. To Douglas, the novel-reading public constituted "a larger parish" with which to share the joys of Christian living.

Magnificent Obsession had its beginnings in two sources. One was a newspaper story reporting the death of a Detroit doctor who could have been saved had his respirator not been lent out to rescue a young man across the lake. The second was a series of sermons Douglas had preached in Los Angeles on the secrets of exultant living. According to his biographer daughter, he had been trying to convince people that their religion could have a practical dynamic effect in their lives if only they would put Jesus' words about secret altruism—let not your left hand know what your right hand is doing—into practice. When his wife remarked that for the first time she understood what he was saying, he admitted that it was his most important message. Then his daughter Betty asked why he did not put in into his novel. So *Magnificent Obsession* came to be, although its early days were not secure. It had originally been sent to *Harper's Magazine* as *Salvage*, rejected, revised as *Magnificent Obsession* and rejected by *Harper's Magazine* and several others before being published by a small religious house in Chicago in 1929. Within eighteen months, however, it was on the best-seller lists, seemingly having hit a nerve of many people whose lives were being buffeted by economic forces beyond their control.

Theme was all-important to Douglas. He considered his novels to be "purpose novels." In a letter, Douglas stated the thesis of *Magnificent Obsession* as "how to get what you want and be what you would like to be through a practice of a Galilean principle of secret philanthropy." To demonstrate such a principle of living, Douglas fleshed it out in the lives of characters, who either act on the principle or who provide a contrast by refraining from acting on the principle. Robert Merrick, the playboy whose life is saved by Dr. Wayne Hudson's secret philanthropy, is skeptical for a long while, even after he reluctantly goes to medical school so that he may take Dr. Hudson's place at the Hudson Clinic. Merrick is skeptical even after he begins to decipher the journal that contains Hudson's philanthropic activities and beliefs. When Hudson's administrative assistant claims that "It's all true, Bobby. You do get what you want that way, if what you want contributes to the larger expression of yourself in constructive service," he could only think that it sounded foolish. Nevertheless, just having helped a fellow medical student out of his financial predicament, and beginning to read the New Testament accounts of how Christ had quietly helped people, Merrick mystically encounters a power that can change lives, thus launching his successful career as a brain surgeon, medical inventor, and philanthropist. Eventually, Merrick does get his heart's desire, Dr. Hudson's young widow as his own wife.

It is no accident that the central figures in this novel are physicians. For Douglas, a doctor rather than a minister is in a better position in society to help people. He is practical, scientific, and compassionate, embodying all the characteristics Douglas admired most. Bobby Merrick himself convinces a popular preacher that the purely intellectual, critical approach to religion that the preacher has been preaching to large crowds each Sunday is bankrupt compared to Merrick's own scientific appropriation of the power of his Major Personality. That power has proved practical in Merrick's own life. He uses it not only to heal the sick but also to invent better ways to do brain surgery and—eventually—to gain his own love's reward.

Although Douglas cloaks his ideas in character and action, his style is not symbolic. Rather, it is direct and vivid, filled with action verbs and many descriptive words and phrases. There is much dialogue, yet little preaching. It is this nonliterary style that put the literary establishment off but attracted a huge reading audience. A direct, accessible style accounts for much of the popularity of Douglas' fiction, along with the appeal of his message to a nation undergoing a spiritual crisis fostered by the economic depression. Carl Bode, a critic writing in the 1950's, claimed that Douglas was the most popular religious writer of the century because he understood America and its religious needs so well.

"Critical Evaluation" by Barbara J. Hampton

Bibliography:
Bode, Carl. "Lloyd Douglas—Loud Voice in the Wilderness." *American Quarterly* 2 (Winter, 1950): 340-352. Argues that "to know Douglas' novels is to understand our country at least a little better."
_____. "Lloyd Douglas and America's Largest Parish." *Religion in Life* 19 (Summer, 1950): 440-447. A professor of English at the University of Maryland concludes that Douglas is important not for his literary contributions but rather for his linking relationship to the American literary and religious scenes.
Dawson, Virginia, and Betty Wilson. *The Shape of Sunday*. London: Peter Davies, 1953. This "intimate biography" of Lloyd Douglas by his daughters gives many anecdotes of his life. Gives the personal background to the writing and reception of *Magnificent Obsession*.
Kunitz, Stanley, ed. *Twentieth Century Authors. First Supplement*. New York: H. W. Wilson, 1955. Basic information about Douglas in a literary dictionary.
Von Gelder, Robert. *Writers and Writing*. New York: Charles Scribner's Sons, 1946. The prolific book reviewer reprints his interview with Douglas about the writing and about the impact of *Magnificent Obsession*.

THE MAGUS

Type of work: Novel
Author: John Fowles (1926-   )
Type of plot: Psychological realism
Time of plot: 1953
Locale: England and Greece
First published: 1965; revised, 1977

Principal characters:
NICHOLAS URFE, a twenty-six-year-old English teacher
ALISON KELLY, his lover
MAURICE CONCHIS, a wealthy Greek-English philosopher
JULIE HOLMES, an actress
LILY DE SEITAS, a friend of Conchis and Julie's mother
JOJO, a Scottish girl

The Story:

Nicholas Urfe, a twenty-six-year-old Englishman looking for something to do with his life, took a teaching job on the Greek island of Phraxos. He had met, romanced, and abandoned an Australian woman, Alison Kelly, at a party in London, and he had little direction or meaning ahead of him.

Discussions with his British predecessor at the Greek school led Urfe to make the acquaintance of Maurice Conchis, a wealthy man who owned an estate near the school. Conchis told Urfe something of his past, and what developed over time was a strange mixture of past and present as characters from Conchis' life appeared during Urfe's visits to the man's villa. One of these was Lily, Conchis' former sweetheart, who, in reality, was Julie Holmes, a British actress. Urfe fell in love with Lily/Julie. Later, Urfe was reunited with Alison in Athens, but, after he told her of his love for Julie, Alison apparently killed herself. Urfe was shaken by the suicide, but he began to pursue Julie.

However, events took a strange turn when Urfe was drugged, taken into a subterranean prison on Phraxos, and forced to judge the people who had appeared in his episodes with Conchis. He was offered the opportunity to punish Julie by whipping her, but he refused. Then Urfe was bound and forced to watch a pornographic film which starred Julie and Joe Harrison, another actor in Conchis' bizarre orchestration of events. Following the film, Julie and Joe appeared and consummated their sexual relationship in front of Urfe.

By now, Urfe was enraged with what had been inflicted on him. When he was released from his imprisonment, he found he had been fired from his teaching job, and he returned to Athens. He discovered that news of Alison's suicide was false. He then went to London in search of Julie and met her mother, Lily de Seitas, a woman who had cooperated with Conchis in Urfe's deception. Lily explained to Urfe that what Conchis and the others did to him was for his own good, to make him a better person. She insisted that he wait for Alison to reappear.

Meanwhile, Urfe met Jojo, an earthy Scottish girl, at a theater. She fell in love with him, and, try as he might, he was unable to keep from hurting her. Despairing of the pain that he caused Jojo, Urfe met Alison in a park, and the story ended as he and she negotiated a resumption of their relationship.

Critical Evaluation:

The Magus is a very involved, appropriately controversial and mystifying novel, made even more so by a revised version of the novel, which John Fowles published in 1977.

The story's fundamental thrust seems to be the moral rehabilitation of its hero-antihero, Nicholas. At the story's outset, Nicholas is a disaffected, rather self-absorbed young man who is unable to find much of value in life. His relationship with an Australian girl, Alison Kelly, is primarily sexual; she, on the other hand, wants a commitment from him that he is not willing to make. Ultimately, the reader is asked to accept the fact that a good deal of time, effort, and expense are devoted to making Nicholas see how cruel he has been to Alison and how important it is to treat other people responsibly.

As the reader finds at the end of the story, the wealthy thinker, Maurice Conchis, has made something of a career of punishing and enlightening wrongdoers such as Nicholas. After Nicholas' arrival at his villa on the Greek island of Phraxos, Conchis orchestrates multilevel real life theater, designed primarily to manipulate and humiliate Nicholas and, finally, to encourage him to come to grips with ethical behavior in a world where God's presence is obscured at best.

While Nicholas is in Conchis' thrall on Phraxos, he is made to fall in love with a British actress named Julie Holmes and, eventually, to be made a fool of because of this. In a particularly crucial part of the story, Nicholas is drugged and held prisoner underground. He sees a number of the characters in the real-life play Conchis has directed and is asked to judge them for what they have done to him. Indeed, he is given a whip and is placed before the naked Julie; those who watch wait to see if Nicholas will punish her.

He chooses not to whip the woman who has so humiliated him, and, in so doing, quickly understands what freedom is. Nicholas sees that Conchis has given him the responsibility to exercise a moral option. Nicholas has evidently realized that what he does in life is entirely his responsibility. Conchis has taught him that in a world where humanity is the source of moral evil, where all things are permitted and anything might happen, each person is nevertheless able to create his or her own values and thereby salvage personal worth and identity.

Conchis had already explained his idea of freedom to Nicholas in one of their many conversations. Conchis tells the story of his own choice when, during the Nazi occupation of Phraxos when he was mayor of the village, the Germans ordered him to execute a group of Greek partisans. In an epiphany, Conchis recalls, he understood that freedom is an absolute, that all are free to commit the most heinous crimes—and to choose to refrain from them.

The basic philosophical focus of the story is reflected in the novel's epigraphs, a passage from a book on the Tarot and three quotations from the Marquis de Sade's *Les Infortunes de la vertu* (*The Misfortunes of Virtue*), a novel published in 1787. Fowles's epigraphs relate to Conchis as a magus, that is, a seer, magician, or juggler, and to Nicholas' passage from irresponsible, reprehensible reprobate to participant in dark affairs to philosophically informed survivor of Conchis' machinations.

The novel's epigraphs constitute only one small dimension of its allusions, symbolism, and cultural resonance. Nicholas' last name, Urfe, is a reference to a seventeenth century French pastoral novel, Honoré d'Urfe's *L'Astrée* (1607-1627), which suggests that Nicholas the young, naïve hero is a suitable target for disillusionment. *The Magus* is full of allusions to the occult, classical mythology, French existentialism, cinema, and twentieth century history. Suitably enough, as the story develops, Nicholas is compared to such mythological heroes as Orpheus, Ulysses, Theseus, all characters who were changed in some ways by extraordinary journeys.

Its literary and cultural baggage shows that *The Magus* can be approached on at least two levels, as little more than a long but interesting thriller and as a complex philosophical novel. As the novel ends, Nicholas has evidently learned that one cannot treat other people selfishly and narcissistically as objects for one's own pleasure. He is also seeing the difference between love and sexual attraction, and he has acquired a sense of guilt for the wrongs he has perpetuated in the past and a resolve to act otherwise in the future.

Many readers will see that *The Magus* is a surprisingly conservative novel from a moral perspective. Its lesson that we will fulfill ourselves and be happy only if we are kind to one another is a direct reaction to the atmosphere of moral permissiveness that certain popular schools of thought expressed in the 1960's. Likewise, where Nicholas only played at being a self-conscious existentialist before he met Conchis, at the end of the novel, he has learned some of the basic lessons one learns from reading such writers and philosophers as Jean-Paul Sartre and Albert Camus. Both Sartre and Camus are preoccupied with how one should conduct oneself in the absence of God and with impressing humanity with its burden of freedom. While Fowles does not deal in *The Magus* explicitly and extensively with humanity's relationship to God or even with God's existence, he stresses the practical nature of intelligent moral choices, as do Sartre and Camus.

Gordon Walters

Bibliography:
Garard, Charles. *Point of View in Fiction and Film: Focus on John Fowles*. New York: Peter Lang, 1991. Important because three of Fowles's novels—*The Collector* (1963), *The Magus*, and *The French Lieutenant's Woman* (1969)—have been made into films and because Fowles's narrative techniques are often cinematic in nature.
Huffaker, Robert. *John Fowles*. Boston: Twayne, 1980. A fine introduction to Fowles and his work, including a critical bibliography.
Onega, Susana. *Form and Meaning in the Novels of John Fowles*. Ann Arbor, Mich.: UMI Research Press, 1989. Includes essays on Fowles's novels of the 1980's. Notes that the structures of the novels always reflect their meanings.
Palmer, William J. *The Fiction of John Fowles*. Columbia: University of Missouri Press, 1974. A brief but stimulating reading of Fowles's novels in the light of philosophical, social, and cultural contexts.
Wolfe, Peter. *John Fowles: Magus and Moralist*. Lewisburg, Pa.: Bucknell University Press, 1976. Especially interesting in that the author applies the concepts of magic and ethical behavior, two concerns of *The Magus*, to all of Fowles's fiction.

THE MAHABHARATA

Type of work: Poetry
Author: Unknown
Type of plot: Epic
Time of plot: Antiquity
Locale: India
First transcribed: Mahābhārata, c. 400 B.C.E.-200 C.E. (English translation, 1834)

Principal characters:
KING DHRITARASHTRA, the father of the Kauravas
KING PANDU, his brother and father of the Pandavas
YUDHISHTHIRA,
BHIMA,
ARJUNA,
NAKULA, and
SAHADEVA, the five sons of King Pandu
DRAUPADI, the Pandavas' wife
DURYODHANA, the oldest son of Dhritarashtra

The Story:

Among the descendants of King Bharata (after whose name India was called Bharata-varsha, land of the Bharatas) there were two successors to the throne of Hastinapura. Of these, the elder, Dhritarashtra, was blind and gave over the reins of government to his younger brother Pandu. Pandu grew weary of his duties and retired to hunt and enjoy himself. Again Dhritarashtra took control, aided by the advice and example of his wise old uncle, Bhishma. Upon Pandu's death, his five sons were put under the care of his younger brother, who had one hundred sons of his own.

At first the king's household was peaceful and free from strife, but gradually it became apparent that Pandu's sons were far more capable of ruling than any of Dhritarashtra's heirs. Of the Pandavas, the name given to the five descendants of Pandu, all were remarkably able, but the oldest, Yudhishthira, was judged most promising and therefore was chosen heir-apparent to the throne of the old blind king. To this selection of their cousin as the future king, the king's own sons took violent exception. Accordingly, they persuaded their father to allow the Pandavas to leave the court and live by themselves. From a trap set by the unscrupulous Duryodhana, leader of the king's sons, the five brothers escaped to the forest with their mother. There they spent some time in rustic exile.

In the meantime King Drupada had announced that the hand of his daughter, Princess Draupadi, would be given to the hero surpassing all others in a feat of strength and skill, and he had invited throngs of noblemen to compete for his daughter's hand. In disguise, the Pandavas set out for King Drupada's court.

More than two weeks were spent in celebrating the approaching nuptials of the princess before the trial of strength which would reveal the man worthy of taking the lovely princess as his wife. The test was to grasp a mighty bow, fit an arrow, bend the bow, and hit a metal target with the arrow. Contestant after contestant failed in the effort to bend the huge bow. Finally Arjuna, third of the sons of Pandu, came forward and performed the feat with little effort to win the hand of the princess. In curious fashion Princess Draupadi became the wife of all five of the brothers. At this time, also, the Pandavas met their cousin on their mother's side, Krishna of

3848

Dvaraka. This renowned Yadava nobleman they accepted as their special counselor and friend, and to him they owed much of their future success and power.

Hoping to avert dissension after his death, King Dhritarashtra decided to divide his kingdom into two parts, giving his hundred sons, the Kauravas, one portion and the Pandavas the other. Thus it came about that Dhritarashtra's sons ruled in Hastinapur and the five sons of Pandu in Indraprastha. The dying king's attempt to settle affairs of government amicably resulted in peace and prosperity for a brief period. Then the wily Duryodhana, leader of the Kauravas, set another trap for the Pandavas. On this occasion he enticed Yudhishthira, the oldest of the brothers, into a game of skill at dice. When the latter lost, the penalty was that the five brothers were to leave the court and spend the next twelve years in the forest. At the end of that time they were to have their kingdom and holdings once again if they could pass another year in disguise, without having anyone recognize them.

The twelve-year period of rustication was one of many romantic and heroic adventures. All five brothers were concerned in stirring events; Arjuna, in particular, traveled far and long, visited the sacred stream of the Ganges, was courted by several noble ladies, and finally married Subhadra, sister of Krishna.

When the long time of exile was over, the Pandavas and Kauravas engaged in a war of heroes. Great armies were assembled; mountains of supplies were brought together. Just before the fighting began, Krishna stepped forth and sang the divine song, the *Bhagavad Gita*, in which he set forth such theological truths as the indestructibility of the soul, the necessity to defend the faith, and other fundamental precepts of the theology of Brahma. By means of this song Arjuna was relieved of his doubts concerning the need to make his trial by battle.

The war lasted for some eighteen consecutive days, each day marked by fierce battles, single combats, and bloody attacks. Death and destruction were everywhere—the battlefields were strewn with broken bodies and ruined weapons and chariots. The outcome was the annihilation of all the pretensions of the Kauravas and their allies to rule over the kingdom. Finally Yudhishthira came to the throne amid great celebrations, the payment of rich tribute, and the ceremonial horse sacrifice.

Later the death of their spiritual and military counselor, Krishna, led the five brothers to realize their weariness with earthly pomp and striving. Accordingly, Yudhishthira gave up his duties as ruler. The five brothers then banded together, clothed themselves as hermits, and set out for Mount Meru, the dwelling place of the gods on high. They were accompanied by their wife Draupadi and a dog that joined them on their journey. As they proceeded, one after the other dropped by the way and perished. At last only Yudhishthira and the faithful dog remained to reach the portals of heaven. When the dog was refused admission to that holy place, Yudhishthira declined to enter without his canine companion. Then the truth was revealed—the dog was in reality the god of justice himself, sent to test Yudhishthira's constancy.

Yudhishthira was not content in heaven, for he soon realized that his brothers and Draupadi had been required to descend to the lower regions and there expiate their mortal sins. Lonely and disconsolate, he decided to join them until all could be united in heaven. After he had spent some time in that realm of suffering and torture, the gods took pity on him. Along with his brothers and Draupadi, he was transported back to heaven, where all dwelt in perpetual happiness.

Critical Evaluation:

In its present form in Sanskrit, the *Mahabharata* runs to some 200,000 verses in couplets (*slokas*), in eighteen sections or books, although there is credible evidence to assume that earlier versions were considerably less extensive. About one-third to one-quarter of the whole relates to the central story, that of a civil war between two great royal houses of India. The *Mahabharata* is a massive collection of fascinating heroic and mythological legends, sermonlike essays, worldly and spiritual advice, material constituting codes of law, popular apothegms and proverbs, and moral tales for the edification of its audience. The *Mahabharata* is a history of prehistoric times and a compendium of materials that throw light on the religious, social, political, ethical, and moral ideals and practices of the people of ancient India.

Western readers who pick up the *Mahabharata* for the first time are often puzzled by the seemingly amorphous nature of this collection. Unlike Homer's *Iliad* (c. 800 B.C.E.) or Vergil's *Aeneid* (c. 29-19 B.C.E.), which have a clear narrative focus, the *Mahabharata* is a rambling account of a war between two factions of Indians, interspersed among a number of treatises that seem only tangentially related to the story. While plot features parallel Western epics and world folk literature (the reluctant warrior, the descent into the underworld, the battles in which gods take part), Western readers may sense that this work is essentially different from those to which they may be more accustomed.

The Western reader may find it helpful to note analogues between the *Mahabharata* and Western literature in order to compare cultural concepts and assumptions. The *Mahabharata* and the Bible share a similar format. The story of Savitri and the story of Ruth have much in common. The polyandry of Princess Draupadi with the Pandavas is reflected in some of the marriages of the Old Testament. The richest source of analogues to the *Mahabharata* is found in Greek mythology. The bow-and-arrow feat of strength for the hand of Princess Draupadi is mirrored in the test of Penelope's suitors. The twelve-year exile and wandering of the Pandavas has its parallel in the *Odyssey*, just as the battle between the Pandavas and the Kauravas is echoed in the *Iliad*.

The *Mahabharata* is classified as a heroic epic to distinguish it from the literary epic and the mock epic. In some formal respects, it does not follow the pattern of the Western epic. Whereas the Greek heroic epic contains twenty-four books and the English literary epic has twelve, the *Mahabharata* consists of eighteen books. The number eighteen does not appear to be arbitrary. The *Bhagavad Gita* section of the *Mahabharata*, for example, is a microcosm of the greater work, and is divided into eighteen chapters. Additionally, the war in which Duryodhana and his forces are defeated lasts eighteen days. Also while most Western heroic epics are nationalistic, the Mahabharata is concerned with a story of conflict primarily for high moral purpose, a struggle between good and evil.

The *Mahabharata* is an accretion of texts from different periods by different hands, assembled perhaps by the person known as Vyasa ("the arranger"). While it lacks the relatively concise plotting one finds in works by Homer and Vergil, the *Mahabharata* is nevertheless carefully constructed to move readers from one point of understanding about human nature to another. There is coherence, too, in the general movement in the poem from an emphasis on action toward a celebration of the principle of *Samkhya*, or renunciation of materialism in favor of a higher spiritual dimension, the attainment of which may provide humans eternal peace.

The *Mahabharata* is a frame story in which various narrators or characters within narratives relate additional stories or discourse on topics such as the proper role of people in society, right behavior for those in authority, or the best course for one to follow in leading a fulfilling life. While they may be read simply as accounts of heroic actions by larger-than-life characters from a bygone era, the individual episodes have long been considered fables intended to vivify for readers a number of important moral, philosophical, and religious doctrines. For example, the war between the Pandavas and the Kauravas may be taken as an allegory of the eternal struggle between good and evil. The struggles of the warrior Arjuna (who shares some affinities with his Western cousin Achilles) can be interpreted as an example of the trials people must go through to discern their proper social and political roles. The adventures of Yudhishthira, whose story concludes the epic, are intended to illustrate the virtues of justice and renunciation of material values.

The frame story is probably based upon a historical event: a war between two neighboring peoples, the Kurus and the Panchalas, who inhabited the west and east points of the Madhyadesa (the "middle land" between the Ganges and the Jumna) respectively, with the war ending in the overthrow of the Kuru dynasty. The *Mahabharata*, however, is best construed on more than one level. For example, the *Bhagavad Gita* is, in one sense, simply a dialogue between Arjuna and Krishna. The circumstances and setting—the impending battle, Arjuna's ethical reservations, and the question-answer format—are merely devices to dramatize Krishna's ethical and metaphysical sermon. On another, allegorical level of interpretation, the *Bhagavad Gita* is about good striving for supremacy over evil: Arjuna is the individual soul, and Krishna is the eternal Supreme Spirit that resides in each heart. Arjuna's chariot stands for the mortal body. King Dhritarashtra's blindness represents ignorance, and his hundred sons are the evil tendencies of humankind. The battle, then, becomes a perennial one between the power of good and the power of evil, and the warrior who heeds the advice of the Supreme Spirit speaking from within will succeed physically in battle and spiritually in attaining the highest good.

While the aggregated collection may seem only loosely tied together, individual sections of the *Mahabharata* are often quite carefully structured and contain some of the most inspiring passages in all of literature. Certainly in Western countries the most widely read section of the poem has been the *Bhagavad Gita*, a treatise on Eastern religious theory and practice presented in the form of a dialogue between the warrior Arjuna and his charioteer, Krishna. The circumstances under which this dialogue takes place are relevant to the story of the war between the Kauravas and the Pandavas. The aim of the discussion is to persuade a despondent Arjuna to take up arms for his people. Since God is doing the persuading, Arjuna listens. The context is often forgotten, however, by readers who become fascinated with the philosophical and religious dimensions of this important section. In the course of this conversation, Arjuna is asked to confront significant moral questions: Should one take up arms in a bloody war even for a just cause? To what end is this action, or any action, justified? The answers are designed to raise the warrior's level of consciousness so that he becomes aware of the limited vision of life possessed by any individual. His mystical experience, told in highly charged poetic language that suggests the possibility of attaining a more profound understanding of human nature than most people reach, has attracted Western readers for over two centuries.

The *Mahabharata* contains many popular tales; one is that of Savitri, whose love for her husband and devotion to her father-in-law triumph over Yama, the god of death. In this legend, a woman has a prominent role as a heroine. This tale gives evidence of the high place women held in ancient Indian culture. The *Mahabharata* also provides ethical guidance and in time became an authoritative treatise on dharma (truth, duty, righteousness), teaching of the divine origin of Brahman institutions, including the caste system.

In an appendix to the *Mahabharata*, called the *Harivamsa*, there is a genealogy of the god Hari (Vishnu), of whom Krishna was the eighth avatar. If considered as an anthology, the *Mahabharata* is structurally comparable to the Bible. Although there is no Bible, as such, in Hinduism, there is still a great quantity of sacred literature, including the *Mahabharata* as well as the *Vedas* (c. 1000-500 B.C.E.), the *Upanishads* (c. 900 B.C.E.), and the *Ramayana* (c. 400 B.C.E.). To the pious Hindu, the most familiar is the *Bhagavad Gita*.

The *Bhagavad Gita* is what is most familiar to Western literature as well. From the earliest English translations in the eighteenth century, the work has exerted strong influence on diverse figures, including Johann Wolfgang von Goethe (who was also enamored with the section of the *Mahabharata* dealing with the exploits of Sakuntala), Ralph Waldo Emerson, and Matthew Arnold.

The *Bhagavad Gita* is, however, only a part of a work whose impact on Eastern literatures has been great. Buddhist and Sanskrit writings, as well as works in Asian countries outside India, have also been influenced by the stories and the philosophy contained in the *Mahabharata*. Two philosophical principles which emerge from the story have universal applicability. First, the work dramatizes the notion that human existence in its material form seems confining, and that a spiritual dimension exists, imprisoned in one's body, waiting for the liberating effect which can come only when one reaches a higher state of consciousness—and eventually through what humankind usually calls death. Second, and equally important, is the lesson that one achieves dignity, power, and esteem only through suffering. This concept, vividly dramatized in the story of the heroes and heroines in this Indian epic and so closely akin to the philosophy that informs Western tragedy, links the *Mahabharata* with great works of literature throughout the world.

"Critical Evaluation" by Joanne G. Kashdan
updated by Laurence W. Mazzeno

Bibliography:
Goldman, Robert P. *Gods, Priests, and Warriors: The Bhrgus of the "Mahabharata."* New York: Columbia University Press, 1977. Analysis of the literary and mythic significance of the tales of the priestly clan known as the Bhrgus, of Bhargavas, whose exploits make up a substantial portion of the text of the *Mahabharata*. Explores the relationship of the epic to historical events which may have inspired it.
Hiltebeitel, Alf. *The Ritual of Battle: Krishna in the "Mahabharata."* Ithaca, N.Y.: Cornell University Press, 1976. Focuses on the role of the Indian god Krishna in the epic; explains the structure of the work and elucidates its relationship to Indian myth and history.
Hopkins, Edward Washburn. *The Great Epic of India*. New York: Charles Scribner's Sons, 1902. Detailed analysis of the *Mahabharata*'s organization, its textual history, and its technical qualities. Still exceptionally helpful for understanding the complexity of the story and themes.
Narasimhan, Chakravarthi V. Introduction to *The Mahabharata*. New York: Columbia University Press, 1965. Outlines the plot of this complex, rambling work. Highlights the human qualities of the epic heroes and notes the underlying emphasis on the necessity for peace to bring about happiness.
Van Nooten, Barend A. *The Mahabharata*. New York: Twayne, 1971. Excellent guidebook to the epic. Includes a detailed summary of the story; explains its mythology, and examines the literary history of the work. Assesses the impact of the *Mahabharata* on modern India and on the West.

THE MAID OF HONOUR

Type of work: Drama
Author: Philip Massinger (1583-1640)
Type of plot: Tragicomedy
Time of plot: Renaissance
Locale: Palermo and Siena, Italy
First performed: c. 1621; first published, 1632

Principal characters:
ROBERTO, king of Sicily
FERDINAND, duke of Urbin
BERTOLDO, a natural brother of Roberto and a Knight of Malta
GONZAGA, a Knight of Malta, general to the duchess of Siena
ASTUTIO, a counselor of state to the king of Sicily
FULGENTIO, the favorite of King Roberto
ADORNI, a Sicilian gentleman, in love with Camiola
AURELIA, duchess of Siena
CAMIOLA, the "Maid of Honour"

The Story:
    At the court of Roberto, king of Sicily, at Palermo, where the arrival of an ambassador from the duke of Urbin was momentarily expected, the conversation of those waiting had turned to discussion of the sinister influence of Fulgentio, the king's unworthy favorite, and of the soldierly qualities of Bertoldo, the king's illegitimate half brother. Upon the arrival of the ambassador, the political situation was explained: The duke of Urbin, in love with the duchess of Siena but rejected by her, had attacked her territories. On the verge of defeat at the hands of the Sienese, he was appealing to Sicily for aid on the basis of a treaty of mutual assistance. King Roberto, however, maintained that the treaty had been rendered void by the aggressive action of the duke and that Sicily was not obligated to come to the rescue. This pacifistic attitude was abhorrent to the king's half brother Bertoldo, who in a fiery speech accused the king of cowardice, claimed that Sicily's honor demanded intervention, and urged the nobles to follow him to the relief of the duke. The king, angered by the speech, replied that any might volunteer who wished, but that they would then cease to be his subjects and could expect no protection from him if fortune went against them.
    On that same day, at the house of Camiola, the maid was being plagued by the suit of one Sylli, a man of almost unbelievable conceit. He, however, left upon the arrival of Bertoldo, who had come to say farewell and to declare his own love. In spite of Camiola's evident love for Bertoldo, she rejected his suit because, as a Knight of Malta, he was vowed to celibacy, nor could she be moved by his suggestion that a dispensation could be obtained. He left for the war with the determination to have honor as his only mistress.
    The next day King Roberto learned of Bertoldo's departure with his volunteers and was displeased at the news. Fulgentio, however, was delighted, for with Bertoldo gone he could pursue his own wooing of Camiola. On his arrival at her house he behaved in an overbearing manner toward all present, particularly her other suitors, Sylli and Adorni. Sylli fainted, but Adorni was prepared to fight until restrained by Camiola. In a series of frank and witty

speeches, Camiola told Fulgentio exactly what she thought of him and outlined his despicable character. He left, vowing to avenge himself by ruining her reputation by spreading scandal about her.

Meanwhile, in the territories of Siena, the forces of the duke of Urbin were still faring badly. Bertoldo and his Sicilian volunteers had arrived, but they could not change the fortunes of war. In the ensuing battle they were captured. When Gonzaga, the Sienese general, recognized Bertoldo as a Knight of Malta, he tore the cross from his prisoner's cloak, for Bertoldo had broken the vows of the order by attacking the duchess in an unjust war. Further, when Astutio came as ambassador from King Roberto to disclaim his sovereign's part in the attack, Gonzaga agreed to accept the usual ransom for all the Sicilian nobles except Bertoldo, for whom he demanded fifty thousand crowns. Astutio bore the news that the king would pay nothing for his half brother and had, in fact, confiscated the unfortunate man's estates. Unable to pay the ransom, Bertoldo faced a lifetime of imprisonment.

In Sicily, Adorni had challenged Fulgentio for his treatment of Camiola, but the cowardly favorite had declined the challenge. On Camiola's birthday, in the midst of the celebration, Adorni entered bleeding. He had been wounded in the fight that he had finally forced upon Fulgentio, but he had compelled the latter to sign a paper repudiating the slanders he had been spreading about Camiola. Adorni then confessed his love for Camiola, but she rejected him with the admonition that he must not aspire so high. Yet when, through the agency of the ransomed Sicilian noblemen, she learned of Bertoldo's plight, she was ready enough to send Adorni with the fifty thousand crowns to ransom the man she loved. Adorni promised to execute the commission faithfully, although he felt that he would not survive for long, and departed for Siena to bring happiness to his rival. Bertoldo, in ecstasies at the goodness of Camiola, gladly agreed to sign the contract of betrothal that she had demanded. It was his tragedy, however, to be sent for by the victorious duchess of Siena, who had heard of his martial prowess. Almost instantly she fell violently in love with him, and he, after a short struggle against the sin of ingratitude, fell equally in love with her and promised to marry her.

While this surprising event was in progress at Siena, an equally unexpected change of fortune was taking place in Sicily. The king and his favorite arrived at Camiola's house; the former, with seeming sternness, rebuked her for disobedience in refusing Fulgentio's suit and for urging Adorni to attack him. Camiola defended her conduct and accused Fulgentio of having slandered her. King Roberto then ordered Fulgentio out of his sight, threatened him with death, and praised the behavior of Camiola. Thus the villain was discomfited.

Camiola, informed by the faithful Adorni of Bertoldo's perfidy, made plans accordingly. At a reunion in the palace at Palermo, the king forgave his half brother and consented to his marriage to the duchess of Siena. Camiola entered and, after promising Fulgentio to try to secure his peace with the king, asked the monarch for justice on Bertoldo. Producing the contract of betrothal that he had signed, she made such a noble plea for her rights that even the love-smitten duchess acknowledged her superiority and yielded Bertoldo to her, while he admitted his falseness and confessed himself branded with disloyalty and ingratitude. Camiola forgave him and announced her approaching marriage. The entrance of a group of friars provided another surprise for the gathering. Camiola announced that she had determined to become the bride of the church; by entering a religious order she was to become, in another sense, a maid of honor. As her last act, she gave Adorni a third of her estate and returned to Bertoldo the cross of the Knights of Malta, bidding him to redeem his honor by fighting against the enemies of the faith. As she departed for the convent, King Roberto stated admiringly that she well deserved her title of Maid of Honor.

Critical Evaluation:

While it is generally accepted that Philip Massinger's *The Maid of Honour* was performed before Henrietta Maria, Queen of Charles I of England in 1630, the precise date of the play's composition is unknown. It has been dated by some scholars as early as 1621 and by others as late as 1630. The earlier date would make it one of Massinger's first independent plays; the latter date would place it during his mature period of authorship. External evidence provides information about the play's performance and publication but gives little or no indication of when it was written. Internal evidence, largely in the form of topical allusions to intrigues at the English court, is subject to various interpretations. What is clear is that the play, whenever it was written, comments upon issues facing English society and politics during the period. The play also transcends these topical issues to touch on enduring themes such as honor, loyalty, and courage.

Philip Massinger, the only son of a family moderately prominent in the cultural and political life of the times, attended Oxford but left without receiving his degree and soon after entered a long and productive life in the theater. His extensive experience included collaboration with many of the most distinguished playwrights of his time, including John Fletcher and Thomas Dekker. He also wrote a number of dramas by himself, and became known as one of the finest of contemporary writers for the stage. In 1620, John Taylor's poem "The Praise of Hemp-Seed" listed Massinger as one of England's premier dramatists, along with notable authors such as John Drayton, Ben Jonson, George Chapman, John Marston, John Middleton, and Thomas Heywood.

The Maid of Honour clearly shows why Massinger was accorded such praise, for it is an excellent display piece for Massinger's talents. It has a clear and fluent style, a deeply felt sense of morality, and a keen appreciation of individual character and motivation, which is seen most clearly in Camiola's renunciation of the world and her fiancé at the moment when she appears to have won both.

The central themes of *The Maid of Honour* are money; the morality involved in the activities of royalty, especially marriages and foreign alliances; and the concept of just versus unjust war. All of these are folded into one overriding theme: the conflict between virtue and expediency. Massinger's play explores this theme in three fashions: through reference to English political life; by correspondences to earlier plays, in particular dramas by William Shakespeare; and in its own original way.

In political terms, *The Maid of Honour* has a double focus. On the one hand, it examines certain general moral and philosophical issues, such as the concept of a just war and the virtue of neutrality during armed conflict, both issues that were of immediate concern at the time and that evoked spirited debate among intellectuals and statesmen. Not infrequently, such debates found expression on the popular stage. The underlying thematic concerns that the play addresses are the role of justice and virtue in political affairs, and how much morality a nation can afford in its relationships with other kingdoms.

In exploring this theme, *The Maid of Honour* echoes specific events of English political life, particularly those which took place during the reign of King James I. A number of critics have commented on the close correspondence between the events in the play and those that took place during the latter years of the reign of James I (1603-1625), in particular his son-in-law's abortive invasion of Bohemia. In fact, so close are the parallels between the play's Roberto, King of Sicily, and his favorite, Fulgentio, and history's James I and the Duke of Buckingham, that some scholars have expressed surprise that the drama was ever authorized for performance and publication.

The Maid of Honour also includes a number of correspondences to other dramas of its own and earlier periods, in particular Shakespeare's *All's Well That Ends Well* (1602-1604). Some critics go so far as to see *The Maid of Honour* as a mirror image of Shakespeare's play, with the ending reversed. In *All's Well That Ends Well*, the heroine Helena leaves a life of seclusion to marry her beloved, Bertram. In *the Maid of Honour*, Camiola leaves her fiancé to enter a convent. There are numerous other parallels between the two dramas in setting, scenes, and even dialogue. Massinger, who was well-versed in the drama of his own and earlier times, is clearly conducting a dialogue with his great predecessor.

Finally, *The Maid of Honour* is an impressive drama in its own right. Although it works within an established pattern—that of the "testing" play, in which the heroine must prove her loyalty and fidelity—it expands beyond the confines of the genre, becoming a meditation on power and statecraft. Its characters, especially Camiola, the maid of honor, are presented as a mix; they are particular individuals and types. They present general and specific truths about human nature.

Massinger's style has been criticized by numerous scholars as lacking in vigor and as not sufficiently poetical. T. S. Eliot, for example, has said that the playwright's verse "without being exactly corrupt, suffers from cerebral anaemia." If such criticisms are just, and there is ample room to dispute the matter, *The Maid of Honour* is an outstanding exception to such charges. In this play, Massinger's use of language is supple and flexible, deploying a blank verse that expresses its meaning clearly, yet carries a level of allusion and symbolism that adds to the depth and richness of the play.

"Critical Evaluation" by Michael Witkoski

Bibliography:
Adler, Doris. *Philip Massinger*. Boston: Twayne, 1987. A brief but thorough overview of Massinger's life and career. Traces his relationships and collaborations with other playwrights of his times. A good introductory volume.
Cruickshank, A. H. *Philip Massinger*. Oxford, England: University Press, 1920. Although dated, it remains one of the scholarly foundations for any study of Massinger and his work. Brief in terms of Massinger's biography, it is much fuller in its assessment of his writings, especially their relationship to the literature of the period.
Edwards, Philip. "Massinger's Men and Women." In *Philip Massinger: A Critical Reassessment*, edited by Douglas Howard. Cambridge, England: Cambridge University Press, 1985. Contains a perceptive and revealing study of Camiola, placing her in the context of drama of the period.
Eliot, T. S. "Philip Massinger." *Times Literary Supplement*, May 27, 1920, 325-326. This influential essay, reprinted in a number of different volumes, contains much thought-provoking commentary on Massinger, especially his artistic and rhetorical abilities. Indispensable reading.
McDonald, Russ. "High Seriousness and Popular Form: The Case of the Maid of Honour." In *Philip Massinger: A Critical Reassessment*, edited by Douglas Howard. Cambridge, England: Cambridge University Press, 1985. A thorough and precise consideration of the drama, displaying clearly how Massinger uses the form of the testing play to present serious ethical and political ideas.

THE MAIDS

Type of work: Drama
Author: Jean Genet (1910-1986)
Type of plot: Surrealism
Time of plot: Indeterminate
Locale: An elegant feminine bedroom
First performed: 1947; first published, 1948 as *Les Bonnes* (English translation, 1954)

> *Principal characters:*
> SOLANGE, a maid approximately thirty-five years of age
> CLAIRE, a maid, Solange's younger sister
> MADAME, their mistress, approximately twenty-five years of age

The Story:

Two women were in a bedroom. One was playing with her rubber gloves, alternately fanning her arms and folding them again. This greatly irritated the other woman. She finally yelled, in an exaggerated fashion, "Those gloves! Those eternal gloves!" She continued yelling at her maid, insulting her, accusing her of trying to seduce the milkman. She told her maid to take the gloves and leave them in the kitchen, which the maid did.

The younger woman—madame—sat at the dressing table, calling for the maid—Claire—to lay out her clothes and jewels. Madame again taunted Claire about the milkman. When Claire spat on the shoes to polish them, Madame expressed her disapproval, and remarked that Claire hated her, that Claire was smothering her with attention and flowers.

Madame then dropped her overexaggerated tragic tone, and briefly spoke to Claire as an equal about the milkman, who despised them. Just as quickly, she recovered her tone, demanding her white dress. Claire refused and explained why. In her explanation, she mentioned Monsieur—Madame's lover—and widowhood. This brought up the fact that Madame had denounced Monsieur in a letter to the police, although he was only imprisoned, not dead. She declared her devotion to him, swearing that she would follow him even to Devil's Island, and therefore she should wear white, to mourn like a queen.

As Claire helped Madame into her dress, Madame complained that Claire smelled like the servants' quarters. Madame said that it was more difficult to be a mistress, because she had to be both a mistress and a servant, containing all the hatred of a servant and her own beauty.

Claire, inspired by Madame's confession, began raving and told Madame how much she hated her. During her tirade, she spat on Madame's dress, and accused her of wanting to steal the milkman. Madame lost control, and Claire slapped her face to prove they were on the same level. Her talk became more and more ominous, as she spoke of rebellion and hatred that emanated from the maids' quarters, from the kitchen.

Suddenly, an alarm clock rang, and the two women grasped each other. The woman who was impersonating Madame started removing her dress. She complained that the woman who was impersonating Claire did not finish. The real Claire put on her maid's outfit. The two began straightening up the room and waiting for the real Madame to return. That night was special, since Claire actually had written the letter leading to Monsieur's arrest.

Solange, Claire's older sister, began taunting Claire about her dressing up at night and pretending to be a queen. Claire countered that Solange was scared of having put Monsieur in jail. Solange declared that no one loved them, but Claire disagreed. She said Madame loved them. Solange said Madame loved them "like her bidet," and that they, the maids, could love no one because filth cannot love filth. She called her spit her spray of diamonds.

Claire wanted to talk of Madame's kindness. Solange pointed out how easy it was to be kind if you were beautiful and rich. Otherwise, you had to act like Claire, dressing up in Madame's clothes and parading around the bedroom. Claire pointed out that it was Solange who was so taken with the idea of following her lover to Devil's Island when it was her turn to play Madame. Claire told Solange that she would not disturb her fantasy; she hated her for other reasons. Claire told Solange that she knew her sister had tried to kill Madame, but symbolically it was Claire she was trying to kill. Solange admitted to the attempt, but claimed she did it to free Claire from Madame's bittersweet kindness, even though she knew Claire would have denounced her. When Solange had seen the figure of Madame, however, she was unable to carry through with her plot. She compared her own dignity to Madame's, and remarked how Madame was transfigured by grief.

The phone rang. It was Monsieur calling to say he had been released on bail. Solange blamed Claire for the failure of their plan, but Claire retorted that it was Solange who had failed to kill Madame earlier, thus forcing Claire to try the letter. Claire called Solange weak and said she would have been able to kill Madame in her sleep. She claimed that where Solange had bungled, she, Claire, would succeed.

Claire compared the act of killing Madame to stories in history of women guided by visions and religion to kill. She would be supported, she said, by her milkman, and they would be saved. The two began to formulate a new plan to kill Madame when she returned home. Solange tried to comfort her, but Madame declared that she would follow Monsieur to Devil's Island if necessary.

Madame started planning her mourning when Claire came in with the drugged tea. Madame pulled the red dress out of the closet and gave it to her as a gift. She gave Solange her fur stole. She was about to go to bed when she noticed the phone was off the hook. When she asked why, Claire and Solange mentioned that Monsieur was out on bail and waiting for Madame. She ordered Solange to get a taxi. While she was waiting, Claire offered to heat up the tea, but Madame was not interested. When Solange finally returned with the taxi, Claire made one final effort to get Madame to drink the tea, but failed.

After Madame had left, Solange reprimanded Claire for failing. She warned that Madame and Monsieur would find out that Claire had written the letters. She was sick that Madame's joy came from the maids' shame. Solange decided it was time for the two to flee, but Claire was exhausted and thought it was too risky. They had already lost control of so much, the slightest mistake would show their guilt. They recommenced their game. Solange told Claire to skip the preliminaries and go straight to the transformation. In Madame's white dress, Claire began insulting the maid right away, comparing maids to gravediggers, scavengers, and police, calling them the distorting mirrors of respectable society.

After more of the bizarre game, during which Solange made "Madame" crawl and whipped her, Claire became sick, and Solange took her to the kitchen. Solange came back to the bedroom alone, speaking to invisible people. She said Madame was dead, strangled by the rubber gloves. She imitated Madame, she spoke to an imaginary detective and to Madame and Monsieur. She spoke of the dignity of servants, which she said the police, as outcasts themselves, would understand but Madame and Monsieur never would. Claire reentered the room as Madame and asked for her tea. She clearly understood what she was doing, as did Solange, who refused. Finally, she relented, and Claire drank the tea while Solange saw in it Madame's death and the maids' assumption.

Critical Evaluation:

Jean Genet, who spent most of his early life in prison, is considered one of the most important French writers of the twentieth century. His writing centers on the themes of illusion versus reality, freedom versus slavery, and the ultimate similarity of good and evil. Throughout his writing, Genet expresses his philosophies: that there can be no evil in evil, since the double negative would make a positive, thus good; that the police and criminals are both outcasts from society and, therefore, equals; and that fiction was too often confused with reality and must be separated. His writings are mostly concerned with criminals, prostitutes, and servants. In *The Maids*, Genet expresses these concepts primarily through the characters of the maids, who begin and end the play pretending to be mistress and servant.

Genet was bothered by the concept of suspension of disbelief upon which most plays and films rely. In his instructions for producing *The Maids*, Genet originally stated that he wanted men to play the roles. His intent, according to his greatest patron, Jean-Paul Sartre, was to show how artificial the play and the players are. If a woman played the role of Claire, she would only have to play a maid and a maid playing her mistress; a man, however, would have to play not only the maid and the maid playing her mistress, but also a woman, thus bringing one more level of artifice to the play.

The falseness of the play is further revealed through the maids' game. They take turns pretending to be the mistress, imitating her. The play has several levels: men playing women, women playing maids, maids playing the mistress, and men playing women playing maids playing the mistress playing a maid. It is when there is a slip in the action, an unexpected intrusion or word, that the levels become confused, such as the time Claire comments on the milkman. The complex circularity of the play goes further, however, when Genet introduces the concept of love. The maids talk about how they love Madame, but, as Solange says, filth cannot love, which must mean they hate Madame—not because she is mean or cruel to them, but because she is good and therefore she can love. It is impossible for her to love, however, because her lover is in prison. In fact, he is the only one of the four characters who never appears. He is also the only man. The circle is completed by the fact that the maids, being outcasts like criminals and the police, were responsible for Monsieur's imprisonment in the first place, thus bringing him to their level and (in Genet's philosophy) making him an outcast, depriving him of the ability to love.

The maids, being outcasts, society's "distorting mirrors" have two ways of becoming a society of their own: through imitating Madame's gestures and words or through her death. Madame is a fake, however, so the maids are doomed to failure. This is why the maids never succeed in killing Madame, and why Claire ends up killing herself while playing Madame—it is the closest she will ever get to becoming the mistress. Solange also knows this and believes that through her sister's-mistress' death, she will be elevated to a higher level, while she only ends up being a criminal and her dead sister a mere servant suicide—in dramatic contrast to Solange's last words: "We are beautiful, joyous, drunk, and free!"

Gregory Harris

Bibliography:

Driver, Tom F. *Jean Genet*. New York: Columbia University Press, 1966. Contains brief but in-depth analyses of most of Genet's works. Aimed primarily at English-speaking college students.

Knapp, Bettina. *Jean Genet*. New York: Twayne, 1968. Analytical look at Genet, geared toward giving U.S. readers a concise understanding of the author's work.

Sartre, Jean-Paul. *Saint Genet: Actor and Martyr*. Translated by Bernard Frechtman. New York: Pantheon Books, 1963. Huge volume of description and philosophy on Genet addresses his life and work, including a long section on *The Maids*, and is central to an understanding of the author.

White, Edmund. *Genet: A Biography*. New York: Alfred A. Knopf, 1993. Definitive English-language biography discusses the chronology behind *The Maids*, as well as Genet's reactions to the play.

_____. *Selected Writings of Jean Genet*. New York: Ecco Press, 1993. Includes excerpts from Genet's works, including *The Maids*, as well as a short synopsis of the play and a discussion of its place in the Genet oeuvre.

THE MAID'S TRAGEDY

Type of work: Drama
Author: Francis Beaumont (c. 1584-1616) and John Fletcher (1579-1625)
Type of plot: Tragedy
Time of plot: Antiquity
Locale: Rhodes
First performed: c. 1611; first published, 1619

> *Principal characters:*
> THE KING OF RHODES
> MELANTIUS, a soldier
> EVADNE, his sister
> AMINTOR, his noble young friend
> CALIANAX, a lord of Rhodes
> ASPATIA, his daughter, betrothed to Amintor

The Story:

Melantius, a military hero, returned to Rhodes from the wars. There he found himself involved in a difficult situation. The king, ostensibly to show his gratitude, had given the hand of Evadne, Melantius' sister, to Amintor, a young courtier and a dear friend of Melantius. The difficulty lay in the fact that Amintor had already promised himself to Aspatia, daughter of Calianax, an old lord.

Preparations were being made for elaborate nuptial festivities. Aspatia grieved. In the royal banqueting hall, just before the presentation of the marriage masque, Melantius encountered Calianax, who insulted him. The King's entrance checked animosities. A masque followed, after which the King, wishing the wedded couple goodnight, asked Amintor to father a boy who would grow up to defend the kingdom.

As Evadne prepared to retire, Aspatia, who was present, could not share the general enthusiastic anticipation of the marriage night, and she expressed her belief that she would soon be dead of a broken heart. Amintor, coming into the apartment, received a kiss from Aspatia before she departed. He suffered momentary misgivings for having forsaken her, but he forgot her when he saw Evadne. His bride, as he soon discovered, did not appear to be interested in the consummation of their marriage. In fact, she told Amintor that she hated him and would never share his bed. Threatened by Amintor, she finally confessed that she had already given herself to the king. Amintor was deeply injured when she revealed to him that the marriage was merely a means to make legitimate any children born of that affair. Determined to make the marriage seem to be normal, however, he slept in her bedchamber, on the floor.

Aspatia, meanwhile, returned to her home, where she warned her maids never to trust their hearts to men and recounted classical stories of women who, much to their distress, gave their hearts away. Old Calianax, always a coward at heart, vowed to be valiant in avenging the slight to his daughter. The next morning Amintor, emerging from the bedchamber, encountered Melantius, whom he puzzled with ambiguous remarks about the virtues of the soldier's family. Later Amintor's assumed manner aroused the king's suspicions; in private he accused Evadne of faithlessness. To prove her steadfastness to the king, Evadne provoked Amintor into revealing that the marriage had not been consummated. Amintor was overcome by the enormity of the way he had been treated, but he refused to draw his sword on the king. Still, he vowed to avenge the insult somehow.

Melantius, meanwhile, pondered on Amintor's peculiar behavior. Dismissing a foolish challenge from Calianax, he encountered Amintor, whom he persuaded to unburden his heart of its troubles. When Amintor revealed that Evadne was the king's mistress, Melantius, incapable of believing Amintor's story, drew his sword and threatened to kill his friend. When Amintor seemed to welcome death, Melantius, convinced, sheathed his sword and swore to avenge his sister's disgrace. Amintor, who felt that it was he who should do the avenging, challenged Melantius to fight. Melantius refused, calmed the youth, and promised that the two could effect a scheme to right the wrongs done them.

Melantius directed his brother Diphilus to prepare his armor for battle. He also asked Calianax, the castellan of Rhodes, to deliver the garrison to him. The old man, promising permission within the hour, hastened to report the rebellion to the king.

Melantius went to Evadne and confronted her with his knowledge of her transgression. Upon asking her to name her seducer, she pretended to be insulted and suggested that he tend to his military affairs. When Melantius threatened to kill her, she confessed the truth. Then, realizing the extent of her disgrace, she promised Melantius that she would kill the king. She also expressed her remorse to Amintor and begged him for forgiveness. Amintor kissed her and cautioned her never to sin again.

Meanwhile, at a dinner in the palace, Calianax told the king of Melantius' scheme to kill him and to escape to the fortress of Rhodes. The king, doubting, called Amintor into the dining chamber, where with leading questions he tested Amintor and Evadne, as well as Melantius, who accompanied them. Melantius maintained his poise. When the king disclosed his knowledge of the plot, Melantius continued to dissemble and stated that Calianax was an irresponsible, foolish old man. The king was convinced that Melantius was innocent. When Melantius, in asides, importuned Calianax about the fortress, the old man tried to convince the king that Melantius was making overtures under his very eyes, but the ruler suggested that someone put the weak-minded old man to bed. The thoroughly confounded lord submitted reluctantly to Melantius' demands for the fortress.

The night for revenge having come, Diphilus took command of the fortress. Amintor, encountering Melantius, asked his assistance in killing the king. Melantius, fearful lest his plans fail, reminded Amintor that the king's person was sacred.

Evadne, going to the king's bedchamber, tied the sleeping monarch to the bed. Awakening, the king thought at first that his bondage was a pretty joke of Evadne's, but he was filled with apprehension when he saw her draw a knife. Reciting his villainy toward her, she stabbed him to death; then she forgave him.

Soon afterward, the death of the king having been discovered, the king's brother Lysippus and his followers went to the citadel, where Melantius and his people were in control. Melantius affirmed his loyalty to Rhodes, but declared that if he were not given amnesty he could very easily destroy the city. Lysippus and Melantius agreed to a general amnesty.

Meanwhile Aspatia, disguised as a man, entered Amintor's apartment, where she told Amintor that she was Aspatia's long-lost brother, returned to avenge his sister. In her disguise, Aspatia challenged Amintor to a duel. When he refused, she struck him. Goaded to action, Amintor drew and wounded Aspatia.

Evadne, bloody dagger in hand, entered and told Amintor that she had killed the king. When she asked Amintor to recognize her as his wife, he, appalled, refused and left her. Evadne stabbed herself to death. Aspatia, meanwhile, had revived long enough to reveal her true identity to Amintor, who declared his unworthiness and his shame for the way that he had treated her. When Aspatia died, Amintor, having nothing more to live for and wishing to be with his true love, stabbed himself.

Melantius, entering, was so overcome by the sight of his dead sister and his dying friend that he attempted to take his own life. Calianax, upon recognizing his daughter, the dead Aspatia, was reconciled to Melantius. Lysippus, the new ruler, looked upon the scene as an object lesson to kings to be chaste.

Critical Evaluation:

Francis Beaumont and John Fletcher's *The Maid's Tragedy* is a typical example of the kind of play written and produced in the Jacobean period (the reign of James I, 1603-1625), which also encompasses the later plays of William Shakespeare and the work of Ben Jonson. Although there were very few theaters at that time, audiences constantly demanded new plays, and there was opportunity for many playwrights to try their hands.

The plays of the Jacobean era are, in the main, very similar and use ideas, motifs, and characters that were interesting to the audiences of the time but are somewhat lacking to a contemporary reader. This is one of the reasons why Jacobean dramas are rarely produced even in Britain, where only Shakespeare and, to a lesser extent, Jonson are regularly presented.

Most Jacobean plays have all the trappings of a Shakespearean play, but little of the content. This play, in which the grandeur of court life and the disastrous, bloody fate of several characters, including a king, are explored, is a rather thin story of the secret love affair of the king of Rhodes and the sister of his greatest general. There is some lack of credibility immediately apparent in his insistence on marrying her to one of his nobles, Amintor, despite the fact that Amintor is betrothed to another noblewoman, Aspatia. The king must marry her off to avoid scandal if she becomes pregnant, but why he marries her off to Amintor, who is engaged, is something of a mystery. One of the marks of a second-rate drama is a tendency to pay little attention to credibility. The audiences of the time liked odd conduct, and they seemed quite prepared to accept arbitrary actions, particularly from monarchs. The historical ironies are clear; the literary legacy is clouded. The higher the rank, the less dependable the characters or their actions.

The characters in the plays also expect questionable conduct from their rulers, and the king of Rhodes is typical. Equally Jacobean is the way in which problems are solved, usually, by violent action. The revenge theme, in which personal or family affronts are not so much solved as aggravated by further affront, in the form of payback, is played out in *The Maid's Tragedy* with some considerable style. Part of the revenge motif is its getting out of hand, often causing the death of those who do not deserve to die. In this play, the king gets what he deserves, but the play does not stop there; instead, it manages to draw in Evadne, who is less guilty than her lover, and Aspatia and Amintor, who are entirely innocent. This element of the play is typical of Jacobean drama.

Beaumont and Fletcher tend to put emphasis upon a love affair as a central theme for their dramas, and they take some care to allow for the poetic expression of amorous feeling. It is generally assumed that Beaumont probably wrote the more lyric passages, and that Fletcher, who is assumed to have had a temperament somewhat less romantic than that of Beaumont, is responsible for the sharper, conversational, sometimes comic material. This play is less comic than others, but the exchanges between Melantius and Calianax, however serious the context, display the kind of smart, combative dialogue enjoyed by the Jacobean audience. Calianax is a typical comic figure, the old man who is the butt of all jokes, however cruel they may be, simply because of his age.

What makes the play difficult for a contemporary reader is its seeming lack of serious substance. It is hardly a tragedy, since the matter at hand is relatively unimportant. The issue has no great import to anyone except for the small handful of intimates, although it does eventually cause the death of a monarch, who is quickly replaced. The matter, however, is somewhat more exclusively personal than is usually the case in tragedy. Certainly in comparison to the psychological, social, and political densities of Shakespeare, the play seems less formidable.

The play is certainly less than consequential in its quick changes of mind. Evadne, seemingly besotted with the king and emotionally committed to deception, needs very little persuasion to reject her lover and to sink immediately into the despair that turns her into a killer. No attempt is made to use her dilemma as an opportunity for extended soliloquy in the Shakespearean style. There are several quick reversals in the play which bother a contemporary reader but that were accepted as part of the convention for this kind of romantic tragedy, which has a ludic aspect to it, since so many of the plays of the time were variations on the pattern. Credibility was unimportant for an audience with a taste for watching the aristocracy, usually in a foreign land, acting arbitrarily, unfairly, and eventually murderously. Characters who are shallow were expected to use language extravagantly and well.

In short, what the Jacobean audience came to see was another version of the old tale of foreign folk of aristocratic power living lives of wild extravagance, lashing about politically, socially, and personally in ways beyond the abilities of the commoners. In this respect, Jacobean plays are not unlike the violent fantasy of late twentieth century adventure films. The obvious difference is the language, which is always intelligent, sophisticated, and often touching.

"Critical Evaluation" by Charles Pullen

Bibliography:
Appleton, William W. *Beaumont and Fletcher: A Critical Study.* Winchester, Mass.: Allen & Unwin, 1956. A short examination of the collaboration, with discussion of this play in the context of the canon. Also some thoughts on the influence of the playwrights on Restoration drama.
Bliss, Lee. *Francis Beaumont.* Boston: Twayne, 1987. Part of a series of short, sensible discussions of authors. Part of the problem of these two authors lies in the difficulty of distinguishing their respective contributions. Also discusses their influences.
Bradbrook, M. C. *Themes and Conventions in Elizabethan Tragedy.* Cambridge, England: Cambridge University Press, 1935. A major text in understanding the peculiar dependence of drama in the Elizabethan and Jacobean period on repeating certain themes, conventions, and motifs.
Ellis-Fermon, Una. *The Jacobean Drama: An Interpretation.* New York: Vintage Books, 1964. Another seminal text with an overall view of the Jacobean drama. Chapter 2 deals with Beaumont and Fletcher, with some discussion of their use of romance and their approach to character and plot.
Fletcher, Ian. *Beaumont and Fletcher.* London: Longmans, Green, 1967. A very short work, but very sensible as a starting point for further study, touching on all the problems involved in understanding the collaborations.
Gayley, Charles Miles. *Beaumont: The Dramatist.* New York: Russell & Russell, 1969. First half is the standard critical biography. Second half deals with specific critical questions, including versification, diction, and critical approaches.

MAIN CURRENTS IN AMERICAN THOUGHT
An Interpretation of American Literature from the Beginnings to 1920

Type of work: History
Author: Vernon L. Parrington (1871-1929)
First published: 1927-1930

Vernon L. Parrington's *Main Currents in American Thought* is generally termed "monumental" for two reasons. First, the detailed tables of contents show an awesome knowledge of literary and political history and the ability to place the major, minor, and insignificant U.S. writers from 1620 to 1900; second, the guide to this imposition of order is a passionate belief in Jeffersonian democracy as the essential philosophy of the United States. Parrington's work had the revolutionary effect of giving U.S. writers a social dimension never seen in histories of English literature or English thought. This dimension made meaningful, and, in turn, greatly accelerated, the study of U.S. literature in schools and colleges, as the work of Frederick Jackson Turner stimulated the study of American history in terms of the United States.

For Parrington, two currents affected the U.S. mind, Romanticism and Realism, with the division between the two coming at 1860. His first problem, however, was to establish the growth and actual existence of that mind itself; this task is accomplished in the historical survey of the first volume, *The Colonial Mind*, where colonial conditions formed a certain way of thinking, which changed during the Revolutionary War into the U.S. mind. The national temper is then studied in the two succeeding volumes, dealing with Romanticism and Realism.

The three books of the first volume are entitled "Liberalism and Puritanism," "The Colonial Mind," and "Liberalism and the Constitution." The first covers the first century of American history, 1620-1720, in which conflict appears between Carolinian liberalism and Puritanism; the new environment comes into play and strengthens the latter so that the first part of this book records the triumph of theocratic oligarchy in Massachusetts up to 1660. The ground for this triumph is prepared for in the growing rigidity of Puritan thought and practice as a result of transplanting European ideas, but Parrington's sympathy is with the Independents, especially Roger Williams, who excites some of his loftiest prose. That triumph led to the twilight of the oligarchy after 1660; Increase Mather is attacked as intolerant and dictatorial, and Cotton Mather is analyzed pitilessly; the fall of Massachusetts is symbolized in the witch trials of Salem and caused by increasing rigidity of thought in the face of growing economic pressure for changes in the social system.

The second book of the first volume is also divided into two parts: the making of the colonial mind and the awakening of the American mind, with the division at 1763. The colonial mind, having lost the Puritan systemization, is at first at the greater mercy of the environment: The eighteenth century influx of Scotch-Irish and Germans—the latter settling mostly in Pennsylvania—develops a consciousness of the hinterland that veers between adulation, in Michel-Guillaume-Jean de Crèvecoeur, and contempt, in Mme Knight, with William Byrd in between. Jonathan Edwards is pushed offstage along with the Great Awakening, and the spotlight given to Benjamin Franklin, the heir to French Physiocratic views and the first American with a truly American mind. The second part is largely political, outlining the mind of the American Tory, Thomas Hutchinson; the American Whig, John Dickinson; and the American Democrat, Samuel Adams. At the conclusion of this part, American literature makes its first appearance as "literary echoes" in the form of Whig and Tory satires.

Literature is better represented in the third part of book 3, which covers the last seventeen years of the eighteenth century and introduces at its close the first novelist, Hugh Henry Brackenridge, and the poets Philip Freneau and Joel Barlow, whom Parrington approves of for their republicanism. He does not think much of the Hartford Wits, whom he labels with his worst stigma, "arch conservatives." The literature in these stirring years takes second place to politics, in which the clash is between the transplanted English ideas of laissez faire and the agrarianism which is, for Parrington, the soundest basis for his cherished liberalism. Agrarianism was defeated in the years between 1783 and 1787, according to Parrington, in spite of Thomas Jefferson, the towering figure who dominates all of Parrington's work and brings the first two centuries of American thought to a fitting close. Jefferson was able to rethink transplanted ideas into an American context and thus establish the American mind as an independent and vital entity.

In the next two volumes, Parrington sets out to trace the fortunes of currents of this mind through the nineteenth century up to 1920, with an even break between them at 1860.

New England comes into its own again in the second volume, *The Romantic Revolution in America.* This pre-eminence is not surprising, for the period covered is the first half of the nineteenth century, the decades of the Transcendentalists. Three "minds" are established as well, those of the Middle East, the South, and New England. The first is treated comparatively briefly under three headings in book 2 of this volume: writers of Philadelphia, such as Charles Brockden Brown, those of New York, the new literary capital, and those who came to New York from New England, William Cullen Bryant, Horace Greeley, and Herman Melville; the treatment of the last is simply headed "Pessimist" and shows at its worst Parrington's inability to analyze literature that does not contain his ideas. Much more sympathetic is his study of James Fenimore Cooper, largely because of the social criticism Parrington discerned in his work. In the New Yorker school, Parrington subdivided Washington Irving and James Kirke Paulding as Knickerbocker Romantics, and preferred the latter on equally bad grounds, labeling Irving an idle man-about-town.

The strength of the second volume is its three parts devoted to "The Mind of the South," with which the volume opens. Howard Mumford Jones has testified, in *The Theory of American Literature* (1948), to the astonishment of young scholars at Parrington's recovery of writers who had gradually been forgotten under the New England ascendancy of the post-Civil War years. The best example is the fourth chapter of part 2, devoted chiefly to the achievements of Charleston as a literary center, best represented by William Gilmore Simms. Perhaps equally surprising is the title of part 1: "The Virginia Renaissance." Although this section begins with the tradition of agrarianism, it passes on to literary matters in the eleven pages devoted to John Pendleton Kennedy and concludes with three on Edgar Allan Poe, literary radicalism (and perhaps insensitivity) could scarcely go further. Parrington is at his best, however, in his scrupulously fair analysis of the Southern defense of slavery, but it must have been with some relief that he concluded the first book with a summary of the positions of Andrew Jackson and Abraham Lincoln as symbols of the West. Parrington also concludes with a summary of the first example of Western literature, Augustus Baldwin Longstreet's *Georgia Scenes* (1835 and 1840). He prefers the realism of the former to the myth of Davy Crockett—"a wastrel."

The third book of the second volume is divided into four parts on the New England mind. The first two parts have remained valuable as summaries of the political and social thought of New England. These two parts include sections on Brook Farm, John Greenleaf Whittier, and Harriet Beecher Stowe, which are largely economic or environmental studies. Literature occupies the third and fourth parts and is somewhat loosely organized as the Transcendental and "other" aspects of the New England mind, the latter including Nathaniel Hawthorne, Oliver Wendell Holmes, and James Russell Lowell, with a brief mention of Henry Wadsworth Longfellow. The "other" writers suffer the stigma of being "genteel," which is interpreted as "unrealistic." This idea allows Parrington to demonstrate the necessary decline in the Romantic movement with which the whole volume is supposed to be concerned, but which is largely evidenced in Henry David Thoreau and Ralph Waldo Emerson. Discussion of the decline closes the volume and prepares the way for Realism to be celebrated in the third.

The third volume, *The Beginnings of Critical Realism in America*, was published after Parrington's death. Of the three books to this volume, the first is almost complete and the second is approximately half complete. Book 1 takes the story of United States' thought through two decades after the Civil War, but the press of economic and political analysis is so great that the writers tend to be sandwiched into the second chapter of part 1—Walt Whitman, Mark Twain, and the local colorists—and the concluding chapter of part 2—Henry James and William Dean Howells. The social and mental background is still Parrington's forte and the information in book 1 and the first half of book 2 is valuable, but it is regrettable that Parrington was unable to complement his accompanying studies of Hamlin Garland and Edward Bellamy with those of other naturalists, such as Frank Norris and Stephen Crane, and frontier writers. All that remains of the third volume are the addenda of scattered notes on writers, the plan, and an unfinished introduction. Perhaps death preserved Parrington from the increasing difficulties of applying his method and purpose to a much greater volume of literature, but one would like to have seen the attempt to fit writers such as Edith Wharton and F. Scott Fitzgerald into his grand design.

Bibliography:

Cowley, Malcolm, and Bernard Smith. *Books That Changed Our Minds*. New York: Doubleday, Doran, 1939. Claims Parrington's book was well received by conservatives as well as liberals; believes the influence exerted by this work places Parrington on par with Oswald Spengler, Alfred North Whitehead, and Vladimir Ilich Lenin.

Gabriel, Ralph W. "Vernon Louis Parrington." In *Pastmasters: Some Essays on American Historians*, edited by Marcus Cunliffe and Robin W. Winks. New York: Harper & Row, 1969. Discusses the publication history of *Main Currents in American Thought* and examines the personal quality of Parrington's approach to history. Reviews the contemporaneous reception of the work, and surveys its influence on later historians.

Hofstadter, Richard. *The Progressive Historians: Turner, Beard, Parrington*. New York: Alfred A. Knopf, 1968. Links Parrington with other important historians who engaged in their profession as a means of influencing contemporary politics. Asserts that *Main Currents in American Thought* helps explain the nature of "the American liberal mind."

Noble, David. *Historians Against History: The Frontier Thesis and the National Covenant in American Historical Writing Since 1830*. Minneapolis: University of Minnesota Press, 1965. Describes *Main Currents in American Thought* as "the single most important book written by a historian of the frontier tradition," synthesizing work by earlier historians and paying tribute to a way of life that would disappear in the coming decades.

Skotheim, Robert Allen. *American Intellectual Histories and Historians*. Princeton, N.J.: Princeton University Press, 1966. Claims that *Main Currents in American Thought* is the first work to offer a systematic view of all U.S. intellectual history. Highlights the contrast of progress and reaction that characterizes Parrington's methodology.

MAIN STREET
The Story of Carol Kennicott

Type of work: Novel
Author: Sinclair Lewis (1885-1951)
Type of plot: Social satire
Time of plot: c. 1910-1920
Locale: A small midwestern town
First published: 1920

> *Principal characters:*
> CAROL KENNICOTT, an idealist
> DR. WILL KENNICOTT, her husband

The Story:

When Carol Milford was graduated from Blodgett College in Minnesota, she thought she could conquer the world. Interested in sociology, and village improvement in particular, she often longed to set out on her own crusade to transform dingy prairie towns into thriving, beautiful communities. When she met Will Kennicott, a doctor from Gopher Prairie, and listened to his praise of his hometown, she agreed to marry him. He had convinced her that Gopher Prairie needed her.

Carol was an idealist. On the train, going to her new home, she deplored the rundown condition of the countryside and wondered whether the northern Midwest had a future. Will told her that the people were happy. As they traveled through town after town, Carol noticed with a sinking heart the shapeless mass of hideous buildings, the dirty depots, the flat wastes of prairie surrounding everything. She knew that Gopher Prairie would be no different from the rest, and she was right. The people were as drab as their houses and as flat as their fields. A welcoming committee met the newlyweds at the train. To Carol, all the men were alike in their colorless clothes and in their overfriendly, overenthusiastic manner. The Kennicott house was a Victorian horror, but Will said he liked it.

At a party held in her honor, Carol heard the men talk of motorcars, train schedules, and "furriners" while they praised Gopher Prairie as God's own country. The women were interested in gossip, sewing, and cooking, and most of them belonged to the two women's clubs, the Jolly Seventeen and the Thanatopsis Club. At the first meeting of the Jolly Seventeen, Carol dismayed everyone when she stated that the duty of a librarian was to get people to read. The town librarian staunchly asserted that her primary trust was to preserve the books.

Carol was unconventional from the start. She hired a maid and paid her the overgenerous sum of six dollars a week. She gave a party with an Oriental motif. She occasionally kicked off a slipper under the table, revealing her arches. Worse, she redecorated the old Kennicott house and got rid of the mildew, the ancient bric-a-brac, and the dark wallpaper. Will protested against her desire to change things.

Carol joined the Thanatopsis Club hoping to use the club as a means of awakening interest in social reform, but the women of Gopher Prairie, while professing charitable intentions, had no idea of improving social conditions. When Carol mentioned that something should be done about the poor people of the town, everyone firmly stated that there was no real poverty in Gopher Prairie. Carol also attempted to raise funds for a new city hall, but no one could see that the ugly old building needed to be replaced. The town voted against appropriating the necessary funds.

Will Kennicott bought a summer cottage on Lake Minniemashie. There Carol enjoyed outdoor life and during the summer months almost lost her desire for reform. When September came, however, she hated the thought of returning to Gopher Prairie.

Carol resolved to study her husband. He was well regarded in the town, and she romanticized herself as the wife of a hardworking, courageous country doctor. She fell in love with Will again on the night she watched him perform a bloody but successful operation on a poor farmer. Carol's praise of her husband, however, had little effect. Will did not fit into any romantic conception. He accepted his duties as a necessary chore, and the thought that he had saved the life of a human being did not occur to him. His interest in medicine was identical with his interest in motorcars. Carol turned her attention back to Gopher Prairie.

Carol, trying to interest the Thanatopsis Club in literature and art, finally persuaded the members to put on an amateur theatrical; but everyone's enthusiasm soon waned. Carol's choice of a play, Shaw's *Androcles*, was vetoed and replaced with *The Girl from Kankakee*. Carol considered even that choice too subtle for Gopher Prairie, but at least that revived the town's interest in theater.

After three years of marriage, Carol discovered that she was pregnant. When her son was born, she resolved that some day she would send little Hugh away from Gopher Prairie, to Harvard, Yale, or Oxford. With her new status of motherhood, Carol found herself more accepted in the town, but because she devoted nine-tenths of her attention to Hugh she had little time to criticize the town. She wanted a new house, but she and Will could not agree on the type of building. He was satisfied with a square frame house. Carol had visions of a Georgian mansion, with stately columns and wide lawns, or a white cottage like those at Cape Cod.

Carol met a tailor in town, an artistic, twenty-five-year-old aesthete with whom she eventually imagined herself in love. She often dropped by his shop to see him, and one day, Will warned her that the gossip in town was growing. Ashamed, Carol promised she would not see him again. The tailor left for Minneapolis.

Carol and Will decided to take a long trip to California. When they returned three months later, Carol realized that her attempt to escape Gopher Prairie had not been a success. For one thing, Will had gone with her, and what she needed was to get away from her husband. After a long argument with Will, Carol took little Hugh and went to Washington, where she planned to do war work. Yet hers was an empty kind of freedom. She found the people in Washington an accumulation of the population of thousands of Gopher Prairies all over the nation. Main Street had been transplanted to the larger city. Though she was disheartened by her discovery, Carol had too much pride to return home.

After thirteen months, Will went to get her. He missed her terribly, he said, and begged her to come back. Hugh was overjoyed to see his father, and Carol realized that she had to return to Gopher Prairie. Home once more, Carol found that her furious hatred for Gopher Prairie had burned itself out. She made friends with the clubwomen and promised herself not to be snobbish in the future. She would go on asking questions—she could never stop herself from doing that—but her questions now would be asked with sympathy rather than with sarcasm. For the first time, she felt serene. In Gopher Prairie, she at last felt that she was wanted. Her neighbors had missed her. For the first time, Carol felt that Gopher Prairie was her home.

Critical Evaluation:
Sinclair Lewis frequently had difficulty in determining in his own mind whether his works

were meant as bitterly comic satires of American life and values or whether they were planned as complex novels centering on the lives of the characters he made famous. One of the difficulties of reading Lewis is that these two conflicting sorts of writing are both present in many of his works, and frequently at odds with each other. This is demonstrably true of *Main Street*. For all his satire of small-town attitudes and values, Lewis is not unequivocal in his attack. He finds a great many things of value in the best *Main Street* has to offer, and he seems to see Carol Kennicott's reconciliation with the town at the end of the novel as a triumph rather than a failure on her part. Though *Main Street* is, as it has been frequently called, a revolt against the village, it is a revolt marked by the complexity of Lewis' attitude toward Gopher Prairie and toward its real-life counterpart, Sauk Center, Minnesota, where Lewis spent his early years.

Lewis' characters, particularly Will and Carol Kennicott, are another complicating factor in this novel that prevents its being simply a satire. Unlike the one-dimensional figures typical of satire, the Kennicotts develop into real people who demand the reader's attention and sympathy. Carol in particular, is developed more novelistically than satirically as Lewis traces her development from a very naïve and foolishly idealistic young women into a more tolerant and understanding human being. Readers who accept only the critical and satiric portrait of the small town that lies at the surface of *Main Street* would be embracing the same overly simplistic attitudes that characterized Carol at the beginning of the novel.

During the early part of the century, Americans tended to accept on faith the premise that all that was best in life was epitomized by the small-town environment. Though by no means the first author to attack this premise, Lewis with *Main Street* achieved the widespread popularity that gave new prominence to this revolt against the small town. Lewis, himself a small-town boy, knew well the discrepancy between the vision of the village as utopia and the actuality of its bleak cultural and moral atmosphere. As Lewis makes clear in his prologue, *Main Street* represents all such towns, and by his treatment of Gopher Prairie, Lewis sought to strike a satiric blow at the very heartland of America. Rather than utopia, Lewis discovers in the provincial mentality of the small town a surfeit of hypocrisy, bigotry, ignorance, cruelty, and, perhaps most damning of all, a crippling dullness and conformity that is essentially hostile to any possibility of intellectual or emotional life. Yet, even while ruthlessly exposing these negative qualities of the small town, Lewis finds, particularly in the matter-of-fact courage and determination of Will Kennicott, some of the very qualities that initially gave the small town its reputation as the strength of America. Lewis himself was ambivalent in his attitude toward the village, and this indecisiveness creeps into the novel to mitigate his criticism.

The action of the novel centers on Carol Kennicott's discovery of the nature of life and society in Gopher Prairie and culminates with her eventual compromise with the town. Carol's growth as a human being is an excellent device through which to expose the bleak heart of the midwestern town, and Lewis does so by contrasting the town's qualities and values with her own. Young, educated, intelligent, and idealistic, Carol can cause Gopher Prairie to see what it lacks. Yet her idealism is accompanied by a naïveté and intolerance, which are poor qualification for accomplishing the reforms she advocates. She can only hope to change Gopher Prairie by becoming part of it. In losing her naïveté, Carol gains a capacity to confront reality and even to change it over a period of time.

Actually, most of Carol's reforms are too superficial to cure what Lewis called the village virus. Her concern is more with manners than values, and she would only substitute the slick sophistication of the city for the provincial dullness she finds so intolerable. The perfect foil to her is Will Kennicott who, while epitomizing all the worst of the town's boorishness, goes about his daily medical practice with quiet efficiency, determination, and even courage, which Lewis clearly admires. Ultimately, it is Gopher Prairie that triumphs when Carol reconciles herself to its full reality.

"Critical Evaluation" by William E. Grant

Bibliography:
Bucco, Martin. *Main Street: The Revolt of Carol Kennicott*. New York: Twayne, 1993. Focuses on Lewis' development of his *Main Street* heroine, especially her unconscious self-perceptions as prairie princess, Carol D'Arc, Lady Bountiful, Mater Dolorosa, Village Intellectual, American Bovary, and Passionate Pilgrim.
Davenport, Garvin F. "Gopher-Prairie-Lake-Wobegon: The Midwest as Mythical Space." In *Sinclair Lewis at One Hundred: Papers Presented at a Centennial Conference*. St. Cloud, Minn.: St. Cloud State University, 1985. Creates connection between fictional places and their peoples. Relates them to Yi-Fu Tuan's theories of the dualities of the fear and possibility of space and the familiarity, comfort, and constrictiveness of place.
Grebstein, Sheldon Norman. *Sinclair Lewis*. New York: Twayne, 1962. A comparison of Lewis' works that concludes that *Main Street* critiques the falseness and shallowness of American life whereas some Lewis novels defend it.
Light, Martin. *The Quixotic Vision of Sinclair Lewis*. West Lafayette, Ind.: Purdue University Press, 1975. Demonstrates Lewis' pattern, especially obvious in *Main Street*, of sending his heroes into the world motivated by heroic chivalric behavior, which results not only in foolish beliefs and behavior but also in kindness, generosity, sympathy, and idealism.
Shorer, Mark, ed. *Sinclair Lewis: A Collection of Critical Essays*. Englewood Cliffs, N.J.: Prentice-Hall, 1962. Places *Main Street* in the context of Lewis' other work.

MAIN-TRAVELLED ROADS
Six Mississippi Valley Stories

Type of work: Short fiction
Author: Hamlin Garland (1860-1940)
Type of plot: Social realism
Time of plot: Late nineteenth century
Locale: Middle West
First published: 1891

In 1887, Hamlin Garland traveled from Boston to South Dakota to visit his mother and father, whom he had not seen in six years. According to his own account, the trip through farming country was a revelation. Although he had been brought up on a farm, he had never realized how wretched farmers' lives were. The farther west he traveled, the more oppressive it became for him to see the bleakness of the landscape and the poverty of its people. When he reached his parents' farm and found his mother living in hopeless misery, Garland's depression turned to bitterness, and in this mood he wrote *Main-Travelled Roads,* a series of short stories about farm life in the Middle West.

In one of these stories, "Up the Coolly," Garland re-creates the mood of his trip under somewhat similar circumstances. Howard McLane, after years spent traveling with his own theatrical troupe, returned to the West for a surprise visit with his mother and brother. He found them living in poverty on a small, unproductive farm, the family property having been sold to pay off a mortgage. Although his mother and his sister-in-law greeted him warmly, Grant, his brother, made it plain that he blamed Howard for the loss of the farm that, had he shared his wealth, could have been saved. Howard's attempt to win his brother's friendship resulted only in alienation until Howard finally admitted his selfishness and neglect and offered to buy the farm back. The brothers were reconciled, but the story ends bleakly with Grant's refusal to accept any assistance.

Not many of Garland's stories end on so despondent a note; in fact, most of them end hopefully and some even happily. Garland spares none of his principal characters a bitter sense of failure, but most of them manage to overcome it. Thus in "A 'Good Fellow's' Wife," Jim Sanford loses the savings of all the farmers who had invested in his bank. In "A Branch Road," Will Hannon loses the beautiful girl he loves and only regains her when she has become prematurely old and wasted. In "Under the Lion's Paw," Tim Haskins is forced to pay twice the former price of a farm whose value he himself had doubled by hard work.

Even in the stories that are lighter in tone, the characters taste the bitterness of life. In "The Creamery Man," which is about a young man's carefree courtship, Claude Williams wins not Lucindy Kennedy, the lovely daughter of a prominent farmer, but Nina Haldeman, the unrefined daughter of an immigrant. In "Mrs. Ripley's Trip," Gran'ma Ripley makes a journey back East, where she had been born, but not without a sense of guilt for leaving her husband, even for so short a time.

Beyond reflecting the bitterness that Garland himself felt, many of his stories set forth a disillusioning contrast between the farm life he remembered and the reality he found when he returned after a long absence. "The Return of a Private," for instance, depicts the return of a Civil War soldier to his farm. Expecting the farm to be as prosperous as when he had left it, Private Smith found it "weedy and encumbered, a rascally renter had run away with his machinery . . . his children needed clothing, the years were coming upon him, he was sick and

3872

emaciated." In "God's Ravens," Robert Bloom, who had moved to the country because he felt stifled by city life, went through an apprenticeship of misery before the country people finally accepted him and made him feel at home.

Garland's disillusionment should not be overemphasized; practically all the stories in *Main-Travelled Roads* have a hopeful ending in that love for and trust in the land are ultimately shown to be justified. It is clear that with hard work Private Smith will restore his farm to its former prosperity. Robert Bloom discovers that the cause of his discontent is within himself, not in the hearts of his farmer neighbors. Tim Haskins, robbed by one man, is set on his feet by another. Garland's realistic portrayal of hardship and poverty did much to shatter romantic illusions about an American pastoral idyll, but the book's somber tone was not enough to discredit the traditional view of the farmer as a doughty, virtuous frontiersman. Rather, it was Garland's accomplishment to expose the pathos, in some cases even tragedy, of people who felt the futility and injustice of farm life but were unable to change that life and so accepted it with fortitude and resignation.

Main-Travelled Roads is more than a social document. The respected author William Dean Howells recognized that it was important in the development of a new American literature. In an essay that was reprinted as an introduction to later editions of *Main-Travelled Roads*, he commended Garland for the social significance of his work and went on to praise his "fine courage to leave a fact with the reader, ungarnished and unvarnished, which is almost the rarest trait in an Anglo-Saxon writer, so infantile and feeble is the custom of our art." Singled out for special praise was the ending of "A Branch Road," in which Will Hannon persuaded Agnes Dingman to leave her husband and the farm to lead a life of comfort and ease. Such an ending Howells deemed immoral but justifiable, since for these characters it was probable and realistic. Howells' judgment was sound. It is because of Garland's contribution to the rise of American literary realism as well as for his social commentary that his works are still read.

Bibliography:
Fiske, Horace S. *Provincial Types in American Fiction*. Port Washington, N.Y.: Kennikat Press, 1968. Includes a detailed critical analysis of Garland's short stories, explaining their realistic style and intent.
Howells, William D. "Editor's Study." In *Critical Essays on Hamlin Garland*, compiled by James Nagel. Boston: G. K. Hall, 1982. Discusses style and themes in the stories "Among the Corn Rows," "A Branch Road," "Mrs. Ripley's Trip," "Up the Coolly," and "Return of a Private."
Knight, Grant C. *American literature and Culture*. New York: Cooper Square Publishers, 1972. Includes a discussion of Garland's collection of short stories as they relate to literary portrayal of rural culture in America. Knight looks specifically at the themes and realistic style in "Up the Coolly" and "Return of a Private."
Parrington, Vernon L. *1860-1920: The Beginnings of Critical Realism in America*. Vol. 3 in *Main Currents in American Thought*. New York: Harcourt, 1958. This authoritative source discusses the factual elements in Garland's stories as well as the kinds of plots and characterizations he used. Explains some of the ways in which Garland's stories compare with other realistic fictional portrayals of American rural life.

MAJOR BARBARA

Type of work: Drama
Author: George Bernard Shaw (1856-1950)
Type of plot: Play of ideas
Time of plot: January, 1906
Locale: London and Middlesex
First performed: 1905; first published, 1907

Principal characters:
    SIR ANDREW UNDERSHAFT, a munitions manufacturer
    LADY BRITOMART, his wife
    BARBARA, their daughter and a major in the Salvation Army
    ADOLPHUS CUSINS, Barbara's fiancé and a professor of Greek

The Story:

    Lady Britomart Undershaft had summoned her children to her house in the fashionable London suburb of Wilton Crescent. Stephen, the first to arrive, greeted his mother in the library. Lady Britomart, a formidable woman of fifty, intended to discuss the family's finances. She reminded Stephen that his sister Sarah's fiancé, Charles Lomax, whose inheritance was still ten years off, was too brainless to support a wife. She objected less to Adolphus Cusins, a professor of Greek, who was engaged to her daughter Barbara, a major in the Salvation Army.

    Stephen timidly mentioned the name of his father, Andrew Undershaft, a wealthy munitions manufacturer who was estranged from his family. Lady Britomart admitted that she had invited Andrew that night to solicit financial help from him. Stephen disdained the tainted Undershaft capital, but his mother informed him that their present income came not from her own father, whose only legacy to his family was an aristocratic name, but from Andrew. She also explained that her separation from Andrew came as a result of her objections to the longstanding Undershaft tradition of turning over the munitions operations to a talented foundling. Seven generations of foundlings had taken the name Andrew Undershaft and run the business, but she had objected against Andrew's disinheriting Stephen.

    The girls and their fiancés arrived shortly before Andrew, who, having been away for twenty years, did not recognize his own children. Barbara's conspicuous Salvation Army uniform turned the conversation to a discussion of personal morality. Andrew's motto, he explained, was "unashamed," and he candidly admitted that he reaped handsome profits from "mutilation and murder." He and Barbara challenged one another to a sort of conversion contest. Andrew agreed to visit Barbara's shelter in the slums if she would visit his weapons factory in Middlesex.

    At the squalid Salvation Army post in West Ham a few days later, two poor Cockneys, Snobby Price and Rummy Mitchens, huddled for shelter from the January cold. In low voices they discussed how they routinely made up dramatic public confessions of sins to get free meals. Jenny Hill, a worker for the Army, brought in Peter Shirley, who had recently lost his job. Unlike Rummy and Snobby, Shirley balked over accepting charity. A loud bully named Bill Walker swaggered in looking for his girlfriend, who had recently converted. When he recognized Jennie as the Salvationist who had helped reform his girlfriend, he angrily wrenched her arm, pulled her hair, and hit her in the face with his fist. Jenny tearfully asked God for strength and ran off.

When Barbara arrived to deal with Bill Walker, her father followed and observed. She awakened Walker's conscience in part by mentioning Todger Fairmile, a former wrestler who was now a sergeant at the Army's Canning Town barracks. Walker offered a sovereign to ease his shame, but Barbara said that she and the Army could not be bought off and would accept nothing less than Walker's repentant soul.

Mrs. Baines, the commissioner, came in to report that the prospect of having to close several shelters because of the lack of money had receded again after a sizable donation from Lord Saxmundham. Barbara was dismayed when Andrew explained that this donor was really Horace Bodger, the whiskey tycoon, whose product had ruined so many of the West Ham destitute. Andrew called Bodger's donation mere conscience money and, not wanting to be outdone, offered to match it with an equal gift of his own. Barbara knew that neither Bodger nor her father had reformed. She was aghast to see Mrs. Baines accept the tainted money. She slowly removed her Salvation badge as Undershaft, Cusins, and Mrs. Baines marched off to celebrate. Bill Walker, having observed the transaction, taunted a disillusioned Barbara by saying, "What price salvation?"

The next day, in Lady Britomart's library, Cusins reported to the family about the fiery religious meeting the day before. Amid music and hysteria, Mrs. Baines had announced the donations and the Army had recorded 117 conversions. Lady Britomart settled the earlier financial question by persuading Andrew to provide support for Charles Lomax and Sarah. Andrew was resolute, however, about upholding the Undershaft tradition and disinheriting Stephen in favor of a foundling. Having seen Stephen's lack of curiosity and intelligence, he suggested a career in politics or journalism for his son.

The entire family later traveled to Andrew's factory in Middlesex, a place that shocked them for being so clean and respectable. They marveled at the nursing home, town hall, libraries, and schools. Peter Shirley, they discovered, had been given a job as a gatekeeper. Andrew proudly bragged that the profits from the bloody business of warfare had eliminated from his community the worst crime of all: poverty. Its byproducts of misery, crime, and hunger were also unknown. Cusins then startled everyone by explaining that technically he himself was a foundling since his Australian parents were not legally married in England. Andrew happily offered him the position of Andrew Undershaft VIII, which he accepted.

Attention returned to Barbara. Andrew invited her to bring her gift for saving souls to his community, telling her that unlike the poor in West Ham the souls of his workers were hungry because their stomachs were full. After considering, Barbara accepted. She announced that she had gotten over the bribe of bread and that "the way of life lies through the factory of death."

Critical Evaluation:

Major Barbara is one of George Bernard Shaw's most stimulating plays. In the early and middle years of his career, he used wit and realism as weapons in his attempt to bestir a complacent society. His iconoclastic nature delighted in overturning accepted morality; one of his famous aphorisms is "all great truths begin as blasphemies." In his second play, *Mrs. Warren's Profession* (1893), he blames prostitution on the men who have no convictions rather than on the poor women without chastity; in *Arms and the Man* (1894), he mocks romantic views of love and war; and in *Candida: A Mystery* (1897), he boldly reversed the emphasis of Henrik Ibsen's *A Doll's House* (1879) by showing that behind the stereotype of the strong male provider lay crippling insecurities and the inability to love. Although *Major Barbara* was written and performed in 1905, Shaw coyly set it in January, 1906—slightly ahead of his time—as if to dramatize an imminent time when his thesis about poverty being the root of all evil could be heard.

Shaw's technique in this play is to use the first act to dramatize the comforts of capitalism and the second to expose its cruelties. In affluent Wilton Crescent, Lady Britomart comically reduces all questions of morality to matters of good and bad taste. To her, polite hypocrisy is a necessary social lubricant. She explains that what infuriated her about Andrew was not that he did wrong things (which he did not) but that he delighted in saying and thinking wrong things and had a type of "religion of wrongness." She scolds Barbara for speaking about religion as if it were something pleasant and not the social drudgery that she knows it to be. Barbara's strong will asserts itself in her language of inversion and paradox. She proves to be a match for her father in their early encounters, showing that she resembles him in being a larger-than-life presence. In the second act, the drawing-room comedy gives way to the realism of the slums.

Many Shavian dramas present mentor-pupil relationships in which a pupil, who starts by believing a set of traditional values, goes through a process of disillusionment and maturation until freed from the artificial trappings of societal values and ready to learn genuine strength. Act II of *Major Barbara* may be Shaw's most compelling example of this formula. Here, the pupil Barbara proves equal to her mentor father. Shaw pivots their clash of values around the soul of Bill Walker, and at first it almost seems as if Barbara may win. When she learns about Horace Bodger's donation, however, and sees Snobby Price sneak off with Bill Walker's unclaimed sovereign, she realizes that Snobby's confessions were manufactured for free meals and that her own work has been futile. The Salvation Army accommodates poverty by merely treating its symptoms and accepting the social status quo. Although the offstage conversions of Todger Fairmile and Walker's girlfriend are presented in earnest, even Snobby Price recognizes that the Army makes more good citizens than true believers: "It combs our air and makes us good little blokes to be robbed and put upon." The Army perpetuates a cycle in which poverty will always have a place. Barbara's disillusionment is genuine and moving.

Its strengths notwithstanding, the play's third act is commonly regarded as flawed. (Shaw himself was still rethinking his ending some thirty-five years later when *Major Barbara* was filmed.) To friends to whom he read his first version of the play, Shaw lamented, "I don't know how to end the thing." In his revision, he sought to balance some of the initial one-sidedness. In the version that now exists, Barbara's disillusionment at the end of Act II is followed by a second conversion in which she sees that "turning our backs on Bodger and Undershaft is turning our backs on life." In Shaw's final design Barbara, Cusins, and Undershaft form a trinity of sorts in which Undershaft's power is matched by Cusins' intelligence and Barbara's spirituality. Shaw's creative evolution thus becomes the utopian fantasy that concludes his drama.

Neat symmetries notwithstanding, the play loses some of its emotional appeal in this improved last act. The concluding Shavian discussion excites the mind more than the emotions, and the fine balance of thought and feeling that Shaw achieved in Acts I and II is dissipated in Act III. The earlier vivid image of Barbara's shattered faith when Mrs. Baines accepts the money of the whiskey king threatens to overshadow her later change of heart. Moreover, details about Barbara's new mission to the workers at Perivale St. Andrews are vague.

All weaknesses aside, *Major Barbara* is a rich and rewarding comedy of ideas. Its insistent realities remain compelling: that all social institutions, even churches, are owned by the captains of industry; that the more destructive war becomes, the more fascinating it is to people; and that any system of morality must fit the facts of life or be scrapped as worthless.

Glenn Hopp

Bibliography:

Bentley, Eric. *Bernard Shaw*. 1947. Reprint. Norfolk, Conn.: New Directions, 1957. One of the best writers about modern drama, Bentley sets forth ideas about Shaw that place later critics in his debt. His study is one of the first important books on Shaw.

Holroyd, Michael. *Bernard Shaw*. 4 vols. New York: Random House, 1987-1992. Authoritative, superbly written, and richly detailed, these books are models of the biographer's art. In the second volume, *The Pursuit of Power 1898-1918*, Holroyd discusses *Major Barbara*, giving particular attention to the troublesome third act and its ambiguities, about which he writes with discernment.

Shaw, George Bernard. *Bernard Shaw's Plays*, edited by Warren S. Smith. New York: W. W. Norton, 1970. This edition of *Major Barbara* and three other Shaw plays includes a useful selection of critical essays, including a reprint of G. K. Chesterton's 1909 objections to the play, Barbara Bellow Watson's 1968 essay that discusses both the play and Chesterton's complaints, and an article that studies Shaw's correspondence with his friend Gilbert Murray, the scholar on whom Adolphus Cusins is based.

_____. *The Collected Screenplays of Bernard Shaw*, edited by Bernard F. Dukore. London: George Prior Publishers, 1980. In his introduction, Dukore devotes twenty-eight pages to a thorough analysis of Shaw's script for the 1941 film version of *Major Barbara* and an informative comparison of that version with the stage version.

Zimbardo, Rose, ed. *Twentieth Century Interpretations of Major Barbara*. Englewood Cliffs, N.J.: Prentice-Hall, 1970. Six complete essays and portions of five others offer differing approaches to the play. Zimbardo's remarks on the play's conformity to the comic paradigm, Joseph Frank's essay on the play's movement toward a Shavian salvation, and Anthony S. Abbott's comments on realism are insightful and accessible to the general reader.

THE MAKING OF AMERICANS
Being a History of a Family's Progress

Type of work: Novel
Author: Gertrude Stein (1874-1946)
Type of plot: Psychological realism
Time of plot: Sixty years, probably during the late nineteenth and early twentieth centuries
Locale: Bridgepoint (Baltimore) and Gossols (Oakland)
First published: 1925; abridged, 1934

> *Principal characters:*
> HENRY DEHNING, a wealthy man
> MRS. DEHNING, his wife
> JULIA DEHNING, their eldest daughter, who marries Alfred Hersland
> DAVID HERSLAND, an immigrant
> DAVID HERSLAND, his son, a rich businessman
> FANNY HISSEN HERSLAND, his ailing, unhappy wife
> MARTHA HERSLAND, the eldest of the Herslands' three children
> ALFRED HERSLAND, their son, a lawyer, who marries Julia Dehning
> DAVID HERSLAND, the youngest son, who dies before middle age
> PHILLIP REDFERN, an intellectual, who marries Martha Hersland
> MADELEINE WYMAN, one of the Hersland children's governesses

The Story:

The Dehning and Hersland families' American history began with their immigrant grandparents' separate journeys to America. Both families settled in Bridgepoint. Years later, the two families came together when Julia Dehning, who was connected with the old world because she was named after her grandmother, wanted to marry Alfred Hersland. Her father cautioned her not to encourage Alfred's advances. Although Julia quietly felt a vague dread about Alfred's plans for her father's money, she resisted Henry Dehning's hesitation and he slowly began to accept their wedding plans. Finally, Julia and Alfred were married after a year's engagement.

A long time before the Dehnings knew the Hersland family, David Hersland's grandparents sold all of their possessions and traveled to America to strike it rich. David's grandfather did not want to leave his home. As the family departed for America, David's grandfather kept returning to take a last look at his old home. Still, he knew that he must begin again in the new world.

David's father made a similar trip a generation later when he moved his family, including his well-to-do wife, Fanny, from Bridgeport to Gossols. Fanny Hissen had been raised by her religious father and dreary mother to feel important in Bridgepoint society. In Bridgepoint, David's sister Martha arranged her brother's marriage, and the family moved out west to Gossols. The Hersland house in Gossols sat on a ten-acre place out in the country, away from the other rich people in town. Although the children felt divided between city living and country living, they identified with the poor country people living around them more than with their own parents. After the Hersland family became established in Gossols, Fanny Hersland, cut off from Bridgepoint society and ignored by her husband and her children, lost all of her important feeling of rich living.

At this time, Madeleine Wyman, the Hersland family governess, had little to do with the children. Instead, she listened to Fanny's stories of her early living in Bridgepoint. This attention made Mrs. Hersland feel important. When Madeleine was pressured by her family to marry a rich man, Mrs. Hersland attempted to persuade her to stay with the family. Fanny commissioned her best dressmakers to make a dress for the governess. Madeleine finally married the rich man, and she realized why Fanny's early life made her feel important.

Martha Hersland, the eldest child, led a particularly uninteresting life until she witnessed a man beating a woman with an umbrella in a city street. This incident prompted her to leave Gossols to pursue her college education. At college, Martha met the young intellectual Phillip Redfern, a student of philosophy, who was her close friend for three years before they were married. The women's college at Farnham invited Phillip to chair the philosophy department. The Redferns accepted; however, Phillip and Martha were not a happy couple. In their marriage, Phillip's elaborate chivalry clashed with his wife's crude intelligence. In spite of compelling evidence, Martha could not admit her husband's marital infidelities or understand why their marriage had failed. They left Farnham around the time of Alfred and Julia's wedding, and never lived together again. Martha believed that she was unworthy of Phillip's love, but she studied and traveled to prepare herself for the time when they might be together again. After Phillip's death, Martha returned to Gossols to stay with her father.

Alfred Hersland's happy childhood was marred only by his confusion about being the eldest son, but the middle child. Alfred thought that he was superior to Martha because she was female. Many times he tried to get her into trouble. He spent his days playing in the orchard with the poor people who lived nearby, until he was old enough to go to Bridgepoint for college. There, he met his Hissen relatives, and with the characteristic Hersland impatience, he developed the urge to marry many years before he knew Julia Dehning.

Like Phillip and Martha's, Alfred and Julia's marriage was unsuccessful. When Alfred faced trouble in his business, Julia's father, Henry, gave him a large loan, even though he knew Alfred to be dishonest. Julia's dread regarding her husband grew, and eventually Alfred and Julia came to love other people. Alfred married Minnie Mason, an acquaintance of his younger brother, and Julia fell in love with a sick man named William Beckling. She never married him.

The youngest Hersland son, David, was obsessed with his own mortality, and he died before he reached middle age. When, like his siblings before him, he arrived in Bridgepoint for his college education, David was introduced to Alfred's friends. He was a remarkably clear thinker and began to advise Julia about his brother. David, the child who offered the most hope for the progress of his family, died before his middle years.

The Hersland and the Dehning families, like all families, contained a range of human nature, which reflected all possibilities and potentialities. Family living continued to exist, since all individuals possessed something of their ancestors. Thus, the dead ones continued to exist in the living ones.

Critical Evaluation:

In America Gertrude Stein is perhaps better known for her eccentric personality and her artistic relationships with Pablo Picasso, Sherwood Anderson, and Ernest Hemingway than for her own literary compositions. Stein's encyclopedic novel, *The Making of Americans*, warrants, however, comparison with other modernist masterworks, such as Marcel Proust's *Remembrance of Things Past* (1913-1927), James Joyce's *Ulysses* (1922), and John Dos Passos' *U.S.A.* (1938). In fact, in *Everybody's Autobiography* (1937), Stein herself recognizes the importance of *The Making of Americans* and insists that "everybody ought to be reading at it or it."

The Making of Americans has had a tortuous publishing history. Although Stein's ambitious project was written and revised sporadically from 1903 to 1911, it was not published until 1924, when about 150 pages of it appeared in serial form in Ford Madox Ford's *Transatlantic Review*. An abridged edition of 416 pages was published in 1934 and republished in 1966. Stein cited this abridged text during her tour of the American lecture circuits, and it offers the most available and penetrable text for students. This article refers exclusively to the 1934 version.

Anyone who has read, or read at, *The Making of Americans* can understand an editor's trepidation when confronted with Stein's excessive book. Its tortuous publishing history is understandable. Its length aside, *The Making of Americans* does not progress according to a plot, but develops laterally by rhythm and repetition. The initial section of the story focuses on the Dehnings and the Herslands, but Stein quickly abandons the Dehnings to concentrate on the Hersland family. Stein deliberately withholds "important" plot information, including the names of several minor characters and the subject of Alfred's dishonesty, in order to investigate the psychology of her characters. Many characters have the same names, signifying the passing on of "bottom natures" from one generation to the next. Some critics even suggest that the novel is flawed because Stein herself became bored with the exhaustive process of outlining the countless permutations of the book's personality types. Stein unravels these variations in long, twisted sentences that stretch the limits of language. The difficulties a reader faces in *The Making of Americans* contribute, however, to Stein's attempt to write "a history of every one and every kind of one and all the nature in every one and all the ways it comes out of them."

The novel's subtitle, *Being a History of a Family's Progress* discloses Stein's intention to make Americans out of a generation of immigrants. On the novel's opening page, she writes: "It has always seemed to me a rare privilege, this, of being an American, a real American, one whose tradition it has taken scarcely sixty years to create. We need only realise our parents, remember our grandparents and know ourselves and our history is complete." *The Making of Americans* goes beyond its autobiographical roots in Stein's family (Martha Hersland is Gertrude) to strive toward a comprehensive, subjective history of Americans.

Stein's family chronicle signals that Victorian ideas of linear, objective history and progress are, as she writes in *Wars I Have Seen* (1945), "dead dead dead." Her interest in describing all personality types requires repetition to establish "kinds" or "types." This shifts the focus away from individual events, which might be organized into a plot sequence, and toward the system she is creating and her psychological creation of her world. Stein's focus simultaneously deconstructs linear history and dismantles the notion of humanity's evolutionary progression. Successive generations of the Hersland and Dehning families in *The Making of Americans* are often more degenerate, more confused, and more dysfunctional than their parents, in part because the parents have passed on the worst part of their "bottom nature" to their children.

The final section of the novel, an abstract coda of twenty pages without any events or characters, moves completely into the dense, unfolding narrative consciousness that is one of Stein's most significant achievements. Stein's making of Americans through this consciousness creates a philosophically complex world, one that challenges her readers to reexamine how they are connected with history. *The Making of Americans* is Stein's most ambitious novel.

Trey Strecker

Bibliography:
Doane, Janice L. "Beginning and Beginning Again: The Discomposing Composition of *The Making of Americans*." In *Silence and Narrative: The Early Novels of Gertrude Stein*.

Westport, Conn.: Greenwood Press, 1986. Details how Stein's novel records her first serious struggle with artistic composition, authorship, origins, and identity. Significant biographical material.

Frieling, Kenneth. "The Becoming of Gertrude Stein's *The Making of Americans*." In *The Twenties: Fiction, Poetry, Drama*, edited by Warren French. Deland, Fla.: Everett/Edwards, 1975. Asserts that Stein overcomes the vision of America as a wasteland in *The Making of Americans* through a unifying consciousness that engulfs her characters' lives in the stream of a continuous present tense.

Katz, Leon. "Weininger and *The Making of Americans*." In *Critical Essays on Gertrude Stein*, edited by Michael J. Hoffman. Boston: G. K. Hall, 1986. Describes the development of Stein's understanding of personality types as influenced by psychologist Otto Weininger's systematization of human nature in *Sex and Character* (1903).

Sutherland, Donald. *Gertrude Stein: A Biography of Her Work*. New Haven, Conn.: Yale University Press, 1951. A good general introduction to Stein's work, despite its overly admiring tone. Acknowledges Stein's debt to artistic and scientific models in *The Making of Americans*.

Walker, Jayne L. "History as Repetition: *The Making of Americans*." In *The Making of a Modernist: Gertrude Stein from "Three Lives" to "Tender Buttons."* Amherst: University of Massachusetts Press, 1984. Demonstrates how Stein's rejection of linear plot in *The Making of Americans* reinforces her commitment to repetition as the source of historical knowledge. Traces how her desire for complete understanding reveals the pitfalls of totalizing systems.

THE MALCONTENT

Type of work: Drama
Author: John Marston (1576-1634)
Type of plot: Tragicomedy
Time of plot: Thirteenth century
Locale: Genoa, Italy
First performed: 1604; first published, 1604

Principal characters:
> GIOVANNI ALTOFRONTO, the Malcontent, at one time the
> duke of Genoa but now disguised as Malevole
> PIETRO JACOMO, the duke of Genoa
> MENDOZA, a court minion
> FERNEZE, a young courtier
> AURELIA, Pietro Jacomo's wife
> MARIA, Altofronto's wife
> BILIOSO, an old marshal
> MAQUERELLE, an old woman and panderer
> CELSO, a friend of Altofronto
> EMILIA and
> BIANCHA, Aurelia's attendants
> PASSARELLO, Bilioso's fool

The Story:

Duke Altofronto had been banished from Genoa. A political coup staged by Mendoza with the help of the Florentines had brought the weak Pietro Jacomo to power through his marriage to Aurelia, the daughter of a powerful Florentine leader. Altofronto, disguised as Malevole, prepared to bide his time until the state wearied of the new duke. Altofronto's devoted duchess, Maria, waited faithfully in prison for his return, and Celso acted as his secret informant on matters of state.

As the Malcontent, Altofronto was described as a likable person of marked intelligence and straightforward honesty. He refused to flatter as others did. On the negative side, however, he was described as more monster than man, more discontented than Lucifer in his fall, a man living on the vexations of others and at variance with his own soul. It was a mixture that made him seem unpredictable and served Altofronto well in plotting against his adversaries. This description of him came from Pietro, who was strangely attracted to the erratic individual known as the Malcontent. It was Altofronto, disguised as Malevole, who told Pietro that he was being cuckolded by Mendoza. This condition, Malevole declared, was most unnatural, for a cuckold was a creation of woman and not of God. In this way, Altofronto tormented Pietro and inflamed him against Mendoza.

Incensed by the thought of a relationship between Mendoza and Aurelia, Pietro confronted the minion with accusations and threats to kill him, but Mendoza placated the duke with disparagement of women and their habits, absolving himself of Pietro's accusations by telling him that Ferneze was the offender against the duke's marital rights. To prove his point, he suggested that Pietro break into Aurelia's room that night; should Ferneze try to escape, Mendoza would kill him. The situation occurred as Mendoza had planned: Ferneze was discovered in Aurelia's room and was, the minion believed, killed in his attempt to flee.

Later, when Mendoza and Aurelia were alone, they planned Pietro's murder. Aurelia promised to use her influence to have Mendoza made duke of Genoa. Unbeknownst to them, however, Ferneze had not been killed. Wounded, he attracted the attention of Altofronto, who revived and hid the young courtier.

Knowing that Pietro had gone hunting, Mendoza hired the Malcontent to pursue and murder the duke. Taken in by Altofronto's apparent willingness to aid him in his villainy, Mendoza outlined the remaining steps to his ultimate goal. With Pietro removed and his alliance with Aurelia established, he would be ready to make his bid for power. The banishment of Aurelia would be an easy step because he would publicize her infidelity to the Florentines. Then he intended to marry Maria, Altofronto's imprisoned wife, whose friends would strengthen Mendoza and his faction.

Reassured by Mendoza's admission that he did not love Maria, that she too was only a pawn to him, Altofronto took heart in his assurance that Maria was still true to him, as Celso had reported. Altofronto suggested to Mendoza that they hire a wretch or holy man to report that he had seen Pietro, bereft of reason because of his wife's infidelity, throw himself into the sea. He also offered to act as Mendoza's emissary in winning Maria's favor.

Instead of murdering Pietro, Altofronto divulged to him the plot against his life and provided him with the disguise of the hermit who was to report his suicide. Pietro, in disguise, gave a vivid description of his own anguished demise while lamenting Aurelia's unfaithfulness. Mendoza immediately banished Aurelia. He then instructed Altofronto to negotiate with Maria.

Duped by the supposed hermit, Mendoza sent him after Altofronto, with orders to poison the Malcontent at supper. When Altofronto returned for a letter that would admit him to Maria's quarters in the citadel, he received Mendoza's instructions to poison the hermit.

Altofronto and Pietro encountered the banished Aurelia in abject grief because of her indiscretions and her love for Pietro. Altofronto eased Pietro's hurt by reminding him that many great men have had unfaithful wives, among them Agamemnon, King Arthur, and Hercules. Maria's faithfulness to Altofronto was proved beyond doubt when Maquerelle and the disguised Altofronto waited on her to deliver Mendoza's offer of marriage. In answer to their proposal and the promise of great riches if she would accept Mendoza, she announced that she already had a husband. Banished or in power, present or absent, Altofronto remained her true lord.

Mendoza's only remaining threat to power was Altofronto, who in the disguise of the Malcontent knew too much of the usurper's malice. To be rid of him, Mendoza planned to use the fumes of one of the two boxes that had been given him by his intended victim. According to the giver, the fumes of one box would put the person who breathed them to sleep for twelve hours; the fumes of the other box would kill him immediately. Unhesitatingly, Mendoza opened what he supposed was the lethal box under Altofronto's nose. The box was, in fact, empty, but Altofronto feigned death. Later, he appeared at a masked ball given by Mendoza to celebrate the deaths he had planned. In the meantime, spurned by Maria, Mendoza accused her of murdering the hermit—the disguised Pietro—whom Altofronto had reported dead. The faithful wife welcomed death as a fate better than that of being married to the usurper.

At the ball, Altofronto chose Maria as his partner. Revealing his identity, he asked her to remain composed so that others would not recognize him. Pietro danced with Aurelia, who repented of her past deeds and vowed her undying devotion to him. At a prearranged signal, Mendoza's three supposed victims—Altofronto, Pietro, and Ferneze—revealed themselves, to the consternation of Mendoza and the joy of the assemblage. Altofronto was immediately restored to his rightful place as duke of Genoa.

Mendoza pleaded for his life, but he was summarily ejected from the court. Aurelia and Pietro were given the blessing of the court. Maquerelle was allowed to carry on her pandering in the suburbs. Bilioso, a sycophant who chose to stand with the wrong rather than fall with the right, was summarily dismissed from any further court favor. Altofronto and Maria were joyously reunited.

Critical Evaluation:

The Malcontent was written during a period of melancholic disillusionment that spanned the turn of the century. This *fin de siècle* mood was similarly expressed in William Shakespeare's *Hamlet* (1600-1601) and John Donne's poems "The First Anniversary" (1611) and "The Second Anniversary" (1612). In the drama of the period, two of the characters "allowed" to express such disillusionment were the fool and the melancholic, or malcontent. Both are to be found in plays as diverse as *Hamlet*, a tragedy, and *As You Like It* (c. 1599-1600), a comedy. *The Malcontent* takes up a middle ground between tragedy and comedy. In the figure of Hamlet, the melancholic becomes the hero. His role is therefore not that of satiric spectator, as is Jaques in *As You Like It*, but he is as active an instrument in restoring justice. The way offered him, though he struggles with it, is revenge. As a Christian response, *Hamlet* is tragic because the revenge ethic is necessarily tragic, doubly so when seen as inauthentic.

Two years after *Hamlet*, John Marston reworked a similar theme quite differently. Retaining the tone of satiric disillusion, though it is possibly closer to Shakespeare's *Timon of Athens* (1607-1608), Marston reworked the melancholic as a specific role and as a specific disguise. Hamlet's disguise of madness was haphazard and probably more an expression of mental disorder than anything deliberately assumed. There are elements of this in Marston's play, too. It is difficult to see Malevole as a mere mask for Altofronto, for there is a genuine expression of personality, an alter ego, expressed in powerful language coming from the heart. Yet Altofronto is clearly in control of his disguise, and he possesses an ability to manipulate events to his advantage that is totally lacking in Hamlet's character.

Marston gives the play an Italian setting, as is very typical of other Jacobean dramatists such as Cyril Tourneur, John Webster, and Thomas Middleton. The Italian influence is also seen in the genre of tragicomedy, which was new to English theater but common in the Italian, and in the language. Whole speeches are taken from Giambattista Guarini's *Il Pastor Fido*, which had been translated into English in 1602. Perhaps even more important, the figure of Mendoza is based on what the English saw as a typical Italian villain, Machiavelli's prince. The Machiavellian villain became typified as a schemer who has no time for conventional morality or religion, is power-hungry, and considers the ends always to justify the means.

Marston created a dramatically well-balanced drama between the two schemers: the deposed duke, who seeks to regain his rightful authority through disguise, and the would-be duke, who seeks power through deceit and violence. In the middle stands the actual duke, Pietro, a weak-willed man and a puppet of the Florentines. Yet, as with much Jacobean drama and unlike Shakespearean tragedy, the plot, such as it is, is motivated, not by political moves, but by sexual passion. Sexual imagery merges with political to give a picture of total immorality and degradation. Maquarelle is the key female character because she plays out the moves of the brothel as the moves of the court. The images are reinforced in the language used by Altofronto in his role as Malevole, Passarello the fool, and in a different way, Bilioso, the biggest panderer of all.

The use of the tragicomic genre is a significant shift away from the more typical Jacobean revenge tragedy. In this genre, the moral conflicts and tensions could be resolved without losing the satiric worldview. Shakespeare likewise experimented with this alternative in *Measure for Measure* (1604), which, like *The Malcontent*, has a supposedly absent duke who watches over the events, and in *The Tempest* (1611), where another deposed duke regains power, but this time by magic. Although *Measure for Measure* is usually not classed as a tragicomedy (the term problem play is sometimes used), *The Tempest* can rightfully be seen as one. All of these plays reject the revenge ethic. Marston's solution must be seen as predominantly successful. Evil overreaches itself and in becoming too confident, becomes too naïve; at the same time, the good learn to become "as wise as a serpent," accept the corrupting nature of power, and seek to bring about repentance and change of heart.

It is in the interpretation of such moral patterning that ambiguity is revealed. Such patterning can be interpreted to be Stoic, representing the return to political and moral equilibrium, the restoration of true authority, and the rejection of extremes of naïveté (folly) and Machiavellianism. It can also be interpreted to be Christian, in which patterns of sin, repentance, restoration, and forgiveness are dominant. Other critical interpretations have suggested that Marston's attacks on the church in the play give rise to the more pessimistic moral that hypocrisy and deceit are everywhere. Altofronto himself is a mask, and his forgiveness of Mendoza will only set the cycle of evil going again. Yet other interpretations, which emphasize the absurd "pretence" motifs and the nature of the play's language, interpret the play in terms of twentieth century absurdism.

Certainly the language of the play has been a source of critical contention. Although the play is dedicated to Ben Jonson, the style bears little resemblance to the controlled, ironic language of Jonsonian drama. In fact, Jonson made fun of Marston's apparently uncontrolled satiric style. Earlier commentators corroborated the Jonsonian censure and pointed to the amount Marston borrowed from other plays. Later critics, however, see energy and creativeness in the "free play" of Marston's language and in its breaking down of the borders of poetry and prose. *The Malcontent* is certainly a play that will continue to attract critical interest and controversy, if only because many of its techniques seem almost designed to illustrate poststructualist and postmodernist modes of reading.

"Critical Evaluation" by David Barratt

Bibliography:

Finkelpearl, Philip. *John Marston of the Middle Temple: An Elizabethan Dramatist in His Social Setting*. Cambridge, Mass.: Harvard University Press, 1969. Covers Marston's biographical and social background and seeks to relate the plays to that background. Bibliography and index.

Geckle, George L. *John Marston's Drama: Themes, Images, Sources*. Rutherford, N.J.: Fairleigh Dickinson University Press, 1980. Chapter 7 discusses *The Malcontent*, dealing in particular with the theme of fortune. Geckle argues that the dominant motif is not disguise but rather the wheel of fortune, and he points to the themes that revolve round this symbol. He agrees that the play is a tragicomedy, but he stresses the tragic aspects of the wheel motif. Includes an index.

Scott, Michael. *John Marston's Plays: Theme, Structure, and Performance*. London: Macmillan, 1978. The plays are not dealt with separately, but under a variety of subject headings. Scott tries to read Marston as an absurdist and looks to typical twentieth century categories. Some discussion of performance tradition. Includes an index.

Tucker, Kenneth. *John Marston: A Reference Guide*. Boston: G. K. Hall, 1985. Follows the standard format and sequencing of the "Reference Guide to Literature" series. Includes bibliography and index.

Wharton, T. F. *The Critical Fall and Rise of John Marston.* Columbia, S.C.: Camden House, 1994. The most recent full-length study of Marston, dealing with the critical debates that have revolved round him. Takes note, among much else, of T. S. Eliot's notable essay on Marston, which sparked off twentieth century critical concern. Includes an index.

MALONE DIES

Type of work: Novel
Author: Samuel Beckett (1906-1989)
Type of plot: Absurdist
Time of plot: 1940's
Locale: A hospital
First published: Malone meurt, 1951 (English translation, 1956)

> *Principal characters:*
> MALONE, a dying old man
> SAPOSCAT/MACMANN, the protagonist of a story Malone tells
> MOLL and
> LEMUEL, other characters in Malone's story

The Story:

Malone, an old man, was sitting in a hospital bed writing. He heard the sounds of other men coming and going; then, he recalled having been brought there in an ambulance. He was bedridden, almost incapable of movement. His memory was unreliable; he did not know whether he was recalling memories or inventing them. Then, abruptly, he began a story about a man named Saposcat. "I wonder if I am not talking yet again about myself," he mused. A page later, however, Malone noted, "Nothing is less like me than this patient, reasonable child."

A family, the Lamberts, had befriended Saposcat, who lived on a farm. Saposcat, known by the nickname of Sapo, helped Mr. Lambert bury a mule. Incest, according to Malone, was in the air in the Lambert home. The Lambert children, a girl and a boy, shared a bedroom and would masturbate in each other's presence.

Malone dropped his pencil, and it took him forty-eight hours to recover it. He said he had spent two unforgettable days of which nothing would ever be known. The pencil was described at some length. It was getting shorter all the time and soon would vanish from wear and tear. Malone was not worried, for he remembered that somewhere in his bed he had another pencil, scarcely used.

Re-encountering the protagonist of his story, Malone changed the name from Saposcat to Macmann. Macmann, caught in a rainstorm, decided to lie flat on the ground, so that at least some portion of himself would stay dry. As the rain went on with unabated violence, he began to roll over and over, until he began to dream of becoming a cylinder and never having to walk upright again.

Malone then interrupted himself to begin an inventory of his possessions. He spoke of the pleasure he used to take in putting his hands deep into his pockets and fingering the "hard shapely" objects that were there and how he loved to fall asleep holding a stone, a horse chestnut, or a cone in his hand.

He interrupted himself once more—or was interrupted by memory—with the thought of Macmann, and Malone said that it looked like he would never finish anything "except perhaps breathing." Malone wondered whether he had died already. No doubt feeling that they would constitute a proof of his continued existence, he imagined taking all of his possessions into the bed with him, his photograph, his stone, his hat, and his buttons.

Malone then wondered if he was hungry. He thought and wrote, "I would gladly eat a little soup, if there was any left. No, even if there was some left I would not eat it." No reason was given for this change of heart.

Having previously lost (and then painstakingly retrieved) his exercise book and his pencil, Malone now lost his stick. Only now did he realize how much it meant to him. Rapidly, however, his thoughts returned to food. He wondered if the hospital workers had fed him while he slept, or if they had withheld soup from him in order to help him die more quickly. He thought that it would have been quicker to poison him and wondered if they feared an autopsy. He then recalled that he had some pills, but he was not sure why. They were either sedatives or laxatives. It would be annoying, he said, to turn to them for calm and to get diarrhea instead. He admitted he could be calmer, but added "enough about me."

One day, much later, Macmann awoke in an asylum, the House of Saint John of God. The person who told him this was a Christlike figure, who handed Macmann the stump of a pencil, requesting that Macmann sign himself into the hospital. He and his attendants left, and a small, ugly old woman called Moll took a chair by his bed. For earrings she wore two long ivory crucifixes. She turned out to be the person charged with his care. She kept bringing him food, emptying his chamberpot, and helping him wash himself. When Macmann one day noticed his clothes were gone, Moll calmed him.

Macmann and Moll became lovers. Moll wrote him love letters. In return, Macmann wrote little love poems, "remarkable for their exaltation of love regarded as a kind of lethal glue." Another kind of writing was done by Lemuel, an attendant, who dutifully noted Macmann's questions in a thick book but never came back with any answers.

Malone interrupted himself to report on a visit from a person unknown to him, who hit him on the head and subsequently scattered his things. This person was malevolent, a characteristic later attributed to Lemuel. He supposed this visitor might be a mourner or a mortician, and himself dead already. Malone made a list of things to say to him. He was cut short by violent symptoms, perhaps fatal ones. His account became even more confused.

The story of Macmann was then resumed with much coherence. The story of his attempted escapes was recounted; he was always thwarted because he hid in the same place each time. From one of these escapades, he fetched back a stick. When Lemuel found it, he had him beaten with it.

Malone concluded with an account of an excursion from the asylum on which Macmann was taken along with fellow inmates. The account, however, failed to conclude, presumably because of the death of its creator, Malone.

Critical Evaluation:

This novel is simultaneously a last will and testament of an old man who knows he is soon to die and a moment-by-moment record of his feelings and impressions as he awaits death. He is talking to himself and writing things while sitting in a bed in some public building. One can deduce from this that he is in a hospital. Beckett's narrative unfolds phenomenologically; the reader is given bits and pieces, glimpses, details from which he or she can derive the bigger picture or watch as Malone derives it.

Malone is indeed writing at least some of these words, because he says at one point, "I fear I must have fallen asleep again. In vain I grope, I cannot find my exercise book. But I still have the pencil in my hand." His musings—typical of this narrative—raise a further question while answering another: Where has he written *those* words?

Such teasing fills this novel. Beckett toys with the frame, always reminding his readers that we are reading words and not seeing through them to an objective reality solidly anchored in some real world. Yet the realities of life and death are ever present. These are not so much called into question as is the ability of words to be their equal, to cope with the facts of mortality and temporality.

Malone "speaks" in the first person. He says, "I, Malone," and whenever he says this, he is also saying, "I'm alone." All Beckett's works, be they drama, poem, or novel, are powered by this single phrase. Such punning is second nature with Samuel Beckett, whose works, like those of his mentor and fellow Irishman James Joyce, are strewn with homonyms both comic and telling.

Absurdly thrown into a universe without appeal, his characters, often suffering from mental and physical diseases, often maimed or physically trapped, keep reminding us of our own humiliating and disgusting limitations, our own failures to realize our potential, our own approaching unceremonious end. Yet Beckett manages to get readers to sit through such unremitting reminders through the use of contradictions and puns. This technique actually appears between, rather than in, each sentence. Nearly every sentence contradicts, qualifies, or undermines the previous sentence. The effect is to keep readers on the edge of their seats and to call the authority of the narrator into question. The embodiment of a mind changing itself before one's very eyes lends authenticity to the book. This impression can be sustained even when Beckett portrays Malone as developmentally challenged to the point of farce.

Malone Dies is an extremely funny book despite its horribly depressing subject matter: disintegration, disease, and death. The way Beckett views human limitations, the human tendency to self-mutilate and self-destruct, can be as humorous as any satire since Jonathan Swift's. Consider Lemuel in this passage:

> One day rolling up the leg of his trousers, he showed Macmann his shin covered with bruises, scars and abrasions. Then producing smartly a hammer from an inner pocket he dealt himself, right in the middle of his ancient wounds, so violent a blow that he fell down backwards, or perhaps I should say forwards. But the part he struck most readily, with his hammer, was the head, and that is understandable, for it too is a bony part, and sensitive, and difficult to miss, and the seat of all the shit and misery, so you rain blows upon it.

Beckett shares with Swift a fascinated disgust with bodily functions, and this disgust frequently drives his sense of humor, as in the description of Macmann and Moll attempting sexual intercourse: "The spectacle was then offered of Macmann trying to bundle his sex into his partner's like a pillow into a pillow-slip." There are also strikingly lyrical passages, as when Malone describes the sensations he has when he is dying. The entire work is moving, all the more so because Beckett is so unsentimental. He refuses to intervene between the reader and the sufferings of his characters by framing their misery in the way that Charles Dickens would. Eventually, the life that springs up in each of Beckett's sentences triumphs over the death of Malone. After all, once dead, Malone can no longer say "I, Malone." He has been taken back into the company of the universe; all of his isolating thinking has been canceled.

David Bromige

Bibliography:
Binns, Ronald. "Beckett, Lowry, and the Anti-Novel." In *The Contemporary English Novel*, edited by John Russell Brown and Bernard Harris. Stratford-upon-Avon studies 18. London: Edward Arnold, 1979. Binns finds that the center of attention is the narrator himself, a garrulous confabulator who undermines confidence in the reality of any world offered by

such writing, suggesting that all writing has credibility problems.

Kenner, Hugh. *Samuel Beckett: A Critical Study*. Berkeley: University of California Press, 1968. The definitive work on Beckett. Kenner reads a text like a detective, uncovering not so much clues as a network of references, literary, historical, and personal. He also provides useful figures to help readers imagine what Beckett's concerns and intentions might be. He places Beckett in relation to James Joyce and Marcel Proust.

Kern, Edith. "Black Humor: The Pockets of Lemuel Gulliver and Samuel Beckett." In *Samuel Beckett Now*, edited by Melvin J. Friedman. Chicago: University of Chicago Press, 1970. Kern ties together a number of Beckett's works by tracing the theme of pockets and the objects they contain. "Yet even the human mind is envisioned by Beckett as a pocket." She helps clarify passages in *Malone Dies* by evoking similar passages in *Waiting for Godot* (1952) and *How It Is, Molloy* (1951). She also suggests precedents for Beckett's satirical vision in Swift's *Gulliver's Travels* (1726).

Lorich, Bruce. "The Accommodating Form of Samuel Beckett." *Southwest Review* 55 (Autumn, 1970): 354-369. Lorich builds his argument around a phrase Beckett stated in an interview: "To find a form that accommodates the mess, that is the task of the artist now." The "mess" is the postmodern world; Beckett's plays, novels, and poems are various formal attempts to contain and depict it. Lorich asserts that Beckett's style counters the absurdity of human beings overwhelmed by technology.

Sachner, Mark J. "The Artist as Fiction: An Aesthetics of Failure in Samuel Beckett's Trilogy." *The Midwest Quarterly* 18, no. 2 (1977): 144-155. Sachner sees Beckett's trilogy as metafiction. The movement away from plot and toward "the acrobatics of language." The protagonist-narrators focus on their own need to be telling the story. He emphasizes Beckett's affinities with Edgar Allan Poe and Fyodor Dostoevski.

THE MALTESE FALCON

Type of work: Novel
Author: Dashiell Hammett (1894-1961)
Type of plot: Detective and mystery
Time of plot: 1928
Locale: San Francisco
First published: 1930

Principal characters:
SAM SPADE, a private detective
EFFIE PERINE, his secretary
BRIGID O'SHAUGHNESSY, his client
CASPER GUTMAN, her employer
WILMER COOK, Gutman's bodyguard
JOEL CAIRO, Gutman's onetime agent
SERGEANT TOM POLHAUS, a police detective
LIEUTENANT DUNDY, a police detective

The Story:

Brigid O'Shaughnessy went to Sam Spade and Miles Archer, detectives, to ask them to trail one Floyd Thursby. Archer, who undertook the job, was murdered. Later that same night, Thursby himself was shot down in front of his hotel. The police suspected Spade of killing Thursby to avenge Archer's murder. Brigid left word at Spade's office that she wanted to see him. She moved out of her hotel because she was afraid. At her new apartment, she said she could not divulge the whole story. She had met Thursby in the Orient. They had arrived in San Francisco the week before. She assumed that Thursby had killed Archer but did not know who killed Thursby.

When Spade returned to his office, Joel Cairo was waiting. He offered Spade five thousand dollars for the recovery of a statuette of a black bird. That night Spade was trailed by a small young man in a gray overcoat. Spade eluded him long enough to slip into Brigid's apartment building. There, he learned that Brigid was connected in some way with a mysterious black bird, a replica of a falcon. Later they went to Spade's apartment to meet Cairo. She told Cairo she did not have the falcon. He would have to wait, possibly a week, before she could sell it to him.

The police learned that Spade was having an illicit affair with Iva Archer and began to suspect Spade may have killed Archer so he could marry his partner's wife. When the police arrived to question Spade about their new line of inquiry, they discovered Cairo and Brigid in a squabble. Spade introduced Brigid as an operator in his employ and said they had been questioning Cairo about the two murders. After Cairo and the policemen had gone, Brigid told Sam she did not know what made the falcon important. She had been hired to steal it from a Russian named Kemidov in Constantinople.

Next morning, before Brigid was awake, Spade went to get groceries and incidentally to search her apartment for the falcon, which he failed to find. He was certain Brigid knew where it was. Brigid was afraid of what Cairo might do, however, and Spade arranged for her to stay at the home of his secretary.

In explaining to Cairo how Thursby was killed, Brigid had outlined the letter *G* in the air; Spade knew that special significance was attached to that letter. He confronted the youth who was trailing him and said that *G* would have to deal with him. Shortly after, a Mr. Gutman called, inviting Spade to his hotel suite. Spade told him that Cairo had offered ten thousand dollars, not five, for the falcon. Gutman laughed derisively; the statuette was obviously worth a fortune. Pretending to be furious because Gutman would reveal no more, Spade stormed out, saying he would give Gutman until five-thirty to talk.

From a taxi driver, Spade learned that instead of going to Effie's house, Brigid had hurried to the waterfront after buying a newspaper. When Gutman summoned him back to his hotel suite, Spade learned that the falcon was an ancient ornament, made in Malta, encrusted with precious gems and later in its bloody history covered with black enamel to conceal its value. Gutman had traced it to the Constantinople home of Kemidov, where Gutman's agents had stolen it but had run off with it.

Next day, Spade searched Cairo's hotel room and found that something had been torn out of Cairo's newspaper the day before. He bought another copy of that paper and saw that the section Cairo had torn out reported the arrival of the ship *La Paloma* from Hong Kong. Remembering that Brigid had mentioned the Orient, he associated her impromptu waterfront errand with the ship's arrival. Later, he learned that Cairo had checked out of his hotel. Meanwhile, Spade had gone aboard *La Paloma* and learned that Gutman, Cairo, the strange young man, and Brigid had held a long conference with Jacobi, the captain.

While Spade was relating his discoveries to his secretary, a man burst in, held out a bundle, and dropped over dead. Spade opened the bundle and discovered the falcon. Spade was sure that the dead man was Captain Jacobi. He had his secretary call the police while he checked the falcon at a nearby bus terminal and mailed the receipt to his own post-office box. He then went to answer a distress call from Brigid, who claimed she was being forcibly held at Gutman's hotel suite. She was not there. Instead, Spade found Gutman's daughter, who sent him on a wild-goose chase. When he returned to his apartment, he met Brigid waiting outside, obviously terrified. Opening the door, he found Gutman, the young man, and Cairo waiting with drawn guns.

Spade realized that his wild-goose chase had been designed to get him out of the way long enough to give these people time to find Jacobi before he returned. Spade said he would relinquish the falcon for ten thousand dollars and someone on whom to blame the murders. He suggested the young man, Wilmer Cook, as the "fall guy." Spade explained that if Wilmer were hanged for Thursby's murder, the district attorney would drop the case, taking it for granted that Jacobi had been killed by the same person. Gutman, sure that Thursby had killed Archer, finally consented to make his young bodyguard the scapegoat.

Gutman produced ten one-thousand-dollar bills. Spade called Effie and asked her to get the claim check from the post office and redeem the falcon. After she had delivered the package, Gutman untied it and found it was a lead imitation. Kemidov had tricked him. Spade gave back nine thousand dollars and the men left in haste, after discovering that Wilmer had slipped away unnoticed. Then Spade called the police and told them that Wilmer had killed Jacobi and Thursby and that Gutman and Cairo were accessories.

Knowing that Gutman would implicate him and Brigid in the affair, Spade made Brigid confess that she had lured Archer into an alley that first night and had shot him with Thursby's revolver. He told Brigid he intended to turn her over to the police. He had to clear himself of suspicion of killing his partner and would not let a woman stand in his way.

Critical Evaluation:

Dashiell Hammett was the leading writer of the so-called hard-boiled school of American mystery writers. Hard-boiled crime fiction began with the pulp magazines, which were exceedingly popular before the new entertainment medium of television began to undermine them in the late 1940's. The magazines, printed on cheap paper, sold for ten or fifteen cents. There were many different kinds of pulp magazines, including true crime, mysteries, romances, westerns, and science fiction. Being directed to a mass audience, they were written in simple English and emphasized action and dialogue. Many of the writers were hacks who were paid a penny a word and did not have the talent or motivation to produce quality literature. From the beginning of his career, Hammett distinguished himself as an exception.

One reason for Hammett's distinction as a mystery writer was that he had actually been a private detective himself for many years. He knew what he was talking about. His early writing career was linked with the legendary *Black Mask*, a pulp magazine featuring male-oriented action and adventure. Hammett was also a gifted writer, although he did not have a great deal of formal education. His practical knowledge, his care and concern about his craft, and his sheer talent made him the leader in his field. *The Maltese Falcon* was originally published as a serial in *Black Mask* and then brought out in hard cover. It is Hammett's best novel. One outstanding stylistic feature is that it is written in a totally objective manner. The author describes a setting and then tells only what the characters say and do. He never attempts to go into any character's mind and explain what he or she is thinking. The story is told entirely from Spade's point of view. The author does not indicate that Spade actually observes everything, but Spade is always present. Nothing happens that he could not have observed.

Hammett deliberately maintains a very fast pace. This was something he learned to do as a *Black Mask* writer. One of the ways he maintains this pace is by crowding several different events into the same chapter. A scene that begins in one chapter often ends in the next, while a new scene begins before that chapter ends. The reader is given the impression that Spade is constantly on the move, conducting his investigation while trying to cope with problems others are creating for him.

Hammett was famous for his ability to write dialogue. Good dialogue sounds realistic and conveys information without doing so too conspicuously. It also characterizes the speaker. Since *The Maltese Falcon* is written in an entirely objective manner and is full of good dialogue, it could easily be turned into a stage play—and Hammett indicated to his publisher that he would like to see such a play produced.

It was obvious that the novel would also make a good motion picture, and it has been adapted to film three times. The most famous version is *The Maltese Falcon* (1941), directed by John Huston and starring Humphrey Bogart as Sam Spade, the role that made him a superstar.

In addition to writing outstanding dialogue, Hammett wrote clean, straightforward, graphic prose that differed radically from the convoluted, affected prose to be found in many of the so-called classic English mystery novels, as well as in much of the other English and Anglo-philic literature produced before writers such as Sherwood Anderson, Ernest Hemingway, Dashiell Hammett and others began writing in the language used by ordinary Americans.

The theme of *The Maltese Falcon* can be summed up in a familiar quotation from the Bible: "The love of money is the root of all evil." A reviewer wrote that Hammett, who had strong socialist sympathies and who admired Karl Marx, "regarded moral evil as economically determined." According to Gutman, the real falcon had a history of bloodshed from its creation in Malta in the sixteenth century. Greed brings out the worst in Gutman, Cairo, and Brigid; it leads directly or indirectly to the deaths of Archer, Thursby, Jacobi, and Gutman. Wilmer will be executed for three murders. Brigid will spend at least twenty years in prison if she avoids execution. The falcon might have led to Spade's own downfall if he had not been shrewd enough to circumvent the traps that everyone, including the police, set for him. When the falcon turns out to be a fake, it symbolizes the futility of materialistic values.

Hammett was responsible for the creation of a distinctively American type of mystery novel, which has come to be called the hard-boiled mystery. He influenced, because of his talent, craftsmanship, and seriousness of purpose, not only American crime writers but also crime writers in other countries. Critics in America, England, France, and Germany acknowledge that Hammett elevated the mystery genre to the rank of quality literature. His influence can be seen in mainstream fiction as well as in genre fiction.

Films based on Hammett's novels influenced filmmakers worldwide. Conversely, the films influenced novelists because few novelists do not dream of selling a book to Hollywood. Hollywood made Hammett rich and famous, but its easy money and notoriously loose living undermined him physically and mentally. His heavy drinking ruined his career and hastened his death. He died a pauper, leaving nothing to posterity but his unique literary creations and his personal legend as a proud, independent individual with a strict code of integrity, one not unlike that of his most famous character, Sam Spade.

"Critical Evaluation" by Bill Delaney

Bibliography:

Chandler, Raymond. *The Simple Art of Murder*. New York: Ballantine, 1972. This interesting essay by another famous American hard-boiled mystery writer discusses the shortcomings of the traditional British mystery novel and the advances in the genre inspired by Hammett. Chandler and Hammett are credited with being the fathers of the modern American mystery novel.

Layman, Richard. *Shadow Man: The Life of Dashiell Hammett*. New York: Harcourt Brace Jovanovich, 1981. The best available biography of Dashiell Hammett, who led a colorful life and resembled Sam Spade in his moral code and unsentimental view of human nature. Discusses the genesis of *The Maltese Falcon*, Hammett's most acclaimed novel, in detail.

Marling, William. *Dashiell Hammett*. Boston: Twayne, 1983. Contains a thorough discussion of Hammett's life and art, with considerable attention to *The Maltese Falcon*. Excellent reference notes and selected bibliography.

Nolan, William F. *Dashiell Hammett: A Casebook*. Santa Barbara, Calif.: McNally & Loftin, 1969. A book about Hammett's life and writing by an author who has established a reputation as an authority on American crime fiction in general and on Dashiell Hammett in particular. Discusses *The Maltese Falcon* thoroughly.

Wolfe, Peter. *Beams Falling: The Art of Dashiell Hammett*. Bowling Green, Ohio: Bowling Green University Press, 1980. An author who has specialized in the study of hard-boiled crime writers presents full-length analyses of Hammett's stories and novels. "Beams Falling" alludes to the much-debated "Flitcraft Episode" in *The Maltese Falcon*.

THE MAMBO KINGS PLAY SONGS OF LOVE

Type of work: Novel
Author: Oscar Hijuelos (1951-   )
Type of plot: Social realism
Time of plot: 1930's-1980's
Locale: Cuba and the United States
First published: 1989

> *Principal characters:*
> CESAR CASTILLO, an immigrant musician from Cuba, living in New York
> NESTOR CASTILLO, his younger brother
> DELORES CASTILLO, Nestor's wife
> EUGENIO and
> LETICIA, Nestor's children

The Story:

Cesar, Nestor, and their three brothers grew up in the sugar-mill town of Las Piñas, in Oriente Province, Cuba. The family moved from the mill to a livestock farm where the father, Pedro Castillo, slaughtered animals; he was proud of his physical strength and demanded respect from his frightened sons with cruel beatings. The powerless mother, Maria, attributed his violent behavior to the fact that he had had a hard life since childhood.

As a child, listening to a music box, Cesar learned to dance, and he enjoyed orchestra performances. When he heard Eusebio Stevenson playing background music for Hollywood silent films in a movie theater, he requested lessons. A mulatto, Pucho, taught him music and magic African chants. Cesar challenged paternal authority when he decided to become a musician.

In 1937, at nineteen, Cesar started his singing career in Santiago de Cuba, invited by the well-known band leader Julián García. Nestor, also musically talented, joined the orchestra. Cesar married the shy schoolteacher Luisa García, Julián's niece; they lived happily until Cesar started drinking, shouting, and cheating on his wife. He loved Luisa and their daughter Mariela, but his macho temperament led him to fear the loss of freedom symbolized by married life. After they were divorced, Luisa married a schoolteacher and had another child.

In Havana, as instrumentalists, composers, and singers, Cesar and Nestor struggled to earn a living at a time when American big brass jazz bands were in vogue. They had met Desi Arnaz in Santiago de Cuba and knew about his fame in the United States. Inspired by stories about Cubans who, since the 1930's, had gotten rich making films in Hollywood or playing in New York, they daydreamed of achieving the same success.

The brothers arrived as immigrants in New York in early 1949, the beginning of the mambo boom. Sponsored by their cousin Pablo, they got a job in a meat-packing plant. At night, playing in clubs and dance halls, they became performing stars, the Mambo Kings, with their own Latin dance band. They lived with Pablo's family near Harlem; his kindhearted wife, Miriam, provided warmth and Cuban home cooking.

Cesar remembered Cuba and missed his daughter, but he liked to look forward to a better future. Nestor thought constantly about the past, tortured by memories of Maria Rivera, a beautiful mulatto dancer in Havana who had abandoned him after a passionate affair and married somebody else. He wanted to believe that she still loved him and, hoping that a song would bring her back, he wrote twenty-two different versions. The mournful tune of "Beautiful Maria of My Soul" caught the attention of Desi Arnaz, who invited the brothers to appear on his television show, *I Love Lucy*, performing the song that would make them famous.

The gregarious Cesar enjoyed music, food, friendship, and women, while the somber Nestor wrote songs expressing torment and sorrow. When Nestor met Delores Fuentes, who cleaned houses and hoped to be a teacher, she represented the prospect of a new love lifting him out of his melancholia. They were married and had two children, Eugenio and Leticia. Nestor felt unprepared for fatherhood; worried about his children's physical health, he relived his own childhood of illness and near-death experiences.

Nestor's wife had arrived from Havana with her father Daniel in 1942, at the age of thirteen. Her mother remained in Cuba with the older sister, Ana Maria. The father's unhappiness increased with the years. When he died on the job, in 1949, Ana Maria came to live with her sister, trying to make her go out instead of staying home, reading books. When Delores married Nestor, her purpose in life was to make him happy; then she noticed his growing distance from her and realized that he could never forget Maria.

One winter night, after a performance, Nestor was driving Cesar's car while Cesar was in the back seat with his girlfriend, Vanna. The car slid over a patch of ice and crushed into a tree, killing Nestor. Cesar was unable to recover from the loss of the beloved brother; tormented by memories and ghosts, he left his band. In 1958, he visited his daughter, who later became a ballet dancer; he saw his relatives for the last time in Cuba. After the Revolution, two of his brothers, Eduardo and Miguel, settled with their families as exiles in Miami.

Cesar tried to change his life by joining the Merchant Marine; upon his return, he held several jobs until his landlady, Mrs. Shannon, offered him the job of superintendent and free rent. He became a musician again, and owned a nightclub until the business failed and his health deteriorated. He searched for lost youth in affairs with younger women; Lydia Santos was his last love. Eugenio, Nestor's son, took care of him at home and in hospitals.

In 1980 Cesar prepared for death at the Hotel Splendour, where he had enjoyed happier times with women. He died drinking, in the company of old letters, photographs, and records, listening to Nestor's song. A year later, Eugenio visited Desi Arnaz and watched the old show's rerun, seeing the Mambo Kings alive again; he re-created the family saga with his own memories of them.

Critical Evaluation:

A native New Yorker of Cuban parentage, Oscar Hijuelos was graduated from the City College of New York. His first novel, *Our House in the Last World*, was published in 1983. *The Mambo Kings Play Songs of Love*, winner of a 1990 Pulitzer Prize, became a major motion picture. *The Fourteen Sisters of Emilio Montez O'Brien* appeared in 1993. The three novels illustrate immigrant life in the United States, with remembrance and nostalgia serving as sources of narrative imagination.

The family saga of *The Mambo Kings Play Songs of Love* is narrated in the first and third person, shifting from one character's story to the next, from one recollection to another, moving back and forth in time, with flashbacks within flashbacks, and foreshadowing the future. The disjointed narrative, with extensive footnotes and inventory-like descriptions, enlivened with monologues and dialogues, finds a focus in the musical career and romantic adventures of Cesar and Nestor Castillo, the Mambo Kings.

The novel is divided into five sections; the first and last, the shortest and untitled, are narrated by Eugenio, providing his own memories of events. The second and third, entitled "Side A" and

"Side B" respectively, recalling a record's two sides, refer in their subtitles to a night in 1980, at the Hotel Splendour, where Cesar spends his last hours, listening to the 1956 record album "The Mambo Kings Play Songs of Love." The fourth section, "Toward the end, while listening to the wistful 'Beautiful María of My Soul,'" includes a Spanish version of the song, handwritten by Cesar, and found next to him after his death.

Hijuelos presents the 1930's and 1940's music scene in Cuba, and then captures the times and spirit of the 1940's and 1950's in New York, when Latin music influenced American jazz, and dancing required expertise in the arts of the mambo, rumba, and cha-cha-cha. The "cu-bop" exemplified the crosscultural fusion of the Afro-Cuban music and hot bebop Harlem jazz. Sociocultural dualism is depicted in the novel with the fluid transition from English to Spanish, including expressions and titles in both languages, and a bilingual version of the bolero "Beautiful María of My Soul" or "Bellísima María de mi alma."

Music is the driving force in the lives of the Mambo Kings. It gives them courage to disobey the father and leave their homeland in search of fame and the American Dream. After rising to stardom with their band in New York, they tour the country. The performance on television with Desi Arnaz and Lucille Ball represents the climax of their career.

At the best and worst times, musical creation allows the expression of feelings and spiritual survival. An epigraph at the beginning of the novel states that music transforms fiction into reality and "will make it all possible." Nestor expresses pure love and desire in his song, hoping that María, possessed magically by it, will return to him. At the end, music brings memories of Cuba to Cesar, and as he listens to the notes, bouncing back and forth in time and places, "swirling inside him like youth," he feels pain and death taken away.

The American Dream of immigrants is often based on Hollywood films and television shows. As with music and literature, miracles are possible on screen; Cesar and Eugenio see the Mambo Kings resurrected and preserved on the rerun of the *I Love Lucy* show. Desi Arnaz and Lucille Ball appear as characters in the novel's fictional world.

Lives are re-created, most of all, through the willful exercise of memory and imagination. In the Hotel Splendour, Cesar relives the glories of the past and the complex relationships with family, friends, women, and age. His encounters with ghosts since Nestor's death provide touches of Magical Realism, denoting the Afro-Cuban influence in his childhood. Sad memories of the abusive father are compensated with images of the loving, religious mother, and caring black women involved with magic. Discrimination is depicted in Cuba and the United States. The prejudiced father is proud to be a white "gallego" from Spain. In the United States, although the brothers have light skin, their Latin look and Spanish language make them "Spics," and black musicians are segregated.

Cesar inherits the father's macho, sexist attitude toward women, acting like a flamboyant Latin lover, ending up with regrets and fears of lifelong loneliness without love. Nestor fears that he could never be a "real macho in the kingdom of machos" and yet, while he adores the mythic Maria, he mistreats his wife, Delores, trying to stop her from going to college. Eugenio inherits his family's melancholia; finally, remembering his father and uncle, he dreams of hearts liberated from pain, reaching "toward the sky, floating away."

Hijuelos' novel represents the Cuban American literary expression. Cuba is experienced through the nostalgic remembrance of immigrants from the island. The younger generation, born in the United States, re-creates the memories, depicting the Cuban culture and its influence in the United States.

Ludmila Kapschutschenko-Schmitt

Bibliography:

Foster, David William, comp. *Handbook of Latin American Literature.* 2d ed. New York: Garland, 1992. The section on Cuban Americans discusses Hijuelos' novel as a text inspired and guided by music, which becomes "the center of the narrative," recalling the influential times in Latin music. Considers the dynamics of the exile experience as a major aspect of the work.

Kanellos, Nicolás. *"The Mambo Kings Play Songs of Love."* Review of *The Mambo Kings Play Songs of Love,* by Oscar Hijuelos. *The Americas Review* 18 (Spring, 1990): 113-114. Praises Hijuelos as an intellectual whose research-based novel is a well-documented chronicle of a period when Hispanic and Afro-Caribbean music strongly influenced popular culture in the United States.

Perez Firmat, Gustavo. *Life on the Hyphen: The Cuban-American Way.* Austin: University of Texas Press, 1994. A scholarly volume of criticism focusing on selected Cuban cultural figures, such as Desi Arnaz and his television show "I Love Lucy." Hijuelos and his Pulitzer Prize-winning novel are also discussed.

Shorris, Earl. "Neither Here nor There." In *Latinos: A Biography of the People.* New York: W. W. Norton, 1992. Refers to the commercial and critical success of Hijuelos' novel, and discusses death as a major theme in the book.

MAN AND SUPERMAN
A Comedy and a Philosophy

Type of work: Drama
Author: George Bernard Shaw (1856-1950)
Type of plot: Play of ideas
Time of plot: c. 1900
Locale: England and Spain
First published: 1903; first performed, 1905

Principal characters:

> JACK TANNER, an eloquent anarchist and social philosopher
> ANN WHITEFIELD, an attractive young woman whose father has just died
> ROEBUCK RAMSDEN, her guardian
> OCTAVIUS ROBINSON, her suitor
> VIOLET ROBINSON, Octavius' sister
> HECTOR MALONE, her husband
> HENRY STRAKER, Jack's chauffeur
> MENDOZA, a bandit
> DON JUAN
> DOÑA ANA DE ULLOA, a Spanish noblewoman
> DON GONZALO, her father
> THE DEVIL

The Story:

Act I. Ramsden and Octavius discussed Ann, whom Octavius wanted to marry, and John Tanner, Octavius' friend and the author of *The Revolutionist's Handbook.* Tanner entered, protesting that he and Ramsden had been named Ann's guardians in her father's will. Ramsden did not wish to serve with Tanner and Tanner did not wish to serve at all, but Ann, entering with her mother, refused to dispense with either guardian. Tanner stated that Ann would do what she liked in any case. When they were left alone, Tanner and Octavius discussed Ann; Tanner predicted that she would eventually marry Octavius. Ann and Ramsden returned with the news that Octavius' unmarried sister, Violet, was pregnant. Ramsden and Octavious went off, leaving Tanner and Ann to engage in a long discussion about their relations when younger. Tanner asserted that he had grown up and no longer played romantic games; now he was concerned to break creeds and demolish ideals. When Violet came in, Tanner approved of her conduct, but Violet said that she was, in fact, married, but she refused to name the man.

Act II. While Henry Straker, the chauffeur, was working on Tanner's car, Octavius announced that he had proposed to Ann and had been put off. Ann came in and discussed why she had forbidden her sister to take a drive with Tanner. Tanner said he was off on a trip to Algiers and jestingly asked Ann if she wished to accompany him. To his horror, she accepted. Ramsden, Octavius, Mrs. Whitefield, and Hector Malone, a rich young American, entered, and Hector said that he would take Violet in his car. All except Hector left for a walk, whereupon Violet returned and kissed Hector. They had been keeping their marriage secret because Hector's rich father wanted him to marry a British aristocrat. After they left, Straker and Tanner came back discussing Ann; Straker insisted that it was Tanner whom Ann was pursuing. At that, Tanner panicked and ordered Straker to make ready to set off on a trip to North Africa.

Act III. In the Sierra Nevada mountains of southern Spain, a group of brigands led by Mendoza captured Straker and Tanner for ransom. Mendoza revealed that he was a former waiter at the Savoy Hotel and hopelessly in love with Louisa, who turned out to be Straker's sister. Tanner tried to talk Mendoza out of his obsession with Louisa. While they slept, Don Juan and the Old Woman appeared in Hell. The woman, who had just died and protested that she did not belong there, turned into a young Doña Ana, a former beloved of Don Juan. She looked much like Ann Whitefield. The Commander, Doña Ana's father, who had once been slain by Don Juan, appeared on a visit from Heaven, after which the Devil appeared. The Commander, who resembled Roebuck Ramsden, wanted to live in Hell because Heaven was so dull. The Devil, the Commander, and Don Juan explained at length to Doña Ana the true nature of Heaven and Hell. Hell was the home of the unreal and of the seekers for happiness, a place of playing and pretending; Heaven was a place of contemplation, where lived the masters of reality, helping the struggle of the Life Force upward. Then followed a long discussion of the Life Force and of its sidetracks in life on earth. Don Juan left for Heaven. The Commander went off with the Devil and mentioned Nietzsche's Superman. Doña Ana asked where she could find the Superman; the Devil said he had not been created yet. Doña Ana was left on a darkening stage, crying out for a father for the Superman. As the scene returned to the Sierras, Ann, Hector, Ramsden, Violet, and Octavius appeared, accompanied by soldiers; the brigands were captured but Tanner saved them from arrest by claiming that they were his escort.

Act IV. In the garden of a villa in Granada, Violet and Hector's father, who had intercepted a note from Violet to Hector, discussed Hector; Malone threatened to disinherit Hector if he married Violet, and when Hector entered, they quarreled. When the fact that Violet and Hector were already married become known, Hector's father capitulated. Ann told Octavius that she could not live up to his ideal of her and that her mother wanted her to marry Tanner. Mrs. Whitefield told Tanner that she had not influenced Ann but did think it would be a good idea because Tanner could handle Ann. When Tanner and Ann were left alone, Tanner protested that he did not want to marry Ann but that everyone else seemed to take it for granted that he would. The Life Force urged Tanner on, and he took Ann, who fainted, in his arms. Everyone returned to find that Tanner had yielded.

"The Story" by Gordon N. Bergquist

Critical Evaluation:

Frequently the subtitles of George Bernard Shaw's plays are just as informative and clever as the prefaces. Certainly they are always more to the point. Such is the case with *Heartbreak House* (1913-1919), which is subtitled *A Fantasia in the Russian Manner on English Themes*; *Fanny's First Play, an Easy Play for a Little Theatre* (1911); and *In Good King Charles's Golden Days, A True History That Never Happened* (1939). So, too, with *Man and Superman*, which is subtitled simply but significantly *A Comedy and a Philosophy*. For *Man and Superman*, though it was written early in Shaw's career, represents the culmination of Shaw's theory that the drama is but a device for getting the public to listen to philosophy—social philosophy, political philosophy, economic philosophy, or Shavian philosophy. With the possible exception of *Back to Methuselah* (1921), *Man and Superman* is Shaw's most philosophical play.

In its simplest terms, the philosophical meaning of the play is that in the war between the sexes, woman always emerges conqueror (even if man, her antagonist, is a superman) and that in a battle between instinct and intelligence, instinct always wins. To develop this theme, Shaw claimed to have written a philosophical interpretation of the Don Juan story, which means that

Don Juan is reincarnated as a Shavian hero in England at the turn of the century. The closest resemblance between Shaw's hero and the libertine celebrated in music and literature lies in their names: John Tanner, Don Juan Tenorio. Any other similarity is purely coincidental, for Shaw transformed literature's most notorious libertine into a man of moral passion, a Nietz-schean superman who lives a life of pure reason in defiance of the traditions of organized society. As a Shavian hero, Tanner is impeccably moral, even chaste. The philosophical meaning of the play arises from the fact that Tanner, representing the good man, is unsuccessful in defending his chastity. Pitted against a scheming female who embodies the sexual, maternal drive, Tanner is forced to surrender his control of sexual instinct. He capitulates and marries. In effect, he commits moral suicide by succumbing to conventionality.

On one level, this theme is worked out in a contrived, almost trivial but nevertheless hilarious plot. On another, more esoteric, level, the philosophical implications of the theme are devel-oped. Tanner has a dream—a play within the play—which turns out to be no less than a Platonic dialogue: "Don Juan in Hell." In this scene, four of the principals are reembodied as historical or mythical personages and are universalized as moral forces. Tanner appears as Don Juan, the man of moral passion; Ann, as Doña Ana de Ulloa, the eternal maternal female; Ramsden, as Don Gonzalo, the man of pleasure; and Mendoza (leader of the bandits), as the Devil. These four engage in a debate that Don Juan, speaking for Shaw, monopolizes with a series of lengthy monologues. Herein the theme of the play is recapitulated in abstract but certain terms. The subject is Man. The end of man, Don Juan argues, is the cultivation of intellect, for only by exercising it dispassionately can man discover his purpose, and discovering it, fulfill it. Therefore, the good man, the man of moral passion, will eschew anything that subverts the life of reason. Woman, however, will not be eschewed, and it is woman, with her relentless desire to propagate, and marriage, the instrument by which she domesticates, that undermine man. If man surrenders to woman, he is doomed.

The conclusion of the play is in that sense a gloomy one. By marrying Ann, Tanner admits that woman, bolstered by the "Life Force," is bound to triumph; that man, even superman, is bound to abandon the pursuit of his own goal to serve woman in her goal of perpetuating the race. Despite the ending and the verbose dream play, the prevailing tone of the play is comic and light. Above all, the drama, despite its philosophy, is eminently playable, principally because Shaw succeeded in making his characters gloriously human and therefore funny. Tanner, for example, is intensely moral, but he is fallible, even a bit ridiculous, and Ann delights in puncturing his eloquent utterances with the charge of political aspiration. Ann herself is as engaging a heroine as any in Shaw's plays. An incorrigible liar, an inveterate hypocrite, she is nevertheless thoroughly charming.

The minor characters were obviously invented to fit into the thematic framework of the drama, but they too contribute to the fun. Both Ramsden and Mrs. Whitefield represent the authority of the old order that Tanner is trying to overthrow; both, however, have distinctly comic personalities. Octavius, who believes that a man's duty lies in protecting the weaker sex, serves primarily as a foil to Tanner and provides many laughs as a lovesick youth. Mendoza, the bandit, Straker, the impudent chauffeur, and Malone, the senile American millionaire, figure in Shaw's design and provide a balance to the underlying seriousness of that design.

Considered as a whole, with the "Epistle Dedicatory," which serves as a preface, and "The Revolutionary's Handbook," which is an appendix of sorts, *Man and Superman* is one of Shaw's most important plays. It is neither Shaw's masterpiece nor his best play, being too obviously a piece of propaganda, but it is central to Shaw's philosophy, and philosophy is always central to Shaw's plays.

Bibliography:
Crompton, Louis. "*Man and Superman*." In *Shaw the Dramatist*. Lincoln: University of Nebraska Press, 1969. Discusses the play's social, philosophical, and historical background. A clear presentation of Shaw's ideas and their sources in the nineteenth century intellectual tradition.

Holroyd, Michael. *Bernard Shaw*. 3 vols. New York: Random House, 1988-1991. In the first two volumes of this detailed and indispensable biography—*The Search for Love* and *The Pursuit of Power*—Holroyd emphasizes Shaw's musical structure in the play and shows how Shaw inverts popular conventions as part of his attack on conventional morals.

Nethercot, Arthur H. *Men and Supermen: The Shavian Portrait Gallery*. 2d ed. New York: Benjamin Blom, 1954. Elaborate treatment of Shaw's ideas on the superman. Discusses *Man and Superman* and its underlying philosophy and relates the work to a number of other plays.

Silver, Arnold. "*Man and Superman*: Erecting a Creed." In *Bernard Shaw: The Darker Side*. Stanford, Calif.: Stanford University Press, 1982. Starts with the premise that the play is a fairly standard romantic comedy and relates it to Shaw's courtship of Charlotte Payne-Townshend at the time he was writing the play.

Wisenthal, J. L. "*Man and Superman*." In *The Marriage of Contraries: Bernard Shaw's Middle Plays*. Cambridge, Mass.: Harvard University Press, 1974. Discusses how Shaw presents and ultimately unifies the varying view and philosophies represented by the play's characters.

A MAN FOR ALL SEASONS

Type of work: Drama
Author: Robert Bolt (1924-1995)
Type of plot: Historical
Time of plot: 1530-1535
Locale: London and environs
First performed: 1954, as a radio play; first published, 1960

Principal characters:
> THE COMMON MAN, part narrator, part character in the play
> SIR THOMAS MORE, scholar and statesman
> LADY ALICE MORE, his wife
> MARGARET MORE, Sir Thomas' daughter
> RICHARD RICH, an ambitious young man, an acquaintance of More
> DUKE OF NORFOLK, a friend of More
> CARDINAL WOLSEY, lord chancellor of England
> THOMAS CROMWELL, Wolsey's unscrupulous secretary
> SIGNOR CHAPUYS, the Spanish ambassador
> HENRY VIII, king of England

The Story:

Richard Rich, eager to find employment at court, came to the manor of his acquaintance, Sir Thomas More, to request aid. When Sir Thomas warned Rich of the bribes and other temptations of court, and offered to help Rich find a position as a teacher, Rich was deeply disappointed. More gave Rich a silver cup that had been sent to More as an attempted bribe. As they were talking, the Duke of Norfolk entered with Lady Alice and Lady Margaret More, and the Duke surprised the gathering by announcing that Thomas Cromwell had become secretary to Cardinal Wolsey. At that moment, a message arrived from the cardinal, summoning More to him, although it was late at night.

When More arrived at the cardinal's chambers, Wolsey rebuked him for having opposed him in council that day. The two men then discussed the dynastic situation. King Henry desperately desired a son to continue the Tudor line, but his wife, Catherine, was barren, and the pope refused to grant a dispensation so that Henry could divorce Catherine to marry again. More was dismissed by the cardinal to return home by boat after they had taken opposing views about what Henry VIII should do.

When More returned, he found William Roper had arrived early in the morning to visit Margaret and ask Sir Thomas for his daughter's hand in marriage. Sir Thomas replied that the answer would be no so long as Roper remained a heretic—that is, a Lutheran. After Roper left, Sir Thomas refused to discuss the political situation with his wife and daughter, except to warn them that times were dangerous and they should be careful.

The Common Man informed the audience that, upon Wolsey's death, Sir Thomas More was appointed lord chancellor. The Spanish ambassador and Cromwell tried to obtain information from Sir Thomas' steward; the man took their bribes, but he evaded giving them any real information.

The king made a visit to Sir Thomas' house and, drawing Thomas aside, asked for his help in securing the divorce from Catherine. The king was reproachful when Thomas said that he could not renounce his obligations to the church. Although Henry expressed his respect for Sir Thomas' conscience, he was clearly disappointed. After the king's departure, William Roper and Richard Rich entered; Roper had returned to belief in the Catholic church and expressed some potentially dangerous opinions regarding the divorce. Rich informed More that Cromwell and others had been after Rich for incriminating evidence against Sir Thomas.

Cromwell and Rich met at a room in a pub, and Cromwell offered Rich the position of collector of revenues for York in return for help in proving a case of bribery against Sir Thomas More. Rich responded by giving information about the cup More had presented him earlier. After the Common Man noted that some two years had passed, More and Roper discussed the momentous changes that had taken place. The king had been declared supreme head of the church in England, but Sir Thomas had found a legal loophole that allowed him safety. More was interrogated by Chapuys, the Spanish ambassador, as to what More would do if the king forced a more definite break with the Catholic church. Roper and the Duke of Norfolk entered with word that the break had indeed taken place. More, with the help of his daughter Margaret, removed the chain of office and handed it to Norfolk. When Norfolk left, More tried to explain to his wife and daughter that his continued silence on the issue was their only hope of safety. Norfolk and Cromwell discussed the situation, and Cromwell explained to the Duke that because of More's reputation for honesty and intelligence, it was necessary that he openly declare his support of the break with Rome. Cromwell announced that he had proof that More had accepted bribes and that this pressure could be used against him. Rich and the woman who had tried to bribe More entered and Norfolk, contemptuous, dismissed the evidence. Cromwell and Rich concluded they must have better evidence against Sir Thomas.

Chapuys came to visit Sir Thomas More with a secret letter from the king of Spain, expressing admiration for the stand More had taken on the matter of the divorce. Sir Thomas pointed out that he had taken no stand and refused to take the letter. After Chapuys left, More again explained to his wife and daughter that in his silence lay their only security.

Cromwell had More brought before him, with Rich as a secretary to record their meeting. Cromwell tried to trip up More on several points, including that More had written a book in defense of Catholic doctrine now repudiated by the king. When More disproved this point and still refused to yield, Cromwell read a short note from the king accusing More of ingratitude and being traitorous as a subject. Then, More was dismissed. On his way home, More encountered Norfolk, and deliberately provoked a quarrel to protect his friend.

When More refused to swear the oath to the Act of Succession passed by Parliament, he was imprisoned, where he was questioned under difficult conditions repeatedly. He was visited by his wife and daughter and learned that Margaret had promised to try to convince him to take the oath. He refused and his wife told him of the hard times the household was suffering, but still More held fast.

More was brought to trial on the charge of high treason. Through wit and logic, he refuted the charges made against him by Cromwell. Richard Rich perjured himself by claiming that More had denied Parliament's authority to declare the king to be the head of the church. More realized his ordeal was over, his battle lost, and he finally broke his silence and affirmed his belief that the laws of man could not supersede the Law of God. Found guilty of treason, he was beheaded.

Critical Evaluation:

A Man for All Seasons (first presented as a stage play in 1960) functions on three separate, related levels. It is first a historical drama which follows, rather closely, the story of Sir Thomas

More's fatal collision of wills with his monarch, Henry VIII of England. The piece is also a representation, almost an allegory, of a struggle between two ways of looking at the world, between a secular and a religious view of life. Finally, it is a play about itself: The Common Man frequently comments, analyzes, and considers the actions that have taken place and that are about to occur; his musings become a play within a play.

Historically, the play remains fairly scrupulously within the boundaries of known facts. The characters, with the exception of the Common Man and a few minor figures, are taken from the historical record. Their actions, and even many of their words, have been adapted by Robert Bolt from contemporary accounts of the period. Where Bolt invents dialogue—as, for example, in conversations between More and his wife or daughter—Bolt has taken special care to maintain the sprightly, witty, yet serious tone unique to the England of the period. England at that time was poised between the Middle Ages and the Renaissance.

The tension between the two periods is revealed within the characters themselves. Sir Thomas More, for example, is a man of learning, representative of the rebirth of classical letters and the birth of experimental science. At the same time, he is a profoundly pious and quite orthodox Catholic, unwilling and perhaps unable to surrender or even compromise his beliefs, even to save his own life. He is easily the most complex and intricate figure in the play, and the character created by Bolt in his drama is one of the most finely drawn and fascinating in English theater.

More is not alone in his vivid complexity. The king (Henry VIII, although he is never referred to by that name during the play) is tugged in conflicting directions. Unlike More, however, the king is a more ambiguous figure. He may or may not be a devout and religious man, convinced that the pope is no more than the bishop of Rome and hence not the supreme ruler of the church. He is willing to grasp this thorny theological problem only when the pope does not grant a divorce. Henry may be read two ways, as principled or as unprincipled.

The conflicts in the play are acted out most strongly in the relationship between More and his monarch. Sir Thomas and the king clearly have an affinity and a bond between them, and the rupture caused by the divorce and the king's remarriage clearly pains both men. This seems historically plausible. Bolt skillfully develops the relationship between the two characters.

This relationship also supports a symbolic interpretation. Sir Thomas and the king, while they represent actual historical figures, are also metaphors. One is the loyal but independent subject and the other is the sometimes gracious but ultimately overbearing monarch. Their clash is not only a clash of wills but also of two differing political and moral views of the world. Is a citizen free to think as he or she will, or must a citizen follow the dictates of the state? Such a question is not restricted to monarchies; it is fully applicable in the modern world as well.

Other characters and relationships also are universal. The Duke of Norfolk, More's superior in feudal rank but his inferior in intellect and faith, bends to the king's will, and is ready to sign an oath of allegiance that he freely, even cheerfully, admits, contains elements that he does not fully understand. Norfolk, a friend of More—first presented in More's house, enjoying the conversation and company—is willing to adapt his conscience and actions to what he sees as political realities. Although the Duke is highly unlikely to have read Niccolò Machiavelli, he clearly understands the Florentine's precepts. The relationship between More and his wife, Lady Alice, is a representation of an actual marriage and a symbolic presentation of such a relationship. Lady Alice, who remains loyal to More to the end, is furious that he throws away all that makes life dear: his position, his income, and, finally, even his family for an ideal. In a sense, she is an innocent bystander caught in a deadly game. She cannot fathom it, so she must make simple fidelity her guide. Finally, there is the element of the play within the play. *A Man for All Seasons* is, in many ways, about itself. The Common Man, who takes a succession of roles, is both a narrator and a guide for the audience. He sets the stage and provides rapid exposition of unfolding events and transposition between scenes. His comments to the audience concern both the action on the stage and their larger, more philosophical meaning. Shrewd, skeptical, yet sympathetic, the Common Man is in many ways the most modern of the play's characters. He is respectful but largely indifferent to the religious concerns that obsess More, and his reaction to figures such as the powerful Thomas Cromwell is one of overt politeness that masks a practical realism.

These three strands of narrative realism, symbolic representation, and self-conscious presentation, together with the vivid portrayal of character and the brilliant, sparkling use of language, combine to make *A Man for All Seasons* a complex and insightful examination of an eternal human situation.

Michael Witkoski

Bibliography:
Garstenauer, Maria. *A Selective Study of English History Plays in the Period Between 1960 and 1977*. Salzburg, Austria: University of Salzburg Press, 1985. A concentrated and extremely thorough study that examines the play from a variety of views. Helpful for placing the drama into the context of its times.
Nightingale, Benedict. *A Reader's Guide to Fifty Modern British Plays*. New York: Barnes & Noble Books, 1982. A brief but informative view of the play, providing the beginning student with an excellent starting point.
Tynan, Kenneth. *A View of the English Stage, 1944-63*. London: Davis-Poynter, 1975. A highly personal, even idiosyncratic view of the play. Since the bulk of the essays in this volume were originally reviews, they provide a clue as to how the play was received during its debut.
Vinson, James, ed. *Contemporary Dramatists*. 3d ed. New York: St. Martin's Press, 1982. There is helpful discussion about *A Man for All Seasons* that places the drama within the scope of Bolt's career.

THE MAN OF FEELING

Type of work: Novel
Author: Henry Mackenzie (1745-1831)
Type of plot: Sentimental
Time of plot: Mid-eighteenth century
Locale: England
First published: 1771

Principal characters:
MR. HARLEY, a sensitive young Englishman
MISS WALTON, a wealthy heiress
EDWARDS, a farmer befriended by Harley
MISS ATKINS, a prostitute befriended by Harley
HARLEY'S AUNT

The Story:

One day in early September, a rural clergyman took a friend from town hunting with him. When they stopped to rest, the friend found some indecipherable initials carved on the bark of a tree. The curate said they were probably the work of a young man named Harley, a former resident of the parish. The clergyman added that he had a manuscript in his possession that told the greater part of Harley's story; he had thought the work of no great value and had used the papers for wadding in his gun. The manuscript had been found among the possessions of a former parishioner, Harley's friend. Upon request, the clergyman gave the bundle of disconnected papers to his friend, who after his return to town pieced together the melancholy story that the rambling narrative unfolded.

Mr. Harley, an orphan reared by a maiden aunt, was descended from a good family among the country gentry in England. Passing years had decreased the family's fortunes, and by the time he reached manhood he had only a very modest income from the small remaining estate. The young man, who was extremely virtuous, did not feel that he needed any more money, but his friends insisted that with very little trouble, he could secure the use of some adjoining lands belonging to the Crown. At his friends' insistence and because he was very much in love with Miss Walton, an heiress, Harley set out for London to attempt to get a lease to the lands, which would give him a handsome increase to his fortunes in return for a low rental fee.

Once in London, Harley had several amazing adventures, partly because he was willing to believe all people good until he found them bad, and partly because he wished to help anyone who needed aid. These adventures took place over several weeks, for Harley found that the baronet who was to help him in his suit for the lease was not an easy man to see. On the occasion of one visit to see the baronet, Harley met someone who pretended to be a man about town. Harley wished to know more about London and spent the evening with the young man, only to learn that the fellow was a former footman who served as a pander for wealthy men.

A short time later, an unnamed friend invited Harley to accompany a party to the asylum at Bedlam. There Harley was much affected by the insane, particularly by a young woman who had gone mad after her lover's death; she touched Harley's heart when she cried out that he resembled her dead lover. As the party left the young lady, a gentleman offered to tell Harley about some of the inmates. Harley assented, only to find within a few minutes that his guide was himself a madman who imagined himself to be an Oriental potentate.

A few evenings later, Harley went for a walk through the park. While there, he met an elderly gentleman who invited him to partake of a glass of cider at a nearby public house. Impressed by the gentleman's attitude of benevolence to a beggar, Harley agreed. Once in the house, Harley was invited to take a hand in a friendly card game, during which the old gentleman and an accomplice swindled the good-hearted Harley out of a substantial sum of money. Leaving the place and still unaware of the swindle, Harley was accosted by a prostitute who begged him for something to eat and drink. Harley hated to see another human in distress and left himself open to severe criticism by taking the girl, a Miss Atkins, to a brothel where she could get some food. When she poured out a tale of seduction to him, he agreed to help her if he could and promised to see her the following day.

The next morning, he went to see Miss Atkins. She told him she wanted only to return to her father, a retired army officer. Just as she had finished telling her story, her father appeared. He misjudged the scene and almost became violent toward Harley and his daughter. A fainting spell on the part of Miss Atkins gave Harley a chance to explain everything to the father, who then forgave his daughter and took her back.

Harley's London adventures were cut short by a notice from the baronet that someone else had been granted the crown lands that Harley sought. The successful petitioner turned out to be the pander Harley had met at the baronet's house. Discouraged, Harley took a coach to return home.

The coach took Harley to within a day's walk of his home. From there, the young man set out for his house on foot rather than wait for a public conveyance. On the way, he met an elderly soldier, who turned out to be a farmer named Edwards, whom Harley had known as a child. Edwards explained to Harley why he was attired as he was. The enclosure acts by Parliament had given Edwards' landlord an excuse to move the farmer and his family from a good farm to a poor one. Bad crops had further decreased the man's ability to make a livelihood, and eventually he and his married son had been forced to become tenants on a tiny, depleted bit of ground. A press gang had seized Edwards' son as well. The only way to secure the younger man's release had been for Edwards himself, an old man, to enter the service in his son's place, after buying off the officials with the little money he had left.

While a soldier in the East Indies, Edwards had befriended an aged Hindu, who made him a present of gold. Upon his release from the service, Edwards had returned to England and was now on his way to visit his son. When he and Harley arrived in Edwards' old neighborhood, they found that his run of disastrous luck had not ended, for his son and daughter-in-law had died, leaving two small children. Harley promised the old man a farm on his own estates, and, taking the two orphans with them, Harley and Edwards continued their journey.

Home once more, Harley saw the old gentleman comfortably established on a small farm. Unhappiness, however, soon overtook Harley. Miss Walton, with whom he was very much in love, was affianced by her father to a rich man. Although he had never declared his love to Miss Walton or anyone else, Harley was heartbroken. He took to his bed with a severe illness. After many weeks of illness, the doctors and his friends feared for his life. Miss Walton heard of his illness and came to visit him, hoping to cheer up the young man for whom she had a great deal of esteem—more, indeed, than anyone had ever guessed.

A tearful and touching scene occurred when Miss Walton appeared at Harley's sickbed. Harley realized that he was near death and told Miss Walton of his love for her. Although she was promised to another, she told of her love for him; she then fainted, and he died. He was buried near his mother, as he had once told his aunt he wished to be. Miss Walton remained single, preferring not to marry after Harley's death. For many years, she was often seen walking or reading near the place where Harley's house had stood.

Critical Evaluation:

In 1745, the year Henry Mackenzie was born, Scotland, uneasily united with England since 1707, was convulsed by an uprising of Highland peasants, who were being driven off the land by English "lairds," much as carpetbaggers attempted to exploit defeated Southerners in America after the Civil War. The clansmen rallied behind Bonnie Prince Charlie (the twenty-five-year-old Charles Edward Stuart) who attempted to instate his father as king of Scotland and England. All Stuart hopes were crushed by defeat at the famous Battle of Culloden Moor, on April 16, 1746. Following the battle, Bonnie Prince Charlie escaped in a female disguise. He ended up in France, and Scotland was forced to endure years of English oppression. The Scots were forbidden to wear the tartan, for example, until 1782.

Though it had become apparent to the Scots that attempts to oppose the English through military force would be futile, their unquenched national pride manifested itself in a remarkable efflorescence of cultural activity. Among prominent contributors to what is sometimes called the Scottish Enlightenment were the chemist Joseph Black; his close friend, the geologist James Hutton; Hutton's followers, John Playfair and James Hall; the economist Adam Smith; the historian William Robertson; the philosopher Adam Ferguson; and the portrait painter who preserved likenesses of them all, Henry Raeburn.

Scottish artists distinguished themselves in their fields, but writers were slow to appear on the scene, primarily because Scottish authors hesitated to write in their own language and did not always feel at home in London English. Philosophers, a term that then included scientists, were more comfortable with English, and by the later eighteenth century, philosophers had been followed by a remarkable group of literary lawyers, who brought to writing the same critical skills that their profession required.

Henry Mackenzie was one such lawyer. When England and Scotland united in 1707, it was stipulated that the Scots would retain their own church (Presbyterian, rather than Anglican) and their own legal system. No group, therefore, remained more aware of the uniqueness of Scottish tradition than did its lawyers. Throughout most of his life, Mackenzie was the most prominent arbiter of literary opinion in Edinburgh. He championed the dialect poetry of Robert Burns, for example, and he strongly encouraged the early literary efforts of Walter Scott, also a lawyer, who dedicated his first novel, *Waverley* (1814), to Mackenzie. Highly regarded as a critic, and an editor, a poet, and a playwright, Mackenzie wrote many essays for literary periodicals, was active in the Highland Society, and oversaw the multidisciplinary *Transactions* of the Royal Society of Edinburgh when they appeared in 1785. A hardheaded, practical opportunist, he had nothing in common with the hero of his most famous book.

The Man of Feeling, a short and fragmentary novel of fewer than one hundred pages, is now the work for which Mackenzie is best remembered. Though often cited as the quintessential sentimental novel, and seemingly a reflection of its times, *The Man of Feeling* remained in manuscript for several years; when it was finally published, however, anonymously, it became extremely popular. Mackenzie went on to write two more novels. Of these, *The Man of the World* (1773) was intended to be a contrastive sequel, its title character, appropriately named Sindall, being as iniquitous as Harley is good. In Mackenzie's third novel, *Julia de Roubigné* (1777), which was strongly influenced by Mackenzie's theatrical aspirations, he attempted to move from melodrama into genuine tragedy; this novel is often considered his best work. It is clearly indebted to a novel with a similar title, *The New Héloïse* (1761), by Jean-Jacques Rousseau.

As a novelist, Mackenzie belongs to an intermediate period in the history of the form. His three works come after the contributions of Samuel Richardson, Henry Fielding, and Tobias

Smollett earlier in the eighteenth century but before the advent of Jane Austen and Walter Scott early in the nineteenth century. He may be a lesser figure than any of these, but he is significant, nevertheless. Mackenzie's experimentation with the form of the novel owed something to Lawrence Sterne's *The Life and Opinions of Tristram Shandy, Gent.* (1759-1767), which is, in addition to its other qualities, an outrageous parody of the structural perfection achieved by Fielding. The tone of *The Man of Feeling*, however, was different from either Sterne or Fielding, both of whom believed in ironic detachment. Sterne also favored a playfulness, and sometimes a naughtiness, entirely foreign to Mackenzie.

Moral seriousness was fundamental to Presbyterianism and eighteenth century Scotland. Indeed, moral seriousness sometimes conflicted with the more general aims of the Enlightenment, a multinational intellectual movement in eighteenth century Europe (the movement later extended to America) that emphasized dispassionate reason rather than emotion, philosophy rather than elaborate religion. Though Scotland contributed a series of distinguished minds to the intellectual history of the eighteenth century, and outstanding skeptical philosophers like David Hume, neither reason nor skeptical philosophy sufficiently assuaged the hunger of its people for satisfying cultural expression.

In both England and Scotland, therefore, it became increasingly necessary to supplant coldhearted logic that too often became callous with deeply felt sympathy for the less fortunate, including such traditional underdogs as the poor, the disgraced, the dispossessed, the unlucky, and the insane. Enlightenment reasoning, which included theological reasoning, had ignored or ridiculed all these unfortunates. Later writers, such as William Wordsworth during the Romantic period, would take these people to heart and insist on the right of all persons—including slaves, criminals, and lunatics—to the prerequisites of humanity. Eventually, these appeals to a moral sense in humankind that transcends logic eventually led to legislative reform, as the indifference of the eighteenth century turned into the humanitarianism of the nineteenth.

"Critical Evaluation" by Dennis R. Dean

Bibliography:
Baker, Ernest A. *The History of the English Novel.* Vol. 5 in *The Novel of Sentiment and the Gothic Romance.* London: H. F. & G. Witherby, 1934. Baker's ten-volume history of the novel is now dated in some of its opinions, but it remains unsurpassed in its scope and is still very helpful on Mackenzie.
Crane, R. S. "Suggestions Toward a Genealogy of *The Man of Feeling.*" *English Literary History* 1, no. 3 (1934): 205-230. This famous essay, often reprinted, explains the intellectual origins of the eighteenth century's belief in the "moral sense."
Foster, James R. *History of the Pre-Romantic Novel in England.* New York: Modern Language Association of America, 1949. An important study that relates "sensibility" to deism, discusses examples from both French and English literature, and comments usefully on all three of Mackenzie's novels.
Thompson, Harold W., ed. *The Anecdotes and Egotisms of Henry Mackenzie, 1745-1831.* London: Oxford University Press, 1927. A very useful collection of autobiographical scraps.
_____. *A Scottish Man of Feeling.* London: Oxford University Press, 1931. The standard biography of Mackenzie. Presents reliable information about his life, but must be supplemented by Mackenzie's more recently published *Letters to Elizabeth Ross of Kilravock* (1967).

THE MAN OF MODE
Or, Sir Fopling Flutter

Type of work: Drama
Author: Sir George Etherege (1635?-1691)
Type of plot: Comedy of manners
Time of plot: 1670's
Locale: London
First performed: 1676; first published, 1676

> *Principal characters:*
> DORIMANT, a young man about town
> LADY LOVEIT, Dorimant's mistress
> BELLINDA, a young woman in love with Dorimant
> YOUNG BELLAIR, Dorimant's friend
> OLD BELLAIR, young Bellair's father
> EMILIA, a young woman in love with young Bellair
> HARRIET WOODVILL, a young countrywoman of fortune
> who loves Dorimant
> SIR FOPLING FLUTTER, a dandy

The Story:

One morning, Dorimant was lounging in his room when an orange-woman made her appearance. In the course of buying some fruit, Dorimant, who had a remarkable reputation as a lover, heard that a young woman of quality and fortune from the country had fallen in love with him at sight, despite her mother's attempts to keep her daughter away from thoughts of loving any heartless man of the fashionable world. Although he was in the process of ending an affair with Lady Loveit and beginning a new one with Bellinda, Dorimant was interested. Shortly afterward he received his friend Bellair, a fop who was very much in love with a young woman named Emilia and wished to marry her instead of the wealthy bride his father had picked out for him. The father's choice was Harriet, the young woman who had been so taken with Dorimant.

To complicate matters for young Bellair, his father had arrived in town to hasten the marriage. Lodging in the same house with Emilia and unaware of his son's affection for her, the old gentleman had fallen in love with her and wished to make her his own bride. Young Bellair, with the help of his aunt, Lady Townley, hoped to win his father's consent to marrying Emilia.

Meanwhile, Lady Loveit was beside herself at the neglect she suffered at the hands of her lover. She complained bitterly to Bellinda, not knowing that it was Bellinda who had won the recent attentions of Dorimant and was about to become his mistress. True to his promise to Bellinda, Dorimant came that afternoon and notified Lady Loveit that he was finished with her. His action frightened Bellinda, although the deed had been done at her request.

At Lady Woodvill's lodgings that day, the lady herself was preparing Harriet to meet young Bellair, for Harriet's mother was as anxious for the match as his father was. That Harriet did not wish to marry him made little difference to the mother. When the two young people met, they quickly confided their dislike of the match to each other. Then they proceeded to play a mock love scene for the benefit of the parents, to throw them off the track.

3911

That same afternoon, Bellinda and Dorimant met at the home of Lady Townley. Dorimant made Bellinda promise to have Lady Loveit walk on the Mall that evening so that Dorimant could confront her with Sir Fopling Flutter, a fool of a fop, and accuse her of being unfaithful. As they spoke, Sir Fopling Flutter entered the company and proceeded to demonstrate what a fool he was by the oddities and fooleries of his dress, deportment, and speech.

That evening, young Bellair and Harriet went walking on the Mall. There they met Dorimant, who was forced to leave when Harriet's mother appeared. Lady Loveit tried to make Dorimant jealous by flirting, but only succeeded in bringing Dorimant's reproaches on her head.

Later that same night there was a party at Lady Townley's house. Dorimant was one of the group, under the alias of Courtage, so that Harriet's mother would not realize that he was the gallant who was trying to woo her daughter. Under his false name, Dorimant succeeded in ingratiating himself with the mother. Harriet, trying to hide her love and admiration from him, showed that her wit was as sharp as Dorimant's. Sir Fopling Flutter joined the party late and showed himself to be even more of a fool than previously.

By the time the party broke up, it was five o'clock in the morning. Dorimant had to hurry home in order to keep a rendezvous he had made with Bellinda, who had promised to spend part of the night with him in his rooms. In the morning, as she was ready to leave, she was almost discovered there by several of Dorimant's friends. Bellinda escaped by going down the back stairs and stepping into a sedan chair. Her danger was not past, however, for the carriers, accustomed to taking Lady Loveit from Dorimant's house, took Bellinda to the former's lodging. Lady Loveit, still awake, saw Bellinda step from the chair. Only quick wit on the part of Bellinda, who told the men to say they had picked her up elsewhere, prevented her assignation with Dorimant from being known to Lady Loveit, who did not suspect that Bellinda was her rival.

A few minutes afterward, Dorimant arrived. He began berating Lady Loveit in a high-handed fashion, only to be embarrassed when Bellinda appeared from an adjoining room. He was so discomfited that he could only mutter excuses and leave the house.

Early that morning, at Lady Townley's house, young Bellair and Emilia were married, the bridegroom taking that drastic step before his father could force him to marry Harriet. As the ceremony was ending, Lady Woodvill, Harriet, old Bellair, and an attorney arrived. They had come to meet with young Bellair and to sign the marriage contract between the two families. Not knowing what to do, Lady Townley temporarily hid the clergyman in a closet. In the confusion of the moment, Emilia asked Harriet if she was in love with Dorimant. Harriet refused still to admit that she was, saying that she only hated to think of leaving the pleasures of the town to be made a prisoner in the country. At that point, while the others were off in another room to go over the terms of the marriage contract, Dorimant himself arrived. When he confessed his love to Harriet, she admitted that she was in love with him.

The others then returned. Old Bellair, anxious to have the marriage celebrated, called for a parson. The clergyman, released from the closet, declared that he had already performed one ceremony when he married young Bellair to Emilia. Old Bellair was thunderstruck. Just then Lady Loveit and Bellinda arrived in pursuit of Dorimant. He made his excuses to Lady Loveit by telling her that he intended to marry Harriet and thus improve his fortunes. Lady Loveit, who knew the value of money, admitted that under the circumstances she could only wish him well. Bellinda was grateful because his excuse concealed her affair with him and kept her honor intact. Lady Woodvill, overhearing the conversation, was furious with Dorimant for capturing Harriet's heart, but when she learned that his intentions were honorable and that he was the same Courtage whom she had admired the evening before, she was mollified to the extent of inviting him to visit the Woodvill estate in Hampshire.

Old Bellair, not to be outdone in graciousness, gave his blessing to his son, who had gone against his will in marrying Emilia. The only person completely dismayed was Lady Loveit, who vowed that she would never again trust a man or go out in society.

Critical Evaluation:

The Man of Mode is, along with William Wycherley's *The Country Wife* (1675) and William Congreve's *The Way of the World* (1700), one of the finest comedies of Restoration theater. It owes its critical acclaim to its etched-in-acid portrait of love rituals in contemporary London high society, the brilliance of its dialogue, and—surprisingly enough—the humanity of its characters.

All of the character types in Sir George's Etherege's last play are the stock-in-trade of Restoration comedy. Dorimant is the fashionably witty rake who enjoys juggling two or three affairs at the same time. In one of the running metaphors of the play, he holds passion in love to be merely a disease, fortunately only a temporary one. "Constancy at my years?" he asks Mrs. Loveit, ". . . you might as well expect the fruit of autumn ripens i' the spring." The heroine is, of course, beautiful, but more important, fully a match in wit for Dorimant. Her ability to discomfit him in their verbal battles is the main reason for his conceding to her the victory over his bachelorhood. Harriet has no intention of becoming one more in the long line of Dorimant's mistresses. Other conventional types include the Frenchified Sir Fopling Flutter, the standard by which all later stage fops were to be judged; the cast-off mistress, the hero's confidant, a couple of foolish older people, and a pair of lovers in the "high" plot, who set off, through their idealized love, the more earth-bound love of Dorimant and Harriet. Basing their relationship on a compromise between passion and social forms, Harriet tells Dorimant: "Though I wish you devout, I would not have you turn fanatic."

Earlier critics of Restoration comedy lamented the pernicious morality of such plays as *The Man of Mode*, which appeared to sanction, or at least accept, libertinism. More recent critics have seen such dramatists as Etherege striving to present an acceptable mean of behavior in matters of love. Dorimant, for instance, is neither as boorishly crude as the country gentleman old Bellair, nor as excessively fastidious about his dress and grooming as Sir Fopling, who finds entertainment in front of a mirror. Harriet, who maintains that "women ought to be no more fond of dressing than fools should be of talking," is similar to Dorimant in this respect. Both hero and heroine prefer to make do with a minimum of affectation and pretense, though complete honesty in love is seen to be either unrealistic in the case of young Bellair and Emilia, or unwise, in the case of Mrs. Loveit, who wears her anguished heart on her passionate sleeve. We may be apprehensive that Dorimant's love for Harriet may be no more permanent than any of his previous inamorata—and indeed, it may not be. What gives their future relationship at least a reasonable chance is their similarity in temperament and wit. Only with Harriet, a woman whose insight into his true nature is penetrating, does Dorimant speak with utter sincerity and feeling.

Audiences like the characters not because they recognize them as types, but because they recognize them as human beings. Dorimant, by all accounts, should be an unsympathetic character: He is callous and cynical in his treatment of people, and his wit may seem inadequate compensation for his larger defects of character. As Bellinda realizes, there is a point beyond which his brutal treatment of women stops being amusing and becomes ugly, even to those who profit by it. Dorimant is, however, just as vulnerable as his victims: His humiliations in the Mall and later, before his former and present mistresses, as well as his awkwardness before the incisive Harriet, reveal a vain man almost pathetically in need of "reputation"; that is, the reputation of being a dispassionate and consummate rake. Etherege's treatment of Mrs. Loveit is also multifaceted. On the one hand, the extravagance and violence of her passion make her a figure to be ridiculed. On the other, she is a figure of pathos. Her only crime, after all, is in having loved Dorimant too much. A careful reading of the play will reveal her not as a caricature but as a woman treated by the playwright with understanding, sympathy, and even dignity: "I would die to satisfy [your love]" she tells Dorimant, "I will not, to save you from a thousand racks, do a shameless thing to please your vanity." Such probing treatment of personal and social behavior, in a genre almost rigidly standardized in its conventions, is a major reason for the continued fascination the play continues to exert in later times.

Bibliography:

Holland, Norman N. *The First Modern Comedies: The Significance of Etherege, Wycherley, and Congreve*. Cambridge, Mass.: Harvard University Press, 1959. This masterful collection of essays underscores the conflict in *The Man of Mode* between personal fulfillment and social expectations. Holland contends that Etherege exposed false sentiments and pretentiousness as agents of hypocrisy.

Huseboe, Arthur R. *Sir George Etherege*. New York: Macmillan, 1987. Even though this is a literary biography, the author devotes nineteen pages and many more cross-references to *The Man of Mode*. Discusses character types and frames the discussion in the context of aristocratic manners and mores as defined by the court of Charles II. Carefully examines Etherege's use of heroic couplets, blank verse, and prose.

Powell, Jocelyn. "George Etherege and the Form of Comedy." In *Restoration Dramatists: A Collection of Critical Essays*, edited by Earl Miner. Englewood Cliffs, N.J.: Prentice-Hall, 1966. This wide-ranging essay links Etherege's realism to the physical action and narrative promise in Anton Chekhov's plays. Emphasizes dramatic technique and the naturalism of details.

Sharma, Ram Chandra. *Themes and Conventions in the Comedy of Manners*. New York: Asia House, 1965. Reinforces the significance of *The Man of Mode* as a groundwork for Restoration themes and patterns. Provides a systematic record of Etherege's career.

Underwood, Dale. *Etherege and the Seventeenth-Century Comedy of Manners*. New Haven, Conn.: Yale University Press, 1957. The author justifies the critical and historical importance of *The Man of Mode* as a masterpiece of English comedy. Highlights Etherege's distinction between nature and reason in terms of pre-Enlightenment idealism. Discusses the "comedy of values" motifs.

THE MAN WHO CAME TO DINNER

Type of work: Drama
Authors: George S. Kaufman (1889-1961) and Moss Hart (1904-1961)
Type of plot: Comedy
Time of plot: Christmas season, late 1930's
Locale: The home of Mr. and Mrs. Stanley in Mesalia, Ohio
First performed: 1939; first published, 1939

> *Principal characters:*
> SHERIDAN WHITESIDE, a radio pundit and bon vivant
> MAGGIE CUTLER, his secretary
> MISS PREEN, his nurse
> DR. BRADLEY, his local physician
> BERT JEFFERSON, a newspaper reporter
> ERNEST W. STANLEY, Whiteside's reluctant host
> DAISY STANLEY, his wife
> RICHARD, their son
> JUNE, their daughter
> LORRAINE SHELDON, an actress
> BEVERLY CARLTON, an actor
> BANJO, a comic actor

The Story:

Just before a Christmas in the late 1930's, Sheridan Whiteside, a noted radio personality, was invited to dinner at the home of Mr. and Mrs. Ernest W. Stanley in Mesalia, Ohio. After slipping on ice and claiming to have dislocated his hip, he became an intrusive and outrageously demanding houseguest. Since he was confined to a wheelchair, he immediately banished his hosts to the second floor and turned the first-floor living room and library into his personal rooms, threatening the none-too-gracious Mr. Stanley with a lawsuit to intimidate him.

An egotistical tyrant, Whiteside browbeat and manipulated everyone who came in range. He treated his nurse, Miss Preen, with caustic insult; on others, like Dr. Bradley, he used self-serving and dissembling flattery. Utterly selfish and shameless, he showed no concern for the feelings of others or any sense of the disruption he caused. At first, it did not seem as if his behavior could have any long-term consequences. Although he was rude to the Stanleys and their neighbors, his demands were manageable: that the Stanleys live on the second floor, keep the mornings quiet, and avoid using the telephone. The Stanleys felt they could put up with the crate of penguins, the cockroach city, and various other oddities delivered to Whiteside at their house. They could even tolerate the steady stream of his outlandish guests, which included inmates from Whiteside's favorite charity, the Crockfield Home, a halfway house for convicts.

As Christmas approached, however, Whiteside began to interfere in the personal lives of the others. Whether his motives in doing so were selfish or merely thoughtless, his interference could have serious and hurtful consequences. One of the first schemes he put in motion was an effort to seduce the Stanleys' servants, John and Sarah, into his service. A gourmand, Whiteside appreciated Sarah's cooking and thought that John, her husband, might be an acceptable butler. He ignored their loyalty to the Stanleys and cajoled and flattered them without a thought of his hosts. He also began to give pseudo-paternal advice to the Stanleys' older children, Richard and June. He encouraged young Richard to follow his dream of becoming a professional photojournalist by just hopping on a boat and steaming off to foreign ports. To June he suggested that she elope with her boyfriend, Sandy, an employee and labor organizer at her father's factory and a young man whom Mr. Stanley intensely disliked and had tried to fire. When, however, his assistant, Maggie Cutler, fell in love with Bert Jefferson, a local newspaper reporter and aspiring playwright, Whiteside's irresponsible, follow-your-star advice would have been inconvenient for him. Instead of trying to help her, Whiteside, unwilling to give Maggie up to anyone, selfishly plotted to undermine her plans. At first, he tried to convince Maggie that the affair was ridiculous, but when she proved stubborn, he was forced to resort to a deceitful scheme. Feigning interest in a new play Jefferson had written, he called the actress and notorious vamp Lorraine Sheldon, who was en route to America on the liner *Normandie* and asked her to come directly to Ohio. It was his plan to distract Jefferson by introducing him to Miss Sheldon as a collaborator and leading lady. Maggie soon realized Whiteside's true intention. After Lorraine arrived, Maggie arranged for Beverly Carlton, an actor and skilled mimic, to call Lorraine pretending to be Lord Bottomley (the English peer whom Lorraine had been hoping to ensnare as a husband) and propose marriage. Unfortunately for Maggie, Whiteside discovered the deception and convinced Lorraine that she had been duped.

Whiteside's scheme threatened to come apart from other complications, however. Dr. Bradley informed him that there was actually nothing wrong with him and that his X-ray had been mixed up with that of another patient. Since disclosure of that fact would have proved inconvenient, Whiteside claimed to be fascinated with the doctor's work-in-progress. Dr. Bradley was easily hoodwinked and entered a conspiracy of silence, bribed by Whiteside's insincere promise to work with him on his manuscript. Mr. Stanley, however, was more intractable. Increasingly outraged by Whiteside's interference in his family's affairs, Mr. Stanley threatened to evict Whiteside, lawsuit or no lawsuit and obtained a warrant and the service of two deputy sheriffs. At the last minute, Whiteside saved himself by using his knowledge that Stanley's mysterious sister was none other than Harriet Sedley, a woman who had murdered her parents with an ax.

On Christmas Day, having finally realized how serious were Maggie's feelings for Jefferson, and prompted by his zany friend Banjo, Whiteside allowed the more generous part of his character to triumph over his selfishness. He and Banjo conspired to get rid of Maggie's competition by trapping Lorraine inside one of Whiteside's bizarre gifts—an Egyptian mummy case. Banjo, assisted by the two deputies, then took her off to an airplane bound for Nova Scotia. That solved Maggie's problem. The Stanleys thought their problems were over, too, as Whiteside was in the process of leaving, but just as Whiteside stepped on the porch, he fell on the ice again and had to be carried back inside. He immediately bellowed for Miss Preen and threatened the Stanleys with a new lawsuit. Mr. Stanley threw his hands up in despair, and his wife sank to the floor in a dead faint.

Critical Evaluation:

George Kaufman and Moss Hart dedicated *The Man Who Came to Dinner* to their friend, the renowned drama critic and radio personality Alexander Woollcott, after whom they modeled the character of Sheridan Whiteside. He is a delightfully outrageous character, a comic parody of Woollcott's traits, especially his notorious gormandizing, cruel wit, and graceless behavior as a houseguest. With the exception of Maggie Cutler, Whiteside dominates everyone around him, using acerbic wit, saccharine cajolery, or threats as the situation seems to call for it. Since he is a massive egotist, he is so caught up in his own conceit as to be completely blind to the harm he can and does do.

The plot of the play is a well-worn one, that of the unwanted intruder who disrupts the normal life and peaceful equanimity of a household. The premise presents a tense situation fraught with comic possibilities that can be mined as long as the intruder remains the play's central figure and driver of the plot. Sheridan Whiteside is the master of comic bluster and an outrageous manipulator who has no qualms about riding roughshod over anyone who stands in his way.

It is hard to sympathize with Whiteside's victims, for the comedy is nonsensical farce, and most of his targets deserve at least some of the comic derision to which they are subjected. Mr. Stanley, for example, is so staid and proper that he is easily intimidated by legal threats. Daisy Stanley, his wife, is one of those society matrons who patronize the arts to bolster their own esteem and be able to crow over their friends. Dr. Bradley and Lorraine Sheldon deserve their treatment because they have an inflated sense of their own talents, Bradley as a writer and Sheldon as a serious actress.

The rapid pace of the play and the stream of oddball characters who flit on and off stage serve to mitigate any real concern the audience might feel for the victims. Only Maggie Cutler and Bert Jefferson, who refuse to be cowed or cajoled by Whiteside, can command much respect. Maggie deftly penetrates Whiteside's bluster, and she is, as he knows, his match. Paradoxically, this is the reason he values her. She is like a daughter to him, and even when he addresses her in insulting terms such as "repulsive" and "sex-ridden hag," his affection for her shapes the insults' subtext.

Most other people are mere toys to Whiteside, and many of them, like Banjo and Beverly Carlton, he values simply because they delight him by being unpredictable or clever. The impression of Whiteside as a rich, willful, spoiled child is reinforced by the physical debris that accumulates during the play as the Stanleys' first floor is turned into Whiteside's personal romper room. Throughout the comedy, gifts for Whiteside pour in from scores of real and fictitious celebrities. By the beginning of the second act, piles of gifts collect under an imposing Christmas tree, put there for Whiteside's exclusive amusement. In the last act, the comic proliferation of things and people includes a radio production crew that turn the Stanleys' living room into Whiteside's private broadcast studio.

Because the play is rich with topical materials and allusions, it has gradually become a bit dated. Throughout, Whiteside talks to or about real personalities of his day, from the great actress Katharine Cornell to the early master of science fiction, H. G. Wells. The frenetic name-dropping is, in fact, part of the fun, and some of the play's characters are even based on well-known celebrities of the day—Banjo, for example, was inspired by Harpo Marx, Lorraine Sheldon by Gertrude Lawrence, and Beverly Carlton by Noël Coward. As pure entertainment, however, *The Man Who Came to Dinner* is hard to fault. It is one of those sparkling, witty, Depression-era comedies that seemed designed to make audiences forget their troubles.

John W. Fiero

Bibliography:
Goldstein, Malcolm. *George S. Kaufman: His Life, His Theater.* New York: Oxford University Press, 1979. An excellent critical biography of Kaufman with insightful discussions of his plays.
_____. *The Political Stage: American Drama and Theater of the Great Depression.* New York: Oxford University Press, 1974. An important study of the theater in America in the Kaufman-Hart era of collaboration. Helpful for understanding the political, social, and artistic context of their work.

Mason, Jeffrey D. *Wisecracks: The Farces of George S. Kaufman*. Ann Arbor, Mich.: UMI Research Press, 1988. Most helpful monograph on the comedies of Kaufman as farce, including those written with Hart. Apt discussion of Whiteside as "clown" and "master of the revels."

Pollack, Rhoda-Gale. *George S. Kaufman*. Boston: Twayne, 1988. A critical biography with a chronology and select bibliography. Gives helpful background information on allusions to Woollcott and others in *The Man Who Came to Dinner*.

Teichmann, Howard. *Smart Aleck: The Wit, World, and Life of Alexander Woollcott*. New York: William Morrow, 1976. Intimate biography of the real person behind Sheridan Whiteside, with a significant chapter on *The Man Who Came to Dinner*.

THE MAN WHO WAS THURSDAY
A Nightmare

Type of work: Novel
Author: G. K. Chesterton (1874-1936)
Type of plot: Allegory
Time of plot: Early twentieth century
Locale: London
First published: 1908

Principal characters:
> LUCIAN GREGORY, an anarchic poet
> GABRIEL SYME, a poet and policeman
> THE SECRETARY, Monday in the council
> GOGOL, Tuesday
> MARQUIS DE ST. EUSTACHE, Wednesday
> PROFESSOR DE WORMS, Friday
> DR. BULL, Saturday
> SUNDAY

The Story:

Lucian Gregory was in the habit of declaiming his anarchistic views to anyone who would listen. He struck others, particularly women, as a thrilling poet, and surely his anarchism was only a pose. By chance, Gabriel Syme happened along and disagreed thoroughly with Gregory. In Syme's view, the real wonder lay in order; anarchists hoped only to shock others and deceive themselves by their nihilistic views.

The dispute grew so intense that Gregory invited Syme to see for himself that there were real anarchists who were intent on destroying the world. However, Syme had to swear never to tell the authorities what Gregory would reveal.

The two took a cab to a restaurant in a poor part of town. There, Syme was surprised to be served an excellent dinner. Then Gregory took him down a subterranean passage lined with firearms to a council room filled with bombs. This room was the meeting place of the group of anarchists to which Gregory belonged. There was to be an election that night, and Gregory confided that he was confident that he would be elected to the post of Thursday on the Central Anarchist Council, the inner ring presided over by the redoubtable Sunday. Before the meeting convened, Syme swore Gregory to silence and confided that he was really a detective. Gregory was filled with confusion and made a poor speech to the assembly. The members grew suspicious of Gregory's private convictions and elected Syme to act as Thursday on the Council.

Syme had become a detective in an unusual way. One day, he met a policeman who had gone to school at Harrow. The policeman said that he was one of the new force recruited to combat intellectuals who were out to destroy law and order. Syme, interested in joining the new force, was taken to a pitch-dark room in Scotland Yard, where a man he could not see gave him a job.

Now, as an elected member of the inner council of the anarchists, he was taken down the Thames River on a tug to a landing, where the Secretary greeted him and took him to the meeting, which was being held on a balcony in open view. Huge, menacing Sunday was presiding at the banquet table. As Syme surveyed the other members, he was struck by how normal they looked.

The business at hand was the assassination of the czar of Russia and the president of France. The bombing was to be done by the dapper Marquis de St. Eustache, called Wednesday. Suddenly, Sunday shut off debate and announced that there was a spy present. He appointed Bull to finalize the plans and then unmasked Gogol as a police spy. Gogol left hurriedly.

As Syme left the meeting, he was shadowed by the aged, decrepit-seeming Professor de Worms. Despite Syme's best efforts to elude him, he was unable to shake de Worms, and they went on an absurd chase all over London. Finally, in a tavern, de Worms told Syme that he was really a young actor disguised as an old professor, another police spy.

Syme and de Worms resolved to visit Bull, since he was the one planning the assassination. When the conversation with Bull seemed to be leading nowhere, Syme suddenly had a brilliant idea and persuaded him to take off his dark spectacles. Seeing the young man's kindly eyes, Symes declared that he could not really be an anarchist, and Bull confessed that he too was a police spy.

The three Scotland Yard men decided to follow St. Eustache to the Continent to try to stop him from bombing the czar and the president. They came upon St. Eustache in a café in Calais. Syme decided that his best chance to delay the Frenchman was to provoke him to a duel by trying to pull his nose. His challenge was accepted, and it was arranged that the duel be fought near a railroad station. Syme thought the place had been chosen so that St. Eustache could board a Paris train immediately afterward. Syme did his best to prolong the duel so that St. Eustache would miss the train, but the Frenchman suddenly offered to end the duel by letting Syme pull his nose. As the train came into the station, St. Eustache pulled off his own nose; he also pulled off his wig and various bits of padding and disguise, revealing that he too was a police spy. Led by the Secretary, a menacing-looking masked mob got off the train and marched toward the men from Scotland Yard. The four confessed spies began to run.

The chase was a mad one. The pursued used horses and a car to seek safety with the police, but the alarmingly well-disciplined mob kept up with them. At last, the spies found themselves crowded together on a pier. Arrayed against them was the mob, firing rifles and pistols. To their horror, they saw that the police too had joined their enemies. As it turned out, however, it was all a misunderstanding, for the Secretary was yet another Scotland Yard man, and he had been attempting to capture the others so as to thwart the bombing. The five policemen returned to London, where they picked up Gogol. They were determined to confront Sunday.

When they found him, Sunday began to run with surprising speed and grace. He used several hansom cabs and a fire engine in his flight, and he even commandeered an elephant from the zoo. On the outskirts of London, he jumped into the basket of a balloon and floated out of their reach.

The six spies pursued Sunday in spite of the rough countryside. When his balloon came to earth, they thought they had overtaken him at last. A servant met them, however, and showed them to a carriage. They were taken to a nearby castle and royally received. A valet laid out costumes for them that symbolized the days of the week and reflected their personalities. Syme was given a gown embellished with a sun and a moon; for according to Genesis, the Lord created the sun and the moon on Thursday.

They learned that Sunday was the Scotland Yard official who had initially employed them all. That evening there was a festive gathering in the garden, with the councilors seated on thrones. Sunday was gowned in pure white, symbolizing the sanctity of the Sabbath. He lectured them on the Sabbath as a holy day; they should use it to gather strength and comfort for the week's work. When Gregory came to the party, he, intellectual anarchist, was denounced as the real enemy.

Critical Evaluation:

One possible clue to the many ambiguities and levels of meaning in *The Man Who Was Thursday* is in the novel's subtitle, "A Nightmare," which implies that after debating poetry and anarchy with his friend Lucian Gregory, Gabriel Syme falls into a reverie in which symbolic events occur and then, the adventure completed, returns to reality. Once this dream structure is accepted, the apparently illogical and progressively symbolic narrative creates no insurmountable difficulties. Nevertheless, it is unlikely that any two readers will arrive at precisely the same interpretation of the meaning behind Syme's adventures and his encounter with the enigmatic Sunday.

Gilbert Keith Chesterton states in his *Autobiography* that *The Man Who Was Thursday* was the product of his intellectually and spiritually unsettled youth: "The whole story is a nightmare of things, not as they are, but as they seemed to the young half-pessimist of the 1890's." Initially, the major targets of the satire are the negative philosophies that seemed to him to dominate the intellectual atmosphere of the late Victorian period. As Chesterton suggested in his poetic dedication to E. C. Bentley, "Science announced nonentity and art admired decay."

Each of the anarchists embodies one possible perversion of intellect: Gogol (Tuesday) is the stereotypical gruff, bearded anarchist; Professor de Worms (Friday) is the perverted scholarly intelligence; Dr. Bull (Saturday) represents cold, scientific rationalism, whereas Marquis de St. Eustache (Wednesday) represents decadent aristocracy and death worship; and the Secretary (Monday) embodies political fanaticism and power madness. This political satire, however, changes into something quite different as each of the supposed anarchists is, in turn, exposed as an upholder of the moral order. "I thought it would be fun," Chesterton commented in an interview, "to make the tearing away of menacing masks reveal benevolence."

Syme prefers the old world of clearly defined good and evil. However disruptive evil may be, it is preferable to moral and spiritual ambiguity. As he runs from a mob that he believes to be in the service of Sunday (they turn out to be good citizens who believe him to be an anarchist), Syme speculates on his new view of reality: "Was not everything, after all, like this bewildering woodland, this dance of dark and light? Everything only a glimpse, the glimpse always unforeseen, and always forgotten. . . . He had found the thing which the modern people call Impressionism, which is another name for that final skepticism which can find no floor to the universe." Thus Syme's nightmare turns from a crusade against tangible evil to a search for reality itself, and that reality—or the absence of it—seems to be embodied in Sunday.

Following a wildly comic chase after Sunday, the search for reality ends in the fantastic, symbolic final scene of the book, where Sunday reveals his identity, only to leave the meaning of the novel more ambiguous than ever. With all the detectives dressed in elaborate costumes that suggest their days in Genesis, Sunday identifies himself. "I am the Sabbath. I am the peace of God." The detectives challenge him to explain and justify his behavior, but the skepticism of the believers is submerged by the negations of the true denier, Lucian Gregory, who presents himself as the authentic anarchist: "I am the destroyer. I would destroy the world if I could."

Gregory issues two challenges that bring the book to its ideological climax. He demands that the five detectives—representatives of human moral order—justify themselves in the light of the fact that they have never suffered. Syme, speaking for Chesterton and humanity, denies the anarchist's charge: "We have been broken upon the wheel," he retorts, "we have descended into Hell!" When the challenge is put directly to Sunday: "Have you ever suffered?" Sunday responds with a question of his own and ends the dream fantasy: "Can ye drink of the cup that I drink of?"

Once when he was questioned about Sunday's identity, Chesterton said: "I think you can take him to stand for Nature as distinguished from God. Huge, boisterous, full of vitality, dancing with a hundred legs, bright with the glare of the sun, and at first sight, somewhat regardless of us and our desires." When asked about Sunday's final question, however, Chesterton admitted that it "seems to mean that Sunday is God. That is the only serious note in the book. The face of Sunday changes, you tear off the mask of Nature and you find God."

The story G. K. Chesterton began as a comic parody of the intrigue-adventure novel ends as a speculation on divine ambiguity. Chesterton suggests that the pessimism of the anarchist is wrong, but the optimism of the pantheist is inadequate. What remains can only be the god behind nature, who embraces both limited views and demands a faith and commitment beyond rationalization and speculation.

Bibliography:

Clipper, Lawrence J. *G. K. Chesterton*. New York: Twayne, 1974. A useful survey of Chesterton's sources of inspiration, works, and themes. Sees *The Man Who Was Thursday* and *Orthodoxy* (both written in 1908) as Chesterton's open declaration of commitment to Christianity as a cure for the problems of twentieth century society. Includes a chronology, a list of works by Chesterton, and a bibliography of critiques.

Conlon, D. J., ed. *G. K. Chesterton: A Half Century of Views*. Oxford, England: Oxford University Press, 1987. A strong collection of critical essays on Chesterton's work by many of the finest critics writing between 1936 and 1985, including Graham Greene, C. S. Lewis, George Orwell, and Dorothy Sayers. Includes two selections specifically discussing *The Man Who Was Thursday*, one by Evelyn Waugh (pp. 72-74) and the other by Gary Wills (pp. 335-342).

Ffinch, Michael. *G. K. Chesterton: A Biography*. San Francisco: Harper & Row, 1986. A lively and lucid biography that provides information on Chesterton's life and literary achievements. Probably the most informative work of its kind since Chesterton's 1936 *Autobiography*. Gives a concise discussion of *The Man Who Was Thursday* (pp. 159-161) as a nightmarish work resembling works of Franz Kafka.

Hollis, Christopher. *The Mind of Chesterton*. London: Hollis & Carter, 1970. A wide-ranging critique of Chesterton's literary accomplishments. Includes a discussion and many references to *The Man Called Thursday* (pp. 54-60).

Kenner, Hugh. *Paradox in Chesterton*. London: Sheed & Ward, 1948. Acknowledges G. K. Chesterton's shortcomings as an artist and craftsman but praises his ability to be consistent in expressing religious convictions and in using paradox as a key to truth and art.

THE MAN WITH THE GOLDEN ARM

Type of work: Novel
Author: Nelson Algren (Nelson Ahlgren Abraham, 1909-1981)
Type of plot: Social realism
Time of plot: Late 1940's
Locale: Chicago
First published: 1949

Principal characters:

FRANCIS MAJCINEK, known as Frankie Machine, war veteran, drug
    addict, card dealer
SOPHIE, nicknamed Zosh, his wife
MOLLY NOVOTNY, Frankie's mistress
DRUNKIE JOHN, Molly's former boyfriend
SPARROW "SOLLY" SALTSKIN, a gambling room steerer
LOUIE FOMOROWSKY, a drug dealer
STASH KOSKOSKA, an icehouse worker
VIOLET, Stash's wife
ZERO SCHWIEFKA, a gambling room owner on West Division Street

The Story:

Twenty-nine-year-old Francis Majcinek, known as Frankie Machine because of his skill in dealing cards, was wounded in World War II, deployed to a hospital with shrapnel in his liver, and sent home for discharge. During his hospitalization, large doses of morphine controlled his pain. He became hooked on drugs, which he had to take regularly in order to function.

Frankie's relationship to his wife, Sophie, was never a healthy one. While dating her, he told her that he needed his freedom. In order to keep him, Sophie lied that she was pregnant. A guilt-ridden Frankie, nineteen years of age, married her. The marriage deteriorated dramatically when Sophie incurred injuries in an accident caused by Frankie's drunk driving.

Sophie was an invalid from that time on, suffering from paralysis that her doctors said had no physical basis. Frankie, again guilt-ridden, was trapped in a loveless relationship. Seeing no way out, he endured a life of futility, scrounging for drug money, and dealing cards at Zero Schwiefka's establishment, where, before his military service, he had gained a reputation as a top dealer.

Sparrow Saltskin, who steered gamblers to Frankie's table, had great admiration for his deftness with cards and, during Frankie's absence in the service, longed for his return. He did not know, when Frankie came home, that Frankie was addicted to drugs, that he had a "monkey on his back," as members of the drug culture would say.

Frankie's supplier, Nifty Louie Fomorowsky, was dedicated to helping Frankie's monkey grow. Nifty Louie used every possible ploy to feed the monkey. He helped Frankie graduate from morphine to a broader panoply of drugs. Frankie's frustration and the guilt that defined his relationship to his wife made him an apt candidate for a huge monkey.

Among those occupying Frankie's world were Stash Koskoska and his wife, Violet, a sexy woman considerably younger than her husband. Stash labored in an icehouse so he could bring Vi bread and sausages that were on sale. While Stash was working, Vi stuffed these goodies into Sparrow, with whom she was having an affair. Vi also attended to Sophie, cleaning her apartment for her and taking her on outings to double features at the motion picture theater.

Among the neighborhood bars was the Tug and Maul, a gathering place for a variety of motley characters. Across the street from the Tug and Maul was the Safari, a sleazy club with an upstairs room in which Nifty Louie gave the community junkies their fixes, regularly adjusting the dosage to make the monkey grow and keep the addicts coming, and paying, for ever-increasing hits.

Molly Novotny, approximately twenty years of age, was the nubile girlfriend of Drunkie John, a never-sober habitué of the Tug and Maul, until he dumped her. She then fell into the welcoming arms of Frankie Machine, with whom she formed a continuing relationship. It took a quarter-grain fix to feed Frankie's monkey at this time.

The Sparrow-Stash-Violet love triangle grew increasingly complicated. Sparrow spent as much time jailed for petty crimes as he spent free. Frankie's life took an ugly turn when he caught Louie cheating in a card game with the Umbrella Man, a Tug and Maul fixture. He exposed Louie, who retaliated by upping the price of the drugs Frankie needed to stay steady enough to deal.

The bad feelings between the two grew until, in a back alley, Frankie, badly in need of a fix, interlocked the fingers of his hands to control their shaking and, in an impassioned moment, brought them down on Louie's neck while he was bending over to pick up Frankie's lucky silver dollar, which Sparrow had dropped deliberately. Louie died instantly.

Frankie and Sparrow concocted an alibi that shifted suspicion from them. Others in the neighborhood fell under suspicion when they showed unexpected signs of affluence. Then Frankie and Sparrow stole some electric irons from a department store. Sparrow fled, but Frankie was caught and imprisoned for the theft.

While Frankie was incarcerated, a feisty prison doctor got him off drugs, helping him to make the long trip "from monkey to zero" as Frankie called it. When he returned to the street, however, he reverted to his old ways, even though Molly Novotny, to whom he had confessed murdering Louie, intermittently helped him to control his drug habit. He needed drugs to give him the steady hands dealers require.

Police captain Bednar was setting up a sting operation in which Sparrow would sell drugs to Frankie while hidden police officers watched. When the drugs were passed, both men were arrested. Frankie, as a user rather than a pusher, was released. Sparrow was detained.

Frankie hid out for three weeks with Molly, whom Drunkie John had been blackmailing. When John came to the apartment, an angry Frankie ordered him to leave. An equally angry John called the police, who shot Frankie's heel as he fled to a flophouse where, cornered by the police and realizing the futility of running, he hanged himself. Molly Novotny, Antek Witwicki, and the investigating officer offered the final report on Frankie's life and death, presented as a Witness Sheet of the State of Illinois in a question-answer format. The book's epitaph is the poem "The Man with the Golden Arm."

Critical Evaluation:

The Man with the Golden Arm, written during Nelson Algren's two years on stipends from the Newberry Library and the American Academy of Arts and with a sixty-dollar-a-week advance from his publisher, is the first novel in the United States to explore fully the drug culture. The novel was an immediate success: In 1950, it was the first book to receive the newly instituted National Book Award. Otto Preminger optioned the book's film rights and eventually produced the first feature-length commercial film to deal openly with drug addiction.

The great difference between the book and the film, released in 1956, is that the book deals respectfully and compassionately with its characters and presents its information factually, bereft of editorializing, whereas the film degenerates into a sensationalized presentation of drug addiction and of the triumph of the forces of right.

Algren's special magic in this landmark novel rests in the fact that he has constructed a sound, viable novel that accommodates what he wanted to say about the drug culture and about the entire culture surrounding West Division Street. Just as John Steinbeck in *Tortilla Flat* (1935) presents Danny and his compadres with respect and even affection, consistently allowing them their personal dignity, Algren deals respectfully and affectionately with his characters in *The Man with the Golden Arm*, a book that grew out of his close association through many years with the sort of people about whom he was writing. His room on Chicago's Wabansia Street was in the midst of the kind of environment about which he writes in this book.

One of the themes Algren explores fully in this novel is guilt, both as it is personified by Frankie and, in a more general sense, as it exists universally in the broader society. The second part of the novel, beginning with Frankie's imprisonment, is entitled "Act of Contrition," clearly suggesting this theme.

Algren's characters are the dispossessed; as such, they experience guilt at being propertyless in a society that values individual progress and possession while providing the means for the ambitious to succeed. These ambitious, successful, up-by-the-bootstraps Americans, however, are not those about whom Algren chooses to write. He focuses on the down-and-outers, whom he understands.

For Frankie, exchanging marriage vows with Sophie when he was nineteen did not really marry the two. The real marriage, the marriage in which Frankie would remain forever trapped, occurred when, through his negligence, Sophie was rendered an invalid. Now he had to endure her endless nagging and whining, complaining and recriminating for the rest of his life because of the special burden of guilt her condition placed upon him.

The value system among Algren's characters has a great deal to do with their continual hustling, their ongoing efforts to turn everything they can to their personal advantage. Sparrow lets Frankie take the rap in the theft of the electric irons. Violet makes her husband a cuckold without a second thought, taking Sparrow into her orb when it suits her but dropping him with equal alacrity when she realizes she can better her lot by giving her sexual favors to the landlord rather than to the hapless, lying Sparrow.

Frankie feels little remorse at killing Louie, nor are readers likely to think ill of Frankie for his lack of remorse. The murder was unpremeditated, a sudden act of passion brought on by drug withdrawal. It is ironic that Frankie is jailed for another crime and, during that incarceration, gets the monkey off his back. Any glimmer of hope that his temporary rehabilitation might suggest is dashed when he returns to Sophie's nagging and belittling and realizes that he cannot do the only job he can do well unless his nerves are soothed by the drugs that Louie can provide.

In *The Man with the Golden Arm*, Algren produces some of his finest female characters, particularly in Molly Novotny and Violet, both multifaceted women caught in the kinds of naturalistic dilemmas that recall the writing of Theodore Dreiser and Frank Norris. Algren's characters emerge, however, as considerably more fulfilled than those earlier heroines and are imbued with comic characteristics that Dreiser's and Norris' women lack.

R. Baird Shuman

Bibliography:
Beauvoir, Simone de. *America Day by Day*. Translated by Patrick Dudley [pseud.]. London: Duckworth, 1952. This book, which displeased Algren, contains considerable detail about

the genesis of *The Man with the Golden Arm*, which Algren had nearly completed when he went on an extended trip with de Beauvoir to New Orleans, Mexico, and Guatemala.

Cox, Martha Heasley, and Wayne Chatterton. *Nelson Algren*. Boston: Twayne, 1975. Material from Algren's letters to and interviews with the authors, who did exhaustive research. Covers Algren's career only to 1970. Accurate, well written, and thorough.

Donohue, H. E. F. *Conversations with Nelson Algren*. New York: Hill & Wang, 1964. Extensive interviews from 1962 and 1963 provide detailed information about Algren's background, childhood, and early years. Valuable information about Algren's wanderings after his graduation from the University of Illinois in 1931.

Drew, Bettina. *Nelson Algren*. New York: G. P. Putnam's Sons, 1989. Detailed, authoritative critical biography of Algren, covering his life up to his death in 1981. Much of the book is based on the extensive collection of Algren papers at the Ohio State University, to which Drew had full access.

Giles, James. "The Harsh Compassion of Nelson Algren." Introduction to *The Man with the Golden Arm*, by Nelson Algren. New York: Four Walls Eight Windows Press, 1990. Provides valuable insights into the pervasive comic element in Algren's writing.

THE MAN WITHOUT A COUNTRY

Type of work: Short fiction
Author: Edward Everett Hale (1822-1909)
Type of plot: Historical
Time of plot: Nineteenth century
Locale: United States and the high seas
First published: 1863

> *Principal character:*
> PHILIP NOLAN, a man convicted of treason and sentenced to
> a life of exile

The Story:

Few people noticed in the newspaper columns of 1863 the report of the death of Philip Nolan. Few people would have recognized his name, in fact, for since Madison's administration went out in 1817, it had never been mentioned in public by any naval officer, and the records concerning his case had been destroyed by fire years before his death.

When he was a young officer in Texas, Philip Nolan met Aaron Burr and became involved in Burr's infamous plot against the United States government. When Burr's treason was revealed and the rebels were brought to trial, Nolan was indicted along with some of the lesser figures of the plot. Asked at his trial whether he had any statement to make concerning his loyalty to the United States, Nolan, in a frenzy, cursed the name of his country. Shocked, Colonel Morgan, who was conducting the court-martial, sentenced Philip Nolan never again to hear the name of his native land.

The secretary of the navy was requested to place the prisoner aboard a naval ship with a letter to the captain explaining Nolan's peculiar punishment. For the remainder of his life, Nolan and this letter went from one ship to another, Nolan traveling alone, speaking only to officers who guarded their country's name from his ears. None of the officers wanted to have him around because his presence prevented any talk of home or of politics. Once in a while, he was invited to the officers' mess, but most of the time, he ate alone under guard. Since he wore an army uniform with perfectly plain buttons, he became known as "Plain Buttons."

The periodicals and books he read had to be edited in order to delete any naming of or allusion to the United States. One incident was marked well by those who witnessed it. Some officers were gathered on deck one day reading aloud to one another Sir Walter Scott's *Lay of the Last Minstrel.* When it came his turn, Nolan took up the poem at the section which contained the lines, "This is my own, my native land!" He colored, choked, and threw the book into the water as he ran to his room. He did not emerge for two months.

Nolan altered considerably as time passed, and he lost the bragging air of unconcern he had assumed at first. After the incident of the poem, he became shy and retiring, conversing with few people and staying in his quarters most of the time. He was transferred from ship to ship, never coming closer than a hundred miles to the land whose name he was forbidden to hear. Once Nolan came close to gaining his freedom from this bondage of silence. It happened during a naval battle with a British ship. A good shot from the enemy struck one of the ship's guns, killing the officer in charge and scattering the men. Unexpectedly, Nolan appeared to take command of the gun, heroically ignoring his own safety and aiding in the defeat of the English ship. He was highly praised by the captain, who promised to mention him in his naval report. Nolan's case had been so forgotten in Washington that there seemed to be no orders concerning him. His punishment was being carried on simply by repetitious habit and naval form.

During his extensive studies, Nolan kept scholarly notebooks. For diversion, he began to collect organic specimens of wildlife, which were brought to him by ship's men who went ashore. He was never known to be ill, and often he nursed those who were. So the expatriate passed his years—nameless, friendless, loveless. If there were any record of him in Washington, no evidence of such papers could ever be uncovered. So far as the government was concerned, Nolan did not exist. Stories about the lonely man circulated through mess halls, but many were untrue.

During the last fifteen years of his life, Nolan aged rapidly. The men whom he had known when he first began his endless journey in 1807 had retired, and younger men took their places on the ships. Nolan became more reserved than ever, but he was always well regarded by those who knew him. It is said that young boys idolized him for his advice and for his interest in them.

Constantly, the men were on guard never to reveal to their prisoner any news about the United States. This secrecy was often difficult to maintain, for the nation was growing rapidly. With the annexation of Texas, there arose a strained incident. The officers puzzled over the removal of that state from Nolan's maps, but they decided that the change would give him a hint of westward expansion. There were other inconvenient taboos. When the states on the West Coast joined the Union, the ships which bore Nolan had to avoid customary landings there. Although Nolan suspected the reason for this change in his habitual itinerary, he kept silent.

When Nolan lay dying, the captain of the ship came to see him. He found that Nolan had draped the stars and stripes around a picture of Washington. On one bulkhead hung the painting of an eagle grasping the entire globe in its claws; at the foot of the bed was a map of the United States which Nolan had drawn from memory. When Nolan asked for news from home, the captain, who liked and pitied Nolan, told him about the progress of the United States during the more than fifty years of Nolan's exile. Seeing Nolan's joy at the news of his country, the captain could not bring himself to tell the dying man that the United States was engaged in a civil war. Philip Nolan died in 1863. His last request was that he be buried at sea, his only home.

Critical Evaluation:

Although Edward Everett Hale lived a long, vigorous, colorful life as a journalist, novelist, editor, historian, reformer, and Christian minister (including a stint as Senate chaplain), his fame rests almost entirely on his first well-known publication, the short story called "The Man Without a Country."

Hale was a young man when he first determined to write a fiction about an "exile" who longs for home, but it took the national trauma of the Civil War and, in particular, the 1863 Ohio gubernatorial campaign to crystallize his idea into "The Man Without a Country." When one candidate proclaimed that he did not want to live in a country led by Abraham Lincoln, Hale became enraged and wrote his short, patriotic fiction as a political polemic. Ironically, Hale's effort had no effect whatsoever on the specific election, since its first publication in the *Atlantic* magazine was delayed until well after the event (the pro-Southern candidate was trounced anyway). Instead, it caught the public fancy and quickly became the great and popular artistic embodiment of American patriotic sentiment.

The factors behind its immediate impact are not hard to understand—the trauma of the Civil War, a roused and committed public opinion, the atmosphere for fervent nationalism and jingoism—but the reasons for its continued popularity are somewhat more difficult to pinpoint. It is easy enough to fault the story for thin characterization, vague scenes, sentimentality, and blatant didacticism, but such a judgment misses the nature and intention of the work. "The Man

Without a Country" is a secular parable. It is not a realistic story that is spoiled by too much rhetoric; it is a didactic story—even a sermon—that is given color and vigor through the use of realistic narrative devices. In the final analysis, the greatness of "The Man Without a Country" lies in its perfect blending of rhetoric and storytelling.

Once the reader accepts Philip Nolan's unlikely sentence as fact, the rest of the story follows believably. The realism of the tale is enhanced by Hale's quasi-documentary approach. In the best nineteenth century tradition, the reality of the tale is certified by the manner of its telling. The narrator of the story claims to be an old naval officer recounting his experiences with Nolan. These experiences are given plausibility through the use of specific details: ships, places, historical events, and naval procedures. Hale is especially skillful in fitting Nolan's fictional story into the real events surrounding the downfall of Aaron Burr. The narrator's reasonable explanation for the "suppression" of Nolan's story, coupled with the fact that Hale originally published the story anonymously, convinced nineteenth century readers that Philip Nolan was a real person; for years, even after Hale acknowledged the piece as his own fiction, the Navy received protests and inquiries on the matter. The device may have long ago been exposed as fictional, but it still gives the story a strong sense of reality and immediacy.

The action of the tale moves swiftly and easily. In each scene, Nolan emerges from his mysterious cabin to confront another reminder of his exile—the reading of Scott's poem on patriotism, a shipboard dance with an old female acquaintance, combat with a British ship, and contact with a slave ship. The climax of the tale occurs when, as Nolan lies dying, the reader is finally admitted to his cabin and encounters a miniature America made out of bits and pieces. Admittedly, the emotions evoked are sentimental and pathetic, rather than tragic, but as a distillation of nationalistic attitudes and evocation of patriotic emotions, "The Man Without a Country" unquestionably realizes the author's stated intention to create a "sensation story with a national moral" directed "towards the formation of a sentiment of love for the nation."

Bibliography:

Adams, John R. *Edward Everett Hale*. Boston: Twayne, 1977. Includes a chapter devoted to *The Man Without a Country*. Discusses the work's analogues and sources—mainly the pro-Confederacy pronouncements of the Ohio politician Clement Laird Vallandigham made early in the Civil War—and its factual background, narrative core, and popularity. Discusses Hale's sequel, *Philip Nolan's Friends* (1876).

Brooks, Van Wyck. Introduction to *The Man Without a Country*, by Edward Everett Hale. New York: Franklin Watts, 1960. Succinctly presents a biography of the versatile, conservative, patriotic Hale, and briefly discusses the political inspiration for the story.

Hale, Edward Everett. "Philip Nolan and the 'Levant.'" *National Geographic Magazine* 16 (March, 1905): 114-116. Hale's cocky, rollicking comments on a possible location of the shipwreck of the *Levant*, a real U.S. Navy sloop-of-war that disappeared in 1860, in the Pacific Ocean east of Hawaii. Because of its disappearance, Hale felt free to use it as the fictional vessel aboard which Nolan dies in 1863.

Oxley, Beatrice. "The Man Who Wasn't There." *English Journal* 38 (September, 1949): 396-397. Explains the care with which Hale provided pseudofactual details and data concerning the life and background of his fictional Philip Nolan.

Van Doren, Carl. Introduction to *The Man Without a Country*, by Edward Everett Hale. New York: Heritage Press, 1936. Defines Hale's motive for writing this unrealistic story as fervent patriotism in the face of the jeopardy in which the nation existed at the time of the work's composition.

MANETTE SALOMON

Type of work: Novel
Author: Edmond de Goncourt (1822-1896) and Jules de Goncourt (1830-1870)
Type of plot: Naturalism
Time of plot: Nineteenth century
Locale: Paris
First published: 1867 (English translation, 1871)

> *Principal characters:*
> NAZ DE CORIOLIS, a young painter
> ANATOLE BAZOCHE, his close friend and a painter
> MANETTE SALOMON, a model and Coriolis' mistress
> GARNOTELLE, a painter of the classical school
> CHASSAGNOL, a painter of the modern school

The Story:

From the Paris zoo there was a magnificent view of the city. Visitors to the zoo were startled one day by a young man, who seemed to be a guide, pointing out landmarks below in terms that might have been used to describe the zoo itself. The young man, Anatole Bazoche, delighted in such pranks; he was studying art at Langibout's studio and kept everyone in a constant uproar. The son of a stolid bourgeois widow, he had become an artist over her protests; although he had talent, he was content to dissipate it in bright, superficial paintings. His gift for farce symbolized the age, which, disillusioned and effete, laughed at everything. Art had become restless eclecticism, turning increasingly to a romanticism that was essentially literary.

In the same studio were Chassagnol, a compulsive talker who hoped for a new vision; Garnotelle, a quiet little peasant who tried earnestly to follow rules for good painting; and Naz de Coriolis. Of Italian and Creole descent, Coriolis was feared for his temper and pride and envied for his money. Caring for nothing but his painting, he remained aloof from all but Anatole.

Coriolis became dissatisfied with this Bohemian world filled with talk and pranks, and he decided to travel in the Near East for a time. As he and Anatole sat talking before his departure, a woman brought her child to his door and asked if he needed a model. Captivated by the child's extraordinary beauty, he caught her up in his arms. As he swung her down again, she pulled his gold watch and chain to the floor. Laughing, he let her keep them.

Garnotelle, who had left the studio, won the Prix de Rome for his careful, if mediocre, academic art. Cut off from his funds by his mother, Anatole experienced a series of ups and downs; he took on any hack jobs that came his way until his uncle invited him to accompany him to Marseilles and from there Constantinople. Unfortunately, the uncle became jealous of Anatole's charm and left him in Marseilles. After helping in a cholera epidemic, Anatole joined a circus. He met Coriolis, now on his way back to Paris, who had inherited great wealth and generously invited Anatole to share a studio with him. There the two began painting. Coriolis had vowed never to marry; he felt that marriage and fatherhood destroy the artist because they attach creativity to a lower order of things. He knew, too, that his lazy, Creole temperament needed even more discipline than most.

Coriolis' first paintings, fruits of his travels, were not favorably received. Volatile and filled with light, they did not conform to the fashionable critical notions of Near Eastern landscapes.

Naïvely astonished, Coriolis discovered that the critics and the public preferred Garnotelle's sterile work. Determined to prove that he was more than an exotic colorist, he began painting nudes.

During his search for a model, he saw a young Jewish girl, Manette Salomon and, through Anatole, obtained her services. Manette was absolute perfection; her body had a pliant beauty that seemed the quintessence of the feminine. Coriolis, obsessed by her beauty, wanted to keep her all to himself, but she was a true Parisian bohemian and wanted only to be free. Her frankness and ignorance delighted him; her serenity gave him peace. In his jealousy, he once followed her, but she went only to the synagogue. This experience made him suddenly aware of her Jewishness—a strange, foreign element akin to something he had found in his travels. One day, however, when he saw a watch chain she had, he realized that she was the child he had admired so long ago. She too remembered her benefactor and vowed tenderly never to leave him.

Coriolis' painting of Manette, in which he captured her glorious flesh tones, was a huge success, and its purchase by a museum restored his faith in himself. Feeling that she too was famous, Manette began to change: The praise of the picture Coriolis had painted of her raised a feeling of pride in her that was almost love, whereas Coriolis, like most artists, thought of his mistress as a charming, necessary little animal.

Soon afterward, when he fell ill, Manette nursed him back to strength, never leaving his side. To speed his convalescence, Coriolis went with Manette and Anatole to the country near Fontainebleau. Manette, completely city bred, was delighted by the strange new world and plunged into it eagerly. Coriolis found nature soothing and inspiring, yet he grew bored and missed the comforts of his studio. Anatole luxuriated in the freshness of the countryside and fell under its spell, but he enlivened his stay by tricking, mocking, and entertaining the other guests at the little inn.

Manette, accepted by this bourgeois group as Coriolis' wife, found her new status attractive, and in her ignorance she believed this bourgeois world worth entering. Then a new arrival, who sensed her true relationship to Coriolis, snubbed her. Hurt and resentful, Manette wanted to leave. The three moved to a small house near the landscapist Crescent and his wife, an ample, friendly woman who took Manette to her heart. The two young artists learned from the old peasant Crescent, but Madame Crescent cooled toward Manette once she learned that she was Jewish; she also sensed (partly through peasant superstition, partly through a kind of animal instinct) something hidden, profound, and destructive in the girl's nature. Shortly thereafter, Coriolis, who could not agree with the moralistic basis of Crescent's art, decided to return to Paris.

After their return to Paris, Manette became pregnant, and her body took on new languor. When Coriolis' son was born, Manette acquired a new outlook on life. The carefree bohemian had become the mother, and her stubborn pride and greed for success came to the fore.

Coriolis had begun to work again, this time on a new kind of painting, an attempt to create art through the truth of life. He did not intend to imitate photography but rather to make of the harmonies available in painting a re-creation unfolding the inner realities of contemporary life. His two paintings, particularly one that depicted a wedding, aroused derision, and Manette, seeing his failure, cooled toward him.

Coriolis doted on his son, watched him play, and sketched him. As time passed, however, he was unable to work and sank into inactivity and despair. He could not understand a world that neglected him in favor of Garnotelle, who was now supremely fashionable with his superficial, heartless paintings.

Manette decided that for the sake of their child and her own growing desire for respectability, Coriolis should rid himself of such bohemian friends as Anatole and Chassagnol and model himself on Garnotelle. She set about arousing Coriolis' suspicions concerning Anatole and herself. She then persuaded Coriolis to go to the country for his lingering cough, taking the child and some new servants, who were her relatives. There was no room for Anatole. Meanwhile, Coriolis had grown increasingly dependent on Manette to run his home, tend his wants, and make his decisions. He was too weak to struggle against her.

Left alone, Anatole became a true bohemian, living from day to day on handouts and forgetting his art entirely. On Coriolis' return, Manette set about alienating his friends in earnest. They ceased to visit him, cutting him off from valid artistic communication. Though Manette understood the artist's life and was able to adapt herself to it, she was fundamentally ignorant. Her ambitions were for money and success. To her, art was a business, to Coriolis, a religion. Yet he did not oppose her. Her mother came to live with them, and feminine domination began to affect his health; as his psychosomatic illness increased, so did his dependence on Manette. He painted as she wanted him to and became filled with self-loathing. Always eager for more money, she persuaded him to sell some of his "failures." Surprisingly, a connoisseur recognized their true artistic merit and purchased them at a fantastically high price. Again Coriolis became successful.

In despair, he turned on Manette, accused her of destroying a number of his canvases, and ordered her out of the house. She calmly went about her business as though she had not heard him. She had beaten him. A broken man, he was still strong enough in his belief to refuse a medal he had won for a wedding picture because he felt he was unworthy of the award. Manette scornfully removed herself still further from him, but he could not leave her.

Sometime later, Anatole heard that Garnotelle had married a princess, with Coriolis as the best man. He saw Coriolis from afar, with Manette and several dreadful bourgeois types following him. Though love had long since waned between Manette and Coriolis, they were married and her ambitions were fulfilled. Coriolis painted almost nothing and became increasingly ill.

Anatole, visiting the zoo again, watched the lions in their cages. He lazed on the grass, feeling himself a part of all nature and completely free.

Critical Evaluation:

Manette Salomon portrays the world of art in Paris during the middle of the nineteenth century. Like most of the Goncourts' works, the novel emerges out of their personal experience. In addition to writing extensive reviews of art exhibitions and salons, both brothers were practicing artists themselves and acquainted with many of the most famous artists of their time. The relationships between artists in *Manette Salomon* reflect the dynamics of the contemporary art world the authors knew.

The main characters represent certain types of artists. Langibout represents the older generation of artist nurtured on officially sponsored schools, and he provides training for younger artists. His stature contrasts with the budding artists under his tutelage. Garnotelle is a parody of the classical academic artist. He compensates for his humble background and lack of training by painting in a formulaic manner. Because Garnotelle enjoys success as a fashionable society portrait painter, he becomes overbearing and pompous.

Bazoche represents an artist who may have talent but is more attracted to the life of an artist than to art itself. He attempts to paint a serious work of art but instead creates a horrendous allegorical tableau of democracy and progress with Christ at its center. In the end, he is haunted by the figure of Pierrot, in whom he sees himself. His alter ego, his pet monkey Vermilion, wears the same mask of levity and even tries painting and fails. When Vermilion dies, Bazoche buries his playfulness and abandons both art and the bohemian life to become an assistant zookeeper.

Crescent represents the successful artist, someone with talent and a stable personality. He has somehow avoided the corrupting influence of civilization. His wife, unlike Manette, helps to further his career. She takes care of the farm and finances while he works. They have no children, so she does not undergo the same unhealthy transformation as Manette. While the Goncourts show Crescent integrating personal and artistic goals, they, like Coriolis, advocated celibacy as the ideal state for an artist.

The principal character is the artist Coriolis, and his developmental struggle is the focus of the novel. Coriolis not only has real talent, he also has the capacity for hard work. While traveling the Continent, he discovers a new approach to painting that resembles impressionist technique. The method is based on the observation of nature in the open air, using detached bits of colors and lighting effects. Coriolis truly comes to life when he strains to achieve absolute beauty in art. The Goncourts themselves keenly sympathized with the quest for the ideal, and they were able vividly to translate the emotional effort and urgency involved in painting, in attempting to capture the ideal. They describe the play of light and color in Coriolis' canvases as appealing more to the senses than the intellect.

The novel opens with a detailed depiction of the artist's world in Paris, after which the Goncourts finally introduce the protagonist and attempt to reconcile the broad social canvas with their protagonist's individual psychology. The love between Coriolis and Manette rapidly disintegrates. At first, Manette does not endanger his career, for she is a professional artist's model dedicated to her own art and seems to Coriolis the incarnation of Beauty. Even when she becomes his mistress, the relationship does not seem serious on either side. Only after Manette appears as an Eastern dancing girl at Coriolis' costume ball, does he become infatuated with the illusion. He had resolved never to marry because the pleasures of family would ruin him as an artist. When Manette becomes a mother however, he yields. Once married, Manette changes entirely. She becomes very greedy for money, which the Goncourts associate with her Jewishness. Her Jewish relatives are caricatures of grasping materialism, and her son is depicted as a monster who is alienated from his father. The Goncourts imply that the true identity of Manette is revealed after marriage and motherhood, and that her character is determined by biological imperative. Yet the layers of illusion that initially mask her character seem too complex for such a simple conclusion.

Manette, by debasing Charles' art and his character, convinces him to pursue money and official honors rather than pure art. As a result, Coriolis finally loses his artistic impulse. The novel dramatizes the clash between two impulses toward creation; man's drive toward artistic creation and woman's drive for maternity. The woman emerges the winner in this struggle because of man's sexual desire and woman's acceptance of lust. Coriolis' suffering, and the accompanying decadent motifs of disintegration and fragmentation, portends the end of a neurotic civilization. Images of winter and nightfall dominate the final chapters, in which Coriolis longs for death. His predicament encapsulates the vain attempt to grasp the ideal. The Goncourts suggest that eternal beauty is masked by the vagaries of popular taste. The theme of the illusive external world opposed to reality extends beyond the question of identity to the nature of art. Not only is true beauty veiled by illusory beauty, but any explanation of beauty is an illusion even though beauty itself is real.

The Goncourts' style transposes painting into literature in a style resembling that of the impressionists, with its attention to nuance of tone. They succeed in creating a picture of an artist's life under Louis-Philippe and in depicting the conflict between the "Ingrists," the etchers who emphasized line, and the colorists. As champions of antiacademic art, the Goncourts thought that the glory of French painting lay in the return to nature. The brothers' styles mesh in *Manette Salomon*. Whereas Jules de Goncourt inclined toward broadly comical sketches and picturesque comparisons, Edmond de Goncourt showed sensitivity toward nuance and was more methodical and pedantic. Their collaborative novel caricatures the Jewish race and indicts women for their pernicious influence over men, but, much more important, *Manette Salomon* depicts in vivid detail the artistic trends of the time and the individual artist's struggle to create pure art.

"Critical Evaluation" by Pamela Pavliscak

Bibliography:
Baldick, Robert. *The Goncourts*. London: Bowes, 1960. A brief but excellent survey of their novels. Concentrates on biographical background to the novels, but also explores major themes and aspects of their literary style. Chronicles their pursuit of an accurate documentary basis for their novels and their ties to the art world.
Billy, Andre. *The Goncourt Brothers*. Translated by Margaret Shaw. New York: Horizon Press, 1960. The standard biography of the Goncourts, which elucidates events in the lives of the brothers that became incorporated in the novels. Also provides contemporary reception of their novels.
Grant, Richard B. *The Goncourt Brothers*. New York: Twayne, 1972. A solid survey of the life and works of Jules and Edmond de Goncourt. Ordered chronologically, the book integrates the lives of the authors with detailed stylistic and thematic analyses of their novels. The chapter on *Manette Salomon* elaborates their involvement in contemporary art and its effect on the novel.
Scott, David. *Pictorialist Poetics: Poetry and the Visual Arts in Nineteenth-Century France.* Cambridge, England: Cambridge University Press, 1988. Argues that aesthetic theory and literary practice of the nineteenth century combine to produce a new conception of literature's potential. Discusses the visual sources that influenced the Goncourts' literary efforts.
Silverman, Deborah. *Art Nouveau in Fin de Siècle France: Politics, Psychology, and Style.* Berkeley: University of California Press, 1989. Although Silverman's book primarily concerns itself with the collecting habits and art criticism of the Brothers Goncourt, it provides some valuable insight into their fictional works from a feminist perspective.

MANFRED

Type of work: Drama
Author: George Gordon, Lord Byron (1788-1824)
Type of plot: Poetic
Time of plot: Indeterminate
Locale: Alps
First published: 1817

> *Principal characters:*
> MANFRED, a lonely, guilt-haunted magician
> A CHAMOIS HUNTER
> THE ABBOT OF ST. MAURICE

The Story:

Alone in a Gothic gallery at midnight, Manfred meditated deeply about his life. He had undergone many experiences, but none had profoundly affected him. When he called on the spirits of the universe to appear before him, none came. Three times he summoned them. At the third call, invoking a mysterious curse on Manfred's soul, voices of the seven spirits were heard. The first voice was that of the Spirit of Air. It was then followed by the voices of the spirits of mountains, ocean, earth, winds, night, and star (all of them identified in line 132). They agree to do his bidding and ask what he would have them do.

Manfred's reply was that he desired forgetfulness. When the Spirit of Air sought further explanation, Manfred could not reveal what he wanted to forget. Surely, he insisted, spirits that controlled earth, sky, water, mountains, winds, night, and destiny, could bring the oblivion he sought. The spirits replied, however, that they had no powers beyond their own realms. When Manfred, failing in his hopes, asked the spirits to take bodily forms, the seventh spirit, the star of his destiny, took the shape of a beautiful woman. At sight of her, Manfred, hinting at a former love, attempted to hold her, but she vanished, leaving him senseless. An unidentified voice then uttered a lengthy incantation (originally published in 1816 as a separate poem), in which Manfred is cursed and seemingly condemned to wander the earth forever with his spiritual agony unassuaged.

Next morning, alone on a cliff of the Jungfrau in the Bernese Alps, Manfred resolved to forego all superhuman aid. He praised the beauty of the nature around him, but he also recognized his alienation from it in a Hamlet-like soliloquy. While thus musing on the relative merits of life and death, a chamois hunter approached unobserved, just in time to restrain Manfred from flinging himself over the cliff. Together, they descended the rocky trail.

In his cottage, the hunter urged Manfred to rest a while before journeying on. Manfred refused guidance and declared that he would go on alone. When the hunter offered Manfred his best wine, Manfred exclaimed in horror that he saw blood, a symbolic transformation in which Manfred turns communion into guilt. The hunter, thinking Manfred mad, suggested that the wretched man seek comfort in contemplation and in the church. Manfred spurned the suggestion, saying that he wished he were mad, for then his mind would be tortured by unrealities instead of the truths which now beset him. He envied the hunter's simple life, but when the hunter, noting Manfred's high-born appearance, wonderingly asked if his guest would wish to change stations in life, Manfred replied that he would not wish any human to suffer his own wretchedness. To this the hunter said that surely a man capable of such tenderness could not harbor a soul belabored by evil. Manfred, departing, protested that the evil was not within himself; he had destroyed those whom he loved.

Below, the Witch of the Alps answered Manfred's summons that she share the loveliness of nature with him. To her he described his past spiritual life, when he had lived among men but not with them. Preferring solitude, he had studied ancient mysteries and had loved and destroyed with love a woman said to resemble him. The witch promised to aid him if he would swear obedience to her, but he refused her offer and she left him.

The three destinies and Nemesis gathered for a festival in the Hall of Arimanes, Spirit of Evil and Prince of Earth and Air. Manfred, daring to approach, was recognized as a magician. He told them he had come in quest of Astarte, the symbol of his sin. When she was summoned from her tomb, she prophesied only that the next day would end his despair.

Back in his castle, Manfred felt a sublime calm. The Abbot of St. Maurice, having heard that Manfred had practiced witchcraft, arrived to save his soul. To Manfred's bitter assurance that his sins lay between heaven and himself, the abbot urged that Manfred turn to the church for help. Manfred explained that he had always lived alone and would remain alone. The abbot mourned that he could not help such a noble man.

While the servants gossiped about their master's strange behavior, Manfred stood alone in his tower. There the abbot came once more in a last vain attempt to save Manfred. Warned that a dangerous spirit was approaching, the abbot insisted that he would confront the spirit, who had come to summon Manfred. Manfred, however, defied the summons; he was willing to die but not to join the spirits of hell, to whom he owed nothing.

As the demon disappeared, Manfred died, still lonely, but unconquerable to all but death itself.

Critical Evaluation:

By 1817, when *Manfred* was published, George Gordon, Lord Byron was both the most famous and the most notorious man of letters in Europe. His fame derived primarily from cantos 1 and 2 of *Childe Harold's Pilgrimage* (1812) whose contemporary attitudes, daring, and originality had made their author the dominant literary figure of his time. By the spring of 1816, however, a series of well-publicized liaisons with highly placed women and his openly expressed affection for his own half sister, Augusta Leigh, had resulted in scandal. These calumnies effectively destroyed Byron's ill-advised marriage to Anne Isabella Milbanke, and forced Byron to leave England for the Continent, from which he was never to return in life.

Byron spent most of the summer of 1816 in a cottage adjacent to the southern shore of Lake Geneva (Lac Leman) in Switzerland, where he had as neighbors Percy and Mary Shelley. In September, after the Shelleys had returned to England, Byron undertook an Alpine excursion, the essentials of which he recorded in a journal later sent to Augusta Leigh. During this twelve-day diversion, he saw many aspects of mountain scenery and several of the most famous peaks, including the Kletsgerberg, the Hockthorn, and the Jungfrau. On September 23, he ascended a lesser mountain, the Wengeren. Byron then returned to his home on Lake Geneva by way of flatter country.

On the evening preceding his return, September 28, he described himself in his Alpine journal as a lover of nature and an admirer of beauty who could still bear fatigue (he was not yet thirty) and welcome privation. Despite having just seen "some of the noblest views in the world," however, he did not escape bitter recollections associated with his recent unhappy past and found none of the glories of Swiss scenery adequate to unburden his heart or free him from the crushing burden of his besmirched name and the enforced separation from Augusta Leigh.

He poured out these feelings in the first two acts of *Manfred*, which were written quickly during the next few days, perhaps even before his departure for Italy on October 5. The "Incantation," which later concluded Act I, was published in London together with other verses written in Switzerland in December.

In February, 1817, Byron wrote John Murray, his publisher in London, to inform him about *Manfred*. Calling it "a kind of poem in dialogue (in blank verse) or drama," Byron described his creation as "very wild, metaphysical, and inexplicable." Except for the chamois hunter, the abbot, and Manfred, all the characters were spirits of nature; Manfred himself was "a kind of magician who is tormented by a species of remorse, the cause of which is left half unexplained." Byron explained that though Manfred summons the various spirits to appear before him, they are of no use in unburdening his mind, and that he at length ventures into "the very abode of the Evil principle," where the summoned ghost of Astarte, the woman he has wronged, informs him that he has only one more day to live. Byron stressed that the predominance of spirits in his work made it unsuitable for the stage.

In letters to various other correspondents, Byron called *Manfred* a "witch drama" or "metaphysical drama" but not really a drama at all except for being in dialogue and acts. He preferred to call it a poem in dialogue rather than a play. Clearly, *Manfred* is in form a closet drama, a play meant to be read rather than staged. Because the real staging takes place in the reader's imagination, the playwright is free to introduce characters beyond normal human experience.

The scenery of the play consists in large part of what Byron saw and noted on his September, 1816, Alpine tour, including mountains, ravines, waterfalls, shepherds, cows, and cow bells. These familiar sights could be expected to have some kind of psychological significance as symbols of conscious or unconscious emotions, and perhaps they do, but Byron's own journal demonstrates that he himself failed to perceive any rapport with the scenery. In *Manfred*, but not in other works by Wordsworth and Shelley, natural beauty and sublimity are insufficient to penetrate Manfred's self-absorption. Neither travel nor nature can in any way be regarded as the theme of *Manfred*, which is ultimately not about the external world at all but very much an internal journey whose unattainable destination is an elysium of self-acceptance for which Byron sought in vain.

The effectiveness of *Manfred* and its validity as self-administered therapy naturally depends on the resolution of its protagonist's dilemma in the third act, which many readers take to be the least successful of the three. In letters to Murray of April 9 and 14, 1817, Byron himself agreed with the criticism. He rewrote the third act, and fundamentally changed the role of the abbot (and hence of sacramental religion). In the earlier version, the abbot had been a self-serving meddler trying to manipulate Manfred by playing on his fear of death; in the revised (and later published) version, he "is become a good man," as Byron tells Murray, and Manfred's death is significantly restaged. Byron completed these changes while he was in Rome.

Readers in Byron's own time and since have found many similarities between *Manfred* and two earlier dramatic versions of the Faust legend, one by the English Renaissance playwright Christopher Marlowe and the other by Byron's older contemporary, the German poet Johann Wolfgang von Goethe. Byron was aware of these charges, which appeared in early reviews of *Manfred*, and he responded to them by denying any knowledge of Marlowe's sixteenth century play. Portions of Goethe's *Faust, Part One* (also a closet drama) had been read to him, as he admitted, shortly before he began writing *Manfred*. In Marlowe's play, Dr. Faustus makes a deal with the devil and is ultimately consigned to spend eternity in hell because of it. In Goethe,

Faust also deals with the devil but gets out of the contract because of his ceaselessly aspiring soul.

Manfred (which inspired important musical treatments in the nineteenth century by Robert Schumann and Pyotr Ilich Tchaikovsky) differs from both the Marlowe and Goethe versions in that its protagonist makes no deals with anyone, whether in Hell or Heaven.

"Critical Evaluation" by Dennis R. Dean

Bibliography:
Butler, E. M. *The Fortunes of Faust.* Cambridge, England: Cambridge University Press, 1952. Traces the Faust theme from its first appearance in 1587 to the present. Includes discussion of *Manfred* and compares Byron's work with Goethe's. For magic more generally, see Butler, *The Myth of the Magus* (1948) and *Ritual Magic* (1949).
Evans, Bertrand. *Gothic Drama from Walpole to Shelley.* Berkeley: University of California Press, 1947. One of the few studies, and certainly the best, on the topic of Gothic drama.
Marchand, Leslie. *Byron: A Biography.* 3 vols. London: John Murray, 1957. It is almost impossible to discuss *Manfred* apart from the unconventional life of its author, particularly because the setting, the hinted-at theme of incest, and the ambiguous treatment of remorse are so obviously central to its meaning. The standard biography of Byron. The author's twelve-volume edition of Byron's letters is equally admirable and should be consulted (volume 5 for *Manfred*), in part because Byron is an extremely interesting letter writer.
Rutherford, Andrew. *Byron: A Critical Study.* Stanford, Calif.: Stanford University Press, 1961. Readable and superficially comprehensive on Byron, but often unsympathetic. Includes a full chapter on *Manfred*, which Rutherford, who believes the work to be a failure, ruthlessly dissolves into a pastiche of stolen references to Goethe's *Faust* and other literary works.
Thorslev, Peter L., Jr. *The Byronic Hero, Types and Prototypes.* Minneapolis: University of Minnesota Press, 1962. One of the most helpful books that a beginning student of British romantic literature can read. Thorslev describes the period as the last great age of heroes. He enumerates seven types of Romantic hero (a very useful classification), as well as the specific heroes that appear in Byron's major works. *Manfred* and *Cain* are analyzed together in chapter 11 as "metaphysical dramas" dealing with the supernatural.

MANHATTAN TRANSFER

Type of work: Novel
Author: John Dos Passos (1896-1970)
Type of plot: Impressionistic realism
Time of plot: 1920's
Locale: New York City
First published: 1925

Principal characters:
ELLEN THATCHER, an actress
CONGO, a French sailor who later became a wealthy bootlegger
GUS MCNIEL, a milkman who later became an assemblyman
JIMMY HERF, a newspaper reporter
GEORGE BALDWIN, a lawyer
JOE HARLAND, a drunk
JOE O'KEEFE, a young labor organizer
STAN EMERY, the beloved of Ellen

The Story:

Ed and Susie Thatcher had their first child, a girl they named Ellen. After the birth of the child, Susie became deeply depressed and wanted to die.

Congo and Emile, two French boys, came to New York to make their fortunes. Emile married a widowed Frenchwoman who owned a delicatessen store. Congo did not like New York and went to sea again.

Gus McNiel, a milkman, was run over by a train. George Baldwin, a young lawyer, took Gus's case against the railroad and obtained a settlement for the injured man. While Gus was in the hospital recovering from the accident, George had an affair with Gus's wife, Nellie.

Jimmy Herf arrived from Europe with his widowed mother, who was in delicate health. One evening, she had a heart attack; not long afterward, she died. Jimmy's rich Uncle Jeff and Aunt Emily Merivale then became his legal guardians. One evening at their house, Jimmy met Joe Harland, the drunken black sheep of the family, who had won and lost several fortunes on Wall Street.

Susie Thatcher died, and Ed worked hard for little Ellen. He stayed at the office until late each evening, working and dreaming of all the fine things he would do for his daughter some day. Ellen grew up, went on the stage, and married John Oglethorpe, a competent but lazy actor. Her married life became unhappy when she discovered that her husband was a homosexual.

Jimmy Herf's Uncle Jeff tried to get him interested in business, but Jimmy would have none of it. He got a job as a reporter and became acquainted with Ruth Prynne, a young actress who lived in the boardinghouse where Ellen and John Oglethorpe stayed.

George Baldwin had forgotten Nellie McNiel and was now interested in Ellen. One afternoon, as he and Ellen sat together at tea, a drunken college boy stopped at their table. George introduced him to Ellen as Stan Emery.

Joe Harland was now age forty-five and almost broke. He spent his last money on a few shots of whiskey to bring back memories of the old prosperous days on Wall Street.

Ellen and Stan fell in love. When she was with him, she was happy, but when she went home to John, she was miserable. Ellen decided that she and John could no longer live together. She packed her belongings and moved to a hotel.

Stan Emery went on a long drunken spree after being expelled from college. He went to Jimmy Herf's room. Later in the day, they met John and Ellen drinking tea together. Stan left, but Jimmy stayed to talk with Ellen.

George Baldwin sat at breakfast with his wife, Cecily, whom he had married for social position. They were not happy, and Cecily knew of his affairs with other women. George did all he could to keep her from leaving him because a scandal would ruin him in the business world.

Ellen moved from her hotel to an apartment. She was supporting herself well now, for she had become a success on Broadway.

Joe Harland had finally got a job as a night watchman. One evening, he was visited by a young labor organizer, Joe O'Keefe. The older man warned him against getting mixed up in labor troubles, but O'Keefe said that Gus McNiel, now an assemblyman, was on the side of labor.

Harry Goldweiser, a rich Broadway producer, fell in love with Ellen and he asked her to marry him. She refused, but in a friendly way, for her career depended upon Goldweiser.

Gus McNiel retained George Baldwin as his lawyer throughout his rise to political power. George warned him against getting mixed up with labor because, as a member of a conservative law firm, George would not be able to help Gus with labor troubles.

Ellen wanted Stan to stop drinking so much, but he would not reform. Drink was the only means by which he could adjust himself to the world.

One evening, Ellen went out to dinner with George Baldwin. Everyone was excited about the beginning of the World War. George, however, could think only of Ellen, and in a fit of rage, he threatened her with a gun. Gus McNiel, who was nearby, took away the gun and hushed up the incident. Jimmy Herf, who had been talking to the bartender, Congo, took Ellen outside and sent her home in a taxi.

Ellen finally obtained a divorce from John, and Harry Goldweiser renewed his attentions. One evening, Ellen and Harry met Stan dancing with a girl named Pearline. Stan revealed that he and Pearline had been on a long drunk and had gotten married. Later, Stan came home drunk, disgusted with his life and with Pearline. He poured kerosene around the apartment and set fire to it. Pearline returned just in time to see the firemen carry Stan from the burning building.

Ellen was crushed by Stan's death, for he was the only man she had really loved. To be with Jimmy Herf gave her some comfort because he had been Stan's friend. Jimmy still loved her, however, and he wanted to be more than a friend. She told him that she was going to have Stan's baby and that she wanted to leave show business and rear the child; instead she had an abortion. Ellen and Jimmy went to Europe to do Red Cross work during the war. They married and returned from France with their baby.

Joe O'Keefe came back from the war with a chip on his shoulder. He thought the veterans deserved a bonus because they had lost out on the big money at home. His other reason for feeling bitter was that he had caught syphilis somewhere overseas.

George Baldwin's home life was still troubled. Having postwar political ambitions, he turned against his old friend, Gus McNiel, and ran for mayor on a reform ticket. Meanwhile, Jimmy and Ellen drifted apart. Jimmy became despondent and quit his job. George Baldwin finally got a divorce. He proposed to Ellen. Too weary of her muddled life to resist him, she accepted his proposal.

One night, Jimmy Herf was walking the streets when a car drew up beside him and stopped. In it was the Frenchman, Congo, now a wealthy bootlegger. He took Jimmy home with him and tried to cheer him up. Late one evening after a party, Jimmy Herf wandered down by the river.

As he waited for a ferry to take him from Manhattan, he realized that he felt happy for the first time in many months. Morning found him walking along a concrete highway, penniless but still happy. He did not know where he was going; he knew only that it would be a long way.

Critical Evaluation:

It was with *Manhattan Transfer*, his third published novel, that John Dos Passos made his first experiments in attempting in a novel to depict an entire society, that of a city that for him embodied the best and worst of American culture. The techniques he began using in this work came to fruition in the trilogy entitled *U.S.A.* (1937). Both *Manhattan Transfer* and *U.S.A.* use the same stripped, staccato style in their narrative passages, and the earlier work foreshadows the later trilogy in its rapid, abrupt shifts among a large and varied cast of characters. The speed of modern life is reflected not only in the style but in those shifts, and the vividly colorful imagery adds to the effect.

Manhattan Transfer also prefigures *U.S.A.* in telling the stories of many characters while lacking a central plot. Such characters as Ellen Thatcher, Jimmy Herf, and George Baldwin receive more attention than others, but the novel can hardly be said to have a main protagonist. In fact, the central character is New York City itself, cruel, indifferent to individuals and their hopes, improbably generous to a few, but above all exciting and glamorous. When Jimmy Herf escapes the clutches of the city at the end, he presumably saves his soul by heading for the hinterlands, but he leaves behind forever the city which made his life worth living.

Like other novels that intend to portray entire societies, *Manhattan Transfer* contains characters from many different economic and social levels (although it reflects the time of its creation in failing to include any African Americans among its major figures). The family that adopts Jimmy Herf is distinctly rich and upper class, and Herf's uncle Jeff Merivale and other members of that family are very disappointed when as a young man he adopts the profession of newspaper reporter, a line of work much less prestigious than banking or the law. It is even worse that Jimmy socializes with theater people and such riffraff and with Joe Harland, whom the Merivales no longer acknowledge as a relation.

In the story of Gus and Nellie McNiel, Dos Passos focuses attention on the laboring class and the political life of the city. The railroad accident that the lawyer George Baldwin turns into a modest fortune for Gus enables the onetime milkman to become a minor elected official and to set himself up as a friend of working men and women. Joe O'Keefe, the union organizer, provides another point of view on the struggles between labor and management.

The strongest thread holding the novel together is the story of Ellen Thatcher. Her birth is the focus of the early part of the novel, and her romances and marriages link such diverse characters as Jimmy Herf, the wealthy theatrical backer Harry Goldweiser, her first husband John Oglethorpe, and the lawyer George Baldwin. In his portrayal of Ellen and her activities, Dos Passos is also able to show the realities of the supposedly glamorous world of the theater. When after a series of ill-fated marriages and romances Ellen marries Jimmy Herf in Europe and returns to this country with him and their baby, Dos Passos is able to repudiate the conventional fictional happy ending. For this marriage is no more successful than the preceding ones, and when Jimmy leaves for the hinterlands, he leaves behind wife and child as well as his career.

Another important aspect of life during the Roaring Twenties is conveyed by the activities of the French sailor named Congo. He jumps ship in New York with a friend, and stays in the city, eventually contracting a marriage of convenience with a woman who owns a restaurant where he was working. Congo eventually becomes a wealthy bootlegger, and in narrating his life, Dos Passos depicts the world of the speakeasies. He also includes an episode in which Congo and the men who work for him engage in an exciting battle with Coast Guardsmen who are trying to stop a shipment of illegal liquor.

Manhattan Transfer is in many ways the most successful novel of Dos Passos' long and productive career, and it conveys as well as any novel of the time the frenetic pace of life in New York City during the 1920's. While its scope is narrower than that of the trilogy *U.S.A.*, (that fact allows Dos Passos to avoid the sprawling structure of the later work and to provide a tighter focus on the cast of characters. It was also easier for him to convey the sense of life in a single city—even one as large and diverse as New York—than, as he later tried, life throughout an entire nation.

Perhaps most important, *Manhattan Transfer* does not carry the strong political message that marks *U.S.A.* The earlier novel makes it clear that Dos Passos' sympathies are with working people rather than with their employers, with those driven to break the law rather than with those who enforce the law, and with outcasts rather than with "pillars of the community." His views, however, are not yet informed by a specific doctrine as they were in later years. For its style, its depiction of city life, and its vigor, *Manhattan Transfer* remains one of the genuine classics of the twentieth century novel.

"Critical Evaluation" by John M. Muste

Bibliography:
Arrington, Philip. "The Sense of an Ending in *Manhattan Transfer*." *American Literature* 54 (October, 1982): 438-443. A brief study of the way in which Dos Passos finds a satisfactory way of concluding his diverse and sometimes incoherent novel.

Clark, Michael. *Dos Passos's Early Fiction, 1912-1938*. Selinsgrove, Pa.: Susquehanna University Press, 1987. A detailed examination of the works leading up to and including *U.S.A.*, with emphasis on *Manhattan Transfer* as the most significant of the early works of the author.

Livingston, Townsend. *John Dos Passos: A Twentieth Century Odyssey*. New York: E. P. Dutton, 1980. A satisfactory and detailed biography, which includes examinations of *Manhattan Transfer* and his other major novels.

Sanders, David. *John Dos Passos: A Comprehensive Bibliography*. New York: Garland, 1985. A thorough compilation of the author's writings and of the major criticism of his work.

Wagner, Linda. *Dos Passos: Artist as American*. A good biography emphasizing Dos Passos' deliberate artistry and showing how his aims, as in the later novels, shaped the structure of *Manhattan Transfer*.

MANIFESTO OF SURREALISM

Type of work: Essays
Author: André Breton (1896-1966)
First published: Manifeste du surréalisme, 1924 (English translation, 1969)

The main goal of André Breton's *Manifesto of Surrealism* is, quite simply, to free one's mind from the past and from everyday reality so one can arrive at truths one has never known. By the time Breton wrote his manifesto, French poets—including Breton himself—and artists had already demonstrated Surrealist techniques in their work. In this sense, Breton was intent on explaining what painters and poets such as Giorgio de Chirico, Joan Miró, Robert Desnos, Max Ernst, and Breton himself had already achieved.

When Breton was a medical student in Nantes, France, before World War I, he had become interested in the theories of Austrian neurologist Sigmund Freud, who has since become widely known as the father of psychoanalysis. Later, during the war, Breton had been an ambulance driver in the French army and had found Freud's ideas useful in helping to treat wounded men. Eventually, Breton and his literary and artistic colleagues contributed to the acceptance in France of Freud and his theories of psychoanalysis, even though Freud's written work itself would not be translated into French until the late 1930's.

In his manifesto, Breton alludes to Freud's ideas about the meaning and significance of dreams and what Freud called the psychopathology of everyday life, those apparently inadvertent slips of the tongue and other "mistakes" that can be traced to states of the subconscious mind. Freud's theories interested Breton largely because they refer to a subconscious life that, Breton believed, constitutes a resource rich in visual and intellectual stimulation.

In Breton's view, one can learn to ascend to perception of a higher reality (the surreal) if one can manage to liberate one's psyche from traditional education, the drudgery of work, and the dullness of what is only useful in modern bourgeois culture. To achieve the heightened consciousness to which Breton wants humanity to aspire, one can also look to the example set by children, poets, and, to a lesser extent, insane persons.

Children, Breton suggests, have not yet learned to stifle their imaginations as most adults have, and successful poets have, similarly, been able to break down barriers erected by reason and tradition and have achieved ways of seeing, understanding, and creating that resemble the free, spontaneous imaginative play of children. On the other hand, as one grows up, one's imagination is dulled by the need to make a living and by concern for practical matters. Hence, in the manifesto's opening paragraphs, Breton calls for a return to the freedom of childhood. Furthermore, if the "insane" are, as Breton suggests, victims of their imaginations, one can learn from the mentally ill that hallucinations and illusions are often a source of considerable pleasure and creativity.

Because of Freud, Breton says, we can think of human beings as heroic explorers who are able to push their investigations beyond the mere facts of reality and the conscious mind and seize dormant strengths buried in the subconscious. Freud's work on the significance of dreams, Breton says, has been particularly crucial in this regard, and the manifesto contains a four-part defense of dreams.

Breton believes that Freud has shown that dreams must be respected as coherent sources of truth and of practical assistance in life. Indeed, despite what is often believed, it may be reality which interferes with dreams rather than the reverse. Hence, Breton recommends that one give oneself up to one's dreams, allowing oneself to be satisfied by what is received from dream states instead of applying the criteria of reason to dreams. Here, Breton's analysis takes on the language of religious fervor when he insists that if one reconciles dreams and reality, one will attain an absolute reality: surreality.

It is important to note, however, that the "surrealist consciousness" about which Breton writes is not uniquely the tool of artists. He believes, to the contrary, that even ordinary people will be happier and will be able to solve heretofore difficult problems once they have regained what he sees as a psychic wholeness.

At this point, Breton's manifesto is seen to divide itself broadly into two general elements: the development of theory and the accounts of practice, or how theory can be used.

One of the ways Surrealist theories can be put into practice is by means of what Breton calls "automatic writing." This process is actually similar to activities of free association or, in the practice of psychology, tests such as the well-known Rorschach test, in which the person being tested is shown various inkblot designs and asked to name objects that he or she thinks those shapes resemble.

As Breton and his friend, poet Robert Desnos, practiced "automatic writing," the activity involved writing as quickly as one could whatever came into one's mind, without any regard for constraints such as punctuation. The point was to bypass the restrictions of the analytical reasoning processes that one has learned and to which one has grown accustomed. As Breton says, the results of the automatic writing exercise included a new awareness of the relationships between things, words, and images. Automatic writing, which Breton calls "spoken thought," therefore stimulates the creative process by allowing one to create new relationships between things, relationships that one never would have seen by means of the customary ways of thinking.

In a section of the manifesto called "Secrets of the Magic Surrealist Art," Breton offers details of how one might participate in the Surrealist experience of automatic writing. One should make oneself as passive and receptive as possible and avoid thinking about literary criteria or items that others have written. Automatic writing must avoid any preconceived subject matter, and one should give oneself up to what Breton calls the inexhaustible flow of one's inner voice.

Out of this experience come Surrealist images, which Breton likens to images that come from drug-induced mental states. Surrealist images result from the fortuitous juxtaposition of two disparate elements, such as "stream" and "song," "daylight" and "white napkin," or "the world" and "a purse." Such juxtapositions, it is to be noted, have nothing to do with reason, which, Breton says, is limited in this process to observing and appreciating the work of the subconscious. Eventually, according to Breton, with the help of automatic writing, one arrives at an ideal realm, a "supreme reality," where even one's reason will recognize that one's knowledge has been extended greatly, opposites have been reconciled, and the mind as a whole has made extraordinary advances. It was the tangible results of this automatic writing that Breton and poet Philippe Soupault called Surrealism. In the manifesto, Breton defines Surrealism as pure psychic automatism which allows one to express—either verbally, in writing, or in some other fashion—the true functioning of thought without regard to any concern for morality or aesthetics.

Breton argues that imaginative literature, such as the novels of British writer Matthew Lewis, is superior to realistic literature, in which the author carefully details physical description and, in effect, tells one too much. Breton thinks that poetry and imaginative literature are worthy means of escape from the chores of daily reality. In fact, Breton says, the poet is like God, proposing and disposing of his own spiritual life and achieving a sense of fulfillment which reality steals from most people. He offers a list of writers, past and present, who have represented or represent Surrealist ideals: Jonathan Swift, the Marquis de Sade, Victor Hugo, and Arthur Rimbaud, as well as Victor Jarry, Leon Fargue, and Pierre Reverdy, among others. In art, Breton points to such painters as Pablo Picasso, Henri Matisse, Gustave Moreau, Georges Seurat, and Marcel Duchamp as major figures in the development of visual Surrealism. Yet it is Desnos, Breton says, who has shown himself to be the ideal Surrealist artist, submitting to numerous experiments and perfecting the ability to follow his train of thought orally, to "speak Surrealist."

While stopping short of recommending the application of the free-association spontaneity of automatic writing to action, Breton nevertheless emphasizes that the great discoveries of science, for example, will be made by truly independent minds, those which have transcended the past by means other than what he calls the "roads of reason." Here, Breton deals with genius, as embodied by those scholars and scientists who work, he suggests, without a clear, preconceived plan of exploration, striking out instead into the unknown. As for crime, where individuals might plead a kind of Surrealist lack of responsibility for what they have done, Breton does imply that a new moral order may one day replace the present ideas of right and wrong. This might happen, he suggests, once Surrealist "methods" gain widespread favor outside the areas of art and science.

Ultimately, Breton's *Manifesto of Surrealism* has perhaps had less influence, especially in the United States, than the ways that Surrealism was expressed in the visual arts. It was Spanish painter Salvador Dalí who came to best represent Surrealism in the popular imagination in the second half of the twentieth century. Dalí's strange paintings, such as the famous *The Persistence of Memory*, feature mirage-like landscapes in which the painter placed, as Breton had suggested, objects that ordinarily have nothing to do with one another or that exhibit bizarre properties. Oddly enough, Dalí's melting watches, dead trees, and insects piqued the imagination of a large group of art lovers, and he became an international celebrity. Breton did not, however, approve of Dalí's courting of public favor in such a theatrical way, and Breton eventually expressed his disdain of Dalí's work and public image. Nevertheless, Dalí's painting and his escapades must surely account in large part for the popular currency of the term "Surrealist," which entered the everyday vocabulary of most Americans as synonymous with the extraordinarily unexpected or shocking in a dreamlike or nightmarish way.

Gordon Walters

Bibliography:
Alquie, Ferdinand. *The Philosophy of Surrealism.* Ann Arbor: University of Michigan Press, 1965. As the book's title indicates, Alquie examines the ideological origins and content of Breton's ideas and those of other Surrealist writers. Chapters 3 and 4 deal in great part with Breton's manifestos and how their ideas relate particularly to poetry.
Balakian, Anna. *André Breton.* New York: Oxford University Press, 1972. Although this book is a biography of Breton, Balakian devotes a long section to Breton's two Surrealist manifestos. Equally thorough studies of Breton's other writings are here as well, along with an entire chapter on Surrealism and painting.
_____. *Surrealism: The Road to the Absolute.* New York: Noonday Press, 1959. Balakian traces the development of Surrealism and considers its application to the visual arts. Even more interesting perhaps is that the author sees a relationship between Surrealism and the hypotheses of nuclear physics.

Charvet, P. E., ed. *The Twentieth Century, 1870-1940.* Vol. 5 in *A Literary History of France.* New York: Barnes & Noble, 1967. In part 2, chapter 10, this history focuses on Surrealism and poetry, beginning with the transition from Dada to Surrealism and Breton's manifesto of 1924. This section includes a brief but pointed reference to Freud and Surrealism.

Cruickshank, John, ed. *The Twentieth Century.* Vol. 6 in *French Literature and Its Background.* New York: Oxford University Press, 1970. This book includes a chapter on Surrealism by R. Short, which is especially good on the historical and literary background of the movement. The volume also includes an extensive bibliography on Breton and Surrealism.

MANON LESCAUT

Type of work: Novel
Author: Abbé Prévost (Antoine-François Prévost d'Exiles, 1697-1763)
Type of plot: Sentimental
Time of plot: 1700
Locale: France and New Orleans
First published: Histoire du chevalier des Grieux et de Manon Lescaut, 1731 (English
translation, 1734); revised, 1753 (English translation, 1786)

> *Principal characters:*
> MANON LESCAUT, a courtesan
> THE CHEVALIER DES GRIEUX, her lover
> TIBERGE, his friend
> MONSIEUR DE G—— M——, a wealthy nobleman
> MONSIEUR LESCAUT, Manon's brother

The Story:
　　When the young Chevalier des Grieux was a student of philosophy in Amiens, he became
friendly with a fellow student named Tiberge. One day, he stood idly with his friend and
watched the arrival of the Arras coach. Among the passengers was a beautiful young woman,
who attracted the chevalier's attention. Politely introducing himself, he learned that her name
was Manon Lescaut and that she had come to Amiens under the protection of an elderly man.
Against her will, she was to enter a convent. She accepted the chevalier's offer to set her free
from that fate, and after skillfully and untruthfully disposing of her escort, she went with the
young student to an inn. They planned to flee to Paris the next day. Tiberge argued with his
friend against this folly, but the chevalier was hopelessly infatuated. In Paris, he and Manon
took a furnished apartment, where for three weeks they were absorbed in each other.
　　The idyll came to an end when the young lover discovered that his mistress had also
bestowed her affections on Monsieur de B——. The chevalier's love for Manon was so great,
however, that he forgave her. Then three lackeys, sent by the chevalier's father, came to the
apartment and took the young man home. There his father tried in vain to persuade him that
Manon had behaved treacherously. Finally the father locked his son in his room for six weeks.
During this time Tiberge came to visit him, bringing him news that Manon was being kept at
the expense of Monsieur de B——. Finally Tiberge persuaded the young man to enroll at the
Seminary of Saint-Supplice as a student of theology. With his father's permission, he entered
the school and became an outstanding student. Manon was present to hear his declamation at
the public disputation at the Sorbonne, and after the ceremonies she came to visit him. A single
passionate embrace made him forget his future in the Church. The chevalier escaped from his
school without any money, and Manon furnished the funds for them to set up quarters at
Chaillot, outside Paris.
　　Then began a life of extravagance and riotous living far beyond their slender means. In Paris,
they met Manon's brother, Monsieur Lescaut of the Royal Guards, who did not scruple to install
himself in their house. When a fire destroyed all of their money and possessions, the brother
suggested that Manon sell her charms to some freehanded nobleman. The chevalier rejected this
proposal but consented to become a professional gambler to support Manon. He borrowed

enough money from Tiberge to begin his career as a card cheat. For a time his luck held, but their period of prosperity ended when a maid and a valet fled with all the valuable possessions of the new household. Urged by her brother, Manon consented to become the mistress of the old and wealthy Monsieur de G—— M——, who had promised her a house, servants, and a large sum of money.

The young couple decided to play on Manon's protector by introducing the chevalier into the household as her brother. Having duped the man to make his settlement on Manon, they ran away with the jewels and money he had given her. They were followed by the police, apprehended, and imprisoned, Manon at the Hôpital Général, the chevalier at Saint-Lazare.

Once lodged at Saint-Lazare, the chevalier began to plan his escape. He cultivated his superiors and made a show of reading theology. M. de G—— M——, hearing of the chevalier's studious habits, came to visit him; but when the young man heard, for the first time, that Manon was also imprisoned, he seized the old man by the throat and tried to throttle him. The monks stopped the fight and saved the old man's life.

The chevalier now wrote to Tiberge, asking his old friend to visit Saint-Lazare. He entrusted to Tiberge a note addressed to M. Lescaut. Using a pistol that Manon's brother brought him soon afterward, the chevalier escaped, killing a turnkey in his flight. Later, by bribing the attendants at the hospital, he was able to arrange for Manon's escape. Wearing men's clothing, Manon was safely conveyed to her brother's house, but just as the happy pair descended from the carriage, M. Lescaut was shot by a man whose fortune the guardsman had won at cards. Manon and the chevalier fled to the inn at Chaillot to escape apprehension for the murder.

In Paris the next day the chevalier borrowed a hundred pistoles from Tiberge. He also met M. de T——, a friend, whom he invited to Chaillot for supper. During the meal the son of old M. de G—— M—— arrived at the inn. The impetuous young chevalier wanted to kill him at once to get revenge on the father, but M. de T—— persuaded him rather to meet young de G—— M—— in a friendly manner over the supper table. The young man was charmed with Manon; like his father, he offered to maintain her handsomely. Manon accepted his rich presents, but she and her lover planned to deceive the gullible young man and avenge themselves on his father. The chevalier planned to have street ruffians capture and hold the infatuated young man while Manon and the chevalier enjoyed the supper and the bed de G—— M—— had arranged for himself and his mistress. The young man's father learned of the scheme, however, and Manon and the chevalier were surprised by the police, who hurried them off to the Chatelet.

The young chevalier now appealed to his father, whose influence was great enough to secure his son's release. He refused to interest himself in Manon, however, and she was sentenced to exile on the next shipload of convicts to be sent to the penal colony in Louisiana. After a bungled attempt to rescue her from the prison guards, the chevalier accompanied his mistress on the trip from the prison to Havre-de-Grace. He also gained permission to accompany her on the voyage to America. On board ship and on their arrival in New Orleans they passed as husband and wife.

In New Orleans, they settled in a rude shelter. After the chevalier secured honorable employment, Manon desired above all things that they become legally husband and wife. The chevalier appealed to the governor for permission to marry and admitted his earlier deceit. The governor refused, for his nephew M. Synnelet, had fallen in love with Manon. As a result, the chevalier fought a duel with Synnelet. Thinking that he had killed his opponent, he and Manon left the colony, but on the journey Manon, ill from fatigue, died in the midst of a vast plain. The chevalier was heartbroken. Tiberge, who had followed his friend to America, persuaded him to return to France. There the chevalier resolved to turn to God in penance.

Critical Evaluation:

Most critics agree that the mercurial life of L'Abbé Antoine-François Prévost d'Exiles contributed to the creation of *Manon Lescaut*. After vacillating between the priesthood and the military and being satisfied with neither, he launched in the 1720's one of the most prolific careers of the century as novelist, editor, translator, journalist, and chronicler of travel accounts.

After completing four volumes of *Le Philosophe anglais: Ou, Les Mémoires de Cleveland* (1732-1739; *The Life and Entertaining Adventures of Mr. Cleveland, Natural Son of Oliver Cromwell,* 1734, 1753), Prévost began to travel between England and Holland. Apparently he was in debt in each country, possibly as the result of an uncertain relationship with a reputed Madame Lenki. In 1734, he was absolved of all clerical transgressions and received a sinecure at Evreux, which he used as a point of departure for Paris and Holland. In 1740, he traveled, again under mysterious circumstances, to Belgium and Germany. In 1746, he settled at Chaillot and continued his remarkable productivity. Church authorities rewarded his efforts by adding to his endowment.

In addition to *Manon Lescaut*, two other works by Prévost—*The Story of a Modern Greek,* (1740) and *The Journal of an Honest Man* (1745)—belong in the genre of the sentimental French novel. Two themes in these novels, which are also present in the English literature that Prévost translated by such writers as Samuel Richardson, Frances Sheridan, and John Dryden, are passionate, tragic love and redemption through suffering.

Histoire du Chevalier Des Grieux et de Manon Lescaut was published in 1731 as the seventh volume of *Mémoires et aventures d'un homme de qualité, qui s'est retiré du monde* (1728-1731; *Memoirs of a Man of Quality After His Retirement from the World,* 1738, a rambling collection of quixotic tales and personal adventures narrated by a Marquis de Renoncour. The commonly used abridged title tends to give Manon an importance she was probably not meant to have. Renoncour introduces the chevalier des Grieux, the protagonist of the story, but he himself does not participate in the events and he merely acts as an impartial observer of the various picaresque adventures—storms at sea, abductions, chance encounters and recognitions, and tranquil moments shattered by action and suspense. All of this is revealed from the marquis' point of view, and it is therefore difficult to ascertain Manon's response to her situation.

Prévost combines realism—his use of the social types, names of places, and the importance of money—with pre-Romantic sentimentality. This combination allows the novel to operate on several levels. Even though Manon is at times promiscuous and des Grieux is an impetuous social deviant, they live without shame in naïve defiance of aristocratic conventions. The spirit of the novel is defined by sensuality, emphasis on living in the present, and restless frivolity. Manon and des Grieux play the following psychological roles: those of jilted lover, faithful husband, provider, brother and sister, mistress-mother, and abandoned child.

Perhaps this explains the magnetism of *Manon Lescaut* to each new generation of readers. Manon was the adopted heroine of the nineteenth century; she was rhapsodized as an image of enigmatic femininity. The idealistic reader might argue that Manon's originally pure love for des Grieux was corrupted by the harmful influence of civilization. Love is dependent on economics in the capitalist marketplace. Manon is not heartless or predatory, but she is mostly interested in maintaining a certain way of life. Perhaps the need for emotional security represents her deepest impulse. She certainly takes enormous risks to attain it. The prison scenes, the deportation of prostitutes, and the gambling dens remind the reader that a heavy penalty awaited those who failed to bargain successfully with fate.

For this reason, *Manon Lescaut* has continued to receive praise from influential writers, and it has inspired a sequel, several dramatic versions, and three famous operas—Daniel-François-

Esprit Auber's *Manon Lescaut* (1856), Jules Massenet's *Manon* (1884), and Giacomo Puccini's *Manon Lescaut* (1893). This cluster of interpretations has crystallized into a composite image of des Grieux and Manon as archetypal lovers.

It is equally instructive to regard *Manon Lescaut* as a product of its times. The age of uncertainty produced by the regency of Louis XV, the South Sea bankruptcy scam in England, and the breakdown of the French economy under John Law had literary repercussions. *Manon Lescaut* promotes love as an innocent passion in a reckless moral climate in which ethical judgment has become dependent on situation. Des Grieux, a second son, is relegated to a choice between the Knights of Malta or the seminary. Manon, not commanding a dowry, is sent to a convent. Des Grieux's infatuation for her leads to criminality, yet his own and Manon's delinquency seems beyond his comprehension. This psychotic indifference to his past is contrasted with Tiberge's personality—the Christian alter ego—and by disastrous interventions through the heavy hand of parental or legal authority.

Prévost's style depends largely on the presentation of contrasting moods and images. The peaceful and retired life is juxtaposed with the Parisian demimonde. Des Grieux's fervor is counterbalanced by Tiberge's spiritual calm. The courtesan and her paramour see their love extinguished in a stark, indeterminate setting, geographically different but emotionally identical to their origins. Prévost develops the timeless motifs of pleasure, luxury, amusement, loss, bereavement, and obsession with economy of language, unaffected lyricism, and classical reserve.

These qualities are even more evident in the 1953 revision of the first edition, which eliminated superfluous language and softened the emotional effect.

The French historian Jules Michelet claimed that *Manon Lescaut* evokes a nostalgia for the manners and mores of the *ancien régime*. In that context, Manon and des Grieux resemble figures in a painting in which the richly polished, cinematic interior scenes are set against the turbulent background of eighteenth century life in Europe and the New World. Whether Manon is viewed as siren or saint, des Grieux as hero or misfit, their literary reputation as quasi-mythical, amoral lovers continues to be affirmed.

"Critical Evaluation" by Robert J. Frail

Bibliography:
Auerbach, Erich. *Mimesis: The Representation of Reality in Western Literature.* Translated by W. R. Trask. Princeton, N.J.: Princeton University Press, 1953. A legendary study of Prévost's artistic technique, this essay uses *Manon Lescaut* as an intellectual springboard to evaluate a wide range of Enlightenment configurations. A vigorous, thought-provoking analysis of erotic sentimentality in literature.
Gilroy, James P. *The Romantic Manon and Des Grieux: Images of Prévost's Heroine and Hero in Nineteenth-Century French Literature.* Sherbrooke, Québec: Éditions Naaman, 1980. A compelling and evocative study that celebrates Manon's status as the enigmatic darling of French literature. Also traces the universality of Manon and des Grieux as archetypal lovers who transcend barriers of time and place.
Kory, Odile A. *Subjectivity and Sensitivity in the Novels of the Abbé Prévost.* Paris: Didier, 1972. Somewhat rambling and discursive, but points out the importance of *Manon Lescaut* as an arranging element in eighteenth century French fiction. Discusses the timeless dimensions of morality, psychology, and the quest for identity.
Rabine, Leslie W. *Reading the Romantic Heroine: Text, History, Idelogy.* Ann Arbor: University

of Michigan Press, 1985. A lively and engaging study that emphasizes the pivotal importance of *Manon Lescaut* in pre-Romantic fiction. Serves as a nice counterpoint to "over-reading" interpretations of the novel.

Segal, Naomi. *The Unintended Reader: Feminism and "Manon Lescaut."* Cambridge, England: Cambridge University Press, 1986. A review of critical reactions to *Manon Lescaut* over a two-hundred-year period, with an emphasis on the phenomenon of seduction by language. The author attempts to apply Freudian Oedipal analogies to issues of female autonomy, identity, and self-esteem.

MAN'S FATE

Type of work: Novel
Author: André Malraux (1901-1976)
Type of plot: Social realism
Time of plot: 1927
Locale: Shanghai, China
First published: La Condition humaine, 1933 (English translation, 1934)

Principal characters:
> CH'EN, a Chinese terrorist
> KYO, a Communist organizer of French and Japanese parentage
> GISORS, Kyo's father
> MAY, Kyo's German wife
> BARON DE CLAPPIQUE, a French adventurer
> KATOV, a Russian revolutionist
> HEMMELRICH, a German revolutionist
> FERRAL, a French businessman
> KONIG, the chief of Chiang Kai-shek's police

The Story:

The Reds, a revolutionary group with a nucleus of Moscow agents, had made a temporary alliance with Chiang Kai-shek, their immediate object being to control Shanghai with the help of the Kuomintang. The alliance, however, was an uneasy one, for neither side trusted the other. The Reds had completed their plans to seize Shanghai, ostensibly as part of Chiang Kai-shek's campaign, but they intended to put a Communist in control before the Blue army arrived. On their part, the Blues hoped to use the Communists to seize the city and afterward disperse the revolutionaries.

Ch'en, the terrorist, stood ready to strike through the mosquito netting and kill the sleeper in the bed. Nerving himself for his first murder, he plunged his dagger into the man's heart. Quickly from the dead man he took a paper which would authorize the delivery of arms now aboard the *Shantung,* at anchor in the harbor. The Reds counted on these arms to seize control of the city before government troops arrived.

Ch'en took the document to Hemmelrich's phonograph shop, where Kyo was waiting. There they all congratulated him—Kyo, Katov, and Hemmelrich. Kyo and Katov tested their new code of paralleled phonograph records. One record gave an innocent language lesson, the other gave a loud hiss which covered all but the key words on the first record. Satisfied with their work, they planned a final check of their revolutionary cells. Hemmelrich refused to go with them; his wife and child were sick.

Kyo and Katov visited their two hundred units. A general strike at noon would paralyze the city. At the same time, saboteurs would wreck the railway so that the government could not send reinforcements from the battlefront. Other groups would take over police stations and army posts and seize all firearms. With the grenades already on hand, they would be equipped to resist even tanks.

Kyo went to the Black Cat, a nightclub where he knew he could find de Clappique. The Frenchman was drunk, but he had to be trusted. De Clappique was commissioned to take a forged order to the *Shantung*, directing her to shift anchorage. Tired and tense, Kyo went home. Gisors, his father, was still awake, and Kyo told him a few details of the plan. Then May, Kyo's wife, came home exhausted from her hospital work. She was one of the few women doctors in all Shanghai, a woman with advanced views on marriage relationships. She and Kyo quarreled because of her affair with another doctor. During the quarrel de Clappique came to report that the *Shantung* had moved. A messenger recalled Kyo to headquarters.

Dressed as government soldiers, Kyo and Katov with ten others boarded the *Shantung* and got the arms, but only after seizing the captain and holding him prisoner. Now the revolutionaries could plan with confidence. Meanwhile Ferral, head of the French Chamber of Commerce, decided to throw his support to Chiang Kai-shek. After giving orders to send funds to the Blues, he returned with his mistress Valerie. It was arranged that she would see him the following night at her hotel. He was to bring her a pet bird in a cage. At the appointed time Ferral asked for Valerie at the hotel desk. To his surprise, she was out. A young Englishman was also waiting for her with a caged bird. To revenge himself, Ferral bought the entire stock of a pet store—forty birds and a kangaroo—and set them loose in Valerie's room.

The uprising took place as planned. Ch'en seized one police station with ease and armed his small band. The second station was better defended, and grenades failed to dislodge officers barricaded on the top floor. Ch'en set fire to the building, killing the resisters as well as his own wounded comrades.

The feeble central government could not fight both Chiang and the Reds at the same time. While the government forces were occupied with the Blues, the Reds easily took control of the city. Two days later, the Blues under Chiang approached Shanghai. The general had been shrewd enough to send his first division, composed largely of Communists, to another front; consequently the Communists found themselves confronting an unsympathetic Blue army which in turn took over the city. Many of the Communists were arrested. When Moscow ordered all armed Communists to surrender their weapons to Chiang's police, dissension broke out among the Reds. Many of the Chinese deserted the Moscow party and embarked on a terroristic campaign of their own.

Ch'en conceived the idea that he must kill Chiang in order to free China. He lay in wait with two companions to throw a bomb into the general's car. His first attempt having failed, Ch'en went to Hemmelrich's shop. Hemmelrich refused to shelter him. In a second attempt, Ch'en threw himself with his bomb under the automobile. The car was wrecked and Ch'en was killed, but Chiang was not in the car.

Chiang's police destroyed Hemmelrich's shop, accidentally killing his wife and baby. Believing his cowardice was the cause of Ch'en's action and the subsequent riot, Hemmelrich seized some grenades and joined the rioters. All were killed except Hemmelrich, who escaped by murdering an officer and fleeing in his uniform.

Now in complete control, Chiang's police chief, Konig, began to round up the Communists, and Katov was among them. When the word went out that Kyo was to be arrested, Gisors begged de Clappique to intervene because the baron was Konig's good friend. Instead of warning Kyo, de Clappique lingered in a gambling house until after Kyo had been arrested. Later de Clappique went to Konig to ask for Kyo's release. The Frenchman was given only forty-eight hours to leave China. In prison, Katov and Kyo each had cyanide tablets. Kyo poisoned himself, but Katov gave half his tablet to each of two panic-stricken prisoners and went to his execution with his revolutionary group.

Each of the survivors sought safety in his own way. Gisors returned to Japan to teach painting. May went to Moscow to practice medicine. By disguising himself, de Clappique got aboard the same French liner that was taking Ferral back to France. So the Communists and their sympathizers were destroyed by relentless Chiang and the vacillating policy of Moscow. Yet there was good news from China for the survivors; the quiet work of revolution had already started again.

Critical Evaluation:

In this novel, depicting the aborted Communist Revolution in China in 1927, André Malraux presents three types of revolutionaries. Each is attracted to the revolution for different reasons and reacts to the events in a distinctive manner.

Ch'en, the terrorist, is shown in the opening scene of the novel in the process of committing his first murder. This experience is so intense that he feels himself separated from those who have been killed. His sense of isolation leads him to believe that individual acts of terrorism are superior to any other form of revolutionary action. He ultimately comes to the conclusion that the only way to have the revolution is to kill Chiang. He initially attempts to perform this act with the aid of two comrades, but the attempt fails. He then decides to perform the deed alone. Ironically, he is killed while throwing himself with a grenade on a car he believes to be occupied by Chiang. Although Chiang is not in the car, Ch'en has died a death consistent with his beliefs, a death that has given his life meaning.

Kyo is the theorist who finds it difficult to reconcile his belief in Marxist theory with the realities of the revolution. For example, although he theoretically believes that no person can be the property of another and that love is free, he is jealous when his wife, May, tells him that she has slept with another man. Kyo is drawn to the revolution because of his belief in the need for human dignity. He loses faith in Communist theory when he finds out (during a trip to Hankow) that the leaders of the Party are willing to betray the people on orders from Moscow. Kyo believes that Communist theory is only of value if it helps the masses to live a more dignified life; he cannot reconcile his beliefs with the political machinations that confront him. During a brief stay in jail, he sees human beings submitted to the most degrading humiliation. When offered a choice of life or death, he chooses death with dignity rather than life with humiliation. His death, although very different from Ch'en's, is consistent with his life. He chooses his death, committing suicide by taking cyanide.

Katov is the most experienced of the three, for he fought in the Russian Revolution. Unlike Ch'en, who cherished his solitude, Katov cherishes his solidarity with his comrades. Like the others, his death is consistent with his life. Although he, like Kyo, has a cyanide pill, Katov chooses to share his pill with two young, frightened comrades. Since there is only enough cyanide to kill two men, his gift of the capsule is the supreme sacrifice, for Katov faces death by being thrown alive into the boiler of a train engine. He believes that his sacrifice gives his life meaning, for through his sacrifice he achieves the fraternity for which he fought in the revolution.

Although these three men are very different, they are similar in joining the revolution in order to give meaning to their lives. Each acts as a revolutionary and dies as a revolutionary in a manner consistent with his beliefs.

Bibliography:

Boak, Denis. "La Condition humaine." In *André Malraux*. Oxford, England: Clarendon Press, 1968. A judicious consideration of the novel within the perspective of Malraux's development as a writer. Emphasizes its metaphysical rather than political aspects. Detailed consideration of imagery and characterization.

Chua, Cheng Lok. "The International Theme in André Malraux's Asian Novels." *Modern Language Quarterly* 39, no. 2 (June, 1978): 169-182. An Asian's view of Malraux's Asian novels, especially *Man's Fate*. Discusses Malraux's cross-fertilization of the European values of individualism and will with Asian values of communal identity and harmony, and his use of irony in plot to create tragic protagonists.

Frohock, W. M. *André Malraux and the Tragic Imagination*. Stanford, Calif.: Stanford University Press, 1952. Classic consideration of Malraux's fictional canon. The chapter on *Man's Fate* analyzes Malraux's style, the rhythm and pattern of the novel's action, its characterization, and the thematic and aesthetic effects of the characters' fates.

Hiddleston, J. A. *Malraux: La Condition humaine*. London: Edward Arnold, 1973. Useful but somewhat critical of Malraux. Focuses on Malraux's concern with the individual's ability to question the world, which leads to his characters' recurrent dilemma of whether to be or to do. Organized into two sections, the first dealing with characters and themes, the second with thought and form. Quite brief.

Leefmans, Bert M.-P. "Malraux and Tragedy: The Structure of *La Condition humaine*." *Romanic Review* 44, no. 3 (October, 1953): 208-214. Pioneering analysis of the formal structure of *Man's Fate*. Shows the seven parts of the novel's action conforming to the classic rise and fall of tragedy, developing in the equally classic pattern of purpose, passion, and perception.

MANSFIELD PARK

Type of work: Novel
Author: Jane Austen (1775-1817)
Type of plot: Domestic realism
Time of plot: Early nineteenth century
Locale: Northamptonshire, England
First published: 1814

Principal characters:
FANNY PRICE, a poor relation at Mansfield Park
SIR THOMAS BERTRAM, the owner of Mansfield Park
LADY BERTRAM, his wife
TOM,
EDMUND,
MARIA, and
JULIA BERTRAM, Fanny's cousins
MRS. NORRIS, a busybody aunt
HENRY CRAWFORD, a self-centered young gentleman
MARY CRAWFORD, his sister
MR. RUSHWORTH, Maria Bertram's suitor
MR. YATES, a young man of fashion

The Story:

The three Ward sisters had each fared differently in marriage. One had married a wealthy baronet, one had married a poor lieutenant of the marines, and the last had married a clergyman. The wealthiest of the sisters, Lady Bertram, agreed at the instigation of her clerical sister, Mrs. Norris, to care for one of the unfortunate sister's nine children. Accordingly, a shy, sensitive, ten-year-old Fanny Price came to make her home at Mansfield Park. Among her four Bertram cousins, Tom, Edmund, Maria, and Julia, Fanny found a real friend only in Edmund. The others usually ignored her except when she could be of use to them, but Edmund comforted and advised her. He alone seemed to recognize that she possessed cleverness, grace, and a pleasant disposition. Besides Edmund's attentions, Fanny received some of a very different kind from her selfish and hypocritical Aunt Norris, who constantly called unnecessary attention to Fanny's dependent position.

When Fanny was fifteen years old, Sir Thomas Bertram went to Antigua to look after some business affairs. His oldest son, who was inclined to extravagance and dissipation, went with him, and the family was left to Edmund's and Lady Bertram's care. During Sir Thomas' absence, his older daughter, Maria, became engaged to Mr. Rushworth, a young man who was rich and well-connected but extremely stupid.

Another event of importance was the arrival in the village of Mary and Henry Crawford, the sister and brother of Mrs. Grant, whose husband had become the rector after the death of Mr. Norris. Both the Bertram girls liked Henry immensely; since Maria was engaged, however, he rightfully "belonged" to Julia. They also became close friends with Mary Crawford, who in turn attracted both Tom, now returned from abroad, and Edmund.

Fanny regretted the Crawfords' arrival, for she saw that Edmund, whom she herself loved, was falling in love with the shallow, worldly Mary, and that her cousin Maria was carrying on a most unseemly flirtation with Henry. The less observant, like Mrs. Norris, saw only what they wished to see and insisted that Henry was paying particular attention to Julia.

At the suggestion of Mr. Yates, a pleasure-loving friend of Tom, the young people decided to put on some private theatricals; they chose for their entertainment the sentimental play *Lovers' Vows* (1798) by Elizabeth Inchbald. Fanny opposed the scheme from the start, for she knew Sir Thomas would have disapproved. Edmund tried to dissuade the others but finally let himself be talked into taking a part because there were not enough men for all the roles. Rehearsals and preparations went forward, and the plan grew more elaborate as it progressed. The unexpected return of Sir Thomas, however, put an end to the rehearsals. The house was soon cleared of all signs of theatrical activity, and of Mr. Yates, whose trifling, affected ways Sir Thomas had disliked immediately.

Maria, who was willing to break her engagement to Mr. Rushworth, had hoped her father's return would bring a declaration from Henry. Instead of declaring himself, however, he announced his departure for a stay in Bath. Maria's pride was hurt, but she resolved that Henry Crawford should never know she had taken their flirtation seriously. She was duly married to Mr. Rushworth.

Julia went to Brighton with the Rushworths. With both the Bertram sisters gone, Henry began an idle flirtation with Fanny, which ended with his falling in love with her. Her beloved brother William had just visited her at Mansfield Park. One of Henry's plans for winning Fanny's favor was a scheme for getting a promotion for William in the navy. Although Fanny was grateful for this favor, she promptly refused him when he proposed. In doing so, she incurred the serious displeasure of her uncle, Sir Thomas, who regarded the sentiments that made her turn down such an advantageous match as sheer perversity. Even Edmund encouraged her to change her mind, for he was too preoccupied with his attachment to Mary Crawford to guess that Fanny had more than a cousinly regard for him. Edmund had just been ordained as a clergyman, a step that Mary Crawford ridiculed, and he was not sure she would accept him as a husband. He persisted in believing, however, that her frivolous dislike of the clergy was only a trait she had acquired from her worldly friends; he believed that he could bring about a change in Mary's opinion.

About this time, Fanny was sent to Portsmouth to visit her family and to be reminded of what poverty is like. The stay was a depressing one, for she found her family, with the exception of William, disorderly and ill-bred by the standards of Mansfield Park. In addition, several catastrophes occurred at Mansfield Park to make her wish she could be of help there. Tom, the oldest son, had such a serious illness that his recovery was uncertain; Maria, now Mrs. Rushworth, had run away with Henry, who forgot his love for Fanny long enough to commit this irrevocable mistake; and Julia eloped with Mr. Yates. Only now, crushed under this series of blows, did the Bertram family at last realize Fanny's value and dearness to them. She was welcomed back to Mansfield Park with a tenderness that touched her deeply.

Mrs. Norris, as spiteful as ever, said that if Fanny had accepted Henry Crawford as she should have, he would never have run away with Maria. Sir Thomas, however, gave Fanny credit for seeing Henry's character more clearly than he had, and he forgave her for having refused Henry. He blamed himself for Maria's downfall, for he realized he had never taken the trouble to know his children well.

Nevertheless, good came from all this evil. Tom's illness sobered him, and he proved a better son thereafter. Although not a great match for Julia, Mr. Yates had more income and fewer debts than Sir Thomas had anticipated, and he seemed inclined to settle down to quiet domesticity. Henry and Maria separated after spending a few unhappy months together. Sir Thomas refused to receive her at Mansfield Park but provided a home for her in another part of the country. Mrs. Norris went to live with her favorite niece, to the great relief of everyone at Mansfield Park.

Edmund finally realized Mary Crawford's frivolous and worldly nature when he saw how lightly she treated the affair of his sister and her brother. Her levity shocked him and made it easier for him to give up thoughts of such an unsuitable marriage. Eventually, he fell in love with the cousin who had loved him for so long a time. Fanny and he were married and moved to the parsonage near Mansfield Park.

Critical Evaluation:

Mansfield Park explores important moral themes woven into a seeming Cinderella story of a poor girl taken in and then neglected by proud, wealthy relatives. Fanny Price is slighted by three of her four confident, energetic cousins. While they pursue their favorite activities, she is required to run endless errands and perform tedious tasks for her aunts. Having little share in the friendships of her cousins, she is happiest alone in her room, a cold, cheerless place furnished with old, cast-off things. Small, timid, and seemingly docile, Fanny does not seem to fit the image of the romantic heroine, but she grows in strength of body and mind as the novel progresses. By the end of the story, her strength of character and unshakable moral convictions win for her the praise, love, and social position she desires.

When the story opens, the unfortunate young cousin from a large, poor family is terrified by the grandeur of Mansfield Park. After she becomes accustomed to life there, she enjoys staying in the background, assisting her aunts and meekly accepting her inferior position in a luxurious household. She feels content with her place in the world. While most of her relatives think her boring and stupid, cousin Edmund, who seeks out her friendship, grows to respect and care for her. With his kind support, she overcomes her timidity to ride horseback for outdoor exercise and to speak up for herself. These instances show that Fanny is capable of a more active life when encouraged.

In fact, Fanny is the only one at Mansfield Park with convictions and character strong enough to refuse to act in the amateur play production, an activity Sir Thomas has forbidden. Her relatives, when tempted by the chance to impress or placate someone they admire, turn away from what they have been taught to believe right and thus betray the values of the family. Fanny alone remains faithful to the routines and rules of the household. Her cousins are amazed by her courage, and Aunt Norris calls her refusal to oblige the others positively wicked.

Later, Fanny is pressured by relatives and friends to accept the marriage proposal of the wealthy, charming Henry Crawford. She again shows surprising strength of character by refusing to follow the wishes of others when they go against her own values. Sir Thomas finds her decision "offensive, and disgusting beyond all common offense." Nevertheless, Fanny prefers staying at Mansfield Park as almost an unpaid servant to marrying someone she does not care for and respect, though by marrying she could have gained approval, security, and social position. Fanny, who is usually obedient and cooperative, proves to be a strongly independent character in matters of importance.

In contrast with Fanny, her Bertram cousins, who at first appear decisive and confident, are swept along in circumstances that bring them shame and disappointment. Tom gambles until he has amassed staggering debts and becomes seriously ill. Maria ruins her marriage and reputation by eloping with Henry Crawford after she has married foolish Rushworth out of spite. Julia, because she is bored, marries a careless, frivolous friend of her brother. Thus the seemingly fortunate cousins spoil their lives by impulsive and thoughtless actions.

Henry and Mary Crawford, the worldly London brother and sister visiting in the neighborhood, are the most intelligent, talented, and attractive characters of the novel. They glow with life and sparkle with wit, making Fanny and her cousins look dull by comparison. The Crawfords, too, understand the true worth of human goodness. Henry so fully recognizes and admires Fanny's purity of heart and inner beauty that he wishes to marry her. Mary begins to fall in love with sincere, good Edmund and to imagine herself as his wife.

The Crawfords bewitch everyone by their charm except Fanny, who finds them dangerous. She envies the attraction the glamorous Mary exerts on Edmund, and she distrusts Henry's flirtatious ways with her female cousins. Even more, she distrusts their opportunistic and scheming ways: Henry callously flirts with both Maria and Julia merely to discover whether he can make them fall in love with him; Mary lies to help her brother have his way and casually overlooks his seducing and ruining of Maria. Flawed as they are, Jane Austen has sketched the Crawfords so brilliantly that they sometimes seem to dominate the story. Some readers have wondered whether Fanny and Henry would not have been excellent marriage partners, each complementing the other's abilities. Some wonder whether Edmund would not have been made happier by vivacious Mary than by his quiet, tender cousin Fanny.

Austen's style and tone in this novel are generally serious and thoughtful. The themes of right conduct and integrity of personal values influence the tone of conversations as well as the delineation of the characters. Lighthearted moments often express frivolous or insincere feelings and thoughts rather than simple enjoyment. When Mary Crawford observes about a career in the navy during wartime, "The profession is well enough under two circumstances; if it make the fortune, and there be discretion in spending it," her sentiment mocks the heroic efforts of sailors fighting against Napoleon.

The role of parents in caring for their children is of particular interest in Mansfield Park. Fanny moves from her parents' chaotic, poverty-stricken home to the well-organized, luxurious home of the Bertrams. There Sir Thomas rigidly oversees the children's upbringing while his agreeable wife, Lady Bertram, sits nodding on the sofa, petting her lap dog, Pug. Family life continues smoothly enough until Sir Thomas is called away on business. Left alone and neglected by their incapable mother, the children rebel against family rules in various ways that lead to pain and misfortune. Sir Thomas returns in time to witness but too late to prevent the disaster. Only Fanny is spared disaster.

"Critical Evaluation" by Patricia H. Fulbright

Bibliography:
Butler, Marilyn. *Jane Austen and the War of Ideas.* Oxford, England: Clarendon Press, 1987. Explores Austen's conservative attitudes toward female education by contrasting Fanny, the "perfect" Christian heroine, with the other female characters. Argues that Fanny is a paradoxical and appealing mixture of feeble passivity and quiet endurance.
Duckworth, Alistair. *The Improvement of the Estate: A Study of Jane Austen's Novels.* Baltimore: The Johns Hopkins University Press, 1971. A crucial study of Austen's treatment of the relation between the individual and society. Asserts that Austen uses the country estate to represent social, political, and moral order. In *Mansfield Park*, contrasts the "improvers," who sacrifice harmony to individual desire, with Fanny, whose individual respect enlivens the communal values of Mansfield Park.
Fleishman, Avrom. *A Reading of "Mansfield Park": An Essay in Critical Synthesis.* Minneapolis: University of Minnesota Press, 1967. A detailed multiperspectival discussion of

the novel. Places the novel in its historical context, examines the psychological realism of Austen's characters, and analyzes the novel's mythical structure. Also contains a helpful bibliography.

Mooneyham, Laura G. *Romance, Language and Education in Jane Austen's Novels.* New York: St. Martin's Press, 1988. Interprets the central issue of *Mansfield Park* as the heroine's education. Sees this, however, as Fanny's progress from the negative, because incomplete, virtues of duty and patience to the positive, active, virtues of judging and directing.

Southam, B. C. *Critical Essays on Jane Austen.* New York: Barnes & Noble Books, 1968. A helpful, introductory collection of ten essays, two of which deal specifically with *Mansfield Park*, exploring the artistry with which Austen conveys the novel's moral and social conservatism.

THE MANSION

Type of work: Novel
Author: William Faulkner (1897-1962)
Type of plot: Social realism
Time of plot: 1908-1948
Locale: Mississippi
First published: 1959

Principal characters:
MINK SNOPES, the protagonist
LINDA SNOPES KOHL, Eula Snopes's daughter
FLEM SNOPES, Linda's "public" father
GAVIN STEVENS, an attorney, Linda's friend
V. K. RATLIFF, Gavin's friend

The Story:

Mink Snopes, convicted of Jack Houston's murder, received a life sentence. Mink killed Houston over a one-dollar pound fee. He learned parole was possible if he behaved and did not attempt escape. Mink accepted that, planning to return in twenty years to murder Flem, who, being close kin and powerful, Mink thought should have helped him.

After seventeen years, through Flem's manipulations, Montgomery Ward Snopes was imprisoned at Parchman prison for possession of bootleg whiskey. Flem told Montgomery to set Mink up to escape and be caught. Montgomery told Mink that Flem wanted him to wear a girl's dress for the escape. Mink, caught and sentenced to twenty additional years, did not fault Flem for tricking him but sent word that "he hadn't ought to used that dress." Two years before Mink's release date, Linda Snopes Kohl initiated a petition, securing his release. With $13.85, he left Parchman and began to hitchhike to Memphis.

Ratliff reviewed the history of Eula, Flem, Manfred de Spain, and himself, interpreting aspects of the story. Eula, de Spain's mistress, stayed with Flem to give Linda respectability, and Flem secured the bank presidency from de Spain after Linda, who, for the chance to get away from the town of Jefferson, had signed over to Flem her part of her maternal grandfather's wealth. Flem went to Will Varner, offering to exchange the paper for the bank presidency. Will's resulting confrontation with de Spain forced Eula to decide between Linda's living as the daughter of a suicide or of a whore; she chose suicide.

Linda left for Greenwich Village, began an affair with a communist, Barton Kohl, married him, and together they went to fight in Spain. Gavin and Ratliff, recently returned to Jefferson from Linda and Barton's wedding, received word that Barton's plane was shot down. Linda, an ambulance driver on the front lines, remained in Spain until a bomb exploded near her, deafening her. Linda returned to Jefferson. Gavin helped her improve her "dead-duck" voice, pleaded with her to quit trying to educate black students, shielded her from the Federal Bureau of Investigation (which had learned she was a card-carrying communist), and got her a job as a riveter with the Pascagoula Shipyards. He married a former sweetheart to please Linda.

After delaying adventures, Mink reached Memphis, haggled at a pawn shop for an old pistol and three rounds, and hitchhiked toward Jefferson. Linda, back in Jefferson, drank bootlegged whiskey and walked incessantly. She had had Gavin initiate a petition to release Mink. Gavin, certain Mink would murder Flem, had tried to dissuade her without telling her his fears. He believed her innocent of any conspiracy, but wanted to avoid complicity in the murder. He had the warden offer Mink the pardon if Mink took $250 (with the promise of $250 quarterly) and never came back into Mississippi. Mink had gone along with the plan but gave the money to a trustee to give back to the warden and left.

Ratliff went to Parchman, missed Mink, and called Gavin to report. Gavin warned Flem, who seemed undisturbed, and alerted the Memphis police. The police discovered the pawn shop, reporting to Gavin that the gun was useless. Mink reached the mansion while Flem was unguarded, entered the house (passing by an open door by which Linda sat), and went into the room where Flem was. Flem swiveled around and watched Mink fumble until the gun fired, killing Flem. Flem and chair fell, Mink ran toward a closed door, and Linda spoke behind him. He threw the gun at her; she told him to take it and leave.

The day of Flem's funeral, Gavin learned that Linda ordered a Jaguar when Mink's pardon was assured. Gavin confronted her, aware, then, that she had maneuvered Flem's murder, making Gavin an accomplice. She agreed, and, perhaps not as contrite as she could have been, assigned Gavin three more tasks: put a monument on Flem's grave, give the deed to the de Spain mansion to the two surviving de Spains, and give Mink $1,000.

Sickened, Gavin left the mansion, not seeing Linda again. Ratliff and Gavin went to Frenchman's Bend, found Mink, and gave him $250. Gavin said he would send him money quarterly. Ratliff and Gavin left. Mink, feeling equal to any and all, stretched himself peaceably upon the ground.

Critical Evaluation:

Criticism often faults *The Mansion* for contradictions and discrepancies, hinting that Faulkner's talent was waning when he wrote it. Faulkner, who said his fiction was only about the "human heart in conflict with itself," wrote that the discrepancies and contradictions resulted from his knowing the characters better, after living with them for thirty-four years. Critics are taking a closer look at Faulkner's later works, seeing them afresh and discovering significant insights overlooked before. This novel shows society its own ugly warts.

The Mansion focuses on the plight of the downtrodden in the hands of the powerful; Faulkner depicts that society artfully. Far from being a faulty work by the Nobel Prize winner, *The Mansion* magnifies what Faulkner meant when he said, in his address to the Nobel academy: "I believe that man will not merely endure, he will prevail." In this last novel of the Snopes trilogy, the reader learns, among much else, what Faulkner had learned about his most interesting "prevailer," Mink Snopes.

The Mansion is divided into three sections: on Mink, Linda, and Flem. The book's main character is Mink. The Linda section foreshadows her as a threat to Gavin, in some way Ratliff cannot fathom, and makes it believable in the end that she, not Mink, is the one who manipulates Flem's murder. The section on Flem makes him a flat character who simply waits on Mink to shoot him. The novel debunks Gavin Stevens, the character critics have often championed as Faulkner's most promising creation, exposing him as a willing pawn, manipulated (in ways Mink would never be) by Linda. He is also a self-confessed coward. From the first sentence to the last, *The Mansion* is Faulkner's monument to Mink Snopes.

Physically, Mink, murderer of two, is "small, almost childlike." Neither his physical appearance nor his physical actions endears him to anyone, but he is thoroughly complex in action, thought, and sentiment. While Flem is impotent, Mink is Faulkner's most sexually potent male. The reader learns this fact in the first novel of the trilogy, and it resonates in the last when, in prison, Mink, thinking of the hardness of the land, recalls the "amazement . . . reverence . . . and incredulous excitement" he felt when he touched his bride, Yettie, on their wedding night.

In the same moment, he regrets how their subsistence lifestyle, warring with earth, wore Yettie to "leather-toughness" and himself to "exhaustion." Mink voices the regret he had when, looking at their two little girls, he saw "what was ahead of that tender and elfin innocence."

In spite of physical smallness, Mink could do hard labor twenty-four hours a day: He paid off his fine to Houston by digging post holes and putting up a fence, simultaneously plowing and planting his own crops far into the night. At Parchman, the warden says Mink worked the cotton "unflaggingly," harder than any man "of his stamp and kind" worked his own crop.

Philosophically, Mink is a self-contained man who lives by a personalized value system. He believes in an indefinite "them" and "they." Life is a test by "them." "They" make him account for any lie he tells, so he counts each lie, keeping rules and accounts carefully. He expects to beat "them." To illustrate, Mink accepts an extra twenty-year prison term without complaint, because he had been warned not to attempt escape.

In prison, he merges "they" and "them" with "Old Moster." He gains first a kind of bravado, then a tenacious faith that Old Moster plays fair with him. Mixed in with Mink's philosophy is his relationship to the land. He expresses the Edenic view that sin makes man earn his food by the sweat of his brow as he wars with earth. He says the land "owned" the sharecroppers, passing "their doomed indigence and poverty from holding to holding."

Mink lives tenaciously on the edges of life, a human being who prevails by remaining true to his inner voice in the face of whatever life deals him. His thoughts are often poetry; he holds to his rules religiously. He also abuses his wife and children verbally and emotionally (although Faulkner makes his heart belie these actions), and he breaks the most serious of laws—committing murder twice.

At each blow from life, he is forced to choose between his values and society's values. From infancy he was on his own, developing his own hard-bought, self-examined, inner light. That evolving light was Mink; to hold to it was to hold to himself. Murder is indefensible, but it came after a lifetime of indefensible treatment perpetrated on those such as Mink by an indefensible society of Flems and Houstons, a society whose wealth is sustained by the Minks of the world. Two men take more than Mink can give and keep his own soul. The first is Jack Houston, the second Flem Snopes.

Houston took too much when, after Mink had worked off his debt to Houston, Houston tacked on a one-dollar pound fee (equal to two days of labor) because Mink figured a day from sunup to sunup (and so left his cow one night more at Houston's) and the law figured it from sundown to sundown, making the pound fee legal. Mink paid the fee off, but for the shame of it, he killed Houston. Legally, he paid twice for that murder. Not much was required of Flem, under Mink's value system, but Montgomery allowed Mink to think that Flem decreed that Mink wear a girl's dress in his attempted escape, and it was for that dress, more than anything else, that Flem is killed. Significantly, Faulkner's ending of book and trilogy exonerates the Minks of the world, leaving them pardoned and peaceful. Near the end of his canon, Faulkner chose Mink as prevailer, because Faulkner had no illusions about human perfectibility. In their complexity, all his characters are wicked and wonderful. Faulkner obviously learned that "damned little murdering bastard," Mink, was both.

The Mansion is not the work of a failing writer. Its complexity invites serious study; if it is a study that horrifies or causes critics to shake their heads at its implications, all the more reason to plumb its depths. If Faulkner ever presented any character that exemplified "the human heart in conflict with itself," that character is Mink Snopes.

Jo Culbertson Davis

Bibliography:

Gwynn, Frederick L., and Joseph L. Blotner, eds. *Faulkner in the University: Class Conference at University of Virginia, 1957-1958*. Charlottesville: University of Virginia Press, 1959. Faulkner's responses to questions about his work. Index provides easy access to pertinent points in *The Mansion* and to its key characters. Faulkner discusses his view of the novel and its "people."

Kirk, Robert W., with Marvin Klotz. *Faulkner's People: A Complete Guide and Index to Characters in the Fiction of William Faulkner*. Berkeley: University of California Press, 1963. This well-indexed source provides a description of all Faulkner's characters, with specific reference to pages on which they appear in his works. Faulkner's many characters are classified and cross-referenced.

McHaney, Thomas L. *William Faulkner: A Reference Guide*. Boston: G. K. Hall, 1976. An index of references and cross-references, providing a helpful, annotated source list for research in *The Mansion*.

Millgate, Michael. *The Achievement of William Faulkner*. New York: Random House, 1966. Millgate presents a compelling view of Mink Snopes, *The Mansion's* primary figure, counteracting the view that Gavin is the central figure in the trilogy of which *The Mansion* is part.

Tuck, Dorothy. *Apollo Handbook of Faulkner*. New York: Crowell, 1964. Draws parallels and distinctions regarding discrepancies between Faulkner's successively presented characters and events. Pertinent, brief, and thorough.

MARAT/SADE

Type of work: Drama
Author: Peter Weiss (1916-1982)
Type of plot: Social morality
Time of plot: 1808
Locale: Charenton asylum, near Paris
First performed: 1964; first published, 1964 as *Die Verfolgung und Ermordung Jean Paul Marats dargestellt durch die Schauspielgruppe des Hospizes zu Charenton unter der Anleitung des Herrn de Sade (Marat/Sade: The Persecution and Assassination of Jean-Paul Marat as Performed by the Inmates of the Asylum of Charenton Under the Direction of the Marquis de Sade,* 1965)

Principal characters:
 MARQUIS DE SADE, a self-centered individualist
 JEAN-PAUL MARAT, a revolutionary
 CHARLOTTE CORDAY, Marat's assassin
 DUPERRET, a Girondist deputy
 JACQUES ROUX, a former priest and radical socialist
 THE HERALD, the stage manager
 COULMIER, the director of the asylum

The Story:
 This two-act play is divided into thirty-three scenes, with the first few setting the stage for the play and the play-within-the-play. At the Charenton clinic, Sade signed to the Herald for the play to begin. Coulmier explained to the audience, seated on the side and consisting of himself, his wife, and his daughter, that Sade had written this historical play portraying the assassination of Marat by Charlotte Corday on July 13, 1793. The performance had two purposes: entertainment for the visitors and therapy for the inmates. The performance was July 13, 1808, exactly fifteen years after the assassination. The Herald then introduced those inmates playing major roles, apologizing for their lack of skill. Sade played himself. Marat was played by a paranoiac. The Marat, in the play, as in life, had a skin disease which necessitated his remaining constantly in a warm bath. Charlotte Corday was played by a woman suffering from sleeping sickness and melancholia.
 The play-within-the-play began with the "Homage to Marat" sung by four balladeers: Kokol, Polpoch, Cucurucu, and Rossignol, represented the attitudes and grievances of the masses. For them, Marat was the only revolutionary, and they wanted to be assured that he would never give up their fight. When Roux elevated their cries for bread and freedom, Coulmier demanded that Sade keep the performers to the approved script so as not to confuse and unsettle the patients.
 Next Charlotte Corday was introduced as both a character in the play and a historical personage. Corday believed Marat had become the evil genius of France and gained an audience with him through deceit, promising to betray the Girondists of her hometown, Caen. Marat was preparing his "fourteenth of July call/ to the people of France." On the street Corday had witnessed the crowd performing a dance of death as they marched to the guillotine. A pantomime, narrated by Marat, portrayed a history of past executions.
 Sade and Marat discussed the meaning of life and death. Sade compared death to the indifference he observed in nature. For him, life and death were purely a matter of the survival

of the fittest, without human compassion. Marat, on the other hand, maintained that it was absolutely essential to intervene whenever injustice occurred, especially when perpetrated in society by the church and the state. When Coulmier objected to this characterization of society, the Herald sarcastically suggested that everything was different now and the comments served only to provide a historical context within the play. Sade expressed his ambivalence about humanity's ability to improve its lot through revolution, while Marat maintained that the time had come to put the writings of the "Declaration of the Rights of Man" into action. The masses, however, demanded an immediate revolution.

Corday continued to believe in her mission, yet now she described Marat, in her somnambulism, as the image of Napoleon. Duperret attempted to dissuade her, believing that Marat and his revolution would soon be conquered and freedom restored. Sade had lost faith in the idealism of the revolution, while Marat believed in it all the more, a viewpoint vigorously supported by Roux and the masses. They sing: "We want our rights and we don't care how/ We want our Revolution now."

Corday and Duperret believed the long-awaited freedom promised by the revolution would soon be realized. Marat, however, delivered a litany exposing those beliefs as lies and attempted to warn the masses against deception. Sade suggested that they were only interested in profiting from the revolution. Sade's views were substantiated when Corday visited Marat a second time and gave him a letter in which she said: "I am unhappy/ and therefore have a right to his aid."

The first act concluded with the scene in which Marat's life was mocked and ridiculed by characters representing his youth, science, the army, the Church, the nouveaux-riches, and even Voltaire and Antoine-Laurent Lavoisier. Roux again came to his defense, asserting that only Marat realized the need for a fundamental change in society.

The second act began with Marat's imaginary speech to the National Assembly attempting to rally the people to continue and conclude the revolution in accordance with his views. Sade, in his haughty and scornful manner, ridiculed Marat's idealism, proposing that he give up since all his writings and speeches had been futile.

Corday, who had dreamed she was saving a corrupt world, approached Marat for the third time that day, to assassinate him. Sade made a final attempt to dissuade Marat from his revolutionary ideas, suggesting the masses would fight only if they perceived a direct and personal reward. Their new cry was now: "And what's the point of a revolution/ without general copulation." The murder was interrupted momentarily by a musical history of the revolution, highlighting political events between Marat's assassination in 1793 and the time of the play in 1808. In the epilogue, Coulmier and the masses sang the glories of their day, with Napoleon ruling the nation as emperor. The final lines, however, were spoken by Roux, admonishing everyone: "When will you learn to see/ When will you learn to take sides."

Critical Evaluation:

With *Marat/Sade*, Peter Weiss became an internationally acclaimed and highly respected dramatist. Prior to writing plays in the 1960's, Weiss had spent many years as a painter, novelist, filmmaker, and translator. Born in Germany, he lived most of his adult life in Sweden, making only short visits to Germany—then both East and West—to lecture, read, and participate in the production of his plays.

He began *Marat/Sade* in 1963 and prepared at least five versions before the play premiered on April 29, 1964, in West Berlin. The East German premiere was on March 26, 1965, in Rostock. In the fall of 1964, Peter Brook produced *Marat/Sade* for the Royal Shakespeare Company in London, making the play an international success in the English-speaking world.

Brook also produced the film version in 1966. An operatic version of *Marat/Sade* premiered in 1984 in Kassel, Germany.

There are many highly complex dramatic devices in the play. Whereas the early German stagings tended to rely on Bertolt Brecht's "epic theater of alienation" for their overall structure, Peter Brook and many English productions were influenced by Antonin Artaud's concept of the "theater of cruelty." Both approaches must deal with the difficulties of presenting a multilayered play and a play-within-a-play, unpunctuated language ranging from doggerel and popular balladry to sophisticated free verse, song, dance, and pantomime, and scenes that are tragic, comical, melodramatic, and highly lyrical.

As Weiss indicated in his "Note on the Historical Background to the Play," certain parts of the drama are based on actual events. The record shows that Sade, now known primarily as the author of erotic novels, was imprisoned at the Charenton asylum from 1801 until his death in 1814. While Sade did write many plays, some performed by the inmates of Charenton, he never wrote a play about Marat. Another historical fact, in no way associated with Sade, is Charlotte Corday's assassination of Marat. Although not a radical agitator, she sympathized with the Girondists in the French Revolution. Corday felt that Marat, as a supporter of the more extremist views of the Jacobins and their waging a deadly war on the Girondists, had become the evil dictator of France. She resolved to emulate the biblical Judith and went to Paris, where she assassinated Marat on July 13, 1793. She was sent to the guillotine shortly thereafter.

With these basic historic facts at hand and a thorough understanding of Marat's and Sade's philosophical viewpoints, Peter Weiss wrote this play. As the title states, the outer framework is a play about Marat's assassination written by Sade and performed by the inmates of Charenton. This dramatic activity becomes the play-within-the-play. Of course, there is a third level to this play, namely the contemporary audience. Thus, three real time periods are presented: 1793 and the assassination of Marat, 1808 with the presentation of Sade's play, and the present.

The actors represent these various time periods. For the present time audience, all actors on the stage play specific roles. Those who play the parts of Coulmier and his family represent France in 1808 as well as in the present time. The actor in the role of Sade is more complex. He plays the historical Sade as playwright and director of this play, and the philosophical sparring partner with the character playing the historical or real Marat. The role of Marat is likewise manifold. The actor must play the role of a paranoiac, play the historical person of Marat, and, occasionally, he must engage the real Sade in philosophical discourse. The other actors have each two roles to perform: the inmates and the historical roles that have been assigned to them.

It is not difficult to understand those aspects of the play that deal with the historical events of either 1793 or 1808. It can be difficult, however, for the present time audience to always know exactly which role the performers playing Marat and Sade are presenting, but that is basically the intent of Peter Weiss. One major purpose in this play is to examine the aims and goals of the French Revolution and why the movement failed despite its noble "Declaration of the Rights of Man" and its advocacy of "Liberty, Equality, Fraternity!"

The battle cry of the masses—"Revolution Revolution/ Copulation Copulation"—epitomizes the conflict and confusion which prevailed after the storming of the Bastille on July 14, 1798, which marked the outbreak of the French Revolution. Neither Marat nor Sade, however, articulated decisive plans that would lead to a successful revolution. Marat, in his idealism, advocated action that was unreasonable for the masses since their most basic needs remained unfulfilled, proclaiming: "The important thing/ is to pull yourself up by your own hair." Sade, on the other hand, believed that humans are by nature incapable of acting beyond themselves.

Both stressed an ideological point of view: Marat believed in the perfectibility of society; Sade was convinced that humanity was impossible to perfect. This is the philosophical dilemma that Weiss presents to the audience. Ultimately he gives the last word to Roux, the most politically aware among the masses, refusing to accept defeat and attempting to continue Marat's revolution.

Weiss's intention in *Marat/Sade* was to provoke and engage the audience in discussion, not to make statements or present answers. His main question centered on the failure of revolutions: the French Revolution, other liberation movements in nineteenth century Germany, the great October Revolution (1917) in Russia, and revolutions and national liberation movements in various Third World nations. In *Marat/Sade*, Weiss investigated the potentiality of establishing a more humane society, a possibility he regarded as feasible in an ideal socialist world.

Thomas H. Falk

Bibliography:

Cohen, Robert. *Understanding Peter Weiss*. Columbia: University of South Carolina Press, 1993. A well-balanced introduction to Weiss's life and works, recommended as a beginner's source.

Ellis, Roger. *Peter Weiss in Exile: A Critical Study of His Works*. Ann Arbor, Mich.: UMI Research Press, 1987. A comprehensive study of Weiss's dramas, with special emphasis on *Marat/Sade*.

Hilton, Ian. *Peter Weiss: A Search for Affinities*. London: Oswald Wolff, 1970. A brief discussion of Weiss's earlier life and works; includes selected translations from essays, novels, and dramas.

Sontag, Susan. "Marat/Sade/Artaud." In *Against Interpretation*. New York: Farrar, Straus & Giroux, 1966. The most important and influential discussion on the reception and performances of *Marat/Sade* in the United States. Also examines how Brecht's and Artaud's dramatic theories can be used in producing this play.

White, John. "History and Cruelty in Peter Weiss's *Marat/Sade*." *Modern Language Review* 63 (1968): 437-448. Outlines Weiss's use of the historical materials in *Marat/Sade*, illustrating how facts and documents of the French Revolution are integrated to reveal later periods in history. Discusses how Artaud's concepts of the "theater of cruelty" were adapted in Brook's first London production.

THE MARBLE FAUN
Or, The Romance of Monte Beni

Type of work: Novel
Author: Nathaniel Hawthorne (1804-1864)
Type of plot: Psychological realism
Time of plot: Mid-nineteenth century
Locale: Rome
First published: 1860

Principal characters:
MIRIAM, an artist
HILDA, another artist and a friend of Miriam
KENYON, an American sculptor
DONATELLO, a young Italian

The Story:

Nothing at all was known about Miriam. In the artistic world of Rome, she lived without revealing anything about herself and without arousing the curiosity or suspicion of those living around her. She enjoyed a friendship with Hilda, a young woman from New England, and Kenyon, a sculptor, which her mysterious origin did not shadow, so complete was their understanding and trust of one another.

One day, the three friends, accompanied by Donatello, a young Italian, saw a statue of the faun by Praxiteles. Struck by Donatello's resemblance to the statue, they asked jokingly to see whether the Italian also had pointed ears under his golden locks. Indeed, Donatello was very much like a faun in his character. He had great agility, cheerfulness, and a sunny nature unclouded by melancholy or care. He was deeply in love with Miriam.

On another occasion, the friends went to visit the catacombs. While there, Miriam disappeared for a moment and returned with a strange individual whom she had met inside one of the tombs. After that, the man followed Miriam wherever she went. No one knew anything about him. He and Miriam had conversations together, and he spoke of the hold he had on her and of their life together in a mysterious past. Miriam became more and more unhappy. She told Donatello, who was ever ready to defend her, that he should go away before she brought doom and destruction upon him. Donatello stayed, however.

One day, Miriam went to Hilda and left a packet with her that Hilda was to deliver on a certain date to the address she would find written on the outside. Shortly afterward, the friends went out one night and climbed the Tarpeian Rock, over which the old Romans used to throw their criminals. As they were getting ready to return home, Miriam's persecutor appeared. Miriam went with him, followed by Donatello, who attacked the man. Grasping her tormentor securely, Donatello looked at Miriam. Her eyes gave him his answer, and he threw the man over a cliff to his death.

United by their crime, Miriam and Donatello also became united in love. They did not, however, know that Hilda had witnessed the murder and was suffering because of it. They had all agreed to visit the Church of the Capuchins the following afternoon in order to see a painting that supposedly bore a resemblance to Miriam's tormentor. Hilda did not keep the appointment. The others went and found a mass for Miriam's persecutor in progress. Later, when Miriam went to see Hilda, the American told Miriam that their friendship was over. Donatello, too, had changed. He was no longer the unworried faun but a person with a guilty conscience. He began to avoid Miriam, even to hate her. He left Rome and went back to his ancestral home. Kenyon visited him there, but Hilda stayed in Rome by herself, lonely and distraught.

At Donatello's country home, Kenyon learned the local legend about his friend's family and that Donatello was, in fact, reputed to be descended from a race of fauns who had inhabited the countryside in remote times. He learned, too, of Donatello's feeling of guilt but, unaware of the murder, did not know the reason for Donatello's changed spirit. When Miriam tried to see Donatello in his home, he would not see her. Kenyon told her that Donatello still loved her, and she agreed to meet both of them later on. When they met in the city square, Miriam stood quietly, waiting for Donatello to speak. When at last he spoke her name, she went to him and they were united once more, but their union continued to be haunted by their sin.

Hilda had in the meantime delivered the packet Miriam had left in her keeping. The address was that of one high in the affairs of the government. After Kenyon returned to Rome, he looked for Hilda everywhere. He had come to realize that he was in love with her and was worried about her disappearance. During the carnival season, he met Donatello and Miriam, and finally on the day the carnival was at its height and the streets were filled with a merrymaking throng, he saw Hilda again. She told him that her knowledge of the crime had weighed so heavily upon her that at last she had gone to confession in St. Peter's and had poured out the tale to a listening priest. When she delivered the packet, as Miriam had requested, she had been detained in a convent until the authorities were satisfied that she had taken no part in the murder on the Tarpeian Rock. She had just been released from her captivity. While they stood talking, there was a commotion in the crowd nearby. The police had seized Donatello and were taking him to jail.

Donatello was sentenced to prison for the murder, but Miriam was not brought to trial, because her only crime had been the look in her eyes telling Donatello to murder her persecutor. Miriam's history, however, was finally revealed. Although she herself was innocent, her family had been involved in a crime that had made the family name infamous. She had gone to Rome and attempted to live down the past, but evil had continued to haunt her; the past had reappeared in the form of the persecutor who had threatened to make her identity known to the world.

After Kenyon and Hilda were married, they saw Miriam once more, kneeling in the Pantheon before the tomb of Raphael. As they passed, she stretched out her hands to them in a gesture that both blessed and repulsed them. They left her to her expiation and her grief.

Critical Evaluation:

Throughout his writing career, Nathaniel Hawthorne was preoccupied with the theme of humanity's fall into sin and mortality. Symbolic representations of Adam and Eden underlie much of his best work. Hawthorne turned to this theme again in his last major romance, where, however, he deploys the idea less skillfully than in some of the earlier stories. His usually subtle symbolic method here becomes a somewhat heavy-handed allegory, and the rather slight, simple story is weighted down with descriptions of Rome and Roman art. These descriptive passages—which he frequently lifted with little alteration straight from his notebooks—have almost no organic relationship to the novel's theme. Yet while *The Marble Faun* may be considered one of Hawthorne's weaker romances, both the faults and the virtues of the work, as in most of his writing, reveal his view of the world. The work features several of the character types that Hawthorne drew on most often and whose interactions he typically used to dramatize the themes that most preoccupied him.

The theme of the story, as the title indicates, centers most particularly around Donatello, the contemporary counterpart of the Faun of Praxiteles. For Hawthorne, Donatello's faunlike qualities are associated with the innocence and animalistic nature of humans before their fall brought the knowledge of sin and death. Donatello's country estate is a counterpart to Eden and suggests a pagan and pre-Christian paradise, bypassed by time, in which primordial innocence has been retained. Though touching in its childlike qualities, Donatello's innocence is not one of which Hawthorne can approve. Because it lacks the knowledge of sin that is part of humankind's humanity, Hawthorne considers it subhuman and incapable of understanding the real nature of the world. Since salvation is a direct result of sin, Donatello, existing outside the world of sin and death, is not a candidate for God's greatest gift to humanity until Miriam, acting the part of an Eve figure, tempts him to murder. She thus becomes the instrument that brings about his fall into humanity. The irony of Hawthorne's scheme is obvious, as the "fall" is in fact a rise from the subhuman condition. Hawthorne is a proponent of the idea of the "fortunate fall" that proves necessary for humans to achieve salvation. The price Donatello is called on to pay in guilt, suffering, and shame is no more than the price of his initiation into the human race with its potential blessing of salvation.

The two women in *The Marble Faun* represent the two extremes of Hawthorne's fictional women: Miriam, the mysterious, dark woman and Hilda, whose innocence and religious faith are everywhere manifest. Yet each becomes a salvation figure by becoming the instrument for humanizing a man. Miriam's tempting of Donatello and her own ambiguous past, with its suggestions of sin and guilt, define her as an Eve figure who tempts the man to the sin that will humanize him. Hilda, described in almost unreal terms of innocence and virtue, is a different sort of salvation figure. She brings Kenyon out of his cold isolation by awakening his ability to love. Ironically, by giving Miriam multilayered complexity of character, readers tend to find her more interesting than Hilda, whom Hawthorne depicts as an incorruptible symbol of Christian goodness. Yet it is clearly Hilda who represents for Hawthorne the moral standard the novel is meant to affirm.

The character in the novel closest to Hawthorne himself is the sculptor, Kenyon. Hawthorne refers to him at one point as "a man of marble," implying that such a description fits his moral nature as well as his profession. Like the light and dark women and the prelapsarian Adamic figure represented by Donatello, Kenyon is a recurrent type in Hawthorne's work. For Hawthorne, the artist and the scientist by their very nature tend to isolate themselves from humanity and to become cold observers who, without emotion of their own, exploit the lives of others for their own ends. In his artist's isolation, Kenyon suppresses what is human in himself for his art until he, in effect, loses his soul to it. Though his moral condition does not exactly parallel Donatello's, Kenyon is equally outside the human community and he, too, needs salvation. Hilda saves Kenyon not through a dramatic temptation to sin but through awakening what is most human in his own heart.

While the flaws of *The Marble Faun* are obvious, its total effect is strengthened by the fact that the characters are among the most important of Hawthorne's creations, while the dual themes of the "fortunate fall" and crime and punishment give the work an honored place within a long tradition of Western literature. Moreover, the novel's setting in Rome anticipated the European novels of Henry James and the literary genre of the international novel that he popularized. For all these reasons, *The Marble Faun* is a significant work of American literature.

"Critical Evaluation" by William E. Grant

Bibliography:

Carton, Evan. *The Marble Faun: Hawthorne's Transformations.* Boston: Twayne, 1992. Discusses biographical details that relate to *The Marble Faun*, indicates the importance of the admittedly flawed novel, and surveys the major literature that deals with the novel.

Herbert, T. Walter, Jr. "The Erotics of Purity: *The Marble Faun* and the Victorian Construction of Sexuality." *Representations* 33 (Fall, 1991): 114-132. Reasons that purity is sometimes not admirable, as when Hilda arouses but frustrates Kenyon, is shocked by Miriam's sensuality, and ignores the representative human being who is stained by knowledge.

Idol, John L. "'A Linked Circle of Three' Plus One: Nonverbal Communication in *The Marble Faun.*" *Studies in the Novel* 23 (April, 1991): 139-151. Analyzes the interactions among Hawthorne's characters through body movements, facial expressions, and maintaining of physical distance. The author's examples include Hilda's avoidance of Miriam's embrace, Miriam's ocular order to Donatello to commit murder, and Kenyon's sculpting Donatello's sin-altered face.

Liebman, Sheldon W. "The Design of *The Marble Faun.*" *New England Quarterly* 40 (March, 1967): 61-78. Dismisses the conclusion of previous critics that the structural principle of *The Marble Faun* is the human "fall" and transformations. Describes the structural principle as residing in the carved sarcophagus, which is symbolic of everybody's "dance, pilgrimage, and corpse."

Stern, Milton R. *Contexts for Hawthorne: "The Marble Faun" and the Politics of Openness and Closure in American Literature.* Urbana: University of Illinois Press, 1991. Analyzes Hawthorne's pull toward closure (as seen in his classical conservativism, preference for past and present, and aesthetic control and unity) and his push toward openness (as reflected by his romanticism, revolutionary tendencies, repudiation of the past, and preference for future expansionism).

MARDI, AND A VOYAGE THITHER

Type of work: Novel
Author: Herman Melville (1819-1891)
Type of plot: Allegory
Time of plot: Mid-nineteenth century
Locale: Islands of the Western Pacific
First published: 1849

Principal characters:

THE NARRATOR, later called Taji, a young American sailor mistaken for a
   god by the islanders
YILLAH, a blonde native, beloved of Taji, and symbolizing Good
HAUTIA, a dark native queen, in love with Taji, and symbolizing Evil
JARL, Taji's sailor companion
SAMOA, a native companion
MEDIA, a native king
YOOMY, Media's minstrel
BABBALANJA, Media's court philosopher

The Story:

The narrator of the story, a young American sailor, was picked up at Ravavai, a Pacific island, by a whaling vessel, the *Arcturion*. The voyage of the *Arcturion* was not a successful one, and when the ship began to head for the cold climate of the Bay of Kamchatka, the young narrator and his special friend in the forecastle, Jarl, decided to leave the ship. Knowing the captain would not land them anywhere, they provisioned a small boat and in it escaped from the ship under cover of darkness.

Heading westward, the two men hoped to reach some hospitable islands. After sailing for many days, they came upon a drifting ship that seemed to be a derelict. Finding it in fairly seaworthy condition, they boarded it. The following morning, a native man and woman were found in the rigging, where they had hidden from the narrator and Jarl. With the help of the natives, who had escaped with the ship from an unfriendly tribe of islanders after the latter had killed the ship's crew, the narrator and Jarl continued their voyage in search of land.

After many days of voyaging, the vessel was becalmed. In the storm that followed, the vessel was wrecked. Jarl and the narrator, with the native man, Samoa, set out in a little whaleboat. The native woman had been killed during the storm. Many days later, they saw a sail in the distance. Taking up their oars to aid the force of the sail, they slowly closed in on the craft they had spotted. As they drew close, they saw it was a strange arrangement of two native canoes with a platform built over them. After some discussion between the native priest in charge of the craft and the narrator, the sailor and Samoa boarded the native vessel. Once aboard the craft, they discovered a beautiful blonde girl, but they had to force a passage through the natives in order to regain the whaleboat. In the scuffle, they took two of the natives prisoners. From the natives, they learned that the blonde girl was the priest's prisoner. Going back aboard the native craft, the sailor and Samoa rescued the girl and escaped with her from the natives.

The girl, whose name was Yillah, wished to return to her native islands. The narrator soon fell in love with her, and the girl, in native fashion, returned his affection. The narrator then decided that he would remain with her on her island home. Sighting a group of islands at last, the party headed for the nearest beach. Before they reached the shore, however, natives swam out to the whaleboat and gave them an excited welcome. Towing the boat into shallow water, the natives picked it up and carried it ashore on their shoulders. The visitors were completely puzzled by their reception until they learned that the narrator had been mistaken for the natives' god, Taji, who, according to an ancient prophecy, would one day revisit them in human form. The natives also thought that the other three occupants of the whaleboat were deities whom Taji had brought from another world for companionship.

Media, king of the atoll, made the guests welcome, and Taji, as the narrator was now called, decided to make the best of his position, as long as his godhood put him under no particular constraints. He and Yillah, housed in a splendid grass house, lived a life of tranquil happiness, doing no more than the islanders, who in their turn had little to do to make life comfortable. Then, suddenly, unhappiness struck the island and Taji. He awoke one morning to find Yillah gone without a trace. Within a few days of Yillah's disappearance, Taji received a visit from a portentously disguised messenger, who gave the young sailor a set of flower symbols from Queen Hautia, the dark queen of a group of distant islands.

The natives interpreted the flower symbols from Hautia to mean that the Queen loved Taji, wished his presence, and bade him not look for Yillah, his lost love. Not to be dissuaded, however, Taji, accompanied by King Media and a party of his courtiers, including Yoomy the poet-singer and Babbalanja the philosopher, set sail in a huge, ornate native canoe in search of Yillah. Before the voyagers had journeyed far on the ocean, they met a black canoe containing more emissaries sent to Taji from Queen Hautia. The messengers, again using flower symbols interpreted by Yoomy, bade Taji forget his quest of the fair love and turn his canoe toward the kingdom of Hautia. Taji refused and continued on his quest.

His first stop was on the island of Juam, where Taji made a friend of King Donjalolo, a monarch who tried to escape reality by moving from one bower to another in his island kingdom and by taking no heed of anyone's happiness but his own and that of people who were in his company. Donjalolo aided Taji in his quest by sending messages throughout his island kingdom to ask for news of Yillah. After the petty princes had come to Donjalolo's court to report that they knew nothing of the girl, Taji decided to set out once more in the canoe, in the company of Media and his courtiers, to continue his search for his lost love. Again, this time in a more menacing fashion, he was accosted at sea by a canoe load of emissaries from Queen Hautia, who demanded that he go to her immediately. Again, Taji refused.

After many days and nights, during which Taji and his companions had lengthy conversations on many branches of knowledge and philosophy, they touched at an island where they visited the temple of Oro and learned of the Polynesian prophet, Alma, who had many years before, according to legend, brought peace, serenity, and love to the islands. Continuing their voyage through the archipelago of Mardi, representing the world and all its ideas, Taji and his party visited Vivenza, modeled on the United States, passed the Cape of Capes, saw many other islands, regaled one another with many philosophical conversations during the long hours at sea, and were finally becalmed. After the calm, a death cloud passed them. Following that adventure, they landed at Serenia, a land that proved too quiet and too good for them.

At last, the only place left to look for Yillah, who had not been found on any one of the many atolls Taji and his companions had visited, was the bower of Queen Hautia herself. Babbalanja the philosopher, who remained in Serenia, told Taji he would never find the unattainable Yillah, but Taji went on until three emissaries from Queen Hautia met him and guided him to her land. Taji found himself entranced by Hautia, who seemed in some strange way connected with Yillah, though she invited him to sin; but still he asked in vain for word of Yillah. He was left in that land by the companions of his travels.

Critical Evaluation:

Perhaps no book by Herman Melville has been the subject of as much negative criticism as *Mardi, and a Voyage Thither*. Having written two books based on his actual experiences in the South Seas—*Typee* (1846) and *Omoo* (1847)—Melville wished in this, his third book, to abandon the travel narrative form for the imaginative freedom of the novel. *Mardi* imagines a map of islands not only unknown to its American narrator but also to the companion islanders who join him in a search for his beloved Yillah throughout the archipelago. Somewhat in the manner of *Gulliver's Travels* (1726), these islands are each allegories of different conditions of humanity. Some, like Dominora (England) and Vivenza (the United States), even represent actual nations. Many critics have objected to the confusion of the numerous symbols in this journey, the hodgepodge of different styles employed by Melville throughout the book, the weak main character, Taji, and the frequent passages of philosophical dialogue between Taji's companions, a Mardian king, philosopher, historian and poet.

On the other hand, *Mardi* in many ways anticipates the concerns of Melville's later master-piece, *Moby Dick* (1851). It has begun to be seen as a great work in its own right, although not without its challenges for the reader. Following Ralph Waldo Emerson's call for an authentic and original American literature, *Mardi*'s display of literary invention was fueled by Melville's ambition to be the author of the great work America awaited. This ambition led to a supremely self-conscious novel in which literary improvisation plays a large role. Several different allegories are at work at once in this complex novel. Alongside Taji's search for Yillah, an embodiment of beauty, is the Mardian philosopher Babbalanja's search for the perfect society. In the meantime, the party flees Hautia, a lustful native queen, who represents possession of the narrator and an end to the quests of all involved. Throughout it all, frequent reflections of the process of writing itself indicate that the novel is first and foremost an allegory about literature and the novelist's attempt to create something new. Tension arises between the knowledge that one learns how to live from the past and the knowledge that one must break with this past if one is to make works that are original and worthwhile. As is true with Ishmael, the narrator of *Moby Dick*, Taji describes the writing of the work as if he were the author himself. Unlike Ishmael (and Melville), however, Taji understands that his book is not fully realized. Nonetheless, he is proud of having risked catastrophe, a possibility only when one has been ambitious enough to risk originality. "Give me, ye gods," he says late in the novel, "an utter wreck, if wreck I do." The reader's ultimate opinion of the novel will rest on whether he or she admires the degree to which Melville chanced something new, or, on the other hand, insists on a more polished finished product.

Even for readers who do not ultimately feel the novel is successful, Melville's brilliance as a novelist and thinker comes through: for instance, in his satirical edge in depicting Vivenza, an allegory of the United States. The natives of Vivenza are loud and jingoistic, braggarts with a high-flown rhetoric of freedom and selective historical memory who ignore the oppression of slaves and the poor, excusing all of their own faults through the singular merit of being without kings. This criticism is half-retracted as the party leaves the island, noting that Vivenza's democratic government may prove a light to the rest of the archipelago in the future, but Melville's points are clear. The United States in the 1840's was a confident nation, growing and pushing ever westward. Melville cautions Americans not to be blind to the national shame of slavery (still an institution when he wrote the novel), nor to trust that a rhetoric of freedom can replace its actual practice. What is called freedom may only be a disguise for misuse of individual authority and responsibility. During the tour of islands, Melville increasingly uses the Mardian philosopher Babbalanja as a didactic mouthpiece, often very effectively. First,

Babbalanja often cites the Mardian epic, *Koztanza*, by Lombardo, composed in much the same improvisational fashion as Melville's own work. Babbalanja's own quest also becomes important, linked with Taji's. His quest is not so much for truth as for peace of mind: a society where he can pursue spirituality with a conscience untroubled by the misery of others. Everywhere else in the archipelago, there is a dark underside to the locals' claims of utopia and right worship of Alma, the Mardian Christ figure. Often, injustice is economic in nature. The Mardian currency is human teeth; thus, the wealth of the rich is often directly composed of the misery of the poor. When the party reaches Serenia, where Alma is worshiped and all goods are shared (a suggestion of the incompatibility of Christianity and free-market capitalism), Babbalanja stays, calling his search complete.

Babbalanja here instructs Taji to give up his own quest, warning him that desire cannot be appeased. Life in Serenia is perfect for one who wishes to give up worldly concerns, but it is unsuitable to those who still want to pursue their desires. Taji's quest throughout has been made problematic by his refusal to see his platonic companionship with Yillah as having any link to the sinful lust expressed by Hautia. Critics have suggested that Melville, recently married as he wrote the novel, projected his own puritanical sexual repression onto Taji in this allegory. Taji is surprised when he discovers, visiting Hautia's bower, that she and Yillah are linked. This means that desire for beauty (humanity's highest pursuit) and sexual expression (humanity's basest instinct) are linked. Taji cannot accept this association between his beloved and the power that he flees. The book ends with Taji still pursued by Hautia and her companions, as much Taji's personal demons as an objective embodiment of evil.

"Critical Evaluation" by Ted Pelton

Bibliography:
Davis, Merrell. *Melville's "Mardi": A Chartless Voyage*. New Haven, Conn.: Yale University Press, 1952. The first book-length study of *Mardi*. Demonstrates Meville's ambition through analysis of letters to publisher John Murray. Asserts that the novel is an important harbinger of *Moby Dick* but in itself a failure.

Moore, Maxine. *That Lonely Game: Melville, "Mardi," and the Almanac*. Columbia: University of Missouri Press, 1975. Argues that Melville wrote *Mardi* as an elaborate riddle based upon the almanac and the recent discovery of planet Neptune, all to get back at British critics' attacks on his first two books. Fascinating but farfetched.

Olson, Charles. *Call Me Ishmael*. San Francisco: City Lights Books, 1947. Poet Olson's analysis of *Moby Dick*, central to understanding Melville's compositional process. Contains several essays that relate Olson's poetic theories to Melville's practice.

Pullin, Faith, ed. *New Perspectives on Melville*. Kent, Ohio: Kent State University Press, 1978. Excellent collection of essays on Melville, including Richard Brodhead's "*Mardi:* Creating the Creative," a strong reply to Davis' thesis.

Rogin, Michael Paul. *Subversive Geneologies: The Politics and Art of Herman Melville*. Berkeley: University of California Press, 1979. Incisive psychological and Marxist reading of Melville's life and work, arguing that Melville was one of the leading thinkers of his age. Its reading of Melville's family's place in the historical context of the 1840's is unparalleled.

MARIA MAGDALENA

Type of work: Drama
Author: Friedrich Hebbel (1813-1863)
Type of plot: Domestic realism
Time of plot: Nineteenth century
Locale: Germany
First published: 1844; first performed, 1846 (English translation, 1935)

> *Principal characters:*
> ANTHONY, a cabinetmaker
> ANTHONY'S WIFE
> CLARA, their daughter
> KARL, their son
> LEONARD, Clara's fiancé
> FRIEDRICH, a secretary and second suitor for Clara's hand

The Story:

After a long illness, from which she was not expected to recover, Anthony's wife, a woman in her fifties, felt that she had been given another chance to make herself worthy of heaven. To show her gratitude for this second chance, she dressed herself in her wedding gown, which was also to be her shroud, and went to church the first Sunday morning she was able. Before she went, she and her daughter Clara had a heart-to-heart talk, during which the mother disclosed her fears about her son Karl, who spent too much time drinking and playing and not enough time working steadily. The mother felt that his attitudes and his conduct were her fault, but still she refused to believe he was really a bad young man.

The mother also raised the subject of Leonard, a poor young clerk who had visited Clara regularly but had not been seen for a while. Shortly after Clara's mother left for church, Leonard came to see Clara and explained that he had not seen her for two weeks for a particular reason. During that time he had been attentive to the mayor's daughter in an effort to get himself a job as clerk for the city. Leonard also accused her of being in love with another man even though, a very short time before, Clara had given herself to Leonard in order to prove her love. After they had straightened out the situation, Leonard told Clara he had come to ask her father for her hand in marriage. Clara assured him that they must soon be married, lest her sin were to show. Even so, she had some misgivings about him when she learned of the chicanery he had executed in securing his position as town clerk.

Her father, when he learned of the proposed marriage and Leonard's prospects, seemed agreeable to the marriage. Then the young man, knowing that old Anthony had loaned out a large sum of money, brought up the question of a dowry. He was surprised to learn, however, that Anthony had called in his money and had used it to help an old man who had befriended him in his youth. When the man had died, Anthony had refused to collect from the widow and had put the dead man's note in his casket. Leonard began to think that, pregnancy or no, Clara was not a desirable wife for him.

At that time, the mother came home from church and told of having seen a newly prepared grave at the churchyard, a grave the sexton dug as an extra, in case it were needed while he was on a holiday. Anthony viewed it as an evil omen. Then the talk turned to a jewel robbery at the home of a rich merchant in town. Anthony recalled that his worthless son Karl had done some work at the house on the day of the robbery. Hardly had he said so when bailiffs knocked at the door and demanded permission to search the house for the stolen goods. The shock was so great that the mother swooned and died. Leonard, who was already none too eager to marry Clara, seized upon the charge as an excuse to break his betrothal to the girl.

As the days passed, Anthony's house was a place of wretchedness. All evidence seemed to point to Karl's guilt in the matter of the theft, even though the jewels were not discovered in the house. Anthony also began to suspect that Clara had strayed from the paths of virtue. He told her that if she also brought shame on the family, he would cut his own throat with a razor. Clara, not wanting to be the cause of her father's death, decided to commit suicide before her father could do away with himself. One day, while Anthony was away visiting a deaf old woodcutter who had not heard of his family's disgrace, the rich merchant appeared at the house with word that Karl was not guilty, that the jewels had been discovered in his own home, where the merchant's own mad wife had hidden them.

Clara, pleased to learn that Karl had been exonerated, believed that something would occur to make her life right again. Her belief seemed to come true when Friedrich, a childhood sweetheart, called to tell her that he still loved her and wished to marry her. Even after Clara told him of her fall from virtue, he said he loved her and would make her his wife. He also swore that he would arrange a duel with Leonard and seek to kill the man who had seduced her. Since Friedrich had a good job as a secretary, Clara knew that her father would be glad to see her married to him. After the secretary left, however, all Clara's doubts again assailed her, and she once more began to think of suicide.

At last, Clara decided to go to see Leonard, whom she found planning to fulfill his ambitions by marrying the mayor's daughter. Clara confronted him with the letter he had written her on the day of her mother's death, a letter telling her that he found it impossible to unite himself with the sister of a thief. Even though her brother had been cleared of the charges, Leonard still did not want to marry her, for he knew that a marriage with the mayor's daughter held greater prospects for him. When Clara told him of her father's plans for suicide, Leonard said the old man thought too well of life to take his own. Even though Clara told him she herself contemplated death, he shrugged off her threat, telling her she was not the first woman to be faced with the prospect of producing an illegitimate child. After Leonard had again refused to marry her, Clara left.

Shortly after her departure, the secretary appeared with a pair of pistols and forced Leonard to leave with him. As they went to fight a duel, Clara, at home, met her brother, who told her of his plans to go to sea. He asked Clara to get him something to eat. She complied and then went to the well, ostensibly to get some fresh water, but actually to drown herself. While she was gone, Anthony returned from his visit with the woodcutter. Soon afterward the secretary, mortally wounded from the duel, staggered to the door. He told how Leonard had been killed and asked old Anthony to forgive the girl. Just as Anthony began to realize Clara's predicament, Karl ran in with the news that she had killed herself by jumping into the well. Friedrich pointed out to Anthony that his own weakness and pride had caused him to talk of suicide and thus send his daughter to her death, lest her sin be a reflection on her father. All Anthony could say was that he no longer understood the world.

Critical Evaluation:

Maria Magdalena was the first bourgeois tragedy in German literature in which all the characters belonged to the lower middle class. Previous bourgeois tragedies had derived their momentum from conflict between the upper and lower classes. For example, a lower-class girl might be seduced and then abandoned by an upper-class lover. Friedrich Hebbel, however, has shown that "one need only be human to have a fate and in certain circumstances a terrible fate."

Written in prose instead of verse, *Maria Magdalena* is the germinal point in the emergence of modern realist drama. As Hebbel points out in his preface, previous authors made mistakes in writing the dialogue of the common people, either giving them beautiful speeches that made them appear as "bewitched princes and princesses" or making them appear so woodenly stupid that it was surprising they could manage to say anything. Hebbel avoids both extremes and lets his characters speak naturally and convincingly.

While introducing the realist style, Hebbel still observed the three unities required by classical drama: the unities of time, place, and action. *Maria Magdalena* takes place within a few days, the encounters are mainly in Anthony's house, and the action centers on Clara's dilemma.

Clara is the main tragic figure in the play. Under duress, she submits to the sexual demands of Leonard, a member of her own class, but is subsequently jilted by him. Rather than bring shame on the family by having an illegitimate child, she commits suicide. The real tragedy, though, lies in the narrow bourgeois mentality that permits no exception to its notion of correctness.

Clara has reached an age where it is no longer acceptable for her to be single. The pressure on her to marry is made evident at the beginning of the drama in her mother's conversation and costume. In a masterful dramatic touch, Hebbel has the mother ask Clara pointedly about Leonard while wearing her own wedding dress. The theme of marriage is presented with strong visual reinforcement.

Significantly, Clara's thoughts are not so much of marriage as of self-sacrifice. Her ideal church scene, described in her closing monologue of Act I, scene iii, was enacted by a little Catholic girl who had been given the first cherries of the year. Rather than eating them, she carried them to the altar as an offering. This vivid image of the cherries that are not eaten foreshadows the drastic fate of Clara and her child. She sacrifices herself to make sure that her family will not be disgraced.

Hebbel's economy of style ensures that every image enhances a major theme. Marriage is suggested by the wedding dress; self-sacrifice, by the cherries. Likewise, death is suggested by the grave digger. In an uncanny touch, the grave he is digging turns out to be for Clara's mother. Her death in turn foreshadows the trio of deaths at the end of the drama: Leonard, Friedrich, and Clara all meet violent ends. Repeated mention of wells and water creates a resonance of expectation in the audience for the circumstances of Clara's death.

The most widely used image in *Maria Magdalena* is the snake, which connotes deception and evil. Leonard is generally perceived as a snake because of his duplicity. He readily reveals his machinations and actually uses the snake image to describe himself. He says to Clara, "You be harmless as a dove, my sweet, and I'll be sly as a snake." Clara later uses the image in a way that stresses Leonard's predatory nature, "I thank you as I would a serpent that had wound itself about me and then suddenly let me go to prey on something else." Leonard, however, is not the only snake in the drama. Hebbel expands his application of the image to include the malicious gossips so dreaded by Anthony. In Friedrich's dying speech he says: "All you thought about was the tongues that would hiss—but not about the worthless snakes they belonged to."

Like Friedrich, many critics place the blame entirely on Anthony, the illiterate, self-righteous father who could tolerate anything but shame. It was his petty bourgeois values and threat of suicide that drove Clara to despair. However, in addition to depicting the destructive side of those values, Hebbel suggests by omission that the reaction Anthony anticipated on the part of the neighbors was grossly exaggerated. Society is not as much to blame as one might think. The neighbors, in fact, say nothing. They are conspicuously absent throughout the drama. Any influence they exert on Anthony's family is purely in Anthony's imagination; he is concerned with the insubstantial. The pastor tells Anthony that he is accountable for no one but himself and that it is "unchristian pride" that makes him want to accept responsibility for his adult son. Yet Anthony persists in his authoritarian and judgmental approach to his own children. Only in the title of the drama does Hebbel suggest the truly Christian alternative of forgiveness. The biblical reference in the title to Mary Magdalen, the fallen woman in need of forgiveness, exemplifies Hebbel's technique of influencing the audience directly without working through the medium of the players.

While it is tempting to follow Friedrich's lead and blame Anthony, one cannot ignore the complexity of the characters and oversimplify the action. Friedrich himself is not guiltless. Although loving Clara since childhood, he did not stay in touch with her during his student years, and, at the crucial moment, gave priority to dueling with Leonard rather than to comforting Clara. Leonard, the supposed blackguard, is also not completely guilty. Seen in his own right, he did have cause to be jealous and to be unenthusiastic about Clara's joyless description of married life. He was also properly disappointed that her dowry had disappeared and wary of the scandal surrounding her brother. As in real life, the distinctions are blurred between good and bad, right and wrong. For such a short drama, *Maria Magdalena* has a tremendous impact. It is thought-provoking and masterfully written, with every detail essential to the whole. Hebbel introduced realism with consummate artistry.

"Critical Evaluation" by Jean M. Snook

Bibliography:
Flygt, Sten G. *Friedrich Hebbel*. New York: Twayne, 1968. A useful plot summary with interpretive observations. Discusses *Maria Magdalena* as Hebbel's first masterpiece; all characters belong to the lower middle class, which is presented as being ripe for change.
Glenn, Jerry H. "The Title of Hebbel's *Maria Magdalena*." *Papers on Language and Literature* 3, no. 2 (Spring, 1967): 122-133. An excellent analysis of the entire play. Like the Pharisees in the Bible, the members of Hebbel's bourgeois society are quick to condemn. The title suggests the Christian message of love and forgiveness that is so conspicuously absent in the play.
Weiss, Hermann F. "Animal and Nature References in F. Hebbel's *Maria Magdalena*." *Seminar* 7, no. 3 (October, 1971): 191-200. Anthony is associated with a hedgehog since he maintains a defensive position. Leonard, the villain of the play, is seen as a snake. The negative animal imagery emphasizes the inhumanity of society's moral standards.
Wells, G. A. "Hebbel's *Maria Magdalena* and Its Critics Past and Present." *Quinquereme* 6, no. 2 (1983): 141-154. Good formal and stylistic analysis of the play, with a critical overview of its reception. The characters Anthony, Leonard, and Friedrich are fatally flawed by their concern with "what people will say." A tragedy of narrow-mindedness.
Wright, J. D. "Hebbel's Klara: The Victim of a Division in Allegiance and Purpose." *Monatshefte* 38 (1946): 304-316. A carefully reasoned analysis of Clara's doubly tragic situation. Although in love with Friedrich, she allows herself to be pressured into premarital sex with Leonard. Then, instead of concentrating on persuading Leonard to marry her, she gets Friedrich involved and loses them both.

MARIUS THE EPICUREAN
His Sensations and Ideas

Type of work: Novel
Author: Walter Pater (1839-1894)
Type of plot: Philosophical
Time of plot: Second century
Locale: Roman Empire
First published: 1885

> *Principal characters:*
> MARIUS, a young Roman of pagan tradition
> FLAVIAN, a close friend of Marius at school
> CORNELIUS, a Roman army officer and friend of Marius
> MARCUS AURELIUS, philosopher-emperor of Rome
> CECILIA, a friend of Cornelius and a Christian leader

The Story:

Marius was a young Roman whose family had for many years lived on Whitenights, an estate in northern Italy. On that estate, Marius had grown to adolescence in an atmosphere of pagan piety and rural simplicity. The family led a relatively simple life because Marius' grandfather had squandered much of the family fortune. In the atmosphere of his childhood, Marius found a great joy in worshiping the household gods and in overseeing the work on the estate. His life was one of contemplation rather than one of activity, and his idealism and religiosity were almost morbid in their extreme.

While still in his teens, young Marius was taken to a temple of Aesculapius in the Etrurian hills for the cure of a childhood disease. There the quiet, fresh atmosphere of the place, as well as the teachings of Galen, the great Roman physician, gave him a new outlook on life. Upon his return home, Marius found his mother's health failing. She died shortly afterward, and the effect of her death on Marius was to turn him into a skeptic, a young man who questioned all aspects of life as they presented themselves to him.

Soon afterward, relatives sent young Marius to Pisa, where he attended school. While there, he conceived the idea of becoming a poet of the intellectual school. His inclination in that direction was stimulated by his friendship with Flavian, a schoolmate. Flavian was three years older than Marius and had great influence over the younger boy. The two read all the literature and philosophy they could find. Among the works they pored over was the *Metamorphoses* of Apuleius; its ornate style was a source of great joy to Marius.

The studies in literature and philosophy that the two young men planned, however, were short-lived. Flavian became sick after an excursion he and Marius made, and he died soon after of a plague brought back to Italy by the armies of Marcus Aurelius, who had just returned from a campaign into the eastern reaches of the Empire. After Flavian's death, Marius needed an intellectual crutch to carry him through the agony of seeing his young friend die, and he became attracted to the study of mysticism. At last, he put aside the desire to look to Oriental mystic lore and turned to early Greek philosophers to find, if he could, some answer to his problems in their writings and thought.

One of the first writers he studied was Heraclitus, who taught him to limit his labors so that he would not lose everything by trying to master all knowledge at once. From Heraclitus, he turned to the teachings of Aristippus of Cyrene, founder of the Epicurean school. From his study of Cyrenaic philosophy, Marius came to the conclusion that knowledge was limited to experiences received through the senses, and he thought that he owed it to himself to have many sensuous experiences in order to reach the highest possible point of wisdom.

The idea appealed to Marius because of the immensely practical ethics that the whole concept implied. Life as the primary end of life was the code that Marius found himself professing; it was, of course, an antimetaphysical metaphysic. Through it, Marius hoped to find, by means of cultural knowledge, the secret of the present in the changing universe; he wanted to discover all the subtle realizations implied in each moment of life. Like Epicureans of that time and since, Marius found there were those who misinterpreted his credo and believed that he sought pleasure as an end in itself; yet hedonism, the search for pleasure as the purpose of life, was farthest from his mind. Such a life would have been too gross for one of Marius' pietistic background. During his search for an answer to life, Marius had turned from poetry to prose, which he felt better fit his nature and his studies.

About the time that his Epicureanism became crystallized in his mind, Marius felt some pangs of regret that his emotional life seemed to have become stunted. He wondered why it was that he felt more inclined to research of the mind than to normal human emotions. He could not feel the necessity of pursuing feminine company and did not regret that he had not found it a matter of urgency that he acquire a wife. Love, in the ordinary sense of the word, did not seem to be a part of his makeup.

At a time when this problem was disturbing him, he had a summons to Rome that interrupted his worries. He was called to become secretary and editor to Emperor Marcus Aurelius, a prolific writer and a patron of the arts and philosophy. Marcus Aurelius had been working for some time on a memoir and a series of disconnected meditations which he wished someone to put into edited form. That task was assigned to Marius.

On the way to Rome, Marius met a young officer of the army named Cornelius, an officer of the famed Twelfth Legion, who was returning to Rome after service in the farther reaches of northern Europe. Under the tutelage of Cornelius, Marius quickly made himself at home in the city. Fortunately, Marius' family had a house in Rome, although it had not been used in many years. To the young Epicurean, Rome was a wonderful place in which to live; for several years, Marius was happy there. Experiences of the richest nature were his; thanks to his family background and the emperor's patronage, he moved in the best of circles.

There was, however, something that Marius could not fathom. His friend Cornelius seemed much happier than he. Since Cornelius was not a simple materialistic person, Marius could not understand why his friend was so much happier. One day as they were returning from a trip away from Rome, Cornelius took Marius into a rich home on the Appian Way. It was the residence of the widow of Cecilius, and Cecilia, who was its mistress, was a Christian, as was Cornelius. From that moment, Marius began to comprehend something of the new religion that was making converts in the Empire. He found a strange kind of happiness in attending mass in the home of Cecilia, and he also noticed that he felt a strange attraction to Cecilia herself.

Some months later, when Cornelius and Marius were once again away from Rome, the small town in which they had stopped was shaken by an earthquake. After the first tremors of the quake had passed, Cornelius, accompanied by Marius, joined a group of Christians who were publicly thanking the Deity for their escape from death. Fearing that the Christians had been the cause of the earthquake, the pagans of the town assaulted them. Marius and Cornelius were arrested because of their rank and sent to Rome. On the way, their captors learned that one of them was not a Christian. In order to save his friend, Marius said that the non-Christian was

Cornelius, who was then set free. Marius himself became violently ill before he and his guards reached Rome. He was left behind to die, but some villagers, who were also Christians, found him and nursed him. He died with Christian prayers in his ears.

Critical Evaluation:

Walter Pater's novel was an answer to those who had misunderstood his views on art and philosophy. The novel is, in great part, a fictional rendering of Pater's own struggle for a philosophical position, and the personality of Marius is a reflection of the author himself. The volume is also an appreciation of the culture of the second century of the Christian era in Roman Italy. Although sharply criticized by historians of fact, Pater's careful study of the environment has caught the spirit of the times and the people. No one who has not some familiarity with the writers of the time, and before, can read with signal success the intellectual adventures and development of the young Roman who is the central figure of the book; the work is, to some extent, a veritable patchwork of ideas and even quotations from the classical authors who would be the basis of knowledge for a young Roman studying seriously during the reign of Marcus Aurelius.

In his portrayal of Marius the Epicurean, Pater shows what might have happened to a young man of Marius' sort during Marcus Aurelius' reign. With precision and accuracy, he also unconsciously delineates the nature of a middle-aged, middle-class bachelor-scholar of about the year 1880. Pater thought that the purpose of higher education was to teach art and poetry, so he incorporates this philosophy into Marius' development. Perhaps this is the reason that *Marius the Epicurean* contains more poetry—not from books and pictures, but from life as Pater saw it—than any of Pater's other works.

The setting of Marius' spiritual journey is chiefly Rome. It is in this, "the most religious city of the world," that readers are given glimpses of many various religions: the religion of Numa, the religion of Isis, the medical cult of Aesculapius, and the new Christianity. It is by mentioning these various religions and having Marius influenced by them that Pater is, from the beginning, able to present a deeply serious tone to the work.

Having chosen the appropriate setting, Pater selected characters that best suited his purpose from the history, philosophy, art, and literature of the age. Such characters as Lucius, Apuleius, Cornelius, Fronto, Marcus Aurelius, and Lucien are leading figures in the Latin literature of Marius' day. The Greek physician Galen is also introduced, and the future patron saint of Christian music, Cecilia, is presented. Ideas of Pliny, Tibullus, Lucretius, Horace, and Vergil are sprinkled throughout the book and add to the philosophical and literary atmosphere. With the imaginary life of Marius as his framework, Pater is able to present what is to him the most important and impressive ideas of the period.

Marius the Epicurean is not easily classified. From its opening pages, one is aware of an unusual reading experience. Pater's writing is often obscure, but is often leisurely and poetic. Interested readers should consult Pater's *Appreciation with an Essay on Style* (1889) for his views on style. Whereas many great Victorian literary artists tend to argue their various doctrines with heavy-handed urgency, Pater whispers and murmurs to his audience, usually in a calm, almost somber tone. It is because each phrase is intricately fashioned that *Marius the Epicurean* is often referred to not only as a philosophical romance (rather than a novel), but also as a prose poem. The many details of the story are easily forgotten, but the overall tonal effect of the work lingers in the mind. It is not the figures, lingering in misty shadows, that capture the attention; the philosophy, aesthetics, and religious doctrines are not easily associated with any concrete individual or personality. The characters serve mainly as vehicles through which

Pater can fulfill his major purpose—exposing his listener to the intellectual and philosophical timbre of ancient Rome.

Bibliography:
Bloom, Harold, ed. *Walter Pater*. New York: Chelsea House, 1985. Includes considerable evaluation of *Marius the Epicurean*, which ranges from detailed stylistic analysis to questions of genre. Pater's work is also evaluated as an inspiration to writers of the early twentieth century.
Crinkley, Richmond. *Walter Pater: Humanist*. Lexington: University Press of Kentucky, 1970. In the chapter analyzing *Marius the Epicurean*, the circular structure of the text and the diminished presence of the author is considered. Also delineates the decorative elements in Pater's prose.
Iser, Wolfgang. *Walter Pater: The Aesthetic Moment*. Translated by David H. Wilson. Cambridge, England: Cambridge University Press, 1987. Examines the narrative structure of Pater's portraits. Finds that significant narrative inconsistencies create a state of flux between past and present. Considers Pater's theories on memory and history.
Monsman, Gerald. *Walter Pater*. Boston: Twayne, 1977. Combines a broad overview of Pater's work with a more focused critique of the novels. The chapter on *Marius the Epicurean* points out the emphasis on inward vision rather than outward events.
Ward, Anthony. *Walter Pater: The Idea in Nature*. London: Macgibbon and Kee, 1966. Traces Pater's explorations of a literary style that expresses the complexity of experience and the inconstancy of meaning. The recurrent quest for beauty in Pater's fictional and nonfictional works is also considered.

MARMION
A Tale of Flodden Field

Type of work: Poetry
Author: Sir Walter Scott (1771-1832)
Type of plot: Historical
Time of plot: Early sixteenth century
Locale: The Scottish border
First published: 1808

Principal characters:
LORD MARMION, an English knight
RALPH DE WILTON, wronged by Marmion, disguised as a palmer
CLARE FITZ-CLARE, loved by de Wilton
CONSTANCE DE BEVERLEY, betrayed by Marmion
ARCHIBALD DOUGLAS, Earl of Angus

The Story:
Wherever Lord Marmion went, he was welcomed and honored as a brave and valiant knight. The English king had sent him to the Scottish court to try to persuade that country's king to end armed raids throughout the Border country. Marmion asked a Scottish lord to furnish him a guide, someone of peaceful appearance, and since there was no one else available the lord sent a palmer, a holy man who had made many pilgrimages to religious shrines.

At the same time an abbess, accompanied by several nuns, was making a sea voyage to Cuthbert Isle to hold an inquisition over two prisoners of the church. One of the young nuns aboard, still a novice, was Clare Fitz-Clare, a lovely young woman who had entered the abbey after her lover, dishonored, had, it was believed, died. One of the accused was Constance de Beverley, a nun who had broken her vows and run away from the convent. Before she was put to death, Constance told the abbess and her other accusers the story of her fall from grace.

Her betrayer had been Lord Marmion. Believing his protestations of love for her, she had escaped from the convent and followed him for three years as his page. Then Marmion met lovely Clare Fitz-Clare, and, because she was an heiress of great wealth, he abandoned Constance to seek Clare for his bride. The king promised him that he should have Clare, but she loved another knight, Ralph de Wilton. Marmion forged papers that offered false proof that Wilton was not true to the king. The two knights fought a duel, and de Wilton was left for dead. Constance, soon to die, gave the papers proving the forgery to the abbess and implored her to get the papers to the king in order to save Clare from a hateful marriage. Although the woman had entered a convent rather than marry Marmion, the king would force the marriage if Clare were found, for Marmion was a great favorite at court. Although her judges pitied her, Constance was put to a horrible death after she had told her story.

Marmion continued on his way to the court. Guilty thoughts of Constance worried him; he had been responsible for her capture by the Church. He soothed his conscience with the belief that she would not be severely punished. One night as they stayed at an inn a young boy sang a ballad about the soul's disquiet of every man who would betray a maid. At the end of the song Marmion thought he heard the tolling of a death bell. When the knight mentioned the tolling sound he heard, the palmer spoke his first words, saying that it was the toll of death for a friend. That night Marmion, unable to sleep, went out into the dark to ride. There he was attacked by what seemed a devil, for the man had the face of de Wilton, long dead. The strangest part was that Marmion's mysterious adversary could have killed him, but instead sheathed his sword and rode off into the night.

As Marmion and his men rode through the Border country, they noticed everywhere huge numbers of armed clansmen readying for battle. On their arrival at the Scottish court, Marmion could not persuade King James to halt preparations for battle. The Scots, claiming that the English had wronged them, demanded vengeance. Courtesy required that Marmion be given safe conduct during his mission, however, and so the king put him in the care of Archibald Douglas, one of the most powerful of all the lords of Scotland. Douglas also was charged with the care of the abbess and her nuns, who were to be returned safely to their convent but who had been taken captive, it being time of war, by the Scots. The abbess feared for Clare's safety if Marmion should learn that she was among the party of nuns. To save Clare from a forced and hated union, the holy woman gave the papers proving Marmion's forgery to the palmer and begged him to deliver them to the English king.

Marmion, learning the woman's identity, secured an order directing him to take Clare to her home, with Douglas for an escort. Separated from the abbess, Clare feared for her safety with Marmion, but he planned not to press his suit until she had been returned to her kinsmen, who would be dominated by the king. Marmion and Clare were quartered in Tantallon Castle, owned by Archibald Douglas, Earl of Angus, to await the impending battle between English and Scottish troops.

Clare, lonely and afraid, walked out onto the battlements of the castle. There she met a young knight who proved to be de Wilton. Clare heard his story. He had not been mortally wounded in his combat with Marmion, but had been healed and cared for by one of his servants. The loyal servant asked one boon for saving his life, that should de Wilton's deadliest enemy fall beneath his sword that enemy should be spared. The young knight wandered far, his name scorned by all who once loved him because he was now branded as a traitor. At last he disguised himself so well that no one recognized in the lowly palmer the once-proud knight. It was de Wilton who had so frightened Marmion during his midnight ride, but he had kept his promise to his old servant and spared the life of the man who had ruined him. The young man had told Douglas his story, which was confirmed by the papers given him by the abbess. That night Douglas restored to de Wilton his knightly honors, and the next day de Wilton would join the English troops.

Marmion, unable to resist the spectacle of troops drawn up for battle, defied Douglas and rode off to join the fight. Having learned from one of his company the palmer's true identity and fearing that he would lose Clare, he took her to a place of safety behind the English lines. When the battle began, Marmion was mortally wounded. Clare, pitying the man she hated, tended him gently. Before he died, Marmion learned of the death of Constance and repented all his sins.

The English defeated the Scots in a bloody battle on Flodden Field. De Wilton was everywhere in the thick of the fighting. After the battle, his lands and his titles were returned to him, and Clare was given to him with the king's blessing. The proud name of de Wilton was known again through the land. Marmion, as he deserved, lay in an unmarked grave.

Critical Evaluation:

In 1488, a group of Scottish nobles rebelled against their king, James III, and defeated him in battle. Following their murder of the monarch, James III was succeeded on the throne by his fifteen-year-old son, James IV, who unified Scotland and led it to new prosperity. During the twenty-five years of James IV's eventful reign, the Spanish Inquisition would establish a well-deserved reputation for intolerance and cruelty, the Star Chamber of England's Henry VII would deprive his subjects of their civil rights, a fanatic Florentine monk named Girolamo Savonarola would preach against the supposed sinfulness of some of the world' greatest art, and Christopher Columbus would discover America. As subsequent explorations revealed hitherto unknown lands in the Americas and Africa and new trade routes to Asia, European powers struggled to adjust.

The opportunities offered by political instability and expanded geographical horizons tempted many to enhance their fortunes through military conquests of various kinds, not only in the New World but also in Europe as well. Anxious to gain influence over his southern neighbor, for example, James IV of Scotland expanded his army and navy, actively supported a young pretender to the English throne named Perkin Warbeck, and threatened to invade England. Scotland had allied itself with France against England, but England defeated them both. James IV's attempt to take England by force came to an abrupt halt September 9, 1513, just south of the border between the two countries. In the Battle of Flodden Field, an army sent from London defeated that of the Scots, killing James IV and most of his nobles. This is also the conflict that climaxes Sir Walter Scott's *Marmion*.

In *Marmion*, Scott makes no attempt to depict the broader aspects of early sixteenth century history, exciting and significant as they certainly were. The world of *Marmion* comprises the English, the Scots, and the church, with the latter represented ambiguously by both the Inquisition and various nuns. As was usual in Scott's work, Marmion himself (supposedly the protagonist or hero) is mostly a spectator to the great historical events of which he is accidentally a part. What was not usual is that he also appears as something of a villain, having forged an important letter dishonoring the real hero of the poem, de Wilton. In the end, he dies and deserves to. If Marmion is compared with any of the characters in Scott's previous long poem, *The Lay of the Last Minstrel* (1805), it is apparent that, unlike them, Marmion embodies complexities, contradictions, and internal torment. Although still somewhat crude, Marmion was the most sophisticated character that Scott had yet created.

In some respects, *Marmion* is also a more well-written poem than its predecessor. Although *Marmion* makes use of several different stanzaic forms, there is less experimentation overall. Interpolated songs and tales are less frequent and generally longer, as with the Host's Tale in canto 3, stanzas 19 to 25. The narrator also emerges as a separate voice in canto 3, stanza 12, but he remains unidentified and has disappeared by the end of the poem. The epigrammatic wisdom of which he is sometimes master emerges most memorably in canto 6, stanza 17 ("Oh! what a tangled web we weave/ When first we practice to deceive," a reference to Marmion's forgery of the letter). The lines on woman in stanza 30 are also famous. Notable, too, is the incisive portrait of James IV in canto 5, stanzas 8 and 9. "Lochinvar," the famous interpolated song, is at canto 5, stanza 12, but is irrelevant to the plot.

Each of the poem's six cantos is preceded by an introduction. These introductions (some of which originated as separate poems before *Marmion* was begun) are verse epistles, or letters, to individuals then living, all of them friends of Scott. Personal, confessional, and often charming, Scott's introductions are more in accord with modern taste than are the cantos they introduce; one can only regret that Scott did not choose to write more often about himself and those he knew at first hand.

In the introduction to canto 1, Scott abandons his usual reticence on contemporary matters to praise the recently deceased English statesmen William Pitt and Charles Fox. He also recalls the grand poetic tradition of England, including the sixteenth and seventeenth century writers

Edmund Spenser, John Milton, and John Dryden, who, although they may have themes in common, are to be contrasted with the "dwindled sons of little men" writing at that time. The introduction to canto 4 similarly recalls William Shakespeare and the eighteenth century poet Thomas Gray. Imitating the latter's artificial diction, Scott humorously refers to his own, less carefully crafted verse as "this rambling strain." The youthful, aspiring poet George Gordon, Lord Byron would fully agree with Scott's self-deprecation and promptly satirized *Marmion* in "English Bards and Scotch Reviewers" (1809). The general strength of canto 6, including the delightful invocations of Christmas now and then, de Wilton's history (stanzas 6-10), the death of Marmion (31-32), and the elegiac regard for defeated Scotland (34-35), set a standard that Byron then could not have met.

"Critical Evaluation" by Dennis R. Dean

Bibliography:
Alexander, J. H. *"Marmion": Studies in Interpretation and Composition.* Salzburg: Institut für Anglistik und Amerikanistik, Universität Salzburg, 1981. Approaches *Marmion* from several different points of view; the most exacting modern appraisal.
Alexander, J. H., and David Hewett, eds. *Scott and His Influence.* Aberdeen, Scotland: Association for Scottish Literary Studies, 1983. Specialized scholarly papers on a variety of Scott topics, including *Marmion.*
Cockshut, A. O. J. *The Achievement of Walter Scott.* London: Collins, 1969. A widely available introduction to the man and his work—reasonable, centrist, and modern. Chapters on Scott's major poems precede those dealing with his novels and other works.
Goslee, Nancy Moore. *Scott the Rhymer.* Lexington: University Press of Kentucky, 1988. Includes separate chapters on *The Lay of the Last Minstrel, Marmion,* and *The Lady of the Lake* (1810). Almost the only serious critique of Scott's long poems since modern techniques of analysis were developed. Deserves to be read in full.
Johnson, Edgar. *Sir Walter Scott: The Great Unknown.* 2 vols. New York: Macmillan, 1970. Intended to commemorate the two hundredth anniversary of Scott's birth, Johnson's critical biography is the most important modern book on Scott. Contains unsurpassed discussions of his major poems, including *The Lay of the Last Minstrel, Marmion,* and *The Lady of the Lake.*

MARRIAGE À LA MODE

Type of work: Drama
Author: John Dryden (1631-1700)
Type of plot: Comedy of manners
Time of plot: Seventeenth century
Locale: Sicily
First performed: 1672; first published, 1673

Principal characters:
    RHODOPHIL, a captain of the king's guards
    DORALICE, his wife
    PALAMEDE, a courtier
    MELANTHA, his betrothed
    POLYDAMAS, king of Sicily
    PALMYRA, his daughter
    LEONIDAS, the true prince

The Story:

Palamede, a courtier who had just returned to Sicily after an absence of five years, overheard Doralice singing a song justifying inconstancy in marriage. Smitten by her great beauty, Palamede promptly declared his love. The information that Doralice was married did not abate his ardor; instead, he confessed that he himself was to be married in three days. The two resolved to meet again. Having been informed that Rhodophil, her husband, was approaching, Doralice abruptly departed.

Rhodophil welcomed Palamede back to court. He sympathized with him over his approaching marriage, complaining that he himself had found no joy in marriage after the first six months. Palamede advised him to take a mistress, a remedy that Rhodophil said he was already trying to effect. He had found a woman whom he desired, but her obsession with court society had prevented her from keeping her assignations. The conversation ended with the approach of Argaleon, the king's favorite, who brought a message summoning Rhodophil to the king.

Amalthea, sister to Argaleon, discussed with a court lady the reason for the king's visit to so remote a section of Sicily. King Polydamas was searching for his son. Many years before, when Polydamas had usurped the throne, the wife of the former king had fled with an infant son. To Polydamas' amazement, his pregnant wife, Eudoxia, fled with the queen. No news had been heard of them until recently, when Polydamas was led to believe that his wife had died but that their child still lived.

Polydamas ordered brought before him a fisherman in company with a youth and a maid whom the fisherman claimed were his children but who looked too noble to be a peasant's offspring. The fisherman turned out to be Hermogenes, who had fled with Eudoxia and the queen. Under threat of torture, Hermogenes asserted that the queen, her son, and Eudoxia had died, but that Polydamas' son still lived and was, in fact, Leonidas, the youth who accompanied him. Hermogenes insisted, however, that the girl Palmyra was his own daughter. The king accepted Leonidas as his son and decreed that Palmyra should live at court so as not to be separated from her foster brother.

Later, Palamede presented himself to Melantha, the woman his father had ordered him to marry. Much to his regret, he found Melantha to be just such an affected lady as Rhodophil had described his mistress to be. Indeed, Palamede soon learned that Melantha was Rhodophil's mistress—at least in name—and that Doralice was Rhodophil's wife. The confusion was compounded when Rhodophil learned that his mistress was to be Palamede's wife.

Royal affairs were also entangled. Polydamas ordered Leonidas to marry Amalthea. When Leonidas refused, Polydamas threatened banishment but was dissuaded by Amalthea from carrying out the threat. Leonidas swore to Palmyra that he would wed none but her. When spies informed the king that Leonidas loved a commoner, Polydamas ordered Palmyra to be set adrift in a boat. Hermogenes saved her from this fate by producing evidence that she, not Leonidas, was the king's child. Although Polydamas offered to confer nobility on Leonidas, the youth chose to live in poverty with Hermogenes.

Palamede had arranged to meet Doralice, and Rhodophil to meet Melantha; both assignations were for the same time and the same place. At the tryst, when the couples converged, all four individuals fabricated excuses that the others pretended to believe. Palamede then left with his intended, and Rhodophil with his wife.

Amalthea informed Leonidas that her brother, Argaleon, had arranged to marry Palmyra and to have Leonidas banished. Although Amalthea loved Leonidas, she agreed to help him see Palmyra by taking him to the masquerade that evening. There Leonidas arranged an assignation with Palmyra at Hermogenes' house, not, however, before being recognized by Argaleon.

Both Doralice and Melantha planned to attend a masquerade dressed as boys, but they got only as far as an eating house where they exchanged insults, much to the delight of their lovers, who hugged and kissed them at each unflattering remark. The game was ended by a message summoning Rhodophil to the king. The two "boys" were left to fend for themselves.

At Hermogenes' house, Eubulus, a former governor who had helped Eudoxia in her escape, informed Palmyra that Leonidas was in reality Theagenes, the son of the late king. Leonidas told Palmyra of a plan to unseat the king, her father, and made her a prisoner when she opposed the plan. Before the conspiracy could be carried out, however, Polydamas arrived with his guards and seized the rebels.

When Palamede was informed that his father expected him to marry Melantha at once, he solicited the advice of Philotis, her maid, as to how best to woo the lady. Philotis supplied him with a list of French words, of which the lady was inordinately fond. Won by these words, Melantha accepted Palamede as her suitor and they agreed to marry. Following this development, Palamede and Rhodophil pledged to respect each other's wives, and Rhodophil and Doralice were reconciled.

Affairs in the royal household ended just as happily for most of those concerned. Suspecting that Leonidas was the true heir to the throne, Argaleon advised the young man's immediate execution, advice that Polydamas decided to follow in spite of Palmyra's pleas for mercy. The sentence would have been carried out had not Amalthea revealed Leonidas' true identity, whereupon Rhodophil and Palamede fought successfully to free the prince. The new king forgave Polydamas and asked for Palmyra's hand in marriage, a request gratefully granted. Having rejected Leonidas' offer of clemency, Argaleon was sentenced to life imprisonment. Amalthea, still in love with Leonidas, declared her intention to spend her life in prayer and mourning.

Critical Evaluation:

John Dryden's *Marriage à la Mode* is a curious mixture of heroic tragedy and comedy of manners. One plot concerns the playful seventeenth century attitude toward married love, another concerns court intrigue. Skillful characterization, especially in the comic plot, has assured a continuing place for the play. In that plot, Dryden illustrates the view of life prevalent in Restoration drama, which sees humans as creatures of appetite constantly searching for new sensations and always battling to steal or conquer the property of others. In both of the play's two plots, the characters play out this view of life through their actions, but in the end, Dryden leads them to a very different conclusion from the one no doubt expected by a Restoration audience.

All the partners in the romantic plot share the belief that a desired love conquest loses its attractiveness the moment it is possessed. In their pursuit of women, Rhodophil and Palamede are like sated, jaded gourmets in frantic search of new delicacies to intrigue their palates. They are caught in a dilemma that seems to have no solution; if love depends on desire, how can love remain after desire has once been been satisfied? Unable to solve this riddle, the characters have accepted the proposition that extramarital affairs are necessary. The opening song in the play states the premise that no one should feel bound to a silly marriage vow once passion has cooled. Operating on this assumption, the characters hopelessly entangle themselves in a confusion of affairs: Palamede, engaged to Melantha, tries to seduce Rhodophil's wife Doralice, while Rhodophil is trying to secure Melantha as his mistress. Their exploits are described in a series of images relating sex to appetite, sport, war, and stolen property, as they fight to conquer someone else's partner while safeguarding their own from like treatment.

The plot dealing with court politics is pervaded with the same belief in the attraction of the forbidden and in the need to dominate. Melantha understands the social hierarchy within which she is battling to ascend, and she knows that manners and dress are the signs by which different classes or castes are identified. Thus she constantly assimilates the ever-changing modes of dress and behavior currently in vogue; she wears the latest fashion as faithfully as she parrots the newest gossip or adheres to the most recent opinion of Leonidas. When she feels discouraged in the daily battle for popularity at court, she can always comfort herself with her vast moral superiority to those lowly creatures not connected with the palace—the women who live in the city, or worse, in the country.

By the end of *Marriage à la Mode*, Dryden has come full circle from the proposal stated in the opening song, by showing that a life of indulged appetites can only lead to satiety and discomfort. Miserable and at the point of fighting, Palamede and Rhodophil agree to halt competition and abide by rules of mutual respect for each other's property. The message of the play is that marital love and peace are possible if humans can curb their greed for greener pastures and enjoy the estate at home.

Bibliography:

Eliot, T. S. *John Dryden: The Poet, the Dramatist, the Critic*. 1932. Reprint. New York: Haskell House, 1966. This classic discussion by a writer who helped to introduce Dryden to twentieth century readers serves as a standard reference. Explains why Dryden's drama continues to interest critics and students.

Hopkins, David. *John Dryden*. Cambridge, England: Cambridge University Press, 1986. An introduction to Dryden and a contextual study of his place among English writers. Hopkins includes a plot summary of *Marriage à la Mode* and discusses marriage and gender relationships in the play.

Hughes, Derek. "The Unity of Dryden's *Marriage à la Mode*." *Philological Quarterly* 61 (1982): 125-142. Besides working to combat the common judgment that the play's two plots are quite separate, this article emphasizes characterization, looking behind the comic dialogue to the disconnections between characters.

Loftis, John. "Chapter Two: Dryden's Comedies." In *Writers and Their Background: John Dryden*, edited by Earl Miner. Athens: Ohio University Press, 1972. Carefully differentiating between the play's comic and serious plots, this discussion calls attention to the sexual play, the witty speeches, and the social distinctions operating in Dryden's most famous comedy.

Wasserman, George R. *John Dryden*. New York: Twayne, 1964. This study covers Dryden's career as well as the political, philosophical, and literary background of his plays for the general reader. The discussion of *Marriage à la Mode* highlights structural problems not developed elsewhere.

THE MARRIAGE OF FIGARO

Type of work: Drama
Author: Pierre-Augustin Caron de Beaumarchais (1732-1799)
Type of plot: Comedy
Time of plot: Eighteenth century
Locale: Spain
First performed: 1784; first published, 1785 as *La Folle Journée: Ou, Le Mariage de Figaro*
  (English translation, 1784)

Principal characters:
>FIGARO, a clever barber and the bridegroom-to-be
>COUNT ALMAVIVA, his lord
>COUNTESS ALMAVIVA, wife of the count
>SUZANNE, Figaro's fiancée and maid to the countess
>MARCELINE, the housekeeper
>DR. BARTHOLO, the former guardian of the countess
>CHÉRUBIN, a page

The Story:

Three years after Figaro, the clever barber, had helped Count Almaviva steal his beloved Rosine from her guardian, Dr. Bartholo, the count had become tired of his wife and had begun to pursue other attractive women, particularly Suzanne, his wife's maid, who was betrothed to Figaro. Suzanne informed Figaro of the count's interest, including his plan to send Figaro on a mission to England so that he could pursue Suzanne undisturbed. Figaro vowed to prevent this.

Figaro also had trouble from another source. Marceline, the count's housekeeper, had Figaro's note for a sum of money she had lent him; if he did not repay the money he would have to marry her. Marceline wanted to marry someone, and Figaro, despite the disparity in their ages, seemed the likeliest prospect, Bartholo was helping her, mostly to revenge himself on Figaro for having outwitted him.

The count's young page, Chérubin, was fascinated by all women, especially the countess. When the count learned of this infatuation, he banished the page from the castle and ordered him to join the count's regiment. Figaro had other ideas. He planned to dress Chérubin in Suzanne's clothing and send him to keep a rendezvous with the count. Figaro hoped that the count would feel so embarrassed and appear so ridiculous when the trick was exposed that he would stop pursuing Suzanne. Figaro also sent the count an anonymous letter hinting that the countess had a lover. When the count burst into his wife's chambers in search of this lover, he found no one but Suzanne, for Chérubin, who had been there moments earlier, had jumped out of a window. After fabricating several stories to account for strange coincidences, Figaro was delighted when the count had to beg his wife's forgiveness for his unfounded suspicions.

Figaro did not have the chance to send Chérubin to keep the tryst with the count because the countess and Suzanne were also plotting to foil the count's plan. After the count told Suzanne that he would not allow her to marry Figaro unless she met him at a pavilion that night, she and the countess concocted a plan to defeat him.

Marceline took her case against Figaro to court. Since he wanted to place obstacles in the way of Figaro's wedding, the count himself presided at the hearing; he ruled that Figaro must either repay the money to Marceline or marry her immediately. The sentence had scarcely been pronounced, however, when Marceline discovered that Figaro was her long-lost illegitimate son by Bartholo. She said the relationship explained the love that had made her want to marry him. Marceline and Bartholo finally agreed to marry, though Bartholo was unhappy that his worst enemy had turned out to be his son. During the dancing to celebrate Suzanne's and Figaro's wedding, Suzanne passed a note to the count to set up their rendezvous. Figaro saw it and was devastated.

That night in the garden, Suzanne and the countess, dressed in one another's clothing, prepared to spring the trap on the count. Figaro, who did not know of the women's plan, had hidden himself in a pavilion to observe Suzanne's treachery; Bartholo and Marceline accompanied him, and he brooded at length about his topsy-turvy destiny and the general injustice of society. The countess, disguised as Suzanne, met the count and permitted him to woo her, accepting money and gifts from him. The count protested his love for her and compared her favorably with his wife. Enraged at Suzanne's apparent duplicity, Figaro approached the supposed countess (Suzanne in disguise) and begged her favor; when he recognized his beloved's voice, he decided to turn her trick around and began to woo her. Suzanne slapped him soundly for his apparent duplicity. Figaro was delighted to learn that Suzanne had not played him false and that the count was actually trying to seduce his own wife.

After much confusion, during which the count discovered that everyone had observed his folly, the situation was untangled. The countess fondly forgave her husband, and the count consented to the marriages of Suzanne and Figaro, Marceline and Bartholo, and Chérubin and the gardener's daughter. Both the count and countess gave a large dowry to Suzanne, and Figaro at last had parents, a fortune, and a beautiful wife. Everyone joined in rejoicing that wit and intelligence can even the social odds.

Critical Evaluation:

In *The Marriage of Figaro* (subtitled *The Crazy Day*), Pierre-Augustin Caron de Beaumarchais takes Figaro through more intrigues and adventures. Again the shrewd barber matches wits with those who would oppress him, again young lovers must overcome obstacles planted by their more powerful enemies, and the high good humor and clever wit of Figaro triumph. Critics have interpreted *The Marriage of Figaro* as everything from a giddy sensual romp to the first rumblings of the French Revolution. Certainly aspects of this delightful play can be used to support a number of interpretations. Beaumarchais claimed about this work, as he did about all his writings, that it was his intention both to entertain and to reform society.

Although Beaumarchais' comic style was often copied by other writers of his day, it was never surpassed. With charm and gaiety, *The Marriage of Figaro* examines love in its many forms and the mad things people do in pursuit of love. Nevertheless, Beaumarchais allows everything to come right in the end: In spite of the lustful lord and predatory spinster, Suzanne and Figaro let nothing keep them from their love match; the estranged count and countess rediscover what had first drawn them together and reconcile under the moonlit chestnut trees; Marceline, who seemed ridiculous in her pursuit of the unwilling Figaro, blooms when she learns she can now love him as her long-lost son—she even gets Bartholo to marry her, albeit thirty years late.

Beaumarchais' meticulous stage directions contribute to the breathless fun. The play teems with examples of the split-second timing and mistaken identities that are so necessary to farce: Chérubin slips behind and then into a chair, only to be discovered as the count mimes finding him; Suzanne and Chérubin switch places in the countess' dressing room; Suzanne loses her composure when she sees Figaro kissing Marceline. The continuing small confusions climax in the total confusion of the last act.

The play revels in a sunny sensuality. Much of the action involves the trappings of feminine apparel; Suzanne and the countess take delight in exchanging clothes and in dressing Chérubin up as a girl (especially droll since Chérubin is usually played by a woman). The dialogue repeatedly refers to soft fabrics, flowers, ribbons, and smooth skin, a subtle reminder that virtually all the characters are thinking about sex.

The play also deals with the social tensions and injustices that would soon destroy the *ancien régime*, particularly in Figaro's long tirade in Act V. He rhetorically asks the absent count "What have you done to deserve so much? You took the trouble to be born, and nothing more." He describes the struggles of his own early life—his poverty, his imprisonment for political "crimes," and controversies with censors. At every step, Figaro learned that society is rigged against men who are intelligent but have no status.

In the character of the count, the play implicitly criticizes those who have and abuse power. The passionate lover in *The Barber of Seville* (1816), the count is, in this work, a bored husband who misuses his power as an aristocrat, especially toward the women in his domain. He and Figaro, formerly allies against the pompous Bartholo, now oppose each other as the count seeks to reclaim the *droit du seigneur* (the right of a lord to take the virginity of a peasant bride on her wedding night). Figaro twice forces him to renounce this right publicly, but even so the count intends to enjoy Suzanne, if necessary by extortion in withholding the dowry needed to pay Figaro's debt to Marceline. The count abuses his power in other ways, too. He feels justified in jealously bullying his wife when he mistakenly suspects her of being as unfaithful as himself. He sends Chérubin off to the army because Chérubin pursues the same women he does. He has the final say in judicial proceedings and, purely out of spite, does his best to force Figaro to marry Marceline.

These actions seem humorous because they all fail, thanks to the efforts of the women and Figaro. Yet the potential for real damage remains, as becomes clear in Beaumarchais' little-known sequel to *The Marriage of Figaro*, *The Guilty Mother* (1791). Here, soon after the reconciliation, the count resumes his habits of unfaithfulness and leaves the unhappy countess to seek consolation in the arms of Chérubin; that liaison results in a child, as does one of the count's liaisons, and the romantic involvement of those half-siblings twenty years later gives a blackmailing lawyer his opening. When the ashamed Chérubin had learned of the countess' pregnancy with his child, he had let himself be killed in battle. Had the count remained a faithful, loving husband, the countess would not have had an affair, and the charming young Chérubin might not have died so young. Though Figaro again manages to foil the count and young love triumphs here, too, this play shows even more clearly than the first two what harm unthinking abuses of power can cause.

Although he roundly criticized the social system of his time, Beaumarchais was, however, not advocating revolutionary change. He strongly supported the American Revolution, contributing generously to the cause and persuading the French government to do the same, but he had too much at stake in the French monarchy and aristocracy to want their downfall. Beaumarchais enjoyed life in the highest circles of French society and even added the title "de Beaumarchais" to his name after marrying a wealthy widow. Like Figaro, he had tried his hand at a wide variety of careers, among them watchmaker, musician, financier, pamphleteer, diplomat, gunrunner, and spy. Also like his creation, he wound up hitching his fortunes to those of the rich and well born. Beaumarchais wrote as an insider who saw the flaws of the system and sought to reform it, not as a radical seeking to destroy it.

"Critical Evaluation" by Susan Wladaver-Morgan

Bibliography:

Cox, Cynthia. *The Real Figaro: The Extraordinary Career of Caron de Beaumarchais*. London: Longmans, 1962. Focuses primarily on Beaumarchais' many activities other than writing. In her discussion of his ventures into diplomacy, Cox notes Beaumarchais' success as an intriguer and interprets the character of Figaro as a self-portrait. Includes illustrations and a good bibliography.

Grendel, Frédéric. *Beaumarchais: The Man Who Was Figaro*. Translated by Roger Greaves. London: MacDonald and Jane's, 1977. Interprets Figaro as Beaumarchais' alter ego and *The Marriage of Figaro* as the pinnacle of his career. Believes Beaumarchais was a reformer, not a revolutionary, and traces his chameleon-like adaptability to the fact that he was secretly a Protestant in Catholic France. Includes illustrations and a selected bibliography.

Ratermanis, J. B., and W. R. Irwin. *The Comic Style of Beaumarchais*. Seattle: University of Washington Press, 1961. Interesting scene-by-scene analysis of *The Barber of Seville* and *The Marriage of Figaro*, analyzing what makes the comedy work on stage, especially in the context of the decline of comic dramatic writing in eighteenth century France. Uses theories of Henri Bergson and others on the nature of humor.

Sungolowsky, Joseph. *Beaumarchais*. New York: Twayne, 1974. Concise biographical treatment, with a useful chronology, notes, selected bibliography, and detailed analysis of all the plays.

Wood, John. Introduction to *"The Barber of Seville" and "The Marriage of Figaro,"* translated by John Wood. Baltimore: Penguin Books, 1964. Excellent concise discussion of the plays and their social context. The edition also includes Beaumarchais' own notes on the characters and their costumes.

MARTIN CHUZZLEWIT

Type of work: Novel
Author: Charles Dickens (1812-1870)
Type of plot: Social realism
Time of plot: Nineteenth century
Locale: England and America
First published: serial, 1843-1844; book, 1844

Principal characters:
 OLD MARTIN CHUZZLEWIT, a selfish old man
 MARTIN CHUZZLEWIT, his grandson
 MARY GRAHAM, old Martin's ward
 ANTHONY CHUZZLEWIT, old Martin's brother
 JONAS CHUZZLEWIT, his son
 MR. PECKSNIFF, a hypocrite
 CHARITY and
 MERCY, his daughters
 TOM PINCH, young Martin Chuzzlewit's friend
 RUTH PINCH, his sister
 MARK TAPLEY, another friend of young Martin
 MRS. SARAH GAMP, a bibulous Cockney

The Story:

Selfishness was a strong family trait in the two aged brothers, Martin and Anthony Chuzzlewit. From his cradle, Anthony's son, Jonas, had been taught to think only of money and gain; in his eagerness to possess his father's wealth, he often grew impatient for the old man to die. Old Martin Chuzzlewit suspected the world of having designs on his fortune; his distrust and lack of generosity turned his grandson, his namesake, into a model of selfishness and obstinacy. The old man's heart was not as hard as it seemed, for he had taken into his house as his companion and ward an orphan named Mary Graham. He told her that she would have a comfortable home as long as he lived but that she should expect nothing at his death. His secret wish, though, was that love might grow between her and his grandson. However, when young Martin told him that he had chosen Mary for his own, he was displeased, afraid that the young couple were acting in their own interests. A disagreement followed, and the old man turned his grandson out.

Thrown on his own resources, young Martin decided to become an architect. He decided to study with Mr. Pecksniff, an architect and land surveyor, who lived in a little Wiltshire village not far from Salisbury. Mr. Pecksniff agreed to train two or three pupils in return for a large premium and exorbitant charges for board and lodging. Mr. Pecksniff thought highly of himself as a moral man, and he had a copybook maxim to quote for every occasion. He and Old Martin Chuzzlewit were cousins, but even though there had been bad feeling between them in the past, Mr. Pecksniff saw in Martin a possible suitor for one of his daughters, and he accepted him as a student without requiring the customary fee.

Mr. Pecksniff had never been known to build anything, a fact that took nothing away from his reputation. With him lived his two affected daughters, Charity and Mercy, as hypocritical and mean-spirited as their father. His assistant was a former pupil named Tom Pinch, a meek, prematurely aged draftsman who looked upon Mr. Pecksniff as a tower of knowledge.

Young Martin arrived in Wiltshire and took the place of John Westlock in Mr. Pecksniff's establishment. Westlock had never been a favorite in the household, his contempt for Mr. Pecksniff having been as great as his regard for honest, loyal Tom Pinch. At first, Martin treated Tom in a patronizing manner. Tom, accustomed to the snubs and ridicule of Charity and Mercy, returned Martin's slights with simple goodwill; before long, the two became friends.

One day, Mr. Pecksniff and his daughters departed suddenly for London, summoned there by Mr. Chuzzlewit. The old man called on them at Mrs. Todgers' shabbily genteel rooming house and accused his grandson of having deceived the worthy man who sheltered him. Mr. Pecksniff pretended to be pained and shocked to learn that Mr. Chuzzlewit had disowned his grandson. When the visitor hinted at future goodwill and expectations if the architect would send the young man away at once, Mr. Pecksniff—even though the old man's proposal was treacherous and his language insulting—agreed eagerly. Returning to Wiltshire, he virtuously announced that Martin had ill-treated the best and noblest of men and taken advantage of his own unsuspecting nature. His humble roof, he declared, could never shelter so base an ingrate and impostor.

Homeless once more, Martin made his way to London in the hope of finding employment. As the weeks passed, his small store of money dwindled steadily. At last, when he had nothing left to pawn, he decided to try his fortunes in America. A twenty-pound note in a letter from an unknown sender gave him the wherewithal for his passage. Mark Tapley, the hostler of the Blue Dragon Inn in Wiltshire, accompanied him on his adventure. Mark was a jolly fellow with a desire to see the world. Martin could not leave London, however, without seeing Mary Graham. He read her a letter he had written to Tom Pinch, in which he asked his friend to show her kindness if the two should ever meet. Martin also arranged to write to Mary in care of Tom.

As passengers in the steerage, Martin and Mark had a miserable voyage to New York. Martin was not fond of the bumptious, tobacco-chewing Americans he met, but he was excited by accounts of the fortunes to be made out West. Taken in by a group of land promoters, he wrote to Mary, telling her of his bright prospects.

Meanwhile old Anthony Chuzzlewit died suddenly in the presence of his son, Mr. Pecksniff, and a faithful clerk, Chuffey. Sarah Gamp was called in to prepare the body for burial. She was a fat, middle-aged Cockney with a fondness for the bottle and the habit of quoting endlessly from the sayings of Mrs. 'Arris, a friend whom none of her acquaintants had ever seen.

After the burial, Jonas went with Mr. Pecksniff to Wiltshire, for his cautious inquiries had revealed that Mr. Pecksniff was prepared to make a handsome settlement on his daughters, and Jonas was ready to court one or the other. A short time later, old Martin Chuzzlewit and Mary Graham arrived to take rooms at the Blue Dragon Inn in the village. There Tom Pinch met Mary and in his humble manner fell deeply in love with her. Only his friendship for Martin kept him from declaring himself.

Mr. Pecksniff had hoped that Jonas would marry Charity, his older daughter, but Mercy was the suitor's choice, much to her sister's chagrin. After the ceremony, Mr. and Mrs. Jonas Chuzzlewit returned to London, but before long he began to treat his bride with ill humor and brutality. Having some business to transact at the office of the Anglo-Bengalee Disinterested Loan and Life Insurance Company, he discovered that Mr. Montague, the president, was in reality Montague Tigg, a flashy speculator whom Jonas had previously known as an associate of his rascally cousin, Chevy Slyme. Lured by the promise of huge profits, Jonas was persuaded to invest in the company and become a director. Tigg, however, had little trust for his new partner. He told Nadgett, his investigator, to learn whatever he could about Jonas.

Jonas had a guilty secret. Before his father's death, he had obtained poison from a debt-ridden young doctor and had mixed it with old Anthony's medicine. Actually, his father had not taken the dose, but the circumstances, of which Chuffey, the clerk, was also aware, would have been incriminating had they become known. This secret was uncovered by Nadgett and gave Tigg a hold over his partner.

In Wiltshire, old Martin Chuzzlewit's condition seemed to deteriorate. When the invalid's mind seemed to fail, Mr. Pecksniff saw the opportunity to get control of his kinsman's fortune. He hoped to make his position doubly secure by marrying Mary Graham, but Mary found his wooing distasteful. When she told Tom Pinch about his employer's unwelcome attentions, Tom, for the first time, realized that Mr. Pecksniff was a hypocrite and a villain. Having overheard the conversation between them, Mr. Pecksniff discharged Tom after telling Mr. Chuzzlewit that the young man had made advances to Mary. Tom went to London to see his sister Ruth. Finding her unhappily employed as a governess, he took her with him to hired lodgings and asked John Westlock, his old friend, to help him in finding work. Before Westlock could go to his assistance, however, an unknown patron hired Tom to catalog a library.

In America, young Martin and Mark fared badly. They had bought land in Eden, but on their arrival, they found nothing more than a huddle of rude cabins in a swamp. Martin fell ill with fever, and when he recovered, Mark became sick. While he nursed his friend, Martin had time to realize the faults of his character and the true reason for the failure of his hopes. More than a year passed before the travelers were able to return to England.

John Westlock, having become interested in Jonas Chuzzlewit, befriended Lewsome, the young doctor from whom Jonas had secured the poison. From Mrs. Gamp, who nursed the physician through an illness, he learned additional details to make him suspect the son's guilt in old Anthony's death.

Old Martin seemed to be in his dotage when his grandson and Mark went to see him at Mr. Pecksniff's house, where by then he was living. Martin attempted to be reconciled with his grandfather and to end the misunderstanding between them, but Mr. Pecksniff broke in to say that the old man knew the young man for a villain and a deceiver, and that he, Mr. Pecksniff, would give his life to protect the sick old man. Old Martin said nothing. Young Martin and Mark thereupon went to London, where they found Tom Pinch and Ruth. They also heard from John Westlock his suspicions of Jonas Chuzzlewit.

Jonas became desperate when Tigg forced him into a scheme to defraud Mr. Pecksniff. On their journey into Wiltshire, Jonas made plans for disposing of the man he hated and feared. After Mr. Pecksniff had agreed to invest his money in the company, Jonas returned to London and left Tigg to handle the transfer of securities. That night, disguised as a workman, he went secretly to the village and assaulted Tigg, who was walking back to his room at the inn. Leaving the body in the woods, he took a coach to London and arrived there at daybreak. Nadgett, ever watchful, had seen Jonas leave and return, and he followed the murderer when he tried to dispose of the clothing he had worn on his journey.

Miraculously restored in body and mind, old Martin Chuzzlewit arrived unexpectedly in London for the purpose of righting many wrongs and turning the tables on hypocritical Mr. Pecksniff. Having heard Westlock's story, he went with him to confront Jonas with their suspicions. A few minutes later, police officers, led by Nadgett, appeared to arrest Jonas for Tigg's murder. The wretched man realized that he was trapped and took the rest of the poison he had obtained from Lewsome. The next day, old Martin met with all concerned. It was he who had hired Tom Pinch, and it was he who now confessed that he had tested his grandson and Mary and found them worthy. When Mr. Pecksniff entered and attempted to shake the hand of his venerable friend, the stern old man struck him to the floor with a cane.

The passing years brought happiness to the deserving. Young Martin and Mary were married, followed a short time later by Westlock and Ruth Pinch. Mark Tapley won the mistress of the Blue Dragon Inn. Old Martin, out of pity, befriended Mercy Chuzzlewit. He himself rejoiced in the happiness of his faithful friends, but there was no joy for Mr. Pecksniff. When news of Tigg's murder had reached the city, another partner in the shady enterprise had run away with the company funds. Mr. Pecksniff was ruined and became a drunken old man who wrote begging letters to Martin and Tom and who had little comfort from Charity, the shrewish companion of his later years.

Critical Evaluation:

Charles Dickens completed *Martin Chuzzlewit* immediately upon his return from a trip to America in 1842, and the novel reflects some of the same concerns as his *American Notes* (1842). Although the novel lagged disappointingly in sales—a situation that ultimately led to Dickens' severing his connection with the publisher Chapman and Hall—he felt himself at the top of his creative powers and believed the book to be his best work yet.

Both in structure and in vividness of character portrayal, *Martin Chuzzlewit* does reveal Dickens at the height of his creative power, and it marks a transition from his rather loosely organized earlier novels to the more structured later works. Yet, while not an absolute failure with the public, it met with perhaps the poorest reception of any of his novels. A number of theories have been forwarded to explain why Dickens' audience did not respond to the book, among them the fact that Dickens treated his characters and themes rather harshly and with less of the previous tongue-in-cheek manner. There is little of the genial warmth and affectionate comedy that had previously mellowed even the bitterest of Dickens' satire.

Another reason put forth for the novel's disappointing initial performance is its biting satire on America and Americans in those portions of the novel in which young Martin seeks his fortune there. In his earlier *American Notes*, Dickens had been careful to balance his criticisms with the many virtues he had found in the young nation; when the American press nevertheless reacted to his polite criticism with hot anger, Dickens felt obliged to pull out all the stops the next time. Indeed, his own enjoyment in creating a scathing portrait of America may perhaps have led him to indulge it to a greater extent than was warranted by the structural importance of the American episodes. The American scenes are an important part of the overall story, if only by the fact that Martin's sufferings in Eden and his grateful appreciation of Mark Tapley are needed to drive home his awareness of his own selfishness. Yet throughout a large part of their American adventures, the focus is less on Mark and Martin than on America itself.

In all fairness, however, Dickens saves an even fiercer scorn for delineating the evils at home. He shows nothing in America to equal the whining insolence of a Chevy Slyme or the greedy meanness of the whole Chuzzlewit family. No American impostor comes close to the insincerity of the hypocritical Pecksniff. The Eden Land Corporation is no more disreputable a swindle than the Anglo-Bengalee Disinterested Loan and Life Assurance Company. It is this deeper inwardness of vision that distinguishes Dickens' handling of evil in his native land from his pictures of trickery and folly in America.

Despite the extraordinary vividness with which he exposes a wide range of American types and their mannerisms, and despite his wit in parodying their methods of speaking, Dickens never gets inside the characters. The British characters, on the other hand, even when they are melodramatically lurid or outrageously satirized, are seen to some degree from within as well as from without, which endows them with an imaginative sympathy lacking for the American portraits. Dickens has no love for Jonas or Montague, but he knows their thoughts, just as he knows Pecksniff, too, to their very depths. It is this difference that makes the hilarious satire of the American scenes appear more sharply hostile than the far deeper condemnation with which Dickens surveys corruption at home.

Perhaps the supreme achievement of the novel is in the characters of Mrs. Gamp and Pecksniff. Mrs. Gamp, with her imaginary friend Mrs. Harris, represents such an almost transcendent vision of character that she threatens to overwhelm the rest of the novel. She has been hailed as one of the greatest comic creations in English literature, an adept in the use of language who would not be surpassed in literature until James Joyce's creation of Molly Bloom. Perhaps even greater is Dickens' achievement with the character of Pecksniff, who has been hailed as a prodigious achievement of imaginative energy, likened to a Tartuffe despoiled of his terrifying and satanic power, and an embodiment of all the bourgeois hypocrisy of Victorian England. Dickens constructs this character with great elaborateness and illustrates him from a thousand angles.

Critical response to *Martin Chuzzlewit* changed significantly after the initial aloofness with which the book was received, and it became recognized as perhaps second only to *The Pickwick Papers* (1836-1837) in the degree of its comic achievement. The work also came to be seen to mark an important stage in Dickens' development as a novelist; his subsequent works became increasingly panoramic, striving toward a coherent overview and sense of totality. He wrote the novel out of the whole available literary tradition as it bore on his chosen subject, and it was in this work that he began to discover the subjects and technique that he eventually made wholly his own.

"Critical Evaluation" by Craig A. Larson

Bibliography:
Adrian, Arthur A. "The Heir of My Bringing-Up." In *Dickens and the Parent-Child Relationship*. Athens: Ohio University Press, 1984. Good study of the parent-child relationship in *Martin Chuzzlewit*, using the example of Anthony and Jonas Chuzzlewit. Adrian argues that the novel explores the harm done by parents in shaping their children's futures.

Gilmour, Robin. *The Novel in the Victorian Age: A Modern Introduction*. London: Edward Arnold, 1986. A good discussion of *Martin Chuzzlewit*, which views it as a transitional novel in Dickens' oeuvre, possessing both the strengths and the weaknesses of his earlier novels at the same time that it anticipates the more complex social vision of his later novels.

Lougy, Robert E. *"Martin Chuzzlewit": An Annotated Bibliography*. Garland Dickens Bibliographies 6. New York: Garland, 1990. An excellent listing of many critical works on the novel, along with reviews by Dickens' contemporaries and a listing of stage and film adaptations. The annotations are invaluable for seeking out further sources.

Miller, J. Hillis. *"Martin Chuzzlewit."* In *Charles Dickens: The World of His Novels*. Cambridge, Mass.: Harvard University Press, 1958. One of the most important essays on the novel. Miller argues that the central problem facing the characters in *Martin Chuzzlewit* is "how to achieve an authentic self, a self which, while resting solidly on something outside of itself, does not simply submit to a definition imposed from without."

Monod, Sylvere. *"Martin Chuzzlewit."* London: Allen and Unwin, 1985. An excellent introduction to the novel, with detailed exploration of its sources and Dickens' experience in writing it. Includes a detailed bibliography.

MARY BARTON

Type of work: Novel
Author: Mrs. Elizabeth Gaskell (1810-1865)
Type of plot: Social realism
Time of plot: First half of the nineteenth century
Locale: Manchester, England
First published: 1848

> *Principal characters:*
> MARY BARTON, a young working-class woman
> JOHN BARTON, her father, a mill worker
> JEM WILSON, the son of John's closest friend
> JANE WILSON, Jem's mother
> ALICE WILSON, Jem's aunt
> MARGARET JENNINGS, a friend of Mary
> JOB LEGH, Margaret's grandfather
> MR. CARSON, a mill owner
> HARRY CARSON, his son

The Story:

John Barton, his pregnant wife Mary, and their thirteen-year-old daughter "little" Mary were on a spring outing with their friends, George and Jane Wilson and their son Jem and twin babies. Mary was extremely worried because her sister Esther had disappeared, probably with a lover. When the group returned to the Barton home for tea, George's sister Alice joined them. Later that night, Mary went into labor, but there were complications and the doctor was unable to save her. John blamed Esther.

The next year, young Mary became an apprentice to a dressmaker. Through Alice Wilson, she met Margaret Jennings, a poor girl blessed with a beautiful voice, and her self-educated grandfather Job Legh. Margaret told Mary that she was going blind. Since she would no longer be able to do needlework, her only hope was to earn a living by singing.

When Carsons' mill caught fire, Jem Wilson became a hero after saving both his father and another workman. The owners thought the fire was a godsend, for with the insurance money they would be able to replace outdated equipment. Their former employees faced starvation, however. When an epidemic raged among the weakened workers, the Wilson twins, always delicate, caught the fever and died.

Although she had strong feelings for Jem, Mary was surreptitiously seeing Harry Carson, with the encouragement of Sally Leadbitter, another apprentice. George Wilson's sudden death shook Mary, but she did not pay a visit of condolence because she could not face Jem. Margaret's future looked brighter after she found work as a singer. John Barton's situation was grim. He had quit his job and gone to London with a group of mill workers to petition Parliament, but the petition was rejected, and no one would hire a Chartist and a union man. He and Mary had to pawn their possessions in order to live. Angry and frustrated, John began taking opium. One night Esther, now a prostitute, came to warn John about his daughter's involvement with Harry, but, still believing Esther responsible for his wife's death, John refused to listen.

Mary had, however, finally realized that all she liked about Harry was his wealth. It was Jem she loved. Yet some time earlier she had firmly rejected Jem's proposal of marriage. At

Margaret's suggestion, Mary called on Jem's mother. There she saw Alice, now deaf and blind, and met Alice's foster-son Will Wilson, a fine, young sailor, who became Margaret's suitor.

Esther told Jem about Mary's involvement with Harry. Shortly thereafter, Jem sought out his rival, and after Carson struck him with his cane, Jem knocked him down. At a trade union meeting, John drew the lot for attacking one of the mill owners. When Harry was shot and killed, Jem was arrested. His gun had been used in the crime, and his relationship with Mary suggested a motive.

After Esther brought Mary a piece of paper she had found at the scene of the crime, Mary realized that her father was the murderer. Margaret remembered that Jem had walked to Liverpool with Will on the night that Harry was shot. Job, Jem, and Mary all set out for Liverpool, where Jem was to be tried. Mary was to find Will, who could establish an alibi for Jem. After taking a boat out to Will's ship and obtaining his promise to appear in court, Mary returned to testify. She publicly admitted her love for Jem and managed not to collapse until Will turned up, along with a pilot who could corroborate his story. Jem was acquitted.

Having been dismissed from his job, Jem began making plans to emigrate to Canada with his mother and Mary. John knew now that he was dying. Calling for Mr. Carson, he confessed to the crime and begged the bereaved father's forgiveness. At first, Carson refused, but after seeing the charitable behavior of a little girl, he returned to the Barton house. John died in his arms. Carson thereafter became a guiding spirit in improving working conditions in Manchester.

Just before Jem, Mary, and Jane were to leave England, Esther came home to die. In a final scene, set in Toronto, Jane was playing with her little grandson. Jem brought home good news. After surgery, Margaret had recovered her sight; she and Will were soon to be married; and when Will made his next voyage, Margaret and Job intended to accompany him and visit their friends.

Critical Evaluation:

In *Chartism* (1839) and *Past and Present* (1843), the great British intellectual Thomas Carlyle voiced his concern about the condition of his country. It was becoming increasingly divided, he said, into two classes, one of which lived in luxury while the other suffered, starved, and died unheeded. Carlyle's works were at least partially responsible for inspiring the novels of social and political criticism that appeared in the 1840's, among them those written by Benjamin Disraeli, who was later to be prime minister, and by Elizabeth Gaskell.

Whereas Carlyle and Disraeli, however, viewed the situation from a comfortable distance, Elizabeth Gaskell, though not a member of the working class, lived with the problems about which she was writing. As the wife of a Unitarian minister in Manchester, one of the industrial capitals of England, she knew the wealthy leaders of her fashionable church, but she also knew the poor. She saw how hard most of them worked, how easily their lives were shattered, and how desperate many of them had become. In *Mary Barton*, her first novel, Gaskell hoped to persuade her middle- and upper-class readers that working men and women were not automatons, but real people who deserved respect, sympathy, and consideration.

Gaskell makes her argument so compelling because she creates individuals for her novel, not types. She does so with marvelous skill. John Barton, for example, is a thoughtful man, an idealist who does not easily accept the difference between the way things are and the way they should be. He seeks for the causes of misfortunes. Essentially, he is a good man, but when Parliament refuses to accept the petition for redress, John's heart hardens. His compassion for others turns into anger toward those who are causing the suffering, and he becomes a killer. His repentance is in character, based as it is on his compassion for the father of his victim, indeed, on his identification with him, since John, too, knew what it was to lose a son.

Gaskell's other working-class characters also challenge her readers' presuppositions. Job Legh, for example, has the mind of a scientist. Jem is not just a stalwart hero, but also a brilliant inventor. The quiet Margaret Jennings turns out to have considerable initiative; instead of just bemoaning her blindness, she breaks into a new field. There is no dullness of mind or lack of ambition in such characters, no justification for their being oppressed and ignored.

Cleverly, Gaskell uses her characters' very imperfections to prove that they are just as human as their supposed betters. Mary is not immune to materialism; when she thinks of Harry, she thinks of his luxurious lifestyle. In the hands of a more sentimental writer, Jane Wilson might have been a pathetic creature, a woman who had lost her twins and her husband and now was facing the loss of her beloved son. However, Gaskell shows her as a spirited woman who insists on going to her son's trial. She is also a sharp-tongued and jealous woman, who has to learn to forgive Mary for taking Jem away from her.

Although characterization is probably Gaskell's most effective means for achieving her purpose, she also incorporates a good many practical observations into her book, primarily through dialogue. She reveals, for example, that most industrial accidents occur in the final hours of a too-long work day, and the ironic truth about the new child labor laws, which, because they did not provide funds to allow poor children to attend school, merely put them out on the street and reduced the incomes of their families.

Gaskell was well aware that the conditions she pointed out and dramatized provided a fertile field for revolution. However, she stopped short of advocating radical political reforms. Instead, she pinned her hopes on personal good will. When John sees in Mr. Carson not an oppressor but a bereaved father, and when Mr. Carson, remembering that he is a Christian, manages to forgive his son's murderer, Gaskell implies that the gap between rich and poor has been bridged. As a result of one influential man's new understanding, improvements thereupon begin to be made.

The social changes mentioned in such vague terms do not affect the principal characters in the novel. John Barton, Alice Wilson, and the unhappy Esther escape from misery by dying; Mary, Jem, and Jane, by emigrating to Canada. Even Job and Margaret loosen their ties to England when they become dependent upon Will, a sailor who can live wherever he likes.

In retrospect, given the rift between rich and poor so graphically described in *Mary Barton*, it is amazing that, unlike France, England was never torn apart by revolution. Historians suggest many reasons that such an event did not occur. Certainly Jem's decision to emigrate was one of the most important releases of tension. As long as there were alternatives elsewhere, people saw no need to stay and fight. Ultimately they helped create new countries with the energy and beliefs that had been rejected by the old one.

Rosemary M. Canfield Reisman

Bibliography:
Lucas, John. "Mrs. Gaskell and Brotherhood." In *Tradition and Tolerance in Nineteenth-Century Fiction: Critical Essays on Some English and American Novels*, edited by David Howard, John Lucas, and John Goode. New York: Barnes & Noble Books, 1967. Concludes that Gaskell was unwilling to deal with the implications of sweeping social change and fell back on the weak suggestion that mere conversation could reconcile master and servant. Points out that she did, however, succeed in showing the masses as being composed of individuals.

Schor, Hilary M. *Scheherezade in the Marketplace: Elizabeth Gaskell and the Victorian Novel.* New York: Oxford University Press, 1992. Discusses Gaskell as a woman writer in Victorian England. In the analysis of *Mary Barton*, Schor explores Gaskell's use of a romantic plot and a marriage-bound heroine to critique an authoritarian political and social structure.

Spencer, Jane. *Elizabeth Gaskell.* New York: St. Martin's Press, 1993. Provides a good overview of the writer and her works. Points out that Gaskell's intention in *Mary Barton* was to provide a voice for the working class and that she was addressing her own group, the largely Unitarian Manchester establishment. Notes, bibliography, and index.

Stoneman, Patsy. *Elizabeth Gaskell.* Bloomington: Indiana University Press, 1987. Notes that in *Mary Barton* the author opposes a working class, with its feminine, nurturing virtues, to a middle class characterized by masculine vices. This anticipates later books that deal specifically with issues of gender. Bibliography and index.

Wheeler, Michael. *The Art of Allusion in Victorian Fiction.* New York: Barnes & Noble Books, 1979. In a chapter on *Mary Barton* entitled "Dives versus Lazarus," Wheeler explains the significance of many of Gaskell's references. The often criticized structure of the novel is justified by Gaskell's basing her work on the biblical Dives-Lazarus story.

THE MASTER AND MARGARITA

Type of work: Novel
Author: Mikhail Bulgakov (1891-1940)
Type of plot: Satire
Time of plot: 30 C.E. and 1920
Locale: First century Jerusalem and postrevolutionary Moscow
First published: Master i Margarita, expurgated, 1966-1967; unexpurgated, 1973 (English translation, 1967)

> *Principal characters:*
> WOLAND THE DEVIL, who arrives in Moscow as a foreign expert in theater
> BERLIOZ, a high-ranking member of the literary elite
> IVAN BEZDOMNY, a poet
> THE MASTER, a Soviet writer who has written a novel about Jesus and Pontius Pilate
> MARGARITA, the Master's beloved and the wife of a successful Soviet scientist
> PONTIUS PILATE, the Roman procurator of Judaea
> YESHUA HA-NOTSRI, an accused rabble-rouser from Galilee

The Story:

On a warm spring afternoon, two Russian writers had met in a Moscow park. One of them, Berlioz, was the editor of a leading literary journal, the other was a poet named Ivan Bezdomny, who had been reviled for writing a poem about Jesus that depicted him as if he had really existed. The two writers were discussing atheism, the official Soviet policy, when they were joined by a strange, foreign-looking person, who asked them provocative questions and gave even more provocative answers to their questions. He even prophesied about their immediate future, telling them, for example, that Berlioz would die before the day was over. In the ensuing philosophical debate, he told them the story of Pontius Pilate. By the end of the afternoon, Berlioz had been decapitated by a streetcar. Bezdomny ended up in a mental hospital because no one would believe his story about the strange visitor.

The visitor, who bore the German-sounding name Woland, professed to be a professor of black magic. He was actually an incarnation of the Devil, and he was accompanied by a black cat named Behemoth, a naked maid, a disreputable clown, and an evil trickster. Woland and his minions proceeded to play tricks on the Soviet literary and theatrical establishments and on the ordinary people of Moscow. Various people were packed off to places thousands of miles away, their vices dramatized, their moribund consciences awakened or called to answer, and their philistine natures exposed.

The unnamed Master, an aspiring writer, had written a novel about Pontius Pilate. When he tried to get the novel published, he was unsuccessful. In fact, the book was criticized severely and the author himself subjected to various forms of persecution from both the literary and the political powers in Moscow. As a result, the author burned his manuscript, resolved never to write again, and then, confirming the judgment of his critics that he was mentally ill, turned himself in at the insane asylum. He was placed in the same ward where Bezdomny was languishing.

The Master's lover, Margarita, was frantic when her lover disappeared. Hoping to find him, she made a Faustian pact with Woland and agreed to preside as queen over the annual Satan's ball, which was to take place in the tiny apartment of the deceased Berlioz. At the ball, Woland demonstrated his links with the supernatural world by producing a copy of the Master's burned manuscript. The Devil knew its contents and declared that he had talked to Pilate himself. In the Master's novel, the New Testament account of the Passion of Jesus, or Yeshua, was retold in fresh terms. Yeshua had been betrayed by Judas. Pilate, while acting as Roman procurator and responding to the political pressure, tried to keep Yeshua from incriminating himself. Yeshua was not eager to suffer or to die, but he refused to admit that any temporal power had jurisdiction over him. As a result, the procurator was unable to release him, and Yeshua was executed. Matthew arrived too late to relieve his pain, just as Margarita had come too late to keep the Master from burning his manuscript.

While presiding over the ball, Margarita observed a parade of human vices and follies as hundreds of dead were brought back to life to answer once more for their deeds. When Margarita showed compassion for a grief-stricken woman who had choked her baby to death, Woland granted her wish for the Master's return and left the lovers in a peaceful life together in death. Soviet agencies found rational explanations for all the irrational events.

Critical Evaluation:

The Master and Margarita was Mikhail Bulgakov's crowning achievement. He had previously written other acclaimed novels, short stories, and plays, but this novel established him as a major writer of the twentieth century. Despite Bulgakov's politically enforced silence in the early 1930's and his debilitating illness and premature death, his work had a significant impact on Russian as well as world literature.

Many of Bulgakov's previous writings anticipate features of *The Master and Margarita*. His telling but nonaggressive satire and a sophisticated humor are evident in his short stories; a flair for dramatics enlivens his plays; and philosophical connotations can be found in almost all his works.

The entire action in *The Master and Margarita* takes place on four days, from Wednesday to Sunday of the Holy Week, a significant choice of days. In addition to being a satire on Soviet life in the late 1920's and the early 1930's and a love story, this "tale of two cities" is also laden with philosophical overtones. This tone is struck at the very outset by Bulgakov's use of a motto borrowed from Johann Wolfgang von Goethe's *Faust*, Part I (1808): "Say at last—who art thou?"/ "That power I serve/ Which wills forever evil/ Yet does forever good." The motto relates to the Devil, commonly recognized as the source of all evil, and to Woland, who, together with his retinue, commits acts of violence and vengeance but also reunites the Master and Margarita and forces the Muscovites to face up to their shortcomings and sins. The basic ethical question of good and evil thus becomes the focal point of the novel, with a Manichaean twist of equality between good and evil. By painting the Devil in colors other than black, and by using Jesus Christ's ethnic name, Yeshua, and making alterations in his age and the account of his crucifixion, Bulgakov urges his readers to abandon the customary, dogmatic, and political way of thinking.

Bulgakov raises another philosophical question, posed by Pontius Pilate to Jesus: What is truth? Without presuming to answer this age-old question, Bulgakov is here addressing the Soviet's usurped monopoly on the truth and their brutality to those who question that truth. To underscore the fact that there is no one truth, Bulgakov tells the Crucifixion story in three narratives—Woland's, the Master's, and Bezdomny's. He shows that everything has more than one side to it, and that looking from only one angle leads to atrophy and death.

Bulgakov poses yet another important question, that of reality, by allowing Woland and his retinue to perform supernatural acts that undermine the Soviet axiom of materialistic reality as the only permissible one. The meaning of the supernatural happenings in the novel lies not in their logical explanation, however, but in the allowance that some other reality—supernatural, spiritual, irrational, or mystical—also exists. To this end, Bulgakov tells the Jerusalem story in a straightforward, realistic manner, without any mythical or supernatural elements, whereas the Moscow story is replete with unreal and supernatural details. Bulgakov seems to ask: If today's reality cannot be explained without resorting to the supernatural, although the events of two thousand years ago are crystal clear, how valid is a reliance on reason and facts? In fact, Bulgakov uses the Jerusalem angle not to give yet another account of the Crucifixion but to entice the reader to abandon dogmatic thinking of any kind.

In this novel, Bulgakov is engaged in an ongoing argument with the Soviet rulers. Nowhere is this clearer than in the statement, repeated in several passages, that cowardice is the greatest sin. This sin lies at the core of Pilate's behavior (hence the emphasis on him, and not on Christ); it figures in the betrayal of Jesus by Matthew; and it constitutes the chief failure of the Master. The author's own stakes in this altercation are obvious from his biography. His long-standing battle with the Soviet bureaucracy and his resignation to his fate lead to a conclusion that Bulgakov was trying to assuage his own guilty feelings for having been bullied into at least superficial submission to the authorities. *The Master and Margarita* was written during the final and most painful period of Bulgakov's life, while he was enduring internal exile. Indeed, at least some aspects of *The Master and Margarita* are based on personal experiences. Like the Master, Bulgakov was hounded into intellectual obscurity by literary and political dogmatists. Margarita is modeled after his second wife, who encouraged him to persevere and did much of the copying work after Bulgakov lost his eyesight in the last years of his life. Just as the Master's novel was rescued from the fire, Bulgakov's novel was preserved after his death by his wife. Both Bulgakov and his character the Master had to rely on faith in basic goodness.

This complex novel has given rise to many equally complex interpretations. Andrew Barratt, for example, has promulgated the theory that the novel's main postulates are based on the Gnostic philosophy of the second century, a precursor of the third century Manichaean movement. According to this philosophy, a supernatural being periodically comes to earth bearing a message which, if properly deciphered, promises the possibility of divine illumination. The message is recognized by only a small number of people in whom the divine spark has not been totally extinguished by the conditions of earthly existence. According to this interpretation, Woland can be regarded as an emissary. His messages are that life is imperfect and must be accepted as such; that good and evil will coexist forever and that evil exists to help human beings recognize what good is; that human striving toward the good leads to suffering and death, but ultimately to life, the only life worth living; and, finally, that cowardice is the greatest sin.

No one interpretation answers all the questions posed by the work, a riddle-novel as the author himself called it. Bulgakov died before giving it its final form, but even as it stands, *The Master and Margarita* remains one of the most thought-provoking, intriguing, and amusing novels in world literature.

Vasa D. Mihailovich

Bibliography:
Barratt, Andrew. *Between Two Worlds: A Critical Introduction to "The Master and Margarita."*

Oxford, England: Clarendon Press, 1987. One of the most astute treatments of the novel, examining many interpretations of it, including that of the Gnostic message and the messenger in the person of Woland. A challenging study.

Curtis, J. A. E. *Bulgakov's Last Decade: The Writer as Hero*. Cambridge, England: Cambridge University Press, 1987. A thoughtful study of Bulgakov's literary profile that includes comparisons with Molière, Alexander Pushkin, and Nikolai Gogol. *The Master and Margarita* is discussed in detail on pp. 129-187.

Ericson, Edward E. Lewiston. *Apocalyptic Vision of Mikhail Bulgakov's "The Master and Margarita."* New York: E. Mellen Press, 1921. An intriguing study of the novel, concluding that an apocalyptic belief is the main underpinning of the novel.

Proffer, Ellendea. *Bulgakov: Life and Work*. Ann Arbor, Mich.: Ardis, 1984. One of the best book-length studies of Bulgakov, discussing both his life and his works in scholarly detail. *The Master and Margarita* is examined at length on pp. 525-566.

Wright, Anthony Colin. *Mikhail Bulgakov: Life and Interpretations*. Toronto: University of Toronto Press, 1978. Includes a solid treatment of *The Master and Margarita*. Good select bibliography.

THE MASTER BUILDER

Type of work: Drama
Author: Henrik Ibsen (1828-1906)
Type of plot: Psychological realism
Time of plot: Nineteenth century
Locale: Norway
First published: Bygmester Solness, 1892; first performed, 1893 (English translation, 1893)

> *Principal characters:*
> HALVARD SOLNESS, the master builder
> ALINE, his wife
> DOCTOR HERDAL, his physician
> KNUT BROVIK, in Solness' employ
> RAGNAR BROVIK, his son
> KAIA FOSLI, Solness' bookkeeper
> HILDA WANGEL, Solness' inspiration

The Story:

Halvard Solness had risen to his high position as a master builder because of a fire that had destroyed the ancestral estate of his wife's family. On the site he had built new homes that won him fame and assured success in his profession. The fire had given him his chance, but he made his own opportunities, too, by crushing all who got in his way.

Knut Brovik, employed by Solness, had once been a successful architect, but Solness had crushed him and then used him as he had many others. Ragnar, Brovik's son, was a draftsman in Solness' office, and it was Brovik's only wish that before his own death his son should have a chance to design something of lasting value. Although Ragnar had drawn plans for a villa that Solness did not wish to bother with, the builder would not give him permission to take the assignment. Ragnar was engaged to Kaia Fosli, Solness' bookkeeper, and he could not marry her until he had established himself. Ragnar did not know that Kaia had come under the spell of the master, as had so many other young women. Solness pretended to Kaia that he could not help Ragnar because that would mean losing her; in reality he needed Ragnar's brain and talent and could not risk having the young man as a competitor.

Solness' physician, Dr. Herdal, and his wife feared that the builder was going mad. He spent much time in retrospection and also seemed to have morbid fears that the younger generation was going to ruin him. Not all of the younger generation frightened Solness. When Hilda Wangel appeared at his home, he was at once drawn to her. He had met Hilda ten years before when he had hung the traditional wreath atop the weather vane on a church he had built. She had been a child at the time. Now she told him that he had called her his princess and had promised to come for her in ten years and carry her off to build her a kingdom. Since he had not kept his promise, she had come to him. Solness, who could not remember the incident, decided that he must have wished it to happen and thus made it come to pass. This, he believed, was another example of his power over people, and it frightened him.

When Hilda asked to see all he had built, especially the high church towers, he told her that he no longer built churches and would never build one again. Now he built homes for mothers and fathers and children. He was building a home for himself and his wife, and on it he was building a high tower. He did not know why he was putting the high tower on the house, but something seemed to be forcing him. Hilda insisted that he complete the tower, for it seemed to her that the tower would have great meaning for her and for him.

Hilda told Solness that his need of her was the kingdom he had promised her and that she would stay near him. She wanted to know why he built nothing but homes, and he told her of the fire that had given him his chance. At the time of the fire, he and his wife had twin baby boys. Although all had been saved from the fire, the babies died soon afterward from the effects of the fevered milk of their mother. Solness knew that his position and his fame were based on the tragedy of the fire and on his wife's heartrending loss, but he believed also that he had willed the fire in order to have his chance. Whatever he willed happened, and afterward he had to pay somehow the horrible price for his almost unconscious desires. So he built homes for others, never able to have a real home himself. He was near madness because his success was based on his and his wife's sorrow.

Solness seemed to have power over human beings as well as events. Brovik was one man who served him, his son Ragnar another. Solness, afraid of Ragnar's younger generation, believed that it would crush him as he had crushed others.

Hilda, begging him to give Ragnar and the other young people a chance, said that he would not be crushed if he himself opened the door to them. She told him that his near-madness was caused by a feeble conscience, that he must overcome this weakness and make his conscience robust, as was hers. She persuaded him to give Ragnar the assignment the young man wanted. She wished Solness to stand completely alone and yet be the master. As final proof of his greatness, she begged Solness to lay the traditional wreath on the high tower of his new home, and she scoffed at a builder who could not climb as high as he could build.

Hilda alone wanted Solness to climb the tower, and only she believed that he would do so. Once she had seen him standing on a church tower, and his magnificence had thrilled her. She must have the thrill again. On that other day she had heard a song in the sky as the master builder shouted into the heavens, but it was not until now that she learned what he had shouted. He told her that as he had stood at the top of the church he had known why God had made the fire that destroyed his wife's estate. It was to make Solness a great builder, a true artist building more and more churches to honor God. God wanted him to have no children, no real home, so that he could give all his time to building churches. Solness, however, had defied God that day. He had shouted his decision to build no more churches, only homes for mothers and fathers and their children.

God had taken his revenge. There was little happiness in the homes Solness built. From now on he would build only castles in the air, with Hilda to help him. He asked Hilda to believe in him, to have faith in him. Hilda, however, demanded proof. She must see him standing again, clear and free, on the top of the tower. Then his conscience would be freed, and he would still be the master builder. He would give her the kingdom he had promised.

Even though his wife and others pleaded with him not to make the ascent, Solness was guided by Hilda's desire. As he climbed higher and higher, she heard a song in the air and thrilled to its crashing music. When he reached the top of the tower, he seemed to be struggling with an invisible being. He toppled and fell to the ground, lifeless. Then Hilda heard music in the sky. Her master builder had given her her kingdom.

Critical Evaluation:

The Master Builder belongs to a series of dramas that are a departure from the earlier types written by Henrik Ibsen. In this play the bitter satire of the social dramas is not present; instead, the play is mysterious, symbolic, lyrical. Ibsen here deals with the human soul and its struggle to rise above its own desires. The idea had been in Ibsen's mind for many years before he actually wrote the play, which is one of the most original of his works.

Ibsen completed *The Master Builder* in 1892, two years after the stormy but mostly favorable reception of *Hedda Gabler*. Whereas he had labored slowly and revised with care the earlier play, his work on *The Master Builder* proceeded smoothly, requiring few major changes from the first draft to the finished manuscript. One year before, Ibsen had left Munich to return to Norway, where he resided in Oslo until his death in 1906. His return to his native land, an event marked by great professional success and personal satisfaction, corresponded with a significant change in his dramatic style. His early romantic plays in verse—*The Vikings at Helgoland* (1858), *Brand* (1866), *Peer Gynt* (1867)—are generally lofty, treating historical or epical subjects. The second period of his creative work, including *The Pillars of Society* (1877), *A Doll's House* (1879), *Ghosts* (1881), *An Enemy of the People* (1882), *The Wild Duck* (1884), consists of social dramas, written in conversational, realistic prose. The last period, beginning with *The Master Builder* and including *Little Eyolf* (1894), *John Gabriel Borkman* (1896), and *When We Dead Awaken* (1900), is noted for qualities often described as metaphysical or spiritual. Confessional plays with a clear autobiographical impulse and written in a style that moves easily from prose to prose-poetry, they break new ground in the history of the late nineteenth century European theater.

Although Ibsen never denied the subjective character of *The Master Builder*, the play should not be studied merely as a symbolic summary of the writer's life. Instead, it is a great work of dramatic art and, judged solely on the basis of its structural values, one of Ibsen's most finely crafted pieces. Nevertheless, as a confessional drama, *The Master Builder* certainly presents some of Ibsen's important ideas and obsessions. For example, like Halvard Solness, Ibsen was impressed with (although not neurotically dismayed by) the success of younger writers. Ibsen himself wrote of Camilla Collett: "A new generation is now ready to welcome and understand you." Also like Solness, Ibsen was attracted to youthful women. Critics generally believe that Hilda Wangel is modeled upon Emilie Bardach, who was also a part-prototype for Hedda Gabler. At any rate, shortly after the production of *The Master Builder*, Emilie sent the author a photograph signed "Princess of Orangia," which apparently annoyed him. If Emilie was not the single inspiration for Hilda, then surely another of Ibsen's young friends might have been part of the composite picture, beginning with Engelcke Friis and continuing with Helene Raff, Hilda Andersen, or, the youngest, Edith Brandes.

In many other ways, the career of the Master Builder parallels Ibsen's own. Solness began by building churches. Later he decided to design "only houses for people to live in." Finally, to please himself and reassert his will to achieve the impossible, he designed a splendid house with a tower, fanciful as a "castle-in-the-air." Ibsen's experience with the theater similarly consisted of three stages: Romantic poetic drama; social drama intended to reform outworn traditions; and at last, personal drama with a special concern for a philosophy of life and death. There are other parallels as well. The high point of Solness' art as a Master Builder was the time he climbed a church tower and, as was the custom among Norwegian builders at that time (much like the christening of a ship), hung a garland at the topmost spire. Hilda had seen the triumph of her hero and remembered the precise date. "It was ten years ago," she said; "on the nineteenth of September." It was on September 20, 1889, that Ibsen wrote on the visitor's ledger at Gossensass: "The great, painful joy of striving for the unattainable." Also, like Solness, Ibsen was troubled by great heights. When he was a youth, he attempted to scale a mountain in Italy but discontinued his ascent in fear, lying flat to the ground clutching a boulder. Finally, like the

Master Builder, he was deeply interested in the power of thought-transference. In fact, Ibsen was an avid follower of studies on hypnotism and spiritualism.

However interesting are the similarities between the author's life and parallel themes of the play, *The Master Builder* is best enjoyed as theater rather than autobiography. The sharply defined conflicts of the play are resolved only at the conclusion. For this reason, the play performs especially well, although within recent decades it has never been quite so popular as *Hedda Gabler, A Doll's House, Ghosts,* or *The Wild Duck.* The central conflict is that between high aspiration—romantic dreams to attain the impossible—and the limitations of reality. As Master Builder, Solness has achieved a measure of financial success and even fame, but, as he discloses to Dr. Herdal and later, more completely, to Hilda, he considers himself a mere shell, a failure. Having defied God at the church tower, he has since feared that he will be cursed for his presumptuousness. At first he believes that the younger generation will be the agent of his destruction. Later, as he allies himself with the idealism of Hilda, he fears that his downfall will come not so much from rivals like Ragnar Brovik, but from the failure of his own will. All his life he has depended upon "Helpers and Servers" to advance his career. Although a genius in his own right, he has nevertheless had to fight the world. His powerful will, like the nearly hypnotic force that controls the affections of Kaia Fosli, has directed the helpers and servers to perform his wishes. Without assistance, however, he loses confidence in his art.

Finally, however, Solness understands that the enemy to his peace lies not outside himself but within. He really has no need to fear the young, and he does not require the blind obedience of servitors. His failings are those of conscience. He believes that he is going insane. So terrible is his sense of guilt—guilt because of his conduct toward his wife; guilt because he has abandoned the dreams of creating great edifices, churches; guilt because he has defied God— that he becomes increasingly isolated, almost paranoid. When Hilda encourages him to perform the impossible, to prove to the world that only he should be allowed to build, his inner conflict breaks. He determines to hazard everything, even his life, to satisfy his princess and provide her with her promised kingdom—to top a wreath on the tower of the new house.

At this point in the drama, the center of conflict shifts from Solness—now that he has made his idealistic decision—to Hilda. Will she allow the Master Builder to risk his life simply to satisfy her own iron will (or from another viewpoint, the passions of a spoiled child)? She knows that Solness experiences giddiness when he is climbing. Ragnar tells her that the Master Builder has always been afraid to place the wreath on the topmost place, that other workmen perform the task. Yet she steadfastly demands her "castle-in-the-air." In a romantic bond with the artist, she has identified her passion with his. Like the Viking women of old, with whom she has declared her kinship, she disdains a bourgeois conscience. For in her sprightly way she, too, is a warrior, and with a "robust" conscience she demands of her hero a sacrifice to prove his manhood.

A modern audience may perhaps judge Hilda more harshly than would Ibsen. As a character of social realism, she is idealistic to the point of folly. Careless, selfish, and willful, she contrasts with the sober, self-sacrificing, dutiful Aline Solness, the Master Builder's wife. Yet when the audience comes to understand Mrs. Solness better, it sees that she has lived too narrow a life, devoid of romantic risks and heroism. She has never dared to confide to her husband the secret of her own guilt—that after the fire that destroyed her ancestral house, she lamented the loss of her nine dolls more grievously than that of her twin sons, who died shortly afterward. While the audience sympathizes with her human frailty (for she is not to be condemned for grasping firmly to such symbols of the past), it also sees in a contrasted light the heroic striving of Hilda. The trolls (hobgoblins that are symbols both of destructive and creative forces) that guide her life are still strong, not diminished by civilization. At the end of the play—when she shrieks with wild intensity, "My—my Master Builder!"—she identifies his romantic achievement with her own. She has willed his triumph. To Ibsen, the death of a mere man, even a genius, is an insignificant price for such a triumph. In his visionary play, the Master Builder lives on in his work and in Hilda.

"Critical Evaluation" by Leslie B. Mittleman

Bibliography:

Clurman, Harold. "Fears and flights." In *Ibsen*. New York: Collier Books, 1977. A discussion of the last four plays, in which Ibsen abandons social polemics to probe his own failures as a man and an artist. Clurman points out biographical parallels in Ibsen's life and the character of Solness.

Knight, G. Wilson. "The Ascent." In *Henrik Ibsen*. New York: Grove Press, 1962. Knight describes the central symbolic action of *The Master Builder* as the climbing of a tower—to live one's art. The play coalesces an external event with spiritual meaning.

Meyer, Michael. "The Master Builder." In *Ibsen: A Biography*. Garden City, N.Y.: Doubleday, 1971. Discusses the inception and writing of the play, its reception by critics, Ibsen's deliberate self-portrayal, and theme of an old man's fear of and longing for youth.

Muir, Kenneth. "Ibsen." In *Last Periods of Shakespeare, Racine, Ibsen*. Detroit: Wayne State University Press, 1961. Discusses how Ibsen's last four plays are linked in theme; each protagonist is a genius facing conflicting claims of vocation and personal life, each is compelled to recognize his guilt, and each expresses Ibsen's own personal conflicts.

Shaw, Bernard. "The Master Builder." In *The Quintessence of Ibsenism*. New York: Hill & Wang, 1957. Shaw's classic introduction of Ibsen remains invaluable. Shaw concludes that old gentlemen and poetic young women are apt to build castles in the air.

"MASTER HAROLD" . . . AND THE BOYS

Type of work: Drama
Author: Athol Fugard (1932-   )
Type of plot: Political realism
Time of plot: 1950
Locale: St. George's Park Tea Room, Port Elizabeth, South Africa
First performed: 1982; first published, 1982

> *Principal characters:*
> WILLIE, a restaurant floor washer
> SAM, a waiter
> HALLY, a student and the son of the restaurant owner

The Story:

Willie Malopo and Sam Semela were forty-five-year-old black men who worked at St. George's Park Tea Room, a restaurant owned by a white family. Since no one was in the restaurant because of heavy rains, Willie practiced his dance steps and Sam coached him. Willie had entered a dance contest, and he needed some advice from Sam, the more experienced dancer.

Sam, who was more educated than Willie, learned that Willie, who had a history of beating women, had hit his dance partner Hilda Samuels. Sam encouraged Willie to apologize to Hilda, even though Willie did not feel he should have to apologize to a woman. Hally, a seventeen-year-old student whose parents owned the restaurant, came into the Tea Room with a school bag and a wet coat as Sam was demonstrating his dancing ability. Hally learned from Sam that the hospital had called and that Hally's mother had gone there to pick up his disabled, alcoholic father. Hally tried to deny that his father was returning home. Later Hally tried to convince Sam that he had not heard his mother's message correctly.

While Sam called the owner's son "Hally," Willie called Hally "Master Harold." Hally treated Sam as if he were a fellow pupil, and they discussed topics such as corporal punishment, social reform, and powerful historical people. Hally shared his problems from school as well as his dreams for writing books, short stories, and novels. Sam, who had created a competition between Hally and himself that helped Hally get better grades, told Hally that he had gone from a fourth-grade to a ninth-grade education because of Hally.

Before they bought the restaurant, Hally's parents had owned the old Jubilee Boarding House. Sam and Willie, then thirty-eight years old, had been tenants there, but they were called "boys" by Hally's mother. Hally recalled his experiences visiting in Sam's room at his parents' boardinghouse. The best memory for Hally was the day Sam created a kite from brown paper, tomato-box wood, glue made from flour and water, and a tail made from Hally's mother's old stockings. Hally was embarrassed about the appearance of the kite, but he loved its flying ability.

Sam explained that the dance was the most important event of the year in New Brighton. Hally became interested in the event as a possible topic for his essay assignment. Hally knew that his English teacher did not like "natives," or blacks, but Hally planned to point out that in "anthropological terms the culture of a primitive black society [included] its dancing and singing." Sam helped Hally with the facts concerning the ballroom dancing contest. When Hally wanted to know more about the dance scoring, Sam compared ballroom dancing to everyday collisions and world politics.

Just when Hally felt a bit optimistic about the future, his mother called with news that his father was coming home. Sam listened to the conversation and told Hally that his conversation with his mother "sounded like a bad bump." Hally became angry at Sam for interfering and realized that there could be no world without collisions. Sam scolded Hally for calling his father a "cripple" and blaming the collisions in his life on his father. Hally's shame toward his father turned to rage against Sam, and he demanded that Sam, like Willie, call him "Master Harold." Hally told Sam an antiblack joke related to the definition of fair that he said he had "learned from [his] father." As a reaction to the punch line in the joke, Sam responded literally and pulled down his pants to show Hally his Basuto buttocks. Hally retaliated by spitting in Sam's face, to which Sam responded by calling him Master Harold.

Sam told Harold that he had made him feel dirtier than he had ever felt in his life because he was not sure how to wash off Harold's and his father's filth. Sam reminded Harold of the time they had had to fetch Harold's drunken father from the floor of the Central Hotel Bar. Harold had had to go into the bar and ask permission for Sam, a black man, to go into the white bar. People crowded around to watch a black man carrying his drunken master on his back. Sam said that Hally had walked with downcast eyes and a heart filled with shame as he carried his father's crutches. Hally had walked behind Sam as he carried his drunken father down the center of the town's main street. Everyone in town watched the strange spectacle of a black servant carrying a drunk master.

Sam retold the story of making the kite because he wanted Hally to look up and stop walking around with his eyes cast on the ground. Sam told Harold that there was a twist to the short story: The bench to which Sam tied the kite was a "Whites Only" bench, and only Hally could sit there.

Sam went back to calling Harold "Hally" and tried to reconcile the differences with Hally, but he was unsuccessful. Hally left Sam and Willie alone in the restaurant to close up. Willie tried to lift Sam's spirits by promising that he would find Hilda and tell her he was sorry. Willie used his bus money to play "Little Man You're Crying" in the jukebox so that he could dance with Sam.

Critical Evaluation:

Athol Fugard's *"MASTER HAROLD"* . . . *and the Boys* is a tightly woven one-act play that examines the author's personal experience as a white South African in troubled times. The play won international acclaim but was considered revolutionary in South Africa because there were black and white actors on the same stage. One of Fugard's close associates was Zakes Mokae, a black actor who studied at Yale and created the role of Sam in the first performance of the play at the Yale Repertory Theatre.

In this perfectly choreographed drama, Fugard illustrates the duplicity in the friendship between the seventeen-year-old white "Master Harold" and the black forty-five-year-old "boys," Sam and Willie, who work for his family. The relationship between Sam and Hally and the interaction between Sam and Willie create a pulsing rhythm of personal conflicts within the play. Hally had taught Sam everything that he himself learned in school, thus creating a verbal sparring partner who could argue with him about topics related to history, literature, and tolerance. To the throbbing beat of historic names from Hally's teachers, texts, and home, Sam offers ideas based on his limited textbook knowledge and his life experience. Willie, who is not as educated, has neither Sam's book knowledge nor his rhythm, but he provides a perfect counterpoint to the beat of the discussion in the Tea Room. Sam's relationship with Hally is intellectual and fatherly, his relationship with Willie is racial and brotherly.

A conflict within one person is Hally's frustration with the dichotomy between his prejudiced, "crippled," drunken father's teaching and Sam's sensible, more educated nonprejudiced teaching. Hally dislikes his father, but he becomes angry when Sam scolds Harold for talking badly about his father. At that point, Sam crosses the fine line of master/servant relationships. While Harold was trying to bring Sam closer to an understanding of the white world, Sam tried to impose a rule of parental respect. This results in the climax of the play, where Hally demands that Sam call him "Master Harold." Hally attributes his superior attitude to his mother, who has said that Sam is only a servant and should not "get too familiar" with the white proprietor. This confrontation illustrates a person versus society conflict.

Several themes create cohesiveness in the play, among them that of the multiple shades of love and hate. Hally loves Sam for his guidance and companionship, yet despises him because he represents the culture he was raised to consider inferior. Male/female relationships are another theme. The relationship between an overbearing male and a submissive female is represented by Hally's father and mother as well as by Willie and Hilda, showing the strong parallel of noncommunication in different cultures. Another theme relates to family and generations. Hally's parents would like him to continue as a biased white person, but his interaction with Sam has caused a split in that prejudiced thinking because Hally sees Sam display an intelligence and insight that Hally had been told blacks did not possess.

Fugard makes use of several symbols in the play. The bench in the park is first mentioned as a starting point from which to fly a kite. New hope of racial cooperation is symbolized by Sam's and Hally's makeshift kite. Only much later in the play is it revealed that the bench was for "Whites Only." At the end of the play, the bench becomes a symbol to discard old prejudices when Sam advises Hally to "stand up and walk away from it." Another symbol is the dancing that flows through the play. Dancing is the symbol of the smooth interaction of people or nations in which no one "bumps" into anyone. Sam, the expert dancer, had integrated white education and black knowledge. Willie was trying to learn to dance to avoid bumps, but Hally refused to learn to dance. The implication is that Sam and Willie are closer to moving toward harmony than Hally and his parents, who would continue to "bump," or fight.

Hally experiences a rite of passage from innocence to experience. All through the play, his immaturity is clear. Once at the beginning, when Sam teases Willie about a "leg trouble" that has a sexual innuendo, Hally takes the remark literally. Earlier, Sam had created the kite to help Hally forget the shame of having seen his drunken father carried through the town streets. While Hally was old enough to appreciate the kite flying, he was not mature enough to understand the implications of the need to distract his sadness, nor did he understand the implications of the "Whites Only" bench. Finally, Hally did not fully understand his father's joke, which concerned white skin versus black skin, until Sam demonstrated the literal and social implications of "fairness" by showing Hally the blackness of his buttocks.

"*MASTER HAROLD*" . . . *and the Boys* illustrates that race has no bearing on intelligence or common sense and that prejudice creates conflicts that education can help to alleviate. Fugard weaves a rich dialogue that illustrates the conflicts between the black and white communities and shows the possibilities of harmony in a vision of the world as a politically smooth ballroom dance.

Annette M. Magid

Bibliography:
Durbach, Errol. " '*MASTER HAROLD*'. . . *and the Boys*': *Athol Fugard and the Psychopathol-*

ogy of Apartheid." Modern Drama 30 (December, 1987): 505-513. A thorough analysis of the political atmosphere of black/white relationships as portrayed by Fugard in comparison with the reality in South Africa.

Freed, Lynn. "Vividly South African: An Interview with Athol Fugard." *Southwest Review* 78 (Summer, 1993): 296-307. A detailed account of apartheid and the interpersonal repercussions it caused. Discusses Fugard's impact as a playwright as well as his antiapartheid themes.

Fuchs, Anne. Review of *Athol Fugard: A Bibliography*, by John Read. *Research in African Literature* 24 (Spring, 1993): 137-139. Reviews Fugard's themes as they relate to the black/white relations in Africa through the 1950's. Includes background information on Fugard.

Post, Robert. "Victims in the Writing of Athol Fugard." *Ariel* 16 (July, 1985): 3-17. Well-written essay that includes a comprehensive interview with the playwright regarding the characters in his work. Excellent analysis of the black "boys" of *"MASTER HAROLD" . . . and the Boys*. Post also analyzes the whites as victims of a society poisoned with prejudice and misinformation.

Richards, Lloyd. "The Art of Theater VIII: Athol Fugard." *The Paris Review* 31 (Summer, 1989): 129-151. Provides a discussion of the playwright's background and analyzes Fugard's talent for character and conflict development.

THE MASTERS

Type of work: Novel
Author: C. P. Snow (1905-1980)
Type of plot: Psychological realism
Time of plot: Mid-twentieth century
Locale: Cambridge, England
First published: 1951

Principal characters:
ELIOT,
BROWN,
CALVERT,
GAY,
NIGHTINGALE,
WINSLOW,
JAGO, and
CHRYSTAL, faculty members at a college of Cambridge University
ALICE JAGO, Jago's wife

The Story:

Eliot, a young tutor at a college of Cambridge University, was informed by Jago, a senior tutor, that the master of the college, Vernon Royce, had been diagnosed with terminal cancer. Jago went on to tell him that a new master would have to be elected within a few months. Jago himself desired the position. Soon after, Eliot was invited to meet with two other fellows of the college, Chrystal and Brown, about influencing a wealthy London businessman, Sir Horace Timberlake, to make a large contribution to the college. The subject of Jago's bid to be master came up, and both Brown and Chrystal agreed that he would make a good candidate. Others, too, agreed, and it seemed that Jago might be elected with a clear majority.

When the faculty of the college were told of Brown's plan to support Jago, a second faction arose supporting Crawford, a senior physicist. The announcement of opposition to Jago's candidacy led to a bitter argument between Eliot and Getliff, one of Crawford's supporters, and the college became divided between the two factions, with each trying to win converts from the other side. Although he was somewhat confident of victory for the party supporting Jago, Brown warned that they consisted mainly of junior, not senior, faculty members.

During the waiting period, a series of political maneuverings took place. Jago's party hoped that securing the large grant from Sir Horace Timberlake might give more clout to their side. Internal problems soon began to take their toll. One of the junior tutors, Nightingale, began to use his support of Jago as a lever to advance himself at Eliot's expense. Later, Nightingale switched his allegiance to Crawford's party. Brown's attempts to win him back were to no avail. With Nightingale's defection, Jago's supporters no longer held a clear majority. Jago contemplated withdrawing his name, but the others advised against it.

As the master of the college wasted away, the contest between Crawford and Jago became increasingly bitter. Insults and insinuations began to circulate about Jago and his wife, and tension grew. Jago and Crawford agreed that it would be proper if they themselves did not cast votes in the contest. Nightingale threatened Luke, a younger faculty member, with loss of position if he did not change sides. Luke dismissed the threat as insubstantial, but both he and Eliot lamented the situation.

The conflict permeated all aspects of college life. When Winslow's son did poorly on his university examinations, Calvert behaved rudely to him. When Eliot visited his old friends Getliff and his wife Katherine, their dinner was spoiled by a bitter argument over Jago's fitness for the position of master.

The stalemate threatened to result in a possibility none of the faculty relished, that the decision would revert to the local bishop, who might even appoint an outsider as master. Calvert suggested that all involved in the election sign a petition instructing Jago and Crawford to vote for themselves to bring about a clear majority for one of them and to prevent the appointment of an outsider; if they failed to do this, all the faculty would switch their votes to favor one of the two. Jago and Crawford were upset by this move, which they considered disrespectful to their rank as senior members. Calvert secretly hoped it would strengthen Jago's position.

When the master of the college died, Gay, an old, eccentric, and sightly senile faculty member, took charge of the election. Brown and his friends learned that they had secured the large grant from Sir Horace Timberlake. Winslow, who was college bursar, resigned because he felt incompetent; he had not done anything to gain the grant and did not feel qualified to manage it.

Though the grant appeared to have strengthened Jago's position, his election was suddenly placed in jeopardy when Pilbrow announced that he could not vote for him. Jago's party was disheartened by this shift and decided to try to persuade Gay to support their side. Before they could do so, a new problem arose. Jago's wife was greatly affected by a flyer Nightingale had written and circulated that attacked her character and abilities. She was so upset that Brown and Eliot put off their plans to visit Gay while they comforted her, and Jago again thought of backing out. At dinner that night, Jago rebuked Crawford for letting his supporters resort to such tactics. At first, Crawford would not acknowledge his responsibility in the matter, but later he agreed to talk to Nightingale about his behavior.

When Brown and Eliot visited Gay, they secured a reasonable assurance that he would vote for Jago. At a final meeting of both parties, Chrystal surprised his friends by announcing that he was satisfied with neither of the two candidates and wished to choose a new one. The group debated his suggestion, then rejected it. At the last minute, Chrystal threw his support to Crawford. This decided the outcome of the election, since, even with Gay's support, Jago could no longer win. The day of the election came. Brown, Crawford, Calvert, Gay, Eliot, and Luke voted for Jago; Chrystal, Desperd-Smith, Getliff, Jago, Nightingale, Pilbrow, and Winslow voted for Crawford, who thus won the election with a clear majority.

Afterward, Eliot's party was glum and wondered how Jago would react. At dinner that night, Jago asked Crawford to be his guest for dinner on the following day, and he participated in a toast to the new master.

Critical Evaluation:

C. P. Snow began his academic career not as a novelist but as a scientist. Unable to gain financial assistance for a university education other than on a scientific scholarship, he earned a Ph.D. in physics. Initially, he worked as a researcher, then as a government official overseeing the hiring of scientists for the British government. His first love, however, was writing, and throughout his life he produced novels, plays, essays, and lectures. His three areas of expertise—science, government, and literature—gave him much of the thematic material for his literary works.

Snow's familiarity with the world of the humanities and of science provided the background of his most famous and controversial work, an essay titled *The Two Cultures and the Scientific Revolution* (1959). In this work, Snow argued that scientists and other educated individuals are out of touch with one another and tend to regard the endeavors of others with suspicion. Snow feared that this condition was resulting in a fragmenting culture that would eventually be disastrous for society. He recommended remedial education—more math and science in the lower grades and more humanities in the upper grades. Snow was also concerned with the technological gap between the developed and developing countries of the world and thought that the more industrialized nations should assist the nonindustrial nations.

In his fictional works, Snow examined the arrangements upon which societies are founded. *The Masters* is one of a series of eight novels, to which he gave the title *Strangers and Brothers* (1940-1970), that trace the life of Lewis Eliot, the narrator of *The Masters*. The book deals with social change, relationships, the nature of power, and the dynamic of human personality. Eliot's life is outlined in these books by the use of two different narrative techniques, one presenting "direct experience," the other "observed experience." The stories are told from Eliot's perspective, but in the works using "observed experience," including *The Masters*, Eliot is principally a reporter who observes and reports the actions of those around him. In other books of the series, Eliot relates his experiences directly.

Strangers and Brothers explores the nature of humanity, recognizing that men live in relative isolation and loneliness but that they are also joined by the sorrows and joys of life that they all experience. This theme is central to *The Masters*. To a large extent, each of the main characters is alone in his private world. They have their own areas of research and their private lives, personal agendas, and hidden aspirations are separate from those of their colleagues. Each of them secretly pursues his goals in isolation. On the other side, they are all members of the same college and function together as a community, forming friendships and allegiances to achieve goals or out of mutual admiration or need.

The Masters examines the dynamic of interpersonal relationships especially as they relate to power, position, and the interworkings of institutional politics. It is an important psychological portrait of the ways in which individuals evaluate one another and the ways in which the private worlds of personal endeavor—the "stranger" aspects of life—come to bear on the public realm, where the "brother" aspect becomes most apparent.

This conjoining of private and public is seen in the lives of all the main characters. Jago, who makes the unsuccessful bid for master, is recognized by Eliot and others as a good man who is humane and accepting. His lack of substantial scholarship, his marriage to a woman who is somewhat emotionally unstable, and his own quick temper and erratic shifts of personality gradually surface and change the opinion of some of his supporters. Nightingale, who shifts his allegiance from Jago to Crawford, is a failure in his academic endeavors and personal relationships; his bitterness and mean spirit result from the disillusionment he feels in his private world. For all the characters, the hidden worlds of their private lives inevitably touch on the public world.

Despite some pessimistic turns, *The Masters*, like Snow's other novels, tends to reflect optimism about the ability of people to get along. The political conflict in the college is resolved, and, with the exception of Nightingale, all the faculty members manage to stay on socially acceptable terms. Snow was deeply concerned about the divisions within society, but he believed in the possibility of reconciliation.

David W. Landrum

Bibliography:

Cooper, William. *C. P. Snow*. London: Longmans, 1959. Part of the British Writers Series, this booklet provides valuable information on Snow, especially on the unifying themes found in his literature.

Davis, Robert Gorham. *C. P. Snow*. New York: Columbia University Press, 1965. A short, concise overview of C. P. Snow intended as a general introduction to his work.

Green, Martin Burgess. *Science and the Shabby Curate of Poetry: Essays About the Two Cultures*. New York: W. W. Norton, 1965. Responses from a variety of scholars to Snow's theory that a "scientific" and a "literary" culture exist in European and world culture.

Karl, Frederick Robert. *C. P. Snow: The Politics of Conscience*. Carbondale: Southern Illinois University Press, 1965. Deals with the themes in Snow's novel, particularly his concerns over class struggle and division in the English society he knew and in society worldwide.

MAUD
A Monodrama

Type of work: Poetry
Author: Alfred, Lord Tennyson (1809-1892)
Type of plot: Melodrama
Time of plot: Early nineteenth century
Locale: England
First published: 1855

> *Principal characters:*
> THE SPEAKER, a young man
> MAUD, whom he loves

The Story:

Speaking in recollection, the speaker told of his despair in the red-ribbed hollow where his father died, of his rapture in Maud's high Hall-garden, of his ostracism from the grand political dinner and dance because of the opposition of Maud's brother, of his killing Maud's brother in a duel, of his exile on the Breton Coast, of his madness in the London asylum, and, finally, of his pursuit of the blood-red blossom of war aboard a British troop ship on its way to the Black Sea.

The speaker, a twenty-five-year-old unnamed youth, angrily lamented the suicide of his father and the failure of his intimate relationship with the sixteen-year-old Maud, whose father's treachery in a business transaction caused the speaker's father to take his life. The grief-stricken youth reacted to his father's death with a savage denunciation of the commercial spirit of the age—one the speaker regarded as responsible for the lust of gain that was running rampant in his era and that had contributed to his family's downfall. The speaker said that his morbid mood mirrored the general madness of the times, one characterized by merchants putting chalk, alum, and plaster in bread for the poor and by mothers selling their infants for burial fees. The speaker argued that in such terrible times, the dignity of war, of action, was preferable to the implicit acquiescence of peace.

The speaker overcame his depressed condition, he related, through a growing involvement with the neighboring squire's daughter Maud, who had returned home with her brother to the family's country estate after having been abroad. Chancing to view Maud's carriage passing, the speaker saw her and eventually met her. Before long, the speaker had fallen in love with her, had wooed her, and had won Maud's love, only to kill her interfering brother thereafter in a duel, an act that necessitated a retreat into exile.

The speaker lived his exile in Brittany, where he heard that Maud had died. Later, he suffered successive phases of insanity and remorse, was confined to a London madhouse, and was haunted by the phantom of Maud. The speaker's nightmares finally yielded to a dream in which Maud was no longer a threatening ghost but was, rather, an angel coming to him with a message of hope. "Sane but shattered," he expiated his crime by joining a noble cause, England's involvement in the Crimean War.

The speaker proclaimed: "I have felt with my native land, I am one with my kind,/ I embrace the purpose of God, and the doom assigned." Sharing a spirit of fellowship with his shipmates, the speaker discovered national togetherness in England's war effort.

Critical Evaluation:

Maud is Alfred, Lord Tennyson's most original and most carefully constructed long poem.

A passionate and violent love story, this lyrical monologue has been called the swan song of the younger Tennyson and the inaugural hymn of the laureate. It was Tennyson's first major venture as poet laureate, his first effort to represent fully the state of contemporary English society, his chief political poem, and his final attempt to convey his social theories in a direct way.

Tennyson called *Maud* "a little *Hamlet*, the history of a morbid poetic soul, under the influence of a recklessly speculative age," and he noted that different phases of passion take the place of different characters in the poem. The poem's central idea, said Tennyson, is "the holy power of love." *Maud* is at once a drama of an individual struggling for self-identity and a drama of human relations between the old landowning caste and the new merchant class.

In January, 1854, Tennyson began adding some one thousand lines to two lyrics he had written in the 1830's, the "O that 'twere possible" lyric (see part 2, section 4 of *Maud*) and the "See what a lovely shell" lyric (part 2, section 2). These are considered the germinal sections of *Maud*. Tennyson wrote the "O that 'twere possible" lyric in 1833 or 1834, soon after the death of Arthur Hallam, and published it in 1837. He did so at the urging of Richard Monckton Milnes, a Cambridge classmate. In 1854, Sir John Simeon, Tennyson's close friend and neighbor on the Isle of Wight, persuaded the poet to compose a narrative around the "O that 'twere possible" verses. This became the full-length poem *Maud*. *Maud* concerns the aftermath of a financial ruin conditioned by the false values of Victorian England's industrial system.

In the first four sections of part 1, a declamatory tone prevails. By section 5, however, the poem's lyrical elements start to predominate and from then on are periodically interrupted by stanzas of social statement. The latter half of part 1 (sections 11-22) consists principally of lyrics, some of the best in *Maud*. In section 11, for example, the speaker rhapsodizes:

> O let the solid ground
> not fall beneath my feet
> Before my life has found
> what some have found so sweet;
> Then let come what come may,
> what matter if I go mad,
> I shall have had my day.

The speaker of *Maud* should be regarded as within the tradition of the confessional Byronic protagonist. *Maud* is thoroughly romantic in the peculiarity of its emotion, in its bitter declamation, in its rebelliousness, in the strangeness of its imagery, and in the fluctuations of its metrics.

The poem's love story is based on Tennyson's memories of Rosa Baring, the principal model for Maud. Like the poem's heroine, Rosa possessed wealth and social prominence. The granddaughter of Sir Francis Baring, chairman of the East India Company and founder of the great financial house of Barings, Rosa lived at Harrington Hall, an exclusive estate two miles from the Tennyson family parsonage at Somersby. Tennyson fell in love with Rosa Baring in 1834 when be was twenty-five and she was twenty. Tennyson's love for Rosa was one of the episodes that most affected his life.

In its most intense passages, the monodrama recalls the realms of sensuous apprehension present in such earlier Tennyson poems as "Mariana," "The Lady of Shalott," "Tithonus," and "The Palace of Art." In these poems, Tennyson deals with states of mind similar to those that the speaker of *Maud* experiences. Moreover, the speaker of *Maud* recalls the speaker of Tennyson's "Locksley Hall," a poem of a love story that is also related to Tennyson's romantic involvement with Rosa Baring. Cousin Amy in "Locksley Hall" is, similarly, the obedient daughter of snobbish gentry who interfere in her personal affairs.

In addition to the autobiographical theme concerning Rosa Baring, *Maud* contains references to much of Tennyson's early life. In *Maud*, Tennyson draws upon the psychological wounds he sustained during his rural childhood years and later. The similarities between the speaker in *Maud* and the young Tennyson are striking. The morbid despondency, the sense of loss, the specter of insanity, and the death wish which are endured by Tennyson's speaker in *Maud* all afflicted the younger Tennyson. Like his hero, Tennyson often struggled to conquer doubt and despair in his pre-1850 years. Tennyson formulated the situation in the monodrama of his young speaker witnessing the suicide of his father and perceiving the death as precipitated by financial disaster from his remembrance of how his father had been disinherited by his grandfather and of how his family had struggled financially.

Some consider Tennyson's poem to be marred by its autobiographical influences. It has what may be seen as an unpleasant emotional dimension that results from Tennyson's inability to distance himself from the experiences about which he was writing. Others note that Tennyson wrote *Maud* during a period of domestic and financial security. He wrote the poem at a time when he was content with the critical acclaim and sales of *In Memoriam* (1850) and happily married to Emily Sellwood.

The public and press of the day were disappointed with *Maud*. Many were bothered by how in the opening sections of *Maud* and in the ending Tennyson conveys so stridently his concerns about the exploitation of the Victorian populace. By the beginning of the 1850's, the people of England were growing tired of being morally improved. This contributed to the mixed reception of the poem.

Readers also found *Maud* obscure. Their troubles resulted from the omissions, gaps, and sharp transitions in the story. For example, the fact of Maud's death is never conveyed explicitly. Tennyson blamed the work's poor reception on the inability of people to read *Maud* properly, but he made some changes in the texts of later editions to make the story more comprehensible.

A number of Victorian reviewers were outraged by the speaker's advocacy of war, which received more discussion than any other aspect of the work. Critics derided Tennyson's idea of war as a remedy for domestic ills. There were also supporters of Tennyson's philosophy of war. They agreed with Tennyson that the Crimean War was assuaging England's moral stagnation.

What Tennyson conveys in part 3 is the attitude of many of his contemporaries at the start of the Crimean War. When England entered the Crimean War on March 28, 1854, the British press and populace were in accord that Russia's machinations had to be checked. On April 15, 1854, the people of England held a general fast to express their spiritual commitment to the cause of war. Tennyson was swept up by the war sentiment raging in England at the start of the war. Public opinion in England later shifted dramatically during the winter of 1854-1855, when dispatches from the front revealed the grim toll in human lives being taken by blunders, bad weather, disease, and unsanitary conditions.

It is notable that Tennyson wrote the prowar ending to the poem in early 1854, a year prior to the infamous blunders in the Crimea, which occurred toward the end of 1854 and during the winter of 1854-1855. *Maud* was published in July, 1855, when the Crimean War was still in midcourse. The publication of the poem, specifically of its prowar ending, should be considered a piece of bad timing. Despite the controversy surrounding its publication, *Maud* was one of Tennyson's great financial successes. With the proceeds from its sales, Tennyson paid for his home on the Isle of Wight.

James Norman O'Neill

Bibliography:

Buckley, Jerome Hamilton. *Tennyson: The Growth of a Poet*. Boston: Houghton Mifflin, 1960. A standard reference, Buckley's critical biography contains an excellent commentary on Tennyson's emotional and intellectual development. Has a brief but perceptive discussion of *Maud*.

Drew, Philip. "Tennyson and the Dramatic Monologue: A Study of *Maud*." In *Tennyson*, edited by D. J. Palmer. Athens: Ohio University Press, 1973. A collection of essays about the poems of Tennyson in their intellectual, social, and artistic contexts. Contains a reader's guide to Tennyson, a chronological table, and a bibliography. Has an excellent article on *Maud*.

O'Neill, James Norman. "Anthem for a Doomed Youth: An Interdisciplinary Study of Tennyson's *Maud* and the Crimean War." *Tennyson Research Bulletin* 5, no. 4 (November, 1990): 166. A thorough treatment of the continuing debate over Tennyson's advocacy of the Crimean War in part 3 of *Maud*. Contains a close reading of the poem's conclusion and includes historical information about the start of the war, the sudden change of public opinion, and the military blunders that occurred.

Rader, Ralph Wilson. *Tennyson's "Maud": The Biographical Genesis*. Berkeley: University of California Press, 1963. An important contribution to Tennyson studies. In his account of the composition of *Maud*, Rader traces Tennyson's involvement with Rosa Baring, Sophy Rawnsley, and Emily Sellwood.

Ricks, Christopher. *Tennyson*. New York: Macmillan, 1972. A standard reference, this study contains close textual analyses of Tennyson's best-known poems. A major Tennyson scholar and the editor of *The Poems of Tennyson*, Ricks provides lucid explanations of Tennyson's central themes and preoccupations.

MAURICE

Type of work: Novel
Author: E. M. Forster (1879-1970)
Type of plot: Bildungsroman
Time of plot: 1903-1913
Locale: Cambridge, London, and Clive Durham's country estate, Penge
First published: 1971

> *Principal characters:*
> MAURICE HALL, the protagonist
> CLIVE DURHAM, Maurice's Cambridge schoolmate
> ALEC SCUDDER, Durham's gamekeeper at Penge

The Story:

At fourteen, Maurice (pronounced "Morris") Hall was sent to the same mediocre public school his dead father had attended. He was not a remarkable student, though he was proficient at his lessons, athletic, and handsome. Mr. Ducie, a schoolmaster, was aware that Maurice had no proper male role model and took it upon himself to instruct Maurice in sexual matters during a walk on the beach. Maurice realized that Ducie's explanation did not explain Maurice's own sexual urges. Maurice was perplexed by his schoolmates' mixture of rude and cruel behavior tempered by tenderness, especially concerning their sexual roles.

When Maurice arrived at one of the less prestigious colleges at Cambridge, he came to understand his sexual inclinations and found them both disgusting and confusing. At Cambridge, Maurice fell under the influence of Greek culture and thought, whose ideals were sexual freedom and tolerance, when he was introduced to Plato's *Symposium* by Clive Durham, a tutor with whom he fell in love and who persuaded Maurice to abandon his conventional religious ideas. A year older than Maurice, Clive became Maurice's first love. Rejecting Christianity and understanding the stirrings of his heart, Maurice began to think about the nature of his identity.

Clive loved Maurice, but in a romantic way that idealized homosexuality. Clive was guilt-ridden by his desires, but liberated by Plato's writings. He derived a freedom to idealize homosexual love from Plato's *Phaedrus*, but not the license to act on his sexual desires. Maurice, taller and more athletic than Clive, desired physical fulfillment of their love. Despite their contrary philosophies, an idyll between the two began. The pair traveled to Italy. After graduation from Cambridge, Maurice and Clive settled in London to fulfill their families' expectations. Maurice was accepted into his father's brokerage firm; Clive studied law in preparation for a career in politics. For two years, the two men spent every Wednesday night and weekend together; however, their relationship remained strictly platonic.

When Maurice refused to accompany Clive on a trip to Greece, their relationship was forever altered. Alone in Greece, Clive concluded that he was mistaken about homosexuality and decided he loved women. Clive returned to London and, wrapped in bandages by Maurice's mother and sisters (who were in training as World War I nurses), saw Maurice again. Clive confessed his choice of a heterosexual identity to Maurice and an argument ensued, causing a rift between the men. Clive married for socioeconomic reasons after Risley, Clive and Maurice's Cambridge friend, had his life ruined after arrest on a morals charge. A rising barrister, Clive rejected Risley's plea for help and warned Maurice that they must forget the past and respect the boundaries of friendship.

Maurice, twenty-three years old, plunged into a deep depression. He experienced guilt over his homosexuality after being rejected by Clive. Desperate and self-loathing, Maurice considered suicide because death seemed preferable to self-denial or the scandal associated with homosexuality. With the distraction of his grandfather's death, Maurice came out of his depression to an extent, but still wanted to be normal. Maurice spent some time with Clive and his wife. Maurice consulted a quack hypnotist who had supposedly helped other men overcome their homosexuality. Science, however—as religion had before—proved what Maurice intuitively knew: He could not change what he was.

A year later, Maurice discovered and accepted his sexual identity when he met Alec Scudder, the gamekeeper of Clive's estate, Penge. Alec's profession kept him outdoors, attuned to nature, in sharp contrast to the indoor world of Maurice and his friends. Maurice broke down class barriers when he entered into a relationship with Alec after a day of playing cricket. Maurice was still conflicted, however, about his homosexuality. Clive believed Maurice's secret trysts were with a girlfriend about whom Maurice had not told Clive. As his relationship with Alec deepened, Maurice became concerned about their class differences and the possibility that Alec might blackmail him. When Clive discovered that Maurice's lover was male, he was appalled—especially by Alec's working-class background—and more than a little jealous.

Alec tried to reconcile with Maurice, but to no avail. Alec decided to emigrate. At the last moment, he decided to stay in England and went to his and Maurice's usual trysting place, where Maurice and a new life together awaited him. Maurice rejected society's standards and accepted his love for another man wholeheartedly. Maurice finally felt as if he were a fully integrated personality. At peace with himself, Maurice convinced Alec to share a life together—a man loving a man, both intellectually and physically. While there was no promise of permanence in Maurice and Alec's relationship, Maurice spoke to Clive one last time with unprecedented eloquence. Maurice told Clive that he, Maurice, loved Alec, that Clive had trapped himself into a dull marriage, and that Maurice was bidding farewell to the life and society in which he had been born and raised. In the manner of earlier bands of English outlaws—those who were alienated from society—Maurice and Alec withdrew to live in the greenwoods where they could find the freedom and happiness necessary to preserve their love. At age twenty-four, Maurice's inner journey to find himself seemed complete.

Critical Evaluation:

During his long life, E. M. Forster distinguished himself with five novels. Two are known as the "Italian novels," *Where Angels Fear to Tread* (1905) and *A Room with a View* (1908), not only because they are set in Italy, but because they share certain qualities and themes, characterizations, and tone. Forster published three other major novels in his lifetime, *The Longest Journey* (1907), *Howards End* (1910), and *A Passage to India* (1924). *Maurice* (1971) was first written between September, 1913, and July, 1914. Because of its homosexual content and the tenor of the times, the novel was not published in Forster's lifetime. During the next fifty years, Forster reworked the novel, and as late as 1960 made substantial revisions, adding a "Terminal Note." This note describes the novel's origins, which can be traced to Forster's visit with the writer Edward Carpenter, who has been called "the first modern writer on sex in England." Edward Carpenter was heavily influenced D. H. Lawrence but is now virtually forgotten. Carpenter's lover, George Merrill, touched Forster's "backside—gently and just above the buttocks. . . . The sensation was unusual and I still remember it." At that moment, Forster began to conceive *Maurice*, a novel that is part autobiography disguised as novel and part novel as wish fulfillment. In *Maurice*, Forster utilizes the epigrammatic theme from

Howards End: "Only connect." In doing so, he writes a novel of a young man's inner journey toward understanding the nature of his sexual identity.

The genius of Forster's novel lies in his creation of Maurice Hall, an Everyman who is "someone handsome, healthy, bodily attractive, mentally torpid, not a bad businessman and rather a snob." Maurice's homosexuality is the "ingredient" that brings Maurice to life: It puzzles him, awakens him, torments him, and finally saves him. In Maurice's efforts to connect, he first meets Clive, whose Hellenic values attract Maurice and awaken his sexual identity. When Maurice determines that he and Clive will never connect physically, only mentally, he is again tormented. When Maurice connects with Alec Scudder, the gamekeeper on Clive's estate, Maurice saves himself by rejecting the conventions of the society in which he was reared.

The character of Alec is loosely based on Stephen Wonham, a man of working-class origins with whom Forster had a relationship. To say, however, that the thematic focus of *Maurice* is finding love despite class hierarchy distinctions would be inaccurate. The theme of *Maurice* is the search for self-fulfillment through realization of sexual and self-identity as well as the homosexual's place in society. Forster thought, by 1960, that the book was dated because it belonged to an era when it was still possible to escape to "the greenwood" and get "lost." This is still possible but unnecessary for homosexuals, given the changing mores that include a greater acceptance of homosexuality. The theme of connection in *Maurice* is still relevant to any confused young man who may be uncertain of his sexual identity and who is experiencing the puzzlement such a discovery brings about.

Change, discovery, and connection are all very much part of *Maurice*. Maurice discovers that his options in life are not limited to those of his deceased father. He does not make this discovery on his own. When Clive speaks openly about his own feelings and platonic ideals, Maurice awakens to the possibility that what had puzzled him about sexuality since his walk on the beach with Mr. Ducie and their discussion of the birds and the bees was the existence of an "other" sexuality. Maurice makes discoveries only when challenged by others; he is as much an "Everyman" as a hero.

The character of Alec is crucial to the novel. He represents nature—a vital life force—feeling free to roam and to satisfy his sexual urges without guilt or shame. In keeping with the tradition of English literature, Forster makes Alec an archetypal dweller in the greenwoods, the places untouched by the corrupt and corrupting values of society, religion, and other institutions. Alec and Maurice move into a darkness that symbolizes fecund nature and the mysteries of love. Alec's presence is—if anything—primal at its best. In a scene in which Maurice moves to the open window at Penge, he knows there is someone or something waiting for him in the darkness to be discovered. Maurice cries out into the night, "Come!," consciously unaware that anyone might hear him, and intuitively aware that someone will. When Alec appears from the darkness, he brings light into Maurice's life—the light of an older, more primitive enlightenment than the so-called enlightened society in which they live.

This concern for the instinct and the subconscious self is one that Forster shared with D. H. Lawrence. By giving Alec primal qualities—like the wild, shining brown eyes of an animal— Forster's sexual theme is linked with Lawrence's sexual themes (Lawrence used some of the same symbolism in *Lady Chatterley's Lover*, 1928). Historically, *Maurice* is important because it establishes a voice contemporaneous with Lawrence that uses an honest, open approach to the body and homosexuality. *Maurice* might provoke less tolerant members of society to question their personal attitudes toward homosexuality. As Forster wrote in the "Terminal Note," "We had not realized that what the public really loathes in homosexuality is not the thing itself but having to think about it."

A faithful film adaptation of the novel, directed by James Ivory and produced by Ismail Merchant, was made available on videotape in 1987.

Thomas D. Petitjean, Jr.

Bibliography:
Colmer, John E. *E. M. Forster: The Personal Voice*. London: Routledge & Kegan Paul, 1975. A full, balanced account of Forster's life and critical assessment of Forster's major works.
Gardner, Philip, ed. *E. M. Forster: The Critical Heritage*. London: Routledge & Kegan Paul, 1973. Dealing with contemporaneous views of Forster and his works, the critical assessment of *Maurice* is balanced and judicious, and includes autobiographical details.
McDowell, Frederick P. W., ed. *E. M. Forster: An Annotated Bibliography of Writings About Him*. DeKalb: Northern Illinois University Press, 1976. A comprehensive bibliography, providing entries on *Maurice* that demonstrate the critical reception of the novel in 1971 and after.
Page, Norman. *E. M. Forster*. New York: St. Martin's Press, 1987. This compact resource charts the life and career of Forster. Page ranks *Maurice* among Forster's minor fiction and is critical of the work, regarding it as an "experiment that misfired," too subtle in its handling of homosexuality.

MAX HAVELAAR

Type of work: Novel
Author: Multatuli (Eduard Douwes Dekker, 1820-1887)
Type of plot: Satire
Time of plot: 1857
Locale: Java
First published: 1860 (English translation, 1868)

Principal characters:
MAX HAVELAAR, a conscientious Dutch colonial administrator
BATAVUS DRYSTUBBLE, a Dutch coffee broker of Amsterdam
MR. VERBRUGGE, an administrator subordinate to Max Havelaar
RADHEN ADHIPATTI KARTA NATTA NEGARA, the native regent of Lebak, Havelaar's district
SHAWLMAN, a schoolmate of Batavus Drystubble and a writer
MR. SLIMERING, Havelaar's superior officer

The Story:

Batavus Drystubble, a self-satisfied coffee broker of Amsterdam, was accosted one day on the street by a former schoolmate who had obviously fallen on bad times. The Shawlman, as Drystubble called him, pressed his prosperous former schoolfellow to look over a bundle of manuscripts, in the hope that Drystubble might be willing to help him have some of them published. Drystubble, thinking he might have a book written about the coffee trade, turned over the manuscripts to a clerk in his firm to edit. The clerk agreed to make a book of the materials, after securing a promise from his employer not to censor the results before publication. Out of the bundle of manuscripts came the story of Max Havelaar, a Dutch administrator in Java, in the Dutch East Indies.

Max Havelaar was an idealist who believed in justice for everyone, even the poor Javanese who labored in the fields. When he arrived at Rangkas-Betoong to take over the post of Assistant Resident of Lebak, a section of the residency of Bantam, in Java, he found the situation much worse than he had anticipated, for the Dutch administrators, despite their oath to protect the poor and lowly, had acquiesced in the robbery and mistreatment of the native Javanese by the Javanese nobility, through whom the Dutch ruled the island. The Adhipatti of Lebak was a relatively poor man because his region did not produce many of the exports that the Dutch wanted. In order to keep up appearances befitting his rank and to support a large and rapacious family, the Adhipatti extorted goods, materials, and services from the people, who felt helpless because of the treatment they would suffer from the native chief if they complained to the Dutch officials.

Max Havelaar, a man who loved a good fight for justice's sake, was glad he had been assigned to Lebak. In his opening speech to the Adhipatti and the lesser chiefs he declared that justice must be done, and he began trying to influence the Adhipatti by advancing him tax money in the hope that the chief would be less exacting on his people. Suggestions and help were of little use, however, for the same evil practices continued. The people, learning that Havelaar wished to see justice done, stole to his home under cover of darkness to lodge their complaints and give the assistant resident information. Havelaar rode many miles to redress complaints. He also gave an example to the chiefs by refusing to use more native labor than the law allowed, even to letting the grounds of the residency go largely untended and revert to jungle. He realized what he was fighting against, for he was a man in his middle thirties who had spent seventeen years in the Dutch colonial service.

His faithful adherent in his battle against injustice was his wife Tine, who was devoted to her husband and knew he was in the right. Of less help was Verbrugge, the controller serving under Havelaar. He knew the Javanese were being exploited, but he hated to risk his job and security by fighting against the tide of complacency of Dutch officialdom. Verbrugge realized that Havelaar's superiors were interested only in keeping peace, in submitting reports that bespoke prosperity, and in providing wealth for the homeland—regardless of what happened to the Javanese.

One example was the story of Saidyah, the son of a Javanese rice farmer. One by one the father's possessions were taken from him by extortion, even the buffalo that had faced a tiger to save the boy's life. Finally Saidyah's father ran away to escape punishment for failing to pay his taxes, and Saidyah himself left his home village to seek work in Batavia, vowing to his beloved that he would return in three years' time to marry her. When he returned as he had promised, however, he found that she and her family had been forced to flee and had joined rebellious Javanese on another island. Saidyah finally found his beloved, but only after she had been killed and mutilated by Dutch troops. Overcome with grief, Saidyah rushed upon the troops and was impaled on their bayonets.

As time went on, Havelaar realized he could expect little help from Mr. Slimering, the Resident of Bantam and his immediate superior. Yet Havelaar hoped optimistically that some support would be forthcoming from that quarter. Havelaar learned that his predecessor had probably been poisoned because he had sought to stop the exploitation of the population by the native chiefs. Havelaar learned this from his predecessor's native wife, who still lived at the official residence.

Having finally gained what he deemed sufficient information against the Adhipatti, Max Havelaar lodged an official protest with Mr. Slimering. He requested that the Adhipatti and his subordinate chiefs be taken into custody and removed from Rangkas-Betoong, lest their presence intimidate the people and prevent their giving testimony of the abuses. Instead of acceding to any part of the request, Mr. Slimering came to Havelaar's district, denounced Havelaar's actions, and even gave money to the Adhipatti. Havelaar, hoping to find support higher up in the administration, appealed to the Governor-General, saying that unless he received some support to eradicate the injustices he had found he would have to resign after seventeen years of faithful service to the colonial administration.

At this point in the manuscript a section was inserted, supposedly written by Batavus Drystubble, who expressed the views of a complacent Dutch businessman in the homeland. Drystubble said that he had been royally entertained by retired colonial officials who assured him that the charges made in Shawlman's manuscripts were groundless. Drystubble also added that he felt as a religious man that the heathen Javanese were given their just deserts for not being Christians and that the Dutch were profiting at the expense of the Javanese because the former were decent, God-fearing, and obedient Christian people who deserved divine favor.

After waiting a month, Max Havelaar learned that he had been relieved of his post in Lebak; he was ordered to another part of Java. He could not accept this official action, knowing that he would have the same fight all over again, a losing battle, in a new assignment. He left Lebak after his successor arrived and went to Batavia to lay his case personally before the Governor-General. That worthy man, too busy to see him, put off Havelaar with one pretext after another. On the eve of the Governor-General's departure for Holland, Havelaar wrote an angry letter as a last hope. That stinging letter did no good; the Governor-General sailed for home, leaving Havelaar poor and forsaken.

At the end of the novel, Multatuli stepped in to break off the story and speak in his own voice, dismissing Shawlman and the clerk from Drystubble's office, who as fictional characters had been writing the novel. Multatuli, after expressing his loathing of the hypocritical, money-grabbing Drystubble, went on to say that he wished to leave an heirloom for Havelaar's children and to bring his appeals to the public. The author said that he knew his book was not well written, but all that mattered was that people learn how the Javanese were being mistreated, thirty million of them, in the name of King William of the Netherlands.

Critical Evaluation:

Max Havelaar is considered the greatest Dutch literary achievement of the latter half of the nineteenth century. This era was a time of literary awakening in many smaller Northern European countries. For example, Norway saw the drama of Henrik Ibsen and Sweden saw that of August Strindberg. These writers, although working in languages spoken by a small minority of the world's population, created works that spoke to the world. The works of Eduard Douwes Dekker, known as Multatuli, are Dutch literature's nearest equivalent to those of Strindberg and of Ibsen. As did the beliefs of Strindberg and Ibsen, Multatuli's liberalism, skepticism, and feminism startled the reading public of his nation. Multatuli's work, however, did not have the impact of the two Scandinavian dramatists. This limited impact is the result of the fact that he wrote comparatively little, in contrast to the voluminous composition of Strindberg and Ibsen. Multatuli's work is also very complex and multilayered, and it deals with specifically Dutch experiences; these factors may well make *Max Havelaar* opaque to the foreign reader.

The most probable interest, though, of *Max Havelaar* to the reader is not its representation of Dutch national literature, although that is still an important concern. *Max Havelaar* is engaging as literature. It is not simply a cultural artifact. *Max Havelaar* seems ahead of its time in terms of formal awareness and self-consciousness. The shifts in levels of reality that the reader encounters in the narrative unsettle conventional expectations. Another element that gives the book a contemporary feel is the book's portrayal of the colonial experience, specifically the Dutch colonial presence in Java. It is often forgotten that the Dutch maintained a considerable colonial empire of their own in the East Indies, in the Caribbean, and in Surinam. Also, until the British seized the territory in the Napoleonic Wars, the Dutch controlled South Africa. Although Multatuli's portrait of the Dutch East Indies in *Max Havelaar* can fruitfully be compared to the portrait of Borneo in Joseph Conrad's novel *Lord Jim* (1900), the books are also different because the Dutch and British colonial experiences were different. Whereas Britain always claimed to be acting in the name of progress and good government, the motives of the Dutch were frankly economic and exploitative. The portrait of the Lebak coffee plantation in *Max Havelaar* shows the greed and brutality associated with the Dutch colonization of Indonesia. The title character, Max Havelaar, struggles to define himself and to adhere to ideals of honor and right conduct amid the squalor he encounters in Java. When Havelaar arrives, virtually the only person of good will he meets is Verbrugge. Verbrugge is clearly a well-intentioned man who is nonetheless ineffectual and powerless in the face of the cold indifference of the Governor-General and the scheming malevolence of Slimering. It is the native Javanese (exemplified in the story of Saidyah) who suffer above all, and this is the lesson the book brings home to its reader.

Multatuli's account of Java is searing. The novel is filled with bitterness and pain on personal and political levels, making the author's pseudonym (which means "I have suffered much" in

Latin) no accident. Most of the material is based on Dekker's own experiences in Java, and the polemical nature of the Javanese passages has led critics to compare the novel to Harriet Beecher Stowe's antislavery work, *Uncle Tom's Cabin* (1851-1852). *Max Havelaar's* polemicism is modified by its ironic narrative structure. The novel is narrated (in a way which is also very reminiscent of the works of Conrad) not by the protagonist, Havelaar, but by Drystubble, who frames Havelaar's story in a web of garrulous deception and self-promotion. A further level of intricacy intrudes when it is hinted that Drystubble is "mirrored" in the colonial world of Lebak by Slimering, while Shawlman is, most probably, Havelaar himself, thus solving the mystery of how the Havelaar manuscript came into his hands. Furthermore, Multatuli comes onstage at the end, proclaiming that Drystubble's illusion-making is but an inadequate reflection of Multatuli's own authorial reality. It is left uncertain how authoritatively the reader is to take this last intervention.

Max Havelaar seems a forerunner of modernist self-conscious text, of a kind of fiction more concerned with the ironies and processes of storytelling than in conveying an external reality. Yet the novel's greatest force comes in its realistic portrait of colonial Java. Furthermore, whatever the games played by Multatuli in the novel, the reader's moral sympathies are meant to lie with Havelaar. The reader's empathy with him is only occasionally made questionable. Part of the contradiction involved in the use of polemical and self-conscious text in one work may be explained by the history of Dutch literature, in which, unlike that of most European countries, Romanticism and realism began more or less at the same time. In other literatures, such as English or German (the two languages closest to Dutch, and the two cultures most influential upon Dutch culture), Romanticism flourished in the early 1800's and was largely associated with poetry, whereas realism flourished in the later 1800's and was largely associated with fiction. In Dutch literature, however, Romanticism began only in the 1880's, with the group of poets known as the "Tachtigers" or "men of the Eighties." *Max Havelaar* was published in 1860, and it is apparent that in Dutch literature the two movements are far more conflated in time than readers may expect. This fact might help to explain what seem to be the many contradictions in the book. *Max Havelaar*, whatever its idiosyncrasies, is a significant contribution to world literature.

"Critical Evaluation" by Nicholas Birns

Bibliography:

King, Peter. *Multatuli*. New York: Twayne, 1972. The most comprehensive study of Multatuli available in English. Gives an overview of the book's complexity as well as its relation to its author's life. An excellent starting place.

_____. "Multatuli: Some Reflections on Perk, Kloos, and Boon." In *European Context: Studies in the History and Literature of the Netherlands, Presented to Theodore Weevers*, edited by P. K. King and P. F. Vincent. Cambridge, England: Modern Humanities Research Association, 1971. Examines Multatuli's relationship to the Dutch Romantic writers, known as "Tachtigers," who wrote in his shadow.

Schreurs, Peter. "Multatuli, a Soul-Brother of Rizal." *Philippine Quarterly of Culture and Society* 14, no. 3 (September, 1986): 189-195. Explores Multatuli's similarities with nineteenth century Filipino poet José Rizal, showing the relevance of *Max Havelaar* to discussions of the colonial and the postcolonial condition.

Van den Berg, H. "Multatuli and Romantic Indecision." *Canadian Journal of Netherlandic Studies* 5, no. 2 (Fall, 1984): 36-47. Discusses the curious mixture of Romanticism and realism in the novel and explores the novel's roots in Dutch literature.

_____. "Multatuli as a Writer of Letters." *Canadian Journal of Netherlandic Studies* 13, no. 2 (Fall, 1992): 17-22. Examines how the private man of Multatuli's letters reveals himself in the fiction.

THE MAXIMS

Type of work: Philosophy
Author: François La Rochefoucauld (1613-1680)
First published: Maximes, 1665-1678 (English translation, 1706)

La Rochefoucauld described his *Maxims* as a "portrait of the human heart." He wrote in the preface to the first edition that these reflections on human conduct would probably offend many persons because the aphorisms were full of truths that are unacceptable to human pride. He suggested that the reader suppose him or herself to be the sole exception to the truth revealed and should avoid the tendency to have his or her opinion influenced by *amour-propre*, or self-love, as that would prejudice his or her mind against the maxims.

The reference to self-love, the basic concern for self by which the value of any action, person, or thing is presumed to be judged, is characteristic of La Rochefoucauld. Critics generally describe this great French writer as a cynic and take as evidence his maxims, in which he attributes to self-love the central role in human conduct. Yet a mere cynic is one who hopes for a better world than the present one; a cynic constantly compares what could be and what ought to be with what is, responding to the disparity with bitterness. Consequently, everything that cynics say is the truth as they see it; as they see it, it is worthy only of a sneer. La Rochefoucauld, on the other hand, takes self-love to be an undeniable fact of human existence and does not hope for anything better. Consequently, his view of the world is that of a man amused to see the difference between what people conceive themselves to be and what they are; his delight is in a witty revelation of the facts of life. Throughout *The Maxims*, as in the refreshing self-portrait with which the collection begins, La Rochefoucauld reveals an intelligent sense of humor that takes the sneer out of what he says.

"My normal expression is somewhat bitter and haughty," he writes in his initial self-portrait, and "makes most people think me supercilious, though I am not the least so really." He goes on to describe himself as "inclined to melancholy" but not from temperament alone: "It is due to . . . many other causes." He calls himself an intellectual who delights in the conversation of cultured persons, in reading, in virtue, and in friendship. His passions are moderate and under control. He is neither ambitious nor afraid of death. He has given up "light amours" and wonders why so many men waste their time paying "pretty compliments." The portrait concludes with the assurance that were he ever to love, he would love with the strong passion that is a sign of noble character; however, he doubts that his knowledge of the value of strong passion will ever "quit my head to find a dwelling in my heart."

The first maxim is important as a summary statement of La Rochefoucauld's central conviction:

> So-called virtue is often merely a compound of varied activities and interests, which good fortune or our own assiduity enables us to display to advantage; so it is not always courage that makes the hero, nor modesty the chaste woman.

With the second maxim, the author names the concern that is essential to the human heart: "Amour-propre is the arch-flatterer."

In many of the maxims, La Rochefoucauld expresses his conviction that virtue is the accidental result of an exercise of the passions; acts undertaken passionately to satisfy the demands of a pervasive self-concern are interpreted in other ways, as signs of nobility of character. In maxim 7, for example, he declares that "Illustrious deeds, of dazzling brilliance, are represented by politicians as the outcome of great aims, whereas they are usually the result of caprice or passion." Similarly, "The clemency of princes is often nothing more than a political artifice designed to secure the goodwill of their subjects" (maxim 15). "Such clemency, though hailed as a virtue, is the product sometimes of vanity, sometimes of indolence, not infrequently of timidity, and generally of all three combined" (maxim 16).

One way of summarizing La Rochefoucauld's philosophy is to point out that, to him, virtue is usually passion misunderstood. People do something because their own irresistible self-love drives them to it; the world observes the power of the act and mistakes it for the grandeur of courageous virtue. Not all of the maxims develop this theme, however. Many of the comments are both wry and true, and the effect is heightened all the more by their pithiness. Examples of this include "The desire to appear clever often prevents our being so" (maxim 199); "We all have enough strength to bear the misfortunes of others" (maxim 19); "Flattery would do us no harm if we did not flatter ourselves" (maxim 152); and "There is no fool so troublesome as a fool with brains" (maxim 451).

There is a positive note to some of the maxims, an appeal to the honesty by which people may lessen the damage caused by their self-love. La Rochefoucauld implies that there is hope for those who find it possible to recognize the worth of others and to do so sincerely, for those who know their own limitations and acknowledge them, and for those who admit that their show of virtue is often an empty show. The author respects such honesty, and it is apparent that *The Maxims* are confessional as well as didactic.

La Rochefoucauld found through his own experience certain truths that writers of all ages have expressed in various ways and that gain power through repetition. In several maxims, he develops the idea that it is doing people an injury to be so much concerned with their welfare as to burden them with the necessity of being grateful. He recognizes that people tend to be free with advice to others but not eager to accept it for themselves. People admit such shortcomings as a poor memory in order to hide something like the lack of intelligence.

La Rochefoucauld's psychology is that of the sophisticated courtier. He was too much aware of his own disguises ever to have acquired the knowledge that would have led to a more objective and more scientific psychology. His psychology, like his philosophy, while not that of the man in the street, was certainly that of the man at court—clever enough to see behind the masks of those who traveled in high society but not tolerant enough of possibilities to be willing to admit that what he called "honest" people were more common than he supposed. When his psychology has the strong ring of truth, it is more by accident than discernment; and when it is false, he seems embittered to distortion—hence the charge of cynicism.

Nevertheless, certain of his maxims do define something of the human character: "To disclaim admiration is to desire it in double measure" (maxim 149); "We easily forget our faults when they are known only to ourselves" (maxim 196); "Excessive eagerness to discharge an obligation is a form of ingratitude" (maxim 226); and "If we were faultless ourselves, we should take less pleasure in commenting on the faults of others" (maxim 31).

Behind the revealing wit of La Rochefoucauld there is the murmur of an injured man. No one can discern the falsity of others better than a timid man who believes himself betrayed, longs for recognition and gratitude, and feels he does not receive enough of either. La Rochefoucauld reveals himself when he reveals the desperate *amour-propre* that moves all human beings.

Bibliography:
Lewis, Philip E. *La Rochefoucauld: The Art of Abstraction.* Ithaca, N.Y.: Cornell University

Press, 1977. Describes the problematic nature of La Rochefoucauld's abstract reflections on the conflict between self-love and love for others. Discusses the psychological and ethical dimensions of *The Maxims*.

Moore, Will G. *La Rochefoucauld: His Mind and Art*. Oxford, England: Clarendon Press, 1969. A clear introduction to the many levels of meaning in La Rochefoucauld's pithy and marvelously ambiguous moral maxims. Discusses the political, social, and religious implications of *The Maxims*.

Mourgues, Odette de. *Two French Moralists: La Rochefoucauld and La Bruyère*. Cambridge, England: Cambridge University Press, 1978. A thoughtful comparison of the Duke of La Rochefoucauld and Jean de La Bruyère, who were the most eminent French moralists in the second half of the seventeenth century. Explores La Rochefoucauld's reflections on subjectivity and contains an excellent bibliography of major critical studies on these two writers.

Thweatt, Vivien. *La Rochefoucauld and the Seventeenth-Century Concept of the Self*. Geneva, Switzerland: Droz, 1980. Discusses the influence of St. Augustine and neo-Stoicism on La Rochefoucauld. Examines La Rochefoucauld's reflections on people's efforts to maintain their individuality in a society that favors and rewards conformity.

Zeller, Mary Francine. *New Aspects of Style in "The Maxims" of La Rochefoucauld*. Washington, D.C.: Catholic University of America Press, 1954. Explains clearly why La Rochefoucauld's *Maxims* permit a wide variety of interpretations. Discusses the refined rhythms and complex structures in many maxims.

THE MAXIMUS POEMS

Type of work: Poetry
Author: Charles Olson (1910-1970)
First published: 1983

The Maximus Poems was Charles Olson's most important work. Sections of *The Maximus Poems*, begun in 1950, were published as Olson produced complete parts. The first volume of the book, called simply *The Maximus Poems*, was published in 1960 by Corinth Books of New York City. A second volume, titled *Maximus Poems IV, V, VI*, was published by London's defunct Cape Goliard Press in 1968. *The Maximus Poems: Volume Three* was published by Viking/Grossman in New York in 1975. Charles Boer, Olson's executor, took on the job of emending the text at the University of Connecticut, producing the final volume published in 1983 by the University of California at Berkeley.

There are only a half dozen or so legitimate long poems published in the United States during the twentieth century, and Olson's is certainly one of the more important. Some of the reason for this has to do with the poet, and some has to do with his teaching at Black Mountain College in North Carolina and his other writing, in particular *The Mayan Letters* (1953) and his famous essay "Projective Verse." They both relate to the business of *The Maximus Poems.*

Olson was born near Gloucester, Massachusetts, the town he adopted as his through the poems in *The Maximus Poems.* He was an imposing figure, standing six feet, ten inches, with penetrating eyes and, during the last twenty years of his life, long white hair. He spent time in Washington, D.C., visiting Ezra Pound at St. Elizabeth's Hospital; time in the Yucatán Peninsula; and time at Harvard University, where he wrote a study of Herman Melville called *Call Me Ishmael: A Study of Melville* (1947). Many of his ideas and discoveries are found in the collected correspondence he kept with American poet Robert Creeley. *The Mayan Letters* are all written to Creeley. Later, Olson became provost of the experimental Black Mountain College, offering his own classes in poetics, in which *The Maximus Poems* and their theories weighed heavily.

Olson conceived of the idea of writing a long poem with a central, larger-than-life figure at its center, a person to be called Maximus. The Maximus of the poems may have been meant to resemble Olson himself, being larger than life and living in Gloucester. Many of the poems are interpretations of events that occurred in Gloucester, from simple daily events, like the fishing boats going out, to a murder that was never solved. The geography of the town was also important to Olson, as were even the smallest details. Many of the poems discuss "the cut," which is a channel between the fishing boats and an inland waterway. A movable bridge was built where Olson's cut used to be.

A fair amount of the population in Olson's time consisted of Portuguese fishermen and their families. They are referred to in the poems, as are surrounding villages. This area is close to Cape Cod and is very popular with tourists. That was not the case when Olson lived in a tiny apartment overlooking the ocean, an apartment crammed with books and his typing materials. He used to walk the streets at night, in the manner of Edgar Allan Poe, absorbing sounds and smells that would become parts of his epic book.

What was Olson about with this book, with which he expressed dissatisfaction near his death? There is no easy answer, but clues can be gleaned from his other writing. "Projective Verse" talked about a kind of poetry that would live on the page, that would be kinetic, that would utilize the entire page and whatever other materials the poet felt called upon to utilize.

The result in his own poetry, including hundreds of pages of *The Maximus Poems*, is a poetry that looks chaotic on the page but that follows his own prescripts in his essay. Many of the poems are spread out across the page in what Olson referred to as "the field of the page," utilizing open parentheticals, sometimes a complete lack of punctuation, and often decisions of how to read the poem that can be answered only by a reader.

Olson was also a student of history, all the way back to the Greeks. One defining element in *The Maximus Poems* is the notion that a man can be a *polis*, or a city, that a man or woman may have the ability to contain knowledge, power, and influence. Olson tried to present his Maximus figure as just such a *polis*. At other times in the poems, Olson seems to acknowledge that a person—most people, anyway—will be incapable of such a feat; then, a literal city, such as Gloucester, becomes *polis*. The best place to see this in action is in the text *Maximus to Gloucester: The Letters and Poems of Charles Olson to the Editor of the "Gloucester Daily Times," 1962-1969*. During this period, Olson lived in Gloucester part of the time, but he kept up his subscription to the newspaper. Olson was not deferential about sending one of his poems, often one that became part of *The Maximus Poems*, to the editor as a commentary on something in the paper. His overall interest in the town newspaper reflects his interest in *polis* and his belief that the body politic is of utmost importance.

Another issue receiving attention in *The Maximus Poems* is Olson's "discovery" in the Yucatán Peninsula. Olson thought that he had come upon the descendants of the people of the area who, very unlike Americans or Europeans, were capable of wearing their insides on their outsides. His poem "A Moebius Strip" uses a mathematical phenomenon to illustrate what he meant. He saw these people as being utterly disingenuous, without pretense: You got what you saw, both inside and outside.

Parts of *The Maximus Poems* do not so much attempt to find or construct such a model as meditate upon it. Stylistically, a good portion of *The Maximus Poems* is rather dry and abstract. Other sections are very difficult to follow, and anyone trying to read and understand all of *The Maximus Poems* at once is taking on a daunting challenge. Olson did not feel a particular debt to his reader; he felt a debt to his muse. Some poems sound like essays, and other poems have allusive qualities that make them very difficult.

Anyone attempting to decipher *The Maximus Poems* should have a good working knowledge of Greek mythology. The work contains a number of references to Aphrodite and Demeter, as sexual goddess and Earth Mother, respectively. It takes some interpreting to develop these ideas. Persephone is in the curl of a wave, and the imagery sounds sexual with proper study. Without some kind of guidance, however, it will just sound like ocean references.

References to Gloucester politics and history emerge in poems such as the famous "The Librarian," in which Olson asks the open question at the end of the poem, "Who lies behind/ Lufkin's Diner?" Presumably, all references would be clear to someone from Gloucester at the time these lines were written, but they pose challenges to anyone reading these poems after Olson's death in 1970.

A reader may also get the impression of speed while reading the poem, a sense that one cannot let up. That response may come from Olson's dictum from "Projective Verse" that "one perception must immediately and directly lead to a further perception." Such was his theory for poetry as a whole, with which many of his poet-friends disagreed. In fact, the writing of *The Maximus Poems* probably at times was a lonely enterprise. Some of his peers appear to have viewed the project as overly ambitious. Olson wanted to write a poem that would include it all and do it all; that may have struck some as being overly ambitious, to put it mildly.

Reading *The Maximus Poems*, one learns about the Native Americans who inhabited the area in the seventeenth century, about the "settling" of the area, and why Gloucester became a fishing village, with very little other trade important to the village. All one need do is glance through George Butterick's *A Guide to "The Maximus Poems" of Charles Olson* (1978) to see the depth and breadth of Olson's knowledge and research.

Another way to view these poems is to see them as mythmaking in the raw, using at their central core the changed figure of Olson himself, Olson become Maximus. If most myth is, as theory has it, based on reality and history, and on stories, then Olson brought into the twentieth century the materials of that construction, or what he called "the materials of the weight,/ of pain," perhaps a reference to what such an enterprise took from him in its twenty years of development.

The evidence is that although Olson was preparing to write a very long poem around 1950, he had already written several poems with the name "Maximus" within them. He seemed ready to start a long poem with a poem titled "Bigmans I," obviously close in statement to "Maximus." He had a corpus of work at hand, and he added "I, Maximus," drawing even tighter his own personal hold on the concept of this long poem that he knew would be based in Gloucester, though Cape Ann figures prominently in the poems. A guiding principle to Olson was John Keats's line, "A man's life of any worth is a continuous allegory," a statement that is in evidence throughout *The Maximus Poems*.

Clearly, Olson had been impressed by his visits with Ezra Pound, and while in the midst of *The Maximus Poems*, Olson visited Pound in seclusion in Italy. Olson had also used Pound's *Cantos* as a text at Black Mountain College. His reverence for the long poem had been long established.

Research shows that "Projective Verse" ends on a note calling for epic and long poems. Early in February of 1950, Olson rejected the long poems of T. S. Eliot, William Carlos Williams, and even Pound, and began on *The Maximus Poems*, a poem that would attempt to fit it all in, a long poem for the twentieth century in all of its complexity and mythmaking.

John Jacob

Bibliography:
Bollobas, Eniko. *Charles Olson.* New York: Twayne, 1992. Although this appears at first to be a biographical study, nothing could be further from the truth. This book studies poetic decisions, the most important of which is *The Maximus Poems*, in relation to Olson's life.
Butterick, George F. *A Guide to "The Maximus Poems" of Charles Olson.* Berkeley: University of California Press, 1978. An indispensable book for anyone who wants to understand the allusions and references in Olson's long poem. Many of the annotations, which took ten years to write, include arcane material, but they give a view into Olson's mind.
Fredman, Stephen. *The Grounding of American Poetry: Charles Olson and the Emersonian Tradition.* New York: Cambridge University Press, 1993. Fredman analyzes Olson's focus on the intellect and on thought processes in his poetry, as opposed to the American tradition of emotional and responsive poetry. *The Maximus Poems* is seen as an abstract, highly intellectual text.
Olson, Charles. *Maximus to Gloucester: The Letters and Poems of Charles Olson to the Editor of the "Gloucester Daily Times," 1962-1969.* Edited by Peter Anastas. Gloucester, Mass.: Ten Pound Island Book Company, 1992. These letters and poems show how the local was important to Olson, particularly the local as applied to Gloucester politics and day-to-day life. The subjects are small, but the book is an interesting view into the thoughts of Charles Olson.

Von Hallberg, Robert. *Charles Olson: The Scholar's Art*. Cambridge, Mass.: Harvard University Press, 1978. Von Hallberg, long an Olson scholar, points out Olson's use of myth and other original contributions to *The Maximus Poems*. He, too, indicates the importance of thought to Olson's poetics. This is a good introduction to the complex parts of Olson's writing.

THE MAYOR OF CASTERBRIDGE
The Life and Death of a Man of Character

Type of work: Novel
Author: Thomas Hardy (1840-1928)
Type of plot: Psychological realism
Time of plot: Nineteenth century
Locale: Wessex, England
First published: 1886

Principal characters:
MICHAEL HENCHARD, the mayor of Casterbridge
SUSAN HENCHARD-NEWSON, his abandoned wife
ELIZABETH-JANE NEWSON, his stepdaughter
RICHARD NEWSON, a sailor
DONALD FARFRAE, a grain merchant
LUCETTA LE SUEUR, Henchard's beloved and later Farfrae's wife

The Story:

On a late summer afternoon in the early nineteenth century, a young farm couple with their baby arrived on foot at the village of Weydon-Priors. A fair was in progress. The couple, tired and dusty, entered a refreshment tent where the husband proceeded to get so drunk that he offered his wife and child for sale. A sailor, a stranger in the village, bought the wife, Susan, and the child, Elizabeth-Jane, for five guineas. The young woman tore off her wedding ring and threw it in her drunken husband's face; then, carrying her child, she followed the sailor out of the tent.

When he awoke sober the next morning, Michael Henchard, the young farmer, realized what he had done. After taking an oath not to touch liquor for twenty years, he searched many months for his wife and child. In a western seaport, he was told that three persons answering his description had emigrated a short time before. He gave up his search and wandered on until he came to the town of Casterbridge. There he decided to seek his fortune.

The sailor, Richard Newson, convinced Susan Henchard that she had no moral obligations to the husband who had sold her and her child. He married her and moved with his new family to Canada. Later, they returned to England. Eventually, Susan learned that her marriage to Newson was illegal, but before she could remedy the situation, Newson was lost at sea. Susan and her attractive eighteen-year-old daughter, Elizabeth-Jane, returned to Weydon-Priors. There they heard that Henchard had gone to Casterbridge.

Henchard had become a prosperous grain merchant and the mayor of Casterbridge. When Susan and her daughter arrived in the town, they heard that Henchard had sold some bad grain to bakers and that restitution was expected. Donald Farfrae, a young Scots corn expert who was passing through Casterbridge, heard of Henchard's predicament and told him a method for partially restoring the grain. Farfrae so impressed Henchard and the people of the town that they prevailed on him to remain. Farfrae became Henchard's manager.

When Susan and Henchard met, they decided that Susan and Elizabeth-Jane would take lodgings and that Henchard would begin to pay court to Susan. Henchard admitted to young Farfrae that he had been philandering with a young woman from Jersey named Lucetta le Sueur. He asked Farfrae to meet Lucetta and prevent her from coming to Casterbridge.

Henchard and Susan were married. Elizabeth-Jane developed into a beautiful young woman for whom Donald Farfrae felt a growing attraction. Henchard wanted Elizabeth-Jane to take his name, but Susan refused his request, much to his mystification. He noticed that Elizabeth-Jane did not possess any of his personal traits.

Henchard and Farfrae fell out over Henchard's harsh treatment of a simpleminded employee. Farfrae had surpassed Henchard in popularity in Casterbridge. The complete break between the two men came when a country dance sponsored by Farfrae drew all the populace, leaving Henchard's dance unattended. Anticipating his dismissal, Farfrae set up his own establishment but refused to take any of Henchard's business away from him. Henchard refused to allow Elizabeth-Jane and Farfrae to see each other.

Henchard received a letter from Lucetta saying she would pass through Casterbridge to pick up her love letters. When Lucetta failed to keep the appointment, Henchard put the letters in his safe. Susan fell sick and wrote a letter for Henchard, to be opened on the day that Elizabeth-Jane was married. Soon afterward she died, and Henchard told the girl that he was her real father. Looking for some documents to corroborate his story, he found the letter his wife had left in his keeping for Elizabeth-Jane. Unable to resist, Henchard read Susan's letter; he learned that Elizabeth-Jane was really the daughter of Newson and Susan and that his own daughter had died in infancy. His wife's reluctance to have the girl take his name was now clear, and Henchard's attitude toward Elizabeth-Jane became distant and cold.

One day, Elizabeth-Jane met a strange woman at the village graveyard. The woman was Lucetta Templeman, formerly Lucetta le Sueur, who had inherited property in Casterbridge from a rich aunt named Templeman. She employed Elizabeth-Jane to make it convenient for Henchard, her old lover, to call on her.

Young Farfrae came to see Elizabeth-Jane, who was away at the time. He and Miss Templeman were immediately attracted to each other, after which Lucetta refused to see Henchard any more. Elizabeth-Jane overheard Henchard berate Lucetta under his breath for refusing to admit him to her house; she became even more uncomfortable when she saw that Farfrae had succumbed to Lucetta's charms. Henchard was now determined to ruin Farfrae. Advised by a weather prophet that the weather would be bad during the harvest, he bought grain heavily. When the weather stayed fair, Henchard was almost ruined by low grain prices. Farfrae was able to buy grain cheap, and when the weather turned bad late in the harvest and prices went up, Farfrae became wealthy.

In the meantime, Farfrae had continued his courtship of Lucetta. When Henchard threatened to expose Lucetta's past unless she married him, Lucetta agreed. An old woman, however, disclosed to the village that Henchard was the man who had sold his wife and child years before. Lucetta was ashamed and left town. On the day of her return, Henchard rescued her and Elizabeth-Jane from an enraged bull. He asked Lucetta to give evidence to a creditor of their engagement. Lucetta confessed that in her absence she and Farfrae had been married. Utterly frustrated, Henchard again threatened to expose her. When Elizabeth-Jane learned of the marriage, she left Lucetta's service.

The news that Henchard had sold his wife and child spread through the village. His creditors closed in, and he became a recluse. Henchard and Elizabeth-Jane were reconciled during his illness. Upon his recovery, he hired out to Farfrae as a common laborer.

Henchard's oath expired, and he began to drink heavily. Farfrae planned to set up Henchard and Elizabeth-Jane in a small seed shop, but the project did not materialize because of a misunderstanding. Despite Lucetta's desire to leave the village, Farfrae became mayor of Casterbridge.

Jopp, a former employee of Henchard, blackmailed his way into Farfrae's employ through

Lucetta, whose past he knew from having lived in Jersey before coming to Casterbridge. Henchard finally took pity on Lucetta and gave Jopp the love letters to return to her. Before delivering them, Jopp read the letters aloud in an inn.

When royalty visited Casterbridge, Henchard wished to retain his old stature in the village and forced himself among the receiving dignitaries; Farfrae pushed him aside. Later, during a fight in a warehouse loft, Henchard had Farfrae at his mercy, but the younger man shamed Henchard by telling him to go ahead and kill him.

The townspeople were excited over the letters they had heard read and devised a mummery employing effigies of Henchard and Lucetta riding back to back on a donkey. Farfrae's friends arranged to have him absent from the village during the mummers' parade, but Lucetta saw it and was prostrated. She died of a miscarriage that night.

Richard Newson was not lost after all; he came to Casterbridge in search of Susan and Elizabeth-Jane. There he met Henchard, who sent him away with the information that both Susan and Elizabeth-Jane were dead.

Elizabeth-Jane joined Henchard in his poverty. They opened a seed shop and began to prosper again in a modest way. Farfrae, to Henchard's dismay, began to pay court to Elizabeth-Jane again, and they planned to marry soon. Newson returned, having realized that he had been duped. Henchard left town but returned for the marriage festivities, bringing with him a goldfinch as a wedding present. When he saw that Newson had completely replaced him as Elizabeth-Jane's father, he sadly went away. Newson was restless and departed for the sea again after Farfrae and his daughter were settled. Henchard pined away and died, ironically enough, in the secret care of the simpleminded old man whom he had once mistreated.

Critical Evaluation:

Despite contrived events, the plot of *The Mayor of Casterbridge* works out well. Descriptions of the countryside are excellent, and Thomas Hardy's simple country people are realistic and sometimes funny, if not always sympathetic. While readers may question the melodramatic and spectacular opening scenes of the novel, Hardy insisted that such events did occur in rural districts during the nineteenth century. He believed that "in fiction it is not improbabilities of incident but improbabilities of character that matter."

This is the first novel in which Hardy focuses his attention on one individual; all other characters are drawn without depth so that by contrast Michael Henchard stands out in all his animal strength and weakness. Although the two women with whom he is intimately involved die, the story is his tragedy. Death is, however, not the main disaster of this narrative; rather, it is the slow downfall and disintegration of a "man of character."

The Mayor of Casterbridge marks a great development in Hardy as an artist. He masterfully delineates Henchard's character and the complex social and economic life of Casterbridge. Both Michael Henchard and his town are governed by the grain market; the mayor's rise and fall are dependent not so much on his personal relations with Susan, Farfrae, Lucetta, and Elizabeth-Jane as on fluctuations of the harvest. The power struggle between Henchard and Farfrae is governed not by their abilities and popularity with the townsfolk but more basically by the supply and demand of grain. Even sexual interests, which figure largely in the story, are dominated by the shifting economies of Casterbridge fortunes.

Also notable are the new dimensions and greater symbolism that Hardy gives both individuals and events. Primitive ritual is suggested, for example, by the marriage transaction that begins Henchard's tragedy, and some critics suggest that the mayor himself has attributes or implicit qualities of a vegetation god or corn king.

Henchard also has affinities with Herman Melville's Ahab in his relentless pursuit of revenge in the face of adverse circumstances and nature's power, although both Ahab and Henchard recognize that such pursuit must lead to their destruction. The story's course also demonstrates supernatural revenge for the hero's violation of moral order—a revenge that demands the violator's atonement and death. This is crime and punishment beyond human control, although ironically Henchard's own character is the instrument of retribution.

The past, whose sinister force Hardy constantly invokes, is best symbolized by the Roman earthworks of Casterbridge, particularly the amphitheater where gladiatorial combats had once been held. For Casterbridge citizens, it is a place of furtive assignations, even murders, because of its obscure location and "dismal privacy." Henchard chooses this spot for a meeting with his long-lost wife, Susan. He also selects another area surrounded by an ancient Roman earthwork for his ill-advised Casterbridge entertainment, which, in contrast to Farfrae's dance in town, turns out to be a failure.

Henchard seems a pawn of the goddess Fortune, who throws him from a position of assured success down to the bottom of her wheel; in this respect, *The Mayor of Casterbridge* is a tragedy in a long *de casibus* tradition, which shows the downfall of a man who possessed inherent greatness and strength. Henchard also resembles the Greek tragic hero who destroys himself through destructive acts arising from his own character. It attests Hardy's artistry that Henchard, in his ruin, seems stronger and more admirable than does the clever Farfrae, his successor as the mayor of Casterbridge.

Bibliography:
Berger, Sheila. *Thomas Hardy and Visual Structures: Framing, Disruption, Process.* New York: New York University Press, 1991. Berger takes a look at the narrative style in Hardy's novels, focusing on acts of storytelling, subjective points of view, and the construction of the "omniscient" narrator.
Enstice, Andrew. *Thomas Hardy: Landscapes of the Mind.* London: Macmillan, 1979. A good historical analysis of the novel, in which Enstice uses a thorough discussion of nineteenth century Dorset and its economic circumstances to interpret Hardy's rendition of Casterbridge's history and society in *The Mayor of Casterbridge.*
Milligate, Michael. *Thomas Hardy: His Career as a Novelist.* London: Bodley Head, 1971. A thorough study of Hardy's life and his concerns, attitudes, values, and problems as they affected his writing and its reception; a critically acclaimed work that offers a fair perspective on Hardy's personal and artistic development.
Widdowson, Peter. *Hardy in History: A Study in Literary Sociology.* New York: Routledge, 1989. An interesting analysis of traditional readings of Hardy's novels that argues that Hardy has been produced as a "rural" novelist in the literary imagination; in reality, his writing deals with his urban vision of Wessex. This work lends a new perspective to the relationship of Casterbridge to the countryside and London, a relationship central to Michael Henchard's fate.
Williams, Raymond. *The Country and the City.* New York: Oxford University Press, 1973. A seminal book on the class relations and rural-urban dislocations that underlie Hardy's representation of Wessex and the lives and fortunes of his "rural" characters.

THE MAYOR OF ZALAMEA

Type of work: Drama
Author: Pedro Calderón de la Barca (1600-1681)
Type of plot: Tragedy
Time of plot: Sixteenth century
Locale: Zalamea, Spain
First performed: El alcalde de Zalamea, 1643; first published, 1651 (English translation, 1853)

> *Principal characters:*
> PHILIP II, the king of Spain
> DON LOPE DE FIGUEROA, the commander of a Spanish regiment
> DON ALVARO DE ATAIDE, a captain
> PEDRO CRESPO, a farmer of Zalamea
> JUAN, his son
> ISABEL, Pedro's daughter
> REBOLLEDO, a soldier
> CHISPA, his mistress

The Story:

As the troops of Don Lope de Figueroa approached the village of Zalamea, old campaigner Rebolledo grumbled in true veteran fashion about the hardships of the march. Quite ready to stop and relax in the village, Rebolledo predicted that the mayor of the village would bribe the officers to march the regiment through and beyond the little community. When he was taken to task by his fellows for this unsoldierly talk, Rebolledo declared that he was mainly concerned for the welfare of his mistress, Chispa, who accompanied the troops. Chispa retorted that, although she was a woman, she could endure the march as well as any man. To cheer up the men, she sang a marching song.

Chispa's song was barely finished when the column reached Zalamea. It was announced that the troops would be billeted in the village to await the imminent arrival of their commander, Don Lope. The captain of the column was pleased to learn that he would be billeted in the home of a proud farmer whose daughter was reputed to be the beauty of the neighborhood.

At the same time that the troops entered Zalamea, an impoverished squire, Don Mendo, accompanied by his servant, Nuno—the pair bore a marked resemblance to Don Quixote and Sancho Panza—came to the village also. Don Mendo sought the favors of Isabel, the daughter of the proud farmer, Pedro Crespo. Isabel banged together the shutters of her window when Don Mendo greeted her in foolishly extravagant terms. Crespo and his son Juan found the presence of Don Mendo highly objectionable.

When the sergeant announced to Crespo that the captain, Don Alvaro de Ataide, would be quartered in Crespo's house, the farmer graciously accepted this imposition; Juan, however, was displeased and suggested to his father that he purchase a patent of gentility so that he might avoid having to billet troops in his home. Crespo declared that as long as he was not of gentle blood he could see no point, even though he was rich, in assuming gentility.

Isabel and her cousin Inés, having learned of the presence of the troops, went to the attic of the house, where they would remain as long as the soldiers were in the town. On the captain's arrival, the sergeant searched the house but was unable to find Isabel. He reported, however, that a servant told him the woman was in the attic and would stay there until the troops departed.

The captain planned to win Isabel by any means.

Rebolledo asked the captain for the privilege of officially conducting gambling among the soldiers. The captain granted the privilege in return for Rebolledo's help in his plan to discover Isabel. The captain and Rebolledo then pretended to fight; Rebolledo, feigning great fright, fled, followed by the captain, up the stairs to the attic. Isabel admitted him to her retreat and, in pleading to the captain for his life, she presented such a charming aspect to the young officer that he was completely smitten.

The clamor of the pretended fight drew Crespo home. He and Juan, with swords drawn, raced upstairs to the attic. Juan sensed the trick and hinted as much, but Crespo, impressed by the captain's courtesy, was duped. Insulted by Juan's innuendoes, the captain was about to come to blows with Juan when Don Lope, the regimental commander, entered. When he demanded an explanation of the scene, the captain said that Rebolledo's insubordination had been the cause. Rebolledo, in denial, explained that the disturbance had been intended to discover Crespo's daughter. Don Lope ordered the captain to change his quarters and the troops to remain in their billets; he himself chose to stay in Crespo's house.

Crespo, jealous of his honor, declared that he would give up all of his worldly goods in submission to the will of the king, but that he would destroy the man who would jeopardize his good name. The captain, stricken with desire for Isabel, courted her under her window; she remained disdainful. Don Mendo, hearing what had happened, armed himself and set out to meet the captain on the field of honor. Meanwhile the captain had prevailed upon Rebolledo to assist him further in his suit. Rebolledo, reconciled, suggested that Isabel could be overcome with song.

At Crespo's, the proud farmer, mollified by Don Lope's seeming gentility, invited the commander to sup in the garden. Don Lope, wounded in the leg in the Flemish wars, so that he was in constant pain, played upon his infirmity in order to arouse Crespo's pity. When he requested the company of Isabel at supper, Crespo readily assented, assuring Don Lope that he would be proud to have his daughter wait on such a fine gentleman. After Isabel had joined Don Lope, the sound of a guitar and a vocal serenade came from the street outside. Those in the garden were so disturbed by the serenade that the supper came abruptly to an end.

Outside, an armed, skinny Don Mendo said he could barely refrain from attacking the captain and his followers, but as long as Isabel did not appear in her window he did not attack. As Chispa sang a particularly vulgar song, Crespo and Don Lope, swords drawn, fell upon the serenaders and scattered them. In the fray, Don Lope belabored Don Mendo, who had somehow become involved. A short time later the captain reappeared with soldiers in an official capacity to maintain the peace. Don Lope commended the captain and assured him that the trouble was of no importance. Since dawn was approaching, Don Lope told the captain to order the regiment out of Zalamea.

The next day, the troops having left, the captain expressed his determination to stay and make a last attempt to enjoy Isabel's favors. Further encouraged by the news that Juan had decided to become a soldier and that he would leave that day with Don Lope, he ordered Rebolledo to accompany him and the sergeant on his mission. Chispa declared that she would go along, disguised as a man.

Toward sundown, Don Lope said his farewell to Crespo and gave Isabel a diamond brooch. Crespo gave fatherly advice to Juan. As father and daughter watched Don Lope and Juan gallop away, Isabel observed that it was the day for the election of municipal officers. Suddenly the captain and his followers came upon them. The captain seized Isabel; the sergeant and Rebolledo seized Crespo.

Later that night, in the forest near Zalamea, a distracted Isabel came upon her father tied to a tree. She told how Juan had come upon the scene of her rape and had fought the captain. Frightened, she had run away from the fight. Crespo, comforting Isabel, vowed revenge. As the old man and his daughter started home, they encountered the town notary, who announced that Crespo had been elected mayor. He added that the wounded captain was in the village.

In Zalamea, Crespo confronted the captain in private. He suggested that the captain, having disgraced the family honor, take Isabel as his wife, but the captain, not fearing a provincial mayor, scoffed at Crespo's request. Crespo then ordered his officers to place the captain and his followers in jail to await the judgment of the king, who was approaching Zalamea.

Returning to his house, Crespo found Juan prepared to take Isabel's life, to wipe out the disgrace she had innocently brought on her family. Crespo, sternly just, ordered his officers to take Juan to jail for having fought his superior officer, the captain. Don Lope, on the highway, was informed that the captain had been jailed by the mayor of Zalamea. He returned to the village, went to Crespo, and, unaware that Crespo had been elected mayor, declared that he would thrash the town official for arresting one of the king's officers. Crespo revealed that he was the mayor and that he fully intended to see the captain hanged. Don Lope ordered the regiment to return to the public square of Zalamea.

The soldiers having returned, a pitched battle between them and the townspeople of Zalamea seemed imminent when King Philip II entered the village with his entourage. Don Lope explained the situation to the king, and Crespo showed his majesty depositions taken from the captain's associates. The king agreed that the captain's crime was vile; he declared, however, that Crespo had authority neither to judge nor to punish an officer of the king. When Crespo revealed that the captain had already been garroted in his cell and that no one knew who had strangled him, the king, unable to deny that Zalamea had meted out true justice upon the captain, appointed Crespo perpetual mayor of the village. Crespo, after declaring that Isabel would take the veil of a nun, released Rebolledo, Chispa, and Juan from jail, and returned Juan to the charge of his military mentor, Don Lope.

Critical Evaluation:

The Mayor of Zalamea is Pedro Calderón de la Barca's reworking of a play by his illustrious predecessor, Lope de Vega Carpio. Calderón, who was himself a soldier, delineates in this play the military life of seventeenth century Spain. He also portrays with sympathy the proud and independent farmer of the provinces. In the tradition of Spanish theater, the play blends comedy and tragedy; the jokes and song at the beginning of the play yield to the terrible crime and punishment at the end. A point of comparison is William Shakespeare's *Romeo and Juliet* (c. 1595-1596), which, one may argue, begins as a comedy and ends as a tragedy. *The Mayor of Zalamea* has achieved a place in the first rank of the world's dramatic masterpieces.

There is a perfect harmony and unity of thought and style. The play, generally assigned to the category of costumbristic drama—that is, drama based partly on history or popular tradition— has become, however, one of Calderón's most popular plays. The theme of *The Mayor of Zalamea* is honor, particularly in the first two acts where it is sharply contrasted with dishonor, as personified in the deeds of Captain Alvaro. The principal cause of the conflicts that drive the plot is the lodging of troops in a house where there is an unmarried woman, Isabel, and the captain's curiosity concerning a beauty he is forbidden to see. The effects of these situations are predictable, and the resultant action is fast moving, with an abduction, a rape, a garroting, and a jurisdictional battle that is resolved by the king. The incidents are structured on a ladder arrangement in that each one develops from the preceding one both logically and psychologically, which escalates into a tide of mounting tension by the end of each act. The play is perfectly constructed.

The conflict is depicted on two levels, exterior and interior. Each level involves a question of jurisdiction. The exterior conflict revolves around the clash between Crespo and Lope over the question of whether the king's justice is to be administered by the military or the civilian authorities. The external conflicts are set forth as debates or arguments and encompass the theme of honor. It may be difficult for the reader to comprehend the importance that honor had in Spain in the seventeenth century. One may find it simply abhorrent and incomprehensible, for example, that a brother may intend to kill his sister, after she has been raped, to preserve the family's honor. Honor as a theme in Calderón's work has manifold faces—honor ranges from a matter of the highest religious principle to a parody of social convention. One should read the play, therefore, with attention toward the importance that honor has in the play, from the first moments (when a starving gentleman discusses the proper way to woo a rich peasant) to the last (when the king decides whether Crespo and the other villagers, whose lives are at stake, have acted honorably).

The interior conflict also evolves from the concept of honor. The internal problem centers on the decision Crespo must make as to whether he should act in his capacity as a father or as the newly elected Mayor of Zalamea. He finally chooses the latter because it embraces a broader sphere of justice than does the personal. The author's style, like the action, is simple and direct. The argumentative aspects of the style are borne out in the aforementioned debates over the concept of honor, but the quaint patter of the lower characters reveals an aspect of Calderón's style that adds a high degree of realism and naturalness to the dialogue. If the debates on honor seem artificial to today's reader, the oaths of Rebolledo, a raw recruit, who curses the officer who forces the troops to march without rest, are timeless bits of dialogue.

Like the style, the characterizations are significant for their attention to variety and detail. A case in point is Pedro Crespo, who represents justice and prudence, but, at the same time, while being symbolic of virtue, is very much a flesh and blood character, with human defects. The soldiers think of him as vain, pompous, and presumptuous. He is proud of his lineage, and he has a sense of honor and personal dignity. Calderón's technique of revealing aspects of one character through the eyes of another is a strong factor in making the character more human and balanced in the eyes of the reader.

The Mayor of Zalamea is an allegory: The Spanish king, as representative of God, finally recalls all of the players to their fixed and rightful positions within the social order. Thus, while Crespo, for example, has an identity as a human being, on another level he is representative of the abstract virtue of justice, while Captain Alvaro is the embodiment of several dishonorable traits. *The Mayor of Zalamea* is Calderón's most popular drama. In critical discussions of this work, it is common to read that it is unlike any of the author's other works. Some critics call it a revolutionary play, while others refer to it as a social drama, or Calderón's only drama of character. In truth, the play does not necessarily occupy an exceptional place in the playwright's canon. It is Calderón's usual kind of play, and it is unusual only in that the protagonist is a common man. Calderón was primarily a man of the theater, and the most significant argument in his selection of material was that of its applicability to the stage. *The Mayor of Zalamea*'s plot is perfectly suited to dramatic presentation. Since its first performance in the seventeenth century, it has perhaps never been out of production.

"Critical Evaluation" by Stephen Hanson

Bibliography:
Calderón de la Barca, Pedro. *Calderón de la Barca: Four Plays*. Translated and with an introduction by Edwin Honig. New York: Hill and Wang, 1961. Honig's introduction and Norman MacColl's appendix provide illuminating context for understanding Spanish drama of the period.

Gerstinger, Heinz. *Pedro Calderón de la Barca*. Translated by Diana Stone Peters. New York: Frederick Ungar, 1973. Discusses another of the play's central themes: order and disorder, and how order is needed to limit human passions. Argues against the play's being unique among Calderón's works. Bibliography.

Hesse, Everett W. *Calderón de la Barca*. New York: Twayne, 1967. Describes *The Mayor of Zalamea* in terms of genre (it is a costumbristic play) and theme (honor). A good starting place for the study of Calderón. Bibliography.

Maraniss, James E. *On Calderón*. Columbia: University of Missouri Press, 1978. Stressing Calderón's sense of "order triumphant," Maraniss moves through the canon examining the structural integrity of each play, the symmetry of the plots, and the repeated ideas of social order.

Parker, Alexander A. *The Mind and Art of Calderón: Essays on the Comedias*. Edited by Deborah Kong. New York: Cambridge University Press, 1988. Discusses historical allusions in the play. Notes and index.

MEASURE FOR MEASURE

Type of work: Drama
Author: William Shakespeare (1564-1616)
Type of plot: Tragicomedy
Time of plot: Sixteenth century
Locale: Vienna
First performed: c. 1604; first published, 1623

Principal characters:
VINCENTIO, the duke of Vienna
ANGELO, the lord deputy
ESCALUS, an ancient counselor
CLAUDIO, a young gentleman
LUCIO, his friend
ISABELLA, Claudio's sister
MARIANA, Angelo's former sweetheart
JULIET, Claudio's fiancée

The Story:

The growing political and moral corruption of Vienna was a great worry to its kindly, temperate ruler, Duke Vincentio. Knowing that he himself was as much to blame for the troubles as anyone because he had been lax in the enforcement of existing laws, the duke tried to devise a scheme to revive the old discipline of civic authority.

Fearing that reforms instituted by himself might seem too harsh for his people to accept without protest, he decided to appoint a deputy governor and to leave the country for a while. Angelo, a respected and intelligent city official, seemed just the man for the job. The duke turned over the affairs of Vienna to Angelo for a certain length of time and appointed Escalus, a trustworthy old official, to be second in command. The duke then pretended to leave for Poland. In reality, he disguised himself as a friar and returned to the city to watch the outcome of Angelo's reforms.

Angelo's first act was to imprison Claudio, a young nobleman who had gotten his betrothed, Juliet, with child. Under an old statute, now revived, Claudio's offense was punishable by death. After being paraded through the streets in disgrace, the young man was sent to prison. He asked his rakish friend Lucio to go to the nunnery where Claudio's sister Isabella was a young novice about to take her vows and to ask her to plead with the new governor for his release. At the same time, Escalus, who had known Claudio's father well, begged Angelo not to execute the young man. The new deputy remained firm, however, in carrying out the duties of his office, and Claudio's well-wishers were given no reason to hope for their friend's release.

The duke, disguised as a friar, visited Juliet and learned that the young couple had been very much in love and had, in fact, been formally engaged; they would have been married but for the fact that Juliet's dowry had become a matter of legal dispute. There was no question of heartless seduction in the case at all.

Isabella, going before Angelo to plead her brother's cause, met with little success at first, even though she had been thoroughly coached by the wily Lucio. Nevertheless, Angelo's cold heart was somewhat touched by Isabella's beauty. By the second interview, he had become so passionately aroused as to forget his reputation for saintly behavior. He told Isabella frankly that she could obtain her brother's release only by yielding herself to his lustful desires, otherwise Claudio would die. Isabella was shocked at these words from the deputy, but when she asserted that she would expose him in public, Angelo, amused, asked who would believe her story. At her wit's end, Isabella rushed to the prison where she told Claudio of Angelo's disgraceful proposition. When he first heard the deputy's proposal, Claudio was outraged, but the thought of death so terrified him that he finally begged Isabella to placate Angelo and give herself to him. Isabella, horrified by her brother's cowardly attitude, lashed out at him with a scornful speech, but she was interrupted by the disguised duke, who had overheard much of the conversation. He drew Isabella aside from her brother and told her that she would be able to save Claudio without shaming herself.

The friar told Isabella that five years earlier Angelo had been betrothed to a high-born lady named Mariana. The marriage had not taken place, however. After Mariana's brother had been lost at sea with her dowry, Angelo had broken the engagement, hinting at supposed dishonor in the young woman. The friar suggested that Isabella plan a rendezvous with Angelo in a dark, quiet place and then let Mariana act as her substitute. Angelo would be satisfied, Claudio released, Isabella still chaste, and Mariana provided with the means to force Angelo to marry her.

Everything went as arranged, with Mariana taking Isabella's place at the assignation. Cowardly Angelo, however, fearing public exposure, broke his promise to release Claudio and instead ordered the young man's execution. Once again the good friar intervened. He persuaded the provost to hide Claudio and then to announce his death by sending Angelo the head of another prisoner who had died of natural causes.

On the day before the execution, a crowd gathered outside the prison. One of the group was Lucio, who accosted the disguised duke as he wandered down the street. Furtively, Lucio told the friar that nothing like Claudio's execution would have taken place if the duke had been ruler. Lucio went on confidentially to say that the duke cared as much for the ladies as any other man and also drank in private. In fact, said Lucio, the duke bedded about as much as any man in Vienna. Amused, the friar protested against this gossip, but Lucio angrily asserted that every word was true.

To arouse Isabella to accuse Angelo publicly of wrongdoing, the duke allowed her to believe that Claudio was dead. Then the duke sent letters to the deputy informing him that the royal party would arrive on the following day at the gates of Vienna and would expect to be welcomed. The command also ordered that anyone who had grievances against the government while the duke was absent should be allowed to make public pronouncement of them at that time and place.

Angelo grew nervous upon receipt of these papers from the duke. The next day, however, he organized a great crowd and a celebration of welcome at the gates of the city. At the prearranged time, Isabella and Mariana, heavily veiled, stepped forward to denounce Angelo. Isabella called him a traitor and violator of virgins; Mariana claimed that he would not admit her as his wife. The duke, pretending to be angry at these tirades against his deputy, ordered the women to prison and asked that someone apprehend the rascally friar who had often been seen in their company.

Then the duke went to his palace and quickly assumed his disguise as a friar. Appearing before the crowd at the gates, he criticized the government of Vienna severely. Escalus, horrified at the fanatical comments of the friar, ordered his arrest, seconded by Lucio, who maintained that the friar had told him only the day before that the duke was a drunkard and a frequenter of bawdy houses. At last, to display his own bravado, Lucio tore away the friar's hood. When the friar stood revealed as Duke Vincentio, the crowd fell back in amazement.

Angelo realized that his crimes would now be exposed, and he asked simply to be put to death without trial. The duke ordered him to marry Mariana first, and he told Mariana that Angelo's goods, once they were legally hers, would secure her a better husband. The duke was surprised when she begged for Angelo's pardon, in which entreaties she was joined by Isabella, but he relented. He did, however, send Lucio to prison. Claudio was released and married to Juliet. The duke himself asked Isabella for her hand.

Critical Evaluation:

Measure for Measure is one of those troubled plays, like *All's Well That Ends Well* (c. 1602-1603) and *Troilus and Cressida* (c. 1601-1602), that William Shakespeare composed during the same years he was writing his greatest tragedies. Yet, though they are dark and often bitter, they are not straightforward tragedy or history or comedy; they have instead frequently been described as problem plays, which generally refers to plays that examine a thesis. The main concern in *Measure for Measure* is a rather grim consideration of the nature of justice and morality in both civic and psychological contexts.

The tone of this play, and of the other problem plays, is so gloomy and pessimistic that critics have tended to try to find biographical or historical causes for their bleakness. Some have argued that they reflect a period of personal disillusionment for the playwright, but there is no external evidence of this. Others have laid the blame on the decadence of the Jacobean period. Although such dramatists as John Marston and Thomas Dekker did write similar plays around the same time, the historical evidence suggests that the period was, on the contrary, rather optimistic. What is clear is that Shakespeare has created a world as rotten as Denmark but without a tragic figure sufficient to purge and redeem it. The result is a threatened world, supported by comic remedies rather than purified by tragic suffering. Consequently, *Measure for Measure* remains a shadowy, ambiguous, and disquieting world even though it ends with political and personal resolutions.

The immediate source of the play seems to be George Whetstone's *History of Promos and Cassandra* (1578), which is based on a narrative and a dramatic version of the tale in Giambattista Giraldi Cinthio's *Hecatommithi* (1527), from whom Shakespeare also derived the plot of *Othello, the Moor of Venice* (1604). However, *Measure for Measure* is such an eclectic amalgamation of items from a wide variety of literary and historical loci that a precise identification of sources is impossible. Indeed, the plot is essentially a conflation of three ancient folktales, which J. W. Lever has identified as the Corrupt Magistrate, the Disguised Ruler, and the Substituted Bedmate. Shakespeare integrates these with disparate other materials into a disturbing, indeterminate analysis of justice, morality, and integrity.

The title of the play comes from the scriptural text: "With what measure ye mete, it shall be measured to you again." As the play develops and expands on this quotation, it becomes clear that a simple but generous resolution "to do unto others what you would have them do unto you" will not suffice to resolve the situation. The play pursues its text so relentlessly that any easy confidence in poetic justice is undermined. In the final analysis, the action tends to support an admonition to "Judge not that ye be not judged," which can be either Christian charity or cynical irresponsibility.

Yet the play takes place in a world in which the civil authorities must judge others. Indeed, that is where the play begins. Vienna, as the duke himself realizes, is a moral morass, and bawdry and licentiousness of all sorts are rampant. The duke accepts responsibility for having been lax in enforcing the law. Corruption seethes throughout society from the nobility down to the base characters who are engaged less in a comic subplot than in a series of vulgar exemplifications of the pervasive moral decay.

The chilling paradox is that when Angelo, renowned for his probity and puritanical stringency, is made responsible for setting things right, he almost immediately falls victim to the sexual license he is supposed to eliminate. Claudio, whom Angelo condemns for making Juliet pregnant, had at least acted out of love and with a full intention to marry. Things do not turn out to be as they seemed. He who is responsible for justice yields to temptation while someone apparently guilty of vice is extenuated by circumstances.

Isabella, called on to intercede for her brother, is faced with an especially nasty dilemma, since her choice is between her honor and her brother's life. Neither is a noble alternative, and Claudio is not strong enough to offer himself up for her and turn the play into a tragedy. Unfortunately, when Claudio shows his reluctance, she behaves petulantly rather than graciously. True, her position is intolerable, but she spends more time speaking in defense of her virtue than in acting virtuously. For all her religious aspirations, which are eventually abandoned, she is not large enough to ennoble her moral context.

Always lurking in the background is the duke, who watches developments and stands ready to intervene to avoid disaster. He seems slow to step in, but then if he had intervened earlier, or had never left in the first place, there would not have been a play that examines the ambiguities of guilt and extenuation, justice and mercy. The duke and Shakespeare allow the characters to act out the complex patterns of moral responsibility that are the heart of the play. When Angelo, thinking he is with Isabella, is in fact with Mariana, his act is objectively less evil than he thinks because he is really with the woman to whom he had earlier plighted his troth. Yet in intention he is more culpable than Claudio, whom he had imprisoned. Such are the intricate complications of behavior in the flawed world of *Measure for Measure*.

The justice that the duke finally administers brings about a comic resolution. Pardons and marriages unravel the complications that varying degrees of evil had occasioned, but no one in the play escapes untainted. The duke, after a period of moral spectatorship that borders on irresponsibility, restores order. Angelo loses his virtue and reputation but gains a wife. Isabella abandons her religious commitment but learns to be more human, for which she is rewarded with a marriage proposal. Everything works out, and justice, tempered with mercy, prevails. The audience is left, however, with an unsettled feeling that tendencies toward corruption and excess may be inextricably blended with what is best and most noble.

"Critical Evaluation" by Edward E. Foster

Bibliography:
Bennett, Josephine Waters. *"Measure for Measure" as Royal Entertainment.* New York: Columbia University Press, 1966. A comprehensive discussion of the play, centering on the way it would have appeared to contemporary audiences. The author rejects earlier criticisms of the work as "dark comedy," and considers instead that in its historical context, it would have been viewed as high entertainment.
Lloyd Evans, Gareth. *The Upstart Crow: An Introduction to Shakespeare's Plays.* London: J. M. Dent and Sons, 1982. A comprehensive discussion of Shakespeare's dramatic works, including information on the plays' critical reviews and sources, as well as on the circumstances surrounding their gestation.
Muir, Kenneth, ed. *Shakespeare—The Comedies: A Collection of Critical Essays.* Englewood Cliffs, N.J.: Prentice-Hall, 1965. An anthology of essays that discuss Shakespeare's comedies from various points of view. The essay on *Measure for Measure*, by R. W. Chambers, emphasizes the violence in the play and its importance in furthering the plot.

Shakespeare, William. *Measure for Measure*. Edited by J. W. Lever. London: Methuen, 1965. In addition to the text of the play, this edition contains more than ninety pages of introductory material about the sources and a critical evaluation of the work. Also includes appendices with the original texts of Shakespeare's sources.

Wheeler, Richard P. *Shakespeare's Development and the Problem Comedies*. Berkeley: University of California Press, 1981. Discusses two of Shakespeare's comedies, *All's Well That Ends Well* and *Measure for Measure*. These two works are considered problem comedies because they do not fit the usual mold of Elizabethan comedy.

MEDEA

Type of work: Drama
Author: Euripides (c. 485-406 B.C.E.)
Type of plot: Tragedy
Time of plot: Antiquity
Locale: Corinth
First performed:Mēdeia, 431 B.C.E. (English translation, 1781)

Principal characters:
MEDEA, a sorceress
JASON, her lover
CREON, the king of Corinth
GLAUCE, the daughter of Creon
AEGEUS, the king of Athens

The Story:

When Medea discovered that Jason had deserted her and married Glauce, the daughter of Creon, she vowed a terrible vengeance. Her nurse, although she loved Medea, recognized that a frightful threat now hung over Corinth, for she knew that Medea would not let the insult pass without some dreadful revenge. She feared especially for Medea's two sons, since the sorceress included her children in the hatred which she now felt for their father.

Her resentment increased still further when Creon, hearing of her vow, ordered her and her children to be banished from Corinth. Slyly, with a plan already in mind, Medea persuaded him to allow her just one day longer to prepare herself and her children for the journey. She had already decided the nature of her revenge; the one problem that remained was a place of refuge afterward.

Then Aegeus, the king of Athens and a longtime friend of Medea, appeared in Corinth on his way home from a journey. Sympathetic with her because of Jason's brutal desertion, he offered her a place of refuge from her enemies in his own kingdom. In this manner Medea assured herself of a refuge, even after Aegeus should learn of the deeds she intended to commit in Corinth.

When the Corinthian women came to visit her, Medea told them of her plan, but only after swearing them to absolute secrecy. At first she had considered killing Jason, his princess, and Creon, and then fleeing with her children. After she had thought about it, however, she felt that revenge would be sweeter should Jason live to suffer long afterward. Nothing could be more painful than to grow old without a lover, without children, and without friends, and so Medea planned to kill the king, his daughter, and her own children.

She called Jason to her and pretended that she forgave him for what he had done, recognizing at last the justice and foresight he had shown in marrying Glauce. She begged his forgiveness for her earlier rage, and asked that she be allowed to send her children with gifts for the new bride, as a sign of her repentance. Jason was completely deceived by her supposed change of heart, and expressed his pleasure at the belated wisdom she was showing.

Medea drew out a magnificent robe and a fillet of gold, presents of her grandfather, Helios, the sun god, but before she entrusted them to her children she smeared them with a deadly drug. Shortly afterward, a messenger came to Medea and told her to flee. One part of her plan had succeeded. After Jason and the children had left, Glauce had dressed herself in her wonderful robe and walked through the palace. As the warmth and moisture of her body came in contact with the drug, the fillet and gown clung to her body and seared her flesh. She tried frantically

4057

to tear them from her, but the garments only wrapped more tightly around her, and she died in a screaming agony of flames. When Creon rushed in and saw his daughter writhing on the floor, he attempted to lift her, but was himself contaminated by the poison. His death was as agonizing as hers had been.

Meanwhile the children had returned to Medea. As she looked at them and felt their arms around her, she was torn between her love for them and her hatred of Jason, between her desire for revenge and the commands of her maternal instinct. The barbarous part of her nature—Medea being not a Greek, but a barbarian from Colchis—triumphed. After reveling in the messenger's account of the deaths of Creon and his daughter, she entered her house with the children and barred the door. While the Corinthian women stood helplessly outside, they listened to the shrieks of the children as Medea killed them with a sword. Jason appeared, frantically eager to take his children away lest they be killed by Creon's followers for having brought the dreadful gifts. When he learned Medea had killed his children, he was almost insane with grief. As he hammered furiously on the barred doors of the house, Medea suddenly appeared above, holding the bodies of her dead children, and drawn in a chariot which Helios, the sun god, had sent her. Jason alternately cursed her and pleaded with her for one last sight of his children as Medea taunted him with the loneliness and grief to which he was doomed. She told him that her own sorrow would be great, but it was mitigated by the sweetness of her revenge.

The chariot, drawn by winged dragons, carried her first to the mountain of the goddess Hera. There she buried her children. Then she journeyed to Athens, where she would spend the remainder of her days feeding on the gall and wormwood of her terrible grief and revenge.

Critical Evaluation:

Commonly regarded as Euripides' greatest work, *Medea* is a powerful study of impassioned love turned into furious hatred. As a tragedy this play is completely unlike the Aristotelian concept of tragedy, but it has a nerve-jarring impact. It also reveals the extent to which Euripides diverges from his fellow tragedians, Aeschylus and Sophocles, in his depiction of human pain. With *Medea* there is no comforting philosophy to put the tragic agony at a safe psychological distance. Instead, Euripides tries to make Medea as close to an actual woman as possible, and to show her fiery lust for vengeance in naked action with nothing to mitigate its effect. The audience is witness to a hideous passion and cannot be certain whether Euripides approves of it or condemns it. He simply presents it objectively so that we understand Medea, but he leaves it to his audience to determine his meaning.

Euripides was probably in his fifties when this play was first produced in 431 B.C.E., an age when a sensitive person is fully aware of the agony that life can inflict on a person. What struck him most was the universality of suffering. Confronted with pain, every other human reality seemed to dissolve. In the face of Medea's consuming hatred, kingship, laws, culture, self-esteem, and even motherly love have become meaningless. In *Medea* Euripides portrays a very important aspect of terrible suffering, namely, the desire of the sufferer to create the identical agony in the person who caused it. The dramatist recognized the crucial link between anguish and hate. Reports of Euripides say that he was a bookish recluse, but it is understandable that a man as vulnerable to human misery as he was should shut himself off from people.

He turned to the old legend of Jason and the Golden Fleece to illustrate his preoccupation. Euripides takes up the story after all of Jason's successes have been accomplished with Medea's help. Jason has deserted Medea to marry the Greek princess, Glauce, leaving Medea with two small sons. As the nurse remarks in her opening monologue, Medea is not one to take such a betrayal lightly. Although Medea is prostrate with bitter grief and hoping to die as the play begins, the nurse knows how murderous her mistress really is, and she fears for the safety of Medea's sons. A common technique of Euripides is to use the opening speech or section to explain the background of the action and to suggest the climactic development.

Medea is a barbarian princess and sorceress who is accustomed to having her own way in everything. Furthermore, as a barbarian she has none of the restraints that civilization imposes. Jason is a Greek, subject to law, rationality, and practical calculation. As a result, he seems cold and indifferent set beside Medea, who is a creature of passion. However, this is merely a surface appearance. Euripides exposes the inner layers of their psyches with unflinching honesty in the course of the play.

As a woman of passion, Medea is wholly committed to Jason as the object of her emotional life, whether in love or hate. When she loved Jason she did not hesitate to kill her brother, betray her father and country, or instigate Pelias' murder for Jason's sake. She is equally amoral in her hatred. The drama consists of the unfolding of her plans for revenge and their ultimate execution. When Medea first appears on stage before a chorus of sympathetic women, she is the image of the wronged woman, and one feels pity for her. At the end of the play, however, after a bloodbath of four persons that includes her sons and that leaves Jason's life a total desolation, one feels only horror.

These murders are as coldly calculated as any in classical tragedy, and Medea feels no penitence at all. It is precisely the icy manner in which she goes about the killings that inspires dread. She caters to Creon in order to gain time to kill him and his daughter, Glauce. Medea plans to kill Jason too, but when she sees Aegeus heartsick at being childless, she determines to render Jason childless, wifeless, and friendless. Medea pretends a reconciliation with Jason to slay Creon and Glauce in a loathsome fashion. Then, after hesitating to kill her sons because of temporary softness, she butchers them without mercy. Medea is a practitioner of black magic, a cold-blooded murderess, and a total monster; but under Euripides' spell the audience understands her.

The passion by which she lives makes her both subhuman and superhuman. When Euripides finally has her escape in a dragon-drawn chariot through the air, one comes to realize that Medea is a piece of raw nature—barbaric, violent, destructive, inhumanly powerful, and beyond all moral standards. Jason becomes entangled with a force that crushes his dignity and detachment, that tears his successes to tatters. At the end, he is in exactly the same position as Medea. Both are bereaved of mate, children, and friends. Both are free to grow old without comfort. Both are utterly empty inside, except that Jason is now filled with the same burning hatred that possessed Medea.

This play operates on several levels. The antagonism between Jason and Medea can be read as the enmity between man and woman, between intelligence and passion, between civilization and barbarism, or between humanity and nature. In each instance, the woman, the passions, the barbarian, the forces of nature—all embodied in Medea—have the power to turn and reduce the masculine elements to nothing. *Medea* is a strong, depressing, fearsome drama in which Euripides presents his vision of life as starkly as possible.

"Critical Evaluation" by James Weigel, Jr.

Bibliography:
McDermott, Emily A. *Euripides' "Medea": The Incarnation of Disorder*. University Park: Pennsylvania State University Press, 1989. McDermott presents Medea as heroic, sympa-

thetic, and morally repugnant. Medea is the incarnation of disorder because of her repeated assaults on family stability and her lack of adherence to the expectations of the parent-child relationship.

Ohlander, Stephen. *Dramatic Suspense in Euripides' and Seneca's "Medea."* New York: Peter Lang, 1989. Scene by scene, Ohlander explores Euripides' sense of dramatic suspense, examining how motifs from mythic tradition are handled and how Euripides manufactures new ones.

Papageorgiou, Vasilis. *Euripides' "Medea" and Cosmetics.* Stockholm: Almqvist & Wiksell, 1986. Papageorgiou discusses Euripides' language, which inspires the audience to think beyond polarities, leading them from Jason's world of light and logic into Medea's, where light cannot reach.

Pucci, Pietro. *The Violence of Pity in Euripides' "Medea."* Ithaca, N.Y.: Cornell University Press, 1980. Pucci examines the painful experience audience members suffer when exposed to the play's violence and the ways Euripides' language moves them from dread to contemplation of the peacefulness of their own existence.

Rabinowitz, Nancy Sorkin. *Anxiety Veiled: Euripides and the Traffic in Women.* Ithaca, N.Y.: Cornell University Press, 1993. Focusing on women in Athens and in tragedy, Rabinowitz explores female desire as a threat to family and the Athenian polis, interpreting Medea as a female victim who, though initially sympathetic to the audience, forfeits that sympathy by indulging in a vengeance made to seem excessive—an act for which she pays no price.

MEDITATIONS

Type of work: Philosophy
Author: Marcus Aurelius (121-180 C.E.)
First transcribed: Tōn eis heauton, c. 171-180 (English translation, 1634)

Although the Greek philosopher Zeno is generally given the credit for creating the school of philosophy called Stoicism, its greatest fame arises from the popularity and widespread influence of the utterances of two later figures: Epictetus, a slave, and Marcus Aurelius, Emperor of Rome. Of the two, Marcus Aurelius, born four years before the death of Epictetus in 125, has probably achieved the greater fame; and this fame results almost entirely from his *Meditations,* one of the most famous philosophical books in the world.

For the average reader, however, there is a disturbing characteristic in the work, which is obscure and often seemingly unrelated; there are passages that suggest that the book has come down to the present time in a disorganized, even careless, form. One widely accepted suggestion to account for this difficulty is the possibility that Marcus intended his writings to be read by no one else, that he recorded his thoughts only for himself. It is certain that the *Meditations* was written during the period between Marcus' accession to the imperial rank in 161 and his death in 180; it is equally certain that the various books were composed during rigorous military campaigns and trying political crises. Although these facts explain in part the irregularity of the book, other scholars feel that there is clear evidence of the emperor's design to publish at least parts of the work.

If this is so, and if Marcus did not merely keep a private journal, then the reason for the present form of the *Meditations* probably lies in errors and misunderstandings by copyists and later editors of the text. In either event, the book contains two generally different styles side by side: a nearly casual, sometimes aphoristic, way of writing, and a more literary, more carefully planned, technique. Throughout the twelve books that make up the whole, there are passages that read like admonitions addressed by the author to himself; in contrast to these are sections that sound as if Marcus were offering philosophical advice to the Romans or to humanity in general.

Despite these irregularities, and in spite of the absence of an organized system of thought, a careful reading reveals that the emperor presents to the world some of the sagest suggestions for leading the good life and some of the most effective expressions of the tenets of later Stoicism to be found anywhere.

To say that Marcus Aurelius can be given credit for profound original thinking is going too far. *Meditations* was not written in a vacuum. It rephrases and reinterprets much of that which is usually considered the best of ancient Greek and Roman philosophy. The author acknowledges his debt to his teachers and his wise forbears; his quotations from, and references to, the leading thinkers of his and earlier times prove his wide reading and careful study, which colors his injunction to throw aside one's books and to live one's philosophy.

Perhaps the fact that Marcus did live by his philosophy, one that was tested by almost continually difficult circumstances, is one of the chief charms of his book. There is very little in the *Meditations* that the emperor probably did not find occasion to think of in relation to his own life. Much of practical philosophic value can be found here. His advice at the opening of book 2, for example, to begin each day with the thought that one will meet during that day men who are arrogant, envious, and deceitful, but to remember that these men are so because of their ignorance of the good and the right, is surely a sound practical application of the Platonic idea that evil is only the absence of knowledge.

Many readers have found the *Meditations* their surest guide to living by Stoic principles. Although happiness must surely come by the pursuit of Stoic virtue, duty is the greatest good in the Stoic view. The word "duty" appears rarely in the book, but the emperor's conviction that a man must face squarely his responsibilities is implicit in almost every paragraph. Often a note of Roman sternness appears, as in the beginning of paragraph 5 of book 2: "Every moment think steadily as a Roman and a man to do what thou hast in hand with perfect and simple dignity, and feeling of affection, and freedom, and justice; and to give thyself relief from all other thoughts."

To achieve true virtue, the emperor says, one must live in accord with both kinds of nature: the nature of humankind and the nature of the universe. The book departs from a commonly held view of the philosopher as an isolated dreamer in its insistence that one must live wisely with one's fellows. One should not be a hermit. Since each individual partakes of the same divinity that informs all people, each must live and work with others; certainly such is the divine intention, and this, then, is one's social duty. The duty one has to the universe is to perceive the informing intelligence that pervades and guides it. Here Marcus is close to pantheism.

With this foundation in mind, the reader can understand the emperor's notion of evil as something that cannot harm or disturb the great plan of the universe; it is simply ignorance and harms only the doer. Thus, no one can be harmed by a force from the outside. Injury comes from within. The advice of the *Meditations*, along with that of other Stoic writings, is to accept calmly what cannot be avoided and to perform to the best of one's ability the duties of a human being in a world of humans. Since one cannot understand the workings of the great force that rules the universe, one must do what can be done in his or her own sphere.

Although he believes the world to be divinely guided, Marcus has no illusions about life; therefore, he scorns fears of death. Life is full of trouble and hardship, and no one should be sorry to leave it. In paragraph 14 of book 2, the author says that however long or short a person's life, a person loses at death only the present moment. No one possesses the past or the future; furthermore, since the progress of time is simply a revolution, and all things have been and will be the same, one loses nothing by an early death. This passage displays something of the occasional coldness of the emperor's thought, but it is one of many sections devoted to the consolation for the hard facts of existence.

Regardless of the varied character of the writing and the thinking in these paragraphs, it is clear that a reasonably consistent philosophy inspired them. Certainly the statement that one rarely comes to grief from not knowing what is in another's soul, that true misery results from not understanding what lies within oneself, is of a piece with the rest of the book.

Some readers have found in Marcus Aurelius a basically Christian spirit and believe that, in many passages, the *Meditations* somewhat foreshadows later religious writings. Considerable doubt exists as to his feeling about the Christians or the extent of his responsibility for their persecution during his reign, but there is little question that a great deal of his thinking is closely allied with that of later spiritual leaders. The readership and influence of *Meditations*, written by perhaps the greatest pagan ruler who ever lived, is as wide as those of other works of its kind, and far greater than those of most.

Bibliography:
Birley, Anthony. *Marcus Aurelius*. London: Eyre & Spottiswoode, 1966. Straightforward, informative chapter on *Meditations* points out that the book was the stoic Emperor Marcus Aurelius' personal diary, and the events surrounding him were intertwined in it. Extensive bibliography.

Brunt, P. A. "Marcus Aurelius in His *Meditations.*" *Journal of Roman Studies* 64 (1974): 1-20. Good breakdown of the books in *Meditations*, and insight into the life of Marcus Aurelius while he was composing *Meditations*. Asserts that Marcus' work was philosophical as well as spiritual.

Farquharson, A. S. L. *Marcus Aurelius: His Life and His World.* Edited by D. A. Rees. Westport, Conn.: Greenwood Press, 1975. Good introduction to serious study. Information on Marcus' upbringing and education, the literature of the era, and Stoicism.

Rutherford, R. B. Introduction and end notes to *The Meditations of Marcus Aurelius Antonius and Selections from Fronto*, by Marcus Aurelius. *Meditations* translated by A. S. L. Farquharson. Oxford, England: Oxford University Press, 1989. Excellent beginner's source. Introduction prepares the reader, and the additional end notes give insight into names, dates, symbolism, and historical meaning. Includes list of additional sources to begin research.

MEDITATIONS ON FIRST PHILOSOPHY

Type of work: Philosophy
Author: René Descartes (1596-1650)
First published: Meditationes de Prima Philosophia, 1641 (English translation, 1680)

The appearance of *Meditations on First Philosophy* marks a dramatic turning point in the history of Western thought. Born in France in 1596, René Descartes was sent to a Jesuit school as a young man and in 1616 obtained a law degree. He spent much of his youth traveling. Like many young Frenchmen of the time, he enlisted as a gentleman volunteer in the army of Prince Maurice of Nassau in Holland during the Thirty Years' War. In November, 1619, when the onset of winter had slowed the fighting, Descartes retired to the village of Ulm on the Danube River to devote himself to study and contemplation. He writes that one day, while trying to escape the cold in a heated room, he had three visions or dreams in which he saw flashes of light and heard thunder. He said it seemed to him that some spirit was revealing a new philosophy to him. He interpreted these visions as a divine sign that it was his destiny to place all of human thought on the firm foundation of mathematics.

In 1637, he published *Discourse on Method,* which roughly outlined that new philosophy. Both *Discourse on Method* and *Meditations on First Philosophy* were written in French rather than Latin, the usual language of scholarly works. Like Galileo before him, who wrote in Italian, Descartes intended to reach beyond the university to a larger educated audience.

The great intellectual tension of Descartes' time was that between belief in traditional Christianity and belief in the potential of the new physical and mathematical sciences. Philosophers before Descartes used a philosophical method called Scholasticism, which was entirely based on comparing and contrasting the views of recognized authorities, especially Aristotle. Since Scholastic philosophy was built on the opinions of many thinkers, it was unable to provide much in the way of certainty on any given subject.

Instead of accepting the traditional views, Descartes believed that people must instead study from "the great book of the world." To know the opinions of others, he said, is history, not science; people should do their own thinking, and the clear and simple process of mathematics would provide the clue for how to proceed on the path to certain knowledge. Descartes turned all questions of human knowledge inward by first thinking about the process of thinking itself, examining the method of knowing as a prerequisite for assuming that certain knowledge has been attained. Descartes was trying to find a body of irrefutable and self-evident truths that every person of common sense and reason could accept. If truths could be established in philosophy as they had been in mathematics, this would end the debates about the existence of God, the immortality of the soul, and the reality of the external world.

In the first meditation, Descartes begins by doubting all knowledge that he has previously accepted as true. Up to the present time, he says, he has accepted the knowledge acquired through sensory experience as the most true and certain knowledge; yet sense perceptions may be illusions, the products of dreams or hallucinations, or the products of an all-powerful being that is causing these sensations or ideas to form. In fact, individuals could be existing in a prolonged "dream state" that seems quite real while in fact there is no way to prove that they are awake. These facts led Descartes to doubt the certainty of everything. The only thing he could not doubt was that he existed.

In the second meditation, Descartes declares that this universal doubt makes him feel like a swimmer who is suddenly plunged into deep water. Unable to touch bottom or see the surface, he cannot find a fixed reference point from which to begin. He therefore must assume that everything is false and that he has no memory, no senses, and no body. Even what he perceives as "reality" could possibly be a deception. Even if, however, he is in a state of universal doubt—even if he is being deceived—he remains a thinking being. He can therefore at least assert that he is "a thing which thinks." At this point he has found the first of what he calls "clear and distinct ideas," ideas so certain that they cannot possibly be denied.

He can now proceed to the more difficult task of proving the existence of the material world. For this purpose, he introduces the famous "wax argument": A piece of wax fresh from the beehive can be seen to have color, size, and smell that present themselves to human senses, but if the wax is placed near a fire it melts and those qualities disappear. Where did they go? Descartes' answer is that there had only been the assumption that the qualities existed in the object, while in fact they were merely intuitions of the mind. The best that humans can do at this point is to speculate that there are material objects outside themselves that cause sensations in the mind.

Descartes' third meditation is devoted to a proof of God's existence, which is also intended to show that the world perceived through the senses is not a deception. Since the existence of the outside world is still in doubt, Descartes begins by examining the ideas present in his mind. He notices that some ideas seem to be "born" with him, while others seem to come from outside; he observes that things seem to be happening around him and independently of his will. For example, as he sits by the fire he feels heat and is persuaded that the heat does not originate from within him; similarly, he has a concept of God, which also does not seem to have come from within him. He asks himself how, given that he himself is not an infinite, all-knowing, all-powerful being, he could produce the idea of a God with these attributes. Because he does not possess these qualities, Descartes argues, they could not have originated within him, and since God is perfect, he could not be a deceiver. Therefore, the world he perceives through his senses must have been created by a being greater than himself, and if God is not a deceiver, the world he perceives must be the "real" world and not an illusion. Thus in establishing the existence of God Descartes established the foundation of all knowledge.

In the fourth meditation, Descartes points out that even though ideas such as the self and God are perceived clearly and distinctly, humans make errors in their thinking because their intellects are finite and they possess free will. This is not an imperfection on God's part but merely a sign of the imperfection of human beings. Since he is not himself the Supreme Being, he says, he should not be surprised that he occasionally falls into error. The power of free will received from God is perfect, but sometimes the will surpasses the understanding, which causes error.

In the fifth meditation, Descartes discusses the essence of material things. To determine further whether anything certain can be known about material things, he presents a second argument for God's existence, which states that just as within the idea of a triangle is contained the concept of "three angles," the idea of "existence" is necessarily contained within the concept of "God." To speak of a "nonexistent God," he says, would be a contradiction, because the property of existence is a part of God's essence. The logical certainty of God's existence means that all other things depend upon God for their existence and that God, being perfect, could not be deceiving us about the external world. Thus Descartes feels assured that the certainty of the existence of the material world is guaranteed by the certainty of God's existence.

In the sixth and final meditation, Descartes completes his argument as to whether material things exist. He begins by differentiating between "extended things" out in the world, and "thinking things" in his mind. Descartes believes that it is certain that material things exist, and the fact that they can be described with the clear and distinct ideas of mathematics supports the certainty that there is an objective reality independent of the human mind. In addition, since God is not a deceiver, Descartes has no reason to believe that what he perceives as the material world is not really there.

What Descartes has established with this line of thinking is that there are actually two realities: "mind" and "matter." In terms of his own existence, his mind is distinct from his body; but if the human body is a material machine, how can the immaterial mind act upon it? Descartes simply answers that it does, like a captain who lives inside his ship. Perhaps, he suggests, God arranges the interaction of mind and body in mysterious ways, beyond our finite understanding.

Descartes was one of the most original thinkers of his time. By using mathematics as his model of certain knowledge, he felt that he had placed all of human knowledge on a firm foundation. Philosophy, he believed, like mathematics, must start with clear and simple truths and then advance toward more complex truths. By showing with absolute certainty that he exists—"I think, therefore I am"—and that God exists, he proceeded to show that the external world exists as well, even though humans may err in their perceptions about the world.

The English philosopher John Locke challenged Descartes' notion of innate ideas, believing instead that at birth human beings' minds are a tabula rasa or "blank slate"—devoid of any ideas of self or God. The German philosopher Immanuel Kant disputed Descartes' proofs for God's existence, especially the proof contained in the fifth meditation. It certainly does not follow, Kant claimed, that something can be asserted to exist merely because it can be conceived.

Descartes acknowledged his critics through his friend and fellow mathematician Marin Mersenne, who sent copies of Descartes' manuscript to contemporary philosophers and theologians. When their criticisms were returned to him, Descartes in turn commented on them and published the entire discussion along with *Meditations on First Philosophy*.

In breaking with Scholasticism, a mode of philosophical thinking that had lasted for almost four hundred years, Descartes was a major influence on every philosopher who came after him. By making a clean sweep of the philosophical landscape and attempting to build it from the foundation up, Descartes' philosophy raised many new difficulties and provoked a host of questions that have continued to challenge philosophers.

Raymond Frey

Bibliography:
Beardsley, Monroe C. *The European Philosophers from Descartes to Nietzsche*. New York: Modern Library, 1960. Contains an excellent introduction to Descartes' work.
"Descartes, René." In *The Encyclopedia of Philosophy*, edited by Paul Edwards. Vol. 2. New York: Macmillan, 1967. This article, in the standard reference work in the field, is clear and informative.
_____. *The Philosophical Works of Descartes*. Translated by Elizabeth S. Haldane and G. R. T. Ross. 2 vols. 1911. Reprint. New York: Cambridge University Press, 1979. An excellent translation of the complete works of Descartes.
Durant, Will. *The Age of Reason Begins*. New York: Simon & Schuster, 1961. Contains an excellent discussion (on pp. 636-647) of the historical significance of Descartes' life and work.
Hampshire, Stuart. *The Age of Reason: The Seventeenth Century Philosophers*. New York: Mentor Books, 1956. A popular work that includes a useful interpretive commentary on Descartes' philosophical method.

MELMOTH THE WANDERER

Type of work: Novel
Author: Charles Robert Maturin (1780-1824)
Type of plot: Gothic
Time of plot: Early nineteenth century
Locale: Ireland
First published: 1820

Principal characters:
JOHN MELMOTH, a young Irishman
MELMOTH THE WANDERER, young Melmoth's ill-starred ancestor
ALONZO MONCADA, a Spaniard shipwrecked in Ireland
YOUNG MELMOTH'S UNCLE

The Story:

In the autumn of 1816, John Melmoth, a student at Trinity College, Dublin, left his school to visit an uncle, his only surviving relative, who was dying. Melmoth's uncle was particularly glad to see his young nephew, for the old man was fearfully afraid of something that he had not revealed to anyone else. The uncle died and left all of his money and property to John Melmoth. A note at the end of the will told John Melmoth to destroy the hidden portrait of an earlier John Melmoth, a painting dated 1646, and also a packet of letters to be found in a secret drawer.

The day after his uncle's death, young John Melmoth made inquiries to learn whether his uncle had been a man of superstitious nature. He was told that the uncle was not a superstitious man, but that in recent months, he had insisted that a strange man appeared and disappeared about the manor house.

Young Melmoth destroyed the portrait as the will requested, but he opened the packet of manuscript, which contained a strange story about the man whose portrait he had destroyed. The document told how the original John Melmoth had been seen many times after his reported death in Germany and had been written of by an Englishman named Stanton, who had met Melmoth the Wanderer in Spain. The Wanderer, apparently angered by Stanton's curiosity, had prophesied that Stanton would be confined in Bedlam, although he was sane. The prediction having come true, the Wanderer appeared to Stanton in his misery and promised the miserable man his freedom if he would sell his soul to the devil. Stanton refused, and the Wanderer disappeared. Stanton wrote down his experiences and left the manuscript with the Melmoth family when he visited Ireland in order to discover more about the man who had tempted him.

After reading the manuscript, young Melmoth went to bed. That night he also saw the Wanderer. His strange ancestor paid the young man a visit and, as proof of his appearance, left a bruise on young Melmoth's wrist. The next night, a ship was wrecked on the Irish coast not far from the Melmoth estate. When young Melmoth and his retainers went to help rescue the sailors, Melmoth saw the Wanderer high on a rock overlooking the ruined ship and heard him laugh derisively. Young Melmoth tried to ascend the rock but fell into the sea, from which he was rescued by Alonzo Moncada, a Spaniard who had escaped from the doomed ship. Young Melmoth and the Spaniard returned to the manor house. A few days later, the Spaniard disclosed that he, too, knew the Wanderer.

Moncada told young Melmoth a series of stories about the activities of the Wanderer in Spain. The first story was about the Spaniard himself, who was an exile from his country, although he was descended from a noble family. Moncada had been born out of wedlock and thus could not inherit the ducal title of his ancestors. As a means of getting him out of the way so that his presence would not tarnish the proud name of his house, his family had destined him for a monastery. Moncada did not want to be a monk, but his wishes in the matter were ignored by his family, including his own mother.

After a few years, Moncada's brother had a change of heart; he tried to secure the monk's release from his vows and thereby called down the hatred of the Church upon both Alonzo and himself. Failing to secure a release legally, the brother then arranged for Moncada's escape. Monastery officials learned of the scheme, had the brother killed, and denounced Moncada to the Inquisition. While he lay in prison, Moncada was visited by Melmoth the Wanderer, who tempted him to secure release by selling his soul to Satan. Moncada refused; he escaped later when the prison of the Inquisition burned.

Moncada found refuge with an old Jewish doctor who had become interested in the history of the Wanderer. From the Jew, Moncada learned the story of still another person whom the Wanderer had tempted. The Jew told how Don Francisco di Aliaga, a Spanish nobleman, had lost his daughter in a shipwreck while she was still a baby. The child and her nurse had been cast upon an unknown and uninhabited island. The nurse died, but the baby grew up alone on the island to become a beautiful young woman. The Wanderer appeared to her on several occasions, each time tempting her to sell her soul to Satan in order to gain knowledge of the world. Strangely enough, the young woman and the Wanderer fell in love. She refused to marry him, however, under any auspices but those of the Church.

Soon afterward, the young woman was found and returned to her family in Spain. There the Wanderer saw her again. Their love was still great, and, unknown to anyone, they were married in what was actually a Satanic ceremony. Meanwhile, the Wanderer was conscience-stricken by fears that he would bring sorrow to the one he loved; he appeared to Don Aliaga and warned him, by stories of the Wanderer's Satanic activities, of dangers surrounding the woman.

The Wanderer told Don Aliaga of the temptation of a father whose children were starving, and of a young woman, during the reign of Charles II of England, who had been tempted in order to have the man she loved. In both cases, however, those tempted had refused to pay the price of damnation in return for earthly happiness. Don Aliaga recognized the meaning of these tales, but pressing business affairs kept him from acting at once.

When Don Aliaga finally returned to his home, he brought with him the young man he had selected to be his daughter's husband. Unknown to her father, however, the woman was about to give birth to a child by the Wanderer. When the Wanderer appeared to claim her at a masked ball, her connection with the accursed guest was revealed, and she was turned over to the Inquisition. She died shortly after giving birth to her child, and her dying words were the wish that she and the Wanderer would enter Heaven.

Such was the tale the Jewish doctor told to Alonzo Moncada, who was escaping from Spain when he was shipwrecked on the Irish coast. The tale ended, and the Wanderer suddenly appeared in the room with them. He told his horrified listeners that he had returned to his ancestral home to end his earthly wanderings. His fate had been to roam the earth for 150 years after his death under a terrible command to win souls for the devil. Everyone he had tempted, however, had refused to exchange earthly happiness for eternal damnation.

The Wanderer then asked that he be left alone to meet his destiny. A short time later, young Melmoth and the Spaniard heard strange voices and horrible noises in the room where they had left the Wanderer. The next morning, the room was empty. The only sign of the Wanderer was a scarf caught on a bush at the place where he had plunged or had been thrown into the sea.

Critical Evaluation:

Charles Robert Maturin's novel has been called by many literary scholars the greatest of the novels of terror that were so popular in English fiction during the early years of the nineteenth century. Other writers have admired and have been influenced by *Melmoth the Wanderer*, partly because of the striking qualities of the plot and partly because of the theme of the never-ending life that it describes. Among the admirers of the novel were Edgar Allan Poe, Dante Gabriel Rossetti, and Charles Baudelaire. Oscar Wilde, after being disgraced in the 1890's, took for himself the name of Sebastian Melmoth, which combined the idea of the wanderer with that of the arrow-pierced saint.

Maturin said in the book's preface that he was ashamed of appearing as a novelist, but that his profession as a clergyman did not pay him enough to avoid such shameful activities as writing novels. Although Maturin lamented the fact that he was forced to write *Melmoth the Wanderer* out of economic necessity (he was out of favor with the Church hierarchy, deeply in debt, and the sole support of eleven people), it would be a mistake to regard *Melmoth the Wanderer* simply as a potboiler written only for money. Even in the "unseemly character as a writer of romances," Maturin remained the preacher, and this novel stands as a profound social, moral, and religious statement—perhaps even a fictionalized sermon.

Structurally, it is the most complex of the important gothic novels. It is actually a series of stories set one into another like a nest of Chinese boxes. In the frame story, young John Melmoth visits his dying uncle and inherits, among other things, a vague story about a demoniac ancestor, also named John Melmoth, a picture of the man, and a manuscript, "The Tale of Stanton," which is the first of the novel's stories. Then he takes in a shipwrecked Spaniard, Alonzo Moncada, who tells his story, "The Tale of the Spaniard," in the center of which "The Tale of the Parricide" occurs. After recounting his own story, Moncada then retells "The Tale of the Indians," a story given to him for translation by an old Jew. Two additional narratives, "The Tale of Guzman's Family" and "The Tale of the Lover" are inserted within "The Tale of the Indians." These finished, Melmoth himself then returns to conclude the novel by paying his debt to the power of darkness.

Although different in substance, each narrative contains similar thematic elements; each tale, except "The Tale of the Parricide," climaxes at the point at which Melmoth intrudes upon the suffering victim and makes his diabolical offer. Maturin presents an elaborate theme and variation structure that continually develops and reinforces his ideas while tantalizing the reader with new and different shocks, torments, and sensations. The brooding presence of Melmoth is always in the background, moving in and out of the narratives; his story and fate are revealed in bits and pieces as the novel progresses.

The overriding thematic motif of the novel concerns the ways in which one's greatest natural inclinations—to worship God and to love—are perverted and distorted by individual weaknesses and institutional corruption. Several other notions reinforce these major ideas: the effects of an unchecked thirst for knowledge, the nature of madness and its relationship to fanaticism, the saving power of love, the family as a moral unit, the line between love and hate, human isolation and alienation, and the relationship between money and happiness.

In "The Tale of Stanton," Maturin introduces a number of these themes. Stanton is made vulnerable to Melmoth's appeal because he, too, has an insatiable curiosity about the forbidden. Fortunately for his soul, he rejects this side of himself when put to the test. As a result of his erratic behavior, Stanton also is made the victim of a familial betrayal when an unscrupulous relative has him committed to Bedlam—the first in a series of such betrayals. All of the stories involve either the destructive cruelties present in a bad family or the positive strengths of a good one.

In the madhouse scenes, Maturin begins his exploration of the moral and psychological nature of insanity that continues throughout the book. Although some of the inmates of the asylum are pure victims, most are fanatics who have simply pushed their religious or political proclivities to their logical conclusions. Maturin shows little sympathy for such madmen, although he recognizes that they differ from the rest of society only in being socially inconvenient; when madness is brought into socially acceptable institutions, Maturin suggests, it becomes not only tolerable but even dominant.

Maturin's analysis of the perversion of the religious impulse and the corruption of institutionalized religion—especially Roman Catholicism in Spain—is developed most completely in "The Tale of the Spaniard." Although anti-Catholicism, especially antimonasticism, had been a staple element of the gothic novel since Matthew Lewis' *The Monk* (1796), Maturin's treatment of the subject is probably the most intense and convincing, because he concentrates on the psychological damage of such institutional confinement rather than the more lurid and sensational accounts rendered by his contemporaries.

Under the rigid, arbitrary, artificial authority of such a life, all natural human capacities are stifled; the firmest faith is dissipated; the kindliest nature is thwarted; and the keenest intellect is stultified. The endlessly repetitive and absurd routine creates an ennui that is poisonous. Petty spite, gossip, and cruelty become the way of life. The smallest infractions of the silliest rules are treated as major crimes, and any person who exhibits the slightest trace of individualism becomes the monastery scapegoat.

The most blatant example of this institutional corruption can be seen in the parricide who is taken into the monastery in spite of, or because of, his criminal nature, and who works out his salvation by instigating the damnation of others. As a parricide, he represents the ultimate betrayal of the familial relationship; because, unlike Melmoth, he enjoys his deeds, he is the most extreme example of human evil. His sadism is the inevitable product of the social system he represents.

The extent of his diabolism and the most gothic scene in the novel is seen in the climax to his story. As he and Moncada wait huddled in the underground tunnel, he gleefully tells how he lured an errant couple into the same subterranean vault, nailed them in, and listened as, without food or water, their love turned to hate: "It was on the fourth night that I heard the shriek of the wretched female—her lover, in the agony of hunger, had fastened his teeth in her shoulder—that bosom on which he had so often luxuriated, became a meal to him now." Nowhere is Maturin's theme of the perversion of the natural into the destructive presented with more gruesome clarity.

Although some of the individual scenes may be impressive, it is the central character of Melmoth that makes the novel memorable. He is, in many ways, the supreme gothic hero-villain. Melmoth is damned, but, like Faustus, his damnation is not the product of an evil nature but of a questing spirit that simply cannot accept human limitations.

In "The Tale of the Indians," Melmoth's character is most clearly presented. The last two stories in the novel, "The Tale of Guzman's Family" and "The Tale of the Lover," add little to Melmoth's saga and are the least gothic, most sentimental, and dramatically weakest in the book. In "The Tale of the Indians," however, Melmoth himself assumes an active role and reveals truly human emotions. It is in this love affair between Melmoth and the native girl, Immalee, which resembles Goethe's "Faust-Margaret" story, that Melmoth's fate is actually decided: only the power of innocent love can save him from his chosen damnation—if he has the strength to accept it.

Since Immalee has grown up in an idyllic state of nature, she is ignorant of society's corrupting influences. It is Melmoth who introduces her to human decadence, although he is ambivalent in his feelings toward her from the beginning. He is reluctant to tempt her consciously, and his teachings are more of a response to her eagerness than an attempt to ensnare her. For her part, Immalee's spontaneous love for him causes her to desire further information about his world, even though this new knowledge proves painful.

Therefore, Melmoth becomes the tormented lover as well as the Satanic tempter. He would love her, but he fears that such love will damn her also. So he alternately woos her and thrusts her away; he entices her and warns her against himself. In the end, he succumbs to his role as tempter, but not before he has struggled desperately with a soul that he no longer believes he possesses. When Melmoth makes his awful proposal to her, he is damned; because Immalee refuses, she is saved.

The central irony is that her love could have saved them both. There is no bargain with the devil that cannot be abrogated by love. Melmoth's damnation comes, finally, not from his formal contract with Satan but from his disbelief in the power of the human spirit. Accepting the corruption he describes as the whole truth, he does not see the evidences of human worth around him: the love exhibited by the Walbergs in "The Tale of Guzman's Family," by Elinor Mortimer in "The Tale of the Lover," and, most of all, by Immalee.

As a result of his embracing evil, Melmoth's condemnation is inevitable; but, because of his lost potential, it is tragic. Therefore, for all the sensationalism and crudity characteristic of the gothic novel, it contains the elements of classical tragedy. No writer of gothic romances came closer to realizing that possibility than Charles Robert Maturin in *Melmoth the Wanderer*.

Keith Neilson

Bibliography:
Coughlan, Patricia. "The Recycling of *Melmoth:* A Very German Story." In *Literary Interrelations: Ireland, England, and the World*, edited by Wolfgang Zach and Heinz Kosok. Vol 2. Tübingen, Germany: Narr, 1987. Demonstrates the imaginative impact of *Melmoth the Wanderer* on contemporary authors. Versions of the story by Honoré de Balzac and James Clarence Mangan are given a detailed analysis. Highlights some of the novel's social and political implications.
Fowler, Kathleen. "Hieroglyphics in Fire: *Melmoth the Wanderer*." *Studies in Romanticism* 25, no. 4 (Winter, 1986): 521-539. Focuses on the novel's artistic methods and the relation between these methods and the novel's religious preoccupations. Discusses the use of the Book of Job in *Melmoth the Wanderer*.
Kiely, Robert. *The Romantic Novel in England*. Cambridge, Mass.: Harvard University Press, 1972. A significant contribution to the study of genres of the novel. Includes a chapter on *Melmoth the Wanderer*, emphasizing its religious and political elements. The novel's psychological interest and cultural implications are also assessed.
Kramer, Dale. *Charles Robert Maturin*. New York: Twayne, 1973. Succinct account of Maturin's life and career, and an extended consideration of *Melmoth the Wanderer*. Discusses the novel's folkloric dimension and the organizational principles governing the cohesiveness of the various tales.

THE MEMBER OF THE WEDDING

Type of work: Novel
Author: Carson McCullers (1917-1967)
Type of plot: Impressionistic realism
Time of plot: 1945
Locale: Georgia
First published: 1946

Principal characters:
> BERENICE SADIE BROWN, the black cook in the Addams household
> FRANKIE ADDAMS, a twelve-year-old girl
> MR. ADDAMS, her father
> JARVIS, her brother and a corporal in the army
> JOHN HENRY WEST, her cousin
> JANICE EVANS, the fiancée of Jarvis
> HONEY CAMDEN BROWN, Berenice's foster brother
> A SOLDIER

The Story:

In the summer of her twelfth year, Frankie Addams felt that she had become isolated and disconnected. She was a lanky girl with a crew haircut and skinned elbows. Some of the older girls she had played with the year before had a neighborhood club, and there were parties with boys on Saturday nights, but Frankie was not a participant. That summer, she got herself into so much trouble that at last she just stayed home with John Henry West, her little cousin, and Berenice Sadie Brown, the black cook. Through long, hot afternoons, they would sit in the dingy, sad Addams kitchen and play cards or talk until their words sounded strange, with little meaning.

Berenice Sadie Brown was short and black and the only mother Frankie had ever known, her own mother having died when she was born. The cook had been married four times, and during one of her marriages, she had lost an eye while fighting with a worthless husband. Now she owned a blue glass eye which always interested John Henry West. He was six and wore gold-rimmed glasses. Sometimes Frankie grew tired of him and sent him home. Sometimes she begged him to stay all night. Everything seemed so mixed up that she seldom knew what she wanted.

Then, on the last Friday in August, something happened that made life wonderful once more. Her brother Jarvis, a soldier home from Alaska, had come to dinner with Janice Evans, a girl who lived at Winter Hill. They were to be married there on Sunday, and Frankie and her father were going to the wedding. After dinner, Janice and Jarvis returned to Winter Hill. Mr. Addams went downtown to his jewelry store. Later, while she sat playing cards with Berenice and John Henry, Frankie thought of her brother and his bride. Winter Hill became all mixed up in her mind with snow and icy glaciers in Alaska.

Jarvis and Janice had brought Frankie a doll, but she had no time for dolls anymore. John Henry could have it. She wished her hair were not so short; she looked like one of the freaks from the Chattahoochee Exposition. Suddenly angry, she chased John Henry home. When Berenice teased her, saying that she was jealous of the wedding, Frankie declared that she was going to Winter Hill and never coming back. For a minute, she wanted to throw a kitchen knife at the black cook. Instead, she hurled it at the stairway door. Berenice went out with Honey Camden Brown, her foster brother, and T. T. Williams, her beau. Honey was not quite right in the head, and Berenice was always trying to keep him out of trouble. T. T. owned a black restaurant. Frankie did not realize that the cook's pity for the unhappy, motherless girl kept her from marrying T. T.

Left alone, Frankie wandered around the block to the house where John Henry lived with Aunt Pet and Uncle Eustace. Somewhere close by, a horn began to play a blues tune. Frankie felt so sad and lonely that she wanted to do something she had never done before. She thought again of Jarvis and Janice. She was going to be a member of the wedding; after the ceremony, the three of them would go away together. She was not plain Frankie Addams any longer. She would call herself F. Jasmine Addams, and she would never feel lonely or afraid again.

The next morning, with Mr. Addams' grunted permission, Frankie went downtown to buy a new dress and shoes. On the way, she found herself telling everyone she met about the wedding. That was how she happened to go into the Blue Moon, a cheap café where she knew children were not allowed. F. Jasmine Addams, however, was no longer a child, and so she went in to tell the Portuguese proprietor about the wedding. The only other person in the café was a red-headed soldier from a nearby army post. Frankie scarcely noticed him at the time, but she remembered him later when she saw him on the street. By that time, he was drunk and trying to buy an organ-grinder's monkey. The soldier bought Frankie a beer and asked her to meet him that night at the Blue Moon.

When Frankie finally arrived home, she learned that Berenice and John Henry were also to attend the wedding. An aged kinsman of the Wests had died, and Aunt Pet and Uncle Eustace were going to the funeral at Opelika. Berenice, dismayed when she saw the orange silk evening dress, the silver hair ribbon, and the silver slippers Frankie had bought to wear at the wedding, tried, without much success, to alter the dress for the gawky young girl. Afterward, they began to talk about the dead people they had known. Berenice told about Ludie Freeman, the first husband she had truly loved. The story of Ludie and the three other husbands made them all feel lonesome and sad. Berenice held the two children on her knees as she tried to explain to them the simple wisdom life had taught her. They began to sing spirituals in the half-dark of the dingy kitchen.

Frankie did meet the soldier that night. First, she went with John Henry to Big Mama's house and had her palm read. Afterward, she told John Henry to go on home; she did not want him to know she was meeting someone at the Blue Moon. The soldier bought two drinks. Frankie was afraid to taste hers. He asked her to go up to his room. Frightened when he tried to pull her down beside him on the bed, she picked up a glass pitcher and hit him over the head. Then she climbed down the fire escape and ran all the way home. She was glad to get into bed with no one but John Henry by her side.

The wedding next day turned into a nightmare for Frankie. Everything was lovely until the time came for the bride and groom to leave. When they carried their bags out to the car, she ran to get her own suitcase. Then they told her, as kindly as possible, that they were going away alone. She grasped the steering wheel and wept until someone dragged her away. Riding home on the bus, she cried all the way. Berenice promised her a bridge party with grown-up refreshments as soon as school opened, but Frankie knew that she would never be happy again. That night, she tried to run away. Not knowing where else to go, she went to the Blue Moon. There a policeman found her and sent for her father.

By November, however, Frankie had almost forgotten the wedding. Other things had happened. John Henry had died of meningitis. Honey Camden Brown, drug-crazed, had tried to hold up a drugstore and was in jail. Mary Littlejohn had become her best, real friend. She and her father were leaving the old house and going to live with Aunt Pet and Uncle Eustace in a new suburb. Berenice, waiting to see the last of the furniture taken away, was sad, for she knew that Frankie would depend on her no longer. Frankie—she wanted to be called Frances—was thirteen.

Critical Evaluation:

All of Carson McCullers' fiction turns on the theme of loneliness and longing as the inescapable condition of humanity. In *The Member of the Wedding*, the issues of the larger world are reflected in the experiences of the twelve-year-old girl trapped in the confusion of her own adolescence. The novel tells the story of several decisive days in the life of Frankie Addams, and much of the meaning of her plight is made clear in her random talk with Berenice Sadie Brown and John Henry West as the three sit around the table in the kitchen of the Addams house. Frankie seizes upon her soldier brother's approaching wedding to will herself into the social community, only to discover that the bride and groom must by necessity reject her and that she must learn to fend for herself. In the story of Frankie Addams, the writer has reduced the total idea of moral isolation to a fable of simple outlines and a few eloquently dramatic scenes, set against a background of adolescent mood and discovery familiar to everyone. It is easy enough to understand why this novel has also been a success in dramatic form. The play of the same name, written by McCullers, is a sympathetic study of inward conflicts. It received two Donaldson Awards and the New York Drama Critics Circle Award in 1950.

Throughout her career as a novelist, short-story writer, and playwright, McCullers explored the human condition from several perspectives, but all with the common focus of loneliness and dissatisfaction. *The Heart Is a Lonely Hunter* (1940) reveals a deaf-mute's isolation in a Southern town, and it draws parallels to the phenomenon of fascism. *Reflections in a Golden Eye* (1941) also takes place in the South, but *The Member of the Wedding* explores anxieties in finer detail. *The Ballad of the Sad Café and Collected Short Stories* (1952), a collection of short stories, includes the famous novella of the title, which was dramatized by Edward Albee in 1963, twenty years after it was first published. Her last two works were *The Square Root of Wonderful* (1957), a play, and a novel, *Clock Without Hands* (1961). McCullers' unpublished works, including some early poetry, appeared posthumously in 1971 under the title *The Mortgaged Heart*.

Although *The Member of the Wedding* certainly deals with themes of loneliness and dissatisfaction, the story is quite interesting as a discussion of the means through which a particular individual attempts to escape these isolating emotions. This psychological novel is enhanced by McCullers' masterful handling of language and point of view. Although the narrative is not in the first person, the language makes it clear that Frankie Addams' viewpoint is of primary concern. The result is that one is able both to observe Frankie objectively and at the same time to appreciate her emotions immediately. Frankie's feelings are, in addition, juxtaposed with the intrusion of adult observation (most often from Berenice and Mr. Addams) so that the reader has a realistic synthesis of information. The structural result is triangular. The adult view cannot comprehend the adolescent because it has grown beyond that stage. The adolescent view, in turn, cannot yet encompass the adult. The reader completes the triangle, gaining the adolescent view through Frankie, and adding the adult view through appreciating the irony of Frankie's observations of adults.

Frankie, Berenice, and John Henry, despite apparent enmities, form a tribunal, sharing experiences and opinions and evaluating them both literally and symbolically, and each is essential in his role in the tribunal. Frankie, literally, is the causing factor of the group's existence: Berenice is hired to care for her, and John Henry is present because Frankie wants juvenile companionship to counter that of Berenice. Yet, although she realizes that she is not yet capable of understanding the activities of the adult world, Frankie, aided by John Henry, symbolizes the almost divine nature often assigned to the child. Frankie knows certain truths, as Berenice occasionally confirms in bewilderment, because the girl's mind has not yet been spoiled by the mundane concerns that obscure those truths. Her almost innate, although selective, knowledge is part of a literary and philosophical ideology most clearly typified by the Wordsworthian view of children. Yet Frankie's strongest understanding is also the most ironic: She realizes that she is incomplete and is terrified by reminders of that fact. In her earnest efforts to belong, to be completed, she is driving herself toward adulthood, in which one loses the innate knowledge she possesses.

Berenice, one of McCullers' most interesting characters, serves multiple functions. Just as she is employed to care for Frankie in many ways, she is also the pivotal character upon whom the novel depends on several levels of development. In simple terms, she is a counterexample of Frankie's search to belong and to love. Although McCullers' familiar theme of such unending search persists in Berenice, she illustrates that love, even when directed toward a vague objective, has the eventual effect of grace. In addition, she is a surrogate mother upon whom Frankie depends, made more credible by being representative of the black parent figure of many Southern novels. Frankie is locked into dependence upon Berenice, but it is dependence from a distance; although she longs to be independent of Berenice and all other authority figures, Frankie knows intuitively that she is not old enough to ignore Berenice. She knows the woman has function in her life, has necessary information to which she has not yet been exposed. She does not want to block Berenice out entirely (while the servant speaks to her, Frankie puts her fingers in her ears, but not enough to prevent Berenice's voice from reaching her) since if Frankie did so she would have to confront life later as an adult without sufficient data. Frankie knows instinctively that ignoring Berenice is only self-defeating. Berenice is, therefore, like an oracle; and she comes from the ancient literary tradition of the blind or one-eyed person who speaks the truth clearly because of his missing vision. Berenice has a glass eye ("glass" and "truth" are related etymologically in Latin); so Berenice sees truth through her glass eye, not through her physically functioning one. McCullers is thus able to elevate the group in the kitchen to mythic dimensions: Berenice is the oracle; John Henry is her acolyte; and Frankie is the pilgrim-initiate.

By emphasizing Frankie's progressive learning and by concentrating primarily on the emotions and experiences of only three days in Frankie's life, Carson McCullers achieves the effect of gradually increasing the reader's expectations. By the end of *The Member of the Wedding*, the reader has been led to believe that the day before the wedding is Frankie's "last afternoon" in town—if not literally, then at least figuratively. This increasing momentum, however, is not followed by a fulfillment of expectation; Frankie is essentially unchanged by the trauma of disappointment. It is suddenly apparent that the initiation of youth into adulthood through artificial, specific rites is a myth. The search for belonging is an unending one; it is simply one's orientation toward that search that can change by the natural process of maturing. In fact, as Berenice's life illustrates, the childlike element of selectively believing in salvation can be concomitantly protective, making both life and the search for social identity not only possible but also bearable.

"Critical Evaluation" by Bonnie Fraser

Bibliography:

Bloom, Harold, ed. *Carson McCullers*. New York: Chelsea House, 1986. Barbara A. White's "Loss of Self in *The Member of the Wedding*" interprets Frankie as a confused tomboy neither wanting to remain a child nor to become a woman. Excellent source for discussion of novella.

Cook, Richard M. *Carson McCullers*. New York: Frederick Ungar, 1975. A biography containing a twenty-two-page chapter on *The Member of the Wedding*, along with a helpful chronology and index. Defends the novelist's concern with human isolation.

Evans, Oliver. *The Ballad of Carson McCullers: A Biography*. New York: Coward, McCann, 1966. Encompasses incisive comments on McCullers' work and a detailed chapter on *The Member of the Wedding*, citing its autobiographical nature and analyzing disparate critical reviews. Valuable for detailing connections between McCullers' life and fiction.

Graver, Lawrence. *Carson McCullers*. Minneapolis: University of Minnesota Press, 1969. Helpfully condensed discussion of the author's life and work. Views *The Member of the Wedding* as a journey of adolescent initiation, combining early dissatisfaction with jubilant hope and disillusionment with wisdom about life's limits.

McDowell, Margaret. *Carson McCullers*. Boston: Twayne, 1980. Insightful discussion of *The Member of the Wedding* that stresses the novelist's thematic concerns with time as it relates to life's stages, and isolation and the fear of independence applied to the novella's three major characters.

MEMED, MY HAWK

Type of work: Novel
Author: Yashar Kemal (Yaşar Kemal Gökçeli, 1922-   )
Type of plot: Folklore
Time of plot: Early twentieth century
Locale: Turkey
First published: İnce Memed, 1955 (English translation, 1961)

> *Principal characters:*
> SLIM MEMED, a brigand
> ABDI AGHA, a cruel landowner
> JABBAR, Memed's comrade
> LAME ALI, a skillful tracker
> HATCHE, Memed's fiancée
> IRAZ, Hatche's cell mate
> SERGEANT ASIM, the police chief

The Story:

In a village called Deyirmenoluk, located in the Taurus Mountains of Turkey, Slim Memed and his mother, Deuneh, lived at the mercy of their cruel landlord, Abdi Agha, who terrorized them and took two-thirds of their crops annually. Unable to endure the Agha's beatings, Memed fled from his village, escaping over the mountains to the ranch of Old Süleyman. For several weeks, he lived as Süleyman's adopted son, herding goats and enjoying himself. One day, however, he drove his goats too far, and encountered a man from his village. News soon spread that Memed was alive, and Abdi Agha went to Süleyman's ranch and forced the boy to return. As punishment for Memed's disobedience, the family had to forfeit three-fourths of their crops, and they nearly starved that winter.

Several years passed, and the oppression continued. As he matured into manhood, Memed grew bitter and callous under the Agha's reign of terror. Only fifteen-year-old Hatche, the most beautiful girl in the village, could inspire tenderness in the young man. Soon after Abdi Agha announced the girl's engagement to his nephew, Memed and Hatche eloped.

They made love in the hollow of a rock during a rainstorm. Furious at Memed's disobedience, the Agha enlisted Lame Ali, a skillful tracker, to find the couple. In a violent encounter in the forest, Memed wounded Abdi Agha and killed his nephew, then fled from the scene. Hatche returned to the village, only to be arrested by the authorities for the nephew's murder. She was taken to the nearest town and imprisoned.

Meanwhile, Memed made his way to Süleyman's ranch, where he received a warm welcome from his old friend. Advised by Süleyman to hide in the mountains, Memed joined Mad Durdu's band of mountain brigands. Durdu was notorious for stopping travelers on the road, ordering them to strip naked, and stealing their money and underclothing. Although Memed did not approve of these tactics, he obeyed his leader. As Durdu grew more reckless, however, Memed began to worry. In one bloody exchange with the police, who had followed the light of Durdu's fire to the camp, several of Durdu's men were killed or wounded, and Memed barely escaped. When Durdu later tried to rob Kerimoghlu, the proud leader of a group of nomads, Memed intervened, and Durdu vowed to avenge the insult.

Accompanied by two comrades, Jabbar and Sergeant Rejep, Memed embarked upon a career as an independent brigand, but he did not have the heart to rob groveling travelers. He decided to return to Deyirmenoluk and punish Abdi Agha. From his mother's friend in the village, Memed learned that the Agha had killed his mother and arranged for Hatche's imprisonment. Memed and his comrades stormed the Agha's house but found only the Agha's two wives and children at home. Sergeant Rejep killed one of the wives and was going to kill the children, but Memed stopped him, preferring to exact revenge on Abdi Agha himself. By sparing the family's lives, Memed earned the respect of the villagers.

Memed then summoned Lame Ali and ordered him to track down Abdi Agha, who had gone into hiding after he had learned that Memed had become a brigand. Feeling guilty for betraying Memed and Hatche, Lame Ali led Memed and his comrades to Abdi Agha's hiding place in a distant village. In an attempt to burn the Agha out of his hiding place, the three brigands set fire to the entire village, destroying it. The villagers pursued them into the mountains, where Sergeant Rejep died from a neck wound that he had received earlier. After returning to Deyirmenoluk to resume his life, Memed learned that Abdi Agha was still alive. He and Jabbar returned to the mountains for their safety.

In the village of Vayvay, Abdi Agha had sought refuge with another powerful Agha, Ali Safa Bey, who controlled a band of mountain brigands led by Kalayji. Ali Safa had promised to use Kalayji to destroy Memed. Kalayji sent Horali, who had been a member of Durdu's gang, to lead the unsuspecting Memed into a trap. Discerning the ploy, however, Memed and Jabbar killed Horali and Kalayji. Across the countryside the news spread that Memed had defeated Ali Safa's man. In the countless retellings of the feat, Memed grew larger than life, until he was a legend. Big Osman from Vayvay started referring to Memed as "my hawk." He collected a large sum of money from his fellow villagers, who were tired of being oppressed by Ali Safa, and delivered it to Memed and Jabbar on their mountaintop.

Jabbar and Memed parted company when Memed decided to visit Hatche in prison. Later, as the police were transporting Hatche to another prison, Memed ambushed them and single-handedly freed his fiancée and her friend Iraz. The three fugitives retreated to a cave on top of Mount Alidagh and were supplied periodically by Lame Ali and Kerimoghlu. At Abdi Agha's prodding, the government sent a former brigand, Black Ibrahim, and a police officer, Sergeant Asim, to arrest Memed. During a shootout on Alidagh, Hatche gave birth to a son, and Memed surrendered to Sergeant Asim, who took pity on the new father and allowed him to escape.

Abdi Agha was furious and frightened. He wrote letters to the government, who then sent Captain Faruk after Memed. In yet another shootout, Faruk killed Hatche. Memed, who managed to escape, gave his son to Iraz and ensured Hatche's proper burial. Then he found Lame Ali and learned about Abdi Agha's hiding place. Despite a general amnesty granted to criminals by the Turkish government, Memed went to the town where Abdi Agha was hiding and killed him. A fugitive once more, Memed returned to the mountains, never to be seen again.

Critical Evaluation:

A translation of the first part of *İnce Memed* (which means "Slim" or "Thin" Memed), *Memed, My Hawk* is important as one of the few Turkish novels to attract attention in Europe and America. In this folktale, Yashar Kemal depicts a low-born man with compassion and respect. His protagonist, Memed, is a larger-than-life folk hero, who has been likened to Robin Hood because he steals from the rich and gives to the poor. Like a majestic hawk, Memed swoops down on the cruel aghas (lords), frustrating their greed. He is able to evade capture for so long because he has the support of the village people. Unlike the other brigands, who rob and humiliate indiscriminately, Memed punishes selectively, never forgetting his roots in the village. Kemal's novel often reads like a courtesy book for brigands. Through example and contrast, and sometimes even dialogue, the reader is shown the proper way to resist institutionalized corruption and oppression. One should not follow the example of the brigand Durdu, who terrorizes not only government officials and powerful landowners, but also farmers, women, and children. He robs his victims of their honor as well as their purses, sending men home naked to their families and kidnapping and raping village women. Kalayji, another brigand, sells himself as a hired gun to a wealthy *agha*, in effect becoming an instrument of oppression. Memed, on the other hand, engages in moral terrorism, never robbing for fun or mere profit, always championing the rights of the poor.

The close association between the people and the land is an important theme in *Memed, My Hawk.* Most of the characters are tenant farmers, whose survival depends on the fickle weather, the quality of the land, and the caprices of the landowners. The farmers are slaves to the *aghas* who own the land. Only by owning the land can the farmers free themselves. Freedom, then, is integrally related to property. Early in the novel, the author proclaims that people, like trees, require rich soil in which to grow strong and tall. The Taurus Mountains consist of dry, rocky soil, covered with thistles, and yield only stunted trees with gnarled branches. The same can be said of Memed, whose growth has been stunted by his meager diet, the constant toil of plowing, and the Agha's physical abuse. Only in rebellion against Abdi Agha does he grow "as tall as a poplar." The harsh terrain of the Taurus Mountains symbolizes the *agha*'s oppressive rule over the villagers. It is significant that when the *agha* dies, the villagers take his property and burn the thistles to make the land more suitable for cultivation.

Western readers may have difficulty understanding the behavior and motivation of the characters, who are products of a different culture. In many Western societies, premarital sex is less uncommon than it is in Turkish society, particularly Turkish rural communities. When Hatche runs away with Memed and yields to him sexually in the woods, her behavior is atypical and extremely courageous, indicating that she must love Memed very much. The concepts of honor and hospitality are also different in Turkey. By forcing his male victims to give him their underpants and sending them home naked, Durdu is not merely embarrassing them, but also impinging upon their honor. It is for this reason that the nomad leader, Kerimoghlu, refuses to strip in front of his family, although he knows that Durdu may kill him. Throughout the novel, Memed encounters strangers who welcome him as if he were a family member. They offer him food and a place to sleep, and become offended if he declines their hospitality. This behavior may be alien to readers who are not accustomed to being treated so warmly by strangers or who are unfamiliar with the role that food plays in Turkish hospitality.

Other cultural differences may prevent Western readers from appreciating the narrator's irony and various nuances in meaning. For example, when Kalayji kills his cousin Bekir during his wedding celebration, "[t]he bride's hands were red with henna, the marriage not yet consummated." It is customary in Turkey for the bride to paint her hands red with henna before her marriage as a sign of her happiness. In this context, however, the red hands ironically become associated with her husband's blood and the tragedy of his death. Later, the old woman Hürü dyes her hair red with henna in celebration of the Agha's death. This, too, is ironic.

Edward A. Malone

Bibliography:
Evin, Ahmet Ö., ed. *Edebiyat: A Journal of Comparative and Middle Eastern Literatures* 5,

nos. 1/2 (1980). The entire issue is devoted to Kemal and his work. Four articles discuss *Memed, My Hawk* in detail.

Prokosch, Frederic. "Robin Hood in Anatolia." *Saturday Review* 44, no. 3 (August 19, 1961): 19, 55. Claims that the novel fails as social criticism but succeeds as myth.

Rau, Santha Rama. "Robin Hood of the Taurus Mountains." *The New York Times Book Review*, June 11, 1961, 6-7. Praises the novel for its romantic and epic qualities.

Theroux, Paul. "Turkish Delight." *The New York Times Book Review*, July 10, 1977, 40. In a review of *They Burn the Thistles* (1972), which is a sequel to *Memed, My Hawk*, Theroux compares Kemal to William Faulkner and laments the Turkish author's relatively small audience in America compared to his audiences in Turkey and Europe.

"Turkish Robin Hood." *Time* 77, no. 25 (June 16, 1961): 90. A representative review of the novel when it was first published in the United States. Touts Memed as a latter-day Robin Hood and speculates about the influence of the author's life on the narrative.

MEMENTO MORI

Type of work: Novel
Author: Muriel Spark (1918-   )
Type of plot: Psychological realism
Time of plot: 1950's
Locale: London, England
First published: 1959

Principal characters:
>DAME LETTIE COLSTON, a pioneer penal reformer
>GODFREY COLSTON, her brother
>CHARMIAN COLSTON, Godfrey's wife
>MISS JEAN TAYLOR, a resident in a nursing home
>MRS. MABEL PETTIGREW, Godfrey's housekeeper
>ALEC WARNER, a retired sociologist
>GUY LEET, a poet
>PERCY MANNERING, a poet
>OLIVE MANNERING, his granddaughter
>HENRY MORTIMER, a retired police inspector

The Story:

Each time Dame Lettie Colston answered the telephone, the anonymous caller announced, "Remember, you must die." Unnerved by the calls, the old woman contacted the police, but they could not identify the caller. Lettie's brother, Godfrey, was too preoccupied with his own problems to be sympathetic. He was exasperated by the mental deterioration his wife, Charmian, had suffered after her stroke.

Miss Jean Taylor, a resident in a nursing home, reflected upon the many years of her work as companion for Charmian Colston, the famous novelist. Now she was trapped in a ward where the other women exhibited signs of memory loss, the staff patronized the residents, and the head nurse brutalized and demoralized the residents.

Godfrey and Dame Lettie attended a memorial service for Lisa Brooke, who had died after suffering a stroke. Godfrey had had an affair with Lisa many years before. He was surprised to see an old acquaintance, Guy Leet, at the service. Guy was now an old man severely afflicted with arthritis. Mrs. Pettigrew, Lisa Brooke's housekeeper, had been named beneficiary of her estate. No one knew that Mrs. Pettigrew had blackmailed Lisa Brooke for many years because of Lisa's affair with Godfrey Colston.

Alec Warner was fascinated with the problems of old age. When he had turned seventy, he had begun the immense project of compiling records of old people's physical condition, routines, attitudes, and tastes. Many years earlier he had loved Jean Taylor, but when he was advised to marry someone of his own class he had ended his relationship with her.

Dame Lettie hired Mrs. Pettigrew to help take care of Charmian. Mrs. Pettigrew planned to blackmail Godfrey just as she had blackmailed Lisa Brooke. She was frustrated when she found out that Guy Leet, who had secretly married Lisa Brooke many years ago, would inherit Lisa's estate.

Jean Taylor faced a new challenge in the nursing home. Although the malicious head nurse was released, her successor admitted eight severely demented residents to the ward. Their wails and bizarre behaviors upset Jean and the other longtime residents.

About six months after that, Godfrey Colston received one of the anonymous calls. Godfrey often visited Olive Mannering, a young woman, in order to satisfy his sexual longings; he paid her for raising her skirt and allowing him to gaze upon her thigh. Godfrey was preoccupied by the threat of Mrs. Pettigrew's blackmail, and he told Olive about it.

Charmian, whose memory had begun to improve over the winter, announced that she wished to move to a nursing home outside London. When she received the anonymous caller's message, "Remember, you must die," she responded cheerfully, saying that she often thought of her death.

Olive Mannering told Alec Warner about Mrs. Pettigrew's plot. When he returned home, Alec became the third person to receive the anonymous telephone message that day. He immediately made notes in his file cards about the event.

Retired Chief Inspector Henry Mortimer welcomed those who had received the telephone calls to his home to review the evidence. He noted that each person who had received a call attributed different characteristics to the caller. Mortimer believed the caller was Death himself, but he didn't reveal that opinion to his guests. Instead, he advised them to make up their own minds as to the identity of the culprit.

Mrs. Pettigrew discovered a newspaper item reporting that Olive Mannering was to marry an old widower, Lisa Brooke's brother-in-law. Mrs. Pettigrew, realizing that Godfrey had been visiting Olive on his mysterious outings, blackmailed him. Feeling helpless, Godfrey allowed her to drag him to his lawyer's office to make changes in his will.

Jean Taylor wanted to free Godfrey from Mrs. Pettigrew's domination, so she told Alec Warner to tell Godfrey that Charmian had had an affair with Guy Leet for many years. Alec did so, and Godfrey dismissed Mrs. Pettigrew.

Dame Lettie became increasingly fearful about the intentions of the anonymous caller and shut herself up in her house. One night, she surprised a burglar and was bludgeoned to death. Her body was not discovered for four days.

Guy Leet visited Charmian in the nursing home outside London. He still expected to inherit Lisa Brooke's estate. When he returned home, Percy Mannering was waiting for him. The two men began to argue about poetry. The telephone rang and the caller asked for Percy Mannering, telling him "Remember, you must die." The two men stopped bickering and spent the evening together. Percy was inspired to write a sonnet on mortality.

During the investigation of Dame Lettie's murder, the police, with the help of Henry Mortimer, discovered that Lisa Brooke had already been married when she married Guy Leet. Her real husband, who had been a patient in a mental hospital for forty years, became the benefactor of Lisa Brooke's estate.

Alec Warner, who had visited patients in that hospital as part of his gerontological research, lost all of his gerontological files when his apartment caught fire. Four months later, he visited Jean Taylor, who encouraged him to begin his research anew. He felt unable to do so. He told Jean that Lisa Brooke's mentally ill husband had died. Now Mrs. Pettigrew would inherit Lisa's fortune.

Critical Evaluation:

Although Muriel Spark's novel about a stern and unyielding schoolteacher, *The Prime of Miss Jean Brodie* (1961), is her most popular and well-known work, many critics consider *Memento Mori* to be her greatest achievement. In this novel Spark creates a diverse cast of characters, almost all of whom are more than seventy years old, and examines the way these individuals face their own mortality. Unlike other novels that treat the experience of aging—

among them John Updike's *The Poorhouse Fair* (1959), William Trevor's *The Old Boys* (1964), and Kingsley Amis' *Ending Up* (1974)—Spark's novel creates a community of older adults who are unified in their response to a particular crisis. Most of the characters have received one or more telephone calls from an anonymous person who says simply, "Remember, you must die."

Spark uses the conventions of the detective story to generate mystery and suspense. Most of the characters think of themselves as targets of harassment. They become uneasy and fearful, and some turn to the police to solve the mystery. Dame Letty, for instance, is sure the caller is a threat to her safety, and she is overcome by terror as the calls continue. Her outcry and the concern the others feel lead to a police investigation, but Chief Inspector Mortimer is unable to solve the case. In fact, he believes the caller to be Death himself and that the purpose of the calls is to remind people to lead a rich, full life while they are alive.

The detective story mystery is the structural underpinning of the novel, but the identity of the anonymous caller is never revealed. Spark is more interested in the moral and ethical dilemmas that face human beings. In the ways her characters respond to the anonymous message, Spark reveals their attitudes toward aging and life in general; she also reveals such human attributes as vanity, piety, mean-spiritedness, self-absorption, loneliness, hardihood, and rebellion. Dame Letty and Godfrey fail to reflect on their own mortality and ignore reminders of their finiteness. They prefer to continue their comfortable existences without inconvenience or interruption. Mrs. Pettigrew is so self-centered and so intent on manipulating others that she succeeds in denying she ever received one of the calls. Percy Mannering responds to his call with intellectual detachment, viewing the message as an opportunity for poetic inspiration and writing a sonnet on mortality. These responses reveal the extent to which some people are unable to face the implications of their mortality.

An important stylistic device in the novel is Spark's use of satire in describing the pompous self-absorption of those characters who take their lives and their old age far too seriously. Alec Warner is an amateur gerontologist, obsessed with recording details of temperature, pulse, and behaviors in old age. Dame Letty Colston devotes her time to revising her will in order to punish her relatives for lapses of affection. The two old poets, Guy Leet and Percy Mannering, harbor grudges against each other. The housekeeper, Mrs. Pettigrew, is determined to make her fortune—by whatever means necessary—before she retires. Godfrey Colston pursues sexual fantasies. Spark deflates these characters' egos by poking fun at their idiosyncracies, foibles, failings, pettiness, fears, insecurities, and manipulative ways.

Religion plays an important role in the novel, though most of the characters in *Memento Mori* lack a specific connection to religious faith. Most of them are officially members of the Anglican faith, but their lives are dominated by secular priorities—making money, finding fame, getting even, seeking comfort and security, and enjoying their leisure. Religious and spiritual concerns are not a part of their daily lives. Two of the characters, Charmian Piper and Jean Taylor, are Roman Catholic—in fact, Jean converted to Catholicism during the time she was a lady's companion to Charmian—and, unlike the other characters, these two women derive comfort and security from their faith. When Charmian receives her telephone call, she admits to the caller that she thinks often of death and is unafraid. Jean Taylor never receives one of the anonymous calls, probably because she is depicted as a woman who does not need a reminder of her mortality. Although she suffers from arthritis and often experiences loneliness as a resident of a nursing home, she does not despair. She tolerates her difficult situation and views the senile old woman in the nursing home as her personal "memento mori."

Charmian Piper and Jean Taylor, along with Chief Inspector Mortimer, are the moral centers of the novel. When Charmian gradually recovers her mental powers and decides to move to a nursing home rather than remain with her husband she expresses both her acceptance of the limitations of old age and her freedom to make decisions about her own welfare. Jean Taylor, too, accepts her fate. She even feels a contentment and appreciation for her life in the nursing home, where she feels a part of a community. Her understanding of the anonymous caller is similar to Mortimer's; he believes that the message is an exhortation to self-enrichment and equanimity in the face of impending mortality.

Robert E. Yahnke

Bibliography:
Hynes, Joseph. *The Art of the Real: Muriel Spark's Novels.* Cranbury, N.J.: Associated University Presses, 1988. Examines the novel's satirical portrayal of old age and the relationships between humor and religious themes.
Kemp, Peter. *Muriel Spark.* London: Paul Elek, 1974. A thorough treatment of the novel's characters and themes. Analyzes the responses of the major characters to the anonymous telephone caller's message and examines the subtlety of the author's depiction of old age.
Page, Norman. *Muriel Spark.* New York: St. Martin's Press, 1990. An excellent overview of the novel's characters, plot, and themes. Compares the novel to others that have treated themes of aging. Considers the novel as a parody of the conventional detective story.
Richmond, Velma Bourgeois. *Muriel Spark.* New York: Frederick Ungar, 1984. Analyzes characters and their relationships. Considers the conflicts of characters as part of tension between the earthly and the eternal, between human desires and God's will. Provides a historical perspective on the remembrance of death since the Middle Ages.
Whittaker, Ruth. *The Faith and Fiction of Muriel Spark.* New York: St. Martin's Press, 1982. A concise survey. Examines the theme of religious faith and the supernatural. Considers *Memento Mori* as a pessimistic treatment of human failings that shows the redemptive power of faith in helping some of the characters to find meaning in their lives.

MEMOIRS OF A PHYSICIAN

Type of work: Novel
Author: Alexandre Dumas, *père* (1802-1870), with Auguste Maquet (1813-1888)
Type of plot: Historical
Time of plot: Eighteenth century
Locale: Paris and environs
First published: Mémoires d'un médecin, 1846-1848 (English translation, 1846)

> *Principal characters:*
> BARON DE TAVERNEY
> PHILIPPE, his son
> ANDRÉE, his daughter
> GILBERT, in love with Andrée
> KING LOUIS XV of France
> MONSIEUR DE CHOISEUL, the king's minister
> MADAME JEANNE DU BARRY, the king's favorite
> ARMAND DE RICHELIEU, a political opportunist
> JOSEPH BALSAMO, also known as COUNT DE FENIX, a sorcerer
>   and revolutionary
> LORENZA FELICIANI, his wife
> ALTHOTAS, his instructor in magic
> MONSIEUR DE SARTINES, a lieutenant of police
> JEAN-JACQUES ROUSSEAU, the philosopher

The Story:

At the court of Louis XV of France, the Duc de Richelieu plotted with Madame du Barry, the king's favorite, to replace Monsieur de Choiseul as the king's minister. They consulted Count de Fenix, who turned out to be the reputed sorcerer Joseph Balsamo; ten years earlier the necromancer had predicted that Madame du Barry would one day be queen of France. Balsamo used his wife Lorenza as an unwilling medium for his sorcery. Through her he was able to give Richelieu and Madame du Barry compromising information contained in a letter sent by the Duchess of Grammont to her brother, de Choiseul, showing that the minister was encouraging the revolt of parliament against the king and attempting to bring about war with England. Fortified with this information, Richelieu forced the king to dismiss his minister.

The philosopher Rousseau, standing in the crowd gathered outside the palace after the king at a "bed of justice" had defied parliament, was urged to attend a secret meeting at which he would be initiated into the mystic order of Freemasonry. Rousseau declared he could do more for the world by not joining the order. The chief of the council, who was Balsamo, read a communication from Swedenborg which warned them of a traitor in their midst.

In order to demonstrate to the surgeon Marat, a member of the secret fraternity, that body and soul can be separated and then reunited and that the soul has a greater knowledge than the body, Balsamo hypnotized one of Marat's patients. As the patient's crushed leg was amputated, Balsamo made the patient sing. He also hypnotized Marat's maid, drew from her an admission of the theft of her master's watch, and, still in the condition of sleep, made her repeat the contents of a letter she could not read while awake.

Andrée, daughter of the impoverished Baron de Taverney, had recently been saved from the violence of a mob by Gilbert, a son of the people, but she was ignorant of this circumstance because Balsamo had brought her home in his carriage. After the woman had been settled at the Trianon through the request of the dauphiness, her beauty charmed the king completely, and he commissioned Richelieu to present her with a necklace worth several million livres, but she declined the gift. Richelieu, escorting de Taverney through the gardens after they had supped with the king, was heard by Gilbert, hidden in a dense thicket, advising the baron to send his daughter to a convent. Philippe, Andrée's brother, who held a commission in the royal army, paid a farewell visit to his sister; she confided to him her fears and forebodings. After his departure, Andrée wept. Gilbert approached and declared his love for her, but Andrée rebuffed him.

In his mansion, Balsamo was summoned to Lorenza's room, where she begged him to release her so that she could retire to a convent. When he refused, she plunged a dagger into her breast. After commanding Lorenza to sleep, Balsamo ascended to the chamber of the alchemist Althotas, who reminded him that in a week the aged man would be one hundred years old, by which time he must have the last three drops of blood of a child or a young female to complete the elixir which would preserve him for another half century. Balsamo, having promised his help, was returning to the sleeping Lorenza when he was interrupted by the arrival of Richelieu, who had come for a special sleeping draught for Andrée. Richelieu had already left instructions that a love potion be given to the king which would cause him to fall in love with the first woman he saw on waking.

Gilbert overheard Nicole, Andrée's maid, tell her lover that Richelieu had arranged for them to escape together after first drugging Andrée and leaving her door unlocked; later he saw them ride off. Andrée, plunged into a hypnotic sleep by the drink, descended the stairs of her apartment in a trance and passed the astounded Gilbert. A flash of lightning disclosed the concealed figure of Balsamo, who ordered Andrée to tell what had happened at his house in Paris after Lorenza had tried to kill herself and he had put her to sleep. Andrée, describing Lorenza's flight, told how she had taken with her a box of papers and, on reaching the street, had inquired the address of the lieutenant of police, Monsieur de Sartines. At this news Balsamo leaped to his horse and without releasing Andrée from her trance, dashed off for Paris.

Andrée, left alone, sank to the ground. Gilbert, a witness of this scene at a distance, rushed toward her, lifted her up, and carried her back to her chamber. As he placed her on the couch, he heard a step. He hastily blew out the candle. Realizing that the visitor was the king, Gilbert fled. King Louis, seeing Andrée lying pale and immobile and thinking her dead, also fled in panic.

Balsamo, riding toward Paris, knew that his only hope of preventing Lorenza from revealing his secrets to the police lay in his magic power over her. Abruptly he reined in his horse and with all the force at his command willed Lorenza to fall asleep wherever she was. From Sevres, he sent a hasty note to Madame du Barry in Paris. Meanwhile, Lorenza had arrived at the office of the police, but before she could give him Balsamo's address, she fell to the floor, overcome by a strange dizziness. A valet carried her into an adjoining room. Monsieur de Sartines burst open the coffer, however, and a clerk deciphered the secret papers which implicated Balsamo in plans affecting the king and the government.

At that moment Balsamo, under the name of the Count de Fenix, was announced. Seeing that the coffer had been opened, he threatened to shoot Monsieur de Sartines. Madame du Barry, acting quickly on receipt of Balsamo's letter, arrived at that moment, and Monsieur de Sartines surrendered the coffer to her. She, in turn, handed it to Balsamo with all the papers intact.

On his return to his chambers, Balsamo found Lorenza there in convulsions. His determination to kill her ebbed as he gazed on her beauty, and an overpowering love for her swept his being and caused him to feel that if he surrendered his control over her he might still earn some heavenly recompense. For three days the very thought plunged him into a happiness he had never before experienced, while in her trance Lorenza dreamed aloud her own mysterious love. On the third day after she had asked him to test if her ability still remained to see through space despite intervening material obstacles, Balsamo willed her to report what Madame du Barry was doing. Lorenza reported that the king's favorite was on her way to see him.

Balsamo put Lorenza into a still deeper sleep. As he was leaving her, he thought he heard a creak. Looking back, he saw only her sleeping form. In her sleep, Lorenza thought she saw part of the ceiling of her room descend and from this moving trap a Caliban-shaped creature creep toward her. Powerless to escape, she felt him place her on the circular trap, which then ascended slowly toward the ceiling.

Madame du Barry, worried because she had been followed, told Balsamo that she had saved him from arrest when Monsieur de Sartines had handed the king the deciphered names from the coffer. In appreciation, Balsamo presented her with a vial containing a draught which would ensure her twenty years of additional youth. After her departure Balsamo returned to Lorenza's couch, only to find her gone. He ascended to his instructor's room and there discovered the body of Lorenza. To his horror he realized that Althotas drained from her the blood needed for his elixir.

Cursing his master, from whose hands the vial with the precious liquid slipped and broke, Balsamo fell unconscious on the lifeless body of his wife. He stirred only when notified by his servant that "the five masters" were waiting to see him. They had come from the secret fraternity to pronounce sentence on him as a traitor. Having watched his movements, they had seen Lorenza leave his home with a coffer which contained secret names in cipher. Later he himself had arrived at the police office, and Lorenza had departed alone; he had left with Madame du Barry, whom he had summoned there to receive the secret information for which he was paid. The paper that had revealed their secrets had been left with the police, they charged, but Balsamo had brought away the coffer in order to avoid implication. As a result of this betrayal, five of their prominent agents had been arrested. Balsamo did not defend himself. When he asked only for a few minutes to bring proof that would speak for him, they let him go. He returned, bearing the body of Lorenza which he let slip from his arms to fall at their feet. In consternation, his judges fled.

Althotas, enraged at his pupil and fearing death for himself, set fire to his precious manuscripts and perished in the flames. All night the fire roared in the rooms above, while Balsamo, stretched beside Lorenza's body, never moved. The vaulted walls were thick, however, and the fire finally burned itself out.

Andrée recovered from her prostration and retired to a convent. Baron de Taverney, repudiated by the king and Richelieu, slunk back to his impoverished estate. Philippe sailed for America, and Gilbert followed. Balsamo vegetated in his mansion, from which he was supposed to have reappeared during the violence of the French Revolution. As for the king, on May 9, 1774, his physician pronounced him suffering from smallpox. His daughter, Madame Louise of France, left her convent cell to attend him, and he was given extreme unction. Madame du Barry was sent to the château of the Duchess d'Aiguillon. The king died the next day, and Louis XVI came to a throne about to be engulfed in the flames of rebellion and anarchy.

Critical Evaluation:

Memoirs of a Physician is an intricate plot of court intrigue in the closing days of the reign of Louis XV, with *dramatis personae* as diverse as the scheming Duc de Richelieu, the philosopher Rousseau, and the favorite-dominated king. Manipulating all these by means of his magical control of natural forces and the power invested in him as a representative of the secret brotherhood of Freemasonry is the mysterious figure of Joseph Balsamo. The climax is as lurid as any modern thriller. For its full historical value this volume should be read as one of a series of five, all concerned with the court life of France at the time of Louis XV and XVI. Called the Marie Antoinette romances, the novels are *Memoirs of a Physician*, *The Chevalier de Maison-Rouge* (1846), *The Queen's Necklace* (1849-1850), *Taking the Bastille* (1853), and *The Countess de Charny* (1853-1855).

Without doubt the most fascinating character in the *Memoirs of a Physician* is that remarkable impostor, Joseph Balsamo. From his first introduction, he is seen as a powerful and contradictory figure, a man of great resources and unscrupulous ambitions. His passion for the unnatural and unexplainable adds to the fascination his personality holds for the reader. The phenomena of occultism had long fascinated Alexandre Dumas, *père*, and it was inevitable that he should work it into one of his novels. The manner in which he used his interest in the *Memoirs of a Physician*, however, is a spectacular success, one of the most remarkable examples of his genius. Dumas dabbled, at different times, in palmistry, phrenology, clairvoyance, and spiritualism. To test the reality of this power, he made several experiments at the time when he was writing the Joseph Balsamo sequences of the novel, and, apparently, with considerable success. In this novel, the possibilities of this and other unusual or unexplainable phenomena were stretched to the furthest demands of his fiction. Dumas' skill, however, was such that the reader willingly suspends disbelief and is drawn into the spell cast by the writer and his sorcerer character.

The arch-quack Joseph Balsamo is presented with all of his quackeries, his schemes and ploys, and his ruthless use of his supernatural powers to exploit the innocent and further his own ends. He believes, however, in himself and in his mission to re-create humanity by destroying the existing order; as the head of a society of nihilists, whose motto is L.P.D. (*lilia pedibus destrus*), he directs the undermining of society's foundations. He loves nothing so much as pulling the strings by which the puppets are made to dance. Balsamo, or the Count of Fenix, as he is also known, is a unique and remarkable character, and he holds the reader's interest even after the virtuous characters are forgotten.

Many famous people appear in the pages of this long novel, some more successfully than others. Jean-Jacques Rousseau is probably the most illustrious member of the cast, but his portrait does not quite come off; one suspects that Dumas held Rousseau in such high esteem that he could not entirely relax while drawing his portrait. Marat, the young surgeon who continually urges prompt and violent methods to cleanse society of its corruption, while less admirable, is realized more successfully than the old philosopher. He pulsates with a vitality and drive almost equal to that which infuses Balsamo with such remarkable life. In some respects, Madame du Barry, with all of her intrigues to keep her position, is a triumph of characterization. Whatever the real du Barry was like, the reader feels that she ought to have been as Dumas describes her. The eminent churchman, the Cardinal de Rohan, shines in that wonderful scene in which he is dazzled by the sight of the alchemist Balsamo "making gold."

With great skill, Dumas weaves into his story the social conditions prevalent in Paris and the country at the time, the conditions that must inevitably lead to revolution. The brilliant opening scene of the families searching for the dead and injured after a great riot quickly sets the tone of the novel. The division of the citizens of France into the revolutionaries and reactionaries is seen to be developing, and the tragic consequences are vividly foreshadowed. While the book is far from a social tract, Dumas seems to take delight in presenting the corruption of the court and the vices of the rich, and, above all, the exploitation of the poor by the powerful. Dumas was always fascinated by power and its various permutations. He explored in novel after novel the schemes and actions of the lovers of power and their ruthless natures. In this novel of intrigue and incipient revolution, Dumas allows himself plenty of room to analyze his favorite subject.

The plot is as complicated and convoluted as most of the plots of Dumas' other novels, but the action moves swiftly, and Dumas' narrative skill keeps the threads traceable; the story is seldom incomprehensible. Even when the plot seems most tangled, the vivid characterizations hold the reader's interest. Perhaps more than many of Dumas' novels, *Memoirs of a Physician* presents some acute character analyses. The principal characters reveal themselves through their actions, as well as through their self-evaluations. The minor characters in the book and the young and idealistic lovers, however, are much less successfully realized and are inclined to be pawns of the plot.

The style of the writing, while vigorous, is not subtle. The dialogue is often completely unrealistic, the characters speaking to inform the reader, rather than one another, of their intentions. The melodrama of the plot carries over into the prose, and many chapters end with cliff-hanging episodes which are lushly overwritten. These scenes are frequently implausible, and the violence of the emotions and the posturing of the characters is sometimes laughable. Yet, despite these flaws, which are, after all, as much the fault of the era of the author as they are of the author's craft, the novel remains a masterpiece. Dumas never tried to write like Gustave Flaubert and was not interested in realism, yet he managed to create a "real" world with his pen. The Paris and France of *Memoirs of a Physician* is as vivid to the reader as the provincial towns of Flaubert's masterpieces, and the breathless narrative drive, for which Dumas is so justly famous, continually holds the reader's attention. The style is consistent throughout, and the prose retains the vigor which characterize the author's earlier books.

"Critical Evaluation" by Bruce D. Reeves

Bibliography:

Bell, A. Craig. *Alexandre Dumas: A Biography and Study*. London: Cassell, 1950. One of the better studies of the works of Dumas, this volume places some emphasis on *The Memoirs of a Physician*. The biography chronicles Dumas' social circle.

Dumas, Alexandre, *père*. *The Road to Monte Cristo: A Condensation from "The Memoirs of Alexandre Dumas."* Translated by Jules Eckert Goodman. New York: Charles Scribner's Sons, 1956. An excellent, abridged translation of Dumas' memoirs that relate to his source material for his novels, including *The Memoirs of a Physician*.

Maurois, André. *The Titans, a Three-Generation Biography of the Dumas*. Translated by Gerard Hopkins. New York: Harper & Row, 1957. Considered the authoritative biography of Dumas *père*, his father, and his son. Includes an excellent bibliography. Discusses *The Memoirs of a Physician* in a cursory fashion.

Schopp, Claude. *Alexandre Dumas: Genius of Life*. Translated by A. J. Koch. New York: Franklin Watts, 1988. A biographical and critical approach to the life and works of Alexandre Dumas, *père*. Contains a discussion on Dumas' problems with the serialization of *The Memoirs of a Physician*.

Stowe, Richard S. *Alexandre Dumas (père)*. Boston: Twayne, 1976. An excellent starting point for an analysis of the life and works of Alexandre Dumas, *père*, probably the best source in English. *The Memoirs of a Physician* is analyzed in the chapter entitled "The Marie-Antoinette Romances," of which the novel is the first of five installments.

MEMOIRS OF HADRIAN

Type of work: Novel
Author: Marguerite Yourcenar (Marguerite de Crayencour, 1903-1987)
Type of plot: Historical realism
Time of plot: Second century C.E.
Locale: Rome and the Roman empire
First published: Mémoires d'Hadrien, 1951 (English translation, 1954)

> *Principal characters:*
> HADRIAN, the Roman emperor
> ANTINOUS, a Bythinian youth
> TRAJAN, the previous Roman emperor
> PLOTINA, Trajan's wife and friend of Hadrian
> ANTONINUS, a virtuous senator and public servant
> SABINA, Hadrian's wife

The Story:

In a book-length letter addressed to Marcus Aurelius, his adopted grandson and heir, the sixty-year-old Emperor Hadrian told of his impending death and meditated upon his life in order to instruct his heir through his accumulated experience, knowledge, and wisdom. The descendant of wealthy aristocratic administrators, Hadrian had been born in Spain. After his father's death, the twelve-year-old boy went to Rome to complete his education, which included science, mathematics, art, literature, and Greek, and to begin his military training. Following his studies, he was named to a series of judgeships, which taught him about human motives and how to listen carefully and organize his time.

Hadrian was promoted to junior officer rank in the army and stationed in Central Europe, where he was exposed to new experiences and ideas. There, he learned that Emperor Nerva had died and that his cousin Trajan had ascended the throne. Although such a family connection, coupled with his own ability and courage, offered new opportunities, advancement was not smooth, for the new emperor and Hadrian often clashed on private and public affairs. Since Trajan wanted to consolidate and increase Roman conquests, he embarked on many campaigns. As a result, Hadrian saw service all over Europe. He acquitted himself daringly and brilliantly and gained both a solid reputation among his colleagues on the battlefield and popularity in Rome. The emperor was so pleased with Hadrian's contribution that he gave him a ring symbolic of imperial favor.

Increasingly influential in the emperor's circle, partly because of Trajan's wife, who shared many of his beliefs, Hadrian performed a variety of administrative functions as well as writing and delivering the emperor's speeches. Gradually, however, this relationship, further strengthened by Hadrian's marriage to Trajan's grandniece Sabina, began to arouse irritation and jealousy in the old sovereign, who resented the successes of his subordinate.

Renewed conflicts in the empire made it necessary that Hadrian visit various fronts to impose discipline on the troops. Several bold strokes on his part defeated Rome's enemies but not without diminishing his humanity and aging him prematurely. With Plotina's help, he continued to rise in the ranks of the administration and army, becoming first a consul, then governor and military legate in Syria. When the emperor wanted to wage war again and conquer the Orient, Hadrian advised him instead to sign advantageous commercial treaties with communities along the Silk Road, for he had realized that Asia, despite some early Roman victories, would be difficult, perhaps impossible, to defeat.

Given his age and illness, Trajan should have officially designated Hadrian as his heir, yet he hesitated. Plotina worked hard to foster his candidacy, however, and shortly before the emperor died, he named Hadrian his successor in his will. In 117 C.E., at the age of forty, Hadrian became ruler of the world. More interested in the betterment of humankind than in the trappings of power, he immediately resolved to seek peace abroad and compromise with senators at home. He instituted reforms to improve life in the empire, ranging from innovative social programs to the granting of new individual freedoms; underlying his reforms was his intent to increase human happiness. To ensure the permanence of Roman peace he encouraged commerce, literature, and the arts and fostered the building of new cities all over the Mediterranean basin. In addition, he civilized Britain and the German plain and continued to experience everything in life to the fullest.

During one of his travels, he became infatuated with a handsome Greek adolescent named Antinous, who began to accompany him everywhere and with whom he shared an unequaled intimacy. This was the beginning of fabulous years. For Hadrian, there was no activity too demanding, no gift too wonderful, as his passion turned into blissful, though not exclusive, adoration. Out of his own overwhelming love for the emperor, Antinous decided, when just short of his twentieth birthday, to commit suicide so that his unlived years could be added to those of Hadrian. Numb with sorrow and guilt, Hadrian, upon his return to Italy devoted time to literary and scientific pursuits while he worked on modifying laws and constitutions so that they would respect local customs and national character. He also continued to build and to improve city services.

The only serious flaw in his otherwise excellent rule concerned the Jews in Judea who, unlike his other non-Roman subjects, attacked Rome for its occupation of their land and its intolerance toward their religious rituals and ways of considering God. Unable and unwilling to accommodate an alternate point of view, Hadrian sent in well-equipped, well-trained troops to crush Simon Bar-Kochba's guerrilla army. The campaign took more than four years and resulted in the resisters' mass suicide.

Suffering from increasingly ill health and wishing to avoid Trajan's imprudent delaying, Hadrian named Antoninus, an honest and virtuous man, to be his successor under the condition that he would agree adopt the philosophical Marcus Aurelius. Having settled all public and private affairs, and surrounded by close friends, Hadrian waited peacefully for death.

Critical Evaluation:

When Marguerite Yourcenar in 1948 began to think of Hadrian, she had already developed her literary gifts in her previous works of fiction. She understood well the first-person narrative form; she had previously evolved themes both human and universal; she was interested in historical research as an aid to conveying eternal ideas; and she had developed an acute understanding of human frailty. In *Memoirs of Hadrian*, her first recognized masterpiece, Yourcenar makes full use of her talents, skills, and knowledge.

The work is divided into six parts, each having a Latin title taken from Hadrian's poetry, philosophical ideas, or coins minted during his reign. Each title describes, and each part is devoted to, different phases of the emperor's life. Each section's title and subject correspond to the development of aspects of Hadrian's power and personality. The first part gives an account of the progress of his illness and his renunciation of many activities as his soul prepares to leave his body. The second describes the variety and complexity of his character, followed by a section dealing with "the stabilized earth." Part 4 equates the golden age with Hadrian, since that age represents the period when his life reached its apogee, a moment when nothing seemed impossible and when all was easy. There follows a section entitled "the august but humane discipline," which is Hadrian's contemplation of life from a different point of view, and the book concludes with a mediation on death.

Yourcenar intends to portray a great historical personage who, thanks to his broad humanist culture and inquiring intelligence, was able, without illusions and with remarkable objectivity and lucidity, to analyze his life and times. Hadrian is at once an aesthete, an art lover, a poet, a tireless traveler, a general, an economist, a master builder, and a political scientist: In other words, he is a man deeply interested in everything.

Yourcenar's book is, however, far more than the autobiography of Emperor Hadrian. It has also been called a learning "manual for princes" that explains how human knowledge and consciousness can be united with imperial knowledge and consciousness to create a better ruler. In his all-encompassing outlook on the world in which he lives, Hadrian is a kind of unique "Everyman," a representative of the people without any elements of demagoguery, who at the same time stands apart from the people and thus allows his rare genius full play in all areas of human endeavor.

He is sufficiently practical and pragmatic that in appreciating the beauty of such treatises as Plato's *Republic* (third century B.C.E.) he is able to take such daring views further and to implement many of them in his rule. Thus he restructures the state to be both less intrusive and more responsive to its citizens and he codifies better, because simpler, laws. His generous nature leads him to improve the status of slaves through proper regulation; he works to modify the ambiguous legal condition of women who "are at one and the same time subjugated and protected, weak and powerful, too much despised and too much respected." Of course, despite his otherwise forward-looking liberalism, he does remain a man of his century, as is evident, for example, in his lack of understanding for women as individual and equal human beings.

His attitude toward his job and position is based on an honest regard for all the people in his care and exemplified by the statement "We emperors are not Caesars; we are functionaries of the State." All of his life he had wanted to better the lot of the people by the wise application of three basic concepts—humanity, happiness, and liberty—tempered by discipline and patience, and he vehemently refuses to believe that the masses are unworthy of such treatment or that such treatment could make them corrupt and complacent.

Memoirs of Hadrian has often been called a historical novel, but it lacks many of the customary attributes of the genre, such as descriptions of local color, period dress, and quaint customs. The Emperor Hadrian characterizes himself partly through accounts of his actions, more often through perspicacious analyses of his thoughts and feelings. If, at times, the book deviates from the recorded truth, it is only because Yourcenar is not presenting the picture of an epoch or an emperor in time, but with a human being out of time and with that collective sensibility or consciousness that had taken this particular and very special Roman for its spokesman.

The style of *Memoirs of Hadrian*, in which the narrator speaks in the first person, is not an interior monologue in the usual sense of the word but rather what has been described as the interior discourse. Through Hadrian's retelling Yourcenar has in fact exposed universal truths and explored archetypes that have their origins in Western culture. She has demonstrated that her Roman emperor not only incarnates the serene Roman patience but also represents the fears and aspirations of thinking readers everywhere.

Pierre L. Horn

Bibliography:

Howard, Joan E. *From Violence to Vision: Sacrifice in the Works of Marguerite Yourcenar.* Carbondale: Southern Illinois University Press, 1992. A scholarly and well-informed study of the role played first by myth and then by sacrificial situations in seven illustrative works, including Yourcenar's 1951 masterpiece.

Shurr, Georgia Hooks. *Marguerite Yourcenar: A Reader's Guide.* Lanham, Md.: University Press of America, 1987. A solid general introduction to Yourcenar's writings and creative process, occasionally marred by irrelevant personal reminiscences.

Taylor, John. "Waiting for Hadrian." *Georgia Review* 42 (1988): 147-151. Brief yet informative. Discusses the slow process between Yourcenar's discovery of a good topic and its full realization in the novel.

Watson-Williams, Helen. "Hadrian's Story Recalled." *Nottingham French Studies* 23 (1984): 35-48. A serious analysis of the novel's central concerns in light of social and historical work on the second-century emperor and his time.

Whatley, Janet. "*Mémoires d'Hadrien:* A Manual for Princes." *University of Toronto Quarterly* 50, no. 2 (Winter, 1980-1981): 221-237. A profound and perceptive essay on the novel's political themes, with special emphasis on the relationship between power and moral knowledge.

MEN AND WOMEN

Type of work: Poetry
Author: Robert Browning (1812-1889)
First published: 1855

The title *Men and Women* was originally appended to two volumes of poems containing fifty-one of Robert Browning's most celebrated works. Beginning with the collected edition of 1863, the number of poems appearing under this title was reduced to thirteen, only eight of which had been in the 1855 edition of *Men and Women*. Of the other forty-three poems, thirty were thereafter grouped by Browning under *Dramatic Lyrics* (the most famous of these being "Love Among the Ruins," "A Toccata of Galuppi's," "Saul," " 'De Gustibus—,' " and "Two in the Campagna"); twelve became *Dramatic Romances* (including " 'Childe Roland to the Dark Tower Came,' " "The Statue and the Bust," "The Last Ride Together," and "A Grammarian's Funeral"); "In a Balcony" came eventually to be listed separately, under its own title. Those poems that remained as belonging to *Men and Women* include several of Browning's greatest dramatic monologues: "Fra Lippo Lippi," "An Epistle Containing the Strange Medical Experience of Karshish, the Arab Physician," "Bishop Blougram's Apology," "The Bishop Orders His Tomb at Saint Praxed's Church," "Andrea del Sarto," and "Cleon."

Men and Women was Browning's only important publication during the period of his marriage to Elizabeth Barrett. These were the years when Browning made Italy his home and when his output of poetry was markedly curtailed by a number of other interests: his family, his dabbling in painting and sculpture, and his study of Italian Renaissance art. The quality of his poetry was never higher than in the poems produced during this period. It was in *Men and Women*, above all, that he brought the dramatic monologue to perfection. His reputation is largely due to his mastery of the dramatic monologue.

Life in Italy suited Browning, and the atmosphere of that land permeates many of the poems in this collection. Some are Italian simply in landscape, such as the humorous "Up at a Villa—Down in the City." In other poems, such as "A Serenade at the Villa," "By the Fire-Side," and "Two in the Campagna," it is apparent that Browning's primary interest is in examining human relationships which could take place anywhere; the setting is Italy but setting is incidental. Other poems, however, owe more to their Italian sources, including curious customs ("Holy-Cross Day"), and local legends ("The Statue and the Bust"). In later years Browning would often say that "Italy was my university"; what he had studied at that university was Italian art. "Old Pictures in Florence" reflects his interest in that art, as do "Fra Lippo Lippi" and "Andrea del Sarto," both of which are imaginary character studies of real Renaissance painters. "The Guardian-Angel" is based on an actual painting (as the subtitle indicates): "A Picture at Fano." " 'De Gustibus—' " contains the clearest statement of Browning's love for Italy; there he writes: "Open my heart and you will see/ Graved inside of it, 'Italy.' " The Italian element is, however, less important than another personal influence, that of the poet's marriage. Although the love poems in *Men and Women* are not necessarily autobiographical, they do reflect, at least indirectly, the relationship between Elizabeth Barrett and Robert Browning. In "By the Fire-Side" communication is complete; love is serene. In "The Last Ride Together," "Andrea del Sarto," "Love in a Life," "Life in a Love," and "Any Wife to Any Husband," communication breaks down and love fails. "Two in the Campagna" deals with "Infinite passion and the pain/ Of finite hearts that yearn." Thus Browning indicates the gap between love in dreams and in reality. Most of these poems dramatize a love situation and are content to evoke it without commenting on it. "The Statue and the Bust," however, includes a flatly stated moral, "Let a man contend to the uttermost/ For his life's set prize," and never miss that prize because of wasted opportunities.

Some have suggested that in examining the vicissitudes of love Browning was revealing flaws in his own marriage. "A Lover's Quarrel," for example, does involve disagreement over two subjects about which he and his wife differed: spiritualism (she believed in it; he scoffed at it) and Napoleon III, Emperor of France (she was an admirer; he was not). The evidence is by no means conclusive, however, and the one poem in *Men and Women* that is openly autobiographical, "One Word More: To E.B.B.," is Browning's dedication to his wife, not only of the book, but of himself.

Many of Browning's favorite themes are broached in the poems of *Men and Women*. The idea that the course of one's life may turn upon a moment's decision is expressed in "The Statue and the Bust." The idea that "A man's reach should exceed his grasp" is the subject of "Andrea del Sarto," as well as "Old Pictures in Florence," and "A Grammarian's Funeral." Browning's attitudes toward religion and religious belief are presented in "Saul," "Cleon," "An Epistle Containing the Strange Medical Experience of Karshish, the Arab Physician," and "Bishop Blougram's Apology."

It must be admitted that the present age may be little interested in most of Browning's opinions per se. People may be no nearer than the Victorians to solving the problems that beset Browning and his contemporaries, but people naturally tend to prefer more recent attempts to solve them, and more recent statements of what the world's problems and solutions are. Browning's ideas about art are, however, perfectly current; they have a bearing not only on art in general but, more particularly, on his own poetry. A number of the poems in *Men and Women* contain, implicitly or explicitly, theories of art that help to explain what Browning was, in his poetry, attempting to do.

"I only knew one poet in my life," says the speaker in "How It Strikes a Contemporary," and the poem itself is in many ways Browning's own description of what a poet should be. The poet, first of all, looks the world full in the face; the poet is no idle dreamer. The poet sees life and sees it whole, taking "such cognizance of men and things" that the poet can truthfully be called "a recording chief-inquisitor." This poem can be seen as a veiled defense of Browning's own tendency to write about characters and events that may not, to one who thinks poetry must be about pretty things, be sufficiently "poetic." If, in Browning's view, the poet's proper sphere is life as it really is, the poet's function is nonetheless an exalted one: The poet writes in the service of God. In "How It Strikes a Contemporary," the poet "walked about and took account/ Of all thought, said and acted, then went home,/ And wrote it fully to our Lord the King."

"Memorabilia," a slight poem, is chiefly remembered because it alludes to Percy Bysshe Shelley—one of Browning's early enthusiasms and the subject of Browning's only important prose essay. "Popularity" is a tribute to another of Browning's favorite poets, John Keats. In this poem there is further allusion to Browning's belief that the poet's role is somehow linked with the divine mission. One of Browning's most explicit statements about what poetry should aim to be is found in "'Transcendentalism': a Poem in Twelve Books." In this work he makes clear his preference for Keatsian or Shelleyan "song" to the over-labored, earnest "thought" that characterizes so much bad Victorian poetry. One poet, speaking to another, says: "'Tis you speak, that's your error. Song's our art:/ Whereas you please to speak these naked thoughts/ Instead of draping them in sights and sounds." Browning has no objection to thought in poetry, but it should not be presented baldly, for its own sake. Rather, it should be draped "in sights and sounds."

In the two dramatic monologues that are generally acknowledged to be the finest poems in *Men and Women*, "Fra Lippo Lippi" and "Andrea del Sarto," Browning gives further insights into his theories of art. It is obvious that, in bringing these two Renaissance painters to life, his own sympathies as an artist lie completely with Lippo Lippi and not at all with Andrea del Sarto. He depicts the latter as a skilled craftsman whose hand and eye are deft, but who has only "something of a heart." His paintings are accomplished, but cold-blooded and uninspired. In the poem Andrea del Sarto comes to realize that he has failed to infuse into his work the quality of a great soul. An artist's success, Browning is saying, resides not merely in technical perfection but also in the ability to give sufficiently of oneself to make the work burn with the true "light of God."

In seeing the creation of a work of art as a moral act Browning is not advocating the kind of art that merely moralizes, although Browning's own late poems, in the years after *The Ring and the Book*, frequently do exactly that. Fra Lippo Lippi's monastic superiors have forced him to paint pious pictures that will "say to folk—remember matins,/ Or, mind you fast next Friday." They have told him that his purpose is not to depict the world but to "forget there's such a thing as flesh" and "to paint the souls of men." Lippi himself, however, is too honest an artist, and too fully a man, to be content with their dictates: ". . . zooks, sir, flesh and blood,/ That's all I'm made of!" Lippi loves the things of the world but not merely in and for themselves. He sees the beauty of the world as God's creation and therefore not to be despised. The artist, he believes (and Browning with him), by portraying finite beauty comes closest to portraying infinite beauty as well. "I never saw," says Lippi, "beauty with no soul at all." In his characterization of this Italian monk Browning has given readers, at a distance, a veritable portrait of himself as an artist.

When readers have sifted Browning's poems for their ideas, even those about art, they have done him less than justice as a poet. His greatness ultimately is to be located in his creation of memorable characters: the Chaucerian Fra Lippo Lippi, the self-pitying Andrea del Sarto, the wily Bishop Blougram, the Greek Cleon, the Arab Karshish, the dying Bishop concerned about his tomb, and a whole gallery of lovers in a splendid variety of moods. Browning's early failures as a writer for the stage taught him a valuable lesson: His abilities were suited for the delineation of "Action in Character, rather than Character in Action." His psychological studies of "Action" within his justly famous characters, particularly in the dramatic monologues, are the main basis for his great reputation.

It is interesting to note that, during his lifetime, Browning's fame came slowly. The sale of so great a collection of poems as *Men and Women* was disappointingly small: No second edition was ever called for. It was not until the publication of *Dramatis Personae*, in 1864, that Browning began to receive the recognition he deserved.

Bibliography:
Auerbach, Nina. "Robert Browning's Last Word." *Victorian Poetry* 22, no. 2 (Summer, 1984): 161-173. Argues that after Elizabeth Barrett Browning's death, Robert Browning incorporated her voice into his dramatic monologues; in doing so, he used her to validate his own authority as a poet.
Erickson, Lee. "The Self and Others in Browning's *Men and Women*." *Victorian Poetry* 21, no. 1 (Spring, 1983): 43-64. Browning exemplified Georg Hegels pattern for romantic art, creating monologists who gained true self-consciousness by interacting with another; frequently, this other was God.
Haigwood, Laura E. "Gender-to-Gender Anxiety and Influence in Robert Browning's *Men and*

Women." *Browning Institute Studies: An Annual Review of Victorian Literary and Cultural History* 14 (1986): 97-118. In order to break ten years of silence and to write in a new style, Robert Browning needed to distance himself from his wife, Elizabeth Barrett Browning, who was a more successful and more popular poet. Suggests that Browning may have respected her editorial judgment too highly.

Willy, Margaret. *A Critical Commentary on Browning's "Men and Women."* New York: Macmillan, 1968. An excellent introduction to *Men and Women*. Defines the dramatic monologue, summarizes Browning's philosophy and style, describes his modernity, and offers analyses of various poems.

Woolford, John. "Periodicals and the Practice of Literary Criticism, 1855-64." In *The Victorian Periodical Press: Samplings and Soundings*, edited by Joanne Shattock and Michael Wolff. Leicester, Toronto: Leicester University Press, 1982. Uses the reception of *Men and Women* at the time of its publication to demonstrate the accuracy of Matthew Arnold's condemnation of the criticism of his age; Woolford shows that it had improved by 1864.

THE MENAECHMI

Type of work: Drama
Author: Plautus (c. 254-184 B.C.E.)
Type of plot: Farce
Time of plot: Third century B.C.E.
Locale: Epidamnum, a city of Macedonia
First performed: Menaechmi, second century B.C.E.

> *Principal characters:*
> MENAECHMUS OF EPIDAMNUM
> MENAECHMUS SOSICLES, his twin brother
> MESSENIO, Menaechmus Sosicles' servant
> WIFE OF MENAECHMUS OF EPIDAMNUM
> EROTIUM, a courtesan, Menaechmus of Epidamnum's mistress
> PENICULUS, a parasite, hanger-on to Menaechmus of Epidamnum

The Story:

When the two Menaechmi were seven years old, one, later to become Menaechmus of Epidamnum, accompanied his merchant father from their home in Syracuse to Tarentum. There, fascinated by the confused activity, the boy wandered away, became lost, and was finally picked up by another merchant who took him to the merchant's own home in Epidamnum and adopted him. The boy's family was so grief-stricken at his loss that his name was given to the remaining son. This boy, Menaechmus Sosicles, grew up, and when he came of age and inherited his father's property, he went out to go on a quest for his brother.

Menaechmus of Epidamnum had by this time inherited his foster father's wealth, married a somewhat shrewish woman, and acquired a mistress. On the day Menaechmus Sosicles arrived in Epidamnum on his undirected search, Menaechmus of Epidamnum had quarreled with his suspicious wife and had parted from her, secretly bearing one of her robes as a gift to Erotium, his mistress. Delivering the robe, he instructed Erotium to prepare an elaborate meal for their evening's entertainment; then he left to attend to some business at the Forum.

Shortly afterward, Menaechmus Sosicles happened to arrive before Erotium's house and, much to his dismay, was addressed familiarly, first by one of her servants and then by Erotium herself. Confusion followed, but Menaechmus Sosicles finally decided that this was merely Erotium's way of trying to seduce him; so he gave his servant Messenio his wallet for safe-keeping and accompanied the courtesan into the house.

When he came back out later, having consumed the food that Menaechmus of Epidamnum had ordered for himself and his parasite, Erotium gave him the robe so that he could have it altered for her. As he walked away, intent on selling the robe for his own gain, he was accosted by Peniculus, Menaechmus of Epidamnum's parasite, indignant at having missed a banquet to which he had been invited only a short time before and convinced that he had been purposely affronted. Menaechmus Sosicles finally dismissed Peniculus with an insult, and the latter, believing himself grievously treated by his erstwhile benefactor, went to Menaechmus of Epidamnum's wife and revealed to her that her husband was not only keeping another woman but had given his mistress his wife's robe as well. When Peniculus had finished, Menaechmus of Epidamnum came by on his way from the Forum to Erotium's house, and, in concealment, the two overheard him soliloquizing in a way that substantiated Peniculus' whole story.

Satisfied with what she heard the wife stepped forward and accosted her husband. There followed a confused argument in which Menaechmus of Epidamnum alternated between dissembled ignorance regarding the theft of the robe and genuine dismay regarding his assumed presence at the banquet Erotium had given. At last, seeing that Peniculus had revealed all, he agreed to get the robe and return it. When he went to Erotium and, unaware that Menaechmus Sosicles had already taken the robe, tried to explain his dilemma, she assumed he was trying to defraud her, grew angry, and slammed her door in his face.

Meanwhile, Menaechmus Sosicles, still carrying the robe, met the angry wife, who assumed that he was Menaechmus of Epidamnum returning the robe as he had promised. While the whole situation was still in confusion, the wife's father arrived to take her part. Menaechmus Sosicles decided to feign madness to get rid of the two and was so successful in his attempt that they went off in search of a physician and men to restrain him.

When these people were assembled, they met Menaechmus of Epidamnum instead of his brother. They would have carried him off if Messenio had not happened along and, mistaking Menaechmus of Epidamnum for his brother, beaten off the assailants. When the others had fled, Messenio asked for his freedom in return for saving his "master's" life; his request was granted by the amazed Menaechmus of Epidamnum, and Messenio went off to collect his master's belongings and return them.

On the way, however, he met Menaechmus Sosicles. Gradually the nature of the confusion came to light. The two brothers finally confronted each other and exchanged their stories. Menaechmus of Epidamnum decided to sell his property and return to Syracuse with his brother. Messenio was freed again, this time by his own master, and was made auctioneer for the sale of the property. Everything was to be converted into cash, including Menaechmus of Epidamnum's wife.

Critical Evaluation:

The Menaechmi can be counted as one of Plautus' most enduring successes. As is often noted, there is a more-or-less direct line of descent from his story of separated twins, almost certainly taken from a Greek play, to William Shakespeare's Renaissance farce of two sets of separated twins to the twentieth century American Broadway musical, *The Boys from Syracuse* (1938). The borrowing may not be over yet.

The history of this mistaken identity plot goes back to the ancient Greeks and most probably to the source of many Latin plays, the Greek New Comedy. It was customary for the Roman playwrights to base their plays on the Greek originals. The plays of Plautus, however, like those of his contemporaries, reflect the Roman society of his day, rather than depicting the lives of the ancient Greeks. The illusion of another time and place supplied by the Greek dress employed on the Roman stage merely enabled playwrights to poke fun at Roman ways under the guise of attacking the Greeks.

Since very few Greek originals have been recovered, it is not easy to evaluate Plautus' originality. Moreover, it is also thought that Latin playwrights combined the Greek New Comedy with the earlier dramatic forms of Italy, which were farcical and included much song and dance. However much he owed to his sources, Plautus is appreciated for his ultimate products, which had a great influence on Western drama.

Three of the achievements that make his plays living theater are Plautus' gift with the Latin language, his memorable characters, and his humor. His language, though certainly hard to appreciate in translation, is well regarded by Latin scholars for being both colloquial and wonderfully fluent: The idiomatic Latin is lively and vulgar, yet the metrics are supple. The vulgarity caused Plautus to fall into disfavor in certain periods, such as the Middle Ages in Europe. Since the rediscovery and reappreciation of all things classical during the Renaissance, Plautus has entertained all those who appreciate Latin.

Equally, in the theater, his gift for farcical situations and his use of song and dance have produced entertaining plays. Whether his plays have a social message remains a matter of debate. Plautus is held in low regard by some critics because his plays seem merely to be wildly amusing. Others, perhaps in response, have found some social commentary in the plays. A third group finds meaning in the social function of plays, whether or not the plays themselves hold any deep meaning.

The Menaechmi is in several respects illustrative of the best Plautine elements of comedy. It is generally admired for its exquisitely balanced and neat construction. Given the basic improbability of the situation, which is that the visiting brother who has set out to find his missing brother with the same name is being mistaken for someone else and yet does not understand his predicament, the swift pace of the play and Plautus' lively language and songs and dance keep it entertaining for the audience.

Beyond its excellence as farce, *The Menaechmi* may be interpreted as a comic wish-fulfillment of its original Roman, mostly male, audiences. As the scholar Erich Segal notes, what Menaechmus Sosicles experiences is, though confusing, a male dream fulfilled: money, sex, and food for nothing. The confusion adds to the dreamlike, fantasy state. A comparison of the dietary restrictions of the times with the food described for the feasts in the play, Segal also notes, is another example of defying social conventions.

Although Plautus' comedies, along with other Latin comedies, have long and often been credited—or perhaps accused—with setting the example for the clichéd, romantic comedy with a happy ending, *The Menaechmi* shows the great range and variety to be found in his works. This range of tone indicates that Plautus is not responsible for the sentimentality of later playwrights. The clearest example of the antiromantic, unsentimental tone in this particular play is the cynical treatment of love. The married brother has a shrewish wife. Part of the plot complication is that he has a mistress to whom he gives what he steals from his wife. Menaechmus of Epidamnum is already bouncing back and forth between duty to a wife he does not love and pleasure with a courtesan when his brother further complicates his life. Further-more, neither woman is portrayed in an attractive light. The wife is a nag and Erotium is greedy and grasping. The ending, in which the brothers go off with each other and leave everyone else behind, is somewhat startling to anyone used to a more conventional happy ending. The right-ness of a traditional family at the end of a comedy is generally reinforced by having errors cleared up. In this play, the brothers decide that the situation is hopeless and simply leave.

On the other hand, some scholars would argue, this ending is also appropriate if one considers the social function of comedy. Comedy often endorses the rebelling against the overturning of too-rigid social customs and the momentary release of inhibitions. Plautus uses the common stock of comedies to win the approval of audiences seeking a momentary change in their ordinary lives.

That *The Menaechmi* has survived so long is a testament to Plautus' great skill in constructing a swiftly moving plot, amusing characters, and entertaining language. Whether he intends social commentary as well is a matter of interpretation. In using much of the local color of his day—the Roman references to places, customs, sayings—he leaves a stamp of his culture on a durable plot of mistaken identity.

"Critical Evaluation" by Shakuntala Jayaswal

Bibliography:

Beare, William. *The Roman Stage*. 3d ed. New York: Barnes & Noble Books, 1965. This introduction to the history of Latin drama has three chapters on Plautus. Provides a quick overview of his life and work. Useful as background.

Candido, Joseph. "Dining Out in Ephesus: Food in *The Comedy of Errors.*" *Studies in English Literature* 30, no. 2 (Spring, 1990): 217-241. Focused on the Shakespeare play based on *The Menaechmi*, this article explains the significance of food in both plays and sheds light on the Plautus play.

Duckworth, George. *The Nature of Roman Comedy: A Study in Popular Entertainment*. Princeton, N.J.: Princeton University Press, 1952. The classic study of Roman comedy. Provides a comprehensive introduction to Latin playwrights, including Plautus.

Plautus. *Menaechmi*. Introduction by A. S. Gratwick. Cambridge, England: Cambridge University Press, 1993. The English language introduction to the Latin language play is comprehensive. Information on Plautus, the play, and how to scan Latin verse.

Segal, Erich. *Roman Laughter: The Comedy of Plautus*. Cambridge, Mass.: Harvard University Press, 1968. Organized by topics, this book presents an argument about Plautus' comedy as a whole: that it was meant to make the Romans laugh by reversing Roman values on stage. This study is often quoted in articles about Plautus.

THE MERCHANT OF VENICE

Type of work: Drama
Author: William Shakespeare (1564-1616)
Type of plot: Tragicomedy
Time of plot: Sixteenth century
Locale: Venice
First performed: c. 1596-1597; first published, 1600

Principal characters:
SHYLOCK, a Jewish moneylender
PORTIA, a wealthy young woman
ANTONIO, an impoverished merchant, Shylock's enemy, who
    is championed by Portia
BASSANIO, Portia's husband and Antonio's friend
NERISSA, Portia's waiting-woman
GRATIANO, Nerissa's husband and Bassanio's friend
JESSICA, Shylock's daughter
LORENZO, Jessica's husband

The Story:

Bassanio, meeting his wealthy friend Antonio, revealed that he had a plan for restoring the fortune he had carelessly spent and for paying the debts he had incurred. In the town of Belmont, not far from Venice, there lived a wealthy young woman named Portia, who was famous for her beauty. If he could secure some money, Bassanio declared, he was sure he could win her as his wife. Antonio replied that he had no funds at hand with which to supply his friend, as they were all invested in the ships he had at sea, but that he would attempt to borrow money for him in Venice.

Portia had many suitors for her hand. According to the strange conditions of her father's will, however, anyone who wished her for his wife had to choose correctly among three caskets of silver, gold, and lead that casket that contained the message that Portia was his. In case of failure, the suitors were compelled to swear never to reveal which casket they had chosen and never to woo another woman. Four of her suitors, seeing they could not win her except under the conditions of the will, had departed. A fifth, a Moor, decided to take his chances. The unfortunate man chose the golden casket, which contained only a skull and a mocking message. The Prince of Arragon was the next suitor to try his luck. He chose the silver casket, only to learn from the note it bore that he was a fool.

True to his promise to Bassanio, Antonio arranged to borrow three thousand ducats from Shylock, a wealthy Jew. Antonio was to have the use of the money for three months. If he found himself unable to return the loan at the end of that time, Shylock was given the right to cut a pound of flesh from any part of Antonio's body. Despite Bassanio's objections, Antonio insisted on accepting the terms, for he was sure his ships would return a month before the payment was due. He was confident that he would never fall into the power of the Jew, who hated Antonio because he often lent money to others without charging the interest Shylock demanded.

That night, Bassanio planned a feast and a masque. In conspiracy with his friend, Lorenzo, he invited Shylock to be his guest. Lorenzo, taking advantage of her father's absence, ran off with the Jew's daughter, Jessica, who took part of Shylock's fortune with her. Shylock was cheated not only of his daughter and his ducats but also of his entertainment, for the wind suddenly changed and Bassanio set sail for Belmont.

As the days passed, the Jew began to hear news of mingled good and bad fortune. In Genoa, Jessica and Lorenzo were lavishly spending the money she had taken with her. The miser flinched at the reports of his daughter's extravagance, but for compensation he had the news that Antonio's ships, on which his continuing fortune depended, had been wrecked at sea.

Portia, much taken with Bassanio when he came to woo her, would have had him wait before he tried to pick the right casket. Sure that he would fail as the others had, she hoped to have his company a little while longer. Bassanio, however, was impatient to try his luck. Not deceived by the ornateness of the gold and silver caskets, and philosophizing that true virtue is inward virtue, he chose the lead box. In it was a portrait of Portia. He had chosen correctly. To seal their engagement, Portia gave Bassanio a ring. She declared he must never part with it, for if he did, it would signify the end of their love.

Gratiano, a friend who had accompanied Bassanio to Belmont, spoke up. He was in love with Portia's waiting-woman, Nerissa. With Portia's delighted approval, Gratiano planned that both couples should be married at the same time.

Bassanio's joy at his good fortune was soon blighted. Antonio wrote that he was ruined, all his ships having failed to return. The time for payment of the loan being past due, Shylock was demanding his pound of flesh. In closing, Antonio declared that he cleared Bassanio of his debt to him. He wished only to see his friend once more before his death. Portia declared that the double wedding should take place at once. Then her husband would be able to set out for Venice in an attempt to buy off the Jew with her dowry of six thousand ducats.

After Bassanio and Gratiano had departed, Portia declared to Lorenzo and Jessica, who had come to Belmont, that she and Nerissa were going to a nunnery, where they would live in seclusion until their husbands returned. She committed the charge of her house and servants to Jessica and Lorenzo.

Instead of taking the course she had described, however, Portia set about executing other plans. She gave her servant, Balthasar, orders to take a note to her cousin, Doctor Bellario, a famous lawyer of Padua, in order to secure a message and some clothes from him. She explained to Nerissa that they would go to Venice disguised as men.

The Duke of Venice, before whom Antonio's case was tried, was reluctant to exact the penalty in Shylock's contract. When his appeals to the Jew's better feelings went unheeded, he could see no course before him but to allow the moneylender his due. Bassanio tried to make Shylock relent by offering him the six thousand ducats, but, like the Duke, he met only a firm refusal.

Portia, dressed as a lawyer, and Nerissa, disguised as her clerk, appeared in the court. Nerissa offered the duke a letter from Doctor Bellario, in which the doctor explained that he was very ill, but that Balthasar, his young representative, would present his opinion in the dispute.

When Portia appealed to the Jew's mercy, Shylock merely demanded the penalty. Portia then declared that the Jew, under the letter of the contract, could not be offered money in exchange for Antonio's release. The only alternative was for the merchant to forfeit his flesh.

Antonio prepared his bosom for the knife, for Shylock was determined to take his portion as close to his enemy's heart as he could cut. Before the operation could begin, however, Portia, examining the contract, declared that it contained no clause stating that Shylock could have any blood with the flesh. The Jew, realizing that he was defeated, offered at once to accept the six thousand ducats, but Portia declared that he was not entitled to the money he had already refused. She stated also that Shylock, an alien, had threatened the life of a Venetian citizen. For that crime Antonio had the right to seize half of his property and the state the remainder.

Antonio refused that penalty, but it was agreed that one half of Shylock's fortune should go at once to Jessica and Lorenzo. Shylock was to keep the remainder, but it was to be willed to the couple after his death. In addition, Shylock was to undergo conversion. The defeated man had no choice but to agree to the terms.

Pressed to accept a reward, Portia took only a pair of Antonio's gloves and the ring that she herself had given Bassanio. Nerissa, likewise, managed to secure Gratiano's ring. Then Portia and Nerissa started back for Belmont, to be there when their husbands returned. They arrived home shortly before Bassanio and Gratiano appeared in company with Antonio. Pretending to discover that their husbands' rings were missing, Portia and Nerissa at first accused Bassanio and Gratiano of unfaithfulness. At last, to the surprise of all, they revealed their secret, which was vouched for by a letter from Doctor Bellario. For Jessica and Lorenzo, they had the good news of their future inheritance, and for Antonio a letter, secured by chance, announcing that some of his ships had arrived safely in port after all.

Critical Evaluation:

Through the years, *The Merchant of Venice* has been one of William Shakespeare's most popular and most frequently performed plays. Not only does the work have an interesting and fast-moving plot, it also evokes an idyllic, uncorrupted world reminiscent of folk tale and romance. From the opening description of Antonio's nameless sadness, the world is bathed in light and music. The insistently improbable plot is complicated only by the evil influence of Shylock, and he is disposed of by the end of Act IV. Yet Shakespeare uses this fragile vehicle to make significant points about justice, mercy, and friendship, three typical Renaissance virtues. Although some critics have suggested that the play contains all of the elements of tragedy only to be rescued by a comic resolution, the tone of the whole play creates a benevolent world in which, despite some opposition, things will always work out for the best.

The story, which is based on ancient tales that could have been drawn from many sources, is actually two stories in one—the casket-plot, involving the choice by the suitor and his reward with Portia, and the bond-plot, involving the loan and the attempt to exact a pound of flesh. Shakespeare's genius is revealed in the way he combines the two. Although they intersect from the start in the character of Bassanio, who occasions Antonio's debt and is a suitor, they fully coalesce when Portia comes to Venice in disguise to make her plea and judgment for Antonio. At that point, the bond-plot is unraveled by the casket-heroine, after which the fifth act brings the celebratory conclusion and joy.

The most fascinating character to both audiences and critics has always been Shylock, the outsider, the anomaly in this felicitous world. Controversy rages over just what kind of villain Shylock is and just how villainous Shakespeare intended him to be. The matter has been complicated by the twentieth century desire to absolve Shakespeare of the common medieval and Renaissance vice of anti-Semitism. Some commentators have argued that in Shylock Shakespeare takes the stock character of the Jew—as personified in Christopher Marlowe's Barabas in his *The Jew of Malta* (1589)—and fleshes him out with complicating human characteristics. Some have gone so far as to argue that even in his villainy, Shylock is presented as a victim of the Christian society, the grotesque product of hatred and ostracism. Regardless of Shakespeare's personal views, the fact remains that in his treatment, Shylock becomes much more than a stock villain.

The more significant dramatic question is just what sort of character Shylock is and what sort of role he is being called upon to play. Certainly he is an outsider in both appearance and action, a stranger to the light and gracious world of Venice and Belmont. His language is full of stridency and materialism, which isolates him from the other characters. He has no part in the network of beautiful friendships that unites the others. He is not wholly a comic character, for despite often appearing ridiculous, he poses too much of a threat to be dismissed lightly. Yet he is too ineffectual and grotesque to be a villain as cold and terrifying as Iago or Edmund, or one as engaging as Richard III. He is a malevolent force, who is finally overcome by the more generous world in which he lives. That he is treated so harshly by the Christians is the kind of irony that ultimately protects Shakespeare from charges of mindless anti-Semitism. Still, on the level of the romantic plot, he is also the serpent in the garden, deserving summary expulsion and the forced conversion that is both a punishment and a charity.

The rest of the major characters have much more in common with each other as sharers in the common civilization of Venice. As they come into conflict with Shylock and form relationships with one another, they act out the ideals and commonplaces of high Renaissance culture. Antonio, in his small but pivotal role, is afflicted with a fashionable melancholy and a gift for friendship. It is his casually generous act of friendship that sets the bond-plot in motion. Bassanio frequently comments on friendship and knows how to accept generosity gracefully, but Bassanio is not just a model Renaissance friend but also a model Renaissance lover. He is quite frankly as interested in Portia's money as in her wit and beauty; he unself-consciously represents a cultural integration of love and gain quite different from Shylock's materialism. When he chooses the leaden casket, he does so for precisely the right traditional reason— a distrust of appearances, a recognition that the reality does not always correspond. Of course, his success as suitor is never really in doubt but is choreographed like a ballet. In any case, it is always the third suitor who is the successful one in folktales. What the ballet provides is another opportunity for the expression of the culturally correct sentiments.

Portia too is a heroine of her culture. She is not merely an object of love but a witty and intelligent woman whose ingenuity resolves the central dilemma. That she, too, is not what she seems to be in the trial scene is another example of the dichotomy between familiar appearance and reality. More important, she has the opportunity to discourse on the nature of mercy as opposed to strict justice and to give an object lesson that he who lives by the letter of the law will perish by it.

With Shylock safely, if a bit harshly, out of the way, the last act is an amusing festival of vindication of cultural values. The characters have had their opportunity to comment on the proper issues—love, friendship, justice, and the disparity between appearances and reality. Now all receive their appropriate reward in marriages and reunions or, in the case of Antonio, with the pleasantly gratuitous recovery of his fortune. There is no more trouble in paradise among the people of grace.

"Critical Evaluation" by Edward E. Foster

Bibliography:
Bulman, James. *Shakespeare in Performance: The Merchant of Venice.* New York: St. Martin's Press, 1992. Provides a survey of nineteenth century productions and a critique of several major twentieth century productions, including a comparison of Jonathan Miller's stage version (featuring Laurence Olivier as Shylock) with the BBC-TV version he produced ten years later.
Danson, Lawrence. *The Harmonies of "The Merchant of Venice."* New Haven, Conn.: Yale University Press, 1978. An excellent full-length study of the play that treats everything from

"The Problem of Shylock" to law and language, miracle and myth, love and friendship, and the "quality of mercy."

Gross, John. *Shylock: Four Hundred Years in the Life of a Legend*. London: Chatto & Windus, 1992. Gross traces Shylock's role and that of the play's in the history of anti-Semitism in the Western world. Also discusses the stage history of *The Merchant of Venice*, including several adaptations.

Levin, Richard A. *Love and Society in Shakespearean Comedy*. Newark: University of Delaware Press, 1985. Levin devotes one chapter to *The Merchant of Venice* and focuses on one of the play's central problems: the ambiguity of Shylock's conflicting motives in Act I, scene iii: The bond proposed may have been "a vicious and deceptive offer" or it may have been an incentive for better treatment from Antonio and others.

Rabkin, Norman. *Shakespeare and the Problem of Meaning*. Chicago: University of Chicago Press, 1981. In a superb essay on *The Merchant of Venice*, Rabkin notes the many significant inconsistencies and contradictions in the play and shows the impossibility of imposing easy, reductivist interpretation on it.

THE MERRY WIVES OF WINDSOR

Type of work: Drama
Author: William Shakespeare (1564-1616)
Type of plot: Comedy
Time of plot: Sixteenth century
Locale: England
First performed: 1597; first published, 1602

> *Principal characters:*
> SIR JOHN FALSTAFF, a rogue
> FENTON, a young gentleman
> SLENDER, a foolish gentleman
> FORD and
> PAGE, two gentlemen living at Windsor
> DOCTOR CAIUS, a French physician
> MISTRESS FORD, Ford's wife
> MISTRESS PAGE, Page's wife
> ANNE PAGE, the daughter of the Pages
> MISTRESS QUICKLY, a servant of Doctor Caius

The Story:

Sir John Falstaff was, without doubt, a rogue. True, he was fat, jolly, and in a way lovable, but he was still a rogue. His men robbed and plundered the citizens of Windsor, but he himself was seldom taken or convicted for his crimes. His fortunes being at low ebb, he hit upon a plan to remedy that situation. He had met Mistress Ford and Mistress Page, two good ladies who held the purse strings in their respective houses. Falstaff wrote identical letters to the two good ladies, letters protesting undying love for each of them.

The daughter of one of the ladies, Anne Page, was the center of a love triangle. Her father wished her to marry Slender, a foolish gentleman who did not love her or anyone else, but who would marry any girl that was recommended to him by his cousin, the justice. Mistress Page, on the other hand, would have her daughter married to Doctor Caius, a French physician then in Windsor. Anne herself loved Fenton, a fine young gentleman who was deeply in love with her. All three lovers paid the doctor's housekeeper, Mistress Quickly, to plead their cause with Anne, for Mistress Quickly had convinced each that she alone could persuade Anne to answer yes to a proposal. Mistress Quickly was, in fact, second only to Falstaff in her plotting and her trickery.

Unknown to poor Falstaff, Mistress Ford and Mistress Page compared the letters received from him, alike except for the lady's name. They decided to cure him of his knavery once and for all. Mistress Ford arranged to have him come to her house that night when her husband would not be there. Mistress Page wrote that she would meet him as soon as she could cautiously arrange it. In the meantime, two former followers of Falstaff had told the two husbands of that knave's designs on their wives. Page refused to believe his wife unfaithful, but Ford became jealous and planned to spy on his wife. Disguising himself as Mr. Brook, he called on Falstaff. His story was that he loved Mistress Ford but could not win her love, and he came to pay Falstaff to court her for him. His stratagem was successful; he learned from Falstaff that the knight already had a rendezvous with the lady that very night.

At the appointed time, having previously arranged to have several servants assist in the plot, the two ladies were ready for Falstaff. While Falstaff was trying to make love to Mistress Ford, Mistress Page rushed in and said that Ford was on his way home. Quickly the ladies put Falstaff in a clothesbasket and had him carried out by the servants, to be dumped into the Thames. Ford did arrive, of course, for, unknown to his wife, he knew Falstaff was to be there. After looking high and low without finding the rogue, he apologized to his wife for his suspicions. Mistress Ford did not know which had been the most sport, having Falstaff dumped into the river or listening to her husband's discomfited apologies.

The ladies had so much fun over their first joke played on Falstaff that they decided to try another. Mistress Ford then sent him another message, this one saying that her husband would be gone all of the following morning, and she asked Falstaff to call on her at that time so that she could make amends for the previous affair of the basket. Again Ford, disguised as Brook, called on Falstaff, and again he learned of the proposed assignation. He learned also of the method of Falstaff's previous escape and vowed the old roisterer should not again slip through his fingers.

When Mistress Ford heard from Mistress Page that Ford was returning unexpectedly, the ladies dressed Falstaff in the clothes of a fat woman whom Ford hated. Ford, finding the supposed woman in his house, drubbed the disguised knight soundly and chased him from the house. Again Ford searched everywhere for Falstaff, and again he was forced to apologize to his wife in the presence of the friends he had brought with him to witness her disgrace. The two ladies thought his discomfiture the funniest part of their joke.

Once more the wives planned to plague poor Falstaff, but this time they took their husbands into their confidence. When Mistress Page and Mistress Ford told about the letters they had received from Falstaff and explained the details of the two previous adventures, Ford felt very contrite over his former suspicions of his wife. Eagerly, the husbands joined their wives in a final scheme intended to bring Falstaff to public shame. The ladies would persuade Falstaff to meet them in the park at midnight. Falstaff was to be disguised as Herne the Hunter, a horned legendary huntsman said to roam the wintry woods each midnight. There he would be surrounded by Anne Page and others dressed as fairies and elves. After he had been frightened half to death, the husbands would accost him and publicly display his knavery.

A quite different event had also been planned for that night. Page plotted to have Slender seize Anne in her disguise as the fairy queen and carry her away to marry her. At the same time, Mistress Page arranged to have Doctor Caius find Anne and take her away to be married. Anne, however, had other plans. She and Fenton agreed to meet in the park and under cover of the dark and confusion flee her parents and her two unwelcome suitors.

All plans were put into effect. Falstaff, after telling the supposed Brook that on this night he would for a certainty win Mistress Ford for him, donned the horns of a stag and met the two ladies at the appointed place. Quickly the fairies and witches surrounded him, and the women ran to join their husbands and watch the fun. Poor Falstaff tried to pretend that he was asleep or dead, but the merry revelers burned his fingers with tapers they carried, and pinched him unmercifully. When Falstaff threw off his disguise, Ford and Page and their wives laid hold of him and soundly scolded him for his silly gallantry and bombast. The wives ridiculed his ungainly body and swore that none would ever have such a fool for a lover. Such was Falstaff's nature, however, that no one could hate him for long. After he had admitted his guilt and his stupidity, they all forgave him.

While all this merriment was going on, Anne and Fenton had stolen away to be married. They returned while the rest were busy with Falstaff. Page and his wife were in such good humor over all that had occurred that they forgave the young lovers and bestowed their blessing on them. Then the whole company, Falstaff included, retired to Page's house to laugh again over the happenings of that night.

Critical Evaluation:

Under public pressure to bring back Sir John Falstaff after Prince Hal's arrogant dismissal of his boyhood friend in *Henry IV, Part II* (1597) and *Henry V* (1598-1599), Shakespeare reintroduces the fat knight in a slapstick romp, *The Merry Wives of Windsor*. On the one hand, the farce can be viewed as a ridiculous satire of the London burghers, the Fords and the Pages, who successfully outwit the not-so-sly fox of an aristocrat, Falstaff, who is trying in his usual way to disrupt the pleasures and the comforts of the conventional.

Another way of approaching the play is by viewing it as a comic resolve of a story similar in some incidents to Shakespeare's earlier play, *Romeo and Juliet* (1594-1596). Unwittingly, Falstaff, in his buffoonery, performs the role of diverting the Pages from the elopement of their daughter, Anne, and Fenton, the comic Romeo. A potential tragedy thus averted, love is allowed to flourish. Falstaff plays the same role which Shakespeare had assigned to him in the histories. As opposed to the deliberate Hal, who orders everything in his life, even his leisure with his cronies, Falstaff devotes his whole life to play, the gratification of the instincts, and the preservation of the self. His dalliance with the Mistresses Page and Ford may be a mockery of good burgher virtue, but he also pursues it with a good deal of pleasure, pleasure for its own sake. Everyone wins in the process. Anne is married to the man she loves, and the Pages, the Fords, and Sir John all have a thoroughly fine time in the romp. The only loser is respectability, which takes a back seat to the loud, vulgar guffaws of "Fat Jack" Falstaff.

Bibliography:

Barton, Ann. "Falstaff and the Comic Community." In *Shakespeare's "Rough Magic": Renaissance Essays in Honor of C. L. Barber*, edited by Peter Erickson and Coppélia Kahn. Newark, N.J.: University of Delaware Press, 1985. An excellent study of Falstaff, the most controversial character in the play. Barton shows that Shakespeare was consciously trying to exclude such self-seeking epicureans from his plays; Falstaff in *The Merry Wives of Windsor* was the last time such a character received such prominence.

Green, William. *Shakespeare's "Merry Wives of Windsor."* Princeton, N.J.: Princeton University Press, 1962. This book follows the history of the play, from its composition to its first performance and audience.

Hemingway, Samuel B. "On Behalf of That Falstaff." *Shakespeare Quarterly* 3 (1952): 307-311. Hemingway attributes Falstaff's controversy to his presence in the *Henry IV* plays as well as in *The Merry Wives of Windsor*. Shakespeare's portrayal of him is different in each.

Roberts, Jeanne Addison. *Shakespeare's English Comedy: "The Merry Wives of Windsor" in Context*. Lincoln: University of Nebraska Press, 1979. Places the play into the context of the development of Shakespeare's career, arguing that the play provided Shakespeare's transition from writing histories to writing tragedies. Roberts also includes chapters on the text, date, sources, and genre.

Wells, Stanley, ed. *The Cambridge Companion to Shakespeare Studies*. Cambridge, England: Cambridge University Press, 1986. This is where all studies of Shakespeare should begin. It includes excellent chapters introducing the poet's biography, conventions and beliefs of Elizabethan England, and reviews of scholarship in the field.

THE METAMORPHOSES

Type of work: Poetry
Author: Ovid (Publius Ovidius Naso, 43 B.C.E.-17 C.E.)
First published: Before 8 C.E. (English translation, 1567)

The Metamorphoses is generally conceded to be Ovid's finest work. In this collection of poems, Ovid managed to draw together artistically most of the stories of Greek and Roman legend. He rendered more than two hundred of the myths of the ancient world into an organic work whose unifying theme was that of transformation. Thus Jove changed himself into a swan, Narcissus was transformed into a flower, Tereus was turned into a bird, and Midas was given the ears of an ass. Ovid arranged these stories into fifteen books, containing in the original Latin version almost twelve thousand lines of sweetly flowing verse in the dactylic hexameter common in classical poetry. The poems were written when Ovid was a mature man of perhaps fifty, shortly before Augustus Caesar banished him far from the city he loved to the little town of Tomi on the shores of the Black Sea. Ovid wrote that he destroyed his own copy of *The Metamorphoses*, apparently because he was dissatisfied with his performance, but he nevertheless seemed to feel that the work would live after him. In his epilogue to *The Metamorphoses*, he wrote:

> Now I have done my work. It will endure,
> I trust, beyond Jove's anger, fire, and sword,
> Beyond Time's hunger. The day will come, I know,
> So let it come, that day which has no power
> Save over my body, to end my span of life
> Whatever it may be. Still, part of me,
> The better part, immortal, will be borne
> Above the stars; my name will be remembered
> Wherever Roman power rules conquered lands,
> I shall be read, and through all centuries,
> If prophecies of bards are ever truthful,
> I shall be living, always.

As if it were necessary for a work of literary art to have some edifying or moral purpose, the poems have sometimes been regarded primarily as a useful handbook on Greek and Roman mythology. Certainly the work does contain a wealth of the ancient legends, and many later writers have become famous in part because they were able to build on the materials Ovid placed at their disposal. However, *The Metamorphoses* is a work of art in its own right.

In later times, stories about the gods of the pagan Pantheon have been viewed in a different light from that in which such tales Ovid's contemporaries regarded them. Where readers in later times could smile, Ovid's light, even facetious, tone was regarded by serious Romans as having more than a little touch of blasphemy. Perhaps his irreverent attitudes may even have been a partial cause for his exile, for Augustus Caesar was at the time attempting moral reforms. Moreover, Ovid had, after having good-humoredly dealt with various gods, turned at the end of *The Metamorphoses* to describe the transformation of Julius Caesar into a god. How seriously he meant this to be taken is not clear from the tone of the poem.

Ovid begins his collection with a description of how the universe came into being with the metamorphosis of Chaos, the unshaped stuff, into Cosmos, the ordered universe. Having described how the Lord of Creation, "Whatever god it was," established order in the universe,

Ovid proceeds to give a picture of the four ages. He begins his account with the Golden Age, when justice and right existed everywhere, and when law and punishment were absent because they were unnecessary. When Saturn was sent to the land of shadowy death, writes Ovid, and Jove became chief of the gods, then came the Age of Silver, when human beings first built houses to guard themselves against the seasons and planted fields to provide themselves with a harvest. Next came the Age of Bronze, when warlike instincts and aggression came into being, to be succeeded in its turn by the Iron Age, when modesty, truth, and righteousness were displaced by trickery, violence, and swindling. So bad was this age that Jove struck down the living and nature brought forth a new race of human beings who were, as Ovid put it, "men of blood." Of this race, all except Deucalion and Pyrrha, a righteous man and woman, were wiped from the face of the earth by Jove, who with Neptune's aid caused a flood to cover the globe. Ovid's stories of the Creation and the Flood, told in a pagan environment, are strikingly similar to the stories of the same phenomena told in the Old Testament.

Much of Ovid's poetry in *The Metamorphoses* deals with love. It is not romanticized, sentimentalized love, however, for the poet recognizes the physical reality that men and women represent to one another, and his gods and goddesses exhibit human passions. In love, as Ovid describes it, there is often a strain of cruelty and brutality; the veneer of civilization is thin enough to let his readers sense the savagery of violence, revenge, and cruelty underlying human nature. In this connection, Ovid recalls Lycaon boiling and broiling the flesh of a human hostage before the altar of Jove; Tereus raping Philomela and then cutting out her tongue to keep the deed a secret; a satyr being flayed alive by Apollo, the son of Latona, for trying to surpass him at playing the flute; sixteen-year-old Athis having his face battered to mere splinters of bone by Perseus; and Pelias' daughters' letting their father's blood at the behest of Medea. In these stories gory details are described in the account of each brutal act; brains, blood, broken bones, and screams of agony and hate fill the lines. Love and hate, both powerful, basic human emotions, are close in Ovid's *Metamorphoses*.

Mere enumeration does not do Ovid's collection the justice it deserves. Practically every phase of the Graeco-Roman mythology is at least represented in the fifteen divisions of the work. The stories are drawn together with consummate skill. Yet the noteworthy fact in assessing Ovid's mastery of his materials and craft is that he himself was a skeptic who did not believe in these stories as having actually happened. Without the sincerity of belief, he nevertheless wrote in such a way as to induce in the reader that mood that Samuel Taylor Coleridge, almost two thousand years later, described as the "willing suspension of disbelief."

Ovid placed believable personalities in his pages. His men and women and his gods and goddesses hate and love as human beings have always done. Later readers have always recognized in themselves the same surges and flows of emotion they find in Ovid's poetry. In this way, later times, despite technological advances, were little different from the Roman empire of Ovid and Augustus.

Ovid's style also includes a large amount of specific detail with which he creates a vivid picture of people or actions. Particularly vital moments include that when Myrrha, in "Cinyras and Myrrha," flings herself, face down, to cry into her pillow; when Pygmalion lavishes gifts of pet birds, sea shells, lilies, and lumps of precious amber on his beloved statue; and when Dorylas, in "The Battle of the Centaurs," is wounded by Peleus and dies trailing his entrails, treading and tangling them with his centaur's hoofs. These details are a reminder that Ovid's Rome was a culture that included not only greatness in art but also the grim and bloody scenes of death by violence within the arena at the Colosseum.

Bibliography:

Gregory, Horace. Introduction to *The Metamorphoses*, by Ovid. Translated by Horace Gregory. New York: New American Library, 1958. Discusses Ovid's play with emotional extremes and conflicting impulses, which infuses *The Metamorphoses* with psychological insight. Discusses Ovid's interest in the subject of women and how this interest illumines his conflict with the Emperor Augustus.

Innes, Mary M. Introduction to *The Metamorphoses of Ovid*. Translated by Mary M. Innes. 1955 Reprint. New York: Penguin, 1975. Includes sections on Ovid's life and works, a commentary on *The Metamorphoses*, a discussion of its influence on later European literature, and a note on Innes' translation.

Mack, Sara. "*The Metamorphoses*." In *Ovid*. New Haven, Conn.: Yale University Press, 1988. Chapters on the reception of Ovid in his own time and later, on his love poetry, on *The Metamorphoses*, and on Ovid the poet. Chapter on *The Metamorphoses* focuses on such difficult aspects of the poem as its structure, transitions, and the inclusion of less appealing tales.

Otis, Brooks. *Ovid as an Epic Poet*. Cambridge, England: Cambridge University Press, 1966. Describes the plan and structure of the poem. Finds the unity of the poem in its order or succession of episodes, motifs, and ideas. Argues that this unity is marred by disharmony between the poem's Roman-Augustan element and its amatory element.

Rand, Edward Kennard. "Poet of Transformations." In *Ovid and His Influence*. New York: Cooper Square, 1963. Devotes a chapter to each of Ovid's major works; analyzes Ovid's influence on medieval and Renaissance authors.

THE METAMORPHOSIS

Type of work: Novella
Author: Franz Kafka (1883-1924)
Type of plot: Allegory
Time of plot: Early twentieth century
Locale: Prague
First published: Die Verwandlung, 1915 (English translation, 1946)

> *Principal characters:*
> GREGOR SAMSA, a man who wakes up to find that he has been
>   transformed into a giant insect
> GRETE SAMSA, his sister
> MR. SAMSA, his father
> MRS. SAMSA, his mother
> THE CHIEF CLERK, his boss
> THREE BOARDERS

The Story:

Gregor Samsa awoke one morning from "uneasy dreams" to find that he had been transformed during the night into a gigantic insect. At first, he tried to remain calm and go back to sleep. His transformed body, however, prevented him from getting comfortable. Regardless of the changes in him, Gregor's thoughts turned to the job he hated, and, as he looked at the clock, he feared being late at the office. Through the locked door to his room, his mother reminded him of the time, and he noticed the change in his voice when he replied. His response alerted the rest of his family that he was still at home, which was unexpected at that time of day.

Still attempting to maintain some semblance of normality, Gregor tried to get out of bed, but it required an unusual effort, rocking back and forth, before he finally fell out of bed onto the floor. When the chief clerk from his office arrived to check on Gregor's whereabouts, he doubled his efforts to return to normal. Gregor's father called to him to allow the clerk to enter his room, but Gregor refused because he was afraid that his job would be jeopardized if the chief clerk discovered his transformation. He was convinced that he could explain his rudeness later, after he had recovered. The clerk threatened him, and Gregor heard the clerk comment about how inhuman his voice sounded. Gregor finally wedged himself against the door and opened the lock with his jaws, but, as he appeared in the doorway, his altered appearance frightened the clerk, who fled the apartment. Gregor's family stared at him, amazed at the metamorphosis he had undergone. Finally, his father forced him back into his room and shut the door.

The next morning, his sister left him food on the floor of his room, but Gregor remained hidden underneath the sofa while she was in the room lest he should frighten her. For the next two days, he overheard his family discussing what they should do about him and the changes that they would have to make in their lives, since he had supplied their only source of income. Gregor worried about his family and mulled over the guilt he felt for losing his job and his place as breadwinner of the household. Night after night, he huddled in the dark and thought about his predicament.

For the first fortnight, his parents could not bear to enter his room, but Grete removed his furniture piece by piece, claiming that he would be more comfortable if he could move around unencumbered by things that were no longer useful to him. His mother argued with her about leaving the room alone, hoping that he would recover from his illness, but his father had lost hope and insisted that he would never recover. One day, his mother entered his room and saw Gregor clinging to the wall by the sticky feet of his many legs. The shock at seeing him behaving like an insect shattered her attachment to him and destroyed forever any hope she had had for his eventual recovery. Despite his changed appearance, Gregor remained lonely for the company of his family and, one night, in a desperate attempt to join his family, ventured out of his room once more. However, his father, angered at Gregor's intrusion into the family's quarters, yelled at him and pelted him with apples, wounding him in the back before forcing Gregor to return to the solitude of his room.

His movements hindered by his injury, Gregor observed the changes his family experienced during his absence through his door, which was inexplicably left open every evening. Even though his father returned to work and they had dismissed the maid, his parents were strained economically, physically exhausted, and increasingly despondent. They largely neglected Gregor and left him alone in his room. He seldom slept and was increasingly haunted by the thought that he would one day recover and once again provide for his family.

In order to increase their income, the family took in three lodgers, and one evening they requested that Grete play her violin. Attracted by the music, which reminded him of the way his life used to be, Gregor left his room once again seeking the warmth and companionship of the others. The lodgers, who did not know of his existence, were outraged by his appearance and threatened to leave, and, for the first time, Gregor heard Grete demand that something be done about him. She called him a creature and denied that he was still her brother. In his weakened condition, it was difficult for him to return for the final time to his room. Once back inside, Gregor realized that he, too, felt the same despair his sister did and longed for death. During the night, he lost consciousness and, the next morning, the charwoman found the husk of Gregor's dead body in the room and swept him up with the trash.

His family seemed little surprised by his death and left the apartment the same day for the first time in months, going into the country to discuss their prospects for the future. They decided to move to a smaller and more convenient apartment. Observing the vivacious change in their daughter, brought about by Gregor's death, her parents realized that it was time to find her a husband.

Critical Evaluation:

Franz Kafka began writing in his early twenties while studying law at the University of Prague from 1901 to 1906. In 1908, he began publishing extracts from his early novel, *Amerika* (1913), and *The Metamorphosis* was written in late 1912, appearing in print in 1915. His working career spans only sixteen years, and, when he died in 1924 at the age of forty-one, many of his major novels had not been published; his work was little known outside of avant-garde German literary circles.

Kafka is now regarded as a central figure in twentieth century literature. The commentary on his writings and his life is extremely large, including scores of books and hundreds of articles. Of all his publications, *The Metamorphosis* is undoubtedly his most famous. The novella has been widely anthologized and is available in several single-volume editions; in addition, the number of articles and portions of books about the story make it the most heavily analyzed of all Kafka's works.

Because it has been so frequently discussed from so many different perspectives—psychological, sociological, political, philosophical, linguistic, and religious—it is difficult to summarize the responses to *The Metamorphosis*. Marxists, psychoanalysts, postmodernists, feminists, Zionists, structuralists, and poststructuralists have all interpreted the story in different ways. However, there does seem to be some general agreement that such overall themes as guilt, judgment, retribution, alienation, and the place of the artist in society are contained in the core of the narrative.

Kafka's writings largely originated from the conflicted relationship he experienced with his family, especially his father. This biographical connection has been much discussed, and it is easily perceived in Gregor Samsa's reaction to his family. Although constrained by his obligations to support his father, mother, and sister, Gregor nevertheless seeks throughout the tale to be reintegrated into the family circle. Made aware of his alienation from them by his transformation, he vainly attempts to ignore it at first and to maintain a semblance of normality, until he is finally abandoned by his sister, with whom he had had a close relationship. It is her firm rejection of him as a person which ultimately causes him to surrender his own sense of self, precipitating his death.

The Metamorphosis is constructed in three acts, each involving an escape by Gregor from his room and a return to it. With each retreat, Gregor becomes noticeably less human and more accepting of his transformative state. With each act, Gregor also becomes physically weaker. As his family abandons its denial of his insectlike appearance and their hope for his full recovery to a normal human condition, they gradually become indifferent to his fate and recognize their need to pursue their lives without him. His father returns to work, his mother learns to operate the house without the help of a maid, even adding the burden of taking in boarders, and his sister assumes the responsibilities of adulthood. Where once he was the center of their lives, he now becomes an unnecessary burden and an embarrassment.

The horror of a tale about a man who transforms into an insect is heightened by Kafka's literary style: a matter-of-fact tone laced with mordant humor. The fact that Gregor initially greets his metamorphosis with a chilling calm suggests that he previously saw himself as verminlike, as somebody who was already less than human. This internal lack of self-esteem and the insecurities it produces are heightened by the change in his body. One of the major problems to reading *The Metamorphosis* is accepting Gregor's transformation as literal and not merely symbolic; he has really turned into an insect. The strangeness of that fact, along with his and his family's reactions to it, is what makes the narrative so fascinating and rich in interpretative possibilities.

The power of Franz Kafka's fiction relies primarily on the uncanny ways he captured the alienation of twentieth century life. Denied the saving grace of religious belief, skeptical of the achievements of modern science, and leery of the significance of art, Kafka's characters are left adrift in a world of their own making over which they seem to have little control. *The Metamorphosis* captures all of the fear and doubt with which human beings face their future.

Charles L. P. Silet

Bibliography:
Bouson, J. Brooks. "The Narcissistic Drama and Reader/Text Transaction in Kafka's Metamorphosis." In *Critical Essays on Franz Kafka*, edited by Ruth V. Gross. Boston: G. K. Hall, 1990. Heinz Kohut's work on narcissistic disorders suggests a new reading of Gregor's hostile world, arguing against the theory of depersonalization.
Eggenschwiler, David. "*The Metamorphosis*, Freud, and the Chains of Odysseus." In *Modern Critical Views: Franz Kafka*, edited by Harold Bloom. New York: Chelsea House, 1986. The

author traces the psychological origins of the story in Kafka's life and encourages a recognition of the tension between parable and interpretation.

Gray, Ronald. *Franz Kafka*. Cambridge, England: Cambridge University Press, 1973. This is the best and most accessible short analysis of Kafka's work, and it furnishes a literary context for the tale.

Hayman, Ronald K. *A Biography of Kafka*. London: Weidenfeld and Nicolson, 1981. This biography is a solid and readable account of Kafka's life.

Karl, Frederick R. *Franz Kafka: Representative Man*. New York: Ticknor & Fields, 1991. Karl's exhaustive study of Kafka's culture extends the possible interpretations of his work.

METAMORPHOSIS

Type of work: Poetry
Author: Edith Sitwell (1887-1964)
First published: 1933 in *Five Variations on a Theme*

The writings of Dame Edith Sitwell sparked both friendly and hostile responses from twentieth century critics. Poets William Butler Yeats and Stephen Spender praised her work, but other critics denounced her work as unpoetic. Sitwell's sharp criticism of those, such as poet Ezra Pound, who did not like her work, led to strongly partisan views of her poetry, with few critics taking time to evaluate the content and genius of her poetry. In the tradition of T. S. Eliot and other symbolist poets, Sitwell enjoyed using sharply contrasting images to evoke emotions in the reader.

Metamorphosis, both in its original 1929 version and even more so in its 1946 revision, represents a transition from Sitwell's earlier, more self-conscious work to her more cohesive, thematically consistent poetry of later years. This poem first appeared in the book *Five Variations on a Theme* (1933), where it was grouped with four other poems, including "Elegy on Dead Fashion" (1926), "Two Songs" ("Come, My Arabia," and "My desert has a noble sun for heart"—both left out of Sitwell's *Collected Works* of 1954), and "Romance" (1933). As with many of Sitwell's other poetry, this set of poems shares several themes, especially that of death overcoming the destructive forces of time and leading to the brightness of eternity. In developing these themes she repeats imagery such as green grass and shadows and shade, along with longer passages of imagery, to emphasize the poems' interrelatedness. Even in this set of five poems, *Metamorphosis* stands as a transitional work, revealing as it does her growing openness to a Christian resolution. By the time she arranged her *Collected Poems* in their 1954 version, she could declare in the preface to that work, "My poems are hymns of praise to the glory of Life." *Metamorphosis* clearly represents a step in this direction.

One of the major debates about the work concerns which version should be considered authoritative or most representative of Sitwell's intentions. In the preface to her *Collected Works*, Sitwell refused to choose between the two versions, simply declaring them both internally consistent with her intended expression of feeling and therefore both satisfactory, though quite different. Consequently, she there presents the two versions side by side without further comment.

The 1946 version is far more precise in expression and has fewer loose ends than does the 1929 version, but even more significant are the differences in tone between the two versions. The earlier poem is decidedly more melancholy than the later one. The 1929 version of *Metamorphosis* begins with a comparison of the snow to the Parthenon as a symbol for the ravages of time, after which the poet introduces the rose as beauty's daughter growing dark with time. Through various images, such as that of the darkening rose, the poem goes on to lament the cruelty of time in contrast to death, which offers a release from suffering and anxiety. As the poem declares, "Death has never worm for heart and brain/ Like that which Time conceives to fill his grave." Sitwell presents death as variously as the climate for living and travel, or as the sun to illumine "our old Dim-Jewelled bones," the topaz, sapphires, and diamonds hidden in the bones. These images of death are woven with images of integration and relating, including the portrayal of the persona's soul as Lazarus come back from the dead, or as the grass growing from the bones of the deceased. One of Sitwell's favorite refrains is that all people are Ethiopian shades of death, or are burned away by the sun's heat, which represents death. In this apparently grim discussion of death, the poem's emphasis falls on unity achieved through death. As the poet notes near the end of the poem,

> Since all things have beginnings; the bright plume
> Was once thin grass in shady winter's gloom,
> And the furred fire is barking for the shape
> Of hoarse-voiced animals.

As this compact section of the poem illustrates, all creation is united in the cycle of life, and each aspect of creation reflects the rest of the created order, even in its mortality.

The conclusion of the poem introduces one more actor, Christ or Heavenly Love, which like the sun will melt the "eternal ice/ Of Death, and crumble the thick centuries." Not only do blades of grass die and become plumes, not only is time overwhelmed by death, at last even death itself will be metamorphosed and life will remain. As the title of the poem implies, metamorphosis is built into creation in such a way as to foreshadow the greater metamorphoses yet to come.

Metamorphosis is rich with allusions from Greco-Roman, Judeo-Christian, and pagan antiquity, as is exemplified by allusions to nymphs, Saturn, Panope, Hector, Parthenon, Jove, Gehenna, and Lazarus. Sitwell thus underscores the universality of the ravages of time that she decries. Although the basic movement of the 1929 version of *Metamorphosis* is fairly consistent and many of the images are striking and intriguing, several of the images seem facile, inappropriate, or racially slighting. Turkeys are for example compared to sultans wearing turbans, an unflattering comparison in which neither image promotes the basic themes of the poem, and in several places people are identified as being as black as Ethiopia or as being like a small Negro page. Such images might be seen as evidence of the nature of metamorphosis, as unlike things are being compared, but the assumptions behind the images are unflattering at best and insensitive at worst. T. S. Eliot had similar problems with his caustic treatment of Jewish people as examples of rootless and unprincipled people in his *The Waste Land* (1922). Such aspects, while reflecting the perceptions current during the author's age, undercut the poem's movement toward unity of humanity and all creation.

By the time of the 1946 version of *Metamorphosis*, with its 132 lines less than half the length of the 1929 version with its 288 lines, the number of racial references has been reduced, and they are usually couched in ambiguous or ironic contexts. For example, shortly after referring to how "Death is the Sun's heat making all men black!," the poet declares again "All men are Ethiopian shades of thee [Death]"; two lines later, there is a reference to the rich and thick Ethiopian herds. In this context the references to Ethiopia are more positive and universal than before. The most significant change between the 1929 and 1946 versions is evident in the way the poet clarifies the essential tension between time and death and more overtly states her Christian resolution to this tension. Whereas this version of the poem still includes allusions to Greek and pagan myths, the allusions to Christian beliefs have been heightened. By stanza 9, the author has already introduced two Judeo-Christian images, the rainbow as a symbol of God's light and promises of mercy, and the dark rose as a symbol of God's love as shown through Christ, the rose of Sharon.

These Christian images of hope and love are linked with the sun, a seventeenth century pun for son or the Son of God, a connection clarified in the closing stanza of this poem. This sun comes to overcome both time and death with the bright hope of eternity expressed through scarlet colored clothing, symbolizing the blood of martyrdom and the flaming blooms of spring. Christ thus comes as a symbol of redemption and resurrection.

The closing two stanzas of the poem are powerful not only for their complex and multifaceted images that encompass the suffering of all time but also for their intriguing metrical variety. Both the 1929 and 1946 versions of this poem make heavy use of iambic pentameter with rhymed couplets, iambic being the natural walking meter in English and rhymed couplets being the easiest to organize. Yet all of these conventions are transformed in the closing stanzas, as if a metamorphosis has taken place that could be described only in a new mode. Here the work reveals some of the rhythmic variety and intensity of contrasting images often found in the writings of Gerard Manley Hopkins, whom Edith Sitwell admired. The penultimate stanza illustrates this pattern well:

> So, out of the dark, see our great Spring begins—
> Our Christ, the new Song, breaking out in the fields and hedgerows,
> The heart of Man! O, the new temper of Christ, in veins and branches.

Here it can be noted how the standard iambic pentameter has been translated into a form of sprung rhythm or accentual verse, verse that depends on a set number of accented syllables and any given number of unaccented syllables between them.

Metamorphosis, especially in its 1946 version, represents a major shift in Sitwell's poetic career. Her early poetic career was characterized by an exacting exploration of human suffering and pain, often in language that seemed somewhat posed and artificial, although certainly learned. Her later poetry, including the superb poem "Still Falls the Rain" (1942), demonstrates a profound sense of balance between her awareness of the suffering of all humanity and her understanding of Christ's sacrifice to bring healing into the world. Her acceptance of the Christian sense of resolution is all the more profound because of her honest acknowledgement of the pervasiveness of suffering in the world. At her best, Edith Sitwell's use of contrasting imagery and lyrical rhythms is as skillful as that of Dylan Thomas. Both poets understood well how truth is born in paradox. Sitwell's sense of suffering as a unifying factor in creation is in her later work carefully balanced with her recognition that divine love is finally greater than suffering and hate and evil. Like the late medieval poet Dante Alighieri, Sitwell brought her work not to the easy resolutions of humanists' praise of the capacity of humankind to endure hardships but to the recognition that all live under the sentence of suffering and death from which only divine love as expressed through Christ's redemptive work can free them. Although some may reject Edith Sitwell's Christian conclusions, her work follows the same line as that of T. S. Eliot, especially in his *Four Quartets* (1942), which Sitwell also admired. *Metamorphosis* demonstrates growth toward a vision of life large enough to swallow all its pain and lead it to the hope of eternal love. Poetically, this work demonstrates considerable maturity in her artistic and theological development.

Daven M. Kari

Bibliography:
Brophy, James D. *Edith Sitwell: The Symbolist Order*. Carbondale: Southern Illinois University Press, 1968. A detailed and skillful analysis of Edith Sitwell's full range of literary achievement. Places *Metamorphosis* in the context of *Five Variations on a Theme*, which deals with the defeat of time.
Cevasco, G. A. *The Sitwells: Edith, Osbert, and Sacheverell*. Boston: Twayne, 1987. A useful review of the biography and literary achievements of the three Sitwell siblings. A very useful

beginning source on Edith Sitwell, although *Metamorphosis* is discussed only briefly. Includes a chronology and an annotated bibliography.

Mills, Ralph J., Jr. *Edith Sitwell: A Critical Essay*. Grand Rapids, Mich.: William B. Eerdmans, 1966. A short and concise treatment of Christian themes in Edith Sitwell's poems, especially as they began to develop in *Metamorphosis* and later blossomed in her poetry of the 1940's.

Sitwell, Edith. *Taken Care Of: The Autobiography of Edith Sitwell*. New York: Atheneum, 1965. An intensely personal and at times painful revelation of the feelings and driving forces behind the poet's work. She has harsh criticism of many of her contemporaries and critics, especially of her parents, who scorned her appearance.

Villa, Jose Garcia, ed. *A Celebration for Edith Sitwell*. New York: New Directions, 1948. A collection of seventeen essays and other observations by such prominent critics as Stephen Spender, John Piper, Gertrude Stein, and John Russell. Includes Kenneth Clark's insightful discussion of both versions of *Metamorphosis*, which he claims present clues to the poet's growing artistic achievements.

MIDAQ ALLEY

Type of work: Novel
Author: Naguib Mahfouz (1911-   )
Type of plot: Historical realism
Time of plot: World War II
Locale: Cairo, Egypt
First published: Zuqaq al-Midaqq, 1947 (English translation, 1966, 1975)

> *Principal characters:*
> UNCLE KAMIL, a confectioner
> ABBAS HILU, a barber
> SALIM ALWAN, the owner of a large retail store
> SHEIKH DARWISH, a "holy man"
> "DR." BUSHI, a quack dentist
> KIRSHA, a coffeehouse owner
> HUSAIN KIRSHA, his son
> RADWAN HUSAINI, a devout Muslim
> HAMIDA, a prostitute
> UMM HAMIDA, her foster mother
> IBRAHIM FARAJ, a pimp

The Story:
  Night fell on Midaq Alley, a small, dead-end street in the ancient Gamaliyya section of Cairo. The entrance to this alley was established by two typical shops: on one side a sweetshop operated by Uncle Kamil, and across the street a barbershop run by Abbas. The men represented the traditional slow and never-changing life of this lower middle-class society at a time when the outside world and wartime were threatening to overwhelm them. Uncle Kamil was an old, lethargic man who spent most of his days asleep on a chair in front of his shop. He was now awakened by Abbas, reminding him that it was time to close. Abbas, although young and energetic, was satisfied with operating his shop and observing the social and religious customs that his society had always practiced.
  The two men joined others from the alley for an evening at Kirsha's coffee house, a typical male gathering place; the men all discussed an old man who had served as the poet in this café for several decades. Times had changed, and customers now preferred the radio to recitations of classical Arabic poetry. Two men came to the aid of this public performer, although neither was able to save his job; the two men were Sheikh Darwish, a "holy man" who made generally incomprehensible pronouncements in English to the group, and Radwan Husaini, the spiritual leader of Midaq Alley.
  Umm Hamida was a matchmaker. Her foster daughter was named Hamida. Hamida prepared herself for her customary afternoon walk outside Midaq Alley, a place she loathed and whose people she loathed. Much to her dismay, however, she did not have a new dress with which to exhibit her beauty.
  Husain Kirsha also felt real repugnance toward the alley and its people. Rather than remain in Midaq Alley, Husain went to work at a British army camp, where he earned much money. He supplemented his income by selling stolen goods. With these ill-gotten funds, Husain bought

fancy foods, wine, and hashish, all of which were forbidden by the Muslim religion. He persuaded his childhood friend, Abbas Hilu, to leave the barbershop and work for the British.

Whenever Hamida left the Alley, she was carefully watched, particularly by Salim Alwan and Abbas, both of whom coveted her. One day, Abbas decided to follow her, to speak to her, and to tell her of his love, a rather bold move for the normally shy and reticent barber. Hamida did not reject her suitor outright, because she believed that he was the only eligible bachelor in Midaq Alley. Abbas interpreted her response as the first sign of love, and he was exhilarated. After many more meetings, Abbas finally asked Hamida to become his wife. He knew of her strong yearning for money and material objects, so he told her that he would work for the British in another town, save his earnings, and give her everything she wanted. The greedy Hamida accepted his proposal and set the traditional engagement procedures into motion: "Dr." Bushi went on Abbas' behalf to ask Umm Hamida for her daughter's hand in marriage. Uncle Kamil brought sweets for a celebration. Finally, the couple read the appropriate verse from the Koran validating their intention to marry. The evening before he left, Abbas and Hamida sealed their vows with their first kiss.

The first problem arose shortly after Abbas' departure. Salim Alwan, the wealthy and sexually frustrated middle-aged owner of the retail store in Midaq Alley, had decided to divorce his wife and marry the young and beautiful Hamida. Umm Hamida and her daughter saw this as an opportunity to acquire great wealth. There was, however, the problem that Hamida was already engaged. Umm sought advice from Radwan Husaini, the most knowledgeable and devout Muslim in the alley. Husaini spoke against the marriage to Salim Alwan, but Husaini's counsel was rejected, and wedding plans were made. That same night, Salim Alwan's scheme was foiled when he had a severe heart attack; the attack devastated Hamida and her mother. Their plot to gain riches was thwarted.

A short time later, another opportunity arose when Ibrahim Faraj began to pursue Hamida. A stranger to Midaq Alley, Faraj wore European clothes and seemed to have considerable wealth; he was the type of man whom Hamida had dreamed of marrying. Hamida ran away with him; she believed that he loved her and that they would soon marry. Faraj's elegant apartment, however, actually served as his "school" for prostitutes, and his intent was to put Hamida to work for him. Her beauty made her a successful and wealthy prostitute, especially among British and American soldiers.

After quite some time, Abbas returned to Cairo. He had worked hard, saved money, and now wanted to marry Hamida. She had left. Neither he nor most others in Midaq Alley knew about Hamida's life as a prostitute. With his friend, Husain Kirsha, Abbas found consolation visiting bars and drinking wine; Abbas had previously never done this. One day, Abbas recognized Hamida as she rode through the streets in an elegant carriage. He pursued her and called out her name, but she was reluctant to acknowledge his presence. He told no one in Midaq Alley about this meeting. People advised him to return to his job and to forget Hamida.

Hamida's life had changed greatly during the period she had been working for her pimp, Ibrahim. She resented the power that he had over her, and she was searching for a way to escape from this enslavement. Now that Abbas had returned and had expressed a willingness to help her, she resolved to have Abbas kill Ibrahim the following Sunday. Husain convinced Abbas that Abbas had to avenge the insult Ibrahim had brought on Abbas' honor. The two men went to a bar where the murder was to take place; they found Hamida surrounded by a group of soldiers. Enraged, Abbas called out to Hamida; however, she rejected him. He hurled a beer glass at her and cut her beautiful face. The angry soldiers attacked Abbas and killed him, while Husain stood by and watched.

The following morning, the news of Abbas' death reached Midaq Alley. There was general mourning; Uncle Kamil wept. After a short while, the crisis subsided, and life in the Alley returned to its tradition-bound, established way of life.

Critical Evaluation:

In 1988, Naguib Mahfouz became the first Arabic-language author to win the Nobel Prize in Literature; he was cited for "works rich in nuance—now clear-sightedly realistic, now evocatively ambiguous—he has formed an Arabic narrative that applies to all mankind."

Mahfouz has been a prolific writer. In addition, he worked for thirty-five years as a full-time civil servant in numerous government ministries until his retirement in 1971. For many years, he also regularly contributed articles on a host of topics to Cairo newspapers.

A man of habit and great discipline, Mahfouz is seen as Egypt's finest writer, and he is credited with making the novel and short story popular in Arabic literature, whereas poetry had been the preferred genre for centuries. His work has been favorably compared to such Western European novelists as Honoré de Balzac, Charles Dickens, Thomas Mann, and John Galsworthy. He became well-known in his native Egypt with the Cairo trilogy (1956-1957), which traces the lives of three generations of a middle-class family between 1917 and 1944, a period of convulsive change in Egyptian society.

Mahfouz established his reputation in the English-speaking world with the translation of *Midaq Alley*, whose characters resemble people he met in the coffee houses he frequented in the neighborhood of his birth. Consequently, his novels portray a realistic world; at the same time, the novels represent a universal social landscape. The novel is divided into thirty-five chapters and includes more than fifty named characters, of which a dozen play major roles. The real character however, is Midaq Alley; the people represent the personalities that make up the life of Midaq Alley. Beyond the main story are numerous parallel and subplots which add seriousness and complexity.

Midaq Alley pictures life in two different worlds—in the alley and away from there—and at two different times—the old time that stands still, and the new time of changes. Each major character is confronted by these conflicts between the old and the new, the here and the there, and each character comes to realize that for survival, life demands a commitment to one or to the other.

It is clear that Hamida has chosen a new life away from Midaq Alley, and it is clear that she will survive. Her primary goal in life is to acquire material luxuries that the poverty of the Alley is unable to provide. Since she is not bound by a traditional ethical code, becoming a prostitute presents no moral conflict for her, especially since she gains the personal power over others that she seeks.

Abbas, however, is a victim of this changing world. His love for Hamida forces him to leave the Alley in order to earn money to provide a life for Hamida outside the only environment in which he can survive. When he finally returns, Hamida rejects him, and she uses him, once more, to fulfill her personal search for power.

Like Abbas, other characters find that they cannot exist in the duality. Salim Alwan is unable to fulfill the sexual fantasies of an elderly man longing for a young and beautiful wife. Umm Hamida has probably lost the riches that her foster daughter could have provided. Husain Kirsha finds his progress toward a life of ease halted when the British no longer employ him as the war comes to an end. Sheikh Darwish and Radwan Husaini have become irrelevant in the alley. Although they attempt to represent positive moral forces, no one accepts their counsel.

Uncle Kamil, the opposite of the character of Hamida, is a survivor because he makes no effort to change his place in the Alley, and he is not affected by the changing times. Hamida willingly prostitutes herself in the new world, and Uncle Kamil is always asleep.

Other characters, although important to the story, do not portray full lives either in or outside Midaq Alley. Their purpose is to enhance and complete the mosaic of a complex society in a critical period of transition.

Thomas H. Falk

Bibliography:

El-Enany, Rasheed. *Naguib Mahfouz: The Pursuit of Meaning*. New York: Routledge, Chapman & Hall, 1993. Major study concentrating on the themes and issues in Mahfouz's novels. Includes a carefully articulated examination of *Midaq Alley*.

Kilpatrick, Hilary. "The Egyptian Novel from *Zaynab* to 1980." In *Modern Arabic Literature*, edited by M. M. Badawi. Cambridge, England: Cambridge University Press, 1992. An important, in-depth examination of contemporary Egyptian literature, with special reference to Mahfouz. Positions him as a significant author of twentieth century prose.

Le Gassick, Trevor, ed. *Critical Perspectives on Naguib Mahfouz*. Washington, D.C.: Three Continents Press, 1991. A collection of essays published between 1971 and 1989 in various journals. Le Gassick translates some essays from Arabic. Articles range from discussions to commentaries on specific works, including a socio-cultural analysis of *Midaq Alley*.

Moosa, Matti. *The Early Novels of Naguib Mahfouz: Images of Modern Egypt*. Gainsville: University Press of Florida, 1994. Concentrates on Mahfouz's work from the formative years in the 1930's, his historical novels, and the novels dealing with contemporary Egypt up to 1959. Includes a detailed analysis of the Cairo trilogy and a thorough examination of *Midaq Alley*.

Somekh, Sasson. *The Changing Rhythm: A Study of Najib Mahfuz's Novels*. Leiden, The Netherlands: E. J. Brill, 1973. This examination, considered by many scholars to be a classic study, remains an important and valuable assessment of Mahfouz's writings, especially his earlier prose works. Includes a useful survey of the development of the Egyptian novel as an emerging literary form in the twentieth century.

MID-CHANNEL

Type of work: Drama
Author: Arthur Wing Pinero (1855-1934)
Type of plot: Psychological realism
Time of plot: Early twentieth century
Locale: London
First performed: 1909, first published, 1910

Principal characters:

ZOE BLUNDELL, an attractive, intelligent woman
THEODORE BLUNDELL, husband of Zoe
THE HONORABLE PETER MOTTRAM, a friend of the Blundells
LEONARD FERRIS, Zoe's lover
ETHEL PIERPOINT, fiancée of Leonard
MRS. PIERPOINT, Ethel's mother
MRS. ALICE ANNERLY, Theodore's lover

The Story:

Mrs. Pierpoint and daughter Ethel visited Zoe Blundell to inquire about the possibility of Leonard Ferris as a suitor for Ethel. Mrs. Pierpoint sought Zoe's opinion because Leonard was one of Zoe's tame robins, a group of male friends and admirers who gathered around Zoe. Unknown to the Pierpoints, Zoe's marriage was breaking up and Leonard was sexually attracted to Zoe. Zoe at first believed her relationship with Leonard was harmless because she felt much, much older than he. Leonard was 32, five years younger than Zoe, but he was a "fresh, boyish young man" and Zoe was a "mature woman." Zoe's husband Theodore is 46. Her perspective reflected society's double standard that an older man may be interested in a younger woman but an older woman should not be interested in a younger man. After the Pierpoints left, Leonard arrived to see Zoe and confessed he did not want to marry anyone, although he was attracted to Ethel because she reminds him of Zoe.

Leonard left and Peter Mottram arrived to discuss Zoe's marriage problems. Peter, who functioned as an informal marriage counselor between the Blundells, told Zoe that her marriage was like some trophies on a shelf. The trophies themselves are not valuable so much as the struggle to win them. Zoe, he thought, had to keep the trophies—like her marriage—new and fresh. Then Theodore arrived, and Peter tried to talk Theodore into mending the marriage. Peter gave another analogy: He described a body of water between Folkestone and Boulogne in which there was a mid-channel, a shoal that caused the passengers of a boat to experience rough travel. Peter said: "Everythin's looked as enticin' as could be; but as we've neared the Ridge—mid-channel—I've begun to feel fidgety, restless, out o' sorts—hatin' myself and hatin' the man who's been sharin' my cabin with me." He told the Blundells the crisis would end if they could wait. After Peter left, the Blundells did not heed his advice. Instead, they fought, and Theodore walked out on Zoe.

Some time later, Leonard and Zoe returned from a tour of Italy. They had a brief affair in Perugia and should have been more discreet. Claud Lowenstein saw them together at the Brufani Hotel. Upon returning to London, Leonard and Zoe learned that Theodore had been dating Alice Annerly, a 30-year-old divorcée. Zoe had a fever, a physical reflection of her declining moral state. Peter reappeared and tried to get Zoe and Theodore to mend their marriage. He again used an analogy. This time it concerned two cracked Ming vases. Would it not, he asked, be better to repair the broken vases than to throw them away? After Peter left, Ethel arrived to discuss her relationship with Leonard. She told Zoe that Leonard had come close to proposing marriage, but that he had changed since Italy and she feared he looked different, as if he had gotten "mixed up with some woman of the wrong sort." Leonard's guilt, like Zoe's, was also having a physical effect on him. Ethel innocently asked Zoe's help in saving him. Zoe said she would. Ethel left, and Leonard returned.

Zoe confronted Leonard about his relationship with Ethel, and he admitted he had been close to proposing marriage. Zoe said they should break up so that he could return to Ethel. Instead, Leonard confessed his love for Zoe and asked her to marry him. Zoe first responded with laughter, then anger. She called him a coward and told him she never wanted to see him again. He left furious.

Theodore and Alice Annerly discussed Theodore's relationship with Zoe. Theodore had discovered that he was still fond of his wife and unhappy with Alice. He told Alice their relationship had ended. Alice told him she felt compromised; Theodore wrote Alice a check for $1,500. Alice left and Peter came back, telling Theodore that Zoe wanted to reunite. Theodore had been miserable without her and was anxious to be with her again. Zoe entered at this point, and Theodore asked her if she could forgive him for Alice. Zoe said she would. Encouraged by Theodore's confessions, she asked him to forgive her for the affair she had had with Leonard. Theodore was outraged. He said he wanted a divorce if Leonard would agree to marry Zoe.

Zoe and Theodore had a showdown. Leonard told Zoe he planned to return to Ethel. Zoe had approached him thinking he would still marry her. Leonard had returned from the meeting with Zoe in which he had proposed to her and ripped apart her pictures. He then went back with Ethel. Talking with Leonard in his room, Zoe found that the pictures of her were no longer there; she was out of his life. When Theodore arrived to ask if Leonard would marry Zoe, she left the room thinking that Leonard belonged with Ethel, and she had no one. Leonard told Theodore, however, that he would still marry Zoe. While the two men conversed, Zoe committed suicide by throwing herself over the balcony.

Critical Evaluation:

Arthur Wing Pinero was one of the pioneers of psychological realism. He addressed the plight of women in unhappy marriages. His best-known play, *The Second Mrs. Tanqueray* (1893), preceded *Mid-Channel* by about twenty years and made Pinero's reputation as a serious playwright. Both plays are examples of the idea play, which centers on a societal issue.

The Second Mrs. Tanqueray deals with a frustrated marriage and ends in the suicide of Paula Tanqueray. The two plays have much in common, especially in their treatment of women. Both plays address the problems women encounter in marriage, but the solution to their problems leaves much to be desired: They both escape the marriage through suicide. This reflects the limited choices of women in England at the time. In *Mid-Channel*, Zoe Blundell has sinned and therefore must die. This illustrates the double standard; Theodore Blundell and Leonard Ferris have also sinned but they are able to redeem themselves. The blame for the unhappy marriage is placed upon Zoe although Theodore walks out on her. Zoe feels that she should have children, and many critics during the first run of the play said this was the primary reason for the Blundells' disastrous marriage. A marriage without children, after all, cannot be happy. The fact that the Blundells had no children was actually Theodore's fault because he told Zoe he did not want any children. Now that the Blundells are comfortable and their struggles are over, they find they cannot rest. They have hit middle age and feel they had accomplished nothing. Zoe is an intelligent, perceptive woman. The men surrounding Zoe—Theodore and Leonard—both love but fail to understand her. Peter is the only one who shows insight into Zoe's predicament, but he does not predict her suicidal reaction. Peter is a catalyst, one who causes changes but remains unchanged himself. Had Peter not arranged the reconciliation of the Blundells, the other events would probably never have happened. Ironically, therefore, Peter's meddling indirectly brings about Zoe's suicide.

Much of the action takes place outside the play—often between acts. The audience learns of events through conversations. At the beginning of the twentieth century, a play about divorce and suicide was daring and shocking; it is not surprising, therefore, that much of the play's action takes place off stage. Pinero was not the only writer of the period to show suicide as the only alternative to an unhappy marriage. The heroines in Henrik Ibsen's *Hedda Gabler* (1890) and Kate Chopin's *The Awakening* (1899) take their own lives rather than stay married and miserable.

Mary C. Bagley

Bibliography:
Cunliffe, John W. *Modern English Playwrights: A Short History of the English Drama from 1825*. Port Washington, N.Y.: Kennikat Press, 1969. Shows how *Mid-Channel* was received in America and Great Britain. Claims the play is overrated by American critics.

Dunkel, Wilbur D. *Sir Arthur Pinero: A Critical Biography with Letters*. Chicago: University of Chicago Press, 1941. Examines Pinero's works in relation to his life.

Fyfe, Hamilton. *Sir Arthur Pinero's Plays and Players*. New York: Macmillan, 1930. Discusses the main characters of *Mid-Channel* as well as the plot and setting of the play. Good for comparative study.

Nicoll, Allardyce. *British Drama: An Historical Survey from the Beginnings to the Present Time*. 5th ed. London: Harrap, 1978. Discusses Pinero's treatment of theme, the lack of sentiment, and cynical point of view. Describes Pinero's views of human weakness and how he acquired the reputation of one of London's master playwrights.

Roy, Emil. *British Drama Since Shaw*. Carbondale: Southern Illinois University Press, 1972. Claims Pinero needed to be more rebellious in his dramatic works. Says Pinero's drama functioned as middle-class escapist theater.

MIDDLEMARCH
A Study of Provincial Life

Type of work: Novel
Author: George Eliot (Mary Ann Evans, 1819-1880)
Type of plot: Psychological realism
Time of plot: Nineteenth century
Locale: England
First published: 1871-1872

> *Principal characters:*
> DOROTHEA BROOKE, an idealistic young woman
> EDWARD CASAUBON, her scholarly husband
> WILL LADISLAW, Casaubon's cousin
> TERTIUS LYDGATE, a doctor
> ROSAMOND VINCY, the woman he married
> CELIA, Dorothea's sister
> SIR JAMES CHETTAM, Celia's husband

The Story:

Dorothea Brooke and her younger sister, Celia, were young women of good birth who lived with their bachelor uncle at Tipton Grange near the town of Middlemarch. So serious was Dorothea's cast of mind that she was reluctant to keep jewelry she had inherited from her dead mother, and she gave all of it to her sister except a ring and a bracelet.

At a dinner party where the middle-aged scholar Edward Casaubon and Sir James Chettam both vied for her attention, she was much more attracted to the serious-minded Casaubon. Casaubon must have had an inkling that his chances with Dorothea were good; for he sought her out the next morning. Celia, who did not like his complexion or his moles, escaped to other interests.

That afternoon, Dorothea considered the scholar's wisdom. While she was out walking, she encountered Sir James by chance; he told her that he was in love with her and, mistaking her silence for agreement, assumed that she loved him in return. When Casaubon made his proposal of marriage by letter, Dorothea accepted him at once. Mr. Brooke, her uncle, thought Sir James a much better match; Dorothea's decision merely confirmed his bachelor views that women were difficult to understand. He decided not to interfere in her plans, but Celia felt that the event would be more like a funeral than a marriage and frankly said so.

Casaubon took Dorothea, Celia, and Mr. Brooke to see his home so that Dorothea might order any necessary changes. Dorothea intended to defer to Casaubon's tastes in all things and said she would make no changes in the house. During the visit, Dorothea met Will Ladislaw, Casaubon's second cousin, who did not seem in sympathy with his elderly cousin's marriage plans.

While Dorothea and her new husband were traveling in Italy, Tertius Lydgate, an ambitious but poor young doctor, was meeting pretty Rosamond Vincy, to whom he was much attracted. Fred Vincy, Rosamond's brother, had indicated that he expected to receive a fine inheritance when his uncle, Mr. Featherstone, died. Meanwhile, Vincy was pressed by a debt he was unable to pay.

Lydgate became involved in petty local politics. When the time came to choose a chaplain for the new hospital of which Lydgate was the head, the young doctor realized that it was in his best interest to vote in accordance with the wishes of Nicholas Bulstrode, an influential banker and founder of the hospital. A clergyman named Tyke received the office.

In Rome, Ladislaw encountered Dorothea and her middle-aged husband. Dorothea had begun to realize how pompous and incompatible she found Casaubon. Seeing her unhappiness, Ladislaw first pitied and then fell in love with his cousin's wife. Unwilling to live any longer on Casaubon's charity, Ladislaw announced his intention of returning to England and finding some kind of gainful occupation.

When Fred Vincy's note came due, he tried to sell a horse at a profit, but the animal turned out to be vicious. Because of Fred's inability to raise the money, Caleb Garth, who had signed his note, now stood to lose one hundred and ten pounds. Fred fell ill, and Lydgate was summoned to attend him. Lydgate used his professional calls to further his suit with Rosamond.

Dorothea and her husband returned from Rome in time to hear of Celia's engagement to Sir James Chettam. Will Ladislaw included a note to Dorothea in a letter he wrote to Casaubon. This attention precipitated a quarrel that was followed by Casaubon's serious illness. Lydgate, who attended him, urged him to give up his studies for the present time. Lydgate confided to Dorothea that Casaubon had a weak heart and must be guarded from all excitement.

Meanwhile, all the relatives of old Mr. Featherstone were waiting impatiently for his death. He hoped to circumvent their desires by giving his fortune to Mary Garth, daughter of the man who had signed Fred Vincy's note. When she refused it, he fell into a rage and died soon afterward. When his will was read, it was learned that he had left nothing to his relatives; most of his money was to go to Joshua Riggs, who was to take the name of Featherstone, and a part of his fortune was to endow the Featherstone Almshouses for old men.

Plans were made for Rosamond's marriage with Lydgate. Fred Vincy was ordered to prepare himself finally for the ministry, since he was to have no inheritance from his uncle. Mr. Brooke had gone into politics; he now enlisted the help of Ladislaw in publishing a liberal paper. Mr. Casaubon had come to dislike his cousin intensely after he rejected further financial assistance, and he had forbidden Ladislaw to enter his house.

After Casaubon died suddenly, a codicil to his will gave Dorothea all of his property as long as she did not marry Ladislaw. This strange provision caused Dorothea's friends and relatives some concern because, if publicly revealed, it would appear that Dorothea and Ladislaw had been indiscreet.

On the advice of his Tory friends, Mr. Brooke gave up his liberal newspaper and cut off his connection with Ladislaw. Ladislaw realized that Dorothea's family was in some way trying to separate him from Dorothea, but he refused to be disconcerted about the matter. He resolved to stay on in Middlemarch until he was ready to leave. When he heard of the codicil to Casaubon's will, he was more than ever determined to remain so that he could eventually disprove the suspicions of the village concerning him and Dorothea.

Meanwhile, Lydgate and Rosamond had married, and the doctor had gone deeply in debt to furnish his house. When he found that his income did not meet his wife's spendthrift habits, he asked her to help him economize. They began to quarrel, and both his practice and his popularity decreased.

A disreputable man named Raffles appeared in Middlemarch. Raffles knew that Ladislaw's grandfather had amassed a fortune as a receiver of stolen goods and that Nicholas Bulstrode, the highly respected banker, had once been the confidential clerk of Ladislaw's ancestor. Moreover, Bulstrode's first wife had been his employer's widow. Bulstrode had built his fortune with money inherited from her, money that should have gone to Ladislaw's mother.

Bulstrode had been blackmailed by Raffles earlier, and he reasoned that the scoundrel would tell Ladislaw the whole story. To forestall trouble, he sent for Ladislaw and offered him an annuity of five hundred pounds and liberal provision in his will. Ladislaw, feeling that his relatives had already tainted his honor, refused; he was unwilling to be associated in any way with the unsavory business and decided to leave Middlemarch and go to London, even though he had no assurance that Dorothea loved him.

Lydgate drifted more deeply into debt. When he wished to sell what he could and take cheaper lodgings, Rosamond managed to persuade him to continue keeping up the pretense of prosperity a little longer. When Bulstrode gave up his interest in the new hospital and withdrew his financial support, the situation grew even worse. Faced at last with the seizure of his goods, Lydgate went to Bulstrode and asked for a loan. The banker advised him to seek aid from Dorothea and abruptly ended the conversation. When Raffles, in the last stages of alcoholism, returned to Middlemarch and Lydgate was called in to attend him, Bulstrode, afraid the doctor would learn the banker's secret from Raffles' drunken ravings, changed his mind and gave Lydgate a check for one thousand pounds. The loan came in time to save Lydgate's goods and reputation. When Raffles died, Bulstrode felt at peace at last. Nevertheless, it soon became common gossip that Bulstrode had given money to Lydgate and that Lydgate had attended Raffles in his final illness. Bulstrode and Lydgate were publicly accused of malpractice in Raffles' death. Only Dorothea took up Lydgate's defense. The rest of the town was busy with gossip over the affair. Rosamond was anxious to leave Middlemarch to avoid public disgrace. Bulstrode too was anxious to leave town, because Raffles had told his secret while drunk in a neighboring village; Bulstrode became ill, however, and his doctors would not permit him to leave his bed.

Feeling sympathy for Lydgate, Dorothea was determined to give her support to the hospital and to try to convince Rosamond that the only way Lydgate could recover his honor was by remaining in Middlemarch. Unfortunately, she came upon Rosamond pouring out her grief to Will Ladislaw. Dorothea, suspecting that Rosamond was involved with Ladislaw, left abruptly. Angered at the false position Rosamond had put him in, Ladislaw told her that he had always loved Dorothea from a distance. When Dorothea forced herself to return to Lydgate's house the following morning, Rosamond told her of Ladislaw's declaration. Dorothea realized she was willing to give up Casaubon's fortune for Ladislaw's affection.

Despite the protests of her family and friends, they were married several weeks later and went to London to live. Lydgate and Rosamond lived together with better understanding and prospects of a happier future. Fred Vincy became engaged to Mary Garth, with whom he had long been in love. For a time, Dorothea's family ignored her, but they were finally reconciled after Dorothea's son was born and Ladislaw was elected to Parliament.

Critical Evaluation:

Modestly subtitled "A Study of Provincial Life," George Eliot's *Middlemarch* has long been recognized as a work of great psychological and moral penetration. Indeed, the novel has been compared with Tolstoy's *War and Peace* (1865-1869) and Thackeray's *Vanity Fair* (1847-1848) for its almost epic sweep and its perspective of early nineteenth century history. These comparisons, however, are partly faulty. Unlike *War and Peace*, *Middlemarch* lacks a philosophical bias, a grand *Weltanschauung* that encompasses the destinies of nations and generations. Unlike *Vanity Fair*, Eliot's novel is not neatly moralistic. In fact, much of *Middlemarch* is morally ambiguous in the twentieth century sense of the term. Eliot's concept of plot and character derives from psychological rather than philosophical or social necessity. This is to say that *Middlemarch*, despite its Victorian trappings of complicated plot and subplot, slow development of character and accumulated detail concerning time and place, and social density in many respects resembles the twentieth century novel that disturbs as well as entertains.

Eliot published *Middlemarch* in eight books between December, 1871, and December, 1872, eight years before her death. She was at the height of her powers and had already achieved a major reputation with *Adam Bede* (1859), *The Mill on the Floss* (1860), and *Silas Marner* (1861). Nevertheless, her most recent fiction, *Felix Holt, the Radical* (1866) and the dramatic poem *The Spanish Gypsy* (1868), had been considered inferior to her best writing and had disappointed her public. *Middlemarch* was, however, received with considerable excitement and critical acclaim. Eliot's publisher, Blackwood, was so caught up with the narrative as he received chapters of her novel by mail that he wrote back to her asking questions about the fates of the characters as though they were real people with real histories. Eliot, in fact, did scrupulous research for the material of her novel. Her discussion of the social climate in rural England directly preceding passage of the Reform Bill of 1832 is convincingly detailed; she accurately describes the state of medical knowledge during Lydgate's time; and she treats the dress, habits, and speech of Middlemarch impeccably, creating the metaphor of a complete world, a piece of provincial England that is a microcosm of the greater world beyond.

The theme of the novel itself, however, revolves around the slenderest of threads: the mating of "unimportant" people. This theme, which engages the talents of such other great writers as Jane Austen, Thomas Hardy, Henry James, and D. H. Lawrence, allows Eliot the scope to examine the whole range of human nature. She is concerned with the mating of lovers because people in love are most vulnerable and most easily the victims of romantic illusions. Each of the three sets of lovers in *Middlemarch*—Dorothea Brooke, Edward Casaubon, and Will Ladislaw; Rosamond Vincy and Tertius Lydgate; and Mary Garth and Fred Vincy—mistake illusion for reality. Eventually, whether or not they become completely reconciled with their mates, all come to understand themselves better. Each undergoes a sentimental education, a discipline of the spirit that teaches the heart its limitations.

Paradoxically, the greater capacity Eliot's characters have for romantic self-deception, the greater their suffering and subsequent tempering of spirit. Mary Garth—plain, witty, honest—is too sensible to arouse psychological curiosity to the same degree as does proud Dorothea, rash Ladislaw, pathetic Casaubon, ambitious Lydgate, or pampered Rosamond. Mary loves simply, directly. Fred, her childhood sweetheart, is basically a good lad who must learn the lessons of thrift and perseverance from his own misfortunes. He "falls" in class, from that of an idle landowner to one of a decent but socially inferior manager of property. In truth, what he seems to lose in social prominence he more than recovers in the development of his moral character. Moreover, he wins as a mate the industrious Mary, who will strengthen his resolve and make of him an admirable provider like her father Caleb.

Dorothea, on the other hand, more idealistic and noble-hearted than Mary, chooses the worst possible mate as her first husband. Edward Casaubon, thirty years her senior, is a dull pedant, cold, hopelessly ineffectual as a scholar, absurd as a lover. Despite his intellectual pretensions, he is too timid, fussy, and dispirited ever to complete his masterwork, "A Key to All Mythologies." Even the title of his project is an absurdity. He conceals as long as possible his "key" from Dorothea, fearing that she will expose him as a sham. Nevertheless, it is possible that she might have endured the disgrace of her misplaced affection were Casaubon only more tender, reciprocating her own tenderness and self-sacrifice; but Casaubon, despotic to the last, tries to blight her spirit when he is alive and, through his will, to restrict her freedom when he is dead.

Dorothea's second choice of a mate, Will Ladislaw, is very nearly the opposite of Casaubon.

A rash, sometimes hypersensitive lover, he is capable of intense affection, above all of self-sacrifice. He is a worthy suitor for Dorothea, who finds greatness in his ardor if not his accomplishments; yet Will, allowing for his greater vitality, is after all a logical successor to Casaubon. Dorothea had favored the elderly scholar because he was unworldly, despised by the common herd. In her imagination, he seemed a saint of intellect. In time, she comes to favor Will because he is also despised by most of the petty-minded bigots of Middlemarch, because he has suffered from injustice, and because he seems to her a saint of integrity. A Victorian St. Theresa, Dorothea is passive, great in aspiration rather than deed. Psychologically, she requires a great object for her own self-sacrifice and therefore chooses a destiny that will allow her the fullest measure of heroism.

Tertius Lydgate is, by contrast, a calculating, vigorous, and ambitious young physician who attempts to bend others to his own iron will. His aggressive energy contrasts with Dorothea's passiveness. Like her, however, he is a victim of romantic illusion. He believes that he can master, through his intelligence and determination, those who possess power. Nevertheless, his choice of a mate, Rosamond Vincy, is a disastrous miscalculation. Rosamond's fragile beauty conceals a petulant, selfish will equal to his own. She dominates him through her weakness. Insensitive except to her own needs, she offers no scope for Lydgate's sensitive intelligence. In his frustration, he can battle only with himself. He comes to realize that he is defeated not only in his dreams of domestic happiness but in his essential judgment of the uses of power.

For Eliot, moral choice does not exist in a sanctified vacuum; it requires an encounter with power. To even the least sophisticated dwellers in Middlemarch, power is represented by wealth and status. As the widow Mrs. Casaubon, Dorothea's social prestige rests on her personal and inherited fortune. When she casts aside her estate under Casaubon's will to marry Ladislaw, she also loses a great measure of status. At the same time, she acquires moral integrity, a superior virtue for Eliot. Similarly, when Mary Garth rejects Mr. Featherstone's dying proposition to seize his wealth before his relatives make a shambles of his will, she chooses morally, justly, and comes to deserve the happiness she eventually wins. Lydgate, whose moral choices are most ambiguous, returns Bulstrode's bribe to save himself from a social embarrassment, but his guilt runs deeper than mere miscalculation. He has associated himself, first through choosing Tyke instead of the worthier Farebrother as vicar, with Bulstrode's manipulation of power. Lydgate's moral defeat is partial, for at least he understands the extent of his compromise with integrity. Bulstrode's defeat is total, for he loses both wealth and social standing. As for Middlemarch, that community of souls is a small world, populated with people of good will and bad, mean spirits and fine, and is the collective agent of moral will. After all, it is the town that endures, the final arbiter of moral judgment in a less than perfect world.

"Critical Evaluation" by Leslie B. Mittleman

Bibliography:
Anderson, Quentin. "George Eliot in *Middlemarch*." In *George Eliot: A Collection of Critical Essays*, edited by George R. Creeger. Englewood Cliffs, N.J.: Prentice-Hall, 1970. Provides a thorough discussion of Eliot's background and preparation of the novel, the provincial panorama she creates, and the plot development that proceeds in an interplay between public opinion and self-regard. Also includes a bibliography.
Beer, Gillian. *George Eliot*. Bloomington: Indiana University Press, 1967. Places *Middlemarch* in the context of the nineteenth century "woman question." Analyzes thoroughly and thoughtfully Eliot's contributions to that issue (especially to questions of education) as

aesthetic, not doctrinal. Concludes that Ladislaw, like Dorothea, needs a blend of vocation with opportunity, but has greater freedom as a male. Includes a bibliography.

Bellringer, Alan W. *George Eliot.* New York: St. Martin's Press, 1993. Detailed discussion of the interactive web of the province. Argues that the novel's morality is scientific, hypothetical, experimental, and provisional. Includes a bibliography.

Heilman, Robert B. "'Stealthy Convergence' in *Middlemarch.*" In *George Eliot: A Centenary Tribute,* edited by Gordon S. Haight and Rosemary T. VanArsdel. New York: Barnes & Noble Books, 1982. Explores attempts to control the past and future as they relate to the plot.

Uglow, Jennifer. *George Eliot.* New York: Pantheon Books, 1987. Shows Eliot in her fiction demolishing gender stereotypes and the illusion of norms, replacing these with insistence on individuality. Analyzes Ladislaw as a figure of light and change who, as the awakener of Dorothea's senses, is an appropriate husband for her.

A MIDSUMMER NIGHT'S DREAM

Type of work: Drama
Author: William Shakespeare (1564-1616)
Type of plot: Comedy
Time of plot: Antiquity
Locale: Athens
First performed: c. 1595-1596; first published, 1600

> *Principal characters:*
> THESEUS, duke of Athens
> LYSANDER and
> DEMETRIUS, in love with Hermia
> BOTTOM, a weaver
> HIPPOLYTA, queen of the Amazons, fiancée of Theseus
> HERMIA, in love with Lysander
> HELENA, in love with Demetrius
> OBERON, king of the fairies
> TITANIA, queen of the fairies
> PUCK, fairy page to Oberon

The Story:

Theseus, the duke of Athens, was to be married in four days to Hippolyta, queen of the Amazons, and he ordered his Master of the Revels to prepare suitable entertainment for the nuptials. Other lovers of ancient Athens, however, were not so happy as their ruler. Hermia, in love with Lysander, was loved also by Demetrius, who had her father's permission to marry her. When she refused his suit, Demetrius took his case to Theseus and demanded that the law be invoked. Theseus upheld the father; by Athenian law, Hermia must either marry Demetrius, be placed in a nunnery, or be put to death. Hermia swore that she would enter a convent before she would consent to become Demetrius' bride.

Faced with this awful choice, Lysander plotted with Hermia to leave Athens. He would take her to the home of his aunt and there marry her. They were to meet the following night in a wood outside the city. Hermia confided the plan to her good friend Helena. Demetrius had formerly been betrothed to Helena, and although he had switched his love to Hermia he was still desperately loved by the scorned Helena. Helena, willing to do anything to gain even a smile from Demetrius, told him of his rival's plan to elope with Hermia.

Unknown to any of the four young people, there were to be others in that same woods on the appointed night, Midsummer Eve. A group of Athenian laborers was to meet there to practice a play the members hoped to present in honor of Theseus and Hippolyta's wedding. The fairies also held their midnight revels in the woods. Oberon, king of the fairies, desired for his page a little Indian foundling, but Oberon's queen, Titania, had the boy. Loving him like a son, she refused to give him up to her husband. In order to force Titania to do his bidding, Oberon ordered his mischievous page, called Puck or Robin Goodfellow, to secure the juice of a purple flower once hit by Cupid's dart. This juice, when placed in the eyes of anyone sleeping, caused that person to fall in love with the first creature seen on awakening. Oberon planned to drop some of the juice in Titania's eyes and then refuse to lift the charm until she gave him the boy.

While Puck was on his errand, Demetrius and Helena entered the woods. Making himself invisible, Oberon heard Helena plead her love for Demetrius and heard the young man scorn and berate her. Demetrius had come to the woods to find the fleeing lovers, Lysander and Hermia, and Helena was following Demetrius. Oberon, pitying Helena, determined to aid her. When Puck returned with the juice, Oberon ordered him to find the Athenian and place some of the juice in his eyes so that he would love the woman who doted on him.

Puck went to do as he was ordered, while Oberon squeezed the juice of the flower into the eyes of Titania as she slept. Puck, coming upon Lysander and Hermia as they slept in the woods, mistook Lysander's Athenian dress for that of Demetrius and poured the charmed juice into Lysander's eyes. Lysander was awakened by Helena, who had been abandoned deep in the woods by Demetrius. The charm worked, although not as intended; Lysander fell in love with Helena. That poor woman, thinking that he was mocking her with his ardent protestations of love, begged him to stop his teasing and return to the sleeping Hermia. Lysander, pursuing Helena, who was running away from him, left Hermia alone in the forest. When she awakened she feared that Lysander had been killed, since she believed that he would never have deserted her otherwise.

Titania, in the meantime, awakened to a strange sight. The laborers, practicing for their play, had paused not far from the sleeping fairy queen. Bottom, the comical but stupid weaver who was to play the leading role, became the butt of another of Puck's jokes. The prankster clapped an ass's head over Bottom's own foolish pate and led the poor fool on a merry chase until the weaver was at the spot where Titania lay sleeping. Thus when she awakened she looked at Bottom, still with the head of an ass. She fell instantly in love with him and ordered the fairies to tend to his every want. This turn pleased Oberon mightily. When he learned of the mistake Puck had made in placing the juice in Lysander's eyes, however, he tried to right the wrong by placing love juice also in Demetrius' eyes, and he ordered Puck to have Helena close by when Demetrius awakened. His act made both women unhappy and forlorn. When Demetrius, who she knew hated her, also began to protest his ardent love to her, Helena thought that both men were taunting and ridiculing her. Poor Hermia, encountering Lysander, could not understand why he tried to drive her away, all the time protesting that he loved only Helena.

Again Oberon tried to set matters straight. He ordered Puck to lead the two men in circles until weariness forced them to lie down and go to sleep. Then a potion to remove the charm and make the whole affair seem like a dream was to be placed in Lysander's eyes. Afterward he would again love Hermia, and all the young people would be united in proper pairs. Titania, too, was to have the charm removed, for Oberon had taunted her about loving an ass until she had given up the prince to him. Puck obeyed the orders and placed the potion in Lysander's eyes.

The four lovers were awakened by Theseus, Hippolyta, and Hermia's father, who had gone into the woods to watch Theseus' hounds perform. Lysander again loved Hermia and Demetrius still loved Helena, for the love juice remained in his eyes. Hermia's father persisted in his demand that his daughter marry Demetrius, but since that young man no longer wanted her and all four were happy with their partners, he ceased to oppose Lysander's suit. Theseus gave them permission to marry on the day set for his own wedding to Hippolyta.

Titania also awakened and, like the others, thought that she had been dreaming. Puck removed the ass's head from Bottom and the bewildered weaver made his way back to Athens, reaching there just in time to save the play, since he was to play Pyramus, the hero. The Master of the Revels tried to dissuade Theseus from choosing the laborer's play for the wedding night. Theseus, however, was intrigued by a play that was announced as tedious, brief, merry, and tragic. So Bottom and his troupe presented an entertainingly awful *Pyramus and Thisbe*, much to the merriment of all the guests.

After the play all the bridal couples retired to their suites, and Oberon and Titania sang a fairy song over them, promising that they and all of their children would be blessed.

Critical Evaluation:

A Midsummer Night's Dream marks the maturation of William Shakespeare's comic form beyond situation and young romantic love. One plot focuses on finding young love and on overcoming obstacles to that love. Shakespeare adds to the richness of comic structure by interweaving the love plot with a cast of rustic guildsmen, who are out of their element as they strive to entertain the ruler with a classic play of their own. The play also features a substructure of fairy forces, whose unseen antics influence the world of humans. With this invisible substructure of dream and chaos, *A Midsummer Night's Dream* not only explores the capriciousness and changeability of love (as the young men switch their affections from woman to woman in the blinking of an eye) but also introduces the question of the psychology of the subconscious.

Tradition held that on midsummer night, people would dream of the one they would marry. As the lovers enter the chaotic world of the forest, they are allowed, with hilarious results, to experience harmlessly the options of their subconscious desires. By focusing in the last act on the play presented by the rustic guildsmen, Shakespeare links the imaginative world of art with the capacity for change and growth within humanity. This capacity is most laughingly realized in the play by the transformation of the enthusiastic actor, Bottom, into half-man, half-ass, an alteration that continues to delight audiences.

The play was originally performed at a marriage ceremony in 1595, and the plot is framed by the four-day suspension of ordinary life in Athens in expectation of the nuptial celebration of Theseus and his queen, Hippolyta. Both characters invoke the moon as they anticipate their union. The lunar spirit of nebulousness, changeability, and lunacy dominates much of the play's action.

A Midsummer Night's Dream is remarkable for its blending of diverse personages into an eventually unified whole. In addition to Theseus and Hippolyta, the cast includes three other categories of society, each distinguished by its own mode of discourse. Theseus and Hippolyta speak high blank verse, filled with leisurely confidence and classical allusion. The four young and mixed-up lovers—Hermia and Lysander, Helena and Demetrius—can also muster blank verse but are typified by rhyming iambic lines that indicate the unoriginal speech of those who woo. The rustic guildsmen are characterized by their prose speech, full of halts and stops, confusions, and malapropisms. The fairies for the most part speak a light rhymed tetrameter, filled with references to nature. Oberon and Titania, as king and queen of the fairies, speak a regal verse similar to that of Theseus and Hippolyta. The roles of the two kings and the two queens are often played by the same actors, since the characters are not on stage at the same time.

In the background of all the love matches is a hint of violence or separation. Theseus conquers Hippolyta. Oberon and Titania feud over a changeling boy. Pyramus and Thisbe, the lovers in the rustics' play, are kept apart by a wall. Demetrius stops loving Helena for no apparent reason and switches his affections to Hermia, who dotes on Lysander. The father of Hermia, supported by Theseus and Athenian law, would keep his daughter from marrying the man of her choosing and instead doom her to death or life in a nunnery.

When Puck addresses the audience in the play's epilogue, he points to a major theme of the badly acted play-within-a-play: art requires an act of imaginative engagement on the part of those who experience it. Art can reveal alternatives, horrible or wonderful turns that life may take. Art's power to transform is only as effective as the audience's capacity to distinguish illusion from reality and to bring the possible into being.

"Critical Evaluation" by Sandra K. Fischer

Bibliography:
Arthos, John. "The Spirit of the Occasion." In *Shakespeare's Use of Dream and Vision*. Totowa, N.J.: Rowman and Littlefield, 1977. Connects nature with the dream world and its dual potential of horror and bliss. Dreams stem from and inform the psyche, and they share a cognitive function with the world of art.

Brown, John Russell. *Shakespeare and His Comedies*. New York: Methuen, 1957. Focuses on Theseus' speech connecting the madman, the lover, and the poet. Reveals how the play negotiates and validates varying responses to the unknown.

Calderwood, James L. *A Midsummer Night's Dream*. New York: Twayne, 1992. Drawing on all the different theoretical approaches to literary interpretation, Calderwood organizes the experience of the play around the topics of patriarchal law, desire and voyeurism, marginality and threshold experiences, the power of naming, performativity, and the illusion of conciliation and unity. An excellent summary of the state of reading Shakespeare.

Patterson, Annabel. "Bottom's Up: Festive Theory." In *Shakespeare and the Popular Voice*. New York: Basil Blackwell, 1989. Reads the presentation of the lower class in political terms. Bottom's malapropisms represent a suppression of voice and class, yet his creative use of language points toward a more synthetic utopian society.

Welsford, Enid. *The Court Masque*. Cambridge, England: Cambridge University Press, 1927. Reads *A Midsummer Night's Dream* in light of the tradition of the court masque, which was a popular form at the time the play was presented. Focuses on the visual and aesthetic qualities of music and dance to try to interpret the play in its cultural context.

THE MIGHTY AND THEIR FALL

Type of work: Novel
Author: Ivy Compton-Burnett (1884-1969)
Type of plot: Domestic realism
Time of plot: Mid-twentieth century
Locale: Unnamed town in England
First published: 1961

Principal characters:
 NINIAN MIDDLETON, a widower and father
 LAVINIA, his oldest daughter
 RANSOM, his brother
 HUGO, his adopted brother
 SELINA, his mother
 EGBERT, his older son
 AGNES, his second daughter
 HENGIST, his second son
 LEAH, his third daughter
 TERESA CHILTON, his second wife
 MISS STARKIE, the children's governess
 AINGER and
 COOK, servants in the house

The Story:

To this polished, stodgy, upper-class British family replete with house servants and a governess, Ninian, the father, who was a widower, announced that he was engaged to marry Teresa Chilton. The news was ill-received by all, because the forthcoming event required redefining family roles and relationships.

The family was visited by Teresa, the fiancée, and conversation was made about such trivial matters as what the children should call their new stepmother. She was made to feel uncomfortable and unwanted by the family. After her visit, she wrote a letter to Ninian saying that if he wanted out of the engagement all he needed to do was to ignore the letter; that is, not reply to it. Lavinia, in a misguided attempt to protect Ninian, hid the letter (not yet read by Ninian), which was not discovered for some ten days, after Teresa's appointed deadline.

Ninian contacted Teresa and the two were married, but it remained a mystery as to which family member had hidden the letter. Eventually, it was revealed that Lavinia was the culprit. Ninian and other family members were ostensibly forgiving, but in truth they were not— Lavinia was to be made to live in her family as a sinner. Ransom, Ninian's younger brother, arrived home and revealed that he was terminally ill. Dying, he had taken a flat near Ninian's house; he wanted one of the children to come and live with him during his last days. He chose Lavinia, because the two of them were the family's appointed reprobates. Before dying, Ransom devised a trick on Ninian that was designed to reveal Ninian's honesty—or lack thereof. Ransom wrote two wills, one in which Ninian was chief benefactor and the other in which Lavinia was. Ransom asked Ninian to burn the will which listed Ninian as chief inheritor of Ransom's estate. Ninian failed the moral test. Ransom revealed all to the family. Thus, it was proved that the father was as morally reprehensible as both Ransom and Lavinia.

Ransom died, leaving his wealth to Lavinia. It was then revealed that Lavinia and Hugo, Ninian's adopted brother and Lavinia's uncle, were to be married. All were in a state of shock, although it was well established that the two were not blood kin. Selina, mother to Ninian and Hugo, then claimed that Hugo was a family member by blood. Specifically, that the dead father had brought Hugo home as a bastard son and that Ninian and Hugo were half-brothers. Hugo, professing his love for the now-rich Lavinia, insisted that the story was not true. He departed to investigate. Shortly, he returned with proof that Selina was lying and that he was, in fact, not a blood member of the family. Thus, all was cleared for the wedding.

Selina devised her own plan to control the event from beyond the grave. She too had become sick to the point of death; she wrote a will in which she made Hugo her chief benefactor. Upon her death, Hugo succeeded to great sums of money. He decided that he did not want to marry, after all, because he liked his life of debauchery and bachelorhood too much. Lavinia was then welcomed back into the family, since it was agreed that her own treachery in hiding the letter was certainly no greater than her father's in burning the will, in Selina's for telling the lie about Hugo's birth, or in Hugo's for being so quickly and manifestly bought off from love with money. All of the mighty family members are fallen, a fact commented upon by the servants in the kitchen.

Critical Evaluation:

Written in the later years of Ivy Compton-Burnett's career and a few years before her death, *The Mighty and Their Fall* has never been considered a work of literature of first quality. Like other novels by this author, the faults are too numerous and too glaring for such ranking. Be that as it may, *The Mighty and Their Fall* does succeed within what may be called the genre of drawing room novel—one written more for diversion and entertainment than for great and involved meaning.

The most noticeable element of the author's style is her use of conversation. Some 90 percent of the work is given in dialogue: short, terse, clipped sentences exchanged between characters with little or no attached explanations to alert the reader as to how the utterances are made, what context they have, or even who the speakers are. It is rather as if one were reading the script of a play with little or no stage directions. Experimental, or at least unique, in this respect, *The Mighty and Their Fall* proceeds with little in common with what is usually identifiable as elements of the novel.

At the same time, the work is structured around moral tension, dilemma, and resolution. In fact, a whole series of such patterns occur, with certain common elements. Lavinia decides to hide her father's letter from his fiancée as a way to protect him from himself but also her hiding the letter is an act of selfishness. She fully believes it would be better for her father if he did not remarry; at the same time, she fully believes that her own lot in life, and that of other family members, will also be better if he does not remarry. She performs the act of treachery and is caught.

The pattern is repeated by her own father. Ninian burns the wrong will not so much because he wants the major portion of Ransom's inheritance upon his death but because, so he reasons, his family will be in better circumstances if Lavinia does not receive the whole lot herself. He, too, is caught and exposed, and therefore must acknowledge his own moral kinship to his daughter Lavinia.

Upon Lavinia and Hugo's announcement that they are engaged to be married, Selina, the matriarch of the family, falls into the same trap. She tells lies about Hugo's parentage in order to prevent the marriage. In claiming that Hugo is actually a biological, illegitimate son to her long-dead husband, Selina, like Lavinia and Ninian, maneuvers to protect others from themselves. At the same time, she does so for selfish reasons, despite being at the point of death. When Hugo exposes his mother's lie, all three family members are now in the same category of moral depravity.

Hugo is bought off from the marriage. Given financial independence, he too is shown to be morally defunct. He does not marry Lavinia because, as his mother understood, his real motivation was for money and not for love. Four of the family members have all lied, cheated, and been immoral, and all have been caught and revealed.

The novel's comment about human nature is centered in that of familial relationships. Those in power abuse those who are dependent upon them. In particular, Ninian and Selina act to repress their children and grandchildren in order to control them, acting in what Ninian and Selina believe is their descendants' best interests. The pattern is reversed when the children (Lavinia and Hugo) respond in a like manner toward the superiors in their family. The author's moral is clear: People have no right to condemn others until they have experienced similar temptations and resisted them. In this case, all four main characters fail the test of morality put before them. Thus, not one is morally superior to the others.

Against the main action of the work is the conversation of the servants in the kitchen. Ainger and Cook, so it would seem, are happy that the affairs of the family are going as they are. It provides them with amusement and a subject for conversation. There is no difference between the morality of the servants and that of the upper-class family. Indeed, the kitchen help is not given to the same whims and silliness as the family. Consequently and fortunately, they do not find themselves given to such moral perplexities.

The Mighty and Their Fall, then, is something of a social satire upon the English upper classes. Their concerns are trivial and petty, their actions are inconsequential (whether they make the correct moral choices or not), their relationships are all shallow and pointless, and the servants are better off, morally. All of the main characters are revealed to act primarily out of selfishness and not from the desire to protect others, as each claims.

Finally, there is a lack of seriousness in the whole work. The "mighty" fall, but they are none the worse for it. Their lives will continue more or less the same regardless of who marries (or does not marry) whom and regardless of who does or does not inherit money from Ransom and Selina. The upper crust of this society survives because of its determination to protect its own regardless of morality or other considerations.

Carl Singleton

Bibliography:
Baldanza, Frank. *Ivy Compton-Burnett.* New York: Twayne, 1964. Set in the context of the author's biography and career, the novel is discussed in terms of characters, plot, and theme.
Karl, Frederick R. *The Contemporary English Novel.* New York: Farrar, Straus & Giroux, 1962. Contains a chapter that delineates all of the important characteristics of Compton-Burnett's novels: problems of Victorian and post-Victorian families, moral choices that involve material values, familial attachments and relationships, drawing room ethics, the roles of governesses and servants, and tragic and semitragic events.
Kiernan, Robert F. *Frivolity Unbound: Six Masters of the Camp Novel.* New York: Continuum, 1990. One of the masters is Compton-Burnett, her ironically formulaic banality is discussed.
Ross, Marlon B. "Contented Spinsters: Governessing and the Limits of Discursive Desire in the Fiction of Ivy Compton-Burnett." In *Old Maids to Radical Spinsters: Unmarried Women in*

the Twentieth-Century Novel, edited by Laura L. Doan. Champaign: University of Illinois Press, 1991. Discusses the role of governesses in the novels of Ivy Compton-Burnett. Miss Starkie and Selina Middleton fill the role in *The Mighty and Their Fall*.

West, Anthony. *Principles and Persuasions: The Literary Essays of Anthony West*. New York: Harcourt, Brace Jovanovich, 1957. An overall discussion of Compton-Burnett's writing style and methodology.

THE MIKADO
Or, The Town of Titipu

Type of work: Drama (opera libretto)
Author: W. S. Gilbert (1836-1911)
Type of plot: Satire
Time of plot: Middle Ages
Locale: Titipu, Japan
First performed: 1885; first published, 1885

Principal characters:
THE MIKADO OF JAPAN
NANKI-POO, his son, disguised as a minstrel
KO-KO, Lord High Executioner of Titipu
POOH-BAH, Lord High Everything Else
YUM-YUM,
PITTI-SING, and
PEEP-BO, wards of Ko-Ko
KATISHA, an elderly lady in love with Nanki-Poo
PISH-TUSH, a noble lord

The Story:

Ko-Ko had become the Lord High Executioner in the town of Titipu in old Japan, and to his courtyard came many knights and lords to flatter and cajole the holder of so dread and august an office. One day a stranger appeared at Ko-Ko's palace, a wandering minstrel who carried his guitar on his back and a sheaf of ballads in his hand. The Japanese lords were curious about his presence there, for he was obviously not of noble birth and therefore could expect no favors from powerful Ko-Ko. At last Pish-Tush questioned him about his business with Ko-Ko. Introducing himself as Nanki-Poo, the minstrel announced that he sought Yum-Yum, the beautiful ward of Ko-Ko, with whom he had fallen in love while playing the second trombone in the Titipu town band a year before. He had heard that Ko-Ko was to be executed for flirting, a capital offense in the land of the Mikado, and since Ko-Ko was to die, he hoped that Yum-Yum would be free to marry him.

Pish-Tush corrected the rash young man, telling him that the Mikado had revoked the death sentence of Ko-Ko and raised him at the same time to the great and noble rank of the Lord High Executioner of Titipu. Nanki-Poo was crestfallen, for he realized that the ward of an official so important would never be allowed to marry a lowly minstrel. Pooh-Bah, another nobleman, secretly resented the fact that he, a man of ancient lineage, had to hold minor office under a man like Ko-Ko, previously a mere tailor. Pooh-Bah, however, was interested in any opportunity for graft; he was even willing to betray the so-called state secret of Ko-Ko's intention to wed his beautiful ward. Pooh-Bah advised Nanki-Poo to leave Titipu and by all means to stay away from Yum-Yum.

Meanwhile, Ko-Ko had been preparing a list of the types of criminals he intended to execute—autograph hunters, people who insist upon spoiling tête-à-têtes, people who eat peppermint and breathe in one's face, the man who praises every country but his own, and apologetic statesmen.

Uncertain of the privileges of his new office, the Lord High Executioner consulted the Lord

High Everything Else about the money to be spent on his impending marriage. Pooh-Bah advised him, first as Private Secretary, and gave one opinion; then as Chancellor of the Exchequer he expressed a contrary point of view. He had a different opinion for every one of his many offices and official titles. They were interrupted, however, by the appearance of Yum-Yum and her sisters Peep-Bo and Pitti-Sing. Ko-Ko attempted to kiss his bride-to-be, but she openly expressed her reluctance and distaste.

When the three sisters saw Nanki-Poo loitering nearby, they rushed to greet him, astonished to find him in Titipu. Ko-Ko, baffled and displeased by their schoolgirl mirth, demanded an introduction to the stranger. When Yum-Yum and Nanki-Poo had a few moments alone with each other, the minstrel revealed his true identity as the son of the Mikado and confessed the reasons for his flight from court. Katisha, a middle-aged woman in the court, had misunderstood acts of Nanki-Poo as overtures of romance. She mentioned them to the Mikado. He in turn misunderstood his son's conduct and requested that Nanki-Poo marry Katisha. Nanki-Poo, already in love with Yum-Yum, fled the court in the disguise of a minstrel and went to Titipu.

That same day Ko-Ko received from the Mikado a communication which instructed him to execute somebody within a month. Otherwise the office of Lord High Executioner would be abolished; Ko-Ko would be beheaded for neglecting his duties, and the city of Titipu would be ranked as only a village. Perplexed by this sudden and unhappy news, Ko-Ko saw no solution until he discovered Nanki-Poo carrying a rope with which to hang himself. Seeing a way of escape, Ko-Ko bargained with Nanki-Poo, promising him a luxuriant life for thirty days, if at the end of that time the minstrel would allow himself to be executed officially. Nanki-Poo agreed on the condition that he could marry Yum-Yum at once.

This acceptable solution was upset, however, by the arrival of Katisha, who recognized Nanki-Poo and tried to claim him for her husband. When she learned that he was to marry Yum-Yum, she attempted to reveal his true identity, but her voice was not heard above the singing and shouting instigated by Yum-Yum. Hearing of the proposed marriage of Yum-Yum and Nanki-Poo, Pooh-Bah informed Ko-Ko that the wife of a beheaded man must be buried alive, a law which would mean Yum-Yum's death if Nanki-Poo were executed. Again lost as to a way out of his problem, Ko-Ko was spurred to action by the unexpected arrival of the Mikado himself. Desperate, he concealed Nanki-Poo and showed the Mikado a forged certificate of Nanki-Poo's execution.

When the Mikado read the name of the victim, he announced that the heir-apparent had been executed. According to law, Ko-Ko's life had to be forfeited. Luckily for Ko-Ko, Nanki-Poo and Yum-Yum appeared at that moment. Man and wife at last, they were ready to start on their honeymoon. Seeing his son happily married and not dead as he had supposed, the Mikado forgave everyone concerned in Ko-Ko's plot—the unfortunate Lord High Executioner, however, only after he had wed the jilted Katisha.

Critical Evaluation:

The Mikado: Or, The Town of Titipu is the work of the most famous collaborators of light opera, Sir William Gilbert and Sir Arthur Sullivan (1842-1900). For about twenty years, they produced many of the most enduring and charming operettas the world has ever known, with Gilbert as librettist and Sullivan as composer. The two began collaborating in 1869, but it was not until they met Richard D'Oyly Carte in 1874 that they started to achieve the fame that continues today. D'Oyly Carte leased an old opera building for their productions, and, in 1881, he built the Savoy Theatre especially for the D'Oyly Carte company to produce Gilbert and Sullivan's comic operas.

Gilbert suggested to Sullivan the subject of *The Mikado* in 1884. The British fashion for things Japanese was at its height as the result of a "Japanese village" exhibition in the London borough of Kensington. (Knightsbridge, in the Kensington area, is mentioned in the dialogue as the place where Nanki-Poo was to have fled.) The opening of Japan to the West by American naval officer Commodore Matthew Calbraith Perry in 1854 created a Victorian fascination for Japanese art and architecture, and wealthier homes displayed expensive Japanese vases, decorated screens and fans, and colorful marionettes, items mentioned in the introductory chorus of nobles. In music, composers experimented with Japanese five-tone scales, rhythmic drums, and the exotic sounds of instruments such as the koto and gongs. The culmination of this musical fascination was Gilbert and Sullivan's *The Mikado*, which ran for more than six hundred nights after it was first presented at the Savoy on March 14, 1885, and Giacomo Puccini's popular Italian opera *Madam Butterfly*, first performed in Milan on February 17, 1904.

The Mikado is not really about Japan. It is about late nineteenth century England, and Japanese kimonos cloak characters whom most Victorian theatergoers would have easily recognized. The Mikado, for instance, is a paternalistic, self-important parliamentarian out to punish "all prosy dull society sinners," a type of politician who remains common. The "criminals" for whom he plans punishment include advertising quacks, music-hall singers, billiard hustlers, and defacers of the windows of railway carriages. Like a true politician, the Mikado labors to make the punishment fit the crime: The billiard sharp is doomed to play with a twisted cue and elliptical billiard balls, the quack is condemned to have all his teeth extracted by amateur dentists, and shrill tenors must exhibit their vocal powers to an audience of wax dummies at Madame Tussaud's museum.

In the same way, others are recognizable Victorian types. Ko-Ko, the Lord High Executioner, and Pooh-Bah, Lord High Everything Else, are deferential small-town English civil servants who would willingly eradicate almost anyone. In Act I, part 2, Ko-Ko's hate list includes autograph seekers, children who memorize historical dates, people with flabby handshakes, those with peppermint on their breath, cross-dressers, and women novelists. None of them would be missed, he assures us. The young lovers, Nanki-Poo and Yum-Yum, are faced, as were many Victorian youths, with a father who forbids flirting and courtship, in this case under penalty of death. Katisha, an aging spinster spurned in love by youthful Nanki-Poo, is a vengeful old maid of Victorian melodrama, albeit a comic one. In the end, she marries Ko-Ko, who takes the lady to prevent himself from being plunged into boiling oil or molten lead, and only after proper assurance that Katisha is old enough to marry—"sufficiently decayed," as Ko-Ko puts it. All of these characters, with names derived from the Victorian nanny-talk of nurseries, were readily identified by Savoy audiences. (Ko-Ko, by the way, means "pickles" in Japanese.)

The essence of *The Mikado*, however, is neither topical nor geographical; it is universal. Gilbert and Sullivan's operas, after all, are enjoyed the world over not because audiences are interested in Victorian England, but because they are willing to laugh at themselves and their fellow human beings. The characters and situations, no matter how exotic the setting, are universal types and patterns found throughout literature. The plot of a prince disguised to escape undesirable consequences recalls similar incidents in many plays, as do the marriage of an unwilling young woman to a villainous suitor and the mistaken identities. The comic songs contain much literary parody, from Nanki-Poo's "The flowers that bloom in the spring" (a parody of sentimental Victorian nature verse) and the song of the three little maids from school (a parody of Victorian notions of the innocence of young girlhood) to Ko-Ko's uncharacteristic song to the titwillow, whose sad warbling is the result of either weak intellect or an undigested worm. Gilbert, in fact, glories in comic words in the same way that film actor W. C. Fields did later. The mere name "titwillow" elicits a smile, more so than, say, the word "sparrow."

Gilbert is also fond of coupling the serious with the ridiculous, and a sense of fun pervades the entire opera. Ko-Ko's comprehensive hate list, for instance, recalls the hit list of many a tyrant, but it includes such a ludicrous array of offenders that it is impossible to take it seriously. In the same way, the Mikado's insistence upon his humane philanthropy is undermined by his ridiculous opinion of wrongdoers, from mystical Germans who preach too much to ladies who dye their hair yellow and puce. Much of Gilbert's comedy also comes from his comic rhymes: "struggled" and "guggled," for example, or "if they do" and "Titipu." Some of Sullivan's tunes, in turn, parody some genuine Japanese music, including the War Song of the Imperial Army. (*The Mikado* was banned in England in 1907 for fear it might give offence to visiting Japanese dignitaries.) Finally, the play parodies the romantic theme of the young lover willing to die rather than live without his beloved and the fact that the couple lives happily ever after is the standard stuff of comedies. Put all this together and one has in *The Mikado* one of the all-time comic masterpieces of the musical stage.

"Critical Evaluation" by Kenneth Seib

Bibliography:

Ayre, Leslie. *The Gilbert and Sullivan Companion.* New York: Dodd, Mead, 1972. A reference book for Gilbert and Sullivan fans, containing anecdotes, details about each opera, and a listing of famous artists who have played leading roles. Foreword by famed D'Oyly Carte star Martyn Green.

Baily, Leslie. *Gilbert and Sullivan: Their Lives and Times.* New York: Viking Press, 1973. Lively biography that puts the two collaborators and their operas in the context of Victorian times. Contains many illustrations and photographs.

Fischler, Alan. *Modified Rapture: Comedy in W. S. Gilbert's Savoy Operas.* Charlottesville: University Press of Virginia, 1991. Brief but informative analysis of Gilbert's comedic techniques and their appeal to the "bourgeois prejudices" of Victorian audiences.

Sullivan, Arthur. *The Complete Plays of Gilbert and Sullivan.* Illustrated by W. S. Gilbert. New York: W. W. Norton, 1976. All of Gilbert's libretti as well as more than seventy amusing illustrations that he drew to illustrate his songs. Contains a brief chronology of Gilbert and Sullivan's career.

Sutton, Max Keith. *W. S. Gilbert.* Boston: Twayne, 1975. Good single-volume introduction to Gilbert's life and works. Sees *The Mikado* as a "ritual" drama, with its emphasis on human sacrifice and absolute law.

Wilson, Robin, and Frederick Lloyd. *Gilbert and Sullivan: The Official D'Oyly Carte Picture History.* New York: Alfred A. Knopf, 1984. One-hundred-year history of the D'Oyly Carte company, with dozens of color illustrations, photographs, drawings, reproductions of paintings, posters, cartoons, and memorabilia.

THE MILL ON THE FLOSS

Type of work: Novel
Author: George Eliot (Mary Ann Evans, 1819-1880)
Type of plot: Domestic realism
Time of plot: Nineteenth century
Locale: England
First published: 1860

Principal characters:
>MR. TULLIVER, the owner of the mill on the Floss
>MRS. TULLIVER, his wife
>TOM TULLIVER, their son
>MAGGIE TULLIVER, their daughter
>AUNT GLEGG and
>AUNT PULLET, the sisters of Mrs. Tulliver
>PHILIP WAKEM, Maggie's suitor
>LUCY DEANE, the cousin of Tom and Maggie
>STEPHEN GUEST, Lucy's fiancé

The Story:

Dorlcote Mill stood on the banks of the River Floss near the village of St. Ogg's. Owned by the ambitious Mr. Tulliver, it provided a good living for him and his family, but he dreamed of the day when his son Tom would achieve a higher station in life.

Mrs. Tulliver's sisters, who had married well, criticized Mr. Tulliver's unseemly ambition and openly predicted the day when his air castles would bring himself and his family to ruin. Aunt Glegg was the richest of the sisters and held a note on his property. After he quarreled with her over his plans for Tom's education, Mr. Tulliver determined to borrow the money and repay her.

Tom had inherited the placid arrogance of his mother's relatives; for him, life was not difficult. He was resolved to be fair in all of his dealings and to deliver punishment to whoever deserved it. His sister Maggie grew up with an imagination that surpassed her understanding. Her aunts predicted she would come to a bad end because she was tomboyish, dark-skinned, dreamy, and indifferent to their commands. Frightened by her lack of success in attempting to please her brother Tom, her cousin Lucy, and her mother and aunts, Maggie ran away, determined to live with the gypsies, but she was glad enough to return. Her father scolded her mother and Tom for abusing her. Her mother was sure Maggie would come to a bad end because of the way Mr. Tulliver humored her.

Tom's troubles began when his father sent him to study at Mr. Stelling's school. Having little interest in spelling, grammar, or Latin, Tom found himself wishing he were back at the mill, where he might dream of someday riding a horse like his father's and giving orders to people around him. Mr. Stelling was convinced that Tom was not just obstinate but stupid. Returning home for the Christmas holidays, Tom learned that Philip Wakem, son of a lawyer who was his father's enemy, was also to enter Mr. Stelling's school.

Philip Wakem was a cripple; Tom, therefore, was not able to beat him up as he should at first have liked. Philip could draw, and he knew Latin and Greek. After they overcame their initial reserve, the two boys became useful to each other. Philip admired Tom's arrogance and

4146

self-possession, and Tom needed Philip to help him in his studies, but their fathers' quarrel kept a gulf between them.

When Maggie came to visit Tom, she met Philip, and the two became close friends. After Maggie had been sent away to school with her cousin Lucy, Mr. Tulliver became involved in a lawsuit. Because Mr. Wakem defended the opposition, Mr. Tulliver said his children should have as little as possible to do with Philip. Mr. Tulliver lost his suit and stood to lose all of his property as well. In order to pay off Aunt Glegg, he had borrowed money on his household furnishings. Now he hoped Aunt Pullet would lend him the money to pay the debt against which those furnishings stood forfeit. He could no longer afford to keep Maggie and Tom in school. When he learned that Mr. Wakem had bought up his debts, the discovery brought on a stroke. Tom made Maggie promise never to speak to Philip Wakem again. Mrs. Tulliver wept because her household possessions were to be put up for sale at auction. In the ruin that followed, Tom and Maggie rejected the scornful offers of help from their aunts.

Bob Jakin, a country lout with whom Tom had fought as a boy, turned up to offer Tom partnership with him in a venture where Tom's education would help Bob's native business shrewdness. Because both of them were without capital, Tom took a job in a warehouse for the time being and studied bookkeeping at night.

Mr. Wakem bought the mill but permitted Mr. Tulliver to act as its manager for wages. It was Wakem's plan eventually to turn the mill over to his son. Not knowing what else to do, Tulliver stayed on as an employee of his enemy, but he asked Tom to sign a statement in the Bible that he would wish the Wakems evil as long as he lived. Against Maggie's entreaties, Tom signed his name. Finally, Aunt Glegg gave Tom money, which he invested with Bob Jakin. Slowly, Tom began to accumulate funds to pay off his father's debts.

Meanwhile, Maggie and Philip had been meeting secretly in the glades near the mill. One day, he asked her if she loved him. She put him off. Later, at a family gathering, she showed feeling for Philip in a manner that aroused Tom's suspicions. He made her swear on the Bible not to have anything more to do with Philip, and then he sought out Philip and ordered him to stay away from his sister.

Shortly afterward, Tom showed his father his profits. The next day, Mr. Tulliver thrashed Mr. Wakem and then suffered another stroke, from which he never recovered.

Two years later, Maggie, now a teacher, went to visit her cousin, Lucy Deane, who was also entertaining young Stephen Guest in her home. One difficulty Lucy foresaw was that Philip, who was friendly with both her and Stephen, might leave during Maggie's visit. Stephen had already decided that Lucy was to be his choice for a wife, but he and Maggie were attracted to each other at first sight. Blind to what was happening, Lucy was pleased that her cousin Maggie and her friend Stephen were becoming good friends.

Maggie asked Tom's permission to see Philip Wakem at a party that Lucy was giving. Tom replied that if Maggie should ever consider Philip as a lover, she must expect never to see her brother again. Tom stood by his oath to his father. He felt his dignity as a Tulliver, and he believed that Maggie was apt to follow the inclination of the moment without giving consideration to the outcome. He was right. Lacking the iron will that characterized so many of her relatives, Maggie loved easily and without restraint.

When Philip learned that Lucy's father had promised to try to buy back the mill for Tom, he hoped to persuade his father to sell the mill. Philip was sure that in return Tom would forget his old hatred.

Stephen Guest tried to kiss Maggie at a dance. She evaded him and the next day avoided Philip Wakem as well. She felt she owed it to Lucy not to allow Stephen to fall in love with her, and she felt that she owed it to her brother not to marry Philip. She let herself be carried along by the tide. Her relatives would not let her go back to teaching, for Tom's good luck continued and he had repossessed his father's mill. Both Stephen and Philip wanted her to marry them, neither knowing about the other's suit. Certainly, Lucy did not suspect Stephen's growing indifference to her.

One day, Stephen took Maggie boating and tried to convince her to run away with him and be married. She refused. Then the tide carried them beyond the reach of shore, and they were forced to spend the night in the boat.

Maggie dared the wrath and judgment of her relatives when she returned and attempted to explain to Lucy and the others what had happened. They refused to listen to her. Tom turned her away from the mill house, with the word that he would send her money but that he never wished to see her again. Mrs. Tulliver resolved to go with Maggie, and Bob Jakin took them in. One by one, people deserted Maggie, and she slowly began to realize what ostracism meant. Only Aunt Glegg and Lucy offered sympathy. Stephen wrote to her in agony of spirit, as did Philip. Maggie wanted to be by herself. She wondered if there could be love for her without pain for others.

That autumn a terrible flood ravaged St. Ogg's. Maggie knew that Tom was at the mill, and she attempted to reach him in a boat. The two were reunited, and Tom took over the rowing of the boat. The full force of the flood, however, overwhelmed them and they drowned, together at the end as they had been when they were children.

Critical Evaluation:

Shortly after George Eliot published *Adam Bede* in 1858, she began to work on a new novel under the tentative title "Sister Maggie." As the book took shape, she considered other possible titles—"The House of Tulliver," "The Tulliver Family," "The Tullivers"—before her editor, Blackwood, suggested *The Mill on the Floss*, a title she approved with some reservations. She objected at first that the "mill is not strictly on the Floss, being on its small tributary" and that the title "is of rather laborious utterance." Having voiced her usual concern for precise details and delicacy of style, she allowed that Blackwood's title was "the only alternate so far as we can see." On March 21, 1860, she completed the book, vacationed in Rome with her husband, George Henry Lewes, and awaited the news of the book's reception, which proved to be almost wholly favorable. Eliot reported with satisfaction: "From all we can gather, the votes are rather on the side of 'The Mill' as a better book than 'Adam.'"

It is certainly the more poignant novel of the two. Although both fictions have as their setting the Warwickshire background that Eliot remembered from her childhood, *The Mill on the Floss* is less genially picturesque, more concerned with psychological truth. *Adam Bede* concludes with a happy marriage for Adam and Dinah, probably contrary to the author's best artistic judgment. Tom and Maggie Tulliver, however, die in the flood, their fate unmitigated by sentimentality. Indeed, much of the novel's power derives from the consistent play of tragic forces that appear early and unify the whole work.

As a boy, Tom entrusts his pet rabbits to his sister Maggie's care. She is preoccupied and allows the creatures to die. Despite her tearful protestations, Tom upbraids her bitterly but finally forgives her. This childhood pattern of close sibling affection, deep hurt and estrangement, and reconciliation determines the structural pattern of the novel. Although Henry James admired the design of *The Mill on the Floss*, he criticized the conclusion for its melodrama. As a matter of fact, the conclusion is implicit in the story from the beginning. The flood that carries the brother and sister to their doom is not an accidental catastrophe. Rather, it is symbolic of the tide that sweeps away two passionate souls divided in conflict yet united by the closest bonds of affection.

Tom Tulliver, like his father, has a tenacious will that is not always under control of his reason. Even as a child, he is fiercely although honorably competitive. He is slow to forgive injury. Robust and vigorous, he despises weakness in others. As a youth, he insults Philip Wakem by drawing attention to the boy's physical deformity. When Maggie demeans, as Tom mistakenly believes, the good name of the Tulliver family through her foreshortened "elopement" with Stephen Guest, he scorns her as a pariah. Nevertheless, his tempestuous nature is also capable of generosity. To redeem his father's good name and restore Dorlcote Mill to the family, he disciplines himself to work purposefully. To this end, he sacrifices his high spirits and love of strenuous excitement, indeed any opportunities for courtship and marriage. He dies as he had lived and labored, the provider of the Tulliver family.

His sister Maggie, many of whose sprightly qualities are drawn from Eliot's memories of her own childhood, is psychologically the more complex character. Whereas Tom is sturdily masculine, Maggie is sensitive, introspective, and tenderly feminine. Quick to tears—to the modern reader perhaps too effusive in her emotions—she cannot control her sensibilities, just as her brother cannot keep his temper. As a youngster, she has the qualities of a tomboy. She is energetic and, unlike the typical Victorian girl, fights for her place in the world. Intelligent, diligent, earnest, she would have made better use of Mr. Stelling's classical schooling than her brother, but girls of her time rarely had the opportunity to advance in education. Therefore, she must content herself, although secretively restive, with the narrow place Victorian society allows for girls of her class. Like Dorothea Brooke in *Middlemarch* (1871-1872), she is attracted to a scholarly but fragile lover, Philip. Her sympathetic nature completes what is lacking in the young man's disposition—courage and self-esteem—and he in turn, offers her a sense of artistic dedication for which she yearns.

Some astute critics of *The Mill on the Floss* have objected to Maggie's other suitor, Stephen Guest, who is Lucy Deane's fiancé. The impetuous Stephen would have been a satisfactory mate for Lucy, a more typical Victorian heroine, sweet but passive. According to Sir Leslie Stephen, Maggie, in her passion for Lucy's betrothed, throws herself away upon a "low creature." His daughter, Virginia Woolf, repeated Sir Leslie's judgment in describing Stephen's "coarseness." Later views of the character did not support such hostile interpretations, considering Stephen neither low nor coarse but instead an ardent lover who rouses a sexual response in Maggie that she does not feel for Philip. Maggie's torment is to be torn between her promises to Philip (who certainly loves and needs her) and her deeper feelings for Stephen. She senses the call of duty and propriety but also feels the sweep of wild emotion. When she masters her feelings and returns to Philip, she betrays her needs as a woman.

For the same reason that some critics refuse to accept Maggie as a mature woman with normal sexual responses, some readers are troubled by the apparent change in her character as she grows from child to adult. The portrait of Maggie the girl is so vital, charming, and convincing that readers may wish to cherish her youthful image, but Maggie the woman does not really change. Within the prudish conventions of the Victorian novel, Eliot can only suggest her heroine's psychological and moral development. Nevertheless, she conveys a sense of Maggie's greater sexual vulnerability with the description of her "highly strung, hungry nature." When she renounces Stephen, she renounces her own happiness. From that point, her tragedy is inevitable. Her mother, Lucy, and Philip have faith in her to the last, but the provincial gossips of St. Ogg's cast her off, and her beloved brother rejects her. Nevertheless, Maggie characteristically determines: "I must not, cannot seek my own happiness by sacrificing others." The floodwaters that carry Maggie and her brother downstream cleanse their guilt and unite them as when they were innocent children. Finally, Eliot tells us, they are "not divided."

"Critical Evaluation" by Leslie B. Mittleman

Bibliography:
Ashton, Rosemary. *"The Mill on the Floss": A Natural History*. Boston: Twayne, 1990. A book-length study useful to beginners. Discusses the novel in relation to Eliot's life, the historical context, natural history, and literary influences. Includes an annotated bibliography.
Barrett, Dorothea. "Demonism, Feminism, and Incest in *The Mill on the Floss*." In *Vocation and Desire: George Eliot's Heroines*. New York: Routledge, 1989. Argues that three elements discussed separately by previous critics work together in *The Mill on the Floss*. Emphasizes a positive view of the novel's "passionate idealism."
Beer, Gillian. *George Eliot*. Bloomington: Indiana University Press, 1986. A reassessment of Eliot's fiction that refutes other feminist criticisms. Asserts that Maggie Tulliver's passion represents her desire for knowledge and freedom as well as sexual love, and that Eliot challenged the boundaries of women's role in Victorian society. Contains an extensive bibliography.
Carroll, David. *"The Mill on the Floss: Growing Up in St. Ogg's."* In *George Eliot and the Conflict of Interpretations: A Reading of the Novels*. Cambridge, England: Cambridge University Press, 1992. Considers the problem of reading the novel as two kinds of narrative: a realistic fiction containing anthropological treatment of the lives of Maggie's relatives and a legend of a unified pastoral world of childhood.
Emery, Laura Comer. *George Eliot's Creative Conflict: The Other Side of Silence*. Berkeley: University of California Press, 1976. Detailed psychoanalytical readings trace the development of George Eliot's creative process from *The Mill on the Floss* (the first detailed expression of Eliot's unconscious conflicts) to *Middlemarch*.

THE MILL ON THE PO

Type of work: Novel
Author: Riccardo Bacchelli (1891-1985)
Type of plot: Historical
Time of plot: 1812-1872
Locale: The region of the Po River, near Ferrara
First published: Il mulino del Po, 1938-1940 (English translation, 1950, 1955)

Principal characters:
LAZZARO SCACERNI, a miller on the Po
DOSOLINA, his wife
GIUSEPPE, his son
CECILIA, his daughter-in-law

The Story:

In 1817, a new water mill appeared on the Po River, near the city of Ferrara. Its owner was young Lazzaro Scacerni, who had become a miller in an odd fashion indeed. Nevertheless, he was no stranger to the river—his father had been a ferryman at Ariano before dying in the peasant uprising of 1807. Shortly afterward the boy Lazzaro had been sent, along with other orphans, to serve as a cabin boy in the navy. When he became older, he went over to the army pontoniers, and in 1812 he found himself a part of Napoleon's ill-fated Russian campaign.

During the terrible retreat, a dying captain gave Lazzaro a mysterious receipt, which the illiterate young man could not read. He guarded it closely, however, as he straggled homeward from a debacle in which fourteen out of every fifteen Italian soldiers perished. Finally returning to the neighborhood of Ferrara, Lazzaro led a hand-to-mouth existence while waiting for a chance to make use of his one mysterious asset. He learned to read well enough to decipher the name and address attached to the receipt, and subsequent search led to Ezekiel the Jew, in Ferrara's ghetto. The receipt was for jewels, plundered from Spanish churches by Lazzaro's benefactor. His windfall once assured, Lazzaro cannily pondered its best use. Millers, he decided, were least affected by times of adversity, and he arranged with a friendly old shipwright to build him a mill. In due time it was finished, christened St. Michael's, and put into operation.

As the years passed, the miller prospered. One, two, and finally three boys were hired for helpers as his trade grew. His success inspired more envy than affection among his neighbors, and a few wives and daughters succumbed to his dashing gallantries. Nearly forty years old and wearying of bachelorhood, Lazzaro fell in love with Dosolina, poor but delicately beautiful and twenty years his junior. Lazzaro bought a house, married Dosolina, and settled down to enjoy his prosperity.

Fate, however, was not always to smile. Floods came, the bane of the Po River millers; smugglers, crossing between Italy and Austria, insolently used his mill for a rendezvous. On the birth night of his son Giuseppe, Lazzaro's troubles reached a climax. While Dosolina was writhing in difficult labor, the desperate Lazzaro fought to save his mill from the swollen menace of the Po. Slipping on the wet deck, he broke a leg but continued to direct his helpers, two of whom worked manfully. The third was malformed Beffa, who secretly hated his master and who had become a tool of the smugglers. Shedding all restraint, Beffa openly exulted over his master's plight and scornfully asserted that the miller had been cuckolded. Lazzaro then reached out with his muscular arms, seized Beffa, and hurled him into the river.

Dosolina recovered, and the mill was saved, but Beffa's damp dismissal caused Lazzaro to receive disturbing threats from Raguseo, king of the smugglers. A gang feud, however, broke out among the outlaws soon afterward, disposing of Raguseo. Lazzaro breathed more easily thereafter. Some dangers were over, but others came, for intermittent floods continued to threaten the mill. One day a large mill washed ashore near Lazzaro's own, its only occupant a girl orphaned by the flood. To Cecilia her mill meant home; she was very happy when the Scacernis befriended her and reestablished her mill alongside theirs. From that time on Lazzaro regarded the girl almost as his own daughter.

He was much less pleased, however, with the character and disposition of his own son. Bandy-legged, crafty, and cowardly, Giuseppe cared nothing about his father's trade except its profit. He early showed great skill, as well as great avarice, in business dealings of any kind, and he was held in contempt by all, except by his mother. During the late 1840's he began successfully trafficking in grain with the hated Austrians, but the same years brought new distress to his family. Roving bands of partisans, Italians or Austrian mercenaries, infested the countryside and disturbed the peace and security of the Scacernis. Finally, both mills were commandeered by the Austrians, and Lazzaro and Cecilia were required to transfer them to the opposite side of the river.

After a few months, the mills were allowed to return, but the political atmosphere was still cloudy and confused among the rival claims and interests of the papacy, the Italian nationalistic movement, and Austria. Lazzaro, who was growing old and querulous, found much to complain about. Only at the mills, in the company of his helpers and Cecilia, did he feel comfortable; even there, he sometimes railed at the smuggling, which carried scarce grain across the river to Austria. He was outraged when he learned that Giuseppe took a leading role in such transactions.

An unexpected family affair suddenly arose which gave concern to both the elder Scacernis. Giuseppe, apparently inattentive to women, had long slyly coveted Cecilia for his wife, in spite of her clear indifference to him. Not daring to risk her mockery by a proposal, he went about winning his goal by characteristic trickery. Meanly playing on her fondness for his father, Giuseppe blandly announced that Lazzaro had broken a law by possessing concealed firearms. His son could exert influence to head off his arrest and punishment—but only for a price— Cecilia's consent to marry him. Cecilia, taken by surprise, was confused, angry, and ignorantly fearful. Her devotion to Lazzaro, however, was greater than her repugnance for his son, and in the end, Giuseppe had his way.

Lazzaro was unaware of Cecilia's sacrifice and felt baffled and hurt by what he considered her poor judgment. In turn, Dosolina regarded her new daughter-in-law as little better than a river gypsy and quite unworthy of her son. Neither of the parents, however, had long to lament the marriage. In 1855 Dosolina was the victim of a wave of cholera that swept all Europe. The next morning Lazzaro was found dead beside her.

The structure of Italy changed: Time was bringing Austrian defeat, the end of papal rule, and the dawn of a united nation. These things, of course, meant little to Cecilia Scacerni, but the small warmth of her nature found, at last, a suitable outlet. Her firstborn and favorite, Lazzarino, was vigorous and intelligent, a reminder of his grandfather in more than name. Even his grasping, mean-natured father openly adored him.

Lazzarino, however, was not destined to match his grandfather in years. Miserable at the general mockery of his father's cowardice, he ran off to join Garibaldi's volunteers. News of his death staggered Cecilia, but its effect on Giuseppe was catastrophic. Grief gnawed at his reason, and the destruction of his house and crops by flood completed his downfall. Howling obscenely, he was carted off to the asylum. Left alone, Cecilia looked about her with calm courage. There was work to do, and she would see that it was done.

Critical Evaluation:

The Mill on the Po is a translation of two volumes of Riccardo Bacchelli's Italian trilogy dealing with the lives and fortunes of the Scacerni family. *Nothing New Under the Sun*, published in 1955, completes the English translation of Bacchelli's novel. The device of the trilogy was quite popular in early twentieth century Italian fiction. It was utilized successfully by Giovanni Verga and Antonio Fogazzaro as well as by Bacchelli as a means to express a grand story without limiting oneself to the confines of a single novel. As is commonly the case, the trilogy itself is almost lost in literary history, and one particular part of the trilogy stands apart as a great work. This is true of *The Mill on the Po*, which was not only the best of this trilogy but also the masterpiece of Bacchelli's literary career.

This novel was written almost at the culmination of Bacchelli's personal victory over his own life's problems. As a youth his inner struggles left marks on all of his works. By the late 1930's, when he wrote *The Mill on the Po*, however, he no longer was compelled to rely on semiauto-biographical themes, and from this point on, his literary output was more prolific and of a higher quality than before.

The novel is set against the background of Italian unification in the late nineteenth century. Bacchelli's work, however, does not depend upon the unification theme for a large part of its thrust. It is merely the stage upon which the drama is set. The major emphasis or theme of the novel is the struggle of common people against life. Bacchelli is able to portray the drama of ordinary people's lives when they are faced with extraordinary circumstances.

Another important aspect of *The Mill on the Po* is the literary device of tracing one family's history from generation to generation. This is a plot scheme that has been particularly popular in the twentieth century, and Bacchelli used it well. The backdrop of the Italian unification is the canvas upon which the family portrait is painted. Italian history moved at a different rate than the lives of the characters and therefore is an effective background for a multigenerational novel such as this.

The Mill on the Po is actually a two-volume story that has episodes held together by history and the Scacerni family line. Though the portions of the novel are different, and indeed even the writing style and mood of the story change from section to section, the historical setting, on the one hand, and the unchanging river Po, on the other, provide pivotal points on which the novel can progress.

Bacchelli was highly influenced by Alessandro Manzoni, the great nineteenth century Italian author of *The Betrothed* (1827). *The Mill on the Po* and several of Bacchelli's other works show large traces of Manzonian influence in the narrative. Bacchelli, like Manzoni, is at his best as a historical novelist. Both wrote monumentally large works about day-to-day characters whose lives take place in a period of historical turmoil. One of the reasons that Bacchelli was so successful was that, like Manzoni, he wrote readable works. In the period of the 1920's, Italy was not known for tremendous literary output. Aside from the works of Grazia Deledda, Italo Svevo, and Bacchelli, Italian literature was at its lowest point of the century. The greats of the early part of the century, such as Giovanni Verga and Gabriele D'Annunzio, were either dead or no longer producing, and the budding authors of the thirties and forties had yet to come into the limelight. Perhaps because of this dry literary period, *The Mill on the Po* was very popular and well received critically. Its popularity has declined somewhat since then, however, especially outside of Italy, but it is still recommended reading for those who enjoy historical fiction, romance, and adventure.

In retrospect, the weakest point of the novel is the characterization. Although well drawn, the characters are stereotypes rather than individuals. Lazzaro and Cecilia represent the strong, pliable personalities who are able to deal with adversities and yet remain true to their ideals and themselves. Dosolina and Giuseppe, on the other hand, personify the weak and the frightened who would make the best out of life only if it were easy and on their own terms. Rather than accept changes, Dosolina gives up, and Giuseppe tries to cheat his way through life. The problems that the characters face are so severe that readers may remember the adventures of the story, however, far more easily than they may recall the details of an individual character's development.

Readers can admire and love Lazzaro, just as they can hate Giuseppe. When a novel portrays such an empathetic central character in such an engaging story, it is likely to be a popular work of fiction for a long time. The historical background and universal theme of one's struggle against the vicissitudes of life, added to its appealing main character, put *The Mill on the Po* on a par with many of the great works of literature.

"Critical Evaluation" by Patricia Ann King

Bibliography:
Bergin, T. G. Review of *The Mill on the Po*, by Riccardo Bacchelli. *The New York Herald Tribune Book Review*, September 17, 1950, p. 5. Points out that Bacchelli, despite the accusations levelled at the lack of subtlety in his writing, is a careful stylist who devotes much attention to the proper word and phrase.
Booklist. Review of *The Mill on the Po*, by Riccardo Bacchelli. 47, no. 136 (December 1, 1950). States that *The Mill on the Po* is regarded in Italy as the Italian *War and Peace* (1865-1869).
Knittel, Robert. Review of *The Mill on the Po*, by Riccardo Bacchelli. *The New York Times*, September 17, 1950, p. 5. Strongly favorable review argues that the novel transcends its historical context and reaches universal truths.
New Yorker, The. Review of *The Mill on the Po*, by Riccardo Bacchelli. 26, no. 118 (September 16, 1950). Criticizes *The Mill on the Po* for being heavy-handed in its presentation of its characters as representatives of the Italian people.
Sandrock, Mary. Review of *The Mill on the Po*, by Riccardo Bacchelli. *Catholic World* 172, no. 153 (November, 1950). Points out that Bacchelli's novel, in portraying the "defects" of the Roman Catholic church and its actions during a tumultuous period of Italian history, nevertheless does not "weaken" the church's "spiritual integrity."

MILTON

Type of work: Poetry
Author: William Blake (1757-1827)
First published: 1804-1808

William Blake composed this brief epic poem to explain Christianity to a troubled England. Geoffrey Chaucer, Edmund Spenser, and John Milton before him had written on that theme, but Blake created a far more personal and highly original myth. As he saw it, England's Christianity had traded supernatural spirituality for scientific rationality. Blake thought scientific rationality, or what he called natural religion, would lead to commercial imperialism, dehumanizing mechanization of work, and worldwide wars. One may say that he was right. He blamed natural religion on Milton's Puritanism with its orthodoxy, dualism, hypocritical moral virtue, militancy, and bondage to law.

Blake wrote *Milton* to correct the errors of this religion, which overvalued reason, undervalued love, and lacked any concept of the Holy Spirit. In his domestic life, Milton was tormented by the sinister aspects of female will. In *Paradise Lost* (1667) he blamed the Fall on Adam's adoration of Eve and depicted their love as dangerous and lustful. Milton's Messiah reminded Blake of Job's Satan, and Blake thought Milton was "of the Devil's party without knowing it." Milton saw man after the Fall struggling under law in fear of punishment until the Last Judgment. Blake's epic follows that cycle of fall, struggle, redemption, and apocalypse. For Blake, the Fall was caused by an usurpation of reason by emotion, and redemption liberates man from laws of moral virtue.

Blake's epic is almost without a plot. Milton finds himself unhappy in heaven. A bard's song moves him to return to earth, where he is reincarnated in Blake. Through mighty struggles with symbolical characters, he purges himself of intellectual error and unites with his female counterpart, Ololon.

Action is spare in this epic because its meanings are revealed not in events but in various unfolding perspectives of characters on those events as Blake presents them throughout the poem. The readers' experience is unlike anything else in literature. Blake puts readers through mental contortions designed to reveal new modes of perception. They must enter Blake's mythical cosmos with the characters interpreting revelations as they happen.

The epic action is actually a single flash of inspiration, and the narrative relates events that are virtually simultaneous. Perspectives shift without warning. Characters are not only personalities but also places, states of mind, systems of thought, and historical epochs. They multiply and divide, travel through time as well as space, and merge with one another to make points about ideas they symbolize. Milton can be discussing philosophy in Beulah at the same time he is falling to earth, struggling with Urizen by the river, and entering Blake. The poet's objective is to take readers' minds completely out of the ordinary, beyond the confines of familiar time and space, in order to comprehend humankind's past and future as a single mental form, eternally human and divine. *Milton* is a poem about how a poet envisions eternal truth with the fourfold power of imagination.

Some background in Blake's cosmic mythology is helpful. Before the fall, Albion (fourfold man) was united with his bride Jerusalem (heaven), and the Four Zoas (aspects of man) presided over their respective realms. The realms are Tharmas (body), Urizen (reason), Luvah (emotion), and Urthona (imagination). But when Luvah encroaches on Urizen, all fall and split asunder. Luvah is divorced from Vala (nature) and turns into Orc (revolt). Urizen casts off his Emanation,

Ahania (pleasure). Tharmas becomes Enion (lust), and Urthona divides into Los (time) and Enitharmon (space). All howl in discord, each claiming to be God. They exist within Albion's bosom and throughout the cosmic vastness beyond the Mundane Shell that encloses earth, where Los labors in Golgonooza, giving form to uncreated things. His four-dimensional gates open onto Eden, Beulah, Generation, and Ulro, places like Milton's heaven, Eden, earth, and hell.

Interestingly, Blake's myth foresees modern psychology, for he portrays fallen man with a split personality: a masculine, reasoning, ravenous, selfish Spectre, and a feminine Emanation, an elusive shadow representing all the Spectre desires. Originally man had fourfold vision, sensory powers that were infinitely expansive and lucid. The fall drops him through successive states of error until he reaches the merciful limits of contraction (Adam) and opacity (Satan). So, symbolically, Milton falls through Luvah, Urizen, and the Mundane Shell, into Albion's bosom, all the way to the limits of contraction (Adam) and opacity for his final confrontation with Satan.

For six thousand years, fallen man has tried to regain the fourfold vision, through seven epochs, each called an Eye of God. First came Lucifer, whose error was egotism. Then came three phases of infernal justice: Molech (execution), Elohim (judgment), and Shaddai (accusation). Next came Pahad, a reign of terror after justice failed, followed by two attempts at order: Jehovah (law) and Jesus (forgiveness). Blake further subdivides history into twenty-seven churches (systems of religious thought) in three groups: from Adam to Lamech, from Noah to Terah, and from Abraham to Luther. Blake sees Milton as the eighth Eye or twenty-eighth church, a new concept of religion without hierarchy, orthodoxy, and other Satanic perversions of faith. Thus, Blake's epic announces a new phase of Christianity liberated from dogma and law.

The personages and machinery of Blake's myth are revealed to characters in the poem through visions that are also witnessed and overheard by readers. Book 1 opens with a bard's song that tells a parable of Satan's fall and the creation of the three classes of men in a story about Los's sons. There is Palamabron, an honest farmer and prophet; Rintrah, an angry prophet; and Satan, the miller, a mild-mannered, respectable prince of this world. They swap places for a day, with catastrophic results. Trying to drive the harrow in pity's path, Satan drives the horses and servants mad. Meanwhile Palamabron revels in wine, song, and dance with workers in the Satanic mills. Satan blames Palamabron, who demands a trial before the Eternals. Rintrah testifies for Palamabron, saying Satan did wrong because "pity divides the soul/ And man unmans." The Eternals refuse to impute guilt to pity, and their judgment falls on Rintrah for his wrath. Enraged, Satan accuses Palamabron of malice and ingratitude. Exiled to Ulro, Satan declares himself God and is worshipped in churches. His daughter Leutha tries but fails to reverse Satan's condemnation by taking the blame on herself. The Eternals rule that Satan must endure among the Elect, unredeemed, until someone dies for him. They create two other classes of men: the Reprobate, like Rintrah, who transgress the law but keep the faith; and the Redeemed, like Palamabron, who labor productively despite being tormented by the Elect.

Milton realizes that the bard's song is about himself. "I in my Selfhood am that Satan," he declares, vowing to descend through a vortex into Ulro, where he can annihilate his Spectre and reunite with his Emanation. Like a falling star, Milton travels to earth and is reincarnated in the poet Blake, entering through his left foot. The fallen Zoas dread Milton's approach. Urizen does battle with him, turning the ground beneath his feet to marble and pouring icy water on his brain. Milton moulds red clay around Urizen's feet to give him new flesh and a human form. Rahab sends her daughters to entice Milton with lust, but he pays no heed and strives onward to Golgonooza.

As Albion stirs in his sleep, Blake starts, noticing something strange on his left foot in the form of a sandal. Though not yet realizing that Milton has come into him, Blake straps on the sandal to stride through Eternity. Los appears and helps him with his sandals, becoming one man with Blake too. At Golgonooza the poet-prophet meets Rintrah and Palamabron, who ask whether Milton comes to let Satan loose, unchain Orc, and raise up Mystery, the Virgin Harlot Mother of War. They see revolution in America and the Covering Cherub advancing from the East. The Covering Cherub represents false dogmas of religion consolidated in the warring churches of Paul, Constantine, Charlemagne, and Luther. Los urges his sons not to flee in fear, for he knows Milton's arrival signals the Last Judgment. Book 1 ends with a glorious account of the redemptive labors of Los in Golgonooza, where material nature and the mental abstractions of Ulro are transformed by imaginative vision and given particularly human forms.

Book 2 opens in Beulah, a dreamy place of respite from the fury of poetic inspiration in Eden. All Beulah laments, for Ololon vows to follow Milton into Ulro. Milton's immortal part converses with the angels, explaining the doctrine of States. According to this doctrine, individual identities never change, but they pass through States that do. Satan, reason, and memory are States to be annihilated; and Milton is about to become a State called Annihilation, where the living go to defeat Death.

Then everything suddenly culminates in a moment of inspiration. Ololon arrives at Blake's garden, and so does Milton. Standing on the sea not far away, Satan thunders. Blake enters Satan's bosom to behold its formless desolation. Milton condemns Satan and his priests for, with their laws and terrors, making men fear death. Satan replies that he is judge of all, God himself in holiness (not mercy). With that, the garden path erupts in flame and the Starry Seven blow trumpets to awaken Albion and the Four Zoas from their slumber of six thousand years. Satan withdraws and Rahab appears, bearing the name of Moral Virtue and revealing herself to be Religion hid in War.

Ololon and Milton discuss times past. They reach the realization that they are contraries who can be reconciled once their inhibiting selfhoods have been expunged. Ololon thereupon sheds her formidable female will, which sinks into the sea with Milton's spectral shadow. Purged, the two are reunited. Milton declares

> I come in Self-annihilation & the grandeur of Inspiration,
> To cast off Rational Demonstration by Faith in the Saviour,
> To cast off the rotten rags of Memory by Inspiration,
> To cast off Bacon, Locke & Newton from Albion's covering,
> To take off his filthy garments & clothe him with Imagination,
> To cast aside from Poetry all that is not Inspiration . . .

Clothed in a garment dipped in blood and inscribed with words of divine revelation, Jesus appears and enters into Albion's bosom. God unites with man. Terror-struck, Blake collapses on the path and is revived by his wife. The lark is heard on high, and all go forth to the Last Judgment.

John L. McLean

Bibliography:
Bloom, Harold. *Blake's Apocalypse: A Study in Poetic Argument.* Garden City, N.Y.: Double-

day, 1963. A comprehensive, virtually line-by-line exposition of Blake's prophetic poems. Sensitively explains the intricate subtleties of Blake's myth and traces its connections to biblical and other literary traditions.

Damon, S. Foster. *A Blake Dictionary: The Ideas and Symbols of William Blake.* Providence, R.I.: Brown University Press, 1965. This handy glossary collects and interprets clues to Blake's terminology, which is scattered through all of his works. There are entries for each character, work, symbol, and geographical or historical reference. Omits most of Blake's contemporaries in the arts. Includes maps, illustrations, and diagrams of difficult concepts such as Golgonooza.

Fox, Susan. *Poetic Form in Blake's "Milton."* Princeton, N.J.: Princeton University Press, 1976. Patiently establishes the structural principle of parallelism beneath the seeming chaos of the poem. Explores the echoes, paired passages, cyclical patterns, and thematic symmetries.

Frye, Northrop. *Fearful Symmetry: A Study of William Blake.* Princeton, N.J.: Princeton University Press, 1947. A brilliant analysis of Blake's poetry and thought, the most important and influential work of Blake criticism. Chapter 10 examines *Milton* in depth.

Howard, John. *Blake's Milton: A Study in the Selfhood.* Madison, N.J.: Fairleigh Dickinson University Press, 1976. A psychological analysis that credits Blake for anticipating twentieth century psychological theories. Focuses on Milton's descent as a journey within the psyche and analyzes Blake's Spectres as models of self-paralyzing inhibition.

THE MINISTRY OF FEAR

Type of work: Novel
Author: Graham Greene (1904-1991)
Type of plot: Psychological realism
Time of plot: World War II
Locale: London and environs
First published: 1943

> *Principal characters:*
> ARTHUR ROWE, a middle-aged Englishman who has killed his wife
> ANNA HILFE, an Austrian refugee
> WILLI HILFE, Anna's brother and a fifth-column leader
> DR. FORESTER, English dupe of Willi Hilfe

The Story:

Arthur Rowe, a middle-aged Englishman, happened one day onto a fete in blitz-torn London. In an effort to recapture some spirit of the brighter past, he entered the grounds. While there, he had his fortune told, and the seer told him the weight of a cake that was to go to the person who guessed the weight correctly. Rowe won the cake and started to leave, but the clergyman who was in charge of the affair tried to get the cake back again. Rowe was angered and donated a pound note to the cause and left.

Just before the German bombers flew up the Thames to terrorize the city that same night, Rowe had his first visitor in months, a man who had just rented a room in the same house. The visitor behaved very oddly. When given a piece of cake by Rowe, he crumbled it as if looking for something. Then, while Rowe was out of the room, the man slipped something into Rowe's tea. Rowe returned and smelled the peculiar odor of the tea, but before he could say or do anything, a bomb fell, wrecking the house. He regained consciousness to find the house demolished.

Because he had few friends to whom he could turn since he had killed his wife in a mercy killing, the worried Rowe went to a detective agency the next day, where he hired a man named Jones to watch after him and discover why someone wished to take his life. Rowe then went to the relief office, which had been in charge of the fete at which he had won the cake. There he found a young woman, Anna Hilfe, and her brother Willi in charge of the office. The two said they were Austrian refugees. Willi Hilfe went with Rowe to the home of the fortune-teller in an effort to uncover the reason for the attempt on Rowe's life.

At the fortune-teller's home, the two men were invited to stay for a séance. During the séance, the man sitting next to Rowe was murdered with Rowe's knife. With Willi's aid, Rowe escaped from the house before the police arrived. He went to an air-raid shelter and there remained through the night. He wrote a letter to the police, but before he posted it, he called Anna, who told him that "they" were still after him. "They" were supposed to be Nazi agents. Rowe still could not understand why he had become a marked man. Anna agreed to aid Rowe and told him to send an address where he could be reached.

After talking to her, Rowe called the detective agency. He then learned that Jones, the man he had hired, had disappeared and that the head of the agency had called the police in on the case. Rowe wandered aimlessly about the city until the afternoon, when he met a man who asked him to take a valise full of books to a Mr. Travers at a hotel. When Rowe arrived at the hotel, he was escorted to Travers' room. There he found Anna waiting for him. In fear of their lives, the two waited for the air raids to begin. They believed that Nazi agents would kill them during the noise and confusion of the raids. Then a bomb fell on the hotel. Rowe awoke in a private nursing home without any memory beyond his eighteenth year.

Anna visited him several times in the nursing home, and Rowe fell in love with her during the visits. She would not tell him of his past and claimed that the head of the institution, Dr. Forester, wanted the recovery to be slow enough to avoid shock. One day, a military officer being treated in the home confided that he had seen someone digging on the island in a pond on the grounds. The officer was immediately put into a straitjacket, and Rowe was confined to his room without newspapers or his clothes on the pretext that he had suffered a mild relapse.

Convinced that some evil was afoot, Rowe escaped from the room and visited the officer. His visit with the officer confirmed his suspicions. Within a few hours, the doctor returned and, extremely angry at Rowe, threatened him, too, with a straitjacket. With the help of an attendant, Rowe escaped and went to Scotland Yard. He turned himself in as the murderer of the victim at the séance; to his surprise, however, he was told that no one had been murdered there. The police turned him over to a counterintelligence agent, who told Rowe that the murder had been a fraud to drive him into hiding and that the nursing home was actually a front for fifth-column activities.

The agent, Rowe, and a man from the hotel where Rowe had been injured went to the tailor shop run by the man who had supposedly been murdered. During the interview, the tailor placed a phone call. After the call was completed, he killed himself. Angry at losing the man before learning any information, the agent told Rowe that he had inadvertently been given a cake containing secret film that had been taken by Nazi agents from British documents.

Rowe and the agent then went to the home of the fortune-teller. They failed to find the film there, and they got no information. The last stop of the trip was at the nursing home. There they found the military officer dead, killed by Dr. Forester, who, as Rowe now remembered, had been at the fortune-teller's home on the night of the supposed murder. The doctor was also dead; he had been killed by the attendant who had helped Rowe to escape.

Without telling the counterintelligence agent, Rowe called the number he had seen the tailor dial. When the call was answered, he found Anna at the other end. Going to her apartment, Rowe discovered that it was her brother Willi who was the head of the fifth-column ring. With Anna's help, Rowe almost got the film. Anna, torn between love for her brother and love for Rowe, allowed Willi to escape. Rowe, whose memory was almost complete, followed Willi and regained the film at the railroad station. He returned Willi's gun to him but with only one bullet in it. Willi then went to the washroom and killed himself, but not before he had revealed the last piece of information that Rowe had failed to remember, the fact that Rowe had killed his first wife to put her out of pain. Rowe was ready to give the film in his possession to the police. He returned to Anna's apartment to tell her of her brother's death and to declare his love to her. Although Rowe had driven her brother to his death, Anna pledged her love for him as well.

Critical Evaluation:

With the publication of *Brighton Rock* in 1938, Graham Greene began to categorize his works as either "novels" or "entertainments," with the latter term suggesting a work of somehow lesser stature. The distinguishing factor between the two appears to be the way in which religion is treated; the novels are set apart by a more serious consideration of religious and ethical problems, while the entertainments focus more on plot, action, and melodrama, with religious problems as secondary concerns.

Yet, despite their overall lack of seriousness, the entertainments often show Greene at his best, committed to keeping his readers in suspense and making the action as exciting as possible, with the goal of telling the best story possible. In some cases, the entertainments even appear to serve as preliminary sketches for the more elaborate treatment of similar themes in the novels that follow them.

This might be argued in the case of *The Ministry of Fear*, the most ambitious, arguably the best, of Greene's entertainments. In its focus on how the emotion of pity can destroy those in which it is overdeveloped, the book is also an obvious precursor to one of Greene's finest achievements, the novel *The Heart of the Matter* (1948).

Moved by an almost corrupting sense of pity, Arthur Rowe, the book's protagonist, has killed his wife, who was suffering from an incurable illness. His sense of pity is corrupting, because it is really a disguised form of contempt for others. To pity other people is to regard them as inferior.

Whether he did it to end her suffering or to free himself from having to watch her endure, he cannot be certain. If he killed her quickly by poison because he could not stand to watch her die slowly from cancer, then his mercy killing sprang from selfishness. This "mercy killing," of which the court acquitted him, has an echo in a childhood memory. As a boy, Rowe had happened upon a struggling rat with a broken back and ended its suffering, an experience which appears to have defined his character.

Rowe is obviously a precursor to Major Scobie, the main character in *The Heart of the Matter*. Like Rowe, Scobie is defined by his pity. Like Rowe's, Scobie's sense of responsibility for his fellow human beings and his concern with their unhappiness imply a lack of trust, a lack of faith in God. It is the treatment of this theme which most separates the two works, as the entertainment chooses to leave it unexplored, whereas the novel treats this lack of trust as one of its primary themes.

In Rowe, pity is overdeveloped to an extreme. In the person of the book's antagonist, the Nazi sympathizer Willi Hilfe, Greene delves into the other extreme: underdeveloped pity or pitilessness. Hilfe is a monstrous villain, an utterly selfish, amoral criminal who has lost the sense of worth of human life.

Arthur Rowe's overwhelming sense of pity makes him capable of bearing pain but equally incapable of causing pain to others. As he unwittingly becomes involved with the activities of an undercover Nazi organization in war-torn London during the air raids of World War II, Rowe ironically becomes the spokesman of humanity as he must face down Hilfe and the threat his group poses. This involvement with Hilfe and his group, however, is necessary for Rowe to achieve self-actualization. To overcome the hurdles that block his rebirth, Rowe must give up both his private life and his safety to help the common cause and rid his country of the threat Hilfe embodies.

The book's structure is notable. *The Ministry of Fear* is divided into four parts. The first, "The Unhappy Man," deals with Rowe, describing the experiences that have combined to create him. As a result of the mercy killing, Rowe has become a solitary man, unable to find a job and without friends. The fact that the murder was a mercy killing does not soften anybody's harsh opinion of Rowe—even Rowe's opinion of himself. He stands condemned just as deeply in his own eyes as in those of others.

Because the story is set during World War II, Rowe is all the more alone because he is cut off from the sense of community engendered by wartime experience. This section sets the stage for the action, portraying the fete at which Rowe wins, ironically, the cake in which the undercover organization has placed a microfilm of secret naval plans.

The second section, "The Happy Man," deals with a Rowe who, as a result of a bomb blast, has lost the memory of his past, along with the sense of pity that has propelled him. Rowe has become Richard Digby and is in a countryside nursing home under the care of the famous Dr. Forester. Rowe is at peace, at least as much as it is possible for him to experience peace. His amnesia allows him to rest and rejuvenate, which eventually leads to thoughts of escape.

In the third section, "Bits and Pieces," Rowe slowly begins his reorientation as he rediscovers his beliefs and convictions. Since he had not yet redeveloped his overdeveloped sense of pity, he is still essentially happy. The fourth section, "The Whole Man," presents Rowe's public and private reintegration as a complete knowledge of his past returns to him.

This structure, which involves Rowe losing touch with himself, only gradually to relearn the painful facts of life, connects *The Ministry of Fear* with the idea of "the divided man," "the man within" of Greene's earlier novels. Were it not for this "man within," an ideal, imagined fantasy self, the ordinary, instinctive man would find it easier to come to terms with actuality.

Yet, surprisingly, Rowe has not entirely lost touch with his sense of pity at the book's end. He has come full circle to a new life with Anna Hilfe but is still so obsessed with his sense of pity at the idea of human suffering that he is willing, at the story's end, to enter into this new relationship with Anna without being entirely honest. Rowe's pity will cause the relationship to be one based entirely in fear and dishonesty, as he attempts to spare her the knowledge that he remembers killing his wife.

Easily one of the strongest of the entertainments, *The Ministry of Fear* falls short of Greene's criteria for his novels only because of the lighter treatment of religious themes. A strong thriller narrative, combined with numerous artistic and thematic complexities, makes *The Ministry of Fear* one of Graham Greene's best works.

"Critical Evaluation" by Craig A. Larson

Bibliography:
Allott, Kenneth, and Miriam Farris. *The Art of Graham Greene*. New York: Russell, 1963. One of the first book-length studies of Greene and still one of the best. Views *The Ministry of Fear* in the terms of Greene's obsessions with "the divided mind" or "the fallen world."
Boardman, Gwenn R. *Graham Greene: The Aesthetics of Exploration*. Gainesville: University Presses of Florida, 1971. Sees the novel as "an ingenious parable on the nature of love." The book is a commentary on the state of the world and "the mess that Western civilization" was in at the time.
Cuoto, Maria. *Graham Greene: On the Frontier*. New York: St. Martin's Press, 1988. An excellent discussion of the book's complexities. Greene's "artistry lies in breaking the mold of the thriller to integrate tragic and spiritual concerns."
DeVitis, A. A. *Graham Greene*. Rev. ed. Edited by Kinley E. Roby. Boston: Twayne, 1986. An excellent starting point for a consideration of Greene's work. Insightful chapter on the "entertainments" as opposed to the "novels."
Wolfe, Peter. *Graham Greene the Entertainer*. Carbondale: Southern Illinois University Press, 1972. Essential book-length study which chiefly addresses those works classified as "entertainments." Devotes an entire chapter to *The Ministry of Fear*.

THE MIRACLE WORKER

Type of work: Drama
Author: William Gibson (1914-   )
Type of plot: Psychological realism
Time of plot: The 1880's
Locale: Tuscumbia, Alabama, and Boston, Massachusetts
First performed: Television play, 1957; stage play, 1960; first published, 1959

Principal characters:
ANNIE SULLIVAN, an obstinate, once-blind teacher
CAPTAIN ARTHUR KELLER, a Southern gentleman
KATE, his second wife
HELEN, their deaf, blind daughter
JAMES, the Captain's indolent son

The Story:

One-and-a-half-year-old Helen Keller was sick with acute congestion and a high fever. She seemed to have made it through the ordeal, but after the doctor left, her parents, Captain Arthur and Kate Keller, were horrified to discover that the illness had left Helen deaf and blind. Five years passed and the Keller family had not been able to find any doctor, teacher, or quack who could do anything to help Helen. The undisciplined, groping, curious girl was left to her own devices, grabbing toys from other children, knocking papers off desks, and eating off other people's plates. When she overturned the cradle, tumbling the baby, Mildred, onto the floor, the Captain agreed to write to yet another rumored specialist in the hope that someone might be able to train Helen.

The Captain's letter eventually found its way to Boston and the Perkins Institute for the Blind, where a governess was found for Helen. Twenty-year-old Annie Sullivan had just completed her own education at Perkins. She had been an abandoned child, left to care for her sickly brother, Jimmie, who died in the state almshouse. Now, after nine eye operations and a turbulent education, Annie was being sent to try to teach Helen. Her teacher, Mr. Anagnos, warned her not to expect miracles.

The Keller family was shocked by Annie's youth and inexperience. It was especially difficult for the Captain's indolent son, James, to see a woman no older than himself given this responsibility. When Annie announced that she intended to teach Helen language, Kate lamented that they had not even been able to teach her to sit still. From the moment of her arrival, Annie began to fingerspell into Helen's hands. The first attempt to impose some structure onto Helen erupted the moment the child did not get her own way. Helen hit Annie in the face with a doll, knocking out a tooth. Helen then locked Annie in Helen's room and groped her way out to the pump in the yard. When James smugly informed the Captain of Annie's plight, the Captain angrily had a ladder fetched and carried the humiliated Annie to the ground. Annie watched the family go in to eat dinner and turned to Helen, who, believing she was alone, gleefully dropped Annie's room key down the well.

The next morning James and the Captain were arguing again, resulting in James comparing Annie to General Grant at the Battle of Vicksburg. At breakfast, when Helen groped her way around the table, Annie refused to allow Helen to eat off her plate. A battle of wills followed, with Annie expelling the family from the dining room and physically forcing Helen to sit down and eat properly. The siege lasted all morning, leaving the room a disaster, but Helen ate breakfast with her own spoon and folded her napkin. Exhausted and discouraged, Annie went upstairs to pack. In the meantime, the Captain informed Kate that the insolent teacher must be fired. Instead of giving up, Annie developed a plan. She convinced the Kellers that in order to succeed, she must have control of every aspect of Helen's life. The Kellers reluctantly agreed to set Annie up in their garden house and leave her in complete charge of Helen for two weeks. After disorienting Helen by driving her around in a wagon, she was delivered into Annie's care. At first Helen refused to have anything to do with the unyielding teacher who demanded personal discipline. Annie finally got Helen to cooperate by fingerspelling into the hand of another child. Helen's jealousy overcame her and she forced herself onto the teacher.

At the end of the two weeks, the wild beast that had been Helen seemed to be tamed. Annie had spelled thousands of words into her hands. Helen had learned eighteen nouns and three verbs. It was all just a finger game, however; Helen had not connected the fingerspelling to the concept of language. Annie begged for more time, but was denied, even though the Kellers were overwhelmed with what she had accomplished. The Captain agreed, at the very least, to maintain the self-control that had been instilled in Helen. The family sat down to eat a celebratory meal, but back in her old environment, Helen immediately tried to revert to her undisciplined ways. When Annie did not tolerate it, Helen threw a tantrum and dumped the water pitcher onto Annie. Ignoring the protests of the Captain, Annie pulled Helen into the yard and forced her to refill the pitcher at the pump. Then the miracle happened. As Annie spelled W-A-T-E-R into her hand, Helen made the connection that the finger game spelled a word which meant the thing. Helen rushed around grasping everything in reach while Annie spelled its name into her hand. She found and hugged her mother, and then turned to find her teacher, whom she embraced and pulled into the house to join the Kellers at the table.

Critical Evaluation:

William Gibson is generally credited with pioneering the modern biographical drama. He did not invent the biographical play; the lives of real people have always supplied playwrights with material. It is how Gibson combined biography with literary and dramatic techniques in *The Miracle Worker* that gives him the distinction of creating the model for biographical drama of the twentieth century. After winning six Tony Awards in 1960, the play has continued as one of the most popular and best-known American plays of the mid-twentieth century. This success is partially the result of the compelling nature of its characters. There is a dramatically rich conflict between a deaf, blind child who, for pity's sake, has been allowed to behave as an animal, and an obstinate, once-blind teacher with a fierce Irish temper. Its success is also attributable to the literary qualities that give the play value as literature as well as theater.

Gibson achieved early recognition as a poet and novelist before writing the first version of *The Miracle Worker* for television. Each facet of his career influenced the play. As a poet, he developed a command of language and imagery. As a novelist, he developed skill in storytelling and theme development. As a writer for television, he developed facility in handling the rigors of succinct dramatic construction, character development, and theatricality. These overlapped as he discovered techniques to develop themes and to explore the thoughts of a character on stage. The end result was the creation of a language for *The Miracle Worker* that is almost without equal in the modern theater, at once literate and dramatic but that does not call undue attention to itself. The script, for example, is replete with religious imagery and metaphor, from the title through James Keller's comparing Annie to the angel who wrestled Jacob, providing a great blessing after causing great pain.

In his book *Shakespeare's Game*, Gibson develops a theory of drama that was greatly influenced by his wife, Margaret Brenman, a psychoanalyst. *The Miracle Worker* is a prime example of Gibson's theory that the roots of dramatic conflict lie in cognitive psychology, specifically examining the struggles of the individual against social and psychological isolation. Helen Keller is isolated by her deafness, her blindness, and her family's inability to discipline her. Discipline would include her in everyday family life. Annie Sullivan is isolated psychologically when the death of her brother, Jimmie, leaves her spiritually dead, looking for a "resurrection"; she is isolated physically as the intruder facing the almost insurmountable obstacle of breaking into Helen's world. Annie also must fight for the right to wage the battle to educate Helen. Annie's chief weapon is language, another recurring theme in Gibson's collective works. For Gibson, language has the power to illuminate the mind even more than eyes illuminate the world. Through Annie, he preaches language, theorizes language, and practices language at every opportunity. Even in the midst of their most physical battles, Annie never stops fingerspelling words, language, into the hands of Helen. At the climax of the play, it is language that bubbles up and out of Helen's mind just as the underground water bubbles up and out of the downstage pump, the play's omnipresent symbol of Helen's miracle. The social and psychological isolation of both teacher and student are resolved through language, and both receive the new life Annie had been seeking.

Each of Gibson's themes is reinforced via a parallel conflict between the Captain and his son, James. The Captain wants desperately to teach James to stand up to the world, but James, who wants to be accepted as a man, fights like a child, wounding with words, throwing a quick barb and retreating. The Captain uses the very techniques on James that he cannot abide to see Annie use on Helen. When the Captain and James debate the Confederate Army's eventual defeat in the Battle for Vicksburg, their own conflict is developed while their argument becomes a metaphor for the teaching of Helen. The Southern General Pemberton represents the Kellers, Vicksburg becomes Helen, and the stubborn General Grant is Annie. Grant won because, despite his lack of training, he never gave up, foreshadowing Annie's eventual victory in the battle to teach Helen. In the end, James also learns to use language to stand up to the Captain and end his own psychological isolation.

The play's climax is both exhilarating and wrenching. *The Miracle Worker* successfully illuminates the human condition while avoiding most of the pitfalls of sentimentality. In the end, it is not the pathos of the characters that wrings emotion from the audience, but the triumph of the human spirit.

Gerald S. Argetsinger

Bibliography:
Brustein, Robert. "Two for the Miracle." *The New Republic* 141, no. 19 (November 9, 1959): 28-29. Argues that Gibson is a gifted writer, with literary and dramatic skills, but that *The Miracle Worker* is merely an essay on interpersonal relations and that Gibson's weakness for the inspirational dooms him to the second rank.
Hayes, Richard. "Images." *Commonwealth* 71, no. 10 (December 4, 1959): 289. Argues that *The Miracle Worker*'s message of goodness is aesthetically irrelevant.
"A Hit at 10: *The Miracle Worker*." *Newsweek* 54, no. 18 (November 2, 1959): 97. Representative of the many favorable reviews when the play opened on Broadway. Focuses on Annie Sullivan as the exemplary teacher and on the themes of love and discipline. Like many

reviews, it expresses surprise that the play succeeds in spite of its first being written for television.

Kerr, Walter. "*The Miracle Worker.*" In *The Theater in Spite of Itself.* New York: Simon & Schuster, 1963. Discusses how *The Miracle Worker* succeeds in spite of some weaknesses.

Tynan, Kenneth. "Ireland Unvanquished." *The New Yorker* 35, no. 37 (October 31, 1959): 131-136. Describes Gibson's juxtaposition of laughter, combat, and pathos. Argues that the play affirms the dignity of the species.

"Who Is Stanislavsky?" *Time* 74, no. 25 (December 21, 1959): 46-52. Discusses the theatrical qualities of *The Miracle Worker*, especially the fight sequences, and examines the development of Annie Sullivan and Helen Keller as characters in the play.

THE MISANTHROPE

Type of work: Drama
Author: Molière (Jean-Baptiste Poquelin, 1622-1673)
Type of plot: Comedy of manners
Time of plot: Seventeenth century
Locale: Paris
First performed: 1666; first published, 1667 as *Le Misanthrope* (English translation, 1709)

Principal characters:
ALCESTE, in love with Célimène
PHILINTE, friend of Alceste
ORONTE, in love with Célimène
CÉLIMÈNE, a young widow
ÉLIANTE, cousin of Célimène
ARSINOÉ, a self-righteous prude

The Story:

Alceste had been called a misanthrope by many of his friends, and he took a rather obstinate delight in the name. This characteristic led him to quarrel heatedly with his good friend Philinte, who accepted uncritically the frivolous manners of the day. When Philinte warmly embraced a chance acquaintance, as was customary, Alceste maintained that such behavior was hypocritical, especially since Philinte hardly knew the man.

Philinte reminded Alceste that his lawsuit was nearly ready for trial, and that he would do well to moderate his attitude toward people in general. His opponents in the suit were doing everything possible to curry favor, but Alceste insulted everyone he met and made no effort to win over the judges. Philinte also taunted Alceste on his love for Célimène, who, as a leader in society, was hypocritical most of the time. Alceste had to admit that his love could not be explained rationally.

Oronte interrupted the quarrel by coming to visit Alceste, who was puzzled by a visit from suave and elegant Oronte. Oronte asked permission to read a sonnet he had lately composed, as he was anxious to have Alceste's judgment of its literary merit. After affecting hesitation, Oronte read his mediocre poem. Alceste at first hedged but then, too honest to give false praise, condemned the verses and even satirized the poor quality of the writing. Oronte took instant offense at this criticism, and a quarrel broke out between them. Although the argument was indecisive, there were hints of a possible duel.

Alceste then went to call on Célimène. As soon as he saw her, he began perversely to upbraid her for her frivolous conduct and her hypocritical attitude toward other people. He pointed out that although Célimène could slander and ridicule with a keen wit and a barbed tongue while a person was absent, she was all flattery and attention when talking with that person. This attitude displeased Alceste.

The servant announced several callers, including Éliante. To Alceste's dismay, they all sat down for an interminable conversation. The men took great delight in naming all their mutual acquaintances, for as each name was mentioned, Célimène made unkind remarks. The only gentle person in the room was Éliante, whose good sense and kind heart were in striking contrast with Célimène's caustic wit. Éliante was overshadowed, however, by the more brilliant Célimène. The men all declared they had nothing to do all day and each swore to outstay the other so as to remain longer with Célimène. Alceste determined to be the last to leave.

A guard appeared, however, to summon Alceste before the tribunal. Astonished, Alceste learned that news of his quarrel with Oronte had reached the authorities, who intended to prevent a possible duel. Loudly protesting that except for an order direct from the king nothing could make him praise the poetry of Oronte, Alceste was led away.

Arsinoé, an austere woman who made a pretense of great virtue, came to call on Célimène, taking the opportunity to warn Célimène that her conduct was creating a scandal and that her many suitors and her sharp tongue were hurting her reputation. Célimène spoke bitingly of Arsinoé's strait-laced character. Arsinoé thereupon decided to talk privately with Alceste, with whom she was half in love. She comforted him as best she could for being so unfortunate as to love Célimène, and complimented him on his plain dealings and forthright character. Carried away by the intimacy of her talk, Arsinoé offered to do much for Alceste by speaking in his favor at court, but the two concluded that Alceste's love for Célimène, though unsuitable from almost every point of view, was a fast tie.

Éliante and Philinte were in the meantime discussing Alceste and his habit of antagonizing his friends with his frankness. Philinte told her of Alceste's hearing before the tribunal, in which he had insisted that Oronte's verses were bad but that he had nothing more to say. Éliante and Philinte began to discover a mutual liking. If Éliante ever lost her fondness for Alceste, Philinte intended to offer himself as her lover.

Alceste received an unflattering letter, purporting to come from Célimène, which described him in malicious terms. After much coy hesitation, Célimène admitted that she had sent the letter and expressed surprise at Alceste's indignation. Other suitors appeared, all much upset and each holding a letter. On comparing notes, they found that they had all been ridiculed and insulted.

Alceste had meanwhile made up his mind to ask Éliante to marry him, but reconsidered when he realized that his proposal would seem to spring from a desire to avenge himself on Célimène. To the misanthrope there seemed to be no solution except to go into exile and live a hermit's life.

When Célimène's suitors clamored for an explanation, she told them that she had written the letters because she was tired of the niceties of polite conversation. For once she had decided to say what she really thought. This confession was shocking to the suitors, who considered frankness and rudeness unpardonable crimes. Hypocrisy, flattery, cajolery, extravagances—these were the marks of a gentle lady. Protesting and disdainful, they left together, never to return.

Only Alceste remained, whereupon even the coquettish and malicious heart of Célimène was touched. When Alceste repeated his vows of fidelity and asked her once more to marry him, she almost consented. When, however, Alceste revealed that he wanted them to go into exile and lead quiet, simple lives, she refused. Célimène could never leave the false, frivolous society she loved.

Now completely the misanthrope, Alceste stalked away with the firm resolve to quit society forever and to become a hermit, far removed from the artificial sham of preciosity. Philinte and Éliante, more moderate in their views, decided that they would marry.

"The Story" by Phyllis Mael

Critical Evaluation:

Although Molière in *The Misanthrope* humorously depicts a frivolous and hypocritical society, Alceste's misperceptions about himself provide the play's most biting humor. Alceste sees himself as the only honest person in his social circle, although he too tries to be tactful sometimes, as when he repeatedly tells Oronte that he had not criticized Oronte's poem when he had, in fact, done so indirectly until disgust and frustration got the better of him. Even more strikingly, Alceste almost begs Célimène to tell him comforting lies rather than unpleasant truths. Arsinoé and Célimène, on the other hand, reveal with vicious honesty what they truly think of one another, even though each wraps her nastiness in assurances that she is criticizing only to help the other. By contrast, Alceste's more moderate friends, Philinte and Éliante, converse frankly, and in the process each finds a loving and trustworthy mate. Molière makes is clear that Alceste cannot recognize honesty when he sees it.

Moreover, for all his much-vaunted independence, Alceste does not take responsibility for his fate or even his day-to-day actions. He has no trouble describing what he dislikes, but he seems hard-pressed to define what would make him happy, much less do it for himself. He says and probably believes that Célimène's exclusive love, far away from the corrupt court, alone with him in his self-imposed exile, would satisfy him. He thus places responsibility for his happiness in the hands of another. In fact, he tends to react to external events instead of consciously choosing his own way. For these reasons, he sees himself as a victim of circumstances. In his view, everything that occurs—losing his lawsuit, antagonizing Oronte, bullying and alienating the woman he loves—happens to him and is the fault of someone else.

Finally, Alceste also considers himself a highly intelligent and astute critic and a perceptive observer. Certainly he can see the faults of everyone around him, and, in truth, this society does deserve criticism. Nevertheless, he errs on two counts, the first being that he allows his emotions to precede his reasoned reaction (he feels, he speaks, then only does he, perhaps, think), and the second that his extremism blinds him to the value of good things right in front of him. While he believes he is offering clear-eyed criticism to a world desperately in need of reform, he is actually merely reacting emotionally to everything around him. His feelings lie so close to the surface that he cannot tell a trivial slight from a serious injury, so he responds with the same vehemence to both.

This last misperception provides the key to the play's power. The eighteenth century English writer Horace Walpole remarked that "This world is a comedy to those that think, a tragedy to those that feel." The clever Célimène basks in the admiration of her many suitors but seems not to care deeply about any of them. Philinte, a moderate, reasonable man, can see the attraction and humor in his society's artificiality and hypocritical flattery. He understands the spiteful wordplay as simply a game of wits; people who play by the rules do not get seriously hurt.

Although Alceste's mistaken perception of himself makes him a fool and a figure of fun to others, his pain is undeniably real. Even when he finally recognizes that his extreme views have forced him to abandon human society, he cannot change. In this, Alceste resembles some of Molière's other great characters, such as Harpagon in *The Miser* (1668). When the miser loses his treasure, he grieves for his "poor money" and weeps as others would for a dead child. His wildly excessive reaction strikes the audience as ridiculous, but he feels his loss as a tragedy. Such characters as Alceste and Harpagon experience the world at the level of pure feeling, which is what most people do when it comes to deeply cherished beliefs. At the same time that audiences laugh at the ludicrous excesses of the characters on stage, they recognize that those poor fools represent painful truths about themselves.

Many comedies aim simply to divert. By contrast, *The Misanthrope*, perhaps because it reflected Molière's own situation so closely, touches a raw nerve. By the time he wrote the play in 1666, he had seen his *Tartuffe* (1664) banned for its supposed attack on religion and *Don Juan* (1665) suddenly withdrawn from production; he himself was virtually excommunicated by the church. Moreover, he and his friend Jean Racine, the great playwright whose earliest works Molière himself had produced, had quarreled bitterly, never to be reconciled. His increasingly frequent work for King Louis XIV had allowed him to observe and experience firsthand the supercilious manners of the court. Perhaps most crucially, the middle-aged Molière and his beautiful young wife, actress Armande Béjart, had just separated, mostly because of her involvement with several young noblemen. Armande both acted the part and provided the model for the casually cruel Célimène, opposite a Molière playing Alceste. At the time Molière was writing the play, he and his wife saw each other only on stage.

Aspects of all these events and circumstances found their way into *The Misanthrope*. Like Molière, Alceste gets into serious legal, economic, and social trouble for speaking the truth as he sees it. He feels betrayed by old friends, beset by two-faced courtiers, and tormented by a frivolous woman he cannot help but love. Yet, miraculously, Molière was able to make his alter ego, Alceste, not a pitiful victim but a believable human being with a full complement of human faults and virtues. Even through his pain, Molière could see a man so like himself as both a hero and a fool. That clear vision makes *The Misanthrope* a comedy of manners that transcends its original time and place, for characters like Alceste remain timeless.

"Critical Evaluation" by Susan Wladaver-Morgan

Bibliography:

Gossman, Lionel. *Men and Masks: A Study of Molière*. Baltimore, Md.: The Johns Hopkins University Press, 1963. Divides Molière's plays into two groups: those, like *The Misanthrope*, that reach a social stalemate and those, like *Les Fourberies de Scapin* (1671), that transcend that apparent dead end. Includes an entire chapter on *The Misanthrope*.

Guicharnaud, Jacques. *Molière: A Collection of Critical Essays*. Englewood Cliffs, N.J.: Prentice-Hall, 1964. Very useful collection that treats *The Misanthrope* in the context of Molière's other plays, of other theatrical and comedic traditions (including Charlie Chaplin), and as a supremely experimental work.

Knutson, Harold C. *The Triumph of Wit: Molière and Restoration Comedy*. Columbus: Ohio State University Press, 1988. Considers Molière's influence on Restoration comedy in England and concludes that, rather than excessive English borrowing from Molière, both sorts of comedy sprang from similar social circumstances.

Lewis, D. B. Wyndham. *Molière: The Comic Mask*. New York: Coward-McCann, 1959. A rich description of Molière's life and works that immerses readers in the world of seventeenth century France. Sees *The Misanthrope* as the greatest of his works and the one closest to his heart.

Mander, Gertrud. *Molière*. Translated by Diana Stone Peters. New York: Frederick Ungar, 1973. Includes descriptions and analyses of fourteen plays and a usefully detailed chronology of Molière's life.

MISCELLANIES

Type of work: Poetry
Author: Abraham Cowley (1618-1667)
First published: 1656 (also published as *Poems*)

The reputation of Abraham Cowley has been affected more than that of many other English poets by the vicissitudes of literary taste. His contemporaries considered him one of their most distinguished poets. John Milton ranked him with William Shakespeare and Edmund Spenser. John Dryden considered him a model, following Cowley's example in writing Pindaric odes. By the end of the eighteenth century, however, Cowley had fallen from favor, largely through the influential judgments rendered against him by Samuel Johnson in *Lives of the Poets* (1779-1781). The first poet to be immortalized in that collection, Cowley is considered too irregular and "specific" a poet to be ranked among the greatest practitioners of the genre. Johnson found Cowley's penchant for irregular versification and his tendency to reach for extraordinary and unusual comparisons disturbing. Johnson described the approach taken by Cowley—and his contemporaries John Donne, Andrew Marvell, Richard Crashaw, and George Herbert—in the term that became a touchstone for classifying many poets of the early seventeenth century: metaphysical. To Johnson, and to many readers of the eighteenth and nineteenth centuries, Cowley's verse displayed more virtuoso learning than it did deep appreciation for that which is important to all humankind.

The charges against Cowley may be accurate in fact, but perhaps erroneous in implication. The verse forms Cowley uses, modeled on Greek writers such as Anacreon and Pindar, are not those that readers in the eighteenth century valued; individual poems contain within them lines of various lengths, irregular rhyme schemes, and varied stanzaic patterns. In addition, Cowley was intensely interested in capturing some of the new learning—scientific discoveries—in his work, and many of his unorthodox comparisons are attempts to integrate scientific learning into his art.

Tastes change, however, and by the middle of the nineteenth century, poets were returning to the practice of irregular versification and stanza patterns; by the twentieth century, the introduction of free verse and other forms of poetry expanded the boundaries of the definition of the genre so that Cowley's works no longer seem so unusual. Readers who take the time to peruse the *Miscellanies* may discover that Cowley displays in his poetry the qualities of seriousness, learning, and imagination that characterize the best of the Metaphysical poets.

Miscellanies is representative of Cowley's work. The volume was published shortly after the poet's return to England from France. Cowley, dispossessed of his fellowship at Cambridge University, had joined friends among the followers of Charles I at Oxford during the early years of the Civil War. When many of the Royalists fled to France, Cowley was among them. In exile, he assisted the English queen in her correspondence with the king in England.

Miscellanies, according to Cowley's preface, represents his attempt to preserve in print all of his poetry that he considered worth keeping for posterity. His avowed motivation was that he intended to write no more verse, and he wished to publish his own edition, so that an edition containing spurious or inferior writings would not be published after his death, as had already happened in the cases of William Shakespeare and Ben Jonson.

The *Miscellanies* consists of four parts. The first is a collection of poems on a variety of themes, some written when Cowley was quite young. The second section includes the poems Cowley had published in 1647 as *The Mistress: Or, Several Copies of Love Verses*, a series dealing with love in various aspects. The third part, he labeled "Pindarique Odes," translations from Pindar and free imitations in English of that poet's work. The final portion of the volume contains the four books of the *Davideis* (1656), an unfinished epic poem, that Cowley completed.

In the first section, there are odes on wit, on the king's return from Scotland, on Prometheus, on the pleasures of wine over the pangs of love, on friendship, and also imitations, in English, of both Horace and Martial. A light but pleasant poem is "The Chronicle," an example of *vers de société* dealing with the experiences of a young man in love with a long series of young women. Of note also is a poem celebrating the publication of the first two books of Sir William Davenant's *Gondibert* (1651). The best, certainly the sincerest, poems of the *Miscellanies* are those written on the deaths of persons the poet had known and respected in life. The most outstanding of these is "On the Death of Mr. William Hervey." Although the poem may seem to the twentieth century reader extravagant in its tone, diction, and imagery, it compares favorably with the best elegiac poetry of the time. Other elegiac poems in the collection are those on Sir Henry Wotton; Mr. Jordan, a master at Westminster School; Sir Anthony Van Dyck, the painter; and Richard Crashaw, the poet. Of little interest, other than for historical purposes, are some English paraphrases of the Greek lyric poet Anacreon.

Most critics have been less inclined to favor *The Mistress*. Like much of the love poetry of the earlier part of the seventeenth century, *The Mistress* is bound too closely by conventions in many respects. It supposedly deals with a courtship and the lady's reception of the suit over a period of three years. That Cowley actually loved a woman of higher social rank and courted her with this poetry is doubtful, for the suffering lover, the standoffish lady of higher degree, and extravagant protestations of love are typical of the love poetry of the time—usually mere convention. Cowley's unusual figures of speech, apparently influenced by John Donne, were the target of critics until the late twentieth century. With the revived interest and renewed sympathy for the metaphysical poets and their techniques, however, Cowley's exercise of his exceptionally learned and fertile fancy was viewed less stringently. In this section, the poem entitled "The Spring" represents Cowley at his best, while "Written in Juice of Lemmon" shows him at a poorer level of performance.

For approximately a century, the ode—particularly the Pindaric ode as it was established by Cowley—was a favorite verse form among English poets and their imitators. In the eighteenth century, however, Dr. Samuel Johnson, literary arbiter of the era, pronounced against it. Undoubtedly the freedom of meter introduced by Cowley and exercised in his "Pindarique Odes" was a decisive factor in the popularity of the form, for, as they were written by Cowley, the odes appear deceptively easy. Twentieth century literary opinion has been negative toward Cowley's odes, declaring them too flat and imitative.

The last portion of the *Miscellanies* is taken up with the unfinished *Davideis*, four of the twelve books originally planned on the model of Vergil's *Aeneid* (30-19 B.C.E.). Cowley's strong religious convictions led him to choose the figure of David, traditional ancestor of Jesus, as the hero for an epic poem. In these four books, he incorporated much of his learning, often in wide and only loosely connected digressions. Critics have argued the fitness of the subject; Cowley himself seems to have changed his mind about its suitability, since he left the work unfinished. What is more, as announced in the preface to the *Miscellanies*, Cowley wrote almost no poetry after publication of that volume.

Bibliography:
Hinman, Robert B. *Abraham Cowley's World of Order*. Cambridge, Mass.: Harvard University

Press, 1960. Lists every book and article on Cowley from the 1930's through the 1950's, and many others before that time. Discusses Cowley's poetic career as it is reflected in his poetry, and Cowley's reputation among contemporaries and moderns.

Martin, L. C. Introduction and notes to *Poetry and Prose*, by Abraham Cowley. Oxford, England: Clarendon Press, 1949. Includes the major commentaries on Cowley and his work from the seventeenth century to 1921. Contains selected poems and Cowley's preface to the *Miscellanies*.

Nethercot, Arthur H. *Abraham Cowley: The Muse's Hannibal*. New York: Russell & Russell, 1967. Biographical study connects the poems in the *Miscellanies* to the events of Cowley's life, thus illuminating both. Helpful bibliography of principal works about Cowley and his work.

Taaffe, James G. *Abraham Cowley*. New York: Twayne, 1972. A convenient survey of Cowley's poetic career. Analyzes and evaluates his major works, including the *Miscellanies*. Helpful notes and annotated bibliography.

Williamson, George. *Six Metaphysical Poets*. New York: Farrar, Straus & Giroux, 1967. Offers a detailed examination of a number of Cowley's poems from the 1656 collection as expressions of metaphysical wit, a concept that Williamson uses to connect Cowley's poetry to that of John Donne and other major poets between the Renaissance and the neoclassical period.

THE MISER

Type of work: Drama
Author: Molière (Jean-Baptiste Poquelin, 1622-1673)
Type of plot: Comedy
Time of plot: Seventeenth century
Locale: Paris, France
First performed: 1668; first published, 1669 as *L'Avare* (English translation, 1672)

> Principal characters:
> HARPAGON, a miser
> CLÉANTE, his son
> ÉLISE, his daughter
> VALÈRE, Élise's lover
> MARIANE, a young woman loved by Cléante and Harpagon
> ANSELME, the father of Valère and Mariane

The Story:

   Valère, the steward of Harpagon's house, was in love with his employer's daughter Élise. Valère was sure that he was of a good family, but until he could find his relatives he had little hope that Harpagon would give his consent to a marriage between his daughter and his steward. Harpagon was a miser of such great avarice and stinginess that he loved nothing but money. He lived in constant fear that someone would rob him of the large sum he had buried in his garden. Valère knew that his only hope lay in gaining Harpagon's affection by flattering the old man shamelessly.

   Harpagon's son Cléante was also in love. The object of his love was Mariane, a poor girl who lived with her widowed mother. Cléante's love was as hopeless as that between his sister Élise and Valère. Since Mariane had no money, Harpagon would not consent to a marriage, and Cléante kept his love for the girl from his father. What he did not know was that his father had seen Mariane and wanted her for himself. He had been a widower for many years, and the young girl's beauty made him desire her. He must first, however, secure a dowry for her; his miserliness was stronger than his love.

   Élise learned from her father that, against her wishes, she was to be married to Anselme, a wealthy man of fifty. The fact that Anselme would take his daughter without a dowry was too good a proposition for Harpagon to miss. Élise appealed to Valère for help. The clever lad pretended to agree with her father while he whispered to her to take heart and trust him to prevent the marriage. If all else failed, he and Élise would flee from the house and be married without her father's consent.

   Cléante was so determined to marry Mariane that he arranged through an agent to borrow from a moneylender. Never was a higher rate of interest demanded. Cléante was to pay twenty-five percent interest and to take part of the loan in goods which he must sell. With no choice but to agree, he went to meet the moneylender. He was horrified to find that the moneylender was his own father. Harpagon was equally angry that his son should be such a spendthrift that he must borrow money at such high rates. The two parted without completing the loan, Cléante to try to arrange a loan elsewhere and Harpagon to try to secure a dowry for Mariane.

Harpagon arranged a party in honor of Mariane, whom he had not as yet met. He cautioned the servants to be very sparing with the food and drink, as it was an injustice to one's guests to stuff them full. Although Mariane found Harpagon repulsive, she was bound by her poor mother's wish that she take a rich husband. When Mariane learned that Harpagon was the father of her beloved Cléante, she detested him more than ever. Cléante got a small measure of revenge on his father by taking a huge diamond ring from his father's finger and presenting it to Mariane after telling her that Harpagon wanted her to have it. The miser was helpless; he could not get it back unless he admitted his stinginess to the girl he wished to marry.

After Harpagon tricked Cléante into admitting his love for Mariane, the old man vowed more than ever to have her for himself. Cléante cursed his father and swore that the old miser should never have the girl, and Harpagon disinherited his son. Then a servant rushed in with the news that Harpagon had been robbed of his buried money. All else was forgotten by the miser as he cried out for help. He suspected everyone of stealing the money, even himself. He would have the whole household hanged, and if the money were not found he would hang himself.

A jealous servant told Harpagon that Valère had taken the money. Harpagon ordered the magistrate to arrest the steward, even though there was no true evidence against him. Anselme arrived in time to hear Valère shouting to Harpagon that he would marry Élise in spite of the miser's objections. Anselme said that he would bow out of the courtship, for he had no desire to take the girl against her wishes. Harpagon was furious. Where else could he find a wealthy son-in-law, particularly one who would demand no dowry? He pressed the magistrate to arrest Valère, but that young man stopped the official with the announcement that he was the son of Don Thomas d'Alburci, a nobleman of Naples who had had to flee his native city.

Valère said that he and a manservant had survived a shipwreck and made their way to Paris. He produced the family seals to prove his identity. Then Mariane rushed to him and told him that she was his sister, that she and her mother had also been saved from the wreck and had thought the rest of the family dead. There was more joy to come for the reunited brother and sister. Anselme was their father, the former Don Thomas d'Alburci, who had also been saved. Thinking his loved ones dead, he had settled in Paris under the name of Anselme.

These revelations made no difference to Harpagon. He still insisted that Valère return his money. While he was ranting, Cléante entered the room and said that he had found the money and would return it to his father as soon as his father gave him permission to marry Mariane. That was no hard choice for Harpagon to make. He would gladly exchange Mariane, even his own children, for his money. Anselme also gave his consent to the marriage. Harpagon insisted that Anselme pay for both weddings. Anselme was willing to do this, and the happy couples and Anselme left to find Mariane and Valère's mother. Harpagon had an errand of his own. He went to examine his cashbox, the true love of his mean and stingy nature.

Critical Evaluation:

Unlike his two greatest contemporaries, Pierre Corneille and Jean Racine, who wrote everything from tragedies based on Greek and Roman history to scathing contemporary satires, Molière concentrated primarily on comedies of manners, particularly those dealing with the urban middle class. The scene is frequently a comfortable bourgeois home, and the plot usually revolves around tensions between husband and wives or parents and children—tensions that arise because at least one member of the family has developed some sort of obsession that disturbs family harmony. It was Molière's genius to weave dark threads of tragedy into his comic vision of this comfortable life, and he never did so more effectively than in *The Misanthrope* (1666) and *The Miser*.

Like *The Misanthrope*, *The Miser* focuses on a monomaniac, but while Alceste the misanthrope directs all his attention outward onto the faults of the courtly society that surrounds him, Harpagon the miser could probably live without any social contact at all, as long as he had his treasure to console him. Though he seeks a new young wife, his motives for doing so remain vague. He definitely hopes to secure a dowry from her family, but he probably wishes to acquire cheap domestic labor; he may also want to beget a new heir, the better to disinherit his two existing children whom he holds in contempt. After all, he curses his only son, and he tells his daughter he would not care if she had drowned. By contrast, he constantly breaks off conversations to go and check his beloved money, and, when it is stolen, he becomes so distraught that he stands ready to kill himself.

Harpagon's monomania affects everyone around him, for, unlike Alceste, he holds considerable power as a father and as a wealthy man. This combination of obsession and power makes Harpagon an irrational tyrant, who can do real damage to the lives of those who should be dearest to him. His single-minded focus on money and his unwillingness to hear any opinion that contradicts his own distort every social interaction in which he participates. His children have no choice but to rebel against him, unless they want to be treated as possessions, not as people. Moreover, as Valère notes early on, the only way to approach Harpagon is through flattery and indirection; other characters, including Frosine and Cléante, soon follow suit. In the presence of such an egocentric fanatic, nearly all the characters have to speak in code, with one message for Harpagon and another hidden message for each other. When Harpagon's faithful old servant dares to tell the truth, he is beaten for his effort. Simply to have the chance to communicate with Harpagon, everyone else must become something of a liar. Harpagon's obsession thus forces hypocrisy on those around him, and even vows of love may become suspect.

Structurally, *The Miser* derives from a classical model, *The Pot of Gold* (c. 195), a farce by the Roman playwright Plautus. That work focused on a poor man who receives a pot of money and becomes terrified of losing it; he finally gives it away so he no longer has to think about it. Molière clearly took this theme in a different direction. Like most farces, however, Molière's work revels in exaggeration, mistaken identities (Valère and Mariane are actually brother and sister, and Anselme, the rival for Élise's hand, is their long-lost father), coincidences (Harpagon is unwittingly the usurious lender to his desperate son), and a massively improbable ending that reunites all the lovers with their loves, including Harpagon with his money box. Molière heightens the contrasts by neatly pairing and balancing all the characters: fathers (one stingy, one munificent), brothers and sisters (extravagant Cléante and cautious Valère, feisty Élise and timid Mariane), and servants and go-betweens. Perhaps to emphasize the relationship between love and money, he cleverly uses economic words in the context of personal and romantic relationships. Love and money may appear to be opposites, he implies, but people need a modicum of both for a happy life, and all the characters except Harpagon realize it.

Molière also experiments with comedy as a form. For instance, at a time when most five-act comedies were written in verse, he wrote *The Miser* in prose. Most strikingly, he flouts the conventions of the theater by having Harpagon break through "the fourth wall" in his great tirade in the fourth act. Harpagon virtually explodes beyond the stage in his anguish, searching the whole audience for the thief and reacting frantically to the spectators' mocking laughter. He weeps for his "poor money," as if it were a living being. In this way, he directly confronts the audience with an appalling vision of unmitigated obsession. Though the audience members laugh at his extreme ideas, they also recognize a man beside himself with grief and panic, a man who cannot tell where he himself ends and his possessions begin. In other words, they see a portrait of madness.

At that point, the play comes close to veering into tragedy, which it would become were the audience to regard events from Harpagon's point of view. After all, from his perspective, he is an old man whose ungrateful children defy him at every turn, whose only security and joy consist of gold that unscrupulous people are forever trying to steal. In his own eyes, he might as well be King Lear. That is why Molière instead concludes the play with a family reunited, lovers requited, and a generous and grateful father lavishing money to obtain happiness for everyone. In spite of the sugar coating, however, a serious, even bitter message remains at the heart of the play: Harpagon has learned nothing from his experiences. He still cares for nothing and no one except his money. The distorting evils of greed and obsession remain alive and well, in the world as in the play. Thus, although *The Miser* works as a cheerful comedy, this brilliant creation never loses its disturbing power.

"Critical Evaluation" by Susan Wladaver-Morgan

Bibliography:
Bermel, Albert. *Molière's Theatrical Bounty: A New View of the Plays*. Carbondale: Southern Illinois University Press, 1990. Original interpretations of the plays, partly designed to help actors think about the characters' motivations, such as why Harpagon seeks a new wife. Sees *The Miser* as a rich and complicated work.
Hall, H. Gaston. *Comedy in Context: Essays on Molière*. Jackson: University Press of Mississippi, 1984. Analyzes *Molière*'s work thematically. Sees Molière's use of comic images as implying both laughter and moral judgment, using the example of Harpagon's soliloquy in Act IV of *The Miser*.
Lewis, D. B. Wyndham. *Molière: The Comic Mask*. New York: Coward-McCann, 1959. Provides a rich description of Molière's life and works, immersing readers in seventeenth century French society. Sees *The Miser* as basically depressing because Harpagon represents a case of clinical obsession totally devoid of normal human feelings.
Mander, Gertrud. *Molière*. Translated by Diana Stone Peters. New York: Frederick Ungar, 1973. Discusses *The Miser*, particularly in terms of its focus on bourgeois family life, seeing the conflicts there as the most bitter in Molière's works. Sets forth the opinion that Harpagon's avarice makes him a monster, forcing others into unnatural or uncharacteristic actions, but he is not a tragic figure.
Walker, Hallam. *Molière*. Boston: Twayne, 1971. Sees *The Miser* as combining issues of sex and power with those of money and greed and, thus, being as much a moral drama as it is a comedy, explaining the ambivalent response of most audiences. Sees the play as satisfying because of the artistic inevitability of the ending and the fitness of all the parts.

LES MISÉRABLES

Type of work: Novel
Author: Victor Hugo (1802-1885)
Type of plot: Social realism
Time of plot: c. 1815-1835
Locale: France
First published: 1862 (English translation, 1862)

Principal characters:

JEAN VALJEAN, also known as Father Madeleine
FANTINE, a woman befriended by Valjean
COSETTE, her daughter
MONSIEUR JAVERT, the inspector of police
MARIUS PONTMERCY, in love with Cosette
MONSIEUR THENARDIER, known also as Jondrette, a rogue
EPONINE THENARDIER, his daughter

The Story:

In 1815, in France, a man named Jean Valjean was released after nineteen years in prison. He had been sentenced to a term of five years because he stole a loaf of bread to feed his starving sister and her family, but the sentence was later increased because of his attempts to escape. During his imprisonment he astonished others by his exhibitions of unusual physical strength.

Freed at last, he started out on foot for a distant part of the country. Innkeepers refused him food and lodging because his yellow passport revealed that he was a former convict. Finally he came to the house of the Bishop of Digne, a saintly man who treated him graciously, fed him, and gave him a bed. During the night Jean stole the bishop's silverware and fled. He was immediately captured by the police, who returned him and the stolen goods to the bishop. Without any censure, the priest not only gave him what he had stolen but also added his silver candlesticks to the gift. The astonished gendarmes released the prisoner. Alone with the bishop, Jean was confounded by the churchman's attitude, for the bishop asked only that he use the silver as a means of living an honest life.

In 1817, a beautiful woman named Fantine lived in Paris. She gave birth to an illegitimate child, Cosette, whom she left with Monsieur and Madame Thenardier to rear with their own children. As time went on, the Thenardiers demanded more and more money for Cosette's support, yet treated the child cruelly and deprived her even of necessities. Meanwhile, Fantine had gone to the town of M—— and obtained a job in a glass factory operated by Father Madeleine, a kind and generous man whose history was known to no one, but whose good deeds and generosity to the poor were public information. He had arrived in M—— a poor laborer, and through a lucky invention he was able to start a business of his own. Soon he built a factory and employed many workers. After five years in the city, he was named mayor and was beloved by all the citizens. He was reported to have prodigious strength. Only one man, Javert, a police inspector, seemed to watch him with an air of suspicion. Javert was born in prison. His whole life was influenced by that fact, and his fanatical attitude toward duty made him a man to be feared. He was determined to discover the facts of Father Madeleine's previous life. One day he found a clue while watching Father Madeleine lift a heavy cart to save an old man who had fallen under it. Javert realized that he had known only one man of such prodigious strength, a former convict named Valjean.

Fantine had told no one of Cosette, but knowledge of her illegitimate child spread and caused Fantine to be discharged from the factory without the knowledge of Father Madeleine. Finally Fantine became a prostitute in an effort to pay the increasing demands of the Thenardiers for Cosette's support. One night Javert arrested her while she was walking the streets. When Father Madeleine heard the details of her plight and learned that she had tuberculosis, he sent Fantine to a hospital and promised to bring Cosette to her. Just before the mayor left to get Cosette, Javert confessed that he had mistakenly reported to the Paris police that he suspected Father Madeleine of being the former convict, Jean Valjean. He said that the real Jean Valjean had been arrested at Arras under an assumed name. The arrested man was to be tried two days later.

That night Father Madeleine struggled with his own conscience, for he was the real Jean Valjean. Unwilling to let an innocent man suffer, he went to Arras for the trial and identified himself as Jean Valjean. After telling the authorities where he could he found, he went to Fantine. Javert came there to arrest him. Fantine was so terrified that she died. After a day in prison, Jean Valjean escaped.

Valjean, some time later, was again imprisoned by Javert. Once more he made his escape. Shortly afterward he was able to take Cosette, a girl of eight, away from the Thenardiers. He grew to love the child greatly, and they lived together happily in the Gorbeau tenement on the outskirts of Paris. When Javert once more tracked them down, Valjean escaped with the child into a convent garden, where they were rescued by Fauchelevant, whose life Valjean had saved when the old peasant had fallen beneath the cart. Fauchelevant was now the convent gardener. Valjean became his helper, and Cosette was put into the convent school.

Years passed. Valjean left the convent and took Cosette, her schooling finished, to live in a modest house on a side street in Paris. The old man and the girl were little noticed by their neighbors. Meanwhile the blackguard Thenardier had brought his family to live in the Gorbeau tenement. He now called himself Jondrette. In the next room lived Marius Pontmercy, a young lawyer estranged from his aristocrat grandfather because of his liberal views. Marius was the son of an officer whose life Thenardier had saved at the battle of Waterloo. The father, now dead, had asked his son someday to repay Thenardier for his deed. Marius never suspected that Jondrette was really his father's benefactor. When the Jondrettes were being evicted from their quarters, however, he paid their rent from his meager resources.

During one of his evening walks, Marius met Cosette and Valjean. He fell in love with the young woman as he continued to see her in the company of her white-haired companion. At last he followed her to her home. Valjean, noticing Marius, took Cosette to live in another house. One morning Marius received a begging letter delivered by Eponine Jondrette. His neighbors were again asking for help, and he began to wonder about them. Peeping through a hole in the wall, he heard Jondrette speak of a benefactor who would soon arrive. When the man came, Marius recognized him as Cosette's companion. He later learned Cosette's address from Eponine, but before he saw Cosette again he overheard the Jondrettes plotting against the man whom he believed to be Cosette's father. Alarmed, he told the details of the plot to Inspector Javert.

Marius was at the wall watching when Valjean returned to give Jondrette money. While they talked, numerous heavily armed men appeared in the room. Jondrette then revealed himself as Thenardier. Horrified, Marius did not know whom to protect, the man his father had requested him to befriend or the father of Cosette. Threatened by Thenardier, Valjean agreed to send to his daughter for more money, but he gave a false address. When this ruse was discovered, the robbers threatened to kill Valjean. Marius threw a note of warning through the hole in the wall as Javert appeared and arrested all but Valjean, who made his escape through a window.

Marius finally located Cosette. One night she told him that she and her father were leaving for England. He tried, unsuccessfully, to get his grandfather's permission to marry Cosette. In despair, he returned to Cosette and found the house where she had lived empty. Eponine met him there and told him that his revolutionary friends had begun a revolt and were waiting for him at the barricades. Cosette had disappeared, so he gladly followed Eponine to the barricades, where Javert had been seized as a spy and bound. During the fighting Eponine gave her life to save Marius. As she died, she gave him a note that Cosette had given her to deliver. In the note, Cosette hold him where she could be found.

In answer to her note, Marius wrote that his grandfather would not permit his marriage, that he had no money, and that he would be killed at the barricades. Valjean discovered the notes and set out for the barricades. Finding Javert tied up by the revolutionists, he freed the inspector. The barricades fell. In the confusion Valjean came upon the wounded Marius and carried him into the Paris sewers.

After hours of wandering, he reached a locked outlet. There Thenardier, unrecognized in the dark, met him and agreed to open the grating in exchange for money. Outside Valjean met Javert, who took him into custody. Valjean asked only that he be allowed to take Marius to his grandfather's house. Javert agreed to wait at the door, but suddenly he turned and ran toward the river. Tormented by his conscientious regard for duty and his reluctance to return to prison the man who had saved his life, he drowned himself in the Seine.

When Marius recovered, he and Cosette were married. Valjean gave Cosette a generous dowry, and for the first time Cosette learned that Valjean was not her real father. Valjean told Marius only that he was an escaped convict, believed dead, and he begged to be allowed to see Cosette occasionally. Gradually Marius banished him from the house. Then Marius learned from Thenardier that it was Valjean who had rescued Marius at the barricades. Marius and Cosette hurried to Valjean's lodgings, to find him on his deathbed. He died knowing that his children loved him and that all his entangling past was now clear. He bequeathed the bishop's silver candlesticks to Cosette, with his last breath saying that he had spent his life in trying to be worthy of the faith of the Bishop of Digne. He was buried in a grave with no name on the stone.

Critical Evaluation:

Essentially a detective story, *Les Misérables* is a unique combination of melodrama and morality. It is filled with unlikely coincidences, with larger-than-life emotions and giantlike human beings, yet it all manages to ring true and to move the reader. An epic of the people of Paris, with a vital and fascinating re-creation of the swarming Parisian underground, the novel suggests the crowded, absorbing novels of Charles Dickens and Fyodor Dostoevski. The main theme of humanity's ceaseless combat with evil clearly emerges from the suspenseful plot, while the book as a whole gives a dramatic picture of the ebb and flow of life.

Victor Hugo claimed that the huge book was a religious work, and certainly religion does play an important part in the story. The struggle between good and evil is foremost in the tale. Another theme that is of equal importance is that of fate or destiny. To whatever extent one attempts to chisel the "mysterious block" of which one's life is made, Hugo writes, the "black vein of destiny" reappears continually. One can never be certain what fate has in store until the last breath of life disappears. Mortals never are safe from the tricks of destiny, from the seemingly endless struggle.

The breathless pace of the novel probably has accounted for its tremendous popularity. The story is filled with dramatic and surprising action, many of the scenes ending with suspenseful episodes. Despite its digressions, the story moves quickly and with excitement, as the characters race across the countryside and through the narrow streets and alleys of Paris. The characterizations, while on a grand—even epic—scale, are lifelike and believable. Many of the characters seem possessed by strange obsessions or hatreds, but Hugo makes it clear that they have been warped by society and their earlier lives. Although a Romantic novel, *Les Misérables* has much in common with the naturalistic school that came into being a few decades later.

Perhaps the most terrifying and fascinating of all the characters who populate the book's pages is Inspector Javert. Javert is clever but not intelligent. He is consumed by the malice that often dwells within the narrow, ignorant individual. He can conceive of no point of view other than his own. Sympathy, mercy, and understanding require an insight that he does not possess. For him there is no such thing as an extenuating circumstance. He clings with mindless, insane tenacity to his belief in duty. At his hands, justice is warped beyond recognition. Through him, Hugo shows the dark side of virtue.

The casual reader may be moved by the author's search for justice in *Les Misérables*, and the more sophisticated may admire the novel's complex structure. Like so many of the greatest literary works, *Les Misérables* can be enjoyed many times by different kinds of readers, and on many different levels.

An important, if implied, theme of *Les Misérables* is the attainment of salvation through good works. Many of the characters of the novel give charity to those less fortunate. The dramatic opening scenes in which the convict Jean Valjean learns of goodness through the charity of the priest establishes the importance of this theme. Later, Jean Valjean and Cosette give anonymous charity to others. Marius, in his goodness, gives charity to the disreputable Thenardier family.

Other biblical virtues are dramatized in the novel, but none so effectively as love. By love, Hugo means not only romantic love but also love of humanity, the love of a kindhearted human being for another human being, the love that must be connected with genuine charity. Jean Valjean learns what love is during the course of the novel. "The bishop has caused the dawn of virtue on Jean's horizon; Cosette worked the dawn of love." Hugo makes it clear that a man cannot exist without love, for if he tries, he becomes warped and less than a man. Jean Valjean grows as a person, becomes a good and honorable man after he has found the love of the helpless little girl. By devoting his life to her, he finds the necessity of a meaning outside of his own life. Jean Valjean comes to value his own existence more because the girl is dependent upon him and loves him.

Victor Hugo knew how to write effectively and with simplicity of the common joys and sorrows of the average man and woman. His poetry and novels have always been popular, although they have at times been out of critical favor. The public mind was much moved by the generosity of his ideas and the warmth of their expression; more than a century after its publication, *Les Misérables* is still a favorite book with many people around the world. Much of Hugo's poetry and drama is no longer read or produced, but *Les Misérables* and *The Hunchback of Notre Dame* (1831) will endure as long as people read.

The novel covers a time span of more than twenty years—from the fall of the first Napoleon to the revolts of a generation later. The most exciting scenes, described with breathless precision and dramatic flair, are those at the barricades. The characters are swept up in an action bigger than they are. Skillfully, Hugo weaves Marius and Javert, Eponine and the others, into the battles along the streets of Paris. Always Hugo's eye catches the details of the passing spectacle, from the old woman who props up a mattress in front of her window to stop the stray bullets to the dynamic flood of humanity coursing down the boulevards. It is here that Hugo's skill as a master of narrative is fully displayed. Never, however, does he lose sight of the pathos of the individuals' struggles; the reader never forgets the principal characters and their plight amid the chaotic scenes. Hugo balances between the two elements that compose his masterpiece. The final scenes of the novel move relentlessly to their conclusion. Perhaps Dostoevski probed deeper or Dickens caught the humor of life more fully, but Hugo was their equal in his ability to portray the individual heartache and tenderness, the human struggle of those caught up in the forces of history.

"Critical Evaluation" by Bruce D. Reeves

Bibliography:

Brombert, Victor. *The Romantic Prison: The French Tradition.* Princeton, N.J.: Princeton University Press, 1978. Points out that in *Les Misérables* the most important reference to hell is its embodiment in the sewers of Paris, through which Jean Valjean carries Marius as the final part of his quest—through death to resurrection.

_____. *Victor Hugo and the Visionary Novel.* Cambridge, Mass.: Harvard University Press, 1984. The most sophisticated study of Hugo's fiction to date. Notes Hugo's use of digressive patterns and impersonal, realistic narration. Draws on a wealth of French criticism.

Grant, Richard B. *The Perilous Quest: Image, Myth, and Prophecy in the Narratives of Victor Hugo.* Durham, N.C.: Duke University Press, 1968. An exhaustive study of Hugo's use of image, myth, and prophecy. Notes—among other images and uses of myth—the Christological references to Jean Valjean, who finds redemption in saving others.

Houston, John Porter. *Victor Hugo.* Rev. ed. Boston: Twayne, 1988. Indispensable starting guide to the works—drama, poetry, and novels—and life of Victor Hugo.

Wellek, René. *A History of Modern Criticism: 1750-1950.* Vol. 2. *The Romantic Age.* New Haven, Conn.: Yale University Press, 1955. Analysis of Hugo's literary theory and its relation to other writers of European romantic works. Discusses Hugo's careful placement of discursive essays throughout the novel.

MISS JULIE

Type of work: Drama
Author: August Strindberg (1849-1912)
Type of plot: Naturalism
Time of plot: Nineteenth century
Locale: A country estate in Sweden
First published: Fröken Julie, 1888 (English translation, 1912); first performed, 1889

> *Principal characters:*
> MISS JULIE, a headstrong young woman of twenty-five
> JEAN, Miss Julie's lover and her father's valet
> CHRISTINE, a cook and Jean's fiancée

The Story:

Miss Julie's broken engagement to the county attorney was quite a scandal to the servants in the house. Miss Julie, daughter of a count, had made the man actually jump over her horsewhip several times, giving him a cut with the whip each time. He had finally put an end to such conduct and the engagement by snatching the whip, breaking it, and striding away from the manor.

A few weeks later, on Midsummer Eve, a great holiday observed throughout the Swedish countryside, Miss Julie entered into the festivities and danced with the servants. She dared to do so because her father had gone to the city and was not expected to return. Although the servants disliked her joining in their fun, they were powerless to stop her or to let her know of their dislike, for she was their mistress. Her father's valet, Jean, left the festivities after dancing once with Miss Julie. He retreated to the kitchen, where his fiancée, Christine the cook, gave him a little supper.

Miss Julie gave Jean no peace, however. She came into the kitchen and dragged him out to dance with her again, even though she knew that he had promised to dance with Christine. After dancing once more with Miss Julie, Jean again escaped to the kitchen. He was afraid that Christine would be angry, but she assured him that she did not blame him for what had happened. Just then Miss Julie returned to the kitchen and demanded that Jean change from his livery into a tailcoat and dance with her again. While he was changing, Christine fell asleep in a chair. When he returned, Miss Julie asked him to get her something to drink. Jean got a bottle of beer for her and another for himself.

After finishing the beer, Miss Julie teased Christine by trying to wake her up. Christine, moving as if asleep, went to her own room. After she had gone, Miss Julie began to ogle Jean, who warned his mistress that it was dangerous to flirt with a man as young as he. Miss Julie paid no attention to him. Jean, falling in with her mood, told about his early life as a cotter's child and how, even as a small child, he had been in love with his young mistress. They talked until the other servants came to look for Jean. Rather than expose themselves to the comments and the scandal of having drunk together in the kitchen, Jean and Miss Julie went into Jean's room. They were there a long time, for the servants stayed in the kitchen and danced and sang. During that time Miss Julie gave herself to Jean.

After the servants had gone, neither Jean nor Miss Julie knew just what to do. They agreed only that it was best for them to leave the country. Jean suggested that they go to Como, Italy, to open a hotel. Miss Julie asked Jean to take her in his arms again. He refused, saying that he could not make love to her a second time in her father's house, where she was the mistress and he the servant. When she reminded him of the extravagant language he had used a little while before, he told her the time had come to be practical.

To comfort her, Jean offered Miss Julie a drink of wine from a bottle he had taken from the count's cellar. She saw whose it was and accused him of stealing. An argument followed, with bitter words on both sides. When they had both calmed a little, Miss Julie tried to tell Jean how she had come to be what she was. She said that she had been brought up to do a man's work by her mother, who hated to be a slave to men. She told also how her mother had revenged herself on Miss Julie's father by taking a brick manufacturer as her lover and how her mother's lover had stolen great sums of money from the count. From her mother, said Miss Julie, she had learned to hate men and to wish to make them her slaves. He understood then why she had treated her fiancé as she had. Miss Julie ended her recital with the recommendation that she and Jean go abroad at once. To her suggestion that when they ceased enjoying one another they should commit suicide, Jean, far more practical, advised her to go away by herself. Miss Julie, helpless in the urgency of the situation, did as Jean suggested and prepared to leave.

While Miss Julie was upstairs dressing, Christine came into the kitchen. It was morning. Seeing the glasses on the table, she knew that Miss Julie and Jean had been drinking together. She guessed the rest, and Jean admitted what had happened. Christine told Jean that fine people did not behave that way with their servants. Christine urged him to go away with her as soon as possible. She loved him and did not intend to lose him to her mistress.

Christine persuaded Jean to get ready to go to church with her, for it was Sunday morning. When they were both dressed, Miss Julie and Jean met in the kitchen. Julie carried a bird cage. When Jean said she could not take her pet finch with her, she ordered him to kill it. While watching her bird die, Miss Julie's love turned to hate. She despised Jean for killing in cold blood the pet she had loved so much, and she raged at him and told him that her father would soon return. She would tell him what had happened. Miss Julie declared that she now wished to die.

When Christine appeared, ready for church, she told Miss Julie bluntly that she would not allow her mistress to run off with the man who had promised to become her husband. Miss Julie tried to persuade Christine to go with them to Como. While the two women talked, Jean left the room. He returned a few moments later with his razor. Christine, refusing to join in the flight, left for church after saying that she had spoken to the men at the stables about not letting anyone have horses until the count's return.

After Christine had departed, Miss Julie asked Jean what he would do if he were in her position. He indicated the razor in his hand. At that moment the valet's bell rang. The count had returned. Jean, answering the bell, received instructions to have boots and coffee ready in half an hour. His master's voice reduced Jean once again to the mental attitudes of a servant. Miss Julie, almost in a state of trance, was filled with ecstasy at the thought of freeing herself by committing suicide. She took the razor Jean had given her and left the kitchen with it in her hand.

Critical Evaluation:

August Strindberg wrote the naturalistic tragedy *Miss Julie*, which is recognized as one of the playwright's greatest, for André Antoine's avant-garde Theatre Libre in Paris. Strindberg's power, complexity, and originality of technique and vision have led such later writers as Eugene O'Neill to see him as the most progressive and influential playwright of his time.

Strindberg's achievements are all the more remarkable in view of the squalor of his upbringing. Born in Stockholm into a bankrupt family, one of twelve children, Strindberg was neglected even by his own mother. After her death when he was thirteen, his new stepmother added harshness to neglect. This early experience developed in him a strong, life-long dislike of any conventional authority figure. In his writing this is evident in his rejection of traditional stage techniques and traditional societal beliefs and conventions. His private life was equally unconventional. Each of his three marriages was characterized by an intense component of love-hate dichotomy. Strindberg was prosecuted for blasphemy upon the publication of his collection of short stories *Married* (1886-1888). The combination of these personal and public tensions led to an unstable psychological state marked by spells of insanity and delusions of persecution. Between the years 1894 and 1896, the increasing violence of his hallucinations led to the crisis known as his Inferno period. His inner torment during this crisis gave rise to a shift in technique from the psychological naturalism of *The Father* (1887) and *Miss Julie* to symbolist and expressionist departures from external reality in the imaginative brilliance of dramas such as *A Dream Play* (1902) and *Ghost Sonata* (1907).

While in Paris in 1883, Strindberg became familiar with the doctrine of literary naturalism espoused by Émile Zola, and he successfully applied this approach to drama. He even sent a copy of his first naturalistic play to Zola for comments. In a long foreword to *Miss Julie*, Strindberg explains his use of naturalistic doctrine in the play, but his definitive formulation of dramatic naturalism is found in his essay "On Modern Drama and Modern Theater" (1889). There he suggests that the true essence of naturalism is a presentation of the polarization of the basic conflicts of life—love and hate, life and death—through the Darwinian principle of survival of the fittest found both in personal relationships and class conflicts. Strindberg's knowledge of psychology contributes to the creation of his powerful authentic dramas, which remain as moving in later times as when they first appeared.

Strindberg introduced a number of important innovations in writing and production in which he was ahead of his time. His dialogue, like that of Anton Chekhov, is meant to reproduce the pauses, wanderings, and flatness of everyday speech. *Miss Julie* is cast in one uninterrupted act so as to capitalize on the emotional involvement of the audience. Strindberg also calls for music, mime, ballet, and improvisation to make use of the full range of actors' talents. He calls for new lighting techniques to illuminate faces better, allowing them to use less make-up and to appear more natural. Finally, he asks for a return to a smaller, more intimate theater with a more intimate relationship between the stage and the audience.

Julie's complex motivations are ample evidence of Strindberg's art. She is presented as a product of both heredity and environment. Her mother was a low-born woman, full of hatred for woman's conventional place in society. She reared Julie as a boy, creating in her a fascination with animals and a loathing for the opposite sex that leads to self-disgust when her natural instincts attract her sexually to men. Her mother suffered from strange attacks of mental instability that seem to have been passed on to Julie. Added to these problems is the biological determinant of Julie's menstrual cycle, which makes her more emotionally unstable than usual. There is also the strong element of chance: Her father's absence frees Julie and Jean from customary restraints. It is chance that leads the couple into the locked room. The sensual excitement of the Midsummer's Eve celebration contributes to the seduction and to Julie's final tragedy.

Jean's motivation, although less complex than Julie's, is also conditioned by his environment, his biological drives, his psychological desires, and his social aspirations. At the same time that he can despise the weaknesses of the old aristocrats, he finds himself unable to break his social conditioning. Only in the count's absence could Jean have brought himself to seduce Julie.

An added complication is the class conflict in which the decaying aristocracy, which Julie represents, must, by law of nature, be destroyed to make way for a stronger lower class that is more fit for the new world. Some things of value, such as aesthetic sensitivity and a sense of personal honor, are lost; these are the qualities that break Julie and her father, whereas brutality and lack of scruples ensure Jean's final triumph. He survives because of his animal virility, his keen physical senses, and his strength of purpose. Religion has been discarded by the aristocracy as meaningless, and it is used by the working class to insure their innocence. Love is seen as no more than a romantic illusion created by the aristocracy to be used, as Julie uses it, to explain animal instincts in an acceptable manner. Jean, the pragmatic realist from the lower class, has no such need for excuses for sexual release.

To underline his themes and characterizations, Strindberg uses recurring animal imagery that links human beings with their animal nature, a technique that may be seen in the dreams of Julie and Jean, the foreshadowing effect of Julie's mother, Julie's attitude toward her dog, and the brutal death of Julie's beautiful, caged bird.

Miss Julie is a naturalistic tragedy that follows the Aristotelian concepts of pity, fear, and catharsis. Pity is aroused in the viewer by the characters' inherent weaknesses and the social class structure they inhabit; fear is aroused when they realize that the same fate could overcome any of them; catharsis results when they realize that the old, decaying order must give way to the newer and stronger order if life is to continue.

"Critical Evaluation" by Ann E. Reynolds

Bibliography:
Gilman, Richard. "Strindberg." In *The Making of Modern Drama.* New York: Farrar, Straus & Giroux, 1974. Posits that Strindberg and Henrik Ibsen restored the presence of personal existence to the drama. In *Miss Julie,* Jean and Julie become the agencies for each other's discovery of their divided selves.
Johnson, Walter. "Master Dramatist." In *August Strindberg.* Boston: Twayne, 1976. Discusses the plays Strindberg wrote from 1882 to 1894. Asserts that in *Miss Julie,* Strindberg achieves the goals of naturalistic drama that he had outlined in the play's preface.
Sprinchorn, Evert. *Strindberg as Dramatist.* New Haven, Conn.: Yale University Press, 1982. Puts Strindberg's drama in context of the dramaturgy of the time and of Strindberg's life and psychology. Argues that *Miss Julie* and *The Father* (1887) move beyond naturalism into tragedy; compares *Miss Julie* with Jean Genet's *The Maids* (1947).
Törnqvist, Egil. "Speech Situations in *Fröken Julie/Miss Julie.*" In *Strindbergian Drama: Themes and Structure.* Atlantic Highlands, N.J.: Humanities Press, 1982. Analyzes the dialogue in the play, dividing it into duologues, triologues, and monologues, and pointing out the significance of each.
Valency, Maurice. "Strindberg." In *The Flower and the Castle: An Introduction to Modern Drama.* 1963. Reprint. New York: Schocken Books, 1982. Valency sees in Strindberg's works a continuous spiritual autobiography styled in the art of the unbalanced and excessive. In *Miss Julie,* the dramatist identifies himself with Jean and characterizes Julie as an iconic femme fatale.

MISS LONELYHEARTS

Type of work: Novel
Author: Nathanael West (Nathan Weinstein, 1903-1940)
Type of plot: Social satire
Time of plot: Late 1920's
Locale: New York City
First published: 1933

Principal characters:
> MISS LONELYHEARTS, an advice-to-the-lovelorn columnist on the
> New York *Post-Dispatch*
> BETTY, his girlfriend
> WILLIE SHRIKE, the paper's feature editor and his boss
> MARY SHRIKE, the boss's wife
> PETER DOYLE, a cripple
> FAY DOYLE, his wife

The Story:

Miss Lonelyhearts found it hard to write his agony column in the New York *Post-Dispatch*: The letters were not funny, and there was no humor in desperate people begging for help. Sick-of-it-all, for example, with seven children in twelve years, was pregnant again and ill, but being a Catholic, she could not consider an abortion and her husband would not let her alone. Desperate, a sixteen-year-old girl, a good dancer with a good figure and pretty clothes, would like boyfriends, but cried all day at the big hole in the middle of her face. She had no nose; should she commit suicide? Harold S., fifteen, wrote that his sister Gracie, thirteen, deaf, mute, and not very smart, had had something dirty done to her by a man, but Harold could not tell their mother that Gracie was going to have a baby because her mother would beat her up. Shrike, the feature editor and Miss Lonelyhearts' tormentor, was no help at all: Instead of the same old stuff, he said, Miss Lonelyhearts ought to give his readers something new and hopeful.

At Delehanty's speakeasy, where Miss Lonelyhearts went to escape his problems, his boss still belabored him about brooding and told him to forget the Crucifixion and remember the Renaissance. Meanwhile, Shrike was trying to seduce Miss Farkis, a long-legged woman with a childish face. He also taunted the columnist by talking of a Western sect which prayed for a condemned slayer with an adding machine, numbers being their idea of the universal language.

Miss Lonelyhearts' bedroom walls were bare except for an ivory Christ nailed with large spikes, and the religious figure combined in a dream with a snake whose scales were tiny mirrors in which the dead world took on a semblance of life. First, he was a magician who could not move his audience by tricks or prayer; then he was on a drunken college spree with two friends. Their attempt to sacrifice a lamb before barbecuing it, with Miss Lonelyhearts chanting the name of Christ, miscarried when the blade broke on the altar, and the lamb slipped out of their bloodied hands. When the others refused to go back to put the lamb out of its misery, Miss Lonelyhearts returned and crushed its head with a stone.

One day, as he tried to put things in order, everything went against him; pencils broke, buttons rolled under the bed, shades refused to stay down, and instead of order, he found chaos. Miss Lonelyhearts remembered Betty, who could bring order into his world, and he went to her apartment. Yet he realized that her world was not the world of, and could never include, the readers of his column; his confusion was significant, and her order was not. Irritated and fidgety, he could neither talk to her nor caress her, although two months before she had agreed to marry him. When she asked if he were sick, he could only shout at her; when she said she loved him, he could only reply that he loved him and her smiling through tears. Sobbing that she felt swell before he came and now felt lousy, she asked him to go away.

At Delehanty's, he listened to talk of raping a woman writer, and as he got drunker, he heard friends mock Shrike's kidding him; but whiskey made him feel good and dreams of childhood made the world dance. Stepping back from the bar, he collided with a man holding a beer. The man punched him in the mouth. With a lump on his head, a loose tooth, and a cut lip, Miss Lonelyhearts walked in the fresh air with Ned Gates. In a comfort station, they met an old man with a terrible cough and no overcoat, who carried a cane and wore gloves because he detested red hands. They forced him to go to an Italian wine cellar. There they told him they were Havelock Ellis and Krafft-Ebing and insultingly mocked him with taunts of his homosexuality. When Miss Lonelyhearts twisted his arm—imagining it was the arm of Desperate, Broken-hearted, or Sick-of-it-all—the old man screamed, and someone hit the columnist with a chair.

Instead of going to the office after Shrike phoned him, Miss Lonelyhearts went to the speakeasy; he knew Shrike found him too perfect a butt for his jokes to fire him. Needing a woman, he phoned Mary, Shrike's wife, whom he had never seduced, although she hated her husband and used Miss Lonelyhearts to arouse Shrike. At a nightclub, in a cab, and at her apartment door, Miss Lonelyhearts tried to talk Mary into sleeping with him; Shrike opened the door, however, ending that scheme.

The next day, Miss Lonelyhearts received a letter from Fay Doyle, unhappily married to a cripple, asking for an appointment. Although he first threw the letter away, he retrieved it, phoned her to meet him in the park, and took her to his apartment. In the intervals of making love, she told of her married life and her child Lucy, whose father was not Doyle.

Physically sick and exhausted in his room for three days, he was comforted by Betty who tried to get him to quit his Lonelyhearts job. He said he had taken the job as a joke, but after several months, the joke had escaped him. Pleas for help made him examine his values, and he became the victim of the joke. While Betty suggested that he go to the country with her, Shrike broke into the room, taunted him to escape to the South Seas, hedonism, art, suicide, or drugs, and ended by dictating an imaginary letter from the columnist to Christ.

After he had been ill for a week, Betty finally persuaded Miss Lonelyhearts to go with her to her aunt's Connecticut farm. They camped in the kitchen, sat near a pond to watch frogs, deer, and a fawn, and slept on a mattress on the floor. They walked in the woods, swam in the nude, and made love in the grass. After several days, they returned to the city. Miss Lonelyhearts knew that Betty had failed to cure him; he could not forget the letters. He vowed to attempt to be humble. In the office, he found a lengthy letter from Broad Shoulders, telling of her troubles with a crazy husband.

About a week later, while Shrike was pulling the same familiar jokes in Delehanty's, the bartender introduced Miss Lonelyhearts to Peter Doyle, a cripple whose wife wanted the columnist to have dinner at their house. After labored conversation, Doyle gave him a letter about his problems: He must pull his leg up and down stairs for $22.50 a week; his wife talked money, money, money; a doctor prescribed a six months' rest. When their hands touched under the table, they were at first embarrassed, but then held hands in silence.

As they left the speakeasy, very drunk, to go to Doyle's, the cripple cursed his wife and his foot. Miss Lonelyhearts was happy in his humility. When Mrs. Doyle tried to seduce the columnist, he failed to respond. Meanwhile, her husband called himself a pimp and, at his wife's request, went out to get gin. Failing to find a message to show Mrs. Doyle that her husband loved her, and disgusted by her obscene attempts to get him to sleep with her, Miss Lonelyhearts struck her again and again before he ran out of the house.

Following three days of illness, Miss Lonelyhearts was awakened by five people, including Shrike and his wife, all drunk, who wanted to take him to a party at the editor's home. Betty was one of the group. Shrike wanted to play a game in which he distributed letters from Miss Lonelyhearts' office file and made taunting comments. When the columnist could stand it no longer, he followed Betty out, dropping unread the letter given him, which Shrike read to the crowd. It was from Doyle, accusing Miss Lonelyhearts of trying to rape his wife.

Miss Lonelyhearts told Betty he had quit the Lonelyhearts job and was going to look for work in an advertising agency. She told him she was going to have a baby. Although he persuaded her to marry him and have the baby instead of an abortion, by the time he left her, he did not feel guilty. In fact, he did not feel, because his feeling, conscience, sense of reality, and self-knowledge were like a rock.

The next morning, he was in a fever. The Christ on his wall was shining, but everything else in the room seemed dead. When the bell rang and he saw Doyle coming up the stairs, he imagined the cripple had come to have Miss Lonelyhearts perform a miracle and make him whole. Misunderstanding the outspread arms, Doyle put his hand in a newspaper-wrapped package as Betty came in the door. In the struggle, the gun Doyle carried went off and Miss Lonelyhearts fell, dragging the cripple with him.

Critical Evaluation:

Nathanael West is a tragic figure of American letters. He published four novels before his death in an automobile accident in 1940, and these novels did not meet with much acclaim during his lifetime. Subsequently, however, they were hailed as works of genius. West's vision of America is one of darkly comic absurdity. His early death robbed American letters of a great talent.

His accidental death by modern, mechanical means has eerie echoes of West's fiction. In his books, the modern world wrecks its inhabitants with a chilling indifference. Traditional orders of society have broken down, norms have vanished. West was criticized by his contemporaries; it was said that his books suffered for want of some "normal" characters to round out the absurd world West's fictions present. In West's fiction, a Murphy's law of human fate rules the roost.

West had a cartoonists' eye that exaggerated human tics, flaws, and failings. His writing is brilliantly focused and his vision intense. West appears to have been a prophet of post-World War II anomie and terror. No doubt this is why he was not appreciated until the 1950's.

West depicts a world made absurd by the disappearance of traditional orders. The paradox of reading West is that one has so much fun while dealing with insoluble miseries and repulsive sufferings. The letters that Miss Lonelyhearts receives are, amazingly, funny. They are also repulsive, depressing, and profound. West thus creates great complexity of feeling in a simple, almost cartoonlike, narrative. His characters, for example, have been termed two-dimensional by detractors. West's characters are sketches of human beings, distorted by simplification. West's technique highlights exactly those qualities that his tragicomedies require. His characters show character as fate; they are trapped in being exactly who they are. They remind readers of the figures of Greek drama, of myth, of biblical personages. West brings ancient concepts of fate into a modern context. Readers read about insoluble human misery, seeing it through the eyes of the compassionate Miss Lonelyhearts, yet at the same time are being made to laugh at it. This keeps readers uneasily aware of the absurdity of human life.

Additionally, *Miss Lonelyhearts* critiques capitalism. Much of the book's cruelty has to do with what the worker suffers. West's critique is also larger, less time-bound than that. It is the human condition readers are being offered, not simply the human condition under late-industrial capitalism.

An indication of the novel's being more than a critique of capitalism is the theme of Miss Lonelyhearts' identification with Jesus Christ. The theme of the novel in a nutshell: Christ will always be killed by those he tries to save. He cannot help himself, any more than they. West sees that it is the very nature of Christ, to be killed for attempting to be the Savior. Miss Lonely-hearts may be suffering delusions of grandeur in identifying with Christ—but then, the book implicitly asks, what was Christ himself suffering from? Miss Lonelyhearts, like Christ, has another name. West is saying that, in his world, one's role is everything—what the workplace does not require, a person does not need. Other names in the book merit examination. Shrike, who tears savagely at Miss Lonelyhearts' idealism, bears the name of a species of fierce bird, and has no other life. Miss Lonelyhearts plays Christ or is Christ, and meets with a similar end.

The alternatives to playing Christ are likewise fatal. Who would want to be Shrike, the soulless mocker? Apart from Miss Lonelyhearts, there is no one with whom readers can identify. Identification itself, as an act, appears to be a mistake in the novel. Yet it appears to be an irresistible human urge. This absurd condition stays unresolved in this novel, except through the power of the novelist's art, which holds the paradox at a certain distance so that it can be recognized for what it is. The author who wrote scripts for the Marx Brothers sees the comedy inherent in the way things go wrong, so that a distancing—and saving—laughter is never far away, even as readers consider the dark side. The callousness with which some critics reproach West is in fact inextricable from his vision and its realization through his masterly technique.

"Critical Evaluation" by David Bromige

Bibliography:

Andreach, Robert. "Nathanael West's *Miss Lonelyhearts:* Between the Dead Pan and the Unborn Christ." In *Twentieth Century Interpretations of "Miss Lonelyhearts": A Collection of Critical Essays*, edited by Thomas H. Jackson. Englewood Cliffs, N.J.: Prentice-Hall, 1971. Analyzes the Pan-Christ antagonism as the unifying principle of West's novel and the central paradox of twentieth century life, in which paganism violates one's conscience and Christianity violates one's nature.

Barnard, Rita. "The Storyteller, the Novelist, and the Advice Columnist." In *The Great Depression and the Culture of Abundance*. Cambridge, England: Cambridge University Press, 1995. Contextualizes *Miss Lonelyhearts* in the mass-media, commercial culture of the 1930's, and discusses West's critique of popular art forms.

Light, James F. *Nathanael West: An Interpretive Study*. 2d ed. Evanston, Ill.: Northwestern University Press, 1971. Claims West's compassion for people whose dreams have been be-trayed fuses form and content in *Miss Lonelyhearts*. Describes the novel's imagistic style, and briefly summarizes its critical reception.

Martin, Jay. *Nathanael West: The Art of His Life*. New York: Farrar, Straus & Giroux, 1970. An indispensable biographical and critical source. Asserts that the dominant issue in West's life and art is the loss of value. An appendix documents West's screenwriting career.

_____, ed. *Nathanael West: A Collection of Critical Essays*. Englewood Cliffs, N.J.: Prentice-Hall, 1971. In addition to West's own essays and reviews by his contemporaries, this volume includes essays that study textual revisions and religious experience in *Miss Lonelyhearts*.

MISTER ROBERTS

Type of work: Novel
Author: Thomas Heggen (1919-1949)
Type of plot: Satire
Time of plot: Last months of World War II
Locale: Southwest Pacific
First published: 1946

' *Principal characters:*
DOUGLAS ROBERTS, the first lieutenant of the USS *Reluctant*
CAPTAIN MORTON, the skipper of the *Reluctant*
ENSIGN KEITH
BOOKSER, a seaman
FRANK THOMPSON, a radioman

The Story:

Douglas Roberts, first lieutenant on the *Reluctant*, a U.S. Navy supply ship in the Pacific, was the guiding spirit of the crew's undeclared war against the skipper, Captain Morton, an officious, childish, and unreasonable officer. The *Reluctant* was noncombatant, plying among islands left in the backwash of the war. None of its complement had seen action, and none wanted action except Roberts, who had applied without success for transfer to a ship of the line.

In the continuously smoldering warfare between the captain and the other officers and the men of the ship, Roberts scored a direct hit on the captain's fundament with a wad of lead-foil shot from a rubber band while Captain Morton was watching motion pictures on board. Ensign Pulver, who spent most of his time devising ways of making the skipper's life unbearable, manufactured a giant firecracker to be thrown into the captain's cabin at night. The premature and violent explosion of the firecracker put the entire *Reluctant* on a momentary battle footing. Ensign Pulver was burned badly.

Ensign Keith came to the *Reluctant* by way of middle-class Boston, Bowdoin College, and accelerated wartime naval officer training. He was piped aboard in the blazing sunshine of Tedium Bay, hot in his blue serge uniform but self-assured because Navy regulations prescribed blues when reporting for duty. Despite the discomfort of a perspiration-soaked shirt and a wilted collar, Ensign Keith immediately showed the crew that they would have to follow naval regulations if he had his way aboard ship. One night, however, while he was on watch, he came upon a drinking and gambling party presided over by Chief Dowdy. Keith was hoodwinked by the men into trying some of their drink. Not much later, under the influence of Chief Dowdy's "pineapple juice," Keith had become roaring drunk, all regulations and service barriers forgotten. His initiation completed, Ensign Keith never again referred to rules and regulations.

At a forward area island base, where the *Reluctant* had docked to unload cargo, the crew quickly learned that the military hospital was staffed by real live nurses. Every available binocular, telescope, and rangefinder on board was soon trained on the nurses' quarters. Interest rose to a fever pitch when it was discovered that a bathroom window shade in the quarters was never lowered. Officers and men soon came to know the nurses by their physical characteristics, if not by formal introduction. One day, a nurse came aboard and overheard two seamen making a wager concerning her physical characteristics. That same day, the bathroom shade was lowered, never to be raised again.

For days in advance, the ship's complement planned their shore leave in Elysium, a civilized port of call. Seaman Bookser, the spiritual type, was the butt of many jokes concerning his liberty plans. At Elysium, half the men were given shore leave. From sundown until the following dawn, they were brought back by jeep and truck. They had fought with army personnel, insulted local citizens, stolen government property, wrecked bars and saloons, and damaged the house of the French consul. Further shore leave was canceled. Bookser, the spiritual seaman, was driven up to the dock in a large car on the day of departure. Beside him was a beautiful young woman whom he kissed long and passionately before leaving her. Astonished at Bookser and proud of him at the same time, the crew made him the hero of the stop at Elysium.

Roberts listened to V-E Day reports on the ship's radio. The apathy of his fellow officers toward events happening in Europe led him to pitch the captain's cherished potted palm overboard late that night. At the same time, Roberts stirred up the noise-hating captain by slamming a lead stanchion against a stateroom bulkhead. Roberts was not caught, nor did he give himself up during the captain's mad search for the culprit. The crew manufactured a medal and presented it to Roberts for valor above and beyond the call of duty—a seaman had seen Roberts in action on V-E night.

Frank Thompson, a radioman and the ship's expert at the game Monopoly, was informed by wire that his baby, whom he had never seen, had died in California. Thompson, anxious to go to the funeral and to be with his wife, applied for permission to fly to the States. The captain refused. Roberts advised him to go to a nearby island to see the chaplain and the flag secretary. Thompson went, but he was told that no emergency leave could be permitted without his captain's approval. He then walked alone in a deserted section of the island for several hours before he returned to the *Reluctant* and took his usual place at the head of the Monopoly table.

Not long after V-E Day, Roberts received orders to report back to the States for reassignment. He spent the night before he left the *Reluctant* with his special friends among officers and men, drinking punch made of crew-concocted raisin brew and grain alcohol from dispensary supplies. The effect of Roberts' leaving was immediate. No longer was there a born leader aboard. All functions and activities in the ship's routine went wrong; no longer was there any one man upon whom the officers could depend to maintain their balance in the tedium of a dull tropic supply run. No longer did the enlisted men have an officer upon whom they could depend as a link between them and the ship's authorities.

Roberts was assigned to duty aboard a destroyer which was part of a task force bombarding the Japanese home islands. Not long before V-J Day, Ensign Pulver received a letter from a friend aboard the same ship. The letter stated that a Japanese kamikaze plane had broken through antiaircraft defenses and had crashed into the bridge of the destroyer. Among those killed in the explosion was Roberts, who had been in the officers' mess drinking coffee with another officer. Mr. Roberts had seen action at last.

Critical Evaluation:

Mister Roberts is an ancestor of such works as Joseph Heller's *Catch-22* (1961). What Mister Roberts embodies—and this has also been absorbed by Heller—is the irreverent tone of the novel and its sometimes stunning mix of the wildly comic and the deeply tragic. The often sudden switch from verbal comedy or even slapstick to dramatic is something many may readily identify with *Catch-22* and the film *M*A*S*H* in which death, pain, passion, and foolishness follow one another very quickly.

Mister Roberts, published in 1946, is certainly one of the first texts to deal with the American military, patriotism, and heroism, in the context of World War II, with something less than rigid respect. At least half of Heggen's novel is comic and satiric, designed to amuse the reader and make fun of military procedure, structures, and what passes for military service in some contexts.

Occasionally, the comedy in *Mister Roberts* is very broad, almost surreal. The name of the ship, the USS *Reluctant*, and the names of Pacific Ocean islands it passes or visits (Apathy, Tedium, Ennui, Elysium, and the Limbo Islands), are conceived as either humorous description or parody of the strange names of the real Pacific islands that figured in campaigns waged during the war.

Many of the comic activities in *Mister Roberts* are things associated with the lighter side of military life: discussions about sex, parties fueled by homemade alcoholic beverages, practical jokes, conspiracies against difficult officers, and gambling. In the novel's last half, Thomas Heggen changes his tone radically in several instances, and this narrative move toward tragedy culminates in the title character's death. Heggen's narrative takes a serious turn with the story of Big Gerhart's bullying of one of the young seamen, Red Stevens, who had shipped out fourteen months after his marriage. Gerhart is a man who delights in being cruel to those weaker than he; in the chapter devoted to the confrontation between him and Stevens, he is first seen mistreating a dog. Later, looking for another target, he picks on Stevens.

Gerhart begins to needle Stevens about being away from his young wife, gradually increasing the suggestiveness of his remarks, asking about Stevens' sexual activities and finally pointing out that Stevens can hardly expect such a pretty young wife to remain faithful while her husband is at sea. To Gerhart's surprise and to the surprise of onlookers, Red hits Gerhart with a wrench. Stevens is given a harmless summary court-martial, but he wins the sympathies of his shipmates and of the reader.

In another moving episode, Frank Thompson receives word that his child has drowned. He asks for emergency leave to attend the funeral and see his wife, but permission is denied. The last image readers have of Thompson is of him maniacally playing Monopoly, as was his frequent custom, the image of a man driven to frantic despair by grief and frustration.

Eventually, in the spring of 1945, Roberts comes to suspect that the war has passed him by, that he has spent his years of service aboard the *Reluctant* while other men elsewhere have seen action and have perhaps distinguished themselves. What worries Roberts is that he has missed his chance at heroism—again. He had tried to join the Lincoln Brigade during the Spanish Civil War in the 1930's, but that war ended before he could participate; he had tried to join the British Royal Air Force in 1940, but had been denied because of a dental problem.

In a conversation with the *Reluctant*'s doctor, Roberts cannot really explain why he wants to fight in the war; he can only indicate that he has a compulsion to do so. While he has no illusions about heroism (he bemoans the fact that people forget too easily those who died in the war), he feels that the best men were those who, through some strange natural-selection process, were good enough to do the fighting. As for Roberts, all he has to show for his service is a medal struck by his friends in recognition of his pitching the captain's beloved palm tree overboard. Nevertheless, he does eventually succeed in being transferred to another ship—a destroyer still active in the Pacific theater.

The terrible irony is that, as *Mister Roberts* ends, Roberts comes to constitute an example of war's tragic waste. He dies in a kamikaze attack on the ship on which he is serving—a perfect example of the fact, as he had thought, that not all casualties are heroes. What is worse is that his death is a horrible accident, a meaningless incident near the end of a war which has already been won and which is being waged by desperate Japanese pilots who hope only to inflict the most damage possible before defeat. In the same attack, another officer on the ship is killed while drinking coffee in the wardroom. Roberts' death has no more significance in the broad picture of the war than that death does.

In the novel's moving denouement, Ensign Pulver creates a memorial for Roberts—by doing what Roberts would do if he were still alive and still aboard the *Reluctant*. He throws the rest of the captain's palm trees over the ship's side.

"Critical Evaluation" by Gordon Walters

Bibliography:
Cohn, Victor. "Mister Heggen." *Saturday Review of Literature* 32 (June 11, 1949): 19. A brief but interesting consideration of Heggen and his work published not long after Heggen's suicide in May of the same year.
Leggett, John. *Ross and Tom: Two American Tragedies*. New York: Simon & Schuster, 1974. Leggett's book is primarily a biographical study of Thomas Heggen and novelist Ross Lockridge (both suicides) rather than a critical work on *Mister Roberts*, it is indispensable to understanding Heggen's state of mind when he wrote the novel.
Schulberg, Budd. "Taps at Reveille." *Esquire* 54 (November, 1960): 101-105. A positive assessment of *Mister Roberts* particularly in the context of other American writing about World War II. Also relevant to the film made of the novel in 1955.

THE MISTRESS OF THE INN

Type of work: Drama
Author: Carlo Goldoni (1707-1793)
Type of plot: Comedy
Time of plot: Mid-eighteenth century
Locale: Florence, Italy
First performed: 1753; first published, 1753 as *La locandiera* (English translation, 1912)

Principal characters:
MIRANDOLINA, the mistress of the inn
THE CAVALIER DI RIPAFRATTA, a woman-hater
THE MARQUIS DI FORLIPOPOLI, in love with Mirandolina
THE COUNT D'ALBAFIORITA, in love with Mirandolina
FABRICIUS, a serving-man who is also in love with Mirandolina

The Story:

A Florentine innkeeper had died and left his young and pretty daughter, Mirandolina, mistress of his inn. The young woman ran the hostelry with much success, for she was as shrewd as she was pretty. On his deathbed, her father had made her promise to marry Fabricius, a faithful young serving-man in the inn. She had promised the father to obey his wishes, but after his death she made excuses for not marrying. She told Fabricius that she was not yet ready to settle down to married life, although she loved him very much. Actually, Mirandolina liked to have men fall in love with her, and she did her best to make fools of them in every way possible. She took all and gave nothing.

A short time after her father's death, two noblemen staying at her inn fell in love with her. One was the Marquis di Forlipopoli, a destitute man who, despite his lack of money, was excessively proud of his empty title. The other love-smitten lodger was the Count d'Albafiorita, a wealthy man who boasted of his money. The two men were constantly at odds with each other, each feeling that Mirandolina should prefer him to his rival. In private she laughed at both of them.

The count gave Mirandolina expensive diamond brooches and earrings, and he also spent a great deal of money as a patron of the inn. The marquis, having no money to spend, tried to impress Mirandolina with his influence in high places and offered her his protection. Occasionally, he gave Mirandolina small gifts, which he openly stated were much better than the count's expensive presents because little gifts were in better taste.

Pleased at the attentions of the count, the marquis, and her faithful Fabricius, Mirandolina was somewhat taken aback when a new guest arrived, the Cavalier di Ripafratta, who professed to be a woman-hater. When he received a letter telling him of a beautiful girl with a great dowry who wished to marry him, he became disgusted and angry and threw away the letter. Although his attitude toward Mirandolina was almost boorish, she seemed much taken with a man who was immune to her charms. More than a little piqued by his attitude, she vowed to make him fall in love with her.

When the cavalier demanded better linens, Mirandolina went to his room and, engaging him in conversation, struck up a friendship of sorts. She told him that she admired him for being truly a man and able to put aside all thoughts of love. The cavalier, struck by her pose, said that he was pleased to know such a forthright woman, and that he desired her friendship.

Mirandolina followed up her initial victory by cooking extra dishes for the cavalier and

4195

serving them to him in his room with her own hands, much to the displeasure of her other two admirers. The marquis was of much greater rank and the count was far more wealthy than the cavalier. Mirandolina's strategy had immediate success. Within twenty-four hours, the cavalier found himself in love with the woman who served him so well and was so agreeable to his ways of thinking.

The cavalier, however, was much disturbed by his new-found love and vowed that he would leave for Leghorn immediately. He believed that out of Mirandolina's sight he would soon forget her. He had already given orders to his servant to pack for his departure when Mirandolina learned of his plans. She herself went to present his bill and had little trouble in beguiling him to stay a little longer. At the end of the interview, during which the cavalier professed his love, Mirandolina fainted. The marquis and the count ran into the room to see what had happened. The cavalier, furious at them for discovering Mirandolina in his room, threw the bottle of restorative at them. The marquis vowed to have satisfaction, but when the cavalier accepted his challenge the marquis showed his cowardice by refusing to fight a duel.

The cavalier, now almost beside himself with love, sent a solid gold flask to Mirandolina, who refused to accept it and threw it into a basket of clothes to be ironed. Fabricius, seeing the flask, became jealous. He was also displeased by the offhanded treatment he had been receiving from the woman who had promised to marry him. Mirandolina finally appeased him by saying that women always treat worst those whom they love best.

Later in the day, while Mirandolina was busy ironing the linen, the cavalier came to her and asked why she had rejected his suit. He refused to believe that she had been playing a game with him, just as she had been doing with the count and the marquis. He became all the more angry because Fabricius continually interrupted the interview, bringing in hot flatirons for Mirandolina to use on the linen. After a lengthy argument, during which the cavalier became furious and refused to let Fabricius bring in the irons, Mirandolina left the room.

The marquis thereupon entered and began to taunt the cavalier for having fallen victim to the innkeeper's charms. The cavalier stormed out of the room. Looking about, the marquis, very much embarrassed for money, saw the gold flask. Intending to sell it, he picked it up and put it in his pocket. At that moment, the count entered and the two began to congratulate themselves on Mirandolina's success in making a fool of their latest rival. They could not help remembering, however, that she had done things for him that she had not done for them: cooked special foods, provided new bed linen, and visited with him in his room. Finally, having come to the conclusion that they were as foolish as the cavalier, they resolved to pay their bills and leave the inn.

While Mirandolina was bidding them goodbye, the cavalier pushed his way into the room and tried to force a duel upon the count. When he seized the marquis' sword, however, and attempted to pull it from the scabbard, he found only the handle. Mirandolina tried to calm him and to send all three away. She bluntly told the cavalier that she had simply used her wiles to make him love her because he had boasted of being a woman-hater. Then, announcing that she had promised her father to marry Fabricius, she took the serving-man by the hand and announced her betrothal to him. The cavalier left angrily, but the count and the marquis received the news more gracefully. The count gave the newly betrothed couple a hundred pounds, and the marquis, poor as he was, gave them six pounds. Both men left the inn wiser in the ways of women than they were when they arrived.

Critical Evaluation:
The humor of Carlo Goldoni's *The Mistress of the Inn* is based on certain assumptions of

class and social structure, as well as on the positions of man and woman relative to each other in society. The heroine's contacts in the play are made possible by virtue of the fact that she is an innkeeper, for, as a rule, women of a nobler class did not encounter large numbers of men in eighteenth century Italy. Although Goldoni underscores Mirandolina's virtue often, her position suggested a certain moral looseness to audiences of the time. Indeed, a woman of mid-eighteenth century Italy would not have conducted herself with Mirandolina's freedom; such behavior toward men would have been judged as being immoral and unfeminine, and such a woman would have lost her social position. Nevertheless, a woman who defied men was an ideal subject for laughter, and Mirandolina's self-assurance and cleverness were considered admirable then as in later times, though for different reasons. Goldoni's contemporaries delighted in seeing Mirandolina triumph over the foolish men in the play, not because her conquests were men, but because they were fools. In truth, Goldoni's audience would not have wanted women to be victorious over men in actuality, or even to challenge long-established male prerogatives. The humor of this battle between the sexes is safe and acceptable in *The Mistress of the Inn* because it is not in any way realistic.

Another way in which Goldoni uses social distinctions for humorous effect is through the opposition between the old gentry and the *nouveau riche*. The count represents the newly moneyed class, whereas the marquis is of the old nobility, impoverished but clinging to his pride in his ancient rank. He scorns the bought title of the count, insisting that lineage cannot be purchased. Yet in the practical world, the man with money has the advantage, and the prestige of an old family is easily swept aside. The marquis babbles about the refinements that come from breeding, about "taste" and "protection" and "honor," but when the count flashes a diamond ring, Mirandolina cannot resist. Eighteenth century Italy was a country in transition, lagging behind the other European countries in economic and political developments, and the contest between these two absurd figures reflects the conditions that existed at the time. Many of the old families were being overwhelmed by the newly affluent commercial families; power was changing hands, being yielded to the ruthless and shrewd, and soon the supreme upstart of them all, Napoleon Bonaparte, would appear on the scene.

In *The Mistress of the Inn*, Goldoni combines old dramatic traditions with his own innovations. The convention of the insolent, shrewd servant, Fabricius, for example goes back to ancient Roman and even Greek comedy, and the character of Mirandolina suggests some of the independent courtesans of the old Roman comedies. On the other hand, the sense of the momentary scene is new to Goldoni; the audience is always aware that life is going on around these characters on the stage and that the events of the comedy are not occurring in a vacuum. Part of the vitality of the play stems from this feeling of the ever-changing quality of human life.

The characters themselves are the primary reason for the play's long success. They are broadly sketched, but each possesses a good-natured vitality. Mirandolina does not marry out of her class, which would have shocked eighteenth century audiences, but the possibility that she might do so tantalizes them until the very end. Her gaiety and cleverness control the proceedings as she plays on the self-centered males as on musical instruments. They, in turn, respond to her efforts according to their personalities, ever-jealous of one another, ridiculing one another, proud and arrogant, yet not one of them is a match for this earthy, witty female.

Carlo Goldoni was a prolific dramatist, and his work completely reformed the comedy of his day. The son of a Venetian doctor, he ran away from school with a company of players. Although he eventually took a degree in law, the theater was always his first love. After making a false start with a lyric tragedy, he found his natural bent with a comedy in verse. Believing that a radical change was necessary in the Italian theater, he followed Molière's example by attempting to depict the realities of social life in as natural a manner as possible. To later audiences, his plays do not seem realistic, but they were a startling departure from what came before him. Goldoni freed his actors from the traditional practice of wearing masks on the stage, and he suppressed improvisation by writing out the parts in full. He eventually replaced the haphazard Italian farces of the day, the *commedia dell'arte*, with his own style of comedy of manners. His plays were both earthy and moral in tone and attempted a faithful "mirror of life." Goldoni's best plays, which reflect the true life of the varied social classes in his native land, have endured and will continue to be enjoyed by audiences around the world. They possess a gaiety and shrewdness unsurpassed in later drama, and they present a tantalizing picture of a dynamic and rapidly changing moment in history.

"Critical Evaluation" by Bruce D. Reeves

Bibliography:
Carlson, Marvin. *The Italian Stage from Goldoni to D'Annunzio.* Jefferson, N.C.: McFarland, 1981. Excellent background for understanding the conditions under which Goldoni produced *The Mistress of the Inn* and other comedies. Also describes the efforts of actress Eleanore Duse in popularizing the play for twentieth century audiences.
Goldoni, Carlo. *Three Comedies.* London: Oxford University Press, 1961. The introduction by Gabriele Baldini discusses Goldoni's abilities as a comic dramatist and examines his use of stock materials in *The Mistress of the Inn.* Also provides an assessment of Mirandolina, "the most fascinating female character" to appear in Italian literature in centuries.
Kennard, Joseph Spencer. *Goldoni and the Venice of His Time.* New York: Macmillan, 1920. Scholarly assessment of the playwright and his influence on Italian theater in the eighteenth century. Remarks on the production of *The Mistress of the Inn* and analyzes Goldoni's development of Mirandolina as the comic seductress.
Riedt, Heinz. *Carlo Goldoni.* Translated by Ursule Molinaro. New York: Frederick Ungar, 1974. General survey of Goldoni's achievements as a dramatist. A chapter on *The Mistress of the Inn* explains it as "a portrayal of feminine psychology," comments on its structure, and remarks on twentieth century productions and adaptations.
Steele, Eugene. *Carlo Goldoni: Life, Work and Times.* Ravenna, Italy: Longo Editore, 1981. Brief comments about the drama, including a general assessment of Goldoni's accomplishments as a playwright. Includes Goldoni's own comments about *The Mistress of the Inn*, and focuses critical attention on the development of Mirandolina.

MITHRIDATES

Type of work: Drama
Author: Jean Baptiste Racine (1639-1699)
Type of plot: Tragedy
Time of plot: First century B.C.E.
Locale: Nymphée, on the Bosphorus
First performed: 1673; first published, 1673 as *Mithridate* (English translation, 1926)

Principai characters:
MITHRIDATES, king of Pontus
MONIME, betrothed to Mithridates and already declared queen
PHARNACE and
XIPHARES, sons of Mithridates by different wives
ARBATE, Mithridates' confidant and governor of Nymphée
PHOEDIME, Monime's confidante
ARCAS, a servant

The Story:

Mithridates, the Pontine king who had been fighting against the Romans for forty years, had just been defeated and was believed dead. Xiphares, the son who was, like his father, an enemy of Rome, deplored sincerely the loss of Mithridates. The other son, Pharnace, favorable to the Romans, was all the more pleased because he was in love with Monime, the old king's betrothed; now he hoped to win her for himself.

Xiphares had told Arbate that he, Xiphares, had no claims to the states Pharnace was to inherit and that his brother's feelings toward the Romans were of little interest to him. His concern for Monime was another matter. The truth was that Xiphares himself had long been in love with Monime, even before his father saw her. Although he had remained silent as long as she was betrothed to his father, he was now convinced that Pharnace would be compelled to kill him in order to have her.

When Monime begged Xiphares to protect her against Pharnace, whom she did not love, Xiphares finally declared his love to her. At first he was afraid that she might receive his avowal with anger. Monime, however, was secretly in love with Xiphares. They might have opened their hearts to each other at that time if Pharnace had not appeared. Pharnace urged Monime to support his cause in Pontus. She thanked him but explained that she could not favor a friend of the Romans who had killed her father. When Pharnace hinted that another interest was prompting her, Xiphares confirmed his suspicions by defending Monime's freedom. The brothers then realized that they were rivals.

At that moment Phoedime, Monime's confidante, arrived to tell them that the report of Mithridates' death was false and that the king was returning. Monime and Xiphares, each having sensed at last the other's feelings, were stunned. Monime deliberately bade them farewell and left. Now Pharnace knew that Monime and Xiphares loved each other, and Xiphares knew that Pharnace loved Monime and was expecting the arrival of the Romans. Both, afraid of their father's anger, would be forced to keep each other's secret when they met him.

After everyone had gone to meet Mithridates at the harbor, Phoedime was surprised to find Monime still in the palace. Monime explained her realization that Xiphares had suffered as much as she did all the time they had been separated after their first meeting in Greece. Aware that she had betrayed her love without even speaking, she felt that she could never see Xiphares again because she also feared Mithridates' anger. She left hurriedly because she heard the noise of Mithridates' arrival and she did not want to face him.

The king was surprised to find his sons in Nymphée instead of in their own states. Suspiciously, he asked whether they were in love with Monime and inquired of Arbate why he had allowed them to enter the city. The governor told him that Pharnace had declared his love to Monime. Arbate said nothing, however, about Xiphares' feelings. Mithridates, relieved that his favorite son had remained faithful, was afraid that Monime might have responded to Pharnace's love. At that moment Monime appeared and he asked to be left alone with her. Mithridates told her that he wished to have their wedding performed as soon as possible. Seeing her sad resignation and suspecting that she was in love with Pharnace, he summoned Xiphares and asked his trusted son to try to turn her affections away from his brother. Xiphares also feared that Monime might love Pharnace. Aware of his fear, Monime was unable to hide her true feelings. At the same time she declared her intention to follow her duty to Mithridates.

A short time later Mithridates called for his two sons and explained to them his plan to attack the Romans in Italy. Pharnace would leave on a mission to the Parthians, his purpose being to marry the daughter of their king, with whom Mithridates wished to make an alliance necessary to his plans. When Pharnace refused, his resistance aroused his father's anger. Pharnace, thinking that his brother had betrayed him, tried to get revenge by disclosing the love of Xiphares for Monime.

At first Mithridates refused to listen to Pharnace. Then, tortured by jealousy, he resorted to a stratagem in order to learn the truth. He announced to Monime his desire to have her marry Xiphares. When she showed surprise, asking if he were trying to test her love, he pretended to believe that she wanted to marry Pharnace instead. He declared that he would go with Xiphares to find death in battle, while she would stay with Pharnace. Monime, misled by the king's apparent sincerity, admitted that she loved Xiphares and was loved by him. After her departure Mithridates prepared to take a terrible revenge on his son.

When Xiphares came to bid Monime farewell, she accused herself of having caused his ruin by her weakness. Hearing the king approaching, he left hurriedly. Monime then reproached Mithridates for his stratagem. Ordered to marry him at once, she gently but firmly refused. At that point Mithridates was in a quandary over killing Xiphares, the son who was not only his rival in love but also his best ally against the Romans. While he was debating with himself, Arbate appeared with the announcement that Pharnace, aided by the Romans, had risen in revolt. Believing that Xiphares had also betrayed him, the king ordered Arcas, his faithful servant, to kill Monime.

Meanwhile, convinced that Xiphares was dead, Monime had attempted to strangle herself, but Phoedime had prevented her. Still wishing to die, she welcomed the poison Arcas brought her. Before she could drink it, however, Arbate came on the run and took the potion away from her. He brought word that Xiphares had routed the Romans and that Mithridates was dying. The king, believing himself defeated, had chosen to die by his own sword. Forgetting all jealousy, Mithridates blessed Monime and Xiphares, the faithful son who would succeed to the throne and avenge his father's death.

Critical Evaluation:

Presenting a theme borrowed from history, *Mithridates* is a tragedy that conforms absolutely to Jean Racine's literary ideal: a simple action with few events. In this work Racine was much more faithful to fact than he had been in his earlier plays. He simply added a love interest to the historical story in order to turn it into a drama. The two main characters are memorable in their complexity. Mithridates offers a contrast between the indomitable willpower of the warrior and the blindness and confusion of the unhappy lover. Monime seems to combine harmoniously all the gentleness and strength of Racine's heroines. The rhetorical style is versatile. Sometimes epic in Mithridates' speech, it also takes on an exquisite softness to express the subtlest shades of sentiments. *Mithridates* is the only one of Racine's tragedies the ending of which is mitigated by a promise of future happiness.

Partly because of his bellicose nature and partly because of the envy inspired by his talent, Racine was regularly involved in one imbroglio or another. In the case of *Mithridates*, however, from its first performance early in 1673, even his adversaries agreed that he had created a triumph. The play was greatly admired at the royal court. Since the seventeenth century, however, *Mithridates* has not maintained a degree of popularity equal to that of others of Racine's tragedies. For example, from 1680 to 1965 *Phèdre* and *Andromache* were each produced slightly in excess of thirteen hundred times, whereas *Mithridates* was played 644 times.

For Racine, particularly adept at portraying the subtleties of the feminine heart, *Mithridates* is an unusually masculine play. The choice of a male historical figure, in this case a despotic Oriental king, as central character in his new play was no doubt influenced by his desire to compete with the allegedly more virile theater of the aging Corneille and to silence those critics prone to blame the softness, or femininity, of plays like *Bérénice* (1670) and *Bajazet* (1672), his two previous tragedies. The plot is more complex than that of Racine's earlier plays. Its basic element is the secret: New revelations serve to develop the plot. Xiphares reveals his love to Monime in the first act. Not until late in the second act does Monime reveal her love for him. In Act III, Mithridates discloses his plan to attack Rome. Then, threatened with imprisonment, Pharnace informs Mithridates of Xiphares' love for Monime. Finally, Monime, tricked by Mithridates, admits that she loves Xiphares. In Act IV, Monime discloses the truth to Xiphares: It was she who revealed their secret to Mithridates. Throughout the play, Pharnace guards his secret: The Roman legions are on the way to Nymphée.

The old king is the central figure whose presence links closely the otherwise disparate elements of the dramatic action. The audience sees him in a double focus: As an implacable enemy of Rome, he is an adversary to his son Pharnace, who seeks conciliation with Rome; as a passionate lover, he becomes a rival of Xiphares, who also is in love with the queen, although otherwise loyal. The entanglement is further complicated by incidents that took place before the action of the play. Xiphares' mother had betrayed Mithridates to the Romans; Mithridates had, as the result of his "cruel suspicions," sacrificed two of his sons.

Mithridates is a complex and ambiguous character. There is a strong hint of fatality in his character, constantly evoked by the king's frequent references to his long series of past misfortunes. These misfortunes, of a sentimental and heroic nature, assure sympathy for the aging warrior. The audience feels a natural sympathy for Monime and Xiphares, young lovers struggling to find a basis on which to approach each other, and so, in this light, Mithridates is hateful in his efforts to coerce the queen into granting him her affection. There is a curious and most delicate balance between, on the one hand, the grandeur of the old king, inspired for the most part by the narration of his past greatness as a warrior, and, on the other hand, the meanness of his present machinations, the duplicity of his dissimulations, and the violence of his outbursts of anger and jealousy.

Mithridates, although imperious and passionate, is really little more than a shell of his former self. His past power has evaporated; the effort to marry Monime represents a last opportunity to reestablish evidence of his manhood. Except for his age—which, were there the slightest hint of anything grotesque in his character or actions, would instantly situate him with Molière's comic lovers, given to infatuations with women much younger than themselves—Mithridates is like Othello. His destruction is brought about by a blind passion that easily, or perhaps inevitably, gives rise to a fatal jealousy. Therein lies the tragic flaw of this king.

The evolution of the dramatic action depends, in a large measure, on the undercurrent of secrecy, intrigue, and deception that informs the play. Mithridates relentlessly strives to determine the hidden motives of others. For example, on his arrival in Nymphée he must know why his sons are not at their assigned posts. There is an unusual amount of misunderstanding. Mithridates, particularly, is constantly manipulating people through ruse. He has a proclivity for expressing himself in ambiguous terms, especially in talking about his sons; instead of naming them, he uses terms such as "treacherous son" and "audacious son." Other characters cannot be sure about whom he is talking. Monime is easily tricked by the duplicity of his language. The result is that Mithridates is a completely isolated figure, having no one in whom he can confide. He has three soliloquies, more than any other Racinian hero.

Unlike other tragedies of Racine, notably *Bajazet*, *Mithridates* does not end in general slaughter. At the end, the doomed king is torn between opposing sentiments: In his decision to unite Xiphares and Monime he triumphs over the base emotions of jealousy and desire for revenge that, at least until then, had appeared to motivate him consistently. The "happy ending" applies, of course, only to the young couple. The king's noble death assures a properly tragic denouement to the play.

"Critical Evaluation" by Robert A. Eisner

Bibliography:
Abraham, Claude. *Jean Racine*. Boston: Twayne, 1977. Contains an excellent introduction to Jean Racine's theater and an annotated bibliography of important critical studies on Racine. The chapter on *Mithridates* explores the contrasts between Mithridates and his two sons.
Barthes, Roland. *On Racine*. Translated by Richard Howard. New York: Hill & Wang, 1964. An influential structuralist study that explores representations of love and tragic space in Racine's tragedies. Barthes' chapter on *Mithridates* examines the death of the title character and the presence of evil and deception in the tragedy.
Goldmann, Lucien. *Racine*. Translated by Alastair Hamilton. Cambridge, England: Rivers Press, 1972. Contains an insightful sociological reading of Racine's tragedies that examines them in the light of French seventeenth century politics and social change. Explains carefully the influence of a Catholic religious movement, Jansenism, on Racine's tragic view of the world.
Maskell, David. *Racine: A Theatrical Reading*. New York: Oxford University Press, 1991. Explores problems involved in staging Racine's eleven tragedies and one comedy. Discusses how different theatrical styles have influenced performances of Racine's plays. Discusses the critical reception of his plays since the seventeenth century.
Weinberg, Bernard. *The Art of Jean Racine*. Chicago: University of Chicago Press, 1963. Examines in chronological order each of Racine's eleven tragedies and describes the significance of each play in the development of Racine's career as a playwright. The chapter on *Mithridates* explores the complex psychological motivation for the behavior of the title character.

MOBY DICK
Or, The Whale

Type of work: Novel
Author: Herman Melville (1819-1891)
Type of plot: Adventure
Time of plot: Early nineteenth century
Locale: High seas
First published: 1851

Principal characters:
ISHMAEL, the narrator, a sailor
QUEEQUEG, a savage and a harpooner
AHAB, the captain of the *Pequod*
STARBUCK, the first mate
STUBB, the second mate
FEDALLAH, Captain Ahab's Parsee servant

The Story:

Ishmael was a schoolmaster who often felt that he must leave his quiet existence and go to sea. Much of his life had been spent as a sailor, and his voyages were a means of ridding himself of the restlessness which frequently seized him. One day, he decided that he would sign on a whaling ship, and packing his carpetbag, he left Manhattan and set out, bound for Cape Horn and the Pacific.

On his arrival in New Bedford, he went to the Spouter Inn near the waterfront to spend the night. There he found he could have a bed only if he consented to share it with a harpooner. His strange bedfellow frightened him when he entered the room, for Ishmael was certain that he was a savage cannibal. After a few moments, however, it became evident that the native, whose name was Queequeg, was a friendly person, for he presented Ishmael with an embalmed head and offered to share his fortune of thirty dollars. The two men quickly became friends and decided to sign on the same ship.

Eventually they signed on the *Pequod*, a whaler out of Nantucket, Ishmael as a seaman, Queequeg as a harpooner. Although several people seemed dubious about the success of a voyage on a vessel such as the *Pequod*, which was reported to be under so strange a man as Captain Ahab, neither Ishmael nor Queequeg had any intention of giving up their plans. They were, however, curious to see Captain Ahab.

For several days after the vessel had sailed, there was no sign of the Captain, as he remained hidden in his cabin. The running of the ship was left to Starbuck and Stubb, two of the mates, and, though Ishmael became friendly with them, he learned very little more about Ahab. One day, as the ship was sailing southward, the Captain strode out on deck. Ishmael was struck by his stern, relentless expression. In particular, he noticed that the Captain had lost a leg and that instead of a wooden leg, he now wore one cut from the bone of the jaw of a whale. A livid white scar ran down one side of his face and was lost beneath his collar, so that it seemed as though he were scarred from head to foot.

For several days, the ship continued south looking for the whaling schools. The sailors began to take turns on masthead watches to give the sign when a whale was sighted. Ahab appeared on deck and summoned all his men around him. He pulled out an ounce gold piece, nailed it to the mast, and declared that the first man to sight the great white whale, known to the sailors as Moby Dick, would have the gold. Everyone expressed enthusiasm for the quest except Starbuck and Stubb, Starbuck especially deploring the madness with which Ahab had directed all his energies to this one end. He told the Captain that he was like a man possessed, for the white whale was a menace to those who would attempt to kill him. Ahab had lost his leg in his last encounter with Moby Dick; he might lose his life in the next meeting, but the Captain would not listen to the mate's warning. Liquor was brought out, and, at the Captain's orders, the crew drank to the destruction of Moby Dick.

Ahab, from what he knew of the last reported whereabouts of the whale, plotted a course for the ship which would bring it into the area where Moby Dick was most likely to be. Near the Cape of Good Hope, the ship came across a school of sperm whales, and the men busied themselves harpooning, stripping, melting, and storing as many as they were able to catch.

When they encountered another whaling vessel at sea, Captain Ahab asked for news about the white whale. The captain of the ship warned him not to attempt to chase Moby Dick, but it was clear by now that nothing could deflect Ahab from the course he had chosen.

Another vessel stopped them, and the captain of the ship boarded the *Pequod* to buy some oil for his vessel. Captain Ahab again demanded news of the whale, but the captain knew nothing of the monster. As the captain was returning to his ship, he and his men spotted a school of six whales and started after them in their rowboats. While Starbuck and Stubb rallied their men into the *Pequod*'s boats, their rivals were already far ahead of them. The two mates, however, urged their crew until they outstripped their rivals in the race, and Queequeg harpooned the largest whale.

Killing the whale was only the beginning of a long and arduous job. After the carcass was dragged to the side of the boat and lashed to it by ropes, the men descended the side and slashed off the blubber. Much of the body was usually demolished by sharks, who streamed around it snapping at the flesh of the whale and at each other. The head of the whale was removed and suspended several feet in the air, above the deck of the ship. After the blubber was cleaned, it was melted in tremendous try-pots and then stored in vats below deck.

The men were kept busy, but their excitement increased as their ship neared the Indian Ocean and the probable sporting grounds of the white whale. Before long, they crossed the path of an English whaling vessel, and Captain Ahab again demanded news of Moby Dick. In answer, the captain of the English ship held out his arm, which from the elbow down consisted of sperm whalebone. Ahab demanded that his boat be lowered at once, and he quickly boarded the deck of the other ship. The captain told him of his encounter and warned Captain Ahab that it was foolhardy to try to pursue Moby Dick. When he told Ahab where he had seen the white whale last, the captain of the *Pequod* waited for no civilities but returned to his own ship to order the course changed to carry him to Moby Dick's new feeding ground. Starbuck tried to reason with the mad Captain, to persuade him to give up this insane pursuit, but Ahab seized a rifle and in his fury ordered the mate out of his cabin.

Meanwhile, Queequeg had fallen ill with a fever. When it seemed almost certain he would die, he requested that the carpenter make him a coffin in the shape of a canoe, according to the custom of his tribe. The coffin was then placed in the cabin with the sick man, but as yet there was no real need for it. Queequeg recovered from his illness and rejoined his shipmates. He used his coffin as a sea chest and carved many strange designs upon it.

The sailors had been puzzled by the appearance early in the voyage of the Parsee servant, Fedallah. His relationship to the Captain could not be determined, but that he was highly regarded was evident. Fedallah had prophesied that the Captain would die only after he had seen two strange hearses for carrying the dead upon the sea, one not constructed by mortal hands, and the other made of wood grown in America. He also said that the Captain himself would have neither hearse nor coffin for his burial.

A terrible storm arose one night. Lightning struck the masts so that all three flamed against the blackness of the night, and the men were frightened by this omen. It seemed to them that the hand of God was motioning them to turn from the course to which they had set themselves and return to their homes. Only Captain Ahab was undaunted by the sight. He planted himself at the foot of the mast and challenged the god of evil, which the fire symbolized for him. He vowed once again his determination to find and kill the white whale.

A few days later, a cry rang through the ship. Moby Dick had been spotted. The voice was Captain Ahab's, for none of the sailors, alert as they had been, had been able to sight him before their captain. Then boats were lowered and the chase began, with Captain Ahab's boat in the lead. As he was about to dash his harpoon into the side of the mountain of white, the whale suddenly turned on the boat, dived under it, and split it into pieces. The men were thrown into the sea, and for some time the churning of the whale prevented rescue. At length, Ahab ordered the rescuers to ride into the whale and frighten him away, so he and his men might be rescued. The rest of that day was spent chasing the whale, but to no avail.

The second day, the men started out again. They caught up with the whale and buried three harpoons in his white flanks, but he so turned and churned that the lines became twisted, and the boats were pulled every way, with no control over their direction. Two of them were splintered, and the men hauled out of the sea, but Ahab's boat had not as yet been touched. Suddenly, it was lifted from the water and thrown high into the air. The Captain and the men were quickly rescued, but Fedallah was nowhere to be found.

When the third day of the chase began, Moby Dick seemed tired, and the *Pequod*'s boats soon overtook him. Bound to the whale's back by the coils of rope from the harpoon poles, they saw the body of Fedallah. The first part of his prophecy had been fulfilled. Moby Dick, enraged by his pain, turned on the boats and splintered them. On the *Pequod*, Starbuck watched and turned the ship toward the whale in the hope of saving the Captain and some of the crew. The infuriated monster swam directly into the *Pequod*, shattering the ship's timbers. Ahab, seeing the ship founder, cried out that the *Pequod*—made of wood grown in America—was the second hearse of Fedallah's prophecy. The third prophecy, Ahab's death by hemp, was fulfilled when rope from Ahab's harpoon coiled around his neck and snatched him from his boat. All except Ishmael perished. He was rescued by a passing ship after clinging for hours to Queequeg's canoe coffin, which had bobbed to the surface as the *Pequod* sank.

Critical Evaluation:

Although his early adventure novels—*Typee* (1846), *Omoo* (1847), *Redburn* (1849), and *White Jacket* (1850)—brought Herman Melville a notable amount of popularity and financial success during his lifetime, it was not until the 1920's and 1930's, nearly fifty years after his death, that he received universal critical recognition as one of the greatest nineteenth century American authors. Melville took part in the first great period of American literature—the period that included Edgar Allan Poe, Ralph Waldo Emerson, Nathaniel Hawthorne, Walt Whitman, and Henry David Thoreau. For complexity, originality, psychological penetration, breadth, and symbolic richness, Melville achieved his greatest artistic expression with the book he wrote when he was thirty, *Moby Dick: Or, The Whale.* Between the time of his birth in New York City and his return there to research and write his masterpiece, Melville had circled the globe of experience—working as a bank messenger, salesman, farmhand, schoolteacher (like his narrator, Ishmael), engineer and surveyor, bowling alley attendant, cabin boy, and whaleman in the Pacific on the *Acushnet*. His involvement in the mutinous Pacific voyage, combined with accounts of a notorious whale called "Mocha Dick" that wrought havoc in the 1840's and 1850's, certainly influenced the creation of *Moby Dick*.

The intertangled themes of this mighty novel express the artistic genius of a mind that, according to Hawthorne, "could neither believe nor be comfortable in unbelief." Many of those themes are characteristic of American Romanticism: the "isolated self" and the pain of self-discovery, the insufficiency of conventional practical knowledge in the face of the "power of blackness," the demoniac center to the world, the confrontation of evil and innocence, the fundamental imperfection of man, Faustian heroism, the search for the ultimate truth, the inadequacy of human perception. *Moby Dick* is, moreover, a unique literary form, combining elements of the psychological and picaresque novel, sea story and allegory, the epic of "literal and metaphorical quest," the satire of social and religious events, the emotional intensity of the lyric genre (both in diction and in metaphor), Cervantian romance, Dantesque mysticism, Rabelaisian humor, Shakespearean drama (both tragedy and comedy), journalistic travel book, and scientific treatise on cetology. Melville was inspired by Hawthorne's example to give his story the unifying quality of a moral parable, although his own particular genius refused to allow that parable an unequivocal, single rendering. Both in style and theme, Melville was also influenced by Edmund Spenser, Shakespeare, Dante, Cervantes, Robert Burton, Sir Thomas Carlyle, Thomas Browne, and vastly miscellaneous reading in the New York Public Library (as witnessed by the two "Etymologies" and the marvelous "Extracts" that precede the text itself, items from the writer's notes and files that he could not bear to discard). It was because they did not know how to respond to its complexities of form and style that the book was "broiled in hell fire" by contemporary readers and critics. Even today, the rich mixture of its verbal texture—an almost euphuistic flamboyance balanced by dry, analytical expository prose—requires a correspondingly unique sensitivity on the part of the reader. The most remarkable thing about the plot is that Moby Dick does not appear physically until after five hundred pages and is not even mentioned by name until nearly two hundred pages have passed.

Whether it be the knowledge of reality, an embodiment of the primitive forces of nature, the deep subconscious energies of humanity, fate or destiny inevitably victorious over illusory free will, or simply the unknown in experience, it is what Moby Dick stands for that occupies the narrator's emphasis and the reader's attention through the greater part of the novel. In many ways, the great white whale may be compared to Spenser's "blatant beast," who, in *The Faerie Queene* (1590-1596), also represents the indeterminable elusive quarry and also escapes at the end to continue haunting the world. Nor is it surprising that *Moby Dick* is often considered to be "the American epic." The novel is replete with the elements characteristic of that genre: the piling up of classical, biblical, historical allusions to provide innumerable parallels and tangents that have the effect of universalizing the scope of action, the narrator's strong sense of the fatefulness of the events he recounts and his corresponding awareness of his own singular importance as the narrator of momentous—otherwise unrecorded—events, Queequeg as Ishmael's "heroic companion," the "folk" flavor provided by countless proverbial statements, the leisurely pace of the narrative with its frequent digressions and parentheses, the epic confrontation of life and death on a suitably grand stage (the sea) with its consequences for the human city (the *Pequod*), the employment of microcosms to explicate the whole (for example, the painting in the Spouter Inn, the Nantucket pulpit, the crow's nest), epithetical characterization, a cyclic notion of time and events, an epic race of heroes (the Nantucket whalers with their biblical and exotic names), the mystical power of objects (Ahab's chair, the gold coin, or the

Pequod itself), the alienated, sulking hero (Ahab), and the use of lists to enhance the impression of an all-inclusive compass. Finally, *Moby Dick* shares the usually didactic purpose of folk epic; on one level, its purpose is to teach the reader about whales; on another level, it is to inspire the reader to become an epic hero.

All this richness of purpose and presentation is somehow made enticing by Melville's masterly invention of his narrator. Ishmael immediately establishes a comfortable rapport with the reader in the unforgettable opening lines of the novel. He is both the objective observer and a participant in the events observed and recounted, both spectator and narrator. Yet he is much more than the conventional wanderer/witness. As a schoolmaster and sometime voyager, he combines his intellectual knowledge with firsthand experience to make him an informed observer and a convincing, moving reporter. Simply by surviving, he transcends the Byronic heroism of Ahab, as the wholesome overcoming the sinister.

"Critical Evaluation" by Kenneth John Atchity

Bibliography:

Brodhead, Richard H., ed. *New Essays on "Moby Dick."* New York: Cambridge University Press, 1986. Contains essays discussing the complexity of *Moby Dick*'s first sentence, its Calvinist themes, and the multiplicity of sources used by Melville, among other subjects.

James, C. L. R. *Mariners, Renegades, and Castaways.* New York: Allison & Busby, 1985. A powerful reading of *Moby Dick* through the context to twentieth century politics, arguing that Ahab's sway over his crew symbolizes the power of totalitarianism.

Matthiessen, F. O. *American Renaissance.* New York: Oxford University Press, 1941. This book gave a title to the period in which Melville lived and wrote and discusses Melville's work alongside that of Nathaniel Hawthorne, Walt Whitman, Ralph Waldo Emerson, Henry David Thoreau, and others.

Miller, Edwin Haviland. *Melville.* New York: George Braziller, 1975. Psychoanalytic biography of Melville, especially attentive to Melville's relationship with Nathaniel Hawthorne during the time he was composing *Moby Dick*.

Olson, Charles. *Call Me Ishmael.* San Francisco: City Lights Books, 1947. A literary work of art in its own right, written by an influential postmodern American poet, this book is also a piece of first-class literary detective work. Olson tracked down Melville's library a half-century after the author's death, upon which he bases his theories of Melville's compositional process and his use of whaling lore and Shakespeare in *Moby Dick*.

A MODERN INSTANCE

Type of work: Novel
Author: William Dean Howells (1837-1920)
Type of plot: Domestic realism
Time of plot: Nineteenth century
Locale: New England
First published: 1882

Principal characters:
    MARCIA GAYLORD, a small-town young woman
    SQUIRE GAYLORD, her father
    BARTLEY HUBBARD, her husband
    ATHERTON, a Boston lawyer
    BEN HALLECK, a moral man
    KINNEY, a vagabond

The Story:

In the little town of Equity, in northern New England, Bartley Hubbard was an up-and-coming young man. An orphan whose life had so far been one of great promise, he had a free and easy way about him and a ready tongue that made him a general favorite. Squire Gaylord was well pleased with his work as editor of the village paper, the *Free Press*, but not so well pleased when Bartley became engaged to Marcia Gaylord, the squire's only daughter.

One afternoon, Bartley and Marcia went for a sleigh ride. In a swamp, they met another cutter that overturned in deep snow while trying to pass them on the narrow trail. The women in the overturned vehicle were Mrs. Morrison and her daughter Hannah, who worked in the office of the Free Press. Bartley jumped out to help them. Mrs. Morrison got into the cutter by herself. Bartley lifted Hannah Morrison to her place, however, and Marcia was angry enough to participate in their first quarrel.

Hannah was the daughter of the town drunkard. Young Bartley encouraged her greatly, thinking to improve the quality of her work, but she interpreted his interest as love. Her father called on Bartley one morning, drunk as usual, and asked Bartley's intentions toward his daughter. The young editor was so vexed and infuriated that he ejected Hannah's father bodily. His foreman, Henry Bird, in his turn accused Bartley of stealing Hannah's affections. When he hit Bartley in the face, the latter retaliated with an openhanded slap. Henry fell, suffering a concussion when his head hit the floor.

The scandal was immense. Squire Gaylord took a legal view of the possibility that Bird might die. Marcia interpreted the fight as proof of an affair between Bartley and Hannah and broke their engagement. Bartley resigned his job, even though Bird soon recovered. Bartley went to stay with Kinney, a crackerbox philosopher who cooked in a nearby logging camp. At the camp Willett, the owner, came to visit with a fashionable party. Mrs. Macallister, one of the guests, flirted with Bartley, and he tried to curry favor by poking fun at the quaint Kinney. That same night, Bartley and Kinney parted in anger, and the young man walked back to town.

After selling his horse and cutter, Bartley went to the station to catch the Boston train. Marcia caught up with him at the depot. Asking his forgiveness, she begged him to take her back. They were married that same day and left for Boston together. In the city, Bartley went to work. He turned his visit to the logging camp into a feature article which he sold for twenty-five dollars. That was the start of his fairly comfortable, although uncertain, income as a freelance writer. Marcia and he could afford only one room, but they were happy together. Marcia's father, Squire Gaylord, came to see her once, to make certain she was married. He refused to meet her husband again.

About the time Marcia learned that she was pregnant, Bartley was offered a job as managing editor of *Events*, whose publisher was a shrewd, unprincipled man named Witherby. With a regular salary at last, Bartley moved his wife into a private house. In college, Bartley had known Ben Halleck, a member of one of Boston's older families. Marcia knew no one at all, and she often wondered why Bartley did not resume his acquaintance with the Hallecks. Now that Bartley had a better job, he did call on the Hallecks, and they at once befriended the Hubbards. Through them, the young couple also got acquainted with Mr. Atherton, a conservative lawyer. Halleck cared no more for Bartley than he ever had, but he was sorry for the trusting Marcia, saddled with a shallow husband. After the birth of her child, Flavia, Marcia saw less and less of Bartley, who spent many of his evenings away from home.

Witherby offered to sell some stock in the newspaper. For this deal, Bartley borrowed fifteen hundred dollars from Halleck. Before long, he had assumed a prosperous air, and his drinking added greatly to his girth. One night, after a quarrel with Marcia, he stayed out late and became quite drunk. Halleck saw him on the street and rescued him from a policeman. When Halleck took the drunken man back to Marcia, his pity for the poor wife increased.

Kinney, visiting the Hubbards, amused Bartley and another newspaperman with stories of his picturesque life. After he left, Bartley wrote up the tales and sold them to another paper without Kinney's permission. Witherby was upset at seeing Bartley's work in a rival newspaper, and when he learned that his managing editor had written the article in violation of ethical considerations, he dismissed Bartley.

Bartley returned to freelancing. Halleck was absent from the city; hence Bartley could not repay him fifteen hundred dollars. He intended to do so, but he gambled with the money and before long lost several hundred dollars. Atherton and Halleck were confirmed in their suspicions of Bartley's moral weakness. Marcia, returning from the Halleck house one evening, saw a drunken woman on the street. To her surprise, she recognized Hannah Morrison. When she tried to talk with Hannah, the latter insisted that Bartley was to blame for her present status in life. Suspecting and believing the worst of Bartley, Marcia rushed home and accused him of having seduced Hannah. During the ensuing quarrel, they separated, and Bartley took a train for Cleveland.

On the train, Bartley's wallet was stolen; in consequence, he was unable to send money back to Halleck. In Boston, Marcia regretted her hasty conclusions and stayed on at their house awaiting her husband's return. When creditors began to hound her, she enlisted Atherton's sympathetic aid. He and Halleck continued to look after the deserted wife. In time, she thought of Bartley as dead, and Halleck wondered when he would be free to speak to her of his love.

By chance, a western newspaper came into Halleck's hands, a paper in which Bartley had given notice of suit for divorce. Marcia, her small daughter, Squire Gaylord, and Halleck took a train to Indiana to contest the suit. They arrived in time to have the divorce set aside, but during the trial, Marcia's father had a stroke from which he never recovered. After the trial, Bartley drifted further west and became the editor of a weekly paper in Whited Sepulchre, Arizona. He was shot there by a citizen of the town. When Bartley's death was reported, Halleck wondered whether he was morally free to ask Marcia to marry him.

Critical Evaluation:

Born the son of a printer in Ohio, in 1837, William Dean Howells pursued a career in printing, journalism, publishing, and fiction. His career began in his teens and eventually established him as the most influential force in American letters in the latter part of the nineteenth century. During the decade he acted as editor of the prestigious *Atlantic Monthly* (1871-1881), Howells shaped the direction of American literature as perhaps no single person before or since has done. Howells resurrected the writings of such great talents as Herman Melville and Emily Dickinson, who had been either forgotten or overlooked. He mentored several gifted young authors, including Hamlin Garland, Bret Harte, and Stephen Crane, helping to introduce their work to the world, and he acted as confidant and valued critic for two of the literary giants of his time, Samuel Clemens and Henry James. Perhaps most important, Howells explicitly defined the style that dominated American literature in the years following the Civil War.

Howells believed that literature should impart a moral message. He argued that the only way it could convincingly do this was to depict life as real people actually lived it. Like Clemens, Howells rejected the fanciful, sentimental, and melodramatic elements associated with Romantic fiction. Howells disliked works that appealed primarily to readers' emotions, that relied on unrealistic or overblown situations, that featured gaudy heroes and heroines, and that suggested that romantic love, or some idealized code of conduct, such as chivalry, was an appropriate basis for values and goals. Howells believed that works based on such romantic ideals had no connection to the lives of ordinary readers and, consequently, offered them no moral message. According to Howells, the best way to impart a moral was to present situations and characters to which readers could relate. He maintained that the story of highly individualized characters could easily have a general moral so long as the story rang true. Howells emphasized character over plot and the commonplace over the unusual. For Howells, such an approach created a more democratic literature, which reflected the needs (and the best interests) of the American reader.

Howells' *A Modern Instance* exemplifies the principles of realism. Its characters are ordinary people with rather modest aspirations, numerous failings, and complex personalities and motivations. Each has a unique view of the world, and all show little ability to see beyond their own narrow perspectives; consequently, they frequently act impulsively, often against their own self-interests. By the same token, the plot of the novel, rather than reflecting some highly structured scheme, seems to evolve naturally, driven by the personalities of its characters and by the sorts of coincidences common to everyday life. For example, Bartley does not really plan to leave Marcia. When he discovers that his wallet has been stolen in Chicago, Bartley reacts to this chance occurrence by choosing a path he almost certainly would not have otherwise taken. Bartley's decision to continue westward, as well as Marcia's stubborn faith in his imminent return, depend on the unique personality traits of these two individualized characters, namely Bartley's desire to avoid conflict and follow the path of least resistance and Marcia's tendency to deny any evidence that threatens her unrealistic image of herself and her marriage.

As an early example of realism, *A Modern Instance* breaks new ground in its techniques and subject matter. Howells' novel is quite innovative in its reliance on psychology, a hallmark of realistic fiction. Howells attempts to portray the processes of perception and judgment; his effort leads to one of the most vivid descriptions of becoming drunk ever penned. Moreover, Howells repeatedly focuses on decision making, depicting it to be often a process beyond his characters' conscious control. For instance, Bartley gives little if any forethought to marrying Marcia. He capriciously decides to propose when he is feeling ill, and she fails to offer the sympathy he craves from her. Howells portrays Bartley's momentous decision as a response to an extremely insignificant and transitory discomfort—but it is exactly the discomfort that Bartley's unique psyche cannot bear.

While Howells is often accused of being overly prudish in his criticism and his fiction, in *A Modern Instance* he tackles a traditionally taboo subject, divorce. Inspired by the ancient play *Medea* and by several arguments he had witnessed between a couple while he was vacationing, Howells determined to deal with this subject, which he thought important to American life. Divorce was not given serious literary treatment again until well into the twentieth century. Moreover, given the strictures of his time, Howells deals as best he might with the more passionate side of human nature. While it is not directly stated, sexual desire clearly forms a major impetus for Bartley and Marcia's decision to marry.

Howell's principles were readily adopted by most of the great writers of his age; however, many soon began moving from Howells' brand of realism into naturalism, a trend that Howells found distasteful and argued vehemently against. Naturalism, while retaining the commonplace situations and ordinary characters of realism, depicts individuals as relatively powerless entities swept along by immense social and natural forces and driven by passions and urges beyond their control. For Howells, such a fatalistic view of life removed the moral component of literature.

Naturalism suggests that people are not responsible for their situations, actions, or even choices. Nevertheless, some of Howells' favorite writers, most notably Crane, were solidly naturalistic, and others, Clemens among them, became more naturalistic as their careers progressed. Howells himself struggled to keep naturalistic themes from creeping into his own fiction. The difficulty of this struggle is evident in *A Modern Instance*, which reveals many naturalistic elements, particularly toward the end of the novel. For example, as the novel progresses, Bartley's drinking increases, causing more difficulties for him and Marcia. Bartley's drinking problem can just as easily be read as an inherited predisposition as it can be read as a flawed moral choice. Indeed, Howells risks denying his characters responsibility by taking such great care to create unique psychological underpinnings for their actions. Many of the characters' personalities—especially those of Marcia, Bartley, and Ben Halleck—seem to have been shaped greatly by the circumstances of their upbringing and events in their early lives. As a result, much of their behavior seems to stem less from conscious choice than from deeply rooted anxieties they cannot control.

"Critical Evaluation" by Tom E. Hockersmith

Bibliography:
Cady, Edwin H. "The Chief American Realist: 1881-1885." In *The Road to Realism: The Early Years, 1837-1885, of William Dean Howells*. Syracuse, N.Y.: Syracuse University Press, 1956. Places the novel in the broader context of Howells' life and work while offering a general critical overview of the novel.
Smith, Geoffrey D. "Bartley Hubbard and Behavioral Art in William Dean Howells's *A Modern Instance*." *Studies in American Fiction* 7 (1979): 83-91. Explores Howells' techniques for depicting psychological processes in the novel.
Spangler, George M. "The Idea of Degeneration in American Fiction, 1880-1940." *English Studies* 70, no. 5 (October, 1989): 407-435. Discusses the novel's place in American literature and identifies it as beginning a reversal of the traditional theme of regeneration. According to Spangler, Bartley Hubbard's degeneration paves the way for a new type of character, one that dominates much of the great fiction of succeeding years.

Tavernier-Courbin, Jacqueline. "Towards the City: Howells' Characterization in *A Modern Instance*." *Modern Fiction Studies* 24, no. 1 (Spring, 1978): 111-127. Examines the novel in the light of the conventions of nineteenth century popular fiction. According to Tavernier-Courbin, Howells uses setting and character in the novel to undermine typical romantic stereotypes.

Wright, Ellen F. "Given Bartley, Given Marcia: A Reconsideration of Howells' *A Modern Instance*." *Texas Studies in Language and Literature* 23, no. 2 (Summer, 1981): 214-231. By examining the many married couples in the novel, Wright argues that Howells does not intend to indict either American culture in general or the institution of marriage in particular.

MODERN LOVE

Type of work: Poetry
Author: George Meredith (1828-1909)
First published: 1862

George Meredith's *Modern Love* is his longest poem, and when it was published (a year after his wife died), it was seen as a disturbed work. It is a sonnet sequence consisting of fifty separate sonnets rhyming *abba cddc effe ghhg*. Meredith's sixteen-line sonnets—a variation on the traditional fourteen-line sonnet—provide an apt structure for presenting interconnected but frequently contradictory feelings and reactions. Noted for their complex imagery, these sonnets present the speaker's diverse emotions, which are constantly shifting, subtly and not so subtly, in both intensity and distance from his subject. The poem is about his love for his wife.

He has discovered that his wife has been unfaithful, and to the husband, like a courtly lover, her faithlessness is unforgivable. Her deception is devastating. If her appearance has nothing to do with reality, he is without any moorings at all. He does not know himself without her. When man is nothing more than clay and discord, death is preferable, but of death and oblivion he wants no part. Unlike May, whose annual glory defies the passage of time, the husband's foot rests precariously on a unique, but unverifiable past that may neither be seen clearly nor blotted out. It remains to mock him, unless he wishes to consign himself and the past that has created him to oblivion.

The brilliance and lucidity of the speaker make it too easy for the reader to forget that although two people are engaged in the most personal of conflicts, only one side, the husband's, is available. The husband, the speaker in *Modern Love*, shifts from third to first person and back as convenience serves ("he" and "I" are mingled throughout the sonnet sequence), and the imagery becomes more densely evocative the more closely it is examined. When the poem was published, Meredith was accused of indecency. The public was not ready to accept the intimate, passionate relationship between a husband and wife as proper subject matter for a writer. The fact that Meredith's first marriage to Mary Peacock Nicolls ended in separation and her death in 1861, complicated critical opinion even more. Since the poem was read biographically, recognition of *Modern Love* as a powerful work of art complete unto itself was hard to win. After the 1862 edition, the poem was not reprinted until 1892. Worse yet, the poem was misread as somehow didactic.

The husband perceives love as the earthly state most nearly divine, the loss of which would be intolerable. Such love is a garden, suggesting both the garden of Eden and the gardens of pagan mythology. When it becomes blighted, however, this garden is most deadly, not only to the lovers (in this case husband and wife, referred to as Madam) but also to any unsuspecting serpents. The golden-haired Lady is a serpent because she is the other woman. The other man, who in this double set of triangles comes first, will undoubtedly meet a serpent's fate and be crushed beneath a heel until he cannot feel or, if he is so unfortunate as to be callous, until he can.

These two, the other man and the other woman, have hearts into which despair can be, and finally is, struck. The wife does not hesitate, but crushes the other woman's rose under her heel as if she were crushing the Lady herself out of her husband's life. Such serpents are, however, innocuous in comparison to the serpent struggle between the wife and the husband (see sonnets 1, 6, 14, 34, and 44), who apostrophizes to Raphael, the Italian painter, whose figures never show signs of inner conflict (sonnet 33). Although the speaker occasionally, briefly, quotes his wife directly (sonnets 9, 34, 35, 42, and 49) and seems to be addressing her at other times (sonnets 6, 8, 9, 11, 14, 24, 25, and 26), *Modern Love* remains the husband's soliloquy, a soliloquy where there should be a dialogue. The husband's passionate, at times violent, intensity leads him to accuse his wife of killing their love (sonnet 11). He shows her love letters she has written, but not all to him (sonnet 15). At another moment, he is aware that he should be able to give charity, when he must ask for charity in return (sonnet 20). In sonnet 43, he recognizes their joint responsibility:

> I see no sin:
> The wrong is mixed. In tragic life, God wot,
> No villain need be! Passions spin the plot:
> We are betrayed by what is false within.

His desperate need to survive the truth, to reconsider his marriage and the love between him and his wife (which he had accepted as the greatest treasure life had to offer), and to escape despair requires some greater absolute than their love. Long ago, he had casually admitted that love dies, but at that time he had never thought much about such a possibility (sonnet 16). The husband, who often tries to assume a position of objectivity, seems to attain compassionate detachment only with his wife's suicide. (That *Modern Love* should be examined as poetry, not biography, is indicated by the fact that there is no evidence that Meredith's first wife committed suicide.)

The husband's struggle with the discouraging truth of self-recognition is revealed. To deny him the ability to describe himself in the third person as well as in the first would not only rob the poem of part of its richness but undercut the variety of the speaker's reactions: noble, ignoble, cruel, compassionate, rigid, yearning, righteous, wrenching. The emotional crisis the speaker is undergoing is such that there is no way to predict how he will react. The husband's approach to the realization that there is no crime—that neither of them is to blame for the other's actions (sonnet 43)—is in no way direct. His lament is that a woman's intellect cannot function independently of her physiology and that the undue subtleties resulting from this given lead to her destruction. He assumes that woman needs "more brain." Such an assertion attests the fact that his own knowledge is still incomplete, his own sense mixed up in his senses (sonnet 48). Initially, the husband saw complete ruin: himself and his wife lying like Tristran and Iseult (sonnet 1). He believes that their love, in spite of all its vicissitudes, is somehow immortal, hence the allusion to Tristan and Iseult, the couple who most exemplifies courtly love.

Husband and wife, however, no longer have a common fate or share a common history. His wife does not know what is going on in his mind, and her lack of awareness, genuine or feigned, infuriates him. When their superficial smiles meet, his inward rage churns until the world he sees is blood-stained (sonnet 2). While he rages against her, she, completely unaware of his inward soliloquy, sits laughing gently with another (sonnet 6). He is still desirous of his wife. She has meaning for him that no one else has. He nevertheless asserts that he knows it is too late to seek the spiritual in love when "the fire is dying in the grate" (sonnet 4), even though the throes of his passion remain anything but cool. Her beauty enables him to see her with the eyes of other men (sonnet 7). The fact that what is familiar to him is currently even more familiar to another man, however, so distorts his perception that he asks himself if they can actually be married. Only later, in the second part of *Modern Love* (sonnets 27-39), does he see her once again as his wife and address her as such (sonnet 33).

The sea imagery in *Modern Love*, including the wreck, is critical. Wrecked or not, wicked or innocent, the speaker will be taken as nothing less than pilot of his own life, no matter what the effect of the wind and the waves. Resolved against ever again leaving his heart in the control of another (sonnet 19), he enters with the Lady in the game of love or sentiment (sonnet 28). There is nothing here to carry him beyond the physical. Even a love seemingly superior in every way to young love has insufficient weight and force (sonnet 39). He is helplessly adrift. Dreading that his original love is still alive prevents him from attending to a new one. How, he asks, can he love one woman and simultaneously be jealous of another (sonnet 40)? Love is increasingly contemplated in the purely earthly realm where a person is nothing but clay. In struggling against his fate, the individual who has become half-serpent, like the Fiend (sonnet 33), may grow again to be half human. From the very beginning of *Modern Love*, as in the courtly love tradition, love is associated with death. Even dead, love is terrible in its effect. Aside from the imagery linking love and death, as the sonnet sequence develops the wife is linked with images of death, losing substance, never joining her husband's present.

Toward the end of the summer, the husband and wife have no shared joys. They are present in the same place and at peace, but not together (sonnet 47). The speaker has learned that passion without love allays no torments (sonnet 32), and the Lady, an asp, is no antidote for the "serpent bites" inflicted by Madam. The husband seeks to salvage his capacity to love. Beneath his agony and frustration, a belief in the reality of his past love is gradually to be perceived. Was this love lost (sonnet 50) because it did not develop in time?

He talks about his wife going among "the children of illusion" (sonnet 12); her illusion is no longer his. He marvels that men should prize the love of woman (sonnet 31), but this feeling is only sour grapes, and he admits that being approved by his Lady is not half as fine as being loved (sonnet 31). Midnight may perhaps be regarded as the hour of truth, or less melodramatically, the moment when pretense may no longer pass for reality. Husband and wife have succeeded in making others envy their love (sonnet 17) but in the country at Christmas, he recognizes that while they have fooled others, the abyss of midnight, in which they will have to recognize themselves as hypocrites, still awaits them (sonnet 23). Later, as the clock approaches midnight (sonnet 41), he can no longer have any doubt about the death of love, and finally, he recalls that it was "the middle of the night" when he heard her call just before she died (sonnet 48).

The fact that there is a reference to spring in sonnet 11, to Christmas in sonnet 23, and to summer in sonnet 45 has lead some critics to assert that *Modern Love* covers a little more than a year, but a chronology of the poem provides no insight into the husband's anguished consciousness that is at issue in this poem. Similarly, seeing the poem as divided into three parts (1-26, 27-39, 40-50) does not provide much insight.

In sonnet 43, the images of love and death and water are synthesized. The force of the wind impels the waves which, forced into hissing serpents, leave their mark far up on the sand that they momentarily devour. The same image is used at the end:

> In tragic hints here see what evermore
> Moves dark as yonder midnight's ocean's force,
> Thundering like ramping hosts of warrior horse,
> To throw that faint thin line upon the shore!

There is an attempt on the speaker's part to draw some kind of moral in the last two sonnets. Only confusion results. The major achievement of this poem is its depiction of the vivid intensity of a husband's failing love for his wife. *Modern Love* remains an oddly undated poem, written one hundred years ahead of its time.

Carol Bishop

Bibliography:
Fletcher, Ian, ed. *Meredith Now: Some Critical Essays*. New York: Barnes & Noble Books, 1971. John Lucas' essay, "Meredith as Poet," is particularly useful.
Priestley, J. B. *George Meredith*. New York: Macmillan, 1970. First published in 1926, contains useful information on Meredith's life and insight into his work. Index.
Trevelyan, G. M. *The Poetry and Philosophy of George Meredith*. New York: Russell & Russell, 1966. First published in 1920, provides helpful commentary on Meredith's poetry from a contemporary admirer.
Williams, Joan, ed. *Meredith: The Critical Heritage*. New York: Barnes & Noble Books, 1971. Provides a lengthy, invaluable record of the early criticism, including Algernon Charles Swinburne's and Robert Louis Stevenson's different statements of defense of Meredith against the charge of indecency.
Wright, Walter F. *Art and Substance in George Meredith: A Study in Narrative*. Lincoln: University of Nebraska Press, 1953. Argues for a congruity between Meredith's emotional life, intellectual life, and creative work. Index.

MOLL FLANDERS

Type of work: Novel
Author: Daniel Defoe (1660-1731)
Type of plot: Picaresque
Time of plot: Seventeenth century
Locale: England and the American colonies
*First published: The Fortunes and Misfortunes of the Famous Moll Flanders, Who Was Born
in Newgate, and During a Life of Continued Variety, for Threescore Years, Besides Her
Childhood, Was Twelve Years a Whore, Five Times a Wife (Thereof Once to Her Own
Brother), Twelve Years a Thief, Eight Years a Transported Felon in Virginia, at Last Grew
Rich, Lived Honest, and Died a Penitent. Written from Her Own Memorandums,* 1722

Principal characters:
MOLL FLANDERS, a rogue
ROBIN, her first husband
A SEA CAPTAIN, Moll's half brother and husband
JEMMY E., a rogue

The Story:

When her mother was transported to the Colonies as a felon, eighteen-month-old Moll
Flanders was left without family or friends to care for her. For a time, she was befriended by a
band of gypsies, who deserted her in Colchester. There the child was a charge of the parish.
Becoming a favorite of the wife and daughters of the mayor, Moll received gentle treatment and
much attention and flattery.

At the age of fourteen, Moll Flanders was again left without a home. When her indulgent
instructor died, she was taken in service by a kindly woman of means, receiving instruction
along with the daughters of the family. Moll was superior to these daughters in all but wealth.
During her residence there, she lost her virtue to the oldest son of the family and secretly became
his mistress. Later, Robin, the youngest son, made her a proposal of marriage, and she accepted
him. Five years later, Robin died. Soon afterward, Moll married a spendthrift draper, who
quickly depleted her savings and was imprisoned. In the meantime, Moll took lodgings at the
Mint. Passing as a widow, she called herself Mrs. Flanders.

Her next venture in matrimony was with a sea captain, with whom she sailed to the Virginia
colony. There she discovered to her extreme embarrassment that she was married to her own
half brother. After eight years of residence in Virginia, she returned to England to take up her
residence at Bath. In due time, she became acquainted with a gentleman whose wife was
demented. Moll helpfully nursed him through a serious illness. Later, she became his mistress.
When she became pregnant, she made arrangements for her lying-in, sent the child to nurse,
and rejoined her companion. During the six years in which they lived together, she gave birth
to three children and saved enough money to support herself after the gentleman had regretted
his indiscretions and left her.

Next, the ambitious woman met a banker, with whom she carried on a mild flirtation, but she
left him to marry an Irishman named Jemmy E., supposedly a very wealthy gentleman of
Lancashire. Moll had allowed him to believe she had means. She soon learned that her new
husband was penniless. He had played the same trick on her that she had used on him. Moll and
Jemmy E. were both rogues and therefore made a congenial couple, but eventually they decided

to separate; he followed his unlawful profession of highway robbery, and she returned to the city. After Jemmy had left her, Moll found that she was again to become a mother. Lying-in at the house of a midwife, Moll delivered a healthy boy, who was boarded out.

In the meantime, Moll Flanders had been receiving letters from her admirer, the bank clerk. They met at an inn and were married there. On the day after the ceremony, she saw her Lancashire husband, the highwayman, in the courtyard of the inn, and she was able to save him from arrest. For five years, until his death, Moll lived with the banker in great happiness. After his death, she sold her property and took lodgings. Forty-eight years old and with two children as dependents, she was prompted by the devil to steal a bundle from an apothecary shop. Next, she stole a necklace from a pretty little girl on her way home from dancing school. Therefore, Moll Flanders embarked on a twelve-year period as a thief. Sometimes she disguised herself in men's clothing. A chance encounter with a gentleman at Bartholomew Fair resulted in an affair, which the two carried on for some time. After a period of apprenticeship, Moll became the richest thief in all England. Her favorite disguise was that of a beggar woman.

Finally, she was seized while trying to steal two pieces of silk brocade and was imprisoned in Newgate prison. There she saw again her former husband, the highwayman, committed at Newgate for a robbery on Hounslow Heath. Before going up for trial and sentence, Moll repented of her sins; nevertheless, she was sentenced to death by the court. Through the kind offices of a minister, however, Moll Flanders, now truly repentant, was given a reprieve. The next day, she watched her fellow prisoners being carried away in carts for the fate that had been spared her. She was finally sentenced to transportation to America.

The highwayman, with whom she had become reconciled, was awarded a like sentence. The pair embarked for Virginia in the same ship; they had made all arrangements for a comfortable journey and stocked themselves with the tools and materials necessary for running a plantation in the new world. Forty-two days after leaving an Irish port, they arrived in Virginia. Once ashore, Moll found that her mother had died. Her half brother, to whom she had once been married, and her son were still living near the spot where she had disembarked.

Not yet wishing to meet her relatives and not desiring to be known as a transported criminal in America, she arranged for transportation to the Carolina colony. After crossing Chesapeake Bay, she and the highwayman found the ship already overloaded. They decided to stay in Maryland and set up a plantation there. With two servants and fifty acres of land under cultivation, they soon prospered. Then Moll arranged an interview with her son in Virginia across the bay.

In due course, she learned that her mother had willed her a plantation on the York River, a plantation complete with stock and servants. She presented one of the stolen watches that she had brought from London to her son. After five weeks, she returned to Maryland, where she and her husband became wealthy and prosperous planters of good repute throughout all the Colonies. This prosperity was augmented by the arrival of a second cargo of goods from England, for which Moll had arranged before she sailed. In the meantime, the man who had been both brother and husband to Moll died, and she was able to see her son without any embarrassment.

At the age of seventy years, Moll returned to England. Her husband soon joined her there, and they resolved to spend the rest of their lives in repentance for their numerous sins.

Critical Evaluation:

As the full original title suggests, the heroine of the story is perhaps the world's best-known female picaro. This book is so convincingly written and contains such a wealth of intimate detail that the reader may conclude that it must be true.

Ever since it was first published in 1722, the reading public has enjoyed *Moll Flanders* as the lusty, energetic tale of a seventeenth century adventuress and manipulator. Many readers have assumed the story is true biography. Daniel Defoe himself rather coyly suggests as much, perhaps because he feared such a scandalous story could not be published or would not be popular if it were seen as the work of the imagination.

In this as in his other great novels, such as *Robinson Crusoe* (1719) and *A Journal of the Plague Year* (1722), Defoe achieves his realistic effect by incorporating a wealth of authentic detail. Having been a pamphleteer and journalist much of his life, Defoe knew how well that the concrete fact and the specific example build plausibility. He has Moll relate her remarkable story simply, thoroughly, and with candor. She is literal-minded and bothers little with description or metaphor. (In his preface, Defoe claims to have cleaned up the language and omitted some of the more "vicious part of her life"; thus Moll's sexual adventures are related in curious, sometimes amusing circumlocutions.) Moll sticks mainly to the stark realities of her life except for passages in which she moralizes about her misdeeds.

Despite the verisimilitude, however, there is a problem of tone that frequently puzzles the modern reader and has stirred a lively controversy among critics. The question may be stated thus: Is the story full of conscious irony, or is it told in utter sincerity? If the former is the case, most scholars agree that *Moll Flanders* is a masterwork of social commentary and of fictional art. If the latter, there are lapses in the author's moral scheme.

The problem centers more on Moll's attitude than her actions. Given her situation—that of a woman of no status but with large ambitions—her behavior is entirely plausible. In her childhood, Moll is dependent for her survival upon the whims and kindnesses of strangers. By the time she is eight years old, she is already determined to be a "gentlewoman"—an ambition very nearly impossible to fulfill in seventeenth century England when one has neither family nor, more important, money. She is quick to recognize the value of money in assuring not only one's physical security but also one's place in the world—and she aims for a comfortable place. Money thus becomes her goal and eventually her god. To attain it, she uses whatever means are at hand; as a beautiful woman, sex is the handiest means available. When, after a number of marriages and other less legitimate alliances, sex is no longer a salable commodity, she turns to thieving and rapidly becomes a master of the trade.

Readers know from other of Defoe's writings that the author sympathized with the plight of women in his society; education and most trades (except the oldest profession) were closed to them. For the most part, their welfare was entirely dependent upon that of their husbands or of other men in their lives. As a hardheaded pragmatist who finds herself in straitened circumstances, Moll is much akin to Becky Sharp of William Makepeace Thackeray's *Vanity Fair* (1847-1848) and Scarlett O'Hara of Margaret Mitchell's *Gone with the Wind* (1936); all three use their ingenuity to survive in a hostile world, and although readers do not entirely condone their behavior, they can understand it.

After Moll has acted, however, she reflects; it is this reflection that poses a problem. For convenience, she marries the younger brother of the man who first seduced her. After he dies, she remarks that "He had been really a very good husband to me, and we lived very agreeably together," but then she quickly complains that because he had not had time to acquire much wealth, she was "not much mended by the match." Another five-year marriage also ends in her widowhood; she wastes not a word in grieving the husband who has given her "an uninterrupted course of ease and content," but laments the loss of his money at excessive length. Soon afterward, she steals a gold necklace from a child and admits that she was tempted to kill the child to prevent any outcry. She rationalizes that "I only thought I had given the parents a just reproof of their negligence in leaving the poor lamb to come home by itself, and it would teach them to take more care another time."

These recollections are told from the point of view of a seventy-year-old woman. She spends a good deal of time explaining that poverty and fear of poverty drove her to all her wickedness; yet, she never admits that even when she is relatively secure, she keeps on scheming and thieving. Like many other entrepreneurs, she has come to find excitement and fulfillment in the turning of the profit, the successful clinching of a deal, the accumulation of wealth for its own sake. Although she repents her flagrant sins—deception, thieving, whoring—she apparently never recognizes the sin of her spirit in basing all human relationships upon their monetary worth. Furthermore, although she closes her account by declaring that she and her husband are "resolved to spend the remainder of our years in sincere penitence for the wicked lives we have lived," they are now free from want, partly because of an inheritance but also because of the proceeds from her years as a thief. Readers see no indication that penitence goes any deeper than a rather gratified feeling that she has made peace with her Maker (a peace made, by the way, in Newgate prison while Moll was under sentence of death). There is no evidence that she intends to make restitution of stolen goods or apply herself in positive good works to offset some of her wicked deeds.

The question, then, is whether Defoe expects readers to see the irony in what one critic has called Moll's moral "muddle"; or whether he is so outraged at what poverty and the lack of opportunity can do that he himself fails to see the lapses in her moral system. A few clues are presented from Defoe's life, but they are contradictory. Like Moll, he was frequently haunted by poverty and spent months in the hell of Newgate. His steadfast stand as a Dissenter (which made him a lifelong outsider in English society); his humane views of the treatment of the poor, of women, of the downtrodden; his dogged and successful efforts to pay every penny of a £17,000 bankruptcy—all give evidence of a man of high and stern principles. On the other hand, he worked for the Tories, then for the Whigs, writing with passion and conviction on both sides of controversial issues; and in his numerous business ventures, he was not above swindling (even his own mother-in-law). His own dreams of status are attested by his love for trade—"the whore I doated on"—and his addition of "De" to his name (his father was James Foe) to provide a touch of gentility.

Critics have not resolved the debate over morality and irony in the novel. Few, however, will dispute that it is a fascinating account. It has held the attention of readers for centuries. Virginia Woolf called *Moll Flanders* one of the "few English novels which we can call indisputably great."

"Critical Evaluation" by Sally Buckner

Bibliography:
Backscheider, Paula R. *Daniel Defoe: Ambition and Innovation.* Louisville: University of Kentucky Press, 1986. Provides biographical data and critical interpretations of Defoe's novels, placing emphasis on his innovative point of view.
Bell, Ian A. *Defoe's Fiction.* New York: Barnes & Noble Books, 1985. Studies the elements of Defoe's writing style and characters. Discusses the problem of morality in *Moll Flanders*.
Boardman, Michael M. *Defoe and the Use of Narrative.* New Brunswick, N.J.: Rutgers University Press, 1985. Discusses Daniel Defoe's narrative technique. Focuses on how Defoe structures his stories.

Defoe, Daniel. *Moll Flanders*. New York: Alfred A. Knopf, 1991. A good version of the original text.

Novak, Maximillian. *Realism, Myth and History in Defoe's Fiction*. Lincoln: University of Nebraska Press, 1983. An excellent starting place. Discusses the author's use of realistic characters, such as Moll Flanders, and discusses how Defoe overcomes the myth of female inferiority by having Moll succeed in realistic situations.

Richetti, John J. *Daniel Defoe*. Boston: Twayne, 1987. Examines Defoe's process of writing and plot development.

Starr, G. A. *Defoe and Causitry*. Princeton, N.J.: Princeton University Press, 1991. Discusses *Moll Flanders* and how Moll creates her many problems by her own choices and bad decisions.

MOLLOY

Type of work: Novel
Author: Samuel Beckett (1906-1989)
Type of plot: Absurdist
Time of plot: Mid-twentieth century
Locale: Indeterminate
First published: 1951 (English translation, 1955)

Principal characters:

MOLLOY, a derelict old man
A and C, two men observed by Molloy
LOUSSE, an old widow
JACQUES MORAN, a man assigned to look for Molloy
JACQUES MORAN, Moran's son
YOUDI, Moran's employer
GABER, Youdi's messenger

The Story:

Chapter 1. Molloy had been in his mother's room, having been brought there after he ceased to walk. He was obliged to write out the story of how he ended there under orders from a thirsty man who collected his pages once a week on Sundays. He had been remembering what happened to bring him to this room. He remembered that he had been on a hilltop from which he watched two men, A and C, walking toward each other along a country road, who met, exchanged a few words, and then went their separate ways. It was after he watched this encounter that Molloy decided to go on a quest for his mother. With his crutches fastened to his bicycle, he set off, but when he reached the walls of his town, he was arrested and questioned by a hostile policeman. After his release, he felt unwell, wandered to the countryside, and then returned to the town, where he ran over a dog. The dog's owner, an old widow called Lousse, decided to adopt him as a replacement for her lost pet. Lousse caused Molloy to recall other love affairs, and he realized they all reminded him of his mother. Although Lousse gave him a haven in her garden, Molloy felt trapped and threatened, and he worried that Lousse was drugging his food. Having lost his bicycle, Molloy escaped Lousse's house on his crutches. He wandered around, considered suicide, and then found himself at the seaside, where he renewed the stock of sucking stones that kept him from feeling hungry. He spent some time trying to devise a mathematical order for the carrying and sucking of the stones. He moved into a forest, but his progress became slower and slower as he became more decrepit. He found a charcoal burner in the forest, whom he assaulted after the charcoal burner made unwanted advances. No longer able to hobble, Molloy crawled and then sank to the bottom of a ditch at the very edge of the forest. It was from this ditch that he was somehow rescued, brought to his mother's room, and ordered to write his story.

Chapter 2. Jacques Moran was a fastidious man, a scrupulous Catholic, and an affluent householder. He had a subservient housekeeper named Martha and a closely monitored young son, Jacques. Moran was employed in an agency by a man named Youdi, who paid him to detect and track down certain individuals. It was Youdi who asked for the report about the events that began one Sunday in summer when Gaber, a thirsty agency messenger, came to him with an urgent assignment. Moran was to leave at once with his son to look for a man named Molloy.

Disquieted and confused by these instructions, Moran rapidly became unwell. Not soon after starting out, he hurt his leg and sent his son to the nearest town to buy a bicycle. When a man with a stick approached Moran, he gave him bread and broke off a heavy stick for himself. The next day, another more respectable-looking man, who was looking for the man with the stick, approached Moran. Moran clubbed him to death. After being away for three days, his son returned with the bicycle; Moran and his son quarreled violently and the son abandoned Moran. Then Gaber appeared with an order for Moran to return home. By this time, Moran had deteriorated to such a degree that he was barely able to get home. He attempted to devise a mathematical order for the wearing of his shirt for his journey and grew even more decrepit, eventually finding it difficult to walk. He subsisted on roots and berries and became such a suspicious character that a farmer accosted him and ordered him off his land. When spring arrived, Moran finally returned home, but he found the house deserted. He began to write his report.

Critical Evaluation:

Samuel Beckett, who was awarded the Nobel Prize in Literature in 1969, is best known for his avant-garde plays, but he is also considered one of the most important experimental novelists of the twentieth century. *Molloy*, the first novel of a trilogy that is followed by *Malone Dies* (1951), and *The Unnamable* (1953), is considered his single greatest work of fiction. Although *Molloy* has lent itself to many interpretations, including Jungian, Freudian, Christian, and existential, Beckett has made it impossible for any one perspective entirely to explain his novel. He has deliberately created an ambiguous text, which, although it includes mythic and philosophical aspects, constantly subverts the attempt to secure clarity and order. Beckett blends irony, despair, lyrical poetry, tragedy, and an anarchic comedy in a narrative that is both realistic and dreamlike. The work can appear to be both about everything that matters and about nothing at all.

Although there are many theories concerning the meaning of the novel, a useful starting point is to explore its structure, which appears to be one of division. The small episode involving the characters of A and C at the beginning of the novel is often seen as an outline for the novel as a whole, because it gives us an image of twoness. The novel itself is divided into two chapters of roughly equal length. Like A and C, who come from opposite directions, the two first-person narratives, one by Molloy and one by Moran, seem to represent opposite points of view.

Each section of this novel is a psychological character study of a different man. The first chapter, narrated by Molloy, dispenses with traditional storytelling, instead using an unpara-graphed, rambling, stream-of-consciousness style. Molloy is a dilapidated vagabond, with little sense of personal worth or significance. Obsessed with excrement and bodily functions, often helpless, moody, and confused, he seems to have entered a second childhood. Miserable, despairing, surrounded by a clutter of unmanageable objects, Molloy finds time to be slow, empty, and punctuated by trivial flurries of fruitless energy. He is filled with anxiety and boredom. Although he still possesses an astute analytical mind, he is utterly convinced that his experience is incomprehensible, and he ends up using his sharp intellect to sort out matters of tremendous inconsequence, such as the order of his sucking stones. Molloy does pursue one real goal, that of being reunited with his mother, with whom he has a love-hate relationship and who is psychologically present in all his relationships with women, but his quest is only ambiguously resolved by his return to his mother's room. Molloy's narrative also touches on the master-narratives of such figures as Ulysses, Aeneas, Christ, and Dante, but Beckett deploys these parallels tentatively or even ironically. Although Molloy represents a kind of life force, eternally ongoing even when only going in circles, the sense of continuation must always take into account the desolate nature of his existence.

Molloy is obsessed with his mother; Moran is a father living in a world of fathers. The sole woman in his life is a servant, Martha. His employer, Youdi, suggests the Hebrew God Yahweh, with Gaber as the angel Gabriel. To further consolidate this hint of a theological order, Moran also consults with the local priest, Father Ambrose. Moran exists within a network of conformity, religious scruples, routines, and material possessions, at the center of which is the authority of the father. Within this patriarchal hierarchy, Moran is an obsessional and paranoid domestic tyrant, punctilious to the point of sadism in his role as a father to his own resentful son. As soon as he is sent on his quest for Molloy, however, Moran begins to undergo an identity crisis. One can interpret Moran's story as that of a psychological breakdown, and, more specifically, a breakdown into the side of himself that is like the hobo Molloy. As his journey unfolds, he fails to do his job and instead kills a man in the forest who closely resembles him. Although Moran's character begins with a sense of distinction between himself and Molloy (Moran is the detective, Molloy the object of his search; Moran is a respectable householder, Molloy is homeless) Moran's narrative ultimately undercuts these surface distinctions as the various meanings that have given shape and coherence to his life fail him. Increasingly, Molloy becomes a reference with which to understand what is happening to Moran. Moran's journey, which can be said to be a journey into his own unconscious, is one of disintegration and loss. It is significant that it is only when Moran has psychically dissolved into Molloy that we find a reference to a mother—the earth-mother or "turdy Madonna." Moran's conventionally successful adult persona is exposed as a false self, and as his identity merges with Molloy's, the division between the two narratives is called into question.

Molloy and Moran can be viewed as one of Beckett's famous "pseudocouples," that is, as two parts of the same psyche. Their narratives features many parallel details: Both Moran and Molloy are in a house writing; both have a visitor who is always thirsty; both assault someone in the forest; both ride a bicycle and use crutches; both follow a pattern of quest, disintegration, and failure; and both circle back home. Moran's search for Molloy and Molloy's search for his mother can be viewed as the same quest pursued on different levels, and for both the creative activity of writing is the end product of their quest. Molloy, however, remains the foundation of the novel, especially since Moran disintegrates, and the style with which he tells his story evolves into that of Molloy. Although Molloy appears to be older and more sickly than Moran, a Moran yet-to-come, he also seems to be archaeologically first, existing in an earlier, repressed layer of Moran's unconscious. Considered in this light, *Molloy* is above all a psychological study.

Margaret Boe Birns

Bibliography:
Abbott, H. Porter. *The Fiction of Samuel Beckett, Form and Effect*. Berkeley: University of California Press, 1973. Examines Beckett as a cunning literary strategist who wrote with an acute awareness of the effect his fiction had on its audience. Includes a useful examination of the parallels in the two stories of Moran and Molloy.
Astro, Alan. *Understanding Samuel Beckett*. Columbia: University of South Carolina Press, 1990. Offers an accessible analysis of *Molloy* and suggests that incomprehensibility is one of the novel's major themes. Includes a useful chronology and a brief bibliography up to 1988.

Ben-Zvi, Linda. *Samuel Beckett*. Boston: Twayne, 1986. Concludes that the fictive process is the central issue and is intimately connected to the novel's quest motif. Includes a useful, simple summary of *Molloy*, a chronology, and a selected bibliography.

Fletcher, John. *The Novels of Samuel Beckett*. London: Chatto & Windus, 1964. Important guide to Beckett's fiction, tracing the evolution of the hero in his novels, and concluding that the question of identity is at the center of Beckett's fiction. Includes a helpful analysis of *Molloy*, which Fletcher suggests is Beckett's greatest work of fiction.

Rabinovitz, Rubin. *Innovation in Samuel Beckett's Fiction*. Champaign: University of Illinois Press, 1992. Suggests that what seems baffling or purposeless in Beckett results from judiciously considered formal strategies. Posits that although the novels may seem chaotic and rambling, they are ingenious works of art that use repetition as a deliberate strategy to create structure and meaning.

A MÖLNA ELEGY
Metamorphoses

Type of work: Poetry
Author: Gunnar Ekelöf (1907-1968)
First published: En Mölna-elegi: Metamorfoser, 1960 (English translation, 1984)

In 1946, Gunnar Ekelöf wrote that his *A Mölna Elegy* has as its theme the relativity of time and experiences in the flow of time. The poet attempted to capture one such moment, a cross-section of time, as it were, in which experiences and re-experiences combine, both remaining separate occasions and becoming a unified instant. In the *A Mölna Elegy*, Ekelöf also questions the idea of identity. The poem's first-person narrator represents a variety of personalities who focus on the lack of constancy in life and on the overwhelming transitory nature of existence. These themes, fragmented in the poem's complex structure, imbue the elegy with a tone of uncertainty and mystery. In that tone and in the disjointed structure, the work clearly echoes the style of American, English, and French surrealists and modernist poets of the early twentieth century. Particularly strong influences were T. S. Eliot's *The Waste Land* (1922) and "The Love Song of J. Alfred Prufrock," a poem Ekelöf translated into Swedish.

For English readers, the complexity of *A Mölna Elegy* is partly due to Ekelöf's use of Swedish settings and history as well as to the poem's dense content and form. The poem functions on a number of levels, for it is a web of allusions, symbols, and points-of-view of many voices inside one character's mind. It is not, however, obvious or necessarily important to know, for example, that the elegy is set at the beginning of World War II, as this information provides no insight into the poem's meaning.

It is important to know the *A Mölna Elegy* takes place in a yellow autumn on a jetty on the Mölna river near Stockholm, Sweden. The setting includes descriptions of old buildings on Lidingo Island, symbolizing the posthumous nature of the past, which is only alive in memory. Through the many Roman and Greek classical allusions, the scope of the setting broadens to include the Mediterranean region, reflecting the places Ekelöf visited in his lifelong travels and his interest in classical mythology. The poem begins and ends speaking to a wanderer, the spokesman first saying "Hail" to him and finally "farewell." These lines echo phrases from Roman gravestones. Other allusions refer to William Shakespeare's *The Tempest* (1611), the Bible, Swedish history, and images borrowed from Ekelöf's favorite writers.

A reader need not be aware of each of these allusions to gain an understanding of the poem; however, some attention to the elegy's difficult structure is required to understand the interconnected themes and subjects throughout the poem's sections and subsections. The poem's structure includes monologues, imagined dialogues, marginal headings, parenthetical asides and stage directions, illustrations, and a graphic layout. Meter and phrasing alternately flow and fragment in stream-of-consciousness images, creating a dense and complex interior monologue that comments on the past, present, and imagined future.

The poem opens with the poet sitting on a "bench of the past," writing of the past, merging what he sees with his memory and imagination. He sees a crazy-eyed fool playing wordless, soundless music and rending the illusion of the past in a swirling, mysterious world of nature. The poet's own life, however, stands still, the frame of reference around which all his images revolve. The repeated image of the "flying moment" is introduced when it robs the poet of his future.

The "Wave Song" section describes waves of tides and winds in an "eternal *then* which is

4226

now"; the eternal now is the past arrested in time. The sun sets beyond the river's canal as the poet describes boating scenes and memories of the past summer. Transformation begins in the cool air as past, present, and future merge, as time runs wild and years equal minutes, in the isolation of the moment.

In "Old Actor," an old man has an appointment with the past, but sleep overtakes him as the narrator remembers the actor as Prospero in Shakespeare's *Tempest*. The poet muses on the past and identity, asking "Who were you yourself?" He remembers singing in the past; in the present, clocks tick, and the poet looks through "a blind window" wondering, in the first of many window images, how Prospero can be alive. The actor awakes, and the poet seems to dream of conversations with dead ancestors who recall his childhood.

Sea imagery dominates the "1809" and "1786" sections, linking the past with the poet's Swedish history; treasured objects from various lands, music, sea travel, and stars and storms lead him to reflect on death and the dead. These memories interact and point to ancient, eternal truths evoking the idea of the interdependence of everything. The poet "remembers Time," "carries it" and "hears it" in his present where it brings together the elements of the past. Time is "complete and unknown" in the poet, ending the first half of *A Mölna Elegy*.

A Swedish "King over all that has gone before" reflects on the autumn of his lineage, himself a vestige of past traditions. He speaks of change and of the importance of action to make change, and he says that one cannot find truth in the rational and must be assimilated into the flow of time to avoid being absurd. Other voices merge hours with seasons. Images of children wanting to "hold tight" to the secure present give way to dream images of grief over the passing of history. The poet sees ancient battles and funeral pyres on the beach of the Mölna river, bringing the distant past into the present setting.

The poet's vision, now reanchored in his riverside setting, expands outward and upward, exploring the elements of nature to dramatize the vastness of time and space. Fire and land imagery, in which fire is a purifying force, is juxtaposed against the earlier water images. The "flames and waves" and land merge in a holy union. The poet sees the fire of the sun in perpetual sunset as a desolate city wind brings the poet back to the present. In a feverish state—bringing the natural elements into his own mind—the past, present, and future fuse in a dizzying, flying moment. The poem ends in a brief, calm remembrance of a near-death experience in childhood, followed by a short reflection that life, in the past or future, is still rarely fully experienced.

A result of twenty years work by Ekelöf and ten by the translators, the first English version of *A Mölna Elegy* helped expand Ekelöf's reputation. He is considered Sweden's most important twentieth century poet, highly regarded for his verse, essays, and studies of European and Middle Eastern languages and literature. As American poet Robert Bly observed, there is no English-language poet like him. Throughout his work, Ekelöf emphasized the importance of the subconscious, and critics praise his cohesiveness and his ability to synthesize varying influences, particularly Eastern and Western philosophies, and to draw on Persian, Indian, and Taoist sources. The Hindu notion that alone is the only place an individual can trust became a very important theme in *A Mölna Elegy*.

Yet Ekelöf maintains a distinctly Swedish voice, largely because of his choice of landscapes and characters. He is considered innovative in his technique, especially in his use of musical forms in his verse. Music, particularly singing, is a central motif in *A Mölna Elegy*, for Ekelöf uses music both as sensory imagery and as a means to evoke the past.

Wesley Britton

Bibliography:
Ekelöf, Gunnar. *Skrifter*. Edited and compiled by Reidar Ekner. Vol. 8. Stockholm: Bonniers, 1993. The complete Swedish edition of Ekelöf's works contains *A Mölna Elegy* with the original illustrations.
Sjoberg, Leif. "The Attempted Reconstruction of a Moment." In *A Mölna Elegy: Metamorphoses*, translated by Muriel Rukeyser and Leif Sjoberg. Greensboro, N.C.: Unicorn Press, 1984. The introduction to the first English translation of *A Mölna Elegy* provides a detailed interpretation of the poem and of specific allusions, sources, and possible meanings in the imagery. Includes comments by Ekelöf and a bibliography.
_____. *A Reader's Guide to Gunnar Ekelöf's "A Mölna Elegy."* New York: Twayne, 1973. A book-length overview of the poem, its sources, and the biographical and historical contexts that helped shape it. Sjoberg analyzes the poem section by section and discusses the critical reception to the 1960 edition.
Thygesen, Erik. *Gunnar Ekelöf's Open-Form Poem "A Mölna Elegy": Problems in Genesis, Structure, and Influence*. Uppsala, Sweden: Almqvist & Wiksell, 1985. Based on the author's dissertation, the study compares *A Mölna Elegy* with Eliot's *The Waste Land* and explores Eliot's influence on the Swedish poet. Describes Ekelöf's poem as a "quotation-mosaic" and refutes critics who find the poem a chaotic, structureless reflection of Ekelöf's contradictory notions of art.

THE MONK

Type of work: Novel
Author: Matthew Gregory Lewis (1775-1818)
Type of plot: Gothic
Time of plot: The Spanish Inquisition
Locale: Madrid, Spain
First published: 1796

Principal characters:
FATHER AMBROSIO, the monk
MATILDA (ROSARIO), his evil mistress
LORENZO DE MEDINA, a young nobleman
AGNES, his sister
ANTONIA, a virtuous maiden
ELVIRA, her mother
THE MARQUIS RAYMOND DE LAS CISTERNAS, a wealthy relative of Elvira
MOTHER ST. AGATHA, the prioress of St. Clare Convent
VIRGINIA DE VILLA FRANCA, a beautiful heiress

The Story:

Whenever Father Ambrosio spoke in the church, all Madrid went to hear him. He was the most learned, the most virtuous, and the most admired monk in the city. Such was his purity that he would tolerate no sin in others, and he berated the worshipers viciously. In the audience one day was a young woman named Antonia, who had come to Madrid with her mother to seek the financial aid of their relative, the Marquis Raymond de las Cisternas. At the church, Antonia met Lorenzo de Medina, a wealthy young nobleman who, charmed by her sweetness, promised to petition Raymond in her behalf. Before he left the church, Lorenzo saw Raymond and learned that he was the man who had supposedly spurned Lorenzo's sister Agnes and caused the heartbroken girl to enter the convent of St. Clare. Lorenzo challenged his former friend, but Raymond begged him to hear the story and then make his judgment.

The marquis did not know the fate at that moment befalling Agnes. Father Ambrosio had intercepted a note written to Agnes by Raymond, acknowledging that the child she would soon bear was his and laying plans for her escape from the convent. Ambrosio summoned Mother St. Agatha, the prioress, and Agnes was carried away to torture and probable death. The young girl begged Ambrosio for mercy, but he was cold to her pleas. Then she cursed him, calling on him to remember her when he himself yielded to temptation.

Ambrosio was to remember Agnes' words when he yielded to the passions of Matilda, an evil woman who had disguised herself as a novice at the monastery and who was known to the monks as Rosario. Ambrosio struggled with his conscience, but his lust overcame him and he surrendered completely to Matilda. He could not let the monks learn that a woman was in the monastery, however, for then he would be exiled and reviled by all who now honored him.

After hearing Raymond's story, Lorenzo forgave his friend for his supposed betrayal of Agnes. Agnes had entered the convent of St. Clare in sorrow after she was persuaded by unscrupulous relatives that Raymond had deserted her. Raymond had found her there and by bribing the gatekeeper had managed to see her each night. When she found that she was to have his child, she sent a note to him; it was his note, in reply, planning the escape and their subsequent marriage, that Ambrosio had intercepted. Neither Raymond nor Lorenzo was aware of the fate that had befallen her, and they planned to rescue her together.

Before the proposed rescue, Lorenzo paid court to Antonia. Her mother, Elvira, feared, however, that his family would not permit his union with a girl without noble family or fortune, and she begged him not to call again until he should secure his family's permission to marry Antonia. He was unable to consult his family until after his sister's rescue. When Agnes did not appear at the appointed time, Lorenzo went to the convent and demanded to see her. For several days, Mother St. Agatha told him that Agnes was too ill to receive him. When he insisted, the prioress told him the girl had died while delivering a stillborn child. Wild with anger, Lorenzo and Raymond swore vengeance on the prioress. Raymond refused to believe that his beloved was really dead.

In the meantime, Ambrosio, satiated by his lust, learned to his horror that Matilda worked magic and consorted with the devil. Although his desire for Matilda was gone, his passion for women was still great, and he turned his attention toward Antonia, who had come to beg him to go to her sick mother. The innocent girl did not suspect his intentions, but her mother did. Elvira came upon them once when the monk was attempting to ravish Antonia, but the girl was so innocent that she did not understand the monk's actions. Matilda came to his aid and cast a spell so that he could ravish Antonia as she slept. The plan would have succeeded if Elvira had not come into the room. When Elvira tried to call out for help, Ambrosio strangled her to death.

Raymond became ill after learning of Agnes' fate. Lorenzo learned from another nun that Mother St. Agatha had murdered Agnes; he then laid plans to have the prioress seized. Ambrosio, meanwhile, had not given up his plan to possess Antonia. With the aid of a magic potion mixed by Matilda, he took the girl to a dungeon in the monastery and ravished her there. Immediately afterward, he was penitent and begged her forgiveness, but she would not hear his pleas and tried to escape from him. Fearing the consequences if she did escape, he plunged a dagger into her heart. She lived only long enough to die in the arms of Lorenzo, who suddenly appeared.

Lorenzo had obtained from the cardinal an order to arrest Mother St. Agatha and to have her tried for the murder of Agnes. News of the arrest turned the fury of the mob against the prioress, and she and several of the other nuns were killed by the crowd. While the mob stormed the convent, Lorenzo was led by screams for help into the cellar of the convent. There in the darkness he found a pitiful figure clutching a baby. The woman's ravings were almost insensible, and she was almost dead of starvation. Lorenzo sent her to the home of Virginia de Villa Franca, a beautiful heiress. Searching the rest of the crypt, he had come upon the dying Antonia.

Ambrosio and Matilda were arrested by the Inquisition. Lorenzo and Raymond learned that the pitiful woman they had saved from death was Agnes, who had been imprisoned and starved by the prioress. Raymond's love and the kind ministering of Virginia restored her to health, and she and Raymond were married. For a long time, Lorenzo lay ill of grief for his lost Antonia, but at last, Virginia's kindness healed his spirit, and they too were married.

The Inquisitors tortured Matilda and Ambrosio to make them confess their crimes and their sorcery. Matilda confessed and was condemned to death by fire. Ambrosio refused to confess and was to be tortured again the following day. That night, Matilda came to his cell a free woman. The devil had released her, and she begged the monk to give his soul to Lucifer and thus escape death. The monk wrestled with his conscience, but his fear of the torture overcame his fears of hell and he sold his soul to the devil.

His freedom was short-lived. Lucifer took him through the sky to a high precipice. There he taunted him with the knowledge that he would have been released by the Inquisition had he been true to his faith. The monk also heard that, through the accident of a mixed-up family relationship, Antonia was his own sister and Elvira his mother. Lucifer, who had promised the monk only release from prison in exchange for his soul—not freedom—held the monk high in the heavens; then he dashed him to death on the rocks below.

Critical Evaluation:

To say that Matthew Gregory Lewis' *The Monk* was a *succès de scandale* when it was first published is an understatement. Edition followed edition, some with alterations, others with variations on the ending. A society for the prevention of vice encouraged England's attorney general to suppress the novel's publication. Samuel Taylor Coleridge thought the novel the "offspring of no common genius" and noted that the face of parents who saw the novel in the hands of a son or daughter would turn pale. A circulating library in Dublin kept the book, but underscored the passages that young ladies might find offensive. The novel shocked the scandalous Lord Byron and was high on the reading list of the Marquis de Sade. Despite all the initial attention, Lewis' work became less popular in the twentieth century, but its place in literature is important.

The Monk is a variation of the gothic novel. Restrained by rationalism, the gothic novel as written by Ann Radcliffe had to have a natural explanation for its supernatural aspects. As written by Lewis, the gothic novel works under no such constraints. The book unfolds with one supernatural encounter after another. Interfering ghosts tamper with human destiny, and magic works as demons and men interact. The plot is resolved in a *deus ex machina* conclusion that involves Satan himself. Lewis, who was first and foremost a playwright, does not present complex characters and motivations in *The Monk*. Because the supernatural is a controlling force in human affairs as of the novel's outset, complex characterization is impossible. Lewis denied his creation some of the elements that make a novel great, but he produced a good story, and the novel is not without moral purpose and lessons.

One such lesson is shown by Antonia's fate, for her innocence was no defense against evil. Another lesson is contained in the major theme of the novel, that pride is a vice that can pervert all virtues, even religious piety. This theme is exemplified in the decline and fall of Ambrosio. Lewis passes moral judgments on characters who transgress. Agnes loses her virginity and suffers a purgatory on earth. The model of virtue, Antonia, is raped by a monk, who then stabs her to death in an attack of panic and conscience.

The most tragic of these characters is Ambrosio, the monk who has dedicated his life to celibacy—something in which he takes pride and that he feels sets him above other men. It is this misplaced pride that makes Ambrosio a prize for the devil, who appears in person to entice the monk to damnation. Satan is unwilling to tempt such a prize with that which damns mere mortals. Ambrosio is directed by lust, rape, perfidy, and murder. This leaves the reader at a loss to understand why the monk is deserving of Satan's attention as a man of high virtue. Satan reveals that Elivira and Antonia (the murdered mother and daughter) were Ambrosio's mother and sister, that Satan threw Matilda in Ambrosio's way (inciting lust), that Satan allowed Ambrosio into Antonia's chamber (inciting him to kill his sister), and that Satan warned Elvira in her dreams of Ambrosio's designs on her daughter, which kept Antonia awake (inciting him to rape his sister and thus adding the charge of incest). Satan's manipulations make plausible the monk's lapsed virtue.

The most intriguing of all the characters is Beatrice, the Bleeding Nun. Early in the novel, Agnes tells Raymond the story of the Bleeding Nun, a ghost that yearly haunts Agnes' family's castle. The family is opposed to Agnes' marriage to Raymond, and the couple arrange for Agnes to masquerade as the Bleeding Nun to escape the castle to marry Raymond. When Raymond comes to fetch Agnes, he carries away the Bleeding Nun instead. In a Freudian view, the nun is a projection of Raymond's guilt. A Jungian reading makes the spectral figure, like the Jungian anima, a being in conflict with a real woman—Agnes. Because she has been unconsciously projected onto Agnes, she seems to emanate from her; Agnes paints her, even though she does not believe in her and ridicules anyone who does. The actual appearance of the ghost, thwarting the elopement, may be Lewis' way of arguing against rationalism.

Of all the characters in this cast of one-dimensional figures, perhaps Agnes stands out as the most human. She loses her virginity (which destroyed her aura of purity for eighteenth century audiences) to her true love, Raymond. That she hopes to marry him redeems her somewhat. Lewis realizes he could not kill off both Antonia and Agnes, so he inflicts a series of terrible events on Agnes in a chamber of horrors before she is allowed to be happily reunited with Raymond.

The female figures in *The Monk* reveal striking archetypal aspects that cannot be dismissed as conventions. Matilda, the Madonna figure, represents the ultimate wish fantasy, that the beloved echo the inner ideal; the Bleeding Nun represents the ultimate dread fantasy, that the beloved turn out to be the worst possible feminine image, an animated corpse; and the character of Ambrosio can be read as an attack on the Catholic practice of celibacy, as the monk cannot overcome his destructive wish fantasy, to make love to the Madonna.

Lewis' *The Monk* relies on the psychological effects of horror and the supernatural, and it flouts the Radcliffean gothic conventions with rational explanations of the supernatural. Plot is privileged over character. This accounts for the assertion that Lewis' true successors are such late twentieth century novelists as Peter Straub and Steven King.

"Critical Evaluation" by Thomas D. Petitjean, Jr.

Bibliography:
Andriano, Joseph. "The Feminine in *The Monk*." In *Our Ladies of Darkness: Feminine Daemonology in Male Gothic Fiction.* University Park: Pennsylvania State University Press, 1993. Provides a Jungian reading of the novel, demonstrating a movement from the sublime (the Madonna in the form of the demoniac Matilda) to the supernatural (the Bleeding Nun).

Conger, Syndy M. "Sensibility Restored: Radcliffe's Answer to Lewis's *The Monk*." In *Gothic Fictions: Prohibition/Transgression*, edited by Kenneth W. Graham. New York: AMS Press, 1989. Notes that *The Monk* stands apart from the norm of the horror fiction of its time because it makes explicit what writers like Radcliffe implied, shocking the sensibilities of both writers and readers.

Kendrick, Walter. *The Thrill of Fear: 250 Years of Scary Entertainment.* New York: Grove Weidenfeld, 1991. Discusses the value of *The Monk* in its own time as a success and scandal. Emphasizes the novel's influence on Nathanial Hawthorne, Mary Shelley, E. T. A. Hoffman, and other writers through the late twentieth century.

Lyndenberg, Robin. "Ghostly Rhetoric: Ambivalence in M. G. Lewis' *The Monk*." *Ariel: A Review of International English Literature* 10, no. 2 (1979): 65-79. Asserts that the use of Beatrice, the Bleeding Nun, suggests that the Bleeding Nun's ghost is a mere stock device and a composite of clichés.

Watkins, Daniel P. "Social Hierarchy in Matthew Lewis's *The Monk*." *Studies in the Novel* 18, no. 2 (Summer, 1986): 115-124. Discusses the social hierarchy that evolves in the novel, using the monastery and the Inquisition as the norm invaded by the supernatural.

MONSIEUR LECOQ

Type of work: Novel
Author: Émile Gaboriau (1832-1873)
Type of plot: Detective and mystery
Time of plot: Nineteenth century
Locale: Paris
First published: 1869 (English translation, 1879)

Principal characters:
MONSIEUR LECOQ, a young detective
FATHER ABSINTHE, an old detective
MONSIEUR D'ESCORVAL, an examining judge
MAY, a suspect
TABARET, a consulting detective

The Story:

A party of police agents left the Barriere d'Italie to make their nightly rounds in a tough, sparsely settled district inhabited by thugs and cheap crooks. In that precinct the police were always careful to go in groups. Their leader was old Gevrol, an unimaginative, fearless inspector. About a hundred yards from Mother Chupin's wineshop they heard some loud cries, and the whole party rushed forward over the rough ground. The house was closed up tight; only bands of light through the shutters gave evidence of life within. One eager young officer climbed up on a box to peer through the shutters, and his evident horror at what he saw caused the officers to hasten their attempt to break into the house.

At Gevrol's order two men battered down the door. Inside on the mud floor were three bodies, two men dead and one wounded. Swaying on his feet was a stocky man with a revolver in his hand. On the stair hysterical Mother Chupin hid her face in her apron. One agent seized the murderer and disarmed him, while another man knelt beside the wounded victim, who was clothed in a soldier's uniform. Murmuring that he had received his just deserts, the man died.

Gevrol diagnosed the affair as a drunken brawl and was pleased that the murderer had been so quickly caught. The young officer who had peered through the shutters, however, expressed doubts about the case. Gevrol patronizingly asked him if he suspected some mystery. When the young man said he did, Gevrol told him he could stay with the bodies until morning and investigate to his heart's content.

After the doctors had gone and a wagon had taken away the accused murderer and Mother Chupin, the young man stayed behind with a stolid, seasoned companion, grizzled Father Absinthe. The young detective was Lecoq, who had decided to join the police force after drifting from one job to another for several years. With Father Absinthe to help him, he eagerly looked around the house.

His first find was an earring, half buried in the mud on the floor. It was a diamond earring, jewelry too expensive to be found in Mother Chupin's establishment. Encouraged, Lecoq went outside. There was enough snow on the ground for him to reconstruct some of the happenings prior to the murders. Two women, one young and one older, had come to the house. They had been running when they left. A man had met them outside the garden and had led them to a cab. There the traces were lost. Lecoq also remembered what the suspect had said when he was captured, "Lost! It is the Prussians who are coming!" Only a man who knew Napoleonic history would have used that allusion. He evidently had been expecting someone to return and help him.

Lecoq presented his lucid report to the examining judge in the morning. Monsieur d'Escorval was greatly impressed with Lecoq's report. Despite Gevrol's insistence that the case was merely a wineshop brawl, Monsieur d'Escorval agreed with Lecoq and prepared to look fully into the affair. Disgruntled and jealous, Gevrol ever afterward was Lecoq's enemy.

As soon as the preliminaries were over, Lecoq hurried to the police station to attend the examination of the prisoner. To his disappointment, M. d'Escorval brusquely ordered him to wait in the corridor. Lecoq overheard enough of the examination to realize that the judge seemed unwell or upset. He asked only a very few routine questions, and the prisoner's answers were almost nonsensical. In a very short time the judge hurried out and drove rapidly away.

Lecoq was curious. Looking into the prisoner's cell, he surprised the man in the act of strangling himself. Lecoq removed the band from the prisoner's throat just in time. Continuing his investigation, he learned that the night before, after the murders, a drunken man had created a disturbance outside the jail. He was locked up for the night in the cell with the murderer. In the morning the police let him go. From the description, Lecoq believed him to be the accomplice, the man who had waited outside the wineshop and helped the two women to their cab.

The next morning Lecoq had a fresh disappointment. M. d'Escorval fell and broke his leg while descending from his carriage. There was more delay while a new judge was assigned to the examination. The new examiner, M. Segmuller, listened attentively to Lecoq's analysis and agreed that there was a mystery behind the case. At last the prisoner was brought in for formal examination.

The murderer, giving his name as May, irritatingly insisted he had no given name. He said he was a circus performer, and he gave convincing imitations of a barker in French, English, and German. His story was that he had been attacked by the three men and had shot them in self-defense. May was returned to his cell, and Lecoq continued his patient investigation.

The quest for the murderer's identity was a long hunt. Lecoq and Father Absinthe, working for weeks on fruitless clues, were never successful in tracing the diamond earring. They found the cab that had picked up two women at the scene of the crime, but the women had left the cab at an apartment house, gone into the courtyard, and disappeared through a back door.

So it went with all clues. A visitor came to see the prisoner and showed a pass issued to a relative of Mother Chupin. Father Absinthe tried to trail the visitor but lost him. Lecoq learned of the visit later. He was sure the man was the drunk who had been locked up with the murderer that first night, the man whose general build Lecoq had reconstructed from the footprints in the snow. Then, by spending six days hidden in the garret above May's cell, Lecoq learned that the prisoner received cipher notes from the outside rolled in bits of bread. Lecoq even suspected Gevrol of helping May, but he could prove nothing.

In despair Lecoq pulled the old trick of letting the prisoner escape; then he followed him closely. May joined his accomplice outside a high wall. Lecoq watched while the accomplice boosted May over the wall into the garden of the Duke of Sairmeuse. The accomplice was captured, but no trace of May could be found, although Lecoq searched the duke's house thoroughly. He learned nothing from May's accomplice, a former convict.

As a last resort Lecoq consulted old Tabaret, the oracle of the force. The sage listened eagerly, and then logically explained Lecoq's errors. M. d'Escorval had conveniently broken his leg because he knew who the prisoner was and did not dare prosecute him. Lecoq could not find May in the Duke of Sairmeuse's house because May was the duke.

Lecoq had to agree; an obscure detective could do nothing against a duke who undoubtedly was engaged in some mysterious intrigue. If he persisted in trying to arrest so great a noble, Lecoq himself would be convicted as a madman. Lecoq gave up the case, but he was determined that sooner or later he would get to the bottom of the whole affair.

Critical Evaluation:

In the development of the modern detective story, Émile Gaboriau's two fictional investigators, Père Tabaret and Monsieur Lecoq, remain, with the possible exception of Wilkie Collins' Sergeant Cuff, the most important transitional figures between Edgar Allan Poe's C. Auguste Dupin and Sir Arthur Conan Doyle's Sherlock Holmes. Further, between them, they represent the two types of detectives that have dominated the genre.

Père Tabaret, the hero of Gaboriau's first crime novel, *L'Affaire Lerouge* (1866), is the talented amateur who, like Sherlock Holmes, fights crime to escape boredom and exercises talents that go unused in the everyday world. He works outside of official channels, entering the proceedings either at the request of the injured party or after the authorities have confessed their bafflement. Monsieur Lecoq, protagonist of Gaboriau's four other detective novels, is the professional policeman who works efficiently within the system but must struggle almost as much with the bureaucratic rigidities of the institution and the mediocrity and jealousy of his colleagues as he does with the criminals. This is especially evident in Gaboriau's most famous novel, *Monsieur Lecoq.*

Although *Monsieur Lecoq* was one of Gaboriau's last novels, it describes Lecoq's first case. He is, therefore, much more believable and human than the remote, mysterious figure who appears and disappears in the other works. *Monsieur Lecoq* is the only book in which he is physically described, minus any disguise, and given a personal history. As a young man from a rich background, Lecoq suddenly found himself penniless and was forced to take a variety of relatively menial jobs. To alleviate boredom, he amused himself by inventing theoretical crimes.

After describing one to his last employer, a famous astronomer, he was promptly fired and advised that "When one has your disposition, and is poor, one will either become a famous thief or a great detective. Choose." Thus, Lecoq has that touch of criminality which many detective writers have found an essential ingredient in the makeup of their fictional heroes. Lecoq is no armchair detective; he follows the evidence actively, sparing himself no discomfort or danger. Unlike many subsequent detective stories, the solution in Gaboriau's novels comes in bits and pieces. There are few moments of sudden revelation, only the dogged tracking down of clues. As one aspect of the case becomes clear to Lecoq, it raises new questions which must, in turn, be laboriously answered.

Lecoq is not only a superlative detective, but he is also a most interesting personality. Observing his reactions to his own investigation is almost as interesting as the investigation itself. Not only must Lecoq deal with the criminal, but he must also deal with the police bureaucracy and especially his supervisor, M. Gevrol. Consequently, he evolves a strategy in dealing with his colleagues that is as subtle and ingenious as that which he uses on the criminals. Lecoq knows that his own ambitions must ultimately conflict with Gevrol's authority and that, as a recent recruit, his career can be stifled by Gevrol before it begins. Thus, he gets permission to investigate the case by manipulating Gevrol's patronizing attitude and lack of imagination; he calls no attention to himself in the early stages of the investigation, turning the report in anonymously to avoid embarrassing his superior; and he selects Father Absinthe, an old officer known more for his drinking than his efficiency, as his partner, because the aged policeman will have no conflicting loyalties or ambitions. Once Lecoq has proven his ability to the department, he is able to stand up to Gevrol's spiteful machinations. Lecoq's emotional fluctuations between elation and depression according to the vicissitudes of the investigation, his barely controlled anger when something goes wrong, especially if it is the result of his own mistakes, his sense of humor and irony all combine to make him a colorful and engrossing figure.

When the detective dominates the action, *Monsieur Lecoq* is a lively, entertaining novel. Unfortunately, Lecoq is not always present. In fact, in all of Gaboriau's crime novels, the detective's investigation occupies only a third to a half of the narrative. For this reason, some historians of the genre have even questioned the validity of *Monsieur Lecoq* as a detective novel. Gaboriau incorporates two structural elements into his novels that obscure the description of the investigation: the interrogation and the family chronicle.

Gaboriau was fascinated by legal procedures and especially by the process of interrogation, which is central to the French judicial system. In *Monsieur Lecoq*, Judge Segmuller's extremely lengthy questioning of the convict May is skillful, ingenious, and frequently witty. Even to a contemporary reader much of it is realistic and interesting. As a result of his own interest, as well as the popularity of courtroom fiction, however, Gaboriau devotes excessive amounts of space to interrogations that reveal little or nothing and do not further the action appreciably.

From the standpoint of the modern reader, a much more serious defect in Gaboriau's work is his insistence on the family chronicle as a central element in his books. Following a premise that has endured from his novels through Doyle to Ross MacDonald, Gaboriau believed that the most interesting and compelling crimes must involve personal, usually familial, relationships, and these become even more engrossing if the family concerned is rich, famous, and aristocratic. The crime committed at the outset of the novel, it ultimately develops, is simply the final effect of a family scandal or crime committed many years previously. Investigating the current crime, therefore, leads the detective back to the original malefaction and threatens not only the present criminal but also the entire clan that he represents.

Unlike later users of this assumption, Gaboriau fails to integrate the investigating side of the novel with the family scandal. Rather, the books divide into two separate parts, the investigation and the exposition. The first part traces the investigation up to the point where the criminal's identity is revealed. Thereupon, Gaboriau shifts his narrative focus to describe all the factors leading up to the crime from the participants' point of view. It is not until this domestic history reaches the point where the crime is committed that the two separate plot lines are joined and the mystery resolved.

This rather disjointed narrative method was popular in the nineteenth century because it allowed Gaboriau to incorporate into his crime novel many of the currently popular motifs and situations at great length. He could include family intrigues, scandals, lengthy, tangled love affairs, victimized aristocratic women, blackmail, long-delayed vengeance, family betrayals, ostentatious displays of wealth, profligacy, complex frauds and hoaxes, all presented with theatrical emphasis and moralistic overtones. For the modern reader, these family chronicles are much too long, ornate, melodramatic, and implausible; by the time they are finished, all the momentum and interest regarding the original investigation has been lost.

Thus the end of the first volume of *Monsieur Lecoq* leaves the detective and the reader frustrated. The criminal May has been identified as the Duke of Sairmeuse, but he seems untouchable, and many questions remain unanswered. Gaboriau added a second volume that answers these questions and leads, finally, to justice for May and vindication for Lecoq. The crime novels of Gaboriau, with their many provocative and exciting moments, will be remembered as important works in the history of detective fiction.

Bibliography:

Mandel, Ernest. *Delightful Murder: A Social History of the Crime Story*. Minneapolis: University of Minnesota Press, 1984. *Monsieur Lecoq*, among other detective and mystery novels, is analyzed as a social commentary. The novel is explored as a statement on the society during which the book was written.

Murch, A. E. *The Development of the Detective Novel*. New York: Kennikat Press, 1968. Explores the influence *Monsieur Lecoq* had on the detective novel genre. Contains an analysis of Lecoq as a character.

Symons, Julian. *Bloody Murder: From the Detective Story to the Crime Novel*. Winchester, Mass.: Faber & Faber, 1972. *Monsieur Lecoq* is analyzed in this work as an exemplary and influential detective novel. Places *Monsieur Lecoq* within the tradition and development of the detective and mystery novel.

Thomson, H. Douglas. *Masters of Mystery: A Study of the Detective Story*. London: Folcroft, 1969. Explores *Monsieur Lecoq* as an influential work. Contains a detailed analysis of the structure and characterizations in the novel.

Wright, Willard Huntington. "The Great Detective Stories." In *The Art of the Mystery Story: A Collection of Critical Essays*, edited by Howard Haycraft. New York: Biblo and Tannen, 1946. Contains an analysis of Monsieur Lecoq as he develops in the novel. Monsieur Lecoq is compared to other great mystery characters.

MONT-ORIOL

Type of work: Novel
Author: Guy de Maupassant (1850-1893)
Type of plot: Satire
Time of plot: Mid-nineteenth century
Locale: Auvergne, France
First published: 1887 (English translation, 1891)

Principal characters:
CHRISTIANE ANDERMATT, a young married woman
PAUL BRETIGNY, Christiane's lover
WILLIAM ANDERMATT, Christiane's husband
GONTRAN DE RAVENEL, Christiane's brother
FATHER ORIOL, a wealthy peasant landowner
CHARLOTTE and
LOUISE, Oriol's daughters

The Story:

The Marquis of Ravenel, who was an enthusiastic patron of the baths at Enval, persuaded his young daughter Christiane and her husband, William Andermatt, to join him. On the advice of one of the doctors at the spring, Christiane agreed to take a series of baths, internal and external, in the hope that they would cure her childlessness. When the young couple arrived, they were joined by Christiane's spendthrift brother Gontran and his friend, Paul Bretigny, who had come to the country to recover from a disappointing love affair. During their stay, learning that Father Oriol, a wealthy peasant landowner of the district, was going to blast out a huge rock that hindered cultivation of his fields, the party went to watch the event.

To everyone's surprise, a spring came gushing from the ground after the explosion. Andermatt decided that if the water were of medicinal value he would make Oriol an offer for it, for he hoped to build an establishment that would give the existing baths heavy competition. That same evening Andermatt, accompanied by Gontran, went to the Oriol house and placed his proposal before the peasant.

Oriol, whose bargaining ability was one to be reckoned with, decided that he would have to be careful not to ask too much for the spring and the fields around it; on the other hand, he would not let the possibility of obtaining great wealth slip from his grasp. To inflame Andermatt's desire, he engaged a beggar named Clovis to help him. Clovis, who engaged in poaching by night and feigned rheumatism by day to escape the attentions of the police, was to bathe in the spring for an hour each day—for a fee. At the end of a month he was to be examined. If he were "cured" of his rheumatism, his condition would prove the medicinal value of the spring.

The unsuspecting Andermatt was enthusiastic about the projected plan, and he agreed to pay Clovis for undergoing treatment. Meanwhile he and Oriol agreed to sign a promise of sale. In order that the Oriol family might be won over to his project, Andermatt decided to hold a charity party and a lottery, in which the Oriol girls and Christiane would participate. Andermatt returned to Paris, leaving Christiane at the baths. She and her family, accompanied by Paul Bretigny and the Oriol girls, made numerous excursions about the countryside. Paul began to confide in her, telling her of his adventures and love affairs. As their conversations became more intimate, she realized that he was paying court to her. To inflame his desire, she held him at arm's length until finally, as they were starting back from a jaunt at nightfall, he caught at her shawl while she walked in front of him and kissed it madly. She had to struggle to master her agitation before she joined the others in the carriage.

Several days later, when the party went to view the ruins of a nearby castle by moonlight, Paul threw himself at Christiane's feet, and she submitted to him. The following morning Andermatt returned. Losing no time, the financier set about reaching an agreement with Oriol. According to the terms decided upon after much discussion, the company that Andermatt had formed was assigned the lands along the newly created stream and the crest and slope of the hill down which it ran. In return, Oriol was to receive one-fourth of the profits to be made.

Andermatt rushed back to Paris after completing his arrangements. That night Paul went to Christiane's room. During Andermatt's absence they had nearly a month for uninterrupted lovemaking. It was a blow to both of them when they learned that Andermatt was arriving within a few days and that he was planning to take Christiane back to Paris with him when he left. The financier brought several members of the newly formed company with him. The terms of the purchase were read and signed before the village notary, and Andermatt was elected president of the company, over the dissenting votes of Oriol and his son. It was agreed that the baths should be known as Mont-Oriol.

That night Paul sorrowfully said good-bye to his love. He felt that, although they might meet later in Paris, part of the enchantment of their affair would be gone forever. Christiane, on the other hand, was full of plans for future meetings and ways of evading the notice of her servants. The first of July in the following year was set as the dedication date for the new baths at Mont-Oriol. Christiane, soon expecting a baby, walked with her father and brother and Paul to watch the dedication of the three new springs. They were to be known as the Christiane, Charlotte, and Louise springs, the latter two named after the Oriol girls, but Clovis, who had seemed so successfully cured the previous summer, was again doubled up by his assumed rheumatism. He threatened to become a serious menace to business because he declared to the guests who would listen that the waters had ultimately done him more harm than good. At last Andermatt was forced to reckon with him, and Clovis finally agreed to undergo treatment every year. It was decided that his return annually for the same treatment would only prove to the public the medicinal value of the baths.

Andermatt had planned an operetta and display of fireworks for that evening. Gontran, observing that his sister was suffering from the heat of the room in which the entertainment was beginning, sneaked out and set off the rocket which was the signal for the fireworks display to start. To Andermatt's disgust, everyone dashed out, but he took advantage of the unexpected interlude to have a serious conversation with Gontran. Having been informed that Oriol intended to give the lands around Mont-Oriol as his daughters' dowries, Andermatt proposed that Gontran, who was deeply in debt, should recoup his finances by marrying either Charlotte or Louise. After meditating for a few moments, Gontran announced that he would open the ball to be held later that evening by dancing with Charlotte Oriol, the younger and prettier of the two sisters.

Christiane, too, made use of the interruption. She proposed to Paul that they walk along the road on which they had said good-bye the previous year. At that time he had fallen to his knees and kissed her shadow. Her hopes that he would repeat the act were dashed, for although the child she was carrying was his, her shadow betrayed too clearly her changed form.

Gontran paid court to Charlotte Oriol at the ball, and the news of his interest in her soon became common gossip at the springs. The innocent girl responded so freely that Christiane and Paul, who were fond of her, began to fear that she would eventually find herself compromised. They were satisfied, however, when Gontran confided to them his intention to ask for her hand. When he asked Andermatt to sound out Oriol, the crafty peasant, realizing that his younger daughter would be easier to dispose of than the older, said that he planned to endow her with the lands on the other side of the mountain. Because those lands were of no use to Andermatt at the moment, Gontran realized that he would have to change his tactics.

He persuaded Louise that he had courted Charlotte only to arouse the older sister's interest. He managed to meet her frequently at the home of one of the doctors and on walks; when the time seemed ripe, he sent Andermatt once more to talk to Oriol. As the reward for his efforts he received a signed statement which assured him a dowry and the promise of the girl's hand. Paul, unaware of Gontran's and Andermatt's schemes, had been incensed by the sudden desertion of Charlotte. Gradually his feeling of sympathy for her grew into love. One day her father found them together. Partly because he was in love and partly because he did not want to compromise Charlotte, his immediate reaction was to propose. When he agreed to sign a statement as to his satisfactory income, the peasant gave his consent to the marriage.

The next morning Christiane learned that Paul was to marry Charlotte. Her informant was the doctor who came to examine her, for she felt ill. As soon as she heard that her lover was to marry, she went into labor from the shock. Fifteen hours later a little girl was born. She would have nothing to do with the baby at first, but when Andermatt brought the child to her, she found the infant irresistible and wanted it kept near her.

There was no one else to nurse the child, so the doctor's wife was chosen to keep Christiane company during her recovery. The talkative woman knew the Oriols well, and Christiane was able to learn from her most of the details of Paul's courtship. Upset by the realization that he had given Charlotte the same attentions she had once received, she fell into a delirium for a day. The next day her condition began to improve.

When the baby was a few days old, Christiane asked that Paul be sent to see her. He went, planning to beg her pardon, but he found there was no need to do so. Christiane, engrossed in the child, had only a few conversational words for him. Although he had hoped to see the infant that was half his, he noted that the curtains of the cradle were significantly fastened in the front with some of Christiane's pins.

Critical Evaluation:

In his chapter on *Mont-Oriol* in *Maupassant the Novelist*, Edward D. Sullivan writes: "In August 1885 Maupassant, visiting Chatel-Guyon in Auvergne, was profoundly impressed by the natural beauty of the region, and determined to use this setting as a background for his next novel." It is an indication of Guy de Maupassant's genius that he was confident of his ability to create a cast of believable characters to people an empty landscape. The imagination that was responsible for Maupassant's fame and fortune tortured him with horrible hallucinations and drove him to attempt suicide before his death in a sanatorium.

Henry James gives an incisive one-sentence evaluation of Maupassant's works in an essay on the French author:

> M. de Maupassant sees human life as a terribly ugly business relieved by the comical, but even the comedy is for the most part the comedy of misery, of avidity, of ignorance, helplessness, and grossness.

This sentence could serve as a capsule summation of the theme and thesis of *Mont-Oriol*. Maupassant's descriptions of the beauty of nature, including those of the pure water gushing from the mountain spring, are contrasted with his depictions of the ugliness of human behavior. He peoples his pristine landscape with fools and hypocrites. Maupassant was a cynic, but always an amusing cynic. His avaricious peasants and hypocritical doctors provide much of the comedy in *Mont-Oriol*.

It is noteworthy that Christiane Andermatt is the only character who changes, indicating that the novel is her story. She loses the girlish innocence, romanticism, and vulnerability that made her so irresistible to the jaded Paul Bretigny. Gontran de Ravenel remains a playboy from beginning to end. William Andermatt remains a greedy businessman. Paul remains an attitudinizing Don Juan. Christiane, however, ends up being cynical, cunning, spiteful, and above all disillusioned. Her disappointment with human nature reflects Maupassant's own disappointment.

Biographers of Maupassant frequently remark on the influence of his contemporary, the pessimistic and misanthropic German philosopher Arthur Schopenhauer. "I admire Schopenhauer madly," Maupassant wrote in a letter. Here is a characteristic passage from one of Schopenhauer's essays:

> . . . how little genuine honesty is to be found in the world and how often injustice and dishonesty sit at the helm, secretly and in the innermost recess, behind all the virtuous outworks, even where we least suspect them.

One by one, Maupassant exhibits the dishonesty, motivated by greed and selfishness, of his characters. The Marquis, an impecunious aristocrat, is willing to marry his tender young daughter to a much older, temperamentally unsuited man of an inferior social class for the sake of money. William Andermatt does not love Christiane but marries her for her family name and the business connections her family can provide. Paul proves to be a faithless lover who not only deceives Christiane's trusting husband but also betrays Christiane.

Christiane's brother Gontran is so dishonest that dishonesty seems as natural to him as breathing: He coldly and deliberately jilts one of Father Oriol's daughters in favor of the other when he finds out where his financial advantage lies. Andermatt, to whom the wastrel Gontran is heavily in debt, encourages his brother-in-law in this heartless deed without regard for the feelings of the trusting young Charlotte Oriol, who is shamefully betrayed, and without regard for the fate of her sister Louise, who will spend a lifetime married to a faithless husband who never loved her.

Maupassant's male peasant characters are just as dishonest as his upper-class characters but do not pretend to be honorable gentlemen, nor do they expect others to be more honest than themselves. Maupassant liked to write about peasants and prostitutes because they were the only people who did not pretend to be other than what they were. The crafty, tightfisted Father Oriol and the totally unscrupulous poacher and malingerer Clovis are two of the most striking characters in the novel. They are human nature in the raw, undisguised by formal clothes and refined manners.

Even Christiane proves to be capable of the grossest dishonesty. She deceives her husband by carrying on an affair with Paul—right under Andermatt's nose. Her dishonesty is more shocking than that of any other character in the novel because of her youth, idealism, and innocence. Ultimately she presents Andermatt with a bastard daughter without showing the slightest remorse as she watches the cuckold cooing over the infant nestled in his arms.

As well as being an admirer of Schopenhauer, Maupassant was an admirer of the Russian novelist Leo Tolstoy, who acknowledged the genius of the younger writer and published an essay about him in which he deplored Maupassant's preoccupation with sexual matters. Maupassant's characterization of Paul and Gontran echoes the negative view of the upper classes that Tolstoy developed in his old age. Tolstoy thought that men and women who did not have to labor for their livelihoods were frustrated and thus exaggerated the importance of love and sex in order to fill their empty lives. Gontran and Paul are examples of leisure-class drones who create tragedy by playing at love.

Maupassant's cynicism about human nature, which he shared with Schopenhauer and Tolstoy, can be seen echoed in many works of modern fiction, perhaps most strikingly in the hard-boiled novels of the American crime writers Dashiell Hammett, Raymond Chandler, James M. Cain, and Jim Thompson. Maupassant may be said to have contributed to this genre in terms of style. He started as a short-story writer and had to learn economy with words. He learned to select the telling detail that could create the scene and the line of dialogue that could bring a character to life.

"Critical Evaluation" by Bill Delaney

Bibliography:
Harris, Trevor A. Le V. "Maupassant's *Mont-Oriol*: Narrative as Declining Noun." *Modern Language Review* 89, no. 3 (July, 1994): 581-594. A close reading of *Mont-Oriol*, with special attention to the meanings in the names of the novel's characters. Emphasizes decline as a major theme and technical device.
James, Henry. *Partial Portraits*. Westport, Conn.: Greenwood Press, 1970. Contains the frequently quoted essay "Guy De Maupassant." Originally published in 1888, this succinct and lucid analysis of Maupassant's literary merits and shortcomings, containing some discussion of *Mont-Oriol*, has never been surpassed by a critic writing in English.
Lerner, Michael G. *Maupassant*. Winchester, Mass.: Allen & Unwin, 1975. Devotes balanced attention to the transmutations of Maupassant's life experiences into material for his short stories and novels, including *Mont-Oriol*. Notes, bibliography, and photographs.
Sullivan, Edward D. *Maupassant the Novelist*. Westport, Conn.: Greenwood Press, 1978. A study of Maupassant's six novels, with a chapter devoted to *Mont-Oriol*. Examines Maupassant's letters, articles, essays, stories, and other works to trace the painful struggle of an acknowledged master of the short story to develop into an equally accomplished novelist.
Wallace, A. H. *Guy de Maupassant*. New York: Twayne, 1973. An excellent introduction to the life and works of Maupassant. One section is devoted to a discussion of *Mont-Oriol*. Chronology, endnotes, and a selected bibliography.

MONT-SAINT-MICHEL AND CHARTRES
A Study of Thirteenth Century Unity

Type of work: Essay
Author: Henry Adams (1838-1918)
First published: private printing, 1904; 1913

Mont-Saint-Michel and Chartres is the study of two great medieval buildings, one a Norman abbey, the other a Gothic cathedral. In the author's mind, however, the book had a far wider purpose. Henry Adams set out to evoke the mood of an era in France, the eleventh to the thirteenth century, in all aspects: art, theology, philosophy, music. Behind this wider purpose was still another. Adams subtitled the book *A Study of Thirteenth Century Unity*, asking that it be read along with his autobiography, *The Education of Henry Adams* (1907), in which he discussed what he called "twentieth century multiplicity."

Adams was a historian, and his two books suggest a theory of history and an attitude toward history. Western civilization had moved from unity to multiplicity, from a God-centered culture in which faith was the major force to an uncentered culture of competing ideologies and conflicting scientific theories. Adams' attitude was one of quiet regret, and his survey of medieval France is informed by an intellectual's poignant yearning.

This emotional longing for the order of a medieval culture is more than balanced, however, by the rigorous intellection Adams exercises. Translations of old French lyrics, incisive summaries of Thomist theories, detailed analyses of architectural subtleties—these are among Adams' self-imposed duties in the book. Scholars agree that Adams fulfilled his duties with grace and considerable accuracy.

His method is deceptively casual. In the preface he announces the desired relationship between himself and the reader: An uncle is speaking to a niece, as guide for a summer's study tour of France. Readers soon see that the genial uncle has planned the course of study quite rigorously. It operates partly in the way that Adams' own mind tended to operate, by emphasizing opposites. Adams concerns himself with contrasts: St. Michel and Chartres, the masculine temperament and the feminine, Norman culture and French culture. All this is within the major contrast of thirteenth century and twentieth. Adams also uses the device of paradox. He insists that his purpose is not to teach. Yet the book is a joy only if the reader's intellect stands alert to follow Adam's careful exposition.

By 1904, when the book was privately printed, Adams had befriended several of the young American scholars who were awakening American universities to the importance of the medieval period. Adams himself had done sporadic writing and study in this realm years before. The book can be usefully thought of as an old man's legacy to a new generation, an unpretentious structure of affectionate scholarship, carefully built with some of Adams' finest prose.

Basically, the book contains three parts. The opening chapters deal with Mont-Saint-Michel on the Normandy coast. A transition chapter enables Adams to traverse the route to the cathedral town of Chartres. Six chapters examine the great cathedral, leading the reader to see its full symbolic meaning. The six concluding chapters then attend to history, poetry, theology, and philosophy—the medieval setting in which the jewel of the cathedral shines.

Adams' focus is medieval France, and his book begins at the offshore hill of St. Michel, where the great abbey was built between 1020 and 1135. Instantly the salient characteristics accumulate, for later contrast with those of Chartres: isolation, height, energy, modest size, utter simplicity, dedication to the archangel St. Michael (representing the Church militant).

As Mont-Saint-Michel "was one of the most famous shrines of northern Europe," so in French song the *Song of Roland* achieved unequaled eminence. How song and shrine complement each other is Adams' theme in the second chapter. The song and the shrine represent the militant temper of the time just before the Battle of Hastings; both exalt simplicity, directness, intensity, and both display a certain naïveté. This was France of the eleventh century.

Next it is the early thirteenth century that draws his attention, "the early and perfect period of Gothic art." On the Mount this period is seen in the ruins of the ancillary buildings (the "Merveille"): great hall, refectory, library, cloisters. The tour of the Mount completed, Adams sums up the meaning of the entire complex, using his key word, "unity": "It expressed the unity of Church and State, God and Man, Peace and War, Life and Death, Good and Bad; it solved the whole problem of the universe."

The uncle goes now to Chartres. As the fenestration of St. Michel's great hall looked ahead to the glass of Chartres, so the choir and façades of Coutances, along the way, prepare the niece for Chartres, as do Bayeux and Saint-Germain-des-Prés. For Adams Chartres is the climactic shrine, the central symbol of its age and of his book.

Readers arrive at Chartres in chapter 5, with a distant glimpse of the two spires. Adams, perhaps at his most genial, explores the façade, especially noting the contrast between the magnificent "old" tower of the twelfth century and the "new" tower completed in 1517. This is a chapter of immense detail perfectly handled. The detail gradually rises into symbolism. For Chartres is the church of the Virgin, "the greatest of all queens, but the most womanly of women." It is her palace, the utter opposite of St. Michel: feminine, elaborate, gracious, a building larger and later than the abbey. Minute examination of the portals and porches concludes chapter 5. Only now, anticipation sufficiently stimulated, does Adams permit entry.

With a bit of the avuncular humor that accounts for the charm of the book, Adams insists on another chapter of delay—"ten minutes to accustom our eyes to the light." This is a ruse. The interior dimness symbolizes the dim past that Adams' literary art seeks to evoke. This chapter characterizes the Queen of Heaven, who demanded light, convenience, and color in her church space.

Next follow a full hundred pages that function on several levels. There is narrative, a progressive tour through the church; description, an examination in detail of windows, apses, chapels; evocation, of an era and its art and faith; symbolism, the meaning of the Lady to the architects and worshipers; the meaning of the iconography; and the significance of the age itself. Adams reaches the high point of his interest and his art, besides demonstrating considerable proficiency as a master of architectural detail.

Adams next, in his chapter on "The Three Queens," turns to one of his favorite doctrines. He has been posing as one of the Virgin's faithful, so that it is no surprise to see him declaring the doctrine of woman's superiority. The twelfth century held this view, insists Adams: Chartres was built for the Virgin. Secular women of the century held power also. These were Eleanor, Queen of France; Mary of Champagne; and Blanche, Queen of France. They created the institution of courtly ("courteous") love.

The subject of courtly love leads Adams on to a lighthearted discussion of thirteenth century song, chiefly a synopsis of *Auscassin et Nicolette*, Adam de la Halle's "Li Gieus de Robin et de Marion," and the famous *Roman de la Rose*. In his discussion of poetry and architecture Adams says that in this period "Art leads always to the woman."

Specifically, art leads to the Virgin. Adams now takes up the miracles of the Virgin. They make up a special branch of literature and demonstrate that the sympathetic Virgin "was by essence illogical, unreasonable and feminine"—a pitying "power above law." Here again is the contrast between the Virgin and St. Michael.

Abruptly turning from the "feel" of the Middle Ages, achieved through study of its art, Adams now attends to its mind. This subject is introduced by way of Abelard, theologian and dialectician at Notre Dame de Paris. Adams constructs an abstract debate between Abelard and his teacher, William of Champeaux, to bring up the issue of unity versus multiplicity, which will concern him through the rest of the book. The problems of unity and multiplicity were several: How can God be One and yet be a Trinity? How can people in their diversity become one with God?

For the moment the focus is on Abelard, the man who sought God by the force of reason. He is the direct opposite of the illogical Virgin and of the equally illogical mystic, Francis of Assisi, whom readers meet also. Adams thus continues his method of displaying the age by means of its opposites.

Whether such opposites as scholasticism and mysticism could be reconciled is part of Adams' problem in the last chapter. The great reconciler was Thomas Aquinas, whose all-encompassing *Summa Theologica* (c. 1265-1274) Adams elaborately compares to the detail and grandeur of the Gothic cathedral. Aquinas showed how to fuse God's trinity with His unity. Even more important, he showed how God, the One, permeates all being, creating the great multiplicity and diversity of humankind and the universe.

Adams sums up some of the paradoxes and polarities he has already dealt with. One unusual thing about the Church of the Middle Ages was its multiplicity: It harbored mystics and rationalists, the holy Virgin and the abject sinners she pitied. Even greater was the Church's unity. Aquinas demonstrated how God and the individual, Creator and created, formed a grand unity that the age celebrated instinctively in art, architecture, and song. Here was the medieval worldview.

Adams' final point is comparison. The Thomist explanation of God's creativity can be compared usefully to a modern dynamo and its production of energy. The dynamo is the key symbol of *The Education of Henry Adams*, the sequel to *Mont-Saint-Michel and Chartres*. The true subject of the autobiography is the century in which multiplicity won.

Bibliography:

Adams, Henry. *Mont-Saint-Michel and Chartres*, with an introduction by Lord Briggs. New York: G. P. Putnam's Sons, 1980. Contains a helpful introduction to this work and its place in the writings of Henry Adams. Illustrations of Mont-Saint-Michel, Chartres, other works of medieval architecture, and scenes of medieval life from illuminated manuscripts aid in visualizing Adams' description of medieval monuments, culture, and society.

Byrnes, Joseph F. *The Virgin of Chartres: An Intellectual and Psychological History of the Work of Henry Adams*. London: Associated University Presses, 1981. Studies the intellectual and psychological development of Henry Adams, particularly regarding women. His ideals culminate in the medieval symbol of the Virgin as expressed in Chartres Cathedral.

McIntyre, John P. "Henry Adams and the Unity of *Chartres*." *Twentieth Century Literature* 7 (January, 1962): 159-171. Explains the historical method that Adams used in writing *Mont-Saint-Michel and Chartres*. Shows how Adams achieves a unified conception of medieval history by utilizing Romanesque and Gothic architectural monuments as documents of social and cultural history.

Mane, Robert. *Henry Adams on the Road to Chartres*. Cambridge, Mass.: Harvard University Press, 1971. Examines *Mont-Saint-Michel and Chartres* by looking at the personal and educational background that led Adams to write on Chartres. Also analyzes the literary work itself.

Samuels, Ernest. *Henry Adams: The Major Phase*. Cambridge, Mass.: The Belknap Press of Harvard University Press, 1964. The third of a three-volume biography of Adams. Contains an extensive examination of *Mont-Saint-Michel and Chartres* within the context of Adams' life.

A MONTH IN THE COUNTRY

Type of work: Drama
Author: Ivan Turgenev (1818-1883)
Type of plot: Psychological realism
Time of plot: 1840's
Locale: Russia
First published: Mesyats v derevne, 1855; first performed, 1872 (English translation, 1924)

Principal characters:
ARKADY ISLAYEV, a wealthy landowner
NATALYA (NATASHA), his wife
KOLYA, their son
VERA, Natalya's ward
LIZAVETA, a companion
RAKITIN, a family friend
BELYAYEV, a young tutor
SHPIGELSKY, a doctor

The Story:

In her drawing room, Natalya, a twenty-nine-year-old wife and mother, was talking confidentially to her good friend Rakitin. She admitted that her husband Islayev had one fault: He went into things too enthusiastically. He was with his workmen constantly, and he himself demonstrated how they should do their work. Her complaint ended, she bade Rakitin to go on reading to her. She really had no interest in the book, but it was being discussed by her friends.

It was read aloud in the big room, where a card game was in progress. Schaaf, the German tutor, had been winning until Lizaveta, companion to Islayev's mother, made a mistake; the German grumbled at her ineptness. The doctor, Shpigelsky, breezed in and, as was his wont, told a long, pointless story. He had really come to talk privately with Natalya about a friend of his who wished to marry Vera. Natalya, claiming that at seventeen Vera was too young, put off a definite answer.

Kolya, Natalya's little son, came running up, full of news about his tutor Belyayev's doings. The energetic young tutor, who had been there nearly a month, was making a kite. Vera, also coming from play, told how Belyayev could climb trees as nimbly as a squirrel. Islayev tried to induce Natalya and Rakitin to look over his new blowing machine, but only Rakitin was interested.

As the room gradually cleared, Natalya had a chance to talk with Belyayev at some length. She complimented him on his good singing voice and asked about his family. She was touched to learn that his mother was dead and that he had a sister also named Natalya. In spite of her friendly attitude, Belyayev was nervous and persisted in being formal and polite with her.

In the garden, Katya, the maid, was listening to the butler's proposal. She had some trouble in fending him off, and the arrival of Schaaf made matters a little more complicated. Schaaf archly sang a love song and tried to kiss her. She escaped by running into a raspberry patch. Vera and Belyayev called her out after Schaaf left. They were working on the kite and, as they worked, they companionably shared Katya's raspberries. Belyayev told Vera much of his past life, of his studies in Moscow, of his poverty. Vera described her loneliness without friends her own age. Interrupted by the arrival of Natalya and Rakitin, they slipped out of the garden.

Natalya professed to Rakitin her uneasiness about Vera; the girl was very young and probably should not be so much alone with Belyayev. Rakitin began to suspect what was happening. Natalya had always been so frank and tender with him. Now she seemed preoccupied and talked distractedly. She even accused him of having a languid mind, and she no longer cared for his descriptions of nature. Rakitin sought out Belyayev to get better acquainted with him. He was troubled when he discovered that the young tutor hid such an engaging manner underneath his gawky exterior. Although Belyayev thought of Natalya only as an older woman and his employer, Rakitin sensed a possible rival for Natalya's affections.

Shpigelsky brought Bolshintsov, a neighbor of forty, to the house and coached him carefully on what he was to say. Bolshintsov was shy with women, but, having decided to make an offer to Vera, he had enlisted the busybody doctor as an intermediary. If the match came off, Shpigelsky was to get three horses as his reward.

When Natalya could not disguise her increasing coldness toward Rakitin, he accused her of being attracted to Belyayev. Although she proclaimed that she still loved Rakitin, she could not deny the young tutor's charms. Rakitin delicately hinted that she owed her love to her husband and suggested that both he and Belyayev should leave the house.

With Vera, Natalya assumed a sisterly air and told her of Bolshintsov's proposal. She did not press the point too much after Vera laughed at the idea of marrying such a funny old man. Instead, with mature skill, she probed into her ward's feelings and got her to confess her love for Belyayev. Her suspicions confirmed, she was torn between her inclinations as a woman and her duty as wife and guardian. Sending for Belyayev, she warned him that Vera was quite immature and that it was easy for her to misinterpret friendship. When the young man finally understood that Vera was in love with him, he was amazed; he had no notions of love at all. He resigned his job and offered to leave the house immediately. Natalya, unable to bear his willingness to leave the house, asked him to defer his decision for a while.

Meanwhile, Shpigelsky was impressing Lizaveta by diagnosing the ills and attitudes of members of the family. He reminded her that she would not want to remain a companion all her life; hence he would make her an offer of marriage. Lizaveta, adopting a coquetish manner, began a coy reply, but the doctor kept talking. He insisted on telling her all his faults and the extent of his fortune and then stated that he had proved to her he was a fine fellow because he had confessed his faults. Lizaveta promised to give him an answer the next day. To her surprise, Shpigelsky sang a peculiar song about a gray goat.

Vera made an effort to save the situation by telling Belyayev that she knew how Natalya had warned him of the girl's love. Bitter over Natalya's efforts to get her married off to Bolshintsov, she hoped that Belyayev would confess his love for her. The young man was unresponsive. Then Vera assured him that Natalya herself was in love with him. When Natalya found them, Vera was openly reproachful. She accused her guardian of treating her as a child when she was a grown woman. Henceforth they would be equals and probably rivals. She left in an emotional state. When they were alone, Natalya confirmed that she was in love with Belyayev. Overwhelmed by her declaration, he could think only of leaving.

Islayev began to suspect that all was not well in his household, for he knew that Rakitin had been much in his wife's company. Being a forthright man, he asked Rakitin outright if he were in love with Natalya. Rakitin admitted that he was, and he added that he was leaving immediately. Islayev did not really want him to leave, but his departure did seem a good solution. Rakitin made no mention of Natalya's infatuation for Belyayev.

Vera told Shpigelsky that she would accept Bolshintsov's offer because she could no longer remain under the same roof with Natalya. Belyayev, not trusting himself to meet Natalya, sent a farewell note by Vera. To Islayev, it seemed peculiar that so many people were leaving at once. Lizaveta also commented to Islayev's mother that she too would be leaving one of these days.

Critical Evaluation:

Ivan Turgenev was one of the first Russian writers to win fame outside Russia. Although best known both inside and outside Russia as a novelist, Turgenev was also a poet, a journalist, and a dramatist. The plays—he wrote about a dozen—came relatively early in his writing career, between 1843 and 1852. Of them, *A Month in the Country*, written in 1850, is generally considered the best, even though *The Lady from the Provinces* (1851) makes a better stage production. *A Month in the Country* was a great favorite of the Moscow Art Theater and its eminent director, Konstantin Stanislavsky. The enduring popularity of the play, however, is less important than its historical position in the evolution of the Russian theater, since Turgenev's contribution anticipated the psychological realism and rather actionless plots of Anton Chekhov's later dramas.

Two of Turgenev's strong points are especially related to what has come to be known as the Chekhovian ambience. One is style; the other is characterization. Because Turgenev was a poet, his residual poetic talents later manifested themselves in the lyrical style which marks both his prose and his drama. The delicate grace of his style in treating nature and love—the incident in the raspberry patch, for instance—anticipates such typically Chekhovian settings as are found in *Uncle Vanya* (1899) and *The Cherry Orchard* (1904). Likewise, in characterization, Turgenev was a trailblazer. He shaped his characters not by asking "How do they look?" or "What are they doing?" but by searching for "What do the characters think and feel?" As a consequence of this method of characterization, the action of the play becomes internalized as mental and emotional events. Physical action, as it is usually understood, is reduced to a minimum. These circumstances were ideal for depicting strong female characters for which Turgenev has rightly been acclaimed. In addition, this technique of characterization was adopted and polished by Chekhov until it became the hallmark of his dramas.

A Month in the Country is a complex play, although the plot merely revolves around a simple love triangle. The theme is also easily stated but more difficult to explain; it is frustration. All of the major characters are frustrated. Their needs and desires are unmet; their attempts at gaining satisfaction are thwarted by the indifference or the insensitivity of second parties, while they, in turn, ignore similar entreaties of third parties. They do not work at cross-purposes; rather, they work along parallel lines that never meet. The interaction, the human relationships of which the plot is made, constitutes an emotional and intellectual pattern best described as undulating, after the manner of ocean waves: High crests are separated by wide troughs. Beneath those wide troughs, life seethes with repression, suppression, and unmet needs which occasionally boil up to the crest of a breaker only to subside again, thwarted by the immutable pattern of frustration, until the next cresting of a breaker signals another emotional crisis. The pattern repeats itself with unremitting regularity. By the end of the play, the reader is emotionally bludgeoned into a resigned submission not unlike that of Natalya or Vera. For a play whose action is psychological rather than physical, *A Month in the Country* has a remarkable impact— and a lasting one, as Belyayev learns from his brief month in the country.

Bibliography:

Fitzlyon, April. *A Month in the Country: An Exhibition Presented by the Theatre Museum.* London: Victoria and Albert Museum, 1983. A useful illustrated presentation of Turgenev's work for theater, with a bibliography of translations of his plays into English and of their productions in Great Britain. Various aspects of *A Month in the Country* are treated in an uncluttered way.

Freeborn, Richard. "Turgenev the Dramatist." In *Critical Essays on Ivan Turgenev*, edited by David A. Lowe. Boston: G. K. Hall, 1989. An excellent survey of Turgenev's dramatic works. Freeborn considers Turgenev's work for the theater a part of his apprenticeship for future works. In *A Month in the Country*, he added a dimension of forceful psychological insight, reinforced by a sharp edge of social criticism.

Magarshack, David. *Turgenev: A Life*. London: Faber and Faber, 1954. An illustrated biography by Turgenev's translator, concentrating on the events shaping his life, his relationships with Russian and foreign writers, and the circumstances surrounding his works, including *A Month in the Country*.

Seeley, Frank Friedeberg. "Poetry, Plays, Criticism." In *Turgenev: A Reading of His Fiction*. New York: Cambridge University Press, 1991. In this survey of Turgenev's poetry and plays, Seeley finds *A Month in the Country* to be a combination of two subtle psychological portraits, that of a woman in crisis and of a Hamlet-type hero. The play marks the full development of the Russian psychological drama a generation before Chekhov.

THE MOON AND SIXPENCE

Type of work: Novel
Author: W. Somerset Maugham (1874-1965)
Type of plot: Biographical
Time of plot: c. 1897-1917
Locale: England, France, and Tahiti
First published: 1919

Principal characters:
  CHARLES STRICKLAND, an artist
  DIRK STROEVE, his friend
  BLANCHE STROEVE, Dirk's wife
  ATA, Strickland's Tahitian wife
  AMY STRICKLAND, Strickland's English wife

The Story:

 Charles Strickland, a dull stockbroker, lived in England with his wife and two children. Mrs. Strickland was a model mother, but her husband seemed bored with her and with his children. To everyone else, it was Strickland who seemed commonplace. The family had spent the summer at the seashore, and Strickland had returned ahead of his wife. When she wrote him that she was coming home, he had answered from Paris, simply stating that he was not going to live with her anymore. With singleness of intention, Mrs. Strickland dispatched a friend to Paris to bring back her husband.

 Strickland was living in a shabby hotel; his room was filthy, but he appeared to be living alone. Much to the discomfort of the friend, he candidly admitted his beastly treatment of his wife, but there was no emotion in his statements concerning her and her future welfare. When asked about the woman with whom he had allegedly run away, he laughed, explaining to Mrs. Strickland's emissary that he had really run off to paint. He knew he could if he seriously tried. The situation was incredible to Mrs. Strickland's friend. Strickland said he did not care what people thought of him.

 Stubbornly, Strickland began to take art lessons. Although his teacher laughed at his work, he merely shrugged his shoulders and continued to paint in his own way. Back in England, the friend tried to explain to Mrs. Strickland the utter hopelessness of trying to reconcile her husband. She could not realize her defeat at first. If Strickland had gone off with a woman, she could have understood him. Mrs. Strickland, however, was not able to cope with his having left her for an idea.

 Dirk Stroeve, a very poor painter with a delicate feeling for art, had married an English-woman and settled in Paris. Impossible as it seemed, Dirk, who had become acquainted with Strickland, thought the redheaded Englishman a great painter. Strickland, however, did not want anyone's opinion. Indifferent to physical discomfort, he had not tried to sell his paintings in order to eat. When he needed money, he found odd jobs in and around Paris.

 It was apparent that the Stroeves were very much in love. A buffoon and a fool, Dirk was constantly berating himself, but Blanche seemed to hold him in high esteem. When Strickland became very ill, Dirk rushed home to Blanche and pleaded with her to nurse the sick artist back to health. She bitterly professed her hatred of the man who had laughed at her husband's paintings, and she tearfully begged Stroeve not to bring the monster near her. Dirk was nevertheless able to persuade her to allow Strickland to come to their home.

Although she and Strickland rarely spoke to each other, Blanche proved a capable nurse. There seemed to be something electrifying in the air when they were together in the same room. Strickland recovered. Dirk admired Strickland's work, and so was anxious that Strickland stay and work in Dirk's studio. Strickland took possession of the studio. When Dirk finally gathered enough courage to ask him to leave, Blanche said that she would also leave. Dirk fell before her, groveling at her feet, and pleaded with her to stay, but his adoring demonstrations only bored her. When he saw that she would indeed return with Strickland to the filthy hovel that was the Englishman's studio, Dirk's generous soul could not bear to think that his beloved Blanche should live in such poverty. He said that she need not leave; he would go. Thanking her for having given him so much happiness, he left her with half of what he owned.

Dirk hung around Paris waiting for the time to come when Blanche would need him again after Strickland had tired of her. Once, he followed her when she went shopping. He walked along with her, telling her of his devotion; she would not speak to him. Suddenly, she slapped him in the face and walked away. One day, the police informed Dirk that Blanche had swallowed oxalic acid. After she died, Dirk felt compelled to return to his studio. There he found a nude portrait of his wife, evidently the work of Strickland. In a mad passion of jealousy, he started to hack at the picture with a knife, but he was arrested by the obvious fact that it was a wonderful piece of art. No matter what he felt, Dirk could not mutilate the painting. He packed his belongings and went back to Holland to live with his mother.

Strickland had chosen Blanche Stroeve as a subject because he thought she had a beautiful body to paint. When he had finished the picture, he was through with her. Thinking that the picture was not satisfactory, he had left it in the studio. The death of Blanche and the misery of Dirk did not move him. He was an artist.

After Blanche's death, Strickland went to Marseilles, and finally, after many wanderings, to Tahiti. There he painted his vivid awkward-looking pictures and left them with people all over the island in payment for lodging and food. No one thought the pictures worth anything, but years later some who had saved the pictures were pleasantly surprised to sell them for enormous sums of money to English and French collectors who came to the island looking for the painter's work.

At one of the hotels in Tahiti, Strickland was befriended by a fat old woman, Tiare, who looked after his health and his cleanliness. She even found him a wife, a seventeen-year-old native girl named Ata. For three years, Ata and her husband lived together in a bungalow just off the main road. These were perhaps the happiest years in Strickland's life. He painted, read, and loafed. Ata had a baby.

One day, Ata sent to the village for a doctor. When the doctor came to the artist's bungalow, he was struck with horror; to his experienced eye, Strickland bore the thickened features of a leper. More than two years passed. No one went near Strickland's plantation, for the natives knew well the meaning of Strickland's disease. Only Ata stayed faithfully with him, and everyone shunned her just as they shunned Strickland. Two more years passed. One of Ata's children died. Strickland was now so crippled by the disease that he would not even permit the doctor to see him. He was painting on the walls of his bungalow when at last he went blind. He sat in the house hour after hour, trying to remember his paintings on the walls—his masterpieces. Strickland was not interested in the fame his art might bring and made Ata promise to destroy his work upon his death, a wish she faithfully carried out.

Years later, a friend of Strickland, just returned from Tahiti, went to call on Mrs. Strickland in London. She seemed little interested in her husband's last years or his death. On the wall were several colored reproductions of Strickland's pictures. They were decorative, she thought, and went well with her Bakst cushions.

Critical Evaluation:

The Moon and Sixpence, W. Somerset Maugham's first novel after his long, autobiographical masterpiece *Of Human Bondage* (1915), marks an important break in style and narrative technique. Instead of being a *Bildungsroman* such as *Of Human Bondage*, the novel portrays the adult life of a genius. The title refers to a saying about a man gazing so intently on the moon that he fails to see the sixpence lying at his feet. Influenced by the life of Paul Gauguin, the French artist, the novel tells of Charles Strickland, whose talent as a painter remains long hidden even from himself. A forty-year-old English stockbroker leading a colorless life, Strickland decides to abandon everything he has known in pursuit of art. He represents the eccentric genius who defies social and moral conventions in pursuit of creativity.

Maugham structures the plot into three major episodes, which from internal evidence can be dated approximately 1897, 1902, and 1917. The first, set in London, introduces the protagonist, his socialite wife, and his children. Strickland's middle-class family is soon broken by his abrupt and seemingly inexplicable decision to become an artist. The London setting—with its upscale apartments, dinner parties, and drawing room conversations—is the conventional one for social comedy, especially for Maugham's earlier dramas. The second section, set in Paris, introduces the mediocre painter Dirk Stroeve and his wife Blanche, whose friendship with Strickland leads to disastrous consequences. The narrative introduces the reader to the Bohemian life in Paris, where Strickland is learning to paint. The third section, which takes place in Tahiti, portrays the exotic setting that marked many of Maugham's later stories and novels. From an assortment of characters who knew Strickland, the narrator learns details of his last years. A return to London for a final interview with Strickland's wife forms an ironic epilogue.

Within the context of Maugham's work, the novel effects a transition between the comic settings of his earlier writing and the exotic settings of the later stories and novels. Significantly, the loosely related episodes are united by the narrative voice, a Maugham persona reminiscent of earlier novels and stories. In later works, he becomes "Willie Ashenden" or "Mr. Maugham." A successful author, this character is primarily but not entirely autobiographical. His interests and attitudes are usually Maugham's, and details of his life often reflect those of the author. It is noteworthy that Maugham was in each of the novel's three major settings at approximately the time of the narrative. The narrator, a first-person speaker, is detached and observant, taking little or no part in the action. Normally he is nonjudgmental, but, after Strickland abandons his wife and children, the narrator risks Strickland's wrath by calling him a cad to his face. On the few occasions when the narrator becomes involved in the action, his participation has little effect on the plot. His futile mission to Paris on behalf of Strickland's wife is a typical example. A reluctant conversationalist, he is a good listener and can induce people to bare their most closely guarded secrets. He relishes travel and art and is fascinated by genius.

The Maugham persona observes self-imposed limitations that at times lead him to appear to be merely reporting what a character is like or what he does. He adopts the tone of ironic objectivity, as if to celebrate the comic incongruity of human beings without bothering to account for them. After seeing Strickland's paintings, the narrator muses on what determined him to make such a drastic change in his life and then adds: "If I were writing a novel, rather than narrating such facts as I know of a curious personality, I should have invented much to account for this change of heart." Maugham was writing a novel, however, and his critics have suggested that it is a novelist's responsibility to show the reader the conflicts and motivation that account for the decisions and actions of the characters created.

Although the narrator claims to know less about painting that Maugham did, he describes Strickland's genius in some detail. He acknowledges that Dirk Stroeve, the ordinary artist, was the first to recognize and appreciate Strickland's genius. Despite Stroeve's enthusiasm, the narrator maintains his skepticism about Strickland's achievement until near the novel's end. What really interests him is the single-minded, ruthless pursuit of his creativity that renders the protagonist callous and cruel to almost everyone he meets. An obscure stockbroker with a comfortable middle-class life, Strickland becomes a Nietzschean superman, living beyond good and evil. He views his wife and Blanche Stroeve as merely means toward his own advancement and discards them when they no longer interest him. Once Blanche has served as a model for a portrait, he no longer wants anything to do with her. Only Ata, the Tahitian girl who gives all and neither asks nor expects anything of him, can live amicably with him.

Remarkably, his attitude toward his own productions is one of almost total indifference; after completing a painting he loses interest in it. He sells paintings if he must to survive, but he shows an icy indifference to anyone else's response to them. Facing death, he orders Ata to burn the house whose walls are adorned with his masterpieces. The novel never resolves Maugham's unstated question—whether genius is its own justification. The epilogue's revelation that Strickland's wife decorates her London apartment with Strickland's prints suggests the answer.

The novel introduces character types that are mainstays of Maugham's fiction, some reappearing with the same name in later writings. Strickland's proper, brave, and resourceful wife reminds one of many other Maugham hostesses in fiction and drama. Tiaré Johnson, the Tahitian hotel keeper, is an energetic, obese, kindhearted woman who is an unfailing friend to those in need. Captain Nichols, who knew Strickland, is an alcoholic seaman who becomes a beachcomber. These characters belong to a group that Maugham portrays with sympathy in his fiction: those whose talents, weaknesses, genius, or vices relegate them to the fringe of society or render them complete outcasts.

"Critical Evaluation" by Stanley Archer

Bibliography:
Brander, Laurence. *Somerset Maugham: A Guide.* Edinburgh, Scotland: Oliver and Boyd, 1963. A chapter devoted to *The Moon and Sixpence* analyzes the novel as an effort to portray genius. It concludes Maugham achieved only a qualified success because his primary talent was in comedy.
Burt, Forrest D. *W. Somerset Maugham.* Boston: Twayne, 1985. This highly accessible book provides a comprehensive introductory critical survey and biography. Treats *The Moon and Sixpence* as one of Maugham's major novels.
Cordell, Richard A. *Somerset Maugham: A Biographical and Critical Study.* Bloomington: Indiana University Press, 1969. Emphasizes the biographical and autobiographical elements in the novel, and places it within the context of Maugham's other fiction.
Curtis, Anthony, and John Whitehead, eds. *W. Somerset Maugham: The Critical Heritage.* London: Routledge & Kegan Paul, 1987. A collection of early Maugham criticism and reviews. Includes three significant early reviews of *The Moon and Sixpence.*
Loss, Archie K. *W. Somerset Maugham.* New York: Frederick Ungar, 1987. Devotes half a chapter to an analysis of *The Moon and Sixpence*, focusing attention on the novel's major characters.

THE MOONSTONE

Type of work: Novel
Author: Wilkie Collins (1824-1889)
Type of plot: Detective and mystery
Time of plot: 1799-1849
Locale: India and England
First published: 1868

Principal characters:

JOHN HERNCASTLE, an adventurer
LADY VERINDER, his sister
RACHEL VERINDER, his niece
FRANKLIN BLAKE, Lady Verinder's nephew
GODFREY ABLEWHITE, a charity worker
DRUSILLA CLACK, Rachel's cousin
GABRIEL BETTEREDGE, the Verinders' old family servant
DR. CANDY, a physician
EZRA JENNINGS, his assistant
SERGEANT CUFF, an inspector from Scotland Yard
ROSANNA SPEARMAN, Rachel's maid

The Story:

In the 1799 storming of Seringapatam, India, John Herncastle, a violent and cruel man, stole the sacred Hindu diamond called the Moonstone. The jewel had been taken years before from the forehead of the Moon-God in its Brahman shrine, and Herncastle's theft was only one of a series. Since the stone had first been stolen, three faithful Hindus had followed its trail, sworn to recovering the gem and returning it to the statue of the Moon-God. Herncastle took the gem to England and kept it in a bank vault. He saved himself from murder by letting the Hindus know that if he were killed the stone would be cut up into smaller gems, thus losing its sacred identity. At his death, Herncastle left the jewel to his niece, Rachel Verinder.

The stone was to be presented to Rachel on her birthday following her uncle's death. Young Franklin Blake, Lady Verinder's nephew, was asked by Herncastle's lawyer to take the gift to his cousin's home several weeks before the event, but he barely missed death at the hands of the Hindus before reaching his destination. On the advice of Gabriel Betteredge, the Verinders' old family servant, Franklin put the gem in the vault of a bank nearby until the birthday arrived, as the Hindus had been seen in the neighborhood. Upon meeting, Franklin and Rachel fell in love. Guests began to arrive for the birthday celebration, including Godfrey Ablewhite, a handsome and accomplished charity worker, Dr. Candy, the town physician, and Mr. Bruff, the family lawyer.

While the guests at the birthday dinner were admiring the beauty of the jewel, they heard the beating of a drum on the terrace and three Hindus appeared, disguised as jugglers. One of the guests, Mr. Murthwaite, who had traveled widely in the Orient, spoke sharply, whereupon the Indians retreated. Watchdogs were released to protect the house that night. All seemed well, but in the morning Rachel announced that the jewel had disappeared from an unlocked cabinet in her dressing room. Despite Rachel's protests, Franklin Blake insisted the police be called. The Hindus were arrested and put in jail, but to everyone's astonishment, they had alibis for the entire night.

Little about the crime was discovered until Sergeant Cuff of Scotland Yard arrived. He decided that fresh paint from the door in Rachel's dressing room must have come off on someone's clothes. Inexplicably, Rachel refused to allow a search for the stained clothing. Sergeant Cuff suspected that Rachel had staged the theft herself, and that Rosanna Spearman, a maid with a criminal record, was a party to the plot, for he learned that Rosanna had made a new nightdress shortly after the theft. Sergeant Cuff guessed that the nightdress was to replace another dress that was stained. Because the Verinders opposed his efforts, he dropped the case. The only other clue he had was that Rosanna might have hidden something in the rocks by the seashore. Rosanna committed suicide soon afterward by throwing herself into a pool of quicksand. She left a letter for Franklin, who had, however, departed from the country by the time the letter was found.

Rachel went to London with her mother. In time, she became engaged to Godfrey Ablewhite. When Mr. Bruff told her, however, that Godfrey had secretly ascertained the terms of her mother's will before asking for her hand, Rachel broke the engagement. Franklin returned to England later in the year and went to visit Betteredge, who told him about Rosanna's letter. From the letter, Franklin learned that she had thought him guilty of the crime; Rosanna also left him directions for recovering a box she had buried by the sea, just as Sergeant Cuff had thought. The box proved to have the stained nightgown in it, but it was not Rosanna's nightgown but rather Franklin's.

Unable to account for this strange fact, Franklin returned to London, where he had a long talk with Mr. Bruff about the case. Mr. Bruff informed Franklin that the Moonstone was thought to be in a bank in London, deposited there by a notorious pawnbroker named Luker. A mysterious attack on the moneylender seemed confirmation. Franklin also told Mr. Bruff of the strange discovery of the nightgown. Mr. Bruff arranged a surprise meeting between Franklin and Rachel, at which Franklin learned that Rachel had actually seen him come into the room and steal the stone. Because she loved him, she had refused to let the investigation continue. Franklin tried to convince her that he had no memory of the deed.

On Mr. Bruff's advice, Franklin returned to the Verinder's country place and tried to discover what had happened to him that night. From Dr. Candy's assistant, Ezra Jennings, he learned that the doctor had secretly given him a dose of laudanum on the night of the theft, so that Franklin, who suffered from insomnia, would get a good night's sleep. Jennings suggested administering a like dose in the same setting, to see what Franklin would do. Mr. Bruff and Rachel came down from London to watch the experiment.

The scene was set with the help of Betteredge, and Franklin was given the laudanum. Under its influence, he repeated his actions on the night of the theft. Rachel watched him come to her room and take out a substitute stone. She was now convinced that his original act had been an attempt to protect her from the Hindus by removing the stone to another room. Before Franklin could recollect what he did with the stone after he left Rachel's room, however, the drug took full effect, and he fell sound asleep.

The experiment explained how the stone had disappeared from Rachel's room but not how it had found its way into a London bank through the hands of Luker. Mr. Bruff suggested that the gem might shortly be redeemed from Luker. Sergeant Cuff was called back into the case, and a watch was set on the bank. One day, Luker came into the bank and claimed the stone. On his way out, the watchers thought he could have passed it to any of three people, all of whom were followed. Two proved to be innocent citizens; the third was a bearded man who looked like a sailor, whom Bruff's office boy trailed to an inn where the suspect took lodgings for the night.

When Franklin and Sergeant Cuff arrived at the inn, they found the sailor dead and the box from the bank empty. Sergeant Cuff examined the dead man closely and then tore away a false wig and beard to expose the features of Godfrey Ablewhite. They learned from Luker that Godfrey had seen Franklin go into Rachel's room the night of the robbery and that Franklin had given Godfrey the stone with instructions to put it in the bank. Since Franklin had remembered nothing of this request the next day, Godfrey kept the jewel. The mystery was solved, and Rachel and Franklin were happily reunited.

Several years later, Mr. Murthwaite, the explorer, told them of a great festival in honor of the Moon-God that he had witnessed in India. When the idol was unveiled, he saw gleaming in the forehead of the stone image the long-lost treasure of the god—the sacred Moonstone.

Critical Evaluation:

T. S. Eliot claimed that "*The Moonstone* is the first, longest, and best of English detective novels," and his praise has been repeated so often as almost to have become a commonplace. This praise, however, if not precisely faint, may yet be perceived as limited, since detective novels are widely regarded as light reading.

Moreover, praise of *The Moonstone* as a detective novel pays tribute to what in Wilkie Collins is both a strength and a weakness. It is commonly believed that detective fiction stands or falls on the coherence and ingenuity of its plot. From the beginning, critics recognized Collins' gifts as a constructor of plots, but they often saw in his narratives a mechanical, manipulative quality they thought limited, if indeed it did not destroy, the human interest of his work.

Critical interest in Collins began to grow, however, as literature began to be less stringently divided into such categories as serious and popular, which would in any case have had little meaning for Collins or his great contemporary and friend Charles Dickens. A renewed appreciation of Collins' plot constructions was accompanied by growing recognition of how much there is in *The Moonstone* besides plot and by the acknowledgment of Collins' achievement in integrating various elements to produce a whole that is both unified and vital.

To begin with, it is no small accomplishment to sustain the readers' interest in the whereabouts of a missing diamond for the entire not inconsiderable length of the novel. That the mystery of the diamond is made to bear on a romantic plot involving Rachel Verinder and Franklin Blake increases the level of narrative complexity. That Collins brings both of these narrative lines of development to resolution in the same moment of discovery is an admirable feat of craft. In fact, Collins' technical mastery, although dazzling in itself, accounts for only part of the satisfaction the novel offers its readers. The focus on the diamond means that we are eager to reach the denouement and learn what has become of the stone, but it is the author's triumph that the readers' eagerness does not become impatience.

The plot emerges from a series of narratives conveyed by a heterogeneous set of narrators. The first, Gabriel Betteredge, is astonished to discover just how difficult it is to stick to the subject; he constantly needs to bring himself back to the point. Yet his digressions are among the greatest delights of the book. In addition to sustaining and intensifying suspense by delaying answers to narrative questions, the digressions reveal the man. In short, while contributing to the effectiveness of the plot, Betteredge's digressions satisfy the readers' interest in character, that other great concern of the novel as a literary form, especially in the nineteenth century. Collins in *The Moonstone* is a master at diverting the readers while making them wait for the denouement.

Betteredge is one of a number of strongly realized characters in *The Moonstone*. Each of the other narrators, perhaps most emphatically the evangelically inclined Miss Clack, expresses an interesting personality while telling part of the tale. Collins is, however, careful to reduce the quantity of digression as he approaches the resolution. Characters other than the narrators achieve a comparable vividness. Rosanna Spearman, the plain and deformed servant who dares to love a gentleman, and Ezra Jennings, the half-caste physician's assistant who is instrumental in solving the mystery, are fascinating characters in their own right. They also provide Collins with an opportunity to engage and extend the sympathies of readers not accustomed to acknowledge the full humanity of Rosannas and Ezras.

While Collins' portrayal of the Brahmins may have about it something of the Orientalism that was a projection of nineteenth century Western fantasies and anxieties, it is a strength of the novel for suggesting thereby a reality beyond the conscious understanding of the English characters. Within the framework of the novel, the Hindus remain the "other," and the reader is not made directly aware of them as characters. Nevertheless, they are never reduced to stock villains. This is all the more impressive given the thorough demonization of Indians in the English imagination following the Indian mutiny of 1857, little more than a decade before the publication of *The Moonstone*. Collins offers an exemplary instance of a popular novelist challenging his readers rather than simply catering to prejudices.

The Moonstone is also remarkable for the range of its thematic concerns. It remains provocative, even if the terms of the argument continue to change with the passage of time, in its exploration of Christianity and its counterfeits. It is both ironic and affectionate in its examination of English values and vigorous in its confrontation of prejudices based on race and class. The novel has even been interpreted, not unpersuasively, as a latent indictment of British imperialism.

What is impressive is not merely that these concerns are there, but that they are integrated within a narrative structure as firm as that of any nineteenth century English novel. At one level, it has been pointed out, *The Moonstone* requires nothing more of its readers than a disposition for solving mysteries and a desire to be entertained. Yet it is also a work of considerable cultural and literary impact that generously rewards the reader's committed investigation.

"Critical Evaluation" by W. P. Kenney

Bibliography:
Heller, Tamar. *Dead Secrets: Wilkie Collins and the Female Gothic*. New Haven, Conn.: Yale University Press, 1992. Applies to Collins' work, including *The Moonstone*, insights derived from feminist criticism, noting the influence on Collins of the gothic novel, one of the major nineteenth century genres associated with women.

Lonoff, Sue. *Wilkie Collins and His Victorian Readers: A Study in the Rhetoric of Authorship*. New York: AMS Press, 1982. In this study of the author's relation to his contemporary audience, Lonoff finds in Collins' work a covert rebellion against public opinion coupled with an overt desire to please. The book includes an extensive, lucid, and persuasive discussion of *The Moonstone*.

Peters, Catherine. *The King of Inventors: A Life of Wilkie Collins*. Princeton, N.J.: Princeton University Press, 1991. A biography that is sensitive to the complexities of the man and appreciative of the accomplishment of the artist.

Taylor, Jenny Bourne. *In the Secret Theatre of Home: Wilkie Collins, Sensation Narrative, and Nineteenth Century Psychology*. London: Routledge, 1988. Explores the ways in which nineteenth century theories of the workings of the mind permeate Collins' fiction. Discusses

The Moonstone as crucially shaped by the process of interplay and transformation between models of the unconscious derived from these theories.

Thoms, Peter. *The Windings of the Labyrinth: Quest and Structure in the Major Novels of Wilkie Collins*. Athens: Ohio University Press, 1992. Posits the quest for design as the thematic link among Collins' major novels. In *The Moonstone*, no governing order is glimpsed behind the apparent disorderedness of life; design can therefore only be constructed out of the needs and desires of the characters.

LE MORTE D'ARTHUR

Type of work: Chronicle
Author: Sir Thomas Malory (1400?-1471)
Type of plot: Arthurian romance
Time of plot: Age of chivalry
Locale: Britain
First transcribed: c. 1469; first printed, 1485

> *Principal characters:*
> ARTHUR, the king of Britain
> QUEEN GUINEVERE, his wife
> SIR MORDRED, his natural son
> SIR LAUNCELOT,
> SIR TRISTRAM, and
> SIR GALAHAD, knights of the Round Table

The Story:

When King Uther Pendragon saw Igraine, the beautiful and chaste duchess of Cornwall, he fell in love with her. Since the obstacle to his desires was Igraine's husband, King Uther made war on Cornwall, and in that war the duke was killed. By means of magic, King Uther caused Igraine to become pregnant, after which the couple married. The child, named Arthur, was raised by a noble knight, Sir Ector. After the death of King Uther, Arthur proved his right to the throne by removing a sword from an anvil that was imbedded in a rock. From the Lady of the Lake, he received his famous sword, Excalibur. When the independent kings of Britain rebelled and made war on the young king, they were defeated. Arthur ruled over all Britain. He married Guinevere, the daughter of King Leodegrance, who presented the Round Table and a hundred knights to Arthur as a wedding gift. Merlin the magician was enticed by one of the Ladies of the Lake into eternal imprisonment under a rock.

Five foreign kings invaded Arthur's realm and were defeated after a long war. To show his gratitude to God for his victory, King Arthur founded the Abbey of the Beautiful Adventure at the scene of his victory.

Sir Accolon was the lover of Morgan Le Fay, enchantress sister of King Arthur. After she procured Excalibur from Arthur by black magic, Sir Accolon fought Arthur and nearly overcame him; only when their swords were accidentally exchanged in the fight, was the king able to defeat Accolon.

King Lucius of Rome sent ambassadors to Britain to demand tribute of King Arthur. When Arthur refused to pay, he was promised aid in war by all the knights of his realm. In the war that followed, the British defeated Lucius and conquered Germany and Italy. Arthur was crowned Emperor of Rome.

Back in England, Sir Launcelot, a knight of the Round Table and Queen Guinevere's favorite, set out on adventures to further his and his queen's honor and glory. After many long and arduous adventures, all of them triumphant, Sir Launcelot returned to Camelot, the seat of King Arthur, and was acclaimed the first knight of all Christendom.

Elizabeth, queen of King Meliodas of Liones, died in giving birth to a son, who was named Tristram because of the sad circumstances surrounding his birth. Young Tristram was sent to France with his preceptor, Gouvernail, where he was trained in all the accomplishments of knighthood. When the king of Ireland demanded tribute from King Mark of Cornwall, Sir Tristram defended the sovereignty of King Mark, his uncle, by slaying the Irish champion, Sir Marhaus, but he was wounded in the contest. He was nursed by Isolde, princess of Ireland. Tristram and Isolde fell in love and promised to remain true to each other. Later, King Mark commissioned Sir Tristram to return to Ireland to bring back Isolde, whom the king had contracted to marry. During the return voyage from Ireland to Cornwall, Tristram and Isolde drank a love potion and swore undying love. Isolde married King Mark, and Sir Tristram later married Isolde La Blanche Mains, daughter of King Howels of Brittany. Unable to remain separated from Isolde of Ireland, Tristram joined her secretly. At last, fearing discovery and out of his mind for love of Isolde, Tristram fled into the forest. In a pitiful condition, he was carried back to the castle, where a faithful hound revealed his identity to King Mark, who then banished him from Cornwall for ten years. The knight went to Camelot, where he won great renown at tournaments and in knightly adventures. King Mark heard of Tristram's honors and went in disguise to Camelot to kill Tristram. Sir Launcelot recognized King Mark and took him to King Arthur, who ordered the Cornish sovereign to allow Sir Tristram to return to Cornwall. In Cornwall, King Mark attempted unsuccessfully to get rid of Tristram, but Tristram managed to avoid all the traps set for him, and he and Isolde escaped to England and took up residence in Castle Joyous Guard.

An old hermit prophesied to King Arthur that a seat that was vacant at the Round Table would be occupied by a knight not yet born—one who would win the Holy Grail.

After Sir Launcelot was tricked into an affair with Elaine, the daughter of King Pelles, the maid gave birth to a boy named Galahad. Some years later, a stone with a sword imbedded in it appeared in a river. A message on the sword stated that the best knight in the world would remove it. All the knights of the Round Table attempted to withdraw the sword without success. Finally, an old man brought a young knight to the Round Table and seated him in the vacant place at which the young knight's name, Sir Galahad, appeared magically after he had been seated. Sir Galahad withdrew the magic sword from the stone and set out, with Arthur's other knights, in quest of the Holy Grail. During his quest, he was joined part of the time by his father, Sir Launcelot. Sir Launcelot tried to enter the Grail chamber and was stricken for twenty-four days as penance for his years of sin. A vision of Christ came to Sir Galahad; he and his comrades received communion from the Grail. They came to a Near-Eastern city where they healed a cripple. Because of this miracle, they were thrown into prison by the pagan king. When the king died, Sir Galahad was chosen king; he saw the miracles of the Grail and died in holiness.

There was great rejoicing in Camelot after the questing knights returned. Sir Launcelot forgot the promises he had made during the quest and began to consort again with Guinevere. One spring while traveling with her attendants, Guinevere was captured by a traitorous knight, Sir Meliagrance. Sir Launcelot rescued the queen and killed the evil knight. Enemies of Launcelot reported Launcelot's love for Guinevere to King Arthur. A party championing the king's cause engaged Launcelot in combat. All members of the party except Mordred, Arthur's natural son, were slain. Guinevere was sentenced to be burned, but Sir Launcelot and his party saved the queen from the stake and retired to Castle Joyous Guard. When King Arthur besieged the castle, the pope commanded a truce between Sir Launcelot and the king. Sir Launcelot and his followers went to France, where they became rulers of that realm. King Arthur invaded France with the intent of overthrowing Sir Launcelot. In Arthur's absence, Mordred seized the throne of Britain and tried to force Guinevere to become his queen. Guinevere escaped to London, where she took refuge in the Tower. Hearing of Sir Mordred's actions, King Arthur returned to England and in a great battle drove the usurper and his false knights back to Canterbury.

At a parley between King Arthur and Sir Mordred, an adder caused a knight to draw his sword. This action brought on a pitched battle in which Mordred was killed and King Arthur mortally wounded. On his deathbed, Arthur asked Sir Bedivere to cast Excalibur back into the lake from which the sword had come. Sir Bedivere hid the sword twice but was reproached by the king each time. Finally, Sir Bedivere threw the sword into the lake, where it was caught by a hand and withdrawn under the water.

King Arthur died and was carried on a barge down the river to the Vale of Avalon. When Sir Launcelot returned from France to avenge his king and queen, he learned that Guinevere had become a nun. Sir Launcelot retired to a hermitage and took holy orders. Sir Constantine of Cornwall was chosen king to succeed King Arthur.

Critical Evaluation:

The authorship of *Le Morte d' Arthur* is controversial, because more than one "Thomas Malory" exists who could have written the work. Many believe the author was most probably the unusual Sir Thomas Malory of Newbold Revel. The strange circumstances of his life contributed significantly to the shape and meaning of his masterwork. Born about 1400, he served with Richard Beauchamp, the earl of Warwick, was knighted in 1442, and was elected a member of Parliament in 1445. After that, Malory turned to a life of irresponsible violence and spent most of his last twenty years in prison until his death in 1471. It was during his imprisonment that Malory composed, translated, and adapted his great rendering of the Arthurian material. Malory lived in the active fifteenth century, just a little past the age of chivalry and at a time when the elegance and leisure of that age had to be rationalized. That accounts for many of the differences between his vigorous narrative and the story's contemplative, ruminative antecedents in chivalric literature.

Malory is the most influential of all Arthurian writers. He was the source and delight of Edmund Spenser and the main wellspring of Alfred, Lord Tennyson's *Idylls of the King* (1859). First printed by William Caxton in one volume in 1485, *Le Morte d'Arthur* has been consistently popular since, except during the Augustan period of the early eighteenth century. Caxton's printing is the source of all extant versions except a manuscript discovered in 1934 in the Fellows' Library of Winchester College. The Winchester manuscript, which seems generally more reliable than Caxton, not only made the identity of the author more certain but also showed that Caxton had condensed the original.

Malory's *Le Morte d'Arthur* is itself a condensation, adaptation, and rearrangement of earlier materials. It is based primarily on the French Arthurian Prose Cycle (1225-1230) known as the Vulgate, a conglomeration of courtly stories of Lancelot that are ostensibly historical accounts of the court of Arthur and stories of the quest for the Holy Grail. Eugène Vinaver, the foremost editor and critic of Malory, has explained that the differences between the Vulgate and Malory's narrative are good indicators of the nature of Malory's achievement.

The primary structure of the Vulgate is episodic, and its narrative movement is largely backwards. Episodes prepare for and elucidate other episodes that may chronologically have preceded them. The work did not grow by accretion; its shape is a reflection of an alternative aesthetic. The result is a web of themes in which forward movement of the narrative is subordinated to the demonstration and clarification of the dominant ideals of the work. Malory took this source, added matter from the fourteenth century English *Alliterative Morte d'Arthur* and, to a lesser extent, from the *Stanzaic Morte*, and fashioned a new kind of fictional structure. The result is not simply condensation but a disentanglement of the elements of the narrative and a recombination of them into an order, an emphasis, and a significance entirely alien to the sources.

Vinaver has identified two primary ways in which Malory transformed the structure of the narrative. First, certain episodes are formed into self-contained units, almost short stories, by detachment from their context and the excision of extraneous detail. In the Vulgate, for example, the incidents grouped together by Malory as the story of the Knight of the Cart appeared long before the Grail quest; Malory puts them long after and organizes them as an exemplum of Lancelot's noble ideals rather than as a prefigurement of his amatory commitment, thus giving the episode a different significance by omission and diminution. Malory's second mode of transformation is to fashion a coherent narrative from bits and pieces scattered throughout his sources. In the story of the Fair Maid of Astolat, he organizes disparate details into a sequential form.

The most striking change in the sources is Malory's imposition of a consistently forward chronological movement. The courtly digressions and the significant configurations of explanatory episodes are gone. Instead, there is a straightforward narrative that alters both the tone and meaning of the original. Malory had no comprehension of or sympathy for the tradition of courtly love that permeated his sources. Where its vestiges cannot be omitted, Malory translates them into something more compatible with his genius. Therefore, Lancelot is no longer the "knight of the cart" because of courtly self-debasement for the beloved but because of a dedication to chivalric ideals. The elegance and controlled artificiality of his antecedents are changed by Malory into directness and moral earnestness. Lancelot becomes a Christianized, somewhat sentimentalized figure who is a model of the moderation that leads to supernatural rewards. Similarly, in the story of Pelleas and Ettard, Malory makes Pelleas' behavior more practical than courtly. After Ettard's infidelity, Malory substitutes the poetic justice of her death and Pelleas' happiness for the courtly self-abnegation demonstrated by Pelleas in the Vulgate.

Sometimes Malory's fiction suffers from the tension between his sources and his rendering of them. As E. K. Chambers has noted, characters are not always sustained on the same level of the narrative. Moreover, not all the courtly and mysterious elements are completely rationalized into the new intention. Some undecipherable oddities result. *Le Morte d'Arthur* remains, however, a vigorous and compelling narrative full of the spirit of adventurous knighthood. As Vinaver has shown in detail, Malory has substituted outdoor images for courtly affectation, the real English countryside for the conventional French, vigorous speech for conventional dialogues, and direct, human relationships for the elaborate rituals of courtly love. All of this is accomplished in a blunt and lively prose that is the antithesis of the intricacies of the French sources and perfectly suited to Malory's more direct structure and more forthright moral attitude.

"Critical Evaluation" by Edward E. Foster

Bibliography:
Adderley, C. M. "Malory's Portrayal of Sir Lancelot." *Language Quarterly* 29, nos. 1-2 (Winter/Spring, 1991): 47-65. Charts the progress of the love between Lancelot and Guinevere and argues that, although the Round Table fails collectively, there remain individuals who excel in virtue and prowess.
Field, P. J. C. *The Life and Times of Sir Thomas Malory.* Cambridge, England: D. S. Brewer, 1993. A convincing biography of Sir Thomas Malory that illustrates his political career during the Wars of the Roses and his several imprisonments.
Lumiansky, R. M., ed. *Malory's Originality: A Critical Study of "Le Morte D'Arthur."* Baltimore, Md.: The Johns Hopkins University Press, 1964. Consists of eight chapters, each of

which deals with a different one of Malory's "tales." The object of the book is to show that the tales are interdependent and the work is therefore single and unified.

Moorman, Charles. *The Book of Kyng Arthur: The Unity of Malory's "Morte Darthur."* Lexington: University of Kentucky Press, 1965. Moorman argues that the success of the Round Table depends on the integration of love, chivalry, and religion. It fails as a result of adultery, feuding, and the failure to find the Holy Grail.

Vinaver, Eugène. "Sir Thomas Malory." In *Arthurian Literature in the Middle Ages*, edited by Roger Sherman Loomis. Oxford, England: Clarendon Press, 1959. An ideal starting point for understanding Malory scholarship. Vinaver sets forth clearly his idea that *Le Morte d'Arthur* is not one book but a series of eight separate tales.

MORTE D'URBAN

Type of work: Novel
Author: J. F. Powers (1917-   )
Type of plot: Social realism
Time of plot: Late 1950's
Locale: Chicago and Minnesota
First published: 1962

Principal characters:
 FATHER URBAN ROCHE, a Roman Catholic priest
 FATHER WILFRID BESTUDIK, a colleague of Urban
 BILLY COSGROVE, a wealthy layman and friend of Urban
 FATHER JACK and
 BROTHER HAROLD, members of a community of Roman Catholic clergy
 BISHOP JAMES CONOR, the head of the local archdiocese
 MONSIGNOR RENTON, another of Urban's superiors
 MRS. THWAITES, an eccentric small-town philanthropist
 SALLY THWAITES HOPWOOD and
 DICKIE, her children
 SYLVIA BEAN, a member of a church that Urban visits

The Story:

Father Urban Roche, who was born Harvey Roche in a small town in Illinois, was fifty-four years old and a longtime member of the Order of Saint Clement, a small order of Roman Catholic priests based in Chicago. Urban had spent a number of years traveling and raising money for the order when, one day after a mass he had said in a suburban Chicago church, he was approached by Billy Cosgrove.

Cosgrove, a wealthy man given to frequent golfing and sailing outings, later met Urban at South Bend, Indiana, after a Notre Dame University football game. Hailing Urban from his chauffeur-driven Rolls Royce, Cosgrove became a mysterious and capricious force in Urban's life. Their relationship, from the beginning, was based on a strange kind of material need—on Billy's need to give Urban money and things, and on Urban's professional courting of a generous and affluent man. Urban gave Billy a load of firewood from the Saint Clement novitiate; later, over the course of time, Cosgrove endowed the Clementines with items for their foundation in Minnesota, built a golf course for the order, and invited Urban on fishing expeditions.

In the meantime, however, Urban was banished by Father Boniface to backwoods Minnesota, where a Clementine priest, Wilfrid "Bunny" Bestudik, presided over a tiny group of men clustered in a former sanatorium. Bunny had the idea of saving the facility, and even the order, from oblivion by transforming the outpost into a retreat center. Much work needed to be done on the buildings, work which, Bunny insisted, could be done by the resident clerics.

Urban had a very difficult time adjusting to his new role and, in fact, did not try very hard to work as a member of the small Clementine team. He complained of the cold and often slept in order to escape the boredom of daily life on the Hill, as the order's facility was called. Wilfrid, in his quiet way, put up with Urban's complaints and did what he thought was best. When the pastor of a nearby church, St. Monica's, suddenly died, Urban managed to persuade Bunny to let him temporarily take the pastor's place. This change in assignment was much to Urban's liking, and he began to build a small empire. He courted the goodwill of Mrs. Thwaites, a reclusive old woman of some wealth. With Billy Cosgrove's suspect help, property adjacent to the Hill was acquired so that the Order might attract retreatants with a golf course. Cosgrove hired an architect to build a fine course; later, he endowed the order with an automobile for its transportation needs.

Fate or Providence intervened in Urban's success. During a golf match with Bishop James Conor on the Hill course, Urban was hit on the head by the Bishop's ball. This proved to be a serious injury, from which Urban recovered after a convalescence, but which caused him recurrent headaches and some temporary short-term memory loss. The injury also set in motion a number of threats to Urban's status and well-being. Urban's brush with death also precipitated a fundamental change in his view of life, faith, and his relationship with others.

Urban found the courage to resist the cruel demands that Billy Cosgrove placed on him. During a fishing trip, in his frustration with not being able to catch a fish, Billy tried to drown a deer in the lake; when Urban objected, Billy simply dumped Urban in the water and left him there. Later, Sally Thwaites Hopwood tried to seduce Urban, not only by undressing in front of him, but by appealing to other worldly pleasures that had tempted Urban for so long in his life.

Ultimately, Urban was elected provincial of the Order of St. Clement, which was perhaps remarkable. Instead of using his new power to achieve what the old Urban might have wanted, however, the post-accident Urban gave repeated evidence that the world and its glories meant nothing to him. Indeed, he gained a reputation for piety, partly because of his ill health, but partly because the reputation was deserved. Moreover, Urban began to think of the Hill as his home—rather than Chicago, which had been his home base in his previous existence as traveling salesman for the order.

Critical Evaluation:

Morte d'Urban is a remarkable wedding of realism, comedy, tragedy, and redemption; indeed, the reader often feels that James Powers has captured much of the spirit of the daily existence of a mid-twentieth century American Roman Catholic priest. Father Urban Roche is consistently torn between piety and commitment to his faith and a desire to engage the world outside the church. Urban is a very worldly, urbane man, gifted with social know-how associated with small town boosters, salesmen, and members of fraternal organizations. Similarly, the other priests whom Powers presents constitute a spectrum of incompetence, foolishness, competitiveness, and sincere intent to do good and to follow the tenets of the faith. Powers shows the delineation of church politics, the petty jealousies and ambitions that motivate priests of various kinds—parish "soldiers," priests in administrative capacities, and priests who are primarily concerned with prayer and meditation. St. Clement's Hill, for example, is run by Bunny Bestudik, who is intent on carving out a small niche of notoriety for the St. Clement order by establishing a retreat house. He and his colleagues, including Urban, however, are worried about competition from the Benedictines and by pressure or indifference from the local archdiocesan bureaucracy.

The thematic focus of the novel is Urban's struggle to determine his own course. The hero's names indicate considerable irony: Urban is not only the name of several popes, but also of a saint, and Roche is one of several French words for rock—which constitutes an oblique reference to the Latin *petrus* and the Greek *petros*, the sources of the name Peter. Saint Peter is the "rock" on which Christ, according to Scripture, built his church. Ultimately then, Urban Roche is the modern rock of the church, Peter's heir. He is also a man who is tempted by what modern culture offers.

The reader may be amused and even appalled by Urban's social sense, his love of cigars, liquor, and fast cars, and by the pleasure he takes in glib verbal salesmanship of his religion and the church. There is a point, however, beyond which he will not go in his spirit of compromise. He argues, for example, against Monsignor Renton's angry denunciation of Mrs. Thwaites, who left the Church and then returned. Renton refuses to forgive Mrs. Thwaites' trespasses; Urban refuses to judge the woman's sincerity. While serving a local parish, Urban is called in the middle of the night to anoint a sick person; he welcomes the experience because it reminds him of his fundamental duties as a priest, something the swim of his social whirl and his concern for personal and professional success tend to obscure. On the other hand, Urban, being convinced that the good to be done in the world counts for a great deal, cannot conceive of the priesthood as a kind of monasticism—nothing more than a prayer and administering the Sacraments. For example, Urban dishonestly distorts facts and figures in order to persuade the Bishop and his parishioners to build a new church at St. Monica's: Certain ends justify certain means. Lest the St. Monica parishioners gain too much control of their church life, Urban institutes and busily involves himself in numerous church social and group religious activities. His goal is, at least in part, to feed his own ego. Similarly, a mission Urban preaches ends with his dramatic, showmanlike flourishes.

Ultimately, however, Urban succeeds in a number of ways at St. Monica's, the most spectacular success being the 150 percent increase in Mass attendance. Powers calls into question the nature. of what passes for faith in modern American society; he suggests that churches that flourish are those which entertain their members and deal in the external, superficial, social appeal of church membership.

It is with the construction of the golf course at St. Clement's Hill that Urban threatens to overstep the limits of good taste and common sense. He had conceived the course as a means to reach the "un-churched," and to enhance the Hill as a retreat site, but the course becomes the focus of his odd change in personality and perspective.

During a tournament at the Hill's golf course, Bishop Conor strokes a ball which hits Urban on the head. As immediately funny as his accident seems, it turns out that Urban is seriously injured. His convalescence takes time, which he spends at Mrs. Thwaites' estate; Urban experiences bad headaches and short-term memory loss; nevertheless, the Bishop decides not to take over the Hill in order to use it as a seminary. Eventually, Urban is abandoned by Billy and by Sally Thwaites Hopwood, Mrs. Thwaites' willful daughter. These apparent setbacks increase readers' admiration of Urban, however, because Urban resists Billy's bullying and Sally's bold attempt to make him give in to his instincts.

An irony surfaces in the story as Urban is elected provincial of the Order of St. Clement, replacing his old nemesis, Father Boniface. What his colleagues see as his disappointing lack of interest in furthering the order's standing is Urban's new lack of interest in jockeying for position in the world. Later, Urban gains a reputation among Clementines for his religious zeal, which may, in part, be disaffection brought about by his poor health. As the novel ends, Powers deliberately leaves readers in doubt—not only about his hero's status as saint or casualty, but about the very nature of faith and God's role in humans' affairs.

Gordon Walters

Bibliography:
Hagopian, John V. *J. F. Powers.* New York: Twayne, 1968. The only book-length study of Powers and his work. Hagopian's reading of *Morte d'Urban* is thorough and intelligent,

although perhaps somewhat intolerant of possible alternative interpretations.

Henault, Marie. "The Saving of Father Urban." *America* 108 (March 2, 1963): 290-292. A study of the Arthurian references in the novel.

Hinchcliffe, Arnold P. "Nightmare of Grace." *Blackfriars* 45 (February, 1964): 61-69. A consideration of what Hinchliffe calls the "Mammon of Iniquity" theme in the novel.

Merton, Thomas. "*Morte d'Urban*: Two Celebrations." *Worship* 36 (November, 1962): 645-650. Defends Powers against charges of anticlericalism and calls the novel a work of genius.

Sisk, John P. "*Morte d'Urban*, by J. F. Powers." *Renascence* 16 (1963): 101. According to Hagopian, Sisk's review of the novel is one of the best early assessments.

THE MOTHER

Type of work: Novel
Author: Grazia Deledda (1871-1936)
Type of plot: Psychological realism
Time of plot: Early twentieth century
Locale: Sardinia
First published: La madre, 1920 (English translation, 1922)

> *Principal characters:*
> PAUL, a priest
> MARIA MADDALENA, his mother
> AGNES, his sweetheart

The Story:

Maria Maddalena had been an orphan, brought up in drudgery by aunts. Part of her work was to bring flour from the mill. If there were no other customers, the old man who waited on her would follow her out and kiss her by force behind the bushes. His whiskers pricked her. When her aunts learned what was happening, they forbade the girl to go near the mill again. To their surprise, the old man came to the house one day and asked for Maria in marriage.

Maria continued to live in her aunts' house, and her husband stayed at the mill. Each day, when she visited him, he would steal flour and give it to her. Widowed shortly after she became pregnant, she supported her son by working as a servant. She refused to become involved with the servants or masters of the places in which she worked, for she wished to make her son a priest and she felt that purity was required of her as well. When her son Paul went to the seminary, Maria worked there to be near him. The bishop often commanded Paul to seek out his sacrificing mother and kiss her hand. During vacations, they sometimes went back to their native village. One summer, Paul visited the town prostitute several times. He was fascinated by her white skin; he thought it was so pale because her house was in constant shade. After that summer, Paul threw off desires of the flesh and felt himself sanctified.

After completing his studies, Paul was assigned to the remote village of Aar, a mountainous town where strong winds blew all the time. Maria was proud that her dreams were coming true as the population gathered in the square to meet the new priest. She settled down placidly in the presbytery to keep house for her son.

Aar had had no priest for some time. The former priest had been a drunkard, a gambler, and, some people said, a sorcerer. They had half-liked him, however, and had never complained to the bishop because they were afraid of his magic. Prudently, Maria had bars in the form of a cross put on the front door to ward off the evil eye, for it was common knowledge that the old priest had sworn to drive away any successor.

One night, Maria was desperately afraid. For some time, Paul had had a mirror in his room; he cleaned his nails and washed with scented soap. He even let his hair grow long and tried to comb it over his tonsure. She knew what was happening. Agnes was the only remaining member of the family in the big house of the village, and Paul had begun to visit her on his parish rounds. From the sounds in his bedroom, Paul was again getting ready to go out that night, and he left hurriedly. Ashamed but desperate, his mother followed him. She saw him go to the side gate of the big house and disappear inside. Finding the gate locked, she circled the grounds, but all the entrances were shut. She returned home to wait for Paul.

Dozing as she waited, she thought the wicked old priest was sitting beside her, leering at her from his whiskered face. He drew off his socks and ordered her to mend them. Calmly enough, she asked him how she could mend socks for a dead man. The priest declared he was not dead; furthermore, he would drive them out of the village. When she called him wicked, he argued with her that God had put people on earth to enjoy themselves.

With a start, she awoke and looked about her for the socks. She thought she heard ghostly footfalls leaving the presbytery. Earlier, she had considered denouncing Paul to the bishop. Not sure of his guilt, however, she resolved to face the problem at once.

When Paul came in, he curtly told his mother that he had been calling on a sick person. Maria was determined, however, to leave the village, never to see him again unless he broke with Agnes. She wondered if her own son could be so selfish that he could not see he was endangering Agnes' soul as well as his own. In his chamber, Paul fell into a troubled sleep after calling on God for help.

In the morning, his mother woke him early, and before he left his room he had written a letter renouncing Agnes. With a pale face, he gave it to his mother and told her to deliver it to the girl in person. After hearing confessions, he said mass. His sermon was cutting. The congregation was growing smaller each day; only on Sunday were the pews filled. After the service, he learned that Agnes had received his letter.

During the morning, word came that King Nicodemus was dying. Nicodemus was a wild hunter who lived far up the mountain, where he had removed himself so he could do no harm to other human beings. His relatives had brought him into the village when he was far gone in sickness. Paul, with his server Antiochus, went to the hut to give the hunter extreme unction. To their surprise, Nicodemus had disappeared. With his last strength, he had left the hated village, to die in his own mountain cabin.

Later, a woman brought a little daughter who was having a tantrum. The mother thought the girl was possessed by a demon, for it took force to get her into the presbytery. Humoring the superstitious mother, Paul read the parable of the Gadarene swine. As he read, the girl became quiet and receptive. Maria and the others were sure Paul had exorcised an evil spirit. The people of the village, believing him a miracle worker who could cast out demons, held a celebration for Paul. He was thankful when some of the merrymakers went home with him. He needed help that night to keep from going to Agnes.

Antiochus lingered after the rest of the company to remind Paul of a promise to visit the boy's mother. Antiochus wanted to be a priest, and Paul had promised to speak about the plan. He wearily set out. While he was impressing on his server's mother the sacrifices demanded of the priesthood, one of Agnes' servants came with the news that Agnes had fallen and was bleeding from her nose. Accepting his fate, Paul went to see her again.

Agnes was pale and looked older but not ill. She reproached him for the letter and inquired about his promise to marry her and take her away. Paul declared that he had only a brother's love for her. Angry, Agnes said that he came at night and seduced young girls. She would so denounce him in church if he did not leave the village before morning.

Paul told his mother of the threat. Both were apprehensive of going to church; they were thankful to see Agnes' pew empty, but toward the end of the service she appeared, looking straight at Paul. As the services were ending, he heard a cry. His mother had dropped dead. Paul went to her side. He saw Agnes staring at him.

Critical Evaluation:

When Grazia Deledda won the Nobel Prize in Literature in 1926, there was controversy because her reputation was not yet international and her prize provided a propaganda victory for Benito Mussolini's government, which she detested. Luigi Pirandello, the Sicilian widely regarded as the leading Italian writer of the twentieth century, was so angry that he dashed off a satirical novella, with a caricatured Deledda as its heroine. Others alleged that Deledda had been chosen by the Scandinavian award committee because her bleak landscapes reminded them of the gloom of their own national authors.

In the late twentieth century, Deledda's writing holds up well, and she appears to be one of the more durable Nobel laureates of the 1920's. A nostalgia for a lost time and place operates in her favor. She evokes her native Sardinia as an island of peasants, small landowners, priests, and bandits. From a safe distance, city dwellers are charmed by this pastoral scene.

Simple statements and clean metaphors not easily lost in translation characterize Deledda's style. She knows how to choose the precise detail to render the flavor of a moment, the personality of a character, or the atmosphere of a place. Italian was not Deledda's native tongue. As a child, she spoke Logudoro, a dialect not even understood throughout her entire island. From Giovanni Verga, the Sicilian novelist, Deledda learned to provide the color of the actual speech of rustic people while writing in the standard literary language of Italy. Like Verga, she became skilled at convincingly converting the rhythms and images of provincial speech into recognizable, dignified, and poetic Italian.

Deledda had little formal education. Although her family had been reasonably affluent by the standards of Nuoro, where they lived, education for women had not been a priority among a people who equated books with laziness and wondered how a "scribbling woman" could ever find a husband. Through a program of self-directed reading, Deledda absorbed the bardic style of Homer and the Bible. Other influences were Giovanni Verga, the realist, and Gabriel d'Annunzio, the decadent romantic. Among the French, English, and Russians, she discovered Victor Hugo, Thomas Hardy, and Fyodor Dostoevski. Her affinities with these sources are evident in her writing.

The Mother is by far Deledda's best known work, although its position as her masterpiece is less clear. The narrative approaches the classicism outlined by Aristotle, and the book is marked by consistency of mood and totality of effect. The action unfolds during a two-day span. The three principals—the priest's mother, Maria Maddalena; Paul, the priest; and Agnes, the woman he covets—are quintessential Deledda characters, whose raw emotions seem appropriate to folk inhabiting Mediterranean islands that have been visited and ravished by Vikings, Arab conquerors, and Vandals. Yet the social and spiritual crises faced by Paul are timeless.

Celibate priesthood originated before the cross was first raised on Sardinia. Paul's tragedy works itself out in a milieu that happens to be Catholic, yet his dilemma is that of the Protestant clergyman in Nathaniel Hawthorne's *The Scarlet Letter* (1850) or of the Druid priestess in Vincenzo Bellini's opera *Norma* (1831). Deledda and her characters are not theologians. They do not concern themselves with the rationale behind the Roman Catholic church demands. They do understand, however, the mystery that surrounds sacred consecration. The dimly understood teachings of Christianity mingle with the older superstitions of the island and the unspoken belief that a grim Providence presides over all.

Paul's pain is intensified by the solitude of his environment. If he had possessed deep spirituality, intellectual interests, companions, or even the opportunities to fraternize with other priests and safe parishioners, his deprivations would have seemed less keen. If the obsessive family ties could have been loosened or his life led under less scrutiny, his burden might have lifted.

Paul's inner resources are further depleted by his never having developed a conscience of his own. His mother remains his conscience, and God speaks in her voice. At one point, he has a vision of her lying on an altar, like a mysterious idol whose hand he is being forced to kiss. He is the victim of this woman, who is equally lonely and lives only through him. His priestly role raises her from servant to madonna status. Having given him to the church before his own age of consent, she has never really given him to God.

A great contrast to Paul is his altar boy, Antiochus. The young man ardently desires to be a priest, even though he must assert his choice against the wishes of his own mother, a usurer who also practices "certain other trades."

Maddalena, a mother who follows her son to assignations and monitors his every act, is as controlling and destructive as Sophia Portnoy in Philip Roth's *Portnoy's Complaint* (1969), which, incidentally, had enormous success in Italy. Yet Deledda does not pass glib judgment on this woman whom the island people view as noble, even heroic, whose struggle is the central focus of the novel.

Operatic adaptations of Deledda's writing have been unsuccessful, but she has an eye and ear for the grand scene. *The Mother* builds to a climax during Sunday mass, in a village church rendered in full sensuous detail. Agnes appears, threatening publicly to expose her relationship with Paul. Although she fails in the end to denounce him, she casts a witchlike spell over his mother, who dies in anticipation of shame and scandal. Agnes is the succubus who has given Maddelena the evil eye, that fearsome glance against which Sardinians wear their horned amulets.

At one time, critics labeled Deledda as a local colorist, because she commemorated Sardinians of her generation much as Berga did Sicilians and Prosper Mérimée did Corsicans. Yet her simple folk are neither the morally depraved country people of an Erskine Caldwell novel nor the noble primitives of a Victor Hugo tale. They are real people, confronting the human situation in a defined time and place, however claustrophobic.

"Critical Evaluation" by Allene Phy-Olsen

Bibliography:
Balducci, Carolyn. *A Self-Made Woman: Biography of Nobel-Prize-Winner Grazia Deledda.* Boston: Houghton Mifflin, 1975. The only book-length study or biography of Deledda in English. Written primarily for young adults in a nonscholarly, novelistic style.
Deledda, Grazia. *The Mother.* Translated by Mary G. Steegmann. New York: Macmillan, 1923. Reprint. Cherokee, 1982. The introduction provides an excellent, nontechnical discussion in English of Deledda's most famous novel.
Lawrence, D. H. *Sea and Sardinia.* London: Heinemann, 1950. A poetic evocation of the Sardinian milieu. An English classic of travel literature, written by one of Deledda's most ardent admirers. Contains an especially pertinent account of a journey inland to Nuoro, identified as Deledda's home town.
Pacifici, Sergio. *The Modern Italian Novel: From Capuana to Tozzi.* Carbondale: Southern Illinois University Press, 1973. Highly readable account of Italian achievements in modern fiction. One chapter is devoted principally to Deledda's work.
Pribic, Rado, ed. *Nobel Laureates in Literature: A Biographical Dictionary.* New York: Garland, 1990. Reviews Deledda's literary achievement, with a concise, pertinent commentary on *The Mother.* Identifies themes the novel shares with Deledda's other books and with representative international works of literary naturalism and existentialism.

MOTHER

Type of work: Novel
Author: Maxim Gorky (Aleksey Maksimovich Peshkov, 1868-1936)
Type of plot: Naturalism
Time of plot: First decade of the twentieth century
Locale: Russia
First published: Mat, serial, 1906; book, 1907 (English translation, 1906)

Principal characters:
    PELAGUEYA VLASOVA, a revolutionary heroine
    PAVEL VLASOV, her son
    ANDREY,
    VYESOVSHCHIKOV,
    RYBIN,
    NIKOLAY IVANOVICH,
    SOFYA,
    SASHENKA, and
    NATASHA, the Vlasovs' revolutionary friends

The Story:
    The factory workers in the small Russian community of Nizhni-Novgorod were an impoverished, soulless, brutal lot. Their work in the factory dehumanized them and robbed them of their energy; as a result, they lived like beasts.
    When the worker Michael Vlasov died, his wife, Pelagueya, feared that her son Pavel would lead the same anguished, brutal life. Gradually, however, she noticed with joy and apprehension that Pavel was turning out differently and that he was given to reading. One day, Pavel informed his mother that he was reading subversive literature and that a group of his socialist friends were coming to visit him. Pelagueya was naturally frightened, but when his friends arrived she noticed that they were much warmer, much more gentle than the people with whom she had lived all of her life. Though they engaged in heated arguments, no one seemed to get angry at the others. Pavel's friends seemed full of hope and vitality, and Pelagueya quickly warmed up to them. In particular, she liked Andrey, who was bighearted and full of laughter, and Natasha, a frail, gentle girl who read aloud during the meetings. Others in the group were Sashenka, a commanding girl who loved Pavel, and Vyesovshchikov, the village misanthropist. They were idealistic young people, hopeful about the future of working people and prepared to put their ideas into action. Pelagueya agreed to take Andrey in as a roomer out of her motherly love for him.
    Gradually Pavel's home became the center of their activities, but at the same time the group became the focus of village suspicion. Pavel and his comrades had printed leaflets and distributed them among the workers, spelling out their miserable condition. Soon afterward, the police dropped in unexpectedly and arrested Andrey and Vyesovshchikov. Several others were arrested as well.
    While the workers were generally hostile to Pavel because of his strangeness, he also inspired a certain confidence in them by virtue of his stern intelligence. Pelagueya was flattered that the sharp peasant, Rybin, an old bear of a man, should go to her son for advice. One day, the workers were notified that their pay would be cut. The workers were behind Pavel when he

made a speech to them and to the manager in protest against the cut; however, because of the speech, Pavel was arrested and sent to jail.

Distressed by her son's arrest, Pelagueya learned that about sixty others had been arrested as well and that Andrey sent her his regards from prison. She thereupon decided to become involved in her son's activities and took a job as a caterer to the factory laborers. Under cover of her work she distributed revolutionary literature. Meanwhile, she continued to see Pavel's socialist friends.

Soon afterward, Andrey was released from prison, and he returned to Pelagueya, who welcomed him with open arms. Rybin, claiming that the peasants were no better off than the workers, went to the country to stir up the peasants against their oppressive masters.

With Andrey living in her house, Pelagueya felt happier. Under his friendly goading, she learned to read and write. She visited Pavel in prison and slyly told him of her activities in distributing leaflets. Pelagueya's world expanded greatly now that she was involved in the socialist cause; she had something to hope for beyond her selfish interests.

In the spring, Pavel was released from prison. The Vlasov household continued to be the hub of the local socialist activities, and Pavel announced his intention of marching with the banner in the coming May Day parade, even though to do so would mean another jail sentence. One day, one of Pavel's friends rushed in to report that a spy had been murdered in the street. At first Pelagueya feared that Vyesovshchikov had committed the crime; later Andrey revealed that he had accidentally killed the spy and felt guilty about his deed. After two weeks of inquiring into the matter, the police gave up the investigation.

May Day arrived, and Pavel and Andrey were up early. The crowds had gathered in the streets, and the two men walked through them with Pelagueya close behind. After they had made an abortive attempt to rouse the workers with speeches and songs, soldiers appeared, forced back the crowd, and arrested Pavel, Andrey, and their companions. Pelagueya felt depressed after their arrest. In answer to her loneliness, Nikolay Ivanovich came to her and invited her to live with him in the city. She accepted his invitation and moved to his apartment. Nikolay and his sister Sofya were well-bred socialists. They treated Pelagueya with affection and respect, and she came to love them as though they were members of her own family.

Pelagueya and Sofya dressed as pilgrims and in that disguise distributed propaganda throughout the city and surrounding countryside. While delivering books to Rybin, Pelagueya saw the hardships of peasant life and the cruelty of the masters. She proved useful in aiding Vyesovshchikov to hide from the police after he had escaped from prison. She nursed a dying comrade, and during a riot at his funeral she helped a wounded boy at some danger to herself. She also visited Pavel in prison.

Learning that many of her comrades had been arrested, she decided to go alone to deliver her pamphlets in the country village. On arriving there she saw that Rybin had been arrested and cruelly beaten. That night, she stayed with sympathetic peasants and gave them copies of her leaflets. Returning to the city, she aided a fugitive peasant and told Nikolay about her trip. Shortly thereafter, she helped a comrade to escape from prison. Her efforts for the workers made her realize how family allegiances could interfere with loyalty to the cause; she understood now why Pavel refused to get married.

After about six months in jail, Pavel and his comrades were finally brought to trial. The judges were cold, impersonal, and aloof. Several of Pavel's friends declined to testify in his defense. As the trial proceeded, Pavel made a rousing speech in which he denounced the decadence of the masters and praised the youth and vision of the socialists. After Andrey had further taunted the judges, Pavel and his companions were sentenced to exile in Siberia.

During this time, the police were hunting down the socialists. Nikolay was arrested shortly after the trial. Pavel's speech had been printed, and Pelagueya had promised to deliver copies to a remote town. On the train, she recognized a police spy and knew she had been trapped. When the police tried to arrest her, she shouted to the other occupants of the train about her mission and their servitude. She opened her bag and handed out the leaflets even while the police were beating her.

Critical Evaluation:

At the turn to the twentieth century, the writings of Maxim Gorky of Russia aroused interest throughout the world for their dramatic presentation of the struggles taking place in that largely unknown country. His representations of the bitter lives of that country's masses caused a sensation whenever they were published or produced on the stage. *Mother* is one of the most famous of these early works, and it is his only long work devoted entirely to the Russian revolutionary movement. Most of Gorky's early novels fail to sustain a continuous, powerful narrative, succumbing instead to frequent and irrelevant philosophical digressions, but *Mother* stands as a vivid and moving portrayal of a bitter struggle. If *Mother* is propaganda, it is propaganda raised to the level of art.

Although Gorky wrote primarily about the proletariat and in a naturalistic vein, he was not fundamentally concerned with politics, and his works exhibit a marked lyric talent that imbues his writing with a haunting poetic quality. Gorky's concern was with strong, vital, memorable characters rather than with dogma or morality. He envisioned a future in which vigorous people would free themselves from their economic degradation and live as free, independent spirits. He was a visionary rather than a dogmatist. This fact is particularly evident in *Mother*, in which Pelagueya Vlasova, through the love of her son, becomes converted to the revolutionary cause and gradually comes to love the people as her children. Gorky was strongly attracted to self-made individuals, to men and women with the courage to carry out their plans, and he makes the reader admire them as well. The lyric sweep of Gorky's vision in this novel is compelling.

Pelagueya's expanding consciousness forms the framework of the novel and serves as the catalyst that unites the parts of the story into a coherent, dynamic vision and raises the book to the level of a masterpiece. In the course of the narrative, the reader experiences the gradual growth of a movement in the radicalization first of the young man Pavel and then of his mother. The mother is only forty years old when the story opens, but already she is an old woman, brutalized by years of poverty and beatings. Yet spiritually she is not dead, and as she painfully learns the truth about herself and her world, she begins to want to help spread this truth. The numbing fatalism that bound her when her husband was alive, her belief that the lot of women must always be despair, is gradually replaced by hope for the future.

The two aspects of love, its pain and its strength, are movingly depicted. The mother wants to protect her son, but she knows that she must let him be free. At the same time, her growing love for the members of the movement gives her the strength to remake her life and to brave hardships in contributing to the struggle. Her love in turn helps the others in the movement, and their united love for the poor, for the masses of humanity as yet unawakened, helps to keep all of them going. The party is called the "spiritual mother" of the working people, and many times it is referred to as helping the masses to be "reborn." The primary task of the mother and her compatriots is to educate the people and to distribute literature that will help them to be "reborn." Awareness must be the first step to revolution. The people are equated with Jesus Christ in several passages, most particularly when the mother washes the feet of the peasant leader Ignaty. The symbolism is unobtrusive yet effective.

The long novel is filled with powerful scenes, from the opening in which the terrified woman is beaten by her husband to the ending when she is killed while carrying on the work of her son. The trial of Pavel, her son, and his close friend Andrey, is effectively handled, as are the several riots and crowd scenes. Gorky's ability to handle large groups of people is remarkable. Each individual stands out distinctly, depicted as having human, believable eccentricities and irrationalities, yet Gorky manages to create a sense of the all-embracing tide of humanity. Human beings are not always consistent to character, and Gorky knew this; his people are realistic, and his characterizations are the principal strength of his mosaic of the early days of the Russian Revolution.

Bibliography:
Borras, F. M. *Maxim Gorky the Writer: An Interpretation*. Oxford, England: Clarendon Press, 1967. One of the more astute interpretations of Gorky's works, especially of his novels and plays. Borras emphasizes Gorky's artistic achievements in such works as *Mother*.

Gifford, Henry. "Gorky and Proletarian Writing." In *The Novel in Russia: From Pushkin to Pasternak*. New York: Harper & Row, 1965. A discussion of Gorky's influence on proletarian writers, with remarks on the role of *Mother* in this respect.

Hare, Richard. *Maxim Gorky: Romantic Realist and Conservative Revolutionary*. London: Oxford University Press, 1962. The first substantial book on Gorky in English since Alexander Kaun's 1932 study. Hare combines the political aspects of Gorky's biography with critical analysis of his works, including *Mother*.

Holtzman, Filia. *The Young Maxim Gorky, 1868-1902*. New York: Columbia University Press, 1948. A detailed survey of the first half of Gorky's life, coinciding with his formation as a person and a writer. *Mother* is discussed at some length.

Levin, Dan. *Stormy Petrel: The Life and Work of Maxim Gorky*. New York: Appleton-Century-Crofts, 1965. A general book that covers Gorky's entire life, thus completing Kaun's book. Includes a discussion of *Mother*.

Weil, Irwin. *Gorky: His Literary Development and Influence on Soviet Intellectual Life*. New York: Random House, 1966. The most scholarly book on Gorky in English, skillfully combining biography with critical analysis, including that of *Mother*. Valuable especially for the discussion of Soviet literary life and Gorky's connection with, and influence on, younger Soviet writers.

MOTHER AND SON

Type of work: Novel
Author: Ivy Compton-Burnett (1884-1969)
Type of plot: Satire
Time of plot: End of the nineteenth century
Locale: An English country house
First published: 1955

>
> *Principal characters:*
> MIRANDA HUME, matriarch of the Hume family
> JULIUS HUME, her husband
> ROSEBERY HUME, their eldest son
> FRANCIS,
> ALICE, and
> ADRIEN, children of Julius Hume
> EMMA GREATHEART, a neighbor of the Humes
> HESTER WOLSEY, Miss Greatheart's companion
> MISS BURKE, Miss Greatheart's housekeeper
> PLAUTUS, Miss Greatheart's cat

The Story:

Miss Burke, who had applied for the post of paid companion to Miranda Hume, found her so rude and overbearing that she felt obliged to refuse to continue the interview with the rigid and autocratic potential employer. Instead Miss Burke blundered into the neighboring house and accepted a position as a housekeeper to Emma Greatheart, who lived alone with her cat Plautus. At the same time, Hester Wolsey, Emma's friend, felt forced by economic necessity to accept the still-available position as companion to the austere and forbidding Miranda.

Although Miranda Hume continued to fail in health, she still found the strength to continue to bully and intimidate her family. Her general hostility excluded, however, her son Rosebery, on whom she doted and who remained a loyal son instead of striking out on his own. Her husband, however, preferred the three children of his late brother, who had become his wards. Francis, Alice, and Adrien's alienation from Miranda's regime, reflected in their bitter jokes, was a marked contrast to the behavior of Rosebery, who basked in his role as his mother's favorite. As Miranda's health declined further, Miss Wolsey was able to cleverly insinuate herself into the family circle.

At a moment when Miranda was particularly unwell, her husband Julius decided to confess that he was in reality not the guardian but the father of the three younger children. Miranda, who had based her life on a belief in her own godlike omniscience, died as a consequence of the shock and fury she felt at the thought of her husband's secret past. The confession of her husband Julius, which can be said to have been a murder weapon, and Miranda's subsequent death were witnessed by both the appalled Rosebery and the keenly interested Hester Wolsey.

The eavesdropping Hester also managed to be there when Rosebery soon learned a second secret—in a letter that Miranda had kept hidden, Rosebery discovered that Julius was not actually his biological father, but that he was the product of an earlier liaison on Miranda's part. In short order, Rosebery saw his respectable Victorian parents exposed as adulterers. On an unconscious level, however, the parents seemed to have known all along. The loyalty of

Miranda and Julius was always to their own gene pools, which they privileged over other bonds, exposing their animal cunning and their human narcissism.

Miranda's death, which allowed Hester to continue to consolidate her position in the household, became the occasion for rejoicing among the younger children and for sorrow on the part of Rosebery. Recovering from his grief with suspicious haste, however, Rosebery immediately proposed to Hester, who declined, hoping instead to marry Julius. Hester became infuriated when Julius proposed to Emma and Rosebery proposed to Miss Burke. Overcome by feelings of jealousy and envy, it suited Hester's purpose at this time to reveal the Hume family secrets concerning the paternity of Rosebery and the other children.. These revelations brought Miss Burke and Emma to their senses.

Emma and Hester returned to their original domestic arrangement, with the addition of the helpful Miss Burke. They remained free from marriages that promised more convenience than love, but they had learned much that was distressing about human nature. The antics of their pet cat Plautus, who brought, as a gift, a mouse he captured, indicated to them the predatory, selfish animal instincts that simmered beneath the respectable appearances of the two households.

At the Hume household, Julius and Rosebery were left without mature female companionship. Instead of having a wife and family of his own, Rosebery continued to live in his mother's house. Rosebery spent his time teaching the children the games his mother taught him. The younger children, whose teasing could be sadistic, especially of their servants, were able to receive from Rosebery some of the affection that had been lacking in their relationship with Miranda. Although Rosebery briefly considered doing so, he did not leave the domestic sphere for a new life in the outside world, and instead took Miranda's place at home.

Critical Evaluation:

Herself the product of a large Victorian family, Ivy Compton-Burnett became one of that institution's foremost critics. Bringing to her study of her Victorian world the critical spirit of modernity, she can be seen as a pioneer in the analysis of the dysfunctional family, exposing the ways in which parents tyrannize their children. Sensitive to the needs and interests of children, Compton-Burnett was ahead of her time in championing their rights and the rights of the individual. Stunned by the tragedies that beset her family, including the suicide of two sisters, the death of two brothers in World War I, and the family's general fragmentation, Compton-Burnett underwent a period of recuperation and reassessment that brought about a transformation of herself and her values, and led to her brilliant and original fiction.

All Compton-Burnett's novels cover the same material—namely, her childhood in a large Victorian family. By her own admission, she never really entered modern life; in a sense, she was haunted by her childhood, which gave her her great subject. The perspective of her novels reflects the deep changes that overcame her psyche and her society in the wake of World War I. Within the narrow confines of her country houses and their old-fashioned denizens, she was able to write telling satires not only of the traditional family but also, by inference, other systems of domination.

Essentially a satiric writer, her novels present her autocratic characters in terms of their potential as figures of jest and ridicule. Such a vision produces an exhilarating sense of liberation from narrow and rigid prejudices and preconceptions, creating space for dissent and critical thought. This farcical examination of troubled families is disconcerting, but Compton-Burnett's ability to present something known to be tragic with an air of high comedy is one of her great achievements. This is not to say that her novels are simply comedies; comedy and tragedy are mingled so that her novels oscillate precariously between farce and serious melodrama.

Another original aspect of Compton-Burnett's work is her dialogue, which constitutes a large component of her narrative. Not simply conversation, her dialogue is in fact a brilliant deployment of modern stream-of-consciousness techniques, indicating thoughts that are usually left unspoken. Although her style is straightforward and economical, its subtleties require and repay concentration. In her dialogue, she indicates half a dozen points of view in rapid succession, moving from one attitude to its opposite and back again. This modernist fragmentation of perspective suggests both the erosion of social consensus and the introduction of a more open, observant, and thoughtful sensibility.

Compton-Burnett's image of human nature is bleak. Twisted emotional attachments such as that between Rosebery and Miranda are the rule rather than the exception in her fiction. This dark view of family relationships is a useful counterweight to sentimental bromides about Victorian family values. Even more, criminality is not uncommon in her domestic world. This perception of criminality combined with her inquisitive intelligence gives her work some kinship with the genre of detective fiction. In addition to exposing the guilty secrets of her Victorian paragons, Compton-Burnett also interrogates the Victorian ideas of women as the conventional "better half" and demystifies motherhood by showing maternal figures who are capable of great cruelty and heartlessness. Miranda is a classic example of the powerful and frightening female characters in Compton-Burnett's work. In the autocratic heroines, one can sense brilliant, heartless individuals whose wily and aggressive natures have been confined in small and domesticated venues.

The ending of *Mother and Son,* in which, against the reader's expectations, there are no marriages, depicts instead the relationship that Compton-Burnett often writes of favorably—that of brother and sister. In addition to this happy picture of brothers and sisters together, she ends with three unmarried women and two unmarried men. The single life, although not perfect, is, for her, preferable to the traditional institution of marriage and family, which is likely to be a venue for loveless power struggles. Compton-Burnett's own happy domestic partnership with the writer Margaret Jourdain may have contributed to her depiction of the three cheerful spinsters at the end of *Mother and Son.*

Reared in an artistic and intellectual atmosphere, Compton-Burnett took her vocation as a novelist quite seriously. From her second novel through her twentieth, her work remained consistent in subject and treatment, so that there appear to be no distinctive phases. All of her novels show her to be a pioneer in the art of modern fiction who broke free of conventional fictional techniques. As time passed, her fiction became more abstract and austere, but the high comedy, the tragic vision, and the deep emotional intelligence remained.

Although she has been compared to authors as diverse as Jane Austen, Nathalie Sarraute, and Aeschylus, in many ways, Ivy Compton-Burnett is sui generis; there is no one quite like her. Although her writing spanned the World Wars, she found her greatest recognition during the Cold War, when she took her place among the generation of writers that include Iris Murdoch, Henry Green, Anthony Powell, Evelyn Waugh, and William Golding. Her recognition by Sarraute, theorist and practitioner of the New Novel that developed in France in the 1950's, ratified her status as an innovative modern author.

Margaret Boe Birns

Bibliography:
Baldanza, Frank. *Ivy Compton-Burnett.* New York: Twayne, 1964. Includes an analysis of each

novel, a chronology, and a bibliography up to 1963, as well as a treatment of Compton-Burnett's techniques.

Burkhart, Charles, ed. *The Art of I. Compton-Burnett*. London: Victor Gollancz, 1972. A compilation of critical essays and interviews by leading critics of Compton-Burnett's work. Examines the theme of domestic tyranny and includes the important essay on Compton-Burnett's dialogue by French novelist Nathalie Sarraute.

Gentile, Kathy Justice. *Ivy Compton-Burnett*. New York: St. Martin's Press, 1991. Establishes Compton-Burnett as a feminist and adds new and important perspectives to her work, including feminist analysis of all of the novels. Excellent bibliography.

Nevius, Blake. *Ivy Compton-Burnett*. New York: Columbia University Press, 1970. A short, appreciative, general book for those unfamiliar with her work. Serves as a lively introduction for those who find her novels difficult and inaccessible.

Spurling, Hilary. *Ivy: The Life of I. Compton-Burnett*. New York: Alfred A. Knopf, 1984. The indispensable biography of Compton-Burnett, with much useful information about her childhood, the source material for all of her novels. Describes her happy and creative years with her companion, Margaret Jourdain.

MOTHER COURAGE AND HER CHILDREN

Type of work: Drama
Author: Bertolt Brecht (1898-1956)
Type of plot: Play of ideas
Time of plot: 1624-1648
Locale: Europe
First performed: 1941 (in German); first published, 1941 (in English); German original,
   1949 as *Mutter Courage und ihre Kinder*

> *Principal characters:*
> MOTHER COURAGE or ANNA FIERLING, owner of a canteen wagon
> KATTRIN, her mute daughter
> EILIF, her older son
> SWISS CHEESE, her younger son
> COOK
> CHAPLAIN
> YVETTE POTTIER, a camp follower

The Story:

In 1624, six years into the Thirty Years' War, a recruiting officer and a sergeant discussed the difficulty of recruiting in Poland, which had been at peace and was not organized for war. Mother Courage's canteen wagon rolled on, drawn by her two sons, Eilif and Swiss Cheese. Mother Courage and her mute daughter, Kattrin, sat on the wagon. Mother Courage sang a song that both criticized war and enticed officers to buy her wares for their soldiers because "cannon is rough on empty bellies." She told the officers she had been given the name "Mother Courage" because she had driven wildly through the bombardment of Riga to sell fifty loaves of bread that were getting moldy.

When the officers tried to recruit Eilif, Mother Courage angrily confronted them. In response to the sergeant's downplaying of the dangers of war, she offered to look into his future by drawing lots. He drew the black cross of death. The recruiting officer persisted, so she had Eilif and Swiss Cheese draw lots, and both drew black crosses. Mother Courage drew for Kattrin, who also got a cross. The sergeant distracted Mother Courage by negotiating to buy a belt, while the recruiting officer convinced Eilif to leave with him.

Two years later, Mother Courage negotiated the sale of a capon to the commander's cook and helped him prepare it for the commander and his guest of honor, Eilif. Angered as she listened to Eilif recounting his daring in capturing twenty bullocks and the commander's praising him, she told the cook that a leader who needs bravery is a bad leader. Eilif and his mother were reunited when she joined his "Song of the Wise Woman and the Soldier," in which the soldier ignored the wise woman's advice and died.

Three years later, Swiss Cheese was paymaster of the retreating Second Protestant Regiment. Yvette, a camp follower, sang "The Fraternization Song," lamenting her first soldier lover, whom she had not seen in five years. The cook and the chaplain brought Eilif's request for money before he left with his regiment. Concerned about the cash box entrusted to Swiss Cheese, Mother Courage paid, complaining that Eilif speculated in mother love.

The cook, the chaplain, and Mother Courage discussed the religious war. Mother Courage noted the Protestant king was unbeatable because, although he waged war from fear of God, he also wanted a good profit, so little fellows backed the war.

The Catholics defeated the Protestant soldiers, who retreated hastily, leaving Mother Courage and the others as prisoners. The group quickly got rid of evidence that tied them to the Protestants, and Catholics ignored the obvious because they needed a canteen. Mother Courage noted, "The defeats and victories of the fellows at the top aren't always defeats and victories for the fellows at the bottom."

Business was good for the canteen and for Yvette, but Swiss Cheese's cashbox remained a concern. He was discovered by Catholic soldiers, confessed under torture, and was put on trial.

Hoping to save Swiss Cheese, Mother Courage negotiated with Yvette, who had formed a liaison with a Catholic colonel willing to buy her a canteen. Mother Courage was unwilling to part with the wagon, arguing for a lease, to which Yvette agreed. When Mother Courage learned Swiss Cheese had thrown the cashbox, from which she had hoped to repay Yvette's loan, into the river, she tried to haggle with her son's captors over the bribe for his release. She failed, and he was condemned and shot. When soldiers brought his body for Mother Courage to identify, she denied knowing him, so his body was thrown into a carrion pit.

Mother Courage went to the officer's tent to complain that soldiers had vandalized her wagon after Swiss Cheese's death. She talked an angry young soldier out of complaining, singing the "Song of the Great Capitulation," then she herself left without lodging a complaint.

Two years later the war had widened. Over Mother Courage's objections, the chaplain, and Kattrin tore up officers' shirts to bind up the peasants' wounds, and Kattrin rescued a baby from its burning home. During the funeral of a fallen commander, Mother Courage, the chaplain, and the clerk argued about the possibility of peace. The chaplain asserted that war would not end, because it satisfied all needs, including the need for peace. Convinced, Mother Courage sent Kattrin and the clerk to stockpile supplies. In their absence, the chaplain unsuccessfully proposed a closer relationship to Mother Courage. Kattrin returned alone with the supplies and a disfiguring wound. They moved on, all three pulling the wagon.

News of peace arrived, and the cook returned. He and Mother Courage berated the chaplain for his reasoning about peace. The argument was interrupted by Yvette's return. She had married the colonel and was now widowed and well off. Recognizing the cook as her first lover, she warned Mother Courage about him. They left, and the cook and the chaplain received Eilif's last visit. During this brief peace, he had acted as if it were still wartime, stealing cattle, and had been sentenced to death. He was taken away before Mother Courage returned with news that the war had resumed. She was told only that Eilif had gone away. The cook and Kattrin pulled the wagon back to the war.

As the war worsened, the cook inherited an inn and invited Mother Courage to run it with him. When he refused to include Kattrin, she started to leave her mother. Mother Courage, who had sent the cook away, assured Kattrin they must stay together.

Mother Courage left Kattrin in the care of a peasant family while she went into the Protestant town of Halle to buy supplies. Catholic soldiers, intent on ambushing Halle while the town slept, forced these peasants to assist them. After the soldiers took the peasant son as their guide, his mother prayed to God to protect her grandchildren, who were sure to be massacred in the ambush. When Kattrin heard the children mentioned, she grabbed a drum and, from the roof, drummed loudly to awaken the town. The soldiers shot her, but the sound of a cannon from the town signaled her success.

Mother Courage returned, mourned Kattrin briefly, then, paying the peasants to bury the body, joined the last regiment leaving Halle to resume her business. At the end, she pulled the wagon alone.

Critical Evaluation:

A major force in modern theater, German playwright Bertolt Brecht is perhaps best known for his concepts of epic theater and *Verfremdungseffekt* (alienation effect). A Marxist, Brecht reacted against what he called culinary theater, which provides its audience with the illusion of reality. Brecht wanted theatrical productions to destroy comforting illusions, so the audience would think rather than feel.

Brecht defined the learning process of alienation as a dialectical progression, moving the audience from its familiar—and false—understanding to an estranging nonunderstanding, achieved by a defamiliarizing theatrical presentation, to the final stage of understanding in a new way. This was to be achieved through productions that used the techniques of epic theater. The ideal was a dispassionate presentation. One means was use of a narrative voice, through projected slogans on stage, to intervene between the audience and events of the play and eliminate audience identification with the character, thus forcing the audience to maintain objectivity.

The plots of epic plays consisted of loosely knit episodes, complete within themselves. The nonliterary elements—stage design, music, choreography—were designed to be autonomous, interrupting the flow of the production. Together, these elements were to create distance, resulting in an audience's viewing the play with a critical eye.

Mother Courage and Her Children, loosely based on Hans Jacob Christoffel von Grimmelshausen's *Courage: The Adventuress* (1670), is Brecht's most successful play. It uses many epic theater techniques. The play is composed of twelve scenes of varying lengths, each introduced by a slogan designed to place it in historical context, eliminate suspense, and clarify the effect of the war on the characters. For example, the slogan for scene three is "Three years pass and Mother Courage, with parts of a Finnish regiment, is taken prisoner. Her daughter is saved, her wagon likewise, but her honest son dies."

Music is also used throughout the play to stop action and comment on it. Mother Courage's first song has a thematically important refrain: "Let all of you who still survive/ Get out of bed and look alive!" This is repeated in several scenes, and sung at the play's conclusion by the soldiers Mother Courage is rushing to join.

Two other songs are thematically important. "The Song of the Great Capitulation," sung by Mother Courage, details her progress in learning to "march in lockstep with the rest." The cook's "Song of the Great Souls of this Earth" notes problems caused by virtues such as Solomon's wisdom, concluding that only vices bring reward. Although Brecht was a Marxist, his pessimism, illustrated in these songs, was difficult for Marxist critics to accept.

Brecht considered *Mother Courage* to be a cautionary tale that shows that those who live on war have to pay. War is a metaphor for capitalistic business; the state of war is analogous to the human condition, poisoned by greed and exploitation. Brecht believed that both war and capitalism made human virtues "fatal even to those who exercise them." He considered Mother Courage to be guilty, a deformed merchant-mother, the hyena of war.

To Brecht's irritation, response to the play generally focused on its emotional impact. Mother Courage has been seen as a complex and tragic character, compared to Niobe. Spectators sympathized with her hard choices. Kattrin, whose love of children, eagerness for motherhood, and compassion make her a life force, is also a profoundly sympathetic character. Ravaged by the war (her muteness resulting from a soldier who "stuck something in her mouth when she was little"), she is normal in an abnormal world that has done its best to deform her. Her act of defiance, drumming to save the children of Halle, has been called the most emotionally moving scene in modern drama.

The emotional depth of this play derives from its ambiguity. Brecht made changes in the play before its second production in post-World War II Berlin, hoping to mitigate the emotional response. The Berlin audience, many of whom had lost relatives in the war, sat weeping at the play's conclusion, and the critics again responded to Mother Courage's Niobe-like qualities. Later critics also have noted its emotional power.

Elsie Galbreath Haley

Bibliography:
Demetz, Peter, ed. *Brecht*. Englewood Cliffs, N.J.: Prentice-Hall, 1962. Essay on *Mother Courage and Her Children* focuses on the "Song of the Great Capitulation," Brecht's Marxism and pessimism, and epic theater.
Esslin, Martin. *Brecht: The Man and His Work*. Garden City, N.Y.: Doubleday, 1960. Critical study of Brecht, including biography, poetry, the theory and practice of Brechtian theater, and Brecht's relationship to the Communists.
Fuegi, John. *Bertolt Brecht: Chaos, According to Plan*. Cambridge, England: Cambridge University Press, 1987. Discusses the theater of Brecht's time and how he changed it. Section on *Mother Courage and Her Children* focuses on the 1949 Berlin production and how Brecht's staging reinforced meaning.
Lyon, Charles R. *Bertolt Brecht: The Despair and the Polemic*. Carbondale: Southern Illinois University Press, 1968. A close reading of seven major Brecht plays, including *Mother Courage and Her Children*.
Speirs, Ronald. *Bertolt Brecht*. New York: St. Martin's Press, 1987. An introduction to Brecht's works, focusing on the balance between the intellect and the emotional response produced by the plays. In-depth analysis of *Mother Courage and Her Children* and four of Brecht's other plays.

MOTHER HUBBERDS TALE

Type of work: Poetry
Author: Edmund Spenser (c. 1552-1599)
Type of plot: Fable
Time of plot: Antiquity
First published: 1591, as *Prosopopoia: Or, Mother Hubberds Tale*

> *Principal characters:*
> REYNOLD, the wily fox of French folk legends
> THE APE, his accomplice

The Story:

August days brought sickness to the poet. His friends visited him and told tales of knights, fairies, and giants to while away his days of illness. What pleased him most, however, was the beast fable recounted by old Mother Hubberd.

In the fable, the fox approached his neighbor, the ape, and proposed that they set out together to seek their fortunes. The ape willingly acquiesced, wanting only to know how his friend planned to improve their sorry lot. The fox suggested a disguise and pointed out that if they pretended to be beggars, they would be free of all obligations and responsibilities. The two dressed themselves in the tattered remains of military uniforms to win confidence and sympathy.

The comrades' first victim was an honest, unintelligent farmer who listened sympathetically to the ape's description of his misfortunes and his wounds. The ape requested employment—something that would not tax his poor, battered body—and soon he was tending the gullible husbandman's sheep with the fox as his trusty dog. The partners in crime feasted lavishly on their charges for several months, then escaped into the night just before they were to produce an accounting of the flock.

Weary of profitless begging, they provided themselves with a gown and a cassock to impersonate learned clergymen. They first encountered an illiterate priest who advised them on their parish duties. All that was necessary was to say the service weekly, to "lay the meat before" the faithful; they had no responsibility for helping their parishioners accept the gospel. The old days when priests prayed daily and sincerely were, fortunately, past:

> Now once a week, upon the Sabbath day,
> It is enough to do our small devotion,
> And then to follow any merry motion.

The priest then suggested that the fox and the ape go to some nobleman, feigning a grave and saintly demeanor, to request a benefice. He could not recommend that they seek preferment at court, for "nothing there is done without a fee."

Heeding this good counsel, the fox assumed the role of priest, and the ape became his parish clerk. They reveled gaily for a time, but the complaints of their abused and exploited parishioners finally brought about their expulsion from their offices. Once more on the road, they almost starved before they met a richly dressed mule who told them that he had just come from the court. He, too, had advice for achieving success. They should appear at court themselves:

> . . . with a good bold face,
> And with big words, and with a stately pace,
> That men may thinke of you, in generall,
> That to be in you, which is not at all:
> For not by that which is, the world now deemeth,
> (As it was wont) but by that same that seemeth.

The fox and the ape easily won the royal favor, being suited by nature and inclination to win acceptance. The ape dressed in outlandish clothes and demonstrated his accomplishments: "For he could play, and daunce, and vault, and spring,/ And all that else pertains to reveling." He was also skilled at fortune-telling, juggling, and sleight of hand. The latter talent was especially profitable, for "what he touched came not to light again."

The ape passed his time gambling, carrying on intrigues, and composing exceedingly bad verses to corrupt the chaste ladies around him. To support his success, the fox, disguised as his confidential servant, practiced all kinds of deceits and, for a large fee, promised favors from his master to poor suitors who came to court looking for preferment.

At length the fox's deceptions were discovered, and he was banished. The ape, left without resources, soon found himself shabby and scorned, and he fled to rejoin his friend. Lamenting their lack of success, they wandered into a wood where they found a lion lying asleep, his crown and scepter beside him. The ape timorously stole the lion's skin and his regalia, then claimed the throne for himself as a reward for his valor. The fox reluctantly agreed, stipulating that he be allowed to make all the decisions of government. They initiated a reign of terror, extorting treasure from all the beasts of the forest.

The fox sold justice, raised the fortunes of his family by his ill-gotten gains, and defended his actions on the grounds of his long experience and his desire to build up the royal treasury. He brought about the downfall of the noblest beasts, scorned scholars and poets, and disdained the common people.

Only divine intervention could put an end to this disastrous reign; Jupiter noticed the turmoil among the wild animals and sent Mercury to humble the usurper ape. Mercury woke the lion from his unnatural sleep, and the latter went to the door of his palace, roaring with such force that most of its inhabitants perished from fear. The ape ran to find a hiding place, and the fox skulked out to the lion, laying all the blame upon his partner. The lion punished both, stripping the fox and casting him out, then clipping the ape's tail and ears; the story ends as a kind of myth of "why the ape has no tail."

Critical Evaluation:

The first three books of Edmund Spenser's masterpiece, *The Faerie Queene*, were published in 1590 and attracted immediate and widespread attention and praise. The next year the publisher William Ponsonby brought out a collection of shorter poems by Spenser titled *Complaints Containing Sundrie Small Poemes of the Worlds Vanitie* containing, among other works, *Prosopopoia: Or, Mother Hubberds Tale*. The *Complaints* was intended to take advantage of the poet's newly found popularity. Unfortunately, the sharp satire of some of the poems, especially *Mother Hubberds Tale*, offended the Elizabethan authorities, and the book was apparently "called in," or censored, shortly after its publication.

The satire in *Mother Hubberds Tale* that caused it to be called in was political in nature, and referred specifically to events surrounding the proposed marriage of Queen Elizabeth I to the French Duc d'Alençon. Although the events had taken place long before the actual publication of the poem, which was probably written in 1579-1580, its offense to high officials in Elizabeth's court, including Lord Burleigh and even the queen herself, was sufficient to have the volume suppressed and Spenser, for all practical purposes, banished to Ireland.

The entire poem is framed as if spoken by Mother Hubberd herself. *Prosopopoeia* refers to the rhetorical device in which an imaginary or absent person speaks or acts out a story. The purpose of the device is to set the satire within an imaginary context, allowing the animal fable that follows to be both believable and understandable.

The central character of *Mother Hubberds Tale*, the wily fox who attempts to defraud the public, comes from the popular French stories of Reynard the Fox, translated and published by England's first printer, William Caxton, in the late fifteenth century.

The format of the poem is that of the "travel tale," specifically that of the picaresque story, which follows the adventures of a clever rogue. (The Spanish word for rogue, *pícaro*, gives the genre its name.) In *Mother Hubberds Tale*, there are two rogues, the fox and the ape. Their travels take them from rustic isolation to palatial splendor, since each deception they perform advances them another step up the social ladder: They begin as beggars and continue their successful trickeries until the ape becomes a king and the fox, his powerful first minister. At that point, Jupiter, a symbol of divine authority, bestirs the rightful monarch, the lion, into reclaiming his throne, and the fox and the ape receive their rightful punishments.

The poem falls into two sections. The largest section of the poem, up to line 950, is a general satire on human society and its ills. The fox and ape meet a succession of stock characters who symbolically represent the various levels of society. First, they encounter and dupe the honest farmer; his failing is that he is credulous to the point of stupidity, mistaking the ape for a shepherd and the fox for his faithful sheepdog. At the same time, Spenser uses this episode to point out an evil of his age, the plight of discharged veterans who were left to wander with no means of livelihood. The two rogues next encounter an illiterate priest, who suggests the benefits of a clerical occupation if religion is not taken too seriously. Spenser's account of their progress in this guise is a scathing condemnation of clerical abuses of his age. Finally, they arrive at court and, after vain efforts to win preference, they chance upon the sleeping lion, steal his skin and crown, and usurp the throne.

The description of the pair's exploits at court is the longest single section of the poem, and it was closest to Spenser's heart, for he had spent many months at court trying without success to win royal favor and patronage. Spenser also contrasts the ape's behavior with that of the true nobleman, whose primary allegiance is to his honor and personal integrity; who spends his days in riding, running, wrestling, preparing himself for military service, playing musical instruments, and writing poetry; who tries to learn enough about the affairs of state to be a wise counselor to his prince; and who endeavors in every way to achieve excellence.

The latter part of the poem is set entirely in the world of animals, as the two adventurers take over the throne of the lion, the traditional king of beasts. Here, the satire becomes pointedly specific. The ape, an animal not native to the land, calls in alien creatures such as griffins, minotaurs, crocodiles, dragons, beavers, and centaurs to support his rule. As the poem notes, "For tyrannie is with strange ayde supported." Spenser is clearly alluding to the proposed marriage of Elizabeth to the Duc d'Alençon. Marriage to a foreigner, Spenser warns, would bring a similar body of unnatural, decidedly un-English figures into the court. Queen Elizabeth, seldom a monarch to seek, and never one to accept, unwanted advice, would have been furious at the poet's presumption, one reason the volume was called back.

There were other reasons. With the ape as king, the fox becomes his powerful chief minister, wielding the real power behind the throne and using the opportunity to advance his own family into positions of influence and riches and ousting the older, more legitimate aristocracy. Just such behavior had been widely alleged against Lord Burleigh, Elizabeth's lord treasurer, and the repetition of such attacks, even in disguised form, would have provided another argument for the authorities to suppress the book.

Beyond the social and political satire of *Mother Hubberds Tale*, however, is the literary and artistic level of the work. *Mother Hubberds Tale* is the most medieval of Spenser's works. As he often did, Spenser turned to the verse of the fourteenth century poet Geoffrey Chaucer for inspiration and pattern. Spenser's debt to the earlier writer includes the use of the beast fable to criticize the politics of the day and stylistic devices. His apology for his plain language, on the grounds that he is simply reproducing the words of an old woman, is reminiscent of Chaucer's excuse for the bawdy vocabulary of some of his characters. Spenser has deliberately tried to reproduce the sentential quality of an old woman's storytelling; however, he occasionally slips out of his persona, especially when he is discussing the evils of the court. Spenser followed Chaucer's example in another important point: that of writing verse with the clarity and simplicity of prose. The action in *Mother Hubberds Tale* is clearly presented and easily grasped. The characters, although sometimes stock figures drawn from conventional morality, are realistic enough to be believable and, the fox and the ape especially, are individuals. The major flaw in the progression of the narrative is probably the personal feeling that overshadows the story in the episode at court, but this adds to the poem's interest for the modern reader.

Taken all in all, *Mother Hubberds Tale* is a minor masterpiece of narrative verse. Spenser has assimilated medieval techniques and the folk tradition brilliantly to produce a work that is still an interesting, amusing narrative, and a powerful religious and political satire. He so success-fully blends the worlds of humans, beasts, and Olympian gods that there is no apparent incongruity.

"Critical Evaluation" by Michael Witkoski

Bibliography:

Cummings, Robert M., ed. *Spenser: The Critical Heritage*. New York: Barnes & Noble Books, 1971. Spenser's reputation as a poet's poet has always been high. This collection of critical opinions on his work traces the course of that reputation from Elizabethan times to the twentieth century.

Fowler, Alastair. "Edmund Spenser." In *British Writers*, edited by Ian Scott-Kilvert. New York: Charles Scribner's Sons, 1979. Excellent introductory piece on Spenser and his works, highlighting his achievements in all poetic genres. Helpful to understanding the place of *Mother Hubberds Tale* in Spenser's career.

Jones, H. S. V. *A Spenser Handbook*. New York: Appleton-Century-Crofts, 1930. One of the most useful works dealing with *Mother Hubberds Tale*. Provides a brief but excellent overview of the work and how it fits into its time.

Nelson, William. *The Poems of Edmund Spenser: A Study*. New York: Columbia University Press, 1963. Well-balanced, evenhanded study of Spenser's poetic achievements. The sec-tions dealing with *Mother Hubberds Tale* are especially helpful.

Sanders, Andrew. *The Short Oxford History of English Literature*. Oxford, England: Clarendon Press, 1994. Good, if brief, introductory articles on Spenser and his contemporary scene that illuminate the particular conditions of Elizabethan England.

MOURNING BECOMES ELECTRA

Type of work: Drama
Author: Eugene O'Neill (1888-1953)
Type of plot: Tragedy
Time of plot: 1860's
Locale: New England
First performed: 1931; first published, 1931

> *Principal characters:*
> EZRA MANNON, a Civil War general
> CHRISTINE, his wife
> ORIN, his son
> LAVINIA, his daughter
> CAPTAIN ADAM BRANT, Christine's lover
> HAZEL NILES and
> PETER NILES, cousins of the Mannons
> SETH, the Mannon caretaker

The Story:

The Civil War was over, and in their New England home Christine and Lavinia Mannon awaited the homecoming of Ezra Mannon and his son, Orin. Lavinia, who adored her father, detested Christine because of Ezra's love for his wife. For her part, Christine was jealous of Orin's love and hated her husband and daughter. In this house of hidden hatred, Seth, the watchful gardener of the old mansion, saw that Lavinia also despised Captain Brant, a regular caller at the Mannon home.

The Mannons, descended from old New England stock, had their family skeleton. Dave Mannon, Ezra's brother, had run off with an Indian woman named Marie Brantome. Seth, seeing the antagonism between Lavinia and her mother, disclosed to Lavinia that Captain Brant was the son of Marie and Dave Mannon.

Embittered by her mother's illicit romance with Brant and jealous of her hold on Ezra, Lavinia forced Christine to send her lover away. Christine was too strong a woman to give in entirely to her daughter's dominance. She urged Brant to send her some poison. It was common knowledge that Ezra had heart trouble, and Christine planned to rid herself of the husband so that she would be free to marry Brant. Lavinia cruelly reminded her mother that Orin, her favorite child, had been born while Ezra was away during the Mexican War.

When Ezra, a kind, just man, came home he realized that Christine shrank from him while pretending concern for his health. That night in their bedroom, Ezra and Christine quarreled over their failing marriage. Ezra had a heart attack, and when he gasped for his medicine Christine gave him the poison instead. As he lay dying in Lavinia's arms, the helpless man feebly but incoherently accused Christine of his murder. Lavinia had no proof, but she did suspect that her mother had had a part in her father's death.

After Ezra's death, Peter and Hazel Niles, cousins of the Mannons, came to the mansion. Peter was a rejected suitor of Lavinia, and Hazel was in love with Orin. Lavinia spied on her mother constantly. When Orin came home, the two women vied for his trust, Lavinia trying to raise suspicion against her mother and Christine attempting to regain her son's close affection. Uncomfortable under her daughter's looks of silent, sneering accusation, Christine finally realized that Lavinia had found the box of poison. While Hazel, Peter, and Christine tried to make a warm welcome for Orin, Lavinia hovered over the group like a specter of gloom. Able to get Orin alone before Lavinia could speak to him, Christine told her son about Lavinia's suspicions concerning Captain Brant and Ezra's death, and she tried to convince him that Lavinia's distraction over Ezra's death had warped her mind.

Orin, whose affection for his mother had made him dislike Ezra, believed Christine, but the returned soldier swore that if he ever discovered that the story about Captain Brant were true, he would kill Brant. Desperate, Christine told Lavinia that Orin's trust had been won and that Lavinia need not try to take advantage of his credulity. Lavinia merely stared at her mother in silent defiance, and under her daughter's cold stare, Christine's triumphant manner collapsed into a pathetic plea that Lavinia not endanger Brant's life, for Orin had threatened to kill him.

When Lavinia slyly hinted the truth to Orin, his childhood trust in her led him, however unwillingly, to believe her story in part. Lavinia hinted that Christine might run to Brant at the first opportunity. Orin agreed to wait for proof, but he repeated that if sufficient proof were offered he would kill Brant. Lavinia instructed Orin to maintain a pretense that he believed her to be mad.

Shortly after Ezra's funeral, Christine went to Brant. Orin and Lavinia had pretended to be paying a call on a nearby estate, but instead they followed their mother to Brant's ship, where they overheard the lovers planning to leave together. Although Orin was consumed with jealous hatred of Brant, Lavinia restrained him from impulsive action. When Christine had gone, Orin went into the cabin and shot Brant. Then the brother and sister rifled the ship's cabin and Brant's pockets to make the death appear to have been a robbery and murder.

Orin and Lavinia returned to the Mannon mansion and told Christine what they had done. Orin saw his mother's grief and fell to his knees, pleading with her to forgive him and to give him her love. Fearing he had lost his mother's affection, the bewildered boy rushed from the room, but Lavinia faced her mother victoriously. Christine went into the house and shot herself. Orin, in a frenzy of grief, accused himself of his mother's murder.

Lavinia took her brother on a long sea trip to help him overcome his guilt. When they returned, Orin was completely under Lavinia's control, reciting in toneless speech the fact that Christine had been an adulteress and a murderess, and that Orin had saved his mother from public hanging. He was changed in appearance and spirit; it was plain that strange thoughts of grief and guilt preyed on his mind. During the trip Lavinia had grown to look and behave like Christine.

Lavinia now accepted Peter's love. When Orin saw his sister in Peter's embrace, he became angry for a brief moment before he congratulated them. When Orin became engaged to Hazel, Lavinia became afraid to leave Orin alone with the girl for fear he would say too much about the past.

Orin began to write a family history, urged by a remorseful desire to leave a record of the family crimes. Jealous of Lavinia's engagement to Peter, he threatened to expose her if she married him. Orin kept hinting to Lavinia that, like Christine, she was planning to poison him as Christine had poisoned the man who held her in bondage. Finally, driven to distraction by Orin's morbid possessive attitude toward her and by his incessantly recurring to their guilt, Lavinia suggested to the crazed Orin that he kill himself. As Peter held Lavinia in his arms, Orin went to the library to clean his pistol. His death was assumed to have been an accident.

Hazel suspected some vile and sinister fact behind Orin's accidental death. She went to Lavinia and pleaded with her not to ruin Peter by marrying him, but Lavinia denied that there was any reason to put off the marriage. While she spoke, however, Lavinia realized that the dead

Mannons would always rule her life. The others had been cowards, and had died. She would live. She sent Peter away. Then she ordered Seth the gardener to board up the windows of the mansion. Alone, the last surviving Mannon, Lavinia entered the old house to spend the rest of her life with the dead.

Critical Evaluation:

Mourning Becomes Electra, a trilogy consisting of *Homecoming*, *The Hunted*, and *The Haunted*, is, though set at the end of the American Civil War, an adaptation of the greatest of Aeschylus' trilogies, the *Oresteia* (458 B.C.E.). It illustrates the struggle between the life force and death, in which human attempts to express natural sensual desires and love of others or even of life itself are overcome by the many forms of death: repression derived from the Puritan religion; death-in-life engendered by society's values; isolation; war; and physical death. This struggle is present not only in the plot structure (each play culminates in a death) but also in the setting, in the actors' faces, stances, and costumes, and in repetitive refrains. Darkness, associated with death, pervades the plays: *Homecoming*, for instance, begins with the sunset, moves into twilight, and ends in the dark of night; *The Hunted* takes place at night; *The Haunted* spans two evenings and a late afternoon and indicates the inevitable coming of night, darkness, and death as Lavinia retreats to rejoin the host of dead Mannons.

The Mannon house itself, seen by the audience at the beginning of each play, stands amid the beauty and abundance of nature. It has a white Greek temple portico that O'Neill directs should resemble "an incongruous white mask fixed on the house to hide its somber grey ugliness." That the house is an ironic inversion of the affirmation and love of life associated with the Greeks is soon obvious. Christine thinks of the house as a tomb of cold, gray stone, and even Ezra compares it to a "white meeting house" of the Puritan Church, a temple dedicated to duty, to the denial of life and love, and to death. The house itself is not only alienated from nature but isolated from the community, built on the foundations of pride and hatred and Puritan beliefs. Its cold façade and isolation symbolize the family that lives within it, whose name indicates their spiritual relationship to Satan's chief helper Mammon. The "curse" of this house stems from the effects of materialism, Puritanism, alienation, and repression of what is natural—a death-in-life state.

The stiff, unnatural military bearing of the Mannons and the masklike look of their faces— on portraits of Orin and Ezra, on Christine's face when she is about to commit suicide, on Lavinia's face after Orin's death—are further evidence that the family is dead in the midst of life. Even the townspeople comment on the Mannons' "secret look." The look indicates the Mannons' denial of life, their repression of their sensual natures, and their refusal or inability to communicate with others. The dark costumes of all the family also indicate the hold that death has on them and accentuates the green satin worn first by Christine and later by Lavinia as they struggle to break out of their tomb and reach life.

The instinct of love and life survives most strongly in the women, but even they are defeated. The search for pure love through a mother-son relationship is futile, for the Oedipal complex, as Orin finally realizes, leads beyond the bounds of a pure relationship. Family love, too, fails, as is evident in the relationships between Christine and Lavinia and Ezra and Orin. Even love between men and women is not sufficient to triumph over the alienation and loneliness of the Mannon world.

The leitmotiv of the South Sea islands, symbols of escape from the death cycle of heredity and environment of New England society, is present throughout the three plays. The islands represent a return to mother earth, a hope of belonging in an environment far removed from

Puritan guilt and materialism. Brant has been to these islands; Ezra wants to have one; Orin, and Christine dream of being on one together, and they do finally travel to the islands but come to realize that they cannot become a permanent part of the island culture, but must return to the society to which they belong by birth and upbringing. Symbols of escape, the islands, too, finally fail the Mannons.

The Mannons try other avenues of escape from their deathly isolation. David Mannon attempted to escape with Marie Brantome but finally turned to drinking and suicide. Ezra "escaped" by concentrating on his business and then on the business of death—war—before he realized the trap of death. Christine focuses her attempts to escape first on her son and then on Brant. Orin tries to escape through his mother's love, then through Hazel's, and finally, in desperation, in an incestuous relationship with Lavinia. Lavinia does not see the dimensions of the death trap and does not desire escape until her trip to the islands, where she experiences the abundance of guilt-free life. After her return, she is willing to let Orin die, just as Christine let Ezra die, in order to be free to love and live. Too late, however, she too feels the curse of the guilt associated with the Puritan beliefs and realizes that she cannot escape. Lavinia learns Orin was right: Those who kill kill part of themselves each time they kill until finally nothing alive is left in them. She underscores this in her last conversation with Peter, remarking, "Always the dead between [us]. . . . The dead are too strong." Death itself is the only real escape for the alienated, guilt-ridden Mannons.

Compared to its source, Aeschylus' *Oresteia*, Eugene O'Neill's themes and characterization seem shallow. Christine, who goads Ezra into a heart attack because of her hatred of his attitude toward their sexual relationship and her love of Brant, is no match for Clytemnestra, who revenges the death of her daughter, her insulted pride, and hatred of Agamemnon with a bloody knife. The neurotic weak Orin is likewise a lesser character than Orestes, whose strong speech of triumphant justice over his mother's slain body breaks only with his horrified vision of the Furies. Yet Ezra is more human than Agamemnon, and Lavinia's complexities far outstrip Electra's: Her recognition and acceptance of her fate is in the noble tradition of the tragic hero.

The radical difference in the intentions of the two playwrights accounts for some of these differences. Aeschylus, whose major themes are concerned with the victory of human and divine laws, concludes his trilogy with the establishment of justice on earth and Orestes' reconciliation with society and the gods; he affirms that good has come out of evil, order from chaos, and wisdom from suffering. In *Mourning Becomes Electra*, the curse is not lifted but confirmed at the end, as Lavinia gives up her futile struggle and succumbs to the psychological "furies" that drive human beings. Although O'Neill's analysis may occasionally be oversimplified, *Mourning Becomes Electra* is one of the few twentieth century American plays that can truly be said to evoke the tragic emotions of pity, fear, and even awe.

"Critical Evaluation" by Ann E. Reynolds

Bibliography:
Berlin, Normand, ed. *Eugene O'Neill, Three Plays: "Mourning Becomes Electra," "The Iceman Cometh," "Long Day's Journey into Night": A Casebook.* Basingstoke, England: Macmillan, 1989. A good introduction. Includes excerpts from O'Neill's working diary, tracing the play's development from inception to second galleys. Contains four reviews of the original production, and seven critical studies dealing with character, theme, and style.
Bogard, Travis. *Contour in Time.* New York: Oxford University Press, 1988. Provides detailed comparison between *Mourning Becomes Electra* and Euripides and Aeschylus, noting the

shift from theological to psychological emphasis. Discusses importance as historical drama, focusing on Calvinist tradition and Puritan repression in New England.

Floyd, Virginia. *The Plays of Eugene O'Neill*. New York: Frederick Ungar, 1985. An excellent introduction. Includes brief biography and interpretive analysis of each play, identifying themes, key words, and ideas. Relates *Mourning Becomes Electra* to its Greek source and to O'Neill's life.

Gelb, Arthur, and Barbara Gelb. *O'Neill*. New York: Harper & Row, 1962. Comprehensive study of O'Neill's life and work based on his writings and over four hundred interviews with family members, friends, and critics. Begins with his ancestors and traces his growth as a man and an artist. Follows the development of *Mourning Becomes Electra* from idea to production.

Moorton, Richard F., ed. *Eugene O'Neill's Century: Centennial Views on America's Foremost Tragic Dramatist*. New York: Greenwood Press, 1991. Presents essays from a variety of perspectives, theatrical arts, psychology, philosophy, classics, which analyze and psychoanalyze character and theme in O'Neill. Includes detailed comparison between *The Haunted* and *Eumenides*.

THE MOUSETRAP

Type of work: Drama
Author: Agatha Christie (1890-1976)
Type of plot: Detective and mystery
Time of plot: Mid-twentieth century
Locale: Berkshire, England
First performed: 1952; first published, 1954

Principal characters:
MOLLIE RALSTON, the owner of Monkswell Manor, a guest house
GILES, her husband
CHRISTOPHER WREN,
MRS. BOYLE,
MAJOR METCALF,
MISS CASEWELL, and
MR. PARAVICINI, the guests at Monkswell Manor
DETECTIVE SERGEANT TROTTER, a police officer

The Story:
Early one winter afternoon, a brutal murder took place on Culver Street in Paddington. Witnesses heard someone whistling the nursery rhyme "Three Blind Mice" just before the victim screamed. Later that afternoon, in the Great Hall of Monkswell Manor, Mollie and Giles Ralston prepared for the opening of their guest house, worrying about the effects of the severe snowstorm outside and their own inexperience in their new venture. Giles left, joking that since they knew so little about their guests some might even be criminals. Alone, Mollie turned on the radio, where a description of the Culver Street murderer was being broadcast. The announcer mentioned the suspect's dark overcoat, light scarf, and felt hat just as Mollie picked up Giles' dark coat, scarf, and hat.

Shortly afterward, the first guest, Christopher Wren, arrived, followed by Mrs. Boyle and Major Metcalf, who had been forced by the weather to share a taxi from the train station. Mrs. Boyle immediately began to criticize the manor and the Ralstons' inexperience, but she refused Giles' offer to take her back to the station. Moments later, the last expected guest, Miss Casewell, rang the bell. After settling the guests in their rooms, Mollie and Giles lamented that they all seemed either peculiar or unpleasant. To their surprise, the doorbell rang once again and an elderly foreign gentleman, Mr. Paravicini, staggered in. He told them that his car was trapped in a snowdrift and that Monkswell Manor would soon be cut off by the snow.

The next morning, Mollie received a call from the Berkshire police, who told her that they had discovered a connection between the Culver Street murder and the manor; because the manor was now snowbound, a Sergeant Trotter would ski there to provide them with protection. When Sergeant Trotter arrived, they learned that the victim in the Culver Street murder, together with her husband, had several years earlier been convicted of criminal neglect after the youngest of three children placed in their protection died. A notebook found near the crime scene held two addresses, one in Culver Street and the other that of Monkswell Manor. Underneath were written the words "This is the first" and the notes of "Three Blind Mice." The police assumed that one of the older children had chosen to avenge the brother. The girl in the case had disappeared long ago, and the eldest boy had deserted from the army after having been diagnosed as schizophrenic. Trotter advised that anyone with a connection to the case should reveal it, since they could be in danger, but no one responded. After Trotter left to search the house, Major Metcalf accused Mrs. Boyle of being the magistrate who had sent the children to the home. She admitted this but denied having done anything wrong.

Trotter, returning to telephone his supervisor, found that the line was dead and went to investigate. Mrs. Boyle entered the empty hall and shut the door. When the door opened again, she turned nervously, but relaxed when she recognized the person. Someone whistled the tune "Three Blind Mice" and the lights went out. There was a quick scuffle, followed by the sound of a fall. Moments later, Mollie found Mrs. Boyle's body.

Trotter questioned the remaining guests, but no one could produce an alibi for the murder. He dismissed the others, but detained Mollie, with whom he discussed his suspicions. Wren was the right age to be the eldest child; Casewell might be the sister; Paravicini was a possibility too, for he walked like a much younger man and was wearing makeup; Metcalf could be the children's father. When Trotter asked about Giles, Mollie revealed they had only known each other for three weeks before they were married. Mollie insisted that Giles had been in the country at the time of the first murder, but Trotter showed her Giles' coat, from the pocket of which he pulled a London paper.

When he discovered that his skis were missing, Trotter reassembled everyone. After examining alibis again, he suddenly announced that he had a clue but needed to reenact Mrs. Boyle's murder. Each person was to duplicate someone else's movements, while Trotter played the victim in the empty Hall. Mollie was assigned to the drawing room. Trotter called her in and told her that he was the oldest child. He planned to kill her because she had not responded when his young brother had written to her, his kind young teacher, for help. Mollie pleaded that she had received the letter too late, but Trotter did not listen to her. He was about to strangle her when Major Metcalf and Miss Casewell entered. Casewell told Trotter that she was his sister. Metcalf revealed that he was the real detective. When Mollie and Giles discussed their both having been in London, they discovered that each had gone there to buy an anniversary present for the other.

Critical Evaluation:

Agatha Christie's name is synonymous with the mystery novel to readers around the globe, for her books have been translated into more than one hundred languages. Almost all of her novels are still in print. Although some critics consider her work to be no more than popular fiction, the mystery novel has become an increasingly respectable literary genre. Critical studies have been devoted to many aspects of the field, in particular to Agatha Christie, one of the finest writers of the classic detective tale.

The traditional mystery story has a particular set of rules, in which the writer sets a puzzle, provides clues for the reader to follow, and then delivers a solution to the puzzle that is both a surprise to the reader and consistent with the accumulated evidence of the story. *The Mousetrap* provides a perfect illustration of how Christie did precisely that and at the same time found new ways to combine those elements.

The Mousetrap, originally a short story entitled "Three Blind Mice" that was adapted first into a radio drama and then into a full-length play, contains many Christie trademarks. One of these is the setting, which, as in most of her works, is the English countryside. Yet this frequently serves as little more than a backdrop. Christie likes to cut the setting—and thus the characters—off from the rest of the world so as to create a closed circle of suspects. In *Ten Little Indians* (1943), the characters are stranded on an island; in *Murder on the Orient Express*

(1934), they are traveling on a train; and in many of the stories, including Christie's first novel, *The Mysterious Affair at Styles: A Detective Story* (1920), they are gathered together in a country house. *The Mousetrap* re-creates this setting with the Great Hall at Monkswell Manor. Christie assembles her characters and then isolates them with a snowstorm; from that point on, the outside world no longer intrudes. There is no mention of politics or names and events in the news. Political realities do not exist, except in the most general of terms; Mrs. Boyle accuses Miss Casewell of being a Socialist, and she laments the lack of responsibility of the lower classes. The play's reality, its true setting, is a tightly closed circle of individuals.

In this world, plot development is paramount. Every narrative detail and character description serves to move the drama forward. In fact, Christie deleted the first nine pages of an early draft of the play, where the murder had been described at greater length, in order to focus more quickly on the narrow circle and the puzzle. The curtain opens on a dark stage and the audience hears shrill whistling, a scream, and police whistles. The lights go up to a radio broadcast account of the murder in an empty room; the announcer adds that a heavy snowstorm is descending on the English countryside. Before a single actor has even been seen, the audience is caught up in the middle of the puzzle.

The stage directions for the play are detailed, since much of the action depends on staging. Red herrings are thrown to the audience with both sight and sound clues. Mollie's glove contains a London bus ticket; Christopher Wren wanders about mysteriously, whistling a succession of nursery rhymes. Gestures, looks, silences, all are designed to focus suspicion on one character after another. These bits of misdirection are carefully designed to hide the clues that reveal the true murderer.

Critics have pointed out the lack of character development in Christie's books, but this is a deliberate device designed to keep attention on the puzzle. Character development would interfere with the play's momentum. Christie's characters are primarily suspects. Every character in *The Mousetrap* is made to seem guilty by at least one gesture or word. Christopher Wren is the most obvious suspect: He has many characteristics that match what has been revealed about the murderer, for he deserted from the Army and suffered from the death of his mother. If Christie had provided further details about his unhappy childhood, she would not only have changed the pace and focus of the play but eliminated one of her more promising suspects.

In her fiction, Christie relies on a set of stock characters that, like her settings, she uses over and over. These stereotypes tend to be defined more by role than by individual personality. Moreover, use of such stereotypes allows Christie to provide frequently humorous insight into the middle- and upper-middle-class social world that predominates in her writing. When personality traits emerge, they often do so as a single or defining characteristic. This is particularly true in *The Mousetrap*, where, for example, Mrs. Boyle establishes herself as an overbearing, fault-finding bully with her first few speeches, and stage directions describe Casewell as a manly young woman.

Although Christie's characters may be stereotypical, they are rare in the world of the classic thriller. Traditionally, the narrator, the detective, and the young lovers are automatically removed from the suspect list. There are no such guarantees with Christie. Her murderer, as in *The Mousetrap*, is often not just the last person to be suspected but the one person who is never considered at all. This clever combination of suspense and humor, which keeps the audience puzzled and entertained until the last page, is the hallmark of a Christie mystery and one of the reasons for her enduring popularity.

Mary Mahony

Bibliography:

Christie, Agatha. *Agatha Christie: An Autobiography*. New York: Dodd, Mead, 1977. Charmingly written memoir in which the author discusses her life and her attitudes about writing. Includes descriptions of incidents that inspired *The Mousetrap* and brief evaluations of characters, as well as insight into methods of plot development.

Keating, H. R. F., ed. *Agatha Christie: First Lady of Crime*. New York: Holt, Rinehart, & Winston, 1977. Informative and entertaining collection of essays by mystery writers and critics. Discusses plot, setting, and character in many of Christie's mysteries. Includes an informative history of the development of *Mousetrap* from short story to stage play.

Osborne, Charles. *The Life and Crimes of Agatha Christie*. New York: Holt, Rinehart, & Winston, 1982. Provides literary evaluations of Christie's fiction. Includes a discussion of the development and production of *The Mousetrap*, as well as interesting statistics. Helpful bibliography of Christie's fiction identifies her writing by type and by detective.

Robyns, Gwen. *The Mystery of Agatha Christie*. Garden City, N.Y.: Doubleday, 1978. Informative biography that provides literary and theatrical evaluation. Includes details about the staging of *The Mousetrap* and interviews with individuals involved in the production.

Wagoner, Mary. *Agatha Christie*. Boston: Twayne, 1986. An extremely helpful beginner's source and the most comprehensive literary analysis of Christie's fiction. Also provides insight into the rules and traditions of the classic detective story. Classifies Christie's main writing styles and humorous analyses of manners. Includes helpful annotated bibliography.

A MOVEABLE FEAST

Type of work: Autobiography
Author: Ernest Hemingway (1899-1961)
First published: 1964

> *Principal personages:*
> ERNEST HEMINGWAY
> HADLEY HEMINGWAY, his first wife
> F. SCOTT FITZGERALD
> ZELDA FITZGERALD
> JAMES JOYCE
> SYLVIA BEACH, the proprietress of the Paris bookshop
> Shakespeare and Company
> EZRA POUND
> GERTRUDE STEIN
> ERNEST WALSH, a poet
> EVAN SHIPMAN, a poet
> JULES PASCIN, a French painter
> WYNDHAM LEWIS
> RALPH CHEEVER DUNNING, an opium-smoking poet
> FORD MADOX FORD

Perhaps more than any other writer of the twentieth century, Ernest Hemingway laid bare the violent realities lurking beneath all human experience. His aim from the very beginning was to represent those realities as precisely as he could, never minimizing their destructive potential. Life, he wrote early in his career, was uncompromising. It punished the fine and the foul impartially, taking its own grim time, choosing its own grim methods. The bleak and simple wisdom is given form in the retreat from Caporetto, the wound of Jake Barnes, the wreckage of the old man's great fish.

In his attempts to render, and thus confront, the desolating facts of life, Hemingway was himself uncompromising. He developed a subdued and stoic prose that betokened what he thought the only meaningful response to the inevitable ruin that time visits on everyone. Through the exercise of control, individuals could confer grace and dignity on defeat, and though time would destroy it need not humiliate. Even Hemingway's symbols reflected this tight dialectic, compressing it into local realities that were images of the eternal shape of the contest, as in his picture of the bullfight. In the rituals of the arena, the bull would always die, and ultimately the man would too. The animal, however, would go down charging, whereas the man at his best performed a ceremony of courage, delicacy, and precision. Though neither would survive, neither would retreat from the confrontation with death.

In *A Moveable Feast*, written in the last years of Hemingway's life and published after his death, there is in one respect a disquieting relaxation of that old standard. Though much of the prose is as fine as ever, Hemingway, in remembering his early years in Paris, engages in nervous battle for first place among his writing contemporaries, those individuals who with the passage of time had gained almost mythic stature. Ezra Pound, James Joyce, Ford Madox Ford, F. Scott and Zelda Fitzgerald had begun to be seen as figures in a novel, endlessly alive on the streets along the Seine, in Gertrude Stein's apartment, at the sidewalk cafés, and in the warm and cluttered interior of Sylvia Beach's bookshop. In *A Moveable Feast*, however, Hemingway reduces these figures not by distortion of facts but by skillful placing of reductive emphases. It is as though Hemingway, before entering the ring, had drugged his bull.

Nevertheless, the writing is so compelling that the reader must make a special effort to remember that this is not an objective account of that literary generation that provoked as much interest in itself as in its works. As historical document, the book adds to an understanding of the past, sometimes striking a comic note, as in clarifying that Gertrude Stein's famous remark, "You are all a generation perdue," originated with an angry garage manager giving a tongue-lashing to an attendant repairing Stein's Model T Ford. More often there is something graceless about Hemingway's selection of detail. A delicate confidence once entrusted to him by Scott Fitzgerald is exposed so casually that one can only conclude Hemingway's intention was to enlarge his own stature by reducing that of his friend. Shaken by Zelda's assertion that he was built too small to satisfy a woman, Fitzgerald had brought himself, with great difficulty, to ask Hemingway's opinion. After a quick inspection in the men's room of a restaurant, Hemingway assured him that he was all right and went on to provide some typical locker-room information on technique. Fitzgerald, of course, remained doubtful. Though this may be precisely the way it all happened, the incident is tilted favorably toward Hemingway, who is clearly meant to represent hero, father, authority, potency figure. There is even a hint that Zelda may not have been entirely wrong and that Hemingway was simply being a good, sympathetic, and protective friend. The passage undercuts itself and gives itself away as not being what it proclaims to be.

An equally private detail from the life of Gertrude Stein is handled in the same callous manner, and Hemingway is similarly self-congratulatory in his treatment of other famous friends. Many of the sketches seem designed exclusively to deflate the competition. Hemingway seldom values someone else valued for something achieved; rather, his most complex friends are treated as though they were equal merely to the worst of their traits. Ford Madox Ford is presented as someone to avoid looking at, in whose presence others must hold their breath and whose arrival at an outdoor café could foul the others' drinks. Wyndham Lewis is presented as unbearably supercilious and gratuitously unkind, the nastiest looking man Hemingway had ever seen, having the eyes of a failed rapist. Sometimes the competition is shown to be downright unsavory, sometimes obtuse, sometimes merely ineffectual (perhaps the unkindest cut of all). There is cynicism in much of this, a failure of sensitivity, and frequently a smell of contrivance.

By contrast, James Joyce is treated with kindness, though he is not often mentioned. Ezra Pound is depicted as a sort of saint, a man who helped other writers by raising money, dispensing advice, and even admiring their works simply because they were friends. There is warmth, too, in the overall treatment of Fitzgerald, though he comes off as somewhat absurd. In the account of Hemingway's friendship with Gertrude Stein, where he writes of helping her proofread her works, she is described serving him fine liqueurs while entertaining, encouraging, and criticizing him. There is a sense throughout, however, that the potency of his friends is limited while his is not.

Beneath these obvious qualities in the sketches runs another current, which is dreamlike and compelling: Hemingway's idyllic remembrance of the time with his first wife in their small apartment over a sawmill on the rue Notre-Dame-des-Champs. This undercurrent is a literature of nostalgia, a beautiful story of crisp winter walks, fire-heated rooms, tender conversation. This quiet world, surely more perfect in recorded memory than in lived reality, is kept apart from the other, that land of tension, celebrity, desecration. Like Huck Finn's river, the apartment over the sawmill is a place of renewal, a sanctified region beyond the touch of ugliness. Hadley is always both lover and mother, their Paris a garden and playground. This is myth, not history. Though built on fact, the tale is transformed by selection and emphasis into a dream of perpetual childhood. In this world, hunger is not pain but a sharpening of the perceptions, an internal signal of one's youth. Poverty is in itself a condition of grace.

Despite descriptions of embarrassingly adolescent talk between Hadley and Hemingway, despite a strange shifting of guilt when the dream is finally betrayed by Hemingway (it is the rich who are responsible), the quiet, lyric power of the romance is irresistible. Even the scraps of wisdom, stripped down, fragmentary, and always too simple, seem impressive and right in their context—on the sense of loss, for instance, which all things, good or bad, evoked after the loss. The loss of the good made demands, required the reconstruction of one's life. It is not the idea here that moves us but the world implied by it, a simplified, manageable world in which good and bad are distinguishable and capable of manifesting their qualities even in their absence. In Hemingway's prose, this is the world of the clean, well-lighted legend from which to look out upon reality, knowing that it will finally destroy what exists but knowing too that it is there.

Bibliography:

Kert, Bernice. *The Hemingway Women.* New York: W. W. Norton, 1983. Biographical details, including for the years 1920-1926, which focus on Hadley Richardson Hemingway and Pauline Pfeiffer.

Lynn, Kenneth S. *Hemingway.* New York: Simon & Schuster, 1987. A standard biography of Hemingway, which places the writing of *A Moveable Feast* in the context of the author's approaching suicide.

Messent, Peter. "Coda: *A Moveable Feast.*" In *Ernest Hemingway.* New York: St. Martin's Press, 1992. Places the work in the context of Hemingway's larger, utopian project of a pure art that would re-create out of the historical world a linguistic one entered at will, that is equally valid and eternally valuable. Shows how, by merging his voice at the end of his career with his voice as a young writer and the voice of his fictional young writer, Nick Adams, Hemingway achieved some of his best literary effects.

Renza, Louis A. "The Importance of Being Ernest." *South Atlantic Quarterly* 88, no. 3 (Summer, 1989): 661-689. Argues that Hemingway felt such a hunger to write true sentences that the very act of writing them created a world as real as the one to which they referred. At the same time, his need to make money threatened his dedication to high artistic standards.

Tavernier-Courbin, Jacqueline. *Ernest Hemingway's "A Moveable Feast": The Making of Myth.* Boston: Northeastern University Press, 1991. Gathering and carefully weighing extensive evidence about the play of imagination and memory in Hemingway's conceptualization and composition, Tavernier-Courbin provides an objective examination of fact and fiction in this work and a balanced analysis of what the book reveals about its author. Includes chronologies, maps, and manuscript revisions.

THE MOVIEGOER

Type of work: Novel
Author: Walker Percy (1916-1990)
Type of plot: Social realism
Time of plot: Early 1960's
Locale: Suburbs of New Orleans
First published: 1961

Principal characters:

JOHN BICKERSON "BINX" BOLLING, an unmarried Southern stockbroker
KATE CUTRER, Binx's beautiful distant cousin
EMILY CUTRER, Binx's great-aunt and Kate's stepmother
JULES CUTRER, Emily's husband and Kate's father
WALTER WADE, Kate's fiancé

The Story:

Binx Bolling was on a "search"—a quest for the meaning of life in modern America. He often visited his great-aunt Emily's home for lunch, where he talked to her about the cosmic importance of the lives of people they knew. She wanted him to go to medical school, but he frequented movies and watched television as a way of distracting himself from domestic realities and from personal involvement with those around him. He was a stockbroker who had affairs with his various secretaries.

At one of Binx's luncheons with his great-aunt, she elicited his help in warding off a "nervous break-down" which was evidently forthcoming for his distant cousin Kate Cutrer. Aunt Emily has found Kate's hidden bottles of whiskey and sodium pentobarbital. Binx agreed to help; that is, he agreed to give Kate attention and keep her distracted. At a subsequent lunch, Walter Wade showed up to talk football and make preparations for Mardi Gras with Uncle Jules. Walter, an old fraternity brother of Binx, and Kate were engaged to marry.

Binx and Kate decided to watch the Mardi Gras parade together, in which they saw Walter and after which they attended a movie. Slowly, over time, they fell in love with each other, and Kate canceled her engagement to Walter. Binx was attracted to his new secretary, Sharon Kincaid, and spent time with her. He came to see, however, that it was Kate whom he really wanted. It was revealed, in turn, that Sharon was in love with another man.

When Binx proposed marriage to Kate, she delayed an answer. At the office the next morning, a Saturday, he invited Sharon to go swimming with him and to have a "date" for the day. She accepted, and they had a minor car accident. They exchanged platitudes of love at the picnic on the beach. Binx took Sharon to meet his mother and other family members; then, predictably, they went to yet another movie.

After going to church with his mother, Binx returned to the home of his aunt Emily, where he learned that Kate, that very morning, had attempted suicide. Emily had discovered Kate before she had died and had telephoned for a doctor, who came to the house and pumped the whiskey and pentobarbital from her stomach. Emily and Binx discussed what was to be done about Kate, with nothing being resolved. Binx then conversed with Kate herself, but toward no immediate end. Even though both had a great understanding of each other, this understanding was self-defeating. Binx could not lie and tell her that life had meaning, for he had found none for himself.

Binx was scheduled to make a business trip to Chicago. At the last moment he decided to take Kate with him, but he did not inform Emily. They traveled by train, and both seemed to be doing fine with each other and with themselves. The trip was somewhat spoiled for Kate because they discovered another couple on the train whom they knew. Binx and Kate discussed the meaning of life and death and their own roles in the universe. Binx returned persistently to thoughts about his search for meaning in life. They made numerous references to movies. They concluded little of importance. Kate muttered: "Losing hope is not so bad. There's something worse: losing hope and hiding it from yourself." Kate and Binx attempted to have sex in the sleeper of the train but failed. In Chicago, Binx perfunctorily took care of his business appointments, leaving Kate at the hotel. The two of them then went to yet another movie. Back at the hotel, Emily telephoned. She was furious because Binx had taken Kate to Chicago without telling anyone. They left Chicago by bus to return home.

Back in New Orleans, Kate and Binx avoided most of the Mardi Gras parade and activities. They returned to Emily's house, where she castigated Binx, excessively, for taking Kate with him without telling anyone. The conversation became rather a social diatribe, with Emily making observations about manners, the class system, history, heritage, literature, art, and responsibility. Binx was dutifully apologetic but obviously could not undo what had been done. Emily claimed that "Ours is the only civilization in history which has enshrined mediocrity as its national ideal." Binx agreed with her. Ironically, it was Binx who understood the source of this "enshrined mediocrity."

Binx escaped his aunt's wrathful gentility. Kate was waiting for him, having overheard every word of the conversation. It was, on that day, Binx's thirtieth birthday. He concluded from his "dark pilgrimage" of thirty years that "Nothing remains but desire"—desire for sex, desire for life, desire to search. The awareness of the futility of such efforts was for him, inevitable.

In the end, Kate and Binx married, as did his secretary Sharon Kincaid and her boyfriend. Two of Binx's family members (his uncle Jules and his brother Scott) died. The two newlyweds were left alone. The search for life had not been concluded, but it had somehow ceased to matter.

Critical Evaluation:

Walker Percy's novel *The Moviegoer* is in many ways the first important novel of the New South. The setting is not agricultural; the characters are not grotesques, larger-than-life figureheads, rednecks, or symbols. The plot does not hinge upon treasure buried in the backyard. Rather, it is a world in which air conditioners, fast living, color televisions, and movies have replaced mint juleps and moss trees.

In this New South, existentialism has arrived. The main character, Binx Bolling, views himself as a character in a movie. He is alienated from nature, society, family, culture, and God. Only movies, those impersonal images on the screen, seem to offer him any vision into the purpose and meaning of his own life. He possesses attention only for his own self as a character. Watching movies becomes, for Binx Bolling, watching life. And watching life becomes living life; or, at least, watching life is a substitute for living it. It is as close as he can get. Binx cannot live life: He cannot go to medical school as his aunt would have it. He cannot fall in love with one of his secretaries, although like characters in a movie, he can have sex with them. He cannot go to church; he cannot even go to Chicago for the week in any meaningful way. He is trapped like a character in a film—unable to control the script, the action, or the projector.

In the opening chapter of the novel, Binx realizes that all the people around him are "dead." They are far more lifeless and immobile than characters on the screen. He is attracted to and repulsed by the Elysian Fields, the nearby suburb of New Orleans. It is a place with a significant name but no substance. It is the new landscape of the South and America.

Much of Binx's efforts center on some sort of self-announced search that he is on. The author toys with this as a literary scheme and device. On the one hand, Binx's search is for the meaning of life, the Holy Grail, the Helen of Troy, the Elysian Fields, the wine of communion—for union with self and God. On the other, it is only a pale imitation of these things in the shadowy no-man's-land of modern life. There is, Percy perhaps implies, not without irony, no Holy Grail in contemporary life unless it is sex. Binx is left to conclude that "Nothing remains but desire."

Binx is on a search for the meaning of life, so the novel proceeds in a formulaic fashion. Binx ponders and thinks; he has sophomoric discussions; he tries to find answers in others and in relationships; he goes to church and studies the arts and literature; he would enter a profession to find meaning in work; he has affairs with women that come to nothing, not even pain. His business trip to Chicago is something of a parody of an odyssey in which a young person leaves home a boy and returns a man. Kate is something of an anti-Helen. Binx leaves home a boy and returns as one. Kate too is emotionally defunct and incapable of love. Her drugs, whiskey, and suicide attempts are also indicative of an alienation that is so complete it amounts to selfishness. It is also a renunciation of the role of women in Percy's New South.

Binx returns home (to Gentilly, Louisiana) to marry Kate, bury the dead in the family, soothe his aunt Emily, and proceed with business, which turns out to be life as usual. He learns that he can do no better than go to movies, for movies are momentary events in which life becomes interesting. The fantasy produced by the screen is more rewarding and fulfilling than the monotony of life at home and work and marriage. Watching movies affords not so much distraction as pretentious involvement with life. Binx cannot be a movie star, which is to say that he cannot have a glamorous, exciting, and rewarding life. What he can do, though, is see himself as a character in a movie and become detached from self, and all the problems that go along with having a role. This detachment is not permanent, but it is one way of dealing with life.

Binx Bolling is the prototype of all the main characters in Percy's later novels. A white, middle-class male suffering from adolescent angst, incipient middle age, distraction, alienation, and paranoia, Binx embodies and foreshadows such characters as Will Barrett in *The Last Gentleman*, Lance Lamar in *Lancelot*, and Tom More in *Love in the Ruins* and *The Thanatos Syndrome*. Binx, a self-defined and self-explained castaway, is representative of persons living in a universe where love and meaning cannot be found.

Carl Singleton

Bibliography:
Hardy, John Edward. "Man, Beast, and Others in Walker Percy." In *Walker Percy: Novelist and Philosopher*. Edited by Jan Nordby Gretlund and Karl-Heinz Westarp. Jackson: University Press of Mississippi, 1991. Discusses Binx Bolling by comparing him to other main characters in Percy's works.
Lawson, Lewis A. "Moviegoing in *The Moviegoer*." *Southern Quarterly* 18, no. 3 (1980): 26-42. The best discussion of the overall metaphor of the novel, moviegoing. Lawson shows how watching movies becomes an alternative to living life.
Thale, Mary. "The Moviegoer of the 1950's." *Twentieth Century Literature* 14, no. 2 (July, 1968): 84-89. Examines the social role of movies in the decade preceding the writing of *The Moviegoer*.
Tharpe, Jac. *Walker Percy*. Boston: Twayne, 1983. Provides all the important information about

Percy's philosophy and essays, as well as biographical and other background information. One chapter is given to *The Moviegoer*.

Wyatt-Brown, Bertram. *The House of Percy*. New York: Oxford University Press, 1994. Primarily a biography of Walker Percy's family, this work reveals connections between Percy's family life and the characters in his novels, particularly Binx Bolling in *The Moviegoer*.

MR. COGITO

Type of work: Poetry
Author: Zbigniew Herbert (1924-   )
First published: Pan Cogito, 1974 (English translation, 1993)

"*Cogito, ergo sum,*" wrote René Descartes, "I think, therefore I am." Mr. Cogito, a twentieth century human being, the citizen of a small European nation, and at least occasionally the alter ego of poet Zbigniew Herbert, does a lot of thinking in this collection of Herbert's poetry from the late 1960's and early 1970's. Mr. Cogito, not surprisingly, confronts the philosophical problem as to precisely what constitutes the self; what makes up human identity in a world full of others, past and present; where Mr. Cogito ends and where others—animal, vegetable, or mineral—begin; and how one individual lives among others.

Herbert's earlier work, including *A String of Light* (1956), *Hermes, a Dog and a Star* (1957), *A Study of the Object* (1961), and *Inscription* (1969), dealt in historical and political ironies, chief among them the question of art (or form) confronted with unspeakable experience. Herbert, like many of his contemporaries throughout Central and Eastern Europe, had a thorough education. During the Nazi occupation, he began writing underground, just as he had studied and fought underground; when the war ended and the Stalinization of Polish life began, that did not essentially change.

Avant-garde in its avoidance of rhyme and punctuation, its use of idiom and casual diction, and classical in its spareness and clarity, Herbert's poetry rarely made direct mention of contemporary events, yet it expresses the collective experience of Poland with unsparing intelligence. The poet often speaks in the first person plural, reserving the "I" for a figure from history or myth, distant in time or space. Yet the speech and sensibility of these figures are as close to the readers of Herbert's time as those of the morning newspaper.

In "Elegy of Fortinbras," one of his best-known pieces, Fortinbras addresses the dead Hamlet with the pragmatic coolness of a twentieth century enlightened tyrant, contemptuous of fancy and as skilled in inventories as he is in invasion:

> Adieu prince I have tasks a sewer project
> and a decree on prostitutes and beggars
> I must also elaborate a better system of prisons
> since as you justly said Denmark is a prison

The irony inherent in conversations between the powerful and powerless underlies much of Herbert's work, and his rejection of both the style and the substance of Poland under Communism made publication difficult for him even after the thaw of 1956. *Report from the Besieged City* (1983), written while Poland was under martial law, was his first work to be published abroad, where it appeared before it appeared in his homeland.

Ironic detachment (not to be confused with moral indifference) has been a hallmark of Herbert's poetry from the beginning, and *Mr. Cogito* is no exception. Mr. Cogito is not a fixed character with a stable point of view, and Herbert himself has called him neither a mask nor a persona but a method for distancing, "objectifying." His points of reference are Herbert's beloved humanist tradition—Greek mythology, ancient history, philosophy—yet the book is clearly more personal than Herbert's earlier ones. This is particularly true of the opening poems, where Mr. Cogito looks at his own reflection, remembers father, mother, and sister, and contemplates returning to his birthplace. In "Mr. Cogito Looks at His Face in the Mirror," he sees features he would rather had not belonged to him: close-set eyes, the better to spy out invading tribes; big ears, the better to hear rumbling mammoths. Those same eyes and ears, he protests, have absorbed Veronese and Mozart, but "the inherited face" shows the descent of the species with all its animal fears and ancient passions, and Mr. Cogito regretfully concludes that it, not he, has won.

"About Mr. Cogito's Two Legs" is an anatomical version of two different attitudes toward life: one leg is boyish, well-shaped, and energetic, ready to dance or run away at any moment, to survive for the love of life; the other is thin, scarred, and rigid. One is not better than the other; rather, they might be compared to Sancho Panza and Don Quixote, and the combination is not crippling. Mr. Cogito simply staggers slightly as he makes his way through the world.

Distressed by the presence of others within himself, he is also surprised and touched by their separateness. Mr. Cogito often feels amazement, as the young boy discovers in "Sister" that he has "remained within the limits of his own skin," or as the grown man wonders at the sudden impenetrability of a dead friend's body. "Others" include things as well as people: In "Sense of Identity" Mr. Cogito looks to a sandstone that, far from being dead and inert, varies according to light and weather, struggles with the elements, and endures changes in its own nature. He is not personifying the stone in any conventional sense; it leads its own opaque, self-enclosed sandstone life, which happens to share much with human existence. Both are always subject to external pressures, to a reality outside themselves—and here is where the self in Herbert's poetry differs from the self-absorbed "I" of many other twentieth century Western poets.

Loss and dislocation lie at the core of Herbert's reality. In "Mr. Cogito Thinks of Returning to the City Where He Was Born," he expects that he would find nothing of his childhood except, and here the speculation turns to nightmarish certainty, a flagstone on which the boy draws a chalk circle. He raises one foot to hop, but finds himself frozen in that pose, unable to grow up, as years pass and wars rage and the circle fills with ash, all the way up to his shoulders and mouth. On one level, the loss is universal—past lost to present, childhood irretrievably lost to the bitter taste of adult experience, lost homes to which one cannot return—but there are more levels as well, on which history and geography cease to be symbolic. After World War II, Herbert's own birthplace of Łwów was suddenly no longer Poland but the Soviet Union, as far removed as if it, like hundreds of other Polish towns and villages, had been razed to the ground. Warfare or camps had killed roughly one-sixth of Poland's entire population, and much of Polish Jewry was indeed reduced to ash. Long used in poetry as a symbol of death and desolation, ash in postwar Poland had a quite specific and horrible meaning.

What is inhuman for Herbert the humanist is not the inanimate object but the perfect system, whether earthly or heavenly. Mr. Cogito is, in his own modest, bemused way, a continuation of what some Herbert commentators have called "the attack on transcendence," and what others have called "the rejection of 'purity.'" Purity was often represented in his earlier works by imperturbable gods or angels bent on creating an unlivable paradise. In "At the Gate of the Valley," for example,

> after a loud whisper of explosion
> after a loud whisper of silence
> this voice resounds like a spring of living water
> it is we are told
> a cry of mothers from whom children are taken
> since as it turns out

we shall be saved each one alone
the guardian angels are unmoved
and let us grant they have a hard job

A philosopher's yearning for absolute perfection prompts "Mr. Cogito Tells About the Temptation of Spinoza," in which God counters Baruch Spinoza's questions about first and final causes with kindly practical advice: take care of yourself, eat better, dress better, buy a new house, forgive flawed mirrors and drunken singers.

—calm
the rational fury
thrones will fall because of it
and stars turn black
—think
about the woman
who will give you a child
—you see Baruch
we are speaking about Great Things

Mr. Cogito may think about great things and great people, but he does not want to be one. In "Mr. Cogito's Game," which is a replay of the escape of Russian anarchist Peter Kropotkin from a Tsarist prison, he delights in the daring flight but prefers the inferior role, preferring to be a helper rather than a hero. This is not cowardice but temperament, as well as a refusal to strike dramatic poses and make grand gestures in the service of a grand abstraction. He clings to his earthly senses of sight, touch, and sound. There is some wistfulness in "Mr. Cogito Laments the Pettiness of Dreams," wherein he envies his grandparents their vividly colored dreams. (His are of the bill collector knocking on his door.) The tone of "Mr. Cogito's Abyss" is low-key and apologetic as he explains that his abyss—his despair, sense of disinheritance, isolation—is persistent and annoying, like a small pet or a skin disease, but hardly the black hole of a Blaise Pascal or a Fyodor Dostoevski.

Even at his most cartoonlike, Mr. Cogito is a small, individual bastion of human values, of the good and the beautiful, fidelity and truth. Mr. Cogito may accept imperfection and defeat; he has his limitations, being an ordinary man. Ordinary men and women are, however, faced with moral choices, and those moral choices are very much present, though Herbert presents them less starkly, more compassionately, than he had in his earlier work. In "Mr. Cogito on Upright Attitudes," the inhabitants of a threatened city have surrendered long before the enemy is at the gates; they are sewing white flags, teaching their children to lie, and practicing their kneeling. Herbert uses an undramatic, ordinary figure of speech for Mr. Cogito's choice, which is "to stand up to the situation," knowing full well that it is simply the choice of position in which to die. Standing up, in fact, simply makes him a better target. He does, and is. Upright attitudes guarantee nothing, most especially not survival. As the biblical language of "The Envoy of Mr. Cogito" argues, however, that is not the point. The point is to bear truthful witness in things great and small, and this is no less heroic than the exploits of a Gilgamesh, a Hector, or a Roland.

Perhaps no other Polish poet except the Nobel laureate Czesław Miłosz has had so wide an appeal to the foreign reader as has Herbert, whose work translates into English with relative ease. The "relative" is important, because he is particularly skilled at using common idioms and clichés, which generally do not translate well, in unexpected contexts. There are allusions to

Polish as well as to Roman history, and associations that non-Polish readers might not make without a footnote. Yet this grounding in the local, the specific, and the individual keeps the poetry from ever seeming abstract and generalized. This, and his balance between austerity and compassion, lucidity and complexity, the ideal and the real, give him a voice that resonates far beyond the borders of his country.

Jane Ann Miller

Bibliography:
Alvarez, A. Introduction to *Selected Poems: Zbigniew Herbert*, translated by Czesław Miłosz and Peter Dale Scott. New York: Ecco, 1968. A brief but eloquent and useful introduction to the first volume of Herbert's poetry to be published in English.
Baranczak, Stanisław. *A Fugitive from Utopia: The Poetry of Zbigniew Herbert*. Cambridge, Mass.: Harvard University Press, 1987. A thorough study of Herbert's poetry, organized around his use of antinomy, or paradox. Baranczak argues that the contradiction between Herbert's attachment to the cultural heritage of the West and his sense of Eastern European disinheritance lies at the core of his work.
Carpenter, Bogdana, and John Carpenter. "The Recent Poetry of Zbigniew Herbert." *World Literature Today* 51, no. 2 (Spring, 1977): 210-214. Refers specifically to *Mr. Cogito*, which the authors later translated. Discusses Herbert's relationship to his persona and the differences between this and his earlier work.
Czerniawski, Adam, ed. *The Mature Laurel: Essays on Modern Polish Poetry*. Bridgend, Mid Glamorgan: Seren Books, 1991. Contains several good essays on Herbert, some devoted to analysis of individual poems. Others discuss his work in relationship to that of such leading contemporaries as Wisława Szymborska and Tadeusz Różewicz.
Heaney, Seamus. "Atlas of Civilization." In *The Government of the Tongue*. New York: Noonday Press, 1990. Heaney sees a direct connection between Herbert and Socrates, Plato and the notion of the examined life.

MR. SAMMLER'S PLANET

Type of work: Novel
Author: Saul Bellow (1915-   )
Type of plot: Social realism
Time of plot: Late twentieth century, specifically during the first moon landing
Locale: New York City and suburbs, Poland, and Israel
First published: 1970

Principal characters:

ARTUR SAMMLER, Holocaust survivor
SHULA (SLAWA) SAMMLER, his eccentric daughter
ELYA GRUNER, Sammler's nephew
ANGELA GRUNER, Elya's daughter
WALLACE GRUNER, Elya's son
DR. GOVINDA LAL, a scientist from whom Shula steals an essay
AFRICAN AMERICAN PICKPOCKET, a nameless, majestic person
EISEN, Shula's abusive former husband
MARGOTTE ARKIN, the niece of Sammler's late wife
LIONEL FEFFER, an associate of Sammler

The Story:

Artur Sammler was a highly introspective, brilliant, and aging Holocaust survivor living in New York City. Loved by those who knew him, he functioned as their gentle, infinitely likable father-confessor. Yet since his experience of crawling out of a mass grave in Poland he had been "dry" inside. His "death" and "rebirth" in a Holocaust killing field had left him with an eye that could only distinguish light and shade, and a spirit that was often myopic and incapacitated. He was slightly confused, bitter, morally indignant, and constantly ready to sit in judgment upon others. Yet he rarely ever expressed these feelings because he nevertheless loved and needed his circle of friends.

In spite of attempts to insulate himself from the modern world that he had reluctantly been born into during the Holocaust, Sammler's life on his planet was presenting him with many problems. His customary existence was upset because of the imminent death of Elya Gruner, the man who had saved Sammler and his daughter from Holocaust Poland and who had supported them in America. Furthermore, he was also involved with the intrigue of spying on an African American pickpocket, and the problem of his daughter, who had stolen the only copy of an important manuscript.

Sammler had been spying for days on an African American male who was pickpocketing the riders of the bus he rode. He was fascinated by this man's grace, his stylish dress, and most of all his audacity in always picking the same bus route for his exploits. Sammler next visited with his daughter Shula, who had changed her name to "Slawa" that month because it was Easter, and Shula, who had been brought up under that name for four years by Catholic nuns during the Holocaust, wanted to participate in Ash Wednesday. Sammler was both amused and repulsed at Shula-Slawa's Jewish-Christian identity, and contemplated the divisions of the modern self.

Sammler then went to Columbia University to give a lecture on H. G. Wells and the Bloomsbury Group on the insistence of a rather irresponsible student named Lionel Feffer.

During the lecture, a bearded Marxist student stood up and violently attacked Sammler's speech as "effete" nonsense. The student then called him an "old man," and even went so far as to question Sammler's sexual prowess. Sammler abruptly left, and on the trip home, once again saw the pickpocket. When the pickpocket caught Sammler watching him, he followed Sammler and cornered Sammler alone in his apartment lobby. Here, rather than mugging Sammler or silencing him with physical violence, the pickpocket calmly displayed his genitalia as a "lesson" to the stupefied Sammler, who almost wanted to watch. After this, he went up to his apartment where Shula had left him a note and a manuscript by Dr. V. Govinda Lal. Its title was "The Future of the Moon."

Next, Sammler visited Angela and Wallace Gruner. Elya Gruner had described Wallace as a "high I.Q. moron," and Angela as "insidious," "an apprentice whore," and a woman who "sent the message of gender everywhere." After talking with these two, Sammler visited Elya in the hospital, where Sammler learned that Gruner was going to die soon, no matter what the doctors did. He spent more time with the Gruner family and noticed their self-centered, casual attitude about their dying father. On the way home from the hospital, Sammler perused Lal's manuscript. He then met Feffer, who tried to apologize for the incident at the university, and then informed him that Shula had stolen Lal's manuscript, and it was the only copy. Sammler immediately jotted off an explanatory letter to Lal, left the manuscript at his home so he could retrieve it, and returned to visit Elya. His anxiety about both the pickpocket and Lal's purloined manuscript caused a flashback to his Holocaust experiences.

Sammler returned to visit Elya at the hospital, then visited with Angela, Wallace, and Eisen, the latter having returned from Israel as a would-be artist. Sammler had a flashback about his experience visiting Israel during the Six-Day War. While at the hospital, Margotte phoned Sammler and informed him that Shula-Slawa had taken the manuscript again, and that Lal was at Sammler's house with a detective. Sammler talked to Lal, complimented his work, and Lal expressed his hopes to publish it before the first lunar landing. After he went to Elya's New Rochelle home with Wallace, he contemplated the thefts and confronted Shula-Slawa. She informed him that the manuscript and a copy she made were then in lockers at Grand Central Station. Sammler and Lal finally met, Sammler gave him the keys to the lockers, and both men engaged in a long, far-reaching dialogue.

They noticed that the floor was wet. In his search for his father's hidden money, Wallace had undone the pipes in the attic. Lal saved the day by turning off the water, and they all retired to bed. Reflecting on the day's madness, Sammler again thought back to the Six-Day War. The next day, Sammler was left stranded in New Rochelle by Wallace and Lal but got a ride into New York with Elya's chauffeur, Emil. Sammler thought deeply about Elya, but as they entered town, Emil pointed a fight out to Sammler, which turned out to involve none other than Feffer and the pickpocket. Feffer had been spying on the man, this time with a hidden camera, and had been caught. Reaching the scene, Sammler spotted Eisen, who, after much confusion and struggle, ended the fight by repeatedly bludgeoning the African American with his art—crude metal figurines. The sheer murderousness of Eisen's blows on the man horrified Sammler, who tried to stop the violence but was too late. The man had fallen to the ground bleeding, his face torn open. At Feffer's insistence, Sammler, weak from experiencing such violence again, left the scene and went to visit Elya.

Entering the hospital, he was once again delayed, this time by Angela. Sammler offended her by asking for her to reconcile with Elya, and intuited that once Elya died, he would probably lose all of his financial support. Sammler then got a phone call from Shula-Slawa, who was ecstatic because she had found money stuffed in a couch at Elya's. He forbade her to take it.

Sammler finally reached Elya's doctor, but was told that Elya had died. Sammler had been distracted too long and had missed Elya's passing.

He found Elya's body and uttered a prayer—almost a Kaddish—over his benefactor, friend, and nephew. Sammler then commended Elya's life to God, and said that Elya had met, in spite of "all the confusion and degraded clowning of life . . . the terms of his contract," and that this was what made any life truly authentic.

Critical Evaluation:

The backdrop for the novel is not only New York's diversity and decay, but also the excitement then in the air about the Apollo moon landing and the potential of a new frontier for humanity. Yet Sammler, a character many have seen to be a thinly disguised Saul Bellow, is not so sure about humanity's potential at all. He is greatly disturbed with the many forms of madness that are destroying the planet. Leaving the planet to inhabit a more pure one is no solution; the notion of purity will do nothing but bring about more violence such as the Holocaust.

Generally in his novels, Bellow allows for a solution, hard-won to be sure, to humanity's problems, and *Mr. Sammler's Planet* is no exception. During his travails in dealing with late twentieth century America, Sammler is still able to come to a moment of peace and rebirth as he stands over Elya's body. His prayer shows that Elya's death has brought about another rebirth in Sammler—this time into a life that can overcome the narrowness of his own modern thinking. Elya's contradictory life of perfect giving to Sammler during the Holocaust and in America, and his imperfection in the taking of Mafia abortion money, have made Sammler aware of the great contradictions in life. He sees in Elya a great life spent living out the knowledge that one must live one's life for others, not only for one's self. Although Elya has shown weakness, his ability to give remains exemplary.

Upon its publication, *Mr. Sammler's Planet* was considered one of Bellow's weaker novels. It is somewhat of a departure for him. Yet Bellow's insights and critiques of the major elements of modern life have made *Mr. Sammler's Planet* one of his more powerful and enduring texts. Its many digressions extend and brilliantly negotiate the more important philosophical and ethical questions about life in the late twentieth century. This partially explains why Bellow received the Nobel Prize in Literature in 1976.

The scenes with the African American pickpocket, Govinda Lal, and Sammler's recollections of the Six-Day War predate many of the current debates about Jewish-African American relations, various postcolonial theories, issues surrounding the Holocaust, and Israel's treatment of Palestinians. Bellow clearly teaches that acts of violence are an affront to all, and are never justified simply by one's history or political stance. For example, when Sammler sees the gashes on the pickpocket's face after he has been viciously beaten by Eisen, his own damaged eye begins to throb in complete sympathy for this new victim of violence.

Angela's characterization, and the lesson taught to Sammler in his apartment lobby each provide valuable insights about regarding the female as other, power, and desire. *Mr. Sammler's Planet* also contains a prolonged investigation about self-construction in late twentieth century America, particularly after such events as the Holocaust and rapid technological advance. Mr. Sammler's planet is the reader's planet, Bellow seems to suggest, and it is a sphere with a movement toward a greater human goal and toward a darker future ripe with brutality, selfishness, and violence. With Sammler, Bellow shows that personal rebirth is still possible on this planet, but always at a cost of great sacrifice and suffering.

James Aaron Stanger

Bibliography:

Cronin, Gloria L., and L. H. Goldman, eds. *Saul Bellow in the 1980's: A Collection of Critical Essays*. East Lansing: Michigan State University Press, 1989. Essential reading for *Mr. Sammler's Planet*. See especially Allan Chavkin's article, "Bellow and English Romanticism," Susan Glickman's "The World as Will and Idea: A Comparative Study of *An American Dream* and *Mr. Sammler's Planet*," and Ellen Pifer's "Two Different Speeches: Mystery and Knowledge in *Mr. Sammler's Planet*."

Dremer, S. Lillian. *Witness Through the Imagination: Jewish-American Holocaust Literature*. Detroit: Wayne State University Press, 1989. An essential discussion of *Mr. Sammler's Planet* as a Holocaust novel.

Fuchs, Daniel. *Saul Bellow: Vision and Revision*. Durham, N.C.: Duke University Press, 1984. Making use of Bellow's collection of unpublished manuscripts, Fuchs details for the reader the evolution of a Bellow novel, from idea through revision. Also examines the literary and intellectual milieus in which Bellow writes.

Kiernan, Robert. *Saul Bellow*. New York: Continuum, 1988. Contains analysis of Bellow's individual works as well as an introduction on his life and career. Chronology, bibliography of works by and about Bellow, index, notes.

Stock, Irvin. *Fiction as Wisdom: From Goethe to Bellow*. University Park: Pennsylvania State University Press, 1974. Has chapter on Saul Bellow that provides an excellent overview of *Mr. Sammler's Planet*'s debt to British Romantic literature.

MRS. DALLOWAY

Type of work: Novel
Author: Virginia Woolf (1882-1941)
Type of plot: Psychological realism
Time of plot: 1920's
Locale: London
First published: 1925

Principal characters:
> CLARISSA DALLOWAY
> RICHARD DALLOWAY, her husband
> PETER WALSH, a former suitor
> ELIZABETH, Mrs. Dalloway's daughter
> MISS KILMAN, Elizabeth's friend
> SALLY SETON, an old friend of Clarissa and Peter

The Story:

Mrs. Clarissa Dalloway went to make last-minute preparations for an evening party. During her day in the city, she enjoyed the summer air, the many sights and people, and the general bustle of London. She met Hugh Whitbread, now a court official and a handsome and sophisticated man. She had known Hugh since her youth, and she also knew his wife, Evelyn, for whom she did not particularly care. Other people came to London to see paintings, to hear music, or to shop, but the Whitbreads came to consult doctors, for Evelyn was always ailing.

Mrs. Dalloway went about her shopping. While she was in a flower shop, a luxurious limousine pulled up outside. Everyone speculated on the occupant behind the drawn curtains of the car, and everywhere the limousine went, it was followed by curious eyes. Mrs. Dalloway, who suspected that the queen was inside, felt that she was right when the car drove into the Buckingham Palace grounds.

The sights and sounds of London reminded Mrs. Dalloway of many things. She thought back to her youth, to the days before her marriage, to her husband, and to her daughter, Elizabeth. Her daughter was a problem, mainly because of her horrid friend Miss Kilman, a religious fanatic who scoffed at the luxurious way the Dalloways lived. Mrs. Dalloway hated her. Miss Kilman was not at all like the friend of her own girlhood, Sally Seton, whom Mrs. Dalloway had truly loved.

Mrs. Dalloway wondered what love really was. She had loved Sally, but she had loved Richard Dalloway and Peter Walsh, too. She had married Richard, and then Peter had left for India. Later, she learned that he had married someone he met on board ship. She had heard little about him since his marriage. The day, however, was wonderful and life was wonderful. The war was over, and she was giving a party.

While Mrs. Dalloway was shopping, Septimus Smith and his wife were sitting in the park. Septimus had married Lucrezia while he was serving in Italy, and she had given up her family and her country for him. Now he frightened her because he acted so strangely and talked of committing suicide. The doctor said that there was nothing physically wrong with him. Septimus, one of the first to have volunteered for war duty, had gone to war to save his country, the England of Shakespeare. When he got back, he was a war hero and was given a good job at the office. They had nice lodgings, and Lucrezia was happy. Septimus began reading Shakespeare again, but he was unhappy and brooded. He and Lucrezia had no children. To Septimus, the world was in such horrible condition that it was unjust to bring children into it.

When Septimus began to experience visitations from Evans, a comrade who had been killed in the war, Lucrezia became even more frightened and she called in Dr. Holmes. Septimus felt almost completely abandoned by that time. Lucrezia could not understand why her husband did not like Dr. Holmes, for he was so kind and so much interested in Septimus. Finally, she took her husband to Sir William Bradshaw, a wealthy and noted psychiatrist. Septimus had had a brilliant career ahead of him, and his employer spoke highly of his work. No one knew why he wanted to kill himself. Septimus said that he had committed a crime, but his wife said that he was guilty of absolutely nothing. Sir William suggested a place in the country where Septimus would be by himself, without his wife. It was not, Sir William said, a question of preference. Since he had threatened suicide, it was a question of law.

Mrs. Dalloway returned home from shopping. Lady Bruton had invited Richard Dalloway to lunch. Mrs. Dalloway had never liked Millicent Bruton because she was far too clever. When Peter Walsh came to call, Mrs. Dalloway was surprised and happy to see him again. She introduced him to Elizabeth, her daughter. He asked Mrs. Dalloway if she were happy; she wondered why. When he left, she called out to him not to forget her party. Peter thought about Clarissa Dalloway and her parties: That was all life meant to her. He had been divorced from his wife and had come to England. Life was far more complicated for him. He had fallen in love with another woman, one who had two children, and he had come to London to arrange for her divorce and to find a job. He hoped Hugh Whitbread would help him find one in government.

That night, Clarissa Dalloway's party was a great success. At first, she was afraid that it might not be, but when the prime minister arrived, her evening was complete. Peter met Lady Rossetter, who turned out to be Sally Seton. She had not been invited but had just dropped in. She had five sons, she told Peter. They chatted. When Elizabeth came in, Peter noticed how beautiful she was.

Later, Sir William Bradshaw and his wife entered. They were late, they explained, because one of Sir William's patients had committed suicide. Feeling altogether abandoned, Septimus Smith had jumped out of a window before they could take him to the country. Clarissa was upset. Although the person who had committed suicide was completely unknown to her, she somehow felt that it was her own disaster, her own disgrace. The poor young man had thrown away his life when it had become useless. Clarissa had never thrown away anything more valuable than a shilling. Once she had stood beside a fountain while Peter Walsh, angry and humiliated, had asked her whether she intended to marry Richard. Richard had never become prime minister. Instead, the prime minister came to her parties. Now she was growing old. Clarissa Dalloway knew herself at last for the beautiful, charming, inconsequential person she was.

Sally and Peter talked on. They thought idly of Clarissa and Richard and wondered whether they were happy together. Sally agreed that Richard had improved. She left Peter and went to talk with Richard. Peter was feeling strange. A sort of terror and ecstasy took hold of him, and he could not be certain what it was that excited him so suddenly. It was Clarissa, he thought. Even after all these years, it must be Clarissa.

Critical Evaluation:

Mrs. Dalloway comes midway in Virginia Woolf's fiction-writing career and near the beginning of her experiments with form and technique, just after *Jacob's Room* (1922), her first experimental novel. The book is really two stories—Clarissa Dalloway's and Septimus Smith's—and the techniques by which Woolf united the two narrative strands are unusual and skillful. While writing the novel, Woolf commented in her diary on her new method of delineating character. Instead of explaining the characters' pasts chronologically, she uses a "tunnelling process": "I dig out beautiful caves behind my characters." The various characters appear in the present without explanation; various sense impressions—a squeaky hinge, a repeated phrase, a particular tree—call to mind a memory, and past becomes present. Such an evocation of the past is reminiscent of Proust, but Woolf's method does not involve the ego of the narrator. Woolf's "caves" reveal both the past and the characters' reactions to present events. Woolf structurally connects the "caves" and her themes by spatial and temporal techniques; her handling of the stream-of-consciousness technique—unlike that of Joyce—is always filtered and indirect; the narrator is in command, telling the reader "Clarissa thought" or "For so it had always seemed to her." This ever-present narrative voice clarifies the characters' inner thoughts and mediates the commentary of the novel; at times, however, it blurs the identity of the speaker. Woolf's use of the "voice" became more prominent in *To the Lighthouse* (1927), then disappeared in *The Waves* (1931).

With its disparate characters and various scenes of street life, the structure of the book seems at first to lack unity. Woolf, however, uses many devices, both technical and thematic, to unite elements. The day, sometime in mid-June, 1923, is a single whole, moving chronologically from early morning to late evening. The book is not divided into chapters or sections headed by titles or numbers, but Woolf notes some of the shifts in time or scene by a short blank space in the manuscript. More often, however, the transition from one group of characters to another is accomplished by the remarking of something public, something common to the experience of both, something seen or heard. The world of Clarissa and her friends alternates with the world of Septimus Smith. The sight of a motorcar, the sight and sound of a skywriting plane, a running child, a woman singing, an omnibus, an ambulance, and the clock striking are the transitions connecting those two worlds. Moreover, the striking of the clocks ("first a warning, musical; then the hour, irrevocable") is noted at various other times to mark a shift from one character's consciousness to another. The exact time, which is given periodically, signals the day's progress (noon comes at almost the exact center of the book) and stresses the irrevocable movement toward death, one of the book's themes. Usually at least two clocks are described as striking— first Big Ben, a masculine symbol, then, a few seconds later, the feminine symbol St. Margaret's; this suggests again the two genders of all existence united in the echoes of the bells, "the leaden circles."

The main thematic devices used to unify the book are the similarity between Clarissa and Septimus and the repetition of key words and phrases in the minds of various characters. The likeness between Clarissa and Septimus is most important, as each helps to explain the other, although they never meet. Both are lonely and contemplate suicide. Both feel guilty for their past lives, Septimus because he "cannot feel" the death of Evans, Clarissa because she rejected Peter and has a tendency to dominate others. Both have homosexual feelings, Septimus for Evans, Clarissa for Sally Seton. More important, both want desperately to bring order into life's chaos. Septimus achieves this momentarily with the making of Mrs. Peters' hat, Clarissa with her successful party. Septimus understands that the chaos will return and so takes his own life to unite himself with Death, the final order. Septimus' suicide forces Clarissa to see herself in a new and more honest way and to understand for the first time her schemings for success. Clarissa "felt somehow very like him"; she does not pity him but identifies with his defiant "embracing" of death.

Certain phrases become thematic because they are so often repeated and thus gain richer overtones of meaning at each use, as different characters interpret differently such phrases as

"Fear no more" and "if it were now to die" and such concepts as the sun and the waves, which appear repeatedly, especially in the thoughts of Septimus and Clarissa.

The disparate strands of the story are joined at Clarissa's party, over which she presides like an artist over her creation. Not inferior to the painter Lily Briscoe as a creator, Clarissa's great talent is "knowing people almost by instinct," and she is able triumphantly to combine the right group of people at her party. Not only Clarissa but Richard and Peter also come to new realizations about themselves at the party. Richard, who has been unable to verbalize his love for Clarissa, is finally able to tell his daughter Elizabeth that he is proud of her. At the end, Peter realizes that the terror and excitement he feels in Clarissa's presence indicate his true feeling for her.

The two figures who are given unfavorable treatment—Sir William, the psychiatrist, and Miss Kilman, the religious fanatic—insist on modes of existence inimical to the passionate desire of Clarissa and Septimus for wholeness. Claiming that Septimus "lacks proportion," Sir William nevertheless uses his profession to gain power over others and, as Clarissa understands, makes life "intolerable" for Septimus. Miss Kilman's life is built on evangelical religion; she considers herself to be better than Clarissa, whom she wants to humiliate. She proudly asserts that she will have a "religious victory," which will be "God's will."

The real action of the story is all within the minds of the characters, but Woolf gives these inner lives a reality and harmony that reveal the excitement and oneness of human existence. Clarissa and Septimus are really two aspects of the same being—the feminine and the masculine—united in Clarissa's ultimate awareness. Mrs. Dalloway remains the best introduction to Woolf's characteristic style and themes.

"Critical Evaluation" by Margaret McFadden-Gerber

Bibliography:

Blackstone, Bernard. *Virginia Woolf: A Commentary*. London: Hogarth Press, 1949. An older but excellent essay on Woolf's use of time, "the insistent hours pressing on," to create a sense of the pressures felt by Septimus and Clarissa. Blackstone claims that the characters' loneliness and the pity they evoke are keys to *Mrs. Dalloway*.

Brower, Reuben Arthur. "Something Central Which Permeated: Virginia Woolf and *Mrs. Dalloway*." In *The Fields of Light: An Experiment in Critical Reading*. Oxford, England: Oxford University Press, 1951. Excellent analysis of Woolf's use of metaphor to convey a sense of suspense and interruption. Woolf creates a sense of the "terror of entering the sea of experience and of living life," so that the reader feels both the loveliness and the frightening truths of reality.

Homans, Margaret, ed. *Virginia Woolf: A Collection of Critical Essays*. Englewood Cliffs, N.J.: Prentice-Hall, 1993. Many of the articles in this collection connect *Mrs. Dalloway* to Woolf's other works. One essay focuses on the web created in *Mrs. Dalloway* and *To the Lighthouse* to explain Woolf's images of space, darkness, and affirmation. In another essay, the structure of the novel is analyzed as it relates to female development. Mirroring and images of death are also examined as a key to understanding the novel.

Warner, Eric, ed. *Virginia Woolf: A Centenary Perspective*. New York: St. Martin's Press, 1984. Includes some of the best available articles on Woolf's symbolism and purpose. The images of reflections in glass, sight, and mirroring are key to her sense of being and to the creation of continuity between people. One article deals with the paradoxes of love and silence, duality and time. Another discusses Woolf's concern with the self and with consciousness.

MRS. DANE'S DEFENCE

Type of work: Drama
Author: Henry Arthur Jones (1851-1929)
Type of plot: Social realism
Time of plot: Early twentieth century
Locale: Near London
First performed: 1900; first published, 1905

> *Principal characters:*
> MRS. DANE, a woman of questionable reputation
> SIR DANIEL CARTERET, a distinguished jurist
> LIONEL CARTERET, his adopted son, in love with Mrs. Dane
> MRS. BULSOM-PORTER, a gossip
> MR. JAMES RISBY, her nephew
> LADY EASTNEY, Mrs. Dane's friend
> JANET COLQUHOUN, her niece

The Story:

Young Lionel Carteret was madly in love with Mrs. Dane, a woman three years older than he. The difference in their ages was not too important to those who loved the young man, but Mrs. Dane's reputation made them try to dissuade Lionel from his attachment. Mrs. Bulsom-Porter, a local gossip, had been told by her nephew, James Risby, that Mrs. Dane was actually one Felicia Hindemarsh.

Miss Hindemarsh had, five years previously, been involved in a horrible scandal in Vienna, when she had had an affair with a married man for whom she worked as a governess. The wife, learning of the affair, had committed suicide, and the man himself was still in an insane asylum. Risby, however, had since told Mrs. Bulsom-Porter that he had been mistaken. Although he had thought that Mrs. Dane was Felicia Hindemarsh, he was now completely convinced that he had been wrong. In fact, he declared that Mrs. Dane hardly resembled the sinful Miss Hindemarsh. His retraction meant little to Mrs. Bulsom-Porter, who knew absolutely nothing of Mrs. Dane except that she was attractive and charming. Those qualities were enough to make Mrs. Bulsom-Porter hate her, and she continued to spread the story about Mrs. Dane's past, without admitting that there might be some doubt about her story.

Lionel had been deeply in love with Janet Colquhoun the year before, but had been persuaded by Sir Daniel Carteret, his foster father, to wait before he asked her to marry him. Sir Daniel tried to make Lionel see that his latest infatuation might also pass away, but Lionel would not listen to that well-meaning advice. He accused Sir Daniel of never having known love. The young man did not know that many years before, Sir Daniel had been in love with a married woman. They had decided to defy the conventions and go away together, but on the night of their departure, her son had become dangerously ill. She had stayed with her child, and she and Sir Daniel had renounced their affections. The woman had been Lionel's mother. After her death, and the subsequent death of her husband, Sir Daniel had adopted Lionel, giving him his name and his love. The young man was so dear to Sir Daniel that he could not stand to see the boy ruin his life by marrying Mrs. Dane, at least while her reputation was clouded.

Sir Daniel and Lady Eastney, Mrs. Dane's friend, set about to try to solve the mystery once and for all. Although Risby had retracted his story, Mrs. Bulsom-Porter would not stop spreading the scandal until she was proved wrong beyond a doubt. Mrs. Dane herself would do nothing to stop the gossip, but at last Sir Daniel persuaded her to tell him enough about her background to allow an investigation. While he was trying to piece together the facts, Mrs. Bulsom-Porter employed a detective to go to Vienna and find evidence to prove Mrs. Dane was Miss Hindemarsh.

When the detective returned from Vienna, Mrs. Dane met him first and begged him to declare her innocence. She offered him any sum not to reveal what he had learned. Consequently, when he was asked by Mrs. Bulsom-Porter and Sir Daniel to reveal his findings, he said that those in Vienna who had known Felicia Hindemarsh swore that there was absolutely no resemblance between her and the photograph of Mrs. Dane that he had shown them. His account satisfied everyone but Mrs. Bulsom-Porter. Sir Daniel, Lady Eastney, and even Mr. Bulsom-Porter insisted that she sign a retraction and a public apology, but she refused. She still hoped to catch Mrs. Dane in a lie.

It might be necessary for Mrs. Dane to sue Mrs. Bulsom-Porter for slander, so Sir Daniel continued his own investigation. He talked again with Mrs. Dane, in an attempt to find out everything about her history. She told him that she had lived in Canada for several years, which made it difficult to trace her past. Then she betrayed herself by mentioning her uncle's name. When Sir Daniel looked up that name and her relative's place of residence, he found a reference to a Reverend Mr. Hindemarsh.

At first, Mrs. Dane claimed that Felicia Hindemarsh was her cousin, and that she had tried to conceal the fact because of the disgrace, but at last she was forced to confess that she was Felicia. Risby and the detective had known the truth but had shielded her because they thought she had suffered enough for her sin.

Mrs. Bulsom-Porter was a troublemaker who needed to be cured of her vicious ways, and no one else wished to make Mrs. Dane suffer more, so Sir Daniel and Lady Eastney forced Mrs. Bulsom-Porter to make a public apology for the scandal she had caused. No one would ever know that she had been right all the time. Lionel wanted to marry Mrs. Dane anyway, but Sir Daniel persuaded her to forsake him, even though she loved him sincerely. Mrs. Dane had had a child as a result of her unfortunate earlier affair, and Sir Daniel knew that, although Lionel loved her, he would forever remember that she had lied once and might lie again. Also, the man in the case was still living, although insane, and the wise Sir Daniel knew that these facts were no foundation for a successful marriage. Since Lionel would never forsake her, Mrs. Dane must use her love for him wisely and disappear from his life forever. She agreed, never doubting the wisdom of Sir Daniel's decision, and left the region without telling Lionel goodbye.

Because Sir Daniel had been so kind and wise in dealing with Mrs. Dane and Lionel, Lady Eastney accepted the proposal that Sir Daniel had made to her some time before. She knew that she would always feel secure with him. Although Lionel thought that he could never be happy or fall in love again, he promised to try to carry out his foster father's wishes. Janet, who had tried hard to pretend that their last year's love was over, kissed Lionel understandingly, promising him better times to come.

Critical Evaluation:

Henry Arthur Jones was one of the early so-called Modern dramatists, the school begun by Henrik Ibsen at the end of the nineteenth century. *Mrs. Dane's Defence* belongs to the period of dramatic literature that saw the introduction of naturalism into the English theater. The attempt to portray people as they really are was coupled with another new tendency in drama—humanitarianism. Although Mrs. Dane's sin was not condoned, her weakness was forgiven by those who were really her friends.

The realistic British "well-made play" provided the transition between the artificial, elaborate, pseudopoetic dramatic spectacles of the early nineteenth century and the realistic, iconoclastic theater of George Bernard Shaw and his successors. On the one hand, the genre brought realism to the English stage—recognizable domestic scenes with actual furniture, doors and windows that opened and closed, functional props, colloquial dialogue, and natural acting. On the other hand, for all its surface realism and apparent concern with serious social issues, the British well-made play typically reflected assumptions and attitudes that reinforced, rather than challenged, the middle-class Victorian society that supported it. If the best of these plays did not actually attack the prevalent social and moral values, they did posit interesting questions and, occasionally, suggested ambiguous difficulties beneath the smug, placid surface of Victorian society. There is no better example of the powers and limits of the British well-made play than Henry Arthur Jones's *Mrs. Dane's Defence*.

For the first three acts *Mrs. Dane's Defence* is a typical well-made play, although the action seems less contrived and the characters more natural than usual. As in most examples of the genre, the action turns on concealed information that is gradually revealed in the course of the play, in this case the true identity and "notorious" past of the heroine, Mrs. Dane. Although her efforts to clear her name seem to be going well, the audience receives several hints that the gossip regarding her is really true. With mechanical precision the play builds to the powerful *scène à faire* (obligatory scene) in which Judge Daniel Carteret cross-examines Mrs. Dane and painfully extracts the truth from her. Having had her true identity revealed and her shady past exposed, Mrs. Dane would normally fall victim to Victorian convention, which demanded punishment (if not death, at least social ostracism) for a woman of Mrs. Dane's sort. In the ambiguous denouement of Act IV, *Mrs. Dane's Defence* veers somewhat from the well-made play pattern and introduces complexities that give the play a modernity that most plays of the genre—including all of Jones's others—conspicuously lack.

Beneath the surface problems of false identity and thwarted romance is a very subtle and interesting battle of the sexes. Sir Daniel Carteret represents the conventional "masculine" view; he demands truth at all costs and insists that the person exposed pay the price of the misdeeds without regard to extenuating circumstances. This attitude clashes with the "feminine" approach advocated by his intended, Lady Eastney, who considers only the "human" aspects of the problem and weighs motive and essential character more heavily than technical fact. Even after she learns Mrs. Dane's actual identity, Lady Eastney says: "Mrs. Dane shall leave this place, if she does leave it, without a stain on her character. And I intend that Mrs. Bulsom-Porter shall stay in it, if she does stay in it, as a self-confessed scandal-monger."

Lady Eastney wins the public battle, in that Mrs. Dane's name is cleared and Mrs. Bulsom-Porter is openly embarrassed. In a sense, she also wins in her conflict with Sir Daniel, since she coerces him into accepting her strategy, even though he knows it is based on false information. On the more important question of Mrs. Dane's engagement to Lionel Carteret, it is the judge's view that prevails.

The central irony is that, in order to impress his view of things on Lionel and Mrs. Dane, Sir Daniel, the apostle of truth at all costs, tells lies. He tells his son that he once made a similar sacrifice, when the opposite was true, and he threatens Mrs. Dane with ultimate exposure, when he knows that the secret is safe. Mrs. Dane analyzes the problem correctly when she says "Only we mustn't get found out. I'm afraid I've broken that part of the law." Thus, the essential hypocrisy and moral self-righteousness of upper middle-class Victorian society is exposed, in the character of its most respectable advocate, to a degree that Jones himself may not fully have intended or realized.

Bibliography:

Cordell, Richard A. *Henry Arthur Jones and the Modern Drama*. Port Washington, N.Y.: Kennikat Press, 1968. Critical study of the playwright's major works. Describes the genesis of *Mrs. Dane's Defence* and comments on its characteristics as a well-made play; claims Jones succumbs to contemporary pressures that upheld a double standard of morality for men and women.

Dietrich, Richard F. *British Drama 1890 to 1950: A Critical History*. Boston: Twayne, 1989. Places Jones in the context of late nineteenth century British drama, highlighting his essential conservatism. Describes *Mrs. Dane's Defence* as a problem play in which the author expertly counterpoints character.

Emeljanow, Victor. *Victorian Popular Dramatists*. Boston: Twayne, 1987. Chapter on Jones explains his popularity with nineteenth century audiences. Comments on the first production of *Mrs. Dane's Defence*; asserts that Jones's characters serve as mouthpieces for conventional British values.

Jenkins, Anthony. "Terrible Leanings Toward Responsibility." In *The Making of Victorian Drama*. Cambridge, England: Cambridge University Press, 1991. Discusses Jones as one of seven influential nineteenth century British dramatists. Accuses him of succumbing to conventional morality in *Mrs. Dane's Defence*; claims his defense of the façade of respectability places him on the side of those who believed in preserving traditional British values at all costs.

Taylor, John Russell. *The Rise and Fall of the Well-Made Play*. London: Methuen, 1967. One chapter discusses Jones's career and the popularity his plays enjoyed at the beginning of the twentieth century. Calls *Mrs. Dane's Defence* "one of the classics of English well-made drama"; analyzes the structure and explains why Jones fails to be convincing in his ending.

MUCH ADO ABOUT NOTHING

Type of work: Drama
Author: William Shakespeare (1564-1616)
Type of plot: Comedy
Time of plot: Thirteenth century
Locale: Italy
First performed: c. 1598-1599; first published, 1600

Principal characters:
DON PEDRO, Prince of Arragon
DON JOHN, his bastard brother
CLAUDIO, a young lord of Florence
BENEDICK, a young lord of Padua
LEONATO, the governor of Messina
HERO, Leonato's daughter
BEATRICE, Leonato's niece
DOGBERRY, a constable

The Story:

Don Pedro, Prince of Arragon, arrived in Messina accompanied by his bastard brother, Don John, and his two friends, the young Italian noblemen Claudio and Benedick. Don Pedro had vanquished his brother in battle. Now, reconciled, the brothers planned to visit Leonato before returning to their homeland. On their arrival in Messina, young Claudio was immediately smitten by the lovely Hero, daughter of Leonato. In order to help his faithful young friend in his suit, Don Pedro assumed the guise of Claudio at a masked ball and wooed Hero in Claudio's name. Then he gained Leonato's consent for Claudio and Hero to marry. The bastard Don John tried to cause trouble by persuading Claudio that Don Pedro meant to betray him and keep Hero for himself, but the villain was foiled in his plot and Claudio remained faithful to Don Pedro.

Benedick, the other young follower of Don Pedro, was a confirmed and bitter bachelor who scorned all men willing to enter the married state. No less opposed to men and matrimony was Leonato's niece, Beatrice. These two constantly sparred with one another, each trying to show intellectual supremacy over the other. Don Pedro, with the help of Hero, Claudio, and Leonato, undertook the seemingly impossible task of bringing Benedick and Beatrice together in matrimony in the seven days before the marriage of Hero and Claudio.

Don John, thwarted in his first attempt to cause disharmony, formed another plot. With the help of a servant, he arranged to make it appear as if Hero was being unfaithful to Claudio. The servant was to gain entrance to Hero's chambers when she was away. In her place would be her attendant, assuming Hero's clothes. Don John, posing as Claudio's true friend, would inform him of her unfaithfulness and lead him to Hero's window to witness her wanton disloyalty.

Don Pedro pursued his plan to persuade Benedick and Beatrice to stop quarreling and fall in love with each other. When Benedick was close by, thinking himself unseen, Don Pedro, Claudio, and Leonato talked of their great sympathy for Beatrice, who loved Benedick but was unloved in return. The three told one another of the love letters Beatrice wrote to Benedick and then tore up, and of the fact that Beatrice beat her breast and sobbed over her unrequited love for Benedick. At the same time, on occasions when Beatrice was nearby but apparently unseen, Hero and her maid told each other that poor Benedick pined and sighed for the heartless Beatrice. The two unsuspecting young people decided not to let the other suffer. Each would sacrifice principles and accept the other's love.

Just as Benedick and Beatrice prepared to admit their love for each other, Don John was successful in his base plot to ruin Hero. He told Claudio that he had learned of Hero's duplicity, and he arranged to take him and Don Pedro to her window that very night to witness her unfaithfulness. Dogberry, a constable, and the watch apprehended Don John's followers and overheard the truth of the plot, but in their stupidity the petty officials could not get their story told in time to prevent Hero's disgrace. Don Pedro and Claudio witnessed the apparent betrayal, and Claudio determined to allow Hero to arrive in church the next day still thinking herself beloved. Then, instead of marrying her, he would shame her before all the wedding guests.

All happened as Don John had hoped. Before the priest and all the guests, Claudio called Hero a wanton and forswore her love for all time. The poor girl protested her innocence, but to no avail. Claudio said that he had seen her foul act with his own eyes. Hero swooned and lay as if dead, but Claudio and Don Pedro left her with her father, who believed the story and wished his daughter really dead in her shame. The priest believed the girl guiltless, however, and he persuaded Leonato to believe in her too. The priest told Leonato to let the world believe Hero dead while they worked to prove her innocent. Benedick, also believing in her innocence, promised to help unravel the mystery. Then Beatrice told Benedick of her love for him and asked him to kill Claudio and so prove his love for her. Benedick challenged Claudio to a duel. Don John had fled the country after the successful outcome of his plot, but Benedick swore that he would find Don John and kill him as well as Claudio.

At last, Dogberry and the watch got to Leonato and told their story. When Claudio and Don Pedro heard the story, Claudio wanted to die and to be with his wronged Hero. Leonato allowed the two sorrowful men to continue to think Hero dead. In fact, they all attended her funeral. Leonato said that he would be avenged if Claudio would marry his niece, a girl who much resembled Hero. Although Claudio still loved the dead Hero, he agreed to marry the other girl so that Leonato should have his wish.

When Don Pedro and Claudio arrived at Leonato's house for the ceremony, all the women were masked. Leonato brought one young woman forward. After Claudio promised to be her husband, she unmasked. She was, of course, Hero. At first Claudio could not believe his senses, but after he was convinced of the truth he took her to the church immediately. Then Benedick and Beatrice declared their true love for each other, and they too went to the church after a dance in celebration of the double nuptials to be performed. Best of all, word came that Don John had been captured and was being brought back to Messina to face his brother, Don Pedro, the next day. On that day, however, all was joy and happiness.

Critical Evaluation:

William Shakespeare's *Much Ado About Nothing* has in fact very much to do with "noting" (an intended pun on "nothing") or half-seeing, with perceiving dimly or not at all. Out of a host of misperceptions arises the comedy of Shakespeare's drama. Indeed, if it can be said that one theme preoccupies Shakespeare more than any other, it is that of perception, which informs not only his great histories and tragedies but his comedies as well. An early history such as *Richard II* (1595-1596), for example, which also involves tragic elements, proceeds not only from the title character's inability to function as a king but also from his failure to apprehend the nature of the new politics. Both *Othello* and *King Lear* are perfect representatives of the tragic consequences of the inability to see. Hindered by their egos, they live in their own restricted worlds oblivious to reality. When they fail to take the real into account, whether it is the nature of evil or their own limitation, they must pay the cost.

Although the blindness of Leonato, Don Pedro, Claudio, and Benedick in *Much Ado About Nothing* very nearly results in tragedy, it is the comic implications of noting rather than seeing that Shakespeare is concerned with here. Yet if his mode is comic, his intention is serious. Besides the characters' inability to perceive Don John's villainy, their superficial grasp of love and their failure to understand the nature of courtship and marriage reveal their moral obtuseness. In fact, the whole society is shot through with a kind of civilized shallowness. The play begins as an unspecified war ends, and the audience is immediately struck by Leonato's and the messenger's lack of response to the casualty report. To the governor of Messina's question, "How many gentlemen have you lost in this action?" the messenger replies, "But few of any sort, and none of name." Leonato comments: "A victory is twice itself, when the achiever brings home full numbers." The heroes of the war, Don Pedro, Claudio, and Benedick, return in a high good humor, seemingly untouched by their experiences and now in search of comfort, games, and diversion.

Only Beatrice is unimpressed with the soldiers' grand entrance, for she knows what they are. Between their "noble" actions, they are are no more than seducers, "valiant trenchermen," gluttons and leeches, or, like Claudio, vain young boys ready to fall in love on a whim. Even the stately Don Pedro is a fool who proposes to Beatrice on impulse after he has wooed the childish Hero for the inarticulate Claudio. In contrast to their behavior, Beatrice's initial cynicism—"I had rather hear my dog bark at a crow, than a man swear he loves me"—is salutary and seems like wisdom.

Yet Beatrice is as susceptible to flattery as is Benedick. Like her eventual lover and husband, she is seduced by Don Pedro's deception, the masque he arranges to lead both Beatrice and Benedick to the altar. Both of them, after hearing that they are adored by the other, pledge their love and devotion. To be sure, the scenes in which they are duped are full of innocent humor, but the comedy does not obscure Shakespeare's rather bitter observations on the foppery of human love and courtship.

Nor is their foppery and foolishness the end of the matter. Don John realizes that a vain lover betrayed is a cruel and indeed inhuman tyrant. With little effort he convinces Claudio and Don Pedro that the innocent Hero is no more than a strumpet. Yet rather than break off the engagement in private, they wait until all meet at the altar to accuse the girl of "savage sensuality." Without compunction they leave her in a swoon, believing her dead. Even the father, Leonato, would have her dead rather than shamed. It is this moment that reveals the witty and sophisticated aristocrats of Messina to be grossly hypocritical, for beneath their glittering and refined manners lies a vicious ethic.

In vivid contrast to the decorous soldiers and politicians are Dogberry and his watchmen, although they certainly function as no more than a slapstick diversion. Hilarious clowns when they attempt to ape their social betters in manners and speech, they are yet possessed by a common sense or—as one critic has observed—by an instinctual morality, which enables them to uncover the villainy of Don John's henchmen, Conrade and Borachio. As the latter says to the nobleman, Don Pedro, "I have deceived even your very eyes: what your wisdoms could not discover, these shallow fools have brought to light." Like the outspoken and bawdy Margaret, who knows that underlying the aristocrats' courtly manners in the game of love is unacknowledged lust, Dogberry and his bumbling followers immediately understand the issue and recognize villainy, though they may use the wrong words to describe it.

Shakespeare does not force the point home in the end. He is not dealing here with characters of great stature, and they could not bear revelations of substantial moral consequence. They may show compunction for their errors, but they exhibit no significant remorse and are ready to get on with the rituals of their class. It does not seem to matter to Claudio whether he marries Hero or someone who looks like her. Even Beatrice has apparently lost her maverick edge as she joins the strutting Benedick in the marriage dance. All ends well for those involved (with the exception of Don John), but through no great fault of their own.

"Critical Evaluation" by David L. Kubal

Bibliography:
Bloom, Harold, ed. *William Shakespeare's "Much Ado About Nothing."* New York: Chelsea House, 1988. Contains eight significant articles from the 1970's and 1980's. See especially the essays by Richard A. Levin, who looks beneath the comedic surface to find unexpected, troubling currents, and Carol Thomas Neely, who contributes an influential feminist interpretation.
Evans, Bertrand. *Shakespeare's Comedies.* Oxford, England: Clarendon Press, 1960. Important critical study. Concludes that Shakespeare's comic dramaturgy is based on different levels of awareness among characters and between them and the audience. The comedy in *Much Ado About Nothing* reflects an intricate game of multiple deceptions and misunderstandings that the audience enjoys from a privileged position.
Hunter, Robert Grams. *Shakespeare and the Comedy of Forgiveness.* New York: Columbia University Press, 1965. Argues persuasively that the thematic core of several Shakespeare comedies derives from the tradition of English morality plays. In *Much Ado About Nothing*, Claudio sins against the moral order by mistrusting Hero and is saved by repentance and forgiveness.
Macdonald, Ronald R. *William Shakespeare: The Comedies.* New York: Twayne, 1992. Compact introduction to Shakespeare's comedy that is both critically sophisticated and accessible to the general reader. Essay on *Much Ado About Nothing* reveals various subtextual relationships of class and gender by probing the characters' semantically complex and ironic verbal behavior.
Ornstein, Robert. *Shakespeare's Comedies: From Roman Farce to Romantic Mystery.* London: Associated University Presses, 1986. Award-winning book by a major Shakespeare scholar. The chapter on *Much Ado About Nothing* offers a sensitive, graceful analysis of the play that focuses primarily on characterization, plot, and moral themes.

MUMBO JUMBO

Type of work: Novel
Author: Ishmael Reed (1938-   )
Type of plot: Satire
Time of plot: 1920's
Locale: Harlem in New York City
First published: 1972

Principal characters:
PAPA LABAS, a conjure man of Jes Grew Kathedral
BERBELANG, LaBas' former assistant and a Mu'tahfikah leader
BLACK HERMAN, a famous African American occultist
HINCKLE VON VAMPTON, the Atonist publisher of *The Benign Monster*
HUBERT "SAFECRACKER" GOULD, Von Vampton's assistant
WOODROW WILSON JEFFERSON, Von Vampton's African American tool
BIFF MUSCLEWHITE, curator for the Center of Art Detention

The Story:
   One night in 1920, the mayor of New Orleans was drinking bootlegged gin with his mistress when a messenger announced the outbreak of Jes Grew, a "psychic epidemic" causing African Americans to thrash in ecstasy and to lust for meaning in life. By the next morning, ten thousand people had contracted the disease, which was spreading rapidly across America.
   PaPa LaBas, a conjure man who carried "Jes Grew in him like most other folk carry genes," ran Jes Grew Kathedral and represented the old ways of Jes Grew, specializing in "Black astrology charts, herbs, potions, candles, talismans." His former assistant, Berbelang, moved away from old ways and worked to expand Jes Grew to other non-Western people such as Native Americans, Asians, and Muslims, as well as to more people of African descent. Berbelang led the Mu'tahfikah, a radical group of Jes Grew Carriers who looted Centers of Art Detention (museums) to return treasures to their native lands in Africa, South America, and Asia.
   Attempting to halt Jes Grew, the Wallflower Order of the Atonist Path (Western culture) formed a two-step plan. Their first step was to install Warren Harding as anti-Jes Grew President of the United States; their next step was to implant a Talking Android within Jes Grew to sabotage the movement. Atonist Biff Musclewhite gave up his job as police commissioner and became a consultant to the Metropolitan Police in order to qualify for a higher paying job as Curator for Art Detention.
   One day, LaBas was in court facing charges that he allowed his "Newfoundland HooDoo dog 3 Cents" to defecate on the altar at St. Patrick's Cathedral. The Manhattan Atonists used charges like this, fire inspections, tax audits, censorship of writings, and other means to deter LaBas and Jes Grew.
   Atonist Hinckle Von Vampton worked in the copy room of the *New York Sun*, a Wallflower Order newspaper. One night, his landlady saw him performing secret rituals. At work, when he forgot to keep a headline in present tense, his boss thought he was "losing his grip." Later, Von Vampton was fired for printing the headline "Voo Doo Generals Surround Marines at Port-au-Prince," violating the paper's policy against mentioning United States military action in Haiti. Their reason was that "Americans will not tolerate wars that can't be explained in simple terms of economics or the White man's destiny." Von Vampton was later seized at gunpoint and taken

to Wallflower Order headquarters, which was buzzing with activity monitoring the Jes Grew epidemic.

The man in charge of the headquarters, Hierophant 1, explained to Von Vampton that the Wallflower Order needed The Text, the sacred Jes Grew writings. Von Vampton had divided The Text into fourteen parts and sent it to fourteen individual Jes Grew Carriers in Harlem. Only Von Vampton had the power to reassemble The Text, so the Wallflower Order agreed to let him control the project. First, he must burn The Text. Second, he must create the Talking Android that would infiltrate and undercut the Jes Grew movement. Von Vampton recruited Hubert "Safecracker" Gould to help run *The Benign Monster*, the magazine he would use to carry out the project.

Woodrow Wilson Jefferson, a young man who left rural Mississippi to begin a journalism career in New York City, was laughed out of the *New York Tribune* because of his ragged, rural appearance and because he wanted to meet Karl Marx and Friedrich Engels. Later, Jefferson saw a sign outside of the offices of *The Benign Monster*, stating, "Negro viewpoint wanted." Von Vampton hired Jefferson and gave him an office in his estate, Spiraling Agony. Jefferson was like putty waiting to be formed and would have made a perfect Talking Android, except Von Vampton thought his skin was too dark. The Talking Android had to be black, but Von Vampton thought people would not accept anyone too dark.

Von Vampton learned that Abdul Hamid had acquired and was trying to publish The Text. Von Vampton, Gould, and Jefferson went to Abdul's office and offered to buy it, but Abdul refused to sell. When Gould pulled out a gun and demanded to see the safe, Abdul resisted, so Von Vampton stabbed him in the back. Gould opened the safe but found it empty. The *Sun* headline distorted the incident by suggesting that Mu'tahfikah was responsible for Abdul's death.

Charlotte, a young French translator at the Kathedral, quit her job to perform Neo HooDoo dances at the Plantation House cabaret, despite LaBas' warning against using The Work for profit. She also entertained customers outside the club.

The Mu'tahfikah—Berbelang, Yellow Jack, Thor Wintergreen, and José Fuentes (whom La Bas had met during an art history class in college)—planned to recover some cultural artifacts. Biff Musclewhite was in Charlotte's apartment when the Mu'tahfikah kidnapped him to gain access to the Center for Art Detention. As ransom, they demanded the return of the Olmec Head, a Central American sculpture.

Left to guard the hostage, Thor Wintergreen was tricked into helping Musclewhite and the police ambush Berbelang, who was shot and killed. Musclewhite convinced Wintergreen that the Mu'tahfikah members were not only taking back their culture but also getting ready to take over the country. Once free, Musclewhite made an appointment to see Charlotte, but before he arrived, she saw the headline announcing Berbelang's death. When she accused Musclewhite of having something to do with the incident, he strangled her.

Making his last run of the night, a trolley operator was seduced by LaBas' assistant Earline, who had picked up a *loa*, the sensuous spirit of the Voodoo goddess Erzulie. When PaPa LaBas went to tell Earline of Berbelang's death, she fainted and LaBas called Black Herman to exorcise the *loa*.

The next morning, Black Herman took LaBas to see Haitian Benoit Battraville aboard the freighter *The Black Plume* in the harbor. Battraville explained the Atonist role in Haiti and revealed the Wallflower Order plot to install a Talking Android. LaBas and Black Herman volunteered to track the Talking Android.

Meanwhile, Von Vampton was still looking for someone to become the Talking Android when he saw an advertisement for skin bleaching cream. He was applying the cream to Jefferson's face when the young man's father rushed in and took his son back home to Mississippi. The skin-lightening plot failed. Instead, Von Vampton settled on an opposite plan when Gould accidentally fell face down into black mud. Gould became the Talking Android.

Concerned about President Harding's political blunderings and alleged black ancestry, the Wallflower Order decided to do away with him by sending him on a train trip to California and slowly poisoning him along the way. Harding died in San Francisco. The Order also took defensive moves to combat the spread of Jes Grew. The federal government seized control of the arts and decentralized art objects away from the Centers for Art Detention to protect them from the Mu'tahfikah.

At a gathering north of New York City, the Talking Android was reading his epic poem "Harlem Tom Toms" when LaBas and Black Herman broke in and exposed Gould as a fake. Asked to defend their charges, LaBas gave an extended history of the mythology behind Jes Grew, dating back thousands of years to ancient Egypt. Having brought Jes Grew history up to the present, LaBas explained how he solved the mystery and located the box which should have held Abdul's copy of The Text underneath the floor of the Cotton Club where Abdul had hidden it. A seal on the box reminded LaBas of Von Vampton's pendant, connecting the Atonist to the mystery. Then Buddy Jackson, operator of several Harlem speakeasies, stepped forward and announced that he had given The Text to Abdul. PaPa LaBas and Black Herman seized Von Vampton and Gould and turned them over to Benoit Battraville.

Jes Grew died down, but PaPa LaBas continued telling its history, giving yearly university lectures. The novel ends with a philosophical discussion of the psychic power of blackness in the American imagination.

Critical Evaluation:

First-time readers of Ishmael Reed's *Mumbo Jumbo* are overwhelmed by the amount of information contained in the novel, including history, mythology, politics, literary history, music, and photography. Critic Henry Louis Gates, Jr., offers the best way to deal with this confusion: Think of it as "gumbo," a complex stew of irregularly shaped chunks and spicy seasonings. Like gumbo, the novel has a cumulative effect, which builds and changes as one reads and lingers long after one has finished the novel.

Mumbo Jumbo is a satire, but the objects of Reed's critiques are not always clear because there are so many. He satirizes politics by having Cab Calloway run against Warren Harding for president of the United States and by naming Hinkle Von Vampton's estate "Spiraling Agony" after Spiro Agnew. He critiques music history by having Moses steal rock lyrics from The Work and by including a photograph of the rock group Black Sabbath. Satires of literary history also flood the book, including a stab at James Baldwin—"King Baldwin 1 grants the Templars his palace as their headquarters"—and a condemnation of *Confessions of the Black Bull God Osiris* by Bilious Styronicus (a stab at William Styron's *The Confessions of Nat Turner*, 1967). Reed even critiques formal education by having PaPa LaBas give university lectures on Jes Grew in the 1960's.

In addition, *Mumbo Jumbo* is a parody of literary form. Reed uses the structure of thriller detective fiction (mystery, clues, whodunits, rational order) but undermines detective fiction's reliance on reason. The discoveries, deductions, and conclusions in *Mumbo Jumbo* are not rational; they defy "order" as defined by Western culture.

Mumbo Jumbo is Reed's most comprehensive study of his "Neo-Hoodoo" aesthetic based on pantheistic voodoo culture rather than on monotheistic Western culture. Reed urges people of color to reclaim their art and culture, a message which echoes the Harlem Renaissance of the 1920's and the Black Arts Movement of the 1960's. *Mumbo Jumbo* creates a history of the Jes Grew movement, a history of African American experience, which stands as an alternative version to the linear grand narrative of Western history. In presenting data, Reed employs devices common to history textbooks: footnotes, definitions, charts, illustrations, and a bibliography. The novel is encyclopedic of African American culture, tracing its origins and roots by examining instances of rapid expansion in the fictional Jes Grew movement.

Reed's resistance of an orderly linear narrative and his technique of bombarding the reader with information place *Mumbo Jumbo* in the realm of postmodern fiction, such as Thomas Pynchon's *Gravity's Rainbow* (1973), Robert Coover's *The Public Burning* (1976), and Salman Rushdie's *Midnight's Children* (1980). All of these works critique history by offering alternatives to a master narrative, and each is a sociopolitical satire.

Geralyn Strecker

Bibliography:
Carter, Steven R. "Ishmael Reed's Neo-Hoodoo Detection." In *Dimensions of Detective Fiction*, edited by Larry N. Landrum, Pat Browne, and Ray B. Browne. Bowling Green, Ohio: Popular Press, 1976. Reed's parody of detective fiction leads readers from the mysteries within the text to the mysteries in life, to consider the culprits in history, to question the alleged truths of Western culture, and to discover distortions of reality in written history.
Gates, Henry Louis, Jr. *The Signifying Monkey: A Theory of Afro-American Literary Criticism.* New York: Oxford University Press, 1988. Includes a valuable discussion of Reed's use of satire and parody. Explains much of the novel's mythology and structure.
Martin, Reginald. *Ishmael Reed and the New Black Aesthetic Critics.* New York: St. Martin's Press, 1988. Relates Reed's "Neo-Hoodoo" aesthetic to trends in African American literature. Contrasts Reed's pantheistic Hoodoo vision with a monotheistic Western worldview.
Mason, Theodore O., Jr. "Performance, History, and Myth: The Problem of Ishmael Reed's *Mumbo Jumbo*." *Modern Fiction Studies* 34, no. 1 (Spring, 1988): 97-109. Reed's use of fiction as performance in showing alternative histories/myths to the Judeo-Christian (Western) tradition is not calm; it is a violent struggle against dominant culture.
Paravisini, Lizabeth. "*Mumbo Jumbo* and the Uses of Parody." *Obsidian II* 1, nos. 1-2 (Spring/Summer, 1986): 113-127. Explores how *Mumbo Jumbo* appropriates the narrative form of a detective novel but undermines Western culture's obsession with rationality and order.

MURDER IN THE CATHEDRAL

Type of work: Drama
Author: T. S. Eliot (1888-1965)
Type of plot: Historical
Time of plot: 1170
Locale: Canterbury, England
First performed: 1935; first published, 1935

> *Principal characters:*
> ARCHBISHOP THOMAS BECKET
> PRIESTS
> TEMPTERS
> KNIGHTS
> CHORUS OF WOMEN OF CANTERBURY

The Story:

The women of Canterbury had been drawn to the cathedral, knowing instinctively that they had been drawn there by danger. There was no safety anywhere, but they had to bear witness. Archbishop Thomas Becket had been gone seven years. He had always been kind to his people, but he should not return. During the periods when the king and the barons ruled alternately, the poor had suffered all kinds of oppression. Like common people everywhere, the women had tried to keep their households in order and to escape the notice of the various rulers. Now they could only wait and witness.

The priests of the cathedral were well aware of the coming struggle for power. The archbishop had been intriguing in France, where he had enlisted the aid of the pope. Henry of Anjou was a stubborn king, however. The priests knew that the strong rule by force, the weak by caprice. The only law was that of seizing power and holding it.

A herald announced that the archbishop was nearing the city and that they were to prepare at once for his coming. Anxiously, they asked whether there would be peace or war, whether the archbishop and the king had been reconciled or not. The herald was of the opinion that there had been only a hasty compromise. He did not know that when the archbishop had parted from the king, the prelate had said that King Henry would not see him again in this life.

After the herald left, one priest expressed the pessimism felt by all. When Thomas Becket was chancellor and in temporal power, courtiers had flattered and fawned over him, but even then he had felt insecure. Either the king should have been stronger or Thomas weaker. For a time, the priests were hopeful that when Thomas returned he would lead them. The women thought the archbishop should return to France. He would still be their spiritual leader, but in France he would be safe. As the priests started to drive out the babbling women, the archbishop arrived and bade them remain. Thomas Becket told his priests of the difficulties he had encountered, and that rebellious bishops and the barons had sworn to have his head. They had sent spies to him and intercepted his letters. At Sandwich he had barely escaped with his life.

The first tempter came to talk with Thomas. When he was chancellor, Thomas had known worldly pleasure and worldly success. Many had been his friends, and at that time he knew how to let friendship dictate over principles. To escape his present hard fate, he needed only to relax his severity and dignity, to be friendly, and to overlook disagreeable principles. Thomas had the strength to give the tempter a strong refusal.

The second tempter reminded Thomas of his temporal power as chancellor. He could be chancellor again and have lasting power. It was well known that the king only commanded, whereas the chancellor ruled. Power was an attribute of the present; holiness was more useful after death. Real power had to be purchased by wise submission, and his present spiritual authority led only to death. Thomas asked about rebellious bishops whom he had excommunicated and barons whose privileges he had curtailed. The tempter was confident that these dissidents would come to heel if Thomas were chancellor with the king's power behind him. Again Thomas had the strength to say no.

The third tempter was even easier to deal with. He represented a clique intent on overthrowing the throne. If Thomas would lead them, they could make the power of the Church supreme. No more would the barons as well as the bishops be ruled by a king. Thomas declined the offer to lead the malcontents.

The fourth tempter was unexpected. He showed Thomas how he could have eternal glory. As plain archbishop, the time would come when men would neither respect nor hate him; he would become a fact of history. So it was with temporal power, too: King succeeds king as the wheel of time turns. Shrines are pillaged and thrones totter. If, however, Thomas would continue in his present course, he would become a martyr and a saint, to dwell forevermore in the presence of God. The archbishop faced a dilemma. No matter whether he acted or suffered, he would sin against his religion.

Early on Christmas morning, Thomas preached a sermon on peace, saying that Christ left people his peace but not peace as the world thinks of it. Spiritual peace did not necessarily mean political peace between England and other countries or between the barons and the king.

After Christmas, four knights came to Canterbury on urgent business. Refusing all hospitality, they began to cite charges against Thomas, saying that he owed all his influence to the king, that he had been ignobly born, and that his eminence was due solely to King Henry's favor. The knights tried to attack Thomas, but the priests and attendants interposed themselves.

The charges were publicly amplified. Thomas had gone to France to stir up trouble in the dominion and to intrigue with the King of France and the pope. In his charity, King Henry had permitted Thomas to return to his see, but Thomas had repaid that charity by excommunicating the bishops who had crowned the young prince; hence the legality of the coronation was in doubt. The knights then pronounced his sentence: He and his retinue must leave English soil.

Thomas answered firmly. In France he had been a beggar of foreign charity; he would never leave England again. He had no dislike for the prince; rather, he had only carried out the pope's orders in excommunicating the bishops. These words availed little. In the cathedral proper, the knights fell on Thomas Becket and slew him.

The knights justified the slaying. It may have looked like four against one, an offense against the English belief in fair play, but before deciding, the people should know the whole story. First, the four knights would not benefit from the murder, for the king, for reasons of state, would deplore the incident, and the knights would be banished.

Second, the king had hoped, in elevating Thomas to the archbishopric, to unite temporal and spiritual rule and to bring order to a troubled kingdom; but as soon as Thomas was elevated, he had become more priestly than the priests and refused to follow the king's orders. Third, he had become an egotistical madman. There was evidence that before leaving France he had clearly prophesied his death in England and that he had been determined to suffer a martyr's fate. In the face of this provocation, the people must conclude that Thomas had committed suicide while of unsound mind. After the knights left, the priests and populace mourned. Their only solace was that so long as men will die for faith the Church will be supreme.

Critical Evaluation:

Unlike those artists who maintain an unchanged view of the world and of the development of their art, T. S. Eliot grew throughout his life. In his youth, he was primarily a satirist, mocking the conventions of society in poems such as "The Love Song of J. Alfred Prufrock" or "Portrait of a Lady." Later, he became a mosaic artist of exquisite sensibility when, fragment by fragment, he pieced together his damning portrait of post-World War I civilization in *The Waste Land* (1922). Still later, finding his ethical pessimism essentially sterile, he climaxed his long interest in philosophy, theology, literary history, and government by becoming a royalist in politics, a classicist in literature, and an Anglo-Catholic in religion.

Born in America and educated at Harvard, Eliot early settled in England. Throughout his early career he had developed more than a casual interest in the drama, not merely as an art form in and of itself, but in the theater as a means of instruction. Such early fragments as *Sweeney Agonistes* (1932) tantalize by their incompleteness, but *Murder in the Cathedral* demonstrates Eliot's mastery of the classic tragic form.

In this remarkably effective play, Eliot links devices derived from the Greeks—the chorus, static action, and Aristotelian purgation—with his profound commitment to the Anglo-Catholic liturgy. *Murder in the Cathedral* in many ways resembles a medieval morality play whose purpose is to enlighten as well as entertain. Yet the work is never merely morally instructive. It rises above didacticism because Archbishop Thomas Becket's internal anguish is made so personal and timeless. Becket's assassination becomes more real by the subsequent political and temporal events it evokes.

Eliot firmly believed that twentieth century drama, to be most effective, had to be written in poetry, a belief he shared with William Butler Yeats, his Irish contemporary. Eliot's poetry is moving without being ostentatiously poetic because it reaches the audience on a level that Eliot himself termed "the auditory imagination." Responding from the unconscious, the spectators are drawn deeply into the drama and begin to share Becket's internal agonies by participating in the almost primitive rhythmic manipulations of Eliot's deceptively simple verse.

What makes Eliot's play so timely is that the four allurements offered to Thomas by the tempters are precisely those faced, whether consciously or unconsciously, by the twentieth century audience: those of worldly pleasure; temporal power; spiritual power; and, finally and most subtly, eternal glory. Thomas refutes all of them, quite directly, but is entranced for a time by the fourth tempter, who indicates that if Thomas were to proceed on his course, he would be deliberately courting martyrdom to achieve eternal happiness with God. Eventually Thomas counters the argument with one of the most effective lines in the play: "The last temptation and the greatest treason/ Is to do the right deed for the wrong reason." Thomas' certainty of the spiritual correctness of his own actions mirrors that of members of the audience, who slowly become aware of their own culpability in acting correctly for insufficient reason in any matter, or even of acting selfishly for a good end. The involvement of the audience so profoundly is another tribute to Eliot's genius.

Eliot also works on still another level, that of the conflict of powers. Each power may perhaps be justified in its own way, and Thomas recognizes that the king and the temporal power he represents have some justification. The king, moreover, had once been Thomas' closest friend and had, in fact, made him archbishop. Thomas ponders on the debts to the temporal realm, to friendship, and to gratitude, but he continues to maintain the primacy of the spiritual order over the temporal. If some things are Caesar's, they are Caesar's only because God permitted that to be so.

Murder in the Cathedral was first staged in Canterbury Cathedral, that magnificent Gothic antiquity providing a most striking setting. Still often produced in a church edifice, the play gains immediacy through the verisimilitude achieved by the combination of setting, liturgy, verse, and chorus. Despite Thomas' brilliant Christmas sermon, which opens the second act, Eliot does not preach. He does not reduce the situation to a simple case of good versus evil. Rather, he creates a conflict of mystiques, each with a well-developed rationale. The choice is between alternatives, not opposites. Thomas, who fears that he may be a victim of the sin of pride, must nevertheless choose either damnation or salvation.

Eliot, always conscious of history, knew that the Shrine of Saint Thomas Becket at Canterbury was among the most famous of medieval objects of devotion and pilgrimage. Thus even the justifications of the knights who slew Thomas deserve serious attention. More than one twentieth century historical critic has wondered if Thomas were not, as it were, "hell-bent" on heaven, a question that Thomas himself ponders. If the knights' justification is to be rejected, the question remains as to how much of their own rationalizations does not continue to be part of what motivates individual action.

Murder in the Cathedral is a compelling drama for celebrating the themes of faith, justification, power, and conflict, which continue to recur through the ages. Eliot has created a timeless work that anticipates his profoundly religious and mystical collection of poems *Four Quartets* (1943) and his later treatments of very similar themes in plays such as *The Cocktail Party* (1949) and *The Confidential Clerk* (1953). All of Eliot's later poetry and plays, however, must be read with *Murder in the Cathedral* in mind, for it represents a pivotal achievement in his distinguished career.

"Critical Evaluation" by Willis E. McNelly

Bibliography:
Ackroyd, Peter. *T. S. Eliot: A Life.* New York: Simon & Schuster, 1984. A very readable biography providing useful and interesting details about the making of this play, its critical reception, and its importance to Eliot's rising career as a playwright. Ackroyd finds the play a success and discusses it in connection with other Eliot works.
Adair, Patricia M. "Mr. Eliot's *Murder in the Cathedral.*" *Cambridge Journal* 4 (November, 1950): 83-95. A full and penetrating study that regards the play not as a tragedy but as a drama paralleling the setting of Canterbury Cathedral in pointing people to God.
Bloom, Harold, ed. *T. S. Eliot's "Murder in the Cathedral."* New York: Chelsea House, 1988. A collection of eleven important essays by prominent literary critics such as Helen Gardner, David Ward, and Stephen Spender. Wide range and balance of approaches, along with a useful chronology and bibliography.
Clark, David R., ed. *Twentieth Century Interpretations of "Murder in the Cathedral": A Collection of Critical Essays.* Englewood Cliffs, N.J.: Prentice-Hall, 1971. A collection of fourteen essays by prominent critics such as E. Martin Browne, Louis L. Martz, Grover Smith, William V. Spanos, and David E. Jones. Includes a substantial chronology of the author's life and a concise bibliography.
Smith, Carol H. *T. S. Eliot's Dramatic Theory and Practice: From "Sweeney Agonistes" to "The Elder Statesman."* Princeton, N.J.: Princeton University Press, 1963. Chapter 3 provides a useful summary of the play's main features and concludes that the play succeeds on the level of poetic rhythm and imagery. A good introduction to the play.

MUTINY ON THE BOUNTY

Type of work: Novel
Author: Charles Nordhoff (1887-1947) and James Norman Hall (1887-1951)
Type of plot: Adventure
Time of plot: Late eighteenth century
Locale: England, South Pacific, and Tahiti
First published: 1932

> *Principal characters:*
> LIEUTENANT WILLIAM BLIGH, the captain of HMS *Bounty*
> ROGER BYAM, a midshipman
> FLETCHER CHRISTIAN, the leader of the mutiny
> GEORGE STEWART, a midshipman friend of Byam
> TEHANI, a Tahitian

The Story:

In 1787, Roger Byam accepted Lieutenant Bligh's offer of a berth as midshipman on HMS *Bounty*, a ship commissioned by the English government to carry the edible breadfruit tree of Tahiti to English possessions in the West Indies, to be used there as a cheap food supply for the black slaves of English planters. Byam's special commission was to work at the task of completing a study of the Tahitian language for the use of English seamen. After filling the ship's roster and getting favorable weather, the *Bounty* set sail, and Midshipman Byam began to learn the ways of a ship at sea. He also began to learn, when only a few days from England, of the many traits of his captain, which were to lead eventually to mutiny. Bligh's fanaticism rested on discipline, which he often enforced at the cost of justice through excessive floggings of the seamen aboard the *Bounty*. However, the principal objection the men had was their captain's exploitation of them and their rations for private graft.

When the *Bounty* arrived in Tahiti, the crew was given the freedom it deserved. Making use of the native custom, each of the men chose for himself a *taio*, or special friend from among the natives, who, during the sailor's stay in Tahiti, would supply him with all the delicacies the island had to offer.

During the stay at Tahiti, Byam, living ashore, collected information for his language study. Most of the sailors found women with whom they lived and to whom some of them were later married. Fletcher Christian chose Maimiti, the daughter of Byam's *taio*. George Stewart chose a Tahitian named Peggy. Byam saw Tehani, later his wife, only once during his stay on the island, but from this one appearance, he was highly impressed with the beauty of the princess.

Captain Bligh, on the *Bounty*, had continued to practice the cruelties which the men considered not only unfair but also illegal. One practice was the confiscation of gifts which the islanders had brought to the men on shipboard and which rightfully belonged to those men. He ordered the gifts to be put into the ship's stores. He had further placed the men on salt pork rations, amid all the plentiful fresh fruits of the island. Just before leaving Tahiti, Bligh falsely accused Christian of stealing his coconuts.

Collection of the breadfruit trees was finally completed, and the *Bounty* left for the West Indies, but not before four of the chagrined crewmen had attempted desertion. They were caught, returned, and flogged before the crew. This was one more incident to add to the already sullen attitude of the sailors. Feeling continued to run high against Bligh during the early part of the voyage, until that fateful night when a sudden impulse led Christian to mutiny. With his mutineering companions, he gained control of the ship and subsequently set Bligh adrift in the *Bounty*'s launch, in the company of as many of the loyal crewmen as that boat would hold. The launch was too small to hold all of the loyal hands so seven had to stay behind, among them Byam and Stewart, his close friend. The mutiny left the *Bounty* manned by twenty-three men, including the seven loyal men.

With Christian in command, the *Bounty* sailed about in the South Seas, the mutineers searching for a suitable island on which to establish a permanent settlement. After several attempts, all balked by hostile natives, Christian returned with the crew to Tahiti. By a show of hands, the crew again split, some of the men continuing with Christian their search for a permanent home, the others, including Byam and Stewart, remaining at Tahiti. They expected eventually to be picked up by an English vessel and returned home to continue their naval careers.

After Christian and his crew had sailed to an unknown destination, Byam and his friend established homes on the island by marrying the natives with whom they had fallen in love during the first visit to the island. Byam went to live in the home of Tehani, his wife, and there continued his language studies. During that idyllic year on the island, children were born to the wives of both Byam and Stewart. Then HMS *Pandora* arrived, searching for the lost *Bounty*. Unaware that Bligh, who had miraculously reached England, had not distinguished between mutineer and loyal sailor among the men who remained on the *Bounty*, Byam and Stewart, anxious for some word of home, eagerly met the newly arrived ship. They were promptly placed in irons and imprisoned. They saw their wives only once after imprisonment, and had it not been for the ship's doctor on the *Pandora*, they would have suffered greater hardship than they had experienced on the *Bounty*. The doctor made it possible for Byam to go on with his studies, a task that gave the prisoners something to do and kept them from losing their minds.

The *Pandora* sailed for England with a total of seven prisoners, four of whom were not guilty of mutiny. They suffered many unnecessary hardships, the greatest occurring during a storm in which the *Pandora* was sunk. The Captain delayed releasing the men from their irons until the last possible moment, an act which cost the life of Stewart, who was unable to get clear of the sinking *Pandora* and drowned.

The survivors, gathered on a small island, were forced into a decision to try to make the voyage to Timor, in the Dutch East Indies, the nearest island of call. Their experiences in open boats, with little or no water and food, were savagely cruel because of the tropic sun, the madness from lack of water, and the foolish attempts of the *Pandora*'s captain to continue to treat the prisoners as prisoners. Eventually, the group reached Timor and there found passage on a Dutch ship bound for England.

Returned to England, the prisoners awaited court-martial for mutiny. The loyal men, falsely accused, were Byam, Morrison, and Muspratt. Three of the mutineers with them were Ellison, Burkitt, and Millward, sailors who were convicted of their crimes and hanged. The evidence concerning the innocent men finally reached a point where the decision rested upon the testimony of Robert Tinkler, another midshipman on the *Bounty*. Tinkler was believed lost at sea, but he turned up in time to save the lives of Byam, Muspratt, and Morrison.

Byam continued his naval career, and eventually, he became the captain of his own ship. In 1810, he returned to Tahiti. Tehani, his wife, was dead. He found his daughter alive and the image of her mother. He saw that he could not make himself known to her, and he left Tahiti without telling her that he was her father. To him, that beautiful green island was a place filled with ghosts of younger men, and young Midshipman Byam was one of them.

Critical Evaluation:

Mutiny on the Bounty is one of the most popular sea stories ever written. It is based on an actual incident that occurred aboard HMS *Bounty* in 1789, when Europeans were still discovering the beauties and riches of the South Pacific, and many of its islands were yet unknown. The contrast between the brutal discipline aboard Captain Bligh's ship and the relaxed, fun-loving lifestyle of the Tahitians is one of the ingredients that makes the novel an effective work of art. It was the warmth, beauty, and sensuality of Tahiti that made the British seaman deplore their miserable existence on board the *Bounty* and led to the famous mutiny.

The authors, Charles Nordhoff and James Norman Hall, saw the dramatic possibilities in this incident. The inflexible, sadistic, yet courageous and dedicated character of the real Captain William Bligh made him potentially as interesting a literary figure as the vindictive Captain Ahab in Herman Melville's *Moby Dick* (1851) or the unscrupulous Captain Wolf Larsen in Jack London's *The Sea-Wolf* (1904). In order to make their fictionalized version of the mutiny truly dramatic and clearly focused, Nordhoff and Hall saw that they needed a strong antagonist to balance their domineering protagonist, Captain Bligh. They realized that the real-life Fletcher Christian, a proud, headstrong aristocrat, was made to order for the role of antagonist. The story of *Mutiny on the Bounty* is largely the story of the conflict of principles and temperaments between these two strong-willed men and how that conflict affected the lives of those who followed them.

The novel opens with several sentences using the word "I," indicating that this story will be told from the point of view of a single participant in the event. The authors wisely chose to use a fictitious narrator, Roger Byam, for several important reasons. The events take place across half the world, all the way from England to the Society Islands. By remaining in a single character's point of view throughout the novel, these thoroughly professional authors are able to achieve a simplification and a focus that would otherwise have been nearly impossible to maintain. By remaining in a single sympathetic character's point of view, the authors are able to involve the reader emotionally with the story. The reader identifies with the young, idealistic, good-natured, ambitious Byam and comes to share his attitude toward the mutiny, the men involved, and the merits and shortcomings of the British Navy.

By remaining in the single point of view of a young man who lived in the eighteenth century, the authors are able to capture more effectively the feeling of mystery and wonder about the vastness of the unexplored world than if they had narrated their story from the objective, retrospective point of view of the twentieth century. Byam makes the reader feel how much bigger the world was in the days of sailing ships. The *Bounty*'s voyage to Tahiti took nearly a year; the modern traveler can fly from London to Sydney, Australia, in a single day.

Some of the characters in the novel are only sketchily drawn, but Byam stands out as a three-dimensional character. He is a child of his times. He is young and feels shocked by the cruelty he witnesses; he does not, however, view the floggings and the loathsome food with the same horror that the modern reader would feel in his place. The ambitious young Byam belongs to the elite; he believes in the necessity of strict discipline and even comes to accept his own condemnation to being hanged as a mutineer. The contrast between the psychology of the eighteenth century and the psychology of today is one of the more interesting features of the novel.

Captain Bligh is a less successful literary creation, and Fletcher Christian is very hard to understand. Christian is a courageous man of principle, but he seems to have initiated the mutiny for reasons of wounded pride rather than out of sympathy for the starved, brutalized HMS *Bounty* crewmen. When Christian assumes command of the ship he becomes as autocratic as Bligh, illustrating a sad truth that revolutions often only replace one form of tyranny with another.

Neither Christian nor Byam is democratic. Byam never expresses any misgivings about the fact that the mission of the *Bounty* is to procure breadfruit trees as a cheap source of food for black slaves who are being worked to death on Jamaican sugar plantations, treated far worse than the sailors aboard the *Bounty*. Byam portrays life on Tahiti as idyllic without showing any concern for the fact that the Polynesian society is based on slavery, exploitation, and ritualized murders. Upper-class Tahitians honor the whites because these visitors bring trade goods and are willing to use their terrifying muskets to support their hosts in wars against other islanders. Byam sees only the easy lives of the Tahitian aristocrats, for whom the island with its bending palm trees and turquoise lagoons was a paradise that still attracts tourists from all over the world.

The story of *Mutiny on the Bounty* is so dramatic and so colorful that it has been made into motion pictures four times, starting with *In the Wake of the Bounty* in 1932. The 1935 production (*Mutiny on the Bounty*), starring Clark Gable as Fletcher Christian and Charles Laughton in a magnificent performance as Captain Bligh, was better. The 1962 version starring Marlon Brando as Christian and Trevor Howard as Bligh was less successful but was enriched by beautiful color photography. There is also a 1984 version, *The Bounty*.

Nordhoff and Hall's stirring novel left at least two questions only very superficially answered in the epilogue. How did Captain Bligh and his companions manage to survive in an overladen 23-foot open boat while traveling 3,618 miles to safety? What happened to Fletcher Christian and the mutineers after Bligh and his loyal companions were set adrift? Both of these questions could not be answered while remaining in the point of view of Roger Byam, who was forced to stay aboard the ship. Nordhoff and Hall answered these questions in the two sequels to *Mutiny on the Bounty*. In *Men Against the Sea* (1933) they describe the incredible voyage of the little launch to the Dutch settlement at Coupang Bay on the island of Timor in the Indian Ocean, where Bligh obtained passage to Batavia (now Djakarta, capital of Indonesia) and eventually back to England. In *Pitcairn's Island* (1934) the authors describe the bloody history of the *Bounty* mutineers, whose descendants, part English and part Polynesian, still maintain a subsistence on bleak, lonely Pitcairn's Island about 1,350 miles southeast of Tahiti.

"Critical Evaluation" by Bill Delaney

Bibliography:
Bone, David W. "The Captain's Cocoanuts." *The Saturday Review of Literature* 9, no. 11 (October 1, 1932): 141, 144. An experienced seaman and writer himself, Bone discusses the accuracy of the authors' descriptions of the sea and sea life. Also examines how they created characters from reading historical documents.
Briand, Paul L., Jr. "Bounty from the Mutiny." In *In Search of Paradise*. New York: Duell, Sloan & Pearce, 1966. A fascinating look at the collaborators' writing process, including their extensive research into the historical incident.
Hall, James Norman. *My Island Home: An Autobiography*. Boston: Little, Brown, 1952. Includes the author's recollections of how the two men came to write *Mutiny on the Bounty*, how they conducted their research, how they set about fictionalizing the historical material, and how they envisioned that material from the beginning as leading to a trilogy of novels.
Roulston, Robert. *James Norman Hall*. Boston: Twayne, 1978. In the first book-length critical study of Hall's work, Roulston examines in some detail the Bounty trilogy. He declares the

novel a melodrama, perhaps something short of true literature, but finds it to be among the best of the genre.

"A Vivid Tale of Maritime Adventure." *The New York Times Book Review*, October 16, 1932, 7. A very favorable review of *Mutiny on the Bounty* as a model of the historical novel. Gives useful background information about the historical basis for the events detailed in the novel.

MY ÁNTONIA

Type of work: Novel
Author: Willa Cather (1873-1947)
Type of plot: Regional
Time of plot: Late nineteenth and early twentieth centuries
Locale: Nebraska prairie land
First published: 1918

Principal characters:
> JIM BURDEN, the narrator and Ántonia's friend
> ÁNTONIA SHIMERDA, a Bohemian peasant girl

The Story:

Jim Burden's father and mother died when he was ten years old, and the boy made the long trip from Virginia to his grandparents' farm in Nebraska in the company of Jake Marpole, a hired hand who was to work for Jim's grandfather. Arriving by train in the prairie town of Black Hawk late at night, the boy noticed an immigrant family huddled on the station platform. He and Jake were met by a lanky, scar-faced cowboy named Otto Fuchs, who drove them in a jolting wagon across the empty prairie to the Burden farm.

Jim grew to love the vast expanse of land and sky. One day, Jim's grandmother suggested that the family pay a visit to the Shimerdas, an immigrant family just arrived in the territory. At first, the newcomers impressed Jim unfavorably. The Shimerdas were poor and lived in a dugout cut into the earth. The place was dirty, and the children were ragged. Although he could not understand her speech, Jim made friends with the oldest girl, Ántonia.

After that, Jim often found his way to the Shimerda home. He did not like Ántonia's surly brother, Ambrosch, or her grasping mother, but Ántonia won an immediate place in Jim's heart with her eager smile and great, warm eyes. One day, her father, with his English dictionary tucked under his arm, cornered Jim and asked him to teach the girl English. She learned rapidly. Jim respected Ántonia's father, a tall, thin, sensitive man who had been a musician in the old country. Now he was worn down by poverty and overwork. He seldom laughed any more.

Jim and Ántonia passed many happy hours on the prairie. Then, during a severe winter, tragedy struck the Shimerdas when Ántonia's father, broken and beaten by the prairie, shot himself. Ántonia had loved her father more than anyone else in her family. After his death, she shouldered his share of the farm work. When spring came, she went with Ambrosch into the fields and plowed like a man. The harvest brought money, and the Shimerdas soon had a house. With the money left over, they bought plowshares and cattle.

Because Jim's grandparents were growing too old to keep up their farm, they dismissed Jake and Otto and moved to the town of Black Hawk. There Jim longed for the open prairie land, the gruff, friendly companionship of Jake and Otto, and the warmth of Ántonia's friendship. He suffered at school and spent his idle hours roaming the barren gray streets of Black Hawk.

At Jim's suggestion, his grandmother arranged with a neighbor, Mrs. Harling, to bring Ántonia into town as her hired girl. Ántonia entered into her tasks with enthusiasm. Jim noticed that she was more feminine and laughed more often; though she never shirked her duties at the Harling house, she was eager for recreation and gaiety.

Almost every night, she went to a dance pavilion with a group of hired girls. There, in new, handmade dresses, the girls gathered to dance with the village boys. Jim Burden went, too, and

4338

the more he saw of the hired girls, the better he liked them. Once or twice, he worried about Ántonia, who was popular and trusting. When she earned a reputation for being a little too loose, she lost her position with the Harlings and went to work for a cruel moneylender, Wick Cutter, who had a licentious eye on her.

One night, Ántonia appeared at the Burdens and begged Jim to stay in her bed for the night and let her remain at the Burdens. Wick Cutter was supposed to be out of town, but Ántonia suspected that, with Mrs. Cutter also gone, he might return and try to harm her. Her fears proved correct, for Wick returned and went to Ántonia's bedroom, where Jake lay.

Ántonia returned to work for the Harlings. Jim studied hard during the summer, passed his entrance examinations, and in the fall left for the state university. Although he found there a whole new world of literature and art, he could not forget his early years under the blazing prairie sun and his friendship with Ántonia. He heard little from Ántonia during those years. One of her friends, Lena Lingard, who had also worked as a hired girl in Black Hawk, visited him one day. He learned from her that Ántonia was engaged to be married to a man named Larry Donovan.

Jim went on to Harvard to study law and for years heard nothing of his Nebraska friends. He assumed that Ántonia was married. When he made a trip back to Black Hawk to see his grandparents, he learned that Ántonia, deceived by Larry Donovan, had left Black Hawk in shame and returned to her family. There she worked again in the fields until her baby was born. When Jim went to see her, he found her the same lovely girl, though her eyes were somber, and she had lost her old gaiety. She welcomed him and proudly showed him her baby.

Jim thought that his visit was probably the last time he would see Ántonia. He told her how much a part of him she had become and how sorry he was to leave her again. Ántonia knew that Jim would always be with her, no matter where he went. He reminded her of her beloved father, who, though he had been dead many years, still lived on in her heart. She told Jim good-bye and watched him walk back toward town along the familiar road.

Jim Burden did not see Ántonia again for twenty years. On a Western trip, he found himself not far from Black Hawk and, on impulse, drove out in an open buggy to the farm where she lived. He found the place swarming with children of all ages. Small boys rushed forward to greet him, then fell back shyly. Ántonia had married well, at last. The grain was high, and the neat farmhouse seemed to be charged with an atmosphere of activity and happiness. Ántonia seemed as unchanged as she was when she and Jim used to whirl over the dance floor together in Black Hawk. Cuzak, her husband, seemed to know Jim before they were introduced, for Ántonia had told all her family about Jim Burden. After a long visit with the Cuzaks, Jim left, promising that he would return the next summer and take two of the Cuzak boys hunting with him.

Waiting in Black Hawk for the train that would take him East, Jim found it hard to realize the long time that had passed since the dark night, years before, when he had seen an immigrant family standing wrapped in their shawls on the same platform. All his memories of the prairie came back to him. Whatever happened now, whatever they had missed, he and Ántonia had shared precious years between them, years that would never be forgotten.

Critical Evaluation:

Perhaps the most beautiful aspect of this book is its disarming simplicity. There are no witty phrases, no complicated characters, indeed, there is scarcely any plot. Yet there is a quiet, probing depth in Willa Cather's writing. The figure of the pioneer woman Ántonia Shimerda concentrates in itself a complex of values, an axis about which *My Ántonia* revolves. The novel illustrates two classical themes of American literature, reaching back into the nineteenth century for its plot and beyond its time for its artistic and moral direction.

Cather, the product of a genteel Virginia upbringing, found herself early in life transplanted to the frontier and forced to confront those vast blank spaces over which humans had not yet succeeded in establishing the dominion of custom and convention. She saw a few brave settlers bearding the wilderness, meeting the physical and moral challenges of having to act straight out of their instincts without benefit of civilized constraints; for her these people, particularly the women, were a race apart. Ántonia, with her noble simplicity, is among other things a monument to that vigorous race.

She is also an embodiment of a long tradition of fictional heroes of British and American romantic tales. At the time the novel was written, literature and criticism in America were undergoing a change. The direction of literature in the new century owed much to the developing sciences; Sinclair Lewis and Theodore Dreiser appeared with their sociological novels that signaled the rise of naturalism. Fictional characters began to be viewed as interpreting in their acts the flaws and beauties of laws, institutions, and social structures. *My Ántonia* fits an older mold, in which the effects of colonial Puritanism can be detected. That mode demanded that the hero overcome or fail to overcome the strictures and hazards of his situation by his own wit, strength, or courage. This convention draws from the very wellspring of American life, the democratic belief in the wholeness and self-sufficiency of the individual, in personal culpability, and in the absolute value of the personal conscience. Cather makes no indictment of the society that scorns and undervalues Ántonia and the other hired girls; the social conventions are, with the land, simply the medium through which she relates the tale. It is the peculiarly American sense of starting afresh in a new land, that sense of moral isolation, that adds poignancy to the struggles of individuals. This theme of American newness and innocence, which R. B. Lewis calls "The Theme of the American Adam," has as a natural concomitant elements of temptation and fortunate fall. The serpent in Ántonia's story is the town of Black Hawk, where she quarrels with her benefactors and runs afoul of Larry Donovan. Seduced and abandoned, she returns to the land, but, as she tells Jim Burden, her experience has made her better able to prepare her own children to face the world.

If the town in one sense represents Ántonia's downfall, it is also the grey backdrop against which she shines; in the same way, the prairie is both her antagonist and the natural force of which she is the flower. Significantly, Jim Burden first finds her actually living in the earth. Early in the novel, she begins to take on characteristics of the land: "Her neck came up strongly out of her shoulders, like the bole of a tree out of the turf"; "But she has such splendid color in her cheeks—like those big dark red plums." She works the land; she makes gardens; she nourishes the Harling children with food and stories. Cather insists on her connection with the fertile earth, the virgin land, which is in this novel the source of physical vigor and the best resource of the soul. Jim Burden describes his first experience of the land as a feeling of cosmic unity: "Perhaps we feel like that when we die and become part of something entire, whether it is sun and air, or goodness and knowledge. At any rate, that is happiness; to be dissolved into something complete and great." The people who live on the prairie seem to him open and giving like the land; he says of Ántonia that "everything she said seemed to come right out of her heart." By contrast, the life of the town is pinched and ungenerous: "People's speech, their voices, their very glances, became furtive and repressed. Every individual taste, every natural appetite, was bridled by caution." Ántonia, in all her acts, shows the naturalness and boundless generosity of the plains; she gives unstintingly of her strength and loyalty to her surly brother, to Jim, and the Harling children, to Larry Donovan, and to her husband Cuzak; and she pours out a flood of love and nurture upon her children. She alludes several times to her dislike of towns and cities and to her feeling of familiar friendship with the country. Toward the end of the book, the figure of Ántonia and the infinite fertility of the land come together symbolically in an extremely vivid and moving image. Ántonia and her children have been showing Jim Burden the contents of their fruit cellar, and as they step outside, the children "all came running up the steps together, big and little, tow heads and gold heads and brown, and flashing little naked legs; a veritable explosion of life out of the dark cave into the sunlight." The cave might be the apotheosis of Ántonia's first home on the prairie, the latter redeeming the former by its fruitfulness.

Above all, the novel celebrates the early life on the plains of which Jim Burden and Ántonia were a part. The long digressions about Peter and Pavel, Blind D'Arnault, the Cutters, and others; the profoundly elegiac descriptions of Jake Marpole and Otto Fuchs; and the sharply caught details of farm life, town life, and landscape are all elements employed in the re-creation of a simpler and better time, a hard life now beyond recall but lovingly remembered.

"Critical Evaluation" by Jan Kennedy Foster

Bibliography:
Bloom, Harold, ed. *Willa Cather's "My Ántonia."* New York: Chelsea House, 1987. Collection of eleven reprinted articles, selected by a leading literary critic. Includes a Cather chronology and bibliography.

Brown, Muriel. "Growth and Development of the Artist: Willa Cather's *My Ántonia*." *Midwest Quarterly* 33, no. 1 (Autumn, 1991): 93-107. Refers to Cather's own ideas about the novel and about creativity. Brown offers her interpretation of the characters of Ántonia and Jim Burden.

Dyck, Reginald. "The Feminist Critique of Willa Cather's Fiction: A Review Essay." *Women's Studies* 22, no. 3 (1993): 263-279. Dyck explains Cather's regained literary reputation as a major writer as a consequence of work by feminist critics since the 1970's. Summarizes some of the conflicting interpretations of Cather, using *My Ántonia* as the primary focus.

Murphy, John J. *"My Ántonia": The Road Home.* Boston: Twayne, 1989. Places the novel in historical and literary context and provides a reading of the text. Also includes a chronology and selected bibliography.

Rosowski, Susan J., ed. *Approaches to Teaching Cather's "My Ántonia."* New York: Modern Language Association, 1989. Interesting and readable essays by both established and newer Cather critics who consider the novel from a wide range of perspectives.

MY BRILLIANT CAREER

Type of work: Novel
Author: Miles Franklin (1879-1954)
Type of plot: Psychological realism
Time of plot: 1890's
Locale: The Australian Bush
First published: 1901

Principal characters:
    SYBYLLA MELVYN, the teenage narrator
    RICHARD MELVYN, Sybylla's father
    LUCY MELVYN, Sybylla's mother
    GERTIE, Sybylla's sister
    AUNT HELEN and
    GRANNIE, with whom Sybylla goes to live
    UNCLE JULIUS (UNCLE JAY-JAY), Aunt Helen's brother
    HAROLD (HARRY) BEECHAM, a wealthy bushman, in love with Sybylla
    EVERARD GREY, a young English aristocrat who befriends Sybylla
    FRANK HAWDEN, suitor to Sybylla
    THE M'SWAT FAMILY, who employ Sybylla as governess

The Story:

Sybylla was the daughter of wealthy cattle station owner Richard Melvyn. When the family fell on hard times, Richard Melvyn sold his three stations and bought Possum Gully, a small farm.

Richard Melvyn's drinking habit undermined his livestock deals. He mortgaged Possum Gully and used the money to set up a dairy farm. The entire family slaved long hours for little return; the family dropped from swelldom to peasantry. Sybylla's previously gentle and refined mother became angry, thin, and careworn, while her father became slovenly and withdrawn; he lost all love for, and interest in, his family. Sybylla, fond of music and literature, longed for something better than the daily grind of work and sleep.

When Sybylla was fifteen, a drought brought the dairy farm to ruin. A dishonest money-lender's agent absconded with Richard Melvyn's repayments, and the bailiffs were sent in; everything the family owned was sold. Their friends and neighbors, however, came to the rescue; they bid low for the family's possessions and returned them.

Since Lucy Melvyn found her daughter's presence a burden to her, Sybylla's grandmother offered to have Sybylla stay with her. Sybylla went to live at Caddagat, the home of Aunt Helen and Grannie. They welcomed Sybylla warmly, in contrast to the cold farewell she had received from her parents. Sybylla thrived in this loving and refined environment; she read and played the piano for hours.

Sybylla felt sad, however, because she was convinced that she was so ugly that she was unlovable. Aunt Helen took pity on Sybylla and took her in hand to bring out her beauty. Sybylla's "coming out" was to meet Uncle Julius (Uncle Jay-Jay) and a young English aristocrat, Everard Grey. Grey, impressed with Sybylla's striking looks and talent for acting and singing, expressed a desire to introduce her to the stage, where, he believed, she would have a brilliant career. The notion of such a career, however, was dismissed by Grannie and Aunt Helen as unsuitable.

Aunt Helen and Grannie were friends of a neighboring wealthy squatter family, the Beechams. Sybylla met Harry Beecham—described as her only real sweetheart—when she was dressed in one of the servant's dresses and a pair of men's boots. Mistaking her for a servant, he tried to kiss her and then tested her mettle by having her stand still while he cracked his stockman's whip around her. When he found out who she was, he was embarrassed, and Sybylla was delighted at having the power to make him so.

Harry and Sybylla continued to spend time together. Perplexed, yet intrigued by her wild nature, Harry proposed to Sybylla. She expressed surprise, because he had never uttered a word of love to her. She accepted the engagement, but she told herself that it would be only for a little while. As he stooped to kiss her, she picked up a riding whip and struck him in the face. He made light of the incident.

When Harry presented her with an engagement ring, she took it, but she refused to put it on; she told him that they would have a three-month probation period to see how they got along, during which time she would sometimes wear the ring.

Harry suddenly lost his money and station property. Sybylla offered to accept his engagement, now that he needed her. She would marry him when she reached twenty-one, whether he was rich or poor. Delighted by her response, Harry left to remake his fortune. Sybylla received a letter from her mother, telling Sybylla that Sybylla must help the family by going as governess to the M'Swat family. Sybylla's father owed money to Peter M'Swat, who was willing to take twenty pounds per year off the debt if Sybylla taught his children.

Sybylla unwillingly left her happy home in order to do her duty by her family. Life with the M'Swats was a kind of hell. The family lived in filth and did not possess a trace of refinement. Sybylla fell ill under the strain and was sent home. Her life had reached a dead end. Her mother was displeased, and Grannie had replaced her with her younger, prettier sister, Gertie. The presents which Uncle Jay-Jay had brought back from his travels were given to Gertie, instead of Sybylla.

Harry Beecham had remade his fortune; he returned to ask for Sybylla's hand, but she could not bring herself to marry him. In his disappointment, Harry set off to travel the world.

Critical Evaluation:

Miles Franklin was the pseudonym for Stella Maria Sarah Miles Franklin, one of Australia's most distinguished novelists. She was born into the "squattocracy," and she was the fifth generation of a pioneering family. Franklin's novels draw on her upbringing in the Australian Bush, and the novels reflect her love for her homeland. They also reveal her iconoclastic nature: her devotion to women's rights and her scorn of marriage as the only viable option for women; her contempt for filial duty; and her irrepressible spirit, which often led to behavior seen as unladylike.

Franklin wrote *My Brilliant Career* at the age of sixteen, though it was not published until she was twenty-two. The novel was greeted by the critic A. G. Stephens as "the very first Australian novel," in the sense that it was the first to embody an Australian outlook in vigorous Australian idiom. Modern critics are still divided over its merit. Some consider it Franklin's best, most original work. Certainly, her characters and her authorial stance were developed in this novel, and they did not progress greatly in future works.

The novel is the first part of the life story of Sybylla Melvyn, the daughter of a once-wealthy squatter family which has fallen on hard times. Franklin continues Melvyn's life story in her later novel, *My Career Goes Bung* (1946). Although *My Brilliant Career* was not intended to be autobiographical, Sybylla's life has some aspects in common with the early life of the author.

The similarities did not escape Franklin's relatives and neighbors. Many took offense at her sardonic portrayal of what they mistakenly believed to be their own lives and characters. Their response caused Franklin great distress, and she forbade the novel's republication until ten years after her death.

The title *My Brilliant Career* is ironic; Franklin initially placed a question mark in parentheses after the word "Brilliant." The high-spirited tomboy narrator, Sybylla, has a more than usual share of intelligence, talent, and maturity. Her ambitions reach far beyond her small-town life in the Australian outback—but she finds no outlet for her gifts, and she is doomed to a frustrated and limited existence of mundane chores and unstimulating company.

This existence could easily be a recipe for a whiny character and a depressing story, but, in fact, Sybylla is a tremendously vital and exhilarating creation. She tells her story with unerring humor and razor-sharp insight. While the storyline of *My Brilliant Career* is slight, and its structure is rambling and inconsequential, the character of Sybylla etches itself indelibly into the memory.

As a feminist, Sybylla is remarkably ahead of her time. Marriage, in her opinion, is "the most horribly tied-down and unfair-to-women existence going." She despises marriage as a "degradation" which she refuses to "perpetuate." She laments that it is only men who can be masters of their fate, whereas women are forced to sit with tied hands and patiently suffer as the waves of fate toss them this way and that.

With her passion for music and literature, with her revolutionary notions of readjusting the wheels of society, and with her determination never to marry, Sybylla is without a sphere. Uncle Jay-Jay gives her a birthday present of a doll, but for a young woman who numbers among her priorities the devising of social and economic solutions to the problems of tramps, this present is inappropriate, to say the least. On another occasion, she tells Uncle Jay-Jay that instead of wasting money on presents, she wishes that he would set her up in an independent profession.

Readers cannot help but cheer Sybylla as her sharp tongue and impetuous nature cut through the conventions and hypocrisies of her world. She is the antithesis of the romantic heroines of the literature of the 1890's; she is plain, difficult, egotistical, and hard to please. Told by her mother that the famous writers whom she idolizes should teach her to be grateful for her lot, Sybylla blasts such homespun philosophy, "It was all very well for great people to point out the greatness of the little, empty, humdrum life. Why didn't they adopt it themselves?" She repeatedly gets into trouble for her "unwomanly" actions, such as her behavior toward Frank Hawden, a despised suitor. When she says that she will drive the buggy to collect the mail, Grannie insists that Hawden accompany her. Sybylla acquiesces, but when he gets out of the buggy to open a gate, she seizes her chance and whips up the horses, leaving an enraged Hawden to walk home in the dust.

Without doubt, Sybylla has acted like a spoiled brat, but Frank's boorish behavior places readers' sympathies firmly on her side. He is an extreme example of the apparent weakness displayed by most of Franklin's male characters. Time and again, it is left to women to provide the strength, the responsibility, and the glue that holds the family units together. Richard Melvyn begins well, but he ends as an irresponsible drunk who shows no love to his family; Everard Grey is revealed as a person without depth of feeling; and even Harry Beecham fails to prove himself exceptional enough to win Sybylla. Sybylla effortlessly dominates and emasculates them all. She picks up her father from his drinking sprees and drives him home like a delinquent child; she scorns Grey; and when Harry proposes to her, she strikes him with a whip. She even sees Harry's restrained response as a weakness, and she seems secretly to long for him to wield power over her.

In spite of her prickly, touch-me-not nature, Sybylla is aware of the value of marriage; she knows that "our greatest heart-treasure" is the knowledge that there is in creation an individual to whom a person's existence is necessary. She asks who can this be but a husband or a wife? This moving passage does a great deal to transform the outcome of the Harry-Sybylla plot. The passage lifts Sybylla's final rejection of Harry out of the region of the wild adolescent perversities which have previously governed her behavior toward him and raises the rejection to the loftier status of a mature affirmation of independence. Despite the inevitable trace of sadness that Sybylla does not ride off into the sunset with her beau, many readers will applaud her courageous decision to journey alone.

Claire J. Robinson

Bibliography:
Barnard, Marjorie. *Miles Franklin*. New York: Twayne, 1967. A lucid and comprehensive guide to Franklin's life and works. An excellent starting point.
Coleman, Verna. *Miles Franklin in America: Her Unknown (Brilliant) Career*. London: Sirius, 1981. Discusses the novels in relation to the author's life.
Green, H. M. *A History of Australian Literature, Pure and Applied*. Vol. 1, *1789-1923*. Sydney, Australia: Angus and Robertson, 1961. Contains a brief but perceptive discussion of Sybylla as heroine.
Hadgraft, Cecil. *Australian Literature: A Critical Account to 1955*. London: Heinemann, 1960. Includes a balanced analysis of Franklin's works.
Mathew, Ray. *Miles Franklin*. Melbourne, Australia: Lansdowne Press, 1963. Psychological study of Franklin's novels. Valuable observations on Sybylla's almost pathological mistrust of emotion.

MY LIFE AND HARD TIMES

Type of work: Wit and humor
Author: James Thurber (1894-1961)
First published: 1933

> *Principal personages:*
> JAMES THURBER
> CHARLES, his father
> MARY, his mother
> HERMAN and
> ROY, his brothers
> HIS GRANDFATHER

To say that there are two worlds—the World of Ordinary Men and the World of Thurber—is a cliché that would never have been tolerated by James Thurber himself, for one of the charms of his style is a scrupulous avoidance of anything resembling the trite. Among his many phobias there must have existed the dread of turning a corner in a sentence and being waylaid with a cliché. His precision of language and careful attention to detail are the qualities that infuse his writing with interest and charm, as is his ability to impose a world of fantasy on a world of reality and to achieve an interrelationship of the external and the internal, the factual and the imaginative.

In his preface to *My Life and Hard Times*, Thurber apologizes for writing an autobiography before he had reached the age of forty and for not conforming to Ford Madox Ford's dictum that one's memoirs should paint a picture of one's time. Thurber more or less admits that there is no time and that all he intends to tell is what happened to this one writer. Since what follows could have happened to no one but Thurber, he thus implicitly admits the existence of the Thurber world.

This world reaches beyond the boundaries of the real or the commonplace and extends into a region of fable, peopled by such figures as the cook Emma Inch and her asthmatic dog Feely; Della, who made cretonnes for the soup and whose brother worked in an incinerator where they burn refuse; Barney Haller, the hired man, whom thunder followed like a dog; and Walter Mitty, that frustrated, comic Prufrock with his dreams of heroism and glory. Strange things happen in this world because James Thurber sees it that way: An old woman with a parasol is seen to walk through a truck, a cat rolls across the street atop a striped barrel, and an admiral in full uniform rides a bicycle across the highway in the path of an oncoming car. That these things are never what they seem but fragments of the ordinary world suddenly revealed in a new light or a different perspective is the secret of Thurber's humor. It is a form of humor little concerned with the conventional or the obvious. It arises quite naturally from a recognition of the inner, emotional chaos of a sensitive, individualistic man trapped in the affairs of the practical, demanding world, with no weapon of defense but his own resistances and inferiorities.

Hence that air of the fabulous that also invests Thurber's drawings: the meek, rotund men with poses of resignation, whose faces reveal long-thwarted efforts to think and act in a positive manner; the aggressive, rather frightening women who never seem disturbed by doubts as to their superiority; the huge, sadly patient dogs. They belong in a world in which life has grown complicated for men and animals, from which one way of escape leads into a Cloud-Cuckoo Land where the illogical becomes the logical and the fantastic reveals the dilemma of people facing the psychological confusion and insecurity of their place in a world almost devoid of sense and meaning.

Nowhere does James Thurber display to better advantage his genius for uncovering the incongruous in everyday human affairs, in the daydream escapes from personal confusion or catastrophe, than in the nine episodes that center on Thurber's youth in Columbus, Ohio, as told in *My Life and Hard Times*.

"The Night the Bed Fell" is about the night the bed did not fall on Thurber's father while he slept in the attic where grandfather was supposed to sleep. Grandfather, who refused to believe that the Army of the Potomac was not still trying to take Richmond, had wandered off some days before; eventually he would turn up with profane criticism of the campaign, its military leaders, and the administration in Washington. Actually, James Thurber rolled out of his cot; his mother was convinced that the bed had fallen on father and he must be pulled from the wreckage; a visiting cousin poured a glass of camphor over himself, and father was sure that the house was on fire. Mother, who always called it the night on which the bed fell on father, was looking on the bright side of things when she said she was glad grandfather had not been there.

"The Car We Had to Push" is about all sorts of things, but mostly about grandfather's brother Zenas, who contracted the chestnut tree blight and died of that strange malady in 1866. "The Day the Dam Broke" is about the day the dam did not break. Expected catastrophes have a way of not happening in the Thurber world, but the effects are very much the same. The citizens of Columbus, thinking it had broken, fled in panic. The police were summoned to the Thurber household on "The Night the Ghost Got In," and grandfather shot one policeman in the shoulder under the hallucinated impression that the men in blue uniforms were deserters from General Meade's army.

"More Alarms at Night" deals with brother Roy's feigned delirium; even at the best of times Roy was likely to sing "Onward, Christian Soldiers" or "Marching Through Georgia" in his sleep. He awakened father in the small hours, called him Buck, and announced that his time had come. Father, a mildly nervous man, aroused his family. Everyone assured him that he had had a bad dream. The sketch also deals with another night when James awoke poor father to get help in remembering the name of a New Jersey city, Perth Amboy. Sure that his son had gone mad, father ran from the room.

"A Sequence of Servants" tells of 162 servants, including Vashti, who told her lover that he must never tangle with her jealous stepfather, who had married her mother just to be near Vashti; it turns out that Vashti had invented her stepfather to pique the lover.

A memorable Airedale named Muggs is "The Dog That Bit People." When he died, after biting almost everybody in Ohio—including Lieutenant-Governor Malloy—mother wanted to bury him in the family plot under "Flights of angels sing thee to thy rest" or some equally misappropriate inscription. The family dissuaded her, however, and Muggs was interred along a lonely road beneath an epitaph of Thurber's choice: "Cave canem." Mother was always quite pleased with the classic dignity of that simple Latin phrase.

"University Days" presents Bolenciecwcz, star tackle on the Ohio State football team, whom an economics professor tried to make eligible for the Illinois game by asking him to name one means of transportation; after hints, prods, and auditory and visual demonstrations by the professor and the whole class, Bolenciecwcz mentioned a train and the day was saved. There is also an agricultural student named Haskins, who wanted to be a journalist and whose beat for campus news covered the cow barns, the horse pavilion, the sheep house, and the animal husbandry department in general.

The final sketch, "Draft Board Nights," describes Thurber being repeatedly called before the draft board, which always turned him down because of poor eyesight, and then, through some repetitive mistake, called him back. He eventually drifted into service, not in the army, but as an unauthorized and undetected examiner of draftees—a pulmonary man, to be exact. What put a merciful end to that was the Armistice.

It is useless for critics to debate the place of Thurber in the literature of his time. His humor, which creates its effects according to the laws of its own logic and yet always with a savoring of common sense, is superbly his own, as his would-be imitators have discovered. His manner is nimble without being racy; it has poignancy without sentimentality. His touch with words is delicate yet precise. Best of all, he illustrates his own books with inimitable drawings that, like his prose pieces, distort the familiar into the fantastic without losing touch with reality.

Bibliography:
Bernstein, Burton. *Thurber: A Biography.* New York: Dodd, Mead, 1975. A thorough treatment, beginning with Thurber's ancestry. Discusses his works in relation to his life. Discussion of *My Life and Hard Times* includes critical reactions of Ernest Hemingway and other contemporaries. The work is also compared to Thurber's other works.
Holmes, Charles S. *The Clocks of Columbus: The Literary Career of James Thurber.* New York: Atheneum, 1972. A thorough and insightful overview of Thurber's works. Chapter 9, "Columbus Remembered: *My Life and Hard Times*," discusses Thurber's autobiography in relation to reality, drawing on news stories and reminiscences of friends and relatives. A scholarly critique of the protagonist, dominant themes, and style.
_____. "James Thurber and the Art of Fantasy." *Yale Review* 55, no. 1 (Autumn, 1965): 17-33. Includes *My Life and Hard Times* in an analysis and overview of fantasy as the hallmark of Thurber's writings. Discusses the evolution of his comic view and observes that his tone shifts over time from celebration, to warning, and finally to faith.
Tanner, Stephen L. "James Thurber and the Midwest." *American Studies* 33, no. 2 (Fall, 1992): 61-72. Compares *My Life and Hard Times* with *The Thurber Album*, which reveals his changing view of Columbus over time. Focuses on the Ohio roots of much of his writing.
Tobias, Richard C. *The Art of James Thurber.* Athens: Ohio University Press, 1970. An excellent appraisal with valuable insights, which compares Thurber's comic writing with that of such writers as Sir Thomas Malory, William Wordsworth, and William Shakespeare. Devotes one chapter to *My Life and Hard Times* and *The Middle-Aged Man on the Flying Trapeze*, viewing both as "comic masks."

MY NAME IS ASHER LEV

Type of work: Novel
Author: Chaim Potok (1929-   )
Type of plot: Domestic realism
Time of plot: Mid-twentieth century
Locale: Crown Heights, Brooklyn, New York
First published: 1972

> *Principal characters:*
> ASHER LEV, a young Hasidic artist
> RIVKEH LEV, Asher's mother
> ARYEH LEV, Asher's father
> YITZCHOK LEV, Asher's uncle, a successful jeweler and watch repairer
> YUDEL KRINSKY, Asher's friend and confidant, a Russian Jew employed
> in a stationery store
> JACOB KAHN, an artist, Asher's mentor
> ANNA SCHAEFFER, art gallery owner who shows Jacob Kahn's and
> Asher Lev's work

The Story:

Asher Lev was the only child of a devout, orthodox Jewish couple, Rivkeh and Aryeh Lev. By the age of four, Asher showed an unusual talent for drawing. His mother urged him repeatedly to make pretty drawings, while his father viewed Asher's preoccupation with suspicion, labeling it "foolishness."

When Asher was six years old, his family received the news of the death of his Uncle Yaakov, Rivkeh's only brother. Yaakov, who had been studying history and Russian affairs, had died in a car accident while traveling for the Rebbe, a religious leader. The death plunged Rivkeh into a prolonged depression. Asher's father worked and traveled for the Rebbe, and Asher was often left alone with a housekeeper.

While visiting Asher's family, Asher's uncle, Yitzchok (Aryeh's brother), noticed his nephew's drawings and proclaimed the boy "A little Chagall." He told Asher that Chagall was the greatest living Jewish artist, and he added that Picasso was the greatest artist of all. Uncle Yitzchok bought one of Asher's drawings so that he could own an "early Lev," but Asher's father opposed this gesture and insisted that Yitzchok return the drawing.

During Rivkeh's depression, Asher began to be haunted by nightmares of his father's great-great-grandfather. Asher came to regard this figure as his mythic ancestor. The figure appeared to him repeatedly at night and came to symbolize Asher's religious and cultural heritage and the accompanying burdens and expectations.

Rivkeh eventually recovered and became convinced that she must continue her brother's work. She received special permission from the Rebbe to attend college and study Russian history, eventually earning a doctorate. With both his parents so involved with the post-World War II affairs of Jews around the world, and particularly in Russia, young Asher was often alone. He stopped drawing for a time and later came to view this period as the time when his gift was taken away. He vowed never to let that happen again.

Asher befriended Yudel Krinsky and often visited the stationery store where Yudel worked. Asher encountered artists' supplies for the first time. Krinsky also answered Asher's many questions about life in Russia.

With the death of Stalin, Asher's father was able to travel more freely in Europe. The Rebbe asked Aryeh to move to Vienna, but Asher refused to move with his family. Asher's attachment to his home and neighborhood was fierce, and he feared that he would lose his artistic gift if he were to leave. Asher began to draw again and sensed that "something was happening to my eyes. . . . I could feel with my eyes."

Asher was doing poorly in school. One day he unconsciously drew a sinister-looking picture of the Rebbe in a religious text. The drawing was discovered, and Asher's instructor and his classmates viewed it as a defilement of a holy book. The rift between Asher, his classmates, and his instructors grew. Asher felt increasingly isolated.

Aryeh's opposition to Asher's preoccupation with art intensified, and Rivkeh frequently found herself caught between her husband and her son. Asher still refused to accompany his parents to Vienna. Eventually Asher's father made the trip alone, leaving Asher and his mother at home together.

Rivkeh took Asher to the museum where Asher began to study the great masterpieces. In his exposure to the history of art, Asher encountered Christian images and themes. Rivkeh bought Asher a set of oil paints from Yudel Krinsky. When Aryeh returned from his travels, he remained unreconciled to his son's gift, and the gulf between father and son widened.

Asher was sent to talk with the Rebbe. The Rebbe told him, "A life is measured by how it is lived for the sake of heaven," and arranged for Asher to meet Jacob Kahn, a successful artist who was a non-practicing Jew. Jacob Kahn was in his seventies. Asher was thirteen. Asher began studying with this great master who had worked with Picasso in Paris and who knew many of the century's great artists. Jacob introduced Asher to gallery owner Anna Schaeffer. Her gallery handled Jacob's art, and Asher learned that Anna would eventually introduce his art to the world.

Asher spent a lot of time with Jacob Kahn and his wife, including summer vacations in Provincetown, Massachusetts. Rivkeh joined Aryeh in Europe, leaving Asher in the care of his uncle Yitzchok, who converted an attic into Asher's first studio. Asher later joined his family in Vienna for a short time, but the stress and the separation from his world and his art proved too great for him. He returned home.

Anna arranged for Asher to have a show, noting that he was "the youngest artist ever to have a one-man show in a Madison Avenue gallery." She billed him as "Asher Lev, Brooklyn Prodigy." Asher's work was well received, leading to subsequent shows and sales. Asher's parents returned after having lived abroad for several years, and Asher moved back home. Asher continued to paint with Jacob and in his own studio in his uncle's home.

After one of his shows, Asher decided that he must go to Europe to study and paint. Following his graduation from college, he traveled alone to Italy and France. He settled in Paris and worked there. Anna Schaeffer visited him in order to arrange for another New York show. She was particularly moved by two paintings Asher had done—crucifixion scenes which depicted his mother's suffering as she was torn between her husband and son. Anna named these paintings "Brooklyn Crucifixion I" and "Brooklyn Crucifixion II." Asher knew these paintings would cause his parents and his religious community great pain. He knew that few in his community would be able to understand his choice of the Crucifixion as a way to depict suffering. He knew, though, that to be true to his artistic calling, he had to paint what he saw and what he felt.

Asher was unable to bring himself to tell his parents about these paintings. His parents saw them for the first time at his show. The impact on them was as Asher had guessed it would be. The show was a critical success. A museum bought the two crucifixion paintings, but the rift now between Asher and his family and his religious community was irreparable. The Rebbe told Asher that he must leave. Asher understood and accepted what was essentially an exile. He left for Europe, taking with him the memory of his parents watching him from their window.

Critical Evaluation:

In writing about orthodox Jewish life, Chaim Potok speaks with considerable authority: He is a rabbi and a respected academic, and he has served as the editor-in-chief of the Jewish Publication Society of America. In *My Name Is Asher Lev*, Potok focuses on the role of the artist in a particular community—a community he locates in Crown Heights, Brooklyn, and calls Ladover Hasidism. Potok models his Ladover Hasidism on Lubavitch Hasidism.

My Name Is Asher Lev, like Potok's other novels including *The Chosen* (1967), *The Promise* (1969), *In the Beginning* (1975), and *Davita's Harp* (1985), probes the specific struggles of one member of a community who comes into conflict with the norms and expectations of that community. Asher Lev's community expects him to follow in his parents' footsteps and to work in some way for the preservation and the betterment of Judaism worldwide. Asher, however, is seen as responding to a radically different calling—art. A very familiar pattern of conflict in the world of the novel—the individual versus society—becomes apparent early in the book. On the first page, Asher lists some of the charges he has had to face. These include "traitor, an apostate, a self-hater, an inflicter of shame upon my family, my friends, my people." Asher's own struggle to come to terms with these labels is also sensed when he adds: "In all honesty, I confess that my accusers are not altogether wrong: I am indeed in some way, all of those things." *My Name Is Asher Lev*, then, becomes a defense. It is at once a defense of the individual and a defense of art.

The particular society to which Asher Lev belongs is bound together by religious beliefs, and the decisions of the individuals and of the corporate body are seen as having eternal consequences. Asher has been taught to view all of his decisions, including those of vocation, not simply in terms of how best to fill his days, but in terms of how best to contribute to eternity. To some, including Asher's father, the world of art is viewed with extreme fear and suspicion; if Asher does not use his art to serve the Master of the Universe, then clearly he has aligned himself with the Other Side. Asher's decision to become an artist ultimately results in the banishment from his home and community. The spiritual parallels of this exile are inescapable.

It is no accident that Asher's father's name means "lion." Aryeh is presented to the reader as a mighty defender of his beliefs and as a protector and rescuer of those with whom he shares beliefs. His opposition to Asher's art becomes as fierce as his devotion to his own causes— causes he sees as incompatible with Asher's worldly pursuits. While both of Asher's parents have devoted their energies to the liberation and resettling of Russian Jews, Asher seeks to master the traditions of Western art, including Christian symbols and images. Asher ultimately establishes a name and place for himself within that tradition—a tradition that Aryeh views as particularly threatening. In borrowing forms from that tradition, particularly the cross, Asher acknowledges the affront this presents to his father: "The Crucifixion had been in a way responsible for his own father's murder on a night before Easter decades ago."

While the role of the artist in society and the relationship of the individual to society are familiar themes in literature, this novel also explores other related themes, including isolation and the search for and creation of identity. The nature of art and suffering, and the artist as exile are explored through the character of Asher Lev as well. The sacrifices inherent in following one's calling are traced not only in the character of the young artist, but through Asher's parents a discussion of Vidal's works, including *Myra Breckinridge*.

Stanton, Robert J. *Gore Vidal: A Primary and Secondary Bibliography*. Boston: G. K. Hall, 1978. An excellent source for Vidal's primary texts and a superb compilation of secondary sources for his works, including *Myra Breckinridge*.

Summers, Claude J. *Gay Fictions: Wilde to Stonewall*. New York: Continuum, 1990. Includes one chapter devoted to Vidal. Discusses primarily *The City and the Pillar*, but refers to the themes in *Myra Breckinridge* with deft understanding.

White, Ray L. *Gore Vidal*. New York: Twayne, 1968. A basic introduction to the life and work of Vidal. Includes a discussion of *Myra Breckinridge*.

In this work, which he saw as a study of obsession, Vidal probed the boundaries of society's sexual tolerance. The novel affected the rest of his career. Some of his readers saw the work as a glorification of homosexuality, for in American fiction until that time homosexual characters had been presented as doomed or bizarre figures. By contrast, the protagonist of *The City and the Pillar* is an average American male confused by his homosexual proclivities and obsessed with the memory of a weekend encounter with another young man. If the protagonist is doomed, it is only because he is obsessed with this past event, not because he prefers men to women. The protagonist tries to revive the affair later, and when he is rejected, he kills his former lover. Vidal later issued a revised edition in which the protagonist comes to realize the sterility of his obsession.

Vidal considers himself a sexual libertarian. He believes that sex between consenting adults is something to be enjoyed, a gift, and that a "heterosexual dictatorship" has distorted human sexuality. He declared that "There is no such thing as a homosexual or heterosexual person. There are only homo- and heterosexual acts. Most people are a mixture of impulses if not practices, and what anyone does with a willing partner is of no social or cosmic significance." However, the reading public in 1948 was not ready for Vidal's message.

Myra Breckinridge in 1968 found a somewhat more receptive audience. The book went through more than twenty printings, although it came out in a censored form in England (with Vidal's cooperation), and it was made into a 1970 feature film. The novel appeared during a burgeoning sexual revolution and the mid-twentieth century women's movement. Beneath the gaiety of Myra's campy narrative is a novel of serious purpose with much to say about popular culture, the mass media, and human sexuality.

Myra's questions about her own—"But who am I? What do I feel? Do I exist at all?"—are not questions limited to homosexual men or women but are germane to the human condition. It is Myra's purpose, as it was the early purpose of the women's movement and of the nascent gay rights movement, subjectively to destroy the masculine principle. Myra achieves her purpose objectively by raping Rusty Godowsky.

In a sequel to *Myra Breckinridge*, *Myron* (1974), Vidal returns to the same theme he approached in the first novel: the struggle for domination of a single body between the personas of Myra and Myron. This struggle can be interpreted both as the struggle for domination between men and women and as the struggle for domination between heterosexuals and homosexuals.

Vidal's novels—especially *The City and the Pillar*, *Myra Breckinridge*, and *Myron*—continue to intrigue, stimulate, and anger a large part of his reading public. Since publishing *The City and the Pillar*, Vidal lived his life and conducted his artistic career on his own terms. To his many admirers, he became a symbol of freedom, just as his character Myra succeeded in liberating women—and by extension, gay men—in *Myra Breckinridge*. Many readers who were once shocked by Vidal's comments on contemporary society eventually realized that Vidal's vision corresponded closely to twentieth century realities.

Thomas D. Petitjean, Jr.

Bibliography:
Dick, Bernard F. *The Apostate Angel: A Critical Study of Gore Vidal*. New York: Random House, 1974. A balanced critical assessment of Vidal's major works, including *Myra Breckinridge*.
Kiernan, Robert F. *Gore Vidal*. New York: Frederick Ungar, 1982. A biographical approach to

through a landscape filled with admiring women. Thrilled that that period of masculine domination had ended, Myra suggested that women were living at the dawn of the age of "Women Triumphant, of Myra Breckinridge!"

Myra revealed that her dead homosexual husband, Myron, had been abused and humiliated by many men. Myra planned to avenge Myron with a three-point plan that called for reviving the "Female Principle"; forcing Buck Loner to submit to her demand that she take over his acting studio; and demeaning the macho, all-American Rusty Godowsky by first breaking up his relationship with his girlfriend, Mary-Ann Pringle, and then raping him with a dildo.

Loner was informed by Flagler and Flagler that the will was valid and that Myra could indeed inherit her dead husband's portion of the acting academy. Myra thereupon assumed her place in the academy. She began to befriend Mary-Ann who was, as Myra put it, "as stupid as she seemed." Mary-Ann, believing everything that Myra said, forced her macho boyfriend to enroll in posture-training classes with Myra. Myra thus had her pawns in place. Buck Loner was lusting after her, Mary-Ann believed her, and Rusty was continually being humiliated in posture-training class.

When Loner hired the Golden State Detective Agency to tape phone calls between Myra and Dr. Randolph Montag in New York, he drew mistaken conclusions from a reference to Dr. Montag's having witnessed a "marriage" in Monterey. He was flabbergasted when the agent, his former lover Letitia Van Allen, took a shine to Myra.

Myra and Letitia went to lunch and became fast friends. Letitia questioned Myra's involvement with Mary-Ann, asking if their relationship was lesbian in nature. Myra denied it and implied, on the contrary, that she was interested in Mary-Ann because of Rusty. Letitia confided about her past, when she had bedded every "stud in town who wants to be an actor," but when she asked Myra if she was shocked, Myra told her that she considered herself the new American woman who "uses men the way they once used women." Myra confided to the reader, however, that she was not so sure of herself. She wondered who she was and how she felt. Eventually she questioned her own existence: "Do I exist at all? That is the unanswerable question."

Myra's plan was put into full effect when she had a nighttime posture lesson with Rusty. She had him strip, ostensibly for a preliminary health examination before referring him to a doctor who specialized in correcting spinal problems. Myra conducted the examination as a professional might. She probed his rectum with a thermometer and questioned him about his sexual history. Finally, she manipulated his genitalia before subjecting him to what she called "the final rite." Myra felt triumphant, believing that she had completed the young man's humiliation. She did not guess that Rusty had enjoyed the experience.

Myra Triumphant was, however, brought down by an automobile accident. Her hormonal balance was upset, her breasts vanished, and she sprouted a beard. Buck Loner discovered that she was, in fact, Myron, who had had a sex-change operation. Rusty became an active homosexual, and Myron/Myra married Rusty's former girlfriend, Mary-Ann, and lived happily ever after.

Critical Evaluation:

Gore Vidal, whose literary oeuvre includes plays and poetry, is best known for his novels. His first novel, *Williwaw* (1946), was written when Vidal was nineteen years old, and his second, *In a Yellow Wood*, came the next year, 1947. With the publication of his third novel, however, *The City and the Pillar* (1948, revised and expanded in 1965 with an essay, "Sex and the Law," and an afterword), Vidal first touched on the subject most important to him, homosexuality.

MYRA BRECKINRIDGE

Type of work: Novel
Author: Gore Vidal (1925-   )
Type of plot: Social realism
Time of plot: 1968
Locale: Hollywood
First published: 1968

Principal characters:

MYRA BRECKINRIDGE, a woman who goes to Hollywood to take over an
acting academy that once belonged to her dead husband

BUCK LONER, Myra's co-owner of the acting academy

RUSTY GODOWSKY, a handsome student at the academy

MARY-ANN PRINGLE, a beautiful student at the academy involved with
Rusty

DR. RANDOLPH SPENSER MONTAG, Myra's analyst

LETITIA VAN ALLEN, an agent

The Story:

Myra Breckinridge was twenty-seven years old when she inherited her dead husband's
portion of an acting academy, which was co-owned by a former "singin', shootin', cowboy"
star of radio and movie fame. Myra, who began her narrative by describing herself as a woman
"whom no man will ever possess," in appearance imitated such former film stars as Fay Wray,
Jean Harlow, and Lana Turner. Myra declared that the novel is dead and that there is no point
"to writing made-up stories." As far as Myra was concerned, the films of the 1940's were the
high point of Western artistic creation, although she believed it was in her time being surpassed
by a higher art form, the television commercial. According to Myra, her real mission in
Hollywood was to fulfill her destiny of reconstructing the sexes.

Myra characterized herself as the "New Woman" whose "astonishing history" she was
recording as part of therapy for her "analyst, friend, and dentist," Dr. Randolph Spenser
Montag. Myra characterized her co-owner in the acting academy, Buck Loner, as "not the man
he had been when he made eighteen low-budget Westerns; now he was huge, disgusting, and
old. He was also trying to seduce Myra, despite the fact that she was the widow of his only
nephew, Myron Breckinridge, who had drowned the previous year while riding on the Staten
Island ferry. Myra implied that Myron had not taken his own life.

In his part of the narrative, Buck Loner detailed his deceased nephew's homosexuality and
career as a movie reviewer. Loner had hired a private investigation agency, Flagler and Flagler,
to examine the deed to the academy and make a careful investigation of his nephew's widow,
Myra; he was hoping to find a loophole that would prevent her from inheriting a property he
felt was his alone, despite the fact that the academy was built with money from Myron's mother,
Gertrude.

Myra considered it her mission in life to teach such aspiring young stars as Rusty Godowsky
and such old cowboy stars as Loner what it meant to be a man in the age of "Woman
Triumphant." As Myra declared, "To be a man in a society of machines is to be an expendable,
soft auxiliary to what is useful and hard." Myra believed there was nothing left for the
old-fashioned male to do, no physical struggle to survive and mate. She defined men as
travesties who can only act out the classic hero who was a law unto himself, moving at ease

as well; the parents must make great personal sacrifices in order to live out their most cherished beliefs.

Potok begins his novel with an epigraph from Picasso: "Art is a lie which makes us realize the truth." This epigraph immediately draws the reader's attention to such philosophical considerations as the nature of truth. The novel is rich in its exploration of paradox and inherent contradictions; on the one hand, we see that Asher pays his parents the highest possible honor by immortalizing them and their struggles in his art; on the other hand, this depiction is viewed as the act of a traitor and blasphemer. Asher's greatest triumph becomes the source of his greatest pain. Potok continues the story of Asher Lev in *The Gift of Asher Lev*, published in 1990.

Beverly J. Matiko

Bibliography:
Abramson, Edward A. *Chaim Potok*. Boston: Twayne, 1986. Chapter four is devoted entirely to *My Name Is Asher Lev* and includes sections on "Judaism and the Visual Arts," "The Individual and the Community," "Ancestors and Fathers," and "Artistic and Stylistic Development." Also of interest are the book's first and last chapters entitled "From Rabbi to Writer" and "The Writer Arrived." Abramson includes a six-page selected bibliography.

Kremer, S. Lillian. "Dedalus in Brooklyn: Influences of *A Portrait of the Artist as a Young Man* on *My Name Is Asher Lev*." *Studies in Jewish American Literature* 4 (1985): 26-38. Finds "the mark of James Joyce indelibly stamped on the third and fourth novels of Chaim Potok," particularly in the use of "monologue, stream of consciousness techniques, and epiphany."

Pinsker, Sanford. "The Crucifixion of Chaim Potok/The Excommunication of Asher Lev: Art and the Hasidic World." *Studies in Jewish American Literature* 4 (1985): 39-51. Calls the novel a *Kunstlerroman*, a novel of an artist's education, and views Asher Lev's departure at the novel's end as "a kind of exile, a kind of excommunication."

Sgan, Arnold D. "*The Chosen, The Promise*, and *My Name Is Asher Lev*." *The English Journal* 66 (March, 1977): 63-64. Erroneously calls Potok a psychologist but offers useful plot summaries and themes for each novel. Discusses Potok's place in high school units on "Ethnic Literature" or "The Search for Identity."

Stern, David. Review of *My Name Is Asher Lev*, by Chaim Potok. *Commentary* 54 (October, 1972): 102, 104. Traces some of the similarities between the main characters in *The Chosen*, *The Promise*, and *My Name Is Asher Lev* and sees in those characters' dilemmas "the dilemma of modern religious Judaism itself."

Walden, Daniel, ed. *Studies in American Jewish Literature* 4 (1985). This issue, entitled "The World of Chaim Potok," contains articles on *My Name Is Asher Lev* cited above and other articles of interest.

now between Asher and his family and his religious community was irreparable. The Rebbe told Asher that he must leave. Asher understood and accepted what was essentially an exile. He left for Europe, taking with him the memory of his parents watching him from their window.

Critical Evaluation:

In writing about orthodox Jewish life, Chaim Potok speaks with considerable authority: He is a rabbi and a respected academic, and he has served as the editor-in-chief of the Jewish Publication Society of America. In *My Name Is Asher Lev*, Potok focuses on the role of the artist in a particular community—a community he locates in Crown Heights, Brooklyn, and calls Ladover Hasidism. Potok models his Ladover Hasidism on Lubavitch Hasidism.

My Name Is Asher Lev, like Potok's other novels including *The Chosen* (1967), *The Promise* (1969), *In the Beginning* (1975), and *Davita's Harp* (1985), probes the specific struggles of one member of a community who comes into conflict with the norms and expectations of that community. Asher Lev's community expects him to follow in his parents' footsteps and to work in some way for the preservation and the betterment of Judaism worldwide. Asher, however, is seen as responding to a radically different calling—art. A very familiar pattern of conflict in the world of the novel—the individual versus society—becomes apparent early in the book. On the first page, Asher lists some of the charges he has had to face. These include "traitor, an apostate, a self-hater, an inflicter of shame upon my family, my friends, my people." Asher's own struggle to come to terms with these labels is also sensed when he adds: "In all honesty, I confess that my accusers are not altogether wrong: I am indeed in some way, all of those things." *My Name Is Asher Lev*, then, becomes a defense. It is at once a defense of the individual and a defense of art.

The particular society to which Asher Lev belongs is bound together by religious beliefs, and the decisions of the individuals and of the corporate body are seen as having eternal consequences. Asher has been taught to view all of his decisions, including those of vocation, not simply in terms of how best to fill his days, but in terms of how best to contribute to eternity. To some, including Asher's father, the world of art is viewed with extreme fear and suspicion; if Asher does not use his art to serve the Master of the Universe, then clearly he has aligned himself with the Other Side. Asher's decision to become an artist ultimately results in the banishment from his home and community. The spiritual parallels of this exile are inescapable.

It is no accident that Asher's father's name means "lion." Aryeh is presented to the reader as a mighty defender of his beliefs and as a protector and rescuer of those with whom he shares beliefs. His opposition to Asher's art becomes as fierce as his devotion to his own causes—causes he sees as incompatible with Asher's worldly pursuits. While both of Asher's parents have devoted their energies to the liberation and resettling of Russian Jews, Asher seeks to master the traditions of Western art, including Christian symbols and images. Asher ultimately establishes a name and place for himself within that tradition—a tradition that Aryeh views as particularly threatening. In borrowing forms from that tradition, particularly the cross, Asher acknowledges the affront this presents to his father: "The Crucifixion had been in a way responsible for his own father's murder on a night before Easter decades ago."

While the role of the artist in society and the relationship of the individual to society are familiar themes in literature, this novel also explores other related themes, including isolation and the search for and creation of identity. The nature of art and suffering, and the artist as exile are explored through the character of Asher Lev as well. The sacrifices inherent in following one's calling are traced not only in the character of the young artist, but through Asher's parents